Judge Antônio A. Cançado Trindade

The Construction of a Humanized International Law

The Judges

VOLUME 7

BOOK 3

INTERNATIONAL COURT OF JUSTICE

The titles published in this series are listed at *brill.com/judg*

Judge
Antônio A. Cançado Trindade

The Construction of a Humanized International Law

A Collection of Individual Opinions (2013–2016)
Volume 3

Preface by Dean Spielmann

General Introduction by Andrew Drzemczewski

BRILL
NIJHOFF

LEIDEN | BOSTON

Library of Congress Cataloging-in-Publication Data

Trindade, Antonio Augusto Cancado, 1947- author.
 The construction of a humanized international law : a collection of individual opinions (1991-2013) / Judge Antonio A. Cancado Trindade ; preface by Dean Spielmann ; general introduction by Andrew Drzemczewski.
 volumes cm. -- (The judges : VOLUME 6)
 Includes bibliographical references and index.
 Contents: Inter-American Court of Human Rights: The right of international individual petition -- The crystallization of the international legal personality of the human person in its new dimension -- The humanization of international law -- The centrality of the suffering of the victims -- Time and law: the projection of human suffering in time -- Origin and basis of the international responsibility of the state -- Incompatibility of self-amnesties with the american convention on human rights -- The jus cogens prohibition of torture -- Enforced disappearance of persons as a continuing violation of human rights in breach of jus cogens --
 ISBN 978-90-04-25102-1 (hardback : alk. paper) -- ISBN 978-90-04-25103-8 (e-book : alk. paper)
 1. International law and human rights--Cases. 2. Judicial opinions. I. Inter-American Court of Human Rights. II. International Court of Justice. III. Title.
 KZ1266.T75 2014
 341.4'8--dc23

2014019953

Typeface for the Latin, Greek, and Cyrillic scripts: "Brill". See and download: brill.com/brill-typeface.

ISSN 0929-6301
ISBN 978-90-04-25102-1 (hardback, set book 1 & 2)
ISBN 978-90-04-34003-9 (hardback, book 3)
ISBN 978-90-04-34004-6 (e-book, book 3)

Copyright 2017 by Koninklijke Brill NV, Leiden, The Netherlands.
Koninklijke Brill NV incorporates the imprints Brill, Brill Hes & De Graaf, Brill Nijhoff, Brill Rodopi and Hotei Publishing.
All rights reserved. No part of this publication may be reproduced, translated, stored in a retrieval system, or transmitted in any form or by any means, electronic, mechanical, photocopying, recording or otherwise, without prior written permission from the publisher.
Authorization to photocopy items for internal or personal use is granted by Koninklijke Brill NV provided that the appropriate fees are paid directly to The Copyright Clearance Center, 222 Rosewood Drive, Suite 910, Danvers, MA 01923, USA. Fees are subject to change.

This book is printed on acid-free paper and produced in a sustainable manner.

Contents

Preface   IX

General Introduction   1

BOOK 3
International Court of Justice

1 **Implied Powers of International Tribunals**   9
   Separate Opinion in the case concerning *Alleged Violations of Sovereign Rights and Maritime Spaces in the Caribbean Sea* (Nicaragua *versus* Colombia, Preliminary Objections, Judgment of 17.03.2016)   10

2 **The Universal Juridical Conscience, Humaneness and the Condemnation of Genocide**   39
   Dissenting Opinion in the case of the *Application of the Convention against Genocide* (Croatia *versus* Serbia, Judgment of 03.02.2015)   40

3 **The Universal Juridical Conscience, Humaneness and the Obligation of Nuclear Disarmament**   235
   1 Dissenting Opinion in the Case of *Obligations Concerning Negotiations Relating to Cessation of the Nuclear Arms Race and to Nuclear Disarmament* (Marshall Islands *versus* India, Jurisdiction, Judgment of 05.10.2016)   236
   2 Dissenting Opinion in the Case of *Obligations Concerning Negotiations Relating to Cessation of the Nuclear Arms Race and to Nuclear Disarmament* (Marshall Islands *versus* United Kingdom, Jurisdiction, Judgment of 05.10.2016)   364
   3 Dissenting Opinion in the Case of *Obligations Concerning Negotiations Relating to Cessation of the Nuclear Arms Race and to Nuclear Disarmament* (Marshall Islands *versus* Pakistan, Jurisdiction, Judgment of 05.10.2016)   490

4 **Victims' Right to Reparations for War Damages**   613
   1 Declaration in the case of *Armed Activities on the Territory of the Congo* (D.R. Congo *versus* Uganda, Order [Reparations] of 01.07.2015)   614

2 Declaration in the case of *Armed Activities on the Territory of the Congo* (D.R. Congo *versus* Uganda, Order [Reparations], of 11.04.2016)   **618**

3 Separate Opinion in the Case of *Armed Activities in the Territory of the Congo* (D.R. Congo *versus* Uganda, Order [Reparations], of 06.12.2016)   **624**

5 The Evolving Law on Conservation of Living Species   **635**
Separate Opinion in the case of *Whaling in the Antarctic* (Australia *versus* Japan, New Zealand intervening, Judgment of 31.03.2014)   **636**

6 The Relevance of General Principles of International Law   **673**
  1 Separate Opinion in the case concerning the *Obligation to Negotiate Access to the Pacific Ocean* (Bolivia *versus* Chile, Preliminary Objections, Judgment of 24.09.2015)   **674**
  2 Separate Opinion in the case of *Questions Relating to the Seizure and Detention of Certain Documents and Data* (Timor-Leste *versus* Australia, Order, Provisional Measures, of 03.03.2014)   **704**

7 The Autonomous Legal Regime of Provisional Measures of Protection   **733**
  1 Separate Opinion in the joined cases of *Certain Activities Carried out by Nicaragua in the Border Area* (Costa Rica *versus* Nicaragua) and *Construction of a Road in Costa Rica along the San Juan River* (Nicaragua *versus* Costa Rica) (Judgment of 16.12.2015)   **734**
  2 Separate Opinion in the case of *Questions Relating to the Seizure and Detention of Certain Documents and Data* (Timor-leste *versus* Australia, Order, Provisional Measures [Modification], of 22.04.2015)   **760**

Index   765

Preface

It is a great honour for me to preface this Collection of Individual Opinions of Judge Antônio A. Cançado Trindade. The first time I came across the name Antônio Augusto Cançado Trindade was during the late 1980s, when I consulted one of his articles on the theme of the exhaustion of local remedies under the European Convention on Human Rights. The article, published in the *Revue des droits de l'homme*, was of considerable help to me. As I was soon to realise, Antônio has truly "exhausted" the topic by many further contributions and he is today the leading authority on this important rule of international law. I was also greatly impressed by his first Hague Lectures on the "Co-existence and Co-ordination of Mechanisms of International Protection of Human Rights (at Global and Regional Levels)" (*Collected Courses of the Hague Academy of International Law*, Volume 202, 1987-II, pp. 9–210).

At Cambridge, where I was reading international law, I then asked the Librarian of the Squire Law Library to show me the original manuscript of Antônio's PhD thesis. Two impressive black leather bound volumes, a total of 1728 pages of dissertation, were produced for my perusal. This seminal work has been published, in an abridged version, in the prestigious series of the *Cambridge Studies in International and Comparative Law* under the title "*The Application of the Rule of Exhaustion of Local Remedies in International Law*" (1983). As a Judge of the European Court of Human Rights, I have found this book to be of the greatest help, as are many of his other contributions composing his immense doctrinal opus.

The first time I met Antônio personally was during a visit to the Inter-American Court of Human Rights in November 1997. As Vice-President of the Court, Judge Cançado Trindade was keen to lay emphasis on the future prospects of the Inter-American system (see D. Spielmann, "Visite officielle d'une délégation de la Cour européenne des droits de l'homme à la Cour interaméricaine des droits de l'homme, San José, Costa Rica, 4 et 5 novembre 1997", *Bulletin des droits de l'homme* (Luxembourg), Vol. 8 (1998), pp. 187–188). Those prospects have always formed a key consideration in many of his separate and dissenting opinions. Andrew Drzemczewski has highlighted this aspect in his General Introduction to the present book. In particular, taking as a starting point the view that human rights belong to the individual and not to the State, Judge Cançado Trindade has been successful in securing a change to that Court's Rules, which now provide the victim with an enhanced role in the proceedings. This is just one illustration of the significant role played by separate opinions in general.

Bringing together the most significant Individual Opinions, in book form, is therefore a commendable initiative. Such Opinions, by their very nature, provide access to the otherwise secret deliberations (see D. Spielmann, "Les opinions séparées: une atténuation de la rigueur du secret des délibérations", *Journal des tribunaux* (Brussels), 2007, at p. 311). Moreover, they provide a valuable insight into different trends and schools of thought. Such a collection not only offers an alternative view on many topics; it also informs the reader, through a *vue d'ensemble*, of a judge's personal choices and above all represents an original way of presenting the consistent legal opinion of a learned author who has had the privilege of shaping, as a member of the international judiciary, the future of the law. This is particularly true in the case of Antônio A. Cançado Trindade, who has been a Member, as Judge, Vice-President and President, of the Inter-American Court of Human Rights, and since 2008 a Judge of the International Court of Justice. Individual opinions are indeed of the greatest interest and importance. As Sir Hersch Lauterpacht put it: "[t]he Statute of the Court in making express provision for the right of Judges to append dissenting or separate opinions made, in a variety of ways, a beneficent contribution to the development of international law and the authority of international justice. Experience has shown that so long as it is clear that the decision of the Court is, within its proper limits, binding and authoritative, the individual Opinions of the Judges, far from detracting from the standing of the Judgments or Advisory Opinions, add to their vitality, comprehension and usefulness and greatly facilitate the fulfilment of the indirect purpose of the Court, which is to develop and to clarify international law" (H. Lauterpacht, *The Development of International Law by the International Court*, London, Stevens and Sons, 1958, at p. 66).

The visionary Opinions featured in this book dwell upon many aspects of the increased humanization of international law. Elevating this body of norms, which have traditionally focused on purely inter-State relations, to a level where individuals and their suffering become a primary concern, is without doubt Antônio A. Cançado Trindade's major doctrinal contribution. He examines international (even aggravated) responsibility of the State in the light of this philosophical approach. For Antônio, focusing on the individual as a starting point has many implications, both procedural and substantive, for a given Case. Revisiting the traditional conceptions of compulsory jurisdiction, provisional measures, *locus standi* and the international legal personality of the human person, limitations of access to justice in the light of *jus cogens*, amnesty laws and principles of reparation are but a few examples of the themes examined in the learned Opinions expressed by Judge Cançado Trindade at the Inter-American Court of Human Rights.

The great achievement of Judge Cançado Trindade at the International Court of Justice has been to draw attention to this dimension and further its development in the Case-law. In a significant number of Cases the World Court acts today as a human rights court, dealing increasingly, albeit under the traditional umbrella of inter-State disputes, with situations that involve human suffering and lead it to find human rights violations. Many of the more recent Opinions of Antônio A. Cançado Trindade echo the views he expressed previously as a Member of the Inter-American Court. Suffice it to mention the delicate issues of provisional measures, the relevance of compromissory clauses in human rights treaties, the primacy of the right to access to justice over State immunities in respect of international crimes, or the *jus cogens* prohibition of torture, among the many subjects that he has addressed.

Judge Antônio A. Cançado Trindade's Opinions, now available in this prestigious collection, will, I am sure, continue to have a significant influence and impact on the development of international law for years to come.

Dean Spielmann
President of the European Court of Human Rights

General Introduction

Even without his name attached, it is always immediately apparent when one is reading an opinion by Judge Antônio Cançado Trindade. Awash with allusions to literature, philosophy and theology and infused with a deep and abiding sense of empathy, Antônio's opinions fuse the intellectual rigour of the academic with the reformist zeal of the advocate. His is an undeniably unique legal personality, and I am privileged to have been his close friend since we first met in the early seventies while studying for our PhDs, he at Cambridge and myself at the London School of Economics and Political Science.

Antônio has played many roles throughout his distinguished career. He has been serving as a Judge successively on two international courts, as President and Vice-President of the Inter-American Court of Human Rights (IACtHR), as an academic at numerous institutions, and as an educator in both Latin America and Europe, amongst other positions. Yet perhaps his greatest accomplishment – besides his two-volume *General Course on Public International Law* delivered at the Hague Academy in 2005 (published in its *Recueil des Cours*, vols. 316–317), and his *Treatise* (*Tratado de Direito International dos Direitos Humanos*, published in Brazil in 3 volumes, in 1999–2003) – has been his remarkable output of Individual Opinions, which are celebrated in this volume.

In the long period between 1991 and 2008, Antônio delivered 103 Individual Opinions in the IACtHR, in its Judgments in contentious cases, in its Advisory Opinions and in its Provisional Measures of Protection. The present volume provides just a sample of those 103 Individual Opinions in the IACtHR (in addition to the more recent ones in the International Court of Justice (ICJ), *infra*) reproduced herein, giving a *vue d'ensemble* of the doctrinal foundations which he maintained throughout those years, which marked an era of "jurisprudential construction" undertaken by the Court in San José. His Individual Opinions encompass a rich collection of his thoughts on the evolution of contemporary International Law of Human Rights, and how this relatively new discipline has profoundly affected developments in "classical" Public International Law.

Most of his Individual Opinions in the IACtHR are not dissents, but rather Separate or Concurring Opinions, in which Antônio sets out the parameters of his legal philosophy and places the case at hand within the broader framework of the history and evolution of international and human rights law. Indeed, Antônio is perhaps the closest living example to Ronald Dworkin's idealised Judge Hercules, who uses his infinite knowledge of legal sources to decide upon the resolution of a particular case in a way that best fits and justifies the seamless web of the law as a whole. While Antônio's knowledge is perhaps not infinite, it is varied and substantial, and he shares with Judge Hercules a rejection of a positivist view of law in favour of focusing upon the broader principles of individual justice that underlie international law in general, and in particular the law of human rights.

His Individual Opinions, both in the IACtHR and more recently in the ICJ, dwell upon general principles of law, the basis of the jurisdiction of the International Court (contentious and advisory functions), international legal personality and the individual's key role therein, the justiciability of human rights, as well as the distinct aspects of the international responsibility of States (including the collective guarantee of conventional obligations). They also address the international *ordre public*, encompassing the direct access (*lato sensu*) of the human person to international justice, the occurrence of crimes of State[1] and the legal consequences for *reparation* in its distinct forms, and the convergence (at normative, hermeneutic and operational levels) between International Law of Human Rights, International Humanitarian Law and the International Law of Refugees. They also address the domain of the international *jus cogens*, in expansion and the obligations or guarantees *erga omnes* of protection (in their horizontal and vertical dimensions, as he perceives them).

Antônio's frequent use of Separate Opinions reflects his perception of the Judge as an educator. He aims at making use of his position not merely to decide the case at hand, but also to inform others – fellow judges, academics, students, and victims of human rights violations – of the intellectual basis of his views in order to promote thought, discussion and possible reform and to provide an alternative to judicial consensus. In the area of law as fluid and relatively nascent as that of international human rights, such a role is invaluable in creating the intellectual foundations for future case-law. These efforts have paid dividends.

At the Inter-American Court, Antônio's strident dissents and Separate Opinions were often, in due course, adopted by the majority of the Court. Antônio was successful, in his position at the Inter-American Court, in changing the Court's view on a number of issues through his consistent pressure. For example, his focus on the importance of providing meaningful non-pecuniary reparation to the victims of human rights abuses, including the families of deceased individuals, was acknowledged by the Court in the paradigmatic

---

1   See his impressive monograph, on the basis of his experience in the international adjudication of cases of massacres: A.A. Cançado Trindade, *State Responsibility in Cases of Massacres: Contemporary Advances in International Justice* (Inaugural Address, 10.11.2011), Utrecht, Universiteit Utrecht, 2011, pp. 1–71.

case of the *"Street Children"* (*Villagrán Morales and Others versus Guatemala*, 1999–2001).

In some ways, the bond of friendship between Antônio and me is emblematic of the broader relationship between the Court in Costa Rica and the Strasbourg Human Rights Convention mechanism. Antônio was greatly inspired by the example of the European Court of Human Rights during his time in Strasbourg at the International Institute for Human Rights (1972 and 1974) – where he and I received our diplomas from the hand of René Cassin – and sought to learn from its successes and failures. The influence of the Strasbourg Court can perhaps best be felt in his longstanding advocacy to ensure a more substantial role for the individual applicant before the IACtHR. His insistence, in cases such as *Castillo Petruzzi and Others versus Peru* (1998), that human rights belong to individuals and not to their States and that it follows from this that individuals themselves must have the capacity to plead their cases before the Court, ultimately resulted in a change in the Regulations of the Court, providing victims with the right to present their grievances themselves before the Court, rather than be represented by the Commission.

One can clearly decipher how influential, not to say daunting, Antônio's role has been. Since the adoption of the American Convention on Human Rights, back in 1969, his "imprint" on human rights developments is unrivaled. In effect, during his tenure as President of the IACtHR, from 1999 to 2004, a number of key developments may be recorded, foremost amongst them being the adoption of the fourth set of Rules of Court (on 24.11.2000, having entered in force on 01.06.2001) which granted *locus standi in judicio* to individual petitioners in *all* stages of the procedure before the Court. Shortly afterwards, in the same vein, Antônio prepared, as *rapporteur* of the Court, and presented as its President to the competent organs of the OAS, in May 2001, his Report titled *Bases para un Proyecto de Protocolo a la Convención Americana sobre Derechos Humanos, para Fortalecer Su Mecanismo de Protección* [*Basis for a Draft Protocol to the American Convention on Human Rights, to Strengthen Its Mechanism of Protection*], aimed at securing the compulsory jurisdiction of the Court and direct access (*jus standi*) to it of individual petitioners, as true subjects of International Law, endowed with full international legal/procedural capacity.

Although petitioners within the Inter-American system are not yet able to directly seize the Court, as is the case in Strasbourg, Antônio's efforts have gone a long way towards ensuring that rights granted under the American Convention are effectively realised. Furthermore, due to the extraordinary influence of judges like Antônio, the Strasbourg Court has been able to "learn" from the case-law of the San José Court in areas such as non-pecuniary reparation (case of the "*Street Children*") and the use of self-amnesties (the historical case of *Barrios Altos versus Peru*, 2001), where the latter Court has had more experience.

In the mid-nineties, Antônio advanced his in-depth research on the direct access of individuals to the Inter-American and European Courts of Human Rights, in primary sources of the archives of the two international tribunals, in San José and Strasbourg. The result of this work was published, in Spain, in 2001.[2] He then developed his research, in the light of new case-law, paying attention to the need to protect individuals in situations of utmost adversity, not to say defenselessness; he delivered a General Course on this theme at the Academy of European Law in Florence in 2007, which again resulted in publication of a book, this time in the United Kingdom.[3]

An enthusiastic promoter of dialogue between international tribunals, I remember Antônio's presence, in the Inter-American Court of Human Rights delegation, at the ceremony inaugurating the new (full-time) European Court of Human Rights at the *Palais des Droits de l'Homme* in Strasbourg, on 1 November 1998, with the entry into force of Protocol n. 11 to the European Convention on Human Rights.[4] From then onwards Antônio set up, on behalf of the Inter-American Court, with the support of his homologue Judge Luzius Wildhaber, the President of the European Court, a permanent dialogue between those two international tribunals, with annual co-ordination meetings, in rotation in the *sièges* of both. Thanks to this initiative, jurisprudential croos-fertilization flourished, and continues to this day.[5]

This cross-fertilization has, as of his election onto the ICJ in 2008, and beginning of work therein in early 2009, been relentlessly pursued by Antônio at The Hague: one need only consult his Separate Opinions, where he stresses (repeatedly in the case *A.S. Diallo*, merits, 2010; Order, 2011; and reparations, 2012) the relevance of such cross-fertilization in the performance by contemporary

---

[2] See A.A. Cançado Trindade, *El Acceso Directo del Individuo a los Tribunales Internacionales de Derechos Humanos*, Bilbao, University of Deusto, 2001, pp. 9–104.

[3] See A.A. Cançado Trindade, *The Access of Individuals to International Justice*, Oxford, Oxford University Press, 2011, pp. 1–236; of particular interest is his analysis, as from some of his Separate Opinions, of the vindication of human rights in cases of massacres and other grave violations of both human rights and International Humanitarian Law.

[4] For an overview, see A. Drzemczewski, "A Major Overhaul of the European Human Rights Convention Control Mechanism: Protocol n. 11", VI-2 *Collection of Courses of the Academy of European Law* (1995–1997) pp. 121–244.

[5] See, recently: European Court of Human Rights, *Research Report: References to the Inter-American Court of Human Rights in the Case-Law of the European Court of Human Rights*, Strasbourg, Council of Europe, 2012, pp. 1–20.

international tribunals of their common mission of the realization of justice. Indeed, in the case of *A.S. Diallo*, the International Court of Justice, for the first time in its history, made express cross-references to the case-law of the European and Inter-American Courts of Human Rights.

The beneficiaries of this development of jurisprudential cross-fertilization, as Antônio points out, are the *justiciables* themselves. As guest speaker on special occasions, he insisted on this point, e.g., at the fiftieth anniversary of the European Court of Human Rights (Rome Conference of 2000), at the fiftieth anniversary of the Court of Justice of the European Communities (European Union, Colloquy of Luxembourg of 2002), at the first joint Seminar of the three human rights tribunals (the European and Inter-American Courts, and the newly-established African Court on Human and Peoples' Rights, held in Strasbourg in 2008).

It is clear from several of his Individual Opinions, both in the International Court of Justice and, earlier on, in the Inter-American Court of Human Rights, that Antônio places particular emphasis on – and is no doubt proud of – the Latin American doctrine of international law, whose influence on the evolution of Public International Law is substantial. This is significant, coming from him, widely regarded as the major contemporary exponent of the Latin American doctrine of Public International Law. Indeed, one could say that he rescued the essence of the historical contribution of this doctrine, e.g., in his address, in representation of Latin America, in the centennial celebration of the II Hague Peace Conference of 1907.[6] At the same time, he has remained always attentive to insert that contribution in the framework of the *universality* of international law, of which he has been a consistent and vigorous supporter.

The recognition of the contribution of his work to a humanized international law has gone well beyond Latin America. Antônio's Opinions have been sought by many, be it, at universal level, by the United Nations (e.g., UNHCR,

---

6   A.A. Cançado Trindade, "The Presence and Participation of Latin America at the II Hague Peace Conference of 1907", in *Actualité de la Conférence de La Haye de 1907, II Conférence de la Paix* (*Colloque de 2007* – ed. Y. Daudet), Leiden/La Haye, Académie de Droit International/Nijhoff, 2008, pp. 51–84, and cf. pp. 110–112, 115–117, 122 and 205–206. Earlier on, while presiding the Inter-American Court of Human Rights, he launched a series of booklets on "Latin American Doctrine of International Law" (*Doctrina Latinoamericana del Derecho Internacional*), paying tribute to the masters of the past. In his Opinions, both in the Inter-American Court as well as in the International Court of Justice, he recalls the legacy of Latin American doctrine, such as, very recently, in the cases opposing Costa Rica to Nicaragua before the ICJ.

UNESCO, UNEP, UNDP), or at the regional level, by the Organization of American States and the Council of Europe. At the request of this latter, he presented an in-depth Opinion, in 1995, titled *Analysis of the Legal Implications for States that Intend to Ratify Both the European Convention on Human Rights and Its Protocols and the Convention on Human Rights of the Commonwealth of Independent States (CIS)*,[7] in which he underlined, in no uncertain terms, that the lack of independence and impartiality of the Minsk Convention's supervisory organ, the Human Rights Commission composed of representatives appointed by States Parties, was "a cause of great concern".[8] He further underlined the need of rendering it possible that the States Parties to the Minsk Convention were to become Parties also to the European Convention on Human Rights itself.

In his Separate Opinions, in the two international jurisdictions he has been successively serving, Antônio has consistently drawn attention to, and stressed, the significance of the general principles of international law. He has done so in the exercise of both the contentious and advisory functions of the two international tribunals. In the ICJ, for example, as to the contentious function, illustrations are lately found in his Separate Opinions in the cases of the *Pulp Mills* (2010), of *A.S. Diallo* (2010–2012) of the *Temple of Preah Vihear* (2011–2013), and in his Dissenting Opinion in the *Georgia versus Russian Federation* case (2011).

And, as to the advisory function, further illustrations are provided by his Separate Opinions in the Advisory Opinions on the *Declaration of Independence of Kosovo* (of 2010), and on a *Judgment of the ILO Administrative Tribunal upon a Complaint Filed against IFAD* (2012) – preceded, in the Inter-American Court, by his Concurring Opinion in the Advisory Opinion on *The Juridical Condition and Rights of Undocumented Migrants* (2003). In Antônio's conception, the necessary attention to those principles brings us closer to the domain of superior *human values* (not sufficiently worked upon in international case-law and doctrine); he warns that such principles (and values) are to safeguarded, as, ultimately, it is those principles that inform and conform the applicable norms, and ultimately any legal system.

It is clear, in reading the Individual Opinions collected in this volume, that Antônio does not only view himself as a Judge and an educator, but also as a person particularly concerned with the need to bring justice to the vulnerable. His is a humanist outlook. He has consistently focused his attention (both in the IACtHR and in the ICJ) to what he perceives as the "centrality" of the role

---

7 Published as Council of Europe document SG/INF (95)17, of 20.12.1995, pp. 1–38.
8 Text also published *in*: 17 *Human Rights Law Journal* (1996) pp. 157–184, at p. 179.

of judicial organs who are duty-bound to bear in mind the suffering of the victims of human rights violations; in his perception, there is a need, always, for what he strongly advocates – the *universal juridical conscience*, as the ultimate *material* source of all law. Reference can be made, for example, *inter alia*, in the IACtHR, to his Separate Opinion in the case of *Bulacio versus Argentina* (2003), and, in the ICJ, to his Dissenting Opinion (Order of 2009) followed by his Separate Opinion (Judgment of 2012) in the case of *Belgium versus Senegal*.

On both occasions (among others), he stressed the importance – to the surviving victims – the *realization of justice* as a form of reparation, so as to alleviate their suffering.

From 1997–1998 onwards, until now, Antônio has patiently and consistently constructed, in the IACtHR and now in the ICJ, a unique body of Separate Opinions on the *humanization* of International Law,[9] which has been a source of inspiration for many others, and has strongly influenced contemporary international legal doctrine.[10] In this respect, his Concurring Opinions in the two landmark Advisory Opinions (nos. 16 and 18) of the IACtHR on *The Right to Information on Consular Assistance in the Framework of the Guarantees of the Due Process of Law* (1999), and on *The Juridical Condition and Rights of Undocumented Migrants* (2003) are widely known on both sides of the Atlantic. His approach has led him to the construction of – as he terms it in his General Course at The Hague Academy of International Law – the new *jus gentium* of our times, which has attracted the attention of a new generation of legal scholars, as reflected in his two recent books published in France.[11]

---

[9] For a general view of this historical process, see A.A. Cançado Trindade, *A Humanização do Direito Internacional*, Belo Horizonte/Brazil, Edit. Del Rey, 2006, pp. 3–409.

[10] Moreover, there have been occasions when international tribunals themselves have taken note of his Separate Opinions and writings; for example, recently, in its Judgment of 13.11.2012 in the case *Margus versus Croatia*, the European Court of Human Rights (First Section) expressly referred (para. 37) to his Concurring Opinion in the case of *Barrios Altos versus Peru* (2001) decided by the Inter-American Court of Human Rights. The same has occurred also within the Inter-American Court itself. For its part, the Special Tribunal for Lebanon has, likewise, in its Order of 15.04.2010, expressly referred (para. 29) to various of his Dissenting and Separate Opinions in the Inter-American Court, in addition to his book (*El Derecho de Acceso a la Justicia en Su Amplia Dimensión*) published in Chile in 2008 (para. 29 n. 31) – now followed by his more recent book (*Los Tribunales Internacionales Contemporáneos y la Humanización del Derecho Internacional*) published in Argentina in 2013.

[11] See A.A. Cançado Trindade, *Le Droit international pour la personne humaine*, Paris, Pédone, 2012, pp. 45–368; A.A. Cançado Trindade, *Évolution du Droit international au droit*

In exploring the philosophical and historical foundations of international law, Antônio has always prioritised the experience of victims of human rights violations. It is perhaps this quality which distinguishes his current position at the International Court of Justice. As the only judge on the Court, in its present composition, who has previously served for a long time on an international human rights tribunal, Antônio's emphasis on the individual's entitlement to justice can be perceived as a breath of fresh air in an institution which has traditionally been concerned with disputes of a solely inter-State nature.[12]

This perspective is present in nearly all of his Separate and Dissenting Opinions at the ICJ, including his Opinions stressing a people-centred view of statehood (the Advisory Opinion on the *Declaration of Independence of Kosovo*, 2010), the need for cases to be resolved in an efficient manner, within a timeframe that accommodates the needs of individuals (*Belgium versus Senegal* case, 2009–2012), the importance of compulsory jurisdiction in the context of human rights treaties (*Georgia versus Russian Federation* case, 2011), and the impact of border disputes upon nomadic populations (*Burkina Faso versus Niger* case, 2013). People and territory go together, as he sustained in his Separate Opinions both in the *Burkina Faso versus Niger* case, 2013, and in the case of the *Temple of Preah Vihear* (Provisional Measures, 2011, and Interpretation of Judgment, 2013).

It has, furthermore, motivated his emphasis on the acknowledgement and the expansion of the material content of *jus cogens* and his refusal to accept impunity for procedural or other reasons when grave violations of human rights and of International Humanitarian Law have been committed: see his dissents, within the ICJ, in the case *Germany versus Italy*, and the IACtHR, especially his Separate Opinions in the cases of *Bámaca Velásquez* and *Myrna Mack Chang versus Guatemala*, 2002–2003. We are all truly fortunate that Antônio's extraordinary career is far from over. It remains to be seen in what ways he will shape the case-law of the ICJ, but it is certain that he will continue to craft illuminating Opinions that will undoubtedly be read for years to come.

Andrew Drzemczewski
Head of Legal Affairs and Human Rights Department, Parliamentary Assembly of the Council of Europe (PACE)

---

des gens – L'accès des particuliers à la justice internationale: le regard d'un juge, Paris, Pédone, 2008, pp. 1–187.

[12] See, in this connection, the comments of the ICJ's former President, Rosalyn Higgins, "Equality of States and Immunity from Suit: A Complex Relationship", 43 *Netherlands Yearbook of International Law* (2012) pp. 129–149, at p. 148.

CHAPTER 1

Implied Powers of International Tribunals

Separate Opinion in the case concerning *Alleged Violations of Sovereign Rights and Maritime Spaces in the Caribbean Sea* (Nicaragua *versus* Colombia, Preliminary Objections, Judgment of 17.03.2016)

Table of Contents Paragraphs

I. *Prolegomena* 1–4
II. Submissions of the Parties and Questions from the Bench 5–6
III. Responses from the Contending Parties 7–15
    1. Response from Nicaragua 7–9
    2. Response from Colombia 10–12
    3. General Assessment 13–15
IV. Inherent Powers beyond State Consent 16–21
V. The Teleological Interpretation (*Ut Res Magis Valeat Quam Pereat*) beyond State Consent 22–27
VI. *Recta Ratio* above *Voluntas*, Human Conscience above the "Will" 28–41
VII. *Competénce de la Compétence / Kompetenz Kompetenz* beyond State Consent 42–47
VIII. Inherent Powers Overcoming *Lacunae*, and the Relevance of General Principles 48–58
IX. Inherent Powers and *Juris Dictio* beyond Transactional Justice 59–66
X. Inherent Powers and Supervision of Compliance with Judgments 67–75
XI. Epilogue 76–82

I *Prolegomena*

1. Once again before this Court, the question of inherent powers of international tribunals has been the object of particular attention in the course of the proceedings in the present case of *Alleged Violations of Sovereign Rights and Maritime Spaces in the Caribbean Sea* (Nicaragua *versus* Colombia). The two contending parties have aptly presented their distinct outlooks of the issue of inherent powers or *facultés*: in their submissions before the Court, they have seen it fit to refer to the relevant case-law of contemporary international

tribunals (in particular international human rights tribunals) in respect, in particular, of the issue of their inherent powers or *facultés*. The issue pertains directly to the fourth preliminary objection raised by Colombia.

2. In the present Judgment, the International Court of Justice (ICJ), having found that it has jurisdiction under the Pact of Bogotá, dismissing Colombia's first preliminary objection, could and should have shed some light on the points made by the contending parties, – Nicaragua's claim of "inherent jurisdiction" and Colombia's fourth preliminary objection, – even if for dismissing this latter as well, rather than, in a minimalist posture, elliptically saying that "there is no ground" for it to deal with the issue (para. 104).

3. Given the importance that I attach to this particular issue, recurrent in the practice of international tribunals, and given the fact that it was brought to the attention of the ICJ in the *cas d'espèce*, not only in the written phase of the proceedings, but also in the course of the hearings before it, I feel obliged to leave on the records, first, the positions of the parties and the treatment dispensed to it, and, secondly, the foundations of my own personal position on it, in its interrelated aspects.

4. It is, after all, an issue of relevance to the operation of contemporary international tribunals, in their common mission of the realization of justice. In my perception, this is an issue which cannot simply be eluded. The aspects which I deem it fit to cover, in the present Separate Opinion, refer to the following successive points: a) inherent powers beyond State consent; b) the teleological interpretation (*ut res magis valeat quam pereat*) beyond State consent; c) *compétence de la compétence / Kompetenz Kompetenz* beyond State consent; d) *recta ratio* above *voluntas*, human conscience above the "will"; e) inherent powers overcoming *lacunae*, and the relevance of general principles; f) inherent powers and *juris dictio*, beyond transactional justice; and g) inherent powers and supervision of compliance with judgments. I shall at last come to my brief epilogue.

II Submissions of the Parties and Questions from the Bench

5. In the course of the proceedings (written and oral phases) in the present case of *Alleged Violations of Sovereign Rights and Maritime Spaces in the Caribbean Sea*, both contending parties, in their submissions, when addressing the issue of inherent powers or *facultés*, referred to the relevant case-law of the Inter-American Court of Human Rights (IACtHR) and of the European Court

of Human Rights (ECtHR). In the written phase of the proceedings in the *cas d'espèce*, both Nicaragua and Colombia referred to the IACtHR's Judgment (of 28.11.2003) in the case of *Baena Ricardo and Others versus Panama*, as well as the ECtHR's (Grand Chamber) Judgment (of 07.02.2003) in the case of *Fabris versus France*.[1] Nicaragua further referred to the ECtHR's (Grand Chamber) Judgments (of 30.06.2009 and 05.02.2015, respectively) in the cases of *Verein gegen Tierfabriken Schweiz (VgT) versus Switzerland*, and of *Bochan versus Ukraine*.[2]

6. Subsequently, towards the end of the oral phase of the proceedings in the *cas d'espèce*, in the public sitting of 02 October 2015 before the Court, I deemed it fit to put the three following questions to the two contending parties, Nicaragua and Colombia:

> In the course of the proceedings along this week, both contending parties referred to the relevant case-law of contemporary international tribunals, in particular in respect of the question of their inherent powers or *facultés*. Having listened attentively to their oral arguments, I have three questions to address to both parties, so as to obtain further precisions, at conceptual level, from both of them, in the context of the *cas d'espèce*.
>
> First: Do the inherent powers or *facultés* of contemporary international tribunals ensue from the exercise itself, by each of them, of their international judicial function?
>
> Second: Do the distinct bases of jurisdiction of contemporary international tribunals have an incidence on the extent of their *compétence de la compétence*?
>
> Third: Do the distinct bases of jurisdiction of contemporary international tribunals condition the operation of the corresponding mechanisms of supervision of compliance with their respective judgments and decisions?[3]

---

1 ICJ, *Memorial of the Republic of Nicaragua*, of 03.10.2014, para. 1.27; and ICJ, *Preliminary Objections of the Republic of Colombia*, of 19.12.2014, paras. 5.22–5.23.
2 ICJ, *Written Statement of the Republic of Nicaragua to the Preliminary Objections of the Republic of Colombia*, of 20.04.2015, para. 5.35.
3 Cf. ICJ, doc. CR 2015/25, of 02.10.2015, p. 47.

III Responses from the Contending Parties

1 *Response from Nicaragua*

7. One week later, on 09 October 2015, both parties provided the Court with their written answers to the questions I had put to them at the end of the Court's hearings in the *cas d'espèce*. In its written reply, Nicaragua stated, in response to my *first question*, that, in its view, the inherent powers of international tribunals ensue, "more widely than from the *exercise* of their judicial function", from "their very *existence* and nature as judicial organs".[4]

8. As to my *second question*, Nicaragua contended that "in all cases", the basis for jurisdiction (statute) of an international tribunal "includes the power or *faculté* to decide on the existence and scope of an inherent power".[5] The *compétence de la compétence* (*Kompetenz Kompetenz*), even if leading to distinct conclusions according to the various Statutes, "can be said to be inherent", it is "a well-established legal principle of general application".[6] This is so, in its view, irrespective of "whether or not it is expressly granted" by the Statute of the international tribunal concerned.[7]

9. And as to my *third question*, Nicaragua was of the view that "all tribunals have the same right to determine the scope of their own (... inherent) powers", it being "indispensable" for them "to exercise some kind of jurisdiction on the implementation of their own judgments".[8] Even if it may vary from one tribunal to another, international tribunals have here an "inherent power" as well, in respect of the implementation of their own judgments (whether they can count or not on the assistance of another organ with supervisory powers).[9]

2 *Response from Colombia*

10. For its part, Colombia, in its written reply, stated, in response to my *first question*, that the ICJ "has such 'inherent powers' as are necessary in the interests of the good administration of justice for the proper conduct of cases over

---

4   ICJ, *Written Reply of Nicaragua to the Questions Put by Judge Cançado Trindade at the Public Sitting Held on the Morning of 02 October 2015*, doc. NICOLC 2015/32, of 09.10.2015, p. 2.
5   *Ibid.*, p. 3.
6   *Ibid.*, p. 2.
7   *Ibid.*, p. 2.
8   *Ibid.*, p. 3.
9   Cf. *ibid.*, pp. 3–4.

which it has jurisdiction".[10] It then added that, yet, there is "no such thing as an 'inherent jurisdiction' enabling the Court to take jurisdiction over new cases, as urged upon the Court by Nicaragua".[11]

11. As to my *second question*, Colombia asserted, as to *compétence de la compétence*, that the Court's deciding as to jurisdiction amounts to "an express power, and in and of itself in no way gives rise to an inherent power or jurisdiction".[12] Colombia added, in this connection, that no such considerations can give rise to "an inherent power or jurisdiction over *the merits* of a case" that an international tribunal "does not otherwise have".[13]

12. And as to my *third question*, Colombia was of the view that a mechanism of supervision of compliance with judgments "must be found in the instrument which created" the international tribunal and "established its jurisdiction"[14] (statutory provisions). In the case of the ICJ, such a mechanism is provided not by its Statute, but by the U.N. Charter ("of which the Statute is an integral part"), which "assigns such competence to the Security Council"; and, in its view, the "Pact of Bogotá (in particular, Article L), reflects the States Parties' understanding that the Court is not the venue for matters of supervision of compliance".[15]

3   *General Assessment*

13. As just seen, Nicaragua sustains a broader scope of inherent powers: irrespective from what is provided distinctly in Statutes of international tribunals, they ensue from their very existence, and they are all endowed with the *compétence de la compétence*; inherent powers, in its view, are indispensable also for them "to exercise some kind of jurisdiction" on the implementation of their own judgments, whether assisted or not by other supervisory organs.

14. For its part, Colombia, rather distinctly, takes the view that inherent powers are exercised when necessary in the interests of the sound administration of justice; it ascribes a stricter scope to them, sustaining that they do not amount

---

10   ICJ, *Written Reply of Colombia to the Questions Put by Judge Cançado Trindade at the Public Sitting Held on the Morning of 02 October 2015*, doc. NICOLC 2015/33, of 09.10.2015, p. 2, para. 3.
11   *Ibid.*, p. 2, para. 4.
12   *Ibid.*, p. 3, para. 6.
13   *Ibid.*, p. 4, para. 6.
14   *Ibid.*, p. 4, para. 7.
15   *Ibid.*, p. 4, para. 7.

to *compétence de la compétence*, that there is no "inherent jurisdiction", and that supervision of compliance with judgments is not expressly provided in the Statute or constitutive Charter (of the U.N., in the case of the ICJ).

15. It is not surprising to see these two distinct conceptions of the scope of inherent powers or *facultés* of international tribunals. I see no reason for the Court not having pronounced upon this issue. Having abstained from doing so, reflects a rather minimalist outlook, which I do not share, of the exercise of the international judicial function. After all, in matters of both admissibility and jurisdiction, as well as of substance, judgments are expected to contain reason and persuasion. In dwelling upon this issue, I propose to address, in the following paragraphs, the interrelated points that I have identified (para. 4, *supra*).

IV   Inherent Powers beyond State Consent

16. The issue of inherent powers or *facultés* has, in effect, been raised time and time again before international tribunals. For some years, I have been dealing with it, in distinct jurisdictions;[16] within the ICJ, I have recently addressed it, *inter alia*, e.g., in my Separate Opinions in other Latin American cases, namely, those of *Certain Activities Carried out by Nicaragua in the Border Area* (Costa Rica *versus* Nicaragua) and *Construction of a Road in Costa Rica along the San Juan River* (Nicaragua *versus* Costa Rica) (Joinder of Proceedings, Orders of 17.04.2013), as well as that of *Obligation to Negotiate Access to the Pacific Ocean* (Bolivia *versus* Chile, Judgment on Preliminary Objections, of 24.09.2015).

17. It is not my intention to reiterate here all that I have already stated in those Separate Opinions, but rather only to summarize it, and then focus briefly on other and related aspects of the matter, of relevance to the present Judgment of the ICJ. In my previous Separate Opinions in the two aforementioned joined cases of *Certain Activities* and *Construction of a Road* (Orders of 2013), I revisited the conceptualization of "implied" and "inherent powers", and pointed out that

> While the doctrinal construction of "implied powers" was intended to set up limits to powers transcending the letter of constitutive charters, – limits found in the purposes and functions of the international

---

[16] For example, almost two decades ago, I addressed it in the IACtHR, in my Dissenting Opinion in the case of *Genie Lacayo versus Nicaragua* (Appeal of Revision of Judgment, Resolution of 13.09.1997), paras. 1–28, esp. para. 7.

organization at issue, – the doctrinal construction of "inherent powers", quite distinctly, was intended to assert the powers of the juridical person at issue for the accomplishment of its goals, as provided for in its constitutive charter. The point I wish here to make is that the same expression – "inherent powers" – has at times been invoked in respect of the operation of international judicial entities; yet, though the expression is the same, its *rationale* and connotation are different, when it comes to be employed by reference to international tribunals. Another precision is here called for, for a proper understanding of the operation of these latter. Understanding and operation go hand in hand: "*ad intelligendum et ad agendum*" (para. 6).[17]

18. I then sought to demonstrate the relevance of Kompetenz Kompetenz (*compétence de la compétence*) to the exercise of the international judicial function (paras. 7–9), and how inherent powers contribute to the sound administration of justice (*la bonne administration de la justice*) (paras. 10–27). Thus, for example, both the PCIJ and the ICJ have "effected joinders *avant la lettre*, even in the absence (before 1978) of a provision to that effect in their *interna corporis*" (para. 25).

19. In effect, most international tribunals have an express power[18] to adopt their own rules of procedure. It may so happen that at times a given situation may not be sufficiently covered by the rules. The application of their rules, and the resolution of issues not sufficiently addressed by them, – with recourse to their inherent powers, – are likewise beyond the "will" or consent of States. Even in the absence of an express provision thereon, international tribunals are entitled to exercise their inherent powers in order to secure the sound administration of justice.

20. In my subsequent Separate Opinion, in the very recent Judgment (as to the merits, of 16.12.2015) in the same two joined cases of *Certain Activities* and *Construction of a Road*, I have retaken my consideration of the matter, expressing my understanding that, if any unforeseeable circumstance should arise, the ICJ is "endowed with inherent powers or *facultés* to take the decision that

---

17 For a study of the conceptualization of "implied powers" of international organizations (distinctly from "inherent powers" of international tribunals), cf. A.A. Cançado Trindade, *Direito das Organizações Internacionais*, 6th. ed., Belo Horizonte/Brazil, Edit. Del Rey, 2014, pp. 7–135 and 645–646.

18 Like the ICJ, in Article 30 of its Statute.

ensures compliance with the provisional measures it has ordered, and thus the safeguard of the rights at stake" (para. 45). And I added:

> In such circumstances, an international tribunal cannot abstain from exercising its inherent power or *faculté* of supervision of compliance with its own Orders, in the interests of the sound administration of justice (*la bonne administration de la justice*). Non-compliance with Provisional Measures of Protection amounts to a breach of international obligations deriving from such measures. (...)
>
> (...) The Court is fully entitled to order *motu proprio* provisional measures which are totally or partially different from those requested by the contending parties. (...) The Court is fully entitled to order further provisional measures *motu proprio*; it does not need to wait for a request by a party to do so. (...) The Court has inherent powers or *facultés* to supervise *ex officio* compliance with Provisional Measures of Protection and thus to enhance their preventive dimension (paras. 63 and 70).

21. In another recent Separate Opinion, in the aforementioned case concerning the *Obligation to Negotiate Access to the Pacific Ocean*, opposing Bolivia to Chile, I have deemed it fit to stress that "the principle of the sound administration of justice (*la bonne administration de la justice*) permeates the considerations of all the (...) incidental proceedings before the Court, namely, preliminary objections, provisional measures of protection, counter-claims and intervention. As expected, general principles mark their presence, and guide, all Court proceedings" (para. 30). The principle of the sound administration of justice (*la bonne administration de la justice*) is always to be kept in mind by an international tribunal (cf. para. 67).

V The Teleological Interpretation (*Ut Res Magis Valeat Quam Pereat*) beyond State Consent

22. This brings me to the question of the teleological interpretation, pursuant to the principle of *effet utile*, or *ut res magis valeat quam pereat*. In my understanding, the teleological interpretation, which I support, covers not only material or substantive law (e.g., the rights vindicated and to be protected) but also jurisdictional issues and procedural law as well. May I briefly recall a couple of points I made, in this respect, in my Dissenting Opinion in the case concerning the *Application of the International Convention on the Elimination of All Forms of Racial Discrimination* (CERD – Georgia *versus* Russian Federation, Judgment

on Preliminary Objections of 01.04.2011). I pondered therein that, by virtue of the principle of *effet utile*,

> widely supported by case-law, States Parties to human rights treaties ought to secure to the conventional provisions *the appropriate effects* at the level of their respective domestic legal orders. Such principle (...) applies not only in relation to *substantive* norms of human rights treaties (that is, those which provide for the protected rights), but also in relation to *procedural* norms, in particular those relating to the right of individual petition and to the acceptance of the compulsory jurisdiction in contentious matters of the international judicial organs of protection. Such conventional norms, essential to the efficacy of the system of international protection, ought to be interpreted and applied in such a way as to render their safeguards truly practical and effective (...). Such has been, as I have already indicated (...), the approach pursued in practice by the ECtHR and the IACtHR (para. 79).

23. I then recalled a couple of relevant examples from the case-law of both international tribunals. For example, I singled out that in the case of *Loizidou versus Turkey* (Judgment on Preliminary Objections, of 23.03.1995), the ECtHR warned that,

> in the light of the letter and the spirit of the European Convention [of Human Rights] the possibility cannot be inferred of restrictions to the optional clause relating to the recognition of the contentious jurisdiction of the ECtHR.[19] In the domain of the international protection of human rights, there are no "implicit" limitations to the exercise of the protected rights; and the limitations set forth in the treaties of ojurisdiction of the international tribunals of human rights does not admit limitations other than those expressly contained in the human rights treaties at issue (para. 80).

24. I further recalled that, in the case of *Castillo Petruzzi and Others versus Peru* (Judgment of Preliminary Objections of 04.09.1998), the IACtHR also stated that it could not be at the mercy of limitations not foreseen in the American

---

[19] Cf. ECtHR, *Case of Loizidou versus Turkey* (Preliminary Objections), Strasbourg, C.E., Judgment of 23.03.1995, p. 25, para. 82, and cf. p. 22, para. 68. On the prevalence of the conventional obligations of the States Parties, cf. also the Court's *obiter dicta* in its previous decision, in the *Belilos versus Switzerland* case (1988).

Convention on Human Rights and invoked by the States Parties for reasons or vicissitudes of domestic order (para. 80).[20] And I added, in the same Dissenting Opinion in the aforementioned case concerning the *Application of the CERD Convention* (2011):

> The clause pertaining to the compulsory jurisdiction of international human rights tribunals constitutes, in my view, a fundamental clause (*cláusula pétrea*) of the international protection of the human being, which does not admit any restrictions other than those expressly provided for in the human rights treaties at issue. This has been so established by the IACtHR in its Judgments on competence in the cases of the *Constitutional Tribunal* and *Ivcher Bronstein versus Peru* (of 24.09.1999).[21] The permissiveness of the insertion of limitations, not foreseen in the human rights treaties, in an instrument of acceptance of an optional clause of compulsory jurisdiction, represents a regrettable historical distortion of the original conception of such clause, in my view unacceptable in the field of the international protection of the rights of the human person
>
> Any understanding to the contrary would fail to ensure that the human rights treaty at issue has the appropiate effects (*effet utile*) in the domestic law of each State Party. The IACtHR's decision in the case of *Hilaire versus Trinidad and Tobago* (preliminary objections, Judgment of 01.09.2001) was clear: the modalities of acceptance, by a State Party to the American Convention on Human Rights, of the contentious jurisdiction of the IACtHR, are expressly stipulated in Article 62 (1) and (2), and are not simply illustrative, but quite *precise*, not authorizing States Parties to interpose any other conditions or restrictions (*numerus clausus*).
>
> In my Concurring Opinion in the (...) *Hilaire versus Trinidad and Tobago* case, I saw it fit to ponder that
>
> > (...) we cannot abide by an international practice which has been subservient to State voluntarism, which has betrayed the spirit and purpose of the optional clause of compulsory jurisdiction, – to the point of entirely denaturalizing it, – and which has led to the perpetuation of a world fragmented into State units which regard themselves as final

---

20   As also upheld in the Concurring Opinion of Judge Cançado Trindade (paras. 36 and 38) appended thereto.

21   IACtHR, case of the *Constitutional Tribunal* (Competence), Judgment of 24.09.1999, p. 44, para. 35; IACtHR, case of *Ivcher Bronstein* (Competence), Judgment of 24.09.1999, p. 39, para. 36.

arbiters of the extent of the contracted international obligations, at the same time that they do not seem truly to believe in what they have accepted: the international justice (paras. 81–83).

25. In concluding my Dissenting Opinion in the case concerning the *Application of the CERD Convention*, I warned that

> This Court cannot keep on privileging State consent above everything, time and time again, even after such consent has already been given by States at the time of ratification of those treaties.
>
> The Court cannot keep on embarking on a literal or grammatical and static interpretation of the terms of compromissory clauses enshrined in those treaties, drawing "preconditions" therefrom for the exercise of its jurisdiction, in an attitude remindful of traditional international arbitral practice (paras. 205–206).

26. I further warned that the goal of the realization of justice "can hardly be attained from a strict State-centered voluntarist perspective, and a recurring search for State consent. This Court cannot, in my view, keep on paying lip service to what it assumes as representing the State's 'intentions' or 'will'" (para. 209). And I finally stated that

> The position and the thesis I sustain in the present Dissenting Opinion is that, when the ICJ is called upon to settle an inter-State dispute on the basis of a human rights treaty, (...) [t]he proper interpretation of human rights treaties (in the light of the canons of treaty interpretation of Articles 31–33 of the two Vienna Conventions on the Law of Treaties, of 1969 and 1986) covers, in my understanding, their *substantive as well as procedural provisions*, thus including a provision of the kind of the compromissory clause set forth in Article 22 of the CERD Convention. This is to the ultimate benefit of human beings, for whose protection human rights treaties have been celebrated, and adopted, by States. The *raison d'humanité* prevails over the old *raison d'État*.
>
> In the present Judgment, the Court entirely missed this point: it rather embarked on the usual exaltation of State consent, labelled, in paragraph 110, as "the fundamental principle of consent". I do not at all subscribe to its view, as, in my understanding, consent is not "fundamental", it is not even a "principle". What is "fundamental", i.e., what lays in the *foundations* of this Court, since its creation, is the imperative of the *realization of justice*, by means of compulsory jurisdiction. State consent is but a rule to be

observed (...). It is a means, not an end, it is a procedural requirement, not an element of treaty interpretation; it surely does not belong to the domain of the *prima principia*. This is what I have been endeavouring to demonstrate in the present Dissenting Opinion (paras. 210–211).

27. May I here again stress that, in my understanding, unlike what the ICJ has usually assumed, State consent is not at all a "fundamental principle", it is not even a "principle"; it is at most a rule (embodying a prerogative or concession to States) to be observed as the *initial* act of undertaking an international obligation. It is surely not an element of treaty interpretation. Once that initial act is performed, it does not condition the exercise of a tribunal's compulsory jurisdiction, which preexisted it and continues to operate unaffected by it.

VI   *Recta Ratio* above *Voluntas*, Human Conscience above the "Will"

28. *Recta ratio* surely stands above *voluntas*, human conscience above the "will". May I here further recall, in historical perspective, that the new *jus gentium*, as conceived by the "founding fathers" of the law of nations (as from the XVIth-century lessons of Francisco de Vitoria), was based on a *lex praeceptiva*, apprehended by human reason, and thus could not possibly derive from the "will" of subjects of law themselves (States and others). The way was thus paved for the apprehension of a true *jus necessarium*, transcending the limitations of the *jus voluntarium*. The lessons of the "founding fathers" of our discipline are perennial, are endowed with an impressive topicality.

29. Contrariwise, the voluntarist conception, obsessed with State consent or "will", has proven flawed, not only in the domain of law, but also in the realms of other branches of human knowledge. The attachment to power, oblivious of values, leads nowhere. As to international law, if, – as voluntarist positivists argue, – it is by the "will" of States that obligations are created, it is also by their "will" that they are violated, and one ends up revolving in vicious circles which are unable to explain the nature of international obligations. As to social sciences, so-called relativists cannot explain anything which does not fit into their *petitio principii*. And as to international relations and political science, so-called realists focus on the present (here and now), and cannot explain – nor forecast anything that suddenly changes in the international scenario; they thus have to readjust their minds to the new "reality". Definitively, it is inescapable that conscience stands above the "will".

30. Turning for a while to international legal doctrine, there were jurists who, throughout the last century, supported the primacy of human conscience over the "will" in the foundations of the law of nations, in the line of jusnaturalist thinking (going back to the lessons of Francisco de Vitoria, Francisco Suárez and Hugo Grotius, in the XVIth–XVIIth centuries). Thus, for example, in his posthumous book *La morale internationale* (1944), Nicolas Politis sustained that legality cannot prescind from justice, they both go together, so as to foster the progressive development of international law.[22]

31. Earlier on, in the same line of thinking, in his course delivered at the *Institut des Hautes Études Internationales* in Paris (1932–1933), Albert de La Pradelle (who had been a member of the Advisory Committee of Jurists which drafted the original Statute of the Permanent Court of International Justice [PCIJ] in 1920), warned that the strictly inter-State dimension is dangerous to the progressive development of international law; one ought to keep in mind also the human person, the peoples and humankind.[23]

32. In A. de La Pradelle's outlook, the *droit des gens* transcends the inter-State dimension, it is a *"droit de la communauté humaine"*, a true *"droit de l'humanité"*.[24] Hence the utmost importance of the general principles of law, which ultimately guide the progressive development of international law.[25] The learned jurist added that there is "surely a natural law", which, nowadays,

> doit être considéré comme étant un droit rationnel qui exprime les réquisitions de la conscience juridique de l'heure. Or, la conscience juridique de l'humanité devient de plus en plus complexe, précise, elle est de plus en plus nuancée, ses exigences deviennent avec le temps de plus en plus fortes. C'est un effet de la culture générale, de la civilisation, du progrès des idées; il ne faut donc pas considérer le droit naturel ou rationnel comme étant un droit immuable qui est fixé dès l'origine et qui ne change pas. Si, il change, mais ces changements ne sont pas des changements

---

22   N. Politis, *La morale internationale*, N.Y., Brentano's, 1944, pp. 157–158, 161 and 165. In invoking the ancient Greeks, in particular Euripides, he pondered that whoever commits an injustice, "est plus malheureux que ne l'est sa victime"; *ibid.*, p. 102.
23   A. de La Pradelle, *Droit international public* [Cours sténographié], Paris, Institut des Hautes Études Internationales, 1932–1933, pp. 25, 33, 37 and 40–41.
24   *Ibid.*, pp. 49, 149 and 264.
25   *Ibid.*, pp. 222 and 413.

de caprice, ces changements constituent une évolution, cette évolution accompagne celle de l'humanité.[26]

33. In the same perspective, Max Huber (a former Judge of the PCIJ), in his book *La pensée et l'action de la Croix Rouge* (1954), wrote that international law is also turned to basic human values, which it ought to protect: this is the true *jus gentium*, from a jusnaturalist, rather than positivist, conception.[27] It thus represents the *"droit de l'humanité"*.[28] This outlook goes well beyond inter-State interests, beholding humankind as a whole.

34. The idea of *civitas maxima gentium*, as conceived by the classic international legal philosophers, – M. Huber proceeded, – is projected into the U.N. Charter itself, which is, on ethical grounds, attentive to peoples and the human person (proper of the *droit des gens*). The international juridical conscience, to his mind, has acknowledged the need to pursue the "humanization" of international law,[29] – a historical process which is, in my own perception, gradually advancing in our times.[30]

35. Likewise, Alejandro Álvarez (a former Judge of the ICJ), in his book *El Nuevo Derecho Internacional en Sus Relaciones con la Vida Actual de los Pueblos* (1962), also wrote that "the universal juridical conscience" plays a very important role in the evolution of international law;[31] it is therefrom that international norms and precepts emanate.[32] In his view, general principles of law much contribute to the formation of a universal international law.[33]

36. Earlier on, in his Dissenting Opinion in the *Anglo-Iranian Oil Company* case (preliminary objections, Judgment of 22.07.1952), Judge Álvarez expressed his

---

26 *Ibid.*, p. 412.
27 M. Huber, *La pensée et l'action de la Croix Rouge*, Genève, CICR, 1954, pp. 26 and 247.
28 *Ibid.*, p. 270.
29 *Ibid.*, pp. 286, 291–293 and 304.
30 Cf. A.A. Cançado Trindade, *A Humanização do Direito Internacional*, 2ª. ed., Belo Horizonte/Brazil, Edit. Del Rey, 2015, pp. 3–789; A.A Cançado Trindade, *La Humanización del Derecho Internacional Contemporáneo*, Mexico, Edit. Porrúa, 2014, pp. 1–324; A.A. Cançado Trindade, *Los Tribunales Internacionales Contemporáneos y la Humanización del Derecho Internacional*, Buenos Aires, Ed. Ad-Hoc, 2013, pp. 7–185.
31 A. Álvarez, *El Nuevo Derecho Internacional en Sus Relaciones con la Vida Actual de los Pueblos* [*The New International Law in Its Relations with the Life of the Peoples*], Santiago de Chile, Editorial Jurídica de Chile, 1962, pp. 49, 57 and 77.
32 *Ibid.*, pp. 155–156 and 356–357.
33 *Ibid.*, pp. 163 and 292.

opposition to a restrictive interpretation of Article 36 of the Statute of the ICJ (pp. 131 and 134) and to the voluntarist conception of international law (pp. 127 and 133). To him, rights under international law "do not result from the will of States", but from human conscience (p. 130).

37. Still in the same line of thinking, in his course delivered at the Hague Academy of International Law in 1960, Stefan Glaser likewise sustained that the norms of the law of nations emanate from human conscience (*recta ratio*), conforming natural justice, independently of the "will" of States. There is an assimilation of moral duties to legal duties, and general principles of law (*pacta sunt servanda, bona fides*) are endowed with the utmost importance; the foundation of international law is essentially ethical.[34] In effect, – may I here add, – *pacta sunt servanda* and *bona fides* are precepts which ensue from natural reason, and are deeply-rooted in natural law thinking.

38. For my part, the present Judgment in the case of *Alleged Violations of Sovereign Rights and Maritime Spaces in the Caribbean Sea* is not the first time when, within the ICJ, I express my concerns as to its undue reliance on State voluntarism. I have likewise done so on earlier occasions as well. Thus, in my extensive Dissenting Opinion in the case of the *Jurisdictional Immunities of the State* (Judgment of 03.02.2012), I cared to rescue some forgotten doctrinal trends nowadays, which, in the mid-XXth century, focused on *fundamental human values*, so as to make the *droit des gens* evolve well beyond the strict inter-State dimension, into a *droit de l'humanité* (paras. 32–40). *Recta ratio* stands above *voluntas*, human conscience stands above the "will".

39. In the same line of thinking, in my lengthy Dissenting Opinion in the aforementioned case concerning the *Application of the CERD Convention* (Judgment of 01.04.2011), I examined the historical development of the professed ideal of compulsory jurisdiction, which originally inspired the optional clause (of Article 36(2) of the ICJ Statute), and the following distorted State practice of inserting, in declarations of its acceptance, restrictions of all kinds, militating against its *rationale*, and, in a display of sheer voluntarism, denaturalizing that clause and depriving it of all efficacy (paras. 37–43 and 45–63).

40. Before moving into compromissory clauses (paras. 64ss.), I then added that, with this distorted practice, and the opportunity missed in the elaboration of

---

34 S. Glaser, "Culpabilité en droit international pénal", 99 *Recueil des Cours de l'Académie de Droit International de La Haye* (1960) pp. 561–563, 566–567, 582–583 and 585.

the Statute of the new ICJ in 1945 to put an end to it and thus to enhance compulsory jurisdiction,

> One abandoned the very basis of the compulsory jurisdiction of the ICJ to an outdated voluntarist conception of International Law, which had prevailed at the beginning of the last century, despite the warnings of lucid jurists of succeeding generations as to its harmful consequences to the conduction of international relations. Yet, a considerable part of the legal profession continued to stress the overall importance of individual State *consent*, regrettably putting it well above the imperatives of the realization of justice at international level (para. 44).

41. It seems most regrettable that, still in our days, the obsession with reliance on State consent remains present in legal practice and international adjudication, apparently by force of mental inertia. In my perception, it is hard to avoid the impression that, if one still keeps on giving pride of place to State voluntarism, we will not move beyond the pre-history of judicial settlement of disputes between States, in which we still live. May I here reiterate that *recta ratio* stands above *voluntas*, human conscience stands above the "will".

VII   *Compétence de la Compétence / Kompetenz Kompetenz* beyond State Consent

42. In the same line of thinking (beholding conscience above the "will"), in my address delivered on 01.11.2000 at the Rome Conference on the Cinquentenary of the European Convention of Human Rights, in recalling the aforementioned decisions of the ECtHR in the case of *Loizidou* (1995), and of the IACtHR in the cases of the *Constitutional Tribunal* and of *Ivcher Bronstein* (1999), I pondered that

> Both the European and Inter-American Courts have rightly set limits to State voluntarism, have safeguarded the integrity of the respective human rights Conventions and the primacy of considerations of *ordre public* over the will of individual States, have set higher standards of State behaviour and established some degree of control over the interposition of undue restrictions by States, and have reassuringly enhanced the position of individuals as subjects of the International Law of Human Rights, with full procedural capacity. [/ Tant la Cour Européenne que la Cour Interaméricaine ont, à juste titre, posé des limites au volontarisme de

l'État, sauvegardé l'intégrité de leurs Conventions des Droits de l'Homme respectives et la primauté des considérations d'ordre public sur la volonté des États individuels, fixé des critères plus élevés de comportement des États et instauré un certain degré de contrôle d'éventuelles restrictions abusives de la part de ces derniers, et amélioré, de manière rassurante, la situation des individus en tant que sujets du Droit International des Droits de l'Homme, les dotant de pleine capacité procédurale].[35]

43. International tribunals have the power to determine their own jurisdiction.[36] And international human rights tribunals (like the IACtHR and the ECtHR), in particular, – the case-law of which has been invoked by the contending parties in the course of the proceedings before the ICJ in the present case of *Alleged Violations of Sovereign Rights and Maritime Spaces in the Caribbean Sea* (cf. *supra*), – have succeeded in liberating themselves from the chains of State consent, and have thereby succeeded in preserving the integrity of their respective jurisdictions. They have consistently pursued a teleological interpretation, have asserted their *compétence de la compétence*, and have exercised their inherent powers.

44. Had they not taken the decisions they took, in the aforementioned cases of *Loizidou*, of the *Constitutional Tribunal* and of *Ivcher Bronstein*, the consequences would have been disastrous for their respective jurisdictions, and they would have deprived the respective Conventions of their *effet utile*. They rightly understood that their *compétence de la compétence*, and their inherent powers, are not constrained by State consent; otherwise, they would simply not be able to impart justice. In the *Loizidou* case, the ECtHR discarded the possibility of inferring restrictions to its jurisdiction. In the *Constitutional Tribunal* and *Ivcher Bronstein* cases,[37] the IACtHR exercised its inherent power to

---

35 A.A. Cançado Trindade, "The Contribution of the Work of the International Human Rights Tribunals to the Development of Public International Law / La contribution de l'oeuvre des Cours internationales des droits de l'homme au développement du Droit international public", in: Council of Europe, *The European Convention of Human Rights at 50* (50 *Human Rights Information Bulletin* (2000) pp. 8–9) / Conseil de l'Europe, *La Convention Européenne des Droits de l'Homme à 50 ans* (50 *Bulletin d'information des droits de l'homme* (2000) pp. 8–9).

36 For a general study, cf., e.g., I.F.I. Shihata, *The Power of the International Court to Determine Its Own Jurisdiction – Compétence de la Compétence*, The Hague, Nijhoff, 1965, pp. 1–304.

37 And also in the *Hilaire, Benjamin and Constantine* case (Preliminary Objections, 2001).

uphold its own jurisdiction, and discarded the respondent State's attempt to "withdraw" unilaterally from it.

45. Those two international tribunals opposed the voluntarist posture, and insisted on their *compétence de la compétence*, as guardians and masters of their respective jurisdictions. The ECtHR and the IACtHR contributed to the primacy of considerations of *ordre public* over the subjective voluntarism of States. They did not hesitate to exercise their inherent powers, and thereby decidedly preserved the integrity of the bases of their respective jurisdictions. In sum, for taking such position of principle, the IACtHR and the ECtHR rightly found that conscience stands above the will.

46. As to international criminal tribunals, it may be recalled that, in the *D. Tadić* case, the *ad hoc* International Criminal Tribunal for the Former Yugoslavia (ICTY – Appeals Chamber) held (Decision of 02.10.1995) that jurisdiction

> is basically – as is visible from the Latin origin of the word itself, *jurisdiction* – a legal power, hence necessarily a legitimate power, "to state the law" (*dire le droit*) within this ambit, in an authoritative and final manner. This is the meaning which it carries in all legal systems (para. 10).

47. The ICTY (Appeals Chamber) added that in international law a narrow concept of jurisdiction is unwarranted; it warned that limitations to an international tribunal cannot be presumed and, "in any case, they cannot be deduced from the concept of jurisdiction itself" (para. 11). In upholding its jurisdiction in a broad sense, it understood that the ICTY's jurisdiction was not limited to those powers the Security Council intended to entrust it with, but it also encompassed the Tribunal's own inherent powers (cf. paras. 14–15). The ICTY relied on its own *compétence de la compétence* in order to assert its power even to review the validity of its own establishment by the Security Council (cf. paras. 18–22).

VIII Inherent Powers Overcoming *Lacunae*, and the Relevance of General Principles

48. International tribunals have made use of their inherent powers or *facultés* in distinct situations. An example, of almost two decades ago, can be found in the decision of the IACtHR in the case of *Genie Lacayo versus Nicaragua*

(Resolution of 13.09.1997), in respect of an appeal for revision of a judgment. In my Dissenting Opinion appended thereto, I pondered that

> The present appeal before the Inter-American Court [IACtHR] is unprecedented in its history: (...) in the present *Genie Lacayo* case the Court is for the first time called upon to pronounce on an appeal of *revision of a judgment*, (...) for which there is no provision either in the American Convention [on Human Rights – ACHR], or in its Statute or Regulations. The silence of these instruments on the question is not to be interpreted as amounting to *vacatio legis*, with the consequence of the inadmissibility of that appeal. (...) The fact that no provision is made for it in the ACHR or in its Statute or Regulations does not prevent the IACtHR from declaring *admissible* an appeal of revision of a judgment: the apparent *vacatio legis* ought in this particular to give way to an imperative of natural justice (paras. 2 and 6).

49. Drawing attention to the importance of general principles of law also in the present context, I then added that

> The Court ought thus to decide (...) on the basis – in application of the principle *jura novit curia* – of general principles of procedural law, and making use of the *powers inherent* to its judicial function. Human beings, and the institutions they integrate, are not infallible, and there is no jurisdiction worthy of this name which does not admit the possibility – albeit exceptional – of revision of a judgment, be it at international law level, or at domestic law level (para. 7).

50. The IACtHR itself acknowledged, in its aforementioned decision in the case *Genie Lacayo*, that its inherent power to consider, in special cases, an appeal for revision of a judgment, is in line with "the general principles of procedural law, both domestic and international" (para. 9). This is just one of the possible situations of recourse to inherent powers; there are several others, pertaining, e.g., *inter alia*, to the due process of law, or else to the award of reparations. The relevant case-law of international criminal tribunals provides illustrations of it.

51. As to the due process of law, the *ad hoc* International Criminal Tribunal for Rwanda (ICTR – Trial Chamber III), for example, in the *A. Rwamakuba* case, upheld (Decision of 31.01.2007) the Tribunal's

inherent power to provide an accused or former accused with an effective remedy for violations of his or her human rights while being prosecuted or tried before this Tribunal. Such power (...) is essential both for the carrying out of its judicial functions and for complying with its obligation to respect generally accepted international human rights norms (para. 49).

In the same *Rwamakuba* case, the ICTR (Appeals Chamber) added (Decision of 13.09.2007) that its inherent power extends, in appropriate circumstances, to ordering compensation, "proportional to the gravity of the harm" suffered (para. 27).

52. For its part, the International Criminal Court (ICC Trial Chamber V-A), in the case of *W.S. Ruto and J.A. Sang* (*Situation in the Republic of Kenya*, Decision of 17.04.2014), observed that it may use such power[38] so as "to preserve its judicial integrity" (para. 80); that power is "essential for the exercise of its primary jurisdiction or the performance of its essential duties and functions" (para. 81). The ICC (Trial Chamber) added that it can make use of that power, e.g., to order the attendance of witnesses.[39]

53. On its turn, in the *J. Bobetko* case, the ICTY (Appeals Chamber) held (Decision of 29.11.2002) that the ICTY "has an inherent power to stay proceedings which are an abuse of process", so as to fulfil the Tribunal's need "to exercise effectively the jurisdiction which it has to dispose of the proceedings" (para. 15). Subsequently, the ICTY (Appeals Chamber) further stated, in its Decision (of 01.09.2005) in the *R. Stanković* case, that the Tribunal's inherent powers encompass the rendering of orders "reasonably related" to the task before it, deriving from the exercise itself of the judicial function (para. 51).

54. More recently, in the *F. Hartmann* case, a specially appointed Chamber of the ICTY recalled (Judgment of 14.09.2009) that the ICTY has the "inherent power" to "hold in contempt those who knowingly and wilfully interfere with its administration of justice" (para. 19). Such inherent power, – it added, – is firmly established in the *jurisprudence constante* of the ICTY, so as to ensure that a "conduct which obstructs, prejudices or abuses the administration of justice" is punished (para. 18).

---

38 Meaning "inherent" power, though using the term "implied" power.
39 Cf. paras. 87–89, 91, 100, 104 and 110–111.

55. For its part, the Special Tribunal for Lebanon (STL Appeals Chamber), likewise, in its Decision (of 10.11.2010) in the matter of *J. El-Sayed*, extensively dwelt upon the exercise of inherent powers,[40] so as to secure the fairness of proceedings (paras. 15, 48 and 52), the equality of arms (para. 17), and, in sum, the due process of law (paras. 49 and 52). As it can be seen, such pronouncements of distinct international criminal tribunals all point to the same direction, in so far as inherent powers are concerned.

56. The relevant international case-law on the matter has lately drawn the attention, also of expert writing, to the use of inherent powers by international tribunals in order to fill *lacunae* of their *interna corporis*.[41] There seems, in effect, to be general acknowledgment nowadays of the multiplicity of possible situations of the use of inherent powers by international tribunals, keeping in mind in particular the distinct functions proper to each international tribunal.

57. Although the International Tribunal for the Law of the Sea (ITLOS), for its part, has not explicitly addressed to date the issue of its inherent powers, it goes without saying that, as an international tribunal, it is vested with them, for the exercise of its judicial function pertaining to the U.N. Convention on the Law of the Sea. In effect, some of its Judges have expressly referred to the inherent powers of ITLOS, in their Separate Opinions appended to its Judgments in two successive cases (namely, the cases of *M/V "SAIGA"* (n. 2), Saint Vincent and Grenadines *versus* Guinea, Judgment of 01.07.1999; and of *M/V "Louisa"*, Saint Vincent and Grenadines *versus* Spain, Judgment of 28.05.2013).

58. In short, contemporary international tribunals have resorted to the inherent powers which appear to them necessary to the proper exercise of their respective judicial functions. They have shown their preparedness to make use of their inherent powers (in deciding on matters of jurisdiction, or handling of evidence, or else merits and reparations), and have not seldom made use of them, in distinct situations, in order to secure a proper and sound administration of justice.

---

40   Cf. paras. 2, 15, 17, 43, 45–49, 52, 54 and 56.
41   Cf., *inter alia*, e.g., P. Gaeta, "Inherent Powers of International Courts and Tribunals", *in Man's Inhumanity to Man – Essays on International Law in Honour of A. Cassese* (eds. L.C. Vohrah, F. Pocar *et alii*), The Hague, Kluwer, 2003, pp. 359 and 364–367; C. Brown, "The Inherent Powers of International Courts and Tribunals", 76 *British Year Book of International Law* (2005) pp. 203, 215, 221, 224 and 244.

IX   Inherent Powers and *Juris Dictio*, beyond Transactional Justice

59. Ultimately, the concern of international tribunals is to endow their own respective judicial functions with the inherent powers needed to ensure the proper and sound administration of justice. Thus, in the case of *Z. Mucić, H. Delić and E. Landžo*, the ICTY (Appeals Chamber, Judgment of 08.04.2003) stated that, besides its express powers, it has also inherent powers, "deriving from its judicial function", so as "to control its proceedings in such a way as to ensure that justice is done" (para. 16). They include the inherent power to reconsider any of its own decisions, so as "to prevent an injustice" (para. 49). In its administration of justice, it has an inherent power "to ensure that its proceedings do not lead to injustice" (para. 50).[42]

60. In the same line of thinking, in the case of *S. Hinga Norman, M. Fofana and A. Kondewa*, the Special Court for Sierra Leone (SCSL – Appeals Chamber) explained (Decision of 17.01.2005) that, although the inherent power of a court cannot be exercised against the express provisions of its Rules, it can be so when the Rules are silent (para. 41). A tribunal – as acknowledged in the jurisprudence of the ICTY – can have recourse to its inherent power "to reconsider *its own decision* to avoid injustice or miscarriage of justice" (para. 40).[43]

61. As it can be seen from the preceding paragraphs (Sections VII–VIII), contemporary international tribunals have made statements in support of their exercise of inherent powers for the proper performance of their international judicial function. This becomes even clearer in the understanding that their task goes beyond peaceful settlement of disputes, as they also *say what the Law is (juris dictio)*. Contemporary international human rights tribunals as well as international criminal tribunals have espoused this outlook in the exercise of their respective judicial functions.

62. In this connection, on the occasion of the commemoration by the ICJ of the centenary of the Peace Palace at The Hague (2013), I had the occasion, in my address, to point out that, parallel to the traditional conception (still prevailing in some circles at the Peace Palace) whereby an international tribunal is "to limit itself to settle the dispute at issue and to handle its resolution of it to the contending parties (a form of transactional justice), addressing only what the parties had put before it", there is another conception,

---

42   And cf. also paras. 52–53.
43   And cf. also para. 34.

a larger one, – the one I sustain, – whereby the tribunal has to go beyond that, and say what the Law is (*juris dictio*), thus contributing to the settlement of other like situations as well, and to the progressive development of international law. In the interpretation itself – or even in the search – of the applicable law, there is space for judicial creativity; each international tribunal is free to find the applicable law, independently of the arguments of the contending parties (*juria novit curia*).[44]

63. There is support for this larger conception in the relevant case-law of international human rights tribunals and international criminal tribunals. Already in its Judgment of 18.01.1978, in the landmark case of *Ireland versus United Kingdom*, the plenary of the ECtHR stated that its functions were not only to decide or settle the cases lodged with it, but more generally also to apply, "elucidate" and "develop" the norms of the European Convention, thus contributing to the observance by States Parties of the engagements undertaken by them (para. 154).

64. Two and a half decades later the ECtHR (First Section) made the same point in its Judgment of 24.07.2003, in the case of *Karner versus Austria*, adding that it could elucidate and develop the *corpus juris* of the European Convention, as its mission, besides settling individual cases, also comprised raising human rights standards of human rights protection and extending its own jurisprudence throughout the community of States Parties to the Convention (para. 26).

65. The IACtHR, likewise going beyond dispute-settlement only, has taken the same wide outlook of its *juris dictio*, in its *jurisprudence constante*. This is significant, considering that there have been circumstances wherein the judgments of international tribunals (particularly the ECtHR and the IACtHR) have had repercussions beyond the States parties to a case, in other States Parties to the respective Conventions.[45]

---

44 A.A. Cançado Trindade, "A Century of International Justice and Prospects for the Future", in: *A Century of International Justice and Prospects for the Future / Rétrospective d'un siècle de justice internationale et perspectives d'avenir* (eds. A.A. Cançado Trindade and D. Spielmann), Oisterwijk, Wolf Publs., 2013, p. 16, para. 40.

45 *Ibid.*, p. 16, para. 41.

66. This is, furthermore, implicit in the notion of "pilot judgments/*arrêts pilotes*" in the work of the ECtHR.[46] This outlook (such as the one pursued by both the IACtHR and the ECtHR) gives greater importance to the reasoning of the tribunals and the exercise of their inherent powers, well beyond the stricter traditional conception of transactional justice. In settling disputes and saying what the Law is, international tribunals have exercised their inherent powers and endeavoured to secure the proper administration of justice, in facing new challenges. International tribunals have thus enabled themselves to contribute to the progressive development of international law.[47]

X   Inherent Powers and Supervision of Compliance with Judgments

67. May I now turn to another point raised in the course of the proceedings of the present case of *Alleged Violations of Sovereign Rights and Maritime Spaces in the Caribbean Sea*, namely, that of inherent powers in relation to compliance with judgments of the ICJ. The point was raised by the two contending parties, on distinct grounds,[48] in relation of Colombia's fifth preliminary objection. The fact that an international tribunal can count on the assistance of another supervisory organ for seeking compliance with its own judgments and decisions, in my view does not mean that, once it renders its judgment or decision, it can remain indifferent as to its compliance. Not at all.

---

46 As from the rendering of its Judgment of 22.06.2004 in the case of *Broniowski versus Poland*.

47 Cf., in this respect, the books by: H. Lauterpacht, *The Development of International Law by the International Court*, London, Stevens, 1958, pp. 3–400; A.A. Cançado Trindade, *Os Tribunais Internacionais e a Realização da Justiça*, Rio de Janeiro, Edit. Renovar, 2015, pp. 1–507; J.G. Merrills, *The Development of International Law by the European Court of Human Rights*, 2nd ed., Manchester, University Press, 1993, pp. 1–255; A.A. Cançado Trindade, *El Ejercicio de la Función Judicial Internacional – Memorias de la Corte Interamericana de Derechos Humanos*, 3rd ed., Belo Horizonte/Brazil, Edit. Del Rey, 2013, pp. 1–409; L.J. van den Herik, *The Contribution of the Rwanda Tribunal to the Development of International Law*, Leiden, Nijhoff, 2005, pp. 1–284; [Various Authors,] *The Development of International Law by the International Court of Justice* (eds. C.J. Tams and J. Sloan), Oxford, Oxford University Press, 2013, pp. 3–396; and cf. M. Lachs, "The Development and General Trends of International Law in Our Time", 169 *Recueil des Cours de l'Académie de Droit International de La Haye* (1980) pp. 245–246, 248–249 and 251.

48 Cf. submissions *in*: ICJ doc. CR 2015/22, of 28.09.2015, pp. 60–62, paras. 1, 3 and 8 (Colombia); ICJ doc. CR 2015/23, of 29.09.2015, pp. 46–50 and 54, paras. 4–5, 9, 12, 14–15 and 23 (Nicaragua); ICJ doc. CR 2015/24, of 30.09.2015, p. 37, para. 23 (Colombia); ICJ doc. CR 2015/25, of 02.10.2015, pp. 37–43, paras. 12–19 and 22 (Nicaragua).

68. The fact, for example, that Article 94(2) of the U.N. Charter entrusts the Security Council with the enforcement of ICJ judgments and decisions, does not mean that compliance with them ceases to be a concern of the Court. Not at all. Moreover, the Security Council has, in practice, very seldom done anything at all in that respect, except in the *Nicaragua versus United States* case (1986).[49] Pursuant to Article 94(1) of the U.N. Charter, non-compliance amounts to an additional breach; hence the importance of avoiding that, and of securing compliance. In my view, compliance with their judgments and decisions remains a concern of the ICJ as well as of all other international tribunals.

69. In the case of the ICJ in particular, it has been mistakenly assumed that it is not the Court's business to secure compliance with its own judgments and decisions. Even if one invokes the silence of the Statute in this respect, or else Article 94(2) of the U.N. Charter, this latter does *not* confer an *exclusive* authority to the Security Council to secure that compliance. On the contrary, a closer look at some provisions of the Statute[50] shows that the Court is entitled to occupy itself with compliance with its own judgments and decisions.[51]

70. What is thus to be criticized, in my view, is not judicial law-making (as often said without reflection), but rather judicial inactivism or absenteeism, – in particular in respect of ensuring compliance with judgments and decisions. In this connection, before considering whether recourse could be made to domestic courts to seek such compliance, further attention should be devoted conceptually to the role of the ICJ itself, and of other international tribunals, in securing compliance with their own judgments and decisions.

71. The practice of the ECtHR (which counts on the assistance of the Committee of Ministers) and of the IACtHR (which has resorted to post-adjudicative hearings, ever since its landmark Judgment, of 28.11.2003, in the case of *Baena Ricardo and Others versus Panama*) provides useful elements to this effect. In the course of the proceedings before the ICJ in the present case of *Alleged*

---

49 Cf. C. Schulte, *Compliance with Decisions of the International Court of Justice*, Oxford, Oxford University Press, 2004, pp. 38–40, 42 and 63, and cf. p. 68 (as to the General Assembly), p. 70 (as to the Secretary-General), and pp. 77 and 79 (as to domestic courts).
50 Articles 41, 57, 60 and 61(3).
51 Cf. M. Al-Qahtani, "The Role of the International Court of Justice in the Enforcement of Its Judicial Decisions", 15 *Leiden Journal of International Law* (2002) pp. 781–783, 786, 792, 796 and 803.

Violations of Sovereign Rights and Maritime Spaces in the Caribbean Sea, the IACtHR's decision in the case of *Blake versus Guatemala* (Order of 27.11.2003) was invoked, when it asserted the Court's inherent powers "to monitor compliance with its decisions" (para. 1).[52]

72. The powers of the Committee of Ministers to supervise the execution of the ECtHR's judgments, in any case, are not exclusive; the Court itself can be concerned with it, as the ECtHR (Grand Chamber) acknowledged in its judgments, e.g., in the cases of *Verein gegen Tierfabriken Schweiz (VgT) versus Switzerland* (of 30.06.2009), and of *Bochan versus Ukraine* (of 05.02.2015). In sum, in my understanding, no international tribunal can remain indifferent to non-compliance with its own judgments. The inherent powers of international tribunals extend to this domain as well, so as to ensure that their judgments and decisions are duly complied with.

73. In doing so, international tribunals are preserving the integrity of their own respective jurisdictions. Surprisingly, international legal doctrine has not yet dedicated sufficient attention to this particular issue. This is regrettable, as compliance with judgments and decisions of international tribunals is a key factor to foster the rule of law in the international community.[53] And, from 2006 onwards, the topic of *"the rule of law at the national and international levels"* has remained present in the agenda of the U.N. General Assembly,[54] and has been attracting increasing attention of member States, year after year.

74. It appears, thus, paradoxical, that a greater general awareness has not yet awakened as to the relevance of compliance with judgments and decisions of international tribunals. The present case, before the ICJ, of *Alleged Violations of Sovereign Rights and Maritime Spaces in the Caribbean Sea*, has, in my perception, brought to the fore the need to dispense much greater attention to the issue of such compliance, as related to the inherent powers of international tribunals. Those jurists who are genuinely concerned with, and engaged in,

---

52   *Cit. in*: ICJ, doc. CR 2015/23, of 29.09.2015, p. 54, para. 23 (Nicaragua).
53   Cf., recently, e.g., A.A. Cançado Trindade, "Prologue: An Overview of the Contribution of International Tribunals to the Rule of Law", *in*: *The Contribution of International and Supranational Courts to the Rule of Law* (eds. G. De Baere and J. Wouters), Cheltenham/Northhampton, E. Elgar, 2015, pp. 3–18.
54   Cf. General Assembly resolutions 61/39, of 04.12.2006; 62/70, of 06.12.2007; 63/128, of 11.12.2008; 64/116, of 16.12.2009; 65/32, of 06.12.2010; 66/102, of 09.12.2011; 67/97, of 14.12.2012; 68/116, of 16.12.2013; 69/123, of 10.12.2014; and 70/118, of 14.12.2015.

the realization of justice (they are not so many), can contribute to it; the legal profession, distinctly, remains more interested in strategies of litigation and "winning cases" only.

75. The path to justice is a long one, and not much has been achieved to date as to the proper conceptualization of the supervision of compliance with judgments and decisions of international tribunals. Instead, the force of mental inertia has persisted throughout decades. It is time to overcome this absenteeism and passiveness. Supervision of such compliance is, after all, a jurisdictional issue. An international tribunal cannot at all remain indifferent as to compliance with its own judgments and decisions.

XI   Epilogue

76. Having addressed this point of inherent powers in relation to compliance with judgments of the ICJ, brought before the Court (on distinct grounds) by Nicaragua and Colombia, I come now to my last words in the present Separate Opinion. As pointed out in the preceding pages, the Court's handling of the question raised by the fourth preliminary objection of Colombia does not reflect the richness of the proceedings in the *cas d'espèce*, and of the arguments presented before the ICJ (in the written and oral phases) by both Nicaragua and Colombia.

77. Their submissions should, in my view, have been fully taken into account expressly in the present Judgment, even if likewise to dismiss the fourth preliminary objection at the end. After all, the parties' submissions in the present case of *Alleged Violations of Sovereign Rights and Maritime Spaces in the Caribbean Sea*, raise an important question, recurrently put before the Court, which continues to require our reflection so as to endeavour to enhance the realization of justice at international level.

78. The fact that the Court has found, in the present Judgment, that it has jurisdiction under the Pact of Bogotá (dismissing Colombia's first preliminary objection) did not preclude it from having considered the arguments of the two contending parties on such an important issue as its inherent powers or *facultés* (to pronounce on the alleged non-compliance with its 2012 Judgment).[55]

---

55   Cf. paras. 16 and 101 of the present Judgment.

I have felt obliged to do so, even if considering that the fourth preliminary objection is unsustainable and was thus to be likewise dismissed, rather than having simply said in an elusive way that "there is no ground" to pronounce upon it.[56]

79. Contemporary international tribunals exercise inherent powers beyond State consent, thus contributing to the sound administration of justice (*la bonne administration de la justice*). There are examples (cf. *supra*) of assertion of their *Kompetenz Kompetenz* (*compétence de la compétence*); this latter has proven of relevance to the exercise of the international judicial function. There are illustrations of their pursuance of the teleological interpretation beyond State consent. The use of inherent powers by contemporary international tribunals beyond State consent, has also aimed at filling *lacunae* in their *interna corporis*, drawing attention to the relevance of general principles.

80. In upholding the exercise of inherent powers for the proper performance of their international judicial function, contemporary international tribunals have given support to the conception of their work – which I sustain – of going beyond dispute-settlement (transactional justice), further *to say what the law is* (*juris dictio*). Moreover, the attention of contemporary international tribunals extends to the monitoring of compliance with their decisions, which is a jurisdictional issue.

81. The inherent powers of international tribunals extend to this particular domain as well, to the supervision of execution of their judgments. In doing so, they are preserving the integrity of their own respective jurisdictions; after all, – as I have pointed out, – no international tribunal can remain indifferent to non-compliance with its own judgments. This is essential, so as to foster the *rule of law* in the international community, – a topic which has remained present, with growing attention on the part of U.N. member States, in the agenda of the U.N. General Assembly throughout the last decade.

82. Last but not least, the consideration, in the present Separate Opinion, of the exercise, in its distinct aspects, by contemporary international tribunals, of their inherent powers or *facultés*, has prompted me to bring to the fore my understanding that *recta ratio* stands above *voluntas*. There is need to overcome the voluntarist conception of international law. There is need of

---

56   Cf. para. 104 and resolutory point 1(e) of the *dispositif* of the present Judgment.

a greater awareness of the primacy of conscience above the "will", and of a constant attention to fundamental human values, so as to secure the progressive development of international law, and, ultimately, to foster the realization of justice at international level.

>(Signed) *Antônio Augusto C̣ançado Trindade*
>Judge

CHAPTER 2

The Universal Juridical Conscience,
Humaneness and the Condemnation of Genocide

Dissenting Opinion in the case of the *Application of the Convention against Genocide* (Croatia *versus* Serbia, Judgment of 03.02.2015)

Table of Contents   Paragraphs

I.   *Prolegomena*..1–5
II. The Regrettable Delays in the Adjudication of the Present Case
     1. Procedural Delays 6–13
     2. *Justitia Longa, Vita Brevis* 14–18
III. Jurisdiction: Automatic Succession to the Genocide Convention as a Human Rights Treaty
     1. Arguments of the Parties as to the Applicability for the Obligations under the Genocide Convention Prior to 27.04.1992 19–21
     2. Continuity of Application of the Genocide Convention (SFRY and FRY)..22–23
     3. Continuity of State Administration and Officials (SFRY and FRY) 24–25
     4. Law Governing State Succession to Human Rights Treaties: *Ipso Jure* Succession to the Genocide Convention..... 26–33
     5. State Conduct in Support of Automatic Succession to, and Continuing Applicability of, the Genocide Convention (to FRY Prior to 27.04.1992) 34–36
     6. *Venire contra Factum Proprium Non Valet* 37–41
     7. Automatic Succession to Human Rights Treaties in the Practice of United Nations Supervisory Organs 42–49
IV. The Essence of the Present Case
     1. Arguments of the Contending Parties............................. 50–52
     2. General Assessment 53–54
V.   Automatic Succession to the Convention against Genocide, and Continuity of Its Obligations, as an Imperative of Humaneness
     1. The Convention against Genocide and the Imperative of Humaneness... 55–64
     2. The Principle of Humanity in Its Wide Dimension 65–72
     3. The Principle of Humanity in the Heritage of Jusnaturalist Thinking...73–76
     4. Judicial Recognition of the Principle of Humanity 77–82
     5. Concluding Observations... 83–84

VI.	The Convention against Genocide and State Responsibility
	1. Legislative History of the Convention (Article IX) 85–91
	2. Rationale, and Object and Purpose of the Convention 92–95
VII.	Standard of Proof in the Case-Law of International Human Rights Tribunals 96
	1. A Question from the Bench: The Evolving Case-Law on the Matter 97–99
	2. Case-Law of the IACtHR
	a) Cases Disclosing a Systematic Pattern of Grave Violations of Human Rights 100–112
	b) Cases Wherein the Respondent State Has the Burden of Proof Given the Difficulty of the Applicant to Obtain It 113–115
	3. Case-Law of the ECtHR 116–121
	4. General Assessment 122–124
VIII.	Standard of Proof in the Case-Law of International Criminal Tribunals 125
	1. Inferring Intent from Circumstantial Evidence (Case-Law of the ICTR and the ICTFY) 126–130
	2. Standards of Proof: Rebuttals of the High Threshold of Evidence
	a) *R. Karadžić* case (2013) 131–133
	b) *Z. Tolimir* case (2012) 134–136
	c) *S. Milošević* case (2004) 137–138
	3. General Assessment 139–148
IX.	Widespread and Systematic Pattern of Destruction: Fact-Finding and Case-Law 149
	1. U.N. (Former Commission on Human Rights) Fact-Finding Reports on Systematic Pattern of Destruction (1992-1993) 150–158
	2. U.N. (Security Council's Commission of Experts) Fact-Finding Reports on Systematic Pattern of Destruction (1993-1994) 159
	a) *Interim Report* (of 10.02.1993) 160–161
	b) *Report of a Mass Grave Near Vukovar* (of 10.01.1993) 162–163
	c) *Second Interim Report* (of 06.10.1993) 164–165
	d) *Final Report* (of 27.05.1994) 166–175
	3. Repercussion of Occurrences in the U.N. II World Conference on Human Rights (1993) 176–179
	4. Judicial Recognition of the Widespread and/or Systematic Attacks against the Croat Civilian Population – Case-Law of the ICTFY 180

	a) *M. Babić* case (2004)	181
	b) *M. Martić* case (2007)	182–186
	c) *Mrkšić and Radić and Šljivančanin* case (2007)	187–190
	d) *Stanišić and Simatović* case (2013)	191–194
X.	Widespread and Systematic Pattern of Destruction: Massive Killings, Torture and Beatings, Systematic Expulsion from Homes and Mass Exodus, and Destruction of Group Culture	195
	1. Indiscriminate Attacks against the Civilian Population	196–205
	2. Massive Killings	206–216
	3. Torture and Beatings	217–226
	4. Systematic Expulsion from Homes and Mass Exodus, and Destruction of Group Culture	227–236
	5. General Assessment	237–241
XI.	Widespread and Systematic Pattern of Destruction: Rape and Other Sexual Violence Crimes Committed in Distinct Municipalities	242
	1. Accounts of Systematic Rape	
	a) Croatia's Claims	243–248
	b) Serbia's Response	249
	2. Systematic Pattern of Rape in Distinct Municipalities	250–259
	3. The Necessity and Importance of a Gender Analysis	260–277
XII.	Systematic Pattern of Disappeared or Missing Persons	
	1. Arguments of the Parties concerning the Disappeared or Missing Persons	278–284
	2. Responses of the Parties to Questions from the Bench	285–291
	3. Outstanding Issues and the Parties' Obligation to Establish the Fate of Missing Persons	292–295
	4. The Extreme Cruelty of Enforced Disappearances of Persons as a Continuing Grave Violation of Human Rights and International Humanitarian Law	296–310
	5. General Assessment	311–320
XIII.	Onslaught, Not Exactly War, in a Widespread and Systematic Pattern of Destruction	
	1. Plan of Destruction: Its Ideological Content	321
	a) Arguments of the Contending Parties	322–329
	b) Examination of Expert Evidence by the ICTFY	330–336
	c) Ideological Incitement and the Outbreak of Hostilities	337–354
	2. The Imposed Obligation of Wearing White Ribbons	355–359

	3. Disposal of Mortal Remains	360–375
	4. The Existence of Mass Graves	376–390
	5. Further Clarifications from the Cross-Examination of Witnesses	391–395
	6. Forced Displacement of Persons and Homelessness	396–407
	7. Destruction of Cultural Goods	408
	a) Arguments of the Contending Parties	409–415
	b) General Assessment	416–422
XIV.	*Actus Reus*: Widespread and Systematic Pattern of Conduct of Destruction: Extreme Violence and Atrocities in Some Municipalities	423
	1. Preliminary Methodological Observations	424–427
	2. The Systematic Pattern of Acts of Destruction	428–429
	3. Killings Members of the Croat Population (Article II(a))	430–440
	4. Causing Serious Bodily or Mental Harm to Members of the Group Article II(b))	441–449
	5. Deliberately Inflicting on the Group Conditions of Life Calculated to Bring about Its Physical Destruction in Whole or in Part (Article II(c))	450–455
	6. General Assessment of Witness Statements and Conclusions	
	a) Witness Statements	456–457
	b) Conclusions	458–459
XV.	Mens Rea: Proof of Genocidal Intent by Inference	460–461
	1. International Case-Law on *Mens Rea*	462–466
	2. General Assessment	467–471
XVI.	The Need of Reparations: Some Reflections	472–485
XVII.	The Difficult Path to Reconciliation	486–493
XVIII.	Concluding Observations: The Need of a Comprehensive Approach to Genocide under the 1948 Convention	494–496
	1. Evidential Assessment and Determination of the Facts	497–507
	2. Conceptual Framework and Reasoning as to the Law	508–524
XIX.	Epilogue: A Recapitulation	525–547

I   *Prolegomena*

1. I regret not to share the position of the Court's majority as to the determination of the facts as well as the reasoning conducive to the three resolutory points, nor to its conclusion of resolutory point n. 2, of the Judgment it has just adopted today, 03 February 2015, in the present case concerning the *Application*

of the Convention against Genocide, opposing Croatia to Serbia. My dissenting position encompasses the adopted methodology, the approach pursued, the whole reasoning in its treatment of issues of evidential assessment as well as of substance, as well as the conclusion on the Applicant's claim. This being so, I care to leave on the records the foundations of my dissenting position, given the considerable importance that I attach to the issues raised by Croatia and Serbia, in the course of the proceedings in the *cas d'espèce*, in respect of the interpretation and application of the 1948 Convention against Genocide, and bearing in mind that the settlement of the dispute at issue is ineluctably linked, as I perceive it, to the imperative of the *realization of justice*.

2. I thus present with the utmost care the foundations of my own entirely dissenting position on those aspects of the matter dealt with by the Court in the Judgment which it has just adopted, out of respect for, and zeal in, the faithful exercise of the international judicial function, guided above all by the ultimate goal precisely of the *realization of justice*. To this effect, I shall dwell upon the relevant aspects concerning the dispute brought before the Court which form the object of its present Judgment, in the hope of thus contributing to the clarification of the issues raised and to the progressive development of international law, in particular in the international adjudication by this Court of a case of the importance of the *cas d'espèce*, under the Convention against Genocide, in the light of fundamental considerations of humanity.

3. Preliminarily, I shall address the regrettable delays in the adjudication of the present case, and, as to jurisdiction, the automatic succession of the 1948 Convention against Genocide as a U.N. human rights treaty, and the continuity of its obligations, as an imperative of humaneness (principle of humanity). Once identified the essence of the present case, I shall consider State responsibility under the Convention against Genocide. My next line of considerations will centre on the standard of proof, in the case-law of contemporary international human rights tribunals as well as international criminal tribunals.

4. I shall then proceed to review the fact-finding and case-law on the factual context of the *cas d'espèce*, disclosing a widespread and systematic pattern of destruction, in relation to: (a) massive killings, torture and beatings, systematic expulsion from homes and mass exodus, and destruction of group culture; (b) rape and other sexual violence crimes committed in distinct municipalities; (c) disappeared or missing persons. Next, I shall review the onslaught (not exactly war), in its multiple aspects, namely: (a) plan of destruction (its ideological content); (b) the imposed obligation of wearing white ribbons;

(c) the disposal of mortal remains; (d) the existence of mass graves; (e) further clarifications from the cross-examination of witnesses; (f) the forced displacement of persons and homelessness; (g) the destruction of cultural goods.

5. In sequence, I shall dwell upon the determination, under the Convention against Genocide, of the *actus reus* of genocide, in the widespread and systematic pattern of conduct of destruction (extreme violence and atrocities) in some devastated municipalities, as well as *mens rea* (proof of genocidal intent by inference). The path will then be paved, last but not least, for my considerations on the need of reparations, and on the difficult path to reconciliation, as well as to the presentation of my concluding observations (on evidential assessment and determination of the facts, as well as conceptual framework and reasoning as to the law), and, last but not least, the epilogue (recapitulation).

II The Regrettable Delays in the Adjudication of the Present Case

1 *Procedural Delays*

6. Looking back in time, I cannot avoid expressing my regret at the considerable delays in the adjudication of the present case concerning the *Application of the Convention against Genocide*, opposing Croatia to Serbia. The *Application Instituting Proceedings* was filed on 02.07.1999. The first time-limits fixed by the Court for the filing by the Parties of the *Memorial* and *Counter-Memorial* were, respectively, 14.03.2000 and 14.09.2000.[1] In a letter dated 25.02.2000, Croatia requested an extension of six months for filing its *Memorial*. The request for extension was not objected by Serbia, who also requested an extension of six months for the filing of its *Counter-Memorial*. The time-limit for filing the *Memorial* was thus extended to 14.09.2000 and, for the *Counter-Memorial*, to 14.09.2001.[2]

7. In a letter dated 26.05.2000, Croatia requested that the Court extend by a further period of six months the time-limit for the filing of the *Memorial*. The request for extension was not objected by Serbia, who also requested an extension of six months for the filing of its *Counter-Memorial*. Thus, the Court further

---

[1] Cf. ICJ, Order of 14.09.1999.
[2] Cf. Order of 10.03.2000.

extended to 14.03.2001 the time-limit for filing the *Memorial* and to 16.09.2002 for the filing of the *Counter-Memorial*.[3] Croatia filed the *Memorial* on 14.03.2001 within the time-limit extended.

8. On 11.09.2002, within the time-limit so extended for the filing of the *Counter-Memorial*, Serbia filed certain *preliminary objections* as to jurisdiction and to admissibility. The proceedings on the merits were suspended, in accordance with Article 79(3) of the Rules of Court, and a time-limit for the filing of a written statement of Croatia's submission on the preliminary objections was fixed for 29.04.2003.[4] Hearings on preliminary objections were held half a decade later, from 26 to 30.05.2008. The Court delivered its Judgment on preliminary objections on 18.11.2008, finding, *inter alia*, that, subject to its finding on the second preliminary objection submitted by Serbia, it has jurisdiction pursuant to Article IX of the Genocide Convention to entertain the *Application* of Croatia.

9. Serbia then requested an equal time-limit of 18 months to file its *Counter-Memorial*, which was the time-limit granted for the filing of the *Memorial* of Croatia. The time-limit for the filing of the *Counter-Memorial* was fixed for 22.03.2010.[5] The *Counter-Memorial* of Serbia was filed, within the time-limit, on 04.01.2010, and it contained *counter-claims*. Croatia indicated (at meeting with the President on 03.02.2010) that it did not intend to raise objections to the admissibility of the counter-claims but wished to respond to the substance of the counter-claims in a *Reply*. Serbia thus indicated that it accordingly wished to file a *Rejoinder*.

10. Given that there were no objections by Croatia as to the admissibility of Serbia's counter-claims, the Court did not consider it necessary to rule definitively at that stage on the question as to whether the counter-claims fulfilled the conditions of Article 80(1) of the Rules of Court. The Court further decided that a *Reply* and *Rejoinder* would be necessary, and to ensure strict equality between the Parties (equality of arms / *égalité des armes*) it reserved the right of Croatia to file an additional pleading relating to the counter-claims. The Court thus fixed the time-limit for the filing of Croatia's *Reply* as 20.12.2010, and 04.11.2011 for the *Rejoinder* of Serbia.[6]

---

3 Cf. Order of 27.06.2000.
4 Cf. Order of 14.11.2002.
5 Cf. Order of 20.01.2009.
6 Cf. Order of 04.02.2010.

11. Croatia filed its *Reply* within the time-limit and Serbia also filed its Rejoinder within the fixed time-limits. Both the *Reply* and *Rejoinder* contained submissions as to the claims and counter-claims. The Court authorized the submission by Croatia of an *Additional Pleading* relating to the counter-claims of Serbia, and fixed for 30.08.2012 the filing of such *Additional Pleading*, which was filed within the time-limit.[7] In light of the foregoing, the hearings on the merits were thus scheduled to take place – as they did – from 03 March to 01 April 2014.

12. These facts speak for themselves, as to the regrettable delays in the adjudication of the present case, keeping in mind in particular those who seek for justice. Unfortunately, as I have pointed out, on other recent occasions within this Court, *the time of human justice is not the time of human beings*. In my Dissenting Opinion in the case of *Questions Relating to the Obligation to Prosecute or Extradite* (provisional measures of protection, Belgium *versus* Senegal, Order of 28.05.2009), I pondered that

> The time of human beings surely does not appear to be the time of human justice. The time of human beings is not long (*vita brevis*), at least not long enough for the full realization of their project of life. The brevity of human life has been commented upon time and time again, along the centuries; in his *De Brevitate Vitae*,[8] Seneca pondered that, except for but a few, most people in his times departed from life while they were still preparing to live. Yet, the time of human justice is prolonged, not seldom much further than that of human life, seeming to make abstraction of the vulnerability and briefness of this latter, even in face of adversities and injustices. The time of human justice seems, in sum, to make abstraction of the time human beings count on for the fulfilment of their needs and aspirations.
>
> Chronological time is surely not the same as biological time. The time of the succession of events does not equate with the time of the briefness of human life. *Tempus fugit*. On its turn, biological time is not the same as psychological time either. Surviving victims of cruelty lose, in moments of deep pain and humiliation, all they could expect of life; the younger lose in a few moments their innocence forever, the elderly suddenly lose their confidence in fellow human beings, not to speak of institutions. Their lives become deprived of meaning, and all that is left, is their hope

---

7 Cf. Order of 23.01.2012.
8 Written sometime between the years 49 and 62.

in human justice. Yet, the time of human justice does not appear to be the time of human beings (paras. 46–47).

13. Shortly afterwards, in my Dissenting Opinion in the case concerning *Jurisdictional Immunities of the State* (counter-claim, Germany *versus* Italy, Order of 06.07.2010), I deemed it fit again to ponder, in relation to the inhuman conditions of the subjection of prisoners of war to forced labour, that

> Not only had those victims to endure inhuman and degrading treatment, but later crossed the final limit of their ungrateful lives living with impunity, without reparation and amidst manifest injustice. The time of human justice is definitively not the time of human beings (para. 118).

This holds true, once again, in the present case concerning the *Application of the Convention against Genocide* (Croatia *versus* Serbia), – involving grave breaches of international law, – where the aforementioned regrettable delays have extended for a virtually unprecedented prolongation of time (1999–2015), of over one and a half decades, despite the *vita brevis* of human beings.

2   *Justitia Longa, Vita Brevis*

14. Paradoxically, the graver the breaches of international law appear to be, the more time-consuming and difficult it becomes to impart justice. To start with, all those who find themselves in this world are then promptly faced with a great enigma posing a life-long challenge to everyone: that of understanding the *passing of time*, and endeavouring to learn how to live *within* it. Already in the late VIIIth or early VIIth century b.C., this mystery surrounding all of us was well captured by Homer in his *Iliad*:

> Like the generations of leaves, the lives of mortal men.
> Now the wind scatters the old leaves across the earth,
> now the living timber bursts with the new buds
> and spring comes round again. And so with men:
> as one generation comes to life, another dies away.[9]

15. As if it were not enough, there is an additional enigma to face, that of the extreme violence and brutality with which human beings got used to relating to each other, century after century:

---

9 Book VI, verses 171–175.

> War – I know it well, and the butchery of men.
> Well I know, shift to the left, shift to the right
> my tough tanned shield. (...) I know it all, (...)
> I know how to stand and fight to the finish,
> twist and lunge in the war-god's deadly dance.[10] (...)
> (...) Now, as it is, the fates of death await us
> thousands poised to strike, and not a man alive
> can flee them or escape (...).[11] (...)
> (...) We must steel our hearts. Bury our dead,
> with tears for the day they die, not one day more.
> And all those left alive, after the hateful carnage,
> (...) wretched mortals...
> like leaves, no sooner flourishing, full of the sun's fire,
> feeding on earth's gifts, than they waste away and die.[12] (...)
> (...) My sons laid low, my daughters dragged away
> and the treasure-chambers looted, helpless babies
> hurled to the earth in the red barbarity of war...
> (...) Ah for a young man
> all looks fine and noble if he goes down in war,
> hacked to pieces under a slashing bronze blade–
> he lies there dead... but whatever death lays bare,
> all wounds are marks of glory. When an old man's killed
> and the dogs go at the grey head and the grey beard
> and mutilate the genitals – that is the cruellest sight
> in all our wretched lives!.[13]

16. Homer's narrative of human cruelty seems endowed with perennial contemporaneity, – especially after the subsequent advent of tragedy. This is the imprint of a true classic. Homer could well be describing the horrors in our times, or in recent times, e.g., in the wars in the former Yugoslavia along the nineties. There are, in the *Iliad*, murders, brutality, rape, pillage, slavery and humiliation; there are, in the present case of the *Application of the Convention against Genocide* (Croatia *versus* Serbia), murders, brutality, torture, beatings, enforced disappearances, looting and humiliation; from the late VIIIth century b.C. to the late XXth century, the propensity of human beings to treat each

---

10   Book VII, verses 275–278 and 280–281.
11   Book XII, verses 378–380.
12   Book XXI, verses 528–530.
13   Book XXII, verses 73–75 and 83–90.

other with extreme violence has remained the same, and has even at times worsened.

17. This suggests that succeeding generations along the centuries, have not learned from the sufferings of their predecessors. The propensity of human beings to do evil to each other has accompanied them from the times of the *Iliad*, through those of the tragedies of Aeschylus and Sophocles and Euripides (IVth century b.C.), until the present, as illustrated by the *cas d'espèce*, concerning the *Application of the Convention against Genocide*. There is a certain distance from epic to tragedy; yet, the former paved the way to the latter, and tragedy was then to find its own expression, and, ever since, has never faded away. Tragedy sought inspiration in the narrative of epic, but added to it something new: the human sentiment, the endurance of living and the human condition. Tragedy has been accompanying the human condition along the centuries.

18. It came to stay, performed throughout the centuries, time and time again, until our days. The war in the Balkans, portrayed in the present case opposing Croatia to Serbia, bears witness of that: it is tragic in its devastation. Yet, tragedy – which gave a new dimension to epic – was not focused only on destructiveness and the lessons to extract therefrom, but also on the *need for justice*. Aeschylus's *Oresteia* trilogy, and in particular the chorus in the *Eumenides*, can be recalled in this connection. Just as the passing of time has not erased the somber propensity of human beings to do evil to each other, the search for justice has likewise been long-lasting, as also illustrated by the *cas d'espèce*. This regrettably appears proper of the human condition, from ancient times to nowadays: perennial evil, *vita brevis*; *justitia longa, vita brevis*.

III Jurisdiction: Automatic Succession to the Genocide Convention as a Human Rights Treaty

1 *Arguments of the Parties as to the Applicability of the Obligations under the Genocide Convention Prior to 27.04.1992*

19. In its Application filed in 1999, Croatia invoked jurisdiction on the basis that the Socialist Federal Republic of Yugoslavia (SFRY) was a party to the Genocide Convention and that Serbia was bound by it as a successor State to the SFRY.[14] Both Parties, according to Croatia, were bound by the Genocide Convention as

---

14 *Application*, para. 28.

successor States of the SFRY.[15] The SFRY had become a Party to the Convention on 29.08.1950. In the light of the ICJ's finding in 2008 that its jurisdiction in the present case arises of succession to the Genocide Convention[16] rather than accession, Croatia has stressed the existence of a continuing obligation, rather than one newly entered into.[17] Croatia has thus submitted that the Genocide Convention accords jurisdiction to the Court over conduct before 27.04.1992; it has put forward an alternative ground for jurisdiction over conduct predating 27.04.1992, namely, Serbia's Declaration on that date.[18]

20. Serbia, for its part, has acknowledged that it succeeded to the Genocide Convention with effect from 27.04.1992; in the light of the 2008 Judgment, it has asserted that it became bound by the Genocide Convention from 27.04.1992 onwards, but not prior to that date.[19] It has submitted that acts and omissions that took place before 27.04.1992 cannot entail its international responsibility, as it only came into existence on that date, and, accordingly, it was not bound by the Genocide Convention before then. Alternatively, it has argued that Croatia only came into existence on 08.10.1991 and cannot raise claims based on facts preceding its coming into existence.[20]

21. It should be recalled that the ICJ, in 2008, examined only the effect of the Declaration and Note to the United Nations of 27.04.1992 (to which it attributed the effect of a notification of succession to treaties), and did not deem it necessary to examine the wider question of the application in this case of the general law relating to succession of States, nor the rules of international law governing State succession to treaties (including the question of *ipso jure* succession to some multilateral treaties).[21] The Court's interpretation of the Declaration of 27.04.1992 was in itself sufficient for the purposes of establishing whether the respondent was bound by the Genocide Convention (with attention to Article IX) at the date of the institution of the proceedings. Be that as it may, now, in the merits phase, the question arises as to the applicability of the Genocide Convention to acts prior to 27.04.1992.

---

15   ICJ, case of the *Application of the Convention against Genocide* (Croatia *versus* Serbia, Preliminary Objections), *ICJ Reports* (2008) para. 37 (hereinafter: "2008 Judgment").
16   2008 Judgment, para. 111.
17   ICJ, doc. CR 2014/12, of 07.03.2014, p. 38, para. 4.
18   *Ibid.*, p. 40, para. 9.
19   ICJ, doc. CR 2014/14, of 11.03.2014, p. 23, para. 4.
20   *Counter-Memorial*, paras. 206, 357–387.
21   2008 Judgment, para. 101.

2 Continuity of Application of the Genocide Convention (SFRY and FRY)

22. In deciding, in its Judgment of 2008 on preliminary objections, that Serbia became bound by the Convention from 27.04.1992 onwards,[22] the Court joined to the merits the question of the applicability of the obligations under the Genocide Convention to the Federal Republic of Yugoslavia (FRY) before 27.04.1992.[23] In this regard, Serbia submitted, in the oral proceedings at the merits stage, that "the Court already decided, at the preliminary objections stage, that Serbia '*only*' became bound by the Convention 'as of April 1992'".[24] However, the Court only dealt with the question of whether the conditions were met under Article 35 of the Statute for the purposes of determining whether the FRY had the capacity to participate in the proceedings before the Court *on the date of the Application*, namely, 02.07.1999.[25]

23. The question was decided not on the basis of whether Serbia succeeded to the Genocide Convention *ipso jure*, but solely on the basis of the historical record and of the Declaration and Note of 27.04.1992.[26] Taking the view that the questions of jurisdiction and admissibility raised by Serbia's preliminary objection *ratione temporis* constituted "two inseparable issues" in that case, the Court expressly left the issue of the applicability of the obligations under the Genocide Convention to the FRY before 27.04.1992 open, to be decided at the merits stage of the *cas d'espèce*.[27]

3 Continuity of the State Administration and Officials (SFRY and FRY)

24. While the FRY formally came into existence as a State on 27.04.1992, this proclamation only formalized a factual situation which had *de facto* arisen during the dissolution of the SFRY. Serbia considers that, until the proclamation of the dissolution of the SFRY, any act performed by individuals in the name of the SFRY may be attributable *only* to that entity. However, as the Badinter Commission recognized in its Opinion n. 1, from mid-1991 the SFRY ceased to operate as a functioning State and was authoritatively recognised as

---

22 *Ibid.*, para. 117.
23 *Ibid.*, para. 129.
24 ICJ, doc. CR 2014/14, of 11.03.2014, p. 14, para. 26.
25 Cf. 2008 Judgment, paras. 60, 67, 69, 71, 78 and 95.
26 *Ibid.*, para. 101.
27 *Ibid.*, paras. 129–130.

in a "process of dissolution". The dissolution was an extended process, completed on 04.07.1992, according to Opinion n. 8 of the Badinter Commission. This implies that, well before April 1992, the territory of the SFRY had already been divided, and Serbian leadership had effectively taken control of the principal organs of the former SFRY. This determination of the control of the political and military apparatus during this whole period is thus relevant.

25. Serbia cannot shift responsibility to an extinct State for the main reason that the personnel controlling the relevant organs in the interim period later assumed similar positions in the new government of the FRY. It was the same leadership which, from October 1991, – when the relevant organs of government and other federal authorities of the SFRY ceased to function, – became *de facto* organs and authorities of the new FRY, acting under Serbian leadership. The former State officials of the SFRY had close ties with the officials of Serbia and Montenegro (FRY). Serbia does not deny that these were the same people carrying out the same policies. In this regard, Croatia provides a list of political and military leaders which illustrates the *personal continuity of the policy and practices from 1991 onwards*, on the part of the Serbian authorities located in Belgrade.[28] Serbia has not challenged the list of political and military leaders which attests this continuity and connections.[29]

4 *Law Governing State Succession to Human Rights Treaties: Ipso Jure Succession to the Genocide Convention*

26. Serbia's conduct – contrary to its allegations – supports the applicability of the Genocide Convention to the FRY before 27.04.1992. It is here important to keep in mind, to start with, the law governing State succession to human rights treaties. In effect, leaving aside State succession in respect of *classic* treaties, it is generally accepted that certain types of treaties – such as human rights treaties – remain in force by reason of their special nature. It can be argued, in this connection, that the application of the Genocide Convention to the FRY, when it was *in statu nascendi*, that is, before 27.04.1992, is justified – to paraphrase the ICJ's Advisory Opinion of 1951 on the *Reservations to the Genocide Convention* (p. 23) – by the Convention's "special and important purpose" to endorse "the most elementary principles of morality", irrespective of questions of formal succession.

---

28   *Memorial*, Appendix 8.
29   One may refer to 7 of the 17 political and military leaders, listed in Appendix 8 to Croatia's *Memorial*.

27. In this respect, the ICJ's understanding of the object and purpose of the Convention, as set out in that *célèbre* Advisory Opinion, may here be recalled:

> The origins of the Convention show that it was the intention of the United Nations to condemn and punish genocide as "a crime under international law" involving a denial of the right of existence of entire human groups, a denial which shocks the conscience of mankind and results in great losses to humanity, and which is contrary to moral law and to the spirit and aims of the United Nations (Resolution 96(I) of the General Assembly, December 11th, 1946). The first consequence arising from this conception is that the principles underlying the Convention are principles which are recognized by civilized nations as binding on States, even without any conventional obligation. A second consequence is the universal character both of the condemnation of genocide and of the Co-operation required "in order to liberate mankind from such an odious scourge" (Preamble to the Convention).[30]

28. Moreover, the Court emphasized that the Convention, as indicated, has a "special and important purpose" to endorse "the most elementary principles of morality".[31] The Court further stated that the principles of the Convention bind States "even without any conventional obligation" and that the Convention was intended to be "definitely universal in scope". In its Judgment on preliminary objections (of 11.07.1996) in the *Bosnia Genocide* case, the ICJ referred no less than three times to the special nature of the Genocide Convention as a universal human rights treaty, in order to found its jurisdiction. There was awareness around the bench as to the needs of protection of the segments of the populations concerned, and automatic succession to the Convention did not pass unnoticed.[32]

29. Nowadays, almost two decades later, it is about time to take this analysis further. It is clear that the Genocide Convention is not a synallagmatic bargain, whereby each State Party would bind itself to the other; it does not simply create rights and obligations between States Parties on a bilateral basis.

---

30 ICJ, Advisory Opinion on *Reservations to the Convention on the Prevention and Punishment of the Crime of Genocide, ICJ Reports* (1951) p. 23.

31 *Ibid.*, p. 23.

32 Cf. ICJ, case concerning the *Application of the Convention against Genocide* (Bosnia-Herzegovina *versus* Yugoslavia), Separate Opinions of Judges Shahabuddeen and Weeramantry, *ICJ Reports* (1996) pp. 634–637 and 645–655, respectively.

As a human rights treaty, it sets up a mechanism of *collective guarantee*.[33] In my view, it is not sufficient to assert (or reassert), as the ICJ did almost two decades ago, that the 1948 Genocide Convention is a human rights treaty: one has, moreover, to extract the legal consequences therefrom (cf. *infra*).

30. In the present case concerning the *Application of the Convention against Genocide* (Croatia *versus* Serbia), the relevant conduct was that of the JNA (or under its direction and control), and the JNA was a *de facto* organ of the nascent Serbian State. It would be utterly artificial to argue that the Convention continued to bind the SFRY until it formally disappeared,[34] becoming thus no longer able to respond for any breach of an international obligation. Such a break in the protection afforded by the Genocide Convention would not be consistent with the precise object of safeguarding the very existence of certain human groups, in pursuance of the most elementary principles of morality.

31. This applies even more cogently in a situation of dissolution of State amidst violence. After all, the consequences of the commission of grave violations of international law will, in most cases, continue to affect and victimize certain human groups even after the date of succession, and even more so when surrounded by violence. In such circumstance, it would be unjust for the victims if no responsibility could be vindicated for the commission of internationally wrongful acts and their consequences extended in time.[35] To argue that responsibility would vanish with the dissolution of the State concerned would render the Genocide Convention irrelevant. An internationally wrongful act and its continuing consequences cannot remain unpunished and without reparation for damages.

32. The Genocide Convention, as a human rights treaty (as generally acknowledged), is concerned with *State* responsibility, besides individual responsibility. It should not pass unnoticed that human rights treaties have a hermeneutics of their own (cf. *infra*), and are endowed with a mechanism of collective guarantee. Moreover, the Genocide Convention implies the undertaking by each

---

33 On the notion of *collective guarantee*, proper to human rights treaties, cf. A.A. Cançado Trindade, *Tratado de Direito Internacional dos Direitos Humanos* [*Treatise of International Law of Human Rights*], vol. II, Porto Alegre/Brazil, S.A. Fabris Ed., 1999, pp. 47–53.

34 In reality, the SFRY, in 1991 and 1992, was no longer exercising any direction or control of the JNA, and was already undergoing an irreversible process of dissolution.

35 Cf., in this sense, e.g., P. Dumberry, *State Succession to International Responsibility*, Leiden, Nijhoff, 2007, pp. 278, 283–284, 297, 366, 409, 411, 424–425 and 428.

State Party to treat successor States as continuing (as from independence) any commitment and status which the predecessor State had as a Party to the Convention.

33. It may be recalled, in this regard, that, in the context of the present proceedings, the Badinter Commission emphasized the need for all human rights treaties to which the SFRY was party to remain in force with respect to all of its territories.[36] I am of the view that there is automatic State succession to universal human rights treaties,[37] and that Serbia has succeeded to the Genocide Convention (under customary law), without the need for any formal confirmation of adherence as the successor State. In light of the declaratory character of the Convention and the need to secure the effective protection of the rights enshrined therein, the *de facto* organs of the nascent Serbia were bound by the Genocide Convention before 27.04.1992.

5 *State Conduct in Support of Automatic Succession to, and Continuing Applicability of, the Genocide Convention (to FRY prior to 27.04.1992)*

34. Serbia's conduct itself evidences the applicability to it of the multilateral conventions to which the SFRY had been a State Party at the time of its dissolution; its conduct itself provides evidence that it remained bound by them. In the particular circumstances of the present case, the FRY had, since 1992, claimed to possess the status of a State Party to the Convention against Genocide; thus, in its Declaration of 27.04.1992,[38] it stated that

---

36 Arbitration Commission, EC Conference on Yugoslavia (Badinter, Chairman), *Opinion n. 1*, of 29.11.1991, 92 *International Law Reports*, p. 162.

37 In relation to international human rights instruments, cf. UN Human Rights Commission resolutions 1993/23, 1994/16 and 1995/18, doc. E/CN4/1995/80 p. 4; Human Rights Committee's *General Comment* 26(61), doc. CCPR/C/21/Rev.1/Add.8/Rev.1. Cf. also, in relation to Bosnia and Herzegovina's succession to the ICCPR, Decision adopted by the Human Rights Committee on 07.10.1992, and discussion thereto, *in Official Records of the Human Rights Committee* 1992/93, vol. 1, p. 15.

38 During the stage of preliminary objections in the present case, Serbia had disputed that the Declaration of 27.04.1992 amounted to a notification of succession. The Court however, rejected that claim and concluded that Serbia did succeed to the Genocide Convention on 27.04.1992: – "The Court, taking into account both the text of the declaration and Note of 27.04.1992, and the consistent conduct of the FRY at the time of its making and throughout the years 1992–2001, considers that it should attribute to those documents precisely the effect that they were, in the view of the Court, intended to have on the face of their terms: namely, that from that date onwards the FRY would be bound by the

THE UNIVERSAL JURIDICAL CONSCIENCE 57

> The [FRY], continuing the state, international legal and political personality of the [SFRY], shall strictly abide by all the commitments that the SFR[Y] assumed internationally.[39]

35. It follows that, by accepting that it was bound by all the obligations assumed by the SFRY, Serbia (the FRY) took expressly the position that the substantive obligations of the Convention against Genocide, like other obligations assumed by the SFRY, continued to apply without any temporal break, including before April 1992. It is important to note that, in its Declaration, the FRY did not expressly or implicitly exclude its intention to be bound by the Convention before the date of the Declaration (27.04.1992). It rather expressed an attitude of continuity at all relevant times, including with regard to obligations emanating from the Convention against Genocide. In this regard, it is useful to highlight that, in its official Note to the United Nations on the same date (27.04.1992), the FRY stated that:

> Strictly respecting the continuity of the international personality of Yugoslavia, the [FRY] shall continue to fulfil all the rights conferred to, and obligations assumed by, the [SFRY] in international relations, including its membership in all international organizations and participation in international treaties ratified or acceded to by Yugoslavia.[40]

36. It thus stems from these two documents (the 1992 Declaration and the official Note to the United Nations) that there was immediate and automatic succession, whereby Serbia (the FRY) deemed itself bound to become the successor State and to assume all obligations of the SFRY, including obligations ensuing from the Genocide Convention. In other words, Serbia (the FRY), by its own Declaration of 27.04.1992, stated clearly its engagement to succeed the SFRY as a State Party to the Convention against Genocide. This entails that

---

obligations of a party in respect of all the multilateral conventions to which the SFRY had been a party at the time of its dissolution, subject of course to any reservations lawfully made by the SFRY limiting its obligations". This was acknowledged by Counsel for Serbia at the hearings in the present proceedings; cf. UN doc. CR 2014/14, of 11.03.2014, p. 23, para. 4.

39 Joint Declaration of the SFRY Assembly, the National Assembly of the Republic of Serbia and the Assembly of the Republic of Montenegro, 27.04.1992, U.N. doc. A/46/915, Annex II.

40 Note to the United Nations (addressed to the Secretary-General), of 27.04.1992, UN doc. A/46/915, Annex I.

Serbia was already bound by the obligations of the Convention in relation to acts that occurred before the date of its Declaration of 1992.

6   *Venire Contra Factum Proprium Non Valet*

37. Thus, in the circumstances of the present case, the ICJ should bear in mind that Serbia (the FRY) itself recognized its commitment to continue its participation in international treaties ratified or acceded to by former Yugoslavia. The FRY's binding declaration strongly supports the continuing applicability of the obligations of the Convention against Genocide to the nascent Serbian State before 27.04.1992. Furthermore, it can be argued that the ICJ appears to have resolved this issue in its 2008 Judgment on preliminary objections in the *cas d'espèce*.[41] When the ICJ stated that "the 1992 declaration and Note had the effect of a notification of succession by the FRY to the SFRY in relation to the Genocide Convention", it seems that it thereby acknowledged that there was continuity as to the conventional obligations (between SFRY and FRY).

38. One decade later, the FRY's notification of accession of 06.03.2001 (deposited on 12.03.2001), after referring to the 1992 Declaration and to the subsequent admission of the FRY to the United Nations as a new Member, stated, however, that

> the [FRY] has not succeeded on April 27, 1992, or on any later date, to treaty membership, rights and obligations of the [SFRY] in the Convention on the Prevention and Punishment of the Crime of Genocide on the assumption of continued membership in the United Nations and continued state, international legal and political personality of the [SFRY] (...).[42]

The notification of accession contained the following reservation:

> The [FRY] does not consider itself bound by Article IX of the Convention (...) and, therefore, before any dispute to which the [FRY] is a party may be validly submitted to the jurisdiction of the International Court of Justice under this Article, the specific and explicit consent of the FRY is required in each case.[43]

39. Be that as it may, this step was inconsistent with the status which Serbia (the FRY), since its Declaration of 1992, had been claiming to possess, namely,

---

41   ICJ, 2008 Judgment, para. 117.
42   *Ibid.*, para. 116.
43   *Ibid.*, para. 116.

that of a State Party to the Convention against Genocide. By the end of the nineties, there remained no doubt that the FRY had assumed all the international obligations that had been entered into by the SFRY, including those pertaining to the respect for human rights.[44] It should further be noted that the FRY never contended before this Court, in the previous proceedings, that it was *not* a Party to the Convention against Genocide.

40. It was only when the FRY, abandoning its claim to continue the U.N. membership of the SFRY, was admitted to the United Nations in 2000, that it advanced the opposite view, initially in its *Written Observations*, filed on 18.12.2002, on the preliminary objections submitted in the *Legality of Use of Force* cases.[45] One cannot avail itself of a position *a contrario sensu* to the one earlier upheld, by virtue of a basic principle going as far back as classic Roman law: *venire contra factum proprium non valet*. In any case, the ICJ, having concluded, at the preliminary objections stage, that the FRY was a Party to the Convention against Genocide, considered that it was not necessary to make a finding as to the legal effect of Serbia's notification of accession to the Convention (dated 06.03.2001).

41. In the light of the aforementioned, in my understanding Serbia's change of attitude can have no bearing upon the jurisdiction of the Court. In this regard, citing its own *jurisprudence constante*, the ICJ stated in 2008 that, if a title of jurisdiction is shown to have existed at the date of institution of proceedings, any subsequent lapse or withdrawal of the jurisdictional instrument is without effect on the jurisdiction of the Court.[46] Accordingly, the FRY, by way of

---

44 The Declaration of 27.04.1992, whereby the formation of the FRY was proclaimed, "est l'acte qui a dans toutes ses dispositions insisté sur la continuité avec la RSFY. Son contenu souligne que le pays garde la subjectivité juridique et politique de l'ancien État et promet de respecter strictement ses obligations internationales"; M. Sahović, "Le droit international et la crise en ex-Yugoslavie", 3 *Cursos Euromediterráneos Bancaja de Derecho Internacional* (1999) p. 392.

45 The FRY requested the ICJ to decide on its jurisdiction considering that the FRY "did not continue the personality and treaty membership of the former Yugoslavia", and was thus "not bound by the Genocide Convention until it acceded to that Convention (with a reservation to Article IX) in March 2001".

46 Cf., e.g., ICJ, *Nottebohm* case (Liechtenstein *versus* Guatemala – Preliminary Objection, Judgment), *ICJ Reports* (1953) p. 122; ICJ, case of *Military and Paramilitary Activities in and against Nicaragua* (Nicaragua *versus* United States of America – Merits, Judgment), *ICJ Reports* (1986) p. 28, para. 36; and ICJ, case concerning the *Application of the Convention on the Prevention and Punishment of the Crime of Genocide* (Croatia *versus*

its Declaration of 1992, bound itself as the successor State of the SFRY; this Declaration operated automatic succession. Serbia remained bound by the Convention against Genocide for acts or omissions having occurred prior to 27.04.1992. The ICJ has jurisdiction under the Convention in relation to those acts or omissions, and Croatia's claims in relation thereto are admissible.

7   Automatic Succession to Human Rights Treaties in the Practice of United Nations Supervisory Organs

42. Already in the early nineties, while the devastation was taking place in the Balkans, there was firm support, on the part of the United Nations supervisory organs, for automatic succession and continuing applicability of human rights treaties to successor States. Thus, in its resolution 1993/23, of 05.03.1993, the (former) U.N. Commission on Human Rights stated that successor States "shall succeed to international human rights treaties to which the predecessor States have been parties and continue to bear responsibilities".[47] After calling upon the continuity by successor States of fulfilment of "international human rights treaty obligations of the predecessor State",[48] the Commission urged successor States "to accede or to ratify those international human rights treaties to which the predecessor States were not parties".[49]

43. The following year, in its resolution 1994/16, of 25.02.1994, the Commission on Human Rights evoked the "relevant decisions of the Human Rights Committee [HRC] and the Committee on the Elimination of Racial Discrimination [CERD] on succession issues, in respect of international obligations in the field of human rights".[50] It further welcomed the recommendation of the Vienna Declaration and Programme of Action, recently adopted by the II World Conference on Human Rights (1993), "to encourage and facilitate the ratification of, and accession or succession to, international human rights treaties and

---

Serbia – Preliminary Objections), p. 445, para. 95. In this sense, as the ICJ stated in its Judgments in 2004 in the *Legality of Use of Force* cases, "the significance of this new development in 2000 is that it has clarified the thus far amorphous legal situation concerning the status of the Federal Republic of Yugoslavia *vis-à-vis* the United Nations" (p. 1191, para. 78).

47   Third preambular paragraph.
48   Fifth preambular paragraph.
49   Operative part, para. 3.
50   Second preambular paragraph. – For an account of this aspect of the practice of the HRC and the CERD Committees in the nineties, cf. A.A. Cançado Trindade, *International Law for Humankind – Towards a New Jus Gentium*, op cit. infra n. (67), pp. 472–475.

protocols".[51] In the operative part of resolution 1994/16, the Commission, after emphasising "the special nature of the human rights treaties"[52] aimed at the protection of the rights of the human person, requested the U.N. supervisory organs of human rights treaties

> to consider further the continuing applicability of the respective international human rights treaties to successor States, with the aim of assisting them in meeting their obligations.[53]

44. Once again, in its following resolution 1995/18, of 24.02.1995, the Commission on Human Rights evoked the relevant decisions and recommendations of HRC and CERD, as well as the aforementioned recommendation of the Vienna Declaration and Programme of Action adopted by the U.N. II World Conference on Human Rights (1993).[54] And it again stressed "the special nature of the human rights treaties",[55] and it reiterated its request to the U.N. supervisory organs of human rights treaties to keep on considering "the continuing applicability of the respective human rights treaties to successor States", so as to assist them "in meeting their obligations".[56] It is clear that, already at the time, in the early nineties, while the wars and devastation in the former Yugoslavia were taking place, the work at the United Nations in the present domain was being guided by basic considerations of humanity, rather than State sovereignty.

45. And it could hardly be otherwise. The "special nature" of human rights treaties – and the Genocide Convention is characterised as such, as a human rights treaty, – requires their continuing applicability, irrespective of the uncertainties of State succession. States themselves have acknowledged the special nature of human rights and humanitarian treaties, and have not objected to the understanding espoused by United Nations supervisory organs of their *continuing applicability, ipso jure*, to successor States. After all, the local populations cannot become suddenly deprived of any protection when they most need it, in cases of turbulent dissolution of a State, when considerations of humanity need to prevail over invocations of State sovereignty.

---

51 Fourth preambular paragraph.
52 Operative part, para. 2.
53 Operative part, para. 3.
54 Second and third preambular paragraphs.
55 Operative part, para. 2.
56 Operative part, para. 3.

46. The U.N. Secretary-General, in his report to the U.N. General Assembly (of 19.10.1994), on the *Implementation of Human Rights Instruments*,[57] recalled that, shortly after the II World Conference on Human Rights (Vienna, 14–25.06.1993), the 4th meeting of persons chairing the U.N. human rights conventional supervisory organs took steps towards the elaboration of "early warning measures and urgent procedures" aiming at the prevention of the occurrence, or recurrence, of grave violations of human rights; the chairpersons, moreover, welcomed the establishment, by the World Conference, of the post of U.N. High Commissioner for Human Rights (para. 12).

47. The U.N. Secretary-General, in his aforementioned report, then turned to the 5th meeting of chairpersons, where they espoused the view that their respective U.N. human rights treaties were "universal in nature and in application" (para. 13), and further stressed that "full and effective compliance" with their conventional obligations "is an essential component of an international order based on the rule of law" (para. 17). The Secretary-General added that the chairpersons endorsed his own initiative to urge States to "ratify, accede or succeed to those principal human rights treaties to which they are not yet a party" (para. 16).

48. It was further reported that their work on prevention of grave violations of human rights, including early warning and urgent procedures, continued (paras. 26–29). And the Secretary-General added, significantly, that the chairpersons were of the view that

> successor States are automatically bound by obligations under international human rights instruments from their respective date of independence and (...) the respect of their obligations should not depend on a declaration of confirmation made by the new Government of the successor State (para. 32).

49. For its part, the U.N. General Assembly, even earlier, in its resolution 47/121, of 18.12.1992, acknowledged, in relation to the "consistent pattern of gross and systematic violations of human rights" in the wars in the former Yugoslavia, – with its concentration camps and "mass expulsions of defenceless civilians from their homes", – that "ethnic cleansing" appeared to be not the consequence of war, "but rather its goal". And the U.N. General Assembly added that "the abhorrent practice of "ethnic cleansing" was "a form of genocide".[58]

---

57 U.N. doc. A/49/537, of 19.10.1994, pp. 1–14.
58 Seventh and ninth preambular paragraphs.

THE UNIVERSAL JURIDICAL CONSCIENCE

The same General Assembly resolution, *inter alia*, urged the Security Council to consider recommending the establishment of an *ad hoc* international war crimes tribunal, – the ICTFY, – to try and punish those responsible for the perpetration of the atrocities.[59]

IV The Essence of the Present Case

1 *Arguments of the Contending Parties*

50. A careful examination of the arguments of the contending parties, in both the written and oral phases of the proceedings as to the merits in the present case of the *Application of the Convention against Genocide* (Croatia *versus* Serbia), reveals that the contending Parties, not surprisingly, devoted considerably more attention to the substance of the case (the merits themselves, in relation to Croatia's *main claim*) than to issues pertaining to jurisdiction/admissibility. These latter occupy only a small portion of the documents submitted by the contending parties, namely: (a) in Croatia's *Memorial*, one chapter out of eight chapters, 7 pages (pp. 317–323) out of a total of 414 pages; (b) in Serbia's *Counter-Memorial*, one chapter out of fourteen chapters, 50 pages (pp. 85–135) out of a total of 478 pages; (c) in Croatia's *Reply*, one chapter out of twelve chapters, 26 pages (pp. 243–269) out of a total of 473 pages; and (d) in Serbia's *Rejoinder*, one chapter out of eight chapters, 55 pages (pp. 39–93) out of a total of 322 pages.

51. As to the oral phase of the present proceedings as to the merits of the *cas d'espèce*, the same picture is disclosed. The arguments of the contending Parties, as expected, were rather brief on issues pertaining to jurisdiction/admissibility; the vast majority of their arguments focused on the substance of the *cas d'espèce* (the merits themselves, in relation to Croatia's *main claim*). May it be recalled that the public sittings before the Court extended for more than one month, having lasted from 03.03.2014 until 01.04.2014. In its first round of oral arguments, Croatia has dedicated not more than a part of one day of its pleadings to discuss in particular the specific question of jurisdiction.[60] And in its second round of oral arguments, Croatia has devoted only a small portion of pleadings to rebutting Serbia's arguments on jurisdiction.[61]

---

59 Operative part, para. 10.
60 Cf. mainly ICJ, doc. CR 2014/12, of 07.03.2014, pp. 37–55. And cf. also ICJ, doc. CR 2014/5, of 03.03.2014, pp. 23–31; and ICJ doc. CR 2014/10, of 06.03.2014, pp. 32–49.
61 Cf. mainly ICJ, doc. CR 2014/20, of 20.03.2014, pp. 63–67. And cf. also ICJ, doc. CR 2014/21, of 21.03.2014, pp. 10–33.

52. For its part, in Serbia's first round of oral arguments, the bulk of the pleadings on questions of jurisdiction took place in just one session.[62] And, in its second round of oral arguments, Serbia has dedicated only a small part of its pleadings to a discussion of questions of jurisdiction.[63] It ensues from an examination of the contending parties' oral pleadings that the vast majority of their arguments concerned questions pertaining to the merits; they have devoted only a small portion of their pleadings (around two sessions each) to the issue of jurisdiction.

2 General Assessment

53. The foregoing shows that the contending Parties, at this stage of the merits of the present case, in the written phase of proceedings, have seen no need to devote more than a very small portion of their arguments to questions of jurisdiction/admissibility. They have rightly focused on the *merits* of the case. Likewise, in the oral phase of proceedings, both Croatia and Serbia have concentrated their pleadings on *substantive* issues; the two contending parties have well captured the essence of the present case, pertaining to the interpretation and application of the Convention against Genocide, and not to State succession.

54. It has been the Court that seems to have misapprehended this, devoting considerable more attention, at this final stage of the adjudication of the present case, again to the issue of jurisdiction, which should have been decided some years ago. The ICJ, in the present Judgment on the merits of the *cas d'espèce*, concerning the *Application of the Convention against Genocide*, has devoted no less than 50 paragraphs to the jurisdiction issue, guarding small proportion in this respect.

V Automatic Succession to the Convention against Genocide, and Continuity of Its Obligations, as an Imperative of Humaneness

1 *The Convention against Genocide and the Imperative of Humaneness*

55. Since the Court has done so in the present Judgment, I feel obliged, in the present Dissenting Opinion, to dwell upon the foundations of my own personal position in support of the automatic succession (*supra*) to the Convention against Genocide. It is generally acknowledged that the Genocide Convention

---

62 Cf. mainly ICJ, doc. CR 2014/14, of 11.03.2014, pp. 10–69.
63 Cf. mainly ICJ, doc. CR 2014/22, of 27.03.2014, pp. 16–47.

is a human rights treaty: one of the legal consequences ensuing therefrom is the automatic succession to it and the continuity of its obligations.

56. As this Court itself indicated in its *célèbre* Advisory Opinion of 1951, States Parties to the 1948 Genocide Convention do not have individual interests of their own, but are rather *jointly* guided by the high ideals and basic considerations of humanity having led the United Nations to condemn and punish the international crime of genocide, which "shocks the conscience of mankind and results in great losses to humanity", being contrary to the spirit and aims of the United Nations.[64] The fundamental principles underlying the Convention are "binding on States, even without any conventional obligation". The condemnation of genocide has a "universal character", with all the cooperation required "to liberate mankind from such an odious scourge", as stated in the preamble to the Convention (cf. *supra*).

57. This calls for the automatic succession to the Genocide Convention, with the continuity of its obligations; international responsibility for the grave wrongs done to segments of the population concerned survives State disruption and succession. To argue otherwise would militate against the object and purpose of the Genocide Convention, depriving it of its *effet utile*; it would thereby deprive the targeted "human groups" of any protection, when they most needed it, thus creating a void of protection which would render the Genocide Convention an almost dead letter.

58. The *corpus juris gentium* for the international safeguard of the rights of the human person is conformed by the converging trends of protection of the International Law of Human Rights, of the International Humanitarian Law, and of the International Law of Refugees.[65] The rights protected thereunder, in any circumstances, are not reduced to those "granted" by the State: they are *inherent to the human person*, and ought thus to be respected by the State. The protected rights are *superior and anterior to the State*, and must thus be respected by this latter, by all States, even in the occurrence of State disruption and succession. It has taken much suffering and sacrifice of succeeding generations to learn this. The aforementioned *corpus juris gentium* is people-oriented, victim-oriented, and not at all State-sovereignty oriented.

---

64   U.N., G.A. resolution 96(1), of 11.12.1946.
65   Cf. A.A. Cançado Trindade, *Derecho Internacional de los Derechos Humanos, Derecho Internacional de los Refugiados y Derecho Internacional Humanitario – Aproximaciones y Convergencias*, Geneva, ICRC, [2000], pp. 1–66.

59. The 1948 Genocide Convention is *people-oriented*, rather than State-centric: it is centred on human groups, whom it aims to protect. As contemporary history shows, in the event of dissolution of States the affected local populations become particularly vulnerable; that is the time when they stand most in need of the protection extended to them by human rights treaties, the Genocide Convention (to which their State had become a Party) being one of them. The fact remains that the *corpus juris gentium* of international protection of the rights of the human person, essentially victim-oriented, has been erected and consolidated along the last decades (almost seven decades) to the benefit of human beings, individually (like under the 1951 Convention on the Status of Refugees, the 1966 U.N. Covenant on Civil and Political Rights, the 1965 U.N. Convention for the Elimination of All Forms of Racial Discrimination) or in groups (like under the 1948 Convention against Genocide).

60. That *corpus juris gentium*, which forms, in my view, the most important legacy of the international legal thinking of the XXth century, cannot be undermined by the vicissitudes of State succession. The population – the most precious constitutive element of statehood – surely cannot be subjected to those vicissitudes, when State succession takes place amidst extreme violence. It is in those circumstances of the disruption of the State that the population concerned stands most in need of protection, such as the one afforded by the core Conventions of the International Law of Human Rights, the International Humanitarian Law, and the International Law of Refugees.

61. To attempt to withdraw their protection, rendering human beings, individually and in groups, extremely vulnerable, if not defenceless, would go against the letter and spirit of those Conventions. Moreover, when it comes to the Convention against Genocide, we find ourselves in the realm not only of conventional international law, but likewise of general or customary international law itself. As the ICJ perspicaciously pondered in its aforementioned Advisory Opinion of 1951, the principles underlying the Convention against Genocide are "binding on States, even without any conventional obligation".[66] And it could not be otherwise, as, in my own conception, the *universal juridical conscience* is the ultimate *material* source of international law, the *jus gentium*.[67]

---

66   *ICJ Reports* (1951) p. 23.
67   A.A. Cançado Trindade, *International Law for Humankind – Towards a New Jus Gentium*, 2nd. rev. ed., Leiden/The Hague, Nijhoff/The Hague Academy of International Law, 2013, Ch. VI, pp. 139–161.

62. It is indeed in times of violent State disruption – as that of the former Yugoslavia – that human beings, individually or in groups, stand in most need of protection. After all, States exist for human beings, and not vice-versa. To deprive human beings of international protection when they most need it, would go against the very foundations of contemporary international law, both conventional and customary, and would make abstraction of the *principle of humanity*, which permeates it. The *corpus juris gentium* of protection of human beings, in any circumstances, is – may I reiterate – essentially victim-oriented, while the outlook of State succession is ineluctably and strictly State-centric.

63. Such outlook cannot at all be made to prevail in violent State disruption, entailing the discontinuity of that protection when it is most needed. The automatic succession to the Convention against Genocide is an *imperative of humaneness*. The *corpus juris gentium* of protection of the human person enshrines rights which are *anterior and superior to the State*. They are listed, *inter alia*, in the *core Conventions* of the United Nations (the two Covenants on Human Rights of 1966; the Conventions for the Elimination of All Forms of Racial Discrimination, and of Discrimination against Women, of 1965 and 1979; the 1984 Convention against Torture; and the 1989 Convention on the Rights of the Child). Moreover, in the last decades international legal doctrine has endeavoured to identify a *hardcore* of universal human rights – non-derogable ones – which admit no restrictions, namely, the fundamental rights to life and to personal integrity, the absolute prohibition of torture and of cruel, inhuman or degrading treatment.

64. Contemporary international law is particularly sensitive to the pressing need of humane treatment of persons, in any circumstances, so as to prohibit inhuman treatment, by reference to humanity as a whole, in order to secure protection to all, even more so when they stand in situations of great vulnerability. *Humaneness* is to orient human behaviour in all circumstances, in times of peace as well as of disturbances and armed conflict. The *principle of humanity* permeates the whole *corpus juris* of protection of the human person, providing one of the illustrations of the approximations or convergences between its distinct and complementary trends (International Humanitarian Law, the International Law of Human Rights, and International Refugee Law), at the hermeneutic level, and also manifested at the normative and the operational levels.[68]

---

68 Cf., on this particular point, e.g., A.A. Cançado Trindade, *Derecho Internacional de los Derechos Humanos, Derecho Internacional de los Refugiados y Derecho Internacional Humanitario – Aproximaciones y Convergencias, op cit. supra* n. (65), pp. 1–66.

2 *The Principle of Humanity in Its Wide Dimension*

65. My own understanding is in the sense that the principle of humanity in endowed with a wide dimension: it applies in the most distinct circumstances, in times both of armed conflict and of peace, in the relations between public power and all persons subject to the jurisdiction of the State concerned. That principle has a notorious incidence when these latter are in a situation of vulnerability or great adversity, or even *defencelessness*, as evidenced by relevant provisions of distinct treaties conforming the International Law of Human Rights.[69]

66. The United Nations Charter itself professes the determination to secure respect for human rights everywhere. Adopted in one of the rare moments of lucidity in the last century, it opens up its preamble by stating that

> We, the peoples of the United Nations, determined to save succeeding generations from the scourge of war; (...) to reaffirm faith in fundamental human rights, in the dignity and worth of the human person (...); to establish conditions under which justice and respect for the obligations arising from treaties and other sources of international law can be maintained; (...) have resolved to combine our efforts to accomplish these aims.

67. And the U.N. Charter includes, among the purposes of the United Nations, to solve problems of humanitarian character, and to promote and encourage respect for human rights for all (Article 1(3)). It determines that the General Assembly shall initiate studies and make recommendations for assisting in the realization of human rights for all (Article 13(1)(b)). It further states that, in order to create the "conditions of stability and well-being which are necessary for peaceful and friendly relations among nations", the United Nations shall promote "universal respect for, and observance of, human rights and fundamental freedoms for all without distinction as to race, sex, language or religion" (Article 55(c)).

---

69 Thus, for example, at U.N. level, the 1990 International Convention on the Protection of the Rights of All Migrant Workers and Members of Their Families, Article 17(1); the 1989 U.N. Convention on the Rights of the Child, (Article 37(b)). Provisions of the kind can also be found in human rights treaties at regional level, e.g., the 1969 American Convention on Human Rights, (Article 5(2); the 1981 African Charter on Human and Peoples' Rights (Article 5).

68. It is clear that the *principle of humanity* permeates the Law of the United Nations. It encompasses the whole *corpus juris* of the international protection of the human person, comprising its converging trends of International Humanitarian Law, International Law of Human Rights, and International Law of Refugees. In effect, when one evokes the principle of humanity, there is a tendency to consider it in the framework of International Humanitarian Law. It is beyond doubt that, in this framework, for example, civilians and persons *hors de combat* are to be treated with humanity. The principle of humane treatment of civilians and persons *hors de combat* is provided for in the 1949 Geneva Conventions on International Humanitarian Law.[70] Such principle, moreover, is generally regarded as one of customary International Humanitarian Law.[71]

69. The principle of humanity, in line with the longstanding thinking of natural law, is an emanation of human conscience, projecting itself into conventional as well as customary international law. The treatment dispensed to human beings, in any circumstances, ought to abide by the *principle of humanity*, which permeates the whole *corpus juris* of the international protection of the rights of the human person (encompassing International Humanitarian Law, the International Law of Human Rights, and International Refugee Law), conventional as well as customary, at global (U.N.) and regional levels. The principle of humanity, usually invoked in the domain of International Humanitarian Law, thus extends itself also to that of International Human Rights Law.[72]

70. In faithfulness to my own conception, I have, in recent decisions of the ICJ (and, earlier on, of the Inter-American Court of Human Rights as well), deemed it fit to develop some reflections on the basis of the principle of humanity *lato sensu*. I have done so, e.g., in my Dissenting Opinion (paras. 24–25 and 61) in the case of the *Obligation to Prosecute or Extradite* (Belgium *versus* Senegal, Request for Provisional Measures, Order of 28.05.2009), and in

---

70 Common Article 3, and Articles 12(1)/12(1)/13/5 and 27(1); and their Additional Protocols I (Article 75(1)) and II (Article 4(1)).

71 For a study in depth, cf. ICRC, *Customary International Humanitarian Law* (eds. J.-M. Henckaerts and L. Doswald-Beck), Geneva/Cambridge, Cambridge University Press, 2005, vol. I: *Rules*, pp. 3–621; vol. II, Part I: *Practice*, pp. 3–1982; vol. II, Part II: *Practice*, pp. 1983–4411.

72 Cf., to this effect, Human Rights Committee, General Comment n. 31 (of 2004), para. 11; and cf. also its General Comments n. 9 (of 1982), para. 3, and n. 21 (of 1992), para. 4. It may further be recalled that, in the aftermath of the II World War, the 1948 Universal Declaration of Human Rights proclaimed that "[a]ll human beings are born free and equal in dignity and rights" (Article 1).

my Dissenting Opinion (paras. 116, 118, 125, 136–139 and 179)[73] in the case of *Jurisdictional Immunities of the State* (Counter-Claim, Germany *versus* Italy, Order of 06.07.2010), as well as in my lengthy Separate Opinion (paras. 67–96 and 169–217) in the Court's Advisory Opinion on *Accordance with International Law of the Declaration of Independence of Kosovo* (of 22.07.2010). I have likewise sustained the wide dimension of the principle of humanity in my lengthy Separate Opinion (paras. 93–106 and 107–142) in the ICJ's Judgment (of 30.11.2010) in the case *A.S. Diallo* (merits, Guinea *versus* D.R. Congo).

71. The ICJ has lately given signs – as I perceive them – of its preparedness to take into account the principle of humanity. Thus, in its Order of Provisional Measures of Protection of 18.07.2011, in the case of the *Temple of Preah Vihear*, the ICJ, in deciding *inter alia* to order the establishment of a provisional demilitarized zone around the Temple (part of the world's cultural and spiritual heritage) and its vicinity, it extended protection (as I pointed out in my Separate Opinion, paras. 66–113) not only to the territory at issue, but also to the local inhabitants, in conformity with the *principle of humanity* in the framework of the new *jus gentium* of our times (paras. 114–117). Territory and people go together.

72. Subsequently, in the recent case of the *Frontier Dispute* (Judgment of 16.04.2013), the contending parties (Burkina Faso and Niger) themselves expressed before the Court their concern, in particular with local nomadic and semi-nomadic populations, and assured that their living conditions would not be affected by the tracing of the frontier. Once again, as I pointed out in my Separate Opinion (paras. 90, 99 and 104–105), the *principle of humanity* seemed to have permeated the handling of the case by the ICJ.

3   *The Principle of Humanity in the Heritage of Jusnaturalist Thinking*

73. It should not pass unnoticed that the principle of humanity is in line with natural law thinking. It underlies classic thinking on humane treatment and the maintenance of sociable relationships, also at international level. Humaneness came to the fore even more forcefully in the treatment of persons in *situation of vulnerability, or even defencelessness*, such as those deprived of

---

73 In this lengthy Dissenting Opinion, my reflections relating to the principle of humanity are found particularly in its Part XII, on human beings as the true bearers (*titulaires*) of the originally violated rights and the pitfalls of State voluntarism (paras 112–123), as well as in its Part XIII, on the incidence of *jus cogens* (paras. 126–146), besides the Conclusions (mainly paras. 178–179).

their personal freedom, for whatever reason. The *jus gentium*, when it emerged as amounting to the law of nations, came then to be conceived by its "founding fathers" (F. de Vitoria, A. Gentili, F. Suárez, H. Grotius, S. Pufendorf, C. Wolff) as regulating the international community constituted by human beings socially organized in the (emerging) States and co-extensive with humankind, thus conforming the *necessary* law of the *societas gentium*.

74. The *jus gentium*, thus conceived, was inspired by the principle of humanity *lato sensu*. Human conscience prevails over the will of individual States. Respect for the human person is to the benefit of the common good.[74] This humanist vision of the international legal order pursued – as it does nowadays – a *people-centred outlook*, keeping in mind the *humane ends of the State*. The precious legacy of natural law thinking, evoking the right human reason (*recta ratio*), has never faded away; this should be stressed time and time again, particularly in face of the indifference and pragmatism of the "strategic" *droit d'étatistes*, so numerous in the legal profession in our days. The principle of humanity may be considered as an expression of the *raison d'humanité* imposing limits on the *raison d'État*.[75]

75. States, created by human beings gathered in their social *milieu*, are bound to protect, and not at all to oppress, all those who are under their respective jurisdictions. This corresponds to the minimum ethical, universally reckoned by the international community of our times. At the time of the adoption of the Universal Declaration on 10.12.1948 (on the day following the adoption of the Convention against Genocide), one could hardly anticipate that a historical process of generalization of the international protection of human rights was being launched, on a truly universal scale.[76] States are bound to safeguard the integrity of the human person from repression and systematic violence, from discriminatory and arbitrary treatment.

---

[74] A.A. Cançado Trindade, *A Humanização do Direito Internacional*, Belo Horizonte/Brazil, Edit. Del Rey, 2006, pp. 9–14, 172, 318–319, 393 and 408.

[75] A.A. Cançado Trindade, *International Law for Humankind – Towards a New Jus Gentium*, op cit. supra n. (67), pp. 150–152 and 275–285.

[76] Throughout almost seven decades, of remarkable historical projection, the Declaration has gradually acquired an authority which its draftsmen could not have foreseen. This happened mainly because successive generations of human beings, from distinct cultures and all over the world, recognized in it a "common standard of achievement" (as originally proclaimed), which corresponded to their deepest and most legitimate aspirations.

76. The conception of fundamental and inalienable human rights is deeply-engraved in the universal juridical conscience; in spite of variations in their enunciation or formulation, their conception marks presence in all cultures, and in the modern history of human thinking of all peoples.[77] The 1948 Universal Declaration warns that "disregard and contempt for human rights have resulted in barbarous acts which have outraged the conscience of mankind" (preamble, para. 2); it further warns that "it is essential, if man is not compelled to have recourse, as a last resort, to rebellion against tyranny and oppression, that human rights should be protected by the rule of law" (preamble, para. 3). Moreover, it acknowledges that "recognition of the inherent dignity and of the equal and inalienable rights of all members of the human family is the foundation of freedom, justice and peace in the world" (preamble, para. 1).

4   Judicial Recognition of the Principle of Humanity

77. May I now turn attention, however briefly, to the acknowledgment of the principle of humanity in the case-law of contemporary international tribunals. The fundamental principle of humanity has indeed met therein with full judicial recognition.[78] Its acknowledgment is found, e.g., in the *jurisprudence constante* of the IACtHR, which holds that it applies even more forcefully when persons are found in an "*exacerbated situation of vulnerability*".[79] In my Separate Opinion in the Judgment of the IACtHR (of 29.04.2004) in the case of the *Massacre of Plan de Sánchez*, concerning Guatemala (one of a pattern of 626 massacres), I devoted a whole section (III, paras. 9–23) of it to the judicial acknowledgement of the principle of humanity in the recent case-law of the IACtHR as well as of the *ad hoc* International Criminal Tribunal for the Former Yugoslavia (ICTFY).

---

77   Cf., e.g., A.A. Cançado Trindade, *Tratado de Direito International dos Direitos Humanos* [*Treatise of International Law of Human Rights*], vol. I, 1st. ed., Porto Alegre/Brazil, S.A. Fabris Ed., 1997, pp. 31–57; [Various Authors,] *Universality of Human Rights in a Pluralistic World* (Proceedings of the 1989 Strasbourg Colloquy), Strasbourg/Kehl, N.P. Engel Verlag, 1990, pp. 45, 57, 103, 138, 143 and 155.

78   Cf. A.A. Cançado Trindade, "Le déracinement et la protection des migrants dans le droit international des droits de l'homme", 19 *Revue trimestrielle des droits de l'homme* – Bruxelles (2008) pp. 289–328, esp. pp. 295 and 308–316.

79   IACtHR, Judgments in the cases of *Maritza Urrutia versus Guatemala*, of 27.11.2003, para. 87; of *Juan Humberto Sánchez versus Honduras*, of 07.06.2003, para. 96; and of *Cantoral Benavides versus Peru*, of 18.08.2000, para. 90; and cf. case of *Bámaca Velásquez versus Guatemala*, of 25.11.2000, para. 150. – For a recent study on the protection of the vulnerable, cf. A.A. Cançado Trindade, *A Proteção dos Vulneráveis como Legado da II Conferência*

78. I pondered therein that the primacy of the principle of humanity is identified with the very end or ultimate goal of the Law, of the whole legal order, both national and international, in recognizing the inalienability of all rights inherent to the human person (para. 17). The same principle of humanity, – I concluded in the aforementioned Separate Opinion in the case of the *Massacre of Plan de Sánchez*, – also has incidence in the domain of International Refugee Law, as disclosed by the facts of the *cas d'espèce*, involving massacres and the State-policy of *tierra arrasada*, i.e., the destruction and burning of homes, which generated a massive forced displacement of persons (para. 23).

79. Likewise, the ICTFY has devoted attention to the principle of humanity in its Judgments, e.g., in the cases of *Mucić et alii* (2001) and of *Čelebići* (1998). In the *Mucić et alii* case (Judgment of 20.02.2001), the ICTFY (Appeals Chamber), pondered that both International Humanitarian Law and the International Law of Human Rights take as a "starting point" their common concern to safeguard human dignity, which forms the basis of their minimum standards of humanity (para. 149).[80]

80. Earlier on, in the *Čelebići* case (Judgment of 16.11.1998), the ICTFY (Trial Chamber) qualified as *inhuman treatment* an intentional or deliberate act or omission which causes serious suffering (or mental or physical damage), or constitutes a serious attack on human dignity; thus, – the Tribunal added, – "inhuman treatment is intentional treatment which does not conform with the fundamental principle of humanity, and forms the umbrella under which the remainder of the listed 'grave breaches' in the Conventions fall".[81] Subsequently, in the *T. Blaškić* case (Judgment of 03.03.2000), the ICTFY (Trial Chamber) reiterated this position.[82]

81. Likewise, in its Judgment of 10.12.2003 in the *Obrenović* case, the ICTFY (Trial Chamber) stated that it is the "abhorrent discriminatory intent" that renders

---

Mundial de Direitos Humanos (1993–2013) [*The Protection of the Vulnerable as Legacy of the II World Conference on Human Rights (1993–2013)*], Fortaleza/Brazil, IBDH, 2014, pp. 13–356.

80   In fact, the principle of humanity can be understood in distinct ways; first, it can be conceived as a principle underlying the prohibition of inhuman treatment, established by Article 3 common to the four Geneva Conventions of 1949; secondly, the principle can be invoked by reference to humankind as a whole, in relation to matters of common, general and direct interest to it; and thirdly, the same principle can be employed to qualify a given quality of human behaviour (humaneness).

81   Paragraph 543 of that Judgment.

82   Paragraph 154 of that Judgment.

crimes against humanity "particularly grave" (para. 65). Evoking the Tribunal (Appeals Chamber)'s finding in the *Erdemović* case (Judgment of 07.10.1997), it added that, because of their "heinousness and magnitude", those crimes (against humanity)

> constitute egregious attacks on human dignity, on the very notion of humaneness. They consequently affect, or should affect, each and every member of [human]kind, whatever his or her nationality, ethnic group and location (para. 65).[83]

82. For its part, the *ad hoc* International Criminal Tribunal for Rwanda (ICTR) pondered, in the case of *J.-P. Akayesu* (Judgment of 02.09.1998), that the concept of crimes against humanity had already been recognized well before the Nuremberg Tribunal itself (1945–1946). The Martens clause contributed to that effect; in fact, expressions similar to that of those crimes, invoking victimized humanity, appeared much earlier in human history.[84] The ICTR further pointed out, in the case *J. Kambanda* (Judgment of 04.09.1998), that in all periods of human history genocide has inflicted great losses to humankind, the victims being not only the persons slaughtered but humanity itself (in acts of genocide as well as in crimes against humanity).[85]

5   *Concluding Observations*

83. There is, in sum, in contemporary (conventional and general) international law, a greater consciousness, in a virtually universal scale, of the principle of humanity. Grave violations of human rights, acts of genocide, crimes against humanity, among other atrocities, are in breach of absolute prohibitions of *jus cogens*. The feeling of *humaneness* permeates the whole *corpus juris* of contemporary international law. I have called this development, – *inter alia* in my Concurring Opinion (para. 35) in the Advisory Opinion (of 01.10.1999), of the IACtHR, on the *Right to Information on Consular Assistance in the Framework of the Guarantees of the Due Process of Law*, – a historical process of a true

---

83   Those words were actually taken by the ICTFY (Trial Chamber) in the *Obrenović* case (para. 65), from a passage of the Joint Separate Opinion (para. 21) of Judges McDonald and Vohrah, in the ICTFY's Appeal Judgment in the aforementioned *Erdemović* case (1997).

84   Paragraphs 565–566 of that Judgment.

85   Paragraphs 15–16 of that Judgment. An equal reasoning is found in the Judgments of the same Tribunal in the aforementioned case *J.-P. Akayesu*, as well as in the case *O. Serushago* (Judgment of 05.02.1999, para. 15).

humanization of International Law. The prevalence of the principle of humanity is identified with the ultimate aim itself of Law, of the legal order, both national and international.

84. By virtue of this fundamental principle, every person ought to be respected (in her honour and in her beliefs) by the simple fact of belonging to humankind, irrespective of any circumstance. In its application in any circumstances (in times both of armed conflict and of peace), in the relations between public power and human beings subject to the jurisdiction of the State concerned, the principle of humanity permeates the whole *corpus juris* of the international protection of the rights of the human person (encompassing International Humanitarian Law, the International Law of Human Rights, and International Refugee Law),[86] conventional as well as customary.[87] And it has further projected itself into the law of international organizations, – and in particular into the Law of the United Nations.

VI   The Convention against Genocide and State Responsibility

1   *Legislative History of the Convention (Article IX)*

85. Turning now, in particular, to the 1948 Convention against Genocide, it appears from its *travaux préparatoires* that State responsibility for breaches of the Convention was in fact considered in the drafting of what was to become its Article X. This occurred in order to cope with amendments to the Draft Convention which seemed to have "weakened" previous views on the responsibility of Heads of State. The insertion of a reference to State responsibility also appeared as an answer to the rejection, during the debates of the *travaux préparatoires*, of a "stronger" form of State liability for genocide related to what then was Draft Article V (and then became Article IV) of the Convention.

86. It may be recalled that, originally, Draft Article X (as prepared by the *Ad Hoc* Committee) did not contain the reference – found later on in what was to become Article IX of the Genocide Convention – to State responsibility for acts of genocide.[88] Article IX of the Genocide Convention, as it now stands,

---

86   Paras. 58, 60, 64, 69 and 79, *supra*.

87   Paras. 60 and 68–69, *supra*.

88   Article X of the Draft Convention, as drawn up by the *Ad Hoc* Committee, used to read as follows: – "Disputes between the High Contracting Parties relating to the interpretation or application of this Convention shall be submitted to the International Court of Justice,

can be traced back to a joint amendment, proposed by Belgium and the United Kingdom, to what was then Article X. The proposed joint amendment to that provision was as follows:

> Any dispute between the High Contracting Parties relating to the interpretation, application or fulfilment of the present Convention, *including disputes relating to the responsibility of a State* for any of the acts enumerated in articles II and IV, shall be submitted to the International Court of Justice at the request of any of the High Contracting Parties.[89]

87. The reasons for this insertion can be found in the discussions on the joint amendment in the VI Committee of the U.N. General Assembly. The Delegate of the United Kingdom (Mr. Fitzmaurice) explained that both the United Kingdom and Belgium considered that the Convention would not be complete if it did not contemplate state liability for genocidal acts and other punishable offences provided for in the Convention.[90] In opposition to this amendment, another joint amendment was proposed by the USSR and France, without providing for obligatory reference to the ICJ with respect to the Convention; it only contemplated an optional reference mechanism.

88. The French Delegate (Mr. Chaumont) did not show any opposition towards the principle of liability, insofar as it was of a civil nature, and not criminal.[91] The Egyptian Delegate (Mr. Rafaat) also supported the principle of State liability, as no international mechanism of punishment existed.[92] But the proposed amendment also faced opposition from a few Delegations.[93] In addition, the

---

provided that no dispute shall be submitted to the International Court of Justice involving an issue which has been referred to and is pending before or has been passed upon by competent international criminal tribunal". U.N. doc. E/794, p. 38.
89 U.N. doc. A/C.6/258, p. 1 [emphasis added].
90 UN doc. A/C.6/SR.103, p. 430.
91 *Ibid.*, p. 431.
92 *Ibid.*, p. 431. The Greek Delegate (Mr. Spiropoulos) raised an issue as to responsibility relating to cases where a State had its liability triggered for genocide: in such cases, responsibility for that State would involve indemnifying itself, as, in his view, individuals were not considered as right-holders in international law at those times; *ibid.*, p. 433.
93 The Philippines Delegate (Mr. Ingles) insisted on his opposition to the principle or criminal liability (which he posited earlier with respect to Article V), and further argued that, although the joint amendment was not explicitly included in the proposition, the very nature of the Convention, purported to punish genocide implied that liability would be criminal; this, in his view, would bring stigmatization of a whole State for acts committed

Canadian Delegate (Mr. Lapointe), for his part, asked clarification from the U.K. Delegation as to the meaning intended to ascribe to "State responsibility", – whether it was criminal or civil, – having in mind in particular that the Committee, in its 93rd meeting, had rejected the idea of criminal State responsibility during discussions related to article V.[94] The Bolivian Delegate (Mr. Medeiros) expressed his support for the U.K./Belgian amendment, finding it necessary.[95]

89. For its part, the Haitian Delegation proposed a consequential amendment to the aforementioned joint amendment, which would add "or of any victims of the crime of genocide (groups of individuals)". This met the opposition of some Delegations, which argued that such amendment would imply a modification of the ICJ Statute. Yet, the Syrian Delegation considered that such consequential amendment was not contrary to the ICJ Statute, as in its view there was no reason for the signatory State to impede groups victims of genocide to seize the ICJ for such breaches. In support of its proposal, the Haitian Delegation asserted, *inter alia*, that States could be liable only directly towards the victims themselves, and not towards other States, for having committed genocide.[96]

90. Some Delegations, such as those of the USSR and Poland, voiced concerns as to the effect of the reference to the ICJ of disputes relating to State liability under the Genocide Convention. The preoccupation was related to the possibility of Draft Article X (as then worded) precluding submission to the U.N. General Assembly or the Security Council of complaints with respect to genocidal acts.[97] The U.K. Delegate replied that submission to the ICJ could not in

---

only by its rulers or officials and not by the State itself, showing that responsibility of the State could not be possible; U.N. doc. A/C.6/SR.103, p. 433. The Delegation of Pakistan also expressed concern about the introduction of State liability in an international instrument which was mainly aimed at a criminal matter; he expressed his preference for the wording of article V when it referred to the "constitutionally responsible leaders"; *ibid.*, p. 438. The Delegation of the USSR argued that the proposed joint amendment was only an intent to submit in a different manner an amendment to article V so as to introduce some form of criminal liability of the State; *ibid.*, p. 441.

94   *Ibid.*, pp. 438–439. The UK representative replied that the amendment was indeed referring to civil liability (international responsibility for violation of the Convention).
95   In the light of the decisions taken up by the Committee in the course its 97th meeting; *ibid.*, p. 439.
96   Cf. U.N. doc. A/C.6/SR.103, p. 436.
97   Cf. U.N. doc. A/C.6/SR.103, *ibid.*, p. 444.

any way preclude submission before other competent organs of the U.N.[98] And the U.K. Delegate concluded that, giving the ICJ jurisdiction for State liability arising out of breaches of the Genocide Convention was necessary in order to ensure an effective enforcement of the Convention, considering in particular the practical difficulties in prosecuting Heads of State.[99]

91. The joint amendment was then adopted by 23 votes to 13, with 8 abstentions.[100] (Then) Article X, with other amendments, was adopted by 18 to 2, with 15 abstentions; it came to read as follows:

> Any dispute between the High Contracting Parties relating to the interpretation, application or fulfilment of the present Convention, including disputes relating to the responsibility of a State for any of the acts enumerated in articles II and IV, shall be submitted to the International Court of Justice at the request of any of the parties to the dispute.[101]

This version of (then) Article X underwent minor changes, leading to the final version of what is now Article IX of the Convention against Genocide, which reads as follows:

> Disputes between the Contracting Parties relating to the interpretation, application or fulfilment of the present Convention, including those relating to the responsibility of a State for genocide or for any of the other acts enumerated in article III, shall be submitted to the International Court of Justice at the request of any of the parties to the dispute.

2   Rationale, and Object and Purpose of the Convention

92. The determination of State responsibility under the Convention against Genocide is well-founded, not only because this was intended by the draftsmen of the Convention, as its *travaux préparatoires* show (*supra*), but also because such determination is in line with the *rationale* of the Convention, as well as its object and purpose. Today, 66 years after its adoption, the Convention

---

98   *Ibid.*, p. 444. Furthermore, in response to the criticism, he asserted that reference to the ICJ might be useless, as that Court would act too late in cases of genocide: genocide is a process, – he added, – and once it started being committed, a State Party could seize the Court; *ibid.*, p. 444.
99   *Ibid.*, p. 444.
100 *Ibid.*, p. 447.
101 U.N. doc. A/C.6/269, p. 1. Cf. also Article IX (as it then became), U.N. doc. A/760, p. 10.

against Genocide counts on 146 States Parties; and the States which have not yet ratified, or acceded to it, are also aware that the prohibition of genocide is one likewise of general or customary international law. It is not conditioned by alterations in State sovereignty or vicissitudes of State succession; it is an absolute prohibition, belonging to the realm of *jus cogens*.

93. The Convention against Genocide is meant to prevent and punish the crime of genocide, – which is contrary to the spirit and aims of the United Nations, – so as to liberate humankind from such an odious scourge. Nowadays, six and a half decades after the adoption of the Convention against Genocide, much more is known about that heinous international crime. "Genocide studies" have been undertaken in recent decades in distinct branches of human learning, attentive to an interdisciplinary perspective (cf. Part XI, *infra*). They have shown that genocide has been committed in modern history in furtherance of State policies.

94. To attempt to make the application of the Genocide Convention to States an impossible task, would render the Convention meaningless, an almost dead letter; it would furthermore create a situation where certain State egregious criminal acts, amounting to genocide, would pass unpunished, – especially as there is at present no international Convention on Crimes against Humanity. Genocide is in fact an egregious crime committed under the direction, or the benign complicity, of the State and its apparatus.[102] Unlike what was assumed by the Nuremberg Tribunal in its *célèbre* Judgment (Part 22, p. 447), States are not "abstract entities"; they have been concretely engaged, together with individual executioners (their so-called "human resources", acting on their behalf), in acts of genocide, in distinct historical moments and places.

95. They have altogether – individuals and States – been responsible for such heinous acts. In this context, individual and State responsibility complement each other. In sum, the determination of State responsibility cannot at all be discarded in the interpretation and application of the Convention against Genocide. When adjudicating a case such as the present one, concerning the *Application of the Convention against Genocide* (Croatia *versus* Serbia), the ICJ should bear in mind the importance of the Convention as a major human

---

[102] The expert evidence examined by the ICTFY, for example, in the *S. Milošević* case (2004), maintained that the knowledge sedimented on the matter shows that State authorities are always responsible for a genocidal process; cf. Part XIII of the present Dissenting Opinion, *infra*.

rights treaty, with all its implications and legal consequences. It should bear in mind the Convention's historic significance for humankind.

VII Standard of Proof in the Case-Law of International Human Rights Tribunals

96. The case-law of international human rights tribunals is of central importance to the determination of the international responsibility of States (rather than individuals) for grave violations of human rights, and cannot pass unnoticed in a case like the present one, concerning the *Application of the Convention against Genocide*, opposing Croatia to Serbia. It cannot thus be overlooked by the ICJ, concerned as it is, like international human rights tribunals, with *State* responsibility, and not individual (criminal) responsibility.

1 *A Question from the Bench: The Evolving Case-Law on the Matter*

97. In the course of the oral proceedings in the present case, the contending parties were, however, referring only to the case-law of international criminal tribunals (concerned with *individual* responsibility), until the moment, in the Court's public sitting of 05.03.2014, that I deemed it fit to put the following question to both of them, on also the case-law of international human rights tribunals:

> My question concerns the international criminal responsibility of individuals, as well as the international responsibility of States, for genocide. References have so far been made only to the case-law of international criminal tribunals (the ICTY and the ICTR), pertaining to individual international criminal responsibility. Do you consider that the case-law of international human rights tribunals is also of relevance here, for the international responsibility of States for genocide, as to standard of proof and attribution?[103]

From then onwards, both Croatia and Serbia started referring, *comme il faut*, to the case-law of international human rights tribunals as well,[104] – concerned as these latter are with the determination of State responsibility.

---

103 Question put by Judge Cançado Trindade, *in*: ICJ, doc. CR 2014/8, of 05.03.2014, p. 59.
104 Croatia's responses, *in*: ICJ, doc. CR 2014/12, of 07.03.2014, p. 44, para. 20; and ICJ, doc. CR 2014/20, of 20.03.2014, pp. 14–16, paras. 8–9; Serbia's response, *in*: ICJ, doc. CR 2014/23, of 28.03.2014, pp. 50–52 para. 27–36.

98. In addition to what the contending Parties argued in the proceedings of the present case concerning the *Application of the Convention against Genocide*, there is, in effect, a wealth of relevant indications as to the standard of proof (and reversal of the burden of proof), which should not pass unnoticed here. This is so, in particular, in the case-law of the Inter-American Court of Human Rights (IACtHR), in cases disclosing a systematic or widespread pattern of gross violations of human rights, where the IACtHR has resorted to factual presumptions.

99. Moreover, the IACtHR has held that it is the respondent State which is to produce the evidence, given the applicant's difficulty to obtain it and the respondent's access to it. There are indications to this effect also in the case-law of the European Court of Human Rights (ECtHR). Given the relevance of the case-law of international human rights tribunals for the determination of international *State* responsibility, it cannot at all be overlooked in the consideration of the *cas d'espèce*, in so far as the key issue of standard of proof is concerned. I thus care to proceed to its review.

2 Case-Law of the IACtHR
a) Cases Disclosing a Systematic Pattern of Grave Violations of Human Rights

100. The case-law of the IACtHR is particularly rich in respect of the standard of proof in cases disclosing a systematic pattern of grave violations of human rights. In the case of *Juan Humberto Sánchez versus Honduras* (Judgment of 07.06.2003), for example, the IACtHR determined the occurrence, in the respondent State, in the eighties and beginning of the nineties, of a systematic pattern of arbitrary detentions, enforced disappearances of persons, and summary or extrajudicial executions committed by the military forces (paras. 70(1) and 96–97), wherein the *cas d'espèce* is inserted (para. 80).

101. The IACtHR thus *inferred*, even in the absence of direct proofs, that the victim suffered cruel and inhuman treatment during the time of his detention (para. 98),[105] before his mortal remains were found. The facts occurred at the time of the pattern of ill-treatment and torture and summary executions, leading the IACtHR to the presumption of the responsibility of the State for those violations in respect of persons under the custody of its agents

---

105 Cf. also, to this effect, IACtHR, case *Bámaca Velásquez versus Guatemala* (Judgment of 25.11.2000), *supra*, para. 150; case *Cantoral Benavides versus Peru* (Judgment of 18.08.2000), paras. 83–84 and 89; and case of the *"Street Children"* (*Villagrán Morales and Others*) *versus Guatemala* (Judgment of 19.11.1999), para. 162.

(para. 99).¹⁰⁶ This being so, – the Court added, – it was incumbent upon the respondent State to provide reasonable explanations on what occurred to the victim (paras. 100 and 135).

102. Other pertinent decisions of the IACtHR can here be recalled.¹⁰⁷ For example, in the case of the *Massacres of Ituango versus Colombia* (Judgment of 01.07.2006), the IACtHR, having found in the municipality at issue a systematic pattern of massacres (in 1996–1997) perpetrated by paramilitary groups, determined the responsibility of the State for "omission, acquiescence and collaboration" of the public forces (para. 132).

103. The IACtHR further found that State agents had "full knowledge" of the activities of paramilitary groups terrorizing the local population, and, far from protecting this latter, they omitted doing so, and even participated in the armed incursion into the municipality and the killings of local inhabitants by the paramilitaries (paras. 133 and 135). Within the context of this systematic pattern of violence, the respondent State incurred into grave violations of the rights of the victims under the American Convention on Human Rights (ACHR – paras. 136–138).

104. In the case of the *Masacre de Mapiripán versus Colombia* (Judgment of 15.09.2005), the IACtHR observed that, although the killings in Mapiripán (in mid-July 1997) were committed by members of paramilitary groups,

> the preparation and execution of the massacre could not have been perpetrated without the collaboration, acquiescence and tolerance, manifested in various actions and omissions, of members of the Armed Forces of State, including of its high officers in the zones. Certainly there are no documental proofs before this Tribunal that demonstrate that the State directed directly the execution of the massacre or that there existed a relation of dependence between the Army and the paramilitary groups or a delegation of public functions from the former to these latter (para. 120).

---

106 Cf. also, in this sense, IACtHR, case *Bámaca Velásquez, cit. supra*, paras. 152–153; and case of the "*Street Children*" (*Villagrán Morales and Others*), *cit. supra*, para. 170.
107 Another example of *inference* of a summary or extrajudicial execution, in a context of a generalized or systematic pattern of crimes against humanity (in the period 1973–1990), victimizing the "civilian population" (with thousands of individual victims), is afforded by the IACtHR's Judgment (of 26.09.2006) in the case of *Almonacid Arellano and Others versus Chile* (paras. 96 and 103–104).

THE UNIVERSAL JURIDICAL CONSCIENCE   83

105. The IACtHR then attributed to the respondent State the conducts of both its own agents and of the members of paramilitary groups in the zones which were "under the control of the State". The incursion of paramilitaries in Mapiripán, – it added, – had been planned for months, and was executed "with full knowledge, logistic previsions and collaboration of the Armed Forces", which facilitated the journey of the paramilitaries from Apartadó and Neclocí until Mapiripán "in zones which were under their control", and, moreover, "left unprotected the civilian population during the days of the massacre with the unjustified moving of the troops to other localities" (para. 120).

106. The "collaboration of members of the Armed Forces with the paramilitaries" was manifested in a pattern of "grave actions and omissions" aiming at allowing the perpetration of the massacre and the cover-up of the facts in search of "the impunity of those responsible" (para. 121). The Court added that the State authorities who knew the intentions of the paramilitary groups to perpetrate a massacre to instil terror in the population, "not only collaborated in the preparation" of the killings, but also left the impression before public opinion that the massacre had been perpetrated by paramilitary groups "without its knowledge, participation and tolerance" (para. 121).

107. The IACtHR, discarding this pretension, and having established the links between the Armed Forces and the paramilitary groups in the perpetration of the massacre, determined that "the international responsibility of the State was generated by a pattern of actions and omissions of State agents and *particuliers*, which took place in a coordinated, parallel or organized way aiming at perpetrating the massacre" (para. 123).

108. In its Judgment (of 22.09.2006) in the case *Goiburú and Others versus Paraguay*, the IACtHR observed that that particular case was endowed with "a particular historical transcendence", as the facts had occurred "in a context of a systematic practice of arbitrary detentions, tortures, executions and disappearances perpetrated by the forces of security and intelligence of the dictatorship of Alfredo Stroessner, in the framework of the Operation Cóndor" (para. 62).

109. That is to say, the grave facts are framed in the flagrant, massive and systematic character of the repression which the population was subjected to, at inter-State scale; in fact, the structures of State security were put into action in a coordinated way against the nations at trans-frontier level by the dictatorial governments concerned (para. 62). The IACtHR thus found that the context in which the facts occurred engaged and conditioned the international

responsibility of the State in relation to its obligation to respect and guarantee the rights set forth in Articles 4, 5, 7, 8 and 25 of the ACHR (para. 63).

110. The illegal and arbitrary detentions or kidnapping, torture and enforced disappearances, – the IACtHR added, – were "product of an operation of policial intelligence", planned and executed, and covered up by members of the national police, "with the knowledge and by the order of the highest authorities of the government of General Stroessner, and, at least in the earlier phases of planification of the detentions or kidnappings, in close collaboration with Argentine authorities" (para. 87). Such was the *modus operandi* of the systematic practice of illegal and arbitrary detentions, torture and enforced disappearances verified in the epoch of the facts, in the framework of the Operation Cóndor (para. 87).

111. There was, moreover, a generalized situation of impunity of the grave violations of human rights that occurred, undermining the protection of the rights at issue. This IACtHR stressed the general obligation to respect and ensure respect for the rights set forth in the American Convention on Human Rights (Article 1(1)), wherefrom ensued the obligation to investigate the cases of violations of the protected rights.

112. Thus, in cases of extra-judicial executions, enforced disappearances and other grave violations of human rights, the IACtHR considered that the prompt and *ex officio* investigation thereof should be undertaken, without delay, as a key element for the guarantee of the protected rights, such as the rights to life, to personal integrity, and to personal freedom (para. 88). In this case, – the IACtHR added, – the lack of investigation of the facts constituted a determining factor of the systematic practice of violations of human rights and led to the impunity of those responsible for them (para. 90).

b) Cases Wherein the Respondent State Has the Burden of Proof Given the Difficulty of the Applicant to Obtain it

113. In the case *Velásquez Rodríguez versus Honduras* (Judgment of 29.07.1988), the IACtHR, in dwelling upon the standards of proof, began by acknowledging the prerogative of international tribunals to evaluate *freely* the evidence produced (para. 127). "For an international tribunal", – the IACtHR added, – "the criteria of assessment of proofs are less formal than in the national legal systems" (para. 128). There is a "special gravity" in the attribution of gross violations of human rights (such as enforced disappearances of persons) to States Parties to the ACHR, and the Court has this in mind (para. 129); yet, in such

circumstances, direct proofs (testimonial or documental) are not the only ones that it can base itself upon. Circumstantial evidence (indicia and presumptions) can also be taken into account, whenever the Court can therefrom "infer consistent conclusions" on the facts (para. 130).

114. Such circumstantial evidence, – the IACtHR proceeded, – may become of special importance in cases of grave violations, such as enforced disappearances of persons, characterized by the intent to suppress "any element which may prove the kidnapping, the whereabouts and the fate of the victims" (para. 131). The IACtHR then warned that the international protection of the rights of the human person "is not to be confused with criminal justice", as States do not appear before the Court as subjects of a criminal legal action (para. 134).

115. Its goal, – it went on, – is not to impose penalties to those held culpable of violations of human rights, but rather provide for reparation to the victims for the damages caused by the States responsible for them (para. 134). In the legal process, here, "the defence of the State cannot rest upon the impossibility of the applicant to produce evidence which, in many cases, cannot be obtained without the cooperation of the State" concerned (para. 135), which "has the control of the means to clarify the facts occurred within its territory" (para. 136).[108]

3   Case-Law of the ECtHR

116. The case-law of the ECtHR, like that of other international tribunals, is built on the understanding of the *free* evaluation of evidence. In recent years, the ECtHR has been pursuing an approach which brings it closer to that of the IACtHR (*supra*). It so happened that, in its earlier decades, and until the late nineties, the ECtHR consistently invoked the standard of proof "beyond reasonable doubt"; yet, by no means the ECtHR understood it as meaning a particularly high threshold of standard of proof as the one required in domestic criminal law, in particular in common-law jurisdictions. The standard of proof "beyond reasonable doubt", as used by the ECtHR, was endowed with an autonomous meaning under the European Convention of Human Rights (ECHR), certainly less stringent than the one applied in national (criminal) proceedings as to the admissibility of evidence.

---

108   In the case *Yatama versus Nicaragua* (Judgment of 23.06.2005), e.g., the IACtHR again deemed it fit to warn that, in cases before an international human rights tribunal, it may well occur that the applicant is faced with the impossibility to produce evidence, "which can only be obtained with the cooperation" of the respondent State (para. 134).

117. Criticisms to applying a high standard of proof were to emerge, within the ECtHR, from the bench itself, from dissenting Judges, as in, e.g., the cases of *Labita versus Italy* (Judgment of 06.04.2000) and *S. Veznedaroglu versus Turkey* (Judgment of 11.04.2000). The point was made therein that, to expect victims of grave violations of their rights to prove their allegations "beyond reasonable doubt" would place an unfair burden upon them, impossible to meet; such standard of proof, applicable only in "*criminal* culpability", is not so in "other fields of judicial enquiry", where "the standard of proof should be proportionate to the aim which the search for truth pursues".[109]

118. In their Joint Partly Dissenting Opinion in the case of *Labita versus Italy*, Judges Pastor Ridruejo, Bonello, Makarczyk, Tulkens, Strážnická, Butkevych, Casadevall and Zupančič lucidly stated that the standard of proof "beyond reasonable doubt" would be "inadequate", if not "illogical and even unworkable", when State authorities fail even to identify the perpetrators of the grave breaches allegedly inflicted upon the individual applicants. This, in their view, would unduly limit State responsibility. Whenever only the State authorities have exclusive knowledge of "some or all the events" that took place, the burden of proof should be shifted upon them (para. 1).

119. The dissenting Judges proceeded that the standard to be met by the applicants is lower if State authorities "have failed to carry out effective investigations and to make the findings available to the Court". And they added:

> Lastly, it should be borne in mind that the standard of proof 'beyond all reasonable doubt' is, in certain legal systems, used in criminal cases. However, this Court is not called upon to judge an individual's guilt or innocence or to punish those responsible for a violation; its task is to protect victims and provide redress for damage caused by the acts of the State responsible. The test, method and standard of proof in respect of responsibility under the Convention are different from those applicable in the various national systems as regards responsibility of individuals for criminal offences (para. 1).

120. Thus, the nature of certain cases – of grave breaches of human rights – brought also before the ECtHR has made it clear that a stringent or too high a standard of proof would be unreasonable, e.g., when respondent States had

---

109   ECtHR, case of *S. Veznedaroglu versus Turkey* (Judgment of 11.04.2000), Partly Dissenting Opinion of Judge Bonello, paras. 12–14.

entire control of the evidence or exclusive knowledge of the facts, and the alleged victims when in a particular adverse situation, of great vulnerability or even defencelessness. The ECtHR, like the IACtHR, admitted shifting the burden of proof (onto the respondent States) whenever necessary, as well as resorting to inferences (from circumstantial evidence) and factual presumptions, so as to secure procedural fairness, in the light of the principle of *equality of arms* (*égalité des armes*).

121. In its Judgment (of 18.09.2009) in the case of *Varnava and Others versus Turkey*, the ECtHR expressly stated that, even if one starts from the test of proof "beyond reasonable doubt", there are cases in which it cannot be applied too rigorously, and has to be mitigated (para. 182). Where the information about the occurrences at issue lie wholly, or in part, within the exclusive knowledge of the State authorities, – the ECtHR proceeded, – strong presumptions of fact will arise in respect of the injuries, the burden of proof then resting on the State authorities to provide a satisfactory and convincing explanation (para. 183). The same takes place if the respondent State has exclusive knowledge of all that has happened (para. 184).

4   *General Assessment*

122. As I have just indicated in the present Dissenting Opinion, international human rights tribunals have not pursued a stringent and high threshold of proof in cases of grave violations of human rights; given the difficulties experienced in the production of evidence, they have resorted to factual presumptions and inferences, and have proceeded to the reversal of the burden of proof. The IACtHR has done so since the beginning of its jurisprudence, and the ECtHR has been doing so in more recent years. They both conduct the free evaluation of evidence.

123. The standard of proof they uphold is surely much less demanding than the corresponding one ("beyond a reasonable doubt") in domestic criminal law. This is so, with all the more reason, when the cases lodged with them disclose a pattern of widespread and systematic gross violations of human rights, and they feel obliged to resort, even more forcefully, to presumptions and inferences, to the ultimate benefit of the individual victims in search of justice. This important issue begins to attract the attention of expert writing in our days.[110]

---

110   For updated studies on the subject, cf., as to the IACtHR, e.g., A.A. Cançado Trindade, *El Ejercicio de la Función Judicial Internacional – Memorias de la Corte Interamericana de Derechos Humanos*, 3rd ed., Belo Horizonte/Brazil, Edit. Del Rey, 2013, pp. 60–79 and

124. Regrettably, none of these jurisprudential developments was taken into account by the ICJ in the present Judgment. It my understanding, it could, and should, have done so, as the issue was addressed by the contending Parties, as from the moment in the proceedings I put a question to both of them in this respect (para. 97, *supra*). The ICJ preferred to stick to a stringent and high threshold of proof in the present case concerning the *Application of the Convention against Genocide* (2015), just as it had done eight years ago in the *Bosnian Genocide* case (2007). May I here only add that expert writing, dwelling upon the complementarity between State and individual responsibility for international crimes (despite their distinct regimes),[111] has likewise been attentive to the orientation and contribution of the case-law of international human rights tribunals (IACtHR and ECtHR, *supra*), particularly on the handling of evidence and the shifting of the burden of proof.[112]

VIII Standard of Proof in the Case-Law of International Criminal Tribunals

125. May I now turn to the case-law of international criminal tribunals as to the standard of proof. Here we find that the intent to commit genocide can be proved by inference, whenever direct evidence is not available. In effect, requiring direct or explicit evidence of genocidal intent in all cases is neither in line with the case-law of international criminal tribunals nor is it practical or realistic. When there is no explicit evidence of intent, it can be inferred from

---

137–142; and cf., as to the ECtHR, e.g., M. O'Boyle and N. Brady, "Investigatory Powers of the European Court of Human Rights", 4 *European Human Rights Law Review* (2013) pp. 378–391.

111 Cf., e.g., B.I. Bonafè, *The Relationship between State and Individual Responsibility for International Crimes*, Leiden, Nijhoff, 2009, pp. 11–255; A.A. Cançado Trindade, "Complementarity between State Responsibility and Individual Responsibility for Grave Violations of Human Rights: The Crime of State Revisited", *in International Responsibility Today – Essays in Memory of O. Schachter* (ed. M. Ragazzi), Leiden, M. Nijhoff, 2005, pp. 253–269; A. Nollkaemper, "Concurrence between Individual Responsibility and State Responsibility in International Law", 52 *International and Comparative Law Quarterly* (2003) pp. 615–640.

112 Cf., e.g., P. Gaeta, "Génocide d'État et responsabilité pénale individuelle", 111 Revue *générale de Droit international public* (2007) pp. 273–284, esp. p. 279; P. Gaeta, "On What Conditions Can a State Be Held Responsible for Genocide?" 18 *European Journal of International Law* (2007) p. 646.

the facts and circumstances. A few examples and references of relevant jurisprudence are provided herein in support of this point.

1   *Inferring Intent from Circumstantial Evidence (Case-Law of the ICTR and the ICTFY)*

126. In the jurisprudence of the *ad hoc* International Criminal Tribunal for Rwanda (ICTR), it has been established that intent to commit genocide can be inferred from facts and circumstances. Thus, in the *Rutaganda* case (Judgment of 06.12.1999), the ICTR (Trial Chamber) stated that "intent can be, on a case-by-case basis, inferred from the material evidence submitted to the Chamber, including the evidence which demonstrates a consistent pattern of conduct by the Accused" (paras. 61–63).[113] Likewise, in the *Semanza* case (Judgment of 15.05.2003), the ICTR (Trial Chamber) stated that a "perpetrator's *mens rea* may be inferred from his actions" (para. 313).

127. Furthermore, in the same line of thinking, in the *Bagilishema* case (Judgment of 07.06.2001), the ICTR (Trial Chamber) found that

> evidence of the context of the alleged culpable acts may help the Chamber to determine the intention of the Accused, especially where the intention is not clear from what that person says or does. The Chamber notes, however, that the use of context to determine the intent of an accused must be counterbalanced with the actual conduct of the Accused. The Chamber is of the opinion that the Accused's intent should be determined, above all, from his words and deeds, and should be evident from patterns of purposeful action (para. 63).

128. In the landmark case *Akayesu* case (Judgment of 02.09.1998), the ICTR (Trial Chamber) found that "intent is a mental factor which is difficult, even impossible to determine", and it held that "in the absence of a confession from the accused", intent may be inferred from the following factors: (a) "general context of the perpetration" of grave breaches "systematically" against the "same group"; (b) "scale of atrocities committed"; (c) "general nature" of the atrocities committed "in a region or a country"; (d) "the fact of deliberately and systematically targeting victims on account of their membership of a particular group, while excluding the members of other groups"; (e) "the general political doctrine which gave rise to the acts"; (f) grave breaches committed

---

113   Cf. also the *Musema* case, ICTR Trial Chamber's Judgment of 27.01.2000, para. 167.

against members of a group specifically because they belong to that group; (g) "the repetition of destructive and discriminatory acts"; and h) the perpetration of acts which violate, or which "the perpetrators themselves consider to violate the very foundation of the group", committed as part of "the same pattern of conduct" (paras. 521 and 523–524).

129. Shortly afterwards, in the *Kayishema and Ruzindana* case (Judgment of 21.05.1999), the ICTR (Trial Chamber) also stated that intent might be difficult to determine and that the accused's "actions, including circumstantial evidence", may "provide sufficient evidence of intent", and that "intent can be inferred either from words or deeds and may be demonstrated by a pattern of purposeful action". The ICTR (Trial Chamber) asserted that the following can be relevant indicators: (a) "the number of group members affected"; (b) "the physical targeting of the group or their property"; (c) "the use of derogatory language toward members of the targeted group"; (d) "the weapons employed and the extent of bodily injury"; (e) "the methodical way of planning"; (f) "the systematic manner of killing"; and (g) "the relative proportionate scale of the actual or attempted destruction of a group" (paras. 93 and 527).

130. Later on, the ICTR (Appeals Chamber), in its Judgment of 07.07.2006 in the *S. Gacumbitsi* case, pondered that, as intent, by its nature, is "not usually susceptible to direct proof", it has to be inferred from relevant facts and circumstances, such as the systematic perpetration of atrocities against the same group, or the repetition of "destructive and discriminatory acts" (paras. 40–41). In a similar vein, the Appeals Chamber of the *ad hoc* International Criminal Tribunal for the former Yugoslavia (ICTFY) also asserted, in the *Jelisić* case (Judgment of 05.07.2001), that,

> As to proof of specific intent, it may, in the absence of direct explicit evidence, be inferred from a number of facts and circumstances, such as the general context, the perpetration of other culpable acts systematically directed against the same group, the scale of atrocities committed, the systematic targeting of victims on account of their membership of a particular group, or the repetition of destructive and discriminatory acts (para. 47).

The ICTFY (Appeals Chamber) further stated, in the *Krstić* case (Judgment of 19.04.2004), that, when proving genocidal intent on the basis of an inference, "that inference must be the only reasonable inference available on the evidence" (para. 41).

2 Standards of Proof: Rebuttals of the High Threshold of Evidence
a) R. Karadžić Case (2013)

131. In its Judgment of 26.02.2007, in the case of the *Application of the Convention against Genocide* (Bosnia and Herzegovina *versus* Serbia and Montenegro), the ICJ, referring to the Keraterm camp in Prijedor, KP Dom in Foča, and Omarska in Prijedor, observed that, having "carefully examined the criminal proceedings of the ICTY and the findings of its Chambers", it appeared that "none of those convicted were found to have acted with specific intent (*dolus specialis*)" (para. 277). Yet the ICTFY (Appeals Chamber), in its recent Judgment (of 11.07.2013) in the *R. Karadžić* case, found that "the question regarding Karadžić's culpability with respect to the crimes of genocide committed in the Municipalities remains open" (para. 116).

132. The ICTFY (Appeals Chamber), in this recent Judgment in the *R. Karadžić* case, reinstated the charges of genocide under count 1 of the indictment; it referred to seven municipalities of Bosnia-Herzegovina claimed as Bosnian Serb territory (para. 57), and mentioned the Keraterm camp in Prijedor, the KP Dom camp in Foča, and the Omarska camp in Prijedor (para. 48). It then observed:

> The Appeals Chamber is satisfied that evidence adduced by the Prosecution, when taken at its highest, indicates that Bosnian Muslims and Bosnian Croats were subjected to conditions of life that would bring about their physical destruction, including severe overcrowding, deprivation of nourishment, and lack of access to medical care (para. 49).

133. Further on, in its same Judgment of 11.07.2013, the ICTFY (Appeals Chamber) significantly stated:

> The Appeals Chamber also recalls that by its nature, genocidal intent is not usually susceptible to direct proof. As recognised by the Trial Chamber, *in the absence of direct evidence, genocidal intent may be inferred from a number of facts and circumstances, such as the general context, the perpetration of other culpable acts systematically directed against the same group, the scale of atrocities committed, the systematic targeting of victims on account of their membership in a particular group, the repetition of destructive and discriminatory acts, or the existence of a plan or policy*[114] (para. 80).

---

114 [Emphasis added].

The ICTFY (Appeals Chamber) then saw it fit to add, in the same Judgment of 11.07.2013 in the *R. Karadžić* case, that, as to "factual findings and evidentiary assessments", that it was bound neither by the decisions of the Trial Chambers of the ICTFY itself, nor by those of the ICJ (para. 94). It thus made clear that it did not support the high threshold of evidence.

b) *Z. Tolimir* Case (2012)

134. In another recent Judgment (of 12.12.2012), in the *Z. Tolimir* case, the ICTFY (Trial Chamber II) sustained that

> Where direct evidence is absent regarding the "conditions of life" imposed on the targeted group and calculated to bring about its physical destruction, a Chamber can be guided by "the objective probability of these conditions leading to the physical destruction of the group in part" and factors like the nature of the conditions imposed, the length of time that members of the group were subjected to them, and characteristics of the targeted group such as its vulnerability (para. 742).

135. The ICTFY (Trial Chamber II) proceeded that, as indications of the intent to destroy (*mens rea* of genocide) are "rarely overt", it is thus "permissible to infer the existence of genocidal intent" on the basis of the whole of the evidence, "taken together". It then added that

> factors relevant to this analysis may include the general context, the perpetration of other culpable acts systematically directed against the same group, the scale of atrocities, the systematic targeting of victims on account of their membership in a particular group, or the repetition of destructive and discriminatory acts. The existence of a plan or policy, a perpetrator's display of his intent through public speeches or meetings with others may also support an inference that the perpetrator had formed the requisite specific intent (para. 745).

136. In sum, even in the absence of direct evidence, genocidal intent may be inferred from circumstantial evidence, and the general context and pattern of extreme violence and destruction. May I add that concern with the needed protection of individuals and groups in situations of vulnerability form today – along the last two decades – the legacy of the II World Conference on Human Rights (1993).[115] It should not pass unnoticed that this points nowadays to a

---

115 Cf. A.A. Cançado Trindade, *A Proteção dos Vulneráveis como Legado da II Conferência Mundial de Direitos Humanos (1993–2013)* [*The Protection of the Vulnerable as Legacy of the II World Conference on Human Rights (1993–2013)*], op. cit. supra n. (79), pp. 13–356.

c) *S. Milošević Case (2004)*

137. In the adjudication of the aforementioned *Bosnian Genocide* case (2007), the ICJ did not react negatively against Serbia's refusal to produce the (unredacted) documents of its Supreme Defence Council (SDC), as the Court apparently did not want to infringe upon Serbia's sovereignty. The ICJ insisted on its high threshold of evidence. For its part, the ICTFY (Trial Chamber), already in its Decision of 16.06.2004 (on motion for judgment of acquittal) in the *S. Milošević* case, had found that

> there is sufficient evidence that genocide was committed in Brčko, Prijedor, Sanski Most, Srebrenica, Bijeljina, Ključ and Bosanski Novi and (…) that the Accused was a participant in a joint criminal enterprise, which included the Bosnian Serb leadership, the aim and intention of which was to destroy a part of the Bosnian Muslims as a group (para. 289, and cf. also para. 288).

138. The final judgment never took place, due to the death of S. Milošević. Yet, although this Decision of the ICTFY Trial Chamber of 16.06.2004 had a bearing on the ICJ Judgment of 26.02.2007, the ICJ preferred not to give any weight to it.[116] The high standard of proof adopted by the ICJ, – criticized by a trend of expert writing, – finds justification in international individual criminal responsibility, facing incarceration, but *not* in international State responsibility, aiming only at declaratory and compensatory relief, where a simple *balance of evidence* would be appropriate, with a lower standard of proof than for international crimes by individuals.[117]

3 *General Assessment*

139. The jurisprudence of international criminal tribunals thus clearly holds that proof of genocidal intent may be inferred from the aforementioned factors (such as, *inter alia*, e.g., the plan or policy of destruction) pertaining to facts and circumstances. Even in the absence of direct proofs, the finding of those factors may lead to the inference of genocidal intent on the part of the perpetrators. In the present case of the *Application of the Convention against*

---

116   Cf. D. Groome, *op cit. infra* n. (117), pp. 964–965.

117   Cf., to this effect, e.g., D. Groome, "Adjudicating Genocide: Is the International Court of Justice Capable of Judging State Criminal Responsibility?" 31 *Fordham International Law Journal* (2008) p. 933.

Genocide, opposing Croatia to Serbia, the contending parties themselves have made arguments in relation to the question whether genocidal intent can be proven by inferences.

140. For example, Croatia argues that "[t]he Parties also appear to be in agreement that the Court (...) can draw proof of genocidal intent from inferences of fact".[118] It further argues that Serbia "acknowledges in the *Counter-Memorial* [para. 135] that it is sometimes difficult to show by direct evidence the intent to commit genocide as the mental element of the crime. The Respondent goes on to refer to the possibility (...) of reliance on indirect evidence and drawing proof from inferences of fact".[119]

141. May it be recalled that, despite all the aforementioned indications from the case-law of the international criminal tribunals, – added to those from the case-law of international human rights tribunals, – the ICJ held, in this respect, in the earlier *Bosnian Genocide* case (2007), opposing Bosnia-Herzegovina to Serbia, that:

> The *dolus specialis*, the specific intent to destroy the group in whole or in part, has to be convincingly shown by reference to particular circumstances, unless a general plan to that end can be convincingly demonstrated to exist; and for a pattern of conduct to be accepted as evidence of its existence, it would have to be such that it could only point to the existence of such intent (para. 373).

142. Keeping in mind the case-law of contemporary international tribunals on the matter (cf. Sections V and VI, *supra*), the ICJ seems to have imposed too high a threshold of evidence (for the determination of genocide), which does not seem to follow the established case-law of international criminal tribunals and of international human rights tribunals on standard of proof (cf. also *infra*). The ICJ seems to have set too high the standard of proof for finding the Serbian regime of the time of the war in Croatia complicit in genocide. Even when direct evidence is not available, the case-law of contemporary international tribunals holds that intent can be inferred on the basis of circumstantial evidence.

---

118   Croatia's *Reply*, para. 2.11.
119   Croatia's *Reply*, para. 2.12.

143. Ultimately, intent can only be inferred, from such factors as the existence of a general plan or policy, the systematic targeting of human groups, the scale of atrocities, the use of derogatory language, among others. The attempts to impose a high threshold for proof of genocide, and to discredit the production of evidence (e.g., witness statements) are most regrettable, ending up in reducing genocide to an almost impossible crime to determine, and the Genocide Convention to an almost dead letter. This can only bring impunity to the perpetrators of genocide, – States and individuals alike, – and make any hope of access to justice on the part of victims of genocide fade away. Lawlessness would replace the rule of law.

144. Another word of caution is to be added here against what may appear as a regrettable deconstruction of the Genocide Convention. One cannot characterize a situation as one of armed conflict, so as to discard genocide. The two do not exclude each other. In this connection, it has been pertinently warned that perpetrators of genocide will almost always allege that they were in an armed conflict, and their actions were taken "pursuant to an ongoing military conflict"; yet, "genocide may be a means for achieving military objectives just as readily as military conflict may be a means for instigating a genocidal plan".[120]

145. In adjudicating the present case, the ICJ should have kept in mind the importance of the Genocide Convention as a major human rights treaty and its historic significance for humankind. A case like the present one can only be decided in the light, not at all of State sovereignty, but rather of the imperative of safeguarding the life and integrity of human groups under the jurisdiction of the State concerned, even more so when they find themselves in situations of utter vulnerability, if not defencelessness. The life and integrity of the population prevail over contentions of State sovereignty, particularly in face of misuses of this latter.

146. History has unfortunately shown that genocide has been committed in furtherance of State policies. Making the application of the Genocide Convention to States Parties an almost impossible task, would render the Convention meaningless. It would also create a situation where certain State egregious criminal acts amounting to genocide would go unpunished, – even more so in the current absence of a Convention on Crimes against Humanity. Genocide is

---

120 R. Park, "Proving Genocidal Intent: International Precedent and ECCC Case 002", 63 *Rutgers Law Review* (2010) pp. 169–170, and cf. pp. 150–152.

indeed an egregious crime committed – more often[121] than one would naively assume – under the direction or the benign complicity of the sovereign State and its apparatus.

147. The repeated mass murders and atrocities, with the extermination of segments of the population, pursuing pre-conceived plans and policies, coldly calculated, have counted on the apparatus of the State public power, with its bureaucracy, with its so-called material and human "resources". Historiography shows that the successive genocides and atrocities along the XXth century have in effect been committed pursuant to a plan, have been organized and

---

121   Cf., in general, *inter alia*, e.g., Y. Ternon, *Guerres et génocides au XXe siècle*, Paris, Éd. Odile Jacob, 2007, pp. 9–379; B. Bruneteau, *Le siècle des génocides*, Paris, Armand Colin, 2004, pp. 5–233; B.A. Valentino, *Final Solutions – Mass Killing and Genocide in the Twentieth Century*, Ithaca/London, Cornell University Press, 2004, pp. 1–309; G. Bensoussan, *Europe – Une passion génocidaire*, Paris, Éd. Mille et Une Nuits, 2006, pp. 7–460; S. Totten, W.S. Parsons and I.W. Charny (eds.), *Century of Genocide – Eyewitness Accounts and Critical Views*, N.Y./London, Garland Publ., 1997, pp. 3–466; B. Kiernan, *Blood and Soil – A World History of Genocide and Extermination from Sparta to Darfur*, New Haven/London, Yale University Press, 2007, pp. 1–697; R. Gellately and B. Kiernan (eds.), *The Specter of Genocide – Mass Murder in Historical Perspective*, Cambridge, Cambridge University Press, 2010 [repr.], pp. 3–380; D. Olusoga and C.W. Erichsen, *The Kaiser's Holocaust – Germany's Forgotten Genocide*, London, Faber & Faber, 2011, pp. 1–379; J.-B. Racine, *Le génocide des Arméniens – Origine et permanence du crime contre l'humanité*, Paris, Dalloz, 2006, pp. 61–102; R.G. Suny, F.M. Göçek and N.M. Naimark (eds.), A *Question of Genocide*, Oxford, Oxford University Press, 2013, pp. 3–414; G. Chaliand and Y. Ternon, *1915, le génocide des Arméniens*, Bruxelles, Éd. Complexe, 2006 (reed.), pp. 3–199; I. Chang, *The Rape of Nanking – The Forgotten Holocaust of World War II*, London, Penguin Books, 1997, pp. 14–220; N.M. Naimark, *Stalin's Genocides*, Princeton/N.J., Princeton University Press, 2012 [repr.], pp. 1–154; E. Kogon, *L'État SS – Le système des camps de concentration allemands* [1947], [Paris,] Éd. Jeune Parque, 1993, pp. 7–447; L. Rees, *El Holocausto Asiático*, Barcelona, Crítica Ed., 2009, pp. 13–212; B. Kiernan, *Le génocide au Cambodge (1975–1979)*, Paris, Gallimard, 1998, pp. 7–702; B. Allen, *Rape Warfare – The Hidden Genocide in Bosnia-Herzegovina and Croatia*, Minneapolis/London, University of Minnesota Press, 1996, pp. 1–162; G. Prunier, *Africa's World War – Congo, the Rwandan Genocide, and the Making of a Continental Catastrophe*, Oxford, Oxford University Press, 2010, pp. 1–468; K. Moghalu, *Rwanda's Genocide The Politics of Global Justice*, N.Y., Palgrave, 2005, pp. 1–236; J.-P. Chrétien and M. Kabanda, *Rwanda – Racisme et genocide – l'idéologie hamitique*, Paris, Éd. Belin, 2013, pp. 7–361; S. Leydesdorff, *Surviving the Bosnian Genocide – The Women of Srebrenica Speak*, Bloomington/Indianapolis, Indiana University Press, 2011, pp. 1–229; M.W. Daly, *Darfur's Sorrow – A History of Destruction and Genocide*, Cambridge, Cambridge University Press, 2007, pp. 1–316.

executed as a State policy, by those who held power, with the use of euphemistic language in the process of *dehumanization* of the victims.[122]

148. Widespread and systematic patterns of destruction have been carried out amidst ideological propaganda, without any moral assessment, blurring the sheer brutality and any responsibility, and erasing any guilt feeling. All was lost in the organic and totalitarian entity. Those mass murders have often been committed without any reparation to the next-of-kin of the fatal victims.[123] Furthermore, not all such mass atrocities have been taken before international tribunals. As to the ones that have been, in an international adjudication of a case concerning the application of the Convention against Genocide, making the elements of genocide too difficult to determine, would maintain the shadow of impunity, and create a situation of lawlessness, contrary to the object and purpose of that Convention.

IX Widespread and Systematic Pattern of Destruction: Fact-Finding and Case-Law

149. May I turn now to the fact-finding that was undertaken, and the reports that were prepared, *at the time those grave breaches of human rights and International Humanitarian Law were being committed*, conforming a systematic practice of destruction. I refer to the fact-finding and *Reports* prepared by the Special *Rapporteur* of the (former) U.N. Commission on Human Rights (1992–1993), as well as the fact-finding and *Reports* prepared by the U.N.

---

122 Cf. further, Part XIII of the present Dissenting Opinion, *infra*.

123 E. Staub, *The Roots of Evil – The Origins of Genocide and Other Group Violence*, Cambridge, Cambridge University Press, 2005 [reimpr.], pp. 7–8, 10, 19, 24, 29, 107, 109, 119, 121–123, 129, 142, 151, 183–187, 221, 225, 227 and 264; D. Muchnik and A. Garvie, *El Derrumbe del Humanismo – Guerra, Maldad y Violencia en los Tiempos Modernos*, Buenos Aires/Barcelona, Edhasa, 2007, pp. 36–37, 116, 128, 135–136, 142, 246 and 250. And cf. also, in general, *inter alia*, e.g., V. Klemperer, *LTI – A Linguagem do Terceiro Reich*, Rio de Janeiro, Contraponto Ed., 2009, pp. 11–424; D.J. Goldhagen, *Worse than War – Genocide, Eliminationism, and the Ongoing Assault on Humanity*, London, Abacus, 2012 [reed.], pp. 6–564; J. Sémelin, *Purificar e Destruir – Usos Políticos dos Massacres e dos Genocídios*, Rio de Janeiro, DIFEL, 2009, pp. 19–532; M. Kullashi, *Effacer l'autre – Identités culturelles et identités politiques dans les Balkans*, Paris, L'Harmattan, 2005, pp. 7–246; S. Matton, *Srebrenica – Un génocide annoncé*, Paris, Flammarion, 2005, pp. 21–420; P. Mojzes, *Balkan Genocides – Holocaust and Ethnic Cleansing in the Twentieth Century*, Lanham, Rowman & Littlefield Publs., 2011, pp. 34–229.

Security Council's Commission of Experts (1993–1994). I shall seek to detect their elements which bear relevance for the consideration of the *cas d'espèce*.

1   U.N. (*Former Commission on Human Rights*) *Fact-Finding Reports on Systematic Pattern of Destruction (1992–1993)*

150. There are passages in the *Reports on the Situation of Human Rights in the Territory of the Former Yugoslavia*, of Special *Rapporteur* of the (former) U.N. Commission on Human Rights (Mr. T. Mazowiecki), which pertain to alleged crimes committed against Croat populations and by the Serb official or paramilitary entities. There are reported facts that assist in evidencing a systematic pattern of destruction during the armed attacks in Croatia in particular. The *Report* of 28.08.1992,[124] for example, referred to the shops and businesses of ethnic Croats that were burned and looted (para. 12).

151. Other forms of intimidation, – it continued, – involved shooting at the houses of other ethnic groups and throwing explosives at them (para. 13). Attacks on churches and mosques were part of the campaign of intimidation (para. 16). Another tactic included "the shelling of population centres and the cutting off of supplies of food and other essential goods" (para. 16). Cultural centres were also targeted, and snipers shot "innocent civilians"; any movement "out of doors" was "hazardous" (paras. 17–18).

152. Detention of civilians was intended to put pressure on them to leave the territory (para. 23). That *Report* also referred to the existence of detention facilities containing between 10 to 100 prisoners in Croatia, and which were "under the control of the Government as well as territories under the control of ethnic Serbs" (para. 34). It added that the situation in which prisoners lived (including poor nutrition overcrowding and poor conditions of detention) was a real threat to their lives, and, in effect, prisoners have died of torture and mistreatment in Croatia (para. 39). The aforementioned *Report* further referred to the massive disappearances occurred in territories under the control of ethnic Serbs; in particular, 3,000 disappearances were reported following the fall of Vukovar, with people allegedly detained in camps before disappearing (para. 41).

153. The subsequent *Report* of 27.10.1992[125] expressed concern as to the need to investigate further the existence of mass graves in Vukovar and surrounding

---

124   U.N., doc. E/CN.4/1992/S-1/9.
125   U.N., doc. E/CN.4/1992/S-1/10.

areas (para. 18). Generally speaking, this report stressed much more on Bosnia and Herzegovina than on Croatia. The following *Report*, of 17.11.1992,[126] addressed the facts occurred in the United Nations Protected Areas (UNPAS). The Special *Rapporteur* stated that in the Krajina parts of UNPA sector South, murders, robberies, looting "and other forms of criminal violence often related to ethnic cleansing" took place (para. 78). People were only allowed to flee upon relinquishment of their properties. As to UNPA sector East, ethnic cleansing was undertaken by Serbian militias and local Serbian authorities, and people were subjected to extremely violent intimidation (para. 83). Furthermore, Catholic churches were destroyed (para. 84).

154. Moreover, that *Report* expressed concern with the disappearance of 2,000 to 3,000 people, following the fall of Vukovar in 1991; it referred to the potential mass grave in Ovčara close to Vukovar. On the site of the potential mass grave referred to, 4 bodies were found, but there might have been many more bodies, including some of the 175 Croatian patients who were evacuated from the Vukovar hospital and then disappeared; there might have been 8 other mass graves in the area (para. 86).

155. Last but not least, the *Report* of 17.11.1992 stated, in its conclusions, that "the continuation of ethnic cleansing is a deliberate effort to create a *fait accompli* in flagrant disregard of international commitments entered into by those who carry out and benefit from ethnic cleansing" (para. 135). It is worth noticing that the *Report* referred to all those identified elements of extreme violence as a "policy" (para. 135).

156. The subsequent *Report* of 10.02.1993[127] likewise referred to an ethnic cleansing policy undertaken by local Serbian authorities and paramilitaries still taking place in some UNPAS, as disclosed by the constant harassment towards the non-Serbs who refused to flee, the destruction of churches and houses (para. 141). The following *Report*, of 17.11.1993,[128] asserted that the organized massive ethnic cleansing of the Croats from the Republic of Krajina then became a *"fait accompli"* (para. 144), and crimes committed against Croats would generally fall into impunity (para. 145). In UNPA Sector South and the Pink Zones, there were only 1,161 Croats left (whereas there were 44,000 of them in the area in 1991. Killings, looting and confiscation of farm equipment were reported.

---

126 U.N., doc. A/47/666/S/24809.
127 U.N., doc. E/CN.4/1993/50.
128 U.N. doc. E/CN.4/1994/47.

Moreover, the same *Report* gave account of disappearances and killings that had been occurring in UNPA Sector North (paras. 151–152).

157. As to UNPA Sector East, the census of 1991 and 1993 evidenced that the Croat population in the area had dropped from 46% to 6%, while the Serb population arose from 36% to approximately 73% (para. 157). Intimidation acts and crimes were often directed at minorities, including killings, robbery and looting, forced recruitment in the armed forces, beatings, among others (para. 158). Furthermore, the *Report* of 17.11.1993 expressed concerns about discrimination against Croats when it comes to medical treatments and food distribution (para. 159). And the *Report* then referred to the "deliberate and systematic shelling of civilian objects in Croatian towns and villages" (para. 161).

158. The *Report* added that, according to Croatian sources, between April 1992 and July 1993, "Serbian shelling" caused "187 civilian deaths and 628 civilian injuries", and, between 1991 and April 1993, an estimated total of 210,00 buildings outside the UNPAs were either seriously damaged or destroyed, primarily as a result of shelling (para. 161). Parts of the Dalmatian coast areas

> have sustained several hundred impacts. There have been numerous civilian deaths and injuries and extensive damage to civilian objects including schools, hospitals and refugee camps, as well as houses and apartments (para. 162).

There were cases of civilian objects, hospitals and refugee camps, seemingly "not situated in the proximity of a military object", which were nevertheless "deliberately shelled from Serbian positions within visual range of the targets" (para. 163). The Special *Rapporteur* received accounts of Croatian forces having also become engaged in "deliberate shelling of civilian areas" (para. 164). Violence breeds violence.

2 U.N. (*Security Council's Commission of Experts*) *Fact-Finding Reports on Systematic Pattern of Destruction (1993–1994)*

159. The Commission established by the U.N. Security Council resolution 780 (1992), of 06.10.1992, started in early November 1992 its fact-finding work on the international crimes perpetrated in the war in Croatia. By the time it concluded its work, by the end of May 1994, the Commission of Experts had issued four reports, namely: *Interim Report* (of 10.02.1993), *Report of a Mass Grave Near Vukovar* (of 10.01.1993), *Second Interim Report* (of 06.10.1993), and *Final Report* (of 27.05.1994). Each of them, and in particular the last one, contains

accounts of the grave breaches of International Humanitarian Law, International Human Rights Law, International Refugee Law and International Criminal Law, committed during the war in Croatia. It is thus important to review the results of the fact-finding work of the Commission of Experts.

a)   *Interim Report* (of 10.02.1993)

160. In his presentation of the first *Interim Report* of the Commission of Experts established by the Security Council, the (then) U.N. Secretary-General (B. Boutros-Ghali) deemed it fit to stress out that, already in that first report, the Commission had already established that

> Grave breaches and other violations of International Humanitarian Law have been committed, including wilful killing, "ethnic cleansing" and mass killings, torture, rape, pillage and destruction of civilian property, destruction of cultural and religious property, and arbitrary arrests.[129]

161. In effect, in its aforementioned *Interim Report*, the Commission of Experts, – bearing in mind the relevant conventional basis for its fact-finding,[130] observed that "ethnic cleansing" – a "relatively new" expression – is "contrary to international law" (para. 55). And it added:

> Based on the many reports describing the policy and practices conducted in the former Yugoslavia, "ethnic cleansing" has been carried out by means of murder, torture, arbitrary arrest and detention, extra-judicial executions, rape and sexual assault, confinement of civilian population in ghetto areas, forcible removal, displacement and deportation of civilian population, deliberate military attacks or threats of attacks on civilians and civilian areas, and wanton destruction of property. Those practices constitute crimes against humanity and can be assimilated to specific war crimes. Furthermore, such acts could also fall within the meaning of the Genocide Convention (para. 56).

---

129 U.N., document S/25274, of 10.02.1993, p. 1.

130 The 1949 Geneva Conventions of International Humanitarian Law (for "grave breaches") and Additional Protocol I, the 1907 Hague Convention IV and the Regulations on the Law and Customs of War on Land, the 1948 Convention on the Prevention and Punishment of the Crime of Genocide, the 1954 Hague Convention for the Protection of Cultural Property in the Event of Armed Conflict, and the 1980 Convention on the Prohibitions and Restrictions on the Use of Certain Conventional Weapons and Protocols (paras. 37, 39 and 47).

The Commission of Experts then reported on "widespread and systematic rape and other forms of sexual assault" throughout the various phases of the armed conflicts (para. 58), as well as on mass executions, disappearances and mass graves during the war in Croatia (paras. 62–63).

b)   *Report of a Mass Grave near Vukovar* (of 10.01.1993)
162. The next report of the Commission of Experts focused specifically on the mass grave near Vukovar. A mass execution took place at the gravesite, and "the executioners sought to bury their victims secretly"; the grave contained some 200 bodies (item I). The mass grave was discovered by members of the UNPROFOR Civilian Police (UNCIVPOL) and an international forensic team, in an area southeast of the farming village of Ovčara, near Vukovar. The Commission of Experts reported that "[t]he discovery of the Ovčara site is consistent with witness testimony of the disappearance of about 200 patients and medical staff members from the Vukovar Hospital during the evacuation of Croatian patients from that facility on 20 November 1991" (item II).

163. JNA soldiers and Serbian paramilitaries loaded a truck with groups of 20 men, beating them, and driving them away (to execution); at "intervals of about 15 to 20 minutes, the truck returned empty and another group was loaded onto it" (item II). A mass execution took place, and the mortal remains (of some 200 bodies) were then put in a clandestine mass grave. The Commission of Experts reiterated that "[t]he remote location of the grave suggests that the executioners intended to bury their victims secretly" (item III).

c)   *Second Interim Report* (of 06.10.1993)
164. In its following report, the Commission of Experts again dwelt upon the mass execution at the grave site in Ovčara (para. 78). Besides mass killings, in its fact-finding missions, it found widespread violations of human rights in detention centres,[131] including torture, beatings, and other forms of physical and psychological mistreatment (paras. 84–85). Furthermore, there was an "overall pattern" of rapes (330 reported cases), suggesting a "systematic rape policy"; among the factors pointing in this direction, – the Commission of Experts proceeded, –

> is the coincidence in time between military action designed to displace civilian populations and widespread rape of the same populations. Group involvement of the members of the same military units in rape

---

[131] There were 353 reported detention centres (para. 35).

suggests command responsibility by commission or omission; in this respect, the manner in which this type of rape was conducted in multiple locations and within a fairly close period of time (mostly between May and December 1992) is also a significant factor. Another factor in this connection is the contemporaneous existence of other violations of international humanitarian law in a given region occurring simultaneously in prison camps, in the battlefield and in the civilian regions of occupied areas (para. 69).

165. The general framework was one of destruction, with findings of mass killings (in the Vukovar area), brutal mistreatment of prisoners, systematic sexual assaults, "ethnic cleansing", and destruction of property (paras. 9–10). There were thousands of "incidents of victimization" (para. 29), mostly against the civilian population (kidnapping or hostage-taking, forced eviction, imprisonment, rapes, torture, killings) (paras. 32 and 35). In the Vukovar area, there was abduction of civilians and personnel (some 200 persons) from the Vukovar Hospital, followed by their execution and burial in a mass grave at Ovčara (paras. 35 and 37). More than a war, it was an onslaught.

d) *Final Report* (of 27.05.1994)

166. The *Final Report* of the Commission of Experts gives a detailed account of the findings of the horrifying atrocities perpetrated against the targeted victims. In its presentation of the *Final Report*, the (then) U.N. Secretary-General (B. Boutros-Ghali) drew attention to the "reported grave breaches" of International Humanitarian Law, committed "on a large scale", and "brutal and ferocious in their execution". He further drew attention to the Commission's "substantive findings on alleged crimes of 'ethnic cleansing', genocide and other massive violations of elementary dictates of humanity".[132] As to "ethnic cleansing" and rape and sexual assault, he added that they have been carried out "so systematically that they strongly appear to be the product of a policy", which "may also be inferred from the consistent failure to prevent the commission of such crimes and to prosecute and punish their perpetrators".[133]

167. Throughout its *Final Report*, the Commission of Experts stressed its findings of *grave* breaches of International Humanitarian Law,[134] mainly in Croatia

---

132 U.N., document S/1994/674, of 27.05.1994, p. 1.
133 *Ibid.*, pp. 1–2.
134 Articles 50/51/130/147 of the 1949 Geneva Conventions on International Humanitarian Law, and Articles 11(4) and 85 of the 1977 Additional Protocol I.

and Bosnia-Herzegovina (paras. 45, 231, 253 and 311). It was attentive to detect the *systematicity* of victimization, disclosing a policy of persecution or discrimination (para. 84). At a certain point, the Commission dwelt upon the Convention against Genocide, adopted, – it recalled, – for "humanitarian and civilizing purposes", in order to safeguard the existence itself of certain human groups and to assert basic "principles of humanity" (para. 88). The Convention, it added, had a "historical evolutionary nature" (para. 89).

168. In the perpetration of those grave breaches, there was ample use of paramilitaries, and the chain of command was thus blurred (paras. 114, 120–122 and 128), so as intentionally to conceal responsibility (para. 124). In this way "ethnic cleansing" was conducted (to build the "Greater Serbia") as a "purposeful policy", terrorizing the civilian population, in order to remove ethnic or religious groups from certain geographic areas, moved at times by a "sense of revenge" (para. 130–131). The areas were strategic, "linking Serbia proper with Serb-inhabited areas in Bosnia and Croatia" (para. 133).

169. The acts of violence, to remove the civilian population from those areas, were carried out with "extreme brutality and savagery", instilling terror, so that the persecuted would flee and never return. They included mass murder, torture and rape, other mistreatment of civilians and prisoners of war, using of civilians as human shields, indiscriminate killings, forced displacement, destruction of cultural property, attacks on hospitals and medical locations, burning and blowing up of houses, destruction of property (paras. 134–137).

170. The Commission of Experts also found frequency of shelling (para. 188) and a pattern of "systematic targeting" (para. 189). Such policy and practices of "ethnic cleansing" were carried out by members of distinct segments of Serbian society, such as members of the Serbian army, militias, special forces, police and individuals (paras. 141–142),[135] as illustrated by the destruction of the city of Vukovar in 1991 (para. 145). The Commission of Experts also singled out the attack on Dubrovnik, a city with no defence: it pondered that the destruction of cultural property therein could not at all be justified as a "military necessity" (paras. 289 and 293–294). The battle of Dubrovnik was criminal (para. 297); there was a deliberate attack on civilians and cultural property (paras. 299–300).

---

135   This generated further violence, – the Commission of Experts added, – and Croatian forces also engaged in such practices, though the Croatian authorities deplored them, indicating that they were not part of a governmental policy (para. 147).

171. The Commission of Experts then turned to the concentration camps: the living conditions in those camps were "appalling", with executions *en masse*, rapes, torture, killings, beatings and deportations (paras. 169–171). Concentration camps were the scene of "the worst inhumane acts", committed by guards, police, special forces and others (para. 223). Those atrocities were accompanied by "purposeful humiliation and degradation", a "common feature in almost all camps" (paras. 229–230(d)).

172. Men of "military age", – between the ages of 16 (or younger) and 60, – were separated from older men, women and children, and transferred to heavily guarded larger camps, where killings and brutal torture were committed (para. 230(i)). Prisoners in all camps were subjected to "mental abuse and humiliation". There was no hygiene, and soon there were epidemics. Prisoners nearly starved to death; "[o]ften sick and wounded prisoners" were "buried alive in mass graves along with the corpses of killed prisoners" (para. 230(p)).

173. The Commission of Experts proceeded, focusing on the practice of rape, not much reported for fear of reprisals, lack of confidence in justice, and the social stigma attached to it (paras. 233–234). The reported cases of rape occurred between the fall of 1991 and the end of 1993, most of them having occurred between April and November 1992 (para. 237). From the reported cases, five patterns of rape emerged, namely: (a) rape as intimidation of the targeted group, involving individuals or small groups (para. 245); (b) rape – sometimes in public – linked to the fighting in an area, involving individuals or small groups (para. 246); (c) rape in detention camps (after the men were killed), followed at times by the murder of the raped women; (d) rape as terror and humiliation, as part of the policy of "ethnic cleansing", keeping pregnant women detained until they could no longer have abortion (para. 248); and e) rape (in hotels or other facilities) for entertainment of soldiers, more often followed by the murder of the raped women (para. 249).

174. Rapes, amidst shame and humiliation, – the Commission proceeded, – were intended "to displace the targeted group from the region"; moreover, "[l]arge groups of perpetrators subject[ed] victims to multiple rapes and sexual assault" (para. 250). They ended up being "committed by all sides to the conflict" (para. 251); the patterns of rape (*supra*) suggest that "a systematic rape policy existed in certain areas" (para. 253).

175. The Commission concluded that practices of "ethnic cleansing", with rapes, were systematic, and appeared as a policy (also by omission – para. 313). Those

grave breaches could thus be reasonably inferred from such "consistent and repeated practices" (para. 314). The Commission of Experts confessed to have been "shocked" by the high level of victimization and the manner in which these crimes were committed (para. 319).

3 Repercussion of Occurrences in the U.N. II World Conference on Human Rights (1993)

176. It should not pass unnoticed that the occurrences in the wars in former Yugoslavia had prompt repercussions in the II World Conference of Human Rights, held in Vienna in June 1993. Having participated in all stages of that U.N. World Conference, I well remember that the original intention was not to single out any country, but soon two exceptions were made, so as to address the situation of the affected populations in the on-going armed conflicts in the former Yugoslavia[136] and in Angola.[137]

177. The special declarations on the two conflicts were adopted therein, on 24.06.1993. As to the former, the concern it expressed was directed to the occurrences in Bosnia and Herzegovina, and in particular at Goražde. An appeal to the U.N. Security Council accompanying the special declaration, referred to the attacks as "genocide". The declaration referred to that "tragedy", as "characterized by the naked Serbian aggression, unprecedented violations of human rights and genocide", being "an affront to the collective conscience of mankind" (3rd preambular paragraph). And it added that

> The World Conference believes that the practice of ethnic cleansing resulting from Serbian aggression against the Muslim and Croat population in the Republic of Bosnia and Herzegovina constitutes genocide in violation of the Convention on the Prevention and Punishment of the Crime of Genocide (8th preambular paragraph).[138]

---

136 "Decision and Special Declaration on Bosnia and Herzegovina", *in Report of the U.N. Secretary-General on the II World Conference on Human Rights* (Vienna, 14–25.06.1993), in A/CONF.157/24 – Part I, of 13.10.1993, p. 47.

137 "Special Declaration on Angola", *in Report of the U.N. Secretary-General on the II World Conference on Human Rights* (Vienna, 14–25.06.1993), in A/CONF.157/24 – Part I, of 13.10.1993, p. 50.

138 "Special Declaration on Bosnia and Herzegovina", *in Report of the U.N. Secretary-General on the II World Conference on Human Rights* (Vienna, 14–25.06.1993), in A/CONF.157/24 – Part I, of 13.10.1993, pp. 47–48.

178. Although the occurrences which attracted the attention of the U.N. World Conference in 1993 were the ones that were taking place in one particular locality, in the European continent, not so far away from Vienna (mainly in Goražde), they occurred likewise, and were to keep on occurring, in other parts of former Yugoslavia. The atrocities at issue formed part of a widespread and systematic pattern of destruction (cf. Sections VIII-X, *infra*). They were committed pursuant to a plan; the chain of command (the Supreme Defence Council) and the perpetrators were the same, engaging State responsibility.

179. The final document adopted by the World Conference, – the Vienna Declaration and Programme of Action (1993), – clearly addressed the problem. The Declaration asserted that

> The World Conference on Human Rights expresses its dismay at massive violations of human rights, especially in the form of genocide, 'ethnic cleansing', and systematic rape of women in war situations, creating mass exodus of refugees and displaced persons. While strongly condemning such abhorrent practices, it reiterates the call that perpetrators of such crimes be punished and such practices immediately stopped (Part I, para. 28).

And the Programme of Action, for its part, added that

> The World Conference on Human Rights calls on all States to take immediate measures, individually and collectively, to combat the practice of ethnic cleansing to bring it quickly to an end. Victims of the abhorrent practice of ethnic cleansing are entitled to appropriate and effective remedies (Part II, para. 24).

4 *Judicial Recognition of the Widespread and/or Systematic Attacks against the Croat Civilian Population – Case-Law of the ICTFY*

180. On successive occasions in its evolving case-law, the ICTFY has addressed the atrocities committed during the war in Croatia (1991–1992), stressing that what occurred was not simply an armed conflict between opposing armed forces, but rather a devastation of villages and mass murder of their populations. References can be made, in this connection, e.g., to the ICTFY's findings in the cases of *M. Babić* (2004), *M. Martić* (2007), *Mrkšić and Radić and Šljivančanin* (2007), *Stanišić and Simatović* (2013).

a)   *M. Babić* Case (2004)

181. Thus, in its Judgment of 29.06.2004 in the *M. Babić* case, the ICTFY (Trial Chamber) found that the regime[139] that launched the armed attacks within Serbia, committed "the extermination or murder of hundreds of Croat and other non-Serb civilians" (para. 15), and did so "in order to transform that territory into a Serb-dominated State" (paras. 8 and 16). And the ICTFY (Trial Chamber) added significantly that

> After the take-over, in cooperation with the local Serb authorities, the Serb forces established a regime of persecutions designed to drive the Croat and other non-Serb civilian populations from these territories. The regime, which was based on political, racial, or religious grounds, included the extermination or murder of hundreds of Croat and other non-Serb civilians in Dubića, Cerovljanji, Baćin, Saborsko, Poljanak, Lipovača, and the neighbouring hamlets of Škabrnja, Nadin, and Bruška in Croatia; the prolonged and routine imprisonment and confinement of several hundred Croat and other non-Serb civilians in inhumane living conditions in the old hospital and the JNA barracks in Knin, which were used as detention facilities; the deportation or forcible transfer of thousands of Croat and other non-Serb civilians from the SAO Krajina; and the deliberate destruction of homes and other public and private property, cultural institutions, historic monuments, and sacred sites of the Croat and other non-Serb populations in Dubića, Cerovljani, Baćin, Saborsko, Poljanak, Lipovača, and the neighbouring hamlets of Vaganac, Škabrnja, Nadin, and Bruška (para. 15).

And the ICTFY (Trial Chamber) then concluded, in the aforementioned *Babić* case, on the basis of the factual statement and other evidence presented to it, that the execution (of the JCE) at issue "entailed a widespread or systematic attack directed against a civilian population", and "was carried out with discriminatory intent, on political, racial, or religious grounds" (para. 35).

b)   *M. Martić* Case (2007)

182. Likewise, in the *M. Martić* case, the ICTFY (Trial Chamber), in its Judgment of 12.06.2007, found that there had been a " widespread and systematic attack"(para. 352) against the Croat population, committed by the JNA,

---

139   Together with Serbian forces, – including the JNA and TO units from Serbia, – in concert with Serbian authorities.

TO, Serbian police and Serbian paramilitaries, acting in concert; that attack involved "the commission of widespread and grave crimes" (para. 443), with "the goal of creating an ethnically Serb State" (para. 342). In its assessment, "[t]here is evidence of Croats being killed in 1991, having their property stolen, having their houses burned, that Croat villages and towns were destroyed, including churches and religious buildings, and that Croats were arbitrarily dismissed from their jobs" (para. 324). The attacks continued in 1992.[140]

183. The ICTFY (Trial Chamber) further found that "numerous attacks were carried out on Croat majority villages by the JNA acting in cooperation with the TO and the Milicija Krajine" (para. 344), and that "[t]hese attacks followed a generally similar pattern, which involved the killing and removal of the Croat population" (para. 443). Moreover, – it added, – hundreds of Croat civilians were imprisoned and subjected to "severe mistreatment" (para. 349). It further determined that "widespread crimes of violence and intimidation and crimes against private and public property were perpetrated against the Croat population, including in detention facilities run by MUP forces of the SAO Krajina and the JNA" (para. 443).

184. By the end of the summer of 1991, – it added, – "the JNA became an active participant in Croatia on the side of the SAO Krajina" (para. 330). The ICTFY (Trial Chamber) also referred to the persecution, forced displacement, deportation and forcible transfer of the Croat population (civilians), and "further evidence that in 1991 Croats were killed by Serb forces in various locations in the SAO Krajina" (para. 426). There was, in sum,

> evidence of a generally similar pattern to the attacks. The area or village in question would be shelled, after which ground unites would enter. After the fighting had subsided, acts of killing and violence would be committed by the forces against the civilian non-Serb population who had not managed to flee during the attack. Houses, churches and property would be destroyed in order to prevent their return and widespread looting would be carried out. (...) Moreover, members of the non-Serb population would be rounded up and taken away to detention facilities (...) (para. 427).

---

140 It proceeded that "[d]uring 1992 on the territory of the RSK, there was a continuation of incidents of killings, harassment, robbery, beatings, burning of houses, theft, and destruction of churches carried out against the non-Serb population" (para. 327).

185. Moreover, the ICTFY (Trial Chamber) referred to the cooperation and assistance with Serbia on the part of Milan Martić (third President of the so-called "RSK"); in this respect, the Trial Chamber stated that, "[t]hroughout 1992, 1993 and 1994, the RSK leadership, including Milan Martić, requested financial, logistical and military support from Serbia on numerous occasions, including directly from Slobodan Milošević" (para. 159). And, as to the political objective of the Serb leadership, the ICTFY (Trial Chamber) stated that,

> [T]he President of Serbia, Slobodan Milošević, (...) covertly intended the creation of a Serb state. Milan Babić testified that Slobodan Milošević intended the creation of such a Serb State through the establishment of paramilitary forces and the provocation of incidents in order to allow for JNA intervention, initially with the aim to separate the warring parties but subsequently in order to secure territories envisaged to be part of a future Serb state (para. 329).

186. The ICTFY (Trial Chamber) added that, as to the period 1991–1995, it had been furnished with "a substantial amount of evidence of massive and widespread acts of violence and intimidation committed against the non-Serb population (...)" (para. 430). It found *inter alia* that there had occurred widespread and systematic attacks "directed against the Croat and other non-Serb civilian population" in Croatia in the period 1991–1995, notwithstanding the presence of Croat forces in some areas (paras. 349–352).

c)   *Mrkšić and Radić and Šljivančanin* Case (2007)

187. In the case of *Mrkšić and Radić and Šljivančanin*, the ICTFY (Trial Chamber) made important findings (Judgment of 27.09.2007) as to the "complete command and full control" exercised by the JNA over the TOs and Serb paramilitaries, in "all military operations" (para. 89). In addressing the "devastation brought on Vukovar over the prolonged military engagement in 1991" (para. 8), the ICTFY (Trial Chamber) described, *inter alia*, how

> in the evening and night hours of 20–21 November 1991 the prisoners of war were taken in groups of 10 to 20 from the hangar at Ovčara to the site where earlier that afternoon a large hole had been dug. There, members of Vukovar TO and paramilitary soldiers executed at least 194 of them. The killings started after 21:00 hours and continued until well after midnight. The bodies were buried in the mass grave and remained undiscovered until several years later (para. 252).

188. In the aforementioned Judgment in the case of *Mrkšić and Radić and Šljivančanin*, the ICTFY (Trial Chamber) again made important findings on the widespread and systematic attack directed against the civilian population in Vukovar. It stated, e.g., that, from 23.08.1991 to 18.11.1991,

> the town of Vukovar and its surroundings were increasingly subjected to shelling and other fire: it came to be almost on a daily basis. The damage to the city of Vukovar was devastating. (...) A large Serb force comprising mainly well armed and equipped troops were involved in far greater numbers than the Croat forces. In essence, the city of Vukovar was encircled and under siege from Serb forces, including air and naval forces, until the Croat forces capitulated on 18 November 1991. By the beginning of November virtually none of the houses along the road from Vukovar to Mitnica were left standing above the cellar. The supply of essential services to the whole of Vukovar was disrupted. Electricity and water supplies and the sewage system all failed. The damage to civilian property was extensive. By 18 November 1991, the city had been more or less totally destroyed. It was absolutely devastated. Those still living in the city had been forced to take shelter in cellars, shelters and the like (para. 465).[141]

189. The ICTFY (Trial Chamber) then stated, in the same Judgment of 27.09.2007 in the *Mrkšić and Radić and Šljivančanin* case, that

> The battle for Vukovar caused a large number of casualties, both dead and wounded, combatants and civilians. There can be no exact number for the wounded treated in Vukovar by Croat services, because the extremely difficult and improvised treatment facilities did not allow the luxury of thorough records. There is no overall evidence of the Serb forces' casualties. What remained of Vukovar hospital, together with a secondary nursing facility in a nearby cellar of a warehouse, dealt with most of the wounded, but there were other facilities in the Vukovar area. (...)

---

141   In its aforementioned Judgment, the ICTFY (Trial Chamber) proceeded that "the Vukovar hospital, schools, public buildings, offices, wells, the water and electricity supply and roads were severely damaged during the conflict. All buildings were shelled, including the hospital, schools and kindergartens. Many wells were also targeted and destroyed. Most of the wells in Vukovar were privately owned, so houses with a water supply were among the first to be destroyed. From September to November 1991 there was no drinking water available, except from the remaining wells" (para. 466).

Civilians, including women and children were amongst the wounded. While precise statistics were not maintained in the circumstances, the Chamber accepts as a reliable estimate that the casualties were 60–75% civilian. A report (...) on 25 October 1991 from the medical director of the hospital noted that 1250 wounded had been admitted since 25 August with a further 300 dead on arrival (para. 468).

190. And the ICTFY (Trial Chamber) significantly added that

There can be no question that the Serb forces were, in part, directing their attack on Vukovar (...). (...) [T]he Serb attack was also consciously and deliberately directed against the city of Vukovar itself and its hapless civilian population, trapped as they were by the Serb military blockade of Vukovar and its surroundings and forced to seek what shelter they could in the basements and other underground structures that survived the ongoing bombardments and assaults. *What occurred was not, in the finding of the Chamber, merely an armed conflict between a military force and an opposing force in the course of which civilians became casualties and some property was damaged. The events, when viewed overall, disclose an attack by comparatively massive Serb forces, well armed, equipped and organised, which slowly and systematically destroyed a city and its civilian and military occupants to the point where there was a complete surrender of those that remained.* While the view is advanced before the Chamber that the Serb forces were merely liberating besieged and wronged Serb citizens who were victims of Croatian oppressiveness and discrimination, this is a significant distortion of the true position as revealed by the evidence, when reviewed impartially (para. 470).[142]

d) *Stanišić and Simatović* Case (2013)

191. Subsequently, in its Judgment of 30.05.2013 in the *Stanišić and Simatović* case, the ICTFY (Trial Chamber) found that, from April 1991 to April 1992, between 80,000 and 100,000 Croat and other non-Serb civilians fled the SAO Krajina, as a result of the situation then prevailing in that region,

which was created by a combination of: the attacks on villages and towns with substantial or completely Croat populations; the killings, use as human shields, detention, beatings, forced labour, sexual abuse,

---

142 [Emphasis added]. And cf., furthermore, Part X(1) of the present Dissenting Opinion, *infra*.

and other forms of harassment (including coercive measures) of Croat persons; and the looting and destruction of property. These actions were committed by the local Serb authorities and the members and units of the JNA (including JNA reservists), the SAO Krajina TO, the SAO Krajina Police (including Milan Martić), and Serb paramilitary units, as well as local Serbs as set out in the Trial Chamber's findings (para. 404, and cf. para. 997).

192. The ICTFY (Trial Chamber) stressed that "[h]arassment and intimidation" of the Croat population were carried out "on a large scale":

> Croats were killed in 1991, their property was stolen, their houses were burned, Croat villages and towns were destroyed, including churches and religious buildings, and Croats were arbitrarily dismissed from their jobs. During 1992 (...) there was a continuation on incidents of killings, harassment, robbery, beatings, burning of houses, theft and destruction of churches carried out against the non-Serb population. Throughout 1993 there were further reports of killings, intimidation and theft (para. 153).

193. There were also cases of deportation and forcible transfer of groups of persons (paras. 996–1054); the ICTFY (Trial Chamber) further found that Serb Forces "committed deportation and forcible transfer of many thousands of Croats"; in such incidents "people were moved against their will or without a genuine choice", as

> Serb Forces created an environment where the victims had no choice but to leave. This included attacks on villages and towns, arbitrary detention, killings, and ill treatment. These conditions prevailed during the days or weeks, and sometimes months, prior to people leaving. The Trial Chamber has also found that the crimes of murder, deportation, and forcible transfer constituted underlying acts of persecution as well (para. 970).

194. It added that, "the persons targeted were primarily members of the civilian population" (para. 971). In the ICTFY (Trial Chamber)'s view, "the requirements of 'attack', 'widespread', and 'civilian population' have been met" (para. 971). The crimes were perpetrated in widespread armed attacks against the non-Serb civilian population, against undefended non-Serb villages, with systematic executions of non-Serb civilians, and destruction of mosques, churches, and homes of non-Serbs and other civilian targets (paras. 969–970). Those attacks, in the ICTFY (Trial Chamber)'s finding, were part of a pattern

of destruction "against a civilian population", and "the perpetrators knew" that their acts were part of it (para. 972). In this widespread and systematic pattern of destruction, all such attacks were, as reckoned in the case-law of the ICTFY (*supra*) deliberate, intentional.

X Widespread and Systematic Pattern of Destruction: Massive Killings, Torture and Beatings, Systematic Expulsion from Homes and Mass Exodus, and Destruction of Group Culture

195. An examination of the factual context, as a whole, of the *cas d'espèce*, discloses a widespread and systematic pattern of destruction, carried out in the villages brought to the attention of the Court in the course of the present proceedings. Such a pattern of destruction, as it will be shown next, encompassed massive killings, torture and beatings, systematic expulsion from homes and mass exodus, and destruction of group culture. After reviewing and assessing the occurrence of those crimes, I shall move on to other manifestations[143] of the widespread and systematic pattern of destruction in the attacked villages in Croatia.

1 *Indiscriminate Attacks against the Civilian Population*

196. In the factual context of the present case of the *Application of the Convention against Genocide* (Croatia *versus* Serbia), the question whether the population attacked was either civilian in its entirety or predominantly civilian, does not raise any jurisdictional issue, as crimes of genocide can be committed against any individual, whether civilian or combatant. In distinct contexts, the ICTFY (Trial Chambers), faced with the jurisdictional requirements also of crimes against humanity and war crimes, has clarified the meaning to be attached to "civilian population": in all instances, it has adopted a wide definition of what constitutes a civilian population, including, *inter alia*, individuals who performed acts of resistance.[144]

---

143 Parts XI, XII and XIII of the present Dissenting Opinion, *infra*.

144 For example, in the *Tadić* case (Judgment of 07.05.1997), the ICTFY (Trial Chamber) held, as to the targeted civilian population, that "[t]he presence of certain non-civilians in their midst does not change the character of the population" (para. 638). It reiterated this point in the case *Kunarac, Kovač and Vuković* (Judgment of 22.02.2001, para. 425). In the case *Blaškić* (Judgment of 03.03.2000), it again held that the presence of individuals bearing arms in a resistance movement did not change the character of the civilian population (paras. 213–214). In the case *Kordić and Čerkez* (Judgment of 26.02.2001), it singled out the consistent adoption, by ICTFY Trial Chambers, of "a wide definition of what constitutes

197. Moreover, in the *cas d'espèce*, the presence of Croatian armed forces and formations should not be used to distort the reality. The events that took place in Vukovar illustrate what was probably the case in other municipalities attacked in Croatia. As the ICTFY (Trial Chamber) stated in case *Mrkšić and Radić and Šljivančanin* ("*Vukovar Hospital*", Judgment of 27.09.2007), there was a "gross disparity between the numbers of the Serb and Croatian forces" engaged in the battle for Vukovar (para. 470).

198. The attack of "massive Serb forces", facing a "comparatively small and very poorly armed and organized Croatian forces", and bringing "devastation on Vukovar and its surroundings", – added the ICTFY, – was "consciously and deliberately directed against the city of Vukovar itself and its hapless civilian population, (...) forced to seek what shelter they could in the basements and other underground structures that survived the ongoing bombardments and assaults" (para. 470).

199. I have already referred, in the present Dissenting Opinion, to the ICTFY's finding of the widespread and systematic attacks by Serb forces against the Croat civilian population.[145] In addition to the passages already quoted of Judgment of 27.09.2007 of the ICTFY (Trial Chamber) in the *Mrkšić and Radić and Šljivančanin* case, may I here recall that, in that same Judgment, the ICTFY (Trial Chamber) proceeded that "[t]he terrible fate that befell the city and the people of Vukovar was but one part of a much more widespread action against

---

a civilian population" (para. 180). In the case *Martić* (Judgment of 12.06.2007), the ICTFY (Trial Chamber I), keeping in mind the size of the attacked civilian population, found that "the presence of Croatian armed forces and formations in the Škabrnja and Saborsko areas does not affect the civilian character of the attacked population" (para. 350). This was confirmed by the ICTFY Appeals Chamber (Judgment of 08.10.2008) in the same case *Martić* (para. 317). In the case *Popović et alii* (Judgment of 10.06.2010), the ICTFY (Trial Chamber II) held that the term "civilian population" is to be "interpreted broadly", referring to a population that is "predominantly civilian in nature", even if there are in in "members of armed resistance groups" (para. 1591). Again in the recent case *Stanišić and Župljanin* (Judgment of 27.03.2013), it pointed out that "the presence within the civilian population of individuals who do not come within the definition of civilians does not deprive the population of its civilian character" (para. 26); it again upheld the test of the "*predominantly* civilian nature" of the population (para. 26). It pursued the same approach in the case *Limaj, Bala and Musliu* (Judgment of 30.11.2005, para. 186), and in the case *Brđanin* (Judgment of 01.09.2004, para. 134).

145 Cf. Part IX(4) of the present Dissenting Opinion, *supra*.

the non-Serb peoples of Croatia and the areas of Croatia in which they were substantial majorities" (para. 471).

200. The ICTFY (Trial Chamber) added that, in its view, "the overall effect of the evidence is to demonstrate that the city and civilian population of and around Vukovar were being punished, and terribly so", for not having accepted "the Serb controlled Federal government in Belgrade", and for Croatia's declaration of independence (para. 471). The ICTFY (Trial Chamber) further stated that, what occurred,

> was not, in the finding of the Chamber, merely an armed conflict between a military force and an opposing force in the course of which civilians became casualties and some property was damaged. The events, when viewed overall, disclose an attack by comparatively massive Serb forces, well armed, equipped and organised, which slowly and systematically destroyed a city and its civilian and military occupants to the point where there was a complete surrender of those that remained. While the view is advanced before the Chamber that the Serb forces were merely liberating besieged and wronged Serb citizens who were victims of Croatian oppressiveness and discrimination, this is a significant distortion of the true position as revealed by the evidence, when reviewed impartially (paras. 470–471).

201. The ICTFY (Trial Chamber) found, in the case of *Mrkšić, Radić and Šljivančanin* ("*Vukovar Hospital*"), that what happened

> was in fact, not only a military operation against the Croat forces in and around Vukovar, but also *a widespread and systematic attack* by the JNA and other Serb forces *directed against the Croat and other non-Serb civilian population* in the wider Vukovar area. The extensive damage to civilian property and civilian infrastructure, *the number of civilians killed or wounded during the military operations and the high number of civilians displaced or forced to flee clearly indicate that the attack was carried out in an indiscriminate way, contrary to international law.* It was an unlawful attack. Indeed it was also directed in part deliberately against the civilian population. The widespread nature of the attack is indicated by the number of villages in the immediate area around Vukovar which was damaged or destroyed and the geographical spread of these villages, as well as by the damage to the city of Vukovar itself. The systematic character of the attack is also evidenced by the JNA's approach to the taking of each

village or town and the damage done therein and the forced displacement of those villagers fortunate enough to survive the taking of their respective villages (para. 472).[146]

202. In effect, in the adjudication of distinct cases pertaining to the war in Croatia, the ICTFY has found a widespread and systematic pattern of extreme violence, victimizing the civilian population. The dossier of the present case of the *Application of the Convention against Genocide* (Croatia *versus* Serbia) contains elements revealing that pattern, planned and premeditated. The extreme violence went far beyond establishing military and administrative hegemony: it involved massive killings, brutal torturing and beatings of Croatian civilians, and the removal by force of the remaining ones from their villages. They were forced to sign documents attesting their "voluntary" consent that all their property should be left to the "SAO Krajina". Moreover, Serbian artillery was used to destroy all traces of Croatian architecture, culture and religion.[147]

203. Such indiscriminate attacks against the civilian population in Croatia formed a pattern of extreme violence and destruction, as follows: (a) first, prior to the occupation of a village, the JNA would send an ultimatum to the Croatian inhabitants to lay down their weapons, or else face the village levelled to the ground; at the same time, promises were made that the Croatian civilians would not be harmed if they did not offer armed resistance; (b) secondly, the JNA would then engage in artillery attack, followed by its infantry of the JNA entering the village together with Serb paramilitary groups; (c) thirdly, they would then, after capturing the village, embark on a campaign of terror, making it physically or psychologically impossible for the surviving Croatians to continue living there.

204. Even where there was not a complete destruction of the village, as, for example, in Poljanak, serious crimes were committed in that village, as the ICTFY recognized in the *M. Martić* case. Yet, those serious crimes have not been extensively depicted in the present Judgement, neither in respect of Poljanak, nor of other villages. As to Poljanak, there were also accounts of killings; for example, B.V. testified that his family was killed and he was heavily beaten, that chetniks searched houses in the village and set them on fire, and captured

---

146 [Emphasis added].
147 Cf. Croatia's *Application Instituting Proceedings*, para. 34, and *Memorial*, paras. 4.8–4.9.

people, and he also witnessed killings.¹⁴⁸ Another witness, M.V., found two victims dead, with their heads smashed and the brains scattered around.¹⁴⁹

205. Similarly to Saborsko, it is significant to note that Serbia acknowledged that the ICTFY (Trial Chamber) in the *Martić* case "confirmed the killings in Poljanak and its hamlet Vuković".¹⁵⁰ There were also accounts of houses having been burned in Poljanak. M.L. testified that prisoners were locked in a room in the camp Manjača, where "they did not get anything to eat or drink for 4 or 5 days, while being interrogated over and over, and were beaten and molested".¹⁵¹ B.V. testified that chetniks searched houses in Poljanak and set them on fire, and captured people.¹⁵²

2 *Massive Killings*

206. At the final stage of the attacks by the Serb armed forces, when a village was captured, a campaign of terror was launched, followed by mass and non-selective executions of Croatian civilians. The smaller remainder of the Croat population was subjected to variants of martial law, imprisonment, forced exile or deportation to camps; in some villages they were forced to display white ribbons, on their sleeves, as armbands, or white sheets attached to the doors of their houses.¹⁵³ During the occupation, many Croatians fled to the neighbouring towns, not yet captured, and some were killed in ambushes by Serb paramilitary units on the way.

207. In its Judgment of 2007 in the previous case of the *Application of the Convention against Genocide* (Bosnia and Herzegovina *versus* Serbia and Montenegro), the ICJ observed, as to the verification of a systematic pattern of destruction, that

> It is not necessary to examine every single incident reported by the Applicant, nor it is necessary to make an exhaustive list of the allegations; the Court finds it sufficient to examine those facts that would illuminate the question of intent, or illustrate the claim by the Applicant of a pattern of acts committed against members of the group, such as to lead to an

---

148 *Memorial*, Annex 387.
149 *Ibid.*, Annex 388.
150 *Counter-Memorial*, para. 861.
151 *Memorial*, Annex 385.
152 *Memorial*, Annex 387.
153 Cf. section XIII, *infra*, of the present Dissenting Opinion.

inference from such pattern of the existence of a specific intent (*dolus specialis*) (para. 242).

208. Bearing in mind this consideration by the Court, I do not purport, nor is it necessary, in this Dissenting Opinion, to proceed to an analysis in depth of individual crimes, as anyway this is not an international criminal court. More important to me is the verification of a widespread and systematic pattern of destruction disclosed by those crimes, all over the villages that were attacked, as brought to the attention of the Court. Numerous crimes – revealing such pattern of destruction – have been described by witnesses, and others have been determined by the ICTFY itself, as indicated throughout the present Dissenting Opinion.

209. In effect, the dossier of the *cas d'espèce* indicates that criminal acts were committed in the various regions occupied by the Serbian forces. In the region of Eastern Slavonia, for example, the following villages are mentioned: Tenja, Dalj, Berak, Bogdanovci, Šarengrad, Ilok, Tompojevci, Bapska, Tovarnik, Sotin, Lovas, Tordinci, and Vukovar.[154] The wrongful acts evidencing the systematic pattern of destruction which occurred in Eastern Slavonia spread to the other regions of Western Slavonia, Banovina, Kordun, Lika and Dalmatia.[155]

210. The first villages and civilian populations to be attacked were those of Dalj, Erdut and Aljmaš, at the beginning of August 1991. Between 28.09.1991 and 17.10.1991, the villages of Sotin, Ilok, Šarengrad, Lovas, Bapska and Tovarnik were captured by the JNA and Serb paramilitary groups. Killings were committed in pursuance of a systematic pattern of brutality, including the perpetration of massacres of entire families, or random murders to force Croats to flee;[156] the campaign culminated in the massacre at Vukovar (after 18.11.1991).[157]

211. Several mass graves were discovered (e.g., in the regions of Banovina, and Kordun and Lika), with little or no indication of who the victims were, or where they were originally from. Such mass graves were found out in the municipalities of Tenja, Dalj, Ilok, Sotin, Lovas, Tordinci, Ovčara, Vukovar,

---

154 Cf. *Memorial*, paras. 4.20–4.30, 4.31–4.37, 4.38–4.46, 4.47–4.55, 4.56–4.61, 4.62–4.72, 4.73–4.80, 4.81–4.93, 4.94–4.106, 4.107–4.115, 4.116–4.132, 4.133–4.138, and 4.139–4.190, respectively.
155 Cf. *ibid.*, paras. 5.3–5.64, 5.65–5.122, 5.123–5.186, and 5.187–5.241, respectively.
156 Cf. *ibid.*, Chapter 4.
157 Cf. *ibid.*, para. 4.19.

Pakrac, Lađevac, and Škabrnja.[158] Croatia pointed out that, by the time of the filing of its *Memorial* (March 2001), 61 mass graves had been found in Eastern Slavonia. Many of the mass graves, which then appeared were used as temporary burial sites only; the JNA often dug up the bodies and moved them to other parts of the occupied territory or of Serbia.[159]

212. For its part, Serbia challenged the evidence presented by Croatia;[160] it contended that the killings of Croats by Serbian forces were not intended to destroy that group, and, accordingly, did not amount to genocide; on the other hand, it added, the killings of Serbs by Croatian forces were committed, in its view, with the intent to destroy the group as such.[161] Croatia replied that Serbia did not dispute that Croats were subjected to torture and to serious bodily and mental harm, on a systematic basis.[162] Serbia, for its part, did not dispute that serious bodily and mental harm was committed by Serbian forces against Croats during the war in Croatia between 1991 and 1995, but it further submitted that serious bodily and mental harm was also committed against Serbs by the Croatian forces.[163]

213. A *"Book of Evidence"* included by Croatia in the *dossier* of the present case, titled *Mass Killing and Genocide in Croatia 1991/92*,[164] identifies *four phases* in the war in Croatia, from the perspective of "civilian casualties and the destruction of Croatian villages and towns", namely:

> In the *first phase* (July-August 1991), the Serbian paramilitary troops armed by JNA had the predominant role. With the aid of JNA they attacked completely unarmed Croatian villages, especially in the area of Banija and in the surrounding of Knin. At that time JNA still pretended to be creating buffer-zones between the "two sides in conflict". However, the examples of Dalj, Kraljevčani, Dragotinci and Kijevo clearly show the active role of JNA using tanks and air force to destroy residential buildings regardless of the fact that there were no Croatian Police (MUP) or National Guard

---

158 *Memorial*, paras. 4.29, 4.35, 4.72, 4.107, 4.116, 4.138, 4.178, 4.188, 5.27, 5.77, 5.137, 5.146, and 5.226, respectively.
159 Cf. *ibid.*, para. 4.07.
160 Cf. *Counter-Memorial*, paras. 660 and 663.
161 Cf. *ibid.*, para. 48.
162 Cf. *Reply*, para. 9.47.
163 Cf. *Counter-Memorial*, para. 81.
164 *Mass Killing and Genocide in Croatia 1991/92: A Book of Evidence*, Zagreb, Ministry of Health of Croatia, 1992, pp. 1–207.

forces (ZNG). In the *second phase* of the war (September 1991), JNA undertook the conquest of larger areas in Croatia, and it conquered Kostajnica, Dubica, Petrinja, Drniš, Jasenovac, Okučani and Stara Gradiška. This is the phase when the Croatian army did not have adequate heavy artillery so that it could not even neutralize the aggressor. This resulted in a number of Croatian defeats, having as a consequence masses of refugees and displaced persons from the areas of Banija, Dalmacija and partly Slavonia. The following *third phase*, took place during October-November 1991, when JNA waged intensive total war using air force, heavy artillery and armored units on the line of the Greater Serbia border Virovitica-Karlovac-Karlobag. Established front-line made possible the stabilization of defense. Still, heavy artillery of JNA produced immense destruction of Croatian cities, including the cities at the seaside which were sealed off. In this period important Croatian cities, e.g., Vukovar, Slunj, Dubrovnik, were surrounded and suffered great damages or total destruction. (...) The last, *fourth phase* of the war, begins after the ceasefire of 03.01.1992. During April 1992 a dramatic escalation of artillery attacks occurred on a number of civilian targets, especially on Osijek, Vinkovci, Slavonski Brod, Županja, Karlovac, Zadar, Gospić and Nova Gradiška. This phase especially threatened the civilians, unprepared for artillery attacks. A new wave of refugees started as well. The endangered population still remains on the occupied territories. They were being forced away from their homes before the U.N. forces arrive.[165]

214. The document singles out, in the first phase of the onslaught, the destruction of homes, forcing the victims to flee away, or else to face death or brutalities. The unarmed residents of the villages attacked were forcefully displaced, and their homes were destroyed or plundered; they moved to more central and safer regions of Croatia. In the second phase, the JNA army itself launched fierce armed attacks, with artillery and fighter jets, against numerous villages and towns (e.g., Vukovar, Osijek, Vinkovci, Sisak, Karlovac, Pakrac, Lipik, Gospić, Otočac, Zadar, Šibenik, Dubrovnik, Petrinja, Nova Gradiška or Novska), with mass killings of civilians. The document adds that

> Many women, children and elderly lost their lives in this manner, as thousands of private residences and public buildings were totally destroyed. Civilians died in their own homes, in schools, kindergartens, churches, hospitals, on their farms, while walking in the streets, riding bicycles or

---

165 *Ibid.*, pp. 1 and 4.

driving their cars. In short, no one was safe anywhere and there was literally no place to take refuge from the bombing and shelling.[166]

215. Systematic destruction of homes by close-range fire occurred extensively in, e.g., Vukovar, Osijek, Petrinja, Vinkovci and Gospić, among others. After the firing, by tanks, of private residences, "first at the upper floors, then at the ground floor (...), hand-grenades were thrown in the basement in which the owners or residents ha[d] sought refuge".[167] Many of the mortal remains were left where they had fallen, and after some time could no longer be recovered (particularly in the regions of Banija, Kordun, Lika, and Eastern Slavonia, as well as the hinterland of Zadar and Šibenik, and Dubrovnik). Massacres of civilians occurred (e.g., in Voćin and Hum near Podravska Slatina, Obrovac, Benkovac, Knin, Škabrnja and Nadin), as "part of a planned genocide", in the occupied territories.[168]

216. The "major cause" of civilian casualties – including children, women and the elderly – was "the indiscriminate and extensive artillery shelling of strictly civilian targets".[169] There were also the "missing persons", – some 8,000–12,000 persons, according to the study. The International Committee of the Red Cross (ICRC) became involved in their search. There was, furthermore, the systematic destruction of "schools, hospitals, monuments, libraries and above all the Catholic churches, a favourite target of the JNA artillery".[170] Libraries, for example, were destroyed all over – for the sake of destruction – during the former Yugoslavia wars, – not only in the attacks in Croatia, but also in those in Bosnia-Herzegovina and in Kosovo,[171] to the detriment of the populations concerned.

3   Torture and Beatings

217. The *dossier* of the present case concerning the *Application of the Convention against Genocide* contains numerous accounts of torture and beatings

---

166   *Ibid.*, p. 4.
167   *Ibid.*, p. 7.
168   *Ibid.*, p. 6.
169   *Ibid.*, p. 6.
170   *Ibid.*, p. 7.
171   For an account, cf., *inter alia*, e.g., L.X. Polastron, *Livros em Chamas – A História da Destruição sem Fim das Bibliotecas* [*Livres en feu*], Rio de Janeiro, J. Olympio Edit., 2013, pp. 236–238.

THE UNIVERSAL JURIDICAL CONSCIENCE

of members of the civilian population, by the time the military offensive was launched by the respondent State, and even before that. The Applicant's *Memorial*, in particular, is permeated with such accounts. There were reported cases of forced labour and torture and beatings (in Dalj, Berak, Bagejci, Bapska, Lovas, Tordinci, Vukovar, Vaganac, Kijevo, Vujići, Tovarnik, Knin);[172] of extreme violence and psychological torture (in Sotin, Josevica, Lipovača, Šarengrad);[173] of abduction and enforced disappearance (in Pakrac);[174] of the use of civilians as "human shields" to "protect" Serb armed forces (in Bapska and Četekovac),[175] among other atrocities (in Kusonje, Podravska Slatina, Kraljevčani, Tovarnik, Joševica).[176]

218. Furthermore, in Poljanak, torture and beatings were likewise reported. According to M.L., in Easter 1991 chetnik groups set an ambush to the workers of the Ministry of the Interior, and there was an armed clash where people were killed. The witness testified that prisoners were locked in a room in the camp "Manjača, where they did not get anything to eat or drink for 4 or 5 days, while being interrogated over and over, and were beaten and molested".[177] B.V. testified that his family members were killed and he was heavily beaten.[178]

219. Beatings occurred in various ways, including with bats, wire, boots, chains, sticks and other objects.[179] On several occasions, torture and humiliation were followed by the murders of the victims (in Bogdanovci, Šarengrad, Tovarnik, Voćin).[180] There were cases of suicides among Croats.[181] Croatia dwells upon a systematic pattern of destruction of the targeted victims, within which occurred physical and psychological torture and beatings, in various ways.

---

172 Cf. *Memorial*, paras. 4.34–4.35, 4.38, 4.40, 4.85, 4.88–4.90, 4.124, 4.135–4.136, 4.168–4.169, 5.175, 5.212, and ICJ doc. CR 2014/10, of 06.03.2014, paras. 20 and 27, respectively.
173 Cf. *Memorial*, paras. 4.111, 4.50, 5.88 and 5.143, respectively.
174 Cf. *ibid.*, para. 5.16, and ICJ doc. CR 2014/10, of 06.03.2014, para. 17.
175 Cf. *Memorial*, paras. 4.85 and 5.43, respectively.
176 Cf. *ibid.*, paras. 5.27, 5.30, 5.98, 4.100, and ICJ doc. CR 2014/10, of 06.03.2014, p. 25, respectively.
177 *Memorial*, Annex 385.
178 *Ibid.*, Annex 387.
179 Cf., e.g., ICJ doc. CR 2014/10, of 06.03.2014, pp. 24–25.
180 *Memorial*, paras. 4.47–4.55, 4.56–4.59, 4.101, and ICJ doc. CR 2014/10, of 06.03.2014, p. 17, respectively.
181 Cf. ICJ doc. CR 2014/10, of 06.03.2014, p. 25.

220. Serbia, for its part, in particular in its *Rejoinder*, acknowledged that many atrocities were committed against Croats during the conflicts,[182] but it challenged the trustworthiness of evidences and documents presented by the applicant State, and in particular the reliability of witnesses statements. In Serbia's view, the tragic events described by the applicant State do not establish genocidal intent and specific intent to destroy; they establish, at most, – it adds, – that war crimes and crimes against humanity were committed, but not genocide.[183]

221. Turning its attention to Vukovar, in the region of Eastern Slavonia, Croatia contended that, after the fall of Vukovar, high-ranking JNA officers aided and abetted the large-scale torture and murder of prisoners,[184] such as those at Velepromet.[185] According to the Applicant, in Vukovar and other towns or villages, Croat civilians, often elderly people, unable or unwilling to flee, were subjected to extreme brutality, were tortured and killed by JNA soldiers, TOs and paramilitaries.[186] In the Applicant's view, those atrocities were committed with the intent to destroy the Croat population in the targeted regions.[187]

222. Croatia further asserted that, in Vukovar, Serbian forces carried out a sustained campaign of bombing and shelling; brutal killings and torture; systematic expulsion; and denial of food, water, electricity, sanitation and medical treatment. It adds that the Serb forces established torture camps to where Croats were taken,[188] – Velepromet and Ovčara. According to the Applicant, the Serb forces had the opportunity to displace and not to destroy the surviving Vukovar Croats, but they were, instead, repeatedly tortured and executed.[189]

223. In the *M. Martić* case, the ICTFY (Trial Chamber I) found (Judgment of 12.06.2007) that, in their attacks on Croat villages in the SAO Krajina, the Serbian armed forces left the villagers with "no choice but to flee", and those who stayed behind were promptly beaten and killed (para. 349). The attacked

---

182   Cf., e.g., ICJ doc CR 2014/13, of 10.03.2014, paras. 3–5; and *Rejoinder*, paras. 349, 360, 367–8, 381, 384 and 386.
183   Cf. *Rejoinder*, paras. 349, 360, 367–368, 381, 284 and 386; and ICJ, doc. CR 2014/13, of 10.03.2014, paras. 3–5.
184   ICJ, doc. CR 2014/5, of 03.03.2014, p. 43.
185   ICJ, doc. CR 2014/6, of 04.03.2014, p. 41.
186   *Ibid.*, 45.
187   *Ibid.*, p. 45.
188   ICJ, doc. CR 2014/8, of 05.03.2014, pp. 29, 31 and 35.
189   *Ibid.*, p. 39.

villages included Potkonije, Vrpolje, Glina, Kijevo, Drniš, Hrvatska Kostajnica, Cerovljani, Hrvatska Dubica, Baćin, Saborsko, Poljanak, Lipovača, Škabrnja, Nadin and Bruška; "grave discriminatory measures were taken against the Croat population" there (para. 349).

224. By and large, – the ICTFY (Trial Chamber I) proceeded in the *M. Martić* case, – there was a "widespread and systematic attack directed against the Croat and other non-Serb civilian population", both in Croatia and in Bosnia and Herzegovina (para. 352). The crimes of torture, and cruel and inhuman treatment, "were carried out with intent to discriminate on the basis of ethnicity" (paras. 411 and 413). There was a pattern of beatings, mistreatment and torture of detainees (paras. 414–416).

225. Six years later, in the *Stanišić and Simatović* case, the ICTFY (Trial Chamber I) likewise found (Judgment of 30.05.2013) that there was a "widespread attack" against the same civilian population to which the targeted persons belonged (paras. 971–972). The perpetrators' "discriminatory intent" was clear (para. 1250). The pattern of extreme violence included arbitrary detention, beatings, sexual assaults, torture, murders, use of derogatory language and insults, deportation and forcible transfer, – all on the basis of the ethnicity of the victims (paras. 970 and 1250). It should be kept in mind – may I add – that the prohibition of torture, in all its forms, is absolute, in any circumstances: it is a prohibition of *jus cogens*.

226. Last but not least, may I here further add that the ICTFY (Appeals Chamber), in its recent Judgment (of 11.07.2013) in the *R. Karadžić* case, rejected an appeal for acquittal, and reinstated genocide charges against Mr. R. Karadžić, for the brutalities committed against detainees: although the atrocities occurred in Bosnian municipalities, the pattern of destruction was the same as the one that took place in Croatian municipalities, and so were the targeted groups: besides Bosnian Muslims, also Bosnian Croats. As to the conditions of detention, the ICTFY (Appeals Chamber) found the occurrences of torture, cruel and inhuman treatment, rape and sexual violence, forced labour, and inhuman living conditions, with "failure to provide adequate accommodation, shelter, food, water, medical care or hygienic facilities" (para. 34). It further noted

> evidence on the record indicating that Bosnian Muslim and/or Bosnian Croat detainees were kicked, and were violently beaten with a range of objects, including, *inter alia,* rifles and rifle butts, truncheons and batons, sticks and poles, bats, chains, pieces of cable, metal pipes and rods, and pieces of furniture. Detainees were often beaten over the course of several

days, for extended periods of time and multiple times a day. Evidence on the record also indicates that in some instances detainees were thrown down flights of stairs, beaten until they lost consciousness, or had their heads hit against walls. These beatings allegedly resulted in serious injuries, including, *inter alia,* rib fractures, skull fractures, jaw fractures, vertebrae fractures, and concussions. Long-term alleged effects from these beatings included, *inter alia,* tooth loss, permanent headaches, facial deformities, deformed fingers, chronic leg pain, and partial paralysis of limbs (para. 35).

4   *Systematic Expulsion from Homes and Mass Exodus, and Destruction of Group Culture*

227. In addition to mass killings, torture, beatings and other mistreatment, unbearable conditions of life were inflicted on the targeted Croat population: there was systematic expulsion from homes, with the imposition of subsistence diet and reduction of essential medical treatment and supplies.[190] The targeted segments of the population were required to display signs of their ethnicity, and were denied food, water, electricity and medical treatment. Their movements were restricted, and they were subjected to repeated looting and to a regime of random and mass killings (*supra*), amidst brutalisation and extreme violence. Their cultural and religious monuments and the signs of their cultural heritage were destroyed or looted; the basis of their education was suppressed, so as to be replaced by education as Serbs.[191]

228. There was expulsion or forced displacement of the Croat population of the villages of Tenja, Dalj, Berak, Bogdanovci, Šarengrad, Ilok, Tompojevci, Bapska, Tovarnik, Sotin, Lovas, and Tordinci, as well as Pakrac, Uskok, Donji, Gornji Varos, Pivare;[192] people were forced to sign statements relinquishing all rights to their property, and to embark on the mass exodus; those who did not do so, were subjected to a brutal regime of extreme violence. Croatia recalled that the ICTFY (Trial Chamber), in its Judgment (of 02.08.2001) in the *Krstić* case, found that

> where there is physical or biological destruction there are often simultaneous attacks on the cultural and religious property and symbols of the

---

190   Cf., e.g., *Memorial*, paras. 4.23 and 5.30.
191   Cf. *ibid.*, paras. 4.60, 4.128, and 5.181.
192   Cf. *ibid.*, paras. 4.30–4.31, 4.37, 4.46–4.47, 4.61–4.64, 4.80, 4.93, 4.105, 4.107, 4.132–4.133, 5.14, 5.49, 5.79, 5.92, 5.93, 5.106, 5.121, 5.140, 5.141, 5.146, 5.148, 5.174, 5.181, 5.196, 5.202, 5.203, 5.204, 5.205, 5.210, 5.223 and 5.225.

targeted group as well, attacks which may legitimately be considered as evidence of an intent to physically destroy the group. In this case [*Krstić*], the Trial Chamber will thus take into account as evidence of intent to destroy the group the deliberate destruction of mosques and houses belonging to members of the group (para. 580).

229. The ICJ itself cited this finding, in its Judgment of 2007 in the previous case of the *Bosnian Genocide* (para. 344). It is clear that the destruction of cultural and religious heritage, as occurred in the present case of the *Application of the Convention against Genocide*, pertaining to the armed attacks in Croatia, can be of significance *within the context* of the widespread and systematic pattern of destruction, as occurred in the *cas d'espèce*, opposing Croatia to Serbia. Such destruction of cultural and religious heritage is not to be simply dismissed *tout court*, as the ICJ has done in the present Judgment (paras. 129, 379, 385–386). It should have taken into due account the aforementioned pattern of destruction *as a whole* (encompassing destruction of cultural and religious sites), – as properly warned by the ICTFY in the *Krstić* case (*supra*).

230. In the present case, Serbia, for its part, retorted that, for the systematic expulsion of people from homes to fall under Article II(c) of the Genocide Convention, it must be part of a "manifest pattern", capable of effecting the physical destruction of the group, and not merely its displacement elsewhere; in its view, the Applicant failed to prove that the expulsion of Croats, where it has occurred, was accompanied by the intent to destroy that population.[193] In addition, Serbia minimized the relevance of the destruction of cultural and religious objects, saying that, in the drafting history of the Genocide Convention, the inclusion of attacks on cultural and religious objects under the rubric "cultural genocide" was discarded in the course of that drafting process.[194]

231. On this point, may I here observe that, in his *Autobiography*, Raphael Lemkin, – who devoted so much energy to the coming into being of the 1948 Convention against Genocide, – warned that genocide has been "an essential part" of world history, it has followed humankind "like a dark shadow from early antiquity to the present".[195] To him, a group can be destroyed as a group even when its members are not all destroyed, but its cultural identity is; genocide, to R. Lemkin, means also the destruction of a culture, impoverishing civilization.

---

193   Cf. *Counter-Memorial*, para. 84; and *Rejoinder*, para. 333.
194   Cf. *Rejoinder*, para. 335.
195   R. Lemkin, *Totally Unofficial – Autobiography* (ed. D.-L. Frieze), New Haven/London, Yale University Press, 2013, pp. 125 and 140.

The destruction of the cultural identity of a group destroys ultimately its "spirit".[196] R. Lemkin confessed that the idea of "cultural genocide" was "very dear" to him:

> It meant the destruction of the cultural pattern of a group, such as language, the traditions, monuments, archives, libraries, and churches. In brief: the shrines of a nation's soul.[197]

232. R. Lemkin much regretted that there was not support for this idea in the *travaux préparatoires* of the Genocide Convention, but he kept nourishing the hope that in the future an Additional Protocol to the Convention, on "cultural genocide", could be adopted. After all, – he added, – "the destruction of a group entails the annihilation of its cultural heritage or the interruption of the cultural contributions coming from the group".[198] R. Lemkin was attentive to the writings of the "founding fathers" of international law (in the XVI XVIIth centuries), and expressed his admiration in particular to those of Bartolomé de Las Casas (and also of Francisco de Vitoria), for his defence, on the basis of natural law, of the rights of native populations against the abuses and brutalities of colonialism in the New World (which R. Lemkin called "colonial genocide").[199]

233. In this connection (destruction of a group's cultural heritage), the ICTFY (Trial Chamber), in its Decision (Review of Indictments, of 11.07.1996) in the case *R. Karadžić and R. Mladić*, observed that, in some cases,

> humiliation and terror serve to dismember the group. The destruction of mosques or Catholic churches is designed to annihilate the centuries-long presence of the group or groups; the destruction of the libraries is intended to annihilate a culture which was enriched through the participation of the various national components of the population (para. 94).

---

196 *Ibid.*, pp. 131, 138 and 168.
197 *Ibid.*, p. 172.
198 *Ibid.*, pp. 172–173.
199 Cf. A. Dirk Moses, "Raphael Lemkin, Culture, and the Concept of Genocide", *in The Oxford Handbook of Genocide Studies* (eds. D. Bloxham and A. Dirk Moses), Oxford, Oxford University Press, 2010, pp. 26–27; and cf. A.A. Cançado Trindade, "Prefacio", *in Escuela Ibérica de la Paz (1511–1694) – La Conciencia Crítica de la Conquista y Colonización de América* (eds. P. Calafate and R.E. Mandado Gutiérrez), Santander, Ed. Universidad de Cantabria, 2014, pp. 72–73 and 98–99.

I shall come back to this point subsequently in the present Dissenting Opinion, when I address the destruction of cultural goods during the bombardments of Dubrovnik (October December 1991).[200]

234. In the already mentioned *Stanišić and Simatović* case, the ICTFY (Trial Chamber I) observed (Judgment of 30.05.2013) that the members of the local civilian population, when not killed, were marginalized, brutalized and forced to flee, "in order to establish a purely Serb territory", so that the attacked villages could afterwards "form part of a Greater Serbia" (para. 1250). The ICTFY (Trial Chamber) recalled "its findings on the actions (including attacks, killings, destruction of houses, arbitrary arrest and detention, torture, harassment, and looting) which occurred in the Saborsko region from June to November 1991" (para. 264). It upheld the initial "evidence of approximately 20,000 to 25,000 Croats and other non-Serbs" who were forcefully displaced from the SAO Krajina region by April 1992 (para. 264).

235. The ICTFY (Trial Chamber) then added, in the aforementioned *Stanišić and Simatović* case, that the total of those forcefully displaced persons considerably raised until April 1992; in its own words, "between 80,000 and 100,000 Croat and other non-Serb civilians fled the SAO Krajina", as a result of the situation created and then prevailing in the region, which was a combination of "the attacks on villages and towns with substantial or completely Croat populations; the killings, use as human shields, detention, beatings, forced labour, sexual abuse, and other forms of harassment of Croat persons; and the looting and destruction of property" (para. 404, and cf. para. 997).[201]

236. Furthermore, in its Judgment of 12.12.2012 in the *Z. Tolimir* case, the ICTFY (Trial Chamber II) drew attention to the need and importance of considering the forcible transfer of segments of the population in connection with other wrongful acts directed against the same targeted groups. It pondered that, proceeding in this way, it becomes clear that the disclosed pattern of destruction, – taking all the wrongful acts together, – is indicative of an intent to destroy all or part of the forcibly displaced population (paras. 739 and 748).

5 General Assessment

237. The evidence produced before the Court in the present case of the *Application of the Convention against Genocide* clearly establishes, in my perception,

---

200   Cf. Part XII(7) of the present Dissenting Opinion, *infra*.
201   And cf. also Part IX(4)(d) of the present Dissenting Opinion, *supra*.

the occurrence of massive killings of targeted members of the Croat civilian population during the armed attacks in Croatia, amidst a systematic pattern of extreme violence, encompassing also torture, arbitrary detention, beatings, sexual assaults, expulsion from homes and looting, forced displacement and transfer, deportation and humiliation, in the attacked villages. It was not exactly a war, it was a devastating onslaught of civilians. It was not only "a plurality of common crimes" that "cannot, in itself, constitute genocide", as Counsel for Serbia argued before the Court in the public sitting of 12.03.2014;[202] it was rather an onslaught, a plurality of atrocities, which, in itself, by its extreme violence and devastation, can disclose the intent to destroy (*mens rea* of genocide).[203]

238. The atrocities were not seldom carried out with the use of derogatory language and hate speech. I find it important to stress the circumstances surrounding the attacked population, which was left in *a situation of the utmost vulnerability, if not defencelessness*; such situation constitutes, in my understanding, an aggravating circumstance. Later on in the present Dissenting Opinion, I shall return to the consideration of the crimes perpetrated, under the relevant parts of the provisions of Article II of the Convention against Genocide.[204]

239. Last but not least, may I here add that, in this factual context, the expression "ethnic cleansing" seems to try to hide the extreme cruelty that it enshrines, in referring to the pursuance with the utmost violence of a forced removal of a targeted group from a given territory. I have already referred to the rather surreptitious way whereby "ethnic cleansing" penetrated legal vocabulary as a breach of international law (para. 47) in my Separate Opinion (para. 47) in the ICJ's Advisory Opinion on the *Declaration of Independence of Kosovo* (of 22.07.2010)

240. It so happens that such coerced or forced removal of a group from a territory, so as to render this latter ethnically "homogeneous", has not seldom been carried out – as the wars in the former Yugoslavia show – by means of killings, torture and beatings, forced labour, rape and other sexual abuses, expulsion from home and forced displacement and deportation (with mass exodus), destruction of cultural and religious sites. Thus, what had initially appeared to

---

202 Cf. ICJ doc. CR 2014/15, of 12.03.2014, p. 18, para. 22. And cf. also *Counter-Memorial*, para. 54.
203 Cf. Part XV of the present Dissenting Opinion, *infra*.
204 Cf. Part XIII of the present Dissenting Opinion, *infra*.

have been an *intent to expel* a group from a territory, may well have become, – as extreme violence breeds more and more violence, – an *intent to destroy* the targeted group.

241. "Ethnic cleansing" and genocide, rather than excluding each other, appear to be somehow overlapping:[205] with the growth of extreme violence, what at first appeared to be "ethnic cleansing" turns out to be genocide: the initial "intent to remove", degenerates into "intent to destroy", the targeted group. In such circumstances, there is no sense in trying to camouflage genocide with the use of the expression "ethnic cleansing". In some circumstances, such expression may well amount to genocide, as reckoned by the ECtHR in the *Jorgić versus Germany* case (Judgment of 12.07.2007).[206] The ECtHR found it fit to ponder that, although there had been "many authorities" who "had favoured a narrow interpretation of the crime of genocide", now that are also "several authorities" who have construed the crime of genocide in a "wider way" (para. 113), as in the *Jorgić* case itself.

XI Widespread and Systematic Pattern of Destruction: Rape and Other Sexual Violence Crimes Committed in Distinct Municipalities

242. May I now dwell upon the widespread and systematic pattern of destruction, in the form of rapes and other sexual violence crimes, systematically

---

205 For a discussion, cf., *inter alia*, e.g., M. Grmek, M. Gjidara and N. Simac (orgs.), *Le nettoyage ethnique – Documents historiques sur une idéologie serbe*, [Paris,] Fayard, 2002, pp. 7–9, 26, 31, 33, 38, 212, 286, 293–294, 311–312, 324–325 and 336–337; J. Quigley, *The Genocide Convention – An International Law Analysis*, Aldershot, Ashgate, 2006, pp. 191–201; N.M. Naimark, *Fires of Hatred – Ethnic Cleansing in the Twentieth-Century Europe*, Cambridge (Mass.)/London, Harvard University Press, 2001, pp. 156–157, 164–165, 168–170, 174 and 183–184; Ph. Spencer, *Genocide since 1945*, London/N.Y., Routledge, 2012, pp. 11–12, 29 and 85–86; N. Cigar, *Genocide in Bosnia – The Policy of "Ethnic Cleansing"*, College Station, Texas A&M University Press, 1995, pp. 3–10, 22–37, 62–85 and 139–180; B. Lieberman, "'Ethnic Cleansing' versus Genocide?" in *The Oxford Handbook of Genocide Studies* (eds. D. Bloxham and A. Dirk Moses), Oxford, Oxford University Press, 2010, pp. 42–60; C. Carmichael, *Ethnic Cleansing in the Balkans – Nationalism and the Destruction of Tradition*, London/N.Y., Routledge, 2002, pp. 2, 66, 112–114.

206 The applicant had alleged that the German courts did not have jurisdiction to convict him of genocide (committed in the villages of Bosnia-Herzegovina); the ECtHR found that the applicant's conviction of genocide by the German courts was not in breach of the ECHR (paras. 113–116).

committed in several municipalities, as from the launching of the military campaign waged by Serbia against Croatia. The *dossier* of the *cas d'espèce*, concerning the *Application of the Convention against Genocide* (Croatia *versus* Serbia), contains in effect several accounts, presented to the ICJ, in the course of both the written and oral phases of the proceedings, of the perpetration of rapes of Croats in a number of municipalities. I shall now dwell upon this particular issue, first addressing the accounts rendered in the oral proceedings, and then those presented earlier on, in the course of the written phase. The path will then be paved for the presentation of my thoughts on other aspects of those atrocities, likewise deserving of close attention.

1   *Accounts of Systematic Rape*
a)   Croatia's Claims

243. In its oral pleadings, Croatia argued that, in their "genocidal campaign" of "extreme brutality", during which "[e]ntire Croat communities were intentionally destroyed", the JNA and subordinate Serb forces "raped more Croat women than can be known", and "destroyed over 100,000 homes and over 1,400 Catholic buildings and places of worship"; they sent over 7,700 detained Croats to "detention camps in occupied parts of Croatia, Serbia, and other parts of the former Yugoslavia, and they forcibly deported over 550,000 others".[207] Croatia next presented a narrative of rapes "accompanied by terrible ethnic abuse" occurred in Berak.[208]

244. Croatia then explained that the first phase of that campaign, – the artillery attacks, – were intended to cause terror and "to compel Croats to abandon their villages"; yet, "the worst atrocities" were reserved for those who refused, or were unable to flee: they were "killed, tortured, raped and abused by the attacking Serb forces", with an intent to destroy the Croat population of the region. There was, in Croatia's perception, "a pattern of attack that was genocidal, in that it intended to destroy a part of the Croat population".[209]

245. Occurrences of torture and rape were reported in the villages of Lovas,[210] Sotin,[211] Bogdanovci – where paramilitaries massacred all or almost all of

---

207   ICJ, doc. CR 2014/6, of 04.03.2014, p. 45, paras. 11 and 13.
208   *Ibid.*, p. 60, para. 22.
209   ICJ, doc. CR 2014/8, of 05.03.2014, p. 17, para. 36.
210   Cf. *ibid.*, p. 17, para. 36, and cf. ICJ, doc. CR 2014/10, of 06.03.2014, p. 23, para. 7.
211   Cf. ICJ, doc. CR 2014/8, of 05.03.2014, p. 22, para. 54.

THE UNIVERSAL JURIDICAL CONSCIENCE 133

Croats remaining in the village,[212] – and Pakrac,[213] and across the region of Eastern Slavonia.[214] Croatia then focused on the raping and other atrocities which victimized the Croat population of Vukovar;[215] it contended that, at Velepromet, women and girls "did not escape brutal rapes",[216] as described in Croatia's pleadings.[217] And it added that

> in the case of *Bosnia versus Serbia*, this Court distinguished between the destruction of a group on the one hand and its "mere dissolution" on the other. To describe the four phases of events at Vukovar in 1991 – the colossal use of force by *overwhelmingly greater Serbian forces* to deprive the trapped inhabitants of their basic conditions of life, the killing, raping and dismembering by the advancing forces of those who remained, the staged removal to torture and death camps and the organized mass killing at Velepromet and Ovčara – to describe that as "mere dissolution" of the Vukovar Croats is so to distort language as to render it meaningless.[218]

246. Croatia argued that "[m]ultiple and gang rapes of Croat women were commonplace", in order to "kill the seed of Croatia", as the perpetrators threatened;[219] this occurred in Siverić, Lovas, Vukovar, Sotin, Doljani, Bapska and Čakovci, Dalj, Gornji Popovac and Tovarnik, among other villages, at times even in the victims' homes. Sexual attacks often took place in the victims' homes, "with their relatives being forced to watch, adding an additional dimension of violation and degradation to the women's ordeals".[220] In Tovarnik, there were also reported cases of castration of men.[221] Croatia added that

---

212 Cf. *ibid.*, p. 24, paras. 62–63.
213 Cf. ICJ, doc. CR 2014/10, of 06.03.2014, p. 13, para. 12.
214 Cf. *ibid.*, pp. 25 and 27, paras. 67 and 71. In Croatia's account, in "different villages and towns across Eastern Slavonia, women were forced to act as 'comfort women' to members of the Serb forces"; ICJ, doc. CR 2014/10, of 06.03.2014, p. 23, para. 7.
215 Cf. ICJ, doc. CR 2014/8, of 05.03.2014, p. 31, para. 11, and cf. ICJ, doc. CR 2014/10, of 06.03.2014, p. 23, para. 7.
216 ICJ, doc. CR 2014/8, of 05.03.2014, p. 42, para. 61.
217 Cf. ICJ, doc. CR 2014/20, of 20.03.2014, p. 33, para. 20, and p. 53, para. 24.
218 ICJ, doc. CR 2014/8, of 05.03.2014, p. 48, para. 88.
219 Cf. ICJ, doc. CR 2014/10, of 06.03.2014, pp. 21–24, para. 4.
220 Cf. *ibid.*, pp. 21–24, paras. 5–6.
221 Cf. *ibid.*, pp. 21–24, para. 8.

Raped women often feel ashamed and they do not even report such attacks. That was the case also in Croatia – the number of reported incidents hides much bigger figures of unreported cases. Those attacks have left an enduring legacy of fear, trauma and shame undiminished by the passage of time.[222]

247. After stressing that "Croat women and girls were frequently the victims of ethnically targeted violence, including rape and gang rape", by members of the JNA, TO, Serbian police and paramilitaries, Croatia recalled that resolution 1820 (2008) of the U.N. Security Council noted that rape and other forms of sexual violence "can constitute war crimes, crimes against humanity or *a constitutive act with respect to genocide*".[223]

248. It further stressed the numerous accounts by numerous witnesses (direct victims or observers of those rapes and gang rapes), in several "towns, villages and hamlets that fell under occupation of the JNA and the Serb paramilitary forces", such as Berše, Brđani, Doljani, Joševica, Korenica, Kostajnički Majur, Kovačevac, Ljubotić and Lisičić, Novo Selo Glinsko, Parčić, Puljane, Šarengrad, Sekulinci, Smilčić, Sotin, Tenja, and Vukovar and many others.[224] Croatia then concluded, on this particular issue, that

> The scale and pattern of killing, torture and rape has been disclosed by the evidence submitted by the Applicant, and that clearly, in our submission, makes out the *actus reus* of genocide within the meaning of Articles II(a) and (b) of the Genocide Convention. To argue otherwise, in our submission, is simply not to be credible.
>
> In addition, the conditions of life which were inflicted on the Croat population remaining in Serb-occupied territory, including systematic expulsion from homes, torture, rape and denial of food, access to water, basic sanitation and medical treatment, were calculated to bring about its physical destruction as a group. This, too, amounted to genocide within the meaning of Article II(c) of the Convention.
>
> Finally, just this morning, you have heard in some detail the evidence of systematic rape of Croatian women and men, the sexual mutilation and castration of Croatian men, and the commission of other sex crimes

---

222   Cf. *ibid.*, pp. 21–24, para. 3.
223   *Ibid.*, p. 21, para. 2 [emphasis added].
224   Cf. *ibid.*, p. 24, para. 9. On the brutalities of sexual abuses, cf. also *ibid.*, p. 27, paras. 22–25 (in Vukovar).

which, when viewed in the context of the broader genocidal policies of the Serb forces, involved the imposition of measures to prevent births within the Croatian population. This, we say, falls squarely within the meaning of Article II(d).[225]

b) Serbia's Response

249. For its part, Serbia, instead of addressing the issue of systematic practice of rape, tried to discredit the evidence produced by Croatia.[226] It did so, largely on the argument that most witness statements were unsigned,[227] – a point already clarified to some extent by Croatia (*supra*). In any case, Serbia admitted, in general terms, the occurrence of "serious crimes" (cf. *supra*); in its own words,

> the fundamental disagreement of the respondent State with the Applicant's approach to the unsigned statements and police reports does not mean that the Serbian Government denies that serious crimes were committed during the armed conflict in Croatia. Yes, the serious crimes were perpetrated against the members of the Croatian national and ethnic group. They were committed by groups and individuals of Serb ethnicity. It goes without saying that Serbia condemns such crimes, regrets that they were committed, and sympathizes profoundly with the victims and their families for the suffering that they have experienced.
>
> The Higher Court in Belgrade has so far convicted and imprisoned 15 Serbs for the war crimes against prisoners of war at the farm Ovčara near Vukovar, and another 14 for the war crimes against civilians in the village of Lovas in Eastern Slavonia. The second judgment has recently been quashed by the Court of Appeal due to the shortcomings concerning the explanation of the individual criminal liability for each accused, and the trial must be held again. An additional ten cases for the war crimes committed by Serbs in Croatia have been concluded before the Higher Court in Belgrade. In total, 31 individuals of Serb nationality have so far been convicted and imprisoned, while there are others being accused. Investigations on several crimes are under way, including the crime in Bogdanovci.

---

225   *Ibid.*, p. 54, paras. 16–18. – For other accounts, cf., e.g., ICJ doc. CR 2014/6, of 04.03.2014, p. 45; ICJ doc. CR 2014/8, of 05.03.2014, pp. 14, 25 and 39; and ICJ doc. CR 2014/10, of 06.03.2014, paras. 23–24.

226   Cf., e.g., ICJ, doc. CR 2014/13, of 10.03.2014, pp. 65–66, para. 43; ICJ, doc. CR 2014/22, of 27.03.2014, pp. 13–14, paras. 10–13.

227   Cf., e.g., ICJ, doc. CR 2014/13, of 10.03.2014, pp. 64–65, paras. 38 and 42.

Thus, despite the careless approach to the presentation of evidence by the Applicant, it is not in dispute that murders of Croatian civilians and prisoners of war took place during the conflict. This was established also in the ICTY Judgment against *Milan Martić*, who was convicted as the former Minister of Interior of the Republic of Serbian Krajina, as well as in the case *Mrkšić et al.*; the last case is also known as 'Ovčara'. In that notorious crime, the ICTY recorded 194 prisoners of war who were killed. This was the gravest mass murder in which Croats were the victims during the entire conflict.[228]

2 *Systematic Pattern of Rape in Distinct Municipalities*

251. As already indicated, the *dossier* of the present case, opposing Croatia to Serbia, contains reports of rapes of Croats in a number of municipalities. Several witnesses testified to having been raped, often multiple times, and by several perpetrators. It is also important to note that the rapes were frequently accompanied by derogatory language and further violence, such as beatings and use of objects.

252. The examples provided, of testimonies regarding the continuous commission of rape in distinct municipalities, evidence a *widespread and systematic pattern of rape* of members of the Croatian population, inflicting humiliation upon the victims. These statements, next referred to, form part of the evidence submitted by Croatia, so as to illustrate the numerous allegations of rape across distinct municipalities and to demonstrate the systematic pattern of those grave breaches.[229]

253. For example, in Lovas, it was alleged that paramilitaries routinely engaged in sexual violence against Croatians.[230] A.M. testified to being raped repeatedly and she reported that paramilitaries made a habit of collecting groups

---

228 Cf. *ibid.*, pp. 64–65, paras. 38–40. And Serbia added: – "If one carefully makes a review of all ICTY indictments in which the crimes against Croats were alleged, he or she will find many victims, indeed. There is no doubt that many Croats also died in the combat activities during the five-year conflict. Yet, from the point of view of the subject-matter of this case, those numbers of victims are of an entirely different magnitude than the many those killed in Srebrenica – or in Krajina – over the course of several days"; *ibid.*, pp. 64–65, para. 41.

229 Cf. also *Memorial*, paras. 5.30, 5.59, 5.88, 5.147, 5.157, 5.175, 5.209–5.210, 5.212 and 5.224; and cf. also *ibid.*, paras. 4.25, 4.44–4.45, 4.60, 4.110, 4.113, 4.129, 4.131, 4.169, 4.185, 4.60, 5.147, 5.157, 5.212, 5.224. And cf. also *Reply*, paras. 5.35, 5.46, 5.54, 5.84.

230 *Memorial*, para. 4.129.

of Croatian women in the village in order to rape them.²³¹ Similarly, P.M. also testified to sexual abuse of Croatian men.²³² In Bapska, P.M. described that a Serbian soldier raped her and her 81 year old mother before he tore her navel with his bare hands.²³³ In this village, there were also accounts of sexual violence against men, according to witness F.K.²³⁴ In Pakrac, H.H. described rape and torture of a victim before her ears were cut off and her skull shattered.²³⁵ In a similar violent vein, there was, in Kraljevčani, a description of rape of a Croat woman, whose breasts were cut off.²³⁶

254. Croatian women in the village of Tenja were routinely raped, along with having to labour in fields and gardens. For example, while K.C. was made to clean the police station, she was indecently assaulted by one of the officers; according to M.M., K.C.'s experience drove her to attempt suicide.²³⁷ In the village of Berak, M.H., thus described her rape: – "(...) I was their special target because I had six sons and they were threatening me because I had delivered six Ustashas".²³⁸ In this village, there were accounts of sexual assault against Croatian women. L.M. and M.H. were raped in front of a group of people, and throughout the night.²³⁹ P.B. testified having been raped with brutality by seven JNA reservists with White Eagle marks.²⁴⁰

255. In the village of Sotin, V.G. describes how on 30.09.1991 two soldiers came into her house and both raped her while holding a gun pointing at her. The next day, one of the soldiers who had raped her came back and raped her mother. After that, V.G. was forced to get down on her knees and was raped from behind.²⁴¹ Furthermore, R.G. described "sexual advantage" being taken of an elderly woman in Sotin, and S.L. also described other sexual abuses in Sotin.²⁴² As to Tovarnik, the document *Mass Killing and Genocide in Croatia*

---

231   *Ibid.*, Annex 108.
232   *Ibid.*, Annex 101.
233   *Memorial*, para. 4.90.
234   *Ibid.*, para. 4.91 and Annex 74.
235   *Ibid.*, para. 5.17 and Annex 175.
236   *Ibid.*, para. 5.98.
237   *Ibid.*, para. 4.25.
238   *Ibid.*, para. 4.44.
239   *Ibid.*, para. 4.44.
240   *Memorial*, para. 4.45.
241   *Ibid.*, para. 4.113, and Annex 94.
242   *Ibid.*, paras. 4.101 and 4.111, respectively.

1991/92: A Book of Evidence (pp. 107–108) also gives account of forced sexual abuses between Croat prisoners.[243]

256. In the *dossier* of the present case, there are many accounts of rape and other sexual violence crimes that occurred, in particular, in the greater Vukovar area. Some examples have been provided by witness testimonies. For example, the Muslim JNA soldier, E.M., described rape and killing in his account of the JNA conduct in Petrova Gora (a suburb of Vukovar).[244] A.S. testified how, on 16.09.1991, M.L., from Vukovar, told her that he was going to kill her: after insulting her, he raped her.[245] T.C. gave likewise an account of what took place in the suburb of Vukovar, Čakovci: R.I. entered her house and, threatening to kill her, tied her hands and raped her.[246]

257. Velepromet was the backdrop of routine executions, torture, and rape often committed by multiple rapists. Women of Croatian nationality that were imprisoned in the Velepromet detention facility in Vukovar were taken to interrogations during which they were exposed to sexual abuse. Group rapes also allegedly took place. B.V. was raped the second day on her arrival in the barracks; four soldiers raped her one after another on the floor of the office while insulting her and hitting her in the face. She testified how 15 Serbian soldiers took M.M. to the room next door to her and raped her in turns.[247]

258. M.M. described how, on 18.11.1991, – the day of the occupation of Central Vukovar, – she and her family were taken to the Velepromet building, and later driven in buses to Šand Šabac (Serbia). Back in Vukovar, she described how she was raped by five men, one after another, from 9 p.m. until the morning. During the rape she was bleeding and was forced to sit on a beer bottle. This happened in front of her little sister, who was also sexually abused during two weeks and was continuously afraid.[248] Likewise, H.E. testified to daily rapes by Serbian police and army upon her arrival to prison. The rapes happened in the cell in front of other female prisoners. She also testified to beatings and mental abuse.[249]

---

243 *Ibid.*, para. 4.101.
244 *Memorial*, para. 4.153, and Annex 127.
245 *Ibid.*, para. 4.155, and Annex 125.
246 *Ibid.*, para. 4.156, and Annex 128.
247 *Ibid.*, para. 4.185.
248 *Memorial*, para. 4.169 and Annex 117.
249 *Ibid.*, Annex 116.

259. Witness T.C. stated that Chetniks "were maltreating, expelling, threatening, beating, raping and killing on a daily basis", and added that "Croats had white ribbons at our gate in order to enable Chetniks who were not from our village to recognize us"; she testified that she was raped.[250] In a similar vein, G.K. testified to having been maltreated and raped,[251] and B.V. likewise testified to killings, rape and maltreatment, and added that she was raped by four men, having used derogatory language during the rape.[252]

3 The Necessity and Importance of a Gender Analysis

260. The present case of the *Application of the Convention against Genocide* (Croatia *versus* Serbia), in my perception, can only be properly adjudicated with *a gender perspective*. This is not the first time that I take this position: in 2006, almost one decade ago, I did the same, in another international jurisdiction,[253] given the circumstances of the case at issue. Now, in 2015, an analysis of gender is, in my perception, likewise unavoidable and essential in the present case before the ICJ, given the incidence of a social-cultural pattern of conduct, disclosing systemic discrimination and extreme violence against women.

261. At the time that the wars in Croatia, and in Bosnia and Herzegovina, were taking place, with their abuses against women, the final documents of the U.N. II World Conference on Human Rights (Vienna, 1993) and the U.N. IV World Conference on Women (Beijing, 1995), paid due attention to the difficulties faced by women in face of cultural patterns of behaviour in distinct situations and circumstances.[254] Attention to the basic *principle of equality and non-discrimination* is of fundamental importance here. In the present case of the *Application of the Convention against Genocide* (Croatia *versus* Serbia), women as well as men, members of the targeted groups, were victimized, but women (of all ages) were brutalized in different ways and in a much greater proportion than men. Hence the great necessity of a gender perspective.

262. The widespread and systematic raping of girls and women, as occurred in the armed attacks in Croatia (and also in those in Bosnia and Herzegovina),

---

250   *Ibid.*, Annex 128.
251   *Ibid.*, Annex 130.
252   *Ibid.*, Annex 151.
253   Cf. IACtHR, case of the *Prison of Castro Castro*, concerning Peru, Judgment of 25.11.2006, Separate Opinion of Judge Cançado Trindade, paras. 58–74.
254   Cf. A.A. Cançado Trindade, *Tratado de Direito Internacional dos Direitos Humanos* [*Treatise of International Law of Human Rights*], vol. III, Porto Alegre/Brazil, S.A. Fabris Ed., 2003, pp. 354–356.

had a devastating effect upon the victims. Girls were suddenly deprived of their innocence and childhood, despite their young age. This is extreme cruelty. Young and unmarried women were suddenly deprived of their project of life. This is extreme cruelty. The victims could no longer cherish any faith or hope in affective relations. This is extreme cruelty. Young or middle-aged women who, after having been raped, became pregnant, could not surround their maternity with care and due respect, given the extreme violence they had been, and continued to be, subjected to. This is extreme cruelty.

263. Middle-aged and older women, who had already constituted a family, had their personal and family life entirely destroyed. Even if they had physically survived, they must have felt like having become walking shadows.[255] This is extreme cruelty. There were also women who kept on being raped until dying. Were the ones who survived this ordeal "luckier" than the ones who passed the last threshold of life? None remained secure from acute pain.[256] The sacrality of life – before birth, during pregnancy, after birth, and along with what remained of human existence, – was destroyed with brutality.

264. What happened later, after the brutal raping with humiliation, to the children who were born of hatred? Do we know? What were the long-term effects of such pattern of destruction victimizing mainly women? Do we know? What happened to the sons and daughters of hatred? Do we know? The widespread and systematic raping of women in the *cas d'espèce* disclosed a pattern of extreme violence *in an inter-temporal dimension*. There were also the women who lost their children, or husbands, in the war, and those who did not have access to their mortal remains, having been thus deprived of their project of after-life.

265. Many centuries ago, Euripides depicted, in his tragedies *Suppliant Women*, *Andromache*, *Hecuba*, and *Trojan Women* (ivth century b.C.), the cruel impact and effects of war particularly upon women. Euripides' *Trojan Women*, for example, came to be regarded, in our times, as one of the greatest anti-war literary pieces of the antiquity, depicting its evil. Over four centuries later, Seneca wrote his own version of the tragedy *Trojan Women* (50–62 A.D.), with a distinct outlook, but portraying likewise the anguish and sufferings that befell upon women. In the last decade of the xxth century, the cruel impact and effects of war upon women marked likewise presence in the facts of the present case

---

255 To paraphrase Shakespeare, *Macbeth* (1605–1606), act v, scene v, verse 24.
256 To paraphrase Sophocles, *Oedipus the King* (428–425 b.C.), verses 1528–1530.

of the *Application of the Convention against Genocide* (Croatia *versus* Serbia), disclosing the projection of evil in time, its perennity and omnipresence.

266. In the *cas d'espèce*, the degradation and humiliation of women by systematic rape and other sexual violence crimes (*supra*) did not exhaust themselves at the level of individual life. The atrocities they were subjected to, caused also (for those who survived) forced separation, and disruption of family life. The terrible sufferings inflicted by rapes allegedly for "ethnic cleansing", went far beyond that, to the destruction of the targeted groups themselves, to which the murdered and brutalized women belonged, – that is, to the realm of genocide.

267. May it be recalled that, in its landmark Judgment (of 02.09.1998) in the case *Akayesu*, the ICTR held precisely that gender-based crimes of rape and sexual violence, disclosing an intent to destroy, constituted genocide, and in fact destroyed the targeted group (para. 731). In determining the occurrence of genocide, the ICTR found that the pattern of rape with public humiliation and mutilation, inflicted serious bodily and mental harm on the women victims, and disclosed an intent to destroy them, their families and communities, the Tutsi group as a whole (paras. 731 and 733–734). The victimized women were degraded, – in the words of the ICTR, – as "sexual objects", and the extreme violence they were subjected to "was a step in the process of destruction" of their social group, – "destruction of the spirit, of the will to live, and of life itself" (para. 732).

268. For its part, the ICTFY (Trial Chamber), in its Decision (Review of Indictments, of 11.07.1996) in the case *R. Karadžić and R. Mladić*, stated that a pattern of sexual assaults began to occur even before the wars in Croatia and Bosnia and Herzegovina broke out, "in a context of looting and intimidation of the population". Concentration camps for rape were established, "with the aim of forcing the birth of Serbian offspring, the women often being interned until it was too late for them to undergo an abortion" (para. 64). Rapes – the ICTFY (Trial Chamber) proceeded – increased "the shame and humiliation of the victims and of the community"; the purpose "of many rapes was enforced impregnation" (para. 64).

269. Such crimes, of "systematic rape of women", purporting "to transmit a new ethnic identity" to the children, undermined "the very foundations of the group", dismembering it (para. 94). They "could have been planned or ordered with a genocidal intent" (para. 95). The ICTFY (Trial Chamber) held that "Radovan Karadžić and Ratko Mladić planned, ordered or otherwise aided and

abetted in the planning, preparation or execution of the genocide perpetrated" in the centres of detention (para. 84).

270. In the present case of the *Application of the Convention against Genocide*, opposing Croatia to Serbia, due to the early mobilization of entities of the civil society, the figures concerning the systematic practice of destruction through rape were soon to become known. By the end of 1992, the estimates were that there had been, in the war in Croatia until then, approximately 12 thousand incidents of rape. Those incidents rose up to 50 to 60 thousand incidents, in the whole period of 1991–1995, in the wars in the former Yugoslavia (both in Croatia and in Bosnia and Herzegovina).

271. But those are only rough estimates, as it was soon realized, – as acknowledged in expert writing,[257] – that it was simply not possible to know with precision the total number of victims (of all ages) of that brutality, and the extent of destruction, perpetrated, with the intent to destroy the victimized families and the targeted social groups, in concentration camps (rape/death camps), in prisons and detention centres, and in brothels. The girls and women victimized were condemned to the utmost humiliation, and were dehumanized by the victimizers, simply because of their ethnic identity, for being who they were.

272. If this systematic pattern of rape was not a plurality of acts of genocide (for the destructive consequences it entailed), what then was it? What is genocide, if that is not? In the present Dissenting Opinion, I have already examined the findings (in 1992–1993), e.g., in the U.N. (former Commission on Human

---

257 Cf., *inter alia*, e.g., B. Allen, *Rape Warfare – The Hidden Genocide in Bosnia-Herzegovina and Croatia*, Minneapolis/London, University of Minnesota Press, 1996, pp. 65, 72, 76–77 and 104; [Various Authors,] *Women, Violence and War – Wartime Victimization of Refugees in the Balkans* (ed. V. Nikolić-Ristanović), Budapest, Central European University Press, 2000, pp. 41, 43, 56–57, 80–82, 142 and 154; S. Fabijanić Gagro, "The Crime of Rape in the ICTY's and the ICTR's Case-Law", 60 *Zbornik Pravnog Fakulteta u Zagrebu* (2010) pp. 1310, 1315–1316 and 1330–1331; M. Ellis, "Breaking the Silence: Rape as an International Crime", 38 *Case Western Reserve Journal of International Law* (2007) pp. 226 and 231–234; S.L. Russell-Brown, "Rape as an Act of Genocide", 21 *Berkeley Journal of International Law* (2003) pp. 351–352, 355, 363–364 and 371; R. Peroomian, "When Death is a Blessing and Life a Prolonged Agony: Women Victims of Genocide", *in Genocide Perspectives II – Essays on Holocaust and Genocide* (eds. C Tatz, P. Arnold and S. Tatz), Sydney, Brandl & Schlesinger / Australian Institute for Holocaust & Genocide Studies, 2003, pp. 314–315 and 327–330.

Rights) *Reports on the Situation of Human Rights in the Territory of the Former Yugoslavia* (*rapporteur*, T. Mazowiecki),[258] which should here be recalled.

273. In effect, those *Reports* contain references, *inter alia*, to the pattern of destruction by means of killings, torture, disappearances, rape and sexual violence. I thus limit myself to add here that the *Report* of 10.02.1993,[259] e.g., states that the "[r]ape of women, including minors, has been widespread in both conflicts" (para. 260) (the wars in Croatia and in Bosnia and Herzegovina). The systematic pattern of rapes was accompanied by other acts of extreme violence.

274. In the subsequent *Report* of 10.06.1994,[260] the Special *Rapporteur* further referred to the "widespread terrorization" of the population by means of killings, destruction of homes, and commission of rapes by soldiers (para. 7) in their "relentless assaults" (para. 11). For its part, the U.N. (Security Council's) Commission of Experts, in its fact-finding reports of 1993–1994, – as I have already indicated in the present Dissenting Opinion, – likewise found the occurrence of a widespread and systematic pattern of rapes, – as well as torture and beatings, often followed by killings, spreading terror, shame and humiliation,[261] disrupting family life and the targeted groups themselves. If this plurality of acts of extreme violence (with all its destructive consequences) was not genocide, what then was it?

275. In its recent Judgment of 11.07.2013, in the *R. Karadžić* case, the ICTFY (Appeals Chamber), in rejecting an appeal for acquittal, and reinstating genocide charges against Mr. R. Karadžić (para. 115), pointed out that it had found that "quintessential examples of serious bodily harm as an underlying act of genocide include torture, rape, and non-fatal physical violence that causes disfigurement or serious injury to the external or internal organs" (para. 33). The ICTFY (Appeals Chamber) took into due account the evidence of "genocidal and other culpable acts" on a large-scale and discriminatory in nature, such as killings, beatings, rape and sexual violence, and inhumane living conditions (paras. 34 and 99).

276. More recently, in its Decision of 15.04.2014, in the *R. Mladić* case, the ICTFY (Trial Chamber I) rejected a defence motion for acquittal, and decided

---

258   Cf. Part IX of the present Dissenting Opinion, *supra*.
259   U.N., doc. E/CN.4/1993/50.
260   U.N., doc. E/CN.4/1995/4.
261   Cf. Part IX of the present Dissenting Opinion, *supra*.

to continue trial on genocide charges. It took due note of the evidence produced on torture and prolonged beatings of detainees (pp. 20937–20938), of "large-scale" expulsions of non-Serbs (p. 20944), and of rape of young women and girls (the youngest one being 12 years old) (pp. 20935–20936 and 20939). Shortly afterwards (Decision of 24.07.2014), the ICTFY (Appeals Chamber) dismissed a defence appeal and confirmed the Trial Chamber I's aforementioned decision (para. 29).

277. Last but not least, as it can be perceived from the selected examples of witness statements in the *cas d'espèce*, reviewed above, as to numerous occurrences of rape and other sexual violence crimes during the armed attacks in Croatia, and also in Bosnia and Herzegovina, that they appear intended to destroy the targeted groups of victims. In my perception, the brutality itself of the numerous rapes perpetrated bears witness of their intent to destroy. The victims were attacked in a situation of *the utmost vulnerability or defencelessness*. As from the launching of the Serbian armed attacks in Croatia, there occurred, in effect, a *systematic pattern of rape*, which can surely be considered under Article II(b) of the Genocide Convention (cf. *infra*).

XII   Systematic Pattern of Disappeared or Missing Persons

1   *Arguments of the Parties Concerning the Disappeared or Missing Persons*

278. During the written phase of the proceedings of the *cas d'espèce*, both Croatia and Serbia referred to the issue of the disappeared or missing persons, persisting to date. In its *Memorial*, Croatia asked the Court to declare the obligation of the FRY to take all steps at its disposal to provide a prompt and full account to it of the whereabouts of each and every one of those missing persons, and, to that end, to work in cooperation with its own authorities.[262] Croatia further stated that "the establishment of the whereabouts of missing persons, often victims of genocide, is a painful process, but a necessary step for the sake of a better future".[263]

279. Croatia claimed that 1,419 persons were, at the date of the filing of its *Memorial* (of 01.03.2009), still missing and unaccounted for.[264] According

---

262   *Memorial*, para. 8.78, and cf. p. 414.
263   *Ibid.*, para. 1.14.
264   *Ibid.*, para. 1.09.

to the information provided in 2009 by Croatia's Government Office for the Detained and Missing Persons, there appeared to be total of at least 886 still "missing persons" from the area of Eastern Slavonia;[265] moreover, the destiny of 511 persons from Vukovar remained still unknown at the time of the filing of its *Memorial*.[266] By an *Agreement on Normalization of Relations*, signed between Croatia and FRY on 23.08.1996, the Parties undertook to "speed up the process of solving the question of missing persons" and to exchange all available information about those missing (Article 6).[267]

280. Subsequently, in its *Reply* (of 20.12.2010), Croatia facilitated an updated *List of Missing Persons* (of 01.09.2010), indicating a total of 1,024 missing persons.[268] According to the Applicant, on 27–28.07.2010, "a meeting on missing persons" was held in Belgrade between Serbia's Commission for Missing Persons and Croatia's Commission for Detained and Missing Persons, under the auspices of the ICRC and the International Commission on Missing Persons. One of the issues then addressed was "the question of those detained on the territory of the Respondent"; in this respect, "representatives of the Respondent gave to the Applicant's representatives a list of 2,786 persons who were detained in Republic of Serbia in the period 1991–1992".[269]

281. Croatia then requested the Court to adjudge and declare that as a consequence of its responsibility for these breaches of the Convention, the Respondent is under the obligations "[t]o provide forthwith to the Applicant all information within its possession or control as to the whereabouts of Croatian citizens who are missing as a result of the genocidal acts for which it is responsible, and generally to cooperate with the authorities of the Applicant to jointly ascertain the whereabouts of the said missing persons or their remains".[270]

282. The two Parties elaborated further the question of the number of still missing persons at the oral proceedings. An expert called by Croatia observed that the data on the missing persons they exhumed "change from day to day", and whenever there is an exhumation, "the number of identified persons increases,

---

265 *Ibid.*, para. 4.06.
266 *Ibid.*, para. 4.190.
267 *Ibid.*, para. 2.160.
268 *Reply*, Annex 41.
269 *Ibid.*, para. 2.54.
270 *Reply*, p. 472.

and the number of missing persons then increases also".²⁷¹ Croatia contended its efforts "to uncover the graves of the genocide victims" have been "hampered by Serbia's practice of removing and reburying victims during its occupation of the region, often in Serbia, in a vain attempt to cover up its atrocities".²⁷²

283. To date, – it proceeded, – 103 bodies have been repatriated from Serbia; furthermore, "whilst many of the victims of the genocide have now been accounted for, and their remains located, hundreds of Croats still remain missing. Twenty-three years later, Croatian families continue to mourn more than 850 missing people. The victims are still denied a proper burial and a dignified final resting place; and their families are still denied the opportunity to lay them to rest".²⁷³ Croatia further stated, with regard to mass graves, that, by July 2013, 142 mass graves had been discovered in Croatia, containing the bodies of 3,656 victims.²⁷⁴

284. For its part, Serbia argued that the Croatian list of missing persons was confusing and unhelpful in clarifying the issues in the dispute. It added that the *Updated List of Missing Persons* (of 01.09.2010) contained data on 1,024 individuals, among whom many "victims of Serb ethnicity". Furthermore, it contained the names of Croats "who were missing in Bosnia and Herzegovina, as well as in some places that were under the full and exclusive control of the Croatian Governmental forces and far away from military operations". The aforementioned list also contained "the names of ethnic Croats who went missing during the offensive criminal Operations *Maslenica* and *Storm* which were undertaken by the Croatian Government".²⁷⁵

2 Responses of the Parties to Questions from the Bench

285. Given the contradictory information provided, Judge Cançado Trindade deemed it fit to put two questions to the contending Parties, in the public sitting before the Court of 14.03.2014. The two questions were formulated as follows:

> 1. Have there been any recent initiatives to identify, and to clarify further the fate of the disappeared persons still missing to date?

---

271 ICJ, doc. CR 2014/9, of 05.03.2014, p. 36.
272 ICJ, doc. CR 2014/10, of 06.03.2014, p. 20, para. 44.
273 *Ibid.*, p. 20, para. 45.
274 *Ibid.*, para. 39.
275 *Rejoinder*, para. 7.

2. Is there any additional and more precise updated information that can be presented to the Court by both Parties on this particular issue of disappeared or missing persons to date?[276]

286. In response to my questions, Croatia elaborated further on the issue of the fate of disappeared persons. In this respect, it recalled that Article II of the Convention enumerates amongst the list of genocidal acts the causing of "serious (...) mental harm to members of the group". The questions I put to both Parties drew the Applicant to the case-law on the disappearance of persons. Recalling the Judgments of the IACtHR in the case of *Velásquez Rodríguez versus Honduras* (of 29.07.1988) and of the ECtHR in the case of *Varnava versus Turkey* (of 18.09.2009), as well as the Decision of the U.N. Human Rights Committee in the case of *C.A. de Quinteros et alii versus Uruguay* (1990), Croatia claimed that disappearance has continuing consequences in several respects. In the light of that jurisprudence, Croatia claims that the

> "serious (...) mental harm" being suffered by the relatives of the disappeared is a direct result of acts for which Serbia is either responsible for its own actions or for which it has a responsibility to punish under the [Genocide] Convention. In this way, the continuing failure of Serbia to account for the whereabouts of some 865 disappeared Croats is an act or acts falling within Article II(b) of the Convention.[277]

287. As for the requested additional, and more precise updated information, on the issue of disappeared or missing persons, Croatia answered that such information can be found in the updated *Book of Missing Persons on the Territory of the Republic of Croatia*, published by Croatia's Directorate for Detained and Missing Persons, in conjunction with the Croatian Red Cross and the ICRC. It informed that the book sets out detailed data on those who were still missing as of April 2012;[278] however, as the figures concerning the disappeared are being constantly updated, the numbers provided in the 2012 book are already out of date.

288. Still in response to my questions to both Parties (*supra*), Croatia further contacted the Directorate for Detained and Missing Persons, on Monday

---

276 Questions put by Judge Cançado Trindade to both Croatia and Serbia, *in*: ICJ, doc. CR 2014/18, of 14.03.2014, p. 69.
277 ICJ, doc. CR 2014/20, of 20.03.2014, p. 15, para. 10.
278 ICJ, doc. CR 2014/20, of 20.03.2014, pp. 34-35, paras. 22-25.

17.03.2014, and provided the ICJ with the most up-to-date figures relating to persons killed during the course of Serbia's attacks on Croatian territory in 1991–1992, namely: (a) the bodies of 3,680 persons who were buried irregularly have been exhumed from 142 mass graves and many more individual graves; (b) of those, the bodies of 3,144 persons have been positively identified; (c) however, 865 persons who disappeared during that period are still missing.[279]

289. For its part, Serbia, in its response to the questions I put to both Parties (*supra*), stated that tracing missing persons "is a complex and long-lasting process of co-operation between two sides", on the basis of the 1995 Bilateral Agreement on Co-operation in Tracing Missing Persons and the 1996 Protocol on Co-operation between two State Commissions.[280] It added that it was "fully aware of its task in the process of tracing missing persons regardless of their nationality and ethnic origin. The interest of families of the missing persons is a joint interest of Serbia and Croatia. It is also the interest of humanity as a whole, and the Republic of Serbia is dedicated to that task".[281] As for the number of missing persons, Serbia claims that the Serbian list of missing persons, received from the Serbian Commission for Missing Persons in the territory of Croatia, today contains 1,748 names.[282]

290. Finally, as regards the argument of continuing violation, – it added, – disappearance itself is not an act of genocide, but it is equivalent to enforced disappearance, a crime against humanity. Serbia relied on the definition of "enforced disappearance" contained in the 2006 U.N. Convention for the Protection of All Persons from Enforced Disappearance, which refers to "abduction or any other form of deprivation of liberty by agents of the State" and then "followed by a refusal to acknowledge the deprivation of liberty or by concealment of the fate or whereabouts of the disappeared person" (Article 2).

291. According to Serbia, enforced disappearance is not a continuing violation of the right to life, with which the acts in Article 2 of the 2006 Convention bear an analogy. The reason why it may be a continuing violation of human

---

279   *Ibid.*, pp. 34–35, paras. 22–25.
280   ICJ, *Preliminary Objections* of Serbia; Annex 53, p. 367.
281   ICJ, doc. CR 2014/24, of 28.03.2014, pp. 60–61, para. 10.
282   However, Serbia did not consider that list to be evidence of the crime, or of State responsibility, and referred to the *Veritas* list of direct victims of "Operation Storm"; cf. ICJ, doc. CR 2014/24, of 28.03.2014, pp. 60–62, paras. 6–10.

THE UNIVERSAL JURIDICAL CONSCIENCE

rights, according to Serbia, is that the family of the victim is subject to ongoing "mental harm", or because of the procedural obligation to investigate the crime. Serbia claims that, if the crime continues today as Croatia asserts, so must the intent. Croatia is "in error to attempt to force this issue into the frame of Article 2 of the Genocide Convention, essentially so that it can bolster its argument on temporal jurisdiction".[283]

3 Outstanding Issues and the Parties' Obligation to Establish the Fate of Missing Persons

292. In the light of the aforementioned, it is clear the issue of missing persons remains one of the key problems raised in the proceedings of the *cas d'espèce*. Admittedly, the Parties had the intention in 1995 to tackle this issue: it may be recalled that in 1995, in Dayton, Croatia and Serbia celebrated an agreement, the purpose of which was to establish the fate of all missing persons and to release the prisoners.[284] In pursuance to that agreement, a Joint Commission was established and some progress was made with respect to missing persons.[285] Yet, there remain a number of outstanding issues that still need to be resolved.

293. For example, the Parties disagree on the role of the Commission. Croatia claims that the Commission, contrary to what was agreed in 1995 that all missing persons who disappeared in Croatia fell within the competence of Croatian authorities, is currently seeking to act as representative of all missing persons of Serb ethnicity, including those who are citizens of Croatia.[286] Serbia responds that this is needed in order to represent the un-reported 1,000 Serbs from Croatia in the list of missing persons provided by Croatia to the Court.[287]

---

283 ICJ, doc. CR 2014/23, of 28.03.2014, pp. 43–45, paras. 10–12.
284 Agreement on Co-operation in Finding Missing Persons (Dayton, 17.11.1995).
285 From August 1996 till 1998 Croatia was given access to information, the so-called protocols, for 1,063 persons who were buried at the Vukovar New Cemetery, and these protocols helped in the identification of 938 people. In 2001, exhumations started with respect to unidentified bodies buried in the Republic of Serbia, at marked gravesites. The remains of 394 persons have been exhumed so far, but, regrettably, only 103 bodies have been handed over to Croatia. In 2013, one mass grave was discovered in Sotin, in Eastern Slavonia, with 13 bodies, as a result of information provided by Serbia. Cf. ICJ, doc. CR 2014/21, of 21.03.2014, pp. 36–38.
286 ICJ, doc. CR 2014/21, of 21.03.2014, p. 37, para. 10.
287 ICJ, doc. CR 2014/24, of 28.03.2014, pp. 60–61, paras. 6–10.

294. Moreover, Croatia contends that Serbia has not yet returned the documents seized by the JNA from the Vukovar hospital in 1991, which are considered essential for the identification of the persons removed from the hospital.[288] Only a small part of those documents was returned, when the President of Serbia (Mr. Boris Tadić) visited Vukovar in November 2010. Both Parties appear unsatisfied with the efforts and activities of each other in this regard.[289] The Court ought thus to ask the Parties to co-operate in good faith in order to resolve those outstanding issues.

295. As the ICJ stated, in this respect, in the *Nuclear Tests* cases (Australia and New Zealand *versus* France, 1974), one of "the basic principles governing the creation and performance of legal obligations, whatever their source, is the principle of good faith. Trust and confidence are inherent in international co-operation" (paras. 46 and 49). On another occasion, in the *North Sea Continental Shelf* cases (F.R. Germany *versus* Denmark and Netherlands, 1969), the ICJ further pondered that the contending Parties "are under an obligation so to conduct themselves that the negotiations are meaningful" (para. 85).

4 *The Extreme Cruelty of Enforced Disappearances of Persons as a Continuing Grave Violation of Human Rights and International Humanitarian Law*

296. The extreme cruelty of the crime of enforced disappearance of persons has been duly acknowledged in international instruments, in international legal doctrine, as well as in international case-law. It goes beyond the confines of the present Dissenting Opinion to dwell at depth on the matter, – what I have done elsewhere.[290] I shall, instead, limit myself to identifying and invoking some pertinent illustrations, with a direct bearing on the proper consideration of the *cas d'espèce*, concerning the *Application of the Convention against Genocide* (Croatia *versus* Serbia).

297. May I begin by recalling that, in 1980, the former U.N. Commission on Human Rights decided to establish its Working Group on Enforced or

---

288 ICJ, doc. CR 2014/21, of 21.03.2014, p. 38, para. 11.
289 *Ibid.*, p. 38, para. 11.
290 A.A. Cançado Trindade, "Enforced Disappearances of Persons as a Violation of *Jus Cogens*: The Contribution of the Jurisprudence of the Inter-American Court of Human Rights", 81 *Nordic Journal of International Law* (2012) pp. 507–536; A.A. Cançado Trindade, *Tratado de Direito International dos Direitos Humanos* [*Treatise of International Law of Human Rights*], vol. II, Porto Alegre/Brazil, S.A. Fabris Ed., 1999, pp. 352–358.

Involuntary Disappearances,[291] to struggle against that international crime,[292] which had already received world attention, in 1978–1979, at both the U.N. General Assembly[293] and ECOSOC,[294] in addition to the former U.N. Sub-Commission for the Prevention of Discrimination and Protection of Minorities.[295] Subsequently, the 1992 U.N. Declaration on the Protection of all Persons from Enforced Disappearance provided (Article 1), *inter alia*, that

> 1. An act of enforced disappearance is an offence to human dignity. It is condemned as a denial of the purposes of the Charter of the United Nations and as a grave and flagrant violation of the human rights and fundamental freedoms proclaimed in the Universal Declaration of Human Rights and reaffirmed and developed in international instruments in this field.
> 2. Any act of enforced disappearance places the persons subjected thereto outside the protection of the law and inflicts severe suffering on them and their families. It constitutes a violation of the rules of international law guaranteeing, *inter alia*, the right to recognition as a person before the law, the right to liberty and security of the person and the right not to be subjected to torture and other cruel, inhuman or degrading treatment or punishment. It also violates or constitutes a grave threat to the right to life.

298. Subsequently, the 2007 U.N. Convention for the Protection of All Persons from Enforced Disappearance referred, in its preamble (5th paragraph) to the "extreme seriousness" of enforced disappearance, which, – it added in Article 5, – when generating a "widespread or systematic practice", constitutes "a crime against humanity in applicable international law", with all legal consequences. The 2007 Convention further referred (3rd preambular paragraph) to relevant (and converging) international instruments of International Human Rights Law, International Humanitarian Law, and International Criminal Law.

299. Parallel to these developments at normative level, the grave violation of enforced disappearance of persons has been attracting growing attention in

---

291 Resolution 20 (XXXVI), of 29.02.1980.
292 For an account of its work, cf. F. Andreu-Guzmán, "Le Groupe de travail sur les disparitions forcées des Nations Unies", 84 *Revue internationale de la Croix-Rouge* (2002) n. 848, pp. 803–818.
293 Resolution 33/173, of 20.12.1978.
294 Resolution 1979/38, of 10.05.1979.
295 Resolution 5B (XXXII), of 05.09.1979.

expert writing,[296] which has characterized it as an extremely cruel and perverse continuing violation of human rights, extending in time, owing to the consequences of the original act (or arbitrary detention or kidnapping), causing a duration in the suffering and anguish, if not agony or despair, of all those concerned (the missing persons and their close relatives), given the non-disclosure of the fate or whereabouts of disappeared or missing persons. The extreme cruelty of enforced disappearances of persons as a continuing grave violation of human rights and International Humanitarian Law has, furthermore, also been portrayed, as widely known, in the final reports of Truth Commissions, in distinct continents.

300. Soon international human rights tribunals (IACtHR and ECtHR) came to be seized of cases on the matter, and began to pronounce on it. The case-law of the IACtHR on the matter is pioneering, and nowadays regarded as the one which has most contributed to the progressive development on international law in respect of the protection of all persons from enforced disappearance.[297] In its early Judgment in the case of *Velásquez Rodríguez versus Honduras* (of 29.07.1988), the IACtHR drew attention to the complexity of enforced disappearance, as bringing about, concomitantly, continuing violations of rights protected under the ACHR, such as the rights to personal liberty and integrity, and often the fundamental right to life itself (Articles 7, 5 and 4).

---

296   Cf., *inter alia*, e.g., R.S. Berliner, "The Disappearance of Raoul Wallenberg: A Resolution is Possible", 11 *New York Law School Journal of International and Comparative Law* (1990) pp. 391–432; R. Broody and F. González, "*Nunca Más*: An Analysis of International Instruments on 'Disappearances'", 19 *Human Rights Quarterly* (1997) pp. 365–405; C. Callejon, "Une immense lacune du droit international comblée des Nations Unies pour la protection de toutes les personnes contre les disparitions forcées", 17 *Revue trimestrielle des droits de l'homme* (2006) pp. 337–358; T. Scovazzi and G. Citroni, *The Struggle against Enforced Disappearance and the 2007 United Nations Convention*, Leiden, Nijhoff, 2007, pp. 1–400; G. Venturini, "International Law and the Offence of Enforced Disappearance", *in*: *Diritti Individuali e Giustizia Internazionale – Liber F. Pocar* (eds. G. Venturini and S. Bariatti), Milano, Giuffrè, 2009, pp. 939–954; L. Ott, *Enforced Disappearance in International Law*, Antwerp, Intersentia, 2011, pp. 1–294; M.L. Vermeulen, *Enforced Disappearance: Determining State Responsibility under the International Convention for the Protection of All Persons from Enforced Disappearance*, Utrecht, Intersentia, 2012, pp. 1–507; I. Giorgou, "State Involvement in the Perpetration of Enforced Disappearance and the Rome Statute", 11 *Journal of International Criminal Justice* (2013) pp. 1001–1021.

297   Cf., to this effect, e.g., T. Scovazzi and G. Citroni, *The Struggle against Enforced Disappearance...*, *op cit. supra* n. (296), pp. 101, 132 and 398.

301. It is, in sum, a grave breach of the States' duty to respect human dignity (paras. 149–158). It was in its landmark Judgments, one decade later, in the case of *Blake versus Guatemala* (of 1996–1999),[298] that the IACtHR dwelt upon, and elaborated, on the legal nature and consequences of enforced disappearances, its characteristic elements, the victimized persons, and the engagement of State responsibility in a temporal dimension.

302. The *Blake* case occurred within a systematic pattern of enforced disappearances of persons, State-planned, and perpetrated not only to "disappear" with persons regarded as "enemies", but also to generate a sense of utter insecurity, anguish and fear; it involved torture, secret execution of the "disappeared" without trial, followed by concealment of their mortal remains, so as to eliminate any material evidence of the crime and to ensure the impunity of the perpetrators.

303. In its Judgment on the merits (of 24.01.1998) in the *Blake* case, the IACtHR asserted that enforced disappearance of persons is a *complex, multiple and continuing violation of a number of rights* protected by the ACHR (rights to life, to personal integrity, to personal liberty), generating the State Party's duty to prevent, investigate and punish such breaches and, moreover, to inform the victim's next of kin of the missing person's whereabouts (paras. 54–58). In the IACtHR's view, the close relatives of the disappeared person were also victims, *in their own right*, of the enforced disappearance, in breach of the relevant provisions of the ACHR.

304. In my Separate Opinion appended to that Judgment of the IACtHR in the *Blake* case, I deemed it fit to stress that enforced disappearance of persons was indeed a grave and complex violation of human rights, besides being a *continuing or permanent violation* until the whereabouts of the missing victims was established, as pointed out in the *travaux préparatoires* of the 1985 Inter-American Convention on Enforced Disappearance of Persons, and as acknowledged in Article III of the Convention itself (para. 9).

305. In the same Separate Opinion, I next warned against the undue fragmentation of the delict of enforced disappearance of persons, drawing attention to the fact that we were here before fundamental or non-derogable rights

---

298   IACtHR, Judgments on preliminary objections (of 02.07.1996), merits (of 24.01.1998) and reparations (of 22.01.1999).

(paras. 12–14), and there was need to preserve the special character and the integrity of human rights treaties (paras. 16–22). And I proceeded:

> We are, definitively, before a particularly *grave* violation of multiple human rights. Among these are *non-derogable* fundamental rights, protected both by human rights treaties as well as by International Humanitarian Law treaties.[299] The more recent doctrinal developments in the present domain of protection disclose a tendency towards the 'criminalization' of grave violations of human rights, – as the practices of torture, of summary and extra-legal executions, and of enforced disappearance of persons. The prohibitions of such practices pave the way for us to enter into the *terra nova* of the international *jus cogens*. The emergence and consolidation of imperative norms of general international law would be seriously jeopardized if one were to decharacterize the crimes against humanity which fall under their prohibition (para. 15).

306. Still in respect to the legal nature and consequences of the enforced disappearance of persons, I added:

> In a continuing situation proper to the enforced disappearance of person, the victims are the disappeared person (main victim) as well as his next of kin; the indefinition generated by the enforced disappearance withdraws all from the protection of the law.[300] The condition of victims cannot be denied also to the next of kin of the disappeared person, who have their day-to-day life transformed into a true calvary, in which the memories of the person dear to them are intermingled with the permanent torment of his enforced disappearance. In my understanding, the complex form of violation of multiple human rights which the crime of enforced disappearance of person represents has as a consequence the *enlargement of the notion of victim* of violation of the protected rights (paras. 32–38).

307. In my subsequent Separate Opinion in the *Blake versus Guatemala* case (reparations, Judgment of 22.01.1999), I insisted on the need to consolidate the

---

299   Cf., e.g., the provisions on fundamental guarantees of Additional Protocol I (of 1977) to the Geneva Conventions on International Humanitarian Law (of 1949), Article 75, and of the Additional Protocol II (of the same year), Article 4.

300   Cf., in this sense, Article 1(2) of the U.N. Declaration on the Protection of All Persons against Enforced Disappearances.

"international regime against *grave* violations of human rights", in the light of the peremptory norms of international law (*jus cogens*) and of the corresponding obligations *erga omnes* of protection of the human being (para. 39). By means of such development, – I added, – one would "overcome the obstacles of the dogmas of the past", and the current inadequacies of the law of treaties, so as to get "closer to the plenitude of the international protection of the human being" (para. 40).

308. Other pertinent decisions of the IACtHR could be recalled, e.g., as to the need to overcome limitations or restrictions ratione temporis, given the legal nature of enforced disappearance (*supra*), the IACtHR's decisions also in the cases of *Trujillo Oroza versus Bolivia* (2000–2002), and of the *Sisters Serrano Cruz versus El Salvador* (2005); and, as to the aggravating circumstances of the grave breach of enforced disappearance, the IACtHR's decisions in the cases of *Bámaca Velásquez versus Guatemala* (2000–2002), of *Caracazo versus Venezuela* (1999–2002), of *Juan Humberto Sánchez versus Honduras* (2003), and of *Servellón-García et alii versus Honduras* (2006).

309. For its part, the ECtHR has also had the occasion to pronounce on aspects the matter at issue. For example, in its Judgment (of 10.05.2001) in the *Cyprus versus Turkey* case, it stressed the endurance of "agony" of the family members of the missing persons, for not knowing their whereabouts (para. 157). Shortly afterwards, in its Judgment (of 18.06.2002) in the *Orhan versus Turkey* case, in again addressed, – as in earlier decisions, – the "vulnerable position" of the individuals concerned (paras. 406–410). Other pronouncements of the kind were made by the ECtHR in the cycle of cases (of last decade) arising out of the armed conflict in Chechnya.

310. In a particularly illustrative decision, the ECtHR, in its Judgment (of 18.09.2009) in the case of *Varnava and Others versus Turkey*, stated that a disappearance is

> characterised by an ongoing situation of uncertainty and unaccountability in which there is a lack of information or even a deliberate concealment and obfuscation of what has occurred [...]. This situation is very often drawn out over time, prolonging the torment of the victim's relatives. It cannot therefore be said that a disappearance is, simply, an 'instantaneous' act or event; the additional distinctive element of subsequent failure to account for the whereabouts and fate of the missing person gives rise to a continuing situation. Thus, the procedural obligation

will, potentially, persist as long as the fate of the person is unaccounted for; the ongoing failure to provide the requisite investigation will be regarded as a continuing violation (...) This is so, even where death may, eventually, be presumed (para. 148).

5   General Assessment

311. In the light of the aforementioned, in so far as the present case of the *Application of the Convention of Genocide* (Croatia *versus* Serbia) is concerned, one cannot thus endorse Serbia's view, expressed during the oral proceedings, whereby enforced disappearance may not be a continuing violation of the right to life as enshrined in Article II of the Genocide Convention. Serbia asserts that the reason why it might be a continuing violation of human rights is that the family of the victim is subject to ongoing mental harm, and this brings into play the prohibition of ill-treatment, or because of the procedural obligation to investigate the crime. According to Serbia, this issue "might belong in Strasbourg, but certainly not in The Hague".[301]

312. Both the ICJ and the ECtHR in Strasbourg are concerned with *State* responsibility. Recent cases (such as the *Georgia versus Russian Federation* case, concerning the fundamental principle of equality and non-discrimination and the corresponding norms in distinct but converging international instruments) have been brought *before both the ICJ and the ECtHR*; the Hague Court and the ECtHR in Strasbourg do not exclude each other, as recent developments in the work of contemporary international tribunals have clearly been showing. This is reassuring for those engaged in the international protection of the rights of the human person, and the *justiciables* themselves.

313. The pioneering and substantial case-law of the IACtHR, together more recently with the case-law of the ECtHR, on the matter at issue, is essential for an understanding of the gravity of the crime of enforced disappearance of persons and of its legal consequences. As to its legal nature, the two aforementioned international human rights tribunals have asserted the complex and continuing violations of the protected rights, while disappearance lasts. In its ground-breaking decisions in the *Blake* case (1996–1998), the IACtHR established the *expansion of the notion of victims* in cases of disappearance, so as to comprise the missing person as well as their close relatives, *in their own*

---

301   ICJ, doc. CR 2014/23, of 28.03.2014, p. 44, para. 12.

right. This has become *jurisprudence constante* of the IACtHR and the ECtHR on the issue.

314. May I add, in this connection, that the provisions of Article 11(b) of the Convention against Genocide, referring to "serious (...) mental harm to members of the group", makes the connection with a continuing violation rather clear. As I pondered in my Dissenting Opinion in the case of the *Jurisdictional Immunities of the State* (Germany versus Italy, Greece intervening), "one cannot take account of inter-temporal law only in a way that serves one's interests in litigation, accepting the passing of time and the evolution of law in relation to certain facts but not to others, of the same *continuing* situation" (para. 17).

315. The fact that a close family member of the missing persons is a member of the same group, and is also subject to a continuing mental harm, prolonging indefinitely in time, together with the State concerned's failure to account for the missing persons, or to take reasonable steps to assist in the location of such persons, in my perception, brings into play the prohibition of acts proscribed by the Genocide Convention, including the obligation to investigate.

316. May I further add, still in this connection, the relevance of the case-law of international human rights tribunals (in particular that of the IACtHR, since its start[302]), to the effect of applying a proper standard of proof, in cases of grave violations (such as enforced disappearances of persons, torture of *incommunicado* detainees, among others), when State authorities hold the monopoly of probatory evidence, and victims have no access to it, thus calling for a shifting of the burden of proof.[303] In cases of grave violations, such as enforced disappearances of persons, the burden of proof cannot certainly be made to fall upon those victimized by those violations (including, of course, the close relatives of the missing persons, who do not know their whereabouts).

317. The effects of enforced disappearances of persons upon the close relatives of missing persons are devastating. They destroy whole families, led into agony or despair. I learned this from my own experience in the international adjudication of cases of this kind. In the present Judgment, the ICJ does not seem to have apprehended the extent of those devastating effects. To require from close relatives, as it does (para. 160), further proof (of serious suffering), so as to

---

[302] Cf. Part VII of the present Dissenting Opinion, *supra*.
[303] Cf. Parts VII-VIII of the present Dissenting Opinion, *supra*.

fall under Article II(b) of the Genocide Convention, amounts to a true *probatio diabolica*!

318. The serious mental harm (Article II(b)) caused to those victimized can surely be presumed, and, in my view, there is no need to demonstrate that the harm itself contributed to the destruction of the targeted group. Yet, the Court requires such additional proof (para. 160 *in fine*). In doing so, it renders the determination of State responsibility for genocide, under Article II(b) of the 1948 Convention, and of its legal consequences (for reparations), an almost impossible task. The Court's outlook, portrayed in its whole reasoning throughout the present Judgment is State sovereignty-oriented, not people-oriented, as it should be under the Convention against Genocide, the applicable law in the *cas d'espèce*.

319. Last but not least, the point I have already made about the absolute prohibition (of *jus cogens*) of torture (para. 225, *supra*), in any circumstances, applies likewise to all the other grave violations of human rights and International Humanitarian Law which occurred in the attacks in Croatia, and that have been examined above, namely: massive killings, rape and other sexual violence crimes, enforced disappearance of persons, systematic expulsion from homes and forced displacement of persons (in mass exodus), destruction of group culture.

320. The prohibition of all those grave violations, like that of torture, in all its forms, is a prohibition belonging to the realm of *jus cogens*,[304] the breach of which entails legal consequences, calling for reparations.[305] This is in line with the idea of *rectitude* (in conformity with the *recta ratio* of natural law), underlying the conception of Law (in distinct legal systems – *Droit / Right / Recht / Direito / Derecho / Diritto*) as a whole.

---

304   Two contemporary international tribunals which, by their evolving case-law, have much contributed to the expansion of the material content of *jus cogens*, have been the IACtHR and the ICTFY; cf. A.A. Cançado Trindade, *International Law for Humankind – Towards a New Jus Gentium*, op cit. supra n. (67), pp. 295–311; A.A. Cançado Trindade, "*Jus Cogens*: The Determination and the Gradual Expansion of Its Material Content in Contemporary International Case-Law", *in XXXV Curso de Derecho Internacional Organizado por el Comité Jurídico Interamericano – 2008*, Washington D.C., General Secretariat of the OAS, 2009, pp. 3–29.

305   Cf. Part XVI of the present Dissenting Opinion, *infra*.

XIII Onslaught, Not Exactly War, in a Widespread and Systematic Pattern of Destruction

1 *Plan of Destruction: Its Ideological Content*

321. The occurrence of a widespread and systematic pattern of destruction has been established in the present case concerning the *Application of the Convention against Genocide*, opposing Croatia to Serbia (cf. *supra*). The devastation pursued a plan of destruction, that was deliberately and methodically carried out: aerial bombardment, shelling, indiscriminate killings, torture and beatings, rape, destruction of homes and looting, forced displacement and deportation. The execution of the plan of destruction has already been reviewed (cf. *supra*), and in my view established in the *cas d'espèce*. The plan of destruction pursued by the Serbian attacks in Croatia had an ideological component, which goes back to the historical origins of the conflict.

a) Arguments of the Contending Parties

322. The point was addressed, to a certain depth in the written phase of the present proceedings, particularly by Croatia. In its *Memorial*, it argued that a catalytic event in relation to the genocide allegedly perpetrated against the Croats was the appearance in 1986 of the *Memorandum by the Serbian Academy of Sciences and Arts* (the "SANU *Memorandum*"). The *Memorandum*, – it added, – which set forth a Serb nationalist reinterpretation of the recent history of the SFRY, carried great weight and reflected the then growing Serbian nationalist movement; it helped to give rise, in its view, to the circumstances for the perpetration of genocide in Croatia.[306]

323. By emphasising the right of the Serbian people "to establish their full national and cultural integrity regardless of which republic or autonomous province they live in", the *Memorandum* provided the idea of a "Greater Serbia", including parts of the territory in Croatia and Bosnia and Herzegovina within which significant Serbian ethnic populations lived. Furthermore, the SANU *Memorandum* provided a detailed analysis of the "crisis" in the SFRY, and it established the idea that Serbia was "the only nation in Yugoslavia without its own state". It bypassed the political and geographical divisions enshrined in the 1974 Constitution.[307]

---

306 *Memorial*, para. 2.43.
307 *Ibid.*, paras. 2.44–2.47.

324. Croatia stressed that the ideas proposed in the *Memorandum* were based on other views expressed by the Serbian intellectual community (including Serbian historians, scientists, writers and journalists) on how Serbs had been "tricked", "stinted", "killed", "persecuted even after being subjected to genocide". The *Memorandum* gained support from militant groups, prompting a nationalist campaign.[308]

325. Croatia further argued that the ideas set out in the SANU *Memorandum* "gave vent to the theory that the Croatian people were collectively to blame for the large number of Serbs that were killed by the Ustashas during the period 1941–1945, and were, accordingly, by their very nature, genocidal in character and adhering to a continuing genocidal intent against the Serbs".[309] Croatia added that the JNA was transformed from an army of the SFRY into a "Serbian Army" promptly after the publication of the *Memorandum*.[310]

326. Serbia, for its part, briefly responded, in its *Counter-Memorial*, to Croatia's arguments concerning the *Memorandum*. It claimed that they amounted to an "enormous exaggeration", given that the Serbs never had the intent to perpetrate genocide against Croats, and that the *Memorandum* never contemplated the occurrence of genocide.[311] Croatia retook the issue in its *Reply*, wherein it reiterated the importance of the SANU *Memorandum* for the perpetration of genocide.

327. It dismissed Serbia's claim of its arguments being an "enormous exaggeration", saying that they are supported by a number of independent sources, which also described the *Memorandum* as a "political bombshell". Croatia further stated that an expert report from the ICTFY, on the use of propaganda in the conflict at issue, came to the conclusion that it was the deliberate leaks of the SANU Memorandum that raised the issue of Serbian nationalism publicly (cf. *infra*).

328. Croatia insisted that the emergence of extreme Serbian nationalism was accompanied by the idea that the Croats had always had a genocidal intent

---

308 According to Croatia, "[a]rticles appeared and speeches were given which promoted Serbian nationalism, demonized the Albanians, the Muslims and the Croats and invoked their genocidal tendencies, and validated the Chetnik movement"; *ibid.*, paras. 2.48–2.51.
309 *Ibid.*, para. 2.52.
310 *Ibid.*, para. 3.03.
311 *Counter-Memorial*, para. 428.

against the Serbs, a theory – articulated in 1986 and then followed by Serbian historians and journalists – that claimed that the Croatian people were collectively to blame for the large number of Serbs who were killed by the "Ustasha" between 1941–45 (e.g., the concentration camp in Jasenovac), during the II world war, pursuant to a plan that had a continuing genocidal intent against the Serbs.[312] According to Croatia, various inflammatory articles published by the media contributed to this idea from 1986 to 1991.[313]

329. Also during the oral phase of the present proceedings, Croatia reiterated its arguments (*supra*), whereas Serbia did not submit any substantial new argument in this respect. Croatia asserted that the publication of the *SANU Memorandum* in 1986 precipitated a period of extreme nationalist propaganda within Serbia, as from the premise that Serbia and the Serbs in the other Republics of the SFRY "were in a uniquely unfavourable position within the SFRY", and from the proposal of a review of the SFRY Constitution, so that autonomous provinces would become an integral part of Serbia, and the Federal State would be strengthened. Croatia also referred to an expert report (by Professor A. Budding), which referred to the *Memorandum* as "a political firestorm" because of its "inflammatory" language.[314]

b)   **Examination of Expert Evidence by the ICTFY**

330. As brought to the attention of the ICJ in the course of the proceedings of the present case (cf. *supra*), the ICTFY, in its decision of 16.06.2004 in the case *S. Milošević*, duly took into account expert evidence concerning the ideological component of the plan of destruction at issue. The first expert report presented to the ICTFY, compiled at the request of its Office of the Prosecutor, was titled "*Political Propaganda and the Plan to Create a 'State for All Serbs' – Consequences of Using the Media for Ultra-Nationalist Ends*" (of 04.02.2003, by R. de la Brosse).

331. According to the expert report, the regime of Slobodan Milošević sought to take "total control over the media owned by the State or public institutions",

---

312   *Reply*, paras. 3.10–3.12.
313   *Ibid.*, paras. 3.12–3.14.
314   ICJ, doc. CR 2014/5, of 03.03.2014, pp. 33–35. The *Memorandum*, Croatia reiterated, paved the way for the publication of articles in the Serbian media, referring to the alleged Croats' genocidal tendencies, and recalling the horrific crimes the Ustasha régime committed against the Serbs during the II world war (e.g., the concentration camp in Jasenovac); ICJ, doc. CR 2014/5, of 03.03.2014, p. 35; and cf. also ICJ, doc. CR 2014/12, of 07.03.2014, pp. 22–23.

restricting its freedom and "using all means to prevent it from informing people". Its control of the audio-visual media "began in 1986–1987 and was complete in the summer of 1991" (para. 27). The expert report proceeded that "[t]he media were used as weapons of war", in order to achieve "strategic objectives", such as "the capture of territories by force, the practice of ethnic cleansing, and the destruction of targets described as symbolic and having priority". The plan combined

> propaganda, partial (and biased) information, false news, manipulation, non-coverage of certain events, etc. This entire arsenal would be mobilised to help justify the creation of a State for all Serbs (…).
>
> (…) [T]he terms "Ustasha fascists" and "cut-throats" were used to stigmatise the Croats and "Islamic Ustashas" and "Djihad fighters" to describe the Bosnian Muslims pejoratively. Systematic recourse to such key words imposed on the media by the Milošević regime undoubtedly provoked and nourished hateful behaviour toward the non-Serbian communities.
>
> (…) Systematic recourse to false, biased information and non-coverage of certain events made it possible to inspire and arouse hatred and fear among the communities. The media prepared the ground psychologically for the rise in nationalist hatred and became a weapon when the war broke out.
>
> (…) Historical facts were imbued with mystical qualities to be used as nationalist objectives so that the Serbian people would feel and express a desire for revenge directed at the prescribed enemies, the Croats and Muslims (…) (paras. 28–31).

332. The expert report went on to state that, by the invocation of "the scars of the 1940 war" (para. 35), "the use of the media for nationalist ends and objectives formed part of a well-thought through plan" (para. 32). It added that the 1986 *SANU Memorandum* constituted an "encouragement" for "Serbian nationalism" (para. 40). The official propaganda drew on the historical sources of "Serbian mystique", with its victims and the injustices they suffered throughout history (paras. 46–49).[315] State authorities sought to condition public opinion in order "to justify the upcoming war with Croatia" (para. 54, and cf. para. 61). "Disinformation" was used in order "to mislead or to conceal and misrepresent facts", and to make up "false news" (paras. 72 and 77).

---

315   The media contributed to "demonising the other communities, especially the Kosovo Albanians, Croats and Bosnian Muslims" (para. 52).

333. The second expert report submitted (by the Prosecution) to the ICTFY in its decision in the case *S. Milošević* (2004), and referred to by Croatia in its oral pleadings in the present case before the ICJ, was titled *"Serbian Nationalism in the Twentieth Century"* (of 29.05.2002, by A. Budding). The expert report provided historical information and the factual context for the understanding of waking Serbian national awareness, and the sequence of events which led to the disintegration of the Yugoslav State and the outbreak of the wars in the region.

334. The expert report also referred to the 1986 *SANU Memorandum* (p. 32), explaining its origins and its consequences for the whole of former Yugoslavia (pp. 36–37). It characterized the *Memorandum* as "by far the most famous document in the modern Serbian national movement" (p. 36). Referring to the expert report, Croatia argued that the *Memorandum* set off "a political firestorm", and that it was "inflammatory because of the contrast between its complaints about the position of Serbia and Serbs within Yugoslavia and its 'vague and elliptical references to a possible post Yugoslav future'".[316] According to the expert report,

> Memorandum nije raspalio debatu u Jugoslaviji zato što je u njemu eksplicitno iznet srpski nacionalni program posle Jugoslavije – pošto i nije – već zbog kontrasta između detaljnih i preteranih primedbi na položaj Srbije unutar postojeće jugoslovenske države, koje su iznete u Memorandumu, kao i neodređenog pozivanja na moguću budućnost posle Jugoslavije (tvrdnja da Srbija mora 'jasno da sagleda svoje privredne i nacionalne interese kako je događaji ne bi iznenadili'). Autori Memoranduma su sugerisali da bi nacionalne alternative višenacionalnoj jugoslovenskoj državi mogle biti poželjne, ali su propustili da priznaju da bi njihovo stvaranje neizbežno podrazumevalo uništenje.[317]

---

316   ICJ, doc. CR 2014/5, pp. 33–35.

317   [Unofficial translation:]
"The Memorandum became an inflammatory element in the Yugoslav debate not because it explicitly set out a post-Yugoslav Serbian national programme – and indeed it did not – but rather because of the contrast between its detailed and exaggerated remarks on the position of Serbia within the existing Yugoslav State, and its vague and elliptical references to a possible post-Yugoslav future (the assertion that Serbia must 'look clearly at its economic and national interests, so as not to be caught by surprise by the course of events'). The authors of the Memorandum suggested that national alternatives to the multinational Yugoslav State would be desirable without acknowledging the destruction that their creation would inevitably entail" (p. 31).

335. In the same case of *S. Milošević*, the ICTFY also took into account the declaration of an expert witness (T. Zwaan), which is summed up in its decision of 16.06.2004. According to the ICTFY, the expert witness testified about "the importance of ideology and use of propaganda" in processes "leading to the commission of genocide, involving various types of radical nationalism, which dehumanise the targeted group", also misusing "collective historical memory" to that end (para. 234). It added that "genocide is a crime of State", as

> genocidal crimes never develop from the "bottom up"; they are "top down" affairs. Such crimes occur with the "knowledge, approval and involvement of the State authorities" (para. 234).

336. Yet a third expert report compiled for the ICTFY (at the request of its Prosecution), for its adjudication of the case of *S. Milošević* (2004), titled *"On the Aetiology and Genesis of Genocides and Other Mass Crimes – Targeting Specific Groups"* (of November 2003, by T. Zwaan), purported to consider, in a condensed way, the learning that exists nowadays in relation to genocide, from an interdisciplinary perspective. The expert report, at the end of the examination of the matter, reached the following findings:

> Firstly, (...) genocide and other mass crimes targeting specific groups should be carefully distinguished from war and civil war, while at the same time one should recognise that situations of war of civil war may contribute in various ways to the development of genocidal processes.
>
> Secondly, it has been pointed out that genocidal crimes only develop and take place under conditions of serious and enduring crisis. A general model of the emergence of such crises has been presented in a very condensed form. Destabilisation of the state-society concerned, polarisation processes, depacification, and increasing use of violence are at the heart of such crises.
>
> Thirdly, in the course of the crisis a radical and ruthless political elite may succeed in taking over the State organisation. The political behaviour and decisions of this political leadership may be considered of decisive importance for the emergence of genocide. It has been argued that a genocidal process does not develop from "bottom up", but that is typically a "top down" development, although the precise involvement of the state may take different forms. One corollary is that the highest state authorities are always responsible for what happens during the genocidal process, another corollary implies that 'single' acts of genocide should

be (also) considered against the background of the prevalent power and authority structure within the state-society concerned.

Fourthly, it has been emphasised that genocides may be best seen as (highly complex) processes, with a beginning, a structured course in which phases can be discerned, and an end – usually brought about by forceful external intervention. Furthermore, in trying to understand a genocidal process attention should be paid to the decision-making, the gradual emergence of planning and organisation, and the division of labour within the category of perpetrators.

Fifthly, it has been argued that ideology is also of crucial importance for genocide to emerge. Usually, varieties of radical nationalism will figure prominently. They contribute to the development of an extremist political climate; to the marking off of the groups or categories to be targeted; they legitimise, rationalise, and justify the genocidal process; and impart to the perpetrators a sense of direction, intent and purpose.

Sixthly, it has been underlined that every genocidal process should also be considered from the angle of the victims, who are typically chosen because of their supposed membership of a group or category targeted for persecution. It has been argued, moreover, that such groups are made increasingly vulnerable and defenceless through the process of persecution itself, that it is usually very difficult for them to foresee what is going to happen, and that their possible courses of (re)action are severely limited. Keeping their fate central in one's mind seems to be the best compass when studying, assessing and judging genocide (pp. 38–39).

c) Ideological Incitement and the Outbreak of Hostilities

337. In effect, in the course of the proceedings, both contending Parties paid special attention to the origins and the factual background of the conflict in the Balkans in the present case concerning the *Application of the Convention against Genocide*. Both Croatia and Serbia expressed their awareness that the historical context helps to understand better the causes that lead to the war in Croatia and its pattern of destruction. They expressed their views, in particular, in the written phase of the *cas d'espèce*. The applicant State contended that the devastation that took place in Croatia was a consequence of the exponential growth of Serbian nationalism in order to build a "Greater Serbia".

338. Thus, in its *Memorial*, Croatia provided an overview of the background of the dispute, deeming it essential to understand what happened, in order to

bring justice and redress to the victims.[318] Focusing on the formation of the FRY, the rise of "Greater-Serbian" nationalism in the eighties and the rise of S. Milošević to power,[319] Croatia argued that, although the inherent tensions (between ethnic groups) had been suppressed for many years, after President Tito's death, federal institutions were usurped by the new Serbian leadership (under S. Milošević), which aimed at establishing a Serb-dominated Yugoslavia, or a "Greater Serbia", to include within its borders more than half of the territory of Croatia.[320]

339. The Serbian State-controlled media – it proceeded – systematically demonized the targeted non-Serb ethnic groups, creating a climate conducive to genocide, inciting and justifying it.[321] After tension grew in Kosovo in 1981, – Croatia claimed, – Serb nationalists began to express their ideas more openly and frequently; it singled out the 1986 SANU Memorandum, as a manifesto setting forth a Serb nationalist reinterpretation of the recent history of the SFRY, which gave rise to a feeling of anger and revenge against Croats.[322] Moreover, according to Croatia, there was a large propaganda validating the Chetnik movement and their goals, and S. Milošević was able to capture such feelings and to promote himself as a defender of Serbian interests.[323]

340. In its *Counter-Memorial*, Serbia submitted that much of what occurred in the Balkans in 1991–1995 was influenced by the atrocities against Serbs in 1941–1945 and the rise of nationalism in the SFRY.[324] The events leading to the conflict of 1991–1995 and the conflict itself, according to Serbia, cannot be understood without taking this into account".[325] Serbia further stated that there was a rise of nationalism in the SFRY, following Tito's death, among Serbians but also Croatians.[326]

---

318   *Memorial*, paras. 2.01–162 and 1.14.
319   *Ibid.*, paras. 2.05–35, 2.36–59 and 2.60–84, respectively. As to the historical background (in the II world war), cf. *ibid.*, paras. 2.08–2.09, and cf. para. 2.53.
320   *Ibid.*, para. 1.26.
321   *Ibid.*, para. 1.26.
322   *Ibid.*, paras. 2.40, 2.43, 2.51–3 and 2.56. – The Croats were demonized and blamed for the deaths of Serbs during the II world war in concentration camps, and an instigated feeling of anger and revenge arose among the Serbs; according to Croatia, the 1986 SANU *Memorandum* was a key element to that end.
323   *Ibid.*, paras. 2.54–6 and 2.60.
324   *Counter-Memorial*, paras. 397–426, and cf. paras. 397, 400, 409 and 419.
325   *Ibid.*, para. 419.
326   *Ibid.*, para. 422.

341. Serbia conceded that there were abundant hate speech and extreme nationalism demonstrations in Serbian media in the late eighties and along the nineties, but it claimed that such was the case also in Croatia. It did not contest that Serbian nationalists misused the recollections of past events, though it contended that the claims made in this regard by Croatia were not always accurate; it finally added that Serbian nationalism could not be held solely accountable for the conflict.[327]

342. In its *Reply*, Croatia stated that, according to an expert report from the ICTFY, the *SANU Memorandum* sparked Serbian nationalism publicly,[328] giving vent to the view that the Croatian people was collectively to blame for the large number of Serbs who had been killed by the Ustashas in 1941–1945.[329] It then rebutted the claims of revival of Croatian nationalism and of hate speech and discriminatory policies against the Serbs.[330] For its part, in its *Rejoinder*, Serbia contended that the historical background helps to understand the events which originated the war. It reaffirmed that the causes were not one-sided and that the claims of Croatia were in its view inaccurate;[331] at last, it requested the ICJ to examine the history of the conflict from both the applicant's and the respondent's perspectives.[332]

343. In the oral phase of the proceedings in the *cas d'espèce*, one of the witness-experts (Ms. S. Biserko) specifically addressed the factual background of the conflict and the developments that led to the atrocities. She singled out the idea of a "Greater Serbia" reviving Serbian nationalism, with its propaganda; the aim of territorial expansion; the rise of S. Milošević and its policies; and the media reports – between 1988 and 1991 – preparing Serbs for the forthcoming armed attacks in Croatia and Bosnia-Herzegovina.[333]

344. The contending Parties themselves, in the course of the proceedings in the *cas d'espèce*, focused – each one in its own way – on the impact of hate speech. Croatia claimed that Serbia sponsored hate speech and propaganda in inciting genocide.[334] Hate speech, in its view, was an important factor in the

---

327 *Ibid.*, paras. 434–435, 420 and 424.
328 *Reply*, para. 3.11.
329 *Ibid.*, para. 3.12.
330 *Ibid.*, paras. 3.17–24.
331 *Rejoinder*, para. 35.
332 *Ibid.*, para. 36.
333 Cf. ICJ, CR 2014/7, of 04.03.2014.
334 *Memorial*, paras. 1.16, 2.04, 2.43–50, 2.51–53, 2.56–59, 2.63–66, 8.16 and 8.23–24.

preparations for the Serbian armed incursions in Croatia.³³⁵ Serbia acknowledged that the media in the country – in the late eighties and along the nineties – constantly broadcasted hate speech, but claimed that such was also the case in Croatia.³³⁶

345. Serbia admitted that hate speech was abundant in Serbian media at the end of the eighties and during nineties,³³⁷ but claimed that it was not confined to Serbia, and also existed in Croatia.³³⁸ Croatia argued that, as from the early eighties, several Serbian newspapers ran inflammatory articles about the Ustasha concentration camp in Jasenovac, during the II world war.³³⁹ Croatia challenged Serbia's claim that it had also promoted hate speech against the Serbs.³⁴⁰ Serbia, for its part, attempted to minimize the proof of incitement to hatred.³⁴¹

346. In its oral arguments, Croatia referred, e.g., to S. Milošević's speech to the Serbian parliament in March 1991,³⁴² and to the hate speech of the extremist Serb nationalist Z. Raznjatović (known as Arkan) against the Croats, constantly referred to as "Ustashas".³⁴³ Serbian newspapers, – it added, – ran inflammatory articles about the Ustasha concentration camp in Jasenovac, as a reference to the II world war crimes committed against the Serbs by the Ustasha regime.³⁴⁴

347. Serbia, in turn, cited statements from Croatian press and politicians.³⁴⁵ Croatia retorted that the examples cited by Serbia were in sharp contrast with the Serbian hate speech that emanated from Serbian State media and its most senior leaders.³⁴⁶ It further insisted that the Serb population's fear

---

335   *Ibid.*, para. 2.58.
336   Cf. *Counter-Memorial*, paras. 434–442.
337   Cf. *ibid.*, paras. 434–437, 439–442 and 953–954.
338   *Ibid.*, para. 439.
339   Cf. *Reply*, paras. 3.10–3.14, 3.26–3.27, 3.31–3.33, 3.131 and 9.52.
340   Cf. *ibid.*, paras. 3.26–3.27, and cf. para. 9.52.
341   Cf. *Rejoinder*, paras. 340–342.
342   Cf. ICJ, doc. CR 2014/5, of 03.03.2014, para. 20.
343   Cf. ICJ, doc. CR 2014/5, of 03.03.2014, para. 30; and cf. also *Memorial*, vol. 5, App. 3, pp. 64–65, paras. 43–45.
344   Cf. ICJ, doc. CR 2014/5, of 03.03.2014, para. 12.
345   Cf. *Counter-Memorial*, para. 438 and 440, and *Rejoinder*, paras. 633–635.
346   Cf. *Additional Pleadings*, para. 2.14.

against Croats was created by the hate-speech campaign against Croats and their demonization as "Ustasha[s]".³⁴⁷

348. In the present Judgment, the ICJ flatly dismissed an examination of the historical origins of the onslaught in the Balkans, in the following terms: – "The Court considers that there is no need to enter into a debate on the political and historical origins of the events that took place in Croatia between 1991 and 1995" (para. 412). Even without embarking on such an examination, the Court, e.g., dismissed the relevance of the *SANU Memorandum*, for having "no official standing" and for not proving *dolus specialis* (para. 412).

349. Yet, in the course of the proceedings in the *cas d'espèce*, that document was cited not to this effect, but only to explain the historical origins of the devastation in Croatia, which the Court found unnecessary to examine in the present Judgment. Once again, I regret not to be able to follow the Court's majority on the handling of this question either, and I lay on the records, in the present Dissenting Opinion, the reasons of my disagreement with the dismissive posture of the Court thereon, particularly bearing in mind that both contending Parties dwelt upon the issue in their arguments before the Court, and expected the Court to address it.

350. It is clear that a nationalistic (ethnic) ideology and propaganda, with their incitement to violence, were at the origins of the outbreak of the former Yugoslavia, having contributed to lead to the hostilities aggravated in the course of the widespread armed conflicts, and then to the "horrors" of the wars in the Balkans, "particularly those in Croatia and Bosnia-Herzegovina".³⁴⁸ In order to understand the factual context of a case under the Genocide Convention such as the present one opposing Croatia to Serbia, it is important to address its causes. They have been addressed, before the Court, by the contending Parties themselves. Already in my Separate Opinion (paras. 46–47 and 220) in the ICJ's Advisory Opinion on the *Declaration of Independence of Kosovo* (2010), I pointed out the need to remain attentive to the historical origins of each humanitarian crisis.

---

347   Cf. ICJ, doc. CR 2014/19, of 18.03.2014, para. 28.
348   S. Letica, "The Genesis of the Current Balkan War", *in Genocide after Emotion – The Postemotional Balkan War* (ed. S.G. Meštrović), London/N.Y., Routledge, 1996, p. 91, and cf. pp. 92–112.

351. An international conflict – a devastation – of the scale and gravity of the wars in the Balkans, *lodged with the ICJ under the Convention against Genocide*, cannot be properly examined in the void. The ICTFY did not do so, and, e.g., in the *S. Milošević* case (Trial Chamber, Decision of 16.06.2004), after studying that conflict as from its historical origins, took into account an expert report, – on the use of propaganda by the media in that conflict, – which determined that

> a comparison between Serbian, Croatian, and Bosnian nationalist propaganda yielded the conclusion that Serbian propaganda surpassed the other two both in the scale and the content of the media messages put out (para. 237).

352. In this way, hatred was widespread, and made its numerous victims. Villagers began to hate each other, sometimes their own former neighbours, solely on the basis of their ethnicity, without knowing exactly why. The consequences of this campaign of hatred were catastrophic, – as on so many other man-made devastations throughout the history of humankind, illustrative of the perennial presence of evil in the human condition (cf. *infra*).

353. Last but not least, with the outbreak of the armed attacks, there is an additional element for the examination of the campaign of extreme nationalism which should not pass unperceived here: the *unredacted Minutes* of the Supreme Defence Council (SDC) of the FRY, – the same unredacted *Minutes* that, in the earlier case concerning the Genocide Convention, were not made available to the ICJ, nor did the ICJ consider them indispensable, for its Judgment in the *Bosnian Genocide* case (2007). Today, eight years later, the unredacted transcripts of the SDC *Minutes* (1992–1996), as lately brought to the attention of the ICTFY, are publicly known.

354. It is not my intention to review them here, but only to refer briefly to two passages, with a direct bearing on the preceding considerations. The (short-hand) unredacted *Minutes* of the SDC, of 07.08.1992, referred to the violence of paramilitary formations, and contained an instruction to dress paramilitaries with "uniforms of Yugoslav soldiers", and to give them weapons. And the unredacted *Minutes* of the SDC, of 09.08.1994, asserted that the Armies of Republika Srpska and of the Serbian Republic of Krajina "are armies of the Serbian people", and, "[t]herefore, they must serve the interests of the Serbian people as a whole".[349]

---

349 FRY/SDC, *Unredacted Transcripts of Minutes* (1992–1996), of 07.08.1992, and of 09.08.1994.

THE UNIVERSAL JURIDICAL CONSCIENCE   171

2   *The Imposed Obligation of Wearing White Ribbons*

355. In my perception, it is clear, from the atrocities already surveyed, that the *cas d'espèce*, concerning the *Application of the Convention against Genocide*, opposing Croatia to Serbia, is not exactly one of war, but rather of onslaught, in a widespread and systematic pattern of destruction (cf. *supra*). There are other aspects of it which, in the course of the proceedings, were also brought to the attention of the Court, and to which I turn attention now. One of them pertains to the obligation imposed upon targeted individuals to wear white ribbons.

356. In the written phase of the proceedings, Croatia claimed, in its *Memorial*, that, in some municipalities, the Croat population was required to identify themselves and their property with white ribbons or other distinctive marks.[350] It submitted various witness statements concerning this practice by Serbia.[351] On the basis of the probatory evidence (and witness statements), it appears that this practice of marking Croats with white ribbons was widespread; its *rationale* was to identify and single out Croats and subject them to varying degrees of humiliation, such as forced labour, violence, and limitation of their freedom of movement (e.g. by imposing curfews). According to Croatia,

> [t]he local Croat population would be required to identify themselves and their property with white ribbons and other distinctive marks; they would be denied access to food, water, electricity and telecommunications and proper medical treatment; their movements would be restricted; they would be put to forced labour; their property would be destroyed or looted; Croatian cultural and religious monuments would be destroyed; and schools and other public utilities would be required to adopt Serbian cultural traditions and language.[352]

357. As to the aims of the practice of marking Croats with white ribbons, Croatia submitted that the local Serb "authorities" would establish their power and "would impose a regime of humiliation and dehumanisation on the remaining Croat population, who would be required to identify themselves and their

---

350   Cf.. *Memorial*, paras. 4.08, 4.60, 4.87 and 4.98. According to Croatia, this obligation to wear white ribbons occurred, e.g., in Šarengrad, Bapska and Sotin; *ibid.*, para. 8.16.8.
351   *Memorial*, vol. 2(I), Annexes 53 (Šarengrad), 66 (Bapska), 76 (Tovarnik), 84 (Tovarnik); 101, 106 and 108 (Lovas), and 128 (Vukovar).
352   *Memorial*, para. 8.60.

property with white ribbons and other distinctive marks".³⁵³ Croatia argued that the majority of the Croat inhabitants of Antin, for instance, left the village, and the 93 Croats that remained there had to wear white ribbons on their sleeves; Croatia added that, at the time of the writing of its *Memorial*, it was still unknown what happened to 15 of them.³⁵⁴ Another example was afforded by the village of Šarengrad, where 412 Croatian inhabitants stayed behind, and all remaining Croats in the village were forced to wear white ribbons.³⁵⁵

358. In its oral pleadings, Croatia reiterated its allegations concerning the marking of the Croatian population. As to the fate of the Croats who were forced to identify themselves by wearing white ribbons, Croatia did not report a common fate, to all of them. It is not clear from its pleadings that absolutely *all* Croats wearing white ribbons were doomed to be exterminated.³⁵⁶ Yet Croatia stated, in this connection, that

> across the occupied communities and regions – not isolated incidents, numerous, set out in the pleadings – Croat civilians were forced to wear white ribbons, and ordered to adorn their homes with white rags. These were measures of ethnic designation. Thus earmarked, *they were ready targets for destruction*. In Bapska, Croats were forced to hang white ribbons on their doors by Serbs who shouted, "Ustasha! We will kill you all" – in the witness statements. The Croat populations in Arapovac, Lovas, Šarengrad, Sotin, Tovarnik and Vukovar, amongst other places, were forced to wear white bands by Serb forces.³⁵⁷

359. Croatia mainly referred to the fact that they were obliged to identify themselves with white ribbons to show that they were Croats; although their fate seems to have been diverse, the targeted individuals, once targeted, became more vulnerable. In this respect, in a response to a question I put, during the public sitting before the Court on 05.03.2014, a Croatia's expert witness stated that Croats

> who were in the camps, were not thus marked (...). Such markings were used in several cases (...) – precisely in Lovas and Tovarnik – where we

---

353   *Ibid.*, para. 373.
354   *Ibid.*, para. 4.17.
355   *Memorial*, para. 4.60.
356   Cf. ICJ, doc. CR 2014/9, of 05.03.2014, p. 35.
357   ICJ, doc. CR 2014/6, of. 04.03.2014, p. 57 [emphasis added].

found victims in mass graves having these markings. And, according to the general information, it is known that in these locations, persons of Croat ethnicity were thus marked with white armbands.[358]

Thus, it appears from the evidence submitted in the present case that some of the Croats who were exterminated, were first marked with white ribbons, or armbands,[359] or white sheets on the doors of their homes.

3 *The Disposal of Mortal Remains*

360. In the course of the proceedings in the present case, Croatia referred to various witness statements describing the mistreatment by Serbs of the mortal remains of the deceased Croats. There were many reported cases of corpses that were burnt, or else thrown into mass graves (cf. *infra*), and also occurrences in which they were shot (in Central Vukovar),[360] dismembered (in Berak),[361] and thrown into wells (in Glina), canals (in Lovas)[362] and rivers.[363] This was a way, – Croatia added, – to conceal the murders; excavators were used to transport the mortal remains.[364]

361. For example, in the written phase of the present proceedings, it was further reported by Croatia that there were mortal remains that were simply burnt (in, e.g., Ervenik, Cerovljani, Hum/Podravska, Joševica).[365] Croatia presented also several accounts of corpses that were disposed of, in a haphazard, if not careless way.[366] Corpses were found everywhere. Mortal remains were reported to have been a problem in Vukovar during the shelling: many corpses remained

---

358 ICJ, doc. CR 2014/9, of 05.03.2014, p. 35.
359 It is not clear from the pleadings of Croatia that absolutely *all* Croats wearing white ribbons were doomed to be exterminated, cf. CR 2014/9, p. 35.
360 Cf. *Memorial*, para. 4.165.
361 Cf. *ibid.*, para. 4.42.
362 Cf. *ibid.*, para. 4.127.
363 Cf. *ibid.*, para. 5.80.
364 Cf. *ibid.*, para. 4.136.
365 Cf. *Memorial*, paras. 5.215, 5.122, 5.41, 5.85 and 5.169–5.170, respectively.
366 A witness stated that he was responsible for collecting of the corpses of the killed Croatian civilians with a tractor; 24 were buried, but it was not possible to identify some of them; *Memorial*, para. 4.102. Another witness reports that he was also responsible for digging graves and transporting the deceased; *ibid.*, para. 4.102. Another witness stated that she saw dead bodies on a trailer driving to the graveyard, where they were dropped into a hole and covered with an excavator; *ibid.*, para. 4.122. It was reported that columns of JNA trucks were used to transport the remains of the deceased; only 5 corpses in Tordinci, and 9 in Antin, were left in the graves; *ibid.*, para. 4.138.

on the streets, in yards and basements; 520 deceased persons were transported by Croatians volunteers and soldiers for identification.[367] In Vukovije, according to a witness three corpses were found on the steps of a house.[368] A witness narrated that, in Tovarnik, there were 48 corpses lying on a road and in yards and their burial was not allowed.[369]

362. I deem it fit to come back to a point I have made earlier on, in the present Dissenting Opinion (Part II, *supra*). This scenario, of the disposal of unburied mortal remains, brings to the fore (at least in my mind), in an inter-temporal dimension, the tragedy of *Antigone*, by Sophocles, some 25 centuries ago. Antigone expresses her determination to defy the tyrannical decision of the powerful Creon to expose the corpse of her brother Polynices so as to rot on the battlefield; she announces that she will give her brother's mortal remains a proper burial, as she looks forward to her reunion one day with her deceased beloved relatives:

> I shall bury him myself.
> And even if I die in the act, that death
> will be a glory. (…) I have longer
> to please the dead than please the living here (…).
> (…) What greater glory could I win
> than to give my own brother decent burial? (…).[370]

363. As self-inflicted death falls upon Antigone, disgrace promptly falls upon the despotic Creon as well. And the chorus limits itself to say that "the sorrows of the house", as in ancient times, piles on "the sorrows of the dead", in such a way that "one generation cannot free the next".[371] Love is "never conquered in battle", and is "alone the victor".[372] And it warns that the "power of fate" is a "terrible wonder, – neither wealth nor armies (…) can save us from that force".[373] At the end, the "mighty blows of fate (…) will teach us wisdom".[374]

---

367 *Memorial*, para. 4.152.
368 *Memorial*, para. 5.62. Elsewhere, a witness saw a corpse on a cargo truck; *ibid.*, para. 5.37.
369 Cf. *Memorial*, para. 4.97; and cf. ICJ, doc. CR 2014/8, of 05.03.2014, para. 51.
370 Verses 85–86, 88–89 and 561–562.
371 Verses 667 and 669–670.
372 Verses 879 and 890.
373 Verses 1045–1047 and 1050.
374 Verses 1469–1470.

364. Sophocles' masterpiece has survived the onslaught of time, and has kept on inspiring literary pieces in distinct ages. With the passing of time, *Antigone* became the symbol of resistance to the omnipotence of the rulers, as well as of the clash between natural law (defended by her) and positive law (represented by Creon). Its lesson has been captured by writers, and has become object of attention of philosophers, along the centuries. In the mid-xxth century, e.g., J. Anouilh wrote his own version of *Antigone*'s tragedy, with a distinct outlook, but likewise portraying the fatality that befell upon Antigone, and the other characters. J. Anouilh's tragedy *Antigone* was originally published in 1942, and first performed in 1944, in Paris under nazi occupation.

365. Along the centuries, the battlefield is full of abandoned corpses, as depicted in so many writings (historical, philosophical and literary). It is against this abandonment that Antigone stands. She shows, from Sophocles' times to date, that the dead and the living are close to each other in many cultures, and ultimately in human conscience. The determination of Antigone to secure a proper burial of her brother's mortal remains brings the beloved dead closer to their living, and the beloved living closer to their dead. This perennial lesson is full of humanism. Against the imposition of calculations of *raison d'État*, Antigone resists and remains faithful to herself, upholding fundamental principles and the superior human values underlying them. She sets up an example to be followed.

366. Nowadays, 25 centuries after Sophocles' *Antigone*, have the "blows of fate" taught us wisdom? I doubt it. Have the lessons of the sufferings of so many preceding generations been learned? I am afraid not. As the present case concerning the *Application of the Convention against Genocide* (Croatia *versus* Serbia) shows, in situations of conflict, mortal remains continue to be treated with disdain (cf. *supra*). And the complaints go on and on. Croatia states that, in 1993, in Tordinci (Eastern Slavonia), corpses were removed from a mass grave and transported to an unknown place in Serbia.[375] In Glina, at least 10 people were killed, but no remains were found by the date of the submission of the *Memorial*.[376] Still in Glina, the mortal remains of 9 civilians were exhumed (on 13.03.1996), but only 6 of them were identified.[377] Other mortal remains remain missing elsewhere.[378]

---

375   *Memorial*, para. 4.138, and cf. also para. 4.07.
376   *Ibid.*, para. 5.93.
377   Cf. *Memorial*, para. 5.83.
378   Cf., e.g., *Memorial*, para 5.179.

367. Furthermore, in Karlovac, – Croatia added, – the corpses of five women and one man were removed to an unknown destination, and by the date of the submission of the *Memorial* they were not found, except the corpse of a woman (which was found in a box on the outskirts of the village of Banski Kovačevac) in the spring of 1992.[379] In its *Reply*, Croatia again evoked witness statements found in the *Memorial*; and it adds that, in Dalj, Croat civilians were prevented to flee (after 01.08.1991), and were forced to collect and bury the mortal remains of those killed in the attack.[380]

368. In its arguments in the written phase of the present proceedings, Serbia did not expressly dismiss Croatia's claims on mortal remains and their mistreatment by Serb forces. It instead challenged the reliability of the evidence produced by Croatia, e.g., as to the number of corpses found in Velepromet (claimed by Croatia to be around a thousand).[381] Then it contended, in its counter-claim, that Croatia was responsible for misdeeds against mortal remains of Serbs and for hiding evidences; it claims, e.g., that Croatian soldiers shot into the corpses of Serbs.[382] It evoked a witness statement that, in Glina, a total of 20 dead bodies were strewn all over the road and on the sides.[383] Another witness described that, near Žirovac, tanks were driven over the dead bodies scattered on the road.[384]

369. Serbia further claimed that, in Knin, bodies were removed from the streets in order to hide them from the U.N.; it added that the United Nations Protection Force (UNPROFOR)'s Canadian battalion witnessed that Croatian forces were removing and burning corpses in order to hide evidences.[385] All this, – it argued, – was aiming at preventing that the precise number of victims could be determined.[386] In its *Rejoinder*, Serbia contended that on the road towards the bridge on the river Sava, there were many dead bodies of Serbs for about 3.5km.[387] It added that Croatian forces removed any traces of dead bodies in order to conceal the extent of the alleged crimes committed,[388] by first burning

---

379 Cf. *ibid.*, para. 5.157.
380 Cf. *Reply*, para. 5.21.
381 Cf. *Counter-Memorial*, para. 736.
382 Cf. *ibid.*, para. 1222.
383 Cf. *ibid.*, para. 1248.
384 Cf. *ibid.*, para. 1249.
385 *Counter-Memorial*, paras. 1262 and 1131.
386 *Ibid.*, para. 1238.
387 Cf. *Rejoinder*, para. 652-4.
388 Cf. *ibid.*, para. 654.

the bodies and then burying them.[389] Many dead bodies were seen, in civilians' columns fleeing Knin, lying on the streets.[390]

370. For its part, Croatia, in the oral phase of the present proceedings, complained that it lacks information on the whereabouts of the remains of more than 840 Croatian citizens, still missing as the result of the attacks on civilians;[391] it added that Serbia still refuses to help locating their mortal remains.[392] It further referred to another witness statement that there were countless bodies lying in the streets in the residential area south of the Vuka river, which could not be buried because of the danger from shelling.[393] In the town centre by the Danube river, – it proceeded, – there were also corpses which remained unburied.[394] In Borovo Selo, – it added, – Serb paramilitaries killed 12 Croat police officers and mutilated their remains.[395]

371. According to the Applicant, after the shelling of the city of Vukovar, dismembered bodies were seen lying in the rubble;[396] corpses lined the street.[397] In Velepromet, a witness describes 15 decapitated bodies by a hole in the ground.[398] Turning to the occurrences in Donji Čaglić, Croatia stated that the corpses of civilians were buried in a trench, dug by a JNA vehicle.[399] In Široka Kula, – it added, – 29 Croats were killed by the SAO Krajina and their corpses were thrown into burning houses.[400] Moreover, – Croatia proceeded, – a witness described that, around Lovas, Croats were used to clear minefields; mines would go off and there were dead bodies lying all over, and Serb forces were firing at them.[401]

---

389   Cf. *ibid.*, para. 654.
390   Cf. *ibid.*, para. 760.
391   ICJ, doc. CR 2014/5, of 03.03.2014, para. 6.
392   ICJ, doc. CR 2014/6, of 04.03.2014, para. 40.
393   Cf. ICJ, doc. CR 2014/8, or 05.03.2014, para. 13.
394   Cf. *ibid.*, para. 14.
395   *Ibid.*, para. 13.
396   *Ibid.*, para. 32.
397   *Ibid.*, para. 38.
398   Cf. ICJ, doc. CR 2014/8, of 05.03.2014, para. 57. Another witness, who was in Vukovar and was taken to Dalj, described a pit of corpses; cf. *ibid.* para. 77.
399   Cf. *Reply*, vol. 1, para. 6.8; and cf. ICJ, doc. CR 2014/10, of 06.03.2014, para. 16.
400   Cf. ICJ, doc. CR 2014/10, of 06.03.2014, para. 27.
401   Cf. ICJ. doc. CR 2014/20, of 20.03.2014, p. 55, para. 33.

372. Croatia cited an agreement between Croatia and Serbia, concluded in 1995, whereby they established a Joint Commission in order, *inter alia*, to exhume and identify mortal remains of unidentified bodies. Croatia contended that the mortal remains of 394 persons have been exhumed, but only 103 bodies have been handed over to it.[402] Serbia retorted that "only 103" corpses have been returned to Croatia because only 103 DNA profiles have matched the DNA samples of the Croatian missing persons.[403]

373. In the oral phase of the present proceedings, Serbia claimed that Croat forces disrespected the mortal remains of Serbs following the Operation *Storm*, and removed traces of the corpses that were lying in the roads.[404] Serbia added that the Croats shot on the bodies of dead Serbs,[405] and also referred to occurrences of corpses having been burned by Croats;[406] five of them were found in Bijeli Klanac.[407] According to Serbia, five tractor drivers were killed by Croatian soldiers and their bodies were thrown into a river.[408]

374. From times immemorial up to the present, the proper disposal of mortal remains, particularly in situations of armed conflicts or extreme violence in the disruption of the social order, has been a perennial concern. It marked presence already in the minds of the "founding fathers" of the law of nations. One decade ago, in another international jurisdiction (IACtHR), in my Separate Opinion in the case of the massacre of the *Moiwana Community versus Suriname* (Judgment of 15.06.2005), I deemed it fit to ponder that

> It cannot pass unnoticed that an acknowledgement of the duties of the living towards their dead was, in fact, present in the very origins, and along the development, of the law of nations. Thus, to refer but to an example, in his treatise *De Jure Belli ac Pacis* (of 1625), H. Grotius dedicated

---

402 ICJ, doc. CR 2014/21, of 21.03.2014, p. 37, para. 9.
403 ICJ, doc. CR 2014/24, of 28.03.2014, pp. 60–61, para. 8.
404 ICJ, doc. CR 2014/16, of 12.03.2014, p. 43, para. 3. Serbia cited statements in support of its claim; cf. *ibid.*, pp. 46–51. It further referred to a witness who was called to recognise his father's dead body but it was torched; the identification was only possible through DNA analysis; *ibid.*, p. 57, para. 52. Another witness found the mortal remains of a deceased beneath a burned family house after six months of the conflict in the area; *ibid.*, p. 59, para. 3.
405 *Ibid.*, pp. 44–45, para. 10.
406 *Ibid.*, p. 60, para. 11.
407 ICJ, doc. CR 2014/17, of 13.03.2014, p. 44, para. 104.
408 Cf. *ibid.*, p. 36, para. 80.

THE UNIVERSAL JURIDICAL CONSCIENCE

Chapter XIX of book II to the *right of burial* (*"derecho de sepultura"*). Therein H. Grotius sustained that the right of burying the dead has its origin in the voluntary law of nations, and all human beings are reduced to an equality by precisely returning to the common dust of the earth.[409]

H. Grotius further recalled that there was no uniformity in the original funeral rites (for example, the ancient Egyptians embalmed, while most of the Greeks burned, the bodies of the dead before committing them to the grave; irrespective of the types of funeral rites, however, the right of burial was ultimately explained by the dignity of the human person.[410] H. Grotius further sustained that all human beings, including "public enemies" (*"enemigos públicos"*) were entitled to burial, this being a precept of "virtue and humanity"[411] (paras. 60–61).

375. Despite this long-lasting concern, mortal remains keep on being disrespected, as the present case concerning the *Application of the Convention against Genocide* (Croatia *versus* Serbia) shows. And this is not the only contemporary example of this sad disdain. This is so – as I further pointed out in my aforementioned Separate Opinion in the *Moiwana Community* case (para. 63) – despite the fact that International Humanitarian Law provides for respect for the remains of the deceased. Article 130 of the 1949 IV Geneva Convention (on the Protection of Civilian Population) requires all due care and respect with mortal remains. Article 34 of Protocol I of 1977 to the four Geneva Conventions of 1949 elaborates on the matter in greater detail; and

> the commentary of the International Committee of the Red Cross on that Article points out that the respect due to the remains of the deceased "implies that they are disposed of as far as possible in accordance with the wishes of the religious beliefs of the deceased, insofar as these are known", and warns that even reasons of overriding public necessity cannot in any case justify a lack of respect for the remains of the deceased[412] (para. 63).

---

409 H. Grotius, *Del Derecho de la Guerra y de la Paz* [1625], vol. III (books II and III), Madrid, Edit. Reus, 1925, p. 39, and cf. p. 55.

410 *Ibid.*, pp. 43 and 45.

411 *Ibid.*, pp. 47 and 49; and cf. Hugonis Grotii, *De Jure Belli ac Pacis* [1625] (ed. B.M. Telders), The Hague, Nijhoff, 1948, p. 88 (abridged version).

412 Y. Sandoz, C. Swinarski and B. Zimmermann (eds.), *Commentary on the Additional Protocols of 08 June 1977 to the Geneva Conventions of 12 August 1949*, Geneva, ICRC/Nijhoff, 1987, pp. 369 and 379.

4 The Existence of Mass Graves

376. In the proceedings in the *cas d'espèce*, Croatia submitted arguments in relation to mass graves discovered in various municipalities, both in its written and in its oral pleadings. It focused on the description of crimes committed in each municipality and the existence of mass graves proving the commission of the crimes. It also submitted material evidence of mass graves, including photographs and colour plates of mass graves, as annexes to its pleadings.

377. The analysis of Croatia's arguments demonstrates that mass graves were common across many of the municipalities that it presented. Croatia submitted photographic and documentary evidence recording the findings made during the excavation of mass graves, as proof of the crimes that it alleges to have been committed. It seems, from the evidence and arguments examined, that the amount of mass graves in various municipalities supports the allegation that mass killings were committed against Croats.

378. In the course of the written phase of the present proceedings, Croatia developed its arguments concerning mass graves in its *Memorial*.[413] It submitted that, in total, 126 mass graves were found (at the time of the writing of the *Memorial*), of which 61 were in Eastern Slavonia.[414] Croatia mentioned mass graves found in various municipalities, including, e.g., villages in Eastern Slavonia: in Banovina, where 39 mass graves were discovered and 241 bodies have been exhumed (of which 175 have been identified);[415] in Kordun and Lika, where 11 mass graves were found;[416] and in the village of Lovas. Croatia submitted arguments and information in relation to each mass grave. In relation to Vukovar, for example, Croatia submitted that most of Vukovar was completely destroyed and that the mass grave at Ovčara, where some 200 Croats were taken by Serbs from the Vukovar Hospital, summarily executed and then left in a shallow mass grave.[417]

---

413 Cf. *Memorial*, Annexes 165 and 166. Cf. also *Memorial*, vol. 3, Section 7 (Identified Mass Graves).
414 *Memorial*, para. 8.11.
415 *Ibid.*, para. 5.77.
416 *Ibid.*, para. 5.137.
417 Cf. *ibid.*, para. 4.175. As to the Ovčara mass grave, Croatia refers to the *Report on Evacuation of the Vukovar Hospital and the Mass Grave at Ovčara*, U.N. Commission of Experts Established Pursuant to Security Council Resolution 780 (1993), and Physicians for Human Rights, *Reports of Preliminary Site Exploration of a Mass Grave Near Vukovar, Former Yugoslavia*, and Appendices A-D (19.01.1993).

THE UNIVERSAL JURIDICAL CONSCIENCE

379. Still in respect of Vukovar, Croatia submitted that three mass graves were found: Ovčara, where 200 corpses were found (and 145 persons were identified); in Novo Groblje, 938 mortal remains were found (and 722 persons were identified); in Nova Street 10 mortal remains were found (and 6 persons were identified). A grave containing three corpses was found in Borovo Selo. Croatia submits that "[t]hese numbers are paralleled only in the Prijedor County in Bosnia and Herzegovina".[418] In total, – Croatia contended, – 1,151 corpses were found in the mass graves in Vukovar.[419]

380. At the time of the writing of the *Memorial*, Croatia further argued that, due to the operations of the Serb paramilitary groups and the JNA in the area of Western Slavonia, 5 mass graves were found, from which 20 bodies were exhumed and identified, and that almost all of the identified corpses were Croats.[420] Croatia added that, at the time of the writing of the *Memorial*,

> 61 mass graves have been found in Eastern Slavonia (...) 2,028 people have been exhumed of whom 1,533 have been identified. In the Osijek-Baranja County, 171 persons were exhumed and 135 of them were identified. In the Vukovar Srijem County 1,857 persons were exhumed, and 1,418 of them were identified. Further mass graves are still being discovered. Moreover, many of the mass graves, which came into being in the relevant period, acted as temporary burial sites only.[421]

381. Croatia further submitted that "[t]he JNA often dug up the bodies and moved them to other parts of the occupied territory or Serbia. For example, dead bodies from the villages Tordinci were taken to Serbia and dead bodies from Tikveš were taken to Beli Manastir".[422] In relation to Eastern Slavonia, for example, Croatia contended, as to the village of Tenja, that a mass grave was exhumed on the farm, and the remains of three persons were identified. In the village of Berak, in the region of Eastern Slavonia, a mass grave between Orolik and Negoslavci, in a valley called "Šarviz", was also found.[423] Croatia also reported exhumations of mass graves in Ilok.[424] In the village of

---

418 *Memorial*, para. 4.188.
419 *Ibid.*, para. 4.188.
420 *Ibid.*, para. 5.04.
421 *Ibid.*, para. 4.07.
422 *Ibid.*, para. 4.07.
423 *Ibid.*, para. 4.41.
424 *Ibid.*, para. 4.72.

Tovarnik, – Croatia added, – it was common for the Serb paramilitary groups to force Croats to bury their fellow dead, and it referred to a witness testimony confirming the existence of mass graves and numerous murders of Croatian civilians.[425]

382. Similarly, at the time of the writing of the *Memorial*, in the village of Lovas, the mass grave of 68 people at the local graveyard was exhumed, and 67 were identified. As to the village of Tordinci, Croatia asserted that the corpses of

> approximately 209 Croats [were] discovered near the Catholic Church. (...) The registrar of Tordinci was to list the people in the mass grave, but because of the number of corpses, he was unable to complete the task. Till today the identity of some of these persons is not known. In 1993, the bodies were removed from the grave and transported to an unknown place in Serbia. (...) Columns of JNA trucks were used to transport the remains of the dead and only 5 bodies of the inhabitants of Tordinci and 9 inhabitants of the village Antin were left in the grave. These were subsequently exhumed and identified, while the others are still registered as missing.[426]

Furthermore, in relation to the village of Saborsko, Croatia submitted that "the village was completely obliterated and the population exterminated. Bodies of the murdered Croats were buried several days later in a mass grave prepared by an excavator".[427]

383. In its *Reply*, Croatia reiterated its arguments and updated the information submitted in its *Memorial*, including information about the location and exhumation of bodies[428] found since the filing of the *Memorial*. In its *Reply*, Croatia relied upon further sites of mass graves "as showing the context and breadth of the killings committed by the Serbian forces".[429] Croatia also retorted Serbia's arguments as to an alleged lack of impartiality of the information obtained: it asserts that international entities, including the Office of the U.N. High Commissioner for Human Rights (UNHCHR), the Organization for Security and Co-operation in Europe (OSCE), and the Observation Commission of the

---

425   *Ibid.*, para. 4.102; and cf. Annex 83.
426   *Memorial*, para. 4.138.
427   *Ibid.*, para. 5.152.
428   Cf. *Reply*, Annexes 43–46.
429   *Reply*, para. 5.12.

European Community (in addition to the ICTFY itself) were invited to observe the exhumation of mass graves in Croatia.[430]

384. Further in its *Reply*, Croatia recalled that the ICTFY also made findings in relation to mass graves in Croatia, in the *Mrkšić and Radić and Šljivančanin* case. In the words of the ICTFY:

> In the Chamber's finding, in the evening and night hours of 20/21 November 1991 the prisoners of war were taken in groups of 10 to 20 from the hangar at Ovčara to the site where earlier that afternoon a large hole had been dug. There, members of Vukovar TO and paramilitary soldiers executed at least 194 of them. The killings started after 2100 hours and continued until well after midnight. The bodies were buried in the mass grave and remained undiscovered until several years later (paras. 215–253).[431]

385. Croatia further referred to the ICTFY (Trial Chamber) findings in the *Martić* case in relation to mass graves. It found, e.g., that some persons from Cerovljani (it names them) were intentionally killed. It then recalled "the manner in which the victims from Hrvatska Dubica were rounded up and detained in the fire station" on 20.10.1991, and then killed on 21.10.1991 at Krečane near Baćin, and "buried in the mass grave at that location". The Trial Chamber considered that the crimes in Cerovljani were "almost identical" to those in Hrvatska Dubica, "including that most of the victims were buried at the mass grave in Krečane". The Trial Chamber considered it "proven beyond reasonable doubt that these victims were civilians and that they were not taking an active part in the hostilities at the time of their deaths" (para. 359).[432]

386. Serbia, for its part, submitted that some of the evidence, especially graphics called "mass graves", were prepared by Croatian official bodies.[433] In its view, evidence of mass graves was of "little worth", considering that "the exhumation reports do not provide evidence of genuinely mass graves of the sort found in Srebrenica, Rwanda and Eastern Europe following World War II. Rather, the burials seemed to be of relatively small clusters of deceased persons, dispersed

---

430 *Ibid.*, para. 2.56.
431 *Cit. in Reply*, para. 5.80.
432 *Cit. in Reply*, para. 6.35. And cf. also ICTFY (Trial Chamber), *Martić* case, paras. 364–367, as to atrocities committed in Baćin; paras. 202–208, as to Lipovača; and paras. 233–234, as to killings in Saborsko.
433 *Rejoinder*, para. 264.

throughout the various regions and municipalities of Slavonia".[434] However, much as it tried to discredit the evidence, Serbia did not come to the point of denying the existence of mass graves.

387. In the course of its oral pleadings, Croatia reiterated its contentions in relation to the existence of mass graves, their location and the bodies found therein. It added that new mass graves were found more recently, e.g., the mass grave in Sotin, containing 13 corpses.[435] Croatia also argued, in relation to Eastern Slavonia, that, within a year of Serbia's occupation, the communities of the region had been destroyed and that "[t]he intent to destroy the Croat population is as clear as the figures are stark (...): 510 mass graves have since been discovered, containing the corpses of nearly 2,300 men, women and children; many others have been discovered in individual graves. More still are being discovered yearly".[436]

388. Croatia further recalled the statement of an expert witness during its oral pleadings (Mr. Grujić), who testified, *inter alia*, about mass graves. He stated that "[a]s regards exhumations and the discovery of mass graves, and the time of their creation", he had to say that "the first mass graves had come into existence as early as July 1991", and "were continually coming into existence still the year 1992".[437] He further asserted that the largest mass grave found is the one at the new Vukovar Cemetery, where there are 938 victims.[438] In an answer to a question posed by Judge Cançado Trindade, the witness stated that, in Lovas and Tovarnik, corpses of victims were found in mass graves having markings such as white bands on their arms, and that, "according to the general information, it is known that in these locations, persons of Croat ethnicity were thus marked with white armbands"[439] (cf. *supra*).

---

434   *Ibid.*, para. 349.
435   ICJ, doc. CR 2014/8, p. 22, para. 55.
436   *Ibid.*, p. 27, para. 71. Croatia then corrected this statement in the following terms: "What I intended to say was that a total of 510 mass and individual graves had been discovered in Eastern Slavonia containing almost 2,300 bodies. We have now checked the most up-to-date figures on the website of the Directorate for Missing and Detained Persons, and it is 71 mass graves, and 432-individual graves in Eastern Slavonia, giving a total of 503"; ICJ, doc. CR 2014/10, of 06.03.2014, p. 10.
437   ICJ, doc. CR 2014/9, of 05.03.2014, p. 28.
438   *Ibid.*, p. 29.
439   *Ibid.*, p. 35.

389. Croatia further stated, in respect of individual and mass graves, that, upon Serbia's withdrawal from the occupied areas of Croatia in 1995, "mass and individual graves containing the remains of Croat victims of the genocide began to be uncovered. These graves have been painstakingly excavated and recorded by [its] Directorate for Detained and Missing Persons".[440] As to the numbers of victims in those graves,[441] Croatia submitted that

> by July 2013, 142 mass graves [plate on] had been discovered in Croatia, containing the bodies of 3,656 victims. Three thousand, one hundred and twenty-one (3,121) of those have been identified. Twenty-seven (27) per cent of these 3,121 bodies were women, and 38.5 per cent of them were older than 60. Thirty-seven (37) minors were also identified.[442]

390. Croatia proceeded that, "[b]y December 2013, over 1,100 such graves have been identified across the formerly occupied territory of Croatia". Croatia added that its efforts to discover the graves have been hindered by "Serbia's practice of removing and reburying victims during its occupation of the region – often in Serbia, – in a vain attempt to cover up its atrocities".[443] In any case, the existence of mass graves had not been denied, and, towards the end of the nineties, such graves – in Croatia as well as in Bosnia and Herzegovina – were fully documented.[444]

5 *Further Clarifications from the Cross-Examination of Witnesses*

391. The information provided to the ICJ in the course of the proceedings of the present case concerning the *Application of the Convention against Genocide* (Croatia *versus* Serbia) leaves it crystal clear, in my perception, that the attacks in Croatia were an onslaught, not exactly a war; there was a widespread and

---

440 ICJ, doc. CR 2014/10, of 06.03.2014, p. 18.

441 As to the definition of mass graves, Croatia contends that, since there is no universally accepted definition of a "mass grave" in international law, it thus follows the definition coined by the U.N. Special *Rapporteur* of the (former) Commission on Human Rights, appointed "to investigate first-hand the human rights situation in the territory of the Former Yugoslavia", who defined mass grave as a grave containing three or more bodies; cf. *ibid.*, p. 19, para. 42.

442 *Ibid.*, p. 19.

443 *Ibid.*, p. 20.

444 On the results of the research on the matter, conducted in both Croatia and Bosnia and Herzegovina from 1992 to 1997, cf., e.g., *The Graves – Srebrenica and Vukovar* (eds. E. Stover and G. Peress), Berlin/Zurich/N.Y., Scalo Ed., 1998, pp. 5–334.

systematic pattern of destruction of the civilian population, of the villagers, on account of their ethnicity. In my perception, as extreme violence intensified, there was, clearly, an intent, not only to displace them forcefully from their homes, but also to destroy them. Further clarifications were provided by the cross-examination of witnesses, that I cared to undertake in the public and closed sittings before the ICJ from 04 to 06 March 2014. Those additional clarifications pertain to three specific topics, namely: a) acts of intimidation and extreme violence; b) marking of Croats with white ribbons; c) burials of mortal remains.

392. As to the first point, in the Court's public sitting of 04.03.2014, I asked the witness (Mr. Kožul) the following question: – "What was the decisive factor for sorting the persons detained in Vukovar? Where and how was the selection carried out?" And he replied that they "knew that the army was coming to different parts of the cities. Because of that, we invited people to come to the hospital. Most of the separations took place in the hospital. The rest of the separations took place where people happened to be".[445] Next, in the Court's closed sitting of 06.03.2014, I asked the following question to the witness (Ms. Milić), and she provided the following response:

– "Did you know of, or do you remember, any initiative to contain, to avoid, or to stop the continued acts of violence reported in your statement? (...) Do you have knowledge of, or do you remember, any initiative to contain, to avoid, or to stop the continued acts of violence narrated in your statement?
– I did not hear that there were any attempts to help or to defend us".[446]

393. In the ICJ public sitting of 05.03.2014, I proceeded to the cross-examination on the issue of the marking of Croats with white ribbons, thus reported:

> *Judge Cançado Trindade*: – I thank the expert witness very much for his testimony. I have one particular question to ask.
> The *Data on Victims* contained in your statement refers, in Part 2 (paragraph 6–9), to victims exhumed from mass and individual graves. And Part 3 (paragraph 10–13) refers to persons detained in camps, subjected, as stated in paragraph 13, to violence with "the utmost level of cruelty".
> In respect of the former, that is, victims exhumed from mass and individual graves, it is mentioned in your statement (paragraph 8) that 'in

---

445   ICJ, doc. CR 2014/7, of 04.03.2014, p. 20.
446   ICJ, doc. CR 2014/11, of 06.03.2014, pp. 23–24.

certain locations in the Croatian Podunavlje, the killing of Croats who remained to live in their homes was preceded by their marking (white bands on the upper arms)". To the best of your knowledge, (...) did this also happen in respect of the latter, that is, of those detained in camps? If so, did all those so marked have the same fate?

Mr. Grujić [witness]: – Persons who were in the camps, were not thus marked as far as I know. Such markings were used in several cases that we have established – precisely in Lovas and Tovarnik – where we found victims in mass graves having these markings. And, according to the general information, it is known that in these locations, persons of Croat ethnicity were thus marked with white armbands.[447]

394. The other point on which further clarifications were obtained from the witnesses, that of burials of mortal remains, was the subject of the cross-examination that I deemed it fit to conduct in the ICJ public sitting of 05.03.2014, reported as follows:

Judge Cançado Trindade: – (...) I thank the witness very much for her testimony, and I proceed to my questions, pertaining to the burying of the murdered people after the fall of Bogdanovci.

At the end of your statement (last paragraph) it is asserted that, after the destruction of the village of Bogdanovci, those who were buried in the so-called School Square were so "in such a way that their bodies were wrapped in tents and buried with a bottle next to their bodies. These bottles contained the data of the dead persons".

Ms. Katić: – Yes, the data were names and surnames of those persons.

Judge Cançado Trindade: – Do you know if the burials described in your statement were attended by the close relatives of the deceased ones? Or were they buried by third persons? In that case, was there a disruption of family life and after-life in Bogdanovci? (...) I wonder whether the funerals were prepared and carried out by persons who belonged to the inner family circles of the deceased ones.

Ms. Katić: – The burials of our dead friends, I was the one to prepare the dead for the burial. In the medical corps, I would remove the clothes, I would put them either in tent halves, or in black sacks, and I would put that bottle containing the names and surnames. There was a young man, Ivica Šimunović is his name, his brother was killed. He would usually say

---

447   ICJ, doc. CR 2014/9, of 05.03.2014, p. 35.

a prayer, because we had no priest. We had some sacred water, we would sprinkle the dead. Branko Krajina was another person who would assist with the burials of those persons. But sometimes, it was not possible to take the dead bodies out of the places where they were, such as basements or garages. So, if it was not possible to remove the dead body, we would cover it with slack lime.

Judge Cançado Trindade: Thank you for this clarification".[448]

395. These further clarifications which ensued from the cross-examination of witnesses in public and closed sittings before the Court, in addition to those lodged with it by means of *affidavits*, are further evidence of the widespread and systematic pattern of destruction which occurred in the attacks against the civilian population in Croatia which form the *dossier* of the *cas d'espèce*. To that evidence we can also add the findings of the ICTFY, of the devastation that took place, in particular in the period 1991–1992, as examined in the course of the present Dissenting Opinion.

6   *Forced Displacement of Persons and Homelessness*

396. The case-law of the ICTR, likewise, contains relevant indications as to the imposition of unbearable conditions of life upon the targeted groups. In the *C. Kayishema and O. Ruzindana* case (Judgment of 21.05.1999), for example, the ICTR adopted the interpretation whereby "deliberately inflicting on the group conditions of life calculated to bring about its physical destruction in whole or in part"[449] includes

> methods of destruction which do not immediately lead to the death of members of the group. (...) [T]he conditions of life envisaged include rape, the starving of a group of people, reducing required medical services below a minimum, and withholding sufficient living accommodation for a reasonable period, provided the above would lead to the destruction of the group in whole or in part (para. 116).

397. In the same vein, in the *S. Gacumbitsi* case (Judgment of 07.07.2006), the ICTR, after recalling that, in accordance with its jurisprudence, genocidal intent can be proven by inference from the facts and circumstances of a case (para. 40), added that these latter could include "the general context", and

---

448   ICJ, doc. CR 2014/9, of 05.03.2014, pp. 22–23.
449   Cf. Part XIII 4 of the present Dissenting Opinion, *supra*.

the perpetration of other culpable acts systematically directed against the same group, the scale of atrocities committed, the systematic targeting of victims on account of their membership of a particular group, or the repetition of destructive and discriminatory acts (para. 41).

398. In effect, in the present case concerning the *Application of the Convention against Genocide* (Croatia *versus* Serbia), those who were forcibly displaced, expelled from their homes (many of them destroyed), were subjected to unbearable conditions of life, or rather, of seeking to survive. It is not surprising that, in the course of the proceedings in the *cas d'espèce*, both Croatia, in its main claim, and Serbia, in its counter-claim, presented arguments in relation to refugees, albeit in different contexts.

399. As to its claim, Croatia contended that many atrocities were committed against refugees by Serb forces. It stated that nearly 7,000 refugees from neighbouring villages were established in Ilok,[450] which was the initial site of refuge for Croats banished from other parts of the region of Eastern Slavonia; according to Croatia, a mass exodus took place from the town on 17.10.1991.[451] During the exodus, the refugees were exposed to humiliation and molestation by the JNA and paramilitary Serbian forces. Many properties were allegedly confiscated.[452] Croats who decided not to leave were subjected to physical and psychological harassment and even killing.[453]

400. Croatia furthermore reports additional cases of harassment against Croatian refugees that were leaving Bapska after its occupation. It contends that around 1,000 Croats fled in the direction of Šid in Serbia, when they were stopped by Serb police and later imprisoned. Croatia states that some of them were used as "human shield" to protect Serb forces and others killed, while some others had to look for refuge in the surrounding woods.[454] According to Croatia, Croat refugees in Serb occupied territories were prevented to return home on a permanent basis.[455] It added that the "RSK" charged Croatian refugees who fought in the Croatian forces with various criminal offences and thus created obstacles to their return.[456]

---

450   *Memorial*, para. 4.64.
451   *Ibid.*, para. 4.62.
452   *Ibid.*, para. 4.65.
453   *Ibid.*, para. 4.66.
454   *Ibid.*, para. 4.85.
455   *Reply*, paras. 10.34 and 10.40.
456   *Ibid.*, para. 10.42.

401. For its part, as to its counter-claim, Serbia also reported on attacks against Serb refugees on the part of Croatia: according to Serbia, refugee columns and fleeing individuals were targeted and attacked by Croatian forces during August 1995.[457] Serbia further claimed that Croatia imposed physical barriers to the return of Serb refugees, mainly by destroying houses and properties,[458] in addition to legal barriers, *inter alia*, by enacting laws to confiscate their properties.[459]

402. Both Croatia and Serbia cited common legal efforts to address the issues of refugees,[460] but each contending Party claimed they were violated by the opposing Party.[461] Thus, it can be concluded that both Parties have addressed, and acknowledged, the issue of attacks against refugees, and in more generic terms, the treatment of refugees by the opposing Party. In the present Judgment, the ICJ referred to evidence produced before it, but in particular in relation to the counter-claim only.[462] Yet, the *dossier* of the present case clearly shows that there were refugees on *both* sides, under attacks or harassment and humiliation, as demonstrated by pleadings of *both* Parties themselves.

403. If one considers, in the course of the proceedings of the present case, the depth of the arguments of the contending Parties in relation to the main claim as a whole, to try to put the counter-claim on an almost equal footing as the claim would seem, to a certain extent, unfair. Nothing would justify it, as there is a lack of proportion between them. In effect, the contending Parties

---

457   *Counter-Memorial*, paras. 1242–1257; cf. also *Rejoinder*, paras. 745–761.
458   *Rejoinder*, paras. 773–774.
459   *Ibid.*, paras. 775–780.
460   Cf., *inter alia*, the role of UNPROFOR in securing the return of refugees and displaced persons to their homes, *in Memorial*, para. 2.125; the signature of the Dayton Agreement of 1995, addressing *inter alia* the issues of refugees, *in Memorial*, para. 2.153–4. Cf. also the role of the U.N. Transitional Administration for Eastern Slavonia (UNTAES – established pursuant to Security Council resolution 1037(1996), which had among its duties to enable all refugees and displaced persons to exercise the right of free return to their homes), *in ibid.*, para. 2.155–158. Cf., moreover, the Agreement on the Procedures for Return (addressing the issue of refugees), signed by Croatia, UNTAES, and the U.N. High Commissioner for Refugees (UNHCR) in 1997, *in ibid.*, para. 2.157; and cf. further the Vance Plan of December 1991, *in Reply*, paras. 10.12–24.
461   Cf. *Memorial*, paras. 2.129 and 2.148; *Counter-Memorial*, para. 570; *Rejoinder*, para. 639–685. As to the Vance Plan, cf. *Reply*, para. 10.39–43. The mandate of the UNTAES, however, was considered a major success; cf. *Memorial*, para. 2.158.
462   Cf. paras. 458, 484 and 492.

have submitted voluminous evidence in relation to the claim, – including witness statements (both in the written and oral phases), photographs, mass graves data, and other important material evidence of the alleged genocide committed in Croatia. In contrast, the evidence submitted in support of the counter-claim does not seem comparable, in quantitative and qualitative terms.

404. In my perception, the evidence submitted by Croatia in support of its main claim is far more convincing in terms of the *actus reus* and *mens rea* of genocide. Likewise, the contending Parties' arguments, at both the written and oral phases of the proceedings, have dedicated far greater attention to the main claim than to the counter-claim. The evidence produced as to this latter[463] is, in contrast, far less convincing; this does not mean that war crimes were not committed, e.g., in the course of the "Operation Storm", with its numerous Serb (civilians) victims. The present Judgment of the ICJ recounts aspects of the counter-claim (Part VI) that could have been considered in less extensive terms,[464] without an apparently superficial attempt to address the claim and the counter-claim on an almost equal footing.

405. Last but not least, it is nowadays widely known that the problem of forced migrations assumed great proportions in the wars in the former Yugoslavia along the nineties, with thousands of refugees and displaced persons from Croatia, Bosnia-Herzegovina and Kosovo, successively. There are accounts and studies of the sufferings and almost unbearable conditions of life to which victims were exposed, not seldom with the separation and dissolution of families, and destruction of homes.[465]

406. The humanitarian crisis of mass forced migrations began with a first wave of internally displaced persons (end of 1991), followed by waves of refugees from Croatia and Bosnia-Herzegovina (early 1992 onwards). It was estimated, half a decade later, that there were 180,000 internally displaced persons in Croatia, as well as 170,000 refugees from Bosnia-Herzegovina (over 80% of them

---

463 E.g., in relation to the "Operation Storm" (August 1995).
464 There would, e.g., hardly be anything to add to what the ICJ found, in the present Judgment, in relation to the transcript of the Brioni meeting of 31.07.1995 (paras. 501–507).
465 Cf., *inter alia*, e.g., N. Mrvić-Petrović, "Separation and Dissolution of the Family", *in Women, Violence and War – Wartime Victimization of Refugees in the Balkans* (ed. V. Nikolić-Ristanović), Budapest, Central European University Press, 2000, pp. 135–149; N. Mrvić-Petrović and I. Stevanović, "Life in Refuge – Changes in Socioeconomic and Familial Status", *in ibid.*, pp. 151–169.

being Bosnian-Croats).[466] Non-governmental organizations (NGOs) were engaged in assisting the voluntary repatriation or return of refugees to Croatia and Bosnia-Herzegovina. Mass forced migrations were another component of the widespread and systematic pattern of extreme violence and destruction in the wars in the Balkans along the nineties.

407. It cannot pass unnoticed here that, in its Decision of 11.07.1996, in the *R. Karadžić and R. Mladić* case, the ICTFY (Trial Chamber), in reviewing the indictments, invoked the charge of genocide (para. 6), and stressed the subhuman conditions of detention of civilians, with the occurrence of crimes (such as torture and rape of women, inside the camps or at other places) (para. 13); it further addressed the devastating effects of forced displacements and abandonment (meant to be definitive) of homes (para. 14), and of expulsion and deportation (paras. 16–17).[467]

7 *Destruction of Cultural Goods*

408. Earlier on in the present Dissenting Opinion, in examining the widespread and systematic pattern of extreme violence and destruction in the factual context of the *cas d'espèce*, I have dwelt upon the destruction of group culture.[468] In addition to the examples already mentioned, I see it fit now to consider the shelling of Dubrovnik (October-December 1991), as it was object of particular attention on the part of the contending Parties in the course of the proceedings of the present case before the ICJ.

a) Arguments of the Contending Parties

409. According to Croatia, Serb politicians were planning to include the city of Dubrovnik into Serbian territory; the JNA carefully planned and premeditated the attacks against the Old Town, and the indiscriminate shelling of Dubrovnik began on the 01.10.1991, and continued until December 1991; under fear, 34,000 were expelled from their homes, and the inhabitants who remained in the occupied surrounding villages were taken to camps and some were tortured.[469] There were also killings.[470] Supplies were cut off, while the town kept being

---

466 Cf., for an account, *inter alia*, P. Stubbs, *Displaced Promises – Forced Migration, Refuge and Return in Croatia and Bosnia-Herzegovina*, Uppsala/Sweden, Life & Peace Institute, 1999, pp. 1 and 21–22.
467 It also addressed the "policy of 'ethnic cleansing'" (paras. 60–62, 90 and 93–95).
468 Cf. Part X(4) of the present Dissenting Opinion, *supra*.
469 *Memorial*, paras. 2.77, 3.90 and 5.237.
470 According to Croatia, some 161 civilians were killed, 272 wounded, and one is still missing; *ibid.*, para 5.237.

bombarded with heavy artillery. Inhabitants were denied access to medical assistance, food and water. Mistreatments, physical and mental intimidation, and house destruction were routinely conducted.[471]

410. Furthermore, – Croatia added, – there was a deliberate intent to destroy important symbols of Croatian culture; many cultural and sacral objects were destroyed in Dubrovnik, mainly in the Old Town: the JNA caused damage to at least 683 monuments, such as churches, chapels, city walls, and others.[472] In its attacks against Dubrovnik, – it proceeded, – the JNA tried to destroy the town in a way that could not be justified by any principle of military necessity or logic, thus pointing to its genocidal intentions.[473] Croatia further referred to the ICTFY (Appeals Chamber) Judgments relating to Dubrovnik, in the *P. Strugar* case (of 17.07.2008) and in the *M. Jokić* case (of 30.08.2005), and claimed that the conduct in Dubrovnik was an attempt to commit genocide.[474]

411. Serbia also referred to the ICTFY's convictions and sentencing of M. Jokić and P. Strugar for the shelling of the Old Town of the city on 06.12.1991,[475] and claimed that Croatia had failed to prove that any of the crimes were committed or attempted with genocidal intent. Serbia challenged the witness statements (for allegedly not fulfilling the requirements of *affidavits*).[476] It added that the ICTFY addressed the alleged crimes in the area of Dalmatia and concluded that they did not fulfil the requirements of extermination as crime against humanity (the killings were allegedly not committed on a large scale).[477] In Serbia's view, no genocidal intent was demonstrated in relation to the events in Dubrovnik.[478]

412. As to the differences concerning the number of victims, Croatia observed that the charges in the *P. Strugar* and the *M. Jokić* cases pertained only to the

---

471   According to Croatia, eleven men from the villages of Bistroće and Beroje were brought to camp Morinje, where they were subjected to mistreatments of all sorts including torture; *ibid.*, para 5.238. Some others were made prisoners and taken in "the camps Morinje, in Boka Kotorska and Bileća in Bosnia and Herzegovina, and some were beaten to death"; *ibid.*, para 5.240.
472   *Ibid.*, para. 5.241.
473   *Memorial*, para 5.236.
474   *Ibid.*, para. 8.27.
475   Cf. *Counter-Memorial*, para. 924.
476   *Ibid.*, para 920.
477   *Ibid.*, paras. 994 and 927, and cf. paras. 923–924.
478   *Ibid.*, para 925.

attacks on Dubrovnik in December 1991 (commencing with the shelling on 06.12.1991), and did not give detailed consideration to the crimes committed in the period between 01.10.1991 and 05.12.1991, other than by way of background context. It added that the deaths in Dubrovnik occurred over a much longer period, and not solely as a result of the December attacks.[479]

413. Croatia acknowledged that the *M. Jokić* and *P. Strugar* cases did not provide the exact number of victims killed by the attacks on Dubrovnik in October and November 1991, since the main focus was on the events of 06.12.1991; the charges in those two cases did not take into account the crimes committed between 01.10.1991 and 05.12.1991.[480] According to Croatia, both cases *Jović* and *Strugar* support its claims that they refer to the factual background of what occurred in Dubrovnik, *i.e.*, to the shelling of the Old Town of Dubrovnik.[481]

414. Moreover, Croatia quoted the ICTFY's *P. Strugar* decision, where it was stated that: (a) "the Old Town was extensively targeted by JNA"; (b) "no military firing points or other objectives, real or believed, in the Old Town were targeted by the JNA"; (c) as a consequence to the previous fact, "in the Chamber's finding, the intent of the perpetrators was to target civilians and civilian objects in the Old Town"; (d) the ICTFY found as a fact that the JNA had carefully planned and premeditated the attack and it was not an spontaneous action.[482]

415. Serbia retorted that M. Jokić and P. Strugar were not charged for crimes against humanity or genocide in those cases, and claimed that the attacks on Dubrovnik do not satisfy the requirements of genocide.[483] It further argued that the attacks were not authorized by the leadership of the JNA, and that there was no policy aimed at the destruction of the Croats.[484] In its view, the *P. Strugar* and *M. Jokić* cases do not contain evidence that the attacks on Dubrovnik were ordered or instructed by the leadership of Serbia.[485]

---

479   Cf. *Reply*, para. 6.97. Croatia further noted that the ICTFY itself referred to the shelling of Dubrovnik in both October and November 1991; cf. *ibid.*, paras. 6.99–105. And, according to the ICTFY, "the evidence establishes that the shelling of the Old Town on 12 November was intense"; cf. *ibid.*, para. 6.100.
480   Cf. *ibid.*, paras. 6.101–102.
481   Cf. *ibid.*, paras. 6.98–6.105.
482   Cf. *ibid.*, paras. 6.103–105.
483   Cf. *Rejoinder*, paras. 408 and 473.
484   Cf. *ibid.*, para. 474.
485   Cf. *ibid.*, para. 475.

THE UNIVERSAL JURIDICAL CONSCIENCE

b) General Assessment

416. As just seen, much of the debate between Croatia and Serbia was around the cases against M. Jokić and P. Strugar – JNA officials alleged to be responsible for the attacks of 06.12.1991 against Dubrovnik – before the ICTFY. Yet, Dubrovnik was under heavy attack by the JNA not only on 06.12.1991, but for a much longer period, during which a number of concomitant occurrences took place during and after the attacks, namely, torture, transfer of prisoners, beatings and killings, disclosing altogether a pattern of extreme violence and destruction.

417. Serbia stated, as to occurrences in Dubrovnik, that there were no charges of genocide in the aforementioned cases in the ICTFY.[486] But what can be the relevance of the absence of the charge of genocide for the present case opposing Croatia to Serbia before the ICJ, as regards the occurrences in Dubrovnik, considering that different standards of proof apply (cf. *supra*) in cases pertaining to individual (domestic) criminal responsibility and to international State responsibility?

418. All groups and peoples have the right to the preservation of their cultural heritage, of their *modus vivendi*, of their human values. The destruction of cultural goods, as occurred in the JNA bombardments of Dubrovnik, shows lack of, and – worse still, – disdain for, human values.[487] There was a deliberate destruction, by the JNA, of cultural goods in the Old City of Dubrovnik (part of UNESCO's World Heritage List, inscription in 1979, extension in 1994); the discriminatory intent against the targeted group was manifest,[488] – as acknowledged in the case-law of the ICTFY.

419. In my perception, this form of destruction is indeed related to physical and biological destruction, as individuals living in groups cannot prescind from their cultural values, and, in any circumstances, in any circumstances (even in isolation), from their spiritual beliefs. Life itself, and the beliefs that help people face the mysteries surrounding it, go together. The right to life and the right to cultural identity go together, they are ineluctably intermingled. Physical and

---

486   Cf. *Rejoinder*, paras. 403–404; and cf. *Reply*, paras. 6.97–6.105.
487   Cf. C. Bories, *Les bombardements serbes sur la vieille ville de Dubrovnik – La protection internationale des biens culturels*, Paris, Pédone, 2005, pp. 145 and 169–170, and cf. pp. 150–154.
488   Cf. *ibid.*, pp. 150–157 and 161–163.

biological destruction is interrelated with the destruction of a group's identity as part of its life, its living conditions.

420. In a factual context disclosing a widespread and systematic pattern of destruction, can we, keeping in mind the victims, really dissociate physical/biological destruction from the cultural one? In my perception, not at all, bearing in mind the relevance of culture, of cultural identity, to the safeguard of the right to life itself, the right to live with dignity. In this respect, I had the occasion to ponder, almost one decade ago, in another international jurisdiction, that

> The concept of culture, – originated from the Roman "*colere*", meaning to cultivate, to consider, to care for and to preserve, – was originally manifested in agriculture (the care with the land). With Cicero, the concept came to be applied to matters of the spirit and the soul (*cultura animi*). With the *passing of time*, it became associated with humanism, with the attitude of preserving and taking care of the things of the world, including those in the past. The peoples – human beings in their social *milieu*, – faced with the mystery of life, develop and preserve their cultures in order to understand and relate with the outside world. Hence the importance of cultural identity, as a component or aggregate of the fundamental right to life itself.[489]

421. I have already pointed out, in the present Dissenting Opinion, that, in its case-law, – e.g., its Decision of 1996 in the *R. Karadžić and R. Mladić* case, – the ICTFY was particularly attentive to the destruction of cultural and religious sites. And, in its Judgment of 2001 in the *Krstić* case, the ICTFY properly warned that the pattern of destruction as a whole (including the destruction of cultural and religious heritage) is to be duly taken into account, as evidence of the intent to destroy the group.[490]

422. The ICJ, contrariwise, has in the present Judgment preferred to close its eyes to it, repeatedly remarking (paras. 136, 388–389), in a dismissive way, that the destruction of cultural and religious heritage does not fall under the categories of acts of genocide set out in Article II of the Convention against

---

489   IACtHR, case of the *Sawhoyamaxa Indigenous Community versus Paraguay* (Judgment of 29.03.2006), Separate Opinion of Judge A.A. Cançado Trindade, para. 4.

490   Cf. Part X(4) of the present Dissenting Opinion, *supra*.

Genocide. To attempt to dissociate physical/biological destruction from the cultural one, for the purpose of the determination of genocide, appears to me an artificiality. Whether one wishes to admit it or not, *body and soul come together*, and it is utterly superficial, clearly untenable, to attempt to dissociate one from the other. Rather than doing so, one has to extract the consequences ensuing therefrom.

XIV *Actus Reus* of Genocide: Widespread and Systematic Pattern of Conduct of Destruction: Extreme Violence and Atrocities in Some Municipalities

423. With the aforementioned considerations, I have completed the examination, in the present Dissenting Opinion, of all the components of the onslaught, in a widespread and systematic pattern of destruction, brought to the attention of the Court in the present case. The time has now come to examine the *actus reus* and the *mens rea*, in the factual context of the present case concerning the *Application of the Convention against Genocide* (Croatia *versus* Serbia).

1 *Preliminary Methodological Observations*

424. Let me turn attention first to the element of *actus reus*. A careful examination of the arguments of the contending Parties, as well as witness statements, presented to the Court, discloses a systematic pattern of conduct of destruction, in the period of the armed attacks of Serb forces in Croatia, in particular in some selected municipalities, – namely, Lovas, Ilok, Bogdanovci and Vukovar (in the region of Eastern Slavonia), and Saborsko (in the region of Lika). The events occurred therein, as narrated in sequence, can, in my perception, be clearly examined in the light of the relevant provisions of the Convention against Genocide (in particular Article 2), to establish the *actus reus* of the crime of genocide (and also, in my understanding, the *mens rea – infra*).

425. In other villages, there was also a wide range of serious crimes committed, for example, in Poljanak, Dalj, Bapska, Tovarnik. I draw attention to these and other villages in other parts of the present Dissenting Opinion. But here, after reviewing the occurrences in all the affected villages, I am focusing only on the five selected villages, – Vukovar, Saborsko, Ilok, Bogdanovci and Lovas, – in view of their complete devastation amidst the extreme violence and the perpetration of atrocities therein, disclosing a widespread and systematic pattern of conduct of destruction (*actus reus,* to my mind together with *mens rea*).

426. It seems regrettable to me that the ICJ did not address all the localities referred to by Croatia, and some villages or municipalities were excluded from the reasoning of the Court. Such is the case, e.g., of Ilok, which was devastated. The Court's Judgment seeks to explain its own approach as follows:

> The Court does not consider it necessary to deal separately with each of the incidents mentioned by the Applicant, nor to compile an exhaustive list of the alleged acts. It will focus on the claims concerning localities put forward by Croatia as representing examples of systematic and widespread acts committed against the protected group, from which an intent to destroy it, in whole or in part, could be inferred. These are the localities cited by Croatia during the oral proceedings or in regard to which it called witnesses to give oral testimony, as well as those where the occurrence of certain acts has been established before the ICTY (para. 203).

427. This outlook of the Court, trying to explain its own selective choice of municipalities, seems unsatisfactory to me, given the Court's overall conclusion as to genocide, dismissing, *tout court, mens rea*, without giving its reasons for it. In this respect, the Court's Judgment should have examined all villages where Croatia claimed that serious crimes were committed. A more comprehensive, if not exhaustive, examination of the systematic pattern of conduct of destruction would have been appropriate – an indeed necessary – in a case of the importance of the *cas d'espèce*.

2 *The Systematic Pattern of Acts of Destruction*

428. The review of the evidence, and in particular witness statements, challenged in general terms by Serbia, reveal that many atrocities were committed in various municipalities. These atrocities range from arbitrary and large-scale killings of members of the Croat population (Article II(a) of the Genocide Convention); causing serious bodily or mental harm to members of the Croat population, including by cruel acts of violence (such as mutilation of limbs), torture and sexual violence (Article II(b) of the Genocide Convention); and deliberately inflicting conditions of life to bring about the destruction of the Croat population and its elimination from the regions concerned, including destruction of towns and villages, systematic expulsion from homes (Article II(c) of the Convention).

429. Witness statements in relation to five municipalities refer to similar events having taken place in those municipalities. These acts, examined closely, demonstrate the consistent and systematic pattern of acts in breach of provisions

of the Convention against Genocide, evidencing a genocidal plan. I thus proceed to a review of those breaches in the selected municipalities, as brought to the Court's attention.

3 Killing Members of the Croat Population (Article II(a))

430. "Killings of members of the group" is an act prohibited by the Genocide Convention, within the meaning of Article II(a). A violation of this provision requires evidence that the victim was killed by an unlawful act, with the intention to kill or to cause serious bodily harm which the perpetrator should reasonably have known might lead to death.[491] The question is thus whether the evidence submitted by the Parties, and in particular witness statements examined in the selected municipalities, support a finding that there were "killings of members of the group". Upon review of the evidence, it stems clearly that there were killings of members of the Croat group in various municipalities in Croatia. Such killings occurred by unlawful acts, with the intention to kill or cause serious bodily harm to the victims.

431. There are statements in the record of eye-witnesses concerning killings of members of the civilian population of Croatian nationality during the occupation of Lovas. The village was invaded and occupied by the JNA on 10.10.1991, after a 10-day heavy shelling by the JNA, causing the death of at least 23 Croat civilians.[492] During the attacks in occupied Lovas, defenceless civilian victims were killed: victims hid in the basements during attacks and Serbs tossed bombs in the basements.[493] Captured Croats were used as human shields to enter Croats' houses.[494] Several men were taken and separated from their families, and were then executed.[495]

432. In an episode which became known as the *"minefield massacre"*, the JNA, on 17.10.1991, singled out all the Croat males in Lovas (around 100, aged between 18 and 65), of whom 50 were taken onto a minefield.[496] On their way, one of them was shot and killed by the Serbs forces because he was unable to keep up with the rest of the group, due to being stabbed in the leg during a session of

---

[491] Cf. *Memorial*, paras. 7.59–7.61, and *Counter-Memorial*, paras. 76–78.
[492] Cf. ICJ, doc. CR 2014/12, of 07.03.2014, para. 59, p. 28; and ICJ, doc. CR 2014/8, of 05.03.2014, para. 23, p. 17.
[493] Cf. witness statement of M.M., *in Memorial*, Annex 99.
[494] *Memorial*, para 4.126.
[495] *Ibid.*, para 4.122.
[496] ICJ, doc. CR 2014/10, of 06.03.2014, para. 24, p. 15.

torture in the previous night.⁴⁹⁷ As soon as the members of the group arrived in the minefield, they were forced to hold each other's hands and to walk forward on the minefield.⁴⁹⁸

433. A witness reported that, at a certain point, they saw some of the mines ahead of them. A young Croat man was pushed onto one of the mines, which immediately exploded and initiated a chain detonation of the mines around the area; according to the Applicant, the explosions immediately killed 21 people and left 12 wounded. Thereafter, Serb soldiers asked for the wounded to shout and raise their hands so that they could be helped. Witnesses described that, as soon as the wounded raised their hands and shouted for help, the Serb soldiers began to shoot and to kill them.⁴⁹⁹ The dead bodies were taken to a mass grave.⁵⁰⁰

434. Serbia acknowledged that "fourteen accused are currently standing trial before the Belgrade District Court for the alleged killing of 68 Croat victims from the village of Lovas".⁵⁰¹ Moreover, in Ilok, for instance, there were also reports of killings of Croats by Serbs: for example, the statement of F.D. (who was kept in custody in Ilok from 01.11.1991 to 31.03.1992), reported brutal killings, including by beating to death.⁵⁰²

435. In Bogdanovci, there were many accounts of killings of Croats during the occupation. Many Croats were allegedly murdered in their houses. Croats were killed while attempting to flee the village.⁵⁰³ According to Croatia, many killings of Croats were committed while they were being forced to go outside their houses, or inside the houses when they would rather stay inside.⁵⁰⁴ The village was occupied by paramilitaries and JNA on 10.11.1991 after it had been attacked by heavy artillery and infantry. Marija Katić,⁵⁰⁵ e.g., testified that the village was completely destroyed, and that "during the destruction ten people were killed, were buried in the so-called School Square in such a way that their

---

497 Cf. *Memorial*, paras. 4.118–4.119 and 4.123–4.126; and witness statements of S.P., Annex 97, and of P.V., Annex 95.

498 Cf. *Memorial*, para. 4.125; and witness statement of Z.T., Annex 102.

499 Cf. *ibid.*, para. 4.125, and witness Statements of Z.T., Annex 102, and of L.S., Annex 98.

500 On the mass grave in Lovas, cf. *Memorial*, Annex 168B.

501 *Counter-Memorial*, para. 720.

502 *Memorial*, Annex 55.

503 Cf. *Memorial*, para. 4.51, and cf. witness statements of A.T., *in Memorial*, Annex 39.

504 *Memorial*, para. 4.52, and Annexes 41 and 45.

505 *Ibid.*, Annex 40.

bodies were wrapped in tents and buried with a bottle next to their bodies. These bottles contained the data of the dead persons"; other witnesses also reported killings of Croats and torture to death.[506]

436. Likewise, in Saborsko, there is evidence of killings of Croats; there are accounts, e.g., of some men who were lined up and shot, and women who were shot in the back.[507] There are also accounts of bodies of Croats being buried in a mass grave.[508] According to M.M., "[a]fter the fall of Saborsko, nobody buried the dead people so they were all left on the places where they died. In the last 15 days, because of the arrival of the blue helmets, the army buried those people with excavators on the places where they got killed and the graves were marked with the crosses that had no names or surnames on them".[509] As to the acts having taken place in Saborsko, Serbia significantly accepted that most of them had been confirmed by the judgment of the ICTFY.[510]

437. There is, moreover, extensive evidence referring to killings of Croats in Vukovar;[511] according to the record, 1,700 persons were allegedly killed (70% civilian), and around 2,000 were killed after the occupation.[512] It stems from the case file that a concentration camp was established in Velepromet, to be later used for organized killings. According to a witness statement, about 50 people were executed in that camp before the final fall of Vukovar. The hospital of Vukovar was bombed with two 250 kg bombs.[513]

438. In central Vukovar, e.g., executions took place:[514] grenades were thrown in houses and streets were covered with dead bodies. According to E.M.,[515] everyday 4–5 people were killed by weapons or slaughtered. He stated that houses were set on fire, and added that, in Velepromet, there were mass executions of people (at least 50 corpses or even more). Another witness, F.G., reported having been cut on the forehead and having seen about 15 decapitated bodies in a hole and a garbage pit in Velepromet, and heads scattered; he also saw a man

---

506 Cf. *Memorial*, Annexes 41 and 45.
507 Cf. *ibid.*, paras. 5.149–5.152.
508 Cf. *ibid.*, Annexes 364 and 365.
509 *Ibid.*, Annex 365.
510 *Counter-Memorial*, para. 841.
511 In relation to Vukovar, cf. *Memorial*, paras. 4.139–4.192.
512 *Ibid.*, para. 4.139.
513 *Ibid.*, para. 4.154.
514 *Ibid.*, paras. 4.164–4.167.
515 *Memorial*, Annex 126.

being decapitated.[516] In Ovčara, an alleged mass execution of 260 people took place, and they were buried in a mass grave.[517] Exhumation took place in 1996 and 145 bodies were identified, but the whereabouts of 60 of the patients taken from the hospital is still unknown.[518]

439. Other civilians were taken from the hospital to Velepromet, – a warehouse which was basically a concentration camp, where 15,000 Croats were sent to during the occupation. In Velepromet, atrocities took place, including decapitation and killings. According to F.J., mass murders occurred in Velepromet.[519] Significantly, in relation to the greater Vukovar area, Serbia acknowledged that "[t]he ICTY has indicted several people for the crimes allegedly committed in Vukovar, but the number of deaths for which the accused are charged is significantly smaller than claimed by [Croatia]".[520]

440. In conclusion, it seems clear from the evidence that there was a consistent and systematic pattern of killings of Croats across the municipalities examined. All witness statements in relation to each village report killings, and the intention to kill, as part of the physical element of the crime. The examination of the case record and the corresponding evidence point to a systematic pattern of killings of Croats. There seems thus to be sufficient evidence of the *actus reus* of "killing members of the group" under Article II(a) of the Genocide Convention.

4 *Causing Serious Bodily or Mental Harm to Members of the Group (Article II(b))*

441. Article II(b) of the Genocide Convention prohibits "causing serious bodily or mental harm to members of the group"; as to the physical element of this prohibited act, the contending parties agree that serious bodily or mental harm does not need to be permanent and irremediable, and that sexual violence crimes can fall within the ambit of this provision.[521] Upon review of the evidence submitted by the Parties, – and in particular witness statements examined in the selected municipalities, – it seems clear that there occurred

---

516 *Memorial*, Annex 121.
517 *Memorial*, para. 4.175.
518 *Ibid.*, para. 4.178.
519 *Memorial*, Annex 129.
520 *Counter-Memorial*, para. 741.
521 Cf. *Memorial*, paras. 7.62–7.64, and *Counter-Memorial*, paras. 79–81.

serious "bodily and mental harm" committed against members of the Croat population across various municipalities in Croatia.

442. Torture, beatings, maltreatment and sexual violence against Croats were common denominators in the evidence produced before the Court. As to Lovas, for example, there were accounts of torture, maltreatment and beatings as well as humiliation suffered therein; those accounts provide evidence of "serious bodily and mental harm" committed against members of the population. An illustration is the statement of witness P.V. concerning events during the occupation of Lovas.[522] She testified that they were held during the day in the "collective yard", and some were kept during the night. The witness reported beatings of those in captivity and torture: she stated that "[t]hey would beat the victims every morning in front of everyone". The witness reported having to disarm mines; she named some of the victims of torture whom she knew personally.[523]

443. There was a series of testimonies of heavy beatings. Stjepan Peulić, e.g., testified about interrogation methods and cruel torture: – "Petronije slapped me repeatedly and then hit me with his boot in the chin, which left a scar and two teeth were broken; he continued beating me. At the same time, Ljuban Devetak started calling people, who were then taken out and beaten with iron tubes and stabbed with bayonets before us".[524] The statements of P.M.[525] and J.K.[526] also referred to heavy beatings.

444. Similar brutalities were reported to have occurred in Ilok; for example, when thousands of Croatian civilians were leaving the city in a convoy, they were exposed to humiliation and molestation by the JNA and paramilitaries, who also robbed them. Croats that did not wish to leave their homes were subject to physical and psychological harassment, robbery and arbitrary detention. Witness P.V., e.g., reported living in fear to have to leave his home.[527] He stated that "[p]eople would work for days without any food or any compensation. The Serbs would humiliate us all the time. (...) We were not allowed to gather publicly. When we walked on the streets, for example, the Serbs (...) would hit

---

522   *Memorial*, Annex 95.
523   *Memorial*, Annexes – vol. II, p. 284.
524   *Memorial*, Annex 97.
525   *Ibid.*, Annex 101.
526   *Ibid.*, Annex 104.
527   *Ibid.*, Annex 58.

us with rocks and insult us".[528] Witness M.V.[529] also reported having been tortured for four years.

445. In Bogdanovci, there were also reported cases of torture and maltreatment of Croats. Heavy attacks causing serious bodily injury were also a common denominator in the witness statements. According to Marija Katić, there were artillery attacks every few days (as in August 1991), destroying family houses and farming objects. Witness M.B. also testified about cases of torture, including the stretching of a Croat on a tree in front of a church until he died.[530] Similar cases of bodily and mental harm were reported in Saborsko. A witness reported, e.g., that, in Saborsko, while the commanders were issuing the orders to kill the civilians, they used to say that these latter were all "Ustashas", and should all be killed.[531]

446. In Vukovar, serious bodily and mental harm was also reported to have been committed. There were accounts of torture in Velepromet; civilians were mistreated and experienced mental distress. There were also accounts of sexual violence, humiliation and cutting of limbs. The narrative of witness Franjo Kožul, e.g., reports of bodily and mental harm having been inflicted upon Croats from Vukovar. He reported that he "could hear" shots, people screaming and sobbing, hits, beating, among other brutalities. He added that

> As we entered the stable, we had to pass through cordon of men who beat us with everything, the cordon was about 30 meters long. They ordered me to make a list of people that were there, so I knew the number, I made a list of 1242 people, in alphabetical order. After some time I found out that in another stable were 480 men. They were offending us, beat us, maltreated us (...). During the first few days we were sitting and sleeping one over the other, on bare concrete. They would give us some water, one little slice of bread and some cheese, twice a day, and they beat us and tortured us 24 hours a day. I cannot describe all kinds of physical and psychological tortures, I would never imagine that people we lived with, and worked with would do that crime.[532]

---

528 *Memorial*, vol. II – Annex 58, p. 165.
529 *Ibid.*, Annex 59.
530 *Ibid.*, Annex 41.
531 *Memorial*, Annex 365, Statement of M.M.
532 *Ibid.*, Annex 114.

447. In a similar vein, witness H.E. testified to daily rapes by Serbian police and army officers upon her arrival to prison. The rapes happened in the cell in front of other female prisoners. She also testified to beatings and mental abuse.[533] Likewise, M.M. also testified to repeated sexual violence, maltreatment and mental distress: she was taken with her two months old baby and six years old sister to Serbia, and then to Vukovar, where they were both raped repeatedly by local Serbs. She testified to the killing of her husband and the mental harm she suffered. She reported that she had to perform forced labour, and, if she did not work, she would not have any food. She also testified about having been tortured, and about repeated rapes by several men, lasting for hours (and in front of her little sister who was very afraid all the time), and with the use of objects causing heavy bleeding.[534]

448. Witness T.C. stated that Chetniks "were maltreating, expelling, threatening, beating, raping and killing on a daily basis. They were harshly terrorizing us. All our men, who were capable of work, were taken to camps". Some of them were ordered to keep on "digging up holes"; they "never returned to their homes", and no one learned anything about them any more. The witness testified that she was raped, and further stated that "Croats had white ribbons at our gate in order to enable Chetniks who were not from our village to recognize us".[535]

449. In conclusion, it stems clearly from the evidence in the case file that, across the municipalities examined, victims suffered serious bodily and mental harm in the form of torture, mistreatment, beatings, sexual violence, psychological distress and forced labour. These accounts were not isolated events; they were repeated in testimonies of witnesses from different municipalities. The aforementioned evidence a systematic pattern of the prohibited acts of destruction, demonstrating the physical element of the acts prohibited under Article II(b) of the Genocide Convention.

5 Deliberately Inflicting on the Group Conditions of Life Calculated to Bring about Its Physical Destruction in Whole or in Part (Article II(c))

450. "Deliberately inflicting on the group conditions of life calculated to bring about its physical destruction in whole or in part" is a prohibited act under

---

533 Ibid., Annex 116.
534 Ibid., Annex 117.
535 Ibid., Annex 128.

Article II(c) of the Genocide Convention. As to the physical element (*actus reus*), Serbia recognized that systematic expulsion from homes can fall within the scope of this provision, if such action is carried out with genocidal intent and forms part of a manifest pattern of conduct that is capable of effecting the physical destruction of the group, and not simply its displacement elsewhere.[536] Thus, the question left is whether, upon analysis of the case file, and in particular witness statements examined in the selected municipalities, it can be concluded that there was a violation of Article II(c) of the Convention.

451. Those witness statements referred to, in addition to rape and sexual violence, also to deprivation of food and basic conditions of life; they also reported on deportation from entire regions. In Lovas, e.g., there were measures which caused the fleeing of Croats, such as the destruction of homes and deportations. According to J.K., before the occupation Lovas had 1700 residents, 94% of whom were Croats; later on, "they settled around 1500 Serbs" there, and, in "the occupied Lovas there remained about 100 Croats, 25 people in mixed marriages and 144 Serbs from Lovas. The settlers arrived in cars or tractors and they moved into our houses with the permission of the housing Commission".[537]

452. In Ilok, the statement of P.V. reported on being forced to leave his house and remaining in fear to have to leave it; he added that

> [p]eople would work for days without any food or any compensation. The Serbs would humiliate us all the time. (...) We were not allowed to gather publicly. When we walked on the streets for example the Serbs would spit on us from the church, they would hit us with rocks and insult us.[538]

In relation to Ilok, it is significant to note that even Serbia itself acknowledged that "[t]he Prosecutor of the ICTY charged Slobodan Milošević for deportation or forcible transfer of inhabitants from Ilok".[539] Likewise, in Bogdanovci, there were accounts of civilians being forced to leave, and the occupation was designed to decimate the population of the village through destruction of the houses, farms and their infrastructure, and churches. It appears that the

---

536   Cf. *Counter-Memorial*, paras. 83–84, and *Rejoinder*, para. 333.
537   *Memorial*, Annex 104, p. 316.
538   *Ibid.*, Annex 58.
539   *Counter-Memorial*, para. 693.

occupation was designed to make the life of Croats impossible. The experience of D.B. is illustrative of how the attack made life in Bogdanovci impossible.[540]

453. The village of Saborsko, likewise, appeared to have been completely destroyed. According to the testimony of M.M., the intention was "to clean" ethnically the village.[541] In the same vein, A.Š. stated that bombs were thrown from a plane on the village and houses and churches were set on fire; the witness further testified to people taking goods from Saborsko.[542] Similarly, M.M. testified that "[a]fter Saborsko was attacked, Nedjeljko Trbojević called 'Kičo', during the action of 'cleaning', went from house to house and he threw bombs", and "burnt a few houses with rocket launchers".[543]

454. It may be recalled that Serbia acknowledged that the Judgment of the ICTFY (Trial Chamber) in the *M. Martić* case confirmed the November 1991 attack on the village, and "most of the acts alleged to have taken place in Saborsko".[544] As to Vukovar, there were, likewise, accounts of attempts to destroy all signs of Croatian life and culture in the city, destruction of property and heavy bombings. The majority of the people of the city stayed in basements for three months and common shelters, and many got killed while trying to get food, water and other supplies.[545]

455. D.K. was in Vukovar until he was wounded; then he was loaded into a bus and deported to Serbia. He testified about the living conditions in Stajićevo and Sremska Mitrovica;[546] victims had inhumane living conditions, with very little supply of food.[547] B.V. reported not having anything to eat day and night.[548] And L.D. stated that "houses were on fire, grenades were falling and killing people. The Serbs had sent their women and children to Serbia earlier and the men stayed in Vukovar to slaughter us Croats".[549] In sum, there is evidence produced before the Court that breaches of Article II(c) of the Genocide

---

540 *Memorial*, Annex 45.
541 *Ibid.*, Annex 365.
542 *Ibid.*, Annex 364.
543 *Ibid.*, Annex 365.
544 *Counter-Memorial*, paras.840–841.
545 *Memorial*, para. 4.151.
546 These are localities in Serbia, where there appears to have been camps where some Croats were taken to.
547 *Ibid.*, Annex 138.
548 *Ibid.*, Annex 151.
549 *Ibid.*, Annex 143.

Convention were committed, within a systematic pattern of extreme violence, aiming at deliberately inflicting conditions of life designed to bring about the physical destruction of the targeted groups of Croats, in whole or in part.

6 *General Assessment of Witness Statements and Conclusions*
a) Witness Statements

456. The witness statements in relation to each of the selected municipalities, – namely, Lovas, Ilok, Bogdanovci, Saborsko and Vukovar, – all refer to similar occurrences in each of those municipalities. All witness statements have been analysed, including those statements that were unsigned by witnesses. All converge to similar occurrences which fall under Article II of the Convention against Genocide. I consider even witness statements that are unsigned relevant for the assessment of events occurred in the aforementioned municipalities, given that they are in the same line as those statements that are signed. The totality of witness testimonies (signed and unsigned), read together, provide substantial evidence of the crimes perpetrated in those municipalities, in breach of Article II of the Convention against Genocide.

457. In the same line of thinking, I have deemed it relevant to examine the acts alleged to have occurred in *all* municipalities for which Croatia submitted evidence – rather than single out one or another specific municipality, – so as to determine whether there was a systematic pattern of destruction. In the present case, the Court, instead of looking at a selected sample of incidents, as it has done, should rather have examined the totality of criminal acts committed during the entire military campaign against Croatia, brought to its attention in the *cas d'espèce*, to determine whether a systematic pattern of conduct of destruction amounting to genocide occurred. The reference to incidents at given municipalities serves to illustrate the general pattern of destruction.

b) Conclusions

458. In my perception, the witness statements in their totality provide evidence of the widespread and systematic pattern of destruction that occurred in those municipalities plagued by extreme violence. The widespread and systematic pattern of destruction, as established in the present case, consisted of the widespread and systematic perpetration of the aforementioned wrongful acts (grave breaches) falling under the Convention against Genocide.

459. They comprised, as seen above, killing members of the Croat (civilian) population (Article II(a)), causing serious bodily or mental harm to members of targeted groups (Article II(b)), and deliberately inflicting on the groups

concerned conditions of life calculated to bring about their physical destruction in whole or in part (Article II(c)). It appears that it can be concluded, on the basis of atrocities committed in the selected municipalities, that the *actus reus* of genocide of Article II(a), (b) and (c) of the Convention against Genocide has been established.

XV *Mens Rea* of Genocide: Proof of Genocidal Intent by Inference

460. May I now, at this stage of my Dissenting Opinion, move from *actus reus* of genocide to the element of *mens rea* (intent to destroy) under the Convention against Genocide, as applied in the present case. In the course of the proceedings of the *cas d'espèce*, the contending Parties themselves presented arguments as to the issue whether genocidal intent can be proven by inferences.[550] From a cumulative analysis of the *dossier* of the *cas d'espèce* as a whole, in my perception the intent to destroy the targeted groups, in whole or in part, can be inferred from the evidence submitted (even if not direct proofs). The extreme violence in the perpetration of atrocities bears witness of such intent to destroy.

461. The widespread and systematic pattern of destruction across municipalities, encompassing massive killings, torture and beatings, enforced disappearances, rape and other sexual violence crimes, systematic expulsion from homes (with mass exodus), provides the basis for inferring a genocidal plan with the intent to destroy the targeted groups, in whole or in part, in the absence of direct evidence. In effect, to require direct evidence of genocidal intent in all cases is not in line with the jurisprudence of international criminal tribunals, as we shall see next.

1   *International Case-Law on* Mens Rea

462. When there is no direct evidence of intent, this latter can be inferred from the facts and circumstances. Thus, in the *Akayesu* case (Judgment of 02.09.1998), the ICTR (Trial Chamber) held that the intent to commit genocide requires that acts must be committed against members of a group specifically because they belong to that group (para. 521). A couple of jurisprudential

---

550 Cf., e.g., Croatia's argument *in Reply*, para. 2.11, invoking Serbia's acknowledgment *in Counter-Memorial*, para. 135 (difficulty to obtain direct evidence, and reliance on indirect evidence, with inferences therefrom); *Reply*, para. 2.12.

illustrations to this effect can here be referred to. For example, the ICTFY (Appeals Chamber) asserted, in the *Jelisić* case (Judgment of 05.07.2001), that,

> As to proof of specific intent, it may, in the absence of direct explicit evidence, be inferred from a number of facts and circumstances, such as the general context, the perpetration of other culpable acts systematically directed against the same group, the scale of atrocities committed, the systematic targeting of victims on account of their membership of a particular group, or the repetition of destructive and discriminatory acts (para. 47).

The ICTFY further stated, in the *Krstić* case (Judgment of 19.04.2004), that, when proving genocidal intent based on an inference, "that inference must be the only reasonable inference available on the evidence" (para. 41).

463. Again, in the jurisprudence of the ICTR, it has been established, in the same vein, that intent to commit genocide can be inferred from facts and circumstances. In the *Rutaganda* case, e.g., the ICTR (Trial Chamber, Judgment of 06.12.1999) stated that: "[I]ntent can be, on a case-by-case basis, inferred from the material evidence submitted to the Chamber, including the evidence which demonstrates a consistent pattern of conduct by the Accused"[551] (paras. 61–63). Likewise, in the *Semanza* case, the ICTR (Trial Chamber, Judgment of 15.05.2003) stated that a "perpetrator's *mens rea* may be inferred from his actions" (para. 313).

459. Furthermore, in the *Bagilishema* case, the ICTR (Trial Chamber, Judgment of 07.06.2001) found that

> evidence of the context of the alleged culpable acts may help the Chamber to determine the intention of the Accused, especially where the intention is not clear from what that person says or does. The Chamber notes, however, that the use of context to determine the intent of an accused must be counterbalanced with the actual conduct of the Accused. The Chamber is of the opinion that the Accused's intent should be determined, above all, from his words and deeds, and should be evident from patterns of purposeful action (para. 63).

464. In this regard, in the landmark case of *Akayesu*, the ICTR (Trial Chamber, Judgment of 02.09.1998) found that "intent is a mental factor which is difficult,

---

551 And cf. also, ICTR, case *Musema*, Judgment of 27.01.2000, para. 167.

even impossible to determine", and it decided that, "in the absence of a confession from the accused", intent may be inferred from the following factors: (a) "the general context of the perpetration of other culpable acts systematically directed against that same group", whether committed "by the same offender or by others"; (b) "the scale of atrocities committed"; (c) the "general nature" of the atrocities committed "in a region or a country"; (d) "the fact of deliberately and systematically targeting victims on account of their membership of a particular group, while excluding the members of other groups"; e) "the general political doctrine which gave rise to the acts"; (f) "the repetition of destructive and discriminatory acts"; and (g) "the perpetration of acts which violate, or which the perpetrators themselves consider to violate the very foundation of the group – acts which are not in themselves covered by the list (...) but which are committed as part of the same pattern of conduct" (paras. 523–524).

465. In the case of *Kayishema and Ruzindana,* the ICTR (Trial Chamber, Judgment of 21.05.1999) stated that intent might be difficult to determine and that the accused's "actions, including circumstantial evidence, however may provide sufficient evidence of intent", and that "intent can be inferred either from words or deeds and may be demonstrated by a pattern of purposeful action". The ICTR (Trial Chamber) affirmed that the following can be relevant indicators: a) the number of group members affected; b) physical targeting of the group or their property; c) use of derogatory language toward members of the targeted group; d) weapons employed and extent of bodily injury; e) methodical way of planning; f) systematic manner of killing; and g) relative proportionate scale of the actual or attempted destruction of a group (paras. 93 and 527).

466. In the light of the foregoing, the jurisprudence of international criminal tribunals holds that proof of genocidal intent may be inferred from facts and circumstances, and provides some guidelines to that effect, even in the absence of documentary evidence. Factual elements which can be taken into account for that inference are, e.g., indications of premeditation, of the existence of a State policy or plan, the repetition of atrocities against the same targeted groups, the systematic pattern of extreme violence against, and destruction of, vulnerable or defenceless groups of individuals.

2   *General Assessment*

467. In the light of the foregoing, the ICJ seems to have imposed too high a threshold for the determination of *mens rea* of genocide, which does not appear in line with the *jurisprudence constante* of international criminal tribunals on the matter. The ICJ has pursued, and insisted upon pursuing, too high

a standard of proof for the determination of the occurrence of genocide or complicity in genocide. In my understanding, *mens rea* cannot simply be discarded, – as the ICJ does in the *cas d'espèce*, – on the basis of an *a priori* adoption of a standard of proof – such as the one the ICJ has adopted – entirely inadequate for the determination of State responsibility for grave violations of the rights of the human person, individually or in groups.

468. The Court cannot simply say, – as is does in the present Judgment, – that there has been no intent to destroy, in the atrocities perpetrated, just because it says so.[552] This is a *Diktat,* not a proper handling of evidence. This *Diktat* goes against the voluminous evidence of the material element of *actus reus* under the Convention against Genocide (Article II), wherefrom the intent to destroy can be inferred. This *Diktat* is unsustainable, it is nothing but a *petitio principii* militating against the proper exercise of the international judicial function. *Summum jus, summa injuria. Mens rea*, the *dolus specialis*, can only be *inferred*, from a number of factors.

469. In my understanding, evidential assessments cannot prescind from axiological concerns. Human values are always present, as acknowledged by the historical emergence of the principle, in process, of the *conviction intime* (*livre convencimento / libre convencimiento / libero convincimento*) of the judge. Facts and values come together, in evidential assessments. The inference of *mens rea / dolus specialis*, for the determination of responsibility for genocide, is undertaken as from the *conviction intime* of each judge, as from human conscience.

470. Ultimately, conscience stands above, and speaks higher than, any wilful *Diktat*. The evidence produced before the ICJ pertains to the *overall conduct* of the State concerned, and not to the conduct only of individuals, in each crime examined in an isolated way. The *dossier* of the present case concerning the *Application of the Convention against Genocide* (Croatia *versus* Serbia) contains irrefutable evidence of a widespread and systematic pattern of extreme violence and destruction, as already examined in the present Dissenting Opinion.

---

552 The Court did the same, eight years ago, in its Judgment of 2007 in the *Bosnian Genocide* case: after finding it "established that massive killings of members of the protected group occurred" (para. 276), it added that it was not "conclusively established" that those "massive killings" had been carried out "with the specific intent (*dolus specialis*) on the part of the perpetrators to destroy, in whole or in part, the group as such" (para. 277), – because it said so, without any explanation. Cf., likewise, paras. 440–441 of the present Judgment.

471. Such widespread and systematic pattern of extreme violence and destruction encompassed massive killings, torture, beatings, rape and other sex crimes, enforced disappearances of persons, expulsion from homes and looting, forced displacement and humiliation[553] (*supra*). The facts conforming this pattern of destruction have been proven, in international case-law and in U.N. fact-finding[554] (*supra*). Even in the absence of direct proofs, genocidal intent (*mens rea*) can reasonably be inferred from such planned and large-scale pattern of destruction, systematically directed against the same targeted groups.

XVI   The Need of Reparations: Some Reflections

472. The widespread and systematic pattern of destruction in the factual context of the *cas d'espèce* discloses, ultimately, the ever-lasting presence of evil, which appears proper to the human condition, in all times. It is thus understandable that it has attracted the concern of, and has presented challenges to, legal thinking, in our times and previous centuries, as well as other branches of knowledge (such as, e.g., history, psychology, anthropology, sociology, philosophy and theology, among others). It has marked presence in literature as well. This long-standing concern, along centuries, has not, however, succeeded to provide an explanation for evil.

473. Despite the endeavours of human thinking, along history, it has not been able to rid humankind of it. Like the passing of time, the ever-lasting presence of evil is yet another mystery surrounding human beings, wherever and while they live. Whenever individuals purport to subject their fellow human beings to their "will", placing this latter above conscience, evil is bound to manifest itself. In one of the most learned writings on the problem of evil, R.P. Sertillanges ponders that the awareness of evil and the anguish emanated therefrom have marked presence in all civilizations. The ensuing threat to the future of humankind has accounted for the continuous presence of that concern throughout the history of human thinking.[555]

474. Religions were the first to dwell upon the problem of evil, which came also to be considered by philosophy, history, psychology, social sciences, and literature. Along the centuries, human thinking has always acknowledged the need

---

553   Parts IX, X and XI of the present Dissenting Opinion, *supra*.
554   Part IX of the present Dissenting Opinion, *supra*.
555   R.P. Sertillanges, *Le problème du mal – l'histoire*, Paris, Aubier, 1948, pp. 5–412.

to examine the problem of evil, its incidence in human relations, in the world wherein we live, without losing faith in human values.[556] Despite the perennial quest of human thinking to find answers to the problem of evil, – going as far back as the *Book of Job*, or even further back, to the *Genesis* itself,[557] – not even theology has found an explanation for it, satisfactory to all.

475. In a devastation, such as the one of the factual context of the present case concerning the *Application of the Convention against Genocide*, the damage done to so many persons, thousands of them, was truly an irreparable one. There is no *restitutio in integrum* at all for the fatal direct victims, the memory of whom is to be honoured. As for the surviving victims, reparations, in their distinct forms, can only *alleviate* their suffering, which defies the passing of time. Yet, such reparations are most needed, so as to render living – or surviving atrocities – bearable. This should be kept constantly in mind.

476. The determination of breaches of Article II of the Convention against Genocide (cf. *supra*) renders inescapable the proper consideration of reparations. In effect, in the course of the proceedings, both contending Parties, in their written and oral arguments, have made claims for reparation for genocide allegedly committed by each other. Croatia's main arguments in this respect are found in its *Memorial*, where it began by arguing that, although the Convention contains no specific provision concerning the consequences of a violation by a Party, breaches of international obligations entail the obligation to make full reparation. In this sense, Croatia claimed that if Serbia[558] was found to be internationally responsible for the alleged violations of the Genocide Convention, it must make full reparation for material and immaterial damage.[559]

---

556 *Ibid.*, pp. 5–412.
557 Cf., *inter alia*, e.g., M. Neusch, *L'énigme du mal*, Paris, Bayard, 2007, pp. 7 193; J. Maritain, *Dio e la Permissione del Male*, 6th. ed., Brescia, Edit. Morcelliana, 2000, pp. 9–100; E. Fromm, *Anatomía de la Destructividad Humana*, Mexico/Madrid/Buenos Aires, Siglo XXI Edit., 2009 [reimpr.], pp. 11–468; P. Ricoeur, *Evil – A Challenge to Philosophy and Theology*, London, Continuum, 2007, pp. 33–72; P. Ricoeur, *Le mal – Un défi à la philosophie et à la théologie*, Genève, Éd. Labor et Fides, 2004, pp. 19–65; C.S. Nino, *Juicio al Mal Absoluto*, Buenos Aires, Emecé Edit., 1997, pp. 7–292; A. Morton, *On Evil*, N.Y./London, Routledge, 2004, pp. 1–148; T. Eagleton, *On Evil*, New Haven/London, Yale University Press, 2010, pp. 1–163; P. Dews, *The Idea of Evil*, Oxford, Wiley-Blackwell, 2013, pp. 1–234.
558 FRY, at the beginning of the proceedings.
559 *Memorial*, para. 8.75.

477. Croatia has in fact requested the Court to reserve this issue "to a subsequent phase of the proceedings", as in previous cases. A declaratory judgment by the ICJ of Serbia's responsibility, – it added, – would already provide a primary means of satisfaction, stressing the importance of the obligations enshrined in the Genocide Convention, and underscoring the rule of law and the respect for fundamental human rights. To Croatia, such declaratory judgment would also "assist in the process of setting the historical record straight", and would thereby "contribute towards reconciliation over the longer term".[560]

478. Croatia has further asked the Court to declare Serbia's obligation to take all steps at its disposal to provide an immediate and full account to Croatia of the whereabouts of missing persons, and to order Serbia to return cultural property which was stolen in the course of the genocidal campaign. Furthermore, Croatia has claimed that, as a consequence of Serbia's illegal conduct, it is entitled to obtain full reparation for the damages caused and for the losses suffered, in particular for the wrongful acts connected to the Serbian genocidal campaign, as described in its *Memorial*.[561]

479. Compensation, – it has added, – is "due for all damage caused to the physical and moral integrity and well-being of the citizens of Croatia". Croatia then concludes that, "in a case relating to genocide, where there has been a massive loss of life and untold human misery has been caused", *restitutio* will never wipe out the consequences of the illegal act; it thus claims also for satisfaction for the damages suffered.[562] At last, in its final submissions read at the end of the oral proceedings, Croatia has repeated its request for reparation.[563]

480. Serbia, for its part, responded briefly to those arguments on reparation, having stated first that they appear hypothetical, as, in its view, its responsibility for genocide cannot be engaged. As to the claim for compensation when *restitutio* in kind is not possible, Serbia has contended that Croatia was trying to get compensation for all possible damages which might have been caused by the war in Croatia. It has added that Croatia's claims for reparation were not to be determined by the ICJ, whose jurisdiction concerns only possible violations of the Convention against Genocide.[564]

---

560   *Ibid.*, paras. 8.75–8.77.
561   *Ibid.*, paras. 8.78–8.79. Cf. also *Application*, pp. 18–20; *Memorial*, p. 414; and *Reply*, p. 472.
562   *Memorial*, paras. 8.80–8.84.
563   Cf. ICJ, doc. CR 2014/21, of 21.03.2014, pp. 40–41.
564   *Counter-Memorial*, paras. 1059–1068.

481. Serbia has also submitted a request for reparation, in relation to its counter-claim, as stated in its *Counter-Memorial*. It has requested the ICJ to adjudge and declare Croatia's responsibility to "redress the consequences of its international wrongful acts" and in particular to provide full compensation for "all damages and losses caused by the acts of genocide".[565] In its final submissions in relation to the counter-claim, read at the end of the oral proceedings, it reiterated its request.[566]

482. It should not pass unnoticed that that both contending Parties have requested that reparation for alleged acts of genocide be determined by the ICJ in a subsequent phase of the case. The ICJ should, in my understanding, have found, in relation to Croatia's claim, that acts of genocide were committed, for the reasons expressed in the present Dissenting Opinion. Accordingly, Croatia's request for reparation should have been entertained by the Court, and the ICJ should thus have reserved the issue of the determination of reparation to a separate phase of the proceedings in this case, as requested by the Applicant.

483. In this respect, it may be recalled that, in the recent case *A.S. Diallo* (Guinea *versus* D.R. Congo, 2010–2012) the ICJ examined, during the merits phase, the violations of the international human rights Conventions invoked by Guinea.[567] In its Judgment of 30.11.2010, the ICJ held that the D.R. Congo had violated certain obligations contained in those Conventions, namely, Articles 9 and 13 of the U.N. Covenant on Civil and Political Rights, and Articles 6 and 12 of the African Charter on Human and Peoples' Rights, in addition to Article 36(1)(b) of the Vienna Convention on Consular Relations.[568] The ICJ accordingly held, in relation to reparation, that:

> In the light of the circumstances of the case, in particular the fundamental character of the human rights obligations breached and Guinea's claim for reparation in the form of compensation, the Court is of the opinion that, in addition to a judicial finding of the violations, reparation due to Guinea for the injury suffered by Mr. Diallo must take the form of compensation.[569]

---

565 *Ibid.*, p. 471; cf. also *Rejoinder*, p. 322.
566 Cf. ICJ, doc. CR 2014/24, of 28.03.2014, p. 64.
567 *A.S. Diallo* (merits, Guinea *versus* D.R. Congo), *ICJ Reports* (2010) p. 639.
568 *Ibid.*, paras. 73, 74, 85 and 97.
569 *Ibid.*, para. 161.

484. In this respect, the Court reserved for a subsequent phase of the proceedings the question of compensation for the injury suffered by Mr. A.S. Diallo.[570] In that phase of reparations, the ICJ then adjudicated the question of the compensation owed by the D.R. Congo to Guinea for the damages suffered by the victim, Mr. A.S. Diallo, and delivered its Judgment on the issue on 19.06.2012.[571] In my extensive Separate Opinion (paras. 1–101), I examined the matter in depth, and upheld, *inter alia*, that the ultimate *titulaire* or beneficiary of the reparations ordered by the ICJ was the human person victimized, rather than his State of nationality.

485. In the present case Judgment in the case relating to the *Application of the Convention against Genocide*, opposing Croatia to Serbia, had the Court found – which it regrettably did not – that the respondent State incurred in breaches of the Genocide Convention, it should have opened a subsequent phase of the proceedings, for the adjudication of the reparations (in its distinct forms) due, ultimately to the victims (human beings) themselves. In recent years, the challenges posed by the determination of reparations in the most complex situations, have begun to attract scholar attention; yet, we are still – surprisingly as it may seem – in the infancy of this domain of international law.

XVII   The Difficult Path to Reconciliation

486. In the violent conflicts which form the factual context of the present case opposing Croatia to Serbia, the numerous atrocities committed (torture and massive killings, extreme violence in concentration camps, rape and other sexual violence crimes, enforced disappearances of persons, expulsions and deportations, unbearable conditions of life and humiliations of various kinds, among others), besides victimizing thousands of persons, made hatred contaminate everyone, and decomposed the *social milieux*. The consequences, in long-term perspective, are, likewise, and not surprisingly, disastrous, given the resentment transmitted from one generation to another.

487. Hence the importance of finding the difficult path to reconciliation. In my understanding, the first step is the acknowledgment that a widespread and systematic pattern of destruction ends up dismantling everyone, the

---

570 Cf. *ibid.*, p. 693, resolutory points 7 and 8.
571 Cf. *ICJ Reports* (2012) p. 324.

oppressed (victims) and the oppressors (victimizers). From the times of the *Iliad* of Homer until nowadays, the impact of war and destruction upon human beings has been constantly warning them as to the perennial evil surrounding humanity, and yet lessons of the past have not been learned.

488. In a penetrating essay (of 1934), Simone Weil, one of the great thinkers of last century, drew attention to the utterly unfair demands of the struggle for power, which ends up victimizing everyone. From Homer's *Iliad* to date, individuals, indoctrinated and conditioned for war and destruction, have become objects of the struggle for domination. There occurs "the substitution of the ends by the means", transforming human life into a simple means, which can be sacrificed; individuals become unable to think, and abandon themselves entirely to "a blind collectivity", struggling for power (the end).[572]

489. The distinction between "oppressors and oppressed", – S. Weil aptly observed, – almost loses meaning, given the "impotence" of all individuals in face of the "social machine" of destruction of the spirit and fabrication of the inconscience.[573] The consequences, as shown by the present case concerning the *Application of the Convention against Genocide*, opposing Croatia to Serbia, are disastrous, and, as I have just pointed out, generate long-lasting resentment.

490. The next step, in the difficult path to reconciliation, lies in the provision of reparations – in all its forms – to the victims. Reparations (*supra*) are, in my understanding, essential for advancing in the long and difficult path to reconciliation, after the tragedy of the wars in the former Yugoslavia in the nineties. In the framework of reparations, besides the judicial (declaratory) acknowledgment of the breaches of the Genocide Convention, there are other measures to pursue the path to reconciliation.

491. In this connection, may I single out that, in a particularly enlightened moment of the long oral proceedings in the present case concerning the *Application of the Convention against Genocide* (Croatia *versus* Serbia), in the public sitting before the Court of 10.03.2014, the Agent of Serbia took the commendable step of making the following statement:

---

[572] S. Weil, *Reflexiones sobre las Causas de la Libertad y de la Opresión Social*, Barcelona, Ed. Paidós/Universidad Autónoma de Barcelona, 1995, pp. 81–82, 84 and 130.

[573] *Ibid.*, pp. 130–131; S. Weil, *Réflexions sur les causes de la liberté et de l'oppression sociale*, Paris, Gallimard, 1955, pp. 124–125, and cf. pp. 114–115 and 144.

> In the name of the Government and the People of the Republic of Serbia, I reiterate the sincere regret for all victims of the war and of the crimes committed during the armed conflict in Croatia, whatever legal characterization of those crimes is adopted, and whatever the national and ethnic origin of the victims. Each victim deserves full respect and remembrance.[574]

492. The path to reconciliation is certainly a difficult one, after the devastation of the wars in the Balkans. The contending parties are surely aware of it. In the same public sitting before the ICJ, of 10.03.2014, the Agent of Serbia further asserted that

> The cases in which Serbia was a party were of an exceptional gravity: these were cases born out of the 1990s conflicts in the former Yugoslavia, which left tragic consequences to all Yugoslav peoples and opened important issues of State responsibility. This case is the final one in that sequence. In this instant case Serbia expects – more than in any of its previous cases – that suffering of the Serb people should also be recognized, get due attention, and a remedy.
>
> Today it is well known that the conflict in Croatia was followed by grave breaches of international humanitarian law. There is no doubt that Croats suffered a lot in that conflict. This case is an opportunity for all of us to remind ourselves of their tragedy (...). However, the Croatian war caused grave sufferings to Serbs as well (...).[575]

493. Croatia, for its part, contends that one of the remedies it seeks is the return of the mortal remains of the deceased to their families.[576] It reports that at least 840 bodies[577] are still missing as the result of the alleged genocidal acts carried out by Serb forces. Croatia claims that Serbia has not been providing the required assistance to carry on the searches for those mortal remains and their identification. The contending parties' identification and return of all the mortal remains to each other is yet another relevant step in the path towards reconciliation. I dare to nourish the hope that the present Dissenting Opinion may somehow, however modestly, serve the purpose of reconciliation.

---

574 ICJ, doc. CR 2014/13, of 10.03.2014, para. 5.
575 *Ibid.*, paras. 2–3.
576 *Memorial*, para. 1.10 and 1.37.
577 ICJ, doc. CR 2014/5, of 03.03.2014, para. 6.

XVIII Concluding Observations: The Need of a Comprehensive Approach to Genocide under the 1948 Convention

494. Contrary to what contemporary disciples of Jean Bodin and Thomas Hobbes may still wish to keep on thinking, the Peace Palace here at The Hague was not built and inaugurated one century ago to remain a sanctuary of State sovereignty. It was meant to become a shrine of international justice, not of State sovereignty. Even if the mechanism of settlement of contentious cases by the PCIJ/ICJ has remained a strictly inter-State one, by force of mental inertia, the nature and subject-matters of certain cases lodged with the Hague Court along the last nine decades have required of it to go beyond the strict inter-State outlook.[578] The artificiality of the exclusively inter-State outlook, resting on a longstanding dogma of the past, has thus been made often manifest, and increasingly so.

495. More recently, the contentious cases wherein the Court's concerns have had to go beyond the strict inter-State outlook have further increased in frequency.[579] The same has taken place in the two more recent Advisory Opinions of the Court.[580] Half a decade ago, for example, in my Separate Opinion in the ICJ's Advisory Opinion on the *Declaration of Independence of Kosovo* (of 22.07.2010), I deemed it fit to warn against the shortcomings of the strict inter-State outlook (para. 191), and stressed the need, in face of a humanitarian crisis in the Balkans, to focus attention on the *people* or *population concerned* (paras. 53, 65–66, 185 and 205–207), in pursuance of a humanist outlook (paras. 75–77 and-190), in the light of the principle of humanity (para. 211).[581]

---

[578] For a study of this issue, cf. A.A. Cançado Trindade, "A Contribuição dos Tribunais Internacionais à Evolução do Direito Internacional Contemporâneo", in: *O Direito Internacional e o Primado da Justiça* (eds. A.A. Cançado Trindade and A.C. Alves Pereira), Rio de Janeiro, Edit. Renovar, 2014, pp. 3–89, esp. pp. 18–20, 46–47, 51, 64 and 68.

[579] E.g., the case on *Questions Relating to the Obligation to Prosecute or Extradite* (2009–2013), pertaining to the principle of universal jurisdiction under the U.N. Convention against Torture; the case of *A.S. Diallo* (2010) on detention and expulsion of a foreigner; the case of the *Jurisdictional Immunities of the State* (2010–2012); the case of the *Application of the International Convention on the Elimination of All Forms of Racial Discrimination* (2011); the case of the *Temple of Preah Vihear* (2011–2013).

[580] On the *Declaration of Independence of Kosovo* (2010), and on a *Judgment of the ILO Administrative Tribunal upon a Complaint Filed against the IFAD* (2012), respectively.

[581] In that same Separate Opinion, I also drew attention to the expansion of international legal personality and capacity, as well as international responsibility (para. 239), in contemporary international law.

496. The present case concerning the *Application of the Convention against Genocide* (Croatia *versus* Serbia) provides yet another illustration of the pressing need to overcome and move away from the dogmatic and strict inter-State outlook, even more cogently. In effect, the 1948 Convention against Genocide, – adopted on the eve of the Universal Declaration of Human Rights, – is not State-centered, but rather *people-centered*. The Convention against Genocide cannot be properly interpreted and applied with a strict State-centered outlook, with attention turned to inter-State susceptibilities. Attention is to be kept on the *justiciables*, on the victims, – real and potential victims, – so as to impart justice under the Genocide Convention.

1   *Evidential Assessment and Determination of Facts*

497. I thus regret not to be able to share at all the Court's reasoning in the *cas d'espèce*, nor its conclusion as to the Applicant's claim. To start with, the Court's *evidential assessment* and *determination of the facts* are atomized and not comprehensive. It chooses some municipalities (cf. para. 203) and describes summarily some occurrences therein. Its examination of the facts is rather aseptic.[582] Not surprisingly, the ICJ fails to characterize the pattern, as a whole, of the atrocities committed, as being widespread and systematic.

498. The Court has taken note of atrocities – such as summary executions and decapitations – perpetrated in Vukovar and its surrounding area, admitted by the Respondent (paras. 212–224). It has taken note of massacres, *inter alia*, e.g., in Lovas (paras. 231–240) and in Bogdanovci, admitted by Serbia (paras. 225–230). It has taken note of other massacres, *inter alia*, e.g., in Saborsko (paras. 268–271), in Poljanak (paras. 272–277), in Hrvatska Dubika and its surrounding area (paras. 257–261). Yet, this is just a sample of the atrocities that were committed in the *cas d'espèce*.

499. In addition to the localities cited by the ICJ in the present Judgment, there are numerous other localities wherein atrocities occurred, – in the regions of Eastern Slavonia, Western Slavonia, Banovina/Banija, Kordun, Lika and Dalmatia, – brought to the attention of the Court by Croatia, which were not cited or addressed directly in the present Judgment of the Court. Not surprisingly, the Court fails to establish a widespread and systematic pattern of destruction

---

[582] Already in my Separate Opinion (para. 219) in the ICJ's Advisory Opinion on the *Declaration of Independence of Kosovo* (2010), I had warned against an aseptic examination of the facts.

with the intent to destroy, without any satisfactory explanation why it has chosen this path for the examination of the facts.

500. In the present Judgment, the ICJ takes note of the findings of the ICTFY (in its Judgments in the cases of *Mrkšić and Radić and Šljivančanin* ["*Vukovar Hospital*"], 2007; and of *M. Martić*, 2007; and of *Stanišić and Simatović*, 2013) that

> from the summer of 1991, the JNA and Serb forces had perpetrated numerous crimes (including killing, torture, ill-treatment and forced displacement) against Croats in the regions of Eastern Slavonia, Banovina/Banija, Kordun, Lika and Dalmatia (para. 208).

Yet, apart from massive killings, the Court fails to characterize other crimes as having been committed also on a large scale, conforming a widespread and systematic pattern of destruction. From time to time the Court minimizes the scale of crimes such as rape and other sexual violence crimes (para. 364), expulsion from homes and forced displacements (para. 376), deprivation of food and medical care (paras. 366 and 370).

501. Even an international criminal tribunal such as the ICTFY, entrusted with the determination of the international criminal responsibility of individuals, has been attentive to a comprehensive approach to evidence in order to determine genocidal intent. This particular point has recently been made by the ICTFY (Appeals Chamber) in the *R. Karadžić* case (Judgment of 11.07.2013), where it warned that

> Rather than considering separately whether an accused intended to destroy a protected group through each of the relevant genocidal acts, a trial chamber should consider whether all of the evidence, taken together, demonstrates a genocidal mental state (para. 56).

502. The ICTFY (Appeals Chamber) further asserted, in the same *R. Karadžić* case, that, "by its nature, genocidal intent is not usually susceptible to direct proof" (para. 80). This being so, – it added, –

> in the absence of direct evidence, genocidal intent may be inferred from a number of facts and circumstances, such as the general context, the perpetration of other culpable acts systematically directed against the same group, the scale of atrocities committed, the systematic targeting of victims on account of their membership in a particular group, the

repetition of destructive and discriminatory acts, or the existence of a plan or policy (para. 80).

503. In face of the task of the determination of the international responsibility of States, – with which the ICJ is entrusted, – with all the more reason one is to pursue a comprehensive approach to evidence. Contemporary international human rights tribunals, – which, like the ICJ, are also entrusted with the determination of the international responsibility of States, – know well, from their own experience, that respondent States tend to withhold the monopoly of evidence of the atrocities perpetrated and attributable to them.

504. It is thus not surprising that, in their evolving case-law, – addressed to by the contending Parties, but entirely overlooked by the ICJ's Judgment in the present case, – international human rights tribunals have rightly avoided a high threshold of proof, and have applied the distribution or shifting of the burden of proof.[583] In the determination of facts in cases of the kind (pertaining to grave breaches), they have remained particularly aware of the primacy of concern with fundamental rights inherent to human beings over concern with State susceptibilities. After all, the *raison d'humanité* prevails over the *raison d'État*.

505. In the present Judgment in the case concerning the *Application of the Convention against Genocide*, the ICJ has seen only what it wanted to see (which is not much), trying to make one believe that the targeted groups were simply forced to leave the territory claimed as Serb (para. 426, and cf. para. 435). As if trying to convince itself of the absence of genocidal intent, the ICJ has further noted – making its own the argument of Serbia[584] – that the ICTFY Prosecutor has never charged any individuals for genocide in the context of the armed attacks in Croatia in the period 1991–1995 (para. 440).

506. This does not at all have a bearing upon State responsibility. Individuals other than the ones charged, could, as State agents, have been responsible; indictments can be confirmed (as in the case of *R. Karadžić*, in mid-2013), so as to encompass genocide; and, in his indictments, the Prosecutor exerts a *discretionary* power, its statute being entirely distinct from that of international judges. In any case, in respect of State responsibility, – as I have already pointed

---

583 Cf. Part VII of the present Dissenting Opinion, *supra*.
584 Cf. *Counter-Memorial*, para. 944.

out, – the standards of proof are not the same as in respect of individual criminal responsibility.

507. Even if we do not know, – and will never know, – the total amount of victims who were tortured or raped (they were numerous), all the facts, taken together, conform, in my perception, a widespread and systematic pattern of destruction, under the Genocide Convention, as examined in the present Dissenting Opinion. They are *facts of common knowledge* (*faits de notoriété publique* / *fatos de conhecimento público e notorio* / *hechos de conocimiento público y notorio* / *fatti notori* [*di comune esperienza*]), which thus do not need to be subjected to a scrutiny pursuant to a high threshold of proof, depriving the Genocide Convention of its *effet utile*, in the determination of State responsibility.

2 Conceptual Framework and Reasoning as to the Law

508. The Court's *conceptual framework* and *reasoning as to the law* are likewise atomized and not comprehensive. First of all, its reading of the categories of acts of genocide under the Convention against Genocide (Article II) is as strict as it can possibly be. The Court, furthermore, considers separately the interrelated elements of *actus reus* and *mens rea* of genocide, applying a high threshold of proof, which finds no parallel in the evolving case-law of international criminal tribunals as well as international human rights tribunals. This ends up rendering, regrettably, the determination of State responsibility for genocide under the Convention an almost impossible task, and the Convention itself an almost dead letter. The way is thus paved for the lack of legal consequences, and for impunity for the atrocities committed.

509. The Court's conceptual framework and reasoning as to the law are, furthermore, atomized also in its perception of each branch of international law on its own, – even those branches that establish regimes of protection of the rights of the human person, – namely, the International Law of Human Rights (ILHR), International Humanitarian Law (IHL), and the International Law of Refugees (ILR). The Court thus insists in approaching even IHL and International Criminal Law (ICL) in a separate and compartmentalized way.

510. In its insistence on its atomized approach, in separating, e.g., the Convention against Genocide from IHL (para. 153), the Court fails to perceive that the Genocide Convention, being a human rights treaty (as generally acknowledged), converges with international instruments which form the *corpus juris* of human rights. They all pertain to the determination of State responsibility.

Some grave breaches of IHL may concomitantly be breaches of the Genocide Convention.

511. This atomized approach, in several aspects, appears static and antihistorical to me, for it fails to grasp the evolution of international legal thinking in respect of the remarkable expansion, along the last decades, of international legal personality and capacity, as well as international responsibility, – a remarkable feature of the contemporary *jus gentium*. Contrary to what the ICJ says in the present Judgment, there are, in my perception, approximations and convergences between the three trends of protection of the rights of the human person (ILHR, IHL, ILR),[585] in addition to contemporary ICL.

512. Moreover, contemporary ICL nowadays is also concerned with the situation of the victims. The Convention against Genocide, for its part, being *people-oriented*, is likewise concerned with the *victims* of extreme human cruelty. The Convention is not separated (as the Court assumes) from other branches of safeguard of the rights of the human person; it rather converges with them, in seeking to protect human dignity. The Genocide Convention, by itself, bears witness of the approximations or convergences between ICL and the ILHR.

513. Last but not least, the Court's reasoning is, moreover, atomized also in its counter-position of customary and conventional IHL itself (paras. 79 and 88–89, *supra*). In my understanding, customary and conventional IHL are to be properly seen in interaction, and are not to be kept separated from each other, as the Court attempts to do. After all, there is no violation of the substantive provisions of the Genocide Convention which is not, at the same time, a violation of customary international law on the matter as well. The atomized approach of the Court, furthermore, fails to recognize the great importance – for both conventional and customary international law – of the general principles of law, and in particular of the principle of humanity.

514. The determination of State responsibility for genocide calls for a comprehensive outlook, rather than an atomized one, as pursued by the ICJ. As I pointed out earlier on, in the present Dissenting Opinion, the Genocide Convention is generally regarded as a human rights treaty, and human rights treaties have a hermeneutics of their own (para. 32), and are endowed with a mechanism of collective guarantee (para. 29). The proper hermeneutics of the Genocide Convention is, in my understanding, necessarily a comprehensive

---

585   Paras. 58, 60, 64, 69, 79 and 84, *supra*.

one, and not an atomized or fragmented one, as pursued by the ICJ in the present Judgment, as well as in its prior Judgment of 2007 in the *Bosnian Genocide* case.

515. Each international instrument is a product of its time, and exerts its function continuously by being applied as a "living instrument". I have carefully addressed this particular point, in detail, in respect of human rights treaties, in my extensive Dissenting Opinion (paras. 167-185) in the case concerning the *Application of the International Convention on the Elimination of All Forms of Racial Discrimination* – CERD (Georgia *versus* Russian Federation, Judgment of 01.04.2011).

516. In that Dissenting Opinion, I warned against the posture of the ICJ in the *CERD Convention* case, – also reflected in the present Judgment of the ICJ (para. 85), as well as in its prior Judgment in the *Bosnian Genocide* case (2007), – of ascribing an "overall importance" to individual State *consent*, "regrettably putting it well above the imperatives of the realization of justice at international level" (para. 44). The CERD Convention, like other human rights treaties, – I continued, – contains obligations of "an essentially objective character, implemented collectively", and showing that, in this domain of protection, international law appears, more than voluntary, as "indeed necessary" (paras. 63 and 72). The protected rights and fundamental human values stand above State "interests" or its "will" (paras. 139 and 162).

517. The proper hermeneutics of human rights treaties, – I proceeded in the same Dissenting Opinion, – moves away from "a strict State-centered voluntarist perspective" and from the "exaltation of State consent", and seeks guidance in fundamental principles (*prima principia*), such as the principle of humanity, which permeates the whole corpus juris of the ILHR, IHL, ILR and ICL (paras. 209-212). Such *prima principia* confer to the international legal order "its ineluctable axiological dimension"; they conform its *substratum*, and convey the idea of an *objective* justice, in the line of jusnaturalist thinking (para. 213).

518. Only in this way, – I added, – can we abide by "the imperative of the *realization of justice* at international level", acknowledging that *"conscience stands above the will"* (para. 214). And I further warned in my aforementioned Dissenting Opinion that

> The Court cannot remain hostage of State consent. It cannot keep displaying an instinctive and continuing search for State consent, (...) to

the point of losing sight of the imperative of realization of justice. The moment State consent is manifested is when the State concerned decides to become a party to a treaty, – such as the human rights treaty in the present case, the CERD Convention. The hermeneutics and proper application of that treaty cannot be continuously subjected to a recurring search for State consent. This would unduly render the letter of the treaty dead, and human rights treaties are meant to be living instruments, let alone their spirit (para. 198).

519. The present Judgment of the Court again misses the point, and fails to render a service to the *Convention against Genocide*. In a case pertaining to the interpretation and application of this latter, the Court even makes recourse to the so-called *Monetary Gold* "principle",[586] which has no place in a case like the present one, and which does not belong to the realm of the *prima principia*, being nothing more than a concession to State consent, within an outdated State voluntarist framework. In face of the pursuance of this outlook, I wonder whether the Genocide Convention has any future at all...

520. The Convention, essentially *people-centered*, will have a future if attention is rightly turned to its *rationale*, to its object and purpose, keeping in mind the principle *ut res magis valeat quam pereat*, so to secure to it the appropriate effects (*effet utile*), and, ultimately, the realization of justice. Already for some time, attention has been drawn to the shortcomings of the Convention against Genocide as originally conceived, namely: a) the narrowing of its scope, excluding cultural genocide and massive slaughter of political and social groups; b) the much lesser attention to prevention of genocide, in comparison with its punishment;[587] c) the weakening of provisions for enforcement, with concern for State sovereignty taking precedence over concern for protection against genocide.[588]

---

586   Even if only to dismiss it (para. 116).
587   As transposed, historically, from domestic into international criminal law.
588   Cf. L. Kuper, *International Action against Genocide*, London, Minority Rights Group (Report n. 53), 1982, pp. 9, 11 and 13–14; G.J. Andreopoulos, "Introduction: The Calculus of Genocide", in *Genocide: Conceptual and Historical Dimensions* (ed. G.J. Andreopoulos), Philadelphia, University of Pennsylvania Press, 1994, pp. 2–3 and 6–17; M. Lippman, "Genocide: The Crime of the Century – The Jurisprudence of Death at the Dawn of the New Millenium", 23 *Houston Journal of International Law* (2001) pp. 477–478, 487, 503–506, 523–526 and 533.

521. From the adoption of the Genocide Convention in 1948 until our days, the vulnerability or defencelessness of targeted groups has continued, just as much as the reluctance of States to deal with the matter and protect them against genocide under the Convention has persisted. This discloses, – as I have already pointed out in the present Dissenting Opinion, – the manifest inadequacy of examining genocide from a strictly inter-State outlook, with undue deferences to State sovereignty. After all, as I have already stressed, the Genocide Convention is *people-oriented*.

522. Genocide, which occurs at intra-State level, calls for a people-centered outlook, focused on the victims, surrounded by extreme vulnerability. There are, among genocide scholars, those who are sensitive enough and support a generic concept, so as not to leave without protection any segment of victims of "genocidal wars" or "genocidal massacres",[589] even beyond the Genocide Convention. It is not my intention here to dwell upon such generic concept or definition; distinctly, I concentrate, more specifically, on the comprehensive outlook, that I sustain, of genocide *under the 1948 Convention*.

523. Such comprehensive outlook takes into due account the *whole factual context* of the present case opposing Croatia to Serbia, – and not only just a sample of selected occurrences in some municipalities, as the Court's majority does. That whole factual context, in my assessment, clearly discloses a widespread and systematic pattern of destruction, – which the Court's majority seems to be at pains with, at times minimizing it, or not even taking it into account. All the aforesaid, in my own understanding, further calls for a comprehensive, rather than atomized, consideration of the matter, faithful to humanist thinking and keeping in mind the principle of humanity,[590] which permeates the whole of the ILHR, IHL, ILR and ICL, including the Genocide Convention.

524. From all the preceding considerations, it is crystal clear that my own position, in respect of the aforementioned points – of evidential assessments as well as of substance – which form the object of the present Judgment of the

---

[589] Cf., e.g., L. Kuper, "Other Selected Cases of Genocide and Genocidal Massacres: Types of Genocide", *in Genocide – A Critical Bibliographic Review* (ed. I.W. Charny), London, Mansell Publ., 1988, pp. 155–171; L. Kuper, "Theoretical Issues Relating to Genocide: Uses and Abuses", *in Genocide: Conceptual and Historical Dimensions, op cit. supra* n. (588), pp. 32–37 and 44; I.W. Charny, "Toward a Generic Definition of Genocide", *in ibid.*, pp. 64–78, 84–85 and 90–92.

[590] Cf. Part V of the present Dissenting Opinion, *supra*.

ICJ on the case concerning the *Application of the Convention against Genocide*, stands in clear opposition to the view espoused by the Court's majority. My dissenting position is grounded not only on the assessment of the arguments produced before the Court by the contending parties (Croatia and Serbia), but above all on issues of principle and on fundamental values, to which I attach even greater importance. I have thus felt obliged, in the faithful exercise of the international judicial function, to lay the foundations of my own dissenting position in the *cas d'espèce* in the present Dissenting Opinion.

XIX Epilogue: A Recapitulation

525. I deem it fit, at this final stage of my Dissenting Opinion, as an epilogue, to recapitulate all the points of my dissenting position, expressed herein, for the sake of clarity, and in order to stress their interrelatedness. *Primus*: Prolonged delays – such as the unprecedented one of 16 years in the *cas d'espèce* – in the international adjudication of cases of the kind are most regrettable, in particular from the perspective of the victims; paradoxically, the graver the breaches of international law appear to be, the more time-consuming and difficult it becomes to impart justice.

526. *Secundus*: In the *cas d'espèce*, opposing Croatia to Serbia, responsibility cannot be shifted to an extinct State; there is personal continuity of policy and practices in the period of occurrences (1991 onwards). *Tertius*: The 1948 Convention against Genocide being a human rights treaty (as generally acknowledged), the law governing State succession to human rights treaties applies (with *ipso jure* succession). *Quartus*: There can be no break in the protection afforded to human groups by the Genocide Convention in a situation of dissolution of State amidst violence, when protection is most needed.

527. *Quintus*: In a situation of this kind, there is automatic succession to, and continuing applicability of, the Genocide Convention, which otherwise would be deprived of its appropriate effects (*effet utile*). *Sextus*: Once the Court's jurisdiction is established in the initiation of proceedings, any subsequent lapse or change of attitude of the State concerned can have no bearing upon such jurisdiction. *Septimus*: Automatic succession to human rights treaties is reckoned in the practice of United Nations supervisory organs.

528. *Octavus*: The essence of the present case lies on substantive issues pertaining to the interpretation and application of the Convention against Genocide,

rather than on issues of jurisdiction/admissibility, as acknowledged by the contending Parties themselves in the course of the proceedings. *Nonus*: Automatic succession to, and continuity of obligations of, the Convention against Genocide, is an imperative of humaneness, so as to secure protection to human groups when they stand most in need of it.

529. *Decimus*: The principle of humanity permeates the whole Convention against Genocide, which is essentially *people-oriented*; it permeates the whole *corpus juris* of protection of human beings, which is essentially *victim-oriented*, encompassing also the International Law of Human Rights (ILHR), International Humanitarian Law (IHL) and the International Law of Refugees (ILR), besides contemporary International Criminal Law (ICL). *Undecimus*: The principle of humanity has a clear incidence in the protection of human beings, in particular in situations of *vulnerability* or *defencelessness*.

530. *Duodecimus*: The United Nations Charter itself professes the determination to secure respect for human rights everywhere; the principle of humanity, – in line with the longstanding jusnaturalist thinking (*recta ratio*), – permeates likewise the Law of the United Nations. *Tertius decimus*: The principle of humanity, furthermore, has met with judicial recognition, on the part of contemporary international human rights tribunals as well as international criminal tribunals.

531. *Quartus decimus*: The determination of State responsibility under the Genocide Convention not only was intended by its draftsmen (as its *travaux préparatoires* show), but also is in line with its *rationale*, as well as its object and purpose. *Quintus decimus*: The Genocide Convention is meant to prevent and punish the crime of genocide, – which is contrary to the spirit and aims of the United Nations, – so as to liberate humankind from this scourge. To attempt to make the application of the Genocide Convention an impossible task, would render the Convention meaningless, an almost dead letter.

532. *Sextus decimus*: International human rights tribunals (IACtHR and ECtHR), in their jurisprudence, have not pursued a stringent and high threshold of proof in cases of grave breaches of the rights of the human person; they have resorted to factual presumptions and inferences, as well as to the shifting or reversal of the burden of proof. *Septimus decimus*: International criminal tribunals (ICTFY and ICTR) have, in their jurisprudence, even in the absence of direct proofs, drawn proof of genocidal intent from inferences of fact.

533. *Duodevicesimus*: The fact-finding undertaken by the United Nations, at the time of the occurrences, contains important elements conforming the widespread and systematic pattern of destruction in the attacks in Croatia: such is the case of the reports of the former U.N. Commission on Human Rights (1992–1993) and of the reports of the Security Council's Commission of Experts (1993–1994). *Undevicesimus*: Those occurrences also had repercussion in the U.N. II World Conference on Human Rights (1993). There has also been judicial recognition (in the case-law of the ICTFY) of the widespread and/or systematic attacks against the Croat civilian population.

534. *Vicesimus*: Such widespread and systematic pattern of destruction, well-established in the present proceedings before the ICJ, encompassed indiscriminate attacks against the civilian population, with massive killings, torture and beatings, systematic expulsion from homes (and mass exodus), and destruction of group culture. *Vicesimus primus*: That widespread and systematic pattern of destruction also comprised rape and other sexual violence crimes, which disclose the necessity and importance of a gender analysis.

535. *Vicesimus secundus*: There was, furthermore, a systematic pattern of disappeared or missing persons. Enforced disappearance of persons is a *continuing* grave breach of human rights and International Humanitarian Law; with its destructive effects, it bears witness of the expansion of the notion of victims (so as to comprise not only the missing persons, but also their close relatives, who do not know their whereabouts). The situation created calls for a proper standard of evidence, and the shifting or reversal of the burden of proof, which cannot be laid upon those victimized.

536. *Vicesimus tertius*: The aforementioned grave breaches of human rights and of International Humanitarian Law amount to breaches of *jus cogens*, entailing State responsibility and calling for reparations to the victims. This is in line with the idea of *rectitude* (in conformity with the *recta ratio* of natural law), underlying the conception of Law (in distinct legal systems – *Droit / Right / Recht / Direito / Derecho / Diritto*) as a whole.

537. *Vicesimus quartus*: In the present case, the widespread and systematic pattern of destruction took place in pursuance of a plan, with an ideological content. In this respect, both contending Parties addressed the historical origins of the armed conflict in Croatia, and the ICTFY examined expert evidence of it. The ICJ did not find it necessary to dwell upon this; yet, the ideological

incitement leading to the outbreak of hostilities was brought to its attention by the contending Parties, as an essential element for a proper understanding of the case.

538. *Vicesimus quintus*: The evidence produced before the Court, concerning the aforementioned widespread and systematic pattern of destruction, shows that the armed attacks in Croatia were not exactly a war, but rather an onslaught. *Vicesimus sextus*: One of its manifestations was the practice of marking Croats with white ribbons, or armbands, or of placing white sheets on the doors of their homes. *Vicesimus septimus*: Another manifestation was the mistreatment by Serb forces of the mortal remains of the deceased Croats, and other successive findings in numerous mass graves, added to further clarifications obtained from the cross-examination of witnesses before the Court (in public and closed sittings).

539. *Vicesimus octavus*: The widespread and systematic pattern of destruction was also manifested in the forced displacement of persons and homelessness, and subjection of the victims to unbearable conditions of life. *Vicesimus nonus*: That pattern of destruction, approached as a whole, also comprised the destruction of cultural and religious heritage (monuments, churches, chapels, city walls, among others). It would be artificial to attempt to dissociate physical/biological destruction from the cultural one.

540. *Trigesimus*: The evidence produced before the Court in respect of selected devastated villages – Lovas, Ilok, Bogdanovci and Vukovar (in the region of Eastern Slavonia), and Saborsko (in the region of Lika), – shows that the *actus reus* of genocide (Article II(a), (b) and (c) of the Genocide Convention) – has been established. *Trigesimus primus*: Furthermore, the intent to destroy (*mens rea*) the targeted groups, in whole or in part, can be inferred from the evidence submitted (even if not direct proofs). The extreme violence in the perpetration of atrocities in the planned pattern of destruction bears witness of such intent to destroy. The inference of *mens rea* cannot prescind from axiological concerns, and is undertaken as from the *conviction intime* (*livre convencimento / libre convencimiento / libero convincimento*) of each judge, as from human conscience.

541. *Trigesimus secundus*: There is thus need of reparations to the victims, – an issue which was duly addressed by the contending Parties themselves before the Court, – to be determined by the ICJ in a subsequent phase of

the case. *Trigesimus tertius*: The difficult path to reconciliation starts with the acknowledgment that the widespread and systematic pattern of destruction ends up victimizing everyone, on both sides. The next step towards reconciliation lies in the provision of reparations (in all its forms). Reconciliation also calls for adequate apologies, honouring the memory of the victims. Another step by the contending Parties in the same direction lies in the identification and return of all mortal remains to each other.

542. *Trigesimus quartus*: The adjudication of a case like the present one shows the need to go beyond the strict inter-State outlook. The Genocide Convention is *people-centered*, and there is need to focus attention on the people or population concerned, in pursuance of a humanist outlook, in the light of the principle of humanity. In interpreting and applying the Genocide Convention, attention is to be turned to the victims, rather than to inter-State susceptibilities.

543. *Trigesimus quintus*: The Court's evidential assessment and determination of the facts of the *cas d'espèce* has to be comprehensive, and not atomized. All the atrocities, presented to the Court, conforming the aforementioned pattern of destruction, have to be taken into account, not only a sample of them, for the determination of State responsibility under the Genocide Convention. *Trigesimus sextus*: Large-scale crimes, such as rape and other sexual violence crimes, expulsion from homes (and homelessness), forced displacements, deprivation of food and medical care, cannot be minimized.

544. *Trigesimus septimus*: The Court's conceptual framework and reasoning as to the law have likewise to be comprehensive, and not atomized, so as to secure the *effet utile* of the Genocide Convention. The branches that conform the *corpus juris* of the international protection of the rights of the human person – ILHR, IHL, ILR and ICL – cannot be approached in a compartmentalized way; there are approximations and convergences among them.

545. The Genocide Convention, which is *victim-oriented*, cannot be approached in a static way, as it is a "living instrument". *Trigesimus octavus*: Customary and conventional IHL are to be properly seen in interaction, and not to be kept separately from each other. A violation of the substantive provisions of the Genocide Convention is bound to be a violation of customary international law on the matter as well. *Trigesimus nonus*: Furthermore, the interrelated elements of *actus reus* and *mens rea* of genocide cannot be approached separately either.

546. *Quadragesimus*: General principles of law (*prima principia*), and in particular the principle of humanity, are of great relevance to both conventional and customary international law. Such *prima principia* confer an ineluctable axiological dimension to the international legal order. *Quadragesimus primus*: Human rights treaties (such as the Genocide Convention) have a hermeneutics of their own, which calls for a comprehensive approach as to the facts and as to the law, and not an atomized or fragmented one.

547. *Quadragesimus secundus*: The imperative of the *realization of justice* acknowledges that conscience (*recta ratio*) stands above the "will". Consent yields to objective justice. *Quadragesimus tertius*: The Genocide Convention is concerned with human groups in situations of vulnerability or defencelessness. In its interpretation and application, fundamental principles and human values exert a relevant role. *Quadragesimus quartus*: There is here the primacy of the concern with the victims of human cruelty, as, after all, the *raison d'humanité* prevails over the *raison d'État*. *Quadragesimus quintus*: These are the foundations of my firm dissenting position in the *cas d'espèce*; in my understanding, this is what the International Court *of Justice* should have decided in the present Judgment on the case concerning the *Application of the Convention against Genocide*.

(Signed) *Antônio Augusto* CANÇADO TRINDADE
Judge

CHAPTER 3

The Universal Juridical Conscience, Humaneness and the Obligation of Nuclear Disarmament

1 Dissenting Opinion in the Case of *Obligations Concerning Negotiations Relating to Cessation of the Nuclear Arms Race and to Nuclear Disarmament* (Marshall Islands *versus* India, Jurisdiction, Judgment of 05.10.2016)

Table of Contents   Paragraphs

I. *Prolegomena* 1–4
II. The Existence of a Dispute before the Hague Court 5
    1. Objective Determination by the Court 5–15
    2. Existence of a Dispute in the *Cas d'Espèce* (case Marshall Islands *versus* India) 16–18
    3. The Threshold for the Determination of the Existence of a Dispute 19–24
    4. Contentions in the Case of Marshall Islands *versus* India 25–28
    5. General Assessment 29–32
III. U.N. General Assembly Resolutions and *Opinio Juris* 33
    1. U.N. General Assembly Resolutions on Nuclear Weapons (1961–1981) 34–39
    2. U.N. General Assembly Resolutions on Freeze of Nuclear Weapons (1982–1992) 40–42
    3. U.N. General Assembly Resolutions on Nuclear Weapons as Breach of the U.N. Charter (Acknowledgment before the ICJ, 1995) 43–46
    4. U.N. General Assembly Resolutions Condemning Nuclear Weapons (1982–2015) 47–52
    5. U.N. General Assembly Resolutions Following up the ICJ's 1996 Advisory Opinion (1996–2015) 53–58
IV. U.N. Security Council Resolutions and *Opinio Juris* 59–65
V. The Saga of the United Nations in the Condemnation of Nuclear Weapons 66–79
VI. U.N. Resolutions and the Emergence of *Opinio Juris*: The Positions of the Contending Parties 80–85
VII. Questions from the Bench and Responses from the Parties 86–92
VIII. Human Wickedness: From the XXIst Century Back to the Book of *Genesis* 93–122

IX.	The Attention of the United Nations Charter to Peoples	123–131
X.	Impertinence of the So-Called *Monetary Gold* "Principle"	132–135
XI.	The Fundamental Principle of the Juridical Equality of States	136–139
XII.	Unfoundedness of the Strategy of "Deterrence"	140–150
XIII.	The Illegality of Nuclear Weapons and the Obligation of Nuclear Disarmament	
	1. The Condemnation of All Weapons of Mass Destruction	151–156
	2. The Prohibition of Nuclear Weapons: The Need of a People-Centred Approach	157–175
	3. The Prohibition of Nuclear Weapons: The Fundamental Right to Life	176–189
	4. The Absolute Prohibitions of *Jus Cogens* and the Humanization of International Law	190–193
	5. The Pitfalls of Legal Positivism: A Rebuttal of the So-Called *Lotus* "Principle"	194–200
XIV.	Recourse to the "Martens Clause" as an Expression of the *Raison d'Humanité*	201–209
XV.	Nuclear Disarmament: Jusnaturalism, the Humanist Conception and the Universality of International Law	210–220
XVI.	The Principle of Humanity and the Universalist Approach: *Jus Necessarium* Transcending the Limitations of *Jus Voluntarium*	221–233
XVII.	NPT Review Conferences	234–249
XVIII.	The Establishment of Nuclear-Weapon-Free Zones	250–262
XIX.	Conferences on the Humanitarian Impact of Nuclear Weapons (2013–2014)	263–265
	1. First Conference on the Humanitarian Impact of Nuclear Weapons	266–270
	2. Second Conference on the Humanitarian Impact of Nuclear Weapons	271–279
	3. Third Conference on the Humanitarian Impact of Nuclear Weapons	280–291
	4. Aftermath: The "Humanitarian Pledge"	292–299
XX.	Final Considerations: *Opinio Juris Communis* Emanating from Conscience (*Recta Ratio*), Well Above the "Will"	300–314
XXI.	Epilogue: A Recapitulation	315–331

I   *Prolegomena*

1. I regret not to be able to accompany the Court's majority in the Judgment of today, 05.10.2016 in the present case of *Obligations Concerning Negotiations Relating to Cessation of the Nuclear Arms Race and to Nuclear Disarmament* (Marshall Islands *versus* India), whereby it has found that the existence of a dispute between the parties has not been established before it, and that the Court has no jurisdiction to consider the Application lodged with it by the Marshall Islands, and cannot thus proceed to the merits of the case. I entirely disagree with the present Judgment. As my dissenting position covers all points addressed in it, in its reasoning as well as in its resolutory points, I feel obliged, in the faithful exercise of the international judicial function, to lay on the records the foundations of my own position thereon.

2. In doing so, I distance myself as much as I can from the position of the Court's majority, so as to remain in peace with my conscience. I shall endeavor to make clear the reasons of my personal position on the matter addressed in the present Judgment, in the course of the present Dissenting Opinion. I shall begin by examining the question of the existence of a dispute before the Hague Court (its objective determination by the Court and the threshold for the determination of the existence of a dispute). I shall then turn attention to the distinct series of U.N. General Assembly resolutions on nuclear weapons and *opinio juris*. After surveying also U.N. Security Council resolutions and *opinio juris*, I shall dwell upon the saga of the United Nations in the condemnation of nuclear weapons. Next, I shall address the positions of the contending parties on U.N. resolutions and the emergence of *opinio juris*, and their responses to questions from the bench.

3. In logical sequence, I shall then, looking well back in time, underline the need to go beyond the strict inter-State dimension, bearing in mind the attention of the U.N. Charter to peoples. Then, after recalling the fundamental principle of the juridical equality of States, I shall dwell upon the unfoundedness of the strategy of "deterrence". My next line of considerations pertains to the illegality of nuclear weapons and the obligation of nuclear disarmament, encompassing: (a) the condemnation of all weapons of mass destruction; (b) the prohibition of nuclear weapons (the need of a people-centred approach, and the fundamental right to life); (c) the absolute prohibitions of *jus cogens* and the humanization of international law; (d) pitfalls of legal positivism.

4. This will bring me to address the recourse to the "Martens clause" as an expression of the *raison d'humanité*. My following reflections, on nuclear

disarmament, will be in the line of jusnaturalism, the humanist conception and the universality of international law; in addressing the universalist approach, I shall draw attention to the principle of humanity and the *jus necessarium* transcending the limitations of *jus voluntarium*. I shall then turn attention to the NPT Review Conferences, to the relevant establishment of nuclear-weapon-free zones, and to the Conferences on the Humanitarian Impact of Nuclear Weapons. The way will then be paved for my final considerations, on *opinio juris communis* emanating from conscience (*recta ratio*), well above the "will", – and, last but not least, to the epilogue (recapitulation).

II   The Existence of a Dispute before the Hague Court

1   *Objective Determination by the Court*

5. May I start by addressing the issue of the existence of a dispute before the Hague Court. In the *jurisprudence constante* of the Hague Court (PCIJ and ICJ), a dispute exists when there is "a disagreement on a point of law or fact, a conflict of legal views or of interests between two persons".[1] Whether there exists a dispute is a matter for "objective determination" by the Court; the "mere denial of the existence of a dispute does not prove its non-existence".[2] The Court must examine if "the claim of one party is positively opposed by the other".[3] The Court further states that "a disagreement on a point of law or fact, a conflict of legal views or interests, or the positive opposition of the claim of one party by the other need not be necessarily be stated *expressis verbis*".[4]

6. Along the last decade, the Court has deemed it fit to insist on its own faculty to proceed to the "objective determination" of the dispute. Thus, in the case of *Armed Activities on the Territory of the Congo* (D.R. Congo *versus* Rwanda, Jurisdiction and Admissibility, Judgment of 03.02.2006), for example, the ICJ has recalled that, as long ago as 1924, the PCIJ stated that "a dispute is a disagreement on a point of law or fact, a conflict of legal views or interests" (case

---

1   PCIJ, case of *Mavrommatis Palestine Concessions*, Judgment of 30.08.1924, p. 11.
2   ICJ, Advisory Opinion (of 30.03.1950) on the *Interpretation of Peace Treaties with Bulgaria, Hungary and Romania*, p. 74.
3   ICJ, *South–West Africa* cases (Ethiopia and Liberia *versus* South Africa, Judgment on Preliminary Objections of 21.12.1962), p. 328; ICJ, case of *Armed Activities on the Territory of the Congo* (New Application – 2002, D.R. Congo *versus* Rwanda, Judgment on Jurisdiction and Admissibility of 03.02.2006), p. 40, para. 90.
4   ICJ, *Land and Maritime Boundary between Cameroon and Nigeria* (Judgment on Preliminary Objections, of 11.06.1998), p. 275, para. 89.

of *Mavrommatis Palestine Concessions,* Judgment of 30.08.1924, p. 11). It then added that

> For its part, the present Court has had occasion a number of times to state the following:
> In order to establish the existence of a dispute, 'it must be shown that the claim of one party is positively opposed by the other' (*South West Africa,* Preliminary Objections, Judgment, *I.C.J. Reports 1962,* p. 328); and further, 'Whether there exists an international dispute is a matter for objective determination' (*Interpretation of Peace Treaties with Bulgaria, Hungary and Romania,* First Phase, Advisory Opinion, *I.C.J. Reports 1950,* p. 74; *East Timor* (Portugal *v.* Australia), Judgment, *I.C.J. Reports 1995,* p. 100, para. 22; *Questions of Interpretation and Application of the 1971 Montreal Convention arising from the Aerial Incident at Lockerbie* (Libyan Arab Jamahiriya *v.* United Kingdom), Preliminary Objections, Judgment, *I.C.J. Reports 1998,* p. 17, para. 22; *Questions of Interpretation and Application of the 1971 Montreal Convention arising from the Aerial Incident at Lockerbie* (Libyan Arab Jamahiriya *v.* United States of America), Preliminary Objections, Judgment, *I.C.J. Reports 1998,* pp. 122–123, para. 21; *Certain Property* (Liechtenstein *v.* Germany), Preliminary Objections, Judgment, *I.C.J. Reports 2005,* p. 18, para. 24) (para. 90).

7. Shortly afterwards, in its Judgment on Preliminary Objections (of 18.11.2008) in the case of the *Application of the Convention against Genocide* (Croatia *versus* Serbia), the ICJ has again recalled that

> In numerous cases, the Court has reiterated the general rule which it applies in this regard, namely: 'the jurisdiction of the Court must normally be assessed on the date of the filing of the act instituting proceedings' (to this effect, cf. *Application of the Convention on the Prevention and Punishment of the Crime of Genocide* (Bosnia and Herzegovina *v.* Yugoslavia), Preliminary Objections, Judgment, *I.C.J. Reports 1996 (II),* p. 613, para. 26; *Questions of Interpretation and Application of the 1971 Montreal Convention arising from the Aerial Incident at Lockerbie* (Libyan Arab Jamahiriya *v.* United Kingdom), Preliminary Objections, Judgment, *I.C.J. Reports 1998,* p. 26, para. 44). (...) (I)t is normally by reference to the date of the filing of the instrument instituting proceedings that it must be determined whether those conditions are met.
> (...) What is at stake is legal certainty, respect for the principle of equality and the right of a State which has properly seised the Court to

see its claims decided, when it has taken all the necessary precautions to submit the act instituting proceedings in time. (....) [T]he Court must in principle decide the question of jurisdiction on the basis of the conditions that existed at the time of the institution of the proceedings.

However, it is to be recalled that the Court, like its predecessor, has also shown realism and flexibility in certain situations in which the conditions governing the Court's jurisdiction were not fully satisfied when proceedings were initiated but were subsequently satisfied, before the Court ruled on its jurisdiction (paras. 79–81).

8. More recently, in its Judgment on Preliminary Objections (of 01.04.2011) in the case of the *Application of the International Convention on the Elimination of All Forms of Racial Discrimination – CERD* (Georgia *versus* Russian Federation), the ICJ has seen it fit, once again, to stress:

The Court recalls its established case law on that matter, beginning with the frequently quoted statement by the Permanent Court of International Justice in the *Mavrommatis Palestine Concessions* case in 1924: 'A dispute is a disagreement on a point of law or fact, a conflict of legal views or of interests between two persons'. (Judgment n. 2, 1924, PCIJ, Series A, n. 2, p. 11). Whether there is a dispute in a given case is a matter for 'objective determination' by the Court (*Interpretation of Peace Treaties with Bulgaria, Hungary and Romania,* First Phase, Advisory Opinion, *I.C.J. Reports 1950,* p. 74). 'It must be shown that the claim of one party is positively opposed by the other' (*South West Africa* (Ethiopia and Liberia *v.* South Africa), Preliminary Objections, Judgment, *I.C.J. Reports 1962*, p. 328); and, most recently, *Armed Activities on the Territory of the Congo* (New Application: 2002, D.R. Congo *v.* Rwanda, Jurisdiction and Admissibility, Judgment, *I.C.J. Reports 2006*, p. 40, para. 90). The Court's determination must turn on an examination of the facts. The matter is one of substance, not of form. As the Court has recognized (for example, *Land and Maritime Boundary between Cameroon and Nigeria,* Cameroon *v.* Nigeria, Preliminary Objections, Judgment, *I.C.J. Reports 1998*, p. 315, para. 89), the existence of a dispute may be inferred from the failure of a State to respond to a claim in circumstances where a response is called for. While the existence of a dispute and the undertaking of negotiations are distinct as a matter of principle, the negotiations may help demonstrate the existence of the dispute and delineate its subject-matter.

The dispute must in principle exist at the time the Application is submitted to the Court (*Questions of Interpretation and Application of the 1971*

Montreal Convention arising from the Aerial Incident at Lockerbie, Libyan Arab Jamahiriya *v.* United Kingdom, Preliminary Objections, *Judgment, I.C.J. Reports 1998*, pp. 25–26, paras. 42–44; *Questions of Interpretation and Application of the 1971 Montreal Convention arising from the Aerial Incident at Lockerbie*, Libyan Arab Jamahiriya *v.* United States of America, Preliminary Objections, Judgment, *I.C.J. Reports 1998*, pp. 130–131, paras. 42–44) (...) (para. 30).

9. This passage of the 2011 Judgment in the case of the *Application of the CERD Convention* reiterates what the ICJ has held in its *jurisprudence constante*. Yet, shortly afterwards in that same Judgment, the ICJ has decided to apply to the facts of the case a higher threshold for the determination of the existence of a dispute, by proceeding to ascertain whether the applicant State had given the respondent State prior notice of its claim and whether the respondent State had opposed it.[5] On this basis, it has concluded that no dispute had arisen between the contending parties (before August 2008). Such new requirement, however, is not consistent with the PCIJ's and the ICJ's *jurisprudence constante* on the determination of the existence of a dispute (cf. *supra*).

10. Now, in the present case of *Obligations Concerning Negotiations Relating to Cessation of the Nuclear Arms Race and to Nuclear Disarmament*, the three respondent States (India, United Kingdom and Pakistan), seek to rely on a requirement of prior notification of the claim, or the test of prior awareness of the claim of the applicant State (the Marshall Islands), for a dispute to exist under the ICJ's Statute or general international law. Yet, nowhere can such a requirement be found in the Court's *jurisprudence constante* as to the existence of a dispute: quite on the contrary, the ICJ has made clear that the position or the attitude of a party can be established by inference.[6] Pursuant to the Court's approach, it is not necessary for the respondent to oppose previously the claim by an express statement, or to express acknowledgment of the existence of a dispute.

---

5 Cf. paras. 50–105, and esp. paras. 31, 61 and 104–105, of the Court's Judgment of 01.04.2011.

6 ICJ, *Land and Maritime Boundary between Cameroon and Nigeria* (Judgment on Preliminary Objections, of 11.06.1998), p. 315, para. 89: "a disagreement on a point of law or fact, a conflict of legal views or interests, or the positive opposition of the claim of one party by the other need not necessarily be stated *expressis verbis*. In the determination of the existence of a dispute, as in other matters, the position or the attitude of a party can be established by inference, whatever the professed view of that party".

11. The respondent States in the present case have made reference to the Court's 2011 Judgment in the case of the *Application of the CERD Convention* in support of their position that prior notice of the applicant's claim is a requirement for the existence of a dispute. Already in my Dissenting Opinion (para. 161) in that case, I have criticized the Court's "formalistic reasoning" in determining the existence of a dispute, introducing a higher threshold that goes beyond the *jurisprudence constante* of the PCIJ and the ICJ itself (cf. *supra*).

12. As I pointed out in that Dissenting Opinion in the case of the *Application of the CERD Convention*,

> As to the first preliminary objection, for example, the Court spent 92 paragraphs to concede that, in its view, a legal dispute at last crystallized, on 10 August 2008 (para. 93), only *after* the outbreak of an open and declared war between Georgia and Russia! I find that truly extraordinary: the emergence of a legal dispute only *after* the outbreak of widespread violence and war! Are there disputes which are quintessentially and ontologically *legal*, devoid of any political ingredients or considerations? I do not think so. The same formalistic reasoning leads the Court, in 70 paragraphs, to uphold the second preliminary objection, on the basis of alleged (unfulfilled) 'preconditions' of its own construction, in my view at variance with its own *jurisprudence constante* and with the more lucid international legal doctrine (para. 161).

13. Half a decade later, I was hopeful that the Court would distance itself from the formalistic approach it adopted in the case of the *Application of the CERD Convention*. As it regrettably has not done so, I feel obliged to reiterate here my dissenting position on the issue, this time in the present case of *Obligations Concerning Negotiations Relating to Cessation of the Nuclear Arms Race and to Nuclear Disarmament*. In effect, there is no general requirement of prior notice of the applicant State's intention to initiate proceedings before the ICJ.[7] It should not pass unnoticed that the *purpose* of the need of determination of the existence of a dispute (and its object) before the Court is to enable this latter to exercise jurisdiction properly: it is not intended to protect the respondent State, but rather and more precisely to safeguard the proper exercise of the Court's judicial function.

---

7 Cf., to this effect, S. Rosenne, *The Law and Practice of the International Court (1920–2005)*, 4th ed., vol. III, Leiden, Nijhoff/Brill, 2006, p. 1153.

14. There is no requirement under general international law that the contending parties must first "exhaust" diplomatic negotiations before lodging a case with, and instituting proceedings before, the Court (as a precondition for the existence of the dispute). There is no such requirement in general international law, nor in the ICJ's Statute, nor in the Court's case-law. This is precisely what the ICJ held in its Judgment on Preliminary Objections (of 11.06.1998) in the case of *Land and Maritime Boundary between Cameroon and Nigeria*: it clearly stated that

> Neither in the Charter nor otherwise in international law is any general rule to be found to the effect that the exhaustion of diplomatic negotiations constitutes a precondition for a matter to be referred to the Court (para. 56).

15. The Court's statement refers to the "exhaustion" of diplomatic negotiations, – to discard the concept. In effect, there is no such a requirement in the U.N. Charter either, that negotiations would need to be resorted to or attempted. May I reiterate that the Court's determination of the existence of the dispute is not designed to protect the respondent State(s), but rather to safeguard the proper exercise of its own judicial function in contentious cases. It is thus a matter for objective determination by the Court, as it recalled in that same Judgment (para. 87), on the basis of its own *jurisprudence constante* on the matter.

2   Existence of a Dispute in the Cas d'Espèce (*Case Marshall Islands versus India*)

16. In the present case opposing the Marshall Islands to India, there were two sustained and distinct courses of conduct of the two contending parties, evidencing their distinct legal positions, which suffice for the determination of the existence of a dispute. The subject-matter of the dispute between the parties is whether India has breached its obligation under customary international law to pursue in good faith and to conclude negotiations leading to nuclear disarmament in all its aspects under effective international control.

17. The Marshall Islands contended, as to India's course of conduct, that, although India repeatedly declared its commitment to the goal of complete nuclear disarmament, having voted consistently in favour of General Assembly resolutions to that effect, when it comes to its actions (or omissions), India has maintained its nuclear arsenal.[8] To the Marshall Islands, India's course of

---

8 *Application Instituting Proceedings* of the M.I., paras. 29–34; *Memorial* of the M.I., para. 19.

conduct is incompatible with the stated objective of nuclear disarmament. The Marshall Islands expressed its opposing position in its declaration of 14.02.2014 at the Conference of Nayarit on the Humanitarian Impact of Nuclear Weapons (cf. Part XIX, *infra*).

18. In its submissions before the ICJ, India confirmed the opposition of legal views.[9] In its *Counter-Memorial*, e.g., India argued that the position of the Marshall Islands "lacks any merit whatsoever".[10] In its oral arguments before the ICJ, India denied the existence of an obligation under customary international law, as invoked by the Marshall Islands.[11] India further contended that "[d]isarmament is a Charter responsibility of the United Nations".[12] Yet, it proceeded, in its view, "the question of a dispute does not arise" in the *cas d'espèce*, as global nuclear disarmament "cannot be litigated between two States or among a handful of States", and has to be supported by, and count on the participation of, all States.[13] India then added that it is "the only State possessing nuclear weapons" that has "co-sponsored and votes for" the U.N. General Assembly resolutions on the follow-up of the 1996 ICJ's Advisory Opinion on the *Threat or Use of Nuclear Weapons*.[14]

3   *The Threshold for the Determination of the Existence of a Dispute*

19. In the present cases of *Obligations Concerning Negotiations Relating to Cessation of the Nuclear Arms Race and to Nuclear Disarmament* (Marshall Islands *versus* India/United Kingdom/Pakistan), the Court's majority has unduly heightened the threshold for establishing the existence of a dispute. Even if dismissing the need for an applicant State to provide notice of a dispute, in practice, the requirement stipulated goes far beyond giving notice: the Court effectively requires an applicant State to set out its legal claim, to direct it specifically to the prospective respondent State(s), and to make the alleged harmful conduct clear. All of this forms part of the "awareness" requirement that the Court's majority has laid down, seemingly undermining its own ability to

---

9   Cf. India's letter of 06.06.2014, *cit. in*: *Memorial* of the M.I., para. 20.
10 *Counter-Memorial* of India, para. 6.
11 Cf., e.g., ICJ doc. CR 2016/8, of 16.03.2016, p. 36, para. 5, for the argument that the M.I. "is attempting to impose a legal obligation on India based on an imaginary principle of parallel customary law distinct from Article VI of the NPT", while providing "no source for this principle".
12 As indicated by its Articles 11, 26 and 47(1); ICJ, doc. 2016/4, of 10.03.2016, p. 13, para. 2 (statement of India).
13 *Ibid.*, p. 19, paras. 11–12.
14 *Ibid.*, p. 19, para. 1; and cf. *ibid.*, p. 16, para. 6.

infer the existence of a dispute from the conflicting courses of conduct of the contending parties.

20. This is not in line with the ICJ's previous *obiter dicta* on inference, contradicting it. For example, in the aforementioned case of *Land and Maritime Boundary between Cameroon and Nigeria* (1998), the ICJ stated that

> [A] disagreement on a point of law or fact, a conflict of legal views or interests, or the positive opposition of the claim of one party by the other need not necessarily be stated *expressis verbis*. In the determination of the existence of a dispute, as in other matters, the position or attitude of a party can be established by inference, whatever the professed view of that party (para. 89).

21. The view taken by the Court's majority in the present case contradicts the Hague Court's (PCIJ and ICJ) own earlier case-law, in which it has taken a much less formalistic approach to the establishment of the existence of a dispute. Early in its life, the PCIJ made clear that it did not attach much importance to "matters of form";[15] it added that it could not "be hampered by a mere defect of form".[16] The PCIJ further stated that "the manifestation of the existence of the dispute in a specific manner, as for instance by diplomatic negotiations, is not required. (...) [T]he Court considers that it cannot require that the dispute should have manifested itself in a formal way".[17]

22. The ICJ has, likewise, in its own case-law, avoided to take a very formalistic approach to the determination of the existence of a dispute.[18] May I recall,

---

15 PCIJ, case of *Mavrommatis Palestine Concessions*, Judgment of 30.08.1924, p. 34.
16 PCIJ, case of *Certain German Interests in Polish Upper Silesia* case (Jurisdiction), Judgment of 25.08.1925, p. 14.
17 PCIJ, case of *Interpretation of Judgments ns. 7 and 8 – Chorzów Factory*, Judgment of 16.12.1927, pp. 10–11.
18 Cf., e.g., ICJ, Advisory Opinion (of 26.04.1988) on the *Applicability of the Obligation to Arbitrate under Section 21 of the U.N. Headquarters Agreement of 26.06.1947*, pp. 28–29, para. 38; ICJ, case of *Nicaragua versus United States* (Jurisdiction and Admissibility), Judgment of 26.11.1984, pp. 428–429, para. 83. Moreover, the critical date for the determination of the existence of a dispute is, "in principle" (as the ICJ says), the date on which the application is submitted to the Court (ICJ, case of *Questions Relation to the Obligation to Prosecute or Extradite*, Judgment of 20.07.2012, p. 20, para. 46; ICJ, case of *Alleged Violations of Sovereign Rights and Maritime Spaces in the Caribbean Sea*, Preliminary Objections, Judgment of 17.03.2016, p. 25, para. 52); the ICJ's phraseology shows that this is not a strict rule, but rather one to be approached with flexibility.

in this respect, *inter alia*, as notable examples, the Court's *obiter dicta* on the issue, in the cases of *East Timor* (Portugal *versus* Australia), of the *Application of the Convention against Genocide* (Bosnia *versus* Yugoslavia), and of *Certain Property* (Liechtenstein *versus* Germany). In those cases, the ICJ has considered that conduct post-dating the critical date (i.e., the date of the filing of the Application) supports a finding of the existence of a dispute between the parties. In the light of this approach taken by the ICJ itself in its earlier case-law, it is clear that a dispute exists in each of the present cases lodged with it by the Marshall Islands.

23. In the case of *East Timor* (1995), in response to Australia's preliminary objection that there was no dispute between itself and Portugal, the Court stated: "Portugal has, rightly or wrongly, formulated complaints of fact and law against Australia which the latter has denied. By virtue of this denial, there is a legal dispute".[19] Shortly afterwards, in the case of the *Application of the Convention against Genocide* (Preliminary Objections, 1996), in response to Yugoslavia's preliminary objection that the Court did not have jurisdiction under Article IX of the Convention against Genocide because there was no dispute between the Parties, the Court, contrariwise, found that there was a dispute between them, on the basis that Yugoslavia had "wholly denied all of Bosnia and Herzegovina's allegations, whether at the stage of proceedings relating to the requests for the indication of provisional measures, or at the stage of the (...) proceedings relating to [...preliminary] objections".[20] Accordingly, "by reason of the rejection by Yugoslavia of the complaints formulated against it",[21] the ICJ found that there was a dispute.

24. In the case of *Certain Property* (Preliminary Objections, 2005), as to Germany's preliminary objection that there was no dispute between the parties, the ICJ found that complaints of fact and law formulated by Liechtenstein were denied by Germany; accordingly, "[i]n conformity with well-established jurisprudence", – the ICJ concluded, – "by virtue of this denial", there was a legal dispute between Liechtenstein and Germany.[22] Now, in the present

---

19 ICJ, case of *East Timor* (Portugal *versus* Australia), *I.C.J. Reports 1995*, p. 100, para. 22 (Judgment of 30.06.1995).

20 ICJ, case of the *Application of the Convention against Genocide* (Bosnia–Herzegovina *versus* Yugoslavia, Preliminary Objections, Judgment of 11.07.1996), *I.C.J. Reports 1996*, pp. 595 and 614–615, paras. 27–29.

21 *Ibid.*, p. 615, para. 29.

22 ICJ, case of *Certain Property* (Liechtenstein *versus* Germany, Preliminary Objections, Judgment of 10.02.2005), *I.C.J. Reports 2005*, p. 19, para. 25, citing the Court's Judgments in the cases of *East Timor*, *I.C.J. Reports 1995*, p. 100, para. 22; and of the *Application of the Convention against Genocide* (Preliminary Objections), *I.C.J. Reports 1996*, p. 615, para. 29.

proceedings before the Court, in each of the three cases lodged with the ICJ by the Marshall Islands (against India, the United Kingdom and Pakistan), the respondent States have expressly denied the arguments of the Marshall Islands. May we now take note of the denials which, on the basis of the Court's aforementioned *jurisprudence constante*, evidence the existence of a dispute between the contending parties.[23]

4 Contentions in the Case of *Marshall Islands* versus *India*

25. The Marshall Islands argues that India has breached the customary international law obligation to negotiate nuclear disarmament in good faith by engaging in a course of conduct that is contrary to the objective of disarmament. The Marshall Islands further argues that India, by its conduct, has breached the customary international law obligation regarding the cessation of the nuclear arms race at an early date.[24] For its part, in its *Counter-Memorial*, India discloses that there is a dispute between the Parties, first, as to whether a customary international law obligation to negotiate disarmament exists, and, secondly, as to whether, by its own conduct, it has breached such an obligation.

26. In effect, India denies the formation of customary international law obligations rooted in the NPT, and also denies the application of any such obligation to itself. The terms in which India does so are very clear:

> In reality the RMI blames India for not complying with Article VI of the NPT on the nature and scope of which there is no agreement within the NPT and with which purportedly there has been no compliance by the States Parties to that Treaty for 45 years. The said obligation therefore cannot acquire customary law character imposing an obligation on a non-State party who has persistently objected to the treaty itself and the obligations contained thereunder (...).[25]

27. Still in its *Counter-Memorial*, India contends that "any suggestion of the existence of a jurisdiction to compel States to accept obligations under a Treaty – in whole or in part – does not vest in this Court, and any invitation to cast upon States obligations other than those that flow from clear and well

---

23 As the present proceedings relate to jurisdiction, the opposition of views is captured in the various jurisdictional objections; it would be even more forceful in pleadings on the merits, which, given the Court's majority decision, will regrettably no longer take place.

24 *Application Instituting Proceedings* of the M.I., pp. 22–23, paras. 58 and 60.

25 *Counter-Memorial* of India, p. 41, para. 93(iii).

defined principles of customary international law would seriously erode the principle of sovereignty of States".[26] India thus makes it clear that it considers that the obligations asserted by the Marshall Islands are not well defined principles of customary international law. This directly contradicts the Marshall Islands' position on the matter.

28. Furthermore, in its oral arguments, India states that "[t]he RMI is attempting to impose a legal obligation on India based on an imaginary principle of parallel customary law distinct from Article VI of the NPT. The RMI provides no source for this principle".[27] As to the contention as to whether India has breached its customary international law obligations by its conduct, in its argument on the absence of a dispute, India argues that it is a supporter of nuclear disarmament; accordingly, it denies the Marshall Islands' arguments regarding its conduct.[28]

5 General Assessment

29. Always attentive and over-sensitive to the position of nuclear-weapon States [NWS] (cf. Part XIII, *infra*), – such as the respondent States in the present cases of *Obligations Concerning Negotiations Relating to Cessation of the Nuclear Arms Race and to Nuclear Disarmament* (India, United Kingdom and Pakistan), – the Court, in the *cas d'espèce*, dismisses the statements made by the Marshall Islands in multilateral *fora* before the filing of the Application, as being, in its view, insufficient to determine the existence of a dispute. Moreover, the Court's majority makes *tabula rasa* of the requirement that "in principle" the date for determining the existence of the dispute is the date of filing of the application (case of *Alleged Violations of Sovereign Rights and Maritime Spaces in the Caribbean Sea*, Nicaragua *versus* Colombia, Preliminary Objections, Judgment of 17.03.2016, para. 52); as already seen, in its case-law the ICJ has taken into account conduct post-dating that critical date (cf. *supra*).

---

26 *Counter-Memorial* of India, p. 15, para. 24.
27 ICJ, doc. CR 2016/8, of 16.03.2016, p. 36, para. 5.
28 For example, India states that:
   "While asserting that RMI's position lacks any merit whatsoever, it is necessary at the outset to set out India's position in the matter of nuclear disarmament and nuclear proliferation.
   India explained in its Letter of 6 June 2014, it is 'committed to the goal of a nuclear weapon free world through global, verifiable and non-discriminatory nuclear disarmament'".
   India's *Counter-Memorial*, p. 4, paras. 6–7, and cf. pp. 4–10, wherein India argues that its conduct supports disarmament.

30. In an entirely formalistic reasoning, the Court borrows the *obiter dicta* it made in the case of the *Application of the* CERD *Convention* (2011), – unduly elevating the threshold for the determination of the existence of a dispute, – in respect of a compromissory clause under that Convention (wrongly interpreted anyway, making abstraction of the object and purpose of the CERD Convention). In the present case, opposing the Marshall Islands to India, worse still, the Court's majority takes that higher standard out of context, and applies it herein, in a case lodged with the Court on the basis of an optional clause declaration, and concerning an obligation under customary international law.

31. This attempt to heighten still further the threshold for the determination of the existence of a dispute (requiring further factual precisions from the applicant) is, besides formalistic, artificial: it does not follow from the definition of a dispute in the Court's *jurisprudence constante*, as being "a conflict of legal views or of interests", as already seen (cf. *supra*). The Court's majority formalistically requires a specific reaction of the respondent State to the claim made by the applicant State (in applying the criterion of "awareness", amounting, in my perception, to an obstacle to access to justice), even in a situation where, as in the *cas d'espèce*, there are two consistent and distinct courses of conduct on the part of the contending parties.

32. Furthermore, and in conclusion, there is a clear denial by the respondent States (India, United Kingdom and Pakistan) of the arguments made against them by the applicant State, the Marshall Islands. By virtue of these denials there is a legal dispute between the Marshall Islands and each of the three respondent States. The formalistic raising, by the Court's majority, of the higher threshold for the determination of the existence of a dispute, is not in conformity with the *jurisprudence constante* of the PCIJ and ICJ on the matter (cf. *supra*). Furthermore, in my perception, it unduly creates a difficulty for the very *access to justice* (by applicants) at international level, in a case on a matter of concern to the whole of humankind. This is most regrettable.

III   U.N. General Assembly Resolutions and *Opinio Juris*

33. In the course of the proceedings in the present cases of *Obligations Concerning Negotiations Relating to Cessation of the Nuclear Arms Race and to Nuclear Disarmament*, both the applicant State (the Marshall Islands) and the respondent States (India, United Kingdom and Pakistan) addressed U.N.

General Assembly resolutions on the matter of nuclear disarmament (cf. Part VI, *infra*). This is the point that I purport to consider, in sequence, in the present Dissenting Opinion, namely, in addition to the acknowledgment before the ICJ (1995) of the authority and legal value of General Assembly resolutions on nuclear weapons as breach of the U.N. Charter, the distinct series of: (a) U.N. General Assembly resolutions on Nuclear Weapons (1961–1981); (b) UN General Assembly Resolutions on Freeze of Nuclear Weapons (1982–1992); (c) U.N. General Assembly Resolutions Condemning Nuclear Weapons (1982–2015); (d) U.N. General Assembly Resolutions Following up the ICJ's 1996 Advisory Opinion (1996–2015).

1 *U.N. General Assembly Resolutions on Nuclear Weapons (1961–1981)*

34. The 1970s was the First Disarmament Decade: it was so declared by General Assembly resolution A/RES/2602 E (XXIV) of 16.12.1969, followed by two other resolutions of 1978 and 1980 on non-use of nuclear weapons and prevention of nuclear war.[29] The General Assembly specifically called upon States to intensify efforts for the cessation of the nuclear arms race, nuclear disarmament and the elimination of other weapons of mass destruction. Even before that, the ground-breaking General Assembly resolution 1653 (XVI), of 24.11.1961, advanced its *célèbre* "Declaration on the Prohibition of the Use of Nuclear and Thermonuclear Weapons" (cf. Part V, *infra*). In 1979, when the First Disarmament Decade was coming to an end, the General Assembly, – disappointed that the objectives of the first Decade had not been realized, – declared the 1980s as a Second Disarmament Decade.[30] Likewise, the 1990s were subsequently declared the Third Disarmament Decade.[31]

35. In this first period under review (1961–1981), the U.N. General Assembly paid continuously special attention to disarmament issues and to nuclear disarmament in particular. May I refer to General Assembly resolutions A/RES/2934 of 29.11.1972; A/RES/2936 of 29.11.1972; A/RES/3078 of 06.12.1973; A/RES/3257 of 09.12.1974; A/RES/3466 of 11.12.1975; A/RES/3478 of 11.12.1975; A/RES/31/66 of 10.12.1976; A/RES/32/78 of 12.12.1977; A/RES/33/71 of 14.12.1978; A/RES/33/72 of 14.12.1978; A/RES/33/91 of 16.12.1978; A/RES/34/83 of 11.12.1979;

---

29 Namely, in sequence, General Assembly resolutions A/RES/33/71B of 14.12.1978, and A/RES/35/152D of 12.12.1980.
30 Cf. General Assembly resolutions A/RES/34/75 of 11.12.1979, and A/RES/35/46 of 03.12.1980.
31 Cf. General Assembly resolutions A/RES/43/78L of 07.12.1988, and A/RES/45/62 A of 04.12.1990.

A/RES/34/84 of 11.12.1979; A/RES/34/85 of 11.12.1979; A/RES/34/86 of 11.12.1979; A/RES/35/152 of 12.12.1980; A/RES/35/155 of 12.12.1980; A/RES/35/156 of 12.12.1980; A/RES/36/81 of 09.12.1981; A/RES/36/84 of 09.12.1981; A/RES/36/92 of 09.12.1981; A/RES/36/94 of 09.12.1981; A/RES/36/95 of 09.12.1981; A/RES/36/97 of 09.12.1981; and A/RES/36/100 of 09.12.1981.

36. In 1978 and 1982, the U.N. General Assembly held two Special Sessions on Nuclear Disarmament (respectively, the 10th and 12th sessions), where the question of nuclear disarmament featured prominently amongst the themes discussed. In fact, it was stressed that the most immediate goal of disarmament is the elimination of the danger of a nuclear war. In a subsequent series of its resolutions (in the following period of 1982–2015), as we shall see, the General Assembly moved on straightforwardly to the condemnation of nuclear weapons (cf. *infra*).

37. In its resolutions adopted during the present period of 1972–1981, the General Assembly repeatedly drew attention to the dangers of the nuclear arms race for humankind and the survival of civilization and expressed apprehension concerning the harmful consequences of nuclear testing for the acceleration of such arms race. Thus, the General Assembly reiterated its condemnation of all nuclear weapon tests, in whatever environment they may be conducted. It called upon States that had not yet done so to adhere to the 1963 Test Ban Treaty (banning nuclear tests in the atmosphere, in outer space and under water) and called for the conclusion of a comprehensive test ban treaty, which would ban nuclear weapons tests in all environments (e.g. underground as well). Pending the conclusion of such treaty, it urged NWS to suspend nuclear weapon tests in all environments.

38. The General Assembly also emphasised that NWS bear a special responsibility for fulfilling the goal of achieving nuclear disarmament, and in particular those nuclear weapon States that are parties to international agreements in which they have declared their intention to achieve the cessation of the nuclear arms race. It further called specifically on the heads of State of the USSR and the United States to implement the procedures for the entry into force of the Strategic Arms Limitation agreement (so-called "SALT" agreement).

39. At the 84th plenary meeting, following the 10th Special Session on Disarmament, the General Assembly declared that the use of nuclear weapons is a "violation of the Charter of the United Nations" and "a crime against humanity", and that the use of nuclear weapons should be prohibited, pending nuclear

disarmament.[32] The General Assembly further noted the aspiration of non-nuclear-weapon States [NNWS] to prevent nuclear weapons from being stationed on their territories through the establishment of nuclear-weapon-free zones, and supported their efforts to conclude an international Convention strengthening the guarantees for their security against the use or threat of use of nuclear weapons. As part of the measures to facilitate the process of nuclear disarmament and the non-proliferation of nuclear weapons, it requested the Committee on Disarmament to consider the question of the cessation and prohibition of the production of fissionable material for weapons purposes.

2   *U.N. General Assembly Resolutions on Freeze of Nuclear Weapons (1982–1992)*

40. Every year in the successive period 1982–1992 (following up on the 10th and 12th Special Sessions on Nuclear Disarmament, held in 1978 and 1982, respectively), the General Assembly adopted resolutions also calling for a nuclear-weapons freeze. May I refer to General Assembly resolutions A/RES/37/100A of 13.12.1982; A/RES/38/73E of 15.12.1983; A/RES/39/63C of 12.12.1984; A/RES/40/151C of 16.12.1985; A/RES/41/60E of 03.12.1986; A/RES/42/39B of 30.11.1987; A/RES/43/76B of 07.12.1988; A/RES/44/117D of 15.12.1989; A/RES/45/59D of 04.12.1990; A/RES/46/37C of 06.12.1991; and A/RES/47/53E of 09.12.1992.

41. These resolutions on freeze of nuclear weapons note that existing arsenals of nuclear weapons are more than sufficient to destroy all life on earth. They express the conviction that lasting world peace can be based only upon the achievement of general and complete disarmament, under effective international control. In this connection, the aforementioned General Assembly resolutions note that the highest priority objectives in the field of disarmament have to be nuclear disarmament and the elimination of all weapons of mass destruction. They at last call upon NWS to agree to reach "a freeze on nuclear weapons", which would, *inter alia*, provide for "a simultaneous total stoppage of any further production of fissionable material for weapons purposes".

42. Such nuclear-weapons freeze is not seen as an end in itself but as the most effective first step towards: (a) halting any further increase and qualitative improvement in the existing arsenals of nuclear weapons; and (b) activating negotiations for the substantial reduction and qualitative limitation of nuclear

---

32   Cf. General Assembly resolutions A/RES/33/71B of 14.12.1978, and A/RES/35/152D of 12.12.1980.

weapons. From 1989 onwards, these resolutions also set out the structure and scope of the prospective joint declaration through which all nuclear-weapons States would agree on a nuclear-arms freeze. Such freeze would encompass: (a) a comprehensive test ban; (b) cessation of the manufacture of nuclear weapons; (c) a ban on all further deployment of nuclear weapons; and (d) cessation of the production of fissionable material for weapons purposes.

3 U.N. *General Assembly Resolutions on Nuclear Weapons as Breach of the U.N. Charter* (*Acknowledgment before the ICJ, 1995*)

43. Two decades ago, when U.N. General Assembly resolutions condemning nuclear weapons were not as numerous as they are today, they were already regarded as authoritative in the views of States from distinct continents. This was made clear, e.g., by States which participated in the advisory proceedings of 30 October to 15 November 1995 before the ICJ, conducive to its Advisory Opinion of 08.07.1996 on the *Threat or Use of Nuclear Weapons*. On the occasion, the view was upheld that those General Assembly resolutions expressed a "general consensus" and had a relevant "legal value".[33] Resolution 1653 (XVI), of 1961, e.g., was invoked as a "law-making" resolution of the General Assembly, in stating that the use of nuclear weapons is contrary to the letter and spirit, and aims, of the United Nations, and, as such, a "direct violation" of the U.N. Charter.[34]

44. It was further stated that, already towards the end of 1995, "numerous" General Assembly resolutions and declarations confirmed the illegality of the use of force, including nuclear weapons.[35] Some General Assembly resolutions (1653 (XVI), of 24.11.1961; 33/71B of 14.12.1978; 34/83G of 11.12.1979; 35/152D of 12.12.1980; 36/92I of 09.12.1981; 45/59B of 04.12.1990; 46/37D of 06.12.1991) were singled out for having significantly declared that the use of nuclear weapons would be a violation of the U.N. Charter itself.[36] The view was expressed that the series of General Assembly resolutions (starting with resolution 1653 (XVI), of 24.11.1961) amounted to "an authoritative interpretation" of humanitarian law treaties as well as the U.N. Charter.[37]

---

33   ICJ, doc. CR 95/25, of 03.11.1995, pp. 52–53 (statement of Mexico).
34   ICJ, doc. CR 95/22, of 30.10.1995, pp. 44–45 (statement of Australia).
35   ICJ, doc. CR 95/26, of 06.11.1995, pp. 23–24 (statement of Iran).
36   ICJ, doc. CR 95/28, of 09.11.1995, pp. 62–63 (statement of the Philippines).
37   ICJ, doc. CR 95/31, of 13.11.1995, p. 46 (statement of Samoa).

45. In the advisory proceedings of 1995 before the ICJ, it was further recalled that General Assembly resolution 1653 (XVI) of 1961 was adopted in the form of a declaration, being thus "an assertion of the law", and, ever since, the General Assembly's authority to adopt such declaratory resolutions (in condemnation of nuclear weapons) was generally accepted; such resolutions declaring the use of nuclear weapons "unlawful" were regarded as ensuing from the exercise of an "inherent" power of the General Assembly.[38] The relevance of General Assembly resolutions has been reckoned by large groups of States[39]

46. Ever since the aforementioned acknowledgment of the authority and legal value of General Assembly resolutions in the course of the pleadings of late 1995 before the ICJ, those resolutions continue to grow in number until today, clearly forming, in my perception, an *opinio juris communis* as to nuclear disarmament. In addition to those aforementioned, may I also review, in sequence, two other series of General Assembly resolutions, extending to the present, namely: the longstanding series of General Assembly resolutions condemning nuclear weapons (1982–2015), and the series of General Assembly resolutions following up the ICJ's 1996 Advisory Opinion (1997–2015).

4   *U.N. General Assembly Resolutions Condemning Nuclear Weapons (1982–2015)*

47. In the period 1982–2015, there is a long series of U.N. General Assembly resolutions condemning nuclear weapons. May I refer to General Assembly resolutions A/RES/37/100C of 09.12.1982; A/RES/38/73G of 15.12.1983; A/RES/39/63H of 12.12.1984; A/RES/40/151F of 16.12.1985; A/RES/41/60F of 03.12.1986; A/RES/42/39C of 30.11.1987; A/RES/43/76E of 07.12.1988; A/RES/44/117C of 15.12.1989; A/RES/45/59B of 04.12.1990; A/RES/46/37D of 06.12.1991; A/RES/47/53C of 09.12.1992; A/RES/48/76B of 16.12.1993; A/RES/49/76E of 15.12.1994; A/RES/50/71E of 12.12.1995; A/RES/51/46D of 10.12.1996; A/RES/52/39C of 09.12.1997; A/RES/53/78D of 04.12.1998; A/RES/54/55D of 01.12.1999; A/RES/55/34G of 20.11. 2000; A/RES/56/25B of 29.11.2001; A/RES/57/94 of 22.11.2002; A/RES/58/64 of 08.12.2003; A/RES/59/102 of 03.12.2004; A/RES/60/88 of 08.12.2005; A/RES/61/97 of 06.12.2006; A/RES/62/51 of 05.12.2007; A/RES/63/75 of 02.02.2008; A/RES/64/59 of 02.12.2009; A/RES/65/80 of 08.12.2010; A/RES/66/57 of 02.12.2011; A/RES/67/64 of 03.12.2012; A/RES/68/58 of 05.12.2013; A/RES/69/69 of 02.12.2014; and A/RES/70/62 of 07.12.2015.

---

38   ICJ, doc. CR 95/27, of 07.11.1995, pp. 58–59 (statement of Malaysia).
39   Cf., e.g., ICJ, doc. CR 95/35, of 15.11.1995, p. 34, and cf. p. 22 (statement of Zimbabwe, on its initiative as Chair of the Non-Aligned Movement).

48. In those resolutions, the General Assembly warned against the threat by nuclear weapons to the survival of humankind. They were preceded by two ground-breaking historical resolutions, namely, General Assembly resolution 1(I) of 24.01.1946, and General Assembly resolution 1653 (XVI), of 24.11.1961 (cf. *infra*). In this new and long series of resolutions condemning nuclear weapons (1982–2015), at the opening of their preambular paragraphs the General Assembly states, year after year, that it is

> *Alarmed* by the threat to the survival of mankind and to the life-sustaining system posed by nuclear weapons and by their use, inherent in the concepts of deterrence,
> *Convinced* that nuclear disarmament is essential for the prevention of nuclear war and for the strengthening of international peace and security,
> *Further convinced* that a prohibition of the use or threat of use of nuclear weapons would be a step towards the complete elimination of nuclear weapons leading to general and complete disarmament under strict and effective international control.

49. Those General Assembly resolutions next significantly *reaffirm*, in their preambular paragraphs, year after year, that

> the use of nuclear weapons would be a violation of the Charter of the United Nations and a crime against humanity, as declared in its resolutions 1653 (XVI) of 24.11.1961, 33/71B of 14.12.1978, 34/83G of 11.12.1979, 35/152D of 12.12.1980 and 36/92I of 09.12.1981.

50. Still in their preambular paragraphs, those General Assembly resolutions further *note with regret* the inability of the Conference on Disarmament to undertake negotiations with a view to achieving agreement on a nuclear disarmament Convention during each previous year. In their operative part, those resolutions reiterate, year after year, the request that the Committee on Disarmament undertakes, on a priority basis, negotiations aiming at achieving agreement on an international Convention prohibiting the use or threat of use of nuclear weapons under any circumstances, taking as a basis the text of the draft Convention on the Prohibition of the Use of Nuclear Weapons.

51. From 1989 (44th session) onwards, those resolutions begin to note specifically that a multilateral agreement prohibiting the use or threat of use of nuclear weapons should strengthen international security and help to create the climate for negotiations leading to the complete elimination of nuclear

weapons. Subsequently, those resolutions come to stress, in particular, that an international Convention would be a step towards the complete elimination of nuclear weapons, leading to general and complete disarmament, under strict and effective international control.

52. Clauses of the kind then evolve, from 1996 onwards,[40] to refer expressly to a time framework, i.e., that an international Convention would be an important step in a phased programme towards the complete elimination of nuclear weapons, within a specific framework of time. More recent resolutions also expressly refer to the determination to achieve an international Convention prohibiting the development, production, stockpiling and use of nuclear weapons, leading to their ultimate destruction.

5 U.N. *General Assembly Resolutions Following up the ICJ's 1996 Advisory Opinion (1996–2015)*

53. Ever since the delivery, on 08.07.1996, of the ICJ's Advisory Opinion on *Nuclear Weapons* to date, the General Assembly has been adopting a series of resolutions (1996–2015), as its follow up. May I refer to General Assembly resolutions A/RES/51/45 of 10.12.1996; A/RES/52/38 of 09.12.1997; A/RES/53/77 of 04.12.1998; A/RES/54/54 of 01.12.1999; A/RES/55/33 of 20.11.2000; A/RES/56/24 of 29.11.2001; A/RES/57/85 of 22.11.2002; A/RES/58/46 of 08.12.2003; A/RES/59/83 of 03.12.2004; A/RES/60/76 of 08.12.2005; A/RES/61/83 of 06.12.2006; A/RES/62/39 of 05.12.2007; A/RES/63/49 of 02.12.2008; A/RES/64/55 of 02.12.2009; A/RES/65/76 of 08.12.2010; A/RES/66/46 of 02.12.2011; A/RES/67/33 of 03.12.2012; A/RES/68/42 of 05.12.2013; A/RES/69/43 of 02.12.2014; and A/RES/70/56 of 07.12.2015. These resolutions make a number of significant statements.

54. The series of aforementioned General Assembly resolutions on follow-up to the 1996 Advisory Opinion of the ICJ (1996–2015) begins by expressing the General Assembly's belief that "the continuing existence of nuclear weapons poses a threat to humanity" and that "their use would have catastrophic consequences for all life on earth", and, further, that "the only defence against a nuclear catastrophe is the total elimination of nuclear weapons and the certainty that they will never be produced again" (2nd preambular paragraph). The General Assembly resolutions reiteratedly reaffirm "the commitment of the international community to the realization of the goal of a nuclear-weapon-free world through the total elimination of nuclear weapons" (3rd preambular paragraph). They recall their request to the Conference on Disarmament to

---

40 Cf., e.g., *inter alia*, General Assembly resolution A/RES/50/71E, of 12.12.1995.

establish an *ad hoc* Committee to commence negotiations on a phased programme of nuclear disarmament, aiming at the elimination of nuclear weapons, within a "time bound framework"; they further reaffirm the role of the Conference on Disarmament as the single multilateral disarmament negotiating forum.

55. The General Assembly then recalls, again and again, that "the solemn obligations of States Parties, undertaken in Article VI of the Treaty on the Non-Proliferation of Nuclear Weapons (NPT), particularly to pursue negotiations in good faith on effective measures relating to cessation of the nuclear arms race at an early date and to nuclear disarmament" (4th preambular paragraph). They express the goal of achieving a legally binding prohibition on the development, production, testing, deployment, stockpiling, threat or use of nuclear weapons, and their destruction under "effective international control". They significantly call upon *all States* to fulfil promptly the obligation leading to an early conclusion of a Convention prohibiting the development, production, testing, deployment, stockpiling, transfer, threat or use of nuclear weapons and providing for their elimination.[41]

56. Those resolutions (from 2003 onwards) express deep concern at the lack of progress made in the implementation of the "thirteen steps" agreed to, at the 2000 Review Conference, for the implementation of Article VI of the NPT. The aforementioned series of General Assembly resolutions include, from 2010 onwards, an additional (6th) preambular paragraph, expressing "deep concern at the catastrophic humanitarian consequences of any use of nuclear weapons", and reaffirming, in this context, "the need for all States at all times to comply with applicable international law, including international humanitarian law". Those follow-up General Assembly resolutions further recognize "with satisfaction that the Antarctic Treaty, the Treaties of Tlatelolco, Rarotonga, Bangkok and Pelindaba, and the Treaty on a Nuclear-Weapon-Free Zone in Central Asia, as well as Mongolia's nuclear-weapon-free status, are gradually freeing the entire southern hemisphere and adjacent areas covered by those treaties from nuclear weapons" (10th preambular paragraph).

57. More recent resolutions (from 2013 onwards) are significantly further expanded. They call upon all NWS to undertake concrete disarmament efforts,

---

41   Note that in earlier resolutions, the following year is explicitly referenced, i.e., States should commence negotiations in "the following year". This reference is removed in later resolutions.

THE UNIVERSAL JURIDICAL CONSCIENCE, HUMANENESS   259

stressing that all States need to make special efforts to achieve and maintain a world without nuclear weapons. They also take note of the "Five-Point Proposal on Nuclear Disarmament" made by the U.N. Secretary-General (cf. Part XVII, *infra*), and recognize the need for a multilaterally negotiated and legally binding instrument to assure that NNWS States stand against the threat or use of nuclear weapons, pending the total elimination of nuclear weapons. In their operative part, the same series of General Assembly resolutions underline the ICJ's unanimous conclusion, in its 1996 Advisory Opinion on the *Threat or Use of Nuclear Weapons*, that "there exists an obligation to pursue in good faith and bring to a conclusion negotiations leading to nuclear disarmament in all its aspects under strict and effective international control" (para. 1).

58. Looking at this particular series of General Assembly follow-up resolutions as a whole, it should not pass unnoticed that they contain paragraphs referring to the obligation to pursue and conclude, in good faith, negotiations leading to nuclear disarmament, without any reference to the NPT or to States Parties to it. They rather refer to that obligation as a general one, not grounded on any treaty provision. *All States*, and not only States Parties to the NPT, are called upon to fulfil promptly that obligation, incumbent upon *all States*, to report (to the Secretary-General) on their compliance with the resolutions at issue. There are, notably, other paragraphs in those resolutions that are specifically directed at nuclear-weapon States, or make specific references to the NPT. In sum, references to *all States* are deliberate, and in the absence of any references to a treaty or other specifically-imposed international obligation, this thus points towards a customary law obligation to negotiate and achieve nuclear disarmament.

IV   U.N. Security Council Resolutions and *Opinio Juris*

59. Like the U.N. General Assembly, the U.N. Security Council has also often dwelt upon the matter at issue. May I refer, *inter alia*, to Security Council resolutions S/23500, of 31.01.1992; S/RES/984, of 11.04.1995; S/RES/1540, of 28.04.2004; S/RES/1673, of 27.04.2006; S/RES/1810, of 25.04.2008; S/RES/1887, of 24.09.2009; and S/RES/1997, of 20.04.2011, – to which others can be added.[42] May I at first

---

42   Cf. also Security Council resolutions S/RES/1695 of 15.07.2006; S/RES/1718 of 14.10.2006; S/RES/1874 of 12.06.2009; S/RES/1928 of 07.06.2010; S/RES/2094 of 07.03.2013; S/RES/2141 of 05.03.2014; S/RES/2159 of 09.06.2014; S/RES/2224 of 09.06.2015; S/RES/2270 of 02.03.2016.

recall that, at a Security Council's meeting at the level of Heads of State and Government, held on 31.01.1992, the President of the U.N. Security Council made a statement on behalf of the members of the Security Council that called upon all member States to fulfil their obligations on matters of arms control and disarmament, and to prevent the proliferation of all weapons of mass destruction[43] (encompassing nuclear, chemical, and biological weapons).

60. The statement expressed the feeling prevailing at the time that the end of the Cold War "has raised hopes for a safer, more equitable and more humane world", giving now to the world "the best chance of achieving international peace and security since the foundation of the United Nations".[44] The members of the Security Council then warned against the threat to international peace and security of all weapons of mass destruction, and expressed their commitment to take appropriate action to prevent "the spread of technology related to the research for or production of such weapons".[45] They further stressed the importance of "the integral role in the implementation" of the NPT of "fully effective IAEA safeguards", and of "effective export controls"; they added that they would take "appropriate measures in the case of any violations notified to them by the IAEA".[46]

61. The proliferation of all weapons of mass destruction is defined in the aforementioned Security Council statement, notably, as a threat to international peace and security, – a point which was to be referred to, in subsequent resolutions of the Security Council, to justify its action under Chapter VII of the U.N. Charter. In three of its subsequent resolutions, in a preambular paragraph (resolutions 1540, of 28.04.2004, para. 2; 1810, of 25.04.2008, para. 3; and 1887, of 24.09.2009, para. 2), the Security Council reaffirms the statement of its President (adopted on 31.01.1992), and, also in other resolutions, further asserts (also in preambular paragraphs) that the proliferation of nuclear, chemical and biological weapons is a threat to international peace and security[47] and that all States need to take measures to prevent such proliferation.

> In preambular paragraphs of all these Security Council resolutions, the Security Council reaffirms, time and time again, that the proliferation of nuclear, chemical and biological weapons, and their means of delivery, constitutes a threat to international peace and security.

43   U.N. doc. S/23500, of 31.01.1992, pp. 1–5.
44   *Ibid.*, pp. 2 and 5.
45   *Ibid.*, p. 4.
46   *Ibid.*, p. 4.
47   Cf. e.g. Security Council resolutions 1540, of 28.04.2004; 1673, of 27.04.2006; 1810, of 25.04.2008; 1977, of 20.04.2011. And cf. also resolutions 1695, of 15.07.2006; 1718, of

62. In resolution 1540/2004 of 28.04.2004, adopted by the Security Council acting under Chapter VII of the U.N. Charter, it sets forth legally binding obligations on all U.N. member States to set up and enforce appropriate and effective measures against the proliferation of nuclear, chemical, and biological weapons, – including the adoption of controls and a reporting procedure for U.N. member States to a Committee of the Security Council (sometimes referred to as the "1540 Committee"). Subsequent Security Council resolutions reaffirm resolution 1540/2004 and call upon U.N. member States to implement it.

63. The U.N. Security Council refers, in particular, in two of its resolutions (984/1995, of 11.04.1995; and 1887/2009 of 24.09.2009), to the obligation to pursue negotiations in good faith in relation to nuclear disarmament. In its preamble, Security Council resolution 984/1995 affirms the need for all States Parties to the NPT "to comply fully with all their obligations"; in its operative part, it further "[u]rges all States, as provided for in Article VI of the Treaty on the Non-Proliferation of Nuclear Weapons, to pursue negotiations in good faith on effective measures relating to nuclear disarmament and on a treaty on general and complete disarmament under strict and effective international control which remains a universal goal" (para. 8). It should not pass unnoticed that Security Council resolution 984/1995 pre-dates the ICJ's 1996 Advisory Opinion on the *Threat or Use of Nuclear Weapons*.

64. And Security Council resolution 1887/2009 of 24.09.2009, in its operative part, again calls upon States Parties to the NPT "to comply fully with all their obligations and fulfil their commitments under the Treaty" (para. 2), and, in particular, "pursuant to Article VI of the Treaty, to undertake to pursue negotiations in good faith on effective measures relating to nuclear arms reduction and disarmament"; furthermore, it calls upon "all other States to join in this endeavour" (para. 5). It should not pass unnoticed that it is a general call, upon all U.N. member States, whether or not Parties to the NPT.

65. In my perception, the aforementioned resolutions of the Security Council, like those of the General Assembly (cf. *supra*), addressing all U.N. member States, provide significant elements of the emergence of an *opinio juris*, in support of the gradual formation of an obligation of customary international law, corresponding to the conventional obligation under Article VI of the NPT. In particular, the fact that the Security Council calls upon *all States*, and not only

---

14.10.2006; 1874, of 12.06.2009; 1928, of 07.06.2010; 2094, of 07.03.2013; 2141, of 05.03.2014; 2159, of 09.06.2014; 2224, of 09.06.2015; and 2270, of 02.03.2016.

States Parties to the NPT, to pursue negotiations towards nuclear disarmament in good faith (or to join the NPT State Parties in this endeavour) is significant. It is an indication that the obligation is incumbent on all U.N. member States, irrespectively of their being or not Parties to the NPT.

V   The Saga of the United Nations in the Condemnation of Nuclear Weapons

66. The U.N. resolutions (of the General Assembly and the Security Council) that I have just reviewed (*supra*) portray the United Nations' longstanding saga in the condemnation of nuclear weapons. This saga goes back to the birth and earlier years of the United Nations. In fact, nuclear weapons were not in the minds of the Delegates to the San Francisco Conference of June 1945, at the time when the United Nations Charter was adopted on 26.06.1945. The U.S. dropping of atomic bombs over Hiroshima and Nagasaki, heralding the nuclear age, occurred on 06 and 09 August 1945, respectively, over ten weeks before the U.N. Charter's entry into force, on 24.10.1945.

67. As soon as the United Nations Organization came into being, it promptly sought to equip itself to face the new challenges of the nuclear age: the General Assembly's very first resolution, – resolution 1(I) of 24.01.1946, – thus, established a Commission to deal with the matter, entrusted with submitting reports to the Security Council "in the interest of peace and security" (para. 2(a)), as well as with making proposals for "control of atomic energy to the extent necessary to ensure its use only for peaceful purposes", and for "the elimination from national armaments of atomic weapons and of all other major weapons adaptable to mass destruction" (para. 5(b)(c)).

68. One decade later, in 1956, the International Atomic Energy Agency (IAEA) was established. And half a decade later, in 1961, the General Assembly adopted a ground-breaking resolution: it would be proper here to recall the precise terms of the historical General Assembly resolution 1653 (XVI), of 24.11.1961, titled *"Declaration on the Prohibition of the Use of Nuclear and Thermo-Nuclear Weapons"*. That *célèbre* resolution 1653 (1961) remains contemporary today, and, 55 years later, continues to require close attention; in it, the General Assembly

> *Mindful* of its responsibility under the Charter of the United Nations in the maintenance of international peace and security, as well as in the consideration of principles governing disarmament,

Gravely concerned that, while negotiations on disarmament have not so far achieved satisfactory results, the armaments race, particularly in the nuclear and thermo-nuclear fields, has reached a dangerous stage requiring all possible precautionary measures to protect humanity and civilization from the hazard of nuclear and thermo-nuclear catastrophe,

Recalling that the use of weapons of mass destruction, causing unnecessary human suffering, was in the past prohibited, as being contrary to the laws of humanity and to the principles of international law, by international declarations and binding agreements, such as the Declaration of St. Petersburg of 1868, the Declaration of the Brussels Conference of 1874, the Conventions of The Hague Peace Conferences of 1899 and 1907, and the Geneva Protocol of 1925, to which the majority of nations are still parties,

Considering that the use of nuclear and thermo-nuclear weapons would bring about indiscriminate suffering and destruction to mankind and civilization to an even greater extent than the use of those weapons declared by the aforementioned international declarations and agreements to be contrary to the laws of humanity and a crime under international law,

Believing that the use of weapons of mass destruction, such as nuclear and thermo-nuclear weapons, is a direct negation of the high ideals and objectives which the United Nations has been established to achieve through the protection of succeeding generations from the scourge of war and through the preservation and promotion of their cultures,

1. *Declares* that:
   (a) The use of nuclear and thermo-nuclear weapons is contrary to the spirit, letter and aims of the United Nations and, as such, a direct violation of the Charter of the United Nations;
   (b) The use of nuclear and thermo-nuclear weapons would exceed even the scope of war and cause indiscriminate suffering and destruction to mankind and civilization and, as such, is contrary to the rules of international law and to the laws of humanity;
   (c) The use of nuclear and thermo-nuclear weapons is a war directed not against an enemy or enemies alone but also against mankind in general, since the peoples of the world not involved in such a war will be subjected to all the evils generated by the use of such weapons;
   (d) Any State using nuclear and thermo-nuclear weapons is to be considered as violating the Charter of the United Nations, as acting contrary to the laws of humanity and as committing a crime against mankind and civilization;

2. *Requests* the Secretary-General to consult the Governments of Member States to ascertain their views on the possibility of convening a Special Conference for signing a Convention on the prohibition of the use of nuclear and thermo-nuclear weapons for war purposes and to report on the results of such consultation to the General Assembly at its XVIIth session.

69. Over half a century later, the lucid and poignant declaration contained in General Assembly resolution 1653 (1961) appears endowed with permanent topicality, as the whole international community remains still awaiting for the conclusion of the propounded general Convention on the prohibition of nuclear and thermo-nuclear weapons: nuclear disarmament remains still a goal to be achieved by the United Nations today, as it was in 1961. The Comprehensive Nuclear-Test-Ban Treaty (CTBT), adopted on 24.09.1996, has not yet entered into force, although 164 States have ratified it to date.

70. It is beyond the scope of the present Dissenting Opinion to dwell upon the reasons why, already for two decades, one remains awaiting for the CTBT's entry into force.[48] Suffice it here to recall that the CTBT provides (Article XIV) that for it to enter into force, the 44 States specified in its Annex 2 need to ratify it;[49] a number of these States have not yet ratified the CTBT, including some NWS, like India and Pakistan. NWS have invoked distinct reasons for their positions conditioning nuclear disarmament (cf. *infra*). The entry into force of the CTBT has thus been delayed.

71. Recently, in a panel in Vienna (on 27.04.2016) in commemoration of the 20th anniversary of the CTBT, the U.N. Secretary-General (Ban Ki-moon) pondered that there have been advances in the matter, but there remains a long way

---

[48] For a historical account and the perspectives of the CTBT, cf., e.g., K.A. Hansen, *The Comprehensive Nuclear Test Ban Treaty*, Stanford, Stanford University Press, 2006, pp. 1–84; [Various Authors,] *Nuclear Weapons after the Comprehensive Test Ban Treaty* (ed. E. Arnett), Stockholm–Solna/Oxford, SIPRI/Oxford University Press, 1996, pp. 1–141; J. Ramaker, J. Mackby, P.D. Marshall and R. Geil, *The Final Test – A History of the Comprehensive Nuclear-Test-Ban Treaty Negotiations*, Vienna, Ed. Prep. Comm. of CTBTO, 2003, pp. 1–265.

[49] Those 44 States, named in Annex 2, participated in the CTBT negotiations at the Conference on Disarmament, from 1994 to 1996, and possessed nuclear reactors at that time.

to go, in the determination "to bring into force a legally binding prohibition against all nuclear tests". He recalled to have

> repeatedly pointed to the toxic legacy that some 2,000 tests left on people and the environment in parts of Central Asia, North Africa, North America and the South Pacific. Nuclear testing poisons water, causes cancers, and pollutes the area with radioactive fall-out for generations and generations to come. We are here to honour the victims. The best tribute to them is action to ban and to stop nuclear testing. Their sufferings should teach the world to end this madness.[50]

He then called on the (eight) remaining CTBT Annex 2 States "to sign and ratify the Treaty without further delay", so as to strengthen its goal of universality; in this way, – he concluded, – "we can leave a safer world, free of nuclear tests, to our children and to succeeding generations of this world".[51]

72. To this one may add the unaccomplished endeavours of the U.N. General Assembly Special Sessions on Disarmament. Of the three Special Sessions held so far (in 1978, 10th Special Session; in 1982, 12th Special Session; and in 1988, 15th Special Session),[52] the first one appears to have been the most significant one so far. The Final Document adopted unanimously (without a vote) by the 1st Special Session on Disarmament sets up a programme of action on disarmament and the corresponding mechanism in its current form.

73. That Final Document of the first General Assembly Special Session on Disarmament (1978) addresses nuclear disarmament in its distinct aspects. In this respect, the General Assembly begins by observing that the accumulation of nuclear weapons constitutes a threat to the future of humankind (para. 1), in effect "the greatest danger" to humankind and to "the survival of civilization" (para. 47). It adds that the arms race, particularly in its nuclear aspect, is incompatible with the principles enshrined in the United Nations Charter (para. 12). In its view, the most effective guarantee against the dangers of nuclear war is the complete elimination of nuclear weapons (paras. 8 and 56).[53]

---

50 U.N. doc. SG/SM/17709-DC/3628, of 27.04.2016, pp. 1–2.
51 *Ibid.*, p. 2.
52 Ever since, several G.A. resolutions have called for a 4th Special Session on Disarmament, but it has not yet taken place.
53 And cf. also paras. 18 and 20.

74. While disarmament is the responsibility of all States, the General Assembly asserts that NWS have the primary responsibility for nuclear disarmament. There is pressing need of "urgent negotiations of agreements" to that end, and in particular to conclude "a treaty prohibiting nuclear-weapon tests" (paras. 50–51). It further stresses the importance of nuclear-weapon-free zones that have been established or are the subject of negotiations in various parts of the globe (paras. 60–64).

75. The Conference on Disarmament, – since 1979 the sole multilateral disarmament-negotiating forum of the international community, – has helped to negotiate multilateral arms-limitation and disarmament agreements.[54] It has focused its work on four main issues, namely: nuclear disarmament, prohibition of the production of fissile material for weapon use, prevention of arms race in outer space, and negative security assurances. Yet, since the adoption of the CTBT in 1996, the Conference on Disarmament has been largely deadlocked, in face of the invocation of divergent security interests, added to the understanding that nuclear weapons require mutuality; furthermore, the Rules of Procedure of the Conference provide that all decisions must be adopted by consensus. In sum, some States blame political factors for causing its long-standing stalemate, while others attribute it to outdated procedural rules.

76. After all, in historical perspective, some advances have been attained in the last decades in respect of other weapons of mass destruction, as illustrated by the adoption of the Convention on the Prohibition of the Development, Production and Stockpiling of Bacteriological (Biological) and Toxin Weapons and on their Destruction (on 10.04.1972), as well as the Convention on the Prohibition of the Development, Production, Stockpiling and Use of Chemical Weapons and on their Destruction (on 13.01.1993); distinctly from the CTBT (*supra*), these two Conventions have already entered into force (on 26.03.1975, and on 29.04.1997, respectively).

77. If we look at conventional international law only, weapons of mass destruction (poisonous gases, biological and chemical weapons) have been outlawed; yet, nuclear weapons, far more destructive, have not been banned yet.

---

54   E.g., the aforementioned NPT, CTBT, the Biological Weapons Convention, and the Chemical Weapons Convention, in addition to the seabed treaties, and the Convention on the Prohibition of Military or Any Other Hostile Use of Environmental Modification Techniques.

This juridical absurdity nourishes the positivist myopia, or blindness, in inferring therefrom that there is no customary international obligation of nuclear disarmament. Positivists only have eyes for treaty law, for individual State consent, revolving in vicious circles, unable to see the pressing needs and aspirations of the international community as a whole, and to grasp the *universality* of contemporary international law – as envisaged by its "founding fathers", already in the XVIth–XVIIth centuries, – with its underlying fundamental principles (cf. *infra*).

78. The truth is that, in our times, the obligation of nuclear disarmament has emerged and crystallized, in both conventional and customary international law, and the United Nations has been giving a most valuable contribution to this along the decades. The matter at issue, the United Nations saga in this domain, was brought to the attention of the ICJ, two decades ago, in the advisory proceedings that led to its Advisory Opinion of 1996 on the *Threat or Use of Nuclear Weapons*, and now again, two decades later, in the present contentious proceedings in the cases of *Obligations Concerning Negotiations Relating to Cessation of the Nuclear Arms Race and to Nuclear Disarmament*, opposing the Marshall Islands to India, Pakistan and the United Kingdom, respectively.

79. The aforementioned U.N. resolutions were in effect object of attention on the part of the contending parties before the Court (Marshall Islands, India, Pakistan and the United Kingdom). In the oral phase of their arguments, they were dealt with by the participating States (Marshall Islands, India and the United Kingdom), and, extensively so, in particular, by the Marshall Islands and India. The key point is the relation of those resolutions with the emergence of *opinio juris*, of relevance to the identification of a customary international law obligation in the present domain. May I turn, first, to the positions sustained by the contending parties, and then, to the questions I put to them in the public sitting of 16.03.2016 before the ICJ in the *cas d'espèce*, and the responses received from them.

VI   U.N. Resolutions and the Emergence of *Opinio Juris*: The Positions of the Contending Parties

80. In their written submissions and oral arguments before the Court in the present case of *Obligations Concerning Negotiations Relating to Cessation of the Nuclear Arms Race and to Nuclear Disarmament*, the Marshall Islands addresses General Assembly resolutions on nuclear disarmament, in relation

to the development of customary international law;⁵⁵ it also refers to Security Council resolutions.⁵⁶ Quoting the ICJ's Advisory Opinion of 1996, it contends (perhaps not as clearly as it could have done) that although General Assembly resolutions lack binding force, they may "sometimes have normative value", and thus contribute to the emergence of an *opinio juris*.⁵⁷

81. In its written submissions and oral arguments before the Court, India addresses U.N. General Assembly resolutions on follow-up to the ICJ's Advisory Opinion of 1996, pointing out that it is the only nuclear weapon State that has co-sponsored and voted in favour of such resolutions.⁵⁸ India supports nuclear disarmament "in a time-bound, universal, non-discriminatory, phased and verifiable manner".⁵⁹ And it criticizes the M.I. for not supporting the General Assembly follow-up resolutions in its own voting pattern (having voted against one of them, in favour once, and all other times abstained).⁶⁰

82. In its *Preliminary Objections* (of 15.06.2015), the United Kingdom, for its part, after recalling the Marshall Islands' position on earlier U.N. General Assembly resolutions, in the sixties and seventies (paras. 21 and 98(c) and (h)), then refers to its own position thereon (paras. 84 and 99(c)). It also refers to U.N. Security Council resolutions (para. 92). It then recalls the Marshall Islands' arguments – e.g., that "the U.K. has always voted against" General Assembly resolutions on the follow-up of the ICJ Advisory Opinion of 1996, and of the U.N. High Level Meetings in 2013 and 2014 (paras. 98(e) and (h)), – in order to rebut them (paras. 99–103).

83. As for Pakistan, though it informed the Court of its decision not to participate in the oral phase of the present proceedings (letter of 02.03.2016), in the submissions in its *Counter-Memorial* it argues that the ICJ 1996 Advisory Opinion nowhere stated that the obligation under Article VI of the NPT was a general obligation or that it was opposable *erga omnes*; in its view, there was no *prima facie* evidence to this effect *erga omnes*.⁶¹ As to the U.N. General Assembly resolutions following up the ICJ's 1996 Advisory Opinion, Pakistan notes

---

55 ICJ, doc. CR 2016/1, of 07.03.2016, para. 7.
56 *Ibid.*, para. 8.
57 *Ibid.*, para. 7.
58 ICJ, doc. CR 2016/4, of 10.03.2016, para. 1, p. 19.
59 *Counter-Memorial* of India, p. 9, para. 13.
60 *Ibid.*, p. 8, para. 12.
61 *Counter-Memorial* of Pakistan., p. 8, para. 2.3.

that it has voted in favour of these resolutions from 1997 to 2015, and by contrast, – it adds, – the Marshall Islands abstained from voting in 2002 and 2003 and again from 2005 to 2012.[62]

84. After recalling that it is not a Party to the NPT,[63] Pakistan further argues that General Assembly resolutions do not have binding force and cannot thus, in its view, give rise to obligations enforceable against a State.[64] Pakistan concludes that the General Assembly resolutions do not support the proposition that there exists a customary international law obligation "rooted" in Article VI of the NPT. Rather, it is the NPT that underpins the Marshall Islands' claims.[65]

85. In sum, the United Kingdom has voted against such resolutions, the Marshall Islands has abstained in most of them, India and Pakistan have voted in favour of them. Despite these distinct patterns of voting, in my view the U.N. General Assembly resolutions reviewed in the present Dissenting Opinion, taken altogether, are not at all deprived of their contribution to the conformation of *opinio juris* as to the formation of a customary international law obligation of nuclear denuclearization. After all, they are resolutions of the U.N. General Assembly itself (and not only of the large majority of U.N. member States which voted in their favour); they are resolutions of the United Nations Organization itself, addressing a matter of common concern of humankind as a whole (cf. Part XX, *infra*).

VII   Questions from the Bench and Responses from the Parties

86. At the end of the public sittings before the Court in the present case of *Obligations Concerning Negotiations Relating to Cessation of the Nuclear Arms Race and to Nuclear Disarmament* (Marshall Islands *versus* India), I deemed it fit to put the following questions (on 16.03.2016, in the morning) to the contending parties:

> I have questions to put to both contending parties, the Marshall Islands and India. My questions are the following:

---

62   *Ibid.*, p. 8, para. 2.4.
63   *Ibid.*, p. 14, para. 4.4; p. 30, para. 7.55.
64   *Ibid.*, p. 38, paras. 7.95–7.97.
65   *Ibid.*, p. 38, para. 7.97.

> In the course of the written submissions and oral arguments, the two contending parties, the Marshall Islands and India, both referred to U.N. General Assembly resolutions on nuclear disarmament. Parallel to the resolutions on the matter which go back to the early 70's (First Disarmament Decade), there have been two more recent series of General Assembly resolutions, namely: those condemning nuclear weapons, extending from 1982 to date, and those adopted as a follow-up to the 1996 ICJ Advisory Opinion on *Nuclear Weapons*, extending so far from 1997 to 2015. In relation to this last series of General Assembly resolutions, – referred to by the contending parties, – I would like to ask both the Marshall Islands and India whether, in their understanding, such General Assembly resolutions are constitutive of an expression of *opinio juris*, and, if so, what in their view is their relevance to the formation of a customary international law obligation to pursue negotiations leading to nuclear disarmament, and what is their incidence upon the question of the existence of a dispute between the parties.[66]

87. One week later (on 23.03.2016), India and the Marshall Islands submitted to the ICJ their written replies to my questions. In its response to them, India began by recalling a passage of the ICJ's 1986 Advisory Opinion on the *Threat or Use of Nuclear Weapons*, whereby the Court acknowledged that

> General Assembly resolutions, even if they are not binding, may sometimes have normative value. They can, in certain circumstances, provide evidence important for establishing the existence of a rule or the emergence of an *opinio juris*. To establish whether this is true of a given General Assembly resolution, it is necessary to look at its content and the conditions of its adoption; it is also necessary to see whether an opinio juris exists as to its normative character.[67]

88. In India's view, the series of General Assembly resolutions advocating measures of restraint, with a view to slowing down vertical proliferation,[68] do not in themselves constitute comprehensive proposals for the global elimination of nuclear weapons; India, thus, focused on the voting pattern relating to two other series of General Assembly resolutions, – those on nuclear

---

66   ICJ, doc. CR 2016/8, of 16.09.2016, pp. 38–39.
67   *I.C.J. Reports 1996*, pp. 254–255, para. 70.
68   Cf. ICJ, *Replies of the Parties [India] to the Questions Put to Them by Judge Cançado Trindade*, doc. MIIND 2016/14, of 23.03.2016, pp. 2–3, paras. 4–8.

THE UNIVERSAL JURIDICAL CONSCIENCE, HUMANENESS   271

disarmament, and those on the follow-up to the ICJ's 1996 Advisory Opinion. As to these latter, India noted that approximately two-thirds of the member States of the United Nations vote in favour, while the others either abstain or vote against;[69] India further noted the lack of consensus on the biennial resolutions following up nuclear disarmament measures agreed to at the Review Conferences of the States Parties to the NPT.

89. India argued that "the lack of unanimity and the abstention or negative vote of States whose interests are specially affected cast doubt on the normative value of these U.N. General Assembly resolutions on the existence of an *opinio juris*".[70] India considered that an *opinio juris* would be facilitated by a number of measures, including reaffirmation of the unequivocal commitment by all nuclear weapon States to the goal of complete elimination of nuclear weapons, and an agreement on a step-by-step process of universal commitment to the global elimination of nuclear weapons.[71] As to the incidence of these resolutions on the existence of a dispute in the *cas d'espèce*, India argued that its own voting record and that of the Marshall Islands indicate that both States support these resolutions and do not hold opposing views on the question of pursuing and bringing to a conclusion negotiations leading tor nuclear disarmament; accordingly, in its view, there is no dispute between them.[72]

90. The Marshall Islands, for its part, also referred to the ICJ's 1996 Advisory Opinion on the *Threat or Use of Nuclear Weapons*, as well as to a number of General Assembly resolutions upholding the obligation to pursue negotiations leading to nuclear disarmament, in support of its position as to the existence of a customary international law obligation to this end. It then also referred to the ICJ's *obiter dictum* in the case of *Nicaragua versus United States*, to the effect that "*opinio juris* may, though with all due caution, be deduced from, *inter alia*, the attitude of the Parties and the attitude of States towards certain General Assembly resolutions" (para. 188).[73]

---

69   *Ibid.*, p. 3, para. 11.
70   *Ibid.*, p. 5, para. 14.
71   *Ibid.*, p. 6, para. 17.
72   *Ibid.*, p. 6, para. 18.
73   The Marshall Islands also cited the U.N. International Law Commission's Draft Conclusions on the *Identification of Customary International Law* (2015), which recognise the importance of the attitude of States towards General Assembly resolutions for establishing State practice and *opinio juris*. ICJ, *Replies of the Parties [Marshall Islands] to the Questions Put to Them by Judge Cançado Trindade*, doc. MIIND 2016/14, of 23.03.2016, pp. 2–3, paras. 2–5.

91. In the perception of the Marshall Islands, the attitude of States towards General Assembly resolutions adopted in the period 1982–1995 indicates an emerging *opinio juris* on the obligation to conduct negotiations in good faith leading to general and complete nuclear disarmament.[74] The Marshall Islands then states that the attitude of States to resolutions following-up the 1996 ICJ's Advisory Opinion, – those affirming the existence of an obligation to pursue negotiations leading to nuclear disarmament, – constitutes an expression of *opinio juris*, in support of a customary international obligation to this end.[75]

92. As to the incidence of General Assembly resolutions on the existence of a dispute in the *cas d'espèce*, the Marshall Islands contends that opposing attitudes of States to such resolutions may contribute to demonstrating the existence of a dispute; however, the importance to be attributed to a State's attitude to resolutions must be determined in the light of the specific circumstances of any given case, as the endorsement of certain resolutions may be contradicted by subsequent conduct of the State at issue.[76] As to the present case opposing the Marshall Islands to India, the Marshall Islands argues that, even if the two States do not show an opposition of legal views as to the relevant General Assembly resolutions, yet they hold divergent views as to whether India is in breach of the customary law obligation to pursue in good faith nuclear disarmament: such divergence is not evidenced by voting records of such resolutions, but rather by other conduct.[77]

VIII   Human Wickedness: From the XXIst Century Back to the Book of *Genesis*

93. Since the beginning of the nuclear age in August 1945, some of the great thinkers of the XXth century started inquiring whether humankind has a future. Indeed, this is a question which cannot be eluded. Thus, already in 1946, for example, deeply shocked by the U.S. atomic bombings of Hiroshima and Nagasaki (on 06 and 09 August 1945, respectively),[78] Mahatma Gandhi, in

---

74   *Ibid.*, p. 4, para. 7.
75   *Ibid.*, p. 4, para. 7.
76   *Ibid.*, p. 4, para. 8.
77   *Ibid.*, p. 4, para. 9.
78   Preceded by a nuclear test undertaken by the United States at Alamagordo, New Mexico, on 16.07.1945.

promptly expressing his worry about the future of human society, wrote, in the Journal *Harijan*, on 07.07.1946, that

> So far as I can see, the atomic bomb has deadened the finest feeling that has sustained mankind for ages. There used to be the so-called laws of war which made it tolerable. Now we know the naked truth. War knows no law except that of might.[79]

94. And M. Gandhi, denouncing its brutality, added that the "atom bomb is the weapon of ultimate force and destruction", evidencing the "futility" of such violence; the development of the atom bomb "represents the most sinful and diabolical use of science".[80] In the same Journal *Harijan*, M. Gandhi further wrote, on 29.09.1946, that non-violence is "the only thing the atom bomb cannot destroy"; and he further warned that "unless now the world adopts non-violence, it will spell certain suicide for mankind".[81]

95. Over a decade later, in the late fifties, Karl Jaspers, in his book *La bombe atomique et l'avenir de l'homme* (1958), regretted that the existence of nuclear weapons seemed to have been taken for granted, despite their capacity to destroy humankind and all life on the surface of earth.[82] One has thus to admit, – he added, – that "cette terre, qui est née d'une explosion de l'atome, soit anéantie aussi par les bombes atomiques".[83] K. Jaspers further regretted that progress had occurred in technological knowledge, but there had been "no progress of ethics nor of reason". Human nature has not changed: "ou l'homme se transforme ou il disparaît".[84]

---

[79] M. Gandhi, "Atom Bomb and Ahimsa", *Harijan* (07.07.1946), reproduced *in*: *Journalist Gandhi – Selected Writings of Gandhi* (org. S. Sharma), 1st ed., Mumbai, Ed. Gandhi Book Center, 1994, p. 104; also *cit. in*: P.F. Power, *Gandhi on World Affairs*, London, Allen & Unwin, 1961, pp. 63–64.

[80] *Cit. in*: *What Mahatma Gandhi Said about the Atom Bomb* (org. Y.P. Anand), New Delhi, National Gandhi Museum, 1998, p. 5.

[81] From the Journal *Harijan* (29.09.1946), *cit. in*: Faisal Devji, *The Impossible Indian – Gandhi and the Temptation of Violence*, London, Hurst & Co., 2012, p. 150.

[82] K. Jaspers, *La bombe atomique et l'avenir de l'homme* [1958], Paris, Buchet/Chastel, 1963, pp. 22 and 336.

[83] *Ibid.*, p. 576.

[84] *Ibid.*, pp. 621 and 640.

96. In the early sixties, for his part, Bertrand Russell, in his book *Has Man a Future?* (1961), likewise regretted that people seemed to have got used to the existence of nuclear weapons, in a world dominated by a "will towards death", prevailing over sanity.[85] Unfortunately, – he proceeded, – "love for power" has enticed States "to pursue irrational policies"; and he added:

> Those who regard *Genesis* as authentic history, may take Cain as the first example: he may well have thought that, with Abel out of the way, he could rule over coming generations.[86]

To B. Russell, it is "in the hearts of men that the evil lies", it is in their minds that "the cure must be sought".[87] He further regretted the discouraging results of disarmament Conferences, and even wrote that ICJ pronouncements on the issue should be authoritative, and it was not "optional" for States "to respect or not international law".[88]

97. For his part, Karl Popper, at the end of his life, in his book (in the form of an interview) *The Lesson of This Century* (1997), in assembling his recollections of the XXth century, expressed the anguish, for example, at the time of the 1962 Cuban missiles crisis, with the finding that each of the 38 warheads at issue had three thousand times more power than the atomic bomb dropped over Hiroshima.[89] Once again, the constatation: human nature has not changed. K. Popper, like other great thinkers of the XXth century, regretted that no lessons seemed to have been learned from the past; this increased the concern they shared, in successive decades, with the future of humankind, in the presence of arsenals of nuclear weapons.

98. A contemporary writer, Max Gallo, in his recent novel *Caïn et Abel – Le premier crime*, has written that the presence of evil is within everyone; "le Mal est au coeur du Bien, et cette réalité ambiguë est le propre des affaires humaines".[90] Writers of the past, – he went on, – eux aussi – "toi Dante, toi Dostoïevski, et ceux

---

85 B. Russell, *Has Man a Future?*, [London], Penguin Books, 1962 [reprint], pp. 27 and 37.
86 *Ibid.*, p. 45.
87 *Ibid.*, pp. 45–46, and cf. 69.
88 *Ibid.*, pp. 97 and 79.
89 K. Popper, *The Lesson of This Century* (interview with G. Bosetti), London/N.Y., Routledge, 1997, pp. 24 and 28. And cf. also, earlier on, K. Popper, *La Responsabilidad de Vivir – Escritos sobre Política, Historia y Conocimiento* [1994], Barcelona, Paidós, 2012 [reed.], p. 242, and cf. p. 274.
90 M. Gallo, *Caïn et Abel – Le premier crime*, [Paris], Fayard, 2011, pp. 112 and 141.

THE UNIVERSAL JURIDICAL CONSCIENCE, HUMANENESS 275

qui vous ont inspiré, Eschyle, Sophocle – attisent le brasier du châtiment et de la culpabilité".[91] And he added:

> Partout, Caïn poignarde ou étrangle Abel. (...) Et personne ne semble voir (...) la mort prochaine de toute humanité. Elle tient entre ses mains l'arme de sa destruction. Ce ne sont plus seulement des villes entières qui seront incendiées, rasées: toute vie sera alors consumée, et la terre vitrifiée.
>
> Deux villes ont déjà connu ce sort, et l'ombre des corps de leurs habitants est à jamais encrustée dans la pierre sous l'effet d'une chaleur de lave solaire.
>
> (...) [P]artout Caïn poursuivra Abel. (...) Les villes vulnérables seront ensanglantées. Les tours les plus hautes seront détruites, leurs habitants ensevelis sous les décombres.[92]

99. As well captured by those and other thinkers, in the Book of *Genesis*, the episode of the brothers Cain and Abel portraying the first murder ever, came to be seen, along the centuries, as disclosing the presence of evil and guilt in the world everyone lives. This called for care, prudence and reflection, as it became possible to realize that human beings were gradually distancing themselves from their Creator. The fragility of civilizations soon became visible. That distancing became manifest in the subsequent episode of the Tower of Babel (*Genesis*, Ch. 11: 9). As they were built, civilizations could be destroyed. History was to provide many examples of that (as singled out, in the XXth century, by Arnold Toynbee). Along the centuries, with the growth of scientific-technological knowledge, the human capacity of self-destruction increased considerably, having become limitless in the present nuclear age.

100. Turning back to the aforementioned book by B. Russell, also in its French edition (*L'homme survivra-t-il?*, 1963), he further warned therein that

> "il faut que nous nous rendions compte que la haine, la perte de temps, d'argent et d'habilité intellectuelle en vue de la création d'engins de destruction, la crainte du mal que nous pouvons nous faire mutuellement, le risque quotidien et permanent de voir la fin de tout ce que l'homme a réalisé, sont le produit de la folie humaine. (...) C'est dans nos

---

91   Ibid., p. 174.
92   Ibid., pp. 236–237.

cœurs que réside le mal, c'est de nos cœurs qu'il doit être extirpé".[93] ["we must become aware that the hatred, the expenditure of time and money and intellectual hability upon weapons of destruction, the fear of what we may do to each other, and the imminent daily and hourly risk of an end to all that man has achieved, (...) all this is a product of human folly. (...) It is in our hearts that the evil lies, and it is from our hearts that it must be plucked out"[94]].

101. Some other great thinkers of the XXth century (from distinct branches of knowledge), expressed their grave common concern with the increased human capacity of destruction coupled with the development of scientific-technological knowledge. Thus, the historian Arnold Toynbee (*A Study in History*, 1934–1954; and *Civilization on Trial*, 1948), regretted precisely the modern tragedy that human iniquity was not eliminated with the development of scientific-technological knowledge, but widely enlarged, without a concomitant advance at spiritual level.[95] And the increase in armaments and in the capacity of destruction, – he added, – became a symptom of the fall of civilizations.[96]

102. For his part, the writer Hermann Hesse, in a posthumous book of essays (*Guerre et paix*, 1946), originally published shortly after the II world war, warned that with the mass killings, not only do we keep on killing ourselves, but also our present and perhaps also our future.[97] The worst destruction, – he added, – was the one organized by the State itself, with its corollary, "the philosophy of the State", accompanied by capital and industry.[98] The philosopher and theologian Jacques Maritain (*Oeuvres Complètes*, 1961–1967), in turn, wrote

---

93   B. Russell, *L'homme survivra-t-il?*, Paris, Éd. J. Didier, 1963, pp. 162–163.
94   B. Russell, *Has Man a Future?*, op. cit. supra n. (85), pp. 109–110. Towards the end of his life, Bertrand Russell again warned against the extreme danger of atomic and hydrogen bombs, and expressed his concern that people seemed to get used to their existence; cf. B. Russell, *Autobiography* [1967], London, Unwin, 1985 [reed.], pp. 554–555.
95   Cf. A.J. Toynbee, *A Study in History*, Oxford, Oxford University Press, 1970 [3rd reprint], pp. 48–558, 559–701, 702–718 and 826–850; A.J. Toynbee, *Civilization on Trial*, Oxford/N.Y., Oxford University Press, 1948, pp. 3–263.
96   A.J. Toynbee, *Guerra e Civilização* [*War and Civilization*], Lisbon, Edit. Presença, 1963, pp. 29, 129 and 178.
97   H. Hesse, *Sobre la Guerra y la Paz* [1946], 5th ed., Barcelona, Edit. Noguer, 1986, pp. 119 and 122.
98   H. Hesse, *Guerre et Paix*, Paris, L'Arche Éd., 2003 [reed.], pp. 127 and 133.

that the atrocities perpetrated in the XXth century had "une importance plus tragique pour la conscience humaine".⁹⁹ In calling for an "integral humanism", he warned that the human person transcends the State, and the realisation of the common good is to be pursued keeping in mind human dignity.¹⁰⁰ In his criticism of the "realists", he stressed the imperatives of ethics and justice, and the importance of general principles of law, in the line of jusnaturalist thinking.¹⁰¹

103. Another writer, the humanist Stefan Zweig, remained always concerned with the fate of humankind. He was impressed with the Scripture's legend of the Tower of Babel, having written an essay on it in 1916, and kept it in mind along the years, as shown in successive essays written in more than the two following decades,¹⁰² taking it as a symbol of the perennial yearning for a unified humanity. In his own words,

> The history of tomorrow must be a history of all humanity and the conflicts between individual conflicts must be seen as redundant alongside the common good of the community. History must then be transformed from the current woeful State to a completely new position; (...) it must clearly contrast the old ideal of victory with the new one of unity and the old glorification of war with a new contempt for it. (...) [T]he only important thing is to push forward under the banner of a community of nations, the mentality of mankind (...).¹⁰³

---

99   J. Maritain, "Dieu et la permission du mal", in Œuvres de Jacques Maritain – 1961–1967 (Jacques et Raissa Maritain – Oeuvres Complètes), vol. XII, Fribourg/Paris, Éd. Universitaires/Éd. Saint-Paul, 1992, p. 17, and cf. p. 41.

100 Cf. J. Maritain, Humanisme intégral, Paris, Aubier, 2000 (reed.), pp. 18, 37, 137 and 230–232; J. Maritain, The Person and the Common Good, Notre Dame, University of Notre Dame Press, 2002 (reed.), pp. 29, 49–50, 92–93 and 104; J. Maritain, O Homem e o Estado, 4th ed., Rio de Janeiro, Livr. Agir Ed., 1966, pp. 96–102; J. Maritain, Los Derechos del Hombre y la Ley Natural, Buenos Aires, Ed. Leviatan, 1982, pp. 38, 44, 50, 69 and 94–95, and cf. pp. 79–82; J. Maritain, Para una Filosofía de la Persona Humana, Buenos Aires, Ed. Club de Lectores, 1984, pp. 164, 176–178, 196–197, 221 and 231.

101 J. Maritain, De la justice politique – Notes sur la présente guerre, Paris, Libr. Plon, 1940, pp. 88, 90–91, 106–107 and 112–114.

102 As shown in his posthumous book of essays: S. Zweig, Messages from a Lost World, London, Pushkin Press, 2016, pp. 55, 88–90, 97, 107 and 176.

103 Ibid., pp. 170 and 175.

104. Yet, in his dense and thoughtful intellectual autobiography (*Le monde d'hier*, 1944), written shortly before putting an end to his own life, Stefan Zweig expressed his deep concern with the fading away of conscience, disclosed by the fact that the world got used to the "dehumanisation, injustice and brutality, as never before in hundreds of centuries";[104] persons had been transformed into simple objects.[105] Earlier on, – before the nuclear age, – his friend the psychologist Sigmund Freud, in a well-known essay (*Civilization and Its Discontents*, 1930), expressed his deep preoccupation with what he perceived as an impulse to barbarism and destruction, which could not be expelled from the human psyche.[106] In face of human hostility and the threat of self-disintegration, – he added, – there is a consequent loss of happiness.[107]

105. Another psychologist, Carl Jung, referring, in his book *Aspects du drame contemporain* (1948), to events of contemporary history of his epoch, warned against subsuming individuals under the State; in his view, collective evil and culpability contaminate everyone everywhere.[108] He further warned against the tragic dehumanization of others[109] and the psychic exteriorizations of mass movements (of the collective inconscient) conducive to destruction.[110]

106. To the writer and theologian Albert Schweitzer (who wrote his *Kulturphilosophie* in 1923), the essence of civilization lies in the respect for life, to the benefit of each person and of humankind.[111] He rejected the "illness" of *Realpolitik*, having stated that good consists in the preservation and exaltation of life, and evil lies in its destruction; nowadays more than ever, – he added, – we need an "ethics of reverence for life", what requires responsibility.[112] He insisted, in

---

104   S. Zweig, *O Mundo que Eu Vi* [1944, *Die Welt von Gestern*], Rio de Janeiro, Edit. Record, 1999, p. 483, and cf. 272–274, 278, 462, 467, 474, 490 and 503–505.
105   *Ibid.*, p. 490.
106   Sigmund Freud, *Civilization and Its Discontents* [1930], N.Y., Norton & Cia., 1962 [reed.], pp. 7–9, 26, 36–37 and 59–63.
107   Cf. *ibid.*, pp. 23 and 67–92.
108   C.G. Jung, *Aspects du drame contemporain*, Genève/Paris, Libr. de l'Univ. Georg/Éd. de la Colonne Vendôme, 1948, pp. 99 and 145.
109   *Ibid.*, pp. 173 and 179.
110   *Ibid.*, pp. 198–200, 208, 218–219 and 223.
111   A. Schweitzer, *Filosofia da Civilização* [1923], São Paulo, Edit. Unesp, 2011 [reed.], pp. 80, 304, 311 and 315.
112   A. Schweitzer, *Pilgrimage to Humanity* [*Weg zur Humanität*], N.Y., Philosophical Library, 1961, pp. 87–88, 99 and 101.

his book *La civilisation et l'éthique* (1923), that respect for life started as from "une prise de conscience" of one's responsibility *vis-à-vis* the life of others.[113]

107. Later on in his life, then in the nuclear age, in his series of lectures *Paix ou guerre atomique* (1958), A. Schweitzer called for an end to nuclear weapons, with their "destructions et anéantissements inimaginables".[114] In his own words,

> La guerre atomique ne connaît pas de vainqueurs, mais uniquement des vaincus. Chaque belligérant subit par les bombes et les projectiles atomiques de l'adversaire les mêmes dégâts qu'il lui inflige par les siens. Il en résulte un anéantissement continu (...). Il peut seulement dire: allons-nous nous suicider tous les deux par une extermination réciproque?.[115]

108. Well before them, by the turn of the XIXth to the XXth century, the writer Leo Tolstoi warned (*The Slavery of Our Times*, 1900) against the undue use of the State monopoly of "organized violence", conforming a new form of slavery of the vulnerable ones;[116] he criticized the recruitment of personnel to be sent to war to kill defenseless persons, perpetrating acts of extreme violence.[117] On his turn, the physician Georges Duhamel warned (in his account *Civilisation – 1914-1917*) against the fact that war had become an industry of killing, with a "barbaric ideology", destroying civilization with its "lack of humanity"; yet, he still cherished the hope that the spirit of humanism could flourish from the ashes.[118]

109. The historian of ideas Isaiah Berlin, for his part, warned (*The Proper Study of Mankind*) against the dangers of the *raison d'État*, and stressed the relevance

---

113 M. Arnold, *Albert Schweitzer – La compassion et la raison*, Lyon, Éd. Olivétan, 2015, pp. 74–75 and 77.
114 *Cit. in ibid.*, p. 111.
115 Extract from his book *Paix ou guerre atomique* (1958), reproduced in his posthumous book of essays: A. Schweitzer, *Respect de la vie* (org. B. Kaempf), Paris, Éd. Arfuyen/CIAL, 1990, p. 98.
116 L. Tolstoi, *La Esclavitud de Nuestro Tiempo* [1900], Barcelona, Littera, 2000 [reed.], pp. 86–87, 89, 91 and 97.
117 *Ibid.*, pp. 101, 103–104 and 121.
118 G. Duhamel, *Civilisation – 1914-1917*, Paris, Mercure de France, 1944, pp. 53 and 274–275; G. Duhamel, *Mémorial de la guerre blanche – 1938*, Paris, Mercure de France, 1945, pp. 41, 95, 100, 102 and 170.

of *values*, in the search of knowledge, of cultures, and of the *recta ratio*.[119] On his turn, the writer Erich Fromm upheld human life in insisting that there could only exist a truly "civilized" society if based on humanist values.[120] Towards the end of his life, in his book *The Anatomy of Human Destructivity* (1974), he warned against destruction and propounded the prevalence of love for life.[121]

110. E. Fromm further warned that the devastation of wars (including the contemporary ones) have led to the loss of hope and to brutalization, amidst the tension of the co-existence or ambivalence between civilization and barbarism, which requires all our endeavours towards the revival of humanism.[122] Likewise, in our days, the philosopher Edgar Morin has also warned that the advances of scientific knowledge disclosed an ambivalence, in that they provided, on the one hand, the means to improve the knowledge of the world, and, on the other hand, with the production (and proliferation) of nuclear weapons, in addition to other weapons (biological and chemical) of mass destruction, the means to destroy the world.[123]

111. Future has thus become unpredictable, and unknown, in face of the confrontation between the forces of life and the forces of death. Yet, – he added, – human beings are endowed with conscience, and are aware that civilizations, as well as the whole of humankind, are mortal.[124] E. Morin further contended the tragic experiences lived in recent times should lead to the repentance of barbarism and the return to humanism; in effect, to think about, and resist to, barbarism, amounts to contributing to recreate humanism.[125]

112. For his part, in the late eighties, in his book of essays *Silences et mémoires d'hommes* (1989), Elie Wiesel stressed the need of memory and attention to the

---

119   I. Berlin, *The Proper Study of Mankind*, N.Y., Farrar & Straus & Giroux, 2000 (reed.), pp. 78, 135, 155, 217, 235–236, 242, 247, 311 and 334; I. Berlin, "Return of the *Volksgeist*: Nationalism, Good and Bad", *in At Century's End* (ed. N.P. Gardels), San Diego/Cal., Alti Publ., 1995, p. 94.
120   Cf. E. Fromm, *Las Cadenas de la Ilusión – Una Autobiografía Intelectual* [1962], Barcelona, Paidós, 2008 [reed.], pp. 78 and 234–239.
121   Cf. E. Fromm, *Anatomía de la Destructividad Humana* [1974], Mexico/Madrid/Buenos Aires, 2009 [reed.], pp. 16–468; and cf. also E. Fromm, *El Amor a la Vida* [1983 – *Über die Liebe zum Leben*], Barcelona, Paidós, 2016 (4th reprint), pp. 15–250.
122   E. Fromm, *Las Cadenas de la Ilusión...*, *op. cit. supra* n. (120), pp. 240 and 250–251.
123   E. Morin, *Vers l'abîme?*, Paris, L'Herne, 2012, pp. 9, 24–25 and 40–41.
124   *Ibid.*, pp. 27, 30, 59, 85, 89, 126 and 181.
125   E. Morin, *Breve Historia de la Barbarie en Occidente*, Barcelona, Paidós, 2009, p. 94, and cf. pp. 60 and 92–93.

world wherein we live, so as to combat the indifference to violence and evil.[126] Looking back to the Book of *Genesis*, he saw it fit to recall that "Caïn et Abel – les premiers enfants sur terre, – se découvrirent ennemis. Bien que frères, l'un devin l'assassin ou la victime de l'autre. L'enseignement que nous devrions en tirer? Deux hommes peuvent être frères et néanmoins désireux de s'entretuer. Et aussi: quiconque tue, tue son frère. Seulement cela, on l'apprend plus tard".[127]

113. Turning attention to the threat of nuclear weapons, E. Wiesel sharply criticized the already prevailing attitude of indifference to it: "le monde, aujourd'hui, nous paraît étonnamment indifférent vis-à-vis de la question nucléaire", – an attitude which he found ununderstandable.[128] And he added that

> L'indifférence (...) peut elle aussi devenir contagieuse. (...) L'indifférence permet également de mesurer la progression du mal que mine la société. (...) Là encore, la mémoire seule peut nous réveiller. Si nous nous souvenons de ce qui s'est passé il y a quarante ans, nous avons une possibilité d'empêcher de nouvelles catastrophes. Sinon, nous risquons d'être les victimes de notre propre indifférence. Car si nous sommes indifférents aux leçons de notre passé, nous le serons aux espoirs inhérents à notre avenir. (...) Voici mon angoisse: si nous oublions, nous serons oubliés. (...) Si nous restons indifférents à notre sort, (...) il ne restera personne pour raconter notre histoire.[129]

114. In effect, already in the early XXth century, Henri Bergson, in his monograph *La conscience et la vie* (1911), devoted attention to the search for meaning in life: to him, to live with conscience is to remember the past (memory) in the present, and to anticipate the future.[130] In his own words,

> Retenir ce qui n'est déjà plus, anticiper sur ce qui n'est pas encore, voilà donc la première fonction de la conscience. (...) [L]a conscience est un trait d'union entre ce qui a été et ce qui sera, un pont jeté entre le passé et l'avenir.[131]

---

126   E. Wiesel, *Silences et mémoires d'hommes*, Paris, Éd. Seuil, 1989, pp. 166, 173 and 175.
127   *Ibid.*, pp. 167–168.
128   *Ibid.*, p. 174, and cf. p. 170.
129   *Ibid.*, pp. 175–176.
130   H. Bergson, *La conscience et la vie* [1911], Paris, PUF, 2012 [reprint], pp. 10–11, 13 and 26.
131   *Ibid.*, pp. 5–6.

115. Also in international legal doctrine, there have been those who have felt the need to move away from State voluntarism and acknowledge the prevalence of conscience over the "will". It is not my intention to dwell upon this point here, as I have dealt with it elsewhere.[132] For the purposes of the present Dissenting Opinion, suffice it to recall a couple of examples. The jurist Gustav Radbruch, at the end of his life, forcefully discarded legal positivism, always subservient to power and the established order, and formulated his moving conversion and profession of faith in jusnaturalism.[133] His lucid message was preserved and has been projected in time,[134] thanks to the devotion of his students and disciples of the School of Heidelberg.

116. There are further examples of doctrinal endeavours to put limits to State voluntarism, such as the jusnaturalist construction of, e.g., Alfred Verdross, – as from the *idée du droit*, – of an objective law finding expression in the general principles of law, preceding positive international law;[135] or else the conception of the *droit spontanée*, of Roberto Ago, upholding the spontaneous formation (emanating from human conscience, well beyond the "will" of individual States) of new rules of international law.[136]

117. In the view of Albert de La Pradelle, the conception of the formation of international law on the strict basis of reciprocal rights and duties only of States is "extremely grave and dangerous".[137] International law is a "droit de la communauté humaine", encompassing, besides States, also peoples and human beings; it is the "droit de toute l'humanité", on the foundations of which are the general principles of law.[138] To A. de La Pradelle, this "droit de

---

[132] Cf. A.A. Cançado Trindade, *International Law for Humankind – Towards a New Jus Gentium*, 2nd rev. ed., Leiden/The Hague, Nijhoff/The Hague Academy of International Law, 2013, pp. 141–147 and 153–161.

[133] Cf. G. Radbruch, *Introducción a la Filosofía del Derecho*, 3rd ed., Mexico/Buenos Aires, Fondo de Cultura Económica, 1965, pp. 9–180.

[134] Cf., e.g., R. Alexy, *The Argument from Injustice – A Reply to Legal Positivism*, Oxford, Oxford University Press, 2010, pp. 3–130.

[135] A. Verdross, *Derecho Internacional Público*, 5th ed., Madrid, Aguilar, 1969 [reprint], pp. 15–19.

[136] R. Ago, "Nouvelles réflexions sur la codification du droit international", 92 *Revue générale de droit international public* (1988) p. 540, and cf. p. 541 on "la nature non volontaire de l'origine du droit coutumier".

[137] A. de La Pradelle, *Droit international public* (cours sténographié), Paris, Institut des Hautes Études Internationales/Centre Européen de la Dotation Carnegie, November 1932/May 1933, p. 33, and cf. pp. 36–37.

[138] *Ibid.*, pp. 49–59, 149, 222 and 264.

l'humanité" is not static, but rather dynamic, attentive to human values, in the line of jusnaturalist thinking.[139]

118. "Juridical conscience" is invoked in lucid criticisms of legal positivism.[140] Thus, in his monograph-plea (of 1964) against nuclear weapons, for example, Stefan Glaser sustained that customary international norms are those that, "according to universal conscience", ought to regulate the international community, for fulfilling common interest and responding to the demands of justice; and he added that

> C'est sur cette conscience universelle que repose la principale caractéristique du droit international: la conviction que ses normes sont indispensables pour le bien commun explique leur reconnaissance en tant que règles obligatoires.[141]

119. This is the position that I also uphold; in my own understanding, it is the universal juridical conscience that is the ultimate material source of international law.[142] In my view, one cannot face the new challenges confronting the whole international community keeping in mind only State susceptibilities; such is the case with the obligation to render the world free of nuclear weapons, an imperative of *recta ratio* and not a derivative of the "will" of States. In effect, to keep hope alive it is necessary to bear always in mind humankind as a whole.

120. For my part, within the ICJ, I have deemed it fit to ponder, in my Dissenting Opinion (paras. 488–489) in the case concerning the *Application of the Convention against Genocide* (Croatia *versus* Serbia, Judgment of 03.02.2015), that, from Homer's *Iliad* (late VIIIth or early VIIth century b.C.) to date, individuals, indoctrinated and conditioned for war and destruction, have become objects of the struggle for domination. I recalled that this has been lucidly warned by Simone Weil, in a penetrating essay (of 1934), to whom this ends up victimizing everyone, there occurring "the substitution of the ends by the means",

---

139   Cf. *ibid.*, pp. 412–413.
140   Such as, e.g., those of Antonio Gómez Robledo, *Meditación sobre la Justicia* [1963], Mexico/Buenos Aires, Fondo de Cultura Económica, 1963, pp. 179 and 185; R. Quadri, "Cours général de droit international public", 113 *Recueil des Cours de l'Académie de Droit International de La Haye* (1964) pp. 326, 332, 336–337, 339 and 350–351.
141   S. Glaser, *L'arme nucléaire à la lumière du droit international*, Paris, Pédone, 1964, p. 18.
142   Cf. A.A. Cançado Trindade, *op. cit. supra* (132), Ch. VI, pp. 139–161.

transforming human life into a simple means, which can be sacrificed; individuals become unable to think, in face of the "social machine" of destruction of the spirit and fabrication of the inconscience.[143]

121. The presence of evil has accompanied and marked human existence along the centuries. In the same aforementioned Dissenting Opinion in the case concerning the *Application of the Convention against Genocide* (2015), after drawing attention to "the ever-lasting presence of evil, which appears proper to the human condition, in all times", I added:

> It is thus understandable that it has attracted the concern of, and has presented challenges to, legal thinking, in our times and previous centuries, as well as other branches of knowledge (such as, e.g., history, psychology, anthropology, sociology, philosophy and theology, among others). It has marked presence in literature as well. This long-standing concern, along centuries, has not, however, succeeded to provide an explanation for evil.
>
> Despite the endeavours of human thinking, along history, it has not been able to rid humankind of it. Like the passing of time, the ever-lasting presence of evil is yet another mystery surrounding human beings, wherever and while they live. Whenever individuals purport to subject their fellow human beings to their 'will', placing this latter above conscience, evil is bound to manifest itself. In one of the most learned writings on the problem of evil, R.P. Sertillanges ponders that the awareness of evil and the anguish emanated therefrom have marked presence in all civilizations. The ensuing threat to the future of human kind has accounted for the continuous presence of that concern throughout the history of human thinking.[144]
>
> Religions were the first to dwell upon the problem of evil, which came also to be considered by philosophy, history, psychology, social sciences, and literature. Along the centuries, human thinking has always acknowledged the need to examine the problem of evil, its incidence in human relations, in the world wherein we live, without losing faith in human values.[145] Despite the perennial quest of human thinking to find answers

---

143   S. Weil, *Reflexiones sobre las Causas de la Libertad y de la Opresión Social*, Barcelona, Ed. Paidós/Universidad Autónoma de Barcelona, 1995, pp. 81–82, 84 and 130–131; S. Weil, *Réflexions sur les causes de la liberté et de l'oppression sociale*, Paris, Gallimard, 1955, pp. 124–125, and cf. pp. 114–115 and 144.
144   R.P. Sertillanges, *Le problème du mal – l'histoire*, Paris, Aubier, 1948, pp. 5–412.
145   *Ibid.*, pp. 5–412.

to the problem of evil, – going as far back as the *Book of Job*, or even further back, to the *Genesis* itself,[146] – not even theology has found an explanation for it, satisfactory to all (paras. 472-474).

122. The Scripture's account of Cain and Abel (*Genesis*, Ch. 4: 8-10) along the centuries came to be regarded as the aetiology of the fragmentation of humankind, as from the indifference of an individual to the fate of another. The increasing disregard for human life was fostered by growing, generalized and uncontrolled violence in search of domination. This was further aggravated by ideological manipulations, and even the dehumanization of the others, the ones to be victimized. The problem of evil continues to be studied, in face of the human capacity for extreme violence and self-destruction on a large scale.[147] The tragic message of the Book of *Genesis*, in my perception, seems perennial, as contemporary as ever, in the current nuclear age.

IX   The Attention of the United Nations Charter to Peoples

123. It should be kept in mind that the United Nations Charter was adopted on 26.06.1945 on behalf of "we, the peoples of the United Nations". In several provisions it expresses its concern with the living conditions of all peoples (preamble, Articles 55, 73(a), 76, 80), and calls for the promotion of, and

---

146   Cf., *inter alia*, e.g., M. Neusch, *L'énigme du mal*, Paris, Bayard, 2007, pp. 7-193; J. Maritain, *Dio e la Permissione del Male*, 6th ed., Brescia, Edit. Morcelliana, 2000, pp. 9-100; E. Fromm, *Anatomía de la Destructividad Humana*, Mexico/Madrid/Buenos Aires, Siglo XXI Edit., 2009 [reprint], pp. 11-468; P. Ricoeur, *Evil – A Challenge to Philosophy and Theology*, London, Continuum, 2007, pp. 33-72; P. Ricoeur, *Le mal – Un défi à la philosophie et à la théologie*, Genève, Éd. Labor et Fides, 2004, pp. 19-65; C.S. Nino, *Juicio al Mal Absoluto*, Buenos Aires, Emecé Edit., 1997, pp. 7-292; A. Morton, *On Evil*, N.Y./London, Routledge, 2004, pp. 1-148; T. Eagleton, *On Evil*, New Haven/London, Yale University Press, 2010, pp. 1-163; P. Dews, *The Idea of Evil*, Oxford, Wiley-Blackwell, 2013, pp. 1-234.

147   Cf., moreover, *inter alia*, e.g., [Various Authors,] *Le Mal* (ed. C. Crignon), Paris, Flammarion, 2000, pp. 11-232; J. Waller, *Becoming Evil*, 2nd ed., Oxford, Oxford University Press, 2007, pp. 3-330; S. Baron-Cohen, *The Science of Evil – On Empathy and the Origins of Cruelty*, N.Y., Basic Books, 2012, pp. 1-243; L. Svendsen, *A Philsophy of Evil*, Champaign/London, Dalkey Archive Press, 2011 [reprint], pp. 9-282; M. Salvioli, *Bene e Male – Variazioni sul Tema*, Bologna, Ed. Studio Domenicano (ESD), 2012, pp. 11-185; D. Livingstone Smith, *Less than Human*, N.Y., St. Martin's Press, 2011, pp. 1-316; R. Safranski, *El Mal, o el Drama de la Libertad*, 4th ed., Barcelona, Tusquets Edit., 2014, pp. 15-281; S. Neiman, *Evil in Modern Thought*, 2nd ed., Princeton/Oxford, Princeton University Press, 2015, pp. 1-359; J.-C. Guillebaud, *Le tourment de la guerre*, Paris, Éd. de l'Iconoclaste, 2016, pp. 9-390.

universal respect for, human rights (Articles 55(c), 62(2), 68, 76(c)). It invokes the "principles of justice and international law" (Article 1(1)), and refers to "justice and respect for the obligations arising from treaties and other sources of international law" (preamble). It further states that the Statute of the ICJ, "the principal judicial organ of the United Nations", forms "an integral part" of the U.N. Charter itself (Article 92).

124. In the mid-fifties, Max Huber, a former Judge of the PCIJ, wrote that international law has to protect also values common to humankind, attentive to respect for life and human dignity, in the line of the jusnaturalist conception of *the jus gentium*; the U.N. Charter, in incorporating human rights into this *droit de l'humanité*, initiated a new era in the development of international law, in a way rescuing the idea of the *civitas maxima*, which marked presence already in the historical origins of the law of nations. The U.N. Charter's attention to peoples, its principled position for the protection of the human person, much transcend positive domestic law and politics.[148]

125. The new vision advanced by the U.N. Charter, and espoused by the Law of the United Nations, has, in my perception, an incidence upon judicial settlement of international disputes. Thus, the fact that the ICJ's mechanism for the handling of contentious cases is an inter-State one, does not mean that its reasoning should also pursue a strictly inter-State dimension; that will depend on the nature and substance of the cases lodged with it. And there have been several cases lodged with the Court that required a reasoning going well beyond the inter-State dimension.[149] Such reasoning beyond the inter-State dimension

---

148 Max Huber, *La pensée et l'action de la Croix-Rouge*, Genève, CICR, 1954, pp. 26, 247, 270, 286 and 291.

149 Cf., e.g., the case of *Nottebohm* (1955, pertaining to double nationality); the cases of the *Trial of Pakistani Prisoners of War* (1973), of the *Hostages (U.S. Diplomatic and Consular Staff) in Teheran* case (1980); of the *Application of the Convention against Genocide* (Bosnia *versus* Serbia, 1996 and 2007); of the *Frontier Dispute between Burkina Faso and Mali* (1998); the triad of cases concerning consular assistance – namely, the cases *Breard* (Paraguay *versus* United States,1998), the case *LaGrand* (Germany *versus* United States, 2001), the case *Avena and Others* (Mexico *versus* United States, 2004); the cases of *Armed Activities in the Territory of Congo* (D.R. Congo *versus* Uganda, 2000, concerning grave violations of human rights and of International Humanitarian Law); of the *Land and Maritime Boundary between Cameroon and Nigeria* (1996); of *Questions Relating to the Obligation to Prosecute or Extradite* (Belgium *versus* Senegal, 2009–2013, pertaining to the principle of universal jurisdiction under the U.N. Convention against Torture); of *A.S. Diallo* (Guinea *versus* D.R. Congo, 2010, on detention and expulsion of a foreigner),

is faithful to the U.N. Charter, the ICJ being "the principal judicial organ of the United Nations" (Article 92).

126. Recently, in one of such cases, that of the *Application of the Convention against Genocide* (Croatia *versus* Serbia, 2015), in my extensive Dissenting Opinion appended thereto, I have deemed it fit, *inter alia*, to warn that

> The present case concerning the *Application of the Convention against Genocide* (Croatia *versus* Serbia) provides yet another illustration of the pressing need to overcome and move away from the dogmatic and strict inter-State outlook, even more cogently. In effect, the 1948 Convention against Genocide, – adopted on the eve of the Universal Declaration of Human Rights, – is not State-centered, but rather *people-centred*. The Convention against Genocide cannot be properly interpreted and applied with a strict State-centered outlook, with attention turned to inter-State susceptibilities. Attention is to be kept on the *justiciables*, on the victims, – real and potential victims, – so as to impart justice under the Genocide Convention (para. 496).

127. In a report in the early nineties, a former U.N. Secretary-General, calling for a "concerted effort" towards complete disarmament, rightly pondered that "[d]ans le monde d'aujourd'hui, les nations ne peuvent plus se permettre de résoudre les problèmes par la force. (...) Le désarmement est l'un des moyens les plus importants de réduire la violence dans les relations entre États".[150] There followed the cycle of World Conferences of the United Nations along the nineties, in a commendable endeavour of the United Nations *to go beyond and transcend the purely inter-State dimension*, imbued of a spirit of solidarity, so as to consider the challenges for the future of humankind.

---

of the *Jurisdictional Immunities of the State* (Germany *versus* Italy, Greece intervening, 2010–2012); of the *Application of the International Convention on the Elimination of All Forms of Racial Discrimination* (Georgia *versus* Russian Federation, 2011); of the *Temple of Preah Vihear* (Cambodia *versus* Thailand, provisional measures, 2011); of the *Application of the Convention against Genocide* (Croatia *versus* Serbia, 2015). To those cases one can add the two most recent Advisory Opinions of the ICJ, on the *Declaration of Independence of Kosovo* (2010); and on a *Judgment of the ILO Administrative Tribunal upon a Complaint Filed against the IFAD* (2012).

150 B. Boutros-Ghali, *Nouvelles dimensions de la réglementation des armements et du désarmement dans la période de l'après-guerre froide – Rapport du Secrétaire Général*, N.Y., Nations Unies, 1993, pp. 21–22.

128. Those U.N. World Conferences disclosed a growing awareness of the international community as a whole, and entered into a continuing universal dialogue between U.N. member States and entities of the civil societies, – which I well remember, having participated in it,[151] – so as to devise the new international agenda in the search of common solutions for the new challenges affecting humankind as a whole. In focusing attention on vulnerable segments of the populations, the immediate concern has been with meeting basic human needs, that memorable cycle of World Conferences disclosed a common concern with the deterioration of living conditions, dramatically affecting increasingly greater segments of the population in many parts of the world nowadays.[152]

129. The common denominator in those U.N. World Conferences – as I have pointed out on distinct occasions along the last two decades[153] – can be found in the recognition of the legitimacy of the concern of the international community as a whole with the conditions of living of all human beings everywhere. The placing of the well-being of peoples and human beings, of the improvement of their conditions of living, at the centre of the concerns of the international community, is remindful of the historical origins of the *droit des gens*.[154]

---

151   E.g., in the U.N. Conference on Environment and Development (Rio de Janeiro, 1992, in its World NGO Forum) and in the II World Conference on Human Rights (Vienna, 1993, in the same Forum and in its Drafting Committee).
152   A growing call was formed for the pursuance of social justice *among* and *within* nations.
153   A.A. Cançado Trindade, *A Proteção dos Vulneráveis como Legado da II Conferência Mundial de Direitos Humanos (1993–2013)*, Fortaleza/Brazil, IBDH/IIDH/SLADI, 2014, pp. 13–356; A.A. Cançado Trindade, "Sustainable Human Development and Conditions of Life as a Matter of Legitimate International Concern: The Legacy of the U.N. World Conferences", *in Japan and International Law – Past, Present and Future* (International Symposium to Mark the Centennial of the Japanese Association of International Law), The Hague, Kluwer, 1999, pp. 285–309; A.A. Cançado Trindade, "The Contribution of Recent World Conferences of the United Nations to the Relations between Sustainable Development and Economic, Social and Cultural Rights", *in Les hommes et l'environnement: Quels droits pour le vingt-et-unième siècle? – Études en hommage à Alexandre Kiss* (eds. M. Prieur and C. Lambrechts), Paris, Éd. Frison-Roche, 1998, pp. 119–146; A.A. Cançado Trindade, "Memória da Conferência Mundial de Direitos Humanos (Viena, 1993)", 87/90 *Boletim da Sociedade Brasileira de Direito Internacional* (1993–1994) pp. 9–57.
154   Those Conferences acknowledged that human rights do in fact permeate all areas of human activity, and contributed decisively to the reestablishment of the central position of human beings in the conceptual universe of the law of nations (*droit des gens*). Cf., on the matter, A.A. Cançado Trindade, *Évolution du Droit international au droit des*

130. At the end of the decade and the dawn of the new millennium, the United Nations Millennium Declaration (adopted by General Assembly's resolution 55/2, of 08.09.2000) stated the determination "to eliminate the dangers posed by weapons of mass destruction" (para. II(8)), and, noticeably,

> To strive for the elimination of weapons of mass destruction, particularly nuclear weapons, and to keep all options open for achieving this aim, including the possibility of convening and international conference to identify ways of eliminating nuclear dangers (para. II(9)).

131. In addition to our responsibilities to our individual societies, – the U.N. Millennium Declaration added, –

> we have a collective responsibility to uphold the principles of human dignity, equality and equity at the global level. (...) [W]e have a duty therefore to all the world's people, especially the most vulnerable and, in particular, the children of the world, to whom the future belongs.
>
> We reaffirm our commitment to the purposes and principles of the Charter of the United Nations, which have proved timeless and universal. Indeed, their relevance and capacity to inspire have increased, as nations and peoples have become increasingly interconnected and interdependent (paras. I(2–3)).

X   Impertinence of the So-Called *Monetary Gold* "Principle"

132. The distortions generated by the obsession with the strict inter-State paradigm are not hard to detect. An example is afforded, in this connection, by the ICJ's handling of the *East Timor* case (1995): the East Timorese people had no *locus standi* to request intervention in the proceedings, not even to present an *amicus curiae*, although the crucial point under consideration was that of sovereignty over their own territory. Worse still, the interests of a third State (which had not even accepted the Court's jurisdiction) were taken for granted and promptly safeguarded by the Court, by means of the application of the so-called *Monetary Gold* "principle", – an assumed "principle" also invoked now, two decades later, in the present case concerning the obligation of elimination of nuclear weapons!

---

gens – L'accès des particuliers à la justice internationale: le regard d'un juge, Paris, Pédone, 2008, pp. 1–187.

133. Attention has to be turned to the *nature* of the case at issue, which may well require a reasoning – as the *cas d'espèce* does – moving away from "a strict State-centred voluntarist perspective" and from the "exaltation of State consent", and seeking guidance in fundamental principles (*prima principia*), such as the principle of humanity. This is what I pointed out in my extensive Dissenting Opinion in the case concerning the *Application of the Convention against Genocide* (Croatia *versus* Serbia, Judgment of 03.02.2015), where I pondered *inter alia* that such *prima principia* confer to the international legal order "its ineluctable axiological dimension"; they "conform its *substratum*, and convey the idea of an *objective* justice, in the line of jusnaturalist thinking" (para. 517).

134. That was not the first time I made such ponderation: I had done the same, in another extensive Dissenting Opinion (para. 213), in the case concerning the *Application of the International Convention on the Elimination of All Forms of Racial Discrimination* – CERD (Georgia *versus* Russian Federation, Judgment of 01.04.2011). In my subsequent aforementioned Dissenting Opinion in the case concerning the *Application of the Convention against Genocide* I expressed my dissatisfaction that in a case pertaining to the interpretation and application of the Convention against Genocide, the ICJ even made recourse to the so-called *Monetary Gold* "principle",[155] which had no place in a case like that, and "which does not belong to the realm of the *prima principia*, being nothing more than a concession to State consent, within an outdated State voluntarist framework" (para. 519).

135. May I, in the present Dissenting Opinion, this time in the case of *Obligations Concerning Negotiations Relating to Cessation of the Nuclear Arms Race and to Nuclear Disarmament*, again leave on the records my dissatisfaction for the same reason. Once again, may I stress that the adjudication of a case like the present one shows the need to go beyond the strict inter-State outlook. The fact that the mechanism for the adjudication of contentious cases before the ICJ is an inter-State one, does not at all imply that the Court's reasoning should likewise be strictly inter State. In the present case concerning nuclear weapons and the obligation of nuclear disarmament, it is necessary to focus attention on peoples, rather than on inter-State susceptibilities. It is imperative to keep in mind the world population, in pursuance of a humanist outlook, in the light of the *principle of humanity*.

---

155 Even if only to dismiss it (para. 116).

XI   The Fundamental Principle of the Juridical Equality of States

136. The present case of *Obligations Concerning Negotiations Relating to Cessation of the Nuclear Arms Race and to Nuclear Disarmament* stresses the utmost importance of the principle of the juridical equality of States. The importance attributed to fundamental principles, the idea of an objective justice, and its incidence upon the laws, go back in time, being deeply-rooted in jusnaturalist thinking. If laws are deprived of justice, they no longer oblige in conscience. Ethics cannot be dissociated from law; in the international scenario, each one is responsible for all the others. To the "founding fathers" of the law of nations (*droit des gens*), like F. de Vitoria and F. Suárez, the principle of equality was fundamental, in the relations among individuals, as well as among nations. Their teachings have survived the erosion of time: today, four and a half centuries later, the basic principle of equality and non-discrimination is in the foundations of the Law of the United Nations itself.

137. The present case of *Obligations Concerning Negotiations Relating to Cessation of the Nuclear Arms Race and to Nuclear Disarmament* is surely not the first one before the ICJ that brings to the fore the relevance of the principle of the juridical equality of States. In the ICJ's Order (of Provisional Measures of Protection) of 03.03.2014, I have deemed it fit to point out, in my Separate Opinion appended thereto, that the case concerning *Questions Relating to the Seizure and Detention of Certain Documents and Data*

> bears witness of the relevance of the principle of the juridical equality of States. The prevalence of this fundamental principle has marked a long-standing presence in the realm of international law, ever since the times of the II Hague Peace Conference of 1907, and then of the drafting of the Statute of the Permanent Court of International Justice by the Advisory Committee of Jurists, in June–July 1920. Recourse was then made, by that Committee, *inter alia*, to general principles of law, as these latter embodied the objective idea of justice. A general principle such as that of the juridical equality of States, enshrined a quarter of a century later in the United Nations Charter (Article 2(1)), is ineluctably intermingled with the quest for justice.
>
> Subsequently, throughout the drafting of the 1970 U.N. Declaration on Principles of International Law concerning Friendly Relations and Co-operation among States in accordance with the Charter of the United Nations (1964–1970), the need was felt to make it clear that stronger States cannot impose their will upon the weak, and that *de facto* inequalities

among States cannot affect the weaker in the vindication of their rights. The principle of the juridical equality of States gave expression to this concern, embodying the *idée de justice*, emanated from the universal juridical conscience (paras. 44–45).

138. And one decade earlier, in my General Course on Public International Law delivered at the Hague Academy of International Law (2005), I pondered that

> On successive occasions the principles of international law have proved to be of fundamental importance to humankind's quest for justice. This is clearly illustrated by the role played, *inter alia*, by the principle of juridical equality of States. This fundamental principle, – the historical roots of which go back to the II Hague Peace Conference of 1907, – proclaimed in the U.N. Charter and enunciated also in the 1970 Declaration of Principles, means ultimately that all States, – factually strong and weak, great and small, – are equal before international law, are entitled to the same protection under the law and before the organs of international justice, and to equality in the exercise of international rights and duties.
>
> Despite successive attempts to undermine it, the principle of juridical equality of States has remained, from the II Hague Peace Conference of 1907 to date, one of the basic pillars of International Law. It has withstood the onslaught of time, and shown itself salutary for the peaceful conduction of international relations, being ineluctably associated – as it stands – with the foundations of International Law. It has been very important for the international legal system itself, and has proven to be a cornerstone of international law in the United Nations era. In fact, the U.N. Charter gave it a new dimension, and the principle developments such as that of the system of collective security, within the ambit of the law of the United Nations.[156]

139. By the turn of the century, the General Assembly's resolution 55/2, of 08.09.2000, adopted the United Nations Millennium Declaration, which *inter alia* upheld the "sovereign equality of all States", in conformity with "the principles of justice and international law" (para. I(4)). Half a decade later, the General Assembly's resolution 60/1, of 16.09.2005, adopted the *World Summit Outcome*, which *inter alia* expressed the determination "to establish a just and lasting peace all over the world in accordance with the purposes and principles

---

156 A.A. Cançado Trindade, *International Law for Humankind – Towards a New Jus Gentium*, op. cit. supra n. (132), pp. 84–85, and cf. pp. 62–63, 65 and 73.

of the [U.N.] Charter", as well as "to uphold the sovereign equality of all States" (para. I(5)). In stressing therein the "vital importance of an effective multilateral system" to face current challenges to international peace and security (paras. 6–7), the international community reiterated its profession of faith in the general principles of international law.

XII   Unfoundedness of the Strategy of "Deterrence"

140. In effect, the strategy of "deterrence", pursued by NWS in the present context of nuclear disarmament in order to attempt to justify their own position, makes abstraction of the fundamental principle of the juridical equality of States, enshrined into the U.N. Charter. Factual inequalities cannot be made to prevail over the juridical equality of States. All U.N. member States are juridically equal. The strategy of a few States pursuing their own "national security interests" cannot be made to prevail over a fundamental principle of international law set forth in the U.N. Charter: factual inequalities between States cannot, and do not prevail over the juridical equality of States.

141. In its 1996 Advisory Opinion on the *Threat or Use of Nuclear Weapons*, permeated with ambiguity, the ICJ gave undue weight to "the still strong adherence to the practice of deterrence" (paras. 67 and 73) by a few NWS, to the point of beholding in it an obstacle to the formation and consolidation of *opinio juris* and a customary rule as to the illegality of nuclear weapons, leading to "a specific and express prohibition" of their use (para. 73). Here the Court assumed its usual positivist posture: in its view, the prohibition must be express, stated in positive law, even if those weapons are capable of destroying all life on earth, the whole of humankind…

142. The ICJ, in its Advisory Opinion of 1996, gave too much weight to the opposition of NWS as to the existence of an *opinio juris* on the unlawfulness of nuclear weapons. And this, despite the fact that in their overwhelming majority, member States of the United Nations stand clearly against nuclear weapons, and in favour of nuclear disarmament. The 1996 Advisory Opinion, notwithstanding, appears unduly influenced by the lack of logic of "deterrence".[157] One cannot conceive, – as the 1996 Advisory Opinion did, – of recourse to nuclear

---

157   Cf. criticisms of such posture in, e.g., A. Sayed, *Quand le droit est face à son néant – Le droit à l'épreuve de l'emploi de l'arme nucléaire*, Bruxelles, Bruylant, 1998, pp. 79–80, 84, 88–89, 96 and 113.

weapons by a hypothetical State in "self-defence" at the unbearable cost of the devastating effects and sufferings inflicted upon humankind as a whole, in an "escalade vers l'apocalypse".[158]

143. The infliction of such devastation and suffering is in flagrant breach of international law, – of the ILHR, IHL and the Law of the United Nations (cf. Part XIII, *infra*). It is, furthermore, in flagrant breach of norms of *jus cogens*.[159] The strategy of "deterrence" seems to make abstraction of all that. The ICJ, as the International Court *of Justice*, should have given, on all occasions when it has been called upon to pronounce on nuclear weapons (in the exercise of its jurisdiction on contentious and advisory matters), far greater weight to the *raison d'humanité*,[160] rather than to the *raison d'État* nourishing "deterrence". We have to keep in mind the human person and the peoples, for which States were created, instead of relying only on what one assumes to be the *raison d'État*. The *raison d'humanité*, in my understanding, prevails surely over considerations of *Realpolitik*.

144. In its 1996 Advisory Opinion, the ICJ, however, at the same time, rightly acknowledged the importance of complete nuclear disarmament, asserted in the series of General Assembly resolutions, and the relevance of the corresponding obligation under Article VI of the NPT to the international community as a whole (paras. 99 and 102). To the Court, this is an obligation of result, and not of mere conduct (para. 99). Yet, it did not extract the consequences of that. Had it done so, it would have reached the conclusion that nuclear disarmament cannot be hampered by the conduct of a few States – the NWS – which maintain and modernize their own arsenals of nuclear weapons, pursuant to their strategy of "deterrence".

145. The strategy of "deterrence" has a suicidal component. Nowadays, in 2016, twenty years after the 1996 ICJ Advisory Opinion, and with the subsequent

---

158 Cf. *ibid.*, p. 147, and cf. pp. 129, 133, 151, 160, 174–175, 197 and 199–200.

159 On the expansion of the material content of this latter, cf. A.A. Cançado Trindade, "*Jus Cogens*: The Determination and the Gradual Expansion of Its Material Content in Contemporary International Case-Law", *in XXXV Curso de Derecho Internacional Organizado por el Comité Jurídico Interamericano – 2008*, Washington D.C., OAS General Secretariat, 2009, pp. 3–29.

160 A.A. Cançado Trindade, "La Humanización del Derecho Internacional y los Límites de la Razón de Estado", *in* 40 *Revista da Faculdade de Direito da Universidade Federal de Minas Gerais* – Belo Horizonte/Brazil (2001), pp. 11–23.

reiteration of the conventional and customary international legal obligation of nuclear disarmament, there is no longer any room for ambiguity. There is an *opinio juris communis* as to the illegality of nuclear weapons, and as to the well-established obligation of nuclear disarmament, which is an obligation of result and not of mere conduct. Such *opinio juris* cannot be erased by the dogmatic positivist insistence on an express prohibition of nuclear weapons; on the contrary, that *opinio juris* discloses that the invocation of the absence of an express prohibition is nonsensical, in relying upon the destructive and suicidal strategy of "deterrence".

146. Such strategy is incompatible with jusnaturalist thinking, always attentive to ethical considerations (cf. Part XV *infra*). Over half a century ago (precisely 55 years ago), the U.N. General Assembly had already stated, in its seminal resolution 1653 (XVI) of 1961, that the use of nuclear weapons was "contrary to the spirit, letter and aims of the United Nations", a "direct violation" of the U.N. Charter, a breach of international law and of "the laws of humanity", and "a crime against mankind and civilization" (operative para. 1). Several subsequent General Assembly resolutions upheld the same understanding of resolution 1653(XVI) of 1961 (cf. Part III, *supra*), leaving thus no room at all for ambiguity or hesitation, or to any concession.

147. Two decades ago, in the advisory proceedings of late 1995 before the ICJ, conducive to its 1996 Advisory Opinion on *Threat or Use of Nuclear Weapons*, fierce criticisms were voiced of the strategy of "deterrence", keeping in mind the inhumane sufferings of victims of nuclear detonation, radiation and contamination.[161] Attention was drawn, on the occasion, to the "distortion of logic" in "deterrence", in trying to rely on so immensely destructive weapons to keep peace, and in further trying to persuade others "to accept that for the last 50 or so years this new and more dangerous and potentially genocidal level or armaments should be credited with keeping peace".[162]

148. In the aforementioned advisory proceedings, "nuclear deterrence" was dismissed as being "simply the maintenance of a balance of fear";[163] it was criticized as seeking to ground itself on a "highly questionable" premise, whereby a handful of NWS feel free to "arrogate to themselves" the faculty "to determine

---

161 Cf., e.g., the testimonies of the Mayors of Hiroshima and Nagasaki, in Part XIII, *infra*.
162 ICJ, doc. CR 95/35, of 15.11.1995, p. 32 (statement of Zimbabwe).
163 ICJ, doc. CR 95/27, of 07.11.1995, p. 37 (statement of the Mayor of Nagasaki).

what is world peace and security, exclusive in the context of their own" national strategies and interests.[164] It was contended that nuclear weapons are in breach of international law by their own nature, as weapons of catastrophic mass destruction; "nuclear deterrence" wrongfully assumes that States and individuals act rationally, leaving the world "under the nuclear sword of Damocles", stimulating "the nuclear ambitions of their countries, thereby increasing overall instability", and also increasing the danger of their being used "intentionally or accidentally".[165]

149. The NWS, in persisting to rely on the strategy of "deterrence", seem to overlook the above-reviewed distinct series of U.N. General Assembly resolutions (cf. Part III, *supra*) condemning nuclear weapons and calling for their elimination. The strategy of "deterrence" has come under strong criticism along the years, for the serious risks it carries with it, and for its indifference to the goal – supported by the United Nations, – of achieving a world free of nuclear weapons. Very recently, e.g., participants in the series of Conferences on the Humanitarian Impact of Nuclear Weapons (2013–2014) have strongly criticized the strategy of nuclear "deterrence". In a statement sent to the 2014 Vienna Conference, for example, the U.N. Secretary-General warned against the dangers of nuclear "deterrence", undermining world stability (cf. Part XIX, *infra*).

150. There is here, in effect, clearly formed, an *opinio juris communis* as to the illegality and prohibition of nuclear weapons. The use or threat of use of nuclear weapons being a clear breach of international law, of International Humanitarian Law and of the International Law of Human Rights, and of the U.N. Charter, renders unsustainable and unfounded any invocation of the strategy of "deterrence". In my view, a few States cannot keep on insisting on "national security interests" to arrogate to themselves indefinitely the prerogative to determine by themselves the conditions of world peace, and to impose them upon all others, the overwhelming majority of the international community. The survival of humankind cannot be made to depend on the "will" of a handful of privileged States. The universal juridical conscience stands well above the "will" of individual States.

---

164   *Ibid.*, p. 45, para. 14 (statement of Malaysia).
165   *Ibid.*, p. 55, para. 8; and cf. pp. 60–61 and 63, paras. 17–20 (statement of Malaysia).

XIII The Illegality of Nuclear Weapons and the Obligation of Nuclear Disarmament

1 *The Condemnation of All Weapons of Mass Destruction*

151. Since the beginning of the nuclear age, it became clear that the effects of nuclear weapons (such as heat and radiation) cannot be limited to military targets only, being thus by nature indiscriminate and disproportionate in their long-term devastation, disclosing the utmost cruelty. The *opinio juris communis* as to the prohibition of nuclear weapons, and of all weapons of mass destruction, has gradually been formed, along the last decades.[166] If weapons less destructive than nuclear weapons have already been expressly prohibited (as is the case of biological and chemical weapons), it would be nonsensical to argue that, those which have not, by positive conventional international law, like nuclear weapons, would not likewise be illicit; after all, they have far greater and long-lasting devastating effects, threatening the existence of the international community as a whole.

152. It may be recalled that, already in 1969, *all* weapons of mass destruction were condemned by the *Institut de Droit International* (I.D.I.). In the debates of its Edinburgh session on the matter, emphasis was placed on the need to respect the principle of distinction (between military and non-military objectives), and the terrifying effects of the use of nuclear weapons were pointed out, – the example of the atomic bombing of Hiroshima and Nagasaki having been expressly recalled.[167] In its resolution of September 1969 on the matter, the *Institut* began by restating, in the preamble, the *prohibition of recourse to force* in international law, and the duty of protection of civilian populations in any armed conflict; it further recalled the general principles of international law, customary rules and conventions, – supported by international case-law and practice, – which "clearly restrict" the extent to which the parties engaged in a conflict may harm the adversary, and warned against

---

166 Cf., e.g., G.E. do Nascimento e Silva, "A Proliferação Nuclear e o Direito Internacional", in *Pensamiento Jurídico y Sociedad Internacional – Libro-Homenaje al Prof. A. Truyol y Serra*, vol. II, Madrid, Universidad Complutense, 1986, pp. 877–886; C.A. Dunshee de Abranches, *Proscrição das Armas Nucleares*, Rio de Janeiro, Livr. Freitas Bastos, 1964, pp. 114–179.

167 Cf. *Annuaire de l'Institut de Droit International* – Session d'Edimbourg (1969)-II, pp. 49–50, 53, 55, 60, 62–63, 66, 88–90 and 99.

the consequences which the indiscriminate conduct of hostilities and particularly the use of nuclear, chemical and bacteriological weapons, may involve for civilian populations and for mankind as a whole.[168]

153. In its operative part, the aforementioned resolution of the *Institut* stressed the importance of the principle of distinction (between military and non-military objectives) as a "fundamental principle of international law" and the pressing need to protect civilian populations in armed conflicts,[169] and added, in paragraphs 4 and 7, that:

> Existing international law prohibits all armed attacks on the civilian population as such, as well as on non-military objects, notably dwellings or other buildings sheltering the civilian population, so long as these are not used for military purposes (...).
>
> Existing international law prohibits the use of all weapons which, by their nature, affect indiscriminately both military objectives and non-military objects, or both armed forces and civilian populations. In particular, it prohibits the use of weapons the destructive effect of which is so great that it cannot be limited to specific military objectives or is otherwise uncontrollable (self-generating weapons), as well as of 'blind' weapons.[170]

154. For its part, the International Law Association (I.L.A.), in its more recent work (in 2014) on nuclear disarmament, after referring to Article VI of the NPT, was of the view that it was not only conventional, but also an evolving customary international obligation with an *erga omnes* character, affecting "the international community as a whole", and not only the States Parties to the NPT.[171] It also referred to the "world-wide public opinion" pointing to "the catastrophic consequences for humankind of any use or detonation of nuclear weapons", and added that reliance on nuclear weapons for "deterrence" was thus unsustainable.[172]

---

168   Text *in*: *Annuaire de l'Institut de Droit International* – Session d'Edimbourg (1969) II, pp. 375–376.
169   Paras. 1–3, 5–6 and 8, *in ibid.*, pp. 376–377.
170   Text *in ibid.*, pp. 376–377.
171   International Law Association (I.L.A.), Committee: *Nuclear Weapons, Non-Proliferation and Contemporary International Law* (2nd Report: *Legal Aspects of Nuclear Disarmament*), I.L.A. Washington Conference, 2014, pp. 2–4.
172   *Ibid.*, pp. 5–6.

155. In its view, "nuclear deterrence" is not a global "umbrella", but rather a threat to international peace and security, and NWS are still far from implementing Article VI of the NPT.[173] To the International Law Association, the provisions of Article VI are not limited to States Parties to the NPT, "they are part of customary international law or at least evolving custom"; they are valid *erga omnes*, as they affect "the international community as a whole", and not only a group of States or a particular State.[174] Thus, as just seen, learned institutions in international law, such as the I.D.I. and the I.L.A., have also sustained the prohibition in international law of all weapons of mass destruction, starting with nuclear weapons, the most devastating of all.

156. A single use of nuclear weapons, irrespective of the circumstances, may today ultimately mean the end of humankind itself.[175] All weapons of mass destruction are illegal, and are prohibited: this is what ineluctably ensues from an international legal order of which the ultimate material source is the *universal juridical conscience*.[176] This is the position I have consistently sustained along the years, including in a lecture I delivered at the University of Hiroshima, Japan, on 20.12.2004.[177] I have done so in the line of jusnaturalist thinking, faithful to the lessons of the "founding fathers" of the law of nations, keeping in mind not only States, but also peoples and individuals, and humankind as a whole.

2 *The Prohibition of Nuclear Weapons: The Need of a People-Centred Approach*

157. In effect, the nuclear age itself, from its very beginning (the atomic blasts of Hiroshima and Nagasaki in August 1945) can be properly studied from a people-centred approach. There are moving testimonies and historical

---

173 *Ibid.*, pp. 8–9.

174 *Ibid.*, p. 18.

175 Nagendra Singh, *Nuclear Weapons and International Law*, London, Stevens, 1959, p. 242.

176 A.A. Cançado Trindade, *International Law for Humankind – Towards a New Jus Gentium*, op. cit. supra n. (132), Ch. VI ("The Material Source of International Law: Manifestations of the Universal Juridical Conscience"), pp. 139–161.

177 Text of my lecture reproduced *in*: A.A. Cançado Trindade, *Le Droit international pour la personne humaine*, Paris, Pédone, 2012, Ch. I ("L'illicéité de toutes les armes de destruction massive au regard du droit international contemporain"), pp. 61–90; A.A. Cançado Trindade, *A Humanização do Direito Internacional*, 2nd ed., Belo Horizonte/Brazil, Edit. Del Rey, 2015, Ch. XVII ("The Illegality under Contemporary International Law of All Weapons of Mass Destruction"), pp. 361–390.

accounts of the devastating effects of nuclear weapons, from surviving victims and witnesses.[178] Yet, even with the eruption of the nuclear age, attention remained focused largely on State strategies: it took some time for it gradually to shift to the devastating effects of nuclear weapons on peoples.

158. As recalled in one of the historical accounts, only at the first Conference against Atomic and Hydrogen Bombs (1955), "the victims had their first opportunity, after ten years of silence, to make themselves heard", in that forum.[179] Along the last decades, there have been endeavours to shift attention from State strategies to the numerous victims and enormous damages caused by nuclear weapons, focusing on "human misery and human dignity".[180] Recently, one significant initiative to this effect has been the series of Conferences on the Humanitarian Impact of Nuclear Weapons (2013–2014), which I shall survey later on in this Dissenting Opinion (cf. Part XIX, *infra*).

159. There has been a chorus of voices of those who have been personally victimized by nuclear weapons in distinct circumstances, – either in the atomic bombings of Hiroshima and Nagasaki (1945), or in nuclear testing (during the cold-war era) in regions such as Central Asia and the Pacific. Focusing on their intensive suffering (e.g., ensuing from radioactive contamination and forced displacement),[181] affecting successive generations, they have drawn attention to the humanitarian consequences of nuclear weapon detonations.

160. In addressing the issue of nuclear weapons, on four successive occasions (cf. *infra*), the ICJ appears, however, to have always suffered from inter-State myopia. Despite the clarity of the formidable threat that nuclear weapons represent, the treatment of the issue of their prohibition under international law has most regrettably remained permeated by ambiguities. The present case of

---

178   Michihiko Hachiya, *Journal d'Hiroshima – 6 août-30 septembre 1945* [1955], Paris, Éd. Tallandier, 2015 [reed.], pp. 25–281; Toyofumi Ogura, *Letters from the End of the World – A Firsthand Account of the Bombing of Hiroshima* [1948], Tokyo/N.Y./London, Kodansha International, 2001 [reed.], pp. 15–173; Naomi Shohno, *The Legacy of Hiroshima – Its Past, Our Future*, Tokyo, Kōsei Publ. Co., 1987 [reed.], pp. 13–140; Kenzaburo Oe, *Notes de Hiroshima* [1965], [Paris,] Gallimard, 1996 [reed.], pp. 17–230; J. Hersey, *Hiroshima* [1946], London, Penguin, 2015 [reprint], pp. 1–98.
179   Kenzaburo Oe, *Hiroshima Notes* [1965], N.Y./London, Marion Boyars, 1997 [reed.], pp. 72 and 159.
180   *Ibid.*, pp. 149 and 162.
181   Cf. J. Borrie, "Humanitarian Reframing of Nuclear Weapons and the Logic of a Ban", 90 *International Affairs* (2014) p. 633, and cf. pp. 637, 643–644 and 646.

Obligations Concerning Negotiations Relating to Cessation of the Nuclear Arms Race and to Nuclear Disarmament is the third time that attempts were made, by means of the lodging of contentious cases with the ICJ, to obtain its pronouncement thereon. On two prior occasions – in the *Nuclear Tests* cases (1974 and 1995),[182] the Court assumed, in both of them, a rather evasive posture, avoiding to pronounce clearly on the substance of a matter pertaining to the very survival of humankind.

161. May I here briefly single out one aspect of those earlier contentious proceedings, given its significance in historical perspective. It should not pass unnoticed that, in the first *Nuclear Tests* case (Australia and New Zealand *versus* France), one of the applicant States contended, *inter alia*, that the nuclear testing undertaken by the French government in the South Pacific region violated not only the right of New Zealand that no radioactive material enter its territory, air space and territorial waters *and* those of other Pacific territories but *also* "the rights of all members of the international community, including New Zealand, that no nuclear tests that give rise to radioactive fall-out be conducted".[183]

162. For its part, the other applicant State contended that it was seeking protection to the life, health and well-being of Australia's population, in common with the populations of other States, against atmospheric nuclear tests by any State.[184] Thus, over three decades ago, the perspective of the *Applications Instituting Proceedings* of both New Zealand and Australia (of 1973) went clearly – and correctly so – beyond the purely inter-State dimension, as the problem at issue concerned the international community as a whole.

163. Both Australia and New Zealand insisted on the people-centred approach throughout the legal proceedings (written and oral phases). New Zealand, for example, in its *Memorial*, invoked the obligation *erga omnes* not to undertake nuclear testing "owed to the international community as a whole" (paras. 207–208), adding that non-compliance with it aroused "the keenest sense of alarm and antagonism among the peoples" and States of the region wherein

---

182 Cf. *I.C.J. Reports 1974*, pp. 63–455; and cf. *I.C.J. Reports 1995*, pp. 4–23, and the position of three dissenting Judges in *ibid.*, pp. 317–421.

183 ICJ, *Application Instituting Proceedings* (of 09.05.1973), *Nuclear Tests* case (New Zealand *versus* France), pp. 8 and 15–16, cf. pp. 4–16.

184 ICJ, *Application Instituting Proceedings* (of 09.05.1973), *Nuclear Tests* case (Australia *versus* France), pp. 12 and 14, paras. 40, 47 and 49(1).

the tests were conducted (para. 212). In its oral arguments in the public sitting of 10.07.1974 in the same *Nuclear Tests* case, New Zealand again invoked "the rights of all members of the international community", and the obligations *erga omnes* owed to the international community as a whole.[185] And Australia, for example, in its oral arguments in the public sitting of 08.07.1974, referring to the 1963 Partial Test Ban Treaty, underlined the concern of "the whole international community" for "the future of mankind" and the responsibility imposed by "the principles of international law" upon "all States to refrain from testing nuclear weapons in the atmosphere".[186]

164. The outcome of the *Nuclear Test* cases, however, was rather disappointing: even though the ICJ issued orders of Provisional Measures of Protection in the cases in June 1973 (requiring the respondent State to cease testing), subsequently, in its Judgments of 1974,[187] in view of the announcement of France's voluntary discontinuance of its atmospheric tests, the ICJ found, yielding to State voluntarism, that the claims of Australia and New Zealand no longer had "any object" and that it was thus not called upon to give a decision thereon.[188] The dissenting Judges in the case rightly pointed out that the legal dispute between the contending parties, far from having ceased, still persisted, since what Australia and New Zealand sought was a declaratory judgment of the ICJ stating that atmospheric nuclear tests were contrary to international law.[189]

---

185   ICJ, *Pleadings, Oral Arguments, Documents – Nuclear Tests cases* (vol. II: New Zealand *versus* France, 1973–1974), pp. 256–257 and 264–266.
186   ICJ, *Pleadings, Oral Arguments, Documents – Nuclear Tests cases* (vol. I: Australia *versus* France, 1973–1974), p. 503.
187   For a critical parallel between the 1973 Orders and the 1974 Judgments, cf. P. Lellouche, "The *Nuclear Tests* Cases: Judicial Silence *versus* Atomic Blasts", 16 *Harvard International Law Journal* (1975) pp. 615–627 and 635; and, for further criticisms, cf. *ibid.*, pp. 614–637.
188   *I.C.J. Reports 1974*, pp. 272 and 478, respectively.
189   ICJ, *Nuclear Tests* case, Joint Dissenting Opinion of Judges Onyeama, Dillard, Jiménez de Aréchaga and Waldock, *I.C.J. Reports 1974*, pp. 319–322, 367–369, 496, 500, 502–504, 514 and 520–521; and cf. Dissenting Opinion of Judge De Castro, *ibid.*, pp. 386–390; and Dissenting Opinion of Judge Barwick, *ibid.*, pp. 392–394, 404–405, 436–437 and 525–528. It was further pointed out that the ICJ should thus have dwelt upon the question of the existence of rules of *customary* international law prohibiting States from causing, through atmospheric nuclear tests, the deposit of radio-active fall-out on the territory of other States; ICJ, *Nuclear Tests* case, Separate Opinion of Judge Petrén, *I.C.J. Reports 1974*, pp. 303–306 and 488–489. It was the existence or otherwise of such customary rules that had to be determined, – a question which unfortunately was left largely unanswered by the Court in that case.

THE UNIVERSAL JURIDICAL CONSCIENCE, HUMANENESS 303

165. The reticent position of the ICJ in that case was even more regrettable if one recalls that the applicants, in referring to the "psychological injury" caused to the peoples of the South Pacific region through their "anxiety as to the possible effects of radioactive fall-out on the well-being of themselves and their descendants", as a result of the atmospheric nuclear tests, ironically invoked the notion of *erga omnes* obligations (as propounded by the ICJ itself in its *obiter dicta* in the *Barcelona Traction* case only four years earlier).[190] As the ICJ reserved itself the right, in certain circumstances, to reopen the case decided in 1974, it did so two decades later, upon an application instituted by New Zealand *versus* France. But in its Order of 22.09.1995, the ICJ dismissed the complaint, as it did not fit into the *caveat* of the 1974 Judgment, which concerned atmospheric nuclear tests; here, the complaint was directed against the underground nuclear tests conducted by France since 1974.[191]

166. The ICJ thus lost two historical opportunities, in both contentious cases (1974 and 1995), to clarify the key point at issue (nuclear tests). And now, with the decision it has just rendered today, 05.10.2016, it has lost a third occasion, this time to pronounce on the *Obligations Concerning Negotiations Relating to Cessation of the Nuclear Arms Race and to Nuclear Disarmament*, at the request of the Marshall Islands. This time the Court has found that the existence of a legal dispute has not been established before it and that it has no jurisdiction to consider the Application lodged with it by the Marshall Islands on 24.04.2014.

167. Furthermore, in the mid-nineties, the Court was called upon to exercise its advisory function, in respect of a directly related issue, that of nuclear weapons: both the U.N. General Assembly and the World Health Organization (WHO) opened those proceedings before the ICJ, by means of requests for an Advisory Opinion. Such requests no longer referred to nuclear tests, but rather to the question of the threat or use of nuclear weapons in the light of international law, for the determination of their illegality or otherwise.

---

190   As recalled in the Joint Dissenting Opinion of Judges Onyeama, Dillard, Jiménez de Aréchaga and Waldock, *I.C.J. Reports 1974*, pp. 362, 368–369 and 520–521; as well as in the Dissenting Opinion of Judge Barwick, *ibid.*, pp. 436–437.

191   Cf. *I.C.J. Reports 1995*, pp. 288–308; once again, there were Dissenting Opinions (cf. *ibid.*, pp. 317–421). Furthermore, petitions against the French nuclear tests in the atoll of Mururoa and in that of Fangataufa, in French Polinesia, were lodged with the European Commission of Human Rights (EComHR); cf. EComHR, case *N.N. Tauira and 18 Others versus France* (appl. n. 28204/95), decision of 04.12.1995, 83-A *Decisions and Reports* (1995) p. 130.

168. In response to only one of the applications, that of the U.N. General Assembly,[192] the Court, in the Advisory Opinion of 08.07.1996 on the *Threat or Use of Nuclear Weapons*, affirmed that neither customary international law nor conventional international law authorizes specifically the threat or use of nuclear weapons; neither one, nor the other, contains a complete and universal prohibition of the threat or use of nuclear weapons as such; it added that such threat or use which is contrary to Article 2(4) of the U.N. Charter and does not fulfil the requisites of its Article 51, is illicit; moreover, the conduct in armed conflicts should be compatible with the norms applicable in them, including those of International Humanitarian Law; it also affirmed the obligation to undertake in good will negotiations conducive to nuclear disarmament in all its aspects.[193]

169. In the most controversial part of its Advisory Opinion (resolutory point 2E), the ICJ stated that the threat or use of nuclear weapons "would be generally contrary to the rules of international law applicable in armed conflict", mainly those of International Humanitarian Law; however, the Court added that, at the present stage of international law "it cannot conclude definitively if the threat or use of nuclear weapons would be lawful or unlawful in an extreme circumstance of self defence in which the very survival of a State would be at stake".[194] The Court therein limited itself to record the existence of a legal uncertainty.

170. In fact, it did not go further than that, and the Advisory Opinion was permeated with evasive ambiguities, not avoiding the shadow of the *non liquet*, in relation to a question which affects, more than each State individually, the whole of humankind. The Advisory Opinion made abstraction of the fact that International Humanitarian Law applies likewise in case of self-defence, always safeguarding the principles of distinction and proportionality (which nuclear weapons simply ignore),[195] and upholding the prohibition of infliction of unnecessary suffering.

---

192 As the ICJ understood, as to the other application, that the WHO was not competent to deal with the question at issue, – despite the purposes of that U.N. specialized agency at issue and the devastating effects of nuclear weapons over human health and the environment...

193 *I.C.J. Reports 1996*, pp. 266–267.

194 *Ibid.*, p. 266.

195 L. Doswald-Beck, "International Humanitarian Law and the Advisory Opinion of the International Court of Justice on the Legality of the Threat or Use of Nuclear Weapons",

171. The Advisory Opinion could and should have given greater weight to a point made before the ICJ in the oral arguments of November 1995, namely, that of the need of a people-centred approach in the present domain. Thus, it was stated, for example, that the "experience of the Marshallese people confirms that unnecessary suffering is an unavoidable consequence of the detonation of nuclear weapons";[196] the effects of nuclear weapons, by their nature, are widespread, adverse and indiscriminate, affecting also future generations.[197] It was further stated that the "horrifying evidence" of the use of atomic bombs in Hiroshima and Nagasaki, followed by the experience and the aftermath of the nuclear tests carried out in the region of the Pacific Island States in the 1950s and the 1960s, have alerted to "the much graver risks to which mankind is exposed by the use of nuclear weapons".[198]

172. The 1996 Opinion, on the one hand, recognized that nuclear weapons cause indiscriminate and durable suffering, and have an enormous destructive effect (para. 35), and that the principles of humanitarian law (encompassing customary law) are "intransgressible" (para. 79); nevertheless, these considerations did not appear sufficient to the Court to discard the use of such weapons also in self-defence, thus eluding to tell what the Law is in all circumstances. It is clear to me that States are bound to respect, and to ensure respect, for International Humanitarian Law (IHL) and the International Law of Human Rights (ILHR) in *any circumstances*; their fundamental principles belong to the domain of *jus cogens*, in prohibition of nuclear weapons.

---

[316] *International Review of the Red Cross* (1997) pp. 35–55; H. Fujita, "The Advisory Opinion of the International Court of Justice on the Legality of Nuclear Weapons", *in ibid.*, pp. 56–64. International Humanitarian Law prevails also over self-defence; cf. M.-P. Lanfranchi and Th. Christakis, *La licéité de l'emploi d'armes nucléaires devant la Cour Internationale de Justice*, Aix-Marseille/Paris, Université d'Aix-Marseille III/Economica, 1997, pp. 111, 121 and 123; S. Mahmoudi, "The International Court of Justice and Nuclear Weapons", 66 *Nordic Journal of International Law* (1997) pp. 77–100; E. David, "The Opinion of the International Court of Justice on the Legality of the Use of Nuclear Weapons", 316 *International Review of the Red Cross* (1997) pp. 21–34.

[196] ICJ, doc. CR 95/32, of 14.11.1995, p. 22 (statement of the Marshall Islands).
[197] *Ibid.*, p. 23.
[198] ICJ, doc. CR 95/32, of 14.11.1995, p. 31 (statement of Solomon Islands). Customary international law and general principles of international law have an incidence in this domain; *ibid.*, pp. 36 and 39–40.

173. Again, in the 1996 Opinion, it were the dissenting Judges, and not the Court's split majority, who drew attention to this,[199] and to the relevance of the Martens clause in the present context[200] (cf. Part XIV, *infra*). Moreover, the 1996 Opinion also minimized (para. 71) the resolutions of the U.N. General Assembly which affirm the illegality of nuclear weapons[201] and condemn their use as a violation of the U.N. Charter and as a crime against humanity. Instead, it took note of the "policy of deterrence", which led it to find that the members of the international community continued "profoundly divided" on the matter, rendering it impossible to determine the existence of an *opinio juris* in this respect (para. 67).

174. It was not incumbent upon the Court to resort to the unfounded strategy of "deterrence" (cf. Part XII, *supra*), devoid of any legal value for the determination of the formation of a customary international law obligation of prohibition of the use of nuclear weapons. The Court did not contribute on this matter. In unduly relying on "deterrence" (para. 73), it singled out a division, in its view "profound", between an extremely reduced group of nuclear powers on the one hand, and the vast majority of the countries of the world on the other; it ended up by favouring the former, by means of an inadmissible *non liquet*.[202]

175. The Court, thus, lost yet another opportunity, – in the exercise of its advisory function as well, – to contribute to the consolidation of the *opinio juris communis* in condemnation of nuclear weapons. Its 1996 Advisory Opinion considered the survival of a hypothetical State (in its resolutory point 2E), rather than that of peoples and individuals, and ultimately of humankind as

---

199   ICJ Advisory Opinion on *Threat or Use of Nuclear Weapons*, *I.C.J Reports 1996*, Dissenting Opinion of Judge Koroma, pp. 573–574 and 578.
200   Cf. *ibid.*, Dissenting Opinions of Judge Shahabuddeen, pp. 386–387, 406, 408, 410–411 and 425; and of Judge Weeramantry, pp. 477–478, 481, 483, 486–487, 490–491, 494, 508 and 553–554.
201   Notably, the ground-breaking General Assembly resolution 1653(XVI), of 24.11.1961.
202   A.A. Cançado Trindade, *International Law for Humankind – Towards a New Jus Gentium*, *op. cit. supra* n. (132), pp. 415–418; L. Condorelli, "Nuclear Weapons: A Weighty Matter for the International Court of Justice – *Jura Novit Curia*?", 316 *International Review of the Red Cross* (1997) pp. 9–20; M. Mohr, "Advisory Opinion of the International Court of Justice on the Legality of the Use of Nuclear Weapons under International Law – A Few Thoughts on Its Strengths and Weaknesses", 316 *International Review of the Red Cross* (1997) pp. 92–102. The Opinion is not conclusive and provides no guidance; J.-P. Queneudec, "E.T. à la C.I.J.: méditations d'un extra-terrestre sur deux avis consultatifs", 100 *Revue générale de Droit international public* (1996) 907–914, esp. p. 912.

a whole. It seemed to have overlooked that the survival of a State cannot have primacy over the right to survival of humankind as a whole.

3   The Prohibition of Nuclear Weapons: The Fundamental Right to Life

176. There is yet another related point to keep in mind. The ICJ's 1996 Advisory Opinion erroneously took IHL as *lex specialis* (para. 25), overstepping the ILHR, oblivious that the maxim *lex specialis derogat generalis*, thus understood, has no application in the present context: in face of the immense threat of nuclear weapons to human life on earth, both IHL and the ILHR apply in a converging way,[203] so as to enhance the much-needed protection of human life. In any circumstances, the norms which best protect are the ones which apply, be them of IHL or of the ILHR, or any other branch of international protection of the human person (such as the International Law of Refugees – ILR). They are all equally important. Regrettably, the 1996 Advisory Opinion unduly minimized the international case-law and the whole doctrinal construction on the right to life in the ambit of the ILHR.

177. It should not pass unnoticed, in this connection, that contemporary international human rights tribunals, such as the European (ECtHR) and the Inter-American (IACtHR) Courts of Human Rights, in the adjudication of successive cases in recent years, have taken into account the relevant principles and norms of both the ILHR and IHL (conventional and customary). For its part, the African Commission of Human and Peoples' Rights (AfComHPR), in its long-standing practice, has likewise acknowledged the approximations and convergences between the ILHR and IHL, and drawn attention to the principles underlying both branches of protection (such as, e.g., the principle of humanity).

178. This has been done, in distinct continents, so as to seek to secure the most effective safeguard of the protected rights, in all circumstances (including in times of armed conflict). Contrary to what was held in the ICJ's 1996 Advisory Opinion, there is no *lex specialis* here, but rather a concerted endeavour to apply the relevant norms (be them of the ILHR or of IHL) that best protect human beings. This is particularly important when they find themselves in a situation of utmost vulnerability, – such as in the present context of threat or use of nuclear weapons. In their case-law, international human rights tribunals

---

203   Cf. A.A. Cançado Trindade, *Derecho Internacional de los Derechos Humanos, Derecho Internacional de los Refugiados y Derecho Internacional Humanitario – Aproximaciones y Convergencias*, Geneva, ICRC, [2000], pp. 1–66.

(like the ECtHR and the IACtHR) have focused attention on the imperative of securing protection, e.g., to the fundamental right to life, of persons in great vulnerability (potential victims).[204]

179. In the course of the proceedings before the ICJ in the present cases of *Obligations Concerning Negotiations Relating to Cessation of the Nuclear Arms Race and to Nuclear Disarmament*, the applicant State draws attention reiteratedly to the devastating effects upon human life of nuclear weapons detonations. Thus, in the case opposing the Marshall Islands to the United Kingdom, the applicant State draws attention, in its Memorial, to the destructive effects of nuclear weapons (testing) in space and time (pp. 12–14). In its oral arguments of 11.03.2016, the Marshall Islands addresses the "tragic losses to the Marshallese", the "dire health consequences suffered by the Marshallese following nuclear contamination, including extreme birth defects and cancers".[205]

180. In the case opposing the Marshall Islands to India, the applicant State, in its *Memorial*, refers to the grave "health and environmental consequences of nuclear testing" upon the Marshallese (pp. 5–6). In its oral arguments of 07.03.2016, the Marshall Islands stated:

> The Marshall Islands has a unique and devastating history with nuclear weapons. While it was designated as a Trust Territory by the United Nations, no fewer than 67 atomic and thermonuclear weapons were deliberately exploded as 'tests' in the Marshall Islands, by the United States. (...) Several islands in my country were vaporized and others are estimated to remain uninhabitable for thousands of years. Many, many Marshallese died, suffered birth defects never before seen and battled cancers resulting from the contamination. Tragically the Marshall Islands thus bears *eyewitness* to the horrific and indiscriminate lethal capacity of these weapons, and the intergenerational and continuing effects that they perpetuate even 60 years later.
>
> One 'test' in particular, called the 'Bravo' test [in March 1954], was one thousand times stronger than the bombs dropped on Hiroshima and Nagasaki.[206]

---

204 Cf. A.A. Cançado Trindade, *The Access of Individuals to International Justice*, Oxford, Oxford University Press, 2012 [reprint], Chs. II–III and VII, pp. 17–62 and 125–131.
205 ICJ, doc. CR 2016/5, of 11.03.2016, p. 9, para. 10.
206 ICJ, doc. CR 2016/1, of 07.03.2016, p. 16, paras. 4–5.

181. And in the case opposing the Marshall Islands to Pakistan, the applicant State, in its *Memorial*, likewise addresses the serious "health and environmental consequences of nuclear testing" upon the Marshallese (pp. 5–6). In its oral arguments of 08.03.2016, the Marshall Islands recalls the 67 atomic and thermonuclear weapons "tests" that it had to endure (since it became a U.N. Trust Territory); it further recalls the reference, in the U.N. Charter, to nations "large and small" having "equal rights" (preamble), and to the assertion in its Article 2 that the United Nations is "based on the principle of the sovereign equality of all its Members".[207]

182. Two decades earlier, in the course of the advisory proceedings before the ICJ of late 1995 preceding the 1996 Advisory Opinion on the *Threat or Use of Nuclear Weapons*, the devastating effects upon human life of nuclear weapons detonations were likewise brought to the Court's attention. It is beyond the purposes of the present Dissenting Opinion to review all statements to this effect; suffice it here to recall two of the most moving statements, from the Mayors of Hiroshima and Nagasaki, who appeared before the Court as members of the Delegation of Japan. The Mayor of Hiroshima (Mr. Takashi Hiraoka) thus began his statement of 07.11.1995 before the ICJ:

> I am here today representing Hiroshima citizens, who desire the abolition of nuclear weapons. More particularly, I represent the hundreds of thousands of victims whose lives were cut short, and survivors who are still suffering the effects of radiation, 50 years later. On their behalf, I am here to testify to the cruel, inhuman nature of nuclear weapons. (...)
>
> The development of the atomic bomb was the product of cooperation among politicians, military and scientists. The nuclear age began the moment the bombs were dropped on human beings.
>
> Their enormous destructive power reduced utterly innocent civilian populations to ashes. Women, the elderly, and the newborn were bathed in deadly radiation and slaughtered.[208]

183. After stressing that the mass killing was "utterly indiscriminate", he added that, even today, "thousands of people struggle daily with the curse of illness caused by that radiation", there being until then "no truly accurate casualty figures".[209] The exposure in Hiroshima to high levels of radiation, – he

---

207 ICJ, doc. CR 2016/2, of 08.03.2016, p. 10, paras. 5–7.
208 ICJ, doc. CR 95/27, of 07.11.1995, pp. 22–23.
209 *Ibid.*, pp. 24–25.

proceeded, – "was the first in human history", generating leukemia, distinct kinds of cancer (of breast, lung, stomach, thyroid, and other), extending for "years or decades", with all the fear generated by such continuing killing "across years or decades".[210]

184. Even half a century later, – added the Mayor of Hiroshima, – "the effects of radiation on human bodies are not thoroughly understood. Medically, we do know that radiation destroys cells in the human body, which can lead to many forms of pathology".[211] The victimized segments of the population have continued suffering "psychologically, physically, and socially from the atomic bomb's after-effects".[212] He further stated that

> The horror of nuclear weapons (...) derives (...) from the tremendous destructive power, but equally from radiation, the effects of which reach across generations. (...) What could be more cruel? Nuclear weapons are more cruel and inhumane than any weapon banned thus far by international law.[213]

185. After singling out the significance of U.N. General Assembly resolution 1653 (XVI) of 1961, the Mayor of Hiroshima warned that "[t]he stockpiles of nuclear weapons on earth today are enough to annihilate the entire human race several times over. These weapons are possessed on the assumption that they can be used".[214] He concluded with a strong criticism of the strategy of "deterrence"; in his own words,

> As long as nuclear weapons exist, the human race faces a real and present danger of self-extermination. The idea based on nuclear deterrence that nuclear war can be controlled and won exhibits a failure of human intelligence to comprehend the human tragedy and global environmental destruction brought about by nuclear war. (...) [O]nly through a treaty that clearly stipulates the abolition of nuclear weapons can the world step toward the future (...).[215]

---

210 *Ibid.*, pp. 25–27.
211 *Ibid.*, p. 25.
212 *Ibid.*, pp. 27–28.
213 *Ibid.*, p. 30.
214 *Ibid.*, pp. 30–31.
215 *Ibid.*, p. 31.

186. For his part, the Mayor of Nagasaki (Mr. Iccho Itoh), in his statement before the ICJ, also of 07.11.1995, likewise warned that "nuclear weapons bring enormous, indiscriminate devastation to civilian populations"; thus, five decades ago, in Hiroshima and Nagasaki, "a single aircraft dropped a single bomb and snuffed out the lives of 140.000 and 74.000 people, respectively. And that is not all. Even the people who were lucky enough to survive continue to this day to suffer from the late effects unique to nuclear weapons. In this way, nuclear weapons bring enormous, indiscriminate devastation to civilian populations".[216]

187. He added that "the most fundamental difference between nuclear and conventional weapons is that the former release radioactive rays at the time of explosion", and the exposure to large doses of radiation generates a "high incidence of disease" and mortality (such as leukaemia and cancer). Descendants of atomic bomb survivors will have, amidst anxiety, "to be monitored for several generations to clarify the genetic impact"; "nuclear weapons are inhuman tools for mass slaughter and destruction", their use "violates international law".[217] The Mayor of Nagasaki concluded with a strong criticism of "nuclear deterrence", characterizing it as "simply the maintenance of a balance of fear" (p. 37), always threatening peace, with its "psychology of suspicion and intimidation"; the Nagasaki survivors of the atomic bombing of 50 years ago, "continue to live in fear of late effects".[218]

188. Those testimonies before the ICJ, in the course of contentious proceedings (in 2016) as well as advisory proceedings (two decades earlier, in 1995), leave it quite clear that the threat or use (including "testing") of nuclear weapons entails an arbitrary deprivation of human life, and is in flagrant breach of the fundamental right to life. It is in manifest breach of the ILHR, of IHL, as well as the Law of the United Nations, and hand an incidence also on the ILR. There are, furthermore, in such grave breach, aggravating circumstances: the harm caused by radiation from nuclear weapons cannot be contained in space, nor can it be contained in time, it is a true inter-generational harm.

189. As pointed out in the pleadings before the ICJ of late 1995, the use of nuclear weapons thus violates the right to life (and the right to health) of "not

---

216   ICJ, doc. CR 95/27, of 07.11.1995, p. 33.
217   *Ibid.*, pp. 36–37.
218   *Ibid.*, p. 39.

only people currently living, but also of the unborn, of those to be born, of subsequent generations".[219] Is there anything quintessentially more cruel? To use nuclear weapons appears like condemning innocent persons to hell on earth, even *before* they are born. That seems to go even further than the Book of *Genesis*'s story of the original sin. In reaction to such extreme cruelty, the consciousness of the rights inherent to the human person has always marked a central presence in endeavours towards complete nuclear disarmament.

4   The Absolute Prohibitions of Jus Cogens *and the Humanization of International Law*

190. The absolute prohibition of arbitrary deprivation of human life (*supra*) is one of *jus cogens*, originating in the ILHR, and with an incidence also on IHL and the ILR, and marking presence also in the Law of the United Nations. The absolute prohibition of inflicting cruel, inhuman or degrading treatment is one of *jus cogens*, originating likewise in the ILHR, and with an incidence also on IHL and the ILR. The absolute prohibition of inflicting unnecessary suffering is one of *jus cogens*, originating in IHL, and with an incidence also on the ILHR and the ILR.

191. In addition to those converging trends (ILHR, IHL, ILR) of international protection of the rights of the human person, those prohibitions of *jus cogens* mark presence also in contemporary International Criminal Law (ICL), as well as in the *corpus juris gentium* of condemnation of all weapons of mass destruction. The absolute prohibitions of *jus cogens* nowadays encompass the threat or use of nuclear weapons, for all the human suffering they entail: in the case of their use, a suffering without limits in space or in time, and extending to succeeding generations.

192. I have been characterizing, along the years, the doctrinal and jurisprudential construction of international *jus cogens* as proper of the new *jus gentium* of our times, the International Law for Humankind. I have been sustaining, moreover, that, by definition, international *jus cogens* goes beyond the law of treaties, extending itself to the law of the international responsibility of the State, and to the whole *corpus juris* of contemporary International Law, and reaching, ultimately, any juridical act.[220]

---

219   ICJ, doc. CR 95/35, of 15.11.1995, p. 28 (statement of Zimbabwe).
220   A.A. Cançado Trindade, *International Law for Humankind – Towards a New Jus Gentium*, op. cit. supra n. (132), Ch. XII, pp. 291–326.

193. In my lectures in an OAS Course of International Law delivered in Rio de Janeiro almost a decade ago, e.g., I have deemed it fit to ponder that

> The fact that the concepts both of the *jus cogens*, and of the obligations (and rights) *erga omnes* ensuing therefrom, already integrate the conceptual universe of contemporary international law, the new *jus gentium* of our days, discloses the reassuring and necessary opening of this latter, in the last decades, to certain superior and fundamental values. This significant evolution of the recognition and assertion of norms of *jus cogens* and obligations *erga omnes* of protection is to be fostered, seeking to secure its full practical application, to the benefit of all human beings. In this way the universalist vision of the founding fathers of the *droit des gens* is being duly rescued. New conceptions of the kind impose themselves in our days, and, of their faithful observance, will depend to a large extent the future evolution of contemporary international law.
>
> This latter does not emanate from the inscrutable 'will' of the States, but rather, in my view, from human conscience. General or customary international law emanates not so much from the practice of States (not devoid of ambiguities and contradictions), but rather from the *opinio juris communis* of all the subjects of international law (States, international organizations, human beings, and humankind as a whole). Above the will stands the conscience. (...)
>
> The current process of the necessary *humanization* of international law stands in reaction to that state of affairs. It bears in mind the universality and unity of the human kind, which inspired, more than four and a half centuries ago, the historical process of formation of the *droit des gens*. In rescuing the universalist vision which marked the origins of the most lucid doctrine of international law, the aforementioned process of humanization contributes to the construction of the new *jus gentium* of the XXIst century, oriented by the general principles of law. This process is enhanced by its own conceptual achievements, such as, to start with, the acknowledgement and recognition of *jus cogens* and the consequent obligations *erga omnes* of protection, followed by other concepts disclosing likewise a universalist perspective of the law of nations.
>
> (...) The emergence and assertion of *jus cogens* in contemporary international law fulfill the necessity of a minimum of verticalization in the international legal order, erected upon pillars in which the juridical and the ethical are merged. The evolution of the concept of *jus cogens* transcends nowadays the ambit of both the law of treaties and the law

of the international responsibility of the States, so as to reach general international law and the very foundations of the international legal order.[221]

5 The Pitfalls of Legal Positivism: A Rebuttal of the So-Called Lotus "Principle"

194. A matter which concerns the whole of humankind, such as that of the existence of nuclear weapons, can no longer be appropriately dealt with from a purely inter-State outlook of international law, which is wholly surpassed in our days. After all, without humankind there is no State whatsoever; one cannot simply have in mind States, apparently overlooking humankind. In its 1996 Advisory Opinion, the ICJ took note of the treaties which nowadays prohibit, e.g., biological and chemical weapons,[222] and weapons which cause excessive damages or have indiscriminate effects (para. 76).[223]

195. But the fact that nowadays, in 2016, there does not yet exist a similar general treaty, of specific prohibition of nuclear weapons, does not mean that these latter are permissible (in certain circumstances, even in self defence).[224] In my understanding, it cannot be sustained, in a matter which concerns the future of humankind, that which is not expressly prohibited is thereby permitted (a classic postulate of positivism). This posture would amount to the traditional – and surpassed – attitude of the *laisser-faire, laisser-passer*, proper of an international legal order fragmented by State voluntarist subjectivism, which in the history of international law has invariably favoured the most powerful ones. *Ubi societas, ibi jus...*

---

221 A.A. Cançado Trindade, "*Jus Cogens*: The Determination and the Gradual Expansion of Its Material Content in Contemporary International Case-Law", *in* XXXV *Curso de Derecho Internacional Organizado por el Comité Jurídico Interamericano – 2008*, Washington D.C., OAS General Secretariat, 2009, pp. 3–29.

222 The Geneva Protocol of 1925, and the Conventions of 1972 and 1993 against Biological and Chemical Weapons, respectively.

223 E.g., the 1980 Convention on Prohibitions or Restrictions on the Use of Certain Conventional Weapons Which May Be Deemed to Be Excessively Injurious or to Have Indiscriminate Effects.

224 The Roman-privatist influence – with its emphasis on the autonomy of the will had harmful consequences in traditional international law; in the public domain, quite on the contrary, conscience stands above the "will", also in the determination of competences.

196. Legal positivists, together with the so-called "realists" of *Realpolitik*, have always been sensitive to the established power, rather than to values. They overlook the time dimension, and are incapable to behold a universalist perspective. They are static, in time and space. Nowadays, in the second decade of the XXIst century, in an international legal order which purports to assert common superior values, amidst considerations of international *ordre public*, and basic considerations of humanity, it is precisely the reverse logic which is to prevail: *that which is not permitted, is prohibited.*[225]

197. Even in the days of the *Lotus* case (1927), the view endorsed by the old PCIJ whereby under international law everything that was not expressly prohibited would thereby be permitted, was object of severe criticisms, not only of a compelling Dissenting Opinion in the case itself[226] but also on the part of expert writing of the time.[227] Such conception could only have flourished in an epoch "politically secure" in global terms, certainly quite different from that of the current nuclear age, in face of the recurrent threat of nuclear weapons and other weapons of mass destruction, the growing vulnerability of territorial States and indeed of the world population, and the increasing complexity in the conduction of international relations. In our days, in face of such terrifying threat, it is the logic opposite to that of the *Lotus* case which imposes itself: all that is not expressly permitted is surely prohibited.[228] All weapons of mass destruction, including nuclear weapons, are illegal and prohibited under contemporary international law.

198. The case of *Shimoda and Others* (District Court of Tokyo, decision of 07.12.1963), with the dismissed claims of five injured survivors of the atomic bombings of Hiroshima and Nagasaki, stands as a grave illustration of the

---

225 A.A. Cançado Trindade, *O Direito Internacional em um Mundo em Transformação*, Rio de Janeiro, Edit. Renovar, 2002, p. 1099.

226 Cf. Dissenting Opinion of Judge Loder, PCIJ, *Lotus* case (France *versus* Turkey), Series A, n. 10, Judgment of 07.09.1927, p. 34 (such conception was not in accordance with the "spirit of international law").

227 Cf. J.L. Brierly, *The Basis of Obligation in International Law and Other Papers*, Oxford, Clarendon Press, 1958, p. 144; H. Lauterpacht, *The Function of Law in the International Community*, Oxford, Clarendon Press, 1933, pp. 409–412 and 94–96; and cf., subsequently, e.g., G. Herczegh, "Sociology of International Relations and International Law", *in Questions of International Law* (ed. G. Haraszti), Budapest, Progresprint, 1971, pp. 69–71 and 77.

228 A.A. Cançado Trindade, *O Direito Internacional em um Mundo em Transformação*, op. cit. supra n. (225), p. 1099.

veracity of the maxim *summum jus, summa injuria*, when one proceeds on the basis of an allegedly absolute submission of the human person to a degenerated international legal order built on an exclusively inter-State basis. May I here reiterate what I wrote in 1981, regarding the *Shimoda and Others* case, namely,

> (...) The whole arguments in the case reflect the insufficiencies of an international legal order being conceived and erected on the basis of an exclusive inter-State system, leaving individual human beings impotent in the absence of express treaty provisions granting them procedural status at international level. Even in such a matter directly affecting fundamental human rights, the arguments were conducted in the case in the classical lines of the conceptual apparatus of the so-called law on diplomatic protection, in a further illustration of international legal reasoning still being haunted by the old Vattelian fiction.[229]

199. There exists nowadays an *opinio juris communis* as to the illegality of all weapons of mass destruction, including nuclear weapons, and the obligation of nuclear disarmament, under contemporary international law. There is no "gap" concerning nuclear weapons; given the indiscriminate, lasting and indescribable suffering they inflict, they are outlawed, as much as other weapons of mass destruction (biological and chemical weapons) are. The positivist outlook purporting to challenge this prohibition of contemporary general international law has long been surpassed. Nor can this matter be approached from a strictly inter-State outlook, without taking into account the condition of peoples and human beings as subjects of international law.

200. All weapons of mass destruction are illegal under contemporary international law. The threat or use of such weapons is condemned in any circumstances by the universal juridical conscience, which in my view constitutes the ultimate material source of International Law, as of all Law. This is in keeping with the conception of the formation and evolution of International Law which I have been sustaining for many years; it transcends the limitations of

---

[229] A.A. Cançado Trindade, "The Voluntarist Conception of International Law: A Re-Assessment", 59 *Revue de droit international de sciences diplomatiques et politiques* – Geneva (1981) p. 214, and cf. pp. 212–213. On the need of a universalist perspective, cf. also Cf. K. Tanaka, "The Character or World Law in the International Court of Justice" [translated from Japanese into English by S. Murase], 15 *Japanese Annual of International Law* (1971) pp. 1–22.

XIV Recourse to the "Martens Clause" as an Expression of the *Raison d'Humanité*

201. Even if there was a "gap" in the law of nations in relation to nuclear weapons, – which there is not, – it is possible to fill it by resorting to general principles of law. In its 1996 Advisory Opinion, the ICJ preferred to focus on self-defence of a hypothetical individual State, instead of developing the rationale of the *Martens clause*, the purpose of which is precisely that of filling gaps[230] in the light of the principles of the law of nations, the "laws of humanity" and the "dictates of public conscience" (terms of the wise premonition of Fyodor Fyodorovich von Martens,[231] originally formulated in the I Hague Peace Conference of 1899).

202. Yet, continuing recourse to the *Martens clause*, from 1899 to our days, consolidates it as an expression of the strength of human conscience. Its historical trajectory of more than one century has sought to extend protection juridically to human beings in all circumstances (even if not contemplated by conventional norms). Its reiteration for over a century in successive international instruments, besides showing that conventional and customary international law in the domain of protection of the human person go together, reveals the Martens clause as an emanation of the *material* source *par excellence* of the whole law of nations (the universal juridical conscience), giving expression to the *raison d'humanité* and imposing limits to the *raison d'État*.[232]

---

[230] J. Salmon, "Le problème des lacunes à la lumière de l'avis 'Licéité de la menace ou de l'emploi d'armes nucléaires' rendu le 8 juillet 1996 par la Cour Internationale de Justice", *in Mélanges en l'honneur de N. Valticos – Droit et justice* (ed. R.-J. Dupuy), Paris, Pédone, 1999, pp. 197–214, esp. pp. 208–209; R. Ticehurst, "The Martens Clause and the Laws of Armed Conflict", 317 *International Review of the Red Cross* (1997) pp. 125–134, esp. pp. 133–134; A. Azar, *Les opinions des juges dans l'Avis consultatif sur la licéité de la menace ou de l'emploi d'armes nucléaires*, Bruxelles, Bruylant, 1998, p. 61.

[231] Which was intended to extend juridically the protection to the civilians and combatants in all situations, even if not contemplated by the conventional norms.

[232] A.A. Cançado Trindade, *Tratado de Direito Internacional dos Direitos Humanos*, vol. II, Porto Alegre/Brazil, S.A. Fabris Ed., 1999, pp. 497–509.

203. It cannot be denied that nuclear weapons are intrinsically indiscriminate, incontrollable, that they cause severe and durable damage and in a wide scale in space and time, that they are prohibited by International Humanitarian Law (Articles 35, 48 and 51 of the Additional Protocol I of 1977 to the 1949 Geneva Conventions on International Humanitarian Law), and are inhuman as weapons of mass destruction.[233] Early in the present nuclear age, the four Geneva Conventions established the *grave violations* of international law (Convention I, Article 49(3); Convention II, Article 50(3); Convention III, Article 129(3); and Convention IV, Article 146(3)). Such *grave violations*, when involving nuclear weapons, victimize not only States, but all other subjects of international law as well, individuals and groups of individuals, peoples, and humankind as a whole.

204. The absence of conventional norms stating specifically that nuclear weapons are prohibited in all circumstances does not mean that they would be allowed in a given circumstance. Two decades ago, in the course of the advisory proceedings of late 1995 before the ICJ leading to its 1996 Advisory Opinion on the *Threat or Use of Nuclear Weapons*, some of the participating States drew attention to the incidence of the Martens clause in the present domain.[234] It was pointed out, on the occasion, that the argument that international instruments do not specifically contain an express prohibition of use of nuclear weapons seems to overlook the Martens clause.[235]

205. Also in rebuttal of that argument, – typical of legal positivism, in its futile search for an express prohibition, – it was further observed that the "principles of humanity" and the "dictates of public conscience", evoked by the Martens clause, permeate not only the law of armed conflict, but "the whole of international law"; they are essentially dynamic, pointing to conduct which may nowadays be condemned as inhumane by the international community,[236] such as recourse to the threat or use of nuclear weapons. It was further stated, in the light of the Martens clause, that the "threat and use of nuclear

---

[233] Cf. comments *in Commentary on the Additional Protocols of 8 June 1977 to the Geneva Conventions of 12 August 1949* (eds. Y. Sandoz, C. Swinarski and B. Zimmermann), Geneva, ICRC/Nijhoff, 1987, pp. 389–420 and 597–600.

[234] Cf. ICJ, doc. CR 95/31, of 13.11.1995, pp. 45–46 (statement of Samoa); ICJ, doc. CR 95/25, of 03.11.1995, p. 55 (statement of Mexico); ICJ, doc. CR 95/27, of 07.11.1995, p. 60 (statement of Malaysia).

[235] ICJ, doc. 95/26, of 06.11.1995, p. 32 (statement of Iran).

[236] ICJ, doc. 95/22, of 30.10.1995, p. 39 (statement of Australia).

weapons violate both customary international law and the dictates of public conscience".[237]

206. The Martens clause safeguards the integrity of Law (against the undue permissiveness of a *non liquet*) by invoking the principles of the law of nations, the "laws of humanity" and the "dictates of the public conscience". Thus, that absence of a conventional norm is not conclusive, and is by no means the end of the matter, – bearing in mind also customary international law. Such absence of a conventional provision expressly prohibiting nuclear weapons does not at all mean that they are legal or legitimate.[238] The evolution of international law[239] points, in our days, in my understanding, towards the construction of the International Law for humankind[240] and, within the framework of this latter, to the outlawing by general international law of all weapons of mass destruction.

207. Had the ICJ, in its 1996 Advisory Opinion on the *Threat or Use of Nuclear Weapons*, made decidedly recourse in great depth to the Martens clause, it would not have lost itself in a sterile exercise, proper of a legal positivism *déjà vu*, of a hopeless search of conventional norms, frustrated by the finding of what it understood to be a lack of these latter as to nuclear weapons specifically, for the purposes of its analysis. The existing arsenals of nuclear weapons, and of other weapons of mass destruction, are to be characterized by what they really are: a scorn and the ultimate insult to human reason, and an affront to the juridical conscience of humankind.

208. The aforementioned evolution of international law, – of which the Martens clause is a significant manifestation, – has gradually moved from an international into a universal dimension, on the basis of fundamental values,

---

237   ICJ, doc. 95/35, of 15.11.1995, p. 33 (statement of Zimbabwe).
238   Stefan Glaser, *L'arme nucléaire à la lumière du Droit international*, Paris, Pédone, 1964, pp. 15, 21, 24–27, 32, 36–37, 41, 43–44 and 62–63, and cf. pp. 18 and 53.
239   If, in other epochs, the ICJ had likewise limited itself to verify a situation of "legal uncertainty" (which, anyway, does not apply in the present context), most likely it would not have issued its *célèbres* Advisory Opinions on *Reparations for Injuries* (1949), on *Reservations to the Convention on the Prevention and Punishment of the Crime of Genocide* (1951), and on *Namibia* (1971), which have so much contributed to the evolution of international law.
240   Cf. A.A. Cançado Trindade, *International Law for Humankind – Towards a New Jus Gentium*, op. cit. supra n. (132), pp. 1–726.

and in the sense of an *objective justice*,[241] which has always been present in jusnaturalist thinking. Human conscience stands above the "will" of individual States. This evolution has, in my perception, significantly contributed to the formation of an *opinio juris communis* in recent decades, in condemnation of nuclear weapons.

209. This *opinio juris communis* is clearly conformed in our days: the overwhelming majority of member States of the United Nations, the NNWS, have been sustaining for years the series of General Assembly resolutions in condemnation of the use of nuclear weapons as illegal under general international law. To this we can add other developments, reviewed in the present Dissenting Opinion, such as, e.g., the NPT Review Conferences, the establishment of regional nuclear-weapon-free zones, and the Conferences on Humanitarian Impact of Nuclear Weapons (cf. parts XVII–XIX, *infra*).

XV Nuclear Disarmament: Jusnaturalism, the Humanist Conception and the Universality of International Law

210. The existence of nuclear weapons, – maintained by the strategy of "deterrence" and "mutually assured destruction" ("MAD", as it became adequately called, since it was devised in the cold-war era), is the contemporary global tragedy of the nuclear age. Death, or self-destruction, haunts everyone everywhere, propelled by human madness. Human beings need protection from themselves, today more than ever,[242] – and this brings our minds to other domains of human knowledge. Law by itself cannot provide answers to this challenge to humankind as a whole.

211. In the domain of nuclear disarmament, we are faced today, within the conceptual universe of international law, with unexplainable insufficiencies,

---

[241] A.A. Cançado Trindade, *Los Tribunales Internacionales Contemporáneos y la Humanización del Derecho Internacional*, Buenos Aires, Ed. Ad-Hoc, 2013, pp. 166–167; and cf. C. Husson-Rochcongar, *Droit international des droits de l'homme et valeurs – Le recours aux valeurs dans la jurisprudence des organes spécialisés*, Bruxelles, Bruylant, 2012, pp. 309–311, 451–452, 578–580, 744–745 and 771–772.

[242] In another international jurisdiction, in my Separate Opinion in the IACtHR's case of the *Massacres of Ituango versus Colombia* (Judgment of 01.07.2006), I devoted part of my reflections to "human cruelty in its distinct manifestations in the execution of State policies" (Part II, paras. 9–13).

or anomalies, if not absurdities. For example, there are fortunately in our times Conventions prohibiting biological and chemical weapons (of 1972 and 1993), but there is to date no such comprehensive conventional prohibition of nuclear weapons, which are far more destructive. There is no such prohibition despite the fact that they are in clear breach of international law, of IHL and the ILHR, as well as of the Law of the United Nations.

212. Does this make any sense? Can international law prescind from ethics? In my understanding, not at all. Just as law and ethics go together (in the line of jusnaturalist thinking), scientific knowledge itself cannot be dissociated from ethics. The production of nuclear weapons is an illustration of the divorce between ethical considerations and scientific and technological progress. Otherwise, weapons which can destroy millions of innocent civilians, and the whole of humankind, would not have been conceived.

213. The principles of *recta ratio*, orienting the *lex praeceptiva*, emanate from human conscience, affirming the ineluctable relationship between law and ethics. Ethical considerations are to guide the debates on nuclear disarmament. Nuclear weapons, capable of destroying humankind as a whole, carry evil in themselves. They ignore civilian populations, they make abstraction of the principles of necessity, of distinction and of proportionality. They overlook the principle of humanity. They have no respect for the fundamental right to life. They are wholly illegal and illegitimate, rejected by the *recta ratio*, which endowed *jus gentium*, in its historical evolution, with ethical foundations, and its character of universality.

214. Already in 1984, in its *general comment* n. 14 (on the right to life), the U.N. Human Rights Committee (HRC – under the Covenant on Civil and Political Rights), for example, began by warning that war and mass violence continue to be "a scourge of humanity", taking the lives of thousands of innocent human beings every year (para. 2). In successive sessions of the General Assembly, – it added, – representatives of States from all geographical regions have expressed their growing concern at the development and proliferation of "increasingly awesome weapons of mass destruction" (para. 3). Associating itself with this concern, the HRC stated that

> (...) It is evident that the designing, testing, manufacture, possession and deployment of nuclear weapons are among the greatest threats to the right to life which confront mankind today. This threat is compounded

by the danger that the actual use of such weapons may be brought about, not only in the event of war, but even through human or mechanical error or failure.

Furthermore, the very existence and gravity of this threat generates a climate of suspicion and fear between States, which is in itself antagonistic to the promotion of universal respect for and observance of human rights and fundamental freedoms in accordance with the Charter of the United Nations and the International Covenants on Human Rights.

The production, testing, possession, deployment and use of nuclear weapons should be prohibited and recognized as crimes against humanity.

The Committee, accordingly, in the interest of mankind, calls upon all States (...) to take urgent steps (...) to rid the world of this menace (paras. 4–7).[243]

215. The absence in contemporary international law of a comprehensive conventional prohibition of nuclear weapons is incomprehensible. Contrary to what legal positivists think, law is not self-sufficient, it needs inputs from other branches of human knowledge for the realisation of justice. Contrary to what legal positivists think, norms and values go together, the former cannot prescind from the latter. Contrary to legal positivism, – may I add, – jusnaturalism, taking into account ethical considerations, pursues a universalist outlook (which legal positivists are incapable of doing), and beholds humankind as entitled to protection.[244]

---

243 "*General Comment*" n. 14 (of 1984) of the HRC, text *in*: United Nations, *Compilation of General Comments and General Recommendations Adopted by Human Rights Treaty Bodies*, doc. HRI/GEN/1/Rev.3, of 15.08.1997, pp. 18–19. The HRC, further stressing that the right to life is a fundamental right which does not admit any derogation not even in time of public emergency, related the current proliferation of weapons of mass destruction to "the supreme duty of States to prevent wars". Cf. also U.N. *Report of the Human Rights Committee*, G.A.O.R. – 40th Session (1985), suppl. n. 40 (A/40/40), p. 162.

244 A.A. Cançado Trindade, *International Law for Humankind – Towards a New Jus Gentium*, op. cit. supra n. (132), pp. 1–726. *Recta ratio* and universalism, present in the jusnaturalist thinking of the "founding fathers" of international law (F. de Vitoria, F. Suárez, H. Grotius, among others), go far back in time to the legacies of Cicero, in his characterization of *recta ratio* in the foundations of *jus gentium* itself, and of Thomas Aquinas, in his conception of *synderesis*, as predisposition of human reason to be guided by principles in the search of the common good; *ibid.*, pp. 10–14.

216. Humankind is subject of rights, in the realm of the new *jus gentium*.[245] As this cannot be visualized from the optics of the State, contemporary international law has reckoned the limits of the State as from the optics of humankind. Natural law thinking has always been attentive to justice, which much transcends positive law. The present case of *Obligations Concerning Negotiations Relating to Cessation of the Nuclear Arms Race and to Nuclear Disarmament* has been lodged with the International Court *of Justice*, and not with an International Court of Positive Law. The contemporary tragedy of nuclear weapons cannot be addressed from the myopic outlook of positive law alone.

217. Nuclear weapons, and other weapons of mass destruction, have no ethics, have no ground on the law of nations (*le droit des gens*): they are in flagrant breach of its fundamental principles, and those of IHL, the ILHR, as well as the Law of the United Nations. They are a contemporary manifestation of evil, in its perennial trajectory going back to the Book of *Genesis* (cf. Part VIII, *supra*). Jusnaturalist thinking, always open to ethical considerations, identifies and discards the disrupting effects of the strategy of "deterrence" of fear creation and infliction[246] (cf. Part XII, *supra*). Humankind is victimized by this.

218. In effect, humankind has been, already for a long time, a *potential victim* of nuclear weapons. To establish such condition of potential victim, one does not need to wait for the actual destruction of life on earth. Humankind has, for the last decades, been suffering psychological harm caused by the existence itself of arsenals of nuclear weapons. And there are peoples, and segments of populations, who have been *actual victims* of the vast and harmful effects of nuclear tests. The existence of *actual and potential victims* is acknowledged

---

245 *Ibid.*, Ch. XI, pp. 275–288; A.A. Cançado Trindade, "Quelques réflexions sur l'humanité comme sujet du droit international", *in Unité et diversité du Droit international – Écrits en l'honneur du Prof. P.-M. Dupuy* (eds. D. Alland, V. Chetail, O. de Frouville and J.E. Viñuales), Leiden, Nijhoff, 2014, pp. 157–173.

246 Cf., to this effect, C.A.J. Coady, "Natural Law and Weapons of Mass Destruction", *in Ethics and Weapons of Mass Destruction – Religious and Secular Perspectives* (eds. S.H. Hashmi and S.P. Lee), Cambridge, Cambridge University Press, 2004, p. 122, and cf. p. 113; and cf. also J. Finnis, J.M. Boyle Jr. and G. Grisez, *Nuclear Deterrence, Morality and Realism*, Oxford, Clarendon Press, 1987, pp. 77–103, 207–237, 275–319 and 367–390. In effect, contemporary expert writing has become, at last, very critical of the "failed strategy" of "deterrence"; cf., *inter alia*, e.g., [Various Authors,] *At the Nuclear Precipice – Catastrophe or Transformation?* (eds. R. Falk and D. Krieger), London, Palgrave/MacMillan, 2008, pp. 162, 209, 218 and 229; A.C. Alves Pereira, *Os Impérios Nucleares e Seus Reféns: Relações Internacionais Contemporâneas*, Rio de Janeiro, Ed. Graal, 1984, pp. 87–88, and cf. pp. 154, 209 and 217.

in international case-law in the domain of the International Law of Human Rights.²⁴⁷ To address this danger from a strict inter-State outlook is to miss the point, to blind oneself. States were created and exist for human beings, and not *vice-versa*.

219. The NPT has a universalist vocation, and counts on everyone, as shown by its three basic principled pillars together. In effect, as soon as it was adopted, the 1968 NPT came to be seen as having been devised and concluded on the basis of those principled pillars, namely: non-proliferation of nuclear weapons (preamble and Articles I–III), peaceful use of nuclear energy (preamble and Articles IV–V), and nuclear disarmament (preamble and Article VI).²⁴⁸ The antecedents of the NPT go back to the work of the U.N. General Assembly in 1953.²⁴⁹ The NPT's three-pillar framework came to be reckoned as the "grand bargain" between its parties, NWS and NNWS. But soon it became a constant point of debate between NWS and NNWS parties to the NPT. In effect, the "grand bargain" came to be seen as "asymmetrical",²⁵⁰ and NNWS began to criticize the very slow pace of achieving nuclear disarmament as one of the three basic principled pillars of the NPT (Article VI).²⁵¹

220. Under the NPT, each State is required to do its due. NWS are no exception to that, if the NPT is not to become dead letter. To achieve the three interrelated

---

247   For an early study on this issue, cf. A.A. Cançado Trindade, "Co-Existence and Co-Ordination of Mechanisms of International Protection of Human Rights (At Global and Regional Levels)", 202 *Recueil des Cours de l'Académie de Droit International de La Haye* (1987), Ch. XI, pp. 271–283. And for subsequent developments on the notion of *potential victims*, cf. A.A. Cançado Trindade, *The Access of Individuals to International Justice*, Oxford, Oxford University Press, 2012 [reprint], Ch. VII, pp. 125–131.
248   Articles VIII–XI, in turn, are procedural in nature.
249   In particular the speech of President D.D. Eisenhower (U.S.) to the U.N. General Assembly in 1953, as part of his plan "Atoms for Peace"; cf., e.g., I. Chernus, *Eisenhower's Atoms for Peace*, [Austin,] Texas A&M University Press, 2002, pp. 3–154.
250   J. Burroughs, *The Legal Framework for Non-Use and Elimination of Nuclear Weapons*, [N.Y.], Greenpeace International, 2006, p. 13.
251   H. Williams, P. Lewis and S. Aghlani, *The Humanitarian Impacts of Nuclear Weapons Initiative: The "Big Tent" in Disarmament*, London, Chatam House, 2015, p. 7; D.H. Joyner, "The Legal Meaning and Implications of Article VI of the Non-Proliferation Treaty", *in: Nuclear Weapons and International Law* (eds. G. Nystuen, S. Casey-Maslen and A.G. Bersagel), Cambridge, Cambridge University Press, 2014, pp. 397, 404 and 417, and cf. pp. 398–399 and 408; and cf. D.H. Joyner, *Interpreting the Nuclear Non-Proliferation Treaty*, Oxford, Oxford University Press, 2013 [reprint], pp. 2, 104 and 126, and cf. pp. 20, 26–29, 31, 97 and 124.

goals (non-proliferation of nuclear weapons, peaceful use of nuclear energy, and nuclear disarmament) is a duty of each and every State towards humankind as a whole. It is a universal duty of conventional and customary international law in the nuclear age. There is an *opinio juris communis* to this effect, sedimented along the recent decades, and evidenced in the successive establishment, in distinct continents, of nuclear-weapon-free zones, and nowadays in the Conferences on the Humanitarian Impact of Nuclear Weapons (cf. parts XVIII–XIX, *infra*).

XVI The Principle of Humanity and the Universalist Approach: *Jus Necessarium* Transcending the Limitations of *Jus Voluntarium*

221. In my understanding, there is no point in keeping attached to an outdated and reductionist inter-State outlook, particularly in view of the revival of the conception of the law of nations (*droit des gens*) encompassing humankind as a whole, as foreseen and propounded by the "founding fathers" of international law[252] (in the XVIth–XVIIth centuries). It would be nonsensical to try to cling to the unduly reductionist inter-State outlook in the international adjudication of a case concerning the contending parties and affecting all States, all peoples and humankind as a whole.

222. An artificial, if not fossilized, strictly inter-State mechanism of dispute-settlement cannot pretend to entail or require a (likewise) entirely inadequate and groundless inter-State reasoning. The law of nations cannot be interpreted and applied in a mechanical way, as from an exclusively inter-State paradigm. To start with, the humane ends of States cannot be overlooked. In relation to nuclear weapons, the *potential victims* are the human beings and peoples, beyond their respective States, for whom these latter were created and exist.

223. As I had the occasion to point out in another international jurisdiction, the law of nations (*droit des gens*), since its historical origins in the XVIth century, was seen as comprising not only States (emerging as they were), but also peoples, the human person (individually and in groups), and humankind as a whole.[253] The strictly inter-State outlook was devised much later on, as

---

[252] A.A. Cançado Trindade, *Évolution du Droit international au droit des gens – L'accès des particuliers à la justice internationale: le regard d'un juge*, Paris, Pédone, 2008, pp. 1–187.

[253] IACtHR, case of the *Community Moiwana versus Suriname* (Judgment of 15.06.2005), Separate Opinion of Judge Cançado Trindade, paras. 6–7.

from the Vattelian reductionism of the mid-XVIIIth century, which became *en vogue* by the end of the XIXth century and beginning of the XXth century, with the well-known disastrous consequences – the successive atrocities victimizing human beings and peoples in distinct regions of world, – along the whole XXth century.[254] In the present nuclear age, extending for the last seven decades, humankind as a whole is threatened.

224. Within the ICJ as well, I have had also the occasion to stress the need to go beyond the inter-State outlook. Thus, in my Dissenting Opinion in the recent case of the *Application of the Convention against Genocide* (Croatia *versus* Serbia, Judgment of 03.02.2015), I have pointed out, *inter alia*, that the 1948 Convention against Genocide is not State-centric, but is rather oriented towards groups of persons, towards the victims, whom it seeks to protect (paras. 59 and 529). The humanist vision of the international legal order pursues an outlook centred on the peoples, keeping in mind the humane ends of States.

225. I have further underlined that the *principle of humanity* is deeply-rooted in the long-standing thinking of natural law (para. 69).

> Humaneness came to the fore even more forcefully in the treatment of persons in *situation of vulnerability, or even defencelessness*, such as those deprived of their personal freedom, for whatever reason. The *jus gentium*, when it emerged as amounting to the law of nations, came then to be conceived by its 'founding fathers' (F. de Vitoria, A. Gentili, F. Suárez, H. Grotius, S. Pufendorf, C. Wolff) as regulating the international community constituted by human beings socially organized in the (emerging) States and co-extensive with humankind, thus conforming the *necessary* law of the *societas gentium*.
>
> The *jus gentium*, thus conceived, was inspired by the principle of humanity *lato sensu*. Human conscience prevails over the will of individual States. Respect for the human person is to the benefit of the common good. This humanist vision of the international legal order pursued – as it does nowadays – a *people-centered outlook*, keeping in mind the *humane ends of the State*. The precious legacy of natural law thinking, evoking the right human reason (*recta ratio*), has never faded away; (paras. 73–74).

The precious legacy of natural law thinking has never vanished; despite the indifference and pragmatism of the "strategic" *droit d'étatistes* (so numerous

---

254 *Ibid.*, paras. 6–7.

in the legal profession nowadays), the *principle of humanity* emerged and remained in international legal thinking as an expression of the *raison d'humanité* imposing limits to the *raison d'État* (para. 74).

226. This is the position I have always taken, within the ICJ and, earlier on, the IACtHR. For example, in the ICJ's Advisory Opinion on *Judgment n. 2867 of the ILO Administrative Tribunal upon a Complaint Filed against IFAD* (of 01.02.2012), I devoted one entire part (n. XI) of my Separate Opinion to the erosion – as I perceive it – of the inter-State outlook of adjudication by the ICJ (paras. 76–81). I warned likewise in my Separate Opinion (paras. 21–23) in the case of *Whaling in the Antarctic* (Australia *versus* Japan, Order of 06.02.2013, on New Zealand's intervention), as well as in my recent Separate Opinion (paras. 16–21 and 28–41) in the case of *Alleged Violations of Sovereign Rights and Maritime Spaces in the Caribbean Sea* (Nicaragua *versus* Colombia, Preliminary Objections, Judgment of 17.03. 2016).

227. Earlier on, within the IACtHR, I took the same position: for example, *inter alia*, in my Concurring Opinions in both the Advisory Opinion n. 16, on the *Right to Information on Consular Assistance in the Framework of the Due Process of Law* (of 01.10.1999), and the Advisory Opinion n. 18, on the *Juridical Condition and Rights of Undocumented Migrants* (of 17.09.2003), of the IACtHR, I deemed it fit to point out, – going beyond the strict inter-State dimension, – that, if non-compliance with Article 36(1)(b) of the 1963 Vienna Convention on Consular Relations takes place, it occurs to the detriment not only of a State Party but also of the human beings at issue. Such pioneering jurisprudential construction, in the line of jusnaturalist thinking, rested upon the evolving concepts of *jus cogens* and obligations *erga omnes* of protection.[255]

228. *Recta ratio* stands firmly above the "will". Human conscience, – the *recta ratio* so cultivated in jusnaturalism, – clearly prevails over the "will" and the strategies of individual States. It points to a universalist conception of the *droit des gens* (the *lex praeceptiva* for the *totus orbis*), applicable to all (States as well as peoples and individuals), given the unity of the human kind. Legal positivism, centred on State power and "will", has never been able to develop such universalist outlook, so essential and necessary to address issues of concern to humankind as a whole, such as that of the obligation of nuclear disarmament. The universal juridical conscience prevails over the "will" of individual States.

---

255 Cf. comments of A.A. Cançado Trindade, *Os Tribunais Internacionais e a Realização da Justiça*, Rio de Janeiro, Edit. Renovar, 2015, pp. 463–468.

229. The "founding fathers" of the law of nations (such as, *inter alii*, F. de Vitoria, F. Suárez and H. Grotius) had in mind humankind as a whole. They conceived a universal *jus gentium* for the *totus orbis*, securing the unity of the *societas gentium*; based on a *lex praeceptiva*, the *jus gentium* was apprehended by the *recta ratio*, and conformed a true *jus necessarium*, much transcending the limitations of the *jus voluntarium*. Law ultimately emanates from the common conscience of what is juridically necessary (*opinio juris communis necessitatis*).[256] The contribution of the "founding fathers" of *jus gentium* found inspiration largely in the scholastic philosophy of natural law (in particular in the stoic and Thomist conception of *recta ratio* and justice), which recognized the human being as endowed with intrinsic dignity.

230. Moreover, in face of the unity of the human kind, they conceived a truly *universal* law of nations, applicable to all – States as well as peoples and individuals – everywhere (*totus orbis*). In thus contributing to the emergence of the *jus humanae societatis*, thinkers like F. de Vitoria and D. de Soto, among others, permeated their lessons with the humanist thinking that preceded them. Four and a half centuries later, their lessons remain contemporary, endowed with perennial validity and aptitude to face, e.g., the contemporary and dangerous problem of the existing arsenals of nuclear weapons. Those thinkers went well beyond the "will" of States, and rested upon the much safer foundation of human conscience (*recta ratio* and justice).

231. The conventional and customary obligation of nuclear disarmament brings to the fore another aspect: the issue of the *validity* of international legal norms is, after all, metajuridical. International law cannot simply remain indifferent to values, general principles of law and ethical considerations; it has, to start with, to identify what is *necessary*, – such as a world free of nuclear weapons, – in order to secure the survival of humankind. This *idée du droit* precedes positive international law, and is in line with jusnaturalist thinking.

232. *Opinio juris communis necessitatis* upholds a customary international law obligation to secure the survival of humankind. Conventional and customary obligations go here together. Just as customary rules may eventually be incorporated into a convention, treaty provisions may likewise eventually enter into the *corpus* of general international law. Customary obligations can

---

256 A.A. Cançado Trindade, *International Law for Humankind – Towards a New Jus Gentium*, op. cit. supra n. (132), pp. 137–138.

either precede, or come after, conventional obligations. They evolve *pari passu*. This being so, the search for an express legal prohibition of nuclear weapons (such as the one undertaken in the ICJ's Advisory Opinion of 1996 on the *Threat or Use of Nuclear Weapons*) becomes a futile, if not senseless, exercise of legal positivism.

233. It is clear to human conscience that those weapons, which can destroy the whole of humankind, are unlawful and prohibited. They are in clear breach of *jus cogens*. And *jus cogens* was reckoned by human conscience well before it was incorporated into the two Vienna Conventions on the Law of Treaties (of 1969 and 1986). As I had the occasion to warn, three decades ago, at the 1986 U.N. Conference on the Law of Treaties between States and International Organizations or between International Organizations, *jus cogens* is "incompatible with the voluntarist conception of international law, because that conception failed to explain the formation of rules of general international law".[257]

XVII   NPT Review Conferences

234. In fact, in the course of the written phase of the proceedings before the Court in the present case of *Obligations Concerning Negotiations Relating to Cessation of the Nuclear Arms Race and to Nuclear Disarmament*, both the Marshall Islands[258] and the United Kingdom[259] addressed, in their distinct arguments, the series of NPT Review Conferences. For its part, India also addressed the Review Conferences,[260] in particular to leave on the records its position on the matter, as explained in a statement made on 09.05.2000.

235. Likewise, in the course of the oral phase of the present proceedings before the Court in *cas d'espèce*, the applicant State, the Marshall Islands, referred to the NPT Review Conferences in its oral arguments in two of the three cases it

---

257   U.N., *United Nations Conference on the Law of Treaties between States and International Organizations or between International Organizations – Official Records*, vol. I (statement by the Representative of Brazil, A.A. Cançado Trindade, of 12.03.1986), pp. 187–188, para. 18.
258   *Application Instituting Proceedings*, p. 24, para. 66; and *Memorial*, pp. 29, 56–60, 61, 63, 68–69, 71 and 73, paras. 50, 123–128, 130, 136, 150, 153, 154, 161–162 and 168; and *Statement of Observations on [U.K.'s] Preliminary Objections*, pp. 15 and 47, paras. 32 and 126.
259   *Preliminary Objections*, pp. 1–2, 10 and 23, paras. 2–3, 21 and 50.
260   *Counter-Memorial*, p. 15, para. 23 n. 49, and Annex 23.

lodged with the Court against India,²⁶¹ and the United Kingdom;²⁶² references to the Review Conferences were also made, for their part, in their oral arguments, by the two respondent States which participated in the public sittings before the Court, namely, India²⁶³ and the United Kingdom.²⁶⁴ Those Review Conferences conform the factual context of the *cas d'espèce*, and cannot pass unnoticed. May I thus proceed to a brief review of them.

236. The NPT Review Conferences, held every five years, started in 1975. The following three Conferences of the kind were held, respectively, in 1980, 1985 and 1990, respectively.²⁶⁵ The fifth of such Conferences took place in 1995, the same year that the Marshall Islands became a party to the NPT (on 30.01.1995). In one of its decisions, the 1995 NPT Conference singled out the vital role of the NPT in preventing the proliferation of nuclear weapons, and warned that the proliferation of nuclear weapons would seriously increase the danger of nuclear war.²⁶⁶ For their part, NWS reaffirmed their commitment, under Article VI of the NPT, to pursue in good faith negotiations on effective measures relating to nuclear disarmament.

237. The 1995 Review Conference prolonged indefinitely the NPT, and adopted its decision on "Principles and Objectives for Nuclear Non-Proliferation and Disarmament". Yet, in its *report*, the Main Committee I (charged with the implementation of the provisions of the NPT) observed with regret that Article VI and preambular paragraphs 8–12 of the NPT had not been wholly fulfilled,²⁶⁷ with the number of nuclear weapons then existing being greater than the one existing when the NPT entered into force; it further regretted "the continuing lack of progress" on relevant items of the Conference on Disarmament, and urged a commitment on the part of NWS on "no-first use and non-use of nuclear weapons with immediate effect".²⁶⁸

---

261 ICJ. doc. CR 2016/1, of 07.03.2016, pp. 26–27 and 50, paras. 9 and 17 (M.I.); ICJ. doc. CR 2016/6, of 14.03.2016, p. 32, para. 10 (M.I.).
262 ICJ. doc. CR 2016/5, of 11.03.2016, p. 47, para. 8 (M.I.).
263 ICJ. doc. CR 2016/4, of 10.03.2016, p. 14, para. 3 (India).
264 ICJ. doc. CR 2016/7, of 09.03.2016, pp. 14–16 and 18–19, paras. 20, 22, 24, 32 and 37 (United Kingdom).
265 For an assessment of these earlier NPT Review Conferences, cf. H. Müller, D. Fischer and W. Kötter, *Nuclear Non-Proliferation and Global Order*, Stockholm–Solna/Oxford, SIPRI/Oxford University Press, 1994, pp. 31–108.
266 Decision 2, NPT/CONF.1995/32 (Part I), Annex, p. 2.
267 *Final Document*, Part II, p. 257, paras. 3–3*ter*., and cf. pp. 258 and 260, paras. 4 and 9.
268 *Ibid.*, pp. 271–273, paras. 36–39.

238. Between the fifth and the sixth Review Conferences, India and Pakistan carried out nuclear tests in 1998. For its part, on several occasions, the Movement of Non-Aligned Countries called for "urgent" measures of nuclear disarmament.[269] To this effect, the 2000 Review Conference agreed to a document containing the "13 Practical Steps" in order to meet the commitments of States Parties under Article VI of the NPT.[270] The "13 Practical Steps" stress the relevance and urgency of ratifications of the CTBT so as to achieve its entry into force, and of setting up a moratorium on nuclear-weapon tests pending such entry into force. Furthermore, they call for the commencement of negotiations on a treaty banning the production of fissile material for nuclear weapons and also call upon NWS to accomplish the total elimination of nuclear arsenals.[271]

239. At the 2005 Review Conference, no substantive decision was adopted, amidst continuing disappointment at the lack of progress on implementation of Article VI of the NPT, particularly in view of the "13 Practical Steps" agreed to at the 2000 Review Conference. Concerns were expressed that new nuclear weapon systems were being developed, and strategic doctrines were being adopted lowering the threshold for the use of nuclear weapons; moreover, regret was also expressed that States whose ratification was needed for the CTBT's entry into force had not yet ratified the CTBT.[272]

240. Between the 2005 and the 2010 Review Conferences, there were warnings that the NPT was "now in danger" and "under strain", as the process of disarmament had "stagnated" and needed to be "revived" in order to prevent the spread of weapons of mass destruction. The concerns addressed what was regarded as the unsatisfactory stalemate in the Conference on Disarmament in Geneva, which had been "unable to adopt an agenda for almost a decade" to identify substantive issues to be discussed and negotiated in the Conference.[273]

---

269 NPT/CONF.2000/4, paras. 12–13.
270 *Final Document*, vol. 1, Part 1, pp. 14–15.
271 The "13 Practical Steps", moreover, affirm that the principle of irreversibility should apply to all nuclear disarmament and reduction measures. At last, the 13 practical steps reaffirm the objective of general and complete disarmament under effective international control, and stress the importance of both regular reports on the implementation of NPT's Article VI obligations, and the further development of verification capabilities.
272 NPT/CONF.2005/57, Part I, and cf. report on the 2005 Review Conference *in*: 30 *U.N. Disarmament Yearbook* (2005) Ch. I, p. 23.
273 Hans Blix, *Why Disarmament Matters*, Cambridge, Mass./London, Boston Review/MIT, 2008, pp. 6 and 63.

241. The "Five-Point Proposal on Nuclear Disarmament", announced by the Secretary-General in an address of 24.10.2008,[274] began by urging all NPT States Parties, in particular the NWS, to fulfil their obligations under the Treaty "to undertake negotiations on effective measures leading to nuclear disarmament" (para. 1).[275] It called upon the permanent members of the Security Council to commence discussions on security issues in the nuclear disarmament process, including by giving NNWS assurances against the use or threat of use of nuclear weapons (para. 5). It stressed the need of "new efforts to bring the CTBT into force", and encouraged NWS to ratify all the Protocols to the Treaties which established Nuclear-Weapon-Free Zones (para. 6). Moreover, it also stressed "the need for greater transparency" in relation to arsenals of nuclear weapons and disarmament achievements (para. 7). And it further called for the elimination also of other types of weapons of mass destruction (para. 8).

242. The "Five-Point Proposal on Nuclear Disarmament" was reiterated by the U.N. Secretary-General in two subsequent addresses in the following three years.[276] In one of them, before the Security Council on 24.09.2009, he stressed the need of an "early entry into force" of the CTBT, and pondered that "disarmament and non-proliferation must proceed together"; he urged "a divided international community" to start moving ahead towards achieving "a nuclear-weapon-free world", and, at last, he expressed his hope in the forthcoming 2010 NPT Review Conference.[277]

243. Both the 2000 and the 2010 Review Conferences made an interpretation of nuclear disarmament under Article VI of the NPT as a "positive disarmament obligation", in line with the *dictum* in the ICJ's 1996 Advisory Opinion of nuclear

---

274 Cf. U.N. Secretary-General (Ban Ki-moon), Address (at a conference at the East–West Institute): "The United Nations and Security in a Nuclear-Weapon-Free World", *in U.N. News Centre*, of 24.10.2008, pp. 1–3.

275 It added that this could be pursued either by an agreement on "a framework of separate, mutually reinforcing instruments", or else by negotiating "a nuclear-weapons convention, backed by a strong system of verification, as has long been proposed at the United Nations" (para. 2).

276 On two other occasions, namely, during a Security Council Summit on Nuclear Non-Proliferation on 24.09.2009, and at a Conference organized by the East–West Institute on 24.10.2011.

277 U.N. Secretary-General (Ban Ki-moon), "Opening Remarks to the Security Council Summit on Nuclear Non-Proliferation and Nuclear Disarmament", *in U.N. News Centre*, of 24.09.2009, pp. 1–2.

disarmament in good faith as an obligation of result.[278] The 2010 Review Conference expressed its deep concern that there remained the continued risk for humankind put by the possibility that nuclear weapons could be used, and the catastrophic humanitarian consequences that would result therefrom.

244. The 2010 Review Conference, keeping in mind the 1995 decision on "Principles and Objectives for Nuclear Non-Proliferation and Disarmament" as well as the 2000 agreement on the "13 Practical Steps", affirmed the vital importance of the universality of the NPT,[279] and, furthermore, took note of the "Five-Point Proposal on Nuclear Disarmament" of the U.N. Secretary-General, of 2008. For the first time in the present series of Review Conferences, the *Final Document* of the 2010 Review Conference recognized "the catastrophic humanitarian consequences that would result from the use of nuclear weapons".[280]

245. The Final Document welcomed the creation of successive nuclear-weapon-free zones,[281] and, in its conclusions, it endorsed the "legitimate interest" of NNWS to receive "unequivocal and legally binding security assurances" from NWS on the matter at issue; it asserted and recognized that "the total elimination of nuclear weapons is the only absolute guarantee against the use or threat of use of nuclear weapons".[282] The aforementioned Final Document reiterated the 2010 Review Conference's "deep concern at the catastrophic humanitarian consequences of any use of nuclear weapons", and "the need for all States at all times to comply with applicable international law, including international humanitarian law".[283] This key message of the 2010 Review Conference triggered the initiative, three years later, of the new series of Conferences on the Humanitarian Impact of Nuclear Weapons (cf. *infra*).

246. The "historic acknowledgement" of "the catastrophic humanitarian consequences of any use of nuclear weapons" was duly singled out by the ICRC, in its

---

278 D.H. Joyner, "The Legal Meaning and Implications of Article VI of the Non-Proliferation Treaty", *in*: *Nuclear Weapons and International Law* (eds. G. Nystuen, S. Casey-Maslen and A.G. Bersagel), Cambridge, Cambridge University Press, 2014, pp. 413 and 417.
279 NPT/CONF.2010/50, vol. I, pp. 12–14 and 19–20.
280 Cf. *2010 Review Conference – Final Document*, vol. I, doc. NPT/CONF.2010/50, of 18.06.2010, p. 12, para. 80.
281 Cf. *ibid.*, p. 15, para. 99.
282 *Ibid.*, p. 21, point (i).
283 *Ibid.*, p. 19, point (v).

statement in the more recent 2015 Review Conference;[284] the ICRC pointed out that that new series of Conferences (2013–2014, in Oslo, Nayarit and Vienna) has given the international community "a much clearer grasp" of the effects of nuclear detonations on peoples around the world. It then warned that, 45 years after the NPT's entry into force, "there has been little or no concrete progress" in fulfilling the goal of elimination of nuclear weapons. As nuclear weapons remain the only weapons of mass destruction not prohibited by a treaty, "filling this gap is a humanitarian imperative", as the "immediate risks of intentional or accidental nuclear detonations" are "too high and the dangers too real".[285]

247. The 2015 Review Conference displayed frustration over the very slow pace of action on nuclear disarmament, in addition to current nuclear modernization programs and reiteration of dangerous nuclear strategies, apparently oblivious of the catastrophic humanitarian consequences of nuclear weapons. At the 2015 Review Conference, the Main Committee I, charged with addressing Article VI of the NPT, stressed the importance of "the ultimate goal" of elimination of nuclear weapons, so as to achieve "general and complete disarmament under effective international control".[286]

248. The 2015 Review Conference reaffirmed that "the total elimination of nuclear weapons is the only absolute guarantee against the use or threat of use of nuclear weapons, including the risk of their unauthorized, unintentional or accidental detonation".[287] It expressed its "deep concern" that, during the period 2010–2015, the Conference on Disarmament did not commence negotiations of an instrument on such nuclear disarmament,[288] and then stressed the "urgency for the Conference on Disarmament" to achieve "an internationally legally binding instrument" to that effect, so as "to assure" NNWS against the use or threat of use of nuclear weapons by all NWS.[289]

249. After welcoming "the increased and positive interaction with civil society" during the cycle of Review Conferences, the most recent 2015 Review Conference stated that

---

284   ICRC, "Eliminating Nuclear Weapons", *Statement – 2015 Review Conference of the Parties to the NPT*, of 01.05.2015, p. 1.
285   *Ibid.*, pp. 2–3.
286   *2015 Review Conference – Working Paper of the Chair of Main Committee I*, doc. NPT/CONF.2015/MC.I/WP.1, of 18.05.2015, p. 3, para. 17.
287   *Ibid.*, p. 5, para. 27.
288   *Ibid.*, p. 5, para. 35.
289   *Ibid.*, p. 6, para. 43.

understandings and concerns pertaining to the catastrophic humanitarian consequences of any nuclear weapon detonation underpin and should compel urgent efforts by all States leading to a world without nuclear weapons. The Conference affirms that, pending the realization of this objective, it is in the interest of the very survival of humanity that nuclear weapons never be used again.[290]

XVIII The Establishment of Nuclear-Weapon-Free Zones

250. In addition to the aforementioned NPT Review Conferences, the *opinio juris communis* on the illegality of nuclear weapons finds expression also in the establishment, along the last half century, of nuclear-weapon-free zones, which has responded to the needs and aspirations of humankind, so as to rid the world of the threat of nuclear weapons. The establishment of those zones has, in effect, given expression to the growing disapproval of nuclear weapons by the international community as a whole. There are, in effect, references to nuclear-weapon-free zones in the arguments, in the written phase of the present proceedings, of the Marshall Islands[291] and of the United Kingdom[292] in the present case *of Obligations Concerning Negotiations Relating to Cessation of the Nuclear Arms Race and to Nuclear Disarmament.*

251. I originally come from the part of the world, Latin America, which, together with the Caribbean, form the first region of the world to have prohibited nuclear weapons, and to have proclaimed itself as a nuclear-weapon-free zone. The pioneering initiative in this domain, of Latin America and the Caribbean,[293] resulted in the adoption of the 1967 Treaty for the Prohibition of Nuclear Weapons in Latin America and the Caribbean and its two Additional Protocols. Its reach transcended Latin America and the Caribbean, as evidenced by its two Additional Protocols,[294] and the obligations set forth in its legal regime were wide in scope:

---

290 *Ibid.*, p. 7, paras. 45–46(1).
291 *Application Instituting Proceedings* of the M.I., p. 26, para. 73; and *Memorial* of the M.I., pp. 40, 53 and 56, paras. 84, 117 and 122.
292 *Preliminary Objections* of the U.K., p. 2, para. 4.
293 On the initial moves in the U.N. to this effect, by Brazil (in 1962) and Mexico (taking up the leading role from 1963 onwards), cf. Naciones Unidas, *Las Zonas Libres de Armas Nucleares en el Siglo XXI, op. cit. infra* n. (298), pp. 116, 20 and 139.
294 The first one concerning the States internationally responsible for territories located within the limits of the zone of application of the Treaty, and the second one pertaining to the nuclear-weapon States.

> Le régime consacré dans le Traité n'est pas simplement celui de non-prolifération: c'est un régime d'absence totale d'armes nucléaires, ce qui veut dire que ces armes seront interdites à perpétuité dans les territoires auxquels s'applique le Traité, quel que soit l'État sous le contrôle duquel pourraient se trouver ces terribles instruments de destruction massive.[295]

252. By the time of the creation of that first nuclear-weapon-free zone by the 1967 Treaty of Tlatelolco, it was pointed out that it came as a response to humanity's concern with its own future (given the threat of nuclear weapons), and in particular with "the survival of the humankind".[296] That initiative[297] was followed by four others of the kind, in distinct regions of the world, conducive to the adoption of the 1985 South Pacific (Rarotonga) Nuclear-Free Zone Treaty, the 1995 Southeast Asia (Bangkok) Nuclear-Weapon-Free Zone Treaty, the 1996 African (Pelindaba) Nuclear Weapon-Free Zone Treaty,[298] as well as the 2006 Central Asian (Semipalatinsk) Nuclear-Weapon-Free Zone Treaty. Basic considerations of humanity have surely been taken into account for the establishment of those nuclear-weapon-free zones.

253. In fact, besides the Treaty of Tlatelolco, also the Rarotonga, Bangkok, Pelindaba, and Semipalatinsk Treaties purport to extend the obligations enshrined therein, by means of their respective Protocols, not only to the States of the regions at issue, but also to nuclear States,[299] as well as States which are internationally responsible, *de jure* or *de facto*, for territories located in the respective regions. The verification of compliance with the obligations regularly engages the IAEA.[300] Each of the five aforementioned treaties (Tlatelolco, Rarotonga, Bangkok, Pelindaba and Semipalatinsk) creating nuclear-weapon-free zones has distinctive features, as to the kinds and extent of obligations

---

295 A. García Robles, "Mesures de désarmement dans des zones particulières: le Traité visant l'interdiction des armes nucléaires en Amérique Latine", 133 *Recueil des Cours de l'Académie de Droit International de La Haye* [RCADI] (1971) p. 103, and cf. p. 71.

296 *Ibid.*, p. 99, and cf. p. 102.

297 Which was originally prompted by a reaction to the *Cuban missiles crisis* of 1962.

298 Naciones Unidas, *Las Zonas Libres de Armas Nucleares en el Siglo XXI*, N.Y./Geneva, U.N.-OPANAL/UNIDIR, 1997, pp. 9, 25, 39 and 153.

299 Those Protocols contain the undertaking not only not to use nuclear weapons, but also not to threaten their use; cf. M. Roscini, *op. cit. infra* (n. 307), pp. 617–618.

300 The Treaty of Tlatelolco has in addition counted on its own regional organism to that end, the Organism for the Prohibition of Nuclear Weapons in Latin America (OPANAL).

THE UNIVERSAL JURIDICAL CONSCIENCE, HUMANENESS 337

and methods of verification,[301] but they share the common ultimate goal of preserving humankind from the threat or use of nuclear weapons.

254. The second nuclear-weapon-free zone, established by the Treaty of Rarotonga (1985), with its three Protocols, came as a response[302] to long-sustained regional aspirations, and increasing frustration of the populations of the countries of the South Pacific with incursions of NWS in the region.[303] The Rarotonga Treaty encouraged the negotiation of a similar zone, – by means of the 1995 Bangkok Treaty, – in the neighbouring region of Southeast Asia, and confirmed the "continued relevance of zonal approaches" to the goal of disarmament and the safeguard of humankind from the menace of nuclear weapons.[304]

255. The third of those treaties, that of Bangkok, of 1995 (with its Protocol), was prompted by the initiative of the Association of South–East Asian Nations (ASEAN) to insulate the region from the policies and rivalries of the nuclear powers. The Bangkok Treaty, besides covering the land territories of all ten Southeast Asian States, is the first treaty of the kind also to encompass their territorial sea, 200-mile exclusive economic zone and continental shelf.[305] The fourth such treaty, that of Pelindaba, of 1996, in its turn, was prompted by the continent's reaction to nuclear tests in the region (as from the French nuclear tests in the Sahara in 1961), and the aspiration – deeply-rooted in African thinking – to keep nuclear weapons out of the region.[306] The Pelindaba Treaty (with its three Protocols) appears to have served the purpose to eradicate nuclear weapons from the African continent.

---

301 Cf., in general, M. Roscini, *Le Zone Denuclearizzate*, Torino, Giappichelli Ed., 2003, pp. 1–410; J. Goldblat, "Zones exemptes d'armes nucléaires: une vue d'ensemble", *in Le droit international des armes nucléaires* (Journée d'études, ed. S. Sur), Paris, Pédone, 1998, pp. 35–55.
302 Upon the initiative of Australia.
303 M. Hamel-Green, "The South Pacific – The Treaty of Rarotonga", *in Nuclear Weapons-Free Zones* (ed. R. Thakur), London/N.Y., MacMillan/St. Martin's Press, 1998, p. 59, and cf. p. 62.
304 *Ibid.*, pp. 77 and 71.
305 This extended territorial scope has generated resistance on the part of nuclear-weapon States to accept its present form; A. Acharya and S. Ogunbanwo, "The Nuclear-Weapon-Free Zones in South–East Asia and Africa", *in Armaments, Disarmament and International Security – SIPRI Yearbook* (1998) pp. 444 and 448.
306 Naciones Unidas, *Las Zonas Libres de Armas Nucleares en el Siglo XXI*, op. cit. supra n. (298), pp. 60–61; and cf. J.O. Ihonvbere, "Africa – The Treaty of Pelindaba", *in Nuclear Weapons-Free Zones*, op. cit. supra n. (303), pp. 98–99 and 109. And, for a general study,

256. The fifth such treaty, that of Semipalatinsk, of 2006, contains, like the other treaties creating nuclear weapon-free zones (*supra*), the basic prohibitions to manufacture, acquire, possess, station or control nuclear explosive devices within the zones.[307] The five treaties at issue, though containing loopholes (e.g., with regard to the transit of nuclear weapons),[308] have as common denominator the practical value of arrangements that transcend the non-proliferation of nuclear weapons.[309]

257. Each of the five treaties (of Tlatelolco, Rarotonga, Bangkok, Pelindaba and Semipalatinsk) reflects the characteristics of each of the five regions, and they all pursue the same cause. The establishment of the nuclear weapon-free zones has been fulfilling the needs and aspirations of peoples living under the fear of nuclear victimization.[310] Their purpose is being served, also in withholding or containing nuclear ambitions, to the ultimate benefit of humankind as a whole.

258. Nowadays, the five aforementioned nuclear weapon-free zones are firmly established in densely populated areas, covering most (almost all) of the landmass of the southern hemisphere land areas (while excluding most sea areas).[311] The adoption of the 1967 Tlatelolco Treaty, the 1985 Rarotonga Treaty, the 1995 Bangkok Treaty, the 1996 Pelindaba Treaty, and the 2006 Semipalatinsk Treaty, have disclosed the shortcomings and artificiality of the posture

---

cf. O. Adeniji, *The Treaty of Pelindaba on the African Nuclear-Weapon-Free Zone*, Geneva, UNIDIR, 2002, pp. 1–169.

307 M. Roscini, "Something Old, Something New: The 2006 Semipalatinsk Treaty on a Nuclear Weapon-Free Zone in Central Asia", 7 *Chinese Journal of International Law* (2008) p. 597.

308 As to their shortcomings, cf., e.g., J. Goldblat, "The Nuclear Non-Proliferation Régime: Assessment and Prospects", 256 *Recueil des Cours de l'Académie de Droit International de La Haye* (1995) pp. 137–138; M. Roscini, *op. cit. supra* n. (307), pp. 603–604.

309 J. Enkhsaikhan, "Nuclear-Weapon-Free Zones: Prospects and Problems", 20 *Disarmament – Periodic Review by the United Nations* (1997) n. 1, p. 74.

310 Cf., e.g., H. Fujita, "The Changing Role of International Law in the Nuclear Age: from Freedom of the High Seas to Nuclear-Free Zones", in *Humanitarian Law of Armed Conflict: Challenges Ahead – Essays in Honour of F. Kalshoven* (eds. A.J.M. Delissen and G.J. Tanja), Dordrecht, Nijhoff, 1991, p. 350, and cf. pp. 327–349.

311 J. Prawitz, "Nuclear-Weapon-Free Zones: Their Added Value in a Strengthened International Safeguards System", in *Tightening the Reins – Towards a Strengthened International Nuclear Safeguards System* (eds. E. Häckel and G. Stein), Berlin/Heidelberg, Springer-Verlag, 2000, p. 166.

of the so-called political "realists",[312] which insisted on the suicidal strategy of nuclear "deterrence", in their characteristic subservience to power politics.

259. The substantial *Final Report* of 1999 of the U.N. Disarmament Commission underlined the relevance of nuclear-weapon-free zones and of their contribution to the achievement of nuclear disarmament,[313] "expressing and promoting common values" and constituting "important complementary" instruments to the NPT and the "international regime for the prohibition" of any nuclear-weapon explosions.[314] Drawing attention to the central role of the United Nations in the field of disarmament,[315] the aforementioned *Report* added:

> Nuclear-weapon-free zones have ceased to be exceptional in the global strategic environment. To date, 107 States have signed or become parties to treaties establishing existing nuclear-weapon-free zones. With the addition of Antarctica, which was demilitarized pursuant to the Antarctic Treaty, nuclear-weapon-free zones now cover more than 50 per cent of the Earth's land mass. (...)
>
> The establishment of further nuclear-weapon-free zones reaffirms the commitment of the States that belong to such zones to honour their legal obligations deriving from other international instruments in force in the area of nuclear non-proliferation and disarmament to which they are parties.[316]

260. Moreover, the 1999 *Final Report* of the U.N. Disarmament Commission further stated that, for their part, NWS should fully comply with their obligations, under the ratified Protocols to the Treaties of treaties on nuclear-weapon-free zones, "not to use or threaten to use nuclear weapons".[317] It went on to encourage member States of those zones "to share experiences" with States of other regions, so as "to establish further nuclear-weapon-free zones".[318] It concluded that the international community, by means of "the creation of nuclear-weapon-free zones around the globe", should aim at "general and complete

---

312 Cf. Naciones Unidas, *Las Zonas Libres de Armas Nucleares en el Siglo XXI, op. cit. supra* n. (298), pp. 27, 33–38 and 134.
313 U.N., *Report of the Disarmament Commission – General Assembly Official Records* (54th Session, supplement n. 42), U.N. doc. A/54/42, of 06.05.1999, Annex I, pp. 6–7, paras. 1, 6 and 9.
314 *Ibid.*, p. 7, paras. 10–11 and 13.
315 *Ibid.*, Annex II, p. 11 3rd preambular paragraph.
316 *Ibid.*, Annex I, p. 7, para. 5; and p. 8, para. 28.
317 *Ibid.*, p. 9, para. 36.
318 *Ibid.*, p. 9, para. 41.

disarmament under strict and effective international control, so that future generations can live in a more stable and peaceful atmosphere".[319]

261. To the establishment of aforementioned five nuclear-weapon-free zones other initiatives against nuclear weapons are to be added, such as the prohibitions of placement of nuclear weapons, and other kinds of weapons of mass destruction, in outer space, on the seabed, on the ocean floor and in the subsoil beyond the outer limit of the territorial seabed zone, – "denuclearized" by the Treaties of Antarctica (1959), Outer Space (1967) and the Deep Sea Bed (1971), respectively, to which can be added the Treaty on the Moon and Other Celestial Bodies (1979), established a complete demilitarization thereon.[320]

262. The fact that the international community counts today on five nuclear-weapon-free zones, in relation to which States that possess nuclear weapons do have a particular responsibility, reveals an undeniable advance of right reason, of the *recta ratio* in the foundations of contemporary international law. Moreover, the initiative of nuclear-weapon-free zones keeps on clearly gaining ground. In recent years, proposals are being examined for the setting up of new denuclearized zones of the kind,[321] as well as of the so-called single-State zone (e.g., Mongolia).[322] That initiative further reflects the increasing disapproval, by the international community as a whole, of nuclear weapons, which, in view of their hugely destructive capability, constitute an affront to right reason (*recta ratio*).

XIX   Conferences on the Humanitarian Impact of Nuclear Weapons (2013–2014)

263. In the course of the proceedings in the present case of *Obligations Concerning Negotiations Relating to Cessation of the Nuclear Arms Race and to*

---

319   *Ibid.*, p. 9, para. 45.
320   Cf. G. Venturini, "Control and Verification of Multilateral Treaties on Disarmament and Non-Proliferation of Weapons of Mass Destruction", 17 *University of California Davis Journal of International Law and Policy* (2011) pp. 359–360.
321   E.g., in Central and Eastern Europe, in the Middle East, in Central and North–East and South Asia, and in the whole of the southern hemisphere.
322   Cf. A. Acharya and S. Ogunbanwo, *op. cit. supra* n. (305), p. 443; J. Enkhsaikhan, *op. cit. supra* n. (309), pp. 79–80. Mongolia in effect declared its territory as a nuclear-weapon-free zone (in 1992), and in February 2000 adopted national legislation defining its status as a nuclear-weapon-free State. This was acknowledged by U.N. General Assembly resolution 55/33S of 20.11.2000.

Nuclear Disarmament, several references were made to the more recent series of Conferences on the Humanitarian Impact of Nuclear Weapons (2013–2014), and in particular to the statement made therein (in the second of those Conferences) by the Marshall Islands, asserting that NWS should fulfill their obligation, "long overdue", of negotiation to achieve complete nuclear disarmament (cf. *infra*). The Marshall Islands promptly referred to its own statement in the Nayarit Conference (2014) in its *Memorial* in the *cas d'espèce*, as well as in its oral arguments before the ICJ.

264. In effect, the Conferences on the Humanitarian Impact of Nuclear Weapons (a series initiated in 2013) were intended to provide a forum for dialogue on, and a better understanding of, the humanitarian consequences of use of nuclear weapons for human beings, societies, and the environment, rather than a substitute of bilateral and multilateral fora for disarmament negotiations. This forum for dialogue and better understanding of the matter has counted on three Conferences to date, held, respectively, in Oslo in March 2013, in Nayarit in February 2014, and in Vienna in December 2014.

265. This recent series of Conferences has drawn attention to the humanitarian effects of nuclear weapons, restoring the central position of the concern for human beings and peoples. It has thus stressed the importance of the human dimension of the whole matter, and has endeavoured to awaken the conscience of the whole international community as well as to enhance the needed humanitarian coordination in the present domain. May I next proceed to a survey of their work and results so far.

1   *First Conference on the Humanitarian Impact of Nuclear Weapons*

266. The first Conference on the Humanitarian Impact of Nuclear Weapons took place in Oslo, Norway, on 04–05 March 2013, having counted on the participation of Delegations representing 127 States, United Nations agencies, the International Committee of the Red Cross (ICRC), the Red Cross and the Red Crescent movement, international organizations, and civil society entities. It should not pass unnoticed that only two of the NWS, India and Pakistan, were present at this Conference (and only India made a statement).[323] On the other hand, neither the Marshall Islands, nor the permanent members of the U.N. Security Council, attended it.

267. The Oslo Conference addressed three key issues, namely: (a) the immediate human impact of a nuclear weapon detonation; (b) the wider economic,

---

323   *In*: https://www.regjeringen.no/globalassets/upload/ud/vedlegg/hum/hum_india.pdf.

developmental and environmental consequences of a nuclear weapon detonation; and (c) the preparedness of States, international organizations, civil society and the general public to deal with the predictable humanitarian consequences that would follow from a nuclear weapon detonation. A wide range of experts made presentations during the Conference.

268. Attention was drawn, e.g., to the nuclear testing's impact during the cold-war period, in particular to the detonation of not less than 456 nuclear bombs in the four decades (between 1949 and 1989) in the testing ground of Semipalatinsk, in eastern Kazakhstan. It was reported (by UNDP) that, according to the Kazakh authorities, up to 1.5 million people were affected by fall-out from the blasts at Semipalatinsk; the nuclear test site was shut down in mid-1991. Other aspects were examined, all from a humanitarian outlook.[324] References were made, e.g., to General Assembly resolutions (such as resolution 63/279, of 25.04.2009), on humanitarian rehabilitation of the region. Such a humanitarian approach proved necessary, as the "historical experience from the use and testing of nuclear weapons has demonstrated their devastating immediate and long-term effects".[325]

269. The key conclusions of the Oslo Conference, as highlighted by Norway's Minister of Foreign Affairs in his closing statement,[326] can be summarized as follows. First, it is unlikely that any state or international body (such as U.N. relief agencies and the ICRC) could address the immediate humanitarian emergency caused by a nuclear weapon detonation in an adequate manner and provide sufficient assistance to those affected. Thus, the ICRC called for the abolition of nuclear weapons as the only effective preventive measure, and several participating States stressed that elimination of nuclear weapons is the only way to prevent their use; some States called for a ban on those weapons.

270. Secondly, the historical experience from the use and testing of nuclear weapons has demonstrated their devastating immediate and long-term effects. While the international scenario and circumstances surrounding it have changed, the destructive potential of nuclear weapons remains. And thirdly,

---

[324] For accounts of the work of the 2013 Oslo Conference, cf., e.g., *Viewing Nuclear Weapons through a Humanitarian Lens* (eds. J. Borrie and T. Caughley), Geneva/N.Y., U.N./UNIDIR, 2013, pp. 81–82, 87, 90–91, 93–96, 99, 105–108 and 115–116.

[325] Norway/Ministry of Foreign Affairs, *Chair's Summary – The Humanitarian Impact of Nuclear Weapons*, Oslo, 05.03.2013, p. 2.

[326] *In*: https://www.regjeringen.no/en/aktuelt/nuclear_summary/id716343/.

the effects of a nuclear weapon detonation, irrespective of its cause, will not be constrained by national borders, and will affect States and peoples in significant ways, in a trans-frontier dimension, regionally as well as globally.

2 Second Conference on the Humanitarian Impact of Nuclear Weapons

271. The second Conference on the Humanitarian Impact of Nuclear Weapons took place in Nayarit, Mexico, on 13–14 February 2014, having counted on the participation of Delegations representing 146 States. The Marshall Islands, India and Pakistan attended it, whereas the United Kingdom did not. In addition to States, other participants included the ICRC, the Red Cross and the Red Crescent movement, international organizations, and civil society entities. During the Nayarit Conference, the Delegate of the Marshall Islands stated that NWS States were failing to fulfill their obligations, under Article VI of the NPT and customary international law, to commence and conclude multilateral negotiations on nuclear disarmament; in his words:

> the Marshall Islands is convinced that multilateral negotiations on achieving and sustaining a world free of nuclear weapons are long overdue. Indeed we believe that states possessing nuclear arsenals are failing to fulfill their legal obligations in this regard. Immediate commencement and conclusion of such negotiations is required by legal obligation of nuclear disarmament resting upon each and every state under Article VI of the Non Proliferation Treaty and customary international law. It also would achieve the objective of nuclear disarmament long and consistently set by the United Nations, and fulfill our responsibilities to present and future generations while honouring the past ones.[327]

272. Earlier on, the Minister of Foreign Affairs of the Marshall Islands stated, at the U.N. High-Level Meeting on Nuclear Disarmament, on 26.09.2013, that the Marshall Islands "has a unique and compelling reason" to urge nuclear disarmament, namely,

> The Marshall Islands, during its time as a UN Trust Territory, experienced 67 large-scale tests of nuclear weapons. At the time of testing, and at

---

[327] Marshall Islands' Statement, Second Conference on the Humanitarian Impact of Nuclear Weapons, Nayarit, Mexico, 13–14 February 2014 (*in*: http://www.reachingcriticalwill.org/images/documents/Disarmament-fora/nayarit-2014/statements/MarshallIslands.pdf). The text is also quoted by the Marshall Islands in its *Memorial* in Marshall Islands *versus* United Kingdom, Annex 72.

every possible occasion in the intervening years, the Marshall Islands has informed UN members of the devastating impacts of these tests – of the deliberate use of our people as unwilling scientific experiments, of ongoing health impacts inherited through generations, of our displaced populations who still live in exile or who were resettled under unsafe circumstances, and then had to be removed. Even today, science remains a moving target and our exiled local communities are still struggling with resettlement.

(...) Perhaps we [the Marshallese] have one of the most important stories to tell regarding the need to avert the use of nuclear weapons, and a compelling story to spur greater efforts for nuclear disarmament (pp. 1–2).[328]

273. The Marshall Islands' statement in the 2014 Nayarit Conference was thus one of a few statements in which the Marshall Islands has articulated its claim, whereon they rely in the *cas d'espèce*, *inter alia*, to substantiate the existence of a dispute, including with the United Kingdom, which was not present at the Conference.[329] The Nayarit Conference participants also heard the poignant testimonies of five *Hibakusha*, – survivors of the atomic bombings of Hiroshima and Nagasaki, – who presented their accounts of the overwhelming devastation inflicted on those cities and their inhabitants by the atomic blasts (including the victims' burning alive, and carbonized or vaporized, as well as the long-term effects of radiation, killing survivors along seven decades).

274. They stressed the "moral imperative" of abolition of nuclear weapons, as humanity and nuclear weapons cannot coexist. A group of Delegations of no less than 20 States called expressly for a ban of nuclear weapons, already long

---

328 *In*: http://www.un.org/en/ga/68/meetings/nucleardisarmament/pdf/MH_en.pdf. And the Marshall Islands' Minister of Foreign Affairs (Ph. Muller) added that

"It should be our collective goal as the United Nations to not only stop the spread of nuclear weapons, but also to pursue the peace and security of a world without them. Further, the Republic of the Marshall Islands has recently ratified the Comprehensive Test Ban Treaty and urges other member states to work towards bringing this important agreement into force.

The Marshall Islands is not the only nation in the Pacific to be touched by the devastation of nuclear weapon testing. (...) We express again our eventual aspirations to join with our Pacific neighbours in supporting a Pacific free of nuclear weapons in a manner consistent with international security" (pp. 1–2).

329 *Memorial* of the M.I. in Marshall Islands *versus* United Kingdom, para. 99.

overdue; this was the sword of Damocles hanging over everyone's heads. The "mere existence" of nuclear weapons was regarded as "absurd"; attention was also drawn to the 2013 U.N. General Assembly High-Level Meeting on Disarmament, and to the obligations under international law, including those deriving from the NPT as well as common Article 1 of the Geneva Conventions on IHL.[330]

275. Furthermore, an association of over 60 entities of the civil society, from more than 50 countries, stated[331] that their own engagement was essential, as responsibilities fell on everyone to prevent the use of nuclear weapons; and prevention required the prohibition and ban of nuclear weapons, in the same way as those of biological and chemical weapons, landmines, and cluster munitions. Both the association, and the *Hibakusha*, condemned the dangerous strategy of nuclear "deterrence".

276. The 2014 Nayarit Conference's conclusions, building on the conclusions of the previous Oslo Conference, can be summarized as follows. First, the immediate and long-term effects of a single nuclear weapon detonation, let alone a nuclear exchange, would be catastrophic. The mere existence of nuclear weapons generates great risks, because the military doctrines of the NWS envisage preparations for the deliberate use of nuclear weapons. Nuclear weapons could be detonated by accident, miscalculation, or deliberately.

277. Delegations of over 50 States from every region of the world made statements unequivocally calling for the total elimination of nuclear weapons and the achievement of a world free of nuclear weapons. At least 20 Delegations of participating States in the Conference (*supra*) expressed the view that the way forward would be a ban on nuclear weapons. Others were equally clear in their calls for a Convention on the elimination of nuclear weapons or a new legally binding instrument.[332]

---

330   Mexico/Gobierno de la República, *Chair's Summary – Second Conference on the Humanitarian Impact of Nuclear Weapons*, Mexico, 14.02.2014, pp. 2–3.
331   On behalf of the International Campaign to Abolish Nuclear Weapons (ICAN), a coalition of over 350 entities in 90 countries.
332   For example, for its part, India favoured a step-by-step approach towards the elimination of nuclear weapons, ultimately leading to "a universal, non-discriminatory Convention on prohibition and elimination of nuclear weapons"; cf. www.reachingcriticalwill.org/images/documents/Disarmament-fora/nayarit-2014/statements/India.pdf.

278. Secondly, some Delegations pointed out the security implications of nuclear weapons, or else expressed skepticism about the possibility of banning nuclear weapons as such. There were those which favoured a "step-by-step" approach to nuclear disarmament (within the framework of the NPT Action Plan), and called for the participation of NWS in this process. For their part, the nuclear-weapon-free States, in their majority, were however of the view that the step-by-step approach had failed to achieve its goal; they thus called for a new approach to nuclear disarmament.

279. Thirdly, for the Chairman of the Conference, a ban on nuclear weapons would be the first step towards their elimination; such a ban would also rectify the anomaly that nuclear weapons are the only weapons of mass destruction that are not subject to an explicit legal prohibition. He added that achieving a world free of nuclear weapons is consistent with States' obligations under international law, including under the NPT and common Article 1 to the Geneva Conventions on IHL. He at last called for the development of new international standards on nuclear weapons, including a legally binding instrument, to be concluded by the 70th anniversary of the atomic bombings of Hiroshima and Nagasaki.[333]

3 Third Conference on the Humanitarian Impact of Nuclear Weapons

280. The third Conference on the Humanitarian Impact of Nuclear Weapons took place in Vienna, Austria, on 08–09 December 2014, having carried forward the momentum created by the previous Conference in Mexico. It counted on the participation of Delegations of 158 States, as well as the U.N., the ICRC, the Red Cross and Red Crescent movement, civil society entities and representatives of the academic world. For the first time, of the NWS, the United Kingdom attended the Conference; Delegates from India, Pakistan, and the Marshall Islands were present as well.

281. Once again, the Conference participants heard the testimonies of survivors, the *Hibakusha*. Speaking of the "hell on earth" experienced in Hiroshima and Nagasaki; the "indiscriminate massacre of the atomic bombing" showed "the illegality and ultimate evil of nuclear weapons".[334] In its statement,

---

333 Cf.http://www.reachingcriticalwill.org/images/documents/Disarmament-fora/nayarit-2014/chairs-summary.pdf.

334 Cf. *Vienna Conference on the Humanitarian Impact of Nuclear Weapons (08–09 December 2014)*, Vienna, Austria's Federal Ministry for Europe, Integration and Foreign Affairs, 2015, p. 19.

the Marshall Islands, addressing the testing in the region of 67 atomic and hydrogen bombs, between 1946 and 1958, – the strongest one having been the Bravo test (of 01.03.1954) of a hydrogen bomb, 1000 times more powerful than the atomic bomb dropped over Hiroshima, – referred to their harmful impacts, such as the birth of "monster-like babies", the continuous suffering from "thyroid cancer, liver cancer and all types of radiogenic cancerous illnesses", extending over the years.[335]

282. For its part, the ICRC stated that nuclear weapons ignore the principle of proportionality, and stand in breach of IHL (both conventional and customary) by causing unnecessary suffering to civilians; it expressed "significant concerns about the eventual spread of radiation to civilian areas and the radiological contamination of the environment" and everyone.[336] The ICRC further observed that, after "decades of focusing on nuclear weapons primarily in technical-military terms and as symbols of power", a fundamental and reassuring change has occurred, as debates on the matter now shift attention to what those weapons "would mean for people and the environment, indeed for humanity".[337]

283. The U.N. Secretary-General (Ban Ki-moon) sent a statement, read at the Conference, wherein he condemned expenditures in the modernization of weapons of mass destruction (instead of meeting the challenges of poverty and climate change). Recalling that the obligation of nuclear disarmament was one of both conventional and customary international law, he further condemned the strategy of nuclear "deterrence"; in his own words,

> Upholding doctrines of nuclear deterrence does not counter proliferation, but it makes the weapons more desirable. Growing ranks of nuclear-armed States does not ensure global stability, but instead undermines it. (...) The more we understand about the humanitarian impacts, the more it becomes clear that we must pursue disarmament as an urgent imperative.[338]

284. The Vienna Conference contributed to a deeper understanding of the consequences and risks of a nuclear detonation, having focused to a larger extent

---

335 *Ibid.*, p. 34.
336 *Ibid.*, p. 58.
337 *Ibid.*, p. 17.
338 Statement reproduced *in ibid.*, p. 16.

on the legal framework (and gaps therein) with regard to nuclear weapons.[339] It was reckoned that the impact of nuclear weapons detonation, irrespective of the cause, would go well beyond national borders, and could have regional and even global consequences, causing destruction, death, diseases and displacement on a very large scale, as well as profound and long-term damage to the environment, climate, human health and well-being, socioeconomic development and social order. They could, in sum, threaten the very survival of humankind. It was acknowledged that the scope, scale and interrelationship of the humanitarian consequences caused by nuclear weapon detonation are catastrophic, and more complex than commonly understood; these consequences can be large scale and potentially irreversible.

285. States expressed various views regarding the ways and means of advancing the nuclear disarmament agenda. The Delegations of 29 States called for negotiations of a legally-binding instrument to prohibit or ban nuclear weapons. A number of Delegations considered that the inability to make progress on any particular step was no reason not to pursue negotiations in good faith on other effective measures to achieve and maintain a nuclear-weapon-free world. Such steps have been taken very effectively in regional contexts in the past, as evidenced by nuclear-weapon-free zones.

286. As the general report of the Vienna Conference observed, the three Conferences on the Humanitarian Impact of Nuclear Weapons (of Oslo, Nayarit and then Vienna), have contributed to a "deeper understanding" of the "actual risks" posed by nuclear weapons, and the "unspeakable suffering", devastating effects, and "catastrophic humanitarian consequences" caused by their use. As "nuclear deterrence entails preparing for nuclear war, the risk of nuclear weapon use is real. (...) The only assurance against the risk of a nuclear weapon detonation is the total elimination of nuclear weapons", in "the interest of the very survival of humanity"; hence the importance of Article VI of the NPT, and of the entry into force of the CTBT.[340]

287. The 2014 Vienna Conference's conclusions can be summarized as follows. First, the use and testing of nuclear weapons have demonstrated their devastating immediate, mid- and long-term effects. Nuclear testing in several parts of the world has left a legacy of serious health and environmental consequences. Radioactive contamination from these tests disproportionately affects women

---

339   Cf. *ibid.* pp. 1–88.
340   *Ibid.*, pp. 5–7.

and children. It contaminated food supplies and continues to be measurable in the atmosphere to this day.

288. Secondly, as long as nuclear weapons exist, there remains the possibility of a nuclear weapon explosion. The risks of accidental, mistaken, unauthorized or intentional use of nuclear weapons are evident due to the vulnerability of nuclear command and control networks to human error and cyber-attacks, the maintaining of nuclear arsenals on high levels of alert, forward deployment and their modernization. The dangers of access to nuclear weapons and related materials by non-state actors, particularly terrorist groups, persist. All such risks, which increase over time, are unacceptable.

289. Thirdly, as nuclear deterrence entails preparing for nuclear war, the risk of the use of nuclear weapons is real. Opportunities to reduce this risk must be taken now, such as de-alerting and reducing the role of nuclear weapons in security doctrines. Limiting the role of nuclear weapons to deterrence does not remove the possibility of their use, nor does it address the risks stemming from accidental use. The only assurance against the risk of a nuclear weapon detonation is the total elimination of nuclear weapons.

290. Fourthly, the existence itself of nuclear weapons raises serious ethical questions, – well beyond legal discussions and interpretations, – which should be kept in mind. Several Delegations asserted that, in the interest of the survival of humankind, nuclear weapons must never be used again, under any circumstances. Fifthly, no State or international organ could adequately address the immediate humanitarian emergency or long-term consequences caused by a nuclear weapon detonation in a populated area, nor provide adequate assistance to those affected. The imperative of prevention as the only guarantee against the humanitarian consequences of nuclear weapons use is thus to be highlighted. Sixthly, participating Delegations reiterated the importance of the entry into force of the CTBT as a key element of the international nuclear disarmament and non-proliferation regime.

291. Seventhly, it is clear that there is no comprehensive legal norm universally prohibiting the possession, transfer, production and use of nuclear weapons, that is, international law does not address today nuclear weapons in the way it addresses biological and chemical weapons. This is generally regarded as an anomaly – or rather, a nonsense, – as nuclear weapons are far more destructive. In any case, international environmental law remains applicable in armed conflict and can pertain to nuclear weapons, even if not specifically regulating

these latter. Likewise, international health regulations would cover effects of nuclear weapons. In the light of the new evidence produced in those two years (2013–2014) about the humanitarian impact of nuclear weapons, it is very doubtful whether such weapons could ever be used in conformity with IHL.

4 Aftermath: The "Humanitarian Pledge"

292. At the 2014 Vienna Conference, although a handful of States expressed scepticism about the effectiveness of a ban on nuclear weapons, the overwhelming majority of NPT States Parties expected the forthcoming 2015 NPT Review Conference to take stock of all relevant developments, including the outcomes of the Conferences on the Humanitarian Impact of Nuclear Weapons (*supra*), and determine the next steps for the achievement and maintenance of a nuclear-weapon-free world. At the end of the Vienna Conference, the host State, Austria, presented a "Pledge" calling upon States parties to the NPT to renew their commitment to the urgent and full implementation of existing obligations under Article VI, and to this end, to identify and pursue effective measures to fill the legal gap for the prohibition and elimination of nuclear weapons.[341]

293. The Pledge further called upon NWS to take concrete interim measures to reduce the risk of nuclear weapons detonations, including by diminishing the role of nuclear weapons in military doctrines. The Pledge also recognised that: (a) the rights and needs of the victims of nuclear weapon use and testing have not yet been adequately addressed; (b) all States share the responsibility to prevent any use of nuclear weapons; and (c) the consequences of nuclear weapons use raise profound moral and ethical questions going beyond debates about the legality of these weapons.

294. Shortly before the Vienna Conference, 66 States had already endorsed the Pledge; by the end of the Conference, 107 States had endorsed it, thus "internationalizing" it and naming it at the end as the "Humanitarian Pledge".[342] On 07.12. 2015, the U.N. General Assembly adopted the substance of the Humanitarian Pledge in the form of its resolution 70/48. As of April 2016, 127 States

---

341 *In*:http://www.bmeia.gv.at/fileadmin/user_upload/Zentrale/Aussenpolitik/Abruestung/-HINW14/HINW14Vienna_Pledge_Document.pdf. The Pledge only refers to States' obligations under the NPT and makes no mention of customary international law.

342 http://www.bmeia.gv.at/fileadmin/user_upload/Zentrale/Aussenpolitik/Abruestung/-HINW14/HINW14.

have formally endorsed the Humanitarian Pledge; unsurprisingly, none of the NWS has done so.

295. Recent endeavours, such as the ones just reviewed of the Conferences on the Humanitarian Impact of Nuclear Weapons have been rightly drawing attention to the grave humanitarian consequences of nuclear weapons detonations. The reframing of the whole matter in a people-centred outlook appears to me particularly lucid, and necessary, keeping in mind the unfoundedness of the strategy of "deterrence" and the catastrophic consequences of the use of nuclear weapons. The "step-by-step" approach, pursued by the NWS in respect to the obligation under Article VI of the NPT, appears essentially State-centric, having led to an apparent standstill or deadlock.

296. The obligation of nuclear disarmament being one of result, the "step-by-step" approach cannot be extended indefinitely in time, with its insistence on the maintenance of the nuclear sword of Damocles. The "step-by-step" approach has produced no significantly concrete results to date, seeming to make abstraction of the numerous pronouncements of the United Nations upholding the obligation of nuclear disarmament (cf. *supra*). After all, the absolute prohibition of nuclear weapons, – which is multifaceted,[343] is one of *jus cogens* (cf. *supra*). Such weapons, as the Conferences on the Humanitarian Impact of Nuclear Weapons have evidenced, are essentially inhumane, rendering the strategy of "deterrence" unfounded and unsustainable (cf. *supra*).

297. Ever since those Conferences (2013–2014), there has been a tendency (in 2014–2016) of slight reduction of nuclear warheads,[344] though NWS have kept on modernizing their respective nuclear armament programs, in an indication that nuclear weapons are likely to remain in the foreseeable future.[345] Yet, the growing awareness of the humanitarian impact of nuclear weapons has raised the question of the possibility of developing "a deontological position according to which the uniquely inhumane suffering that nuclear weapons inflict on their victims makes it inherently wrongful to use them".[346]

---

343 Encompassing measures relating to any use, threat of use, development, production, acquisition, possession, stockpiling and transfer of nuclear weapons.
344 From around 16.300 nuclear warheads in 2014 to 15,850 in 2015, and to 15,395 in early 2016.
345 Cf. *SIPRI Yearbook 2016: Armaments, Disarmament and International Security*, Stockholm-Solna, SIPRI, 2016, Ch. 16, pp. 609–667.
346 ILPI, *Evidence of Catastrophe – A Summary of the Facts Presented at the Three Conferences on the Humanitarian Impact of Nuclear Weapons*, Oslo, ILPI, 2015, p. 15.

298. *Tempus fugit.* There remains a long way to go to achieve a nuclear-weapon-free world. The United Nations itself has been drawing attention to the urgency of nuclear disarmament. It has done so time and time again, and, quite recently, in the convocation in October 2015, of a new Open-Ended Working Group (OEWG), as a subsidiary body of the U.N. General Assembly, to address concrete and effective legal measures to attain and maintain a world without nuclear weapons.[347] It draws attention therein to the importance of multilateralism, to the relevance of "inclusiveness" (participation of all U.N. member States) and of the contribution, in addition to that of States, also of international organizations, of entities of the civil society, and of the academia.[348] And it reaffirms "the urgency of securing substantive progress in multilateral nuclear disarmament negotiations", in order "to attain and maintain a world without nuclear weapons".[349]

299. It should not pass unnoticed that all the initiatives that I have just reviewed in the present Dissenting Opinion (NPT Review Conferences, the establishment of nuclear-weapon-free zones, and the Conferences on the Humanitarian Impact of Nuclear Weapons), referred to by the contending parties in the course of the proceedings before the ICJ in the present case of *Obligations Concerning Negotiations Relating to Cessation of the Nuclear Arms Race and to Nuclear Disarmament*, have gone beyond the inter-State outlook. In my perception, there is great need, in the present domain, to keep on looking beyond States, so as to behold peoples' and humankind's quest for survival in our times.

XX   Final Considerations: *Opinio Juris Communis* Emanating from Conscience (*Recta Ratio*), Well above the "Will"

300. Nuclear weapons, as from their conception, have been associated with overwhelming destruction. It may be recalled that the first atomic bombs were fabricated in an epoch of destruction and devastation, – the II world war, – of the abominable "total war", in flagrant breach of IHL and of the ILHR.[350]

---

347   U.N. General Assembly, doc. A/C.1/70/L.13/Rev.1, of 29.10.2015, pp. 1–3.
348   Preamble, paras. 8 and 14–15.
349   Operative part, para. 2.
350   For an account, cf., e.g., *inter alia*, J. Lukacs, *L'héritage de la Seconde Guerre Mondiale*, Paris, Ed. F.-X. de Guibert, 2011, pp. 38–39, 55, 111 and 125–148; and cf. I. Kershaw, *To Hell and Back – Europe 1914–1949*, London, Penguin, 2016, pp. 7, 356, 407, 418, 518 and 521.

The fabrication of nuclear weapons, followed by their use, made abstraction of the fundamental principles of international law, moving the world into lawlessness in the current nuclear age. The strategy of "deterrence", in a "dialectics of suspicion", leads to an unforeseeable outcome, amidst complete destruction. Hence the utmost importance of negotiations conducive to general disarmament, which, – as warned by Raymond Aron already in the early sixties, – had "never been taken seriously" by the super-powers.[351]

301. Last but not least, may I come back to a key point which I have dwelt upon in the present Dissenting Opinion pertaining to the *opinio juris communis* as to the obligation of nuclear disarmament (cf. Part XVI, *supra*). In the evolving law of nations, basic considerations of humanity have an important role to play. Such considerations nourish *opinio juris* on matters going well beyond the interests of individual States. The ICJ has, on more than one occasion, taken into account resolutions of the United Nations (in distinct contexts) as a means whereby international law manifests itself.

302. In its *célèbre* Advisory Opinion (of 21.06.1971) on *Namibia*, for example, the ICJ dwelt upon, in particular, two U.N. General Assembly resolutions relevant to the formation of *opinio juris*.[352] Likewise, in its Advisory Opinion (of 16.10.1975) on the *Western Sahara*, the ICJ considered and discussed in detail some U.N. General Assembly resolutions.[353] In this respect, references can further be made to the ICJ's Advisory Opinions on *Legal Consequences of the Construction of a Wall in the Occupied Palestinian Territory* (of 09.07.2004),[354] and on the *Declaration of Independence of Kosovo* (of 22.07.2010).[355] In its 1996 Advisory Opinion on the *Threat or Use of Nuclear Weapons*, the ICJ admitted, – even if in a rather restrictive way, – the emergence and gradual evolution of an

---

351 R. Aron, *Paz e Guerra entre as Nações* [1962], Brasília, Edit. Universidade de Brasília, 1979, pp. 413, 415, 421–422 and 610. R. Aron's book contains his reflections on the new age of nuclear weapons, amidst the tensions of the cold-war era, and the new challenges and dangers it imposed, – persisting to date, – for the future of humankind; cf., for the French edition, R. Aron, *Paix et guerre entre les nations*, 8th ed., Paris, Éd. Calmann-Levy, 2015, pp. 13–770.

352 On the principle of self-determination of peoples, namely, G.A. resolutions 1514(XV) of 14.12.1960, and 2145(XXI) of 27.10.1966; cf. *I.C.J Reports 1971*, pp. 31, 45 and 49–51.

353 Cf. *I.C.J. Reports 1975*, pp. 20, 23, 26–37, 40, 57 and 67–68.

354 Cf. *I.C.J. Reports 1975*, pp. 171–172, paras. 86–88.

355 Cf. *I.C.J. Reports 2010*, p. 437, para. 80 (addressing a General Assembly resolution "which reflects customary international law").

opinio juris as reflected in a series of resolutions of the U.N. General Assembly (para. 70). But the ICJ could have gone (much) further than that.

303. After all, *opinio juris* has already had a long trajectory in legal thinking, being today endowed with a wide dimension. Thus, already in the XIXth century, the so-called "historical school" of legal thinking and jurisprudence (of F.K. von Savigny and G.F. Puchta) in reaction to the voluntarist conception, gradually discarded the "will" of the States by shifting attention to *opinio juris*, requiring practice to be an authentic expression of the "juridical conscience" of nations and peoples. With the passing of time, the acknowledgment of conscience standing above the "will" developed further, as a reaction against the reluctance of some States to abide by norms addressing matters of general or common interest of the international community.

304. This had an influence on the formation of rules of customary international law, a much wider process than the application of one of its formal "sources". *Opinio juris communis* came thus to assume "a considerably broader dimension than that of the subjective element constitutive of custom".[356] *Opinio juris* became a key element in the *formation* itself of international law, a *law of conscience*. This diminished the unilateral influence of the most powerful States, fostering international law-making in fulfilment of the public interest and in pursuance of the common good of the international community as a whole.

305. The foundations of the international legal order came to be reckoned as independent from, and transcending, the "will" of individual States; *opinio juris communis* came to give expression to the "juridical conscience", no longer only of nations and peoples – sustained in the past by the "historical school" – but of the international community as a whole, heading towards the universalization of international law. It is, in my perception, this international law of

---

356   A.A. Cançado Trindade, *International Law for Humankind – Towards a New Jus Gentium*, *op. cit. supra* n. (132), p. 137, and cf. p. 138; and cf. R. Huesa Vinaixa, *El Nuevo Alcance de la "Opinio Juris" en el Derecho Internacional Contemporáneo*, Valencia, Tirant lo Blanch, 1991, pp. 30–31 and 36–38, and cf. pp. 76–77, 173, 192, 194, 199 and 204–205; R.E. Piza Escalante, "La '*Opinio Juris*' como Fuente Autónoma del Derecho Internacional ('*Opinio Juris*' y '*Jus Cogens*')", 39 *Relaciones Internacionales* – Heredia/C.R. (1992) pp. 61–74; J.I. Charney, "International Lawmaking – Article 38 of the ICJ Statute Reconsidered", *in New Trends in International Lawmaking – International "Legislation" in the Public Interest* (Proceedings of the Kiel Symposium, March 1996), Berlin, Duncker & Humblot, 1997, pp. 180–183 and 189–190.

conscience that turns in particular towards nuclear disarmament, for the sake of the survival of humankind.

306. In 1983, Wang Tieya wrote against minimizing the legal significance of resolutions of General Assembly, in particular the declaratory ones. As they clarify principles and rules of international law, he contended that they "cannot be said to have no law-making effect at all merely because they are not binding in the strict sense. At the very least, since they embody the convictions of a majority of States, General Assembly resolutions can indicate the general direction in which international law is developing".[357] He added that those General Assembly resolutions, reflecting the position of "an overwhelming majority of States", have "accelerated the development of international law", in helping to crystallize emerging rules into "clearly defined norms".[358] In the same decade, it was further pointed out that General Assembly resolutions have been giving expression, along the years, to "basic concepts of equity and justice, or of the underlining spirit and aims" of the United Nations.[359]

307. Still in the eighties, in the course I delivered at the Institute of Public International Law and International Relations of Thessaloniki, in 1988, I began by pondering that customary and conventional international law are interrelated, – as acknowledged by the ICJ itself[360] – and U.N. General Assembly resolutions contribute to the emergence of *opinio juris communis*.[361] I stood

---

[357] Wang Tieya, "The Third World and International Law", *in The Structure and Process of International Law: Essays in Legal Philosophy Doctrine and Theory* (eds. R.St.J. Macdonald and D.M. Johnston), The Hague, M. Nijhoff, 1983, p. 964.

[358] *Ibid.*, pp. 964–965.

[359] B. Sloan, "General Assembly Resolutions Revisited (Forty Years Later)", 58 *British Year Book of International Law* (1987) p. 80, and cf. pp. 116, 137 and 141.

[360] For example, in the course of the proceedings in the *Nuclear Tests* cases (1973–1974), one of the applicant States (Australia) recalled, in the public sitting of 08.07.1974, that the ICJ had held, in the *North Sea Continental Shelf* cases (*I.C.J. Reports 1969*, p. 41), that a conventional norm can pass into the general *corpus* of international law thus becoming also a rule of customary international law; cf. ICJ, *Pleadings, Oral Arguments, Documents – Nuclear Tests cases* (vol. I: Australia *versus* France, 1973–1974), p. 503. In effect, – may I add, – just as a customary rule may later crystallize into a conventional norm, this latter can likewise generate a customary rule. International law is not static (as legal positivists wrongfully assume); it is essentially dynamic.

[361] A.A. Cançado Trindade, "Contemporary International Law-Making: Customary International Law and the Systematization of the Practice of States", *in Sources of International Law* (Thesaurus Acroasium, vol. XIX), Thessaloniki, Institute of Public International Law and International Relations, 1992, pp. 68 and 71.

against the "strictly voluntarist position" underlying the unacceptable concept of so-called "persistent objector", and added that dissent from "one or another State individually cannot prevent the creation of new customary rules" or obligations, ensuing from *opinio juris communis* and not from *voluntas*.[362]

308. In the evolution of international law in time, – I proceeded, – voluntarist positivism has shown itself "entirely incapable" of explaining the consensual formation of customary international obligations; contrary to "the pretensions of positivist voluntarism" (with its stubborn emphasis on the consent of individual States), "freedom of spirit is the first to rebel" against immobilism, in devising responses to new challenges affecting the international community as a whole, and acknowledging obligations incumbent upon all States.[363]

309. In my "repudiation of voluntarist positivism", I concluded on this point that the attention to customary international law ("incomparably less vulnerable" than conventional international law to voluntarist temptations) is in line with the progressive development (moved by conscience) of international law, so as to provide a common basis for the fulfilment of the needs and aspirations of all peoples.[364] Today, almost three decades later, I firmly restate, in the present Dissenting Opinion, my own position on the matter, in respect of the customary and conventional international obligation to put an end to nuclear weapons, so as to rid the world of their inhuman threat.

310. May I here, furthermore, ponder that U.N. General Assembly or Security Council resolutions are adopted on behalf not of the States which voted in favour of them, but more precisely on behalf of the United Nations Organization itself (its respective organs), being thus *valid for all U.N. member States*. This applies to the resolutions surveyed in the present Dissenting Opinion. It should be kept in mind that the U.N. is endowed with an international legal personality of its own, which enables it to act at international level as a distinct entity, independently of individual member States; in this way, it upholds the juridical equality of all States, and mitigates the worrisome vulnerability of factually weaker States, such as the NNWS; in doing so, it aims – by

---

362 *Ibid.*, pp. 78–79.
363 *Ibid.*, pp. 126–129.
364 *Ibid.*, pp. 128–129. And cf., more recently, in general, A.A. Cançado Trindade, "The Contribution of Latin American Legal Doctrine to the Progressive Development of International Law", 376 *Recueil des Cours de l'Académie de Droit International de La Haye* (2014) pp. 9–92, esp. pp. 75–76.

multilateralism – at the common good, at the realization of common goals of the international community as a whole,[365] such as nuclear disarmament.

311. A small group of States – such as the NWS – cannot overlook or minimize those reiterated resolutions, extended in time, simply because they voted against them, or abstained. Once adopted, they are valid for all U.N. member States. They are resolutions of the United Nations Organization itself, and not only of the large majority of U.N. member States which voted in favour of them. U.N. General Assembly resolutions, reiteratedly addressing matters of concern to humankind as a whole (such as existing nuclear weapons), are in my view endowed with normative value. They cannot be properly considered from a State voluntarist perspective; they call for another approach, away from the strict voluntarist-positivist one.

312. Conscience stands above the "will". The universal juridical conscience stands well above the "will" of individual States, and resonates in resolutions of the U.N. General Assembly, which find inspiration in general principles of international law, which, for their part, give expression to values and aspirations of the international community as a whole, of all humankind.[366] This – may I reiterate – is the case of General Assembly resolutions surveyed in the present Dissenting Opinion (cf. *supra*). The values which find expression in those *prima principia* inspire every legal order and, ultimately, lie in the foundations of this latter.

313. The general principles of law (*prima principia*), in my perception, confer upon the (national and international) legal order its ineluctable axiological dimension. Notwithstanding, legal positivism and political "realism", in their characteristic subservience to power, incur into their basic mistake of minimizing those principles, which lie in the foundations of any legal system, and which inform and conform the norms and the action pursuant to them, in the search for the realization of justice. Whenever that minimization of principles has prevailed the consequences have been disastrous.[367]

---

365 Cf., in this sense, A.A. Cançado Trindade, *Direito das Organizações Internacionais*, 6th rev. ed., Belo Horizonte/Brazil, Edit. Del Rey, 2014, pp. 51 and 530–531.

366 A.A. Cançado Trindade, *International Law for Humankind – Towards a New Jus Gentium*, op. cit. supra n. (132), pp. 129–138.

367 A.A. Cançado Trindade, *A Humanização do Direito Internacional*, 2nd rev. ed., Belo Horizonte/Brazil, 2015, pp. 6–24; A.A. Cançado Trindade, *Os Tribunais Internacionais e a Realização da Justiça*, op. cit. supra n. (255), pp. 410–418.

314. They have been contributing, in the last decades, to a vast *corpus juris* on matters of concern to the international community as a whole, such as nuclear disarmament. Their contribution to this effect has overcome the traditional inter-State paradigm of the international legal order.[368] This can no longer be overlooked in our days. The inter-State mechanism of the *contentieux* before the ICJ cannot be invoked in justification for an inter-State reasoning. As "the principal judicial organ" of the United Nations (U.N. Charter, Article 92), the ICJ has to bear in mind not only States, but also "we, the peoples", on whose behalf the U.N. Charter was adopted. In its international adjudication of contentious cases, like the present one of *Obligations Concerning Negotiations Relating to Cessation of the Nuclear Arms Race and to Nuclear Disarmament*, the ICJ has to bear in mind basic considerations of humanity, with their incidence on questions of admissibility and jurisdiction, as well as of substantive law.

XXI   Epilogue: A Recapitulation

315. Coming to the end of the present Dissenting Opinion, I feel in peace with my conscience: from all the preceding considerations, I trust to have made it crystal clear that my own position, in respect of all the points which form the object of the present Judgment on the case of *Obligations Concerning Negotiations Relating to Cessation of the Nuclear Arms Race and to Nuclear Disarmament*, stands in clear and entire opposition to the view espoused by the Court's majority that the existence of a legal dispute has not been established before it, and that the Court has no jurisdiction to consider the Application lodged with it by the Marshall Islands, and cannot thus proceed to the merits of the case. Not at all: in my understanding, there is a dispute before the Court, which has jurisdiction to decide the case. There is a conventional and customary international law obligation of nuclear disarmament. Whether there has been a concrete breach of this obligation, the Court could only decide on the merits phase of the present case.

316. My dissenting position is grounded not only on the assessment of the arguments produced before the Court by the contending parties, but above all on issues of principle and on fundamental values, to which I attach even greater importance. As my dissenting position covers all points addressed in

---

368 A.A. Cançado Trindade, *Direito das Organizações Internacionais, op. cit. supra* n. (365), pp. 530–537.

the present Judgment, in its reasoning as well as in its conclusion, I have thus felt obliged, in the faithful exercise of the international judicial function, to lay on the records, in the present Dissenting Opinion, the foundations of my dissenting position thereon. I deem it fit, at this last stage, to recapitulate all the points of my dissenting position, expressed herein, for the sake of clarity, and in order to stress their interrelatedness.

317. *Primus*: According to the *jurisprudence constante* of the Court, a dispute is a disagreement on a point of law or fact, a conflict of legal views or interests; The existence of an international dispute (at the time of lodging a claim) is a matter for the objective determination of the Court. The existence of a dispute may be inferred. *Secundus*: The objective determination of a dispute by the Court is not intended to protect respondent States, but rather and more precisely to secure the proper exercise of the Court's judicial function. *Tertius*: There is no requirement of prior notice of the applicant State's intention to initiate proceedings before the ICJ, nor of prior "exhaustion" of diplomatic negotiations, nor of prior notification of the claim; it is, in sum, a matter for objective determination of the Court itself.

318. *Quartus*: The Marshall Islands and the United Kingdom/India/Pakistan have pursued distinct arguments and courses of conduct on the matter at issue, evidencing their distinct legal positions, which suffice for the Court's objective determination of the existence of a dispute. *Quintus*: There is no legal ground for attempting to heighten the threshold for the determination of the existence of a dispute; in its *jurisprudence constante*, the Court has expressly avoided a formalistic approach on this issue, which would affect access to justice itself. The Court has, instead, in its *jurisprudence constante*, upheld its own *objective determination* of the existence of a dispute, rather than relying – as it does in the present case – on the subjective criterion of "awareness" of the respondent States.

319. *Sextus*: The distinct series of U.N. General Assembly resolutions on nuclear disarmament along the years (namely, warning against nuclear weapons, 1961–1981; on freeze of nuclear weapons, 1982–1992; condemning nuclear weapons, 1982 2015; following-up the ICJ's 1996 Advisory Opinion, 1996–2015) are endowed with authority and legal value. *Septimus*: Their authority and legal value have been duly acknowledged before the ICJ in its advisory proceedings in 1995. *Octavus*: Like the General Assembly, the Security Council has also expressed its concern on the matter at issue, in its work and its resolutions on nuclear disarmament.

320. *Nonus*: The aforementioned United Nations resolutions, in addition to other initiatives, portray the longstanding saga of the United Nations in the condemnation of nuclear weapons. *Decimus*: The fact that weapons of mass destruction (poisonous gases, biological and chemical weapons) have been outlawed, and nuclear weapons, far more destructive, have not been banned yet, is a juridical absurdity. The obligation of nuclear disarmament has emerged and crystallized nowadays in both conventional and customary international law, and the United Nations has, along the decades, been giving a most valuable contribution to this effect.

321. *Undecimus*: In the *cas d'espèce*, the issue of United Nations resolutions and the emergence of *opinio juris communis* in the present domain of the obligation of nuclear disarmament has grasped the attention of the contending parties in submitting their distinct arguments before the Court. *Duodecimus*: The presence of evil has marked human existence along the centuries. Ever since the eruption of the nuclear age in August 1945, some of the world's great thinkers have been inquiring whether humankind has a future, and have been drawing attention to the imperative of respect for life and the relevance of humanist values. *Tertius decimus*: Also in international legal doctrine there have been those who have been stressing the needed prevalence of human conscience, the universal juridical conscience, over State voluntarism.

322. *Quartus decimus*: The U.N. Charter is attentive to peoples; the recent cycle of World Conferences of the United Nations has had, as a common denominator, the recognition of the legitimacy of the concern of the international community as a whole with the conditions of living and the well-being of peoples everywhere. *Quintus decimus*: General principles of law (*prima principia*) rest in the foundations of any legal system. They inform and conform its norms, guide their application, and draw attention to the prevalence of *jus necessarium* over *jus voluntarium*.

323. *Sextus decimus*: The nature of a case before the Court may well require a reasoning going beyond the strictly inter-State outlook; the present case concerning the obligation of nuclear disarmament requires attention to be focused on peoples, in pursuance of a humanist outlook, rather than on inter-State susceptibilities. *Septimus decimus*: The inter-State mechanism of adjudication of contentious cases before the ICJ does not at all imply that the Court's reasoning should likewise be strictly inter-State. Nuclear disarmament is a matter of concern to humankind as a whole.

324. *Duodevicesimus*: The present case stresses the utmost importance of fundamental principles, such as that of the juridical equality of States, following the principle of humanity, and of the idea of an objective justice. *Undevicesimus*: Factual inequalities and the strategy of "deterrence" cannot be made to prevail over the juridical equality of States. *Vicesimus*: "Deterrence" cannot keep on overlooking the distinct series of U.N. General Assembly resolutions, expressing an *opinio juris communis* in condemnation of nuclear weapons. *Vicesimus primus*: As also sustained by general principles of international law and international legal doctrine, nuclear weapons are in breach of international law, of IHL and the ILHR, and of the U.N. Charter.

325. *Vicesimus secundus*: There is need of a people-centred approach in this domain, keeping in mind the fundamental right to life; the *raison d'humanité* prevails over the *raison d'État*. Attention is to be kept on the devastating and catastrophic consequences of the use of nuclear weapons. *Vicesimus tertius*: In the path towards nuclear disarmament, the peoples of the world cannot remain hostage of individual State consent. The universal juridical conscience stands well above the "will" of the State. *Vicesimus quartus*: The absolute prohibitions of arbitrary deprivation of human life, of infliction of cruel, inhuman or degrading treatment, and of infliction of unnecessary suffering, are prohibitions of *jus cogens*, which have and incidence on ILHR and IHL and ILR, and foster the current historical process of humanization of international law.

326. *Vicesimus quintus*: The positivist outlook unduly overlooks the *opinio juris communis* as to the illegality of all weapons of mass destruction, including [and starting with] nuclear weapons, and the obligation of nuclear disarmament, under contemporary international law. *Vicesimus sextus*: Conventional and customary international law go together, in the domain of the protection of the human person, as disclosed by the Martens clause, with an incidence on the prohibition of nuclear weapons. *Vicesimus septimus*: The existence of nuclear weapons is the contemporary tragedy of the nuclear age; today, more than ever, human beings need protection from themselves. Nuclear weapons have no ethics, and ethics cannot be separated from law, as taught by jusnaturalist thinking.

327. *Vicesimus octavus*: Humankind, a subject of rights, has been a potential victim of nuclear weapons already for a long time. *Vicesimus nonus*: The law of nations encompasses, among its subjects, humankind as a whole (as propounded by the "founding fathers" of international law). *Trigesimus*: This

humanist vision is centred on peoples, keeping in mind the humane ends of States. *Trigesimus primus*: *Opinio juris communis necessitatis*, upholding a customary and conventional obligation of nuclear disarmament, has been finding expression in the NPT Review Conferences, in the relevant establishment of nuclear-weapon-free zones, and in the recent Conferences of the Humanitarian Impact of Nuclear Weapons, – in their common cause of achieving and maintaining a nuclear-weapon-free world. *Trigesimus secundus*: Those initiatives have gone beyond the State-centric outlook, duly attentive to peoples' and humankind's quest for survival in our times.

328. *Trigesimus tertius*: *Opinio juris communis* – to which U.N. General Assembly resolutions have contributed – has a much broader dimension than the subjective element of custom, being a key element in the formation of a law of conscience, so as to rid the world of the inhuman threat of nuclear weapons. *Trigesimus quartus*: U.N. (General Assembly and Security Council) resolutions are adopted on behalf of the United Nations Organization itself (and not only of the States which voted in their favour); they are thus valid for *all* U.N. member States.

329. *Trigesimus quintus*: The United Nations Organization, endowed with an international legal personality of its own, upholds the juridical equality of States, in striving for the realization of common goals such as nuclear disarmament. *Trigesimus sextus*: Of the main organs of the United Nations, the contributions of the General Assembly, the Security Council and the Secretary-General to nuclear disarmament have been consistent and remarkable along the years.

330. *Trigesimus septimus*: United Nations resolutions in this domain address a matter of concern to humankind as a whole, which cannot thus be properly approached from a State voluntarist perspective. The universal juridical conscience stands well above the "will" of individual States. *Trigesimus octavus*: The ICJ, as the principal judicial organ of the United Nations, is to keep in mind basic considerations of humanity, with their incidence on questions of admissibility and jurisdiction, as well as of substantive law. *Trigesimus nonus*: In sum, the ICJ has jurisdiction to consider the *cas d'espèce*, and there is a conventional and customary international law obligation of nuclear disarmament; whether there has been a breach of this obligation, the Court could only decide on the merits phase of the present case.

331. *Quadragesimus*: A world with arsenals of nuclear weapons, like ours, is bound to destroy its past, dangerously threatens the present, and has no future

at all. Nuclear weapons pave the way into nothingness. In my understanding, the International Court *of Justice*, as the principal judicial organ of the United Nations, should, in the present Judgment, have shown sensitivity in this respect, and should have given its contribution to a matter which is a major concern of the vulnerable international community, and indeed of humankind as a whole.

(Signed) *Antônio Augusto* CANÇADO TRINDADE
Judge

2 Dissenting Opinion in the Case of *Obligations Concerning Negotiations Relating to Cessation of the Nuclear Arms Race and to Nuclear Disarmament* (Marshall Islands *versus* United Kingdom, Jurisdiction, Judgment of 05.10.2016)

Table of Contents   Paragraphs

I. *Prolegomena* 1–4
II. The Existence of a Dispute before the Hague Court 5
   1. Objective Determination by the Court 5–15
   2. Existence of a Dispute in the *Cas d'Espèce* (case Marshall Islands versus United Kingdom) 16–19
   3. The Threshold for the Determination of the Existence of a Dispute 20–25
   4. Contentions in the Case of Marshall Islands *versus* United Kingdom 26
   5. General Assessment 27–30
III. U.N. General Assembly Resolutions and *Opinio Juris* 31
   1. U.N. General Assembly Resolutions on Nuclear Weapons (1961–1981) 32–37
   2. U.N. General Assembly Resolutions on Freeze of Nuclear Weapons (1982–1992) 38–40
   3. U.N. General Assembly Resolutions on Nuclear Weapons as Breach of the U.N. Charter (Acknowledgment before the ICJ, 1995) 41–44
   4. U.N. General Assembly Resolutions Condemning Nuclear Weapons (1982–2015) 45–50
   5. U.N. General Assembly Resolutions Following up the ICJ's 1996 Advisory Opinion (1996–2015) 51–56
IV. U.N. Security Council Resolutions and *Opinio Juris* 57–63
V. The Saga of the United Nations in the Condemnation of Nuclear Weapons 64–77
VI. U.N. Resolutions and the Emergence of *Opinio Juris*: The Positions of the Contending Parties 78–83
VII. Questions from the Bench and Responses from the Parties 84–88
VIII. Human Wickedness: From the XXIst Century Back to the Book of *Genesis* 89–118

IX.	The Attention of the United Nations Charter to Peoples	119–127
X.	Impertinence of the So-Called *Monetary Gold* "Principle"	128–131
XI.	The Fundamental Principle of the Juridical Equality of States	132–135
XII.	Unfoundedness of the Strategy of "Deterrence"	136–146
XIII.	The Illegality of Nuclear Weapons and the Obligation of Nuclear Disarmament	
	1. The Condemnation of All Weapons of Mass Destruction	147–152
	2. The Prohibition of Nuclear Weapons: The Need of a People-Centred Approach	153–171
	3. The Prohibition of Nuclear Weapons: The Fundamental Right to Life	172–185
	4. The Absolute Prohibitions of *Jus Cogens* and the Humanization of International Law	186–189
	5. Pitfalls of Legal Positivism: A Rebuttal of the So-Called *Lotus* "Principle"	190–196
XIV.	Recourse to the "Martens Clause" as an Expression of the *Raison d'Humanité*	197–205
XV.	Nuclear Disarmament: Jusnaturalism, the Humanist Conception and the Universality of International Law	206–216
XVI.	The Principle of Humanity and the Universalist Approach: *Jus Necessarium* Transcending the Limitations of *Jus Voluntarium*	217–229
XVII.	NPT Review Conferences	230–245
XVIII.	The Establishment of Nuclear-Weapon-Free Zones	246–258
XIX.	Conferences on the Humanitarian Impact of Nuclear Weapons (2013–2014)	259–261
	1. First Conference on the Humanitarian Impact of Nuclear Weapons	262–266
	2. Second Conference on the Humanitarian Impact of Nuclear Weapons	267–275
	3. Third Conference on the Humanitarian Impact of Nuclear Weapons	276–287
	4. Aftermath: The "Humanitarian Pledge"	288–295
XX.	Final Considerations: *Opinio Juris Communis* Emanating from Conscience (*Recta Ratio*), Well Above the "Will"	296–310
XXI.	Epilogue: A Recapitulation	311–327

I *Prolegomena*

1. I regret not to be able to accompany the Court's majority in the Judgment of today, 05.10.2016 in the present case of *Obligations Concerning Negotiations Relating to Cessation of the Nuclear Arms Race and to Nuclear Disarmament* (Marshall Islands *versus* United Kingdom), whereby it has found that the existence of a dispute between the parties has not been established before it, and that the Court has no jurisdiction to consider the Application lodged with it by the Marshall Islands, and cannot thus proceed to the merits of the case. I entirely disagree with the present Judgment. As my dissenting position covers all points addressed in it, in its reasoning as well as in its resolutory points, I feel obliged, in the faithful exercise of the international judicial function, to lay on the records the foundations of my own position thereon.

2. In doing so, I distance myself as much as I can from the position of the Court's split majority, so as to remain in peace with my conscience. I shall endeavor to make clear the reasons of my personal position on the matter addressed in the present Judgment, in the course of the present Dissenting Opinion. I shall begin by examining the question of the existence of a dispute before the Hague Court (its objective determination by the Court and the threshold for the determination of the existence of a dispute). I shall then turn attention to the distinct series of U.N. General Assembly resolutions on nuclear weapons and *opinio juris*. After surveying also U.N. Security Council resolutions and *opinio juris*, I shall dwell upon the saga of the United Nations in the condemnation of nuclear weapons. Next, I shall address the positions of the contending parties on U.N. resolutions and the emergence of *opinio juris*, and their responses to questions from the bench.

3. In logical sequence, I shall then, looking well back in time, underline the need to go beyond the strict inter-State dimension, bearing in mind the attention of the U.N. Charter to peoples. Then, after recalling the fundamental principle of the juridical equality of States, I shall dwell upon the unfoundedness of the strategy of "deterrence". My next line of considerations pertains to the illegality of nuclear weapons and the obligation of nuclear disarmament, encompassing: (a) the condemnation of all weapons of mass destruction; (b) the prohibition of nuclear weapons (the need of a people-centred approach, and the fundamental right to life); (c) the absolute prohibitions of *jus cogens* and the humanization of international law; (d) pitfalls of legal positivism.

4. This will bring me to address the recourse to the "Martens clause" as an expression of the *raison d'humanité*. My following reflections, on nuclear disarmament, will be in the line of jusnaturalism, the humanist conception and the universality of international law; in addressing the universalist approach, I shall draw attention to the principle of humanity and the *jus necessarium* transcending the limitations of *jus voluntarium*. I shall then turn attention to the NPT Review Conferences, to the relevant establishment of nuclear-weapon-free zones, and to the Conferences on the Humanitarian Impact of Nuclear Weapons. The way will then be paved for my final considerations, on *opinio juris communis* emanating from conscience (*recta ratio*), well above the "will", – and, last but not least, to the epilogue (recapitulation).

II The Existence of a Dispute before the Hague Court

1 *Objective Determination by the Court*

5. May I start by addressing the issue of the existence of a dispute before the Hague Court. In the *jurisprudence constante* of the Hague Court (PCIJ and ICJ), a dispute exists when there is "a disagreement on a point of law or fact, a conflict of legal views or of interests between two persons".[1] Whether there exists a dispute is a matter for "objective determination" by the Court; the "mere denial of the existence of a dispute does not prove its non-existence".[2] The Court must examine if "the claim of one party is positively opposed by the other".[3] The Court further states that "a disagreement on a point of law or fact, a conflict of legal views or interests, or the positive opposition of the claim of one party by the other need not be necessarily be stated *expressis verbis*".[4]

6. Along the last decade, the Court has deemed it fit to insist on its own faculty to proceed to the "objective determination" of the dispute. Thus, in the case

---

1 PCIJ, case of *Mavrommatis Palestine Concessions*, Judgment of 30.08.1924, p. 11.
2 ICJ, Advisory Opinion (of 30.03.1950) on the *Interpretation of Peace Treaties with Bulgaria, Hungary and Romania*, p. 74.
3 ICJ, *South–West Africa* cases (Ethiopia and Liberia *versus* South Africa, Judgment on Preliminary Objections of 21.12.1962), p. 328; ICJ, case of *Armed Activities on the Territory of the Congo* (New Application – 2002, D.R. Congo *versus* Rwanda, Judgment on Jurisdiction and Admissibility of 03.02.2006), p. 40, para. 90.
4 ICJ, *Land and Maritime Boundary between Cameroon and Nigeria* (Judgment on Preliminary Objections, of 11.06.1998), p. 275, para. 89.

of *Armed Activities on the Territory of the Congo* (D.R. Congo *versus* Rwanda, Jurisdiction and Admissibility, Judgment of 03.02.2006), for example, the ICJ has recalled that, as long ago as 1924, the PCIJ stated that "a dispute is a disagreement on a point of law or fact, a conflict of legal views or interests" (case of *Mavrommatis Palestine Concessions,* Judgment of 30.08.1924, p. 11). It then added that

> For its part, the present Court has had occasion a number of times to state the following:
>> In order to establish the existence of a dispute, 'it must be shown that the claim of one party is positively opposed by the other' (*South West Africa,* Preliminary Objections, Judgment, *I.C.J. Reports 1962,* p. 328); and further, 'Whether there exists an international dispute is a matter for objective determination' (*Interpretation of Peace Treaties with Bulgaria, Hungary and Romania,* First Phase, Advisory Opinion, *I.C.J. Reports 1950,* p. 74; *East Timor* (Portugal v. Australia), Judgment, *I.C.J. Reports 1995,* p. 100, para. 22; *Questions of Interpretation and Application of the 1971 Montreal Convention arising from the Aerial Incident at Lockerbie* (Libyan Arab Jamahiriya v. United Kingdom), Preliminary Objections, Judgment, *I.C.J. Reports 1998,* p. 17, para. 22; *Questions of Interpretation and Application of the 1971 Montreal Convention arising from the Aerial Incident at Lockerbie* (Libyan Arab Jamahiriya v. United States of America), Preliminary Objections, Judgment, *I.C.J. Reports 1998,* pp. 122–123, para. 21; *Certain Property* (Liechtenstein v. Germany), Preliminary Objections, Judgment, *I.C.J. Reports 2005,* p. 18, para. 24) (para. 90).

7. Shortly afterwards, in its Judgment on Preliminary Objections (of 18.11.2008) in the case of the *Application of the Convention against Genocide* (Croatia *versus* Serbia), the ICJ has again recalled that

> In numerous cases, the Court has reiterated the general rule which it applies in this regard, namely: 'the jurisdiction of the Court must normally be assessed on the date of the filing of the act instituting proceedings' (to this effect, cf. *Application of the Convention on the Prevention and Punishment of the Crime of Genocide* (Bosnia and Herzegovina v. Yugoslavia), Preliminary Objections, Judgment, *I.C.J. Reports 1996 (II),* p. 613, para. 26; *Questions of Interpretation and Application of the 1971 Montreal Convention arising from the Aerial Incident at Lockerbie* (Libyan Arab Jamahiriya v.

United Kingdom), Preliminary Objections, Judgment, *I.C.J. Reports 1998*, p. 26, para. 44). (...) (I)t is normally by reference to the date of the filing of the instrument instituting proceedings that it must be determined whether those conditions are met.

(...) What is at stake is legal certainty, respect for the principle of equality and the right of a State which has properly seised the Court to see its claims decided, when it has taken all the necessary precautions to submit the act instituting proceedings in time. (....) [T]he Court must in principle decide the question of jurisdiction on the basis of the conditions that existed at the time of the institution of the proceedings.

However, it is to be recalled that the Court, like its predecessor, has also shown realism and flexibility in certain situations in which the conditions governing the Court's jurisdiction were not fully satisfied when proceedings were initiated but were subsequently satisfied, before the Court ruled on its jurisdiction (paras. 79–81).

8. More recently, in its Judgment on Preliminary Objections (of 01.04.2011) in the case of the *Application of the International Convention on the Elimination of All Forms of Racial Discrimination – CERD* (Georgia *versus* Russian Federation), the ICJ has seen it fit, once again, to stress:

The Court recalls its established case law on that matter, beginning with the frequently quoted statement by the Permanent Court of International Justice in the *Mavrommatis Palestine Concessions* case in 1924: 'A dispute is a disagreement on a point of law or fact, a conflict of legal views or of interests between two persons'. (Judgment n. 2, 1924, PCIJ, Series A, n. 2, p. 11). Whether there is a dispute in a given case is a matter for 'objective determination' by the Court (*Interpretation of Peace Treaties with Bulgaria, Hungary and Romania,* First Phase, Advisory Opinion, *I.C.J. Reports 1950,* p. 74). 'It must be shown that the claim of one party is positively opposed by the other' (*South West Africa* (Ethiopia and Liberia *v.* South Africa), Preliminary Objections, Judgment, *I.C.J. Reports 1962,* p. 328); and, most recently, *Armed Activities on the Territory of the Congo* (New Application: 2002, D.R. Congo *v.* Rwanda, Jurisdiction and Admissibility, Judgment, *I.C.J. Reports 2006,* p. 40, para. 90). The Court's determination must turn on an examination of the facts. The matter is one of substance, not of form. As the Court has recognized (for example, *Land and Maritime Boundary between Cameroon and Nigeria,* Cameroon *v.* Nigeria, Preliminary Objections, Judgment, *I.C.J. Reports*

1998, p. 315, para. 89), the existence of a dispute may be inferred from the failure of a State to respond to a claim in circumstances where a response is called for. While the existence of a dispute and the undertaking of negotiations are distinct as a matter of principle, the negotiations may help demonstrate the existence of the dispute and delineate its subject-matter.

The dispute must in principle exist at the time the Application is submitted to the Court (*Questions of Interpretation and Application of the 1971 Montreal Convention arising from the Aerial Incident at Lockerbie*, Libyan Arab Jamahiriya *v.* United Kingdom, Preliminary Objections, *Judgment, I.C.J. Reports 1998*, pp. 25–26, paras. 42–44; *Questions of Interpretation and Application of the 1971 Montreal Convention arising from the Aerial Incident at Lockerbie*, Libyan Arab Jamahiriya *v.* United States of America, Preliminary Objections, Judgment, *I.C.J. Reports 1998*, pp. 130–131, paras. 42–44) (...) (para. 30).

9. This passage of the 2011 Judgment in the case of the *Application of the CERD Convention* reiterates what the ICJ has held in its *jurisprudence constante*. Yet, shortly afterwards in that same Judgment, the ICJ has decided to apply to the facts of the case a higher threshold for the determination of the existence of a dispute, by proceeding to ascertain whether the applicant State had given the respondent State prior notice of its claim and whether the respondent State had opposed it.[5] On this basis, it has concluded that no dispute had arisen between the contending parties (before August 2008). Such new requirement, however, is not consistent with the PCIJ's and the ICJ's *jurisprudence constante* on the determination of the existence of a dispute (cf. *supra*).

10. Now, in the present case of *Obligations Concerning Negotiations Relating to Cessation of the Nuclear Arms Race and to Nuclear Disarmament*, the three respondent States (India, United Kingdom and Pakistan), seek to rely on a requirement of prior notification of the claim, or the test of prior awareness of the claim of the applicant State (the Marshall Islands), for a dispute to exist under the ICJ's Statute or general international law. Yet, nowhere can such a requirement be found in the Court's *jurisprudence constante* as to the existence of a dispute: quite on the contrary, the ICJ has made clear that the position or the attitude of a party can be established by inference.[6] Pursuant to the Court's

---

5 Cf. paras. 50–105, and esp. paras. 31, 61 and 104–105, of the Court's Judgment of 01.04.2011.

6 ICJ, *Land and Maritime Boundary between Cameroon and Nigeria* (Judgment on Preliminary Objections, of 11.06.1998), p. 315, para. 89: "a disagreement on a point of law or fact, a conflict

approach, it is not necessary for the respondent to oppose previously the claim by an express statement, or to express acknowledgment of the existence of a dispute.

11. The respondent States in the present case have made reference to the Court's 2011 Judgment in the case of the *Application of the CERD Convention* in support of their position that prior notice of the applicant's claim is a requirement for the existence of a dispute. Already in my Dissenting Opinion (para. 161) in that case, I have criticized the Court's "formalistic reasoning" in determining the existence of a dispute, introducing a higher threshold that goes beyond the *jurisprudence constante* of the PCIJ and the ICJ itself (cf. *supra*).

12. As I pointed out in that Dissenting Opinion in the case of the *Application of the CERD Convention*,

> As to the first preliminary objection, for example, the Court spent 92 paragraphs to concede that, in its view, a legal dispute at last crystallized, on 10 August 2008 (para. 93), only *after* the outbreak of an open and declared war between Georgia and Russia! I find that truly extraordinary: the emergence of a legal dispute only *after* the outbreak of widespread violence and war! Are there disputes which are quintessentially and ontologically *legal*, devoid of any political ingredients or considerations? I do not think so. The same formalistic reasoning leads the Court, in 70 paragraphs, to uphold the second preliminary objection, on the basis of alleged (unfulfilled) 'preconditions' of its own construction, in my view at variance with its own *jurisprudence constante* and with the more lucid international legal doctrine (para. 161).

13. Half a decade later, I was hopeful that the Court would distance itself from the formalistic approach it adopted in the case of the *Application of the CERD Convention*. As it regrettably has not done so, I feel obliged to reiterate here my dissenting position on the issue, this time in the present case of *Obligations Concerning Negotiations Relating to Cessation of the Nuclear Arms Race and to Nuclear Disarmament*. In effect, there is no general requirement of prior

---

of legal views or interests, or the positive opposition of the claim of one party by the other need not necessarily be stated *expressis verbis*. In the determination of the existence of a dispute, as in other matters, the position or the attitude of a party can be established by inference, whatever the professed view of that party".

notice of the applicant State's intention to initiate proceedings before the ICJ.[7] It should not pass unnoticed that the *purpose* of the need of determination of the existence of a dispute (and its object) before the Court is to enable this latter to exercise jurisdiction properly: it is not intended to protect the respondent State, but rather and more precisely to safeguard the proper exercise of the Court's judicial function.

14. There is no requirement under general international law that the contending parties must first "exhaust" diplomatic negotiations before lodging a case with, and instituting proceedings before, the Court (as a precondition for the existence of the dispute). There is no such requirement in general international law, nor in the ICJ's Statute, nor in the Court's case-law. This is precisely what the ICJ held in its Judgment on Preliminary Objections (of 11.06.1998) in the case of *Land and Maritime Boundary between Cameroon and Nigeria*: it clearly stated that

> Neither in the Charter nor otherwise in international law is any general rule to be found to the effect that the exhaustion of diplomatic negotiations constitutes a precondition for a matter to be referred to the Court (para. 56).

15. The Court's statement refers to the "exhaustion" of diplomatic negotiations, – to discard the concept. In effect, there is no such a requirement in the U.N. Charter either, that negotiations would need to be resorted to or attempted. May I reiterate that the Court's determination of the existence of the dispute is not designed to protect the respondent State(s), but rather to safeguard the proper exercise of its own judicial function in contentious cases. It is thus a matter for objective determination by the Court, as it recalled in that same Judgment (para. 87), on the basis of its own *jurisprudence constante* on the matter.

2 Existence of a Dispute in the Cas d'Espèce (*Case Marshall Islands versus United Kingdom*)

16. In the present case opposing the Marshall Islands to the United Kingdom, there were two sustained and quite distinct courses of conduct of the two contending parties, evidencing their distinct legal positions (as to the duty of negotiations leading to nuclear disarmament in all its aspects under strict

---

7 Cf., to this effect, S. Rosenne, *The Law and Practice of the International Court (1920–2005)*, 4th ed., vol. III, Leiden, Nijhoff/Brill, 2006, p. 1153.

and effective international control), which suffice for the determination of the existence of a dispute. The Marshall Islands drew attention to the fact that the United Kingdom has consistently opposed the commencement of multilateral negotiations on nuclear disarmament,[8] and has voted against General Assembly resolutions reaffirming the obligations recognized in the 1996 ICJ Advisory Opinion and calling for negotiations on nuclear disarmament.[9]

17. There were thus opposing views of the contending parties as to their divergent voting records in respect of the aforementioned General Assembly resolutions.[10] The primary articulation of the Marshall Islands' claim was its declaration in the Conference of Nayarit on 14.02.2014, wherein the Marshall Islands contested the legality of the conduct of the nuclear-weapon States [NWS], (including the United Kingdom), under the NPT and customary international law. The fact that the Marshall Islands' declaration was addressed to a plurality of States (namely "all States possessing nuclear arsenals"), and not to the United Kingdom individually, in my perception does not affect the existence of a dispute.

18. States possessing nuclear weapons are a small and easily identifiable group of States – to which the United Kingdom belongs – of the international community. The Marshall Islands' declaration was made with sufficient clarity to enable all NWS, including the United Kingdom, to consider the existence of a dispute concerning the theme; the Marshall Islands' declaration clearly identified the legal basis of the claim and the conduct complained of. Likewise, the fact that the United Kingdom was not present at the Conference of Nayarit of 2014 does not prejudice the opposition of legal views between the Marshall Islands and the United Kingdom.

19. There is a consistent course of distinct conducts by the two contending parties. This is followed by a claim, as to the substance of the matter at issue. This is sufficient for a dispute to crystallize; nothing more is required. The United Kingdom's subsequent submissions before the ICJ confirm the opposition of legal views: suffice it to mention that the United Kingdom stated that

---

8 Cf. W[ritten Statement] of the M.I., para. 40.
9 Cf. resolutions A/RES/68/32, A/RES/68/42, and A/RES/68/47 of 05.12.2013; A/RES/69/58, A/RES/69/43, and A/RES/69/48 of 02.12.2014; A/RES/70/34, A/RES/70/56, and A/RES/70/52 of 07.12.2015.
10 Response of the Marshall Islands to the questions addressed by Judge Cançado Trindade to both Parties, in: ICJ doc. CR 2016/13, para. 9.

the allegations brought by the Marshall Islands are "manifestly unfounded on the merits":[11] this is a clear opposition to the Marshall Islands' claim. A dispute already existed on the date of filing of the Application in the *cas d'espèce*, and the subsequent arguments of the parties before the Court confirm that.

3   The Threshold for the Determination of the Existence of a Dispute

20. In the present cases of *Obligations Concerning Negotiations Relating to Cessation of the Nuclear Arms Race and to Nuclear Disarmament* (Marshall Islands versus India/United Kingdom/Pakistan), the Court's majority has unduly heightened the threshold for establishing the existence of a dispute. Even if dismissing the need for an applicant State to provide notice of a dispute, in practice, the requirement stipulated goes far beyond giving notice: the Court effectively requires an applicant State to set out its legal claim, to direct it specifically to the prospective-respondent State(s), and to make the alleged harmful conduct clear. All of this forms part of the "awareness" requirement that the Court's majority has laid down, seemingly undermining its own ability to infer the existence of a dispute from the conflicting courses of conduct of the contending parties.

21. This is not in line with the ICJ's previous *obiter dicta* on inference, contradicting it. For example, in the aforementioned case of *Land and Maritime Boundary between Cameroon and Nigeria* (1998), the ICJ stated that

> [A] disagreement on a point of law or fact, a conflict of legal views or interests, or the positive opposition of the claim of one party by the other need not necessarily be stated *expressis verbis*. In the determination of the existence of a dispute, as in other matters, the position or attitude of a party can be established by inference, whatever the professed view of that party (para. 89).

22. The view taken by the Court's majority in the present case contradicts the Hague Court's (PCIJ and ICJ) own earlier case-law, in which it has taken a much less formalistic approach to the establishment of the existence of a dispute. Early in its life, the PCIJ made clear that it did not attach much importance to "matters of form";[12] it added that it could not "be hampered by a mere defect

---

11   *Preliminary Objections* of the U.K., para. 5.
12   PCIJ, case of *Mavrommatis Palestine Concessions*, Judgment of 30.08.1924, p. 34.

of form".[13] The PCIJ further stated that "the manifestation of the existence of the dispute in a specific manner, as for instance by diplomatic negotiations, is not required. (...) [T]he Court considers that it cannot require that the dispute should have manifested itself in a formal way".[14]

23. The ICJ has, likewise, in its own case-law, avoided to take a very formalistic approach to the determination of the existence of a dispute.[15] May I recall, in this respect, *inter alia*, as notable examples, the Court's *obiter dicta* on the issue, in the cases of *East Timor* (Portugal *versus* Australia), of the *Application of the Convention against Genocide* (Bosnia *versus* Yugoslavia), and of *Certain Property* (Liechtenstein *versus* Germany). In those cases, the ICJ has considered that conduct post-dating the critical date (i.e., the date of the filing of the Application) supports a finding of the existence of a dispute between the parties. In the light of this approach taken by the ICJ itself in its earlier case-law, it is clear that a dispute exists in each of the present cases lodged with it by the Marshall Islands.

24. In the case of *East Timor* (1995), in response to Australia's preliminary objection that there was no dispute between itself and Portugal, the Court stated: "Portugal has, rightly or wrongly, formulated complaints of fact and law against Australia which the latter has denied. By virtue of this denial, there is a legal dispute".[16] Shortly afterwards, in the case of the *Application of the Convention against Genocide* (Preliminary Objections, 1996), in response to Yugoslavia's preliminary objection that the Court did not have jurisdiction under Article IX

---

13   PCIJ, case of *Certain German Interests in Polish Upper Silesia* case (Jurisdiction), Judgment of 25.08.1925, p. 14.
14   PCIJ, case of *Interpretation of Judgments ns. 7 and 8 – Chorzów Factory*, Judgment of 16.12.1927, pp. 10–11.
15   Cf., e.g., ICJ, Advisory Opinion (of 26.04.1988) on the *Applicability of the Obligation to Arbitrate under Section 21 of the U.N. Headquarters Agreement of 26.06.1947*, pp. 28–29, para. 38; ICJ, case of *Nicaragua versus United States* (Jurisdiction and Admissibility), Judgment of 26.11.1984, pp. 428–429, para. 83. Moreover, the critical date for the determination of the existence of a dispute is, "in principle" (as the ICJ says), the date on which the application is submitted to the Court (ICJ, case of *Questions Relation to the Obligation to Prosecute or Extradite*, Judgment of 20.07.2012, p. 20, para. 46; ICJ, case of *Alleged Violations of Sovereign Rights and Maritime Spaces in the Caribbean Sea*, Preliminary Objections, Judgment of 17.03.2016, p. 25, para. 52); the ICJ's phraseology shows that this is not a strict rule, but rather one to be approached with flexibility.
16   ICJ, case of *East Timor* (Portugal *versus* Australia), *I.C.J. Reports 1995*, p. 100, para. 22 (Judgment of 30.06.1995).

of the Convention against Genocide because there was no dispute between the Parties, the Court, contrariwise, found that there was a dispute between them, on the basis that Yugoslavia had "wholly denied all of Bosnia and Herzegovina's allegations, whether at the stage of proceedings relating to the requests for the indication of provisional measures, or at the stage of the (...) proceedings relating to [...preliminary] objections".[17] Accordingly, "by reason of the rejection by Yugoslavia of the complaints formulated against it",[18] the ICJ found that there was a dispute.

25. In the case of *Certain Property* (Preliminary Objections, 2005), as to Germany's preliminary objection that there was no dispute between the parties, the ICJ found that complaints of fact and law formulated by Liechtenstein were denied by Germany; accordingly, "[i]n conformity with well-established jurisprudence", – the ICJ concluded, – "by virtue of this denial", there was a legal dispute between Liechtenstein and Germany.[19] Now, in the present proceedings before the Court, in each of the three cases lodged with the ICJ by the Marshall Islands (against India, the United Kingdom and Pakistan), the respondent States have expressly denied the arguments of the Marshall Islands. May we now take note of the denials which, on the basis of the Court's aforementioned *jurisprudence constante*, evidence the existence of a dispute between the contending parties.[20]

4   Contentions in the Case of *Marshall Islands* versus *United Kingdom*

26. The Marshall Islands argues that the United Kingdom has violated its obligations under Article VI of the NPT as well as its obligations under customary international law with regard to nuclear disarmament and the cessation of the nuclear arms race.[21] Although the United Kingdom's *Preliminary Objections* do

---

17   ICJ, case of the *Application of the Convention against Genocide* (Bosnia–Herzegovina *versus* Yugoslavia, Preliminary Objections, Judgment of 11.07.1996), *I.C.J. Reports 1996*, pp. 595 and 614–615, paras. 27–29.
18   *Ibid.*, p. 615, para. 29.
19   ICJ, case of *Certain Property* (Liechtenstein *versus* Germany, Preliminary Objections, Judgment of 10.02.2005), *I.C.J. Reports 2005* p. 19, para. 25, citing the Court's Judgments in the cases of *East Timor, I.C.J. Reports 1995*, p. 100, para. 22; and of the *Application of the Convention against Genocide* (Preliminary Objections), *I.C.J. Reports 1996*, p. 615, para. 29.
20   As the present proceedings relate to jurisdiction, the opposition of views is captured in the various jurisdictional objections; it would be even more forceful in pleadings on the merits, which, given the Court's majority decision, will regrettably no longer take place.
21   *Application Instituting Proceedings* of the Marshall Islands, pp. 35–36, paras. 100–109.

THE UNIVERSAL JURIDICAL CONSCIENCE, HUMANENESS 377

not address the merits of the dispute, there is one statement by the United Kingdom that reveals a dispute between the Parties:

> The silence by the Marshall Islands *vis-à-vis* the UK on nuclear disarmament issues comes against a backdrop of both a progressive unilateral reduction by the UK of its own nuclear arsenal, (...), and of active UK engagement in efforts, *inter alia*, to secure and extend nuclear-weapon-free zones around the world. The UK is a party to the Protocols to the Treaty of Tlatelolco, the Treaty of Rarotonga and the Treaty of Pelindaba, addressing, respectively, nuclear-weapon-free zones in Latin America and the Caribbean, the South Pacific, and Africa. The UK has ratified the Protocol to the Treaty on a Nuclear-Weapon-Free Zone in Central Asia and continues to engage with the States Parties to the Treaty on the Southeast Asia Nuclear-Weapon-Free Zone. The UK signed the Comprehensive Nuclear Test Ban Treaty on the first day it was opened for signature and was, alongside France, the first nuclear-weapon State to become a party to it. Beyond this, the UK is leading efforts to develop verification technologies to ensure that any future nuclear disarmament treaty will apply under strict and effective international control.
>
> Against this background, the Marshall Islands' Application instituting proceedings against the UK alleging a breach *inter alia* of Article VI of the NPT, and of asserted parallel obligations of customary international law, came entirely out of the blue. The United Kingdom considers the allegations to be manifestly unfounded on the merits.[22]

5   *General Assessment*

27. Always attentive and over-sensitive to the position of nuclear-weapon States [NWS] (cf. part XIII, *infra*), – such as the respondent States in the present cases of *Obligations Concerning Negotiations Relating to Cessation of the Nuclear Arms Race and to Nuclear Disarmament* (India, United Kingdom and Pakistan), – the Court, in the *cas d'espèce*, dismisses the statements made by the Marshall Islands in multilateral *fora* before the filing of the Application, as being, in its view, insufficient to determine the existence of a dispute. Moreover, the Court's split majority makes *tabula rasa* of the requirement that "in principle" the date for determining the existence of the dispute is the date of filing of the application (case of *Alleged Violations of Sovereign Rights and Maritime Spaces in the Caribbean Sea*, Nicaragua *versus* Colombia, Preliminary

---

22   *Preliminary Objections* of the United Kingdom, pp. 2–3, paras. 4–5.

Objections, Judgment of 17.03.2016, para. 52); as already seen, in its case-law the ICJ has taken into account conduct post-dating that critical date (cf. *supra*).

28. In an entirely formalistic reasoning, the Court borrows the *obiter dicta* it made in the case of the *Application of the CERD Convention* (2011), – unduly elevating the threshold for the determination of the existence of a dispute, – in respect of a compromissory clause under that Convention (wrongly interpreted anyway, making abstraction of the object and purpose of the CERD Convention). In the present case, opposing the Marshall Islands to the United Kingdom, worse still, the Court's majority takes that higher standard out of context, and applies it herein, in a case lodged with the Court on the basis of an optional clause declaration, even though also concerning a conventional obligation (under the NPT).

29. This attempt to heighten still further the threshold for the determination of the existence of a dispute (requiring further factual precisions from the applicant) is, besides formalistic, artificial: it does not follow from the definition of a dispute in the Court's *jurisprudence constante*, as being "a conflict of legal views or of interests", as already seen (cf. *supra*). The Court's majority formalistically requires a specific reaction of the respondent State to the claim made by the applicant State (in applying the criterion of "awareness", amounting, in my perception, to an obstacle to access to justice), even in a situation where, as in the *cas d'espèce*, there are two consistent and distinct courses of conduct on the part of the contending parties.

30. Furthermore, and in conclusion, there is a clear denial by the respondent States (India, United Kingdom and Pakistan) of the arguments made against them by the applicant State, the Marshall Islands. By virtue of these denials there is a legal dispute between the Marshall Islands and each of the three respondent States. The formalistic raising, by the Court's majority, of the higher threshold for the determination of the existence of a dispute, is not in conformity with the *jurisprudence constante* of the PCIJ and ICJ on the matter (cf. *supra*). Furthermore, in my perception, it unduly creates a difficulty for the very *access to justice* (by applicants) at international level, in a case on a matter of concern to the whole of humankind. This is most regrettable.

III   U.N. General Assembly Resolutions and *Opinio Juris*

31. In the course of the proceedings in the present cases of *Obligations Concerning Negotiations Relating to Cessation of the Nuclear Arms Race and to Nuclear*

Disarmament, both the applicant State (the Marshall Islands) and the respondent States (India, United Kingdom and Pakistan) addressed U.N. General Assembly resolutions on the matter of nuclear disarmament (cf. Part VI, *infra*). This is the point that I purport to consider, in sequence, in the present Dissenting Opinion, namely, in addition to the acknowledgment before the ICJ (1995) of the authority and legal value of General Assembly resolutions on nuclear weapons as breach of the U.N. Charter, the distinct series of: (a) U.N. General Assembly resolutions on Nuclear Weapons (1961–1981); (b) UN General Assembly Resolutions on Freeze of Nuclear Weapons (1982–1992); (c) U.N. General Assembly Resolutions Condemning Nuclear Weapons (1982–2015); (d) U.N. General Assembly Resolutions Following up the ICJ's 1996 Advisory Opinion (1996–2015).

1   *U.N. General Assembly Resolutions on Nuclear Weapons (1961–1981)*

32. The 1970s was the First Disarmament Decade: it was so declared by General Assembly resolution A/RES/2602 E (XXIV) of 16.12.1969, followed by two other resolutions of 1978 and 1980 on non-use of nuclear weapons and prevention of nuclear war.[23] The General Assembly specifically called upon States to intensify efforts for the cessation of the nuclear arms race, nuclear disarmament and the elimination of other weapons of mass destruction. Even before that, the ground-breaking General Assembly resolution 1653 (XVI), of 24.11.1961, advanced its *célèbre* "Declaration on the Prohibition of the Use of Nuclear and Thermonuclear Weapons" (cf. Part V, *infra*). In 1979, when the First Disarmament Decade was coming to an end, the General Assembly, – disappointed that the objectives of the first Decade had not been realized, – declared the 1980s as a Second Disarmament Decade.[24] Likewise, the 1990s were subsequently declared the Third Disarmament Decade.[25]

33. In this first period under review (1961–1981), the U.N. General Assembly paid continuously special attention to disarmament issues and to nuclear disarmament in particular. May I refer to General Assembly resolutions A/RES/2934 of 29.11.1972; A/RES/2936 of 29.11.1972; A/RES/3078 of 06.12.1973; A/RES/3257 of 09.12.1974; A/RES/3466 of 11.12.1975; A/RES/3478 of 11.12.1975; A/RES/31/66 of 10.12.1976; A/RES/32/78 of 12.12.1977; A/RES/33/71 of 14.12.1978; A/RES/33/72 of 14.12.1978; A/RES/33/91 of 16.12.1978; A/RES/34/83 of 11.12.1979;

---

23   Namely, in sequence, General Assembly resolutions A/RES/33/71B of 14.12.1978, and A/RES/35/152D of 12.12.1980.
24   Cf. General Assembly resolutions A/RES/34/75 of 11.12.1979, and A/RES/35/46 of 03.12.1980.
25   Cf. General Assembly resolutions A/RES/43/78L of 07.12.1988, and A/RES/45/62 A of 04.12.1990.

A/RES/34/84 of 11.12.1979; A/RES/34/85 of 11.12.1979; A/RES/34/86 of 11.12.1979; A/RES/35/152 of 12.12.1980; A/RES/35/155 of 12.12.1980; A/RES/35/156 of 12.12.1980; A/RES/36/81 of 09.12.1981; A/RES/36/84 of 09.12.1981; A/RES/36/92 of 09.12.1981; A/RES/36/94 of 09.12.1981; A/RES/36/95 of 09.12.1981; A/RES/36/97 of 09.12.1981; and A/RES/36/100 of 09.12.1981.

34. In 1978 and 1982, the U.N. General Assembly held two Special Sessions on Nuclear Disarmament (respectively, the 10th and 12th sessions), where the question of nuclear disarmament featured prominently amongst the themes discussed. In fact, it was stressed that the most immediate goal of disarmament is the elimination of the danger of a nuclear war. In a subsequent series of its resolutions (in the following period of 1982–2015), as we shall see, the General Assembly moved on straightforwardly to the condemnation of nuclear weapons (cf. *infra*).

35. In its resolutions adopted during the present period of 1972–1981, the General Assembly repeatedly drew attention to the dangers of the nuclear arms race for humankind and the survival of civilization and expressed apprehension concerning the harmful consequences of nuclear testing for the acceleration of such arms race. Thus, the General Assembly reiterated its condemnation of all nuclear weapon tests, in whatever environment they may be conducted. It called upon States that had not yet done so to adhere to the 1963 Test Ban Treaty (banning nuclear tests in the atmosphere, in outer space and under water) and called for the conclusion of a comprehensive test ban treaty, which would ban nuclear weapons tests in all environments (e.g. underground as well). Pending the conclusion of such treaty, it urged NWS to suspend nuclear weapon tests in all environments.

36. The General Assembly also emphasised that NWS bear a special responsibility for fulfilling the goal of achieving nuclear disarmament, and in particular those nuclear weapon States that are parties to international agreements in which they have declared their intention to achieve the cessation of the nuclear arms race. It further called specifically on the heads of State of the USSR and the United States to implement the procedures for the entry into force of the Strategic Arms Limitation agreement (so-called "SALT" agreement).

37. At the 84th plenary meeting, following the 10th Special Session on Disarmament, the General Assembly declared that the use of nuclear weapons is a "violation of the Charter of the United Nations" and "a crime against humanity", and that the use of nuclear weapons should be prohibited, pending

nuclear disarmament.[26] The General Assembly further noted the aspiration of non-nuclear-weapon States [NNWS] to prevent nuclear weapons from being stationed on their territories through the establishment of nuclear-weapon-free zones, and supported their efforts to conclude an international Convention strengthening the guarantees for their security against the use or threat of use of nuclear weapons. As part of the measures to facilitate the process of nuclear disarmament and the non-proliferation of nuclear weapons, it requested the Committee on Disarmament to consider the question of the cessation and prohibition of the production of fissionable material for weapons purposes.

2   U.N. General Assembly Resolutions on Freeze of Nuclear Weapons (1982–1992)

38. Every year in the successive period 1982–1992 (following up on the 10th and 12th Special Sessions on Nuclear Disarmament, held in 1978 and 1982, respectively), the General Assembly adopted resolutions also calling for a nuclear-weapons freeze. May I refer to General Assembly resolutions A/RES/37/100A of 13.12.1982; A/RES/38/73E of 15.12.1983; A/RES/39/63C of 12.12.1984; A/RES/40/151C of 16.12.1985; A/RES/41/60E of 03.12.1986; A/RES/42/39B of 30.11.1987; A/RES/43/76B of 07.12.1988; A/RES/44/117D of 15.12.1989; A/RES/45/59D of 04.12.1990; A/RES/46/37C of 06.12.1991; and A/RES/47/53E of 09.12.1992.

39. These resolutions on freeze of nuclear weapons note that existing arsenals of nuclear weapons are more than sufficient to destroy all life on earth. They express the conviction that lasting world peace can be based only upon the achievement of general and complete disarmament, under effective international control. In this connection, the aforementioned General Assembly resolutions note that the highest priority objectives in the field of disarmament have to be nuclear disarmament and the elimination of all weapons of mass destruction. They at last call upon NWS to agree to reach "a freeze on nuclear weapons", which would, *inter alia*, provide for "a simultaneous total stoppage of any further production of fissionable material for weapons purposes".

40. Such nuclear-weapons freeze is not seen as an end in itself but as the most effective first step towards: (a) halting any further increase and qualitative improvement in the existing arsenals of nuclear weapons; and (b) activating

---

26   Cf. General Assembly resolutions A/RES/33/71B of 14.12.1978, and A/RES/35/152D of 12.12.1980.

negotiations for the substantial reduction and qualitative limitation of nuclear weapons. From 1989 onwards, these resolutions also set out the structure and scope of the prospective joint declaration through which all nuclear-weapons States would agree on a nuclear-arms freeze. Such freeze would encompass: (a) a comprehensive test ban; (b) cessation of the manufacture of nuclear weapons; (c) a ban on all further deployment of nuclear weapons; and (d) cessation of the production of fissionable material for weapons purposes.

3   U.N. *General Assembly Resolutions on Nuclear Weapons as Breach of the U.N. Charter (Acknowledgment before the ICJ, 1995)*

41. Two decades ago, when U.N. General Assembly resolutions condemning nuclear weapons were not as numerous as they are today, they were already regarded as authoritative in the views of States from distinct continents. This was made clear, e.g., by States which participated in the advisory proceedings of 30 October to 15 November 1995 before the ICJ, conducive to its Advisory Opinion of 08.07.1996 on the *Threat or Use of Nuclear Weapons*. On the occasion, the view was upheld that those General Assembly resolutions expressed a "general consensus" and had a relevant "legal value".[27] Resolution 1653 (XVI), of 1961, e.g., was invoked as a "law-making" resolution of the General Assembly, in stating that the use of nuclear weapons is contrary to the letter and spirit, and aims, of the United Nations, and, as such, a "direct violation" of the U.N. Charter.[28]

42. It was further stated that, already towards the end of 1995, "numerous" General Assembly resolutions and declarations confirmed the illegality of the use of force, including nuclear weapons.[29] Some General Assembly resolutions (1653 (XVI), of 24.11.1961; 33/71B of 14.12.1978; 34/83G of 11.12.1979; 35/152D of 12.12.1980; 36/92I of 09.12.1981; 45/59B of 04.12.1990; 46/37D of 06.12.1991) were singled out for having significantly declared that the use of nuclear weapons would be a violation of the U.N. Charter itself.[30] The view was expressed that the series of General Assembly resolutions (starting with resolution 1653 (XVI), of 24.11.1961) amounted to "an authoritative interpretation" of humanitarian law treaties as well as the U.N. Charter.[31]

---

27   ICJ, doc. CR 95/25, of 03.11.1995, pp. 52–53 (statement of Mexico).
28   ICJ, doc. CR 95/22, of 30.10.1995, pp. 44–45 (statement of Australia).
29   ICJ, doc. CR 95/26, of 06.11.1995, pp. 23–24 (statement of Iran).
30   ICJ, doc. CR 95/28, of 09.11.1995, pp. 62–63 (statement of the Philippines).
31   ICJ, doc. CR 95/31, of 13.11.1995, p. 46 (statement of Samoa).

43. In the advisory proceedings of 1995 before the ICJ, it was further recalled that General Assembly resolution 1653 (XVI) of 1961 was adopted in the form of a declaration, being thus "an assertion of the law", and, ever since, the General Assembly's authority to adopt such declaratory resolutions (in condemnation of nuclear weapons) was generally accepted; such resolutions declaring the use of nuclear weapons "unlawful" were regarded as ensuing from the exercise of an "inherent" power of the General Assembly.[32] The relevance of General Assembly resolutions has been reckoned by large groups of States[33]

44. Ever since the aforementioned acknowledgment of the authority and legal value of General Assembly resolutions in the course of the pleadings of late 1995 before the ICJ, those resolutions continue to grow in number until today, clearly forming, in my perception, an *opinio juris communis* as to nuclear disarmament. In addition to those aforementioned, may I also review, in sequence, two other series of General Assembly resolutions, extending to the present, namely: the longstanding series of General Assembly resolutions condemning nuclear weapons (1982–2015), and the series of General Assembly resolutions following up the ICJ's 1996 Advisory Opinion (1997–2015).

4   U.N. *General Assembly Resolutions Condemning Nuclear Weapons (1982–2015)*

45. In the period 1982–2015, there is a long series of U.N. General Assembly resolutions condemning nuclear weapons. May I refer to General Assembly resolutions A/RES/37/100C of 09.12.1982; A/RES/38/73G of 15.12.1983; A/RES/39/63H of 12.12.1984; A/RES/40/151F of 16.12.1985; A/RES/41/60F of 03.12.1986; A/RES/42/39C of 30.11.1987; A/RES/43/76E of 07.12.1988; A/RES/44/117C of 15.12.1989; A/RES/45/59B of 04.12.1990; A/RES/46/37D of 06.12.1991; A/RES/47/53C of 09.12.1992; A/RES/48/76B of 16.12.1993; A/RES/49/76E of 15.12.1994; A/RES/50/71E of 12.12.1995; A/RES/51/46D of 10.12.1996; A/RES/52/39C of 09.12.1997; A/RES/53/78D of 04.12.1998; A/RES/54/55D of 01.12.1999; A/RES/55/34G of 20.11. 2000; A/RES/56/25B of 29.11.2001; A/RES/57/94 of 22.11.2002; A/RES/58/64 of 08.12.2003; A/RES/59/102 of 03.12.2004; A/RES/60/88 of 08.12.2005; A/RES/61/97 of 06.12.2006; A/RES/62/51 of 05.12.2007; A/RES/63/75 of 02.02.2008; A/RES/64/59 of 02.12.2009; A/RES/65/80 of 08.12.2010; A/RES/66/57 of 02.12.2011; A/RES/67/64 of 03.12.2012;

---

32   ICJ, doc. CR 95/27, of 07.11.1995, pp. 58–59 (statement of Malaysia).
33   Cf., e.g., ICJ, doc. CR 95/35, of 15.11.1995, p. 34, and cf. p. 22 (statement of Zimbabwe, on its initiative as Chair of the Non-Aligned Movement).

A/RES/68/58 of 05.12.2013; A/RES/69/69 of 02.12.2014; and A/RES/70/62 of 07.12.2015.

46. In those resolutions, the General Assembly warned against the threat by nuclear weapons to the survival of humankind. They were preceded by two ground-breaking historical resolutions, namely, General Assembly resolution 1(I) of 24.01.1946, and General Assembly resolution 1653 (XVI), of 24.11.1961 (cf. infra). In this new and long series of resolutions condemning nuclear weapons (1982–2015), at the opening of their preambular paragraphs the General Assembly states, year after year, that it is

> *Alarmed* by the threat to the survival of mankind and to the life-sustaining system posed by nuclear weapons and by their use, inherent in the concepts of deterrence,
> *Convinced* that nuclear disarmament is essential for the prevention of nuclear war and for the strengthening of international peace and security,
> *Further convinced* that a prohibition of the use or threat of use of nuclear weapons would be a step towards the complete elimination of nuclear weapons leading to general and complete disarmament under strict and effective international control.

47. Those General Assembly resolutions next significantly *reaffirm*, in their preambular paragraphs, year after year, that

> the use of nuclear weapons would be a violation of the Charter of the United Nations and a crime against humanity, as declared in its resolutions 1653 (XVI) of 24.11.1961, 33/71B of 14.12.1978, 34/83G of 11.12.1979, 35/152D of 12.12.1980 and 36/92I of 09.12.1981.

48. Still in their preambular paragraphs, those General Assembly resolutions further *note with regret* the inability of the Conference on Disarmament to undertake negotiations with a view to achieving agreement on a nuclear disarmament Convention during each previous year. In their operative part, those resolutions reiterate, year after year, the request that the Committee on Disarmament undertakes, on a priority basis, negotiations aiming at achieving agreement on an international Convention prohibiting the use or threat of use of nuclear weapons under any circumstances, taking as a basis the text of the draft Convention on the Prohibition of the Use of Nuclear Weapons.

49. From 1989 (44th session) onwards, those resolutions begin to note specifically that a multilateral agreement prohibiting the use or threat of use of nuclear weapons should strengthen international security and help to create the climate for negotiations leading to the complete elimination of nuclear weapons. Subsequently, those resolutions come to stress, in particular, that an international Convention would be a step towards the complete elimination of nuclear weapons, leading to general and complete disarmament, under strict and effective international control.

50. Clauses of the kind then evolve, from 1996 onwards,[34] to refer expressly to a time framework, i.e., that an international Convention would be an important step in a phased programme towards the complete elimination of nuclear weapons, within a specific framework of time. More recent resolutions also expressly refer to the determination to achieve an international Convention prohibiting the development, production, stockpiling and use of nuclear weapons, leading to their ultimate destruction.

5 U.N. General Assembly Resolutions Following up the ICJ's 1996 Advisory Opinion (1996–2015)

51. Ever since the delivery, on 08.07.1996, of the ICJ's Advisory Opinion on *Nuclear Weapons* to date, the General Assembly has been adopting a series of resolutions (1996–2015), as its follow up. May I refer to General Assembly resolutions A/RES/51/45 of 10.12.1996; A/RES/52/38 of 09.12.1997; A/RES/53/77 of 04.12.1998; A/RES/54/54 of 01.12.1999; A/RES/55/33 of 20.11.2000; A/RES/56/24 of 29.11.2001; A/RES/57/85 of 22.11.2002; A/RES/58/46 of 08.12.2003; A/RES/59/83 of 03.12.2004; A/RES/60/76 of 08.12.2005; A/RES/61/83 of 06.12.2006; A/RES/62/39 of 05.12.2007; A/RES/63/49 of 02.12.2008; A/RES/64/55 of 02.12.2009; A/RES/65/76 of 08.12.2010; A/RES/66/46 of 02.12.2011; A/RES/67/33 of 03.12.2012; A/RES/68/42 of 05.12.2013; A/RES/69/43 of 02.12.2014; and A/RES/70/56 of 07.12.2015. These resolutions make a number of significant statements.

52. The series of aforementioned General Assembly resolutions on follow-up to the 1996 Advisory Opinion of the ICJ (1996–2015) begins by expressing the General Assembly's belief that "the continuing existence of nuclear weapons poses a threat to humanity" and that "their use would have catastrophic consequences for all life on earth", and, further, that "the only defence against a nuclear catastrophe is the total elimination of nuclear weapons and the

---

[34] Cf., e.g., *inter alia*, General Assembly resolution A/RES/50/71E, of 12.12.1995.

certainty that they will never be produced again" (2nd preambular paragraph). The General Assembly resolutions reiteratedly reaffirm "the commitment of the international community to the realization of the goal of a nuclear-weapon-free world through the total elimination of nuclear weapons" (3rd preambular paragraph). They recall their request to the Conference on Disarmament to establish an *ad hoc* Committee to commence negotiations on a phased programme of nuclear disarmament, aiming at the elimination of nuclear weapons, within a "time bound framework"; they further reaffirm the role of the Conference on Disarmament as the single multilateral disarmament negotiating forum.

53. The General Assembly then recalls, again and again, that "the solemn obligations of States Parties, undertaken in Article VI of the Treaty on the Non-Proliferation of Nuclear Weapons (NPT), particularly to pursue negotiations in good faith on effective measures relating to cessation of the nuclear arms race at an early date and to nuclear disarmament" (4th preambular paragraph). They express the goal of achieving a legally binding prohibition on the development, production, testing, deployment, stockpiling, threat or use of nuclear weapons, and their destruction under "effective international control". They significantly call upon *all States* to fulfil promptly the obligation leading to an early conclusion of a Convention prohibiting the development, production, testing, deployment, stockpiling, transfer, threat or use of nuclear weapons and providing for their elimination.[35]

54. Those resolutions (from 2003 onwards) express deep concern at the lack of progress made in the implementation of the "thirteen steps" agreed to, at the 2000 Review Conference, for the implementation of Article VI of the NPT. The aforementioned series of General Assembly resolutions include, from 2010 onwards, an additional (6th) preambular paragraph, expressing "deep concern at the catastrophic humanitarian consequences of any use of nuclear weapons", and reaffirming, in this context, "the need for all States at all times to comply with applicable international law, including international humanitarian law". Those follow-up General Assembly resolutions further recognize "with satisfaction that the Antarctic Treaty, the Treaties of Tlatelolco, Rarotonga, Bangkok and Pelindaba, and the Treaty on a Nuclear-Weapon-Free Zone in

---

35   Note that in earlier resolutions, the following year is explicitly referenced, i.e., States should commence negotiations in "the following year". This reference is removed in later resolutions.

Central Asia, as well as Mongolia's nuclear-weapon-free status, are gradually freeing the entire southern hemisphere and adjacent areas covered by those treaties from nuclear weapons" (10th preambular paragraph).

55. More recent resolutions (from 2013 onwards) are significantly further expanded. They call upon all NWS to undertake concrete disarmament efforts, stressing that all States need to make special efforts to achieve and maintain a world without nuclear weapons. They also take note of the "Five-Point Proposal on Nuclear Disarmament" made by the U.N. Secretary-General (cf. Part XVII, *infra*), and recognize the need for a multilaterally negotiated and legally binding instrument to assure that NNWS stand against the threat or use of nuclear weapons, pending the total elimination of nuclear weapons. In their operative part, the same series of General Assembly resolutions underline the ICJ's unanimous conclusion, in its 1996 Advisory Opinion on the *Threat or Use of Nuclear Weapons*, that "there exists an obligation to pursue in good faith and bring to a conclusion negotiations leading to nuclear disarmament in all its aspects under strict and effective international control" (para. 1).

56. Looking at this particular series of General Assembly follow-up resolutions as a whole, it should not pass unnoticed that they contain paragraphs referring to the obligation to pursue and conclude, in good faith, negotiations leading to nuclear disarmament, without any reference to the NPT or to States Parties to it. They rather refer to that obligation as a general one, not grounded on any treaty provision. *All States*, and not only States Parties to the NPT, are called upon to fulfil promptly that obligation, incumbent upon *all States*, to report (to the Secretary-General) on their compliance with the resolutions at issue. There are, notably, other paragraphs in those resolutions that are specifically directed at nuclear-weapon States, or make specific references to the NPT. In sum, references to *all States* are deliberate, and in the absence of any references to a treaty or other specifically-imposed international obligation, this thus points towards a customary law obligation to negotiate and achieve nuclear disarmament.

IV   U.N. Security Council Resolutions and *Opinio Juris*

57. Like the U.N. General Assembly, the U.N. Security Council has also often dwelt upon the matter at issue. May I refer, *inter alia*, to Security Council resolutions S/23500, of 31.01.1992; S/RES/984, of 11.04.1995; S/RES/1540, of 28.04.2004; S/RES/1673, of 27.04.2006; S/RES/1810, of 25.04.2008; S/RES/1887, of 24.09.2009;

and S/RES/1997, of 20.04.2011, – to which others can be added.³⁶ May I at first recall that, at a Security Council's meeting at the level of Heads of State and Government, held on 31.01.1992, the President of the U.N. Security Council made a statement on behalf of the members of the Security Council that called upon all member States to fulfil their obligations on matters of arms control and disarmament, and to prevent the proliferation of all weapons of mass destruction³⁷ (encompassing nuclear, chemical, and biological weapons).

58. The statement expressed the feeling prevailing at the time that the end of the Cold War "has raised hopes for a safer, more equitable and more humane world", giving now to the world "the best chance of achieving international peace and security since the foundation of the United Nations".³⁸ The members of the Security Council then warned against the threat to international peace and security of all weapons of mass destruction, and expressed their commitment to take appropriate action to prevent "the spread of technology related to the research for or production of such weapons".³⁹ They further stressed the importance of "the integral role in the implementation" of the NPT of "fully effective IAEA safeguards", and of "effective export controls"; they added that they would take "appropriate measures in the case of any violations notified to them by the IAEA".⁴⁰

59. The proliferation of all weapons of mass destruction is defined in the aforementioned Security Council statement, notably, as a threat to international peace and security, – a point which was to be referred to, in subsequent resolutions of the Security Council, to justify its action under Chapter VII of the U.N. Charter. In three of its subsequent resolutions, in a preambular paragraph (resolutions 1540, of 28.04.2004, para. 2; 1810, of 25.04.2008, para. 3; and 1887, of 24.09.2009, para. 2), the Security Council reaffirms the statement of its

---

36   Cf. also Security Council resolutions S/RES/1695 of 15.07.2006; S/RES/1718 of 14.10.2006; S/RES/1874 of 12.06.2009; S/RES/1928 of 07.06.2010; S/RES/2094 of 07.03.2013; S/RES/2141 of 05.03.2014; S/RES/2159 of 09.06.2014; S/RES/2224 of 09.06.2015; S/RES/2270 of 02.03.2016. In preambular paragraphs of all these Security Council resolutions, the Security Council reaffirms, time and time again, that the proliferation of nuclear, chemical and biological weapons, and their means of delivery, constitutes a threat to international peace and security.
37   U.N. doc. S/23500, of 31.01.1992, pp. 1–5.
38   Ibid., pp. 2 and 5.
39   Ibid., p. 4.
40   Ibid., p. 4.

President (adopted on 31.01.1992), and, also in other resolutions, further asserts (also in preambular paragraphs) that the proliferation of nuclear, chemical and biological weapons is a threat to international peace and security[41] and that all States need to take measures to prevent such proliferation.

60. In resolution 1540/2004 of 28.04.2004, adopted by the Security Council acting under Chapter VII of the U.N. Charter, it sets forth legally binding obligations on all U.N. member States to set up and enforce appropriate and effective measures against the proliferation of nuclear, chemical, and biological weapons, – including the adoption of controls and a reporting procedure for U.N. member States to a Committee of the Security Council (sometimes referred to as the "1540 Committee"). Subsequent Security Council resolutions reaffirm resolution 1540/2004 and call upon U.N. member States to implement it.

61. The U.N. Security Council refers, in particular, in two of its resolutions (984/1995, of 11.04.1995; and 1887/2009 of 24.09.2009), to the obligation to pursue negotiations in good faith in relation to nuclear disarmament. In its preamble, Security Council resolution 984/1995 affirms the need for all States Parties to the NPT "to comply fully with all their obligations"; in its operative part, it further "[u]rges all States, as provided for in Article VI of the Treaty on the Non-Proliferation of Nuclear Weapons, to pursue negotiations in good faith on effective measures relating to nuclear disarmament and on a treaty on general and complete disarmament under strict and effective international control which remains a universal goal" (para. 8). It should not pass unnoticed that Security Council resolution 984/1995 pre-dates the ICJ's 1996 Advisory Opinion on the *Threat or Use of Nuclear Weapons*.

62. And Security Council resolution 1887/2009 of 24.09.2009, in its operative part, again calls upon States Parties to the NPT "to comply fully with all their obligations and fulfil their commitments under the Treaty" (para. 2), and, in particular, "pursuant to Article VI of the Treaty, to undertake to pursue negotiations in good faith on effective measures relating to nuclear arms reduction and disarmament"; furthermore, it calls upon "all other States to join in this endeavour" (para. 5). It should not pass unnoticed that it is a general call, upon all U.N. member States, whether or not Parties to the NPT.

---

41 Cf. e.g. Security Council resolutions 1540, of 28.04.2004; 1673, of 27.04.2006; 1810, of 25.04.2008; 1977, of 20.04.2011. And cf. also resolutions 1695, of 15.07.2006; 1718, of 14.10.2006; 1874, of 12.06.2009; 1928, of 07.06.2010; 2094, of 07.03.2013; 2141, of 05.03.2014; 2159, of 09.06.2014; 2224, of 09.06.2015; and 2270, of 02.03.2016.

63. In my perception, the aforementioned resolutions of the Security Council, like those of the General Assembly (cf. *supra*), addressing all U.N. member States, provide significant elements of the emergence of an *opinio juris*, in support of the gradual formation of an obligation of customary international law, corresponding to the conventional obligation under Article VI of the NPT. In particular, the fact that the Security Council calls upon *all States*, and not only States Parties to the NPT, to pursue negotiations towards nuclear disarmament in good faith (or to join the NPT State Parties in this endeavour) is significant. It is an indication that the obligation is incumbent on all U.N. member States, irrespectively of their being or not Parties to the NPT.

V   The Saga of the United Nations in the Condemnation of Nuclear Weapons

64. The U.N. resolutions (of the General Assembly and the Security Council) that I have just reviewed (*supra*) portray the United Nations' longstanding saga in the condemnation of nuclear weapons. This saga goes back to the birth and earlier years of the United Nations. In fact, nuclear weapons were not in the minds of the Delegates to the San Francisco Conference of June 1945, at the time when the United Nations Charter was adopted on 26.06.1945. The U.S. dropping of atomic bombs over Hiroshima and Nagasaki, heralding the nuclear age, occurred on 06 and 09 August 1945, respectively, over ten weeks before the U.N. Charter's entry into force, on 24.10.1945.

65. As soon as the United Nations Organization came into being, it promptly sought to equip itself to face the new challenges of the nuclear age: the General Assembly's very first resolution, – resolution 1(I) of 24.01.1946, – thus, established a Commission to deal with the matter, entrusted with submitting reports to the Security Council "in the interest of peace and security" (para. 2(a)), as well as with making proposals for "control of atomic energy to the extent necessary to ensure its use only for peaceful purposes", and for "the elimination from national armaments of atomic weapons and of all other major weapons adaptable to mass destruction" (para. 5(b)(c)).

66. One decade later, in 1956, the International Atomic Energy Agency (IAEA) was established. And half a decade later, in 1961, the General Assembly adopted a ground-breaking resolution: it would be proper here to recall the precise terms of the historical General Assembly resolution 1653 (XVI), of 24.11.1961, titled *"Declaration on the Prohibition of the Use of Nuclear and Thermo-Nuclear*

Weapons". That *célèbre* resolution 1653 (1961) remains contemporary today, and, 55 years later, continues to require close attention; in it, the General Assembly

> *Mindful* of its responsibility under the Charter of the United Nations in the maintenance of international peace and security, as well as in the consideration of principles governing disarmament,
>
> *Gravely concerned* that, while negotiations on disarmament have not so far achieved satisfactory results, the armaments race, particularly in the nuclear and thermo-nuclear fields, has reached a dangerous stage requiring all possible precautionary measures to protect humanity and civilization from the hazard of nuclear and thermo-nuclear catastrophe,
>
> *Recalling* that the use of weapons of mass destruction, causing unnecessary human suffering, was in the past prohibited, as being contrary to the laws of humanity and to the principles of international law, by international declarations and binding agreements, such as the Declaration of St. Petersburg of 1868, the Declaration of the Brussels Conference of 1874, the Conventions of The Hague Peace Conferences of 1899 and 1907, and the Geneva Protocol of 1925, to which the majority of nations are still parties,
>
> *Considering* that the use of nuclear and thermo-nuclear weapons would bring about indiscriminate suffering and destruction to mankind and civilization to an even greater extent than the use of those weapons declared by the aforementioned international declarations and agreements to be contrary to the laws of humanity and a crime under international law,
>
> *Believing* that the use of weapons of mass destruction, such as nuclear and thermo-nuclear weapons, is a direct negation of the high ideals and objectives which the United Nations has been established to achieve through the protection of succeeding generations from the scourge of war and through the preservation and promotion of their cultures,
>
> 1. *Declares* that:
>   (a) The use of nuclear and thermo-nuclear weapons is contrary to the spirit, letter and aims of the United Nations and, as such, a direct violation of the Charter of the United Nations;
>   (b) The use of nuclear and thermo-nuclear weapons would exceed even the scope of war and cause indiscriminate suffering and destruction to mankind and civilization and, as such, is contrary to the rules of international law and to the laws of humanity;
>   (c) The use of nuclear and thermo-nuclear weapons is a war directed not against an enemy or enemies alone but also against mankind

in general, since the peoples of the world not involved in such a war will be subjected to all the evils generated by the use of such weapons;

(d) Any State using nuclear and thermo-nuclear weapons is to be considered as violating the Charter of the United Nations, as acting contrary to the laws of humanity and as committing a crime against mankind and civilization;

2. *Requests* the Secretary-General to consult the Governments of Member States to ascertain their views on the possibility of convening a Special Conference for signing a Convention on the prohibition of the use of nuclear and thermo-nuclear weapons for war purposes and to report on the results of such consultation to the General Assembly at its XVIIth session.

67. Over half a century later, the lucid and poignant declaration contained in General Assembly resolution 1653 (1961) appears endowed with permanent topicality, as the whole international community remains still awaiting for the conclusion of the propounded general Convention on the prohibition of nuclear and thermo-nuclear weapons: nuclear disarmament remains still a goal to be achieved by the United Nations today, as it was in 1961. The Comprehensive Nuclear-Test-Ban Treaty (CTBT), adopted on 24.09.1996, has not yet entered into force, although 164 States have ratified it to date.

68. It is beyond the scope of the present Dissenting Opinion to dwell upon the reasons why, already for two decades, one remains awaiting for the CTBT's entry into force.[42] Suffice it here to recall that the CTBT provides (Article XIV) that for it to enter into force, the 44 States specified in its Annex 2 need to ratify it;[43] a number of these States have not yet ratified the CTBT, including some NWS, like India and Pakistan. NWS have invoked distinct reasons for their positions conditioning nuclear disarmament (cf. *infra*). The entry into force of the CTBT has thus been delayed.

---

42 For a historical account and the perspectives of the CTBT, cf., e.g., K.A. Hansen, *The Comprehensive Nuclear Test Ban Treaty*, Stanford, Stanford University Press, 2006, pp. 1–84; [Various Authors,] *Nuclear Weapons after the Comprehensive Test Ban Treaty* (ed. E. Arnett), Stockholm-Solna/Oxford, SIPRI/Oxford University Press, 1996, pp. 1–141; J. Ramaker, J. Mackby, P.D. Marshall and R. Geil, *The Final Test – A History of the Comprehensive Nuclear-Test-Ban Treaty Negotiations*, Vienna, Ed. Prep. Comm. of CTBTO, 2003, pp. 1–265.

43 Those 44 States, named in Annex 2, participated in the CTBT negotiations at the Conference on Disarmament, from 1994 to 1996, and possessed nuclear reactors at that time.

69. Recently, in a panel in Vienna (on 27.04.2016) in commemoration of the 20th anniversary of the CTBT, the U.N. Secretary-General (Ban Ki-moon) pondered that there have been advances in the matter, but there remains a long way to go, in the determination "to bring into force a legally binding prohibition against all nuclear tests". He recalled to have

> repeatedly pointed to the toxic legacy that some 2,000 tests left on people and the environment in parts of Central Asia, North Africa, North America and the South Pacific. Nuclear testing poisons water, causes cancers, and pollutes the area with radioactive fall-out for generations and generations to come. We are here to honour the victims. The best tribute to them is action to ban and to stop nuclear testing. Their sufferings should teach the world to end this madness.[44]

He then called on the (eight) remaining CTBT Annex 2 States "to sign and ratify the Treaty without further delay", so as to strengthen its goal of universality; in this way, – he concluded, – "we can leave a safer world, free of nuclear tests, to our children and to succeeding generations of this world".[45]

70. To this one may add the unaccomplished endeavours of the U.N. General Assembly Special Sessions on Disarmament. Of the three Special Sessions held so far (in 1978, 10th Special Session; in 1982, 12th Special Session; and in 1988, 15th Special Session),[46] the first one appears to have been the most significant one so far. The Final Document adopted unanimously (without a vote) by the 1st Special Session on Disarmament sets up a programme of action on disarmament and the corresponding mechanism in its current form. In the present case before the ICJ, the Marshall Islands refers to this document in its Memorial, singling out its relevance for the interpretation of Article VI of the NPT and the corresponding customary international law obligation of nuclear disarmament (paras. 129–132).

71. That Final Document of the first General Assembly Special Session on Disarmament (1978) addresses nuclear disarmament in its distinct aspects. In this respect, the General Assembly begins by observing that the accumulation of nuclear weapons constitutes a threat to the future of humankind (para. 1), in

---

44 U.N. doc. SG/SM/17709-DC/3628, of 27.04.2016, pp. 1–2.
45 *Ibid.*, p. 2.
46 Ever since, several G.A. resolutions have called for a 4th Special Session on Disarmament, but it has not yet taken place.

effect "the greatest danger" to humankind and to "the survival of civilization" (para. 47). It adds that the arms race, particularly in its nuclear aspect, is incompatible with the principles enshrined in the United Nations Charter (para. 12). In its view, the most effective guarantee against the dangers of nuclear war is the complete elimination of nuclear weapons (paras. 8 and 56).[47]

72. While disarmament is the responsibility of all States, the General Assembly asserts that NWS have the primary responsibility for nuclear disarmament. There is pressing need of "urgent negotiations of agreements" to that end, and in particular to conclude "a treaty prohibiting nuclear-weapon tests" (paras. 50–51). It further stresses the importance of nuclear-weapon-free zones that have been established or are the subject of negotiations in various parts of the globe (paras. 60–64).

73. The Conference on Disarmament, – since 1979 the sole multilateral disarmament-negotiating forum of the international community, – has helped to negotiate multilateral arms-limitation and disarmament agreements.[48] It has focused its work on four main issues, namely: nuclear disarmament, prohibition of the production of fissile material for weapon use, prevention of arms race in outer space, and negative security assurances. Yet, since the adoption of the CTBT in 1996, the Conference on Disarmament has been largely deadlocked, in face of the invocation of divergent security interests, added to the understanding that nuclear weapons require mutuality; furthermore, the Rules of Procedure of the Conference provide that all decisions must be adopted by consensus. In sum, some States blame political factors for causing its longstanding stalemate, while others attribute it to outdated procedural rules.

74. After all, in historical perspective, some advances have been attained in the last decades in respect of other weapons of mass destruction, as illustrated by the adoption of the Convention on the Prohibition of the Development, Production and Stockpiling of Bacteriological (Biological) and Toxin Weapons and on their Destruction (on 10.04.1972), as well as the Convention on the Prohibition of the Development, Production, Stockpiling and Use of Chemical

---

47   And cf. also paras. 18 and 20.
48   E.g., the aforementioned NPT, CTBT, the Biological Weapons Convention, and the Chemical Weapons Convention, in addition to the seabed treaties, and the Convention on the Prohibition of Military or Any Other Hostile Use of Environmental Modification Techniques.

THE UNIVERSAL JURIDICAL CONSCIENCE, HUMANENESS   395

Weapons and on their Destruction (on 13.01.1993); distinctly from the CTBT (*supra*), these two Conventions have already entered into force (on 26.03.1975, and on 29.04.1997, respectively).

75. If we look at conventional international law only, weapons of mass destruction (poisonous gases, biological and chemical weapons) have been outlawed; yet, nuclear weapons, far more destructive, have not been banned yet. This juridical absurdity nourishes the positivist myopia, or blindness, in inferring therefrom that there is no customary international obligation of nuclear disarmament. Positivists only have eyes for treaty law, for individual State consent, revolving in vicious circles, unable to see the pressing needs and aspirations of the international community as a whole, and to grasp the *universality* of contemporary international law – as envisaged by its "founding fathers", already in the XVIth–XVIIth centuries, – with its underlying fundamental principles (cf. *infra*).

76. The truth is that, in our times, the obligation of nuclear disarmament has emerged and crystallized, in both conventional and customary international law, and the United Nations has been giving a most valuable contribution to this along the decades. The matter at issue, the United Nations saga in this domain, was brought to the attention of the ICJ, two decades ago, in the advisory proceedings that led to its Advisory Opinion of 1996 on the *Threat or Use of Nuclear Weapons*, and now again, two decades later, in the present contentious proceedings in the cases of *Obligations Concerning Negotiations Relating to Cessation of the Nuclear Arms Race and to Nuclear Disarmament*, opposing the Marshall Islands to India, Pakistan and the United Kingdom, respectively.

77. The aforementioned U.N. resolutions were in effect object of attention on the part of the contending parties before the Court (Marshall Islands, India, Pakistan and the United Kingdom). In the oral phase of their arguments, they were dealt with by the participating States (Marshall Islands, India and the United Kingdom), and, extensively so, in particular, by the Marshall Islands and India. The key point is the relation of those resolutions with the emergence of *opinio juris*, of relevance to the identification of a customary international law obligation in the present domain. May I turn, first, to the positions sustained by the contending parties, and then, to the questions I put to them in the public sitting of 16.03.2016 before the ICJ in the *cas d'espèce*, and the responses received from them.

VI U.N. Resolutions and the Emergence of *Opinio Juris*: The Positions of the Contending Parties

78. In their written submissions and oral arguments before the Court in the present case(s) of *Obligations Concerning Negotiations Relating to Cessation of the Nuclear Arms Race and to Nuclear Disarmament*, the Marshall Islands addresses General Assembly resolutions on nuclear disarmament, in relation to the development of customary international law;[49] it also refers to Security Council resolutions.[50] Quoting the ICJ's Advisory Opinion of 1996, it contends (perhaps not as clearly as it could have done) that although General Assembly resolutions lack binding force, they may "sometimes have normative value", and thus contribute to the emergence of an *opinio juris*.[51]

79. In its written submissions and oral arguments before the Court, India addresses U.N. General Assembly resolutions on follow-up to the ICJ's Advisory Opinion of 1996, pointing out that it is the only nuclear weapon State that has co-sponsored and voted in favour of such resolutions.[52] India supports nuclear disarmament "in a time-bound, universal, non-discriminatory, phased and verifiable manner".[53] And it criticizes the M.I. for not supporting the General Assembly follow-up resolutions in its own voting pattern (having voted against one of them, in favour once, and all other times abstained).[54]

80. In its *Preliminary Objections* (of 15.06.2015), the United Kingdom, after recalling the Marshall Islands' position on earlier U.N. General Assembly resolutions, in the sixties and seventies (paras. 21 and 98(c) and (h)), then refers to its own position thereon (paras. 84 and 99(c)). It also refers to U.N. Security Council resolutions (para. 92). It then recalls the Marshall Islands' arguments – e.g., that "the U.K. has always voted against" General Assembly resolutions on the follow-up of the ICJ Advisory Opinion of 1996, and of the U.N. High Level Meetings in 2013 and 2014 (paras. 98(e) and (h)), – in order to rebut them (paras. 99–103).

81. As for Pakistan, though it informed the Court of its decision not to participate in the oral phase of the present proceedings (letter of 02.03.2016), in

---

49 ICJ, doc. CR 2016/1, of 07.03.2016, para. 7.
50 *Ibid.*, para. 8.
51 *Ibid.*, para. 7.
52 ICJ, doc. CR 2016/4, of 10.03.2016, para. 1, p. 19.
53 *Counter-Memorial* of India, p. 9, para. 13.
54 *Ibid.*, p. 8, para. 12.

the submissions in its *Counter-Memorial* it argues that the ICJ 1996 Advisory Opinion nowhere stated that the obligation under Article VI of the NPT was a general obligation or that it was opposable *erga omnes*; in its view, there was no *prima facie* evidence to this effect *erga omnes*.[55] As to the U.N. General Assembly resolutions following up the ICJ's 1996 Advisory Opinion, Pakistan notes that it has voted in favour of these resolutions from 1997 to 2015, and by contrast, – it adds, – the Marshall Islands abstained from voting in 2002 and 2003 and again from 2005 to 2012.[56]

82. After recalling that it is not a Party to the NPT,[57] Pakistan further argues that General Assembly resolutions do not have binding force and cannot thus, in its view, give rise to obligations enforceable against a State.[58] Pakistan concludes that the General Assembly resolutions do not support the proposition that there exists a customary international law obligation "rooted" in Article VI of the NPT. Rather, it is the NPT that underpins the Marshall Islands' claims.[59]

83. In sum, the United Kingdom has voted against such resolutions, the Marshall Islands has abstained in most of them, India and Pakistan have voted in favour of them. Despite these distinct patterns of voting, in my view the U.N. General Assembly resolutions reviewed in the present Dissenting Opinion, taken altogether, are not at all deprived of their contribution to the conformation of *opinio juris* as to the formation of a customary international law obligation of nuclear denuclearization. After all, they are resolutions of the U.N. General Assembly itself (and not only of the large majority of U.N. member States which voted in their favour); they are resolutions of the United Nations Organization itself, addressing a matter of common concern of humankind as a whole (cf. part XX, *infra*).

VII   Questions from the Bench and Responses from the Parties

84. At the end of the public sittings before the Court in the present case of *Obligations Concerning Negotiations Relating to Cessation of the Nuclear Arms Race and to Nuclear Disarmament* (Marshall Islands *versus* United Kingdom),

---

55   *Counter-Memorial* of Pakistan., p. 8, para. 2.3.
56   *Ibid.*, p. 8, para. 2.4.
57   *Ibid.*, p. 14, para. 4.4; p. 30, para. 7.55.
58   *Ibid.*, p. 38, paras. 7.95–7.97.
59   *Ibid.*, p. 38, para. 7.97.

I deemed it fit to put the following questions (on 16.03.2016, in the afternoon) to the contending parties:

> I have questions to put to both contending parties, the Marshall Islands and the United Kingdom. My questions are the following:
> The Marshall Islands, in the course of the written submissions and oral arguments, and the United Kingdom, in its document on Preliminary Objections (of 15 June 2015), have both referred to U.N. General Assembly resolutions on nuclear disarmament. Parallel to the resolutions on the matter which go back to the early 70s (First Disarmament Decade), there have been two more recent series of General Assembly resolutions, namely: those condemning nuclear weapons, extending from 1982 to date, and those adopted as a follow-up to the 1996 ICJ Advisory Opinion on Nuclear Weapons, extending so far from 1997 to 2015. In relation to this last series of General Assembly resolutions, – referred to by the contending parties, – I would like to ask both the Marshall Islands and the United Kingdom whether, in their understanding, such General Assembly resolutions are constitutive of an expression of *opinio juris*, and, if so, what in their view is their relevance to the formation of a customary international law obligation to pursue negotiations leading to nuclear disarmament, and what is their incidence upon the question of the existence of a dispute between the parties.[60]

85. One week later (on 23.03.2016), the United Kingdom and the Marshall Islands submitted to the ICJ their written replies to my questions. In its response to them, the United Kingdom stated that resolutions adopted by international organizations may, in some circumstances, be evidence of customary international law or contribute to its development; however, they do not constitute an expression of customary international law in and of themselves. In the *cas d'espèce*, the United Kingdom deems it unnecessary to assess whether the General Assembly resolutions following up on the ICJ's 1996 Advisory Opinion on the *Threat or Use of Nuclear Weapons* constitute evidence of custom, as the obligation set forth in Article VI of the NPT is binding upon the United Kingdom anyway, irrespective of whether there is a corresponding obligation in customary international law.[61]

---

60   ICJ, doc. CR 2016/9, of 16.09.2016, pp. 33–34.
61   ICJ, *Reply of the United Kingdom to the Questions Addressed by Judge Cançado Trindade to Both Parties*, doc. MIUK 2016/13, of 23.03.2016, pp. 1–2, para. 3.

86. The Marshall Islands, for its part, recalls the ICJ's 1996 Advisory Opinion on the *Threat or Use of Nuclear Weapons*, as well as a number of General Assembly resolutions upholding the obligation to pursue negotiations leading to nuclear disarmament, in support of its position as to the existence of a customary international law obligation to this end. It also refers to the ICJ's *obiter dictum* in the case of *Nicaragua versus United States*, to the effect that "*opinio juris* may, though with all due caution, be deduced from, *inter alia*, the attitude of the Parties and the attitude of States towards certain General Assembly resolutions".[62]

87. In the perception of the Marshall Islands, the attitude of States towards General Assembly resolutions adopted in the period 1982–1995 indicates an emerging *opinio juris* on the obligation to conduct negotiations in good faith leading to general and complete nuclear disarmament. The Marshall Islands then states that the attitude of States to resolutions following up the 1996 ICJ's Advisory Opinion, – those affirming the existence of an obligation to pursue negotiations leading to nuclear disarmament, – constitutes an expression of *opinio juris*, in support of a customary international obligation to this end.[63]

88. As to the incidence of General Assembly resolutions on the existence of a dispute in the *cas d'espèce*, the Marshall Islands contends that opposing attitudes of States to such resolutions may contribute to demonstrating the existence of a dispute.[64] As to the present case opposing the Marshall Islands to the United Kingdom, the Marshall Islands contends that the diverging voting records of the Marshall Islands and the United Kingdom are a clear indication of the opposing views of the parties concerning the obligations enshrined in Article VI of the NPT (and the corresponding obligation of customary international law).[65]

---

62 The Marshall Islands also cites the International Law Commission's Draft Conclusions on the *Identification of Customary International Law* (2015), which recognise the importance of the attitude of States towards General Assembly resolutions for establishing State practice and *opinio juris*. ICJ, *Reply of the Marshall Islands to the Questions Addressed by Judge Cançado Trindade to Both Parties*, doc. MIUK 2016/13, of 23.03.2016, pp. 2–3, paras. 2–5.
63 *Ibid.*, p. 4, para. 7.
64 *Ibid.*, p. 4, para. 8.
65 *Ibid.*, p. 4, para. 9.

VIII Human Wickedness: From the XXIst Century Back to the Book of *Genesis*

89. Since the beginning of the nuclear age in August 1945, some of the great thinkers of the XXth century started inquiring whether humankind has a future. Indeed, this is a question which cannot be eluded. Thus, already in 1946, for example, deeply shocked by the U.S. atomic bombings of Hiroshima and Nagasaki (on 06 and 09 August 1945, respectively),[66] Mahatma Gandhi, in promptly expressing his worry about the future of human society, wrote, in the Journal *Harijan*, on 07.07.1946, that

> So far as I can see, the atomic bomb has deadened the finest feeling that has sustained mankind for ages. There used to be the so-called laws of war which made it tolerable. Now we know the naked truth. War knows no law except that of might.[67]

90. And M. Gandhi, denouncing its brutality, added that the "atom bomb is the weapon of ultimate force and destruction", evidencing the "futility" of such violence; the development of the atom bomb "represents the most sinful and diabolical use of science".[68] In the same Journal *Harijan*, M. Gandhi further wrote, on 29.09.1946, that non-violence is "the only thing the atom bomb cannot destroy"; and he further warned that "unless now the world adopts non-violence, it will spell certain suicide for mankind".[69]

91. Over a decade later, in the late fifties, Karl Jaspers, in his book *La bombe atomique et l'avenir de l'homme* (1958), regretted that the existence of nuclear weapons seemed to have been taken for granted, despite their capacity to destroy humankind and all life on the surface of earth.[70] One has thus to

---

[66] Preceded by a nuclear test undertaken by the United States at Alamagordo, New Mexico, on 16.07.1945.

[67] M. Gandhi, "Atom Bomb and Ahimsa", *Harijan* (07.07.1946), reproduced *in: Journalist Gandhi – Selected Writings of Gandhi* (org. S. Sharma), 1st ed., Mumbai, Ed. Gandhi Book Center, 1994, p. 104; also *cit. in*: P.F. Power, *Gandhi on World Affairs*, London, Allen & Unwin, 1961, pp. 63–64.

[68] *Cit. in: What Mahatma Gandhi Said about the Atom Bomb* (org. Y.P. Anand), New Delhi, National Gandhi Museum, 1998, p. 5.

[69] From the Journal *Harijan* (29.09.1946), *cit. in*: Faisal Devji, *The Impossible Indian – Gandhi and the Temptation of Violence*, London, Hurst & Co., 2012, p. 150.

[70] K. Jaspers, *La bombe atomique et l'avenir de l'homme* [1958], Paris, Buchet/Chastel, 1963, pp. 22 and 336.

admit, – he added, – that "cette terre, qui est née d'une explosion de l'atome, soit anéantie aussi par les bombes atomiques".⁷¹ K. Jaspers further regretted that progress had occurred in technological knowledge, but there had been "no progress of ethics nor of reason". Human nature has not changed: "ou l'homme se transforme ou il disparaît".⁷²

92. In the early sixties, for his part, Bertrand Russell, in his book *Has Man a Future?* (1961), likewise regretted that people seemed to have got used to the existence of nuclear weapons, in a world dominated by a "will towards death", prevailing over sanity.⁷³ Unfortunately, – he proceeded, – "love for power" has enticed States "to pursue irrational policies"; and he added:

> Those who regard *Genesis* as authentic history, may take Cain as the first example: he may well have thought that, with Abel out of the way, he could rule over coming generations.⁷⁴

To B. Russell, it is "in the hearts of men that the evil lies", it is in their minds that "the cure must be sought".⁷⁵ He further regretted the discouraging results of disarmament Conferences, and even wrote that ICJ pronouncements on the issue should be authoritative, and it was not "optional" for States "to respect or not international law".⁷⁶

93. For his part, Karl Popper, at the end of his life, in his book (in the form of an interview) *The Lesson of This Century* (1997), in assembling his recollections of the XXth century, expressed the anguish, for example, at the time of the 1962 Cuban missiles crisis, with the finding that each of the 38 warheads at issue had three thousand times more power than the atomic bomb dropped over Hiroshima.⁷⁷ Once again, the constatation: human nature has not changed. K. Popper, like other great thinkers of the XXth century, regretted that no lessons seemed to have been learned from the past; this increased the concern they

---

71 *Ibid.*, p. 576.
72 *Ibid.*, pp. 621 and 640.
73 B. Russell, *Has Man a Future?*, [London], Penguin Books, 1962 [reprint], pp. 27 and 37.
74 *Ibid.*, p. 45.
75 *Ibid.*, pp. 45–46, and cf. 69.
76 *Ibid.*, pp. 97 and 79.
77 K. Popper, *The Lesson of This Century* (interview with G. Bosetti), London/N.Y., Routledge, 1997, pp. 24 and 28. And cf. also, earlier on, K. Popper, *La Responsabilidad de Vivir – Escritos sobre Política, Historia y Conocimiento* [1994], Barcelona, Paidós, 2012 [reed.], p. 242, and cf. p. 274.

shared, in successive decades, with the future of humankind, in the presence of arsenals of nuclear weapons.

94. A contemporary writer, Max Gallo, in his recent novel *Caïn et Abel – Le premier crime*, has written that the presence of evil is within everyone; "le Mal est au coeur du Bien, et cette réalité ambiguë est le propre des affaires humaines".[78] Writers of the past, – he went on, – "eux aussi – toi Dante, toi Dostoïevski, et ceux qui vous ont inspiré, Eschyle, Sophocle – attisent le brasier du châtiment et de la culpabilité".[79] And he added:

> Partout, Caïn poignarde ou étrangle Abel. (...) Et personne ne semble voir (...) la mort prochaine de toute humanité. Elle tient entre ses mains l'arme de sa destruction. Ce ne sont plus seulement des villes entières qui seront incendiées, rasées: toute vie sera alors consumée, et la terre vitrifiée.
>
> Deux villes ont déjà connu ce sort, et l'ombre des corps de leurs habitants est à jamais encrustée dans la pierre sous l'effet d'une chaleur de lave solaire.
>
> (...) [P]artout Caïn poursuivra Abel. (...) Les villes vulnérables seront ensanglantées. Les tours les plus hautes seront détruites, leurs habitants ensevelis sous les décombres.[80]

95. As well captured by those and other thinkers, in the Book of *Genesis*, the episode of the brothers Cain and Abel portraying the first murder ever, came to be seen, along the centuries, as disclosing the presence of evil and guilt in the world everyone lives. This called for care, prudence and reflection, as it became possible to realize that human beings were gradually distancing themselves from their Creator. The fragility of civilizations soon became visible. That distancing became manifest in the subsequent episode of the Tower of Babel (*Genesis*, Ch. 11: 9). As they were built, civilizations could be destroyed. History was to provide many examples of that (as singled out, in the XXth century, by Arnold Toynbee). Along the centuries, with the growth of scientific-technological knowledge, the human capacity of self-destruction increased considerably, having become limitless in the present nuclear age.

96. Turning back to the aforementioned book by B. Russell, also in its French edition (*L'homme survivra-t-il?*, 1963), he further warned therein that

---

78   M. Gallo, *Caïn et Abel – Le premier crime*, [Paris], Fayard, 2011, pp. 112 and 141.
79   *Ibid.*, p. 174.
80   *Ibid.*, pp. 236–237.

"il faut que nous nous rendions compte que la haine, la perte de temps, d'argent et d'habilité intellectuelle en vue de la création d'engins de destruction, la crainte du mal que nous pouvons nous faire mutuellement, le risque quotidien et permanent de voir la fin de tout ce que l'homme a réalisé, sont le produit de la folie humaine. (...) C'est dans nos cœurs que réside le mal, c'est de nos cœurs qu'il doit être extirpé".[81] ["we must become aware that the hatred, the expenditure of time and money and intellectual hability upon weapons of destruction, the fear of what we may do to each other, and the imminent daily and hourly risk of an end to all that man has achieved, (...) all this is a product of human folly. (...) It is in our hearts that the evil lies, and it is from our hearts that it must be plucked out"[82]].

97. Some other great thinkers of the XXth century (from distinct branches of knowledge), expressed their grave common concern with the increased human capacity of destruction coupled with the development of scientific-technological knowledge. Thus, the historian Arnold Toynbee (*A Study in History*, 1934–1954; and *Civilization on Trial*, 1948), regretted precisely the modern tragedy that human iniquity was not eliminated with the development of scientific-technological knowledge, but widely enlarged, without a concomitant advance at spiritual level.[83] And the increase in armaments and in the capacity of destruction, – he added, – became a symptom of the fall of civilizations.[84]

98. For his part, the writer Hermann Hesse, in a posthumous book of essays (*Guerre et paix*, 1946), originally published shortly after the II world war, warned that with the mass killings, not only do we keep on killing ourselves, but also our present and perhaps also our future.[85] The worst destruction, – he added, – was the one organized by the State itself, with its corollary,

---

81   B. Russell, *L'homme survivra-t-il?*, Paris, Éd. J. Didier, 1963, pp. 162–163.
82   B. Russell, *Has Man a Future?*, op. cit. supra n. (73), pp. 109–110. Towards the end of his life, Bertrand Russell again warned against the extreme danger of atomic and hydrogen bombs, and expressed his concern that people seemed to get used to their existence; cf. B. Russell, *Autobiography* [1967], London, Unwin, 1985 [reed.], pp. 554–555.
83   Cf. A.J. Toynbee, *A Study in History*, Oxford, Oxford University Press, 1970 [3rd reprint], pp. 48–558, 559–701, 702–718 and 826–850; A.J. Toynbee, *Civilization on Trial*, Oxford/N.Y., Oxford University Press, 1948, pp. 3–263.
84   A.J. Toynbee, *Guerra e Civilização* [*War and Civilization*], Lisbon, Edit. Presença, 1963, pp. 29, 129 and 178.
85   H. Hesse, *Sobre la Guerra y la Paz* [1946], 5th ed., Barcelona, Edit. Noguer, 1986, pp. 119 and 122.

"the philosophy of the State", accompanied by capital and industry.[86] The philosopher and theologian Jacques Maritain (*Oeuvres Complètes*, 1961–1967), in turn, wrote that the atrocities perpetrated in the XXth century had "une importance plus tragique pour la conscience humaine".[87] In calling for an "integral humanism", he warned that the human person transcends the State, and the realisation of the common good is to be pursued keeping in mind human dignity.[88] In his criticism of the "realists", he stressed the imperatives of ethics and justice, and the importance of general principles of law, in the line of jusnaturalist thinking.[89]

99. Another writer, the humanist Stefan Zweig, remained always concerned with the fate of humankind. He was impressed with the Scripture's legend of the Tower of Babel, having written an essay on it in 1916, and kept it in mind along the years, as shown in successive essays written in more than the two following decades,[90] taking it as a symbol of the perennial yearning for a unified humanity. In his own words,

> The history of tomorrow must be a history of all humanity and the conflicts between individual conflicts must be seen as redundant alongside the common good of the community. History must then be transformed from the current woeful State to a completely new position; (...) it must clearly contrast the old ideal of victory with the new one of unity and the old glorification of war with a new contempt for it. (...) [T]he only important thing is to push forward under the banner of a community of nations, the mentality of mankind (...).[91]

---

86 H. Hesse, *Guerre et Paix*, Paris, L'Arche Éd., 2003 [reed.], pp. 127 and 133.
87 J. Maritain, "Dieu et la permission du mal", in *Œuvres de Jacques Maritain – 1961–1967* (*Jacques et Raïssa Maritain – Oeuvres Complètes*), vol. XII, Fribourg/Paris, Éd. Universitaires/Éd. Saint-Paul, 1992, p. 17, and cf. p. 41.
88 Cf. J. Maritain, *Humanisme intégral*, Paris, Aubier, 2000 (reed.), pp. 18, 37, 137 and 230–232; J. Maritain, *The Person and the Common Good*, Notre Dame, University of Notre Dame Press, 2002 (reed.), pp. 29, 49–50, 92–93 and 104; J. Maritain, *O Homem e o Estado*, 4th ed., Rio de Janeiro, Livr. Agir Ed., 1966, pp. 96–102; J. Maritain, *Los Derechos del Hombre y la Ley Natural*, Buenos Aires, Ed. Leviatan, 1982, pp. 38, 44, 50, 69 and 94–95, and cf. pp. 79–82; J. Maritain, *Para una Filosofía de la Persona Humana*, Buenos Aires, Ed. Club de Lectores, 1984, pp. 164, 176–178, 196–197, 221 and 231.
89 J. Maritain, *De la justice politique – Notes sur la présente guerre*, Paris, Libr. Plon, 1940, pp. 88, 90–91, 106–107 and 112–114.
90 As shown in his posthumous book of essays: S. Zweig, *Messages from a Lost World*, London, Pushkin Press, 2016, pp. 55, 88–90, 97, 107 and 176.
91 *Ibid.*, pp. 170 and 175.

100. Yet, in his dense and thoughtful intellectual autobiography (*Le monde d'hier*, 1944), written shortly before putting an end to his own life, Stefan Zweig expressed his deep concern with the fading away of conscience, disclosed by the fact that the world got used to the "dehumanisation, injustice and brutality, as never before in hundreds of centuries";[92] persons had been transformed into simple objects.[93] Earlier on, – before the nuclear age, – his friend the psychologist Sigmund Freud, in a well-known essay (*Civilization and Its Discontents*, 1930), expressed his deep preoccupation with what he perceived as an impulse to barbarism and destruction, which could not be expelled from the human psyche.[94] In face of human hostility and the threat of self-disintegration, – he added, – there is a consequent loss of happiness.[95]

101. Another psychologist, Carl Jung, referring, in his book *Aspects du drame contemporain* (1948), to events of contemporary history of his epoch, warned against subsuming individuals under the State; in his view, collective evil and culpability contaminate everyone everywhere.[96] He further warned against the tragic dehumanization of others[97] and the psychic exteriorizations of mass movements (of the collective inconscient) conducive to destruction.[98]

102. To the writer and theologian Albert Schweitzer (who wrote his *Kulturphilosophie* in 1923), the essence of civilization lies in the respect for life, to the benefit of each person and of humankind.[99] He rejected the "illness" of *Realpolitik*, having stated that good consists in the preservation and exaltation of life, and evil lies in its destruction; nowadays more than ever, – he added, – we need an "ethics of reverence for life", what requires responsibility.[100] He insisted, in his

---

92   S. Zweig, *O Mundo que Eu Vi* [1944, *Die Welt von Gestern*], Rio de Janeiro, Edit. Record, 1999, p. 483, and cf. 272–274, 278, 462, 467, 474, 490 and 503–505.

93   *Ibid.*, p. 490.

94   Sigmund Freud, *Civilization and Its Discontents* [1930], N.Y., Norton & Cia., 1962 [reed.], pp. 7–9, 26, 36–37 and 59–63.

95   Cf. *ibid.*, pp. 23 and 67–92.

96   C.G. Jung, *Aspects du drame contemporain*, Genève/Paris, Libr. de l'Univ. Georg/Éd. de la Colonne Vendôme, 1948, pp. 99 and 145.

97   *Ibid.*, pp. 173 and 179.

98   *Ibid.*, pp. 198–200, 208, 218–219 and 223.

99   A. Schweitzer, *Filosofia da Civilização* [1923], São Paulo, Edit. Unesp, 2011 [reed.], pp. 80, 304, 311 and 315.

100 A. Schweitzer, *Pilgrimage to Humanity* [*Weg zur Humanität*], N.Y., Philosophical Library, 1961, pp. 87–88, 99 and 101.

book *La civilisation et l'éthique* (1923), that respect for life started as from "une prise de conscience" of one's responsibility *vis-à-vis* the life of others.[101]

103. Later on in his life, then in the nuclear age, in his series of lectures *Paix ou guerre atomique* (1958), A. Schweitzer called for an end to nuclear weapons, with their "destructions et anéantissements inimaginables".[102] In his own words,

> La guerre atomique ne connaît pas de vainqueurs, mais uniquement des vaincus. Chaque belligérant subit par les bombes et les projectiles atomiques de l'adversaire les mêmes dégâts qu'il lui inflige par les siens. Il en résulte un anéantissement continu (...). Il peut seulement dire: allons-nous nous suicider tous les deux par une extermination réciproque?[103]

104. Well before them, by the turn of the XIXth to the XXth century, the writer Leo Tolstoi warned (*The Slavery of Our Times*, 1900) against the undue use of the State monopoly of "organized violence", conforming a new form of slavery of the vulnerable ones;[104] he criticized the recruitment of personnel to be sent to war to kill defenseless persons, perpetrating acts of extreme violence.[105] On his turn, the physician Georges Duhamel warned (in his account *Civilisation – 1914–1917*) against the fact that war had become an industry of killing, with a "barbaric ideology", destroying civilization with its "lack of humanity"; yet, he still cherished the hope that the spirit of humanism could flourish from the ashes.[106]

105. The historian of ideas Isaiah Berlin, for his part, warned (*The Proper Study of Mankind*) against the dangers of the *raison d'État*, and stressed the relevance

---

101   M. Arnold, *Albert Schweitzer – La compassion et la raison*, Lyon, Éd. Olivétan, 2015, pp. 74–75 and 77.
102   *Cit. in ibid.*, p. 111.
103   Extract from his book *Paix ou guerre atomique* (1958), reproduced in his posthumous book of essays: A. Schweitzer, *Respect de la vie* (org. B. Kaempf), Paris, Éd. Arfuyen/CIAL, 1990, p. 98.
104   L. Tolstoi, *La Esclavitud de Nuestro Tiempo* [1900], Barcelona, Littera, 2000 [reed.], pp. 86–87, 89, 91 and 97.
105   *Ibid.*, pp. 101, 103–104 and 121.
106   G. Duhamel, *Civilisation – 1914–1917*, Paris, Mercure de France, 1944, pp. 53 and 274–275; G. Duhamel, *Mémorial de la guerre blanche – 1938*, Paris, Mercure de France, 1945, pp. 41, 95, 100, 102 and 170.

of *values*, in the search of knowledge, of cultures, and of the *recta ratio*.¹⁰⁷ On his turn, the writer Erich Fromm upheld human life in insisting that there could only exist a truly "civilized" society if based on humanist values.¹⁰⁸ Towards the end of his life, in his book *The Anatomy of Human Destructivity* (1974), he warned against destruction and propounded the prevalence of love for life.¹⁰⁹

106. E. Fromm further warned that the devastation of wars (including the contemporary ones) have led to the loss of hope and to brutalization, amidst the tension of the co-existence or ambivalence between civilization and barbarism, which requires all our endeavours towards the revival of humanism.¹¹⁰ Likewise, in our days, the philosopher Edgar Morin has also warned that the advances of scientific knowledge disclosed an ambivalence, in that they provided, on the one hand, the means to improve the knowledge of the world, and, on the other hand, with the production (and proliferation) of nuclear weapons, in addition to other weapons (biological and chemical) of mass destruction, the means to destroy the world.¹¹¹

107. Future has thus become unpredictable, and unknown, in face of the confrontation between the forces of life and the forces of death. Yet, – he added, – human beings are endowed with conscience, and are aware that civilizations, as well as the whole of humankind, are mortal.¹¹² E. Morin further contended the tragic experiences lived in recent times should lead to the repentance of barbarism and the return to humanism; in effect, to think about, and resist to, barbarism, amounts to contributing to recreate humanism.¹¹³

108. For his part, in the late eighties, in his book of essays *Silences et mémoires d'hommes* (1989), Elie Wiesel stressed the need of memory and attention to the

---

107   I. Berlin, *The Proper Study of Mankind*, N.Y., Farrar & Straus & Giroux, 2000 (reed.), pp. 78, 135, 155, 217, 235–236, 242, 247, 311 and 334; I. Berlin, "Return of the *Volksgeist*: Nationalism, Good and Bad", *in At Century's End* (ed. N.P. Gardels), San Diego/Cal., Alti Publ., 1995, p. 94.
108   Cf. E. Fromm, *Las Cadenas de la Ilusión – Una Autobiografía Intelectual* [1962], Barcelona, Paidós, 2008 [reed.], pp. 78 and 234–239.
109   Cf. E. Fromm, *Anatomía de la Destructividad Humana* [1974], Mexico/Madrid/Buenos Aires, 2009 [reed.], pp. 16–468; and cf. also E. Fromm, *El Amor a la Vida* [1983 – *Über die Liebe zum Leben*], Barcelona, Paidós, 2016 (4th reprint), pp. 15–250.
110   E. Fromm, *Las Cadenas de la Ilusión...*, op. cit. supra n. (120), pp. 240 and 250–251.
111   E. Morin, *Vers l'abîme?*, Paris, L'Herne, 2012, pp. 9, 24–25 and 40–41.
112   *Ibid.*, pp. 27, 30, 59, 85, 89, 126 and 181.
113   E. Morin, *Breve Historia de la Barbarie en Occidente*, Barcelona, Paidós, 2009, p. 94, and cf. pp. 60 and 92–93.

world wherein we live, so as to combat the indifference to violence and evil.[114] Looking back to the Book of *Genesis*, he saw it fit to recall that "Caïn et Abel – les premiers enfants sur terre, – se découvrirent ennemis. Bien que frères, l'un devin l'assassin ou la victime de l'autre. L'enseignement que nous devrions en tirer? Deux hommes peuvent être frères et néanmoins désireux de s'entre-tuer. Et aussi: quiconque tue, tue son frère. Seulement cela, on l'apprend plus tard".[115]

109. Turning attention to the threat of nuclear weapons, E. Wiesel sharply criticized the already prevailing attitude of indifference to it: "le monde, aujourd'hui, nous paraît étonnamment indifférent vis-à-vis de la question nucléaire", – an attitude which he found ununderstandable.[116] And he added that

> L'indifférence (...) peut elle aussi devenir contagieuse. (...) L'indifférence permet également de mesurer la progression du mal que mine la société. (...) Là encore, la mémoire seule peut nous réveiller. Si nous nous souvenons de ce qui s'est passé il y a quarante ans, nous avons une possibilité d'empêcher de nouvelles catastrophes. Sinon, nous risquons d'être les victimes de notre propre indifférence. Car si nous sommes indifférents aux leçons de notre passé, nous le serons aux espoirs inhérents à notre avenir. (...) Voici mon angoisse: si nous oublions, nous serons oubliés. (...) Si nous restons indifférents à notre sort, (...) il ne restera personne pour raconter notre histoire.[117]

110. In effect, already in the early XXth century, Henri Bergson, in his monograph *La conscience et la vie* (1911), devoted attention to the search for meaning in life: to him, to live with conscience is to remember the past (memory) in the present, and to anticipate the future.[118] In his own words,

> Retenir ce qui n'est déjà plus, anticiper sur ce qui n'est pas encore, voilà donc la première fonction de la conscience. (...) [L]a conscience est un trait d'union entre ce qui a été et ce qui sera, un pont jeté entre le passé et l'avenir.[119]

---

114 E. Wiesel, *Silences et mémoires d'hommes*, Paris, Éd. Seuil, 1989, pp. 166, 173 and 175.
115 *Ibid.*, pp. 167–168.
116 *Ibid.*, p. 174, and cf. p. 170.
117 *Ibid.*, pp. 175–176.
118 H. Bergson, *La conscience et la vie* [1911], Paris, PUF, 2012 [reprint], pp. 10–11, 13 and 26.
119 *Ibid.*, pp. 5–6.

111. Also in international legal doctrine, there have been those who have felt the need to move away from State voluntarism and acknowledge the prevalence of conscience over the "will". It is not my intention to dwell upon this point here, as I have dealt with it elsewhere.[120] For the purposes of the present Dissenting Opinion, suffice it to recall a couple of examples. The jurist Gustav Radbruch, at the end of his life, forcefully discarded legal positivism, always subservient to power and the established order, and formulated his moving conversion and profession of faith in jusnaturalism.[121] His lucid message was preserved and has been projected in time,[122] thanks to the devotion of his students and disciples of the School of Heidelberg.

112. There are further examples of doctrinal endeavours to put limits to State voluntarism, such as the jusnaturalist construction of, e.g., Alfred Verdross, – as from the *idée du droit*, – of an objective law finding expression in the general principles of law, preceding positive international law;[123] or else the conception of the *droit spontanée*, of Roberto Ago, upholding the spontaneous formation (emanating from human conscience, well beyond the "will" of individual States) of new rules of international law.[124]

113. In the view of Albert de La Pradelle, the conception of the formation of international law on the strict basis of reciprocal rights and duties only of States is "extremely grave and dangerous".[125] International law is a "droit de la communauté humaine", encompassing, besides States, also peoples and human beings; it is the "droit de toute l'humanité", on the foundations of which are the general principles of law.[126] To A. de La Pradelle, this "droit de

---

120 Cf. A.A. Cançado Trindade, *International Law for Humankind – Towards a New Jus Gentium*, 2nd rev. ed., Leiden/The Hague, Nijhoff/The Hague Academy of International Law, 2013, pp. 141–147 and 153–161.
121 Cf. G. Radbruch, *Introducción a la Filosofía del Derecho*, 3rd ed., Mexico/Buenos Aires, Fondo de Cultura Económica, 1965, pp. 9–180.
122 Cf., e.g., R. Alexy, *The Argument from Injustice – A Reply to Legal Positivism*, Oxford, Oxford University Press, 2010, pp. 3–130.
123 A. Verdross, *Derecho Internacional Público*, 5th ed., Madrid, Aguilar, 1969 [reprint], pp. 15–19.
124 R. Ago, "Nouvelles réflexions sur la codification du droit international", 92 *Revue générale de droit international public* (1988) p. 540, and cf. p. 541 on "la nature non volontaire de l'origine du droit coutumier".
125 A. de La Pradelle, *Droit international public* (cours sténographié), Paris, Institut des Hautes Études Internationales/Centre Européen de la Dotation Carnegie, November 1932/May 1933, p. 33, and cf. pp. 36–37.
126 *Ibid.*, pp. 49–59, 149, 222 and 264.

l'humanité" is not static, but rather dynamic, attentive to human values, in the line of jusnaturalist thinking.[127]

114. "Juridical conscience" is invoked in lucid criticisms of legal positivism.[128] Thus, in his monograph-plea (of 1964) against nuclear weapons, for example, Stefan Glaser sustained that customary international norms are those that, "according to universal conscience", ought to regulate the international community, for fulfilling common interest and responding to the demands of justice; and he added that

> C'est sur cette conscience universelle que repose la principale caractéristique du droit international: la conviction que ses normes sont indispensables pour le bien commun explique leur reconnaissance en tant que règles obligatoires.[129]

115. This is the position that I also uphold; in my own understanding, it is the universal juridical conscience that is the ultimate material source of international law.[130] In my view, one cannot face the new challenges confronting the whole international community keeping in mind only State susceptibilities; such is the case with the obligation to render the world free of nuclear weapons, an imperative of *recta ratio* and not a derivative of the "will" of States. In effect, to keep hope alive it is necessary to bear always in mind humankind as a whole.

116. For my part, within the ICJ, I have deemed it fit to ponder, in my Dissenting Opinion (paras. 488–489) in the case concerning the *Application of the Convention against Genocide* (Croatia *versus* Serbia, Judgment of 03.02.2015), that, from Homer's *Iliad* (late VIIIth or early VIIth century b.C.) to date, individuals, indoctrinated and conditioned for war and destruction, have become objects of the struggle for domination. I recalled that this has been lucidly warned by Simone Weil, in a penetrating essay (of 1934), to whom this ends up victimizing everyone, there occurring "the substitution of the ends by the means",

---

127 Cf. *ibid.*, pp. 412–413.
128 Such as, e.g., those of Antonio Gómez Robledo, *Meditación sobre la Justicia* [1963], Mexico/Buenos Aires, Fondo de Cultura Económica, 1963, pp. 179 and 185; R. Quadri, "Cours général de droit international public", 113 *Recueil des Cours de l'Académie de Droit International de La Haye* (1964) pp. 326, 332, 336–337, 339 and 350–351.
129 S. Glaser, *L'arme nucléaire à la lumière du droit international*, Paris, Pédone, 1964, p. 18.
130 Cf. A.A. Cançado Trindade, *op. cit. supra* (120), ch. VI, pp. 139–161.

transforming human life into a simple means, which can be sacrificed; individuals become unable to think, in face of the "social machine" of destruction of the spirit and fabrication of the inconscience.[131]

117. The presence of evil has accompanied and marked human existence along the centuries. In the same aforementioned Dissenting Opinion in the case concerning the *Application of the Convention against Genocide* (2015), after drawing attention to "the ever-lasting presence of evil, which appears proper to the human condition, in all times", I added:

> It is thus understandable that it has attracted the concern of, and has presented challenges to, legal thinking, in our times and previous centuries, as well as other branches of knowledge (such as, e.g., history, psychology, anthropology, sociology, philosophy and theology, among others). It has marked presence in literature as well. This long-standing concern, along centuries, has not, however, succeeded to provide an explanation for evil.
>
> Despite the endeavours of human thinking, along history, it has not been able to rid humankind of it. Like the passing of time, the ever-lasting presence of evil is yet another mystery surrounding human beings, wherever and while they live. Whenever individuals purport to subject their fellow human beings to their 'will', placing this latter above conscience, evil is bound to manifest itself. In one of the most learned writings on the problem of evil, R.P. Sertillanges ponders that the awareness of evil and the anguish emanated therefrom have marked presence in all civilizations. The ensuing threat to the future of human kind has accounted for the continuous presence of that concern throughout the history of human thinking.[132]
>
> Religions were the first to dwell upon the problem of evil, which came also to be considered by philosophy, history, psychology, social sciences, and literature. Along the centuries, human thinking has always acknowledged the need to examine the problem of evil, its incidence in human relations, in the world wherein we live, without losing faith in human values.[133] Despite the perennial quest of human thinking to find answers

---

131   S. Weil, *Reflexiones sobre las Causas de la Libertad y de la Opresión Social*, Barcelona, Ed. Paidós/Universidad Autónoma de Barcelona, 1995, pp. 81–82, 84 and 130–131; S. Weil, *Réflexions sur les causes de la liberté et de l'oppression sociale*, Paris, Gallimard, 1955, pp. 124–125, and cf. pp. 114–115 and 144.

132   R.P. Sertillanges, *Le problème du mal – l'histoire*, Paris, Aubier, 1948, pp. 5–412.

133   *Ibid.*, pp. 5–412.

to the problem of evil, – going as far back as the *Book of Job*, or even further back, to the *Genesis* itself,[134] – not even theology has found an explanation for it, satisfactory to all (paras. 472–474).

118. The Scripture's account of Cain and Abel (*Genesis*, Ch. 4: 8–10) along the centuries came to be regarded as the aetiology of the fragmentation of humankind, as from the indifference of an individual to the fate of another. The increasing disregard for human life was fostered by growing, generalized and uncontrolled violence in search of domination. This was further aggravated by ideological manipulations, and even the dehumanization of the others, the ones to be victimized. The problem of evil continues to be studied, in face of the human capacity for extreme violence and self-destruction on a large scale.[135] The tragic message of the Book of *Genesis*, in my perception, seems perennial, as contemporary as ever, in the current nuclear age.

IX   The Attention of the United Nations Charter to Peoples

119. It should be kept in mind that the United Nations Charter was adopted on 26.06.1945 on behalf of "we, the peoples of the United Nations". In several provisions it expresses its concern with the living conditions of all peoples (preamble, Articles 55, 73(a), 76, 80), and calls for the promotion of, and universal

---

134   Cf., *inter alia*, e.g., M. Neusch, *L'énigme du mal*, Paris, Bayard, 2007, pp. 7–193; J. Maritain, *Dio e la Permissione del Male*, 6th ed., Brescia, Edit. Morcelliana, 2000, pp. 9–100; E. Fromm, *Anatomía de la Destructividad Humana*, Mexico/Madrid/Buenos Aires, Siglo XXI Edit., 2009 [reprint.], pp. 11–468; P. Ricoeur, *Evil – A Challenge to Philosophy and Theology*, London, Continuum, 2007, pp. 33–72; P. Ricoeur, *Le mal – Un défi à la philosophie et à la théologie*, Genève, Éd. Labor et Fides, 2004, pp. 19–65; C.S. Nino, *Juicio al Mal Absoluto*, Buenos Aires, Emecé Edit., 1997, pp. 7–292; A. Morton, *On Evil*, N.Y./London, Routledge, 2004, pp. 1–148; T. Eagleton, *On Evil*, New Haven/London, Yale University Press, 2010, pp. 1–163; P. Dews, *The Idea of Evil*, Oxford, Wiley-Blackwell, 2013, pp. 1–234.

135   Cf., moreover, *inter alia*, e.g., [Various Authors,] *Le Mal* (ed. C. Crignon), Paris, Flammarion, 2000, pp. 11–232; J. Waller, *Becoming Evil*, 2nd ed., Oxford, Oxford University Press, 2007, pp. 3–330; S. Baron-Cohen, *The Science of Evil – On Empathy and the Origins of Cruelty*, N.Y., Basic Books, 2012, pp. 1–243; L. Svendsen, *A Philsophy of Evil*, Champaign/London, Dalkey Archive Press, 2011 [reprint], pp. 9–282; M. Salvioli, *Bene e Male – Variazioni sul Tema*, Bologna, Ed. Studio Domenicano (ESD), 2012, pp. 11–185; D. Livingstone Smith, *Less than Human*, N.Y., St. Martin's Press, 2011, pp. 1–316; R. Safranski, *El Mal, o el Drama de la Libertad*, 4th ed., Barcelona, Tusquets Edit., 2014, pp. 15–281; S. Neiman, *Evil in Modern Thought*, 2nd ed., Princeton/Oxford, Princeton University Press, 2015, pp. 1–359; J.-C. Guillebaud, *Le tourment de la guerre*, Paris, Éd. de l'Iconoclaste, 2016, pp. 9–390.

respect for, human rights (Articles 55(c), 62(2), 68, 76(c)). It invokes the "principles of justice and international law" (Article 1(1)), and refers to "justice and respect for the obligations arising from treaties and other sources of international law" (preamble). It further states that the Statute of the ICJ, "the principal judicial organ of the United Nations", forms "an integral part" of the U.N. Charter itself (Article 92).

120. In the mid-fifties, Max Huber, a former Judge of the PCIJ, wrote that international law has to protect also values common to humankind, attentive to respect for life and human dignity, in the line of the jusnaturalist conception of *the jus gentium*; the U.N. Charter, in incorporating human rights into this *droit de l'humanité*, initiated a new era in the development of international law, in a way rescuing the idea of the *civitas maxima*, which marked presence already in the historical origins of the law of nations. The U.N. Charter's attention to peoples, its principled position for the protection of the human person, much transcend positive domestic law and politics.[136]

121. The new vision advanced by the U.N. Charter, and espoused by the Law of the United Nations, has, in my perception, an incidence upon judicial settlement of international disputes. Thus, the fact that the ICJ's mechanism for the handling of contentious cases is an inter-State one, does not mean that its reasoning should also pursue a strictly inter-State dimension; that will depend on the nature and substance of the cases lodged with it. And there have been several cases lodged with the Court that required a reasoning going well beyond the inter-State dimension.[137] Such reasoning beyond the inter-State dimension

---

136   Max Huber, *La pensée et l'action de la Croix-Rouge*, Genève, CICR, 1954, pp. 26, 247, 270, 286 and 291.
137   Cf., e.g., the case of *Nottebohm* (1955, pertaining to double nationality); the cases of the *Trial of Pakistani Prisoners of War* (1973), of the *Hostages* (*U.S. Diplomatic and Consular Staff*) *in Teheran* case (1980); of the *Application of the Convention against Genocide* (Bosnia *versus* Serbia, 1996 and 2007); of the *Frontier Dispute between Burkina Faso and Mali* (1998); the triad of cases concerning consular assistance – namely, the cases *Breard* (Paraguay *versus* United States,1998), the case *LaGrand* (Germany *versus* United States, 2001), the case *Avena and Others* (Mexico *versus* United States, 2004); the cases of *Armed Activities in the Territory of Congo* (D.R. Congo *versus* Uganda, 2000, concerning grave violations of human rights and of International Humanitarian Law); of the *Land and Maritime Boundary between Cameroon and Nigeria* (1996); of *Questions Relating to the Obligation to Prosecute or Extradite* (Belgium *versus* Senegal, 2009–2013, pertaining to the principle of universal jurisdiction under the U.N. Convention against Torture); of *A.S. Diallo* (Guinea *versus* D.R. Congo, 2010, on detention and expulsion of a foreigner), of the *Jurisdictional*

is faithful to the U.N. Charter, the ICJ being "the principal judicial organ of the United Nations" (Article 92).

122. Recently, in one of such cases, that of the *Application of the Convention against Genocide* (Croatia *versus* Serbia, 2015), in my extensive Dissenting Opinion appended thereto, I have deemed it fit, *inter alia*, to warn that

> The present case concerning the *Application of the Convention against Genocide* (Croatia *versus* Serbia) provides yet another illustration of the pressing need to overcome and move away from the dogmatic and strict inter-State outlook, even more cogently. In effect, the 1948 Convention against Genocide, – adopted on the eve of the Universal Declaration of Human Rights, – is not State-centered, but rather *people-centred*. The Convention against Genocide cannot be properly interpreted and applied with a strict State-centered outlook, with attention turned to inter-State susceptibilities. Attention is to be kept on the *justiciables*, on the victims, – real and potential victims, – so as to impart justice under the Genocide Convention (para. 496).

123. In a report in the early nineties, a former U.N. Secretary-General, calling for a "concerted effort" towards complete disarmament, rightly pondered that "[d]ans le monde d'aujourd'hui, les nations ne peuvent plus se permettre de résoudre les problèmes par la force. (...) Le désarmement est l'un des moyens les plus importants de réduire la violence dans les relations entre États".[138] There followed the cycle of World Conferences of the United Nations along the nineties, in a commendable endeavour of the United Nations *to go beyond and transcend the purely inter-State dimension*, imbued of a spirit of solidarity, so as to consider the challenges for the future of humankind.

Immunities of the State (Germany *versus* Italy, Greece intervening, 2010–2012); of the *Application of the International Convention on the Elimination of All Forms of Racial Discrimination* (Georgia *versus* Russian Federation, 2011); of the *Temple of Preah Vihear* (Cambodia *versus* Thailand, provisional measures, 2011); of the *Application of the Convention against Genocide* (Croatia *versus* Serbia, 2015). To those cases one can add the two most recent Advisory Opinions of the ICJ, on the *Declaration of Independence of Kosovo* (2010); and on a *Judgment of the ILO Administrative Tribunal upon a Complaint Filed against the IFAD* (2012).

138 B. Boutros-Ghali, *Nouvelles dimensions de la réglementation des armements et du désarmement dans la période de l'après-guerre froide – Rapport du Secrétaire Général*, N.Y., Nations Unies, 1993, pp. 21–22.

124. Those U.N. World Conferences disclosed a growing awareness of the international community as a whole, and entered into a continuing universal dialogue between U.N. member States and entities of the civil societies, – which I well remember, having participated in it,[139] – so as to devise the new international agenda in the search of common solutions for the new challenges affecting humankind as a whole. In focusing attention on vulnerable segments of the populations, the immediate concern has been with meeting basic human needs, that memorable cycle of World Conferences disclosed a common concern with the deterioration of living conditions, dramatically affecting increasingly greater segments of the population in many parts of the world nowadays.[140]

125. The common denominator in those U.N. World Conferences – as I have pointed out on distinct occasions along the last two decades[141] – can be found in the recognition of the legitimacy of the concern of the international community as a whole with the conditions of living of all human beings everywhere. The placing of the well-being of peoples and human beings, of the improvement of their conditions of living, at the centre of the concerns of the international community, is remindful of the historical origins of the *droit des gens*.[142]

---

139 E.g., in the U.N. Conference on Environment and Development (Rio de Janeiro, 1992, in its World NGO Forum) and in the II World Conference on Human Rights (Vienna, 1993, in the same Forum and in its Drafting Committee).

140 A growing call was formed for the pursuance of social justice *among* and *within* nations.

141 A.A. Cançado Trindade, *A Proteção dos Vulneráveis como Legado da II Conferência Mundial de Direitos Humanos (1993–2013)*, Fortaleza/Brazil, IBDH/IIDH/SLADI, 2014, pp. 13–356; A.A. Cançado Trindade, "Sustainable Human Development and Conditions of Life as a Matter of Legitimate International Concern: The Legacy of the U.N. World Conferences", *in Japan and International Law – Past, Present and Future* (International Symposium to Mark the Centennial of the Japanese Association of International Law), The Hague, Kluwer, 1999, pp. 285–309; A.A. Cançado Trindade, "The Contribution of Recent World Conferences of the United Nations to the Relations between Sustainable Development and Economic, Social and Cultural Rights", *in Les hommes et l'environnement: Quels droits pour le vingt-et-unième siècle? – Études en hommage à Alexandre Kiss* (eds. M. Prieur and C. Lambrechts), Paris, Éd. Frison-Roche, 1998, pp. 119–146; A.A. Cançado Trindade, "Memória da Conferência Mundial de Direitos Humanos (Viena, 1993)", 87/90 *Boletim da Sociedade Brasileira de Direito Internacional* (1993–1994) pp. 9–57.

142 Those Conferences acknowledged that human rights do in fact permeate all areas of human activity, and contributed decisively to the reestablishment of the central position of human beings in the conceptual universe of the law of nations (*droit des gens*). Cf., on the matter, A.A. Cançado Trindade, *Évolution du Droit international au droit des*

126. At the end of the decade and the dawn of the new millennium, the United Nations Millennium Declaration (adopted by General Assembly's resolution 55/2, of 08.09.2000) stated the determination "to eliminate the dangers posed by weapons of mass destruction" (para. II(8)), and, noticeably,

> To strive for the elimination of weapons of mass destruction, particularly nuclear weapons, and to keep all options open for achieving this aim, including the possibility of convening and international conference to identify ways of eliminating nuclear dangers (para. II(9)).

127. In addition to our responsibilities to our individual societies, – the U.N. Millennium Declaration added, –

> we have a collective responsibility to uphold the principles of human dignity, equality and equity at the global level. (...) [W]e have a duty therefore to all the world's people, especially the most vulnerable and, in particular, the children of the world, to whom the future belongs.
>
> We reaffirm our commitment to the purposes and principles of the Charter of the United Nations, which have proved timeless and universal. Indeed, their relevance and capacity to inspire have increased, as nations and peoples have become increasingly interconnected and interdependent (paras. I(2–3)).

X   Impertinence of the So-Called *Monetary Gold* "Principle"

128. The distortions generated by the obsession with the strict inter-State paradigm are not hard to detect. An example is afforded, in this connection, by the ICJ's handling of the *East Timor* case (1995): the East Timorese people had no *locus standi* to request intervention in the proceedings, not even to present an *amicus curiae*, although the crucial point under consideration was that of sovereignty over their own territory. Worse still, the interests of a third State (which had not even accepted the Court's jurisdiction) were taken for granted and promptly safeguarded by the Court, by means of the application of the so-called *Monetary Gold* "principle", – an assumed "principle" also invoked now, two decades later, in the present case concerning the obligation of elimination of nuclear weapons!

---

gens – *L'accès des particuliers à la justice internationale: le regard d'un juge*, Paris, Pédone, 2008, pp. 1–187.

129. Attention has to be turned to the *nature* of the case at issue, which may well require a reasoning – as the *cas d'espèce* does – moving away from "a strict State-centred voluntarist perspective" and from the "exaltation of State consent", and seeking guidance in fundamental principles (*prima principia*), such as the principle of humanity. This is what I pointed out in my extensive Dissenting Opinion in the case concerning the *Application of the Convention against Genocide* (Croatia *versus* Serbia, Judgment of 03.02.2015), where I pondered *inter alia* that such *prima principia* confer to the international legal order "its ineluctable axiological dimension"; they "conform its *substratum*, and convey the idea of an *objective* justice, in the line of jusnaturalist thinking" (para. 517).

130. That was not the first time I made such ponderation: I had done the same, in another extensive Dissenting Opinion (para. 213), in the case concerning the *Application of the International Convention on the Elimination of All Forms of Racial Discrimination – CERD* (Georgia *versus* Russian Federation, Judgment of 01.04.2011). In my subsequent aforementioned Dissenting Opinion in the case concerning the *Application of the Convention against Genocide* I expressed my dissatisfaction that in a case pertaining to the interpretation and application of the Convention against Genocide, the ICJ even made recourse to the so-called *Monetary Gold* "principle",[143] which had no place in a case like that, and "which does not belong to the realm of the *prima principia*, being nothing more than a concession to State consent, within an outdated State voluntarist framework" (para. 519).

131. May I, in the present Dissenting Opinion, this time in the case of *Obligations Concerning Negotiations Relating to Cessation of the Nuclear Arms Race and to Nuclear Disarmament*, again leave on the records my dissatisfaction for the same reason. Once again, may I stress that the adjudication of a case like the present one shows the need to go beyond the strict inter-State outlook. The fact that the mechanism for the adjudication of contentious cases before the ICJ is an inter-State one, does not at all imply that the Court's reasoning should likewise be strictly inter State. In the present case concerning nuclear weapons and the obligation of nuclear disarmament, it is necessary to focus attention on peoples, rather than on inter-State susceptibilities. It is imperative to keep in mind the world population, in pursuance of a humanist outlook, in the light of the *principle of humanity*.

---

143 Even if only to dismiss it (para. 116).

XI   The Fundamental Principle of the Juridical Equality of States

132. The present case of *Obligations Concerning Negotiations Relating to Cessation of the Nuclear Arms Race and to Nuclear Disarmament* stresses the utmost importance of the principle of the juridical equality of States. The importance attributed to fundamental principles, the idea of an objective justice, and its incidence upon the laws, go back in time, being deeply-rooted in jusnaturalist thinking. If laws are deprived of justice, they no longer oblige in conscience. Ethics cannot be dissociated from law; in the international scenario, each one is responsible for all the others. To the "founding fathers" of the law of nations (*droit des gens*), like F. de Vitoria and F. Suárez, the principle of equality was fundamental, in the relations among individuals, as well as among nations. Their teachings have survived the erosion of time: today, four and a half centuries later, the basic principle of equality and non-discrimination is in the foundations of the Law of the United Nations itself.

133. The present case of *Obligations Concerning Negotiations Relating to Cessation of the Nuclear Arms Race and to Nuclear Disarmament* is surely not the first one before the ICJ that brings to the fore the relevance of the principle of the juridical equality of States. In the ICJ's Order (of Provisional Measures of Protection) of 03.03.2014, I have deemed it fit to point out, in my Separate Opinion appended thereto, that the case concerning *Questions Relating to the Seizure and Detention of Certain Documents and Data*

> bears witness of the relevance of the principle of the juridical equality of States. The prevalence of this fundamental principle has marked a long-standing presence in the realm of international law, ever since the times of the II Hague Peace Conference of 1907, and then of the drafting of the Statute of the Permanent Court of International Justice by the Advisory Committee of Jurists, in June-July 1920. Recourse was then made, by that Committee, *inter alia*, to general principles of law, as these latter embodied the objective idea of justice. A general principle such as that of the juridical equality of States, enshrined a quarter of a century later in the United Nations Charter (Article 2(1)), is ineluctably intermingled with the quest for justice.
>
> Subsequently, throughout the drafting of the 1970 U.N. Declaration on Principles of International Law concerning Friendly Relations and Co-operation among States in accordance with the Charter of the United Nations (1964–1970), the need was felt to make it clear that stronger States cannot impose their will upon the weak, and that *de facto* inequalities

among States cannot affect the weaker in the vindication of their rights. The principle of the juridical equality of States gave expression to this concern, embodying the *idée de justice*, emanated from the universal juridical conscience (paras. 44–45).

134. And one decade earlier, in my General Course on Public International Law delivered at the Hague Academy of International Law (2005), I pondered that

> On successive occasions the principles of international law have proved to be of fundamental importance to humankind's quest for justice. This is clearly illustrated by the role played, *inter alia*, by the principle of juridical equality of States. This fundamental principle, – the historical roots of which go back to the II Hague Peace Conference of 1907, – proclaimed in the U.N. Charter and enunciated also in the 1970 Declaration of Principles, means ultimately that all States, – factually strong and weak, great and small, – are equal before international law, are entitled to the same protection under the law and before the organs of international justice, and to equality in the exercise of international rights and duties.
>
> Despite successive attempts to undermine it, the principle of juridical equality of States has remained, from the II Hague Peace Conference of 1907 to date, one of the basic pillars of International Law. It has withstood the onslaught of time, and shown itself salutary for the peaceful conduction of international relations, being ineluctably associated – as it stands – with the foundations of International Law. It has been very important for the international legal system itself, and has proven to be a cornerstone of international law in the United Nations era. In fact, the U.N. Charter gave it a new dimension, and the principle developments such as that of the system of collective security, within the ambit of the law of the United Nations.[144]

135. By the turn of the century, the General Assembly's resolution 55/2, of 08.09.2000, adopted the United Nations Millennium Declaration, which *inter alia* upheld the "sovereign equality of all States", in conformity with "the principles of justice and international law" (para. I(4)). Half a decade later, the General Assembly's resolution 60/1, of 16.09.2005, adopted the *World Summit Outcome*, which *inter alia* expressed the determination "to establish a just and lasting peace all over the world in accordance with the purposes and principles

---

144 A.A. Cançado Trindade, *International Law for Humankind – Towards a New Jus Gentium*, op. cit. supra n. (120), pp. 84–85, and cf. pp. 62–63, 65 and 73.

of the [U.N.] Charter", as well as "to uphold the sovereign equality of all States" (para. I(5)). In stressing therein the "vital importance of an effective multilateral system" to face current challenges to international peace and security (paras. 6–7), the international community reiterated its profession of faith in the general principles of international law.

XII   Unfoundedness of the Strategy of "Deterrence"

136. In effect, the strategy of "deterrence", pursued by NWS in the present context of nuclear disarmament in order to attempt to justify their own position, makes abstraction of the fundamental principle of the juridical equality of States, enshrined into the U.N. Charter. Factual inequalities cannot be made to prevail over the juridical equality of States. All U.N. member States are juridically equal. The strategy of a few States pursuing their own "national security interests" cannot be made to prevail over a fundamental principle of international law set forth in the U.N. Charter: factual inequalities between States cannot, and do not prevail over the juridical equality of States.

137. In its 1996 Advisory Opinion on the *Threat or Use of Nuclear Weapons*, permeated with ambiguity, the ICJ gave undue weight to "the still strong adherence to the practice of deterrence" (paras. 67 and 73) by a few NWS, to the point of beholding in it an obstacle to the formation and consolidation of *opinio juris* and a customary rule as to the illegality of nuclear weapons, leading to "a specific and express prohibition" of their use (para. 73). Here the Court assumed its usual positivist posture: in its view, the prohibition must be express, stated in positive law, even if those weapons are capable of destroying all life on earth, the whole of humankind...

138. The ICJ, in its Advisory Opinion of 1996, gave too much weight to the opposition of NWS as to the existence of an *opinio juris* on the unlawfulness of nuclear weapons. And this, despite the fact that, in their overwhelming majority, member States of the United Nations stand clearly against nuclear weapons, and in favour of nuclear disarmament. The 1996 Advisory Opinion, notwithstanding, appears unduly influenced by the lack of logic of "deterrence".[145] One cannot conceive, – as the 1996 Advisory Opinion did, – of recourse to nuclear

---

145   Cf. criticisms of such posture in, e.g., A. Sayed, *Quand le droit est face à son néant – Le droit à l'épreuve de l'emploi de l'arme nucléaire*, Bruxelles, Bruylant, 1998, pp. 79–80, 84, 88–89, 96 and 113.

weapons by a hypothetical State in "self-defence" at the unbearable cost of the devastating effects and sufferings inflicted upon humankind as a whole, in an "escalade vers l'apocalypse".[146]

139. The infliction of such devastation and suffering is in flagrant breach of international law, – of the ILHR, IHL and the Law of the United Nations (cf. Part XIII, *infra*). It is, furthermore, in flagrant breach of norms of *jus cogens*.[147] The strategy of "deterrence" seems to make abstraction of all that. The ICJ, as the International Court *of Justice*, should have given, on all occasions when it has been called upon to pronounce on nuclear weapons (in the exercise of its jurisdiction on contentious and advisory matters), far greater weight to the *raison d'humanité*,[148] rather than to the *raison d'État* nourishing "deterrence". We have to keep in mind the human person and the peoples, for which States were created, instead of relying only on what one assumes to be the *raison d'État*. The *raison d'humanité*, in my understanding, prevails surely over considerations of *Realpolitik*.

140. In its 1996 Advisory Opinion, the ICJ, however, at the same time, rightly acknowledged the importance of complete nuclear disarmament, asserted in the series of General Assembly resolutions, and the relevance of the corresponding obligation under Article VI of the NPT to the international community as a whole (paras. 99 and 102). To the Court, this is an obligation of result, and not of mere conduct (para. 99). Yet, it did not extract the consequences of that. Had it done so, it would have reached the conclusion that nuclear disarmament cannot be hampered by the conduct of a few States – the NWS – which maintain and modernize their own arsenals of nuclear weapons, pursuant to their strategy of "deterrence".

141. The strategy of "deterrence" has a suicidal component. Nowadays, in 2016, twenty years after the 1996 ICJ Advisory Opinion, and with the subsequent

---

146   Cf. *ibid.*, p. 147, and cf. pp. 129, 133, 151, 160, 174–175, 197 and 199–200.
147   On the expansion of the material content of this latter, cf. A.A. Cançado Trindade, "*Jus Cogens*: The Determination and the Gradual Expansion of Its Material Content in Contemporary International Case-Law", *in XXXV Curso de Derecho Internacional Organizado por el Comité Jurídico Interamericano – 2008*, Washington D.C., OAS General Secretariat, 2009, pp. 3–29.
148   A.A. Cançado Trindade, "La Humanización del Derecho Internacional y los Límites de la Razón de Estado", *in 40 Revista da Faculdade de Direito da Universidade Federal de Minas Gerais – Belo Horizonte/Brazil* (2001), pp. 11–23.

reiteration of the conventional and customary international legal obligation of nuclear disarmament, there is no longer any room for ambiguity. There is an *opinio juris communis* as to the illegality of nuclear weapons, and as to the well-established obligation of nuclear disarmament, which is an obligation of result and not of mere conduct. Such *opinio juris* cannot be erased by the dogmatic positivist insistence on an express prohibition of nuclear weapons; on the contrary, that *opinio juris* discloses that the invocation of the absence of an express prohibition is nonsensical, in relying upon the destructive and suicidal strategy of "deterrence".

142. Such strategy is incompatible with jusnaturalist thinking, always attentive to ethical considerations (cf. Part XV, *infra*). Over half a century ago (precisely 55 years ago), the U.N. General Assembly had already stated, in its seminal resolution 1653 (XVI) of 1961, that the use of nuclear weapons was "contrary to the spirit, letter and aims of the United Nations", a "direct violation" of the U.N. Charter, a breach of international law and of "the laws of humanity", and "a crime against mankind and civilization" (operative para. 1). Several subsequent General Assembly resolutions upheld the same understanding of resolution 1653(XVI) of 1961 (cf. Part III, *supra*), leaving thus no room at all for ambiguity or hesitation, or to any concession.

143. Two decades ago, in the advisory proceedings of late 1995 before the ICJ, conducive to its 1996 Advisory Opinion on *Threat or Use of Nuclear Weapons*, fierce criticisms were voiced of the strategy of "deterrence", keeping in mind the inhumane sufferings of victims of nuclear detonation, radiation and contamination.[149] Attention was drawn, on the occasion, to the "distortion of logic" in "deterrence", in trying to rely on so immensely destructive weapons to keep peace, and in further trying to persuade others "to accept that for the last 50 or so years this new and more dangerous and potentially genocidal level or armaments should be credited with keeping peace".[150]

144. In the aforementioned advisory proceedings, "nuclear deterrence" was dismissed as being "simply the maintenance of a balance of fear";[151] it was criticized as seeking to ground itself on a "highly questionable" premise,

---

149 Cf., e.g., the testimonies of the Mayors of Hiroshima and Nagasaki, in Part XIII, *infra*.
150 ICJ, doc. CR 95/35, of 15.11.1995, p. 32 (statement of Zimbabwe).
151 ICJ, doc. CR 95/27, of 07.11.1995, p. 37 (statement of the Mayor of Nagasaki).

whereby a handful of NWS feel free to "arrogate to themselves" the faculty "to determine what is world peace and security, exclusive in the context of their own" national strategies and interests.[152] It was contended that nuclear weapons are in breach of international law by their own nature, as weapons of catastrophic mass destruction; "nuclear deterrence" wrongfully assumes that States and individuals act rationally, leaving the world "under the nuclear sword of Damocles", stimulating "the nuclear ambitions of their countries, thereby increasing overall instability", and also increasing the danger of their being used "intentionally or accidentally".[153]

145. The NWS, in persisting to rely on the strategy of "deterrence", seem to overlook the above-reviewed distinct series of U.N. General Assembly resolutions (cf. Part III, *supra*) condemning nuclear weapons and calling for their elimination. The strategy of "deterrence" has come under strong criticism along the years, for the serious risks it carries with it, and for its indifference to the goal – supported by the United Nations, – of achieving a world free of nuclear weapons. Very recently, e.g., participants in the series of Conferences on Humanitarian Impact of Nuclear Weapons (2013–2014) have strongly criticized the strategy of nuclear "deterrence". In a statement sent to the 2014 Vienna Conference, for example, the U.N. Secretary-General warned against the dangers of nuclear "deterrence", undermining world stability (cf. Part XIX, *infra*).

146. There is here, in effect, clearly formed, an *opinio juris communis* as to the illegality and prohibition of nuclear weapons. The use or threat of use of nuclear weapons being a clear breach of international law, of International Humanitarian Law and of the International Law of Human Rights, and of the U.N. Charter, renders unsustainable and unfounded any invocation of the strategy of "deterrence". In my view, a few States cannot keep on insisting on "national security interests" to arrogate to themselves indefinitely the prerogative to determine by themselves the conditions of world peace, and to impose them upon all others, the overwhelming majority of the international community. The survival of humankind cannot be made to depend on the "will" of a handful of privileged States. The universal juridical conscience stands well above the "will" of individual States.

---

152 *Ibid.*, p. 45, para. 14 (statement of Malaysia).
153 *Ibid.*, p. 55, para. 8; and cf. pp. 60–61 and 63, paras. 17–20 (statement of Malaysia).

XIII The Illegality of Nuclear Weapons and the Obligation of Nuclear Disarmament

1 *The Condemnation of All Weapons of Mass Destruction*

147. Since the beginning of the nuclear age, it became clear that the effects of nuclear weapons (such as heat and radiation) cannot be limited to military targets only, being thus by nature indiscriminate and disproportionate in their long-term devastation, disclosing the utmost cruelty. The *opinio juris communis* as to the prohibition of nuclear weapons, and of all weapons of mass destruction, has gradually been formed, along the last decades.[154] If weapons less destructive than nuclear weapons have already been expressly prohibited (as is the case of biological and chemical weapons), it would be nonsensical to argue that, those which have not, by positive conventional international law, like nuclear weapons, would not likewise be illicit; after all, they have far greater and long-lasting devastating effects, threatening the existence of the international community as a whole.

148. It may be recalled that, already in 1969, *all* weapons of mass destruction were condemned by the *Institut de Droit International* (I.D.I.). In the debates of its Edinburgh session on the matter, emphasis was placed on the need to respect the principle of distinction (between military and non-military objectives), and the terrifying effects of the use of nuclear weapons were pointed out, – the example of the atomic bombing of Hiroshima and Nagasaki having been expressly recalled.[155] In its resolution of September 1969 on the matter, the *Institut* began by restating, in the preamble, the *prohibition of recourse to force* in international law, and the duty of protection of civilian populations in any armed conflict; it further recalled the general principles of international law, customary rules and conventions, – supported by international case-law and practice, – which "clearly restrict" the extent to which the parties engaged in a conflict may harm the adversary, and warned against

---

154 Cf., e.g., G.E. do Nascimento e Silva, "A Proliferação Nuclear e o Direito Internacional", in *Pensamiento Jurídico y Sociedad Internacional – Libro-Homenaje al Prof. A. Truyol y Serra*, vol. II, Madrid, Universidad Complutense, 1986, pp. 877–886; C.A. Dunshee de Abranches, *Proscrição das Armas Nucleares*, Rio de Janeiro, Livr. Freitas Bastos, 1964, pp. 114–179.

155 Cf. *Annuaire de l'Institut de Droit International* – Session d'Edimbourg (1969)-II, pp. 49–50, 53, 55, 60, 62–63, 66, 88–90 and 99.

the consequences which the indiscriminate conduct of hostilities and particularly the use of nuclear, chemical and bacteriological weapons, may involve for civilian populations and for mankind as a whole.[156]

149. In its operative part, the aforementioned resolution of the *Institut* stressed the importance of the principle of distinction (between military and non-military objectives) as a "fundamental principle of international law" and the pressing need to protect civilian populations in armed conflicts,[157] and added, in paragraphs 4 and 7, that:

> Existing international law prohibits all armed attacks on the civilian population as such, as well as on non-military objects, notably dwellings or other buildings sheltering the civilian population, so long as these are not used for military purposes (...).
>
> Existing international law prohibits the use of all weapons which, by their nature, affect indiscriminately both military objectives and non-military objects, or both armed forces and civilian populations. In particular, it prohibits the use of weapons the destructive effect of which is so great that it cannot be limited to specific military objectives or is otherwise uncontrollable (self-generating weapons), as well as of 'blind' weapons.[158]

150. For its part, the International Law Association (I.L.A.), in its more recent work (in 2014) on nuclear disarmament, after referring to Article VI of the NPT, was of the view that it was not only conventional, but also an evolving customary international obligation with an *erga omnes* character, affecting "the international community as a whole", and not only the States Parties to the NPT.[159] It also referred to the "world-wide public opinion" pointing to "the catastrophic consequences for humankind of any use or detonation of nuclear weapons", and added that reliance on nuclear weapons for "deterrence" was thus unsustainable.[160]

---

156   Text *in: Annuaire de l'Institut de Droit International* – Session d'Edimbourg (1969) II, pp. 375–376.
157   Paras. 1–3, 5–6 and 8, *in ibid.*, pp. 376–377.
158   Text *in ibid.*, pp. 376–377.
159   International Law Association (I.L.A.), Committee: *Nuclear Weapons, Non-Proliferation and Contemporary International Law* (2nd Report: *Legal Aspects of Nuclear Disarmament*), I.L.A. Washington Conference, 2014, pp. 2–4.
160   *Ibid.*, pp. 5–6.

151. In its view, "nuclear" deterrence is not a global "umbrella", but rather a threat to international peace and security, and NWS are still far from implementing Article VI of the NPT.¹⁶¹ To the International Law Association, the provisions of Article VI are not limited to States Parties to the NPT, "they are part of customary international law or at least evolving custom"; they are valid *erga omnes*, as they affect "the international community as a whole", and not only a group of States or a particular State.¹⁶² Thus, as just seen, learned institutions in international law, such as the I.D.I. and the I.L.A., have also sustained the prohibition in international law of all weapons of mass destruction, starting with nuclear weapons, the most devastating of all.

152. A single use of nuclear weapons, irrespective of the circumstances, may today ultimately mean the end of humankind itself.¹⁶³ All weapons of mass destruction are illegal, and are prohibited: this is what ineluctably ensues from an international legal order of which the ultimate material source is the *universal juridical conscience*.¹⁶⁴ This is the position I have consistently sustained along the years, including in a lecture I delivered at the University of Hiroshima, Japan, on 20.12.2004.¹⁶⁵ I have done so in the line of jusnaturalist thinking, faithful to the lessons of the "founding fathers" of the law of nations, keeping in mind not only States, but also peoples and individuals, and humankind as a whole.

2 *The Prohibition of Nuclear Weapons: The Need of a People-Centred Approach*

153. In effect, the nuclear age itself, from its very beginning (the atomic blasts of Hiroshima and Nagasaki in August 1945) can be properly studied from a people-centred approach. There are moving testimonies and historical accounts of the devastating effects of nuclear weapons, from surviving victims

---

161 *Ibid.*, pp. 8–9.
162 *Ibid.*, p. 18.
163 Nagendra Singh, *Nuclear Weapons and International Law*, London, Stevens, 1959, p. 242.
164 A.A. Cançado Trindade, *International Law for Humankind – Towards a New Jus Gentium*, *op. cit. supra* n. (132), Ch. VI ("The Material Source of International Law: Manifestations of the Universal Juridical Conscience"), pp. 139–161.
165 Text of my lecture reproduced *in*: A.A. Cançado Trindade, *Le Droit international pour la personne humaine*, Paris, Pédone, 2012, Ch. I ("L'illicéité de toutes les armes de destruction massive au regard du droit international contemporain"), pp. 61–90; A.A. Cançado Trindade, *A Humanização do Direito Internacional*, 2nd ed., Belo Horizonte/Brazil, Edit. Del Rey, 2015, Ch. XVII ("The Illegality under Contemporary International Law of All Weapons of Mass Destruction"), pp. 361–390.

and witnesses.¹⁶⁶ Yet, even with the eruption of the nuclear age, attention remained focused largely on State strategies: it took some time for them gradually to shift to the devastating effects of nuclear weapons on peoples.

154. As recalled in one of the historical accounts, only at the first Conference against Atomic and Hydrogen Bombs (1955), "the victims had their first opportunity, after ten years of silence, to make themselves heard", in that forum.¹⁶⁷ Along the last decades, there have been endeavours to shift attention from State strategies to the numerous victims and enormous damages caused by nuclear weapons, focusing on "human misery and human dignity".¹⁶⁸ Recently, one significant initiative to this effect has been the series of Conferences on the Humanitarian Impact of Nuclear Weapons (2013–2014), which I shall survey later on in this Dissenting Opinion (cf. Part XIX, *infra*).

155. There has been a chorus of voices of those who have been personally victimized by nuclear weapons in distinct circumstances, – either in the atomic bombings of Hiroshima and Nagasaki (1945), or in nuclear testing (during the cold-war era) in regions such as Central Asia and the Pacific. Focusing on their intensive suffering (e.g., ensuing from radioactive contamination and forced displacement),¹⁶⁹ affecting successive generations, they have drawn attention to the humanitarian consequences of nuclear weapon detonations.

156. In addressing the issue of nuclear weapons, on four successive occasions (cf. *infra*), the ICJ appears, however, to have always suffered from inter-State myopia. Despite the clarity of the formidable threat that nuclear weapons represent, the treatment of the issue of their prohibition under international law has most regrettably remained permeated by ambiguities. The present case of *Obligations Concerning Negotiations Relating to Cessation of the Nuclear Arms*

---

166 Michihiko Hachiya, *Journal d'Hiroshima – 6 août-30 septembre 1945* [1955], Paris, Éd. Tallandier, 2015 [reed.], pp. 25–281; Toyofumi Ogura, *Letters from the End of the World – A Firsthand Account of the Bombing of Hiroshima* [1948], Tokyo/N.Y./London, Kodansha International, 2001 [reed.], pp. 15–173; Naomi Shohno, *The Legacy of Hiroshima – Its Past, Our Future*, Tokyo, Kösei Publ. Co., 1987 [reed.], pp. 13–140; Kenzaburo Oe, *Notes de Hiroshima* [1965], [Paris,] Gallimard, 1996 [reed.], pp. 17–230; J. Hersey, *Hiroshima* [1946], London, Penguin, 2015 [reprint], pp. 1–98.
167 Kenzaburo Oe, *Hiroshima Notes* [1965], N.Y./London, Marion Boyars, 1997 [reed.], pp. 72 and 159.
168 *Ibid.*, pp. 149 and 162.
169 Cf. J. Borrie, "Humanitarian Reframing of Nuclear Weapons and the Logic of a Ban", 90 *International Affairs* (2014) p. 633, and cf. pp. 637, 643–644 and 646.

Race and to Nuclear Disarmament is the third time that attempts were made, by means of the lodging of contentious cases with the ICJ, to obtain its pronouncement thereon. On two prior occasions – in the *Nuclear Tests* cases (1974 and 1995),[170] the Court assumed, in both of them, a rather evasive posture, avoiding to pronounce clearly on the substance of a matter pertaining to the very survival of humankind.

157. May I here briefly single out one aspect of those earlier contentious proceedings, given its significance in historical perspective. It should not pass unnoticed that, in the first *Nuclear Tests* case (Australia and New Zealand *versus* France), one of the applicant States contended, *inter alia*, that the nuclear testing undertaken by the French government in the South Pacific region violated not only the right of New Zealand that no radioactive material enter its territory, air space and territorial waters *and* those of other Pacific territories but *also* "the rights of all members of the international community, including New Zealand, that no nuclear tests that give rise to radioactive fall-out be conducted".[171]

158. For its part, the other applicant State contended that it was seeking protection to the life, health and well-being of Australia's population, in common with the populations of other States, against atmospheric nuclear tests by any State.[172] Thus, over three decades ago, the perspective of the *Applications Instituting Proceedings* of both New Zealand and Australia (of 1973) went clearly – and correctly so – beyond the purely inter-State dimension, as the problem at issue concerned the international community as a whole.

159. Both Australia and New Zealand insisted on the people-centred approach throughout the legal proceedings (written and oral phases). New Zealand, for example, in its *Memorial*, invoked the obligation *erga omnes* not to undertake nuclear testing "owed to the international community as a whole" (paras. 207–208), adding that non-compliance with it aroused "the keenest sense of alarm and antagonism among the peoples" and States of the region wherein the tests were conducted (para. 212). In its oral arguments in the public sitting

---

170 Cf. *I.C.J. Reports 1974*, pp. 63–455; and cf. *I.C.J. Reports 1995*, pp. 4–23, and the position of three dissenting Judges in *ibid.*, pp. 317–421.
171 ICJ, *Application Instituting Proceedings* (of 09.05.1973), *Nuclear Tests* case (New Zealand *versus* France), pp. 8 and 15–16, cf. pp. 4–16.
172 ICJ, *Application Instituting Proceedings* (of 09.05.1973), *Nuclear Tests* case (Australia *versus* France), pp. 12 and 14, paras. 40, 47 and 49(1).

of 10.07.1974 in the same *Nuclear Tests* case, New Zealand again invoked "the rights of all members of the international community", and the obligations *erga omnes* owed to the international community as a whole.[173] And Australia, for example, in its oral arguments in the public sitting of 08.07.1974, referring to the 1963 Partial Test Ban Treaty, underlined the concern of "the whole international community" for "the future of mankind" and the responsibility imposed by "the principles of international law" upon "all States to refrain from testing nuclear weapons in the atmosphere".[174]

160. The outcome of the *Nuclear Test* cases, however, was rather disappointing: even though the ICJ issued orders of Provisional Measures of Protection in the cases in June 1973 (requiring the respondent State to cease testing), subsequently, in its Judgments of 1974,[175] in view of the announcement of France's voluntary discontinuance of its atmospheric tests, the ICJ found, yielding to State voluntarism, that the claims of Australia and New Zealand no longer had "any object" and that it was thus not called upon to give a decision thereon.[176] The dissenting Judges in the case rightly pointed out that the legal dispute between the contending parties, far from having ceased, still persisted, since what Australia and New Zealand sought was a declaratory judgment of the ICJ stating that atmospheric nuclear tests were contrary to international law.[177]

---

[173] ICJ, *Pleadings, Oral Arguments, Documents – Nuclear Tests cases* (vol. II: New Zealand *versus* France, 1973–1974), pp. 256–257 and 264–266.

[174] ICJ, *Pleadings, Oral Arguments, Documents – Nuclear Tests cases* (vol. I: Australia *versus* France, 1973–1974), p. 503.

[175] For a critical parallel between the 1973 Orders and the 1974 Judgments, cf. P. Lellouche, "The *Nuclear Tests* Cases: Judicial Silence *versus* Atomic Blasts", 16 *Harvard International Law Journal* (1975) pp. 615–627 and 635; and, for further criticisms, cf. *ibid.*, pp. 614–637.

[176] *I.C.J. Reports 1974*, pp. 272 and 478, respectively.

[177] ICJ, *Nuclear Tests* case, Joint Dissenting Opinion of Judges Onyeama, Dillard, Jiménez de Aréchaga and Waldock, *I.C.J. Reports 1974*, pp. 319–322, 367–369, 496, 500, 502–504, 514 and 520–521; and cf. Dissenting Opinion of Judge De Castro, *ibid.*, pp. 386–390; and Dissenting Opinion of Judge Barwick, *ibid.*, pp. 392–394, 404–405, 436–437 and 525–528. It was further pointed out that the ICJ should thus have dwelt upon the question of the existence of rules of *customary* international law prohibiting States from causing, through atmospheric nuclear tests, the deposit of radio-active fall-out on the territory of other States; ICJ, *Nuclear Tests* case, Separate Opinion of Judge Petrén, *I.C.J. Reports 1974*, pp. 303–306 and 488–489. It was the existence or otherwise of such customary rules that had to be determined, – a question which unfortunately was left largely unanswered by the Court in that case.

161. The reticent position of the ICJ in that case was even more regrettable if one recalls that the applicants, in referring to the "psychological injury" caused to the peoples of the South Pacific region through their "anxiety as to the possible effects of radioactive fall-out on the well-being of themselves and their descendants", as a result of the atmospheric nuclear tests, ironically invoked the notion of *erga omnes* obligations (as propounded by the ICJ itself in its *obiter dicta* in the *Barcelona Traction* case only four years earlier).[178] As the ICJ reserved itself the right, in certain circumstances, to reopen the case decided in 1974, it did so two decades later, upon an application instituted by New Zealand *versus* France. But in its Order of 22.09.1995, the ICJ dismissed the complaint, as it did not fit into the *caveat* of the 1974 Judgment, which concerned atmospheric nuclear tests; here, the complaint was directed against the underground nuclear tests conducted by France since 1974.[179]

162. The ICJ thus lost two historical opportunities, in both contentious cases (1974 and 1995), to clarify the key point at issue (nuclear tests). And now, with the decision it has just rendered today, 05.10.2016, it has lost a third occasion, this time to pronounce on the *Obligations Concerning Negotiations Relating to Cessation of the Nuclear Arms Race and to Nuclear Disarmament*, at the request of the Marshall Islands. This time the Court has found that the existence of a legal dispute has not been established before it and that it has no jurisdiction to consider the Application lodged with it by the Marshall Islands on 24.04.2014.

163. Furthermore, in the mid-nineties, the Court was called upon to exercise its advisory function, in respect of a directly related issue, that of nuclear weapons: both the U.N. General Assembly and the World Health Organization (WHO) opened those proceedings before the ICJ, by means of requests for an Advisory Opinion. Such requests no longer referred to nuclear tests, but rather to the question of the threat or use of nuclear weapons in the light of international law, for the determination of their illegality or otherwise.

---

178   As recalled in the Joint Dissenting Opinion of Judges Onyeama, Dillard, Jiménez de Aréchaga and Waldock, *I.C.J. Reports 1974*, pp. 362, 368–369 and 520–521; as well as in the Dissenting Opinion of Judge Barwick, *ibid.*, pp. 436–437.

179   Cf. *I.C.J. Reports 1995* pp. 288–308; once again, there were Dissenting Opinions (cf. *ibid.*, pp. 317–421). Furthermore, petitions against the French nuclear tests in the atoll of Mururoa and in that of Fangataufa, in French Polinesia, were lodged with the European Commission of Human Rights (EComHR); cf. EComHR, case *N.N. Tauira and 18 Others versus France* (appl. n. 28204/95), decision of 04.12.1995, 83-A *Decisions and Reports* (1995) p. 130.

164. In response to only one of the applications, that of the U.N. General Assembly,[180] the Court, in the Advisory Opinion of 08.07.1996 on the *Threat or Use of Nuclear Weapons*, affirmed that neither customary international law nor conventional international law authorizes specifically the threat or use of nuclear weapons; neither one, nor the other, contains a complete and universal prohibition of the threat or use of nuclear weapons as such; it added that such threat or use which is contrary to Article 2(4) of the U.N. Charter and does not fulfil the requisites of its Article 51, is illicit; moreover, the conduct in armed conflicts should be compatible with the norms applicable in them, including those of International Humanitarian Law; it also affirmed the obligation to undertake in good will negotiations conducive to nuclear disarmament in all its aspects.[181]

165. In the most controversial part of its Advisory Opinion (resolutory point 2E), the ICJ stated that the threat or use of nuclear weapons "would be generally contrary to the rules of international law applicable in armed conflict", mainly those of International Humanitarian Law; however, the Court added that, at the present stage of international law "it cannot conclude definitively if the threat or use of nuclear weapons would be lawful or unlawful in an extreme circumstance of self defence in which the very survival of a State would be at stake".[182] The Court therein limited itself to record the existence of a legal uncertainty.

166. In fact, it did not go further than that, and the Advisory Opinion was permeated with evasive ambiguities, not avoiding the shadow of the *non liquet*, in relation to a question which affects, more than each State individually, the whole of humankind. The Advisory Opinion made abstraction of the fact that International Humanitarian Law applies likewise in case of self-defence, always safeguarding the principles of distinction and proportionality (which nuclear weapons simply ignore),[183] and upholding the prohibition of infliction of unnecessary suffering.

---

180 As the ICJ understood, as to the other application, that the WHO was not competent to deal with the question at issue, – despite the purposes of that U.N. specialized agency at issue and the devastating effects of nuclear weapons over human health and the environment...

181 *I.C.J. Reports 1996*, pp. 266-267.

182 *Ibid.*, p. 266.

183 L. Doswald-Beck, "International Humanitarian Law and the Advisory Opinion of the International Court of Justice on the Legality of the Threat or Use of Nuclear Weapons", 316 *International Review of the Red Cross* (1997) pp. 35-55; H. Fujita, "The Advisory Opinion

167. The Advisory Opinion could and should have given greater weight to a point made before the ICJ in the oral arguments of November 1995, namely, that of the need of a people-centred approach in the present domain. Thus, it was stated, for example, that the "experience of the Marshallese people confirms that unnecessary suffering is an unavoidable consequence of the detonation of nuclear weapons";[184] the effects of nuclear weapons, by their nature, are widespread, adverse and indiscriminate, affecting also future generations.[185] It was further stated that the "horrifying evidence" of the use of atomic bombs in Hiroshima and Nagasaki, followed by the experience and the aftermath of the nuclear tests carried out in the region of the Pacific Island States in the 1950s and the 1960s, have alerted to "the much graver risks to which mankind is exposed by the use of nuclear weapons".[186]

168. The 1996 Opinion, on the one hand, recognized that nuclear weapons cause indiscriminate and durable suffering, and have an enormous destructive effect (para. 35), and that the principles of humanitarian law (encompassing customary law) are "intransgressible" (para. 79); nevertheless, these considerations did not appear sufficient to the Court to discard the use of such weapons also in self-defence, thus eluding to tell what the Law is in all circumstances. It is clear to me that States are bound to respect, and to ensure respect, for International Humanitarian Law (IHL) and the International Law of Human Rights (ILHR) in *any circumstances*; their fundamental principles belong to the domain of *jus cogens*, in prohibition of nuclear weapons.

169. Again, in the 1996 Opinion, it were the dissenting Judges, and not the Court's split majority, who drew attention to this,[187] and to the relevance of the

---

of the International Court of Justice on the Legality of Nuclear Weapons", *in ibid.*, pp. 56–64. International Humanitarian Law prevails also over self-defence; cf. M.-P. Lanfranchi and Th. Christakis, *La licéité de l'emploi d'armes nucléaires devant la Cour Internationale de Justice*, Aix-Marseille/Paris, Université d'Aix-Marseille III/Economica, 1997, pp. 111, 121 and 123; S. Mahmoudi, "The International Court of Justice and Nuclear Weapons", 66 *Nordic Journal of International Law* (1997) pp. 77–100; E. David, "The Opinion of the International Court of Justice on the Legality of the Use of Nuclear Weapons", 316 *International Review of the Red Cross* (1997) pp. 21–34.

184 ICJ, doc. CR 95/32, of 14.11.1995, p. 22 (statement of the Marshall Islands).
185 *Ibid.*, p. 23.
186 ICJ, doc. CR 95/32, of 14.11.1995, p. 31 (statement of Solomon Islands). Customary international law and general principles of international law have an incidence in this domain; *ibid.*, pp. 36 and 39–40.
187 ICJ Advisory Opinion on *Threat or Use of Nuclear Weapons, I.C.J Reports 1996*, Dissenting Opinion of Judge Koroma, pp. 573–574 and 578.

Martens clause in the present context[188] (cf. Part XIV, *infra*). Moreover, the 1996 Opinion also minimized (para. 71) the resolutions of the U.N. General Assembly which affirm the illegality of nuclear weapons[189] and condemn their use as a violation of the U.N. Charter and as a crime against humanity. Instead, it took note of the "policy of deterrence", which led it to find that the members of the international community continued "profoundly divided" on the matter, rendering it rendered impossible to determine the existence of an *opinio juris* in this respect (para. 67).

170. It was not incumbent upon the Court to resort to the unfounded strategy of "deterrence" (cf. Part XII, *supra*), devoid of any legal value for the determination of the formation of a customary international law obligation of prohibition of the use of nuclear weapons. The Court did not contribute on this matter. In unduly relying on "deterrence" (para. 73), it singled out a division, in its view "profound", between an extremely reduced group of nuclear powers on the one hand, and the vast majority of the countries of the world on the other; it ended up by favouring the former, by means of an inadmissible *non liquet*.[190]

171. The Court, thus, lost yet another opportunity, – in the exercise of its advisory function as well, – to contribute to the consolidation of the *opinio juris communis* in condemnation of nuclear weapons. Its 1996 Advisory Opinion considered the survival of a hypothetical State (in its resolutory point 2E), rather than that of peoples and individuals, and ultimately of humankind as a whole. It seemed to have overlooked that the survival of a State cannot have primacy over the right to survival of humankind as a whole.

3 The Prohibition of Nuclear Weapons: The Fundamental Right to Life

172. There is yet another related point to keep in mind. The ICJ's 1996 Advisory Opinion erroneously took IHL as *lex specialis* (para. 25), overstepping the ILHR,

---

188 Cf. *ibid.*, Dissenting Opinions of Judge Shahabuddeen, pp. 386–387, 406, 408, 410–411 and 425; and of Judge Weeramantry, pp. 477–478, 481, 483, 486–487, 490–491, 494, 508 and 553–554.

189 Notably, the ground-breaking General Assembly resolution 1653(XVI), of 24.11.1961.

190 A.A. Cançado Trindade, *International Law for Humankind – Towards a New Jus Gentium*, op. cit. supra n. (120), pp. 415–418; L. Condorelli, "Nuclear Weapons: A Weighty Matter for the International Court of Justice – *Jura Novit Curia*?", 316 *International Review of the Red Cross* (1997) pp. 9–20; M. Mohr, "Advisory Opinion of the International Court of Justice on the Legality of the Use of Nuclear Weapons under International Law – A Few Thoughts on Its Strengths and Weaknesses", 316 *International Review of the Red Cross* (1997) pp. 92–102. The Opinion is not conclusive and provides no guidance; J.-P. Queneudec, "E.T. à la C.I.J.: méditations d'un extra-terrestre sur deux avis consultatifs", 100 *Revue générale de Droit international public* (1996) 907–914, esp. p. 912.

oblivious that the maxim *lex specialis derogat generalis*, thus understood, has no application in the present context: in face of the immense threat of nuclear weapons to human life on earth, both IHL and the ILHR apply in a converging way,[191] so as to enhance the much-needed protection of human life. In any circumstances, the norms which best protect are the ones which apply, be them of IHL or of the ILHR, or any other branch of international protection of the human person (such as the International Law of Refugees – ILR). They are all equally important. Regrettably, the 1996 Advisory Opinion unduly minimized the international case-law and the whole doctrinal construction on the right to life in the ambit of the ILHR.

173. It should not pass unnoticed, in this connection, that contemporary international human rights tribunals, such as the European (ECtHR) and the Inter-American (IACtHR) Courts of Human Rights, in the adjudication of successive cases in recent years, have taken into account the relevant principles and norms of both the ILHR and IHL (conventional and customary). For its part, the African Commission of Human and Peoples' Rights (AfComHPR), in its long-standing practice, has likewise acknowledged the approximations and convergences between the ILHR and IHL, and drawn attention to the principles underlying both branches of protection (such as, e.g., the principle of humanity).

174. This has been done, in distinct continents, so as to seek to secure the most effective safeguard of the protected rights, in all circumstances (including in times of armed conflict). Contrary to what was held in the ICJ's 1996 Advisory Opinion, there is no *lex specialis* here, but rather a concerted endeavour to apply the relevant norms (be them of the ILHR or of IHL) that best protect human beings. This is particularly important when they find themselves in a situation of utmost vulnerability, – such as in the present context of threat or use of nuclear weapons. In their case-law, international human rights tribunals (like the ECtHR and the IACtHR) have focused attention on the imperative of securing protection, e.g., to the fundamental right to life, of persons in great vulnerability (potential victims).[192]

---

191   Cf. A.A. Cançado Trindade, *Derecho Internacional de los Derechos Humanos, Derecho Internacional de los Refugiados y Derecho Internacional Humanitario – Aproximaciones y Convergencias*, Geneva, ICRC, [2000], pp. 1–66.

192   Cf. A.A. Cançado Trindade, *The Access of Individuals to International Justice*, Oxford, Oxford University Press, 2012 [reprint], Chs. II–III and VII, pp. 17–62 and 125–131.

175. In the course of the proceedings before the ICJ in the present cases of *Obligations* Concerning Negotiations Relating to Cessation of the Nuclear Arms Race and to Nuclear Disarmament, the applicant State draws attention reiteratedly to the devastating effects upon human life of nuclear weapons detonations. Thus, in the case opposing the Marshall Islands to the United Kingdom, the applicant State draws attention, in its Memorial, to the destructive effects of nuclear weapons (testing) in space and time (pp. 12–14). In its oral arguments of 11.03.2016, the Marshall Islands addresses the "tragic losses to the Marshallese", the "dire health consequences suffered by the Marshallese following nuclear contamination, including extreme birth defects and cancers".[193]

176. In the case opposing the Marshall Islands to India, the applicant State, in its *Memorial*, refers to the grave "health and environmental consequences of nuclear testing" upon the Marshallese (pp. 5–6). In its oral arguments of 07.03.2016, the Marshall Islands stated:

> The Marshall Islands has a unique and devastating history with nuclear weapons. While it was designated as a Trust Territory by the United Nations, no fewer than 67 atomic and thermonuclear weapons were deliberately exploded as 'tests' in the Marshall Islands, by the United States. (...) Several islands in my country were vaporized and others are estimated to remain uninhabitable for thousands of years. Many, many Marshallese died, suffered birth defects never before seen and battled cancers resulting from the contamination. Tragically the Marshall Islands thus bears *eyewitness* to the horrific and indiscriminate lethal capacity of these weapons, and the intergenerational and continuing effects that they perpetuate even 60 years later.
>
> One 'test' in particular, called the 'Bravo' test [in March 1954], was one thousand times stronger than the bombs dropped on Hiroshima and Nagasaki.[194]

177. And in the case opposing the Marshall Islands to Pakistan, the applicant State, in its *Memorial*, likewise addresses the serious "health and environmental consequences of nuclear testing" upon the Marshallese (pp. 5–6). In its oral arguments of 08.03.2016, the Marshall Islands recalls the 67 atomic and thermonuclear weapons "tests" that it had to endure (since it became a U.N. Trust Territory); it further recalls the reference, in the U.N. Charter, to nations

---

193 ICJ, doc. CR 2016/5, of 11.03.2016, p. 9, para. 10.
194 ICJ, doc. CR 2016/1, of 07.03.2016, p. 16, paras. 4–5.

"large and small" having "equal rights" (preamble), and to the assertion in its Article 2 that the United Nations is "based on the principle of the sovereign equality of all its Members".[195]

178. Two decades earlier, in the course of the advisory proceedings before the ICJ of late 1995 preceding the 1996 Advisory Opinion on the *Threat or Use of Nuclear Weapons*, the devastating effects upon human life of nuclear weapons detonations were likewise brought to the Court's attention. It is beyond the purposes of the present Dissenting Opinion to review all statements to this effect; suffice it here to recall two of the most moving statements, from the Mayors of Hiroshima and Nagasaki, who appeared before the Court as members of the Delegation of Japan. The Mayor of Hiroshima (Mr. Takashi Hiraoka) thus began his statement of 07.11.1995 before the ICJ:

> I am here today representing Hiroshima citizens, who desire the abolition of nuclear weapons. More particularly, I represent the hundreds of thousands of victims whose lives were cut short, and survivors who are still suffering the effects of radiation, 50 years later. On their behalf, I am here to testify to the cruel, inhuman nature of nuclear weapons. (...)
>
> The development of the atomic bomb was the product of cooperation among politicians, military and scientists. The nuclear age began the moment the bombs were dropped on human beings.
>
> Their enormous destructive power reduced utterly innocent civilian populations to ashes. Women, the elderly, and the newborn were bathed in deadly radiation and slaughtered.[196]

179. After stressing that the mass killing was "utterly indiscriminate", he added that, even today, "thousands of people struggle daily with the curse of illness caused by that radiation", there being until then "no truly accurate casualty figures".[197] The exposure in Hiroshima to high levels of radiation, – he proceeded, – "was the first in human history", generating leukemia, distinct kinds of cancer (of breast, lung, stomach, thyroid, and other), extending for "years or decades", with all the fear generated by such continuing killing "across years or decades".[198]

---

195 ICJ, doc. CR 2016/2, of 08.03.2016, p. 10, paras. 5–7.
196 ICJ, doc. CR 95/27, of 07.11.1995, pp. 22–23.
197 *Ibid.*, pp. 24–25.
198 *Ibid.*, pp. 25–27.

180. Even half a century later, – added the Mayor of Hiroshima, – "the effects of radiation on human bodies are not thoroughly understood. Medically, we do know that radiation destroys cells in the human body, which can lead to many forms of pathology".[199] The victimized segments of the population have continued suffering "psychologically, physically, and socially from the atomic bomb's after-effects".[200] He further stated that

> The horror of nuclear weapons (...) derives (...) from the tremendous destructive power, but equally from radiation, the effects of which reach across generations. (...) What could be more cruel? Nuclear weapons are more cruel and inhumane than any weapon banned thus far by international law.[201]

181. After singling out the significance of U.N. General Assembly resolution 1653 (XVI) of 1961, the Mayor of Hiroshima warned that "[t]he stockpiles of nuclear weapons on earth today are enough to annihilate the entire human race several times over. These weapons are possessed on the assumption that they can be used".[202] He concluded with a strong criticism of the strategy of "deterrence"; in his own words,

> As long as nuclear weapons exist, the human race faces a real and present danger of self-extermination. The idea based on nuclear deterrence that nuclear war can be controlled and won exhibits a failure of human intelligence to comprehend the human tragedy and global environmental destruction brought about by nuclear war. (...) [O]nly through a treaty that clearly stipulates the abolition of nuclear weapons can the world step toward the future (...).[203]

182. For his part, the Mayor of Nagasaki (Mr. Iccho Itoh), in his statement before the ICJ, also of 07.11.1995, likewise warned that "nuclear weapons bring enormous, indiscriminate devastation to civilian populations"; thus, five decades ago, in Hiroshima and Nagasaki, "a single aircraft dropped a single bomb and snuffed out the lives of 140.000 and 74.000 people, respectively. And that is not all. Even the people who were lucky enough to survive continue

---

199   Ibid., p. 25.
200   Ibid., pp. 27–28.
201   Ibid., p. 30.
202   Ibid., pp. 30–31.
203   Ibid., p. 31.

to this day to suffer from the late effects unique to nuclear weapons. In this way, nuclear weapons bring enormous, indiscriminate devastation to civilian populations".[204]

183. He added that "the most fundamental difference between nuclear and conventional weapons is that the former release radioactive rays at the time of explosion", and the exposure to large doses of radiation generates a "high incidence of disease" and mortality (such as leukaemia and cancer). Descendants of atomic bomb survivors will have, amidst anxiety, "to be monitored for several generations to clarify the genetic impact"; "nuclear weapons are inhuman tools for mass slaughter and destruction", their use "violates international law".[205] The Mayor of Nagasaki concluded with a strong criticism of "nuclear deterrence", characterizing it as "simply the maintenance of a balance of fear" (p. 37), always threatening peace, with its "psychology of suspicion and intimidation"; the Nagasaki survivors of the atomic bombing of 50 years ago, "continue to live in fear of late effects".[206]

184. Those testimonies before the ICJ, in the course of contentious proceedings (in 2016) as well as advisory proceedings (two decades earlier, in 1995), leave it quite clear that the threat or use (including "testing") of nuclear weapons entails an arbitrary deprivation of human life, and is in flagrant breach of the fundamental right to life. It is in manifest breach of the ILHR, of IHL, as well as the Law of the United Nations, and hand an incidence also on the ILR. There are, furthermore, in such grave breach, aggravating circumstances: the harm caused by radiation from nuclear weapons cannot be contained in space, nor can it be contained in time, it is a true inter-generational harm.

185. As pointed out in the pleadings before the ICJ of late 1995, the use of nuclear weapons thus violates the right to life (and the right to health) of "not only people currently living, but also of the unborn, of those to be born, of subsequent generations".[207] Is there anything quintessentially more cruel? To use nuclear weapons appears like condemning innocent persons to hell on earth, even *before* they are born. That seems to go even further than the Book of *Genesis*'s story of the original sin. In reaction to such extreme cruelty, the

---

204 ICJ, doc. CR 95/27, of 07.11.1995, p. 33.
205 *Ibid.*, pp. 36–37.
206 *Ibid.*, pp. 39.
207 ICJ, doc. CR 95/35, of 15.11.1995, p. 28 (statement of Zimbabwe).

consciousness of the rights inherent to the human person has always marked a central presence in endeavours towards complete nuclear disarmament.

4   The Absolute Prohibitions of Jus Cogens and the Humanization of International Law

186. The absolute prohibition of arbitrary deprivation of human life (*supra*) is one of *jus cogens*, originating in the ILHR, and with an incidence also on IHL and the ILR, and marking presence also in the Law of the United Nations. The absolute prohibition of inflicting cruel, inhuman or degrading treatment is one of *jus cogens*, originating likewise in the ILHR, and with an incidence also on IHL and the ILR. The absolute prohibition of inflicting unnecessary suffering is one of *jus cogens*, originating in IHL, and with an incidence also on the ILHR and the ILR.

187. In addition to those converging trends (ILHR, IHL, ILR) of international protection of the rights of the human person, those prohibitions of *jus cogens* mark presence also in contemporary International Criminal Law (ICL), as well as in the *corpus juris gentium* of condemnation of all weapons of mass destruction. The absolute prohibitions of *jus cogens* nowadays encompass the threat or use of nuclear weapons, for all the human suffering they entail: in the case of their use, a suffering without limits in space or in time, and extending to succeeding generations.

188. I have been characterizing, along the years, the doctrinal and jurisprudential construction of international *jus cogens* as proper of the new *jus gentium* of our times, the International Law for Humankind. I have been sustaining, moreover, that, by definition, international *jus cogens* goes beyond the law of treaties, extending itself to the law of the international responsibility of the State, and to the whole *corpus juris* of contemporary International Law, and reaching, ultimately, any juridical act.[208]

189. In my lectures in an OAS Course of International Law delivered in Rio de Janeiro almost a decade ago, e.g., I have deemed it fit to ponder that

> The fact that the concepts both of the *jus cogens*, and of the obligations (and rights) *erga omnes* ensuing therefrom, already integrate the conceptual universe of contemporary international law, the new *jus gentium* of

---

208   A.A. Cançado Trindade, *International Law for Humankind – Towards a New Jus Gentium*, op. cit. supra n. (120), Ch. XII, pp. 291–326.

our days, discloses the reassuring and necessary opening of this latter, in the last decades, to certain superior and fundamental values. This significant evolution of the recognition and assertion of norms of *jus cogens* and obligations *erga omnes* of protection is to be fostered, seeking to secure its full practical application, to the benefit of all human beings. In this way the universalist vision of the founding fathers of the *droit des gens* is being duly rescued. New conceptions of the kind impose themselves in our days, and, of their faithful observance, will depend to a large extent the future evolution of contemporary international law.

This latter does not emanate from the inscrutable 'will' of the States, but rather, in my view, from human conscience. General or customary international law emanates not so much from the practice of States (not devoid of ambiguities and contradictions), but rather from the *opinio juris communis* of all the subjects of international law (States, international organizations, human beings, and humankind as a whole). Above the will stands the conscience. (...)

The current process of the necessary *humanization* of international law stands in reaction to that state of affairs. It bears in mind the universality and unity of the human kind, which inspired, more than four and a half centuries ago, the historical process of formation of the *droit des gens*. In rescuing the universalist vision which marked the origins of the most lucid doctrine of international law, the aforementioned process of humanization contributes to the construction of the new *jus gentium* of the XXIst century, oriented by the general principles of law. This process is enhanced by its own conceptual achievements, such as, to start with, the acknowledgement and recognition of *jus cogens* and the consequent obligations *erga omnes* of protection, followed by other concepts disclosing likewise a universalist perspective of the law of nations.

(...) The emergence and assertion of *jus cogens* in contemporary international law fulfill the necessity of a minimum of verticalization in the international legal order, erected upon pillars in which the juridical and the ethical are merged. The evolution of the concept of *jus cogens* transcends nowadays the ambit of both the law of treaties and the law of the international responsibility of the States, so as to reach general international law and the very foundations of the international legal order.[209]

---

[209] A.A. Cançado Trindade, "*Jus Cogens*: The Determination and the Gradual Expansion of Its Material Content in Contemporary International Case-Law", in XXXV *Curso de Derecho Internacional Organizado por el Comité Jurídico Interamericano – 2008*, Washington D.C., OAS General Secretariat, 2009, pp. 3–29.

5 *Pitfalls of Legal Positivism: A Rebuttal of the So-Called* Lotus *"Principle"*

190. A matter which concerns the whole of humankind, such as that of the existence of nuclear weapons, can no longer be appropriately dealt with from a purely inter-State outlook of international law, which is wholly surpassed in our days. After all, without humankind there is no State whatsoever; one cannot simply have in mind States, apparently overlooking humankind. In its 1996 Advisory Opinion, the ICJ took note of the treaties which nowadays prohibit, e.g., biological and chemical weapons,[210] and weapons which cause excessive damages or have indiscriminate effects (para. 76).[211]

191. But the fact that nowadays, in 2016, there does not yet exist a similar general treaty, of specific prohibition of nuclear weapons, does not mean that these latter are permissible (in certain circumstances, even in self defence).[212] In my understanding, it cannot be sustained, in a matter which concerns the future of humankind, that which is not expressly prohibited is thereby permitted (a classic postulate of positivism). This posture would amount to the traditional – and surpassed – attitude of the *laisser-faire, laisser-passer*, proper of an international legal order fragmented by State voluntarist subjectivism, which in the history of international law has invariably favoured the most powerful ones. *Ubi societas, ibi jus...*

192. Legal positivists, together with the so-called "realists" of *Realpolitik*, have always been sensitive to the established power, rather than to values. They overlook the time dimension, and are incapable to behold a universalist perspective. They are static, in time and space. Nowadays, in the second decade of the XXIst century, in an international legal order which purports to assert common superior values, amidst considerations of international *ordre public*, and basic considerations of humanity, it is precisely the reverse logic which is to prevail: *that which is not permitted, is prohibited.*[213]

---

210 The Geneva Protocol of 1925, and the Conventions of 1972 and 1993 against Biological and Chemical Weapons, respectively.

211 E.g., the 1980 Convention on Prohibitions or Restrictions on the Use of Certain Conventional Weapons Which May Be Deemed to Be Excessively Injurious or to Have Indiscriminate Effects.

212 The Roman-privatist influence – with its emphasis on the autonomy of the will had harmful consequences in traditional international law; in the public domain, quite on the contrary, conscience stands above the "will", also in the determination of competences.

213 A.A. Cançado Trindade, *O Direito Internacional em um Mundo em Transformação*, Rio de Janeiro, Edit. Renovar, 2002, p. 1099.

193. Even in the days of the *Lotus* case (1927), the view endorsed by the old PCIJ whereby under international law everything that was not expressly prohibited would thereby be permitted, was object of severe criticisms, not only of a compelling Dissenting Opinion in the case itself[214] but also on the part of expert writing of the time.[215] Such conception could only have flourished in an epoch "politically secure" in global terms, certainly quite different from that of the current nuclear age, in face of the recurrent threat of nuclear weapons and other weapons of mass destruction, the growing vulnerability of territorial States and indeed of the world population, and the increasing complexity in the conduction of international relations. In our days, in face of such terrifying threat, it is the logic opposite to that of the *Lotus* case which imposes itself: all that is not expressly permitted is surely prohibited.[216] All weapons of mass destruction, including nuclear weapons, are illegal and prohibited under contemporary international law.

194. The case of *Shimoda and Others* (District Court of Tokyo, decision of 07.12.1963), with the dismissed claims of five injured survivors of the atomic bombings of Hiroshima and Nagasaki, stands as a grave illustration of the veracity of the maxim *summum jus, summa injuria*, when one proceeds on the basis of an allegedly absolute submission of the human person to a degenerated international legal order built on an exclusively inter-State basis. May I here reiterate what I wrote in 1981, regarding the *Shimoda and Others* case, namely,

> (...) The whole arguments in the case reflect the insufficiencies of an international legal order being conceived and erected on the basis of an exclusive inter-State system, leaving individual human beings impotent in the absence of express treaty provisions granting them procedural status at international level. Even in such a matter directly affecting fundamental human rights, the arguments were conducted in the case in the

---

214 Cf. Dissenting Opinion of Judge Loder, PCIJ, *Lotus* case (France *versus* Turkey), Series A, n. 10, Judgment of 07.09.1927, p. 34 (such conception was not in accordance with the "spirit of international law").

215 Cf. J.L. Brierly, *The Basis of Obligation in International Law and Other Papers*, Oxford, Clarendon Press, 1958, p. 144; H. Lauterpacht, *The Function of Law in the International Community*, Oxford, Clarendon Press, 1933, pp. 409–412 and 94–96; and cf., subsequently, e.g., G. Herczegh, "Sociology of International Relations and International Law", *in Questions of International Law* (ed. G. Haraszti), Budapest, Progresprint, 1971, pp. 69–71 and 77.

216 A.A. Cançado Trindade, *O Direito Internacional em um Mundo em Transformação, op. cit. supra* n. (213), p. 1099.

classical lines of the conceptual apparatus of the so-called law on diplomatic protection, in a further illustration of international legal reasoning still being haunted by the old Vattelian fiction.[217]

195. There exists nowadays an *opinio juris communis* as to the illegality of all weapons of mass destruction, including nuclear weapons, and the obligation of nuclear disarmament, under contemporary international law. There is no "gap" concerning nuclear weapons; given the indiscriminate, lasting and indescribable suffering they inflict, they are outlawed, as much as other weapons of mass destruction (biological and chemical weapons) are. The positivist outlook purporting to challenge this prohibition of contemporary general international law has long been surpassed. Nor can this matter be approached from a strictly inter-State outlook, without taking into account the condition of peoples and human beings as subjects of international law.

196. All weapons of mass destruction are illegal under contemporary international law. The threat or use of such weapons is condemned in any circumstances by the universal juridical conscience, which in my view constitutes the ultimate material source of International Law, as of all Law. This is in keeping with the conception of the formation and evolution of International Law which I have been sustaining for many years; it transcends the limitations of legal positivism, seeking to respond effectively to the needs and aspirations of the international community as a whole, and, ultimately, of all humankind.

XIV Recourse to the "Martens Clause" as an Expression of the *Raison d'Humanité*

197. Even if there was a "gap" in the law of nations in relation to nuclear weapons, – which there is not, – it is possible to fill it by resorting to general principles of law. In its 1996 Advisory Opinion, the ICJ preferred to focus on self-defence of a hypothetical individual State, instead of developing the rationale of the *Martens clause*, the purpose of which is precisely that of filling

---

217 A.A. Cançado Trindade, "The Voluntarist Conception of International Law: A Re-Assessment", 59 *Revue de droit international de sciences diplomatiques et politiques* – Geneva (1981) p. 214, and cf. pp. 212–213. On the need of a universalist perspective, cf. also Cf. K. Tanaka, "The Character or World Law in the International Court of Justice" [translated from Japanese into English by S. Murase], 15 *Japanese Annual of International Law* (1971) pp. 1–22.

gaps[218] in the light of the principles of the law of nations, the "laws of humanity" and the "dictates of public conscience" (terms of the wise premonition of Fyodor Fyodorovich von Martens,[219] originally formulated in the I Hague Peace Conference of 1899).

198. Yet, continuing recourse to the *Martens clause*, from 1899 to our days, consolidates it as an expression of the strength of human conscience. Its historical trajectory of more than one century has sought to extend protection juridically to human beings in all circumstances (even if not contemplated by conventional norms). Its reiteration for over a century in successive international instruments, besides showing that conventional and customary international law in the domain of protection of the human person go together, reveals the Martens clause as an emanation of the *material* source *par excellence* of the whole law of nations (the universal juridical conscience), giving expression to the *raison d'humanité* and imposing limits to the *raison d'État*.[220]

199. It cannot be denied that nuclear weapons are intrinsically indiscriminate, incontrollable, that they cause severe and durable damage and in a wide scale in space and time, that they are prohibited by International Humanitarian Law (Articles 35, 48 and 51 of the Additional Protocol I of 1977 to the 1949 Geneva Conventions on International Humanitarian Law), and are inhuman as weapons of mass destruction.[221] Early in the present nuclear age, the four Geneva Conventions established the *grave violations* of international law (Convention I, Article 49(3); Convention II, Article 50(3); Convention III, Article 129(3); and Convention IV, Article 146(3)). Such *grave violations*, when involving nuclear weapons, victimize not only States, but all other subjects of international law

---

218 J. Salmon, "Le problème des lacunes à la lumière de l'avis 'Licéité de la menace ou de l'emploi d'armes nucléaires' rendu le 8 juillet 1996 par la Cour Internationale de Justice", *in Mélanges en l'honneur de N. Valticos – Droit et justice* (ed. R.-J. Dupuy), Paris, Pédone, 1999, pp. 197–214, esp. pp. 208–209; R. Ticehurst, "The Martens Clause and the Laws of Armed Conflict", 317 *International Review of the Red Cross* (1997) pp. 125–134, esp. pp. 133–134; A. Azar, *Les opinions des juges dans l'Avis consultatif sur la licéité de la menace ou de l'emploi d'armes nucléaires*, Bruxelles, Bruylant, 1998, p. 61.

219 Which was intended to extend juridically the protection to the civilians and combatants in all situations, even if not contemplated by the conventional norms.

220 A.A. Cançado Trindade, *Tratado de Direito Internacional dos Direitos Humanos*, vol. II, Porto Alegre/Brazil, S.A. Fabris Ed., 1999, pp. 497–509.

221 Cf. comments *in Commentary on the Additional Protocols of 8 June 1977 to the Geneva Conventions of 12 August 1949* (eds. Y. Sandoz, C. Swinarski and B. Zimmermann), Geneva, ICRC/Nijhoff, 1987, pp. 389–420 and 597–600.

as well, individuals and groups of individuals, peoples, and humankind as a whole.

200. The absence of conventional norms stating specifically that nuclear weapons are prohibited in all circumstances does not mean that they would be allowed in a given circumstance. Two decades ago, in the course of the advisory proceedings of late 1995 before the ICJ leading to its 1996 Advisory Opinion on the *Threat or Use of Nuclear Weapons*, some of the participating States drew attention to the incidence of the Martens clause in the present domain.[222] It was pointed out, on the occasion, that the argument that international instruments do not specifically contain an express prohibition of use of nuclear weapons seems to overlook the Martens clause.[223]

201. Also in rebuttal of that argument, – typical of legal positivism, in its futile search for an express prohibition, – it was further observed that the "principles of humanity" and the "dictates of public conscience", evoked by the Martens clause, permeate not only the law of armed conflict, but "the whole of international law"; they are essentially dynamic, pointing to conduct which may nowadays be condemned as inhuman by the international community,[224] such as recourse to the threat or use of nuclear weapons. It was further stated, in the light of the Martens clause, that the "threat and use of nuclear weapons violate both customary international law and the dictates of public conscience".[225]

202. The Martens clause safeguards the integrity of Law (against the undue permissiveness of a *non liquet*) by invoking the principles of the law of nations, the "laws of humanity" and the "dictates of the public conscience". Thus, that absence of a conventional norm is not conclusive, and is by no means the end of the matter, – bearing in mind also customary international law. Such absence of a conventional provision expressly prohibiting nuclear weapons does not at all mean that they are legal or legitimate.[226] The evolution of international

---

222 Cf. ICJ, doc. CR 95/31, of 13.11.1995, pp. 45–46(statement of Samoa); ICJ, doc. CR 95/25, of 03.11.1995, p. 55 (statement of Mexico); ICJ, doc. CR 95/27, of 07.11.1995, p. 60 (statement of Malaysia).
223 ICJ, doc. 95/26, of 06.11.1995, p. 32 (statement of Iran).
224 ICJ, doc. 95/22, of 30.10.1995, p. 39 (statement of Australia).
225 ICJ, doc. 95/35, of 15.11.1995, p. 33 (statement of Zimbabwe).
226 Stefan Glaser, *L'arme nucléaire à la lumière du Droit international*, Paris, Pédone, 1964, pp. 15, 21, 24–27, 32, 36–37, 41, 43–44 and 62–63, and cf. pp. 18 and 53.

law[227] points, in our days, in my understanding, towards the construction of the International Law for humankind[228] and, within the framework of this latter, to the outlawing by general international law of all weapons of mass destruction.

203. Had the ICJ, in its 1996 Advisory Opinion on the *Threat or Use of Nuclear Weapons*, made decidedly recourse in great depth to the Martens clause, it would not have lost itself in a sterile exercise, proper of a legal positivism *déjà vu*, of a hopeless search of conventional norms, frustrated by the finding of what it understood to be a lack of these latter as to nuclear weapons specifically, for the purposes of its analysis. The existing arsenals of nuclear weapons, and of other weapons of mass destruction, are to be characterized by what they really are: a scorn and the ultimate insult to human reason, and an affront to the juridical conscience of humankind.

204. The aforementioned evolution of international law, – of which the Martens clause is a significant manifestation, – has gradually moved from an international into a universal dimension, on the basis of fundamental values, and in the sense of an *objective justice*,[229] which has always been present in jusnaturalist thinking. Human conscience stands above the "will" of individual States. This evolution has, in my perception, significantly contributed to the formation of an *opinio juris communis* in recent decades, in condemnation of nuclear weapons.

205. This *opinio juris communis* is clearly conformed in our days: the overwhelming majority of member States of the United Nations, the NNWS,

---

227   If, in other epochs, the ICJ had likewise limited itself to verify a situation of "legal uncertainty" (which, anyway, does not apply in the present context), most likely it would not have issued its *célèbres* Advisory Opinions on *Reparations for Injuries* (1949), on *Reservations to the Convention on the Prevention and Punishment of the Crime of Genocide* (1951), and on *Namibia* (1971), which have so much contributed to the evolution of international law.

228   Cf. A.A. Cançado Trindade, *International Law for Humankind – Towards a New Jus Gentium*, op. cit. supra n. (120), pp. 1–726.

229   A.A. Cançado Trindade, *Los Tribunales Internacionales Contemporáneos y la Humanización del Derecho Internacional*, Buenos Aires, Ed. Ad-Hoc, 2013, pp. 166–167; and cf. C. Husson-Rochcongar, *Droit international des droits de l'homme et valeurs – Le recours aux valeurs dans la jurisprudence des organes spécialisés*, Bruxelles, Bruylant, 2012, pp. 309–311, 451–452, 578–580, 744–745 and 771–772.

have been sustaining for years the series of General Assembly resolutions in condemnation of the use of nuclear weapons as illegal under general international law. To this we can add other developments, reviewed in the present Dissenting Opinion, such as, e.g., the NPT Review Conferences, the establishment of regional nuclear-weapon-free zones, and the Conferences on Humanitarian Impact of Nuclear Weapons (cf. parts XVII–XIX, *infra*).

XV Nuclear Disarmament: Jusnaturalism, the Humanist Conception and the Universality of International Law

206. The existence of nuclear weapons, – maintained by the strategy of "deterrence" and "mutually assured destruction" ("MAD", as it became adequately called, since it was devised in the cold-war era), is the contemporary global tragedy of the nuclear age. Death, or self-destruction, haunts everyone everywhere, propelled by human madness. Human beings need protection from themselves, today more than ever,[230] – and this brings our minds to other domains of human knowledge. Law by itself cannot provide answers to this challenge to humankind as a whole.

207. In the domain of nuclear disarmament, we are faced today, within the conceptual universe of international law, with unexplainable insufficiencies, or anomalies, if not absurdities. For example, there are fortunately in our times Conventions prohibiting biological and chemical weapons (of 1972 and 1993), but there is to date no such comprehensive conventional prohibition of nuclear weapons, which are far more destructive. There is no such prohibition despite the fact that they are in clear breach of international law, of IHL and the ILHR, as well as of the Law of the United Nations.

208. Does this make any sense? Can international law prescind from ethics? In my understanding, not at all. Just as law and ethics go together (in the line of jusnaturalist thinking), scientific knowledge itself cannot be dissociated from ethics. The production of nuclear weapons is an illustration of the divorce

---

230 In another international jurisdiction, in my Separate Opinion in the IACtHR's case of the *Massacres of Ituango versus Colombia* (Judgment of 01.07.2006), I devoted part of my reflections to "human cruelty in its distinct manifestations in the execution of State policies" (Part II, paras. 9–13).

between ethical considerations and scientific and technological progress. Otherwise, weapons which can destroy millions of innocent civilians, and the whole of humankind, would not have been conceived and produced.

209. The principles of *recta ratio*, orienting the *lex praeceptiva*, emanate from human conscience, affirming the ineluctable relationship between law and ethics. Ethical considerations are to guide the debates on nuclear disarmament. Nuclear weapons, capable of destroying humankind as a whole, carry evil in themselves. They ignore civilian populations, they make abstraction of the principles of necessity, of distinction and of proportionality. They overlook the principle of humanity. They have no respect for the fundamental right to life. They are wholly illegal and illegitimate, rejected by the *recta ratio*, which endowed *jus gentium*, in its historical evolution, with ethical foundations, and its character of universality.

210. Already in 1984, in its *general comment* n. 14 (on the right to life), the U.N. Human Rights Committee (HRC – under the Covenant on Civil and Political Rights), for example, began by warning that war and mass violence continue to be "a scourge of humanity", taking the lives of thousands of innocent human beings every year (para. 2). In successive sessions of the General Assembly, – it added, – representatives of States from all geographical regions have expressed their growing concern at the development and proliferation of "increasingly awesome weapons of mass destruction" (para. 3). Associating itself with this concern, the HRC stated that

> (...) It is evident that the designing, testing, manufacture, possession and deployment of nuclear weapons are among the greatest threats to the right to life which confront mankind today. This threat is compounded by the danger that the actual use of such weapons may be brought about, not only in the event of war, but even through human or mechanical error or failure.
>
> Furthermore, the very existence and gravity of this threat generates a climate of suspicion and fear between States, which is in itself antagonistic to the promotion of universal respect for and observance of human rights and fundamental freedoms in accordance with the Charter of the United Nations and the International Covenants on Human Rights.
>
> The production, testing, possession, deployment and use of nuclear weapons should be prohibited and recognized as crimes against humanity.

The Committee, accordingly, in the interest of mankind, calls upon all States (...) to take urgent steps (...) to rid the world of this menace (paras. 4–7).[231]

211. The absence in contemporary international law of a comprehensive conventional prohibition of nuclear weapons is incomprehensible. Contrary to what legal positivists think, law is not self-sufficient, it needs inputs from other branches of human knowledge for the realisation of justice. Contrary to what legal positivists think, norms and values go together, the former cannot prescind from the latter. Contrary to legal positivism, – may I add, – jusnaturalism, taking into account ethical considerations, pursues a universalist outlook (which legal positivists are incapable of doing), and beholds humankind as entitled to protection.[232]

212. Humankind is subject of rights, in the realm of the new *jus gentium*.[233] As this cannot be visualized from the optics of the State, contemporary international law has reckoned the limits of the State as from the optics of humankind. Natural law thinking has always been attentive to justice, which much transcends positive law. The present case of *Obligations Concerning Negotiations Relating to Cessation of the Nuclear Arms Race and to Nuclear Disarmament* has been lodged with the International Court *of Justice*, and not with

---

231 "*General Comment*" n. 14 (of 1984) of the HRC, text *in*: United Nations, *Compilation of General Comments and General Recommendations Adopted by Human Rights Treaty Bodies*, doc. HRI/GEN/1/Rev.3, of 15.08.1997, pp. 18–19. The HRC, further stressing that the right to life is a fundamental right which does not admit any derogation not even in time of public emergency, related the current proliferation of weapons of mass destruction to "the supreme duty of States to prevent wars". Cf. also U.N. *Report of the Human Rights Committee*, G.A.O.R. – 40th Session (1985), suppl. n. 40 (A/40/40), p. 162.

232 A.A. Cançado Trindade, *International Law for Humankind – Towards a New Jus Gentium*, *op. cit. supra* n. (120), pp. 1–726. *Recta ratio* and universalism, present in the jusnaturalist thinking of the "founding fathers" of international law (F. de Vitoria, F. Suárez, H. Grotius, among others), go far back in time to the legacies of Cicero, in his characterization of *recta ratio* in the foundations of *jus gentium* itself, and of Thomas Aquinas, in his conception of *synderesis*, as predisposition of human reason to be guided by principles in the search of the common good; *ibid.*, pp. 10–14.

233 *Ibid.*, Ch. XI, pp. 275–288; A.A. Cançado Trindade, "Quelques réflexions sur l'humanité comme sujet du droit international", *in Unité et diversité du Droit international – Écrits en l'honneur du Prof. P.-M. Dupuy* (eds. D. Alland, V. Chetail, O. de Frouville and J.E. Viñuales), Leiden, Nijhoff, 2014, pp. 157–173.

an International Court of Positive Law. The contemporary tragedy of nuclear weapons cannot be addressed from the myopic outlook of positive law alone.

213. Nuclear weapons, and other weapons of mass destruction, have no ethics, have no ground on the law of nations (*le droit des gens*): they are in flagrant breach of its fundamental principles, and those of IHL, the ILHR, as well as the Law of the United Nations. They are a contemporary manifestation of evil, in its perennial trajectory going back to the Book of *Genesis* (cf. Part VIII, *supra*). Jusnaturalist thinking, always open to ethical considerations, identifies and discards the disrupting effects of the strategy of "deterrence" of fear creation and infliction[234] (cf. Part XII, *supra*). Humankind is victimized by this.

214. In effect, humankind has been, already for a long time, a *potential victim* of nuclear weapons. To establish such condition of potential victim, one does not need to wait for the actual destruction of life on earth. Humankind has, for the last decades, been suffering psychological harm caused by the existence itself of arsenals of nuclear weapons. And there are peoples, and segments of populations, who have been *actual victims* of the vast and harmful effects of nuclear tests. The existence of *actual and potential victims* is acknowledged in international case-law in the domain of the International Law of Human Rights.[235] To address this danger from a strict inter-State outlook is to miss the point, to blind oneself. States were created and exist for human beings, and not *vice-versa*.

---

[234] Cf., to this effect, C.A.J. Coady, "Natural Law and Weapons of Mass Destruction", *in Ethics and Weapons of Mass Destruction – Religious and Secular Perspectives* (eds. S.H. Hashmi and S.P. Lee), Cambridge, Cambridge University Press, 2004, p. 122, and cf. p. 113; and cf. also J. Finnis, J.M. Boyle Jr. and G. Grisez, *Nuclear Deterrence, Morality and Realism*, Oxford, Clarendon Press, 1987, pp. 77–103, 207–237, 275–319 and 367–390. In effect, contemporary expert writing has become, at last, very critical of the "failed strategy" of "deterrence"; cf., *inter alia*, e.g., [Various Authors,] *At the Nuclear Precipice – Catastrophe or Transformation?* (eds. R. Falk and D. Krieger), London, Palgrave/MacMillan, 2008, pp. 162, 209, 218 and 229; A.C. Alves Pereira, *Os Impérios Nucleares e Seus Reféns: Relações Internacionais Contemporâneas*, Rio de Janeiro, Ed. Graal, 1984, pp. 87–88, and cf. pp. 154, 209 and 217.

[235] For an early study on this issue, cf. A.A. Cançado Trindade, "Co-Existence and Co-Ordination of Mechanisms of International Protection of Human Rights (At Global and Regional Levels)", 202 *Recueil des Cours de l'Académie de Droit International de La Haye* (1987), ch. XI, pp. 271–283. And for subsequent developments on the notion of *potential victims*, cf. A.A. Cançado Trindade, *The Access of Individuals to International Justice*, Oxford, Oxford University Press, 2012 [reprint], Ch. VII, pp. 125–131.

215. The NPT has a universalist vocation, and counts on everyone, as shown by its three basic principled pillars together. In effect, as soon as it was adopted, the 1968 NPT came to be seen as having been devised and concluded on the basis of those principled pillars, namely: non-proliferation of nuclear weapons (preamble and Articles I–III), peaceful use of nuclear energy (preamble and Articles IV–V), and nuclear disarmament (preamble and Article VI).[236] The antecedents of the NPT go back to the work of the U.N. General Assembly in 1953.[237] The NPT's three-pillar framework came to be reckoned as the "grand bargain" between its parties, NWS and NNWS. But soon it became a constant point of debate between NWS and NNWS parties to the NPT. In effect, the "grand bargain" came to be seen as "asymmetrical",[238] and NNWS began to criticize the very slow pace of achieving nuclear disarmament as one of the three basic principled pillars of the NPT (Article VI).[239]

216. Under the NPT, each State is required to do its due. NWS are no exception to that, if the NPT is not to become dead letter. To achieve the three interrelated goals (non-proliferation of nuclear weapons, peaceful use of nuclear energy, and nuclear disarmament) is a duty of each and every State towards humankind as a whole. It is a universal duty of conventional and customary international law in the nuclear age. There is an *opinio juris communis* to this effect, sedimented along the recent decades, and evidenced in the successive establishment, in distinct continents, of nuclear-weapon-free zones, and nowadays in the Conferences on the Humanitarian Impact of Nuclear Weapons (cf. parts XVIII–XIX, *infra*).

---

236   Articles VIII–XI, in turn, are procedural in nature.
237   In particular the speech of President D.D. Eisenhower (U.S.) to the U.N. General Assembly in 1953, as part of his plan "Atoms for Peace"; cf., e.g., I. Chernus, *Eisenhower's Atoms for Peace*, [Austin,] Texas A&M University Press, 2002, pp. 3–154.
238   J. Burroughs, *The Legal Framework for Non-Use and Elimination of Nuclear Weapons*, [N.Y.], Greenpeace International, 2006, p. 13.
239   H. Williams, P. Lewis and S. Aghlani, *The Humanitarian Impacts of Nuclear Weapons Initiative: The "Big Tent" in Disarmament*, London, Chatam House, 2015, p. 7; D.H. Joyner, "The Legal Meaning and Implications of Article VI of the Non-Proliferation Treaty", *in: Nuclear Weapons and International Law* (eds. G. Nystuen, S. Casey-Maslen and A.G. Bersagel), Cambridge, Cambridge University Press, 2014, pp. 397, 404 and 417, and cf. pp. 398–399 and 408; and cf. D.H. Joyner, *Interpreting the Nuclear Non-Proliferation Treaty*, Oxford, Oxford University Press, 2013 [reprint], pp. 2, 104 and 126, and cf. pp. 20, 26–29, 31, 97 and 124.

XVI   The Principle of Humanity and the Universalist Approach: *Jus Necessarium* Transcending the Limitations of *Jus Voluntarium*

217. In my understanding, there is no point in keeping attached to an outdated and reductionist inter-State outlook, particularly in view of the revival of the conception of the law of nations (*droit des gens*) encompassing humankind as a whole, as foreseen and propounded by the "founding fathers" of international law[240] (in the XVIth–XVIIth centuries). It would be nonsensical to try to cling to the unduly reductionist inter-State outlook in the international adjudication of a case concerning the contending parties and affecting all States, all peoples and humankind as a whole.

218. An artificial, if not fossilized, strictly inter-State mechanism of dispute-settlement cannot pretend to entail or require a (likewise) entirely inadequate and groundless inter-State reasoning. The law of nations cannot be interpreted and applied in a mechanical way, as from an exclusively inter-State paradigm. To start with, the humane ends of States cannot be overlooked. In relation to nuclear weapons, the *potential victims* are the human beings and peoples, beyond their respective States, for whom these latter were created and exist.

219. As I had the occasion to point out in another international jurisdiction, the law of nations (*droit des gens*), since its historical origins in the XVIth century, was seen as comprising not only States (emerging as they were), but also peoples, the human person (individually and in groups), and humankind as a whole.[241] The strictly inter-State outlook was devised much later on, as from the Vattelian reductionism of the mid-XVIIIth century, which became *en vogue* by the end of the XIXth century and beginning of the XXth century, with the well-known disastrous consequences – the successive atrocities victimizing human beings and peoples in distinct regions of world, – along the whole XXth century.[242] In the present nuclear age, extending for the last seven decades, humankind as a whole is threatened.

220. Within the ICJ as well, I have had also the occasion to stress the need to go beyond the inter-State outlook. Thus, in my Dissenting Opinion in the recent

---

240   A.A. Cançado Trindade, *Évolution du Droit international au droit des gens – L'accès des particuliers à la justice internationale: le regard d'un juge*, Paris, Pédone, 2008, pp. 1–187.
241   IACtHR, case of the *Community Moiwana versus Suriname* (Judgment of 15.06.2005), Separate Opinion of Judge Cançado Trindade, paras. 6–7.
242   *Ibid.*, paras. 6–7.

case of the *Application of the Convention against Genocide* (Croatia *versus* Serbia, Judgment of 03.02.2015), I have pointed out, *inter alia*, that the 1948 Convention against Genocide is not State-centric, but is rather oriented towards groups of persons, towards the victims, whom it seeks to protect (paras. 59 and 529). The humanist vision of the international legal order pursues an outlook centred on the peoples, keeping in mind the humane ends of States.

221. I have further underlined that the *principle of humanity* is deeply-rooted in the long-standing thinking of natural law (para. 69).

> Humaneness came to the fore even more forcefully in the treatment of persons in *situation of vulnerability, or even defencelessness*, such as those deprived of their personal freedom, for whatever reason. The *jus gentium*, when it emerged as amounting to the law of nations, came then to be conceived by its 'founding fathers' (F. de Vitoria, A. Gentili, F. Suárez, H. Grotius, S. Pufendorf, C. Wolff) as regulating the international community constituted by human beings socially organized in the (emerging) States and co-extensive with humankind, thus conforming the *necessary* law of the *societas gentium*.
>
> The *jus gentium*, thus conceived, was inspired by the principle of humanity *lato sensu*. Human conscience prevails over the will of individual States. Respect for the human person is to the benefit of the common good. This humanist vision of the international legal order pursued – as it does nowadays – a *people-centered outlook*, keeping in mind the *humane ends of the State*. The precious legacy of natural law thinking, evoking the right human reason (*recta ratio*), has never faded away; (paras. 73–74).

The precious legacy of natural law thinking has never vanished; despite the indifference and pragmatism of the "strategic" *droit d'étatistes* (so numerous in the legal profession nowadays), the *principle of humanity* emerged and remained in international legal thinking as an expression of the *raison d'humanité* imposing limits to the *raison d'État* (para. 74).

222. This is the position I have always taken, within the ICJ and, earlier on, the IACtHR. For example, in the ICJ's Advisory Opinion on *Judgment n. 2867 of the ILO Administrative Tribunal upon a Complaint Filed against IFAD* (of 01.02.2012), I devoted one entire part (n. XI) of my Separate Opinion to the erosion – as I perceive it – of the inter-State outlook of adjudication by the ICJ (paras. 76–81). I warned likewise in my Separate Opinion (paras. 21–23) in the case of *Whaling in the Antarctic* (Australia *versus* Japan, Order of 06.02.2013, on

New Zealand's intervention), as well as in my recent Separate Opinion (paras. 16–21 and 28–41) in the case of *Alleged Violations of Sovereign Rights and Maritime Spaces in the Caribbean Sea* (Nicaragua *versus* Colombia, Preliminary Objections, Judgment of 17.03. 2016).

223. Earlier on, within the IACtHR, I took the same position: for example, *inter alia*, in my Concurring Opinions in both the Advisory Opinion n. 16, on the *Right to Information on Consular Assistance in the Framework of the Due Process of Law* (of 01.10.1999), and the Advisory Opinion n. 18, on the *Juridical Condition and Rights of Undocumented Migrants* (of 17.09.2003), of the IACtHR, I deemed it fit to point out, – going beyond the strict inter-State dimension, – that, if non-compliance with Article 36(1)(b) of the 1963 Vienna Convention on Consular Relations takes place, it occurs to the detriment not only of a State Party but also of the human beings at issue. Such pioneering jurisprudential construction, in the line of jusnaturalist thinking, rested upon the evolving concepts of *jus cogens* and obligations *erga omnes* of protection.[243]

224. *Recta ratio* stands firmly above the "will". Human conscience, – the *recta ratio* so cultivated in jusnaturalism, – clearly prevails over the "will" and the strategies of individual States. It points to a universalist conception of the *droit des gens* (the *lex praeceptiva* for the *totus orbis*), applicable to all (States as well as peoples and individuals), given the unity of the human kind. Legal positivism, centred on State power and "will", has never been able to develop such universalist outlook, so essential and necessary to address issues of concern to humankind as a whole, such as that of the obligation of nuclear disarmament. The universal juridical conscience prevails over the "will" of individual States.

225. The "founding fathers" of the law of nations (such as, *inter alii*, F. de Vitoria, F. Suárez and H. Grotius) had in mind humankind as a whole. They conceived a universal *jus gentium* for the *totus orbis*, securing the unity of the *societas gentium*; based on a *lex praeceptiva*, the *jus gentium* was apprehended by the *recta ratio*, and conformed a true *jus necessarium*, much transcending the limitations of the *jus voluntarium*. Law ultimately emanates from the common conscience of what is juridically necessary (*opinio juris communis necessitatis*).[244] The contribution of the "founding fathers" of *jus gentium* found inspiration

---

243   Cf. comments of A.A. Cançado Trindade, *Os Tribunais Internacionais e a Realização da Justiça*, Rio de Janeiro, Edit. Renovar, 2015, pp. 463–468.
244   A.A. Cançado Trindade, *International Law for Humankind – Towards a New Jus Gentium*, op. cit. supra n. (120), pp. 137–138.

largely in the scholastic philosophy of natural law (in particular in the stoic and Thomist conception of *recta ratio* and justice), which recognized the human being as endowed with intrinsic dignity.

226. Moreover, in face of the unity of the human kind, they conceived a truly *universal* law of nations, applicable to all – States as well as peoples and individuals – everywhere (*totus orbis*). In thus contributing to the emergence of the *jus humanae societatis*, thinkers like F. de Vitoria and D. de Soto, among others, permeated their lessons with the humanist thinking that preceded them. Four and a half centuries later, their lessons remain contemporary, endowed with perennial validity and aptitude to face, e.g., the contemporary and dangerous problem of the existing arsenals of nuclear weapons. Those thinkers went well beyond the "will" of States, and rested upon the much safer foundation of human conscience (*recta ratio* and justice).

227. The conventional and customary obligation of nuclear disarmament brings to the fore another aspect: the issue of the *validity* of international legal norms is, after all, metajuridical. International law cannot simply remain indifferent to values, general principles of law and ethical considerations; it has, to start with, to identify what is *necessary*, – such as a world free of nuclear weapons, – in order to secure the survival of humankind. This *idée du droit* precedes positive international law, and is in line with jusnaturalist thinking.

228. *Opinio juris communis necessitatis* upholds a customary international law obligation to secure the survival of humankind. Conventional and customary obligations go here together. Just as customary rules may eventually be incorporated into a convention, treaty provisions may likewise eventually enter into the *corpus* of general international law. Customary obligations can either precede, or come after, conventional obligations. They evolve *pari passu*. This being so, the search for an express legal prohibition of nuclear weapons (such as the one undertaken in the ICJ's Advisory Opinion of 1996 on the *Threat or Use of Nuclear Weapons*) becomes a futile, if not senseless, exercise of legal positivism.

229. It is clear to human conscience that those weapons, which can destroy the whole of humankind, are unlawful and prohibited. They are in clear breach of *jus cogens*. And *jus cogens* was reckoned by human conscience well before it was incorporated into the two Vienna Conventions on the Law of Treaties (of 1969 and 1986). As I had the occasion to warn, three decades ago, at the 1986 U.N. Conference on the Law of Treaties between States and International

Organizations or between International Organizations, *jus cogens* is "incompatible with the voluntarist conception of international law, because that conception failed to explain the formation of rules of general international law".[245]

XVII   NPT Review Conferences

230. In fact, in the course of the written phase of the proceedings before the Court in the present case of *Obligations Concerning Negotiations Relating to Cessation of the Nuclear Arms Race and to Nuclear Disarmament*, both the Marshall Islands[246] and the United Kingdom[247] addressed, in their distinct arguments, the series of NPT Review Conferences. For its part, India also addressed the Review Conferences,[248] in particular to leave on the records its position on the matter, as explained in a statement made on 09.05.2000.

231. Likewise, in the course of the oral phase of the present proceedings before the Court in *cas d'espèce*, the applicant State, the Marshall Islands, referred to the NPT Review Conferences in its oral arguments in two of the three cases it lodged with the Court against India,[249] and the United Kingdom;[250] references to the Review Conferences were also made, for their part, in their oral arguments, by the two respondent States which participated in the public sittings before the Court, namely, India[251] and the United Kingdom.[252] Those Review Conferences conform the factual context of the *cas d'espèce*, and cannot pass unnoticed. May I thus proceed to a brief review of them.

---

245   U.N., *United Nations Conference on the Law of Treaties between States and International Organizations or between International Organizations – Official Records*, vol. I (statement by the Representative of Brazil, A.A. Cançado Trindade, of 12.03.1986), pp. 187–188, para. 18.
246   *Application Instituting Proceedings*, p. 24, para. 66; and *Memorial*, pp. 29, 56–60, 61, 63, 68–69, 71 and 73, paras. 50, 123–128, 130, 136, 150, 153, 154, 161–162 and 168; and *Statement of Observations on [U.K.'s] Preliminary Objections*, pp. 15 and 47, paras. 32 and 126.
247   *Preliminary Objections*, pp. 1–2, 10 and 23, paras. 2–3, 21 and 50.
248   *Counter-Memorial*, p. 15, para. 23 n. 49, and Annex 23.
249   ICJ. doc. CR 2016/1, of 07.03.2016, pp. 26–27 and 50, paras. 9 and 17 (M.I.); ICJ. doc. CR 2016/6, of 14.03.2016, p. 32, para. 10 (M.I.).
250   ICJ. doc. CR 2016/5, of 11.03.2016, p. 47, para. 8 (M.I.).
251   ICJ. doc. CR 2016/4, of 10.03.2016, p. 14, para. 3 (India).
252   ICJ. doc. CR 2016/7, of 09.03.2016, pp. 14–16 and 18–19, paras. 20, 22, 24, 32 and 37 (United Kingdom).

232. The NPT Review Conferences, held every five years, started in 1975. The following three Conferences of the kind were held, respectively, in 1980, 1985 and 1990, respectively.[253] The fifth of such Conferences took place in 1995, the same year that the Marshall Islands became a party to the NPT (on 30.01.1995). In one of its decisions, the 1995 NPT Conference singled out the vital role of the NPT in preventing the proliferation of nuclear weapons, and warned that the proliferation of nuclear weapons would seriously increase the danger of nuclear war.[254] For their part, NWS reaffirmed their commitment, under Article VI of the NPT, to pursue in good faith negotiations on effective measures relating to nuclear disarmament.

233. The 1995 Review Conference prolonged indefinitely the NPT, and adopted its decision on "Principles and Objectives for Nuclear Non-Proliferation and Disarmament". Yet, in its *report*, the Main Committee I (charged with the implementation of the provisions of the NPT) observed with regret that Article VI and preambular paragraphs 8–12 of the NPT had not been wholly fulfilled,[255] with the number of nuclear weapons then existing being greater than the one existing when the NPT entered into force; it further regretted "the continuing lack of progress" on relevant items of the Conference on Disarmament, and urged a commitment on the part of NWS on "no-first use and non-use of nuclear weapons with immediate effect".[256]

234. Between the fifth and the sixth Review Conferences, India and Pakistan carried out nuclear tests in 1998. For its part, on several occasions, the Movement of Non-Aligned Countries called for "urgent" measures of nuclear disarmament.[257] To this effect, the 2000 Review Conference agreed to a document containing the "13 Practical Steps" in order to meet the commitments of States Parties under Article VI of the NPT.[258] The "13 Practical Steps" stress the relevance and urgency of ratifications of the CTBT so as to achieve its entry into force, and of setting up a moratorium on nuclear-weapon tests pending such entry into force. Furthermore, they call for the commencement of negotiations

---

253   For an assessment of these earlier NPT Review Conferences, cf. H. Müller, D. Fischer and W. Kötter, *Nuclear Non-Proliferation and Global Order*, Stockholm-Solna/Oxford, SIPRI/Oxford University Press, 1994, pp. 31–108.
254   Decision 2, NPT/CONF.1995/32 (Part I), Annex, p. 2.
255   *Final Document*, Part II, p. 257, paras. 3–3*ter*., and cf. pp. 258 and 260, paras. 4 and 9.
256   *Ibid.*, pp. 271–273, paras. 36–39.
257   NPT/CONF.2000/4, paras. 12–13.
258   *Final Document*, vol. 1, Part I, pp. 14–15.

on a treaty banning the production of fissile material for nuclear weapons and also call upon NWS to accomplish the total elimination of nuclear arsenals.[259]

235. At the 2005 Review Conference, no substantive decision was adopted, amidst continuing disappointment at the lack of progress on implementation of Article VI of the NPT, particularly in view of the "13 Practical Steps" agreed to at the 2000 Review Conference. Concerns were expressed that new nuclear weapon systems were being developed, and strategic doctrines were being adopted lowering the threshold for the use of nuclear weapons; moreover, regret was also expressed that States whose ratification was needed for the CTBT's entry into force had not yet ratified the CTBT.[260]

236. Between the 2005 and the 2010 Review Conferences, there were warnings that the NPT was "now in danger" and "under strain", as the process of disarmament had "stagnated" and needed to be "revived" in order to prevent the spread of weapons of mass destruction. The concerns addressed what was regarded as the unsatisfactory stalemate in the Conference on Disarmament in Geneva, which had been "unable to adopt an agenda for almost a decade" to identify substantive issues to be discussed and negotiated in the Conference.[261]

237. The "Five-Point Proposal on Nuclear Disarmament", announced by the Secretary-General in an address of 24.10.2008,[262] began by urging all NPT States Parties, in particular the NWS, to fulfil their obligations under the Treaty "to undertake negotiations on effective measures leading to nuclear disarmament" (para. 1).[263] It called upon the permanent members of the Security Council to

---

259 The "13 Practical Steps", moreover, affirm that the principle of irreversibility should apply to all nuclear disarmament and reduction measures. At last, the 13 practical steps reaffirm the objective of general and complete disarmament under effective international control, and stress the importance of both regular reports on the implementation of NPT's Article VI obligations, and the further development of verification capabilities.

260 NPT/CONF.2005/57, Part I, and cf. report on the 2005 Review Conference *in*: 30 *U.N. Disarmament Yearbook* (2005) ch. I, p. 23.

261 Hans Blix, *Why Disarmament Matters*, Cambridge, Mass./London, Boston Review/MIT, 2008, pp. 6 and 63.

262 Cf. U.N. Secretary-General (Ban Ki-moon), Address (at a conference at the East-West Institute): "The United Nations and Security in a Nuclear-Weapon-Free World", *in* U.N. *News Centre*, of 24.10.2008, pp. 1–3.

263 It added that this could be pursued either by an agreement on "a framework of separate, mutually reinforcing instruments", or else by negotiating "a nuclear-weapons convention, backed by a strong system of verification, as has long been proposed at the United Nations" (para. 2).

commence discussions on security issues in the nuclear disarmament process, including by giving NNWS assurances against the use or threat of use of nuclear weapons (para. 5). It stressed the need of "new efforts to bring the CTBT into force", and encouraged NWS to ratify all the Protocols to the Treaties which established Nuclear-Weapon-Free Zones (para. 6). Moreover, it also stressed "the need for greater transparency" in relation to arsenals of nuclear weapons and disarmament achievements (para. 7). And it further called for the elimination also of other types of weapons of mass destruction (para. 8).

238. The "Five-Point Proposal on Nuclear Disarmament" was reiterated by the U.N. Secretary-General in two subsequent addresses in the following three years.[264] In one of them, before the Security Council on 24.09.2009, he stressed the need of an "early entry into force" of the CTBT, and pondered that "disarmament and non-proliferation must proceed together"; he urged "a divided international community" to start moving ahead towards achieving "a nuclear-weapon-free world", and, at last, he expressed his hope in the forthcoming 2010 NPT Review Conference.[265]

239. Both the 2000 and the 2010 Review Conferences made an interpretation of nuclear disarmament under Article VI of the NPT as a "positive disarmament obligation", in line with the *dictum* in the ICJ's 1996 Advisory Opinion of nuclear disarmament in good faith as an obligation of result.[266] The 2010 Review Conference expressed its deep concern that there remained the continued risk for humankind put by the possibility that nuclear weapons could be used, and the catastrophic humanitarian consequences that would result therefrom.

240. The 2010 Review Conference, keeping in mind the 1995 decision on "Principles and Objectives for Nuclear Non-Proliferation and Disarmament" as well as the 2000 agreement on the "13 Practical Steps", affirmed the vital importance of the universality of the NPT,[267] and, furthermore, took note of the "Five-Point

---

264 On two other occasions, namely, during a Security Council Summit on Nuclear Non-Proliferation on 24.09.2009, and at a Conference organized by the East-West Institute on 24.10.2011.
265 U.N. Secretary-General (Ban Ki-moon), "Opening Remarks to the Security Council Summit on Nuclear Non-Proliferation and Nuclear Disarmament", *in U.N. News Centre*, of 24.09.2009, pp. 1–2.
266 D.H. Joyner, "The Legal Meaning and Implications of Article VI of the Non-Proliferation Treaty", *in: Nuclear Weapons and International Law* (eds. G. Nystuen, S. Casey-Maslen and A.G. Bersagel), Cambridge, Cambridge University Press, 2014, pp. 413 and 417.
267 NPT/CONF.2010/50, vol. I, pp. 12–14 and 19–20.

Proposal on Nuclear Disarmament" of the U.N. Secretary-General, of 2008. For the first time in the present series of Review Conferences, the *Final Document* of the 2010 Review Conference recognized "the catastrophic humanitarian consequences that would result from the use of nuclear weapons".[268]

241. The Final Document welcomed the creation of successive nuclear-weapon-free zones,[269] and, in its conclusions, it endorsed the "legitimate interest" of NNWS to receive "unequivocal and legally binding security assurances" from NWS on the matter at issue; it asserted and recognized that "the total elimination of nuclear weapons is the only absolute guarantee against the use or threat of use of nuclear weapons".[270] The aforementioned Final Document reiterated the 2010 Review Conference's "deep concern at the catastrophic humanitarian consequences of any use of nuclear weapons", and "the need for all States at all times to comply with applicable international law, including international humanitarian law".[271] This key message of the 2010 Review Conference triggered the initiative, three years later, of the new series of Conferences on Humanitarian Impact of Nuclear Weapons (cf. *infra*).

242. The "historic acknowledgement" of "the catastrophic humanitarian consequences of any use of nuclear weapons" was duly singled out by the ICRC, in its statement in the more recent 2015 Review Conference;[272] the ICRC pointed out that that new series of Conferences (2013–2014, in Oslo, Nayarit and Vienna) has given the international community "a much clearer grasp" of the effects of nuclear detonations on peoples around the world. It then warned that, 45 years after the NPT's entry into force, "there has been little or no concrete progress" in fulfilling the goal of elimination of nuclear weapons. As nuclear weapons remain the only weapons of mass destruction not prohibited by a treaty, "filling this gap is a humanitarian imperative", as the "immediate risks of intentional or accidental nuclear detonations" are "too high and the dangers too real".[273]

243. The 2015 Review Conference displayed frustration over the very slow pace of action on nuclear disarmament, in addition to current nuclear modernization

---

268 Cf. *2010 Review Conference – Final Document*, vol. I, doc. NPT/CONF.2010/50, of 18.06.2010, p. 12, para. 80.
269 Cf. *ibid.*, p. 15, para. 99.
270 *Ibid.*, p. 21, point (i).
271 *Ibid.*, p. 19, point (v).
272 ICRC, "Eliminating Nuclear Weapons", *Statement – 2015 Review Conference of the Parties to the NPT*, of 01.05.2015, p. 1.
273 *Ibid.*, pp. 2–3.

programs and reiteration of dangerous nuclear strategies, apparently oblivious of the catastrophic humanitarian consequences of nuclear weapons. At the 2015 Review Conference, the Main Committee I, charged with addressing Article VI of the NPT, stressed the importance of "the ultimate goal" of elimination of nuclear weapons, so as to achieve "general and complete disarmament under effective international control".[274]

244. The 2015 Review Conference reaffirmed that "the total elimination of nuclear weapons is the only absolute guarantee against the use or threat of use of nuclear weapons, including the risk of their unauthorized, unintentional or accidental detonation".[275] It expressed its "deep concern" that, during the period 2010–2015, the Conference on Disarmament did not commence negotiations of an instrument on such nuclear disarmament,[276] and then stressed the "urgency for the Conference on Disarmament" to achieve "an internationally legally binding instrument" to that effect, so as "to assure" NNWS against the use or threat of use of nuclear weapons by all NWS.[277]

245. After welcoming "the increased and positive interaction with civil society" during the cycle of Review Conferences, the most recent 2015 Review Conference stated that

> understandings and concerns pertaining to the catastrophic humanitarian consequences of any nuclear weapon detonation underpin and should compel urgent efforts by all States leading to a world without nuclear weapons. The Conference affirms that, pending the realization of this objective, it is in the interest of the very survival of humanity that nuclear weapons never be used again.[278]

XVIII The Establishment of Nuclear-Weapon-Free Zones

246. In addition to the aforementioned NPT Review Conferences, the *opinio juris communis* on the illegality of nuclear weapons finds expression also in

---

274 *2015 Review Conference – Working Paper of the Chair of Main Committee* I, doc. NPT/CONF.2015/MC.I/WP.1, of 18.05.2015, p. 3, para. 17.
275 *Ibid.*, p. 5, para. 27.
276 *Ibid.*, p. 5, para. 35.
277 *Ibid.*, p. 6, para. 43.
278 *Ibid.*, p. 7, paras. 45–46(1).

the establishment, along the last half century, of nuclear-weapon-free zones, which has responded to the needs and aspirations of humankind, so as to rid the world of the threat of nuclear weapons. The establishment of those zones has, in effect, given expression to the growing disapproval of nuclear weapons by the international community as a whole. There are, in effect, references to nuclear-weapon-free zones in the arguments, in the written phase of the present proceedings, of the Marshall Islands[279] and of the United Kingdom[280] in the present case *of Obligations Concerning Negotiations Relating to Cessation of the Nuclear Arms Race and to Nuclear Disarmament*.

247. I originally come from the part of the world, Latin America, which, together with the Caribbean, form the first region of the world to have prohibited nuclear weapons, and to have proclaimed itself as a nuclear-weapon-free zone. The pioneering initiative in this domain, of Latin America and the Caribbean,[281] resulted in the adoption of the 1967 Treaty for the Prohibition of Nuclear Weapons in Latin America and the Caribbean and its two Additional Protocols. Its reach transcended Latin America and the Caribbean, as evidenced by its two Additional Protocols,[282] and the obligations set forth in its legal regime were wide in scope:

> Le régime consacré dans le Traité n'est pas simplement celui de non-prolifération: c'est un régime d'absence totale d'armes nucléaires, ce qui veut dire que ces armes seront interdites à perpétuité dans les territoires auxquels s'applique le Traité, quel que soit l'État sous le contrôle duquel pourraient se trouver ces terribles instruments de destruction massive.[283]

248. By the time of the creation of that first nuclear-weapon-free zone by the 1967 Treaty of Tlatelolco, it was pointed out that it came as a response to humanity's concern with its own future (given the threat of nuclear weapons),

---

279 *Application Instituting Proceedings* of the M.I., p. 26, para. 73; and *Memorial* of the M.I., pp. 40, 53 and 56, paras. 84, 117 and 122.

280 *Preliminary Objections* of the U.K., p. 2, para. 4.

281 On the initial moves in the U.N. to this effect, by Brazil (in 1962) and Mexico (taking up the leading role from 1963 onwards), cf. Naciones Unidas, *Las Zonas Libres de Armas Nucleares en el Siglo XXI, op. cit. infra* n. (298), pp. 116, 20 and 139.

282 The first one concerning the States internationally responsible for territories located within the limits of the zone of application of the Treaty, and the second one pertaining to the nuclear-weapon States.

283 A. García Robles, "Mesures de désarmement dans des zones particulières: le Traité visant l'interdiction des armes nucléaires en Amérique Latine", 133 *Recueil des Cours de l'Académie de Droit International de La Haye* [RCADI] (1971) p. 103, and cf. p. 71.

THE UNIVERSAL JURIDICAL CONSCIENCE, HUMANENESS 463

and in particular with "the survival of the humankind".[284] That initiative[285] was followed by four others of the kind, in distinct regions of the world, conducive to the adoption of the 1985 South Pacific (Rarotonga) Nuclear-Free Zone Treaty, the 1995 Southeast Asia (Bangkok) Nuclear-Weapon-Free Zone Treaty, the 1996 African (Pelindaba) Nuclear Weapon-Free Zone Treaty,[286] as well as the 2006 Central Asian (Semipalatinsk) Nuclear-Weapon-Free Zone Treaty. Basic considerations of humanity have surely been taken into account for the establishment of those nuclear-weapon-free zones.

249. In fact, besides the Treaty of Tlatelolco, also the Rarotonga, Bangkok, Pelindaba, and Semipalatinsk Treaties purport to extend the obligations enshrined therein, by means of their respective Protocols, not only to the States of the regions at issue, but also to nuclear States,[287] as well as States which are internationally responsible, *de jure* or *de facto*, for territories located in the respective regions. The verification of compliance with the obligations regularly engages the IAEA.[288] Each of the five aforementioned treaties (Tlatelolco, Rarotonga, Bangkok, Pelindaba and Semipalatinsk) creating nuclear-weapon-free zones has distinctive features, as to the kinds and extent of obligations and methods of verification,[289] but they share the common ultimate goal of preserving humankind from the threat or use of nuclear weapons.

250. The second nuclear-weapon-free zone, established by the Treaty of Rarotonga (1985), with its three Protocols, came as a response[290] to long-sustained regional aspirations, and increasing frustration of the populations of the countries of the South Pacific with incursions of NWS in the region.[291] The Rarotonga Treaty encouraged the negotiation of a similar zone, – by means

---

284   *Ibid.*, p. 99, and cf. p. 102.
285   Which was originally prompted by a reaction to the *Cuban missiles crisis* of 1962.
286   Naciones Unidas, *Las Zonas Libres de Armas Nucleares en el Siglo XXI*, N.Y./Geneva, U.N.-OPANAL/UNIDIR, 1997, pp. 9, 25, 39 and 153.
287   Those Protocols contain the undertaking not only not to use nuclear weapons, but also not to threaten their use; cf. M. Roscini, *op. cit. infra* (n. 307), pp. 617–618.
288   The Treaty of Tlatelolco has in addition counted on its own regional organism to that end, the Organism for the Prohibition of Nuclear Weapons in Latin America (OPANAL).
289   Cf., in general, M. Roscini, *Le Zone Denuclearizzate*, Torino, Giappichelli Ed., 2003, pp. 1–410; J. Goldblat, "Zones exemptes d'armes nucléaires: une vue d'ensemble", *in Le droit international des armes nucléaires* (Journée d'études, ed. S. Sur), Paris, Pédone, 1998, pp. 35–55.
290   Upon the initiative of Australia.
291   M. Hamel-Green, "The South Pacific – The Treaty of Rarotonga", *in Nuclear Weapons-Free Zones* (ed. R. Thakur), London/N.Y., MacMillan/St. Martin's Press, 1998, p. 59, and cf. p. 62.

of the 1995 Bangkok Treaty, – in the neighbouring region of Southeast Asia, and confirmed the "continued relevance of zonal approaches" to the goal of disarmament and the safeguard of humankind from the menace of nuclear weapons.[292]

251. The third of those treaties, that of Bangkok, of 1995 (with its Protocol), was prompted by the initiative of the Association of South–East Asian Nations (ASEAN) to insulate the region from the policies and rivalries of the nuclear powers. The Bangkok Treaty, besides covering the land territories of all ten Southeast Asian States, is the first treaty of the kind also to encompass their territorial sea, 200-mile exclusive economic zone and continental shelf.[293] The fourth such treaty, that of Pelindaba, of 1996, in its turn, was prompted by the continent's reaction to nuclear tests in the region (as from the French nuclear tests in the Sahara in 1961), and the aspiration – deeply-rooted in African thinking – to keep nuclear weapons out of the region.[294] The Pelindaba Treaty (with its three Protocols) appears to have served the purpose to eradicate nuclear weapons from the African continent.

252. The fifth such treaty, that of Semipalatinsk, of 2006, contains, like the other treaties creating nuclear weapon-free zones (*supra*), the basic prohibitions to manufacture, acquire, possess, station or control nuclear explosive devices within the zones.[295] The five treaties at issue, though containing loopholes (e.g., with regard to the transit of nuclear weapons),[296] have as common denominator the practical value of arrangements that transcend the non-proliferation of nuclear weapons.[297]

---

292   *Ibid.*, pp. 77 and 71.
293   This extended territorial scope has generated resistance on the part of nuclear-weapon States to accept its present form; A. Acharya and S. Ogunbanwo, "The Nuclear-Weapon-Free Zones in South-East Asia and Africa", in *Armaments, Disarmament and International Security – SIPRI Yearbook* (1998) pp. 444 and 448.
294   Naciones Unidas, *Las Zonas Libres de Armas Nucleares en el Siglo XXI*, op. cit. supra n. (286), pp. 60–61; and cf. J.O. Ihonvbere, "Africa – The Treaty of Pelindaba", in *Nuclear Weapons-Free Zones*, op. cit. supra n. (291), pp. 98–99 and 109. And, for a general study, cf. O. Adeniji, *The Treaty of Pelindaba on the African Nuclear-Weapon-Free Zone*, Geneva, UNIDIR, 2002, pp. 1–169.
295   M. Roscini, "Something Old, Something New: The 2006 Semipalatinsk Treaty on a Nuclear Weapon-Free Zone in Central Asia", 7 *Chinese Journal of International Law* (2008) p. 597.
296   As to their shortcomings, cf., e.g., J. Goldblat, "The Nuclear Non-Proliferation Régime: Assessment and Prospects", 256 *Recueil des Cours de l'Académie de Droit International de La Haye* (1995) pp. 137–138; M. Roscini, op. cit. supra n. (295), pp. 603–604.
297   J. Enkhsaikhan, "Nuclear-Weapon-Free Zones: Prospects and Problems", 20 *Disarmament – Periodic Review by the United Nations* (1997) n. 1, p. 74.

253. Each of the five treaties (of Tlatelolco, Rarotonga, Bangkok, Pelindaba and Semipalatinsk) reflects the characteristics of each of the five regions, and they all pursue the same cause. The establishment of the nuclear weapon-free zones has been fulfilling the needs and aspirations of peoples living under the fear of nuclear victimization.[298] Their purpose is being served, also in withholding or containing nuclear ambitions, to the ultimate benefit of humankind as a whole.

254. Nowadays, the five aforementioned nuclear weapon-free zones are firmly established in densely populated areas, covering most (almost all) of the landmass of the southern hemisphere land areas (while excluding most sea areas).[299] The adoption of the 1967 Tlatelolco Treaty, the 1985 Rarotonga Treaty, the 1995 Bangkok Treaty, the 1996 Pelindaba Treaty, and the 2006 Semipalatinsk Treaty, have disclosed the shortcomings and artificiality of the posture of the so-called political "realists",[300] which insisted on the suicidal strategy of nuclear "deterrence", in their characteristic subservience to power politics.

255. The substantial *Final Report* of 1999 of the U.N. Disarmament Commission underlined the relevance of nuclear-weapon-free zones and of their contribution to the achievement of nuclear disarmament,[301] "expressing and promoting common values" and constituting "important complementary" instruments to the NPT and the "international regime for the prohibition" of any nuclear-weapon explosions.[302] Drawing attention to the central role of the United Nations in the field of disarmament,[303] the aforementioned *Report* added:

---

[298] Cf., e.g., H. Fujita, "The Changing Role of International Law in the Nuclear Age: from Freedom of the High Seas to Nuclear-Free Zones", *in Humanitarian Law of Armed Conflict: Challenges Ahead – Essays in Honour of F. Kalshoven* (eds. A.J.M. Delissen and G.J. Tanja), Dordrecht, Nijhoff, 1991, p. 350, and cf. pp. 327–349.

[299] J. Prawitz, "Nuclear-Weapon-Free Zones: Their Added Value in a Strengthened International Safeguards System", *in Tightening the Reins – Towards a Strengthened International Nuclear Safeguards System* (eds. E. Häckel and G. Stein), Berlin/Heidelberg, Springer-Verlag, 2000, p. 166.

[300] Cf. Naciones Unidas, *Las Zonas Libres de Armas Nucleares en el Siglo XXI*, op. cit. supra n. (286), pp. 27, 33–38 and 134.

[301] U.N., *Report of the Disarmament Commission – General Assembly Official Records* (54th Session, supplement n. 42), U.N. doc. A/54/42, of 06.05.1999, Annex I, pp. 6–7, paras. 1, 6 and 9.

[302] *Ibid.*, p. 7, paras. 10–11 and 13.

[303] *Ibid.*, Annex II, p. 11 3rd preambular paragraph.

> Nuclear-weapon-free zones have ceased to be exceptional in the global strategic environment. To date, 107 States have signed or become parties to treaties establishing existing nuclear-weapon-free zones. With the addition of Antarctica, which was demilitarized pursuant to the Antarctic Treaty, nuclear-weapon-free zones now cover more than 50 per cent of the Earth's land mass. (...)
>
> The establishment of further nuclear-weapon-free zones reaffirms the commitment of the States that belong to such zones to honour their legal obligations deriving from other international instruments in force in the area of nuclear non-proliferation and disarmament to which they are parties.[304]

256. Moreover, the 1999 *Final Report* of the U.N. Disarmament Commission further stated that, for their part, NWS should fully comply with their obligations, under the ratified Protocols to the Treaties of treaties on nuclear-weapon-free zones, "not to use or threaten to use nuclear weapons".[305] It went on to encourage member States of those zones "to share experiences" with States of other regions, so as "to establish further nuclear-weapon-free zones".[306] It concluded that the international community, by means of "the creation of nuclear-weapon-free zones around the globe", should aim at "general and complete disarmament under strict and effective international control, so that future generations can live in a more stable and peaceful atmosphere".[307]

257. To the establishment of aforementioned five nuclear-weapon-free zones other initiatives against nuclear weapons are to be added, such as the prohibitions of placement of nuclear weapons, and other kinds of weapons of mass destruction, in outer space, on the seabed, on the ocean floor and in the subsoil beyond the outer limit of the territorial seabed zone, – "denuclearized" by the Treaties of Antarctica (1959), Outer Space (1967) and the Deep Sea Bed (1971), respectively, to which can be added the Treaty on the Moon and Other Celestial Bodies (1979), established a complete demilitarization thereon.[308]

304　*Ibid.*, Annex I, p. 7, para. 5; and p. 8, para. 28.
305　*Ibid.*, p. 9, para. 36.
306　*Ibid.*, p. 9, para. 41.
307　*Ibid.*, p. 9, para. 45.
308　Cf. G. Venturini, "Control and Verification of Multilateral Treaties on Disarmament and Non-Proliferation of Weapons of Mass Destruction", 17 *University of California Davis Journal of International Law and Policy* (2011) pp. 359–360.

258. The fact that the international community counts today on five nuclear-weapon-free zones, in relation to which States that possess nuclear weapons do have a particular responsibility, reveals an undeniable advance of right reason, of the *recta ratio* in the foundations of contemporary international law. Moreover, the initiative of nuclear-weapon-free zones keeps on clearly gaining ground. In recent years, proposals are being examined for the setting up of new denuclearized zones of the kind,[309] as well as of the so-called single-State zone (e.g., Mongolia).[310] That initiative further reflects the increasing disapproval, by the international community as a whole, of nuclear weapons, which, in view of their hugely destructive capability, constitute an affront to right reason (*recta ratio*).

XIX Conferences on the Humanitarian Impact of Nuclear Weapons (2013–2014)

259. In the course of the proceedings in the present case of *Obligations Concerning Negotiations Relating to Cessation of the Nuclear Arms Race and to Nuclear Disarmament*, several references were made to the more recent series of Conferences on the Humanitarian Impact of Nuclear Weapons (2013–2014), and in particular to the statement made therein (in the second of those Conferences) by the Marshall Islands, asserting that NWS should fulfill their obligation, "long overdue", of negotiation to achieve complete nuclear disarmament (cf. *infra*). The Marshall Islands promptly referred to its own statement in the Nayarit Conference (2014) in its *Memorial* in the *cas d'espèce*, as well as in its oral arguments before the ICJ.

260. In effect, the Conferences on the Humanitarian Impact of Nuclear Weapons (a series initiated in 2013) were intended to provide a forum for dialogue on, and a better understanding of, the humanitarian consequences of use of nuclear weapons for human beings, societies, and the environment, rather than a substitute of bilateral and multilateral fora for disarmament

---

309 E.g., in Central and Eastern Europe, in the Middle East, in Central and North-East and South Asia, and in the whole of the southern hemisphere.

310 Cf. A. Acharya and S. Ogunbanwo, *op. cit. supra* n. (293), p. 443; J. Enkhsaikhan, *op. cit. supra* n. (297), pp. 79–80. Mongolia in effect declared its territory as a nuclear-weapon-free zone (in 1992), and in February 2000 adopted national legislation defining its status as a nuclear-weapon-free State. This was acknowledged by U.N. General Assembly resolution 55/33S of 20.11.2000.

negotiations. This forum for dialogue and better understanding of the matter has counted on three Conferences to date, held, respectively, in Oslo in March 2013, in Nayarit in February 2014, and in Vienna in December 2014.

261. This recent series of Conferences has drawn attention to the humanitarian effects of nuclear weapons, restoring the central position of the concern for human beings and peoples. It has thus stressed the importance of the human dimension of the whole matter, and has endeavoured to awaken the conscience of the whole international community as well as to enhance the needed humanitarian coordination in the present domain. May I next proceed to a survey of their work and results so far.

1 *First Conference on the Humanitarian Impact of Nuclear Weapons*

262. The first Conference on the Humanitarian Impact of Nuclear Weapons took place in Oslo, Norway, on 04–05 March 2013, having counted on the participation of Delegations representing 127 States, United Nations agencies, the International Committee of the Red Cross (ICRC), the Red Cross and the Red Crescent movement, international organizations, and civil society entities. It should not pass unnoticed that only two of the NWS, India and Pakistan, were present at this Conference (and only India made a statement).[311] On the other hand, neither the Marshall Islands, nor the permanent members of the U.N. Security Council, attended it.

263. The Oslo Conference addressed three key issues, namely: (a) the immediate human impact of a nuclear weapon detonation; (b) the wider economic, developmental and environmental consequences of a nuclear weapon detonation; and (c) the preparedness of States, international organizations, civil society and the general public to deal with the predictable humanitarian consequences that would follow from a nuclear weapon detonation. A wide range of experts made presentations during the Conference.

264. Attention was drawn, e.g., to the nuclear testing's impact during the cold-war period, in particular to the detonation of not less than 456 nuclear bombs in the four decades (between 1949 and 1989) in the testing ground of Semipalatinsk, in eastern Kazakhstan. It was reported (by UNDP) that, according to the Kazakh authorities, up to 1.5 million people were affected by fall-out from the blasts at Semipalatinsk; the nuclear test site was shut down in mid-1991.

---

311 *In*: https://www.regjeringen.no/globalassets/upload/ud/vedlegg/hum/hum_india.pdf.

Other aspects were examined, all from a humanitarian outlook.[312] References were made, e.g., to General Assembly resolutions (such as resolution 63/279, of 25.04.2009), on humanitarian rehabilitation of the region. Such a humanitarian approach proved necessary, as the "historical experience from the use and testing of nuclear weapons has demonstrated their devastating immediate and long-term effects".[313]

265. The key conclusions of the Oslo Conference, as highlighted by Norway's Minister of Foreign Affairs in his closing statement,[314] can be summarized as follows. First, it is unlikely that any state or international body (such as U.N. relief agencies and the ICRC) could address the immediate humanitarian emergency caused by a nuclear weapon detonation in an adequate manner and provide sufficient assistance to those affected. Thus, the ICRC called for the abolition of nuclear weapons as the only effective preventive measure, and several participating States stressed that elimination of nuclear weapons is the only way to prevent their use; some States called for a ban on those weapons.

266. Secondly, the historical experience from the use and testing of nuclear weapons has demonstrated their devastating immediate and long-term effects. While the international scenario and circumstances surrounding it have changed, the destructive potential of nuclear weapons remains. And thirdly, the effects of a nuclear weapon detonation, irrespective of its cause, will not be constrained by national borders, and will affect States and peoples in significant ways, in a trans-frontier dimension, regionally as well as globally.

2 Second Conference on the Humanitarian Impact of Nuclear Weapons

267. The second Conference on the Humanitarian Impact of Nuclear Weapons took place in Nayarit, Mexico, on 13–14 February 2014, having counted on the participation of Delegations representing 146 States. The Marshall Islands, India and Pakistan attended it, whereas the United Kingdom did not. In addition to States, other participants included the ICRC, the Red Cross and the Red Crescent movement, international organizations, and civil society entities.

---

312 For accounts of the work of the 2013 Oslo Conference, cf., e.g., *Viewing Nuclear Weapons through a Humanitarian Lens* (eds. J. Borrie and T. Caughley), Geneva/N.Y., U.N./UNIDIR, 2013, pp. 81–82, 87, 90–91, 93–96, 99, 105–108 and 115–116.

313 Norway/Ministry of Foreign Affairs, *Chair's Summary – Humanitarian Impact of Nuclear Weapons*, Oslo, 05.03.2013, p. 2.

314 *In*: https://www.regjeringen.no/en/aktuelt/nuclear_summary/id716343/.

During the Nayarit Conference, the Delegate of the Marshall Islands stated that NWS States were failing to fulfill their obligations, under Article VI of the NPT and customary international law, to commence and conclude multilateral negotiations on nuclear disarmament; in his words:

> the Marshall Islands is convinced that multilateral negotiations on achieving and sustaining a world free of nuclear weapons are long overdue. Indeed we believe that states possessing nuclear arsenals are failing to fulfill their legal obligations in this regard. Immediate commencement and conclusion of such negotiations is required by legal obligation of nuclear disarmament resting upon each and every state under Article VI of the Non Proliferation Treaty and customary international law. It also would achieve the objective of nuclear disarmament long and consistently set by the United Nations, and fulfill our responsibilities to present and future generations while honouring the past ones.[315]

268. Earlier on, the Minister of Foreign Affairs of the Marshall Islands stated, at the U.N. High-Level Meeting on Nuclear Disarmament, on 26.09.2013, that the Marshall Islands "has a unique and compelling reason" to urge nuclear disarmament, namely,

> The Marshall Islands, during its time as a UN Trust Territory, experienced 67 large-scale tests of nuclear weapons. At the time of testing, and at every possible occasion in the intervening years, the Marshall Islands has informed UN members of the devastating impacts of these tests – of the deliberate use of our people as unwilling scientific experiments, of ongoing health impacts inherited through generations, of our displaced populations who still live in exile or who were resettled under unsafe circumstances, and then had to be removed. Even today, science remains a moving target and our exiled local communities are still struggling with resettlement.
> (...) Perhaps we [the Marshallese] have one of the most important stories to tell regarding the need to avert the use of nuclear weapons,

---

315 Marshall Islands' Statement, Second Conference on the Humanitarian Impact of Nuclear Weapons, Nayarit, Mexico, 13–14 February 2014 (*in*: http://www.reachingcriticalwill.org/images/documents/Disarmament-fora/nayarit-2014/statements/MarshallIslands.pdf). The text is also quoted by the Marshall Islands in its *Memorial* in Marshall Islands *versus* United Kingdom, Annex 72.

and a compelling story to spur greater efforts for nuclear disarmament (pp. 1–2).[316]

269. The Marshall Islands' statement in the 2014 Nayarit Conference was thus one of a few statements in which the Marshall Islands has articulated its claim, whereon they rely in the *cas d'espèce*, *inter alia*, to substantiate the existence of a dispute, including with the United Kingdom, which was not present at the Conference.[317] The Nayarit Conference participants also heard the poignant testimonies of five *Hibakusha*, – survivors of the atomic bombings of Hiroshima and Nagasaki, – who presented their accounts of the overwhelming devastation inflicted on those cities and their inhabitants by the atomic blasts (including the victims' burning alive, and carbonized or vaporized, as well as the long-term effects of radiation, killing survivors along seven decades).

270. They stressed the "moral imperative" of abolition of nuclear weapons, as humanity and nuclear weapons cannot coexist. A group of Delegations of no less than 20 States called expressly for a ban of nuclear weapons, already long overdue; this was the sword of Damocles hanging over everyone's heads. The "mere existence" of nuclear weapons was regarded as "absurd"; attention was also drawn to the 2013 U.N. General Assembly High-Level Meeting on Disarmament, and to the obligations under international law, including those deriving from the NPT as well as common Article 1 of the Geneva Conventions on IHL.[318]

---

316 *In*: http://www.un.org/en/ga/68/meetings/nucleardisarmament/pdf/MH_en.pdf. And the Marshall Islands' Minister of Foreign Affairs (Ph. Muller) added that

"It should be our collective goal as the United Nations to not only stop the spread of nuclear weapons, but also to pursue the peace and security of a world without them. Further, the Republic of the Marshall Islands has recently ratified the Comprehensive Test Ban Treaty and urges other member states to work towards bringing this important agreement into force.

The Marshall Islands is not the only nation in the Pacific to be touched by the devastation of nuclear weapon testing. (...) We express again our eventual aspirations to join with our Pacific neighbours in supporting a Pacific free of nuclear weapons in a manner consistent with international security" (pp. 1–2).

317 *Memorial* of the M.I. in Marshall Islands *versus* United Kingdom, para. 99.

318 Mexico/Gobierno de la República, *Chair's Summary – Second Conference on the Humanitarian Impact of Nuclear Weapons*, Mexico, 14.02.2014, pp. 2–3.

271. Furthermore, an association of over 60 entities of the civil society, from more than 50 countries, stated[319] that their own engagement was essential, as responsibilities fell on everyone to prevent the use of nuclear weapons; and prevention required the prohibition and ban of nuclear weapons, in the same way as those of biological and chemical weapons, landmines, and cluster munitions. Both the association, and the *Hibakusha*, condemned the dangerous strategy of nuclear "deterrence".

272. The 2014 Nayarit Conference's conclusions, building on the conclusions of the previous Oslo Conference, can be summarized as follows. First, the immediate and long-term effects of a single nuclear weapon detonation, let alone a nuclear exchange, would be catastrophic. The mere existence of nuclear weapons generates great risks, because the military doctrines of the NWS envisage preparations for the deliberate use of nuclear weapons. Nuclear weapons could be detonated by accident, miscalculation, or deliberately.

273. Delegations of over 50 States from every region of the world made statements unequivocally calling for the total elimination of nuclear weapons and the achievement of a world free of nuclear weapons. At least 20 Delegations of participating States in the Conference (*supra*) expressed the view that the way forward would be a ban on nuclear weapons. Others were equally clear in their calls for a Convention on the elimination of nuclear weapons or a new legally binding instrument.[320]

274. Secondly, some Delegations pointed out the security implications of nuclear weapons, or else expressed skepticism about the possibility of banning nuclear weapons as such. There were those which favoured a "step-by-step" approach to nuclear disarmament (within the framework of the NPT Action Plan), and called for the participation of NWS in this process. For their part, the nuclear-weapon-free States, in their majority, were however of the view that the step-by-step approach had failed to achieve its goal; they thus called for a new approach to nuclear disarmament.

---

319   On behalf of the International Campaign to Abolish Nuclear Weapons (ICAN), a coalition of over 350 entities in 90 countries.

320   For example, for its part, India favoured a step-by-step approach towards the elimination of nuclear weapons, ultimately leading to "a universal, non-discriminatory Convention on prohibition and elimination of nuclear weapons"; cf. www.reachingcriticalwill.org/images/documents/Disarmament-fora/nayarit-2014/statements/India.pdf.

275. Thirdly, for the Chairman of the Conference, a ban on nuclear weapons would be the first step towards their elimination; such a ban would also rectify the anomaly that nuclear weapons are the only weapons of mass destruction that are not subject to an explicit legal prohibition. He added that achieving a world free of nuclear weapons is consistent with States' obligations under international law, including under the NPT and common Article 1 to the Geneva Conventions on IHL. He at last called for the development of new international standards on nuclear weapons, including a legally binding instrument, to be concluded by the 70th anniversary of the atomic bombings of Hiroshima and Nagasaki.[321]

3 Third Conference on the Humanitarian Impact of Nuclear Weapons

276. The third Conference on the Humanitarian Impact of Nuclear Weapons took place in Vienna, Austria, on 08–09 December 2014, having carried forward the momentum created by the previous Conference in Mexico. It counted on the participation of Delegations of 158 States, as well as the U.N., the ICRC, the Red Cross and Red Crescent movement, civil society entities and representatives of the academic world. For the first time, of the NWS, the United Kingdom attended the Conference; Delegates from India, Pakistan, and the Marshall Islands were present as well.

277. Once again, the Conference participants heard the testimonies of survivors, the *Hibakusha*. Speaking of the "hell on earth" experienced in Hiroshima and Nagasaki; the "indiscriminate massacre of the atomic bombing" showed "the illegality and ultimate evil of nuclear weapons".[322] In its statement, the Marshall Islands, addressing the testing in the region of 67 atomic and hydrogen bombs, between 1946 and 1958, – the strongest one having been the Bravo test (of 01.03.1954) of a hydrogen bomb, 1000 times more powerful than the atomic bomb dropped over Hiroshima, – referred to their harmful impacts, such as the birth of "monster-like babies", the continuous suffering from "thyroid cancer, liver cancer and all types of radiogenic cancerous illnesses", extending over the years.[323]

---

321 Cf. http://www.reachingcriticalwill.org/images/documents/Disarmament-fora/nayarit-2014/chairs-summary.pdf.
322 Cf. *Vienna Conference on the Humanitarian Impact of Nuclear Weapons (08–09 December 2014)*, Vienna, Austria's Federal Ministry for Europe, Integration and Foreign Affairs, 2015, p. 19.
323 *Ibid.*, p. 34.

278. For its part, the ICRC stated that nuclear weapons ignore the principle of proportionality, and stand in breach of IHL (both conventional and customary) by causing unnecessary suffering to civilians; it expressed "significant concerns about the eventual spread of radiation to civilian areas and the radiological contamination of the environment" and everyone.[324] The ICRC further observed that, after "decades of focusing on nuclear weapons primarily in technical-military terms and as symbols of power", a fundamental and reassuring change has occurred, as debates on the matter now shift attention to what those weapons "would mean for people and the environment, indeed for humanity".[325]

279. The U.N. Secretary-General (Ban Ki-moon) sent a statement, read at the Conference, wherein he condemned expenditures in the modernization of weapons of mass destruction (instead of meeting the challenges of poverty and climate change). Recalling that the obligation of nuclear disarmament was one of both conventional and customary international law, he further condemned the strategy of nuclear "deterrence"; in his own words,

> Upholding doctrines of nuclear deterrence does not counter proliferation, but it makes the weapons more desirable. Growing ranks of nuclear-armed States does not ensure global stability, but instead undermines it. (...) The more we understand about the humanitarian impacts, the more it becomes clear that we must pursue disarmament as an urgent imperative.[326]

280. The Vienna Conference contributed to a deeper understanding of the consequences and risks of a nuclear detonation, having focused to a larger extent on the legal framework (and gaps therein) with regard to nuclear weapons.[327] It was reckoned that the impact of nuclear weapons detonation, irrespective of the cause, would go well beyond national borders, and could have regional and even global consequences, causing destruction, death, diseases and displacement on a very large scale, as well as profound and long-term damage to the environment, climate, human health and well-being, socioeconomic development and social order. They could, in sum, threaten the very survival of humankind. It was acknowledged that the scope, scale and interrelationship

---

324 *Ibid.*, p. 58.
325 *Ibid.*, p. 17.
326 Statement reproduced *in ibid.*, p. 16.
327 Cf. *ibid.* pp. 1–88.

of the humanitarian consequences caused by nuclear weapon detonation are catastrophic, and more complex than commonly understood; these consequences can be large scale and potentially irreversible.

281. States expressed various views regarding the ways and means of advancing the nuclear disarmament agenda. The Delegations of 29 States called for negotiations of a legally-binding instrument to prohibit or ban nuclear weapons. A number of Delegations considered that the inability to make progress on any particular step was no reason not to pursue negotiations in good faith on other effective measures to achieve and maintain a nuclear-weapon-free world. Such steps have been taken very effectively in regional contexts in the past, as evidenced by nuclear-weapon-free zones.

282. As the general report of the Vienna Conference observed, the three Conferences on the Humanitarian Impact of Nuclear Weapons (of Oslo, Nayarit and then Vienna), have contributed to a "deeper understanding" of the "actual risks" posed by nuclear weapons, and the "unspeakable suffering", devastating effects, and "catastrophic humanitarian consequences" caused by their use. As "nuclear deterrence entails preparing for nuclear war, the risk of nuclear weapon use is real. (...) The only assurance against the risk of a nuclear weapon detonation is the total elimination of nuclear weapons", in "the interest of the very survival of humanity"; hence the importance of Article VI of the NPT, and of the entry into force of the CTBT.[328]

283. The 2014 Vienna Conference's conclusions can be summarized as follows. First, the use and testing of nuclear weapons have demonstrated their devastating immediate, mid- and long-term effects. Nuclear testing in several parts of the world has left a legacy of serious health and environmental consequences. Radioactive contamination from these tests disproportionately affects women and children. It contaminated food supplies and continues to be measurable in the atmosphere to this day.

284. Secondly, as long as nuclear weapons exist, there remains the possibility of a nuclear weapon explosion. The risks of accidental, mistaken, unauthorized or intentional use of nuclear weapons are evident due to the vulnerability of nuclear command and control networks to human error and cyber-attacks, the maintaining of nuclear arsenals on high levels of alert, forward deployment and their modernization. The dangers of access to nuclear weapons and

---

328   *Ibid.*, pp. 5–7.

related materials by non-state actors, particularly terrorist groups, persist. All such risks, which increase over time, are unacceptable.

285. Thirdly, as nuclear deterrence entails preparing for nuclear war, the risk of the use of nuclear weapons is real. Opportunities to reduce this risk must be taken now, such as de-alerting and reducing the role of nuclear weapons in security doctrines. Limiting the role of nuclear weapons to deterrence does not remove the possibility of their use, nor does it address the risks stemming from accidental use. The only assurance against the risk of a nuclear weapon detonation is the total elimination of nuclear weapons.

286. Fourthly, the existence itself of nuclear weapons raises serious ethical questions, – well beyond legal discussions and interpretations, – which should be kept in mind. Several Delegations asserted that, in the interest of the survival of humankind, nuclear weapons must never be used again, under any circumstances. Fifthly, no State or international organ could adequately address the immediate humanitarian emergency or long-term consequences caused by a nuclear weapon detonation in a populated area, nor provide adequate assistance to those affected. The imperative of prevention as the only guarantee against the humanitarian consequences of nuclear weapons use is thus to be highlighted. Sixthly, participating Delegations reiterated the importance of the entry into force of the CTBT as a key element of the international nuclear disarmament and non-proliferation regime.

287. Seventhly, it is clear that there is no comprehensive legal norm universally prohibiting the possession, transfer, production and use of nuclear weapons, that is, international law does not address today nuclear weapons in the way it addresses biological and chemical weapons. This is generally regarded as an anomaly – or rather, a nonsense, – as nuclear weapons are far more destructive. In any case, international environmental law remains applicable in armed conflict and can pertain to nuclear weapons, even if not specifically regulating these latter. Likewise, international health regulations would cover effects of nuclear weapons. In the light of the new evidence produced in those two years (2013–2014) about the humanitarian impact of nuclear weapons, it is very doubtful whether such weapons could ever be used in conformity with IHL.

4   Aftermath: The "Humanitarian Pledge"

288. At the 2014 Vienna Conference, although a handful of States expressed scepticism about the effectiveness of a ban on nuclear weapons, the overwhelming majority of NPT States Parties expected the forthcoming 2015 NPT

Review Conference to take stock of all relevant developments, including the outcomes of the Conferences on the Humanitarian Impact of Nuclear Weapons (*supra*), and determine the next steps for the achievement and maintenance of a nuclear-weapon-free world. At the end of the Vienna Conference, the host State, Austria, presented a "Pledge" calling upon States parties to the NPT to renew their commitment to the urgent and full implementation of existing obligations under Article VI, and to this end, to identify and pursue effective measures to fill the legal gap for the prohibition and elimination of nuclear weapons.[329]

289. The Pledge further called upon NWS to take concrete interim measures to reduce the risk of nuclear weapons detonations, including by diminishing the role of nuclear weapons in military doctrines. The Pledge also recognised that: (a) the rights and needs of the victims of nuclear weapon use and testing have not yet been adequately addressed; (b) all States share the responsibility to prevent any use of nuclear weapons; and (c) the consequences of nuclear weapons use raise profound moral and ethical questions going beyond debates about the legality of these weapons.

290. Shortly before the Vienna Conference, 66 States had already endorsed the Pledge; by the end of the Conference, 107 States had endorsed it, thus "internationalizing" it and naming it at the end as the "Humanitarian Pledge".[330] On 07.12.2015, the U.N. General Assembly adopted the substance of the Humanitarian Pledge in the form of its resolution 70/48. As of April 2016, 127 States have formally endorsed the Humanitarian Pledge; unsurprisingly, none of the NWS has done so.

291. Recent endeavours, such as the ones just reviewed of the Conferences on the Humanitarian Impact of Nuclear Weapons have been rightly drawing attention to the grave humanitarian consequences of nuclear weapons detonations. The reframing of the whole matter in a people-centred outlook appears to me particularly lucid, and necessary, keeping in mind the unfoundedness of the strategy of "deterrence" and the catastrophic consequences of the use of nuclear weapons. The "step-by-step" approach, pursued by the NWS in respect

---

329 *In*:http://www.bmeia.gv.at/fileadmin/user_upload/Zentrale/Aussenpolitik/Abruestung/ -HINW14/HINW14Vienna_Pledge_Document.pdf. The Pledge only refers to States' obligations under the NPT and makes no mention of customary international law.

330 http://www.bmeia.gv.at/fileadmin/user_upload/Zentrale/Aussenpolitik/Abruestung/ -HINW14/HINW14.

to the obligation under Article VI of the NPT, appears essentially State-centric, having led to an apparent standstill or deadlock.

292. The obligation of nuclear disarmament being one of result, the "step-by-step" approach cannot be extended indefinitely in time, with its insistence on the maintenance of the nuclear sword of Damocles. The "step-by-step" approach has produced no significantly concrete results to date, seeming to make abstraction of the numerous pronouncements of the United Nations upholding the obligation of nuclear disarmament (cf. *supra*). After all, the absolute prohibition of nuclear weapons, – which is multifaceted,[331] is one of *jus cogens* (cf. *supra*). Such weapons, as the Conferences on the Humanitarian Impact of Nuclear Weapons have evidenced, are essentially inhumane, rendering the strategy of "deterrence" unfounded and unsustainable (cf. *supra*).

293. Ever since those Conferences (2013–2014), there has been a tendency (in 2014–2016) of slight reduction of nuclear warheads,[332] though NWS have kept on modernizing their respective nuclear armament programs, in an indication that nuclear weapons are likely to remain in the foreseeable future.[333] Yet, the growing awareness of the humanitarian impact of nuclear weapons has raised the question of the possibility of developing "a deontological position according to which the uniquely inhumane suffering that nuclear weapons inflict on their victims makes it inherently wrongful to use them".[334]

294. *Tempus fugit*. There remains a long way to go to achieve a nuclear-weapon-free world. The United Nations itself has been drawing attention to the urgency of nuclear disarmament. It has done so time and time again, and, quite recently, in the convocation in October 2015, of a new Open-Ended Working Group (OEWG), as a subsidiary body of the U.N. General Assembly, to address concrete and effective legal measures to attain and maintain a world without nuclear weapons.[335] It draws attention therein to the importance of multilateralism, to the relevance of "inclusiveness" (participation of all U.N. member States) and of the contribution, in addition to that of States,

---

331   Encompassing measures relating to any use, threat of use, development, production, acquisition, possession, stockpiling and transfer of nuclear weapons.
332   From around 16.300 nuclear warheads in 2014 to 15,850 in 2015, and to 15,395 in early 2016.
333   Cf. *SIPRI Yearbook 2016: Armaments, Disarmament and International Security*, Stockholm-Solna, SIPRI, 2016, Ch. 16, pp. 609–667.
334   ILPI, *Evidence of Catastrophe – A Summary of the Facts Presented at the Three Conferences on the Humanitarian Impact of Nuclear Weapons*, Oslo, ILPI, 2015, p. 15.
335   U.N. General Assembly, doc. A/C.1/70/L.13/Rev.1, of 29.10.2015, pp. 1–3.

THE UNIVERSAL JURIDICAL CONSCIENCE, HUMANENESS 479

also of international organizations, of entities of the civil society, and of the academia.³³⁶ And it reaffirms "the urgency of securing substantive progress in multilateral nuclear disarmament negotiations", in order "to attain and maintain a world without nuclear weapons".³³⁷

295. It should not pass unnoticed that all the initiatives that I have just reviewed in the present Dissenting Opinion (NPT Review Conferences, the establishment of nuclear-weapon-free zones, and the Conferences on Humanitarian Impact of Nuclear Weapons), referred to by the contending parties in the course of the proceedings before the ICJ in the present case of *Obligations Concerning Negotiations Relating to Cessation of the Nuclear Arms Race and to Nuclear Disarmament*, have gone beyond the inter-State outlook. In my perception, there is great need, in the present domain, to keep on looking beyond States, so as to behold peoples' and humankind's quest for survival in our times.

XX Final Considerations: *Opinio Juris Communis* Emanating from Conscience (*Recta Ratio*), Well above the "Will"

296. Nuclear weapons, as from their conception, have been associated with overwhelming destruction. It may be recalled that the first atomic bombs were fabricated in an epoch of destruction and devastation, – the II world war, – of the abominable "total war", in flagrant breach of IHL and of the ILHR.³³⁸ The fabrication of nuclear weapons, followed by their use, made abstraction of the fundamental principles of international law, moving the world into lawlessness in the current nuclear age. The strategy of "deterrence", in a "dialectics of suspicion", leads to an unforeseeable outcome, amidst complete destruction. Hence the utmost importance of negotiations conducive to general disarmament, which, – as warned by Raymond Aron already in the early sixties, – had "never been taken seriously" by the super-powers.³³⁹

---

336 Preamble, paras. 8 and 14–15.
337 Operative part, para. 2.
338 For an account, cf., e.g., *inter alia*, J. Lukacs, *L'héritage de la Seconde Guerre Mondiale*, Paris, Ed. F.-X. de Guibert, 2011, pp. 38–39, 55, 111 and 125–148; and cf. I. Kershaw, *To Hell and Back – Europe 1914–1949*, London, Penguin, 2016, pp. 7, 356, 407, 418, 518 and 521.
339 R. Aron, *Paz e Guerra entre as Nações* [1962], Brasília, Edit. Universidade de Brasília, 1979, pp. 413, 415, 421–422 and 610. R. Aron's book contains his reflections on the new age of nuclear weapons, amidst the tensions of the cold-war era, and the new challenges and dangers it imposed, – persisting to date, – for the future of humankind; cf., for the French edition, R. Aron, *Paix et guerre entre les nations*, 8th ed., Paris, Éd. Calmann-Lévy, 2015, pp. 13–770.

297. Last but not least, may I come back to a key point which I have dwelt upon in the present Dissenting Opinion pertaining to the *opinio juris communis* as to the obligation of nuclear disarmament (cf. Part XVI, *supra*). In the evolving law of nations, basic considerations of humanity have an important role to play. Such considerations nourish *opinio juris* on matters going well beyond the interests of individual States. The ICJ has, on more than one occasion, taken into account resolutions of the United Nations (in distinct contexts) as a means whereby international law manifests itself.

298. In its *célèbre* Advisory Opinion (of 21.06.1971) on *Namibia*, for example, the ICJ dwelt upon, in particular, two U.N. General Assembly resolutions relevant to the formation of *opinio juris*.[340] Likewise, in its Advisory Opinion (of 16.10.1975) on the *Western Sahara*, the ICJ considered and discussed in detail some U.N. General Assembly resolutions.[341] In this respect, references can further be made to the ICJ's Advisory Opinions on *Legal Consequences of the Construction of a Wall in the Occupied Palestinian Territory* (of 09.07.2004),[342] and on the *Declaration of Independence of Kosovo* (of 22.07.2010).[343] In its 1996 Advisory Opinion on the *Threat or Use of Nuclear Weapons*, the ICJ admitted, – even if in a rather restrictive way, – the emergence and gradual evolution of an *opinio juris* as reflected in a series of resolutions of the U.N. General Assembly (para. 70). But the ICJ could have gone (much) further than that.

299. After all, *opinio juris* has already had a long trajectory in legal thinking, being today endowed with a wide dimension. Thus, already in the XIXth century, the so-called "historical school" of legal thinking and jurisprudence (of F.K. von Savigny and G.F. Puchta) in reaction to the voluntarist conception, gradually discarded the "will" of the States by shifting attention to *opinio juris*, requiring practice to be an authentic expression of the "juridical conscience" of nations and peoples. With the passing of time, the acknowledgment of conscience standing above the "will" developed further, as a reaction against the reluctance of some States to abide by norms addressing matters of general or common interest of the international community.

---

340 On the principle of self-determination of peoples, namely, G.A. resolutions 1514(XV) of 14.12.1960, and 2145(XXI) of 27.10.1966; cf. *I.C.J. Reports 1971* pp. 31, 45 and 49–51.
341 Cf. *I.C.J. Reports 1975* pp. 20, 23, 26–37, 40, 57 and 67–68.
342 Cf. *I.C.J. Reports 1975* pp. 171–172, paras. 86–88.
343 Cf. *I.C.J. Reports 2010* p. 437, para. 80 (addressing a General Assembly resolution "which reflects customary international law").

300. This had an influence on the formation of rules of customary international law, a much wider process than the application of one of its formal "sources". *Opinio juris communis* came thus to assume "a considerably broader dimension than that of the subjective element constitutive of custom".[344] *Opinio juris* became a key element in the *formation* itself of international law, a *law of conscience*. This diminished the unilateral influence of the most powerful States, fostering international law-making in fulfilment of the public interest and in pursuance of the common good of the international community as a whole.

301. The foundations of the international legal order came to be reckoned as independent from, and transcending, the "will" of individual States; *opinio juris communis* came to give expression to the "juridical conscience", no longer only of nations and peoples – sustained in the past by the "historical school" – but of the international community as a whole, heading towards the universalization of international law. It is, in my perception, this international law of conscience that turns in particular towards nuclear disarmament, for the sake of the survival of humankind.

302. In 1983, Wang Tieya wrote against minimizing the legal significance of resolutions of General Assembly, in particular the declaratory ones. As they clarify principles and rules of international law, he contended that they "cannot be said to have no law-making effect at all merely because they are not binding in the strict sense. At the very least, since they embody the convictions of a majority of States, General Assembly resolutions can indicate the general direction in which international law is developing".[345] He added that those General Assembly resolutions, reflecting the position of "an overwhelming majority of States", have "accelerated the development of international

---

[344] A.A. Cançado Trindade, *International Law for Humankind – Towards a New Jus Gentium*, op. cit. supra n. (132), p. 137, and cf. p. 138; and cf. R. Huesa Vinaixa, *El Nuevo Alcance de la "Opinio Juris" en el Derecho Internacional Contemporáneo*, Valencia, Tirant lo Blanch, 1991, pp. 30–31 and 36–38, and cf. pp. 76–77, 173, 192, 194, 199 and 204–205; R.E. Piza Escalante, "La '*Opinio Juris*' como Fuente Autónoma del Derecho Internacional ('*Opinio Juris*' y '*Jus Cogens*')", 39 *Relaciones Internacionales* – Heredia/C.R. (1992) pp. 61–74; J.I. Charney, "International Lawmaking – Article 38 of the ICJ Statute Reconsidered", *in New Trends in International Lawmaking – International "Legislation" in the Public Interest* (Proceedings of the Kiel Symposium, March 1996), Berlin, Duncker & Humblot, 1997, pp. 180–183 and 189–190.

[345] Wang Tieya, "The Third World and International Law", *in The Structure and Process of International Law: Essays in Legal Philosophy Doctrine and Theory* (eds. R.St.J. Macdonald and D.M. Johnston), The Hague, M. Nijhoff, 1983, p. 964.

law", in helping to crystallize emerging rules into "clearly defined norms".[346] In the same decade, it was further pointed out that General Assembly resolutions have been giving expression, along the years, to "basic concepts of equity and justice, or of the underlining spirit and aims" of the United Nations.[347]

303. Still in the eighties, in the course I delivered at the Institute of Public International Law and International Relations of Thessaloniki, in 1988, I began by pondering that customary and conventional international law are interrelated, – as acknowledged by the ICJ itself[348] – and U.N. General Assembly resolutions contribute to the emergence of *opinio juris communis*.[349] I stood against the "strictly voluntarist position" underlying the unacceptable concept of so-called "persistent objector", and added that dissent from "one or another State individually cannot prevent the creation of new customary rules" or obligations, ensuing from *opinio juris communis* and not from *voluntas*.[350]

304. In the evolution of international law in time, – I proceeded, – voluntarist positivism has shown itself "entirely incapable" of explaining the consensual formation of customary international obligations; contrary to "the pretensions of positivist voluntarism" (with its stubborn emphasis on the consent of individual States), "freedom of spirit is the first to rebel" against immobilism, in devising responses to new challenges affecting the international community as a whole, and acknowledging obligations incumbent upon all States.[351]

---

346   *Ibid.*, pp. 964–965.
347   B. Sloan, "General Assembly Resolutions Revisited (Forty Years Later)", 58 *British Year Book of International Law* (1987) p. 80, and cf. pp. 116, 137 and 141.
348   For example, in the course of the proceedings in the *Nuclear Tests* cases (1973–1974), one of the applicant States (Australia) recalled, in the public sitting of 08.07.1974, that the ICJ had held, in the *North Sea Continental Shelf* cases (*I.C.J. Reports 1969*, p. 41), that a conventional norm can pass into the general *corpus* of international law thus becoming also a rule of customary international law; cf. ICJ, *Pleadings, Oral Arguments, Documents – Nuclear Tests cases* (vol. I: Australia *versus* France, 1973–1974), p. 503. In effect, – may I add, – just as a customary rule may later crystallize into a conventional norm, this latter can likewise generate a customary rule. International law is not static (as legal positivists wrongfully assume); it is essentially dynamic.
349   A.A. Cançado Trindade, "Contemporary International Law-Making: Customary International Law and the Systematization of the Practice of States", *in Sources of International Law* (Thesaurus Acroasium, vol. XIX), Thessaloniki, Institute of Public International Law and International Relations, 1992, pp. 68 and 71.
350   *Ibid.*, pp. 78–79.
351   *Ibid.*, pp. 126–129.

305. In my "repudiation of voluntarist positivism", I concluded on this point that the attention to customary international law ("incomparably less vulnerable" than conventional international law to voluntarist temptations) is in line with the progressive development (moved by conscience) of international law, so as to provide a common basis for the fulfilment of the needs and aspirations of all peoples.[352] Today, almost three decades later, I firmly restate, in the present Dissenting Opinion, my own position on the matter, in respect of the customary and conventional international obligation to put an end to nuclear weapons, so as to rid the world of their inhuman threat.

306. May I here, furthermore, ponder that U.N. General Assembly or Security Council resolutions are adopted on behalf not of the States which voted in favour of them, but more precisely on behalf of the United Nations Organization itself (its respective organs), being thus *valid for all U.N. member States*. This applies to the resolutions surveyed in the present Dissenting Opinion. It should be kept in mind that the U.N. is endowed with an international legal personality of its own, which enables it to act at international level as a distinct entity, independently of individual member States; in this way, it upholds the juridical equality of all States, and mitigates the worrisome vulnerability of factually weaker States, such as the NNWS; in doing so, it aims – by multilateralism – at the common good, at the realization of common goals of the international community as a whole,[353] such as nuclear disarmament.

307. A small group of States – such as the NWS – cannot overlook or minimize those reiterated resolutions, extended in time, simply because they voted against them, or abstained. Once adopted, they are valid for all U.N. member States. They are resolutions of the United Nations Organization itself, and not only of the large majority of U.N. member States which voted in favour of them. U.N. General Assembly resolutions, reiteratedly addressing matters of concern to humankind as a whole (such as existing nuclear weapons), are in my view endowed with normative value. They cannot be properly considered from a State voluntarist perspective; they call for another approach, away from the strict voluntarist-positivist one.

---

352   *Ibid.*, pp. 128–129. And cf., more recently, in general, A.A. Cançado Trindade, "The Contribution of Latin American Legal Doctrine to the Progressive Development of International Law", 376 *Recueil des Cours de l'Académie de Droit International de La Haye* (2014) pp. 9–92, esp. pp. 75–76.

353   Cf., in this sense, A.A. Cançado Trindade, *Direito das Organizações Internacionais*, 6th rev. ed., Belo Horizonte/Brazil, Edit. Del Rey, 2014, pp. 51 and 530–531.

308. Conscience stands above the "will". The universal juridical conscience stands well above the "will" of individual States, and resonates in resolutions of the U.N. General Assembly, which find inspiration in general principles of international law, which, for their part, give expression to values and aspirations of the international community as a whole, of all humankind.[354] This – may I reiterate – is the case of General Assembly resolutions surveyed in the present Dissenting Opinion (cf. *supra*). The values which find expression in those *prima principia* inspire every legal order and, ultimately, lie in the foundations of this latter.

309. The general principles of law (*prima principia*), in my perception, confer upon the (national and international) legal order its ineluctable axiological dimension. Notwithstanding, legal positivism and political "realism", in their characteristic subservience to power, incur into their basic mistake of minimizing those principles, which lie in the foundations of any legal system, and which inform and conform the norms and the action pursuant to them, in the search for the realization of justice. Whenever that minimization of principles has prevailed the consequences have been disastrous.[355]

310. They have been contributing, in the last decades, to a vast *corpus juris* on matters of concern to the international community as a whole, such as nuclear disarmament. Their contribution to this effect has overcome the traditional inter-State paradigm of the international legal order.[356] This can no longer be overlooked in our days. The inter-State mechanism of the *contentieux* before the ICJ cannot be invoked in justification for an inter-State reasoning. As "the principal judicial organ" of the United Nations (U.N. Charter, Article 92), the ICJ has to bear in mind not only States, but also "we, the peoples", on whose behalf the U.N. Charter was adopted. In its international adjudication of contentious cases, like the present one of *Obligations Concerning Negotiations Relating to Cessation of the Nuclear Arms Race and to Nuclear Disarmament*, the

---

354 A.A. Cançado Trindade, *International Law for Humankind – Towards a New Jus Gentium*, op. cit. supra n. (120), pp. 129–138.

355 A.A. Cançado Trindade, *A Humanização do Direito Internacional*, 2nd rev. ed., Belo Horizonte/Brazil, 2015, pp. 6–24; A.A. Cançado Trindade, *Os Tribunais Internacionais e a Realização da Justiça*, op. cit. supra n. (243), pp. 410–418.

356 A.A. Cançado Trindade, *Direito das Organizações Internacionais*, op. cit. supra n. (353), pp. 530–537.

ICJ has to bear in mind basic considerations of humanity, with their incidence on questions of admissibility and jurisdiction, as well as of substantive law.

XXI   Epilogue: A Recapitulation

311. Coming to the end of the present Dissenting Opinion, I feel in peace with my conscience: from all the preceding considerations, I trust to have made it crystal clear that my own position, in respect of all the points which form the object of the present Judgment on the case of *Obligations Concerning Negotiations Relating to Cessation of the Nuclear Arms Race and to Nuclear Disarmament*, stands in clear and entire opposition to the view espoused by the Court's split majority that the existence of a legal dispute has not been established before it, and that the Court has no jurisdiction to consider the Application lodged with it by the Marshall Islands, and cannot thus proceed to the merits of the case. Not at all: in my understanding, there is a dispute before the Court, which has jurisdiction to decide the case. There is a conventional and customary international law obligation of nuclear disarmament. Whether there has been a concrete breach of this obligation, the Court could only decide on the merits phase of the present case.

312. My dissenting position is grounded not only on the assessment of the arguments produced before the Court by the contending parties, but above all on issues of principle and on fundamental values, to which I attach even greater importance. As my dissenting position covers all points addressed in the present Judgment, in its reasoning as well as in its conclusion, I have thus felt obliged, in the faithful exercise of the international judicial function, to lay on the records, in the present Dissenting Opinion, the foundations of my dissenting position thereon. I deem it fit, at this last stage, to recapitulate all the points of my dissenting position, expressed herein, for the sake of clarity, and in order to stress their interrelatedness.

313. *Primus*: According to the *jurisprudence constante* of the Court, a dispute is a disagreement on a point of law or fact, a conflict of legal views or interests; The existence of an international dispute (at the time of lodging a claim) is a matter for the objective determination of the Court. The existence of a dispute may be inferred. *Secundus*: The objective determination of a dispute by the Court is not intended to protect respondent States, but rather and more precisely to secure the proper exercise of the Court's judicial function. *Tertius*:

There is no requirement of prior notice of the applicant State's intention to initiate proceedings before the ICJ, nor of prior "exhaustion" of diplomatic negotiations, nor of prior notification of the claim; it is, in sum, a matter for objective determination of the Court itself.

314. *Quartus*: The Marshall Islands and the United Kingdom/India/Pakistan have pursued distinct arguments and courses of conduct on the matter at issue, evidencing their distinct legal positions, which suffice for the Court's objective determination of the existence of a dispute. *Quintus*: There is no legal ground for attempting to heighten the threshold for the determination of the existence of a dispute; in its *jurisprudence constante*, the Court has expressly avoided a formalistic approach on this issue, which would affect access to justice itself. The Court has, instead, in its *jurisprudence constante*, upheld its own *objective determination* of the existence of a dispute, rather than relying – as it does in the present case – on the subjective criterion of "awareness" of the respondent States.

315. *Sextus*: The distinct series of U.N. General Assembly resolutions on nuclear disarmament along the years (namely, warning against nuclear weapons, 1961–1981; on freeze of nuclear weapons, 1982–1992; condemning nuclear weapons, 1982 2015; following-up the ICJ's 1996 Advisory Opinion, 1996–2015) are endowed with authority and legal value. *Septimus*: Their authority and legal value have been duly acknowledged before the ICJ in its advisory proceedings in 1995. *Octavus*: Like the General Assembly, the Security Council has also expressed its concern on the matter at issue, in its work and its resolutions on nuclear disarmament.

316. *Nonus*: The aforementioned United Nations resolutions, in addition to other initiatives, portray the longstanding saga of the United Nations in the condemnation of nuclear weapons. *Decimus*: The fact that weapons of mass destruction (poisonous gases, biological and chemical weapons) have been outlawed, and nuclear weapons, far more destructive, have not been banned yet, is a juridical absurdity. The obligation of nuclear disarmament has emerged and crystallized nowadays in both conventional and customary international law, and the United Nations has, along the decades, been giving a most valuable contribution to this effect.

317. *Undecimus*: In the *cas d'espèce*, the issue of United Nations resolutions and the emergence of *opinio juris communis* in the present domain of the obligation of nuclear disarmament has grasped the attention of the contending parties in

submitting their distinct arguments before the Court. *Duodecimus*: The presence of evil has marked human existence along the centuries. Ever since the eruption of the nuclear age in August 1945, some of the world's great thinkers have been inquiring whether humankind has a future, and have been drawing attention to the imperative of respect for life and the relevance of humanist values. *Tertius decimus*: Also in international legal doctrine there have been those who have been stressing the needed prevalence of human conscience, the universal juridical conscience, over State voluntarism.

318. *Quartus decimus*: The U.N. Charter is attentive to peoples; the recent cycle of World Conferences of the United Nations has had, as a common denominator, the recognition of the legitimacy of the concern of the international community as a whole with the conditions of living and the well-being of peoples everywhere. *Quintus decimus*: General principles of law (*prima principia*) rest in the foundations of any legal system. They inform and conform its norms, guide their application, and draw attention to the prevalence of *jus necessarium* over *jus voluntarium*.

319. *Sextus decimus*: The nature of a case before the Court may well require a reasoning going beyond the strictly inter-State outlook; the present case concerning the obligation of nuclear disarmament requires attention to be focused on peoples, in pursuance of a humanist outlook, rather than on inter-State susceptibilities. *Septimus decimus*: The inter-State mechanism of adjudication of contentious cases before the ICJ does not at all imply that the Court's reasoning should likewise be strictly inter-State. Nuclear disarmament is a matter of concern to humankind as a whole.

320. *Duodevicesimus*: The present case stresses the utmost importance of fundamental principles, such as that of the juridical equality of States, following the principle of humanity, and of the idea of an objective justice. *Undevicesimus*: Factual inequalities and the strategy of "deterrence" cannot be made to prevail over the juridical equality of States. *Vicesimus*: "Deterrence" cannot keep on overlooking the distinct series of U.N. General Assembly resolutions, expressing an *opinio juris communis* in condemnation of nuclear weapons. *Vicesimus primus*: As also sustained by general principles of international law and international legal doctrine, nuclear weapons are in breach of international law, of IHL and the ILHR, and of the U.N. Charter.

321. *Vicesimus secundus*: There is need of a people-centred approach in this domain, keeping in mind the fundamental right to life; the *raison d'humanité*

prevails over the *raison d'État*. Attention is to be kept on the devastating and catastrophic consequences of the use of nuclear weapons. *Vicesimus tertius*: In the path towards nuclear disarmament, the peoples of the world cannot remain hostage of individual State consent. The universal juridical conscience stands well above the "will" of the State. *Vicesimus quartus*: The absolute prohibitions of arbitrary deprivation of human life, of infliction of cruel, inhuman or degrading treatment, and of infliction of unnecessary suffering, are prohibitions of *jus cogens*, which have and incidence on ILHR and IHL and ILR, and foster the current historical process of humanization of international law.

322. *Vicesimus quintus*: The positivist outlook unduly overlooks the *opinio juris communis* as to the illegality of all weapons of mass destruction, including [and starting with] nuclear weapons, and the obligation of nuclear disarmament, under contemporary international law. *Vicesimus sextus*: Conventional and customary international law go together, in the domain of the protection of the human person, as disclosed by the Martens clause, with an incidence on the prohibition of nuclear weapons. *Vicesimus septimus*: The existence of nuclear weapons is the contemporary tragedy of the nuclear age; today, more than ever, human beings need protection from themselves. Nuclear weapons have no ethics, and ethics cannot be separated from law, as taught by jusnaturalist thinking.

323. *Vicesimus octavus*: Humankind, a subject of rights, has been a potential victim of nuclear weapons already for a long time. *Vicesimus nonus*: The law of nations encompasses, among its subjects, humankind as a whole (as propounded by the "founding fathers" of international law). *Trigesimus*: This humanist vision is centred on peoples, keeping in mind the humane ends of States. *Trigesimus primus*: *Opinio juris communis necessitatis*, upholding a customary and conventional obligation of nuclear disarmament, has been finding expression in the NPT Review Conferences, in the relevant establishment of nuclear-weapon-free zones, and in the recent Conferences of Humanitarian Impact of Nuclear Weapons, – in their common cause of achieving and maintaining a nuclear-weapon-free world. *Trigesimus secundus*: Those initiatives have gone beyond the State-centric outlook, duly attentive to peoples' and humankind's quest for survival in our times.

324. *Trigesimus tertius*: *Opinio juris communis* – to which U.N. General Assembly resolutions have contributed – has a much broader dimension than the subjective element of custom, being a key element in the formation of a law of conscience, so as to rid the world of the inhuman threat of nuclear weapons.

Trigesimus quartus: U.N. (General Assembly and Security Council) resolutions are adopted on behalf of the United Nations Organization itself (and not only of the States which voted in their favour); they are thus valid for *all* U.N. member States.

325. *Trigesimus quintus*: The United Nations Organization, endowed with an international legal personality of its own, upholds the juridical equality of States, in striving for the realization of common goals such as nuclear disarmament. *Trigesimus sextus*: Of the main organs of the United Nations, the contributions of the General Assembly, the Security Council and the Secretary-General to nuclear disarmament have been consistent and remarkable along the years.

326. *Trigesimus septimus*: United Nations resolutions in this domain address a matter of concern to humankind as a whole, which cannot thus be properly approached from a State voluntarist perspective. The universal juridical conscience stands well above the "will" of individual States. *Trigesimus octavus*: The ICJ, as the principal judicial organ of the United Nations, is to keep in mind basic considerations of humanity, with their incidence on questions of admissibility and jurisdiction, as well as of substantive law. *Trigesimus nonus*: In sum, the ICJ has jurisdiction to consider the *cas d'espèce*, and there is a conventional and customary international law obligation of nuclear disarmament; whether there has been a breach of this obligation, the Court could only decide on the merits phase of the present case.

327. *Quadragesimus*: A world with arsenals of nuclear weapons, like ours, is bound to destroy its past, dangerously threatens the present, and has no future at all. Nuclear weapons pave the way into nothingness. In my understanding, the International Court *of Justice*, as the principal judicial organ of the United Nations, should, in the present Judgment, have shown sensitivity in this respect, and should have given its contribution to a matter which is a major concern of the vulnerable international community, and indeed of humankind as a whole.

(Signed) *Antônio Augusto* CANÇADO TRINDADE
Judge

3 Dissenting Opinion in the Case of *Obligations Concerning Negotiations Relating to Cessation of the Nuclear Arms Race and to Nuclear Disarmament* (Marshall Islands *versus* Pakistan, Jurisdiction, Judgment of 05.10.2016)

Table of Contents	Paragraphs
I. *Prolegomena*	1–4
II. The Existence of a Dispute before the Hague Court	5
1. Objective Determination by the Court	5–15
2. Existence of a Dispute in the *Cas d'Espèce* (case Marshall Islands *versus* Pakistan)	16–17
3. The Threshold for the Determination of the Existence of a Dispute	18–23
4. Contentions in the Case of Marshall Islands *versus* Pakistan	24–25
5. General Assessment	26–29
III. U.N. General Assembly Resolutions and *Opinio Juris*	30
1. U.N. General Assembly Resolutions on Nuclear Weapons (1961–1981)	31–36
2. U.N. General Assembly Resolutions on Freeze of Nuclear Weapons (1982–1992)	37–39
3. U.N. General Assembly Resolutions on Nuclear Weapons as Breach of the U.N. Charter (Acknowledgment before the ICJ, 1995)	40–43
4. U.N. General Assembly Resolutions Condemning Nuclear Weapons (1982–2015)	44–49
5. U.N. General Assembly Resolutions Following up the ICJ's 1996 Advisory Opinion (1996–2015)	50–55
IV. U.N. Security Council Resolutions and *Opinio Juris*	56–62
V. The Saga of the United Nations in the Condemnation of Nuclear Weapons	63–76
VI. U.N. Resolutions and the Emergence of *Opinio Juris*: The Positions of the Contending Parties	77–82
VII. Human Wickedness: From the XXIst Century Back to the Book of *Genesis*	83–112

VIII.	The Attention of the United Nations Charter to Peoples	113–121
IX.	Impertinence of the So-Called *Monetary Gold* "Principle"	122–125
X.	The Fundamental Principle of the Juridical Equality of States	126–129
XI.	Unfoundedness of the Strategy of "Deterrence"	130–140
XII.	The Illegality of Nuclear Weapons and the Obligation of Nuclear Disarmament	
	1. The Condemnation of All Weapons of Mass Destruction	141–146
	2. The Prohibition of Nuclear Weapons: The Need of a People-Centred Approach	147–165
	3. The Prohibition of Nuclear Weapons: The Fundamental Right to Life	166–179
	4. The Absolute Prohibitions of *Jus Cogens* and the Humanization of International Law	180–183
	5. The Pitfalls of Legal Positivism: A Rebuttal of the So-Called *Lotus* "Principle"	184–190
XIII.	Recourse to the "Martens Clause" as an Expression of the *Raison d'Humanité*	191–199
XIV.	Nuclear Disarmament: Jusnaturalism, the Humanist Conception and the Universality of International Law	200–210
XV.	The Principle of Humanity and the Universalist Approach: *Jus Necessarium* Transcending the Limitations of *Jus Voluntarium*	211–223
XVI.	NPT Review Conferences	224–239
XVII.	The Establishment of Nuclear-Weapon-Free Zones	240–252
XVIII.	Conferences on the Humanitarian Impact of Nuclear Weapons (2013–2014)	253–255
	1. First Conference on the Humanitarian Impact of Nuclear Weapons	256–260
	2. Second Conference on the Humanitarian Impact of Nuclear Weapons	261–269
	3. Third Conference on the Humanitarian Impact of Nuclear Weapons	270–281
	4. Aftermath: The "Humanitarian Pledge"	282–289
XIX.	Final Considerations: *Opinio Juris Communis* Emanating from Conscience (*Recta Ratio*), Well Above the "Will"	290–304
XX.	Epilogue: A Recapitulation	305–321

I   Prolegomena

1. I regret not to be able to accompany the Court's majority in the Judgment of today, 05.10.2016 in the present case of *Obligations Concerning Negotiations Relating to Cessation of the Nuclear Arms Race and to Nuclear Disarmament* (Marshall Islands *versus* Pakistan), whereby it has found that the existence of a dispute between the parties has not been established before it, and that the Court has no jurisdiction to consider the Application lodged with it by the Marshall Islands, and cannot thus proceed to the merits of the case. I entirely disagree with the present Judgment. As my dissenting position covers all points addressed in it, in its reasoning as well as in its resolutory points, I feel obliged, in the faithful exercise of the international judicial function, to lay on the records the foundations of my own position thereon.

2. In doing so, I distance myself as much as I can from the position of the Court's majority, so as to remain in peace with my conscience. I shall endeavor to make clear the reasons of my personal position on the matter addressed in the present Judgment, in the course of the present Dissenting Opinion. I shall begin by examining the question of the existence of a dispute before the Hague Court (its objective determination by the Court and the threshold for the determination of the existence of a dispute). I shall then turn attention to the distinct series of U.N. General Assembly resolutions on nuclear weapons and *opinio juris*. After surveying also U.N. Security Council resolutions and *opinio juris*, I shall dwell upon the saga of the United Nations in the condemnation of nuclear weapons. Next, I shall address the positions of the contending parties on U.N. resolutions and the emergence of *opinio juris*.

3. In logical sequence, I shall then, looking well back in time, underline the need to go beyond the strict inter-State dimension, bearing in mind the attention of the U.N. Charter to peoples. Then, after recalling the fundamental principle of the juridical equality of States, I shall dwell upon the unfoundedness of the strategy of "deterrence". My next line of considerations pertains to the illegality of nuclear weapons and the obligation of nuclear disarmament, encompassing: (a) the condemnation of all weapons of mass destruction; (b) the prohibition of nuclear weapons (the need of a people-centred approach, and the fundamental right to life); (c) the absolute prohibitions of *jus cogens* and the humanization of international law; (d) pitfalls of legal positivism.

4. This will bring me to address the recourse to the "Martens clause" as an expression of the *raison d'humanité*. My following reflections, on nuclear

disarmament, will be in the line of jusnaturalism, the humanist conception and the universality of international law; in addressing the universalist approach, I shall draw attention to the principle of humanity and the *jus necessarium* transcending the limitations of *jus voluntarium*. I shall then turn attention to the NPT Review Conferences, to the relevant establishment of nuclear-weapon-free zones, and to the Conferences on the Humanitarian Impact of Nuclear Weapons. The way will then be paved for my final considerations, on *opinio juris communis* emanating from conscience (*recta ratio*), well above the "will", – and, last but not least, to the epilogue (recapitulation).

II   The Existence of a Dispute before the Hague Court

1   *Objective Determination by the Court*

5. May I start by addressing the issue of the existence of a dispute before the Hague Court. In the *jurisprudence constante* of the Hague Court (PCIJ and ICJ), a dispute exists when there is "a disagreement on a point of law or fact, a conflict of legal views or of interests between two persons".[1] Whether there exists a dispute is a matter for "objective determination" by the Court; the "mere denial of the existence of a dispute does not prove its non-existence".[2] The Court must examine if "the claim of one party is positively opposed by the other".[3] The Court further states that "a disagreement on a point of law or fact, a conflict of legal views or interests, or the positive opposition of the claim of one party by the other need not be necessarily be stated *expressis verbis*".[4]

6. Along the last decade, the Court has deemed it fit to insist on its own faculty to proceed to the "objective determination" of the dispute. Thus, in the case of *Armed Activities on the Territory of the Congo* (D.R. Congo *versus* Rwanda, Jurisdiction and Admissibility, Judgment of 03.02.2006), for example, the ICJ has recalled that, as long ago as 1924, the PCIJ stated that "a dispute is a

---

1   PCIJ, case of *Mavrommatis Palestine Concessions*, Judgment of 30.08.1924, p. 11.
2   ICJ, Advisory Opinion (of 30.03.1950) on the *Interpretation of Peace Treaties with Bulgaria, Hungary and Romania*, p. 74.
3   ICJ, *South-West Africa* cases (Ethiopia and Liberia *versus* South Africa, Judgment on Preliminary Objections of 21.12.1962), p. 328; ICJ, case of *Armed Activities on the Territory of the Congo* (New Application – 2002, D.R. Congo *versus* Rwanda, Judgment on Jurisdiction and Admissibility of 03.02.2006), p. 40, para. 90.
4   ICJ, *Land and Maritime Boundary between Cameroon and Nigeria* (Judgment on Preliminary Objections, of 11.06.1998), p. 275, para. 89.

disagreement on a point of law or fact, a conflict of legal views or interests" (case of *Mavrommatis Palestine Concessions,* Judgment of 30.08.1924, p. 11). It then added that

> For its part, the present Court has had occasion a number of times to state the following:
>> In order to establish the existence of a dispute, 'it must be shown that the claim of one party is positively opposed by the other' (*South West Africa,* Preliminary Objections, Judgment, *I.C.J. Reports 1962,* p. 328); and further, 'Whether there exists an international dispute is a matter for objective determination' (*Interpretation of Peace Treaties with Bulgaria, Hungary and Romania,* First Phase, Advisory Opinion, *I.C.J. Reports 1950,* p. 74; *East Timor* (Portugal v. Australia), Judgment, *I.C.J. Reports 1995,* p. 100, para. 22; *Questions of Interpretation and Application of the 1971 Montreal Convention arising from the Aerial Incident at Lockerbie* (Libyan Arab Jamahiriya v. United Kingdom), Preliminary Objections, Judgment, *I.C.J. Reports 1998,* p. 17, para. 22; *Questions of Interpretation and Application of the 1971 Montreal Convention arising from the Aerial Incident at Lockerbie* (Libyan Arab Jamahiriya v. United States of America), Preliminary Objections, Judgment, *I.C.J. Reports 1998,* pp. 122–123, para. 21; *Certain Property* (Liechtenstein v. Germany), Preliminary Objections, Judgment, *I.C.J. Reports 2005,* p. 18, para. 24) (para. 90).

7. Shortly afterwards, in its Judgment on Preliminary Objections (of 18.11.2008) in the case of the *Application of the Convention against Genocide* (Croatia *versus* Serbia), the ICJ has again recalled that

> In numerous cases, the Court has reiterated the general rule which it applies in this regard, namely: 'the jurisdiction of the Court must normally be assessed on the date of the filing of the act instituting proceedings' (to this effect, cf. *Application of the Convention on the Prevention and Punishment of the Crime of Genocide* (Bosnia and Herzegovina v. Yugoslavia), Preliminary Objections, Judgment, *I.C.J. Reports 1996 (II),* p. 613, para. 26; *Questions of Interpretation and Application of the 1971 Montreal Convention arising from the Aerial Incident at Lockerbie* (Libyan Arab Jamahiriya v. United Kingdom), Preliminary Objections, Judgment, *I.C.J. Reports 1998,* p. 26, para. 44). (...) (I)t is normally by reference to the date of the filing of the instrument instituting proceedings that it must be determined whether those conditions are met.

(...) What is at stake is legal certainty, respect for the principle of equality and the right of a State which has properly seised the Court to see its claims decided, when it has taken all the necessary precautions to submit the act instituting proceedings in time. (....) [T]he Court must in principle decide the question of jurisdiction on the basis of the conditions that existed at the time of the institution of the proceedings.

However, it is to be recalled that the Court, like its predecessor, has also shown realism and flexibility in certain situations in which the conditions governing the Court's jurisdiction were not fully satisfied when proceedings were initiated but were subsequently satisfied, before the Court ruled on its jurisdiction (paras. 79–81).

8. More recently, in its Judgment on Preliminary Objections (of 01.04.2011) in the case of the *Application of the International Convention on the Elimination of All Forms of Racial Discrimination – CERD* (Georgia *versus* Russian Federation), the ICJ has seen it fit, once again, to stress:

The Court recalls its established case law on that matter, beginning with the frequently quoted statement by the Permanent Court of International Justice in the *Mavrommatis Palestine Concessions* case in 1924: 'A dispute is a disagreement on a point of law or fact, a conflict of legal views or of interests between two persons'. (Judgment n. 2, 1924, PCIJ, Series A, n. 2, p. 11). Whether there is a dispute in a given case is a matter for 'objective determination' by the Court (*Interpretation of Peace Treaties with Bulgaria, Hungary and Romania,* First Phase, Advisory Opinion, *I.C.J. Reports 1950,* p. 74). 'It must be shown that the claim of one party is positively opposed by the other' (*South West Africa* (Ethiopia and Liberia *v.* South Africa), Preliminary Objections, Judgment, *I.C.J. Reports 1962,* p. 328); and, most recently, *Armed Activities on the Territory of the Congo* (New Application: 2002, D.R. Congo *v.* Rwanda, Jurisdiction and Admissibility, Judgment, *I.C.J. Reports 2006,* p. 40, para. 90). The Court's determination must turn on an examination of the facts. The matter is one of substance, not of form. As the Court has recognized (for example, *Land and Maritime Boundary between Cameroon and Nigeria,* Cameroon *v.* Nigeria, Preliminary Objections, Judgment, *I.C.J. Reports 1998,* p. 315, para. 89), the existence of a dispute may be inferred from the failure of a State to respond to a claim in circumstances where a response is called for. While the existence of a dispute and the undertaking of negotiations are distinct as a matter of principle, the negotiations may help demonstrate the existence of the dispute and delineate its subject-matter.

The dispute must in principle exist at the time the Application is submitted to the Court (*Questions of Interpretation and Application of the 1971 Montreal Convention arising from the Aerial Incident at Lockerbie*, Libyan Arab Jamahiriya v. United Kingdom, Preliminary Objections, *Judgment, I.C.J. Reports 1998*, pp. 25–26, paras. 42–44; *Questions of Interpretation and Application of the 1971 Montreal Convention arising from the Aerial Incident at Lockerbie*, Libyan Arab Jamahiriya v. United States of America, Preliminary Objections, Judgment, *I.C.J. Reports 1998*, pp. 130–131, paras. 42–44) (...) (para. 30).

9. This passage of the 2011 Judgment in the case of the *Application of the CERD Convention* reiterates what the ICJ has held in its *jurisprudence constante*. Yet, shortly afterwards in that same Judgment, the ICJ has decided to apply to the facts of the case a higher threshold for the determination of the existence of a dispute, by proceeding to ascertain whether the applicant State had given the respondent State prior notice of its claim and whether the respondent State had opposed it.[5] On this basis, it has concluded that no dispute had arisen between the contending parties (before August 2008). Such new requirement, however, is not consistent with the PCIJ's and the ICJ's *jurisprudence constante* on the determination of the existence of a dispute (cf. *supra*).

10. Now, in the present case of *Obligations Concerning Negotiations Relating to Cessation of the Nuclear Arms Race and to Nuclear Disarmament*, the three respondent States (India, United Kingdom and Pakistan), seek to rely on a requirement of prior notification of the claim, or the test of prior awareness of the claim of the applicant State (the Marshall Islands), for a dispute to exist under the ICJ's Statute or general international law. Yet, nowhere can such a requirement be found in the Court's *jurisprudence constante* as to the existence of a dispute: quite on the contrary, the ICJ has made clear that the position or the attitude of a party can be established by inference.[6] Pursuant to the Court's approach, it is not necessary for the respondent to oppose previously the claim

---

[5] Cf. paras. 50–105, and esp. paras. 31, 61 and 104–105, of the Court's Judgment of 01.04.2011.

[6] ICJ, *Land and Maritime Boundary between Cameroon and Nigeria* (Judgment on Preliminary Objections, of 11.06.1998), p. 315, para. 89: "a disagreement on a point of law or fact, a conflict of legal views or interests, or the positive opposition of the claim of one party by the other need not necessarily be stated *expressis verbis*. In the determination of the existence of a dispute, as in other matters, the position or the attitude of a party can be established by inference, whatever the professed view of that party".

by an express statement, or to express acknowledgment of the existence of a dispute.

11. The respondent States in the present case have made reference to the Court's 2011 Judgment in the case of the *Application of the CERD Convention* in support of their position that prior notice of the applicant's claim is a requirement for the existence of a dispute. Already in my Dissenting Opinion (para. 161) in that case, I have criticized the Court's "formalistic reasoning" in determining the existence of a dispute, introducing a higher threshold that goes beyond the *jurisprudence constante* of the PCIJ and the ICJ itself (cf. *supra*).

12. As I pointed out in that Dissenting Opinion in the case of the *Application of the CERD Convention*,

> As to the first preliminary objection, for example, the Court spent 92 paragraphs to concede that, in its view, a legal dispute at last crystallized, on 10 August 2008 (para. 93), only *after* the outbreak of an open and declared war between Georgia and Russia! I find that truly extraordinary: the emergence of a legal dispute only *after* the outbreak of widespread violence and war! Are there disputes which are quintessentially and ontologically *legal*, devoid of any political ingredients or considerations? I do not think so. The same formalistic reasoning leads the Court, in 70 paragraphs, to uphold the second preliminary objection, on the basis of alleged (unfulfilled) 'preconditions' of its own construction, in my view at variance with its own *jurisprudence constante* and with the more lucid international legal doctrine (para. 161).

13. Half a decade later, I was hopeful that the Court would distance itself from the formalistic approach it adopted in the case of the *Application of the CERD Convention*. As it regrettably has not done so, I feel obliged to reiterate here my dissenting position on the issue, this time in the present case of *Obligations Concerning Negotiations Relating to Cessation of the Nuclear Arms Race and to Nuclear Disarmament*. In effect, there is no general requirement of prior notice of the applicant State's intention to initiate proceedings before the ICJ.[7] It should not pass unnoticed that the *purpose* of the need of determination of the existence of a dispute (and its object) before the Court is to enable this latter to exercise jurisdiction properly: it is not intended to protect the

---

7 Cf., to this effect, S. Rosenne, *The Law and Practice of the International Court (1920–2005)*, 4th ed., vol. III, Leiden, Nijhoff/Brill, 2006, p. 1153.

respondent State, but rather and more precisely to safeguard the proper exercise of the Court's judicial function.

14. There is no requirement under general international law that the contending parties must first "exhaust" diplomatic negotiations before lodging a case with, and instituting proceedings before, the Court (as a precondition for the existence of the dispute). There is no such requirement in general international law, nor in the ICJ's Statute, nor in the Court's case-law. This is precisely what the ICJ held in its Judgment on Preliminary Objections (of 11.06.1998) in the case of *Land and Maritime Boundary between Cameroon and Nigeria*: it clearly stated that

> Neither in the Charter nor otherwise in international law is any general rule to be found to the effect that the exhaustion of diplomatic negotiations constitutes a precondition for a matter to be referred to the Court (para. 56).

15. The Court's statement refers to the "exhaustion" of diplomatic negotiations, – to discard the concept. In effect, there is no such a requirement in the U.N. Charter either, that negotiations would need to be resorted to or attempted. May I reiterate that the Court's determination of the existence of the dispute is not designed to protect the respondent State(s), but rather to safeguard the proper exercise of its own judicial function in contentious cases. It is thus a matter for objective determination by the Court, as it recalled in that same Judgment (para. 87), on the basis of its own *jurisprudence constante* on the matter.

2 Existence of a Dispute in the Cas d'Espèce (*Case Marshall Islands* versus *Pakistan*)

16. In the present case opposing the Marshall Islands to Pakistan, there were two sustained and distinct courses of conduct of the two contending parties, evidencing their distinct legal positions (as to the duty of negotiations leading to nuclear disarmament in all its aspects under strict and effective international control), which suffice for the determination of the existence of a dispute. This dispute concerns Pakistan's compliance with its obligation under customary international law to pursue in good faith, and bring to a conclusion, negotiations leading to nuclear disarmament in all its aspects under strict and effective international control.

17. On 14.02.2014, in its declaration at the aforementioned Conference of Nayarit, the Marshall Islands publicly expressed its view concerning the

obligation on nuclear disarmament. Pakistan did not react to that declaration, nor did it change its conduct. Thus, one can already infer an opposition of legal views. In its subsequent submissions to the ICJ, Pakistan sustained its position, opposing that of the Marshall Islands in its *Note Verbale* of 09.07.2014, Pakistan challenged the Marshall Islands' arguments, referring to what it regarded as an exaggerated and unfounded interpretation of Article VI of the NPT, which is in its view inapplicable to States that are not parties to the NPT, and which does not have an *erga omnes* character. In its *Counter-Memorial*, Pakistan submits that the Marshall Islands' claims are manifestly without legal merit or substance (paras. 4.1–4.6), clearly challenging the legal basis of the Marshall Islands' claim (para. 4.5).

3 *The Threshold for the Determination of the Existence of a Dispute*

18. In the present cases of *Obligations Concerning Negotiations Relating to Cessation of the Nuclear Arms Race and to Nuclear Disarmament* (Marshall Islands *versus* India/United Kingdom/Pakistan), the Court's majority has unduly heightened the threshold for establishing the existence of a dispute. Even if dismissing the need for an applicant State to provide notice of a dispute, in practice, the requirement stipulated goes far beyond giving notice: the Court effectively requires an applicant State to set out its legal claim, to direct it specifically to the prospective-respondent State(s), and to make the alleged harmful conduct clear. All of this forms part of the "awareness" requirement that the Court's majority has laid down, seemingly undermining its own ability to infer the existence of a dispute from the conflicting courses of conduct of the contending parties.

19. This is not in line with the ICJ's previous *obiter dicta* on inference, contradicting it. For example, in the aforementioned case of *Land and Maritime Boundary between Cameroon and Nigeria* (1998), the ICJ stated that

> [A] disagreement on a point of law or fact, a conflict of legal views or interests, or the positive opposition of the claim of one party by the other need not necessarily be stated *expressis verbis*. In the determination of the existence of a dispute, as in other matters, the position or attitude of a party can be established by inference, whatever the professed view of that party (para. 89).

20. The view taken by the Court's majority in the present case contradicts the Hague Court's (PCIJ and ICJ) own earlier case-law, in which it has taken a much less formalistic approach to the establishment of the existence of a dispute.

Early in its life, the PCIJ made clear that it did not attach much importance to "matters of form";[8] it added that it could not "be hampered by a mere defect of form".[9] The PCIJ further stated that "the manifestation of the existence of the dispute in a specific manner, as for instance by diplomatic negotiations, is not required. (...) [T]he Court considers that it cannot require that the dispute should have manifested itself in a formal way".[10]

21. The ICJ has, likewise, in its own case-law, avoided to take a very formalistic approach to the determination of the existence of a dispute.[11] May I recall, in this respect, *inter alia*, as notable examples, the Court's *obiter dicta* on the issue, in the cases of *East Timor* (Portugal *versus* Australia), of the *Application of the Convention against Genocide* (Bosnia *versus* Yugoslavia), and of *Certain Property* (Liechtenstein *versus* Germany). In those cases, the ICJ has considered that conduct post-dating the critical date (i.e., the date of the filing of the Application) supports a finding of the existence of a dispute between the parties. In the light of this approach taken by the ICJ itself in its earlier case-law, it is clear that a dispute exists in each of the present cases lodged with it by the Marshall Islands.

22. In the case of *East Timor* (1995), in response to Australia's preliminary objection that there was no dispute between itself and Portugal, the Court stated: "Portugal has, rightly or wrongly, formulated complaints of fact and law against Australia which the latter has denied. By virtue of this denial, there is a legal dispute".[12] Shortly afterwards, in the case of the *Application of the Convention*

---

8   PCIJ, case of *Mavrommatis Palestine Concessions*, Judgment of 30.08.1924, p. 34.

9   PCIJ, case of *Certain German Interests in Polish Upper Silesia* case (Jurisdiction), Judgment of 25.08.1925, p. 14.

10 PCIJ, case of *Interpretation of Judgments ns. 7 and 8 – Chorzów Factory*, Judgment of 16.12.1927, pp. 10–11.

11 Cf., e.g., ICJ, Advisory Opinion (of 26.04.1988) on the *Applicability of the Obligation to Arbitrate under Section 21 of the U.N. Headquarters Agreement of 26.06.1947*, pp. 28–29, para. 38; ICJ, case of *Nicaragua versus United States* (Jurisdiction and Admissibility), Judgment of 26.11.1984, pp. 428–429, para. 83. Moreover, the critical date for the determination of the existence of a dispute is, "in principle" (as the ICJ says), the date on which the application is submitted to the Court (ICJ, case of *Questions Relation to the Obligation to Prosecute or Extradite*, Judgment of 20.07.2012, p. 20, para. 46; ICJ, case of *Alleged Violations of Sovereign Rights and Maritime Spaces in the Caribbean Sea*, Preliminary Objections, Judgment of 17.03.2016, p. 25, para. 52); the ICJ's phraseology shows that this is not a strict rule, but rather one to be approached with flexibility.

12 ICJ, case of *East Timor* (Portugal *versus* Australia), *I.C.J. Reports 1995*, p. 100, para. 22 (Judgment of 30.06.1995).

against Genocide (Preliminary Objections, 1996), in response to Yugoslavia's preliminary objection that the Court did not have jurisdiction under Article IX of the Convention against Genocide because there was no dispute between the Parties, the Court, contrariwise, found that there was a dispute between them, on the basis that Yugoslavia had "wholly denied all of Bosnia and Herzegovina's allegations, whether at the stage of proceedings relating to the requests for the indication of provisional measures, or at the stage of the (…) proceedings relating to […preliminary] objections".[13] Accordingly, "by reason of the rejection by Yugoslavia of the complaints formulated against it",[14] the ICJ found that there was a dispute.

23. In the case of *Certain Property* (Preliminary Objections, 2005), as to Germany's preliminary objection that there was no dispute between the parties, the ICJ found that complaints of fact and law formulated by Liechtenstein were denied by Germany; accordingly, "[i]n conformity with well-established jurisprudence", – the ICJ concluded, – "by virtue of this denial", there was a legal dispute between Liechtenstein and Germany.[15] Now, in the present proceedings before the Court, in each of the three cases lodged with the ICJ by the Marshall Islands (against India, the United Kingdom and Pakistan), the respondent States have expressly denied the arguments of the Marshall Islands. May we now take note of the denials which, on the basis of the Court's aforementioned *jurisprudence constante*, evidence the existence of a dispute between the contending parties.[16]

4 Contentions in the Case of *Marshall Islands* versus *Pakistan*

24. The Marshall Islands argues that Pakistan has breached the customary international law obligation to negotiate nuclear disarmament in good faith by engaging in a course of conduct that is contrary to the objective of disarmament. The Marshall Islands further contends that Pakistan, by its conduct, has

---

13 ICJ, case of the *Application of the Convention against Genocide* (Bosnia-Herzegovina *versus* Yugoslavia, Preliminary Objections, Judgment of 11.07.1996), *I.C.J. Reports 1996*, pp. 595 and 614–615, paras. 27–29.
14 *Ibid.*, p. 615, para. 29.
15 ICJ, case of *Certain Property* (Liechtenstein *versus* Germany, Preliminary Objections, Judgment of 10.02.2005), *I.C.J. Reports 2005*, p. 19, para. 25, citing the Court's Judgments in the cases of *East Timor*, *I.C.J. Reports 1995*, p. 100, para. 22; and of the *Application of the Convention against Genocide* (Preliminary Objections), *I.C.J. Reports 1996*, p. 615, para. 29.
16 As the present proceedings relate to jurisdiction, the opposition of views is captured in the various jurisdictional objections; it would be even more forceful in pleadings on the merits, which, given the Court's majority decision, will regrettably no longer take place.

breached the customary international law obligation regarding the cessation of the nuclear arms race at an early date.[17] For its part, in its *Counter-Memorial*, Pakistan discloses a dispute about the existence of the customary international law obligations asserted by the Marshall Islands as well as its own compliance with such obligations.[18]

25. In Part 4 of its *Counter-Memorial*, e.g., Pakistan states that it emerges from the *Application Instituting Proceedings* and the *Memorial* of the Marshall Islands that its "claims are based upon: (1) multilateral treaties to which Pakistan is not a party; (2) non-binding General Assembly resolutions; and (3) a non-binding Advisory Opinion of the Court". And it adds:

> As to (1), although the RMI seeks to present its claims as founded in customary international law, the obligations which it identifies are said to be 'rooted' and 'enshrined' in Article VI of the NPT, a treaty provision to which the 22-page *Application* refers at least 15 times. Pakistan is not a party to the NPT. As to (2) and (3), due to their non-binding status, these cannot give rise to obligations binding on Pakistan. None of the above-referenced sources invoked by the RMI is opposable to Pakistan.
>
> Even if Pakistan (and the Court) were to accept the facts as alleged by the RMI to be true, these do not give rise to any breach by Pakistan and, as explained below, the RMI's asserted injuries and claims are not redressable. As a result, the RMI's case against Pakistan is inadmissible and manifestly without any legal merit or substance and the Court must decline jurisdiction.[19]

5   *General Assessment*

26. Always attentive and over-sensitive to the position of nuclear-weapon States [NWS] (cf. Part XII, *infra*), – such as the respondent States in the present cases of *Obligations Concerning Negotiations Relating to Cessation of the Nuclear Arms Race and to Nuclear Disarmament* (India, United Kingdom and Pakistan), – the Court, in the *cas d'espèce*, dismisses the statements made by the Marshall Islands in multilateral *fora* before the filing of the Application,

---

17   *Application Instituting Proceedings* of the Marshall Islands, pp. 20–21, paras. 52–55.
18   For example, Part 4 of the *Counter-Memorial* of Pakistan is titled "The RMI's Claims against Pakistan are Manifestly without Legal Merit or Substance"; cf. *Counter-Memorial*, p. 14.
19   *Counter-Memorial* of Pakistan, p. 14, paras. 4.4–4.6.

as being, in its view, insufficient to determine the existence of a dispute. Moreover, the Court's majority makes *tabula rasa* of the requirement that "in principle" the date for determining the existence of the dispute is the date of filing of the application (case of *Alleged Violations of Sovereign Rights and Maritime Spaces in the Caribbean Sea*, Nicaragua *versus* Colombia, Preliminary Objections, Judgment of 17.03.2016, para. 52); as already seen, in its case-law the ICJ has taken into account conduct post-dating that critical date (cf. *supra*).

27. In an entirely formalistic reasoning, the Court borrows the *obiter dicta* it made in the case of the *Application of the CERD Convention* (2011), – unduly elevating the threshold for the determination of the existence of a dispute, – in respect of a compromissory clause under that Convention (wrongly interpreted anyway, making abstraction of the object and purpose of the CERD Convention). In the present case, opposing the Marshall Islands to Pakistan, worse still, the Court's majority takes that higher standard out of context, and applies it herein, in a case lodged with the Court on the basis of an optional clause declaration, and concerning an obligation under customary international law.

28. This attempt to heighten still further the threshold for the determination of the existence of a dispute (requiring further factual precisions from the applicant) is, besides formalistic, artificial: it does not follow from the definition of a dispute in the Court's *jurisprudence constante*, as being "a conflict of legal views or of interests", as already seen (cf. *supra*). The Court's majority formalistically requires a specific reaction of the respondent State to the claim made by the applicant State (in applying the criterion of "awareness", amounting, in my perception, to an obstacle to access to justice), even in a situation where, as in the *cas d'espèce*, there are two consistent and distinct courses of conduct on the part of the contending parties.

29. Furthermore, and in conclusion, there is a clear denial by the respondent States (India, United Kingdom and Pakistan) of the arguments made against them by the applicant State, the Marshall Islands. By virtue of these denials there is a legal dispute between the Marshall Islands and each of the three respondent States. The formalistic raising, by the Court's majority, of the higher threshold for the determination of the existence of a dispute, is not in conformity with the *jurisprudence constante* of the PCIJ and ICJ on the matter (cf. *supra*). Furthermore, in my perception, it unduly creates a difficulty for the very *access to justice* (by applicants) at international level, in a case on a matter of concern to the whole of humankind. This is most regrettable.

III U.N. General Assembly Resolutions and *Opinio Juris*

30. In the course of the proceedings in the present cases of *Obligations Concerning Negotiations Relating to Cessation of the Nuclear Arms Race and to Nuclear Disarmament*, both the applicant State (the Marshall Islands) and the respondent States (India, United Kingdom and Pakistan) addressed U.N. General Assembly resolutions on the matter of nuclear disarmament (cf. Part VI, *infra*). This is the point that I purport to consider, in sequence, in the present Dissenting Opinion, namely, in addition to the acknowledgment before the ICJ (1995) of the authority and legal value of General Assembly resolutions on nuclear weapons as breach of the U.N. Charter, the distinct series of: (a) U.N. General Assembly resolutions on Nuclear Weapons (1961–1981); (b) UN General Assembly Resolutions on Freeze of Nuclear Weapons (1982–1992); (c) U.N. General Assembly Resolutions Condemning Nuclear Weapons (1982–2015); (d) U.N. General Assembly Resolutions Following up the ICJ's 1996 Advisory Opinion (1996–2015).

1 *U.N. General Assembly Resolutions on Nuclear Weapons (1961–1981)*

31. The 1970s was the First Disarmament Decade: it was so declared by General Assembly resolution A/RES/2602 E (XXIV) of 16.12.1969, followed by two other resolutions of 1978 and 1980 on non-use of nuclear weapons and prevention of nuclear war.[20] The General Assembly specifically called upon States to intensify efforts for the cessation of the nuclear arms race, nuclear disarmament and the elimination of other weapons of mass destruction. Even before that, the ground-breaking General Assembly resolution 1653 (XVI), of 24.11.1961, advanced its *célèbre* "Declaration on the Prohibition of the Use of Nuclear and Thermonuclear Weapons" (cf. Part V, *infra*). In 1979, when the First Disarmament Decade was coming to an end, the General Assembly, – disappointed that the objectives of the first Decade had not been realized, – declared the 1980s as a Second Disarmament Decade.[21] Likewise, the 1990s were subsequently declared the Third Disarmament Decade.[22]

---

[20] Namely, in sequence, General Assembly resolutions A/RES/33/71B of 14.12.1978, and A/RES/35/152D of 12.12.1980.

[21] Cf. General Assembly resolutions A/RES/34/75 of 11.12.1979, and A/RES/35/46 of 03.12.1980.

[22] Cf. General Assembly resolutions A/RES/43/78L of 07.12.1988, and A/RES/45/62 A of 04.12.1990.

32. In this first period under review (1961–1981), the U.N. General Assembly paid continuously special attention to disarmament issues and to nuclear disarmament in particular. May I refer to General Assembly resolutions A/RES/2934 of 29.11.1972; A/RES/2936 of 29.11.1972; A/RES/3078 of 06.12.1973; A/RES/3257 of 09.12.1974; A/RES/3466 of 11.12.1975; A/RES/3478 of 11.12.1975; A/RES/31/66 of 10.12.1976; A/RES/32/78 of 12.12.1977; A/RES/33/71 of 14.12.1978; A/RES/33/72 of 14.12.1978; A/RES/33/91 of 16.12.1978; A/RES/34/83 of 11.12.1979; A/RES/34/84 of 11.12.1979; A/RES/34/85 of 11.12.1979; A/RES/34/86 of 11.12.1979; A/RES/35/152 of 12.12.1980; A/RES/35/155 of 12.12.1980; A/RES/35/156 of 12.12.1980; A/RES/36/81 of 09.12.1981; A/RES/36/84 of 09.12.1981; A/RES/36/92 of 09.12.1981; A/RES/36/94 of 09.12.1981; A/RES/36/95 of 09.12.1981; A/RES/36/97 of 09.12.1981; and A/RES/36/100 of 09.12.1981.

33. In 1978 and 1982, the U.N. General Assembly held two Special Sessions on Nuclear Disarmament (respectively, the 10th and 12th sessions), where the question of nuclear disarmament featured prominently amongst the themes discussed. In fact, it was stressed that the most immediate goal of disarmament is the elimination of the danger of a nuclear war. In a subsequent series of its resolutions (in the following period of 1982–2015), as we shall see, the General Assembly moved on straightforwardly to the condemnation of nuclear weapons (cf. *infra*).

34. In its resolutions adopted during the present period of 1972–1981, the General Assembly repeatedly drew attention to the dangers of the nuclear arms race for humankind and the survival of civilization and expressed apprehension concerning the harmful consequences of nuclear testing for the acceleration of such arms race. Thus, the General Assembly reiterated its condemnation of all nuclear weapon tests, in whatever environment they may be conducted. It called upon States that had not yet done so to adhere to the 1963 Test Ban Treaty (banning nuclear tests in the atmosphere, in outer space and under water) and called for the conclusion of a comprehensive test ban treaty, which would ban nuclear weapons tests in all environments (e.g. underground as well). Pending the conclusion of such treaty, it urged NWS to suspend nuclear weapon tests in all environments.

35. The General Assembly also emphasised that NWS bear a special responsibility for fulfilling the goal of achieving nuclear disarmament, and in particular those nuclear weapon States that are parties to international agreements in which they have declared their intention to achieve the cessation of the nuclear

arms race. It further called specifically on the heads of State of the USSR and the United States to implement the procedures for the entry into force of the Strategic Arms Limitation agreement (so-called "SALT" agreement).

36. At the 84th plenary meeting, following the 10th Special Session on Disarmament, the General Assembly declared that the use of nuclear weapons is a "violation of the Charter of the United Nations" and "a crime against humanity", and that the use of nuclear weapons should be prohibited, pending nuclear disarmament.[23] The General Assembly further noted the aspiration of non-nuclear weapon States [NNWS] to prevent nuclear weapons from being stationed on their territories through the establishment of nuclear-weapon-free zones, and supported their efforts to conclude an international Convention strengthening the guarantees for their security against the use or threat of use of nuclear weapons. As part of the measures to facilitate the process of nuclear disarmament and the non-proliferation of nuclear weapons, it requested the Committee on Disarmament to consider the question of the cessation and prohibition of the production of fissionable material for weapons purposes.

2 U.N. General Assembly Resolutions on Freeze of Nuclear Weapons (1982–1992)

37. Every year in the successive period 1982–1992 (following up on the 10th and 12th Special Sessions on Nuclear Disarmament, held in 1978 and 1982, respectively), the General Assembly adopted resolutions also calling for a nuclear-weapons freeze. May I refer to General Assembly resolutions A/RES/37/100A of 13.12.1982; A/RES/38/73E of 15.12.1983; A/RES/39/63C of 12.12.1984; A/RES/40/151C of 16.12.1985; A/RES/41/60E of 03.12.1986; A/RES/42/39B of 30.11.1987; A/RES/43/76B of 07.12.1988; A/RES/44/117D of 15.12.1989; A/RES/45/59D of 04.12.1990; A/RES/46/37C of 06.12.1991; and A/RES/47/53E of 09.12.1992.

38. These resolutions on freeze of nuclear weapons note that existing arsenals of nuclear weapons are more than sufficient to destroy all life on earth. They express the conviction that lasting world peace can be based only upon the achievement of general and complete disarmament, under effective international control. In this connection, the aforementioned General Assembly resolutions note that the highest priority objectives in the field of disarmament have to be nuclear disarmament and the elimination of all weapons of mass

---

23   Cf. General Assembly resolutions A/RES/33/71B of 14.12.1978, and A/RES/35/152D of 12.12.1980.

destruction. They at last call upon NWS to agree to reach "a freeze on nuclear weapons", which would, *inter alia*, provide for "a simultaneous total stoppage of any further production of fissionable material for weapons purposes".

39. Such nuclear-weapons freeze is not seen as an end in itself but as the most effective first step towards: (a) halting any further increase and qualitative improvement in the existing arsenals of nuclear weapons; and (b) activating negotiations for the substantial reduction and qualitative limitation of nuclear weapons. From 1989 onwards, these resolutions also set out the structure and scope of the prospective joint declaration through which all nuclear-weapons States would agree on a nuclear-arms freeze. Such freeze would encompass: (a) a comprehensive test ban; (b) cessation of the manufacture of nuclear weapons; (c) a ban on all further deployment of nuclear weapons; and (d) cessation of the production of fissionable material for weapons purposes.

3 *U.N. General Assembly Resolutions on Nuclear Weapons as Breach of the U.N. Charter (Acknowledgment before the ICJ, 1995)*

40. Two decades ago, when U.N. General Assembly resolutions condemning nuclear weapons were not as numerous as they are today, they were already regarded as authoritative in the views of States from distinct continents. This was made clear, e.g., by States which participated in the advisory proceedings of 30 October to 15 November 1995 before the ICJ, conducive to its Advisory Opinion of 08.07.1996 on the *Threat or Use of Nuclear Weapons*. On the occasion, the view was upheld that those General Assembly resolutions expressed a "general consensus" and had a relevant "legal value".[24] Resolution 1653 (XVI), of 1961, e.g., was invoked as a "law-making" resolution of the General Assembly, in stating that the use of nuclear weapons is contrary to the letter and spirit, and aims, of the United Nations, and, as such, a "direct violation" of the U.N. Charter.[25]

41. It was further stated that, already towards the end of 1995, "numerous" General Assembly resolutions and declarations confirmed the illegality of the use of force, including nuclear weapons.[26] Some General Assembly resolutions (1653 (XVI), of 24.11.1961; 33/71B of 14.12.1978; 34/83G of 11.12.1979; 35/152D of 12.12.1980; 36/92I of 09.12.1981; 45/59B of 04.12.1990; 46/37D of 06.12.1991) were singled out for having significantly declared that the use of nuclear weapons

---

24   ICJ, doc. CR 95/25, of 03.11.1995, pp. 52–53 (statement of Mexico).
25   ICJ, doc. CR 95/22, of 30.10.1995, pp. 44–45 (statement of Australia).
26   ICJ, doc. CR 95/26, of 06.11.1995, pp. 23–24 (statement of Iran).

would be a violation of the U.N. Charter itself.[27] The view was expressed that the series of General Assembly resolutions (starting with resolution 1653 (XVI), of 24.11.1961) amounted to "an authoritative interpretation" of humanitarian law treaties as well as the U.N. Charter.[28]

42. In the advisory proceedings of 1995 before the ICJ, it was further recalled that General Assembly resolution 1653 (XVI) of 1961 was adopted in the form of a declaration, being thus "an assertion of the law", and, ever since, the General Assembly's authority to adopt such declaratory resolutions (in condemnation of nuclear weapons) was generally accepted; such resolutions declaring the use of nuclear weapons "unlawful" were regarded as ensuing from the exercise of an "inherent" power of the General Assembly.[29] The relevance of General Assembly resolutions has been reckoned by large groups of States[30]

43. Ever since the aforementioned acknowledgment of the authority and legal value of General Assembly resolutions in the course of the pleadings of late 1995 before the ICJ, those resolutions continue to grow in number until today, clearly forming, in my perception, an *opinio juris communis* as to nuclear disarmament. In addition to those aforementioned, may I also review, in sequence, two other series of General Assembly resolutions, extending to the present, namely: the longstanding series of General Assembly resolutions condemning nuclear weapons (1982–2015), and the series of General Assembly resolutions following up the ICJ's 1996 Advisory Opinion (1997–2015).

4 U.N. General Assembly Resolutions Condemning Nuclear Weapons (1982–2015)

44. In the period 1982–2015, there is a long series of U.N. General Assembly resolutions condemning nuclear weapons. May I refer to General Assembly resolutions A/RES/37/100C of 09.12.1982; A/RES/38/73G of 15.12.1983; A/RES/39/63H of 12.12.1984; A/RES/40/151F of 16.12.1985; A/RES/41/60F of 03.12.1986; A/RES/42/39C of 30.11.1987; A/RES/43/76E of 07.12.1988; A/RES/44/117C of 15.12.1989; A/RES/45/59B of 04.12.1990; A/RES/46/37D of 06.12.1991; A/RES/47/53C of 09.12.1992; A/RES/48/76B of 16.12.1993; A/RES/49/76E of 15.12.1994; A/RES/50/71E of 12.12.1995; A/RES/51/46D of 10.12.1996; A/RES/52/39C

---

27 ICJ, doc. CR 95/28, of 09.11.1995, pp. 62–63 (statement of the Philippines).
28 ICJ, doc. CR 95/31, of 13.11.1995, p. 46 (statement of Samoa).
29 ICJ, doc. CR 95/27, of 07.11.1995, pp. 58–59 (statement of Malaysia).
30 Cf., e.g., ICJ, doc. CR 95/35, of 15.11.1995, p. 34, and cf. p. 22 (statement of Zimbabwe, on its initiative as Chair of the Non-Aligned Movement).

of 09.12.1997; A/RES/53/78D of 04.12.1998; A/RES/54/55D of 01.12.1999; A/RES/55/34G of 20.11. 2000; A/RES/56/25B of 29.11.2001; A/RES/57/94 of 22.11.2002; A/RES/58/64 of 08.12.2003; A/RES/59/102 of 03.12.2004; A/RES/60/88 of 08.12.2005; A/RES/61/97 of 06.12.2006; A/RES/62/51 of 05.12.2007; A/RES/63/75 of 02.02.2008; A/RES/64/59 of 02.12.2009; A/RES/65/80 of 08.12.2010; A/RES/66/57 of 02.12.2011; A/RES/67/64 of 03.12.2012; A/RES/68/58 of 05.12.2013; A/RES/69/69 of 02.12.2014; and A/RES/70/62 of 07.12.2015.

45. In those resolutions, the General Assembly warned against the threat by nuclear weapons to the survival of humankind. They were preceded by two ground-breaking historical resolutions, namely, General Assembly resolution 1(I) of 24.01.1946, and General Assembly resolution 1653 (XVI), of 24.11.1961 (cf. infra). In this new and long series of resolutions condemning nuclear weapons (1982–2015), at the opening of their preambular paragraphs the General Assembly states, year after year, that it is

> *Alarmed* by the threat to the survival of mankind and to the life-sustaining system posed by nuclear weapons and by their use, inherent in the concepts of deterrence,
> *Convinced* that nuclear disarmament is essential for the prevention of nuclear war and for the strengthening of international peace and security,
> *Further convinced* that a prohibition of the use or threat of use of nuclear weapons would be a step towards the complete elimination of nuclear weapons leading to general and complete disarmament under strict and effective international control.

46. Those General Assembly resolutions next significantly *reaffirm*, in their preambular paragraphs, year after year, that

> the use of nuclear weapons would be a violation of the Charter of the United Nations and a crime against humanity, as declared in its resolutions 1653 (XVI) of 24.11.1961, 33/71B of 14.12.1978, 34/83G of 11.12.1979, 35/152D of 12.12.1980 and 36/92I of 09.12.1981.

47. Still in their preambular paragraphs, those General Assembly resolutions further *note with regret* the inability of the Conference on Disarmament to undertake negotiations with a view to achieving agreement on a nuclear disarmament Convention during each previous year. In their operative part, those resolutions reiterate, year after year, the request that the Committee on Disarmament undertakes, on a priority basis, negotiations aiming at achieving

agreement on an international Convention prohibiting the use or threat of use of nuclear weapons under any circumstances, taking as a basis the text of the draft Convention on the Prohibition of the Use of Nuclear Weapons.

48. From 1989 (44th session) onwards, those resolutions begin to note specifically that a multilateral agreement prohibiting the use or threat of use of nuclear weapons should strengthen international security and help to create the climate for negotiations leading to the complete elimination of nuclear weapons. Subsequently, those resolutions come to stress, in particular, that an international Convention would be a step towards the complete elimination of nuclear weapons, leading to general and complete disarmament, under strict and effective international control.

49. Clauses of the kind then evolve, from 1996 onwards,[31] to refer expressly to a time framework, i.e., that an international Convention would be an important step in a phased programme towards the complete elimination of nuclear weapons, within a specific framework of time. More recent resolutions also expressly refer to the determination to achieve an international Convention prohibiting the development, production, stockpiling and use of nuclear weapons, leading to their ultimate destruction.

5   *U.N. General Assembly Resolutions Following up the ICJ's 1996 Advisory Opinion (1996–2015)*

50. Ever since the delivery, on 08.07.1996, of the ICJ's Advisory Opinion on *Nuclear Weapons* to date, the General Assembly has been adopting a series of resolutions (1996–2015), as its follow up. May I refer to General Assembly resolutions A/RES/51/45 of 10.12.1996; A/RES/52/38 of 09.12.1997; A/RES/53/77 of 04.12.1998; A/RES/54/54 of 01.12.1999; A/RES/55/33 of 20.11.2000; A/RES/56/24 of 29.11.2001; A/RES/57/85 of 22.11.2002; A/RES/58/46 of 08.12.2003; A/RES/59/83 of 03.12.2004; A/RES/60/76 of 08.12.2005; A/RES/61/83 of 06.12.2006; A/RES/62/39 of 05.12.2007; A/RES/63/49 of 02.12.2008; A/RES/64/55 of 02.12.2009; A/RES/65/76 of 08.12.2010; A/RES/66/46 of 02.12.2011; A/RES/67/33 of 03.12.2012; A/RES/68/42 of 05.12.2013; A/RES/69/43 of 02.12.2014; and A/RES/70/56 of 07.12.2015. These resolutions make a number of significant statements.

51. The series of aforementioned General Assembly resolutions on follow-up to the 1996 Advisory Opinion of the ICJ (1996–2015) begins by expressing the General Assembly's belief that "the continuing existence of nuclear weapons

---

31   Cf., e.g., *inter alia*, General Assembly resolution A/RES/50/71E, of 12.12.1995.

poses a threat to humanity" and that "their use would have catastrophic consequences for all life on earth", and, further, that "the only defence against a nuclear catastrophe is the total elimination of nuclear weapons and the certainty that they will never be produced again" (2nd preambular paragraph). The General Assembly resolutions reiteratedly reaffirm "the commitment of the international community to the realization of the goal of a nuclear-weapon-free world through the total elimination of nuclear weapons" (3rd preambular paragraph). They recall their request to the Conference on Disarmament to establish an *ad hoc* Committee to commence negotiations on a phased programme of nuclear disarmament, aiming at the elimination of nuclear weapons, within a "time bound framework"; they further reaffirm the role of the Conference on Disarmament as the single multilateral disarmament negotiating forum.

52. The General Assembly then recalls, again and again, that "the solemn obligations of States Parties, undertaken in Article VI of the Treaty on the Non-Proliferation of Nuclear Weapons (NPT), particularly to pursue negotiations in good faith on effective measures relating to cessation of the nuclear arms race at an early date and to nuclear disarmament" (4th preambular paragraph). They express the goal of achieving a legally binding prohibition on the development, production, testing, deployment, stockpiling, threat or use of nuclear weapons, and their destruction under "effective international control". They significantly call upon *all States* to fulfil promptly the obligation leading to an early conclusion of a Convention prohibiting the development, production, testing, deployment, stockpiling, transfer, threat or use of nuclear weapons and providing for their elimination.[32]

53. Those resolutions (from 2003 onwards) express deep concern at the lack of progress made in the implementation of the "thirteen steps" agreed to, at the 2000 Review Conference, for the implementation of Article VI of the NPT. The aforementioned series of General Assembly resolutions include, from 2010 onwards, an additional (6th) preambular paragraph, expressing "deep concern at the catastrophic humanitarian consequences of any use of nuclear weapons", and reaffirming, in this context, "the need for all States at all times to comply with applicable international law, including international humanitarian law". Those follow-up General Assembly resolutions further recognize "with

---

32   Note that in earlier resolutions, the following year is explicitly referenced, i.e., States should commence negotiations in "the following year". This reference is removed in later resolutions.

satisfaction that the Antarctic Treaty, the Treaties of Tlatelolco, Rarotonga, Bangkok and Pelindaba, and the Treaty on a Nuclear-Weapon-Free Zone in Central Asia, as well as Mongolia's nuclear-weapon-free status, are gradually freeing the entire southern hemisphere and adjacent areas covered by those treaties from nuclear weapons" (10th preambular paragraph).

54. More recent resolutions (from 2013 onwards) are significantly further expanded. They call upon all NWS to undertake concrete disarmament efforts, stressing that all States need to make special efforts to achieve and maintain a world without nuclear weapons. They also take note of the "Five-Point Proposal on Nuclear Disarmament" made by the U.N. Secretary-General (cf. Part XVI, *infra*), and recognize the need for a multilaterally negotiated and legally binding instrument to assure that NNWS stand against the threat or use of nuclear weapons, pending the total elimination of nuclear weapons. In their operative part, the same series of General Assembly resolutions underline the ICJ's unanimous conclusion, in its 1996 Advisory Opinion on the *Threat or Use of Nuclear Weapons*, that "there exists an obligation to pursue in good faith and bring to a conclusion negotiations leading to nuclear disarmament in all its aspects under strict and effective international control" (para. 1).

55. Looking at this particular series of General Assembly follow-up resolutions as a whole, it should not pass unnoticed that they contain paragraphs referring to the obligation to pursue and conclude, in good faith, negotiations leading to nuclear disarmament, without any reference to the NPT or to States Parties to it. They rather refer to that obligation as a general one, not grounded on any treaty provision. *All States*, and not only States Parties to the NPT, are called upon to fulfil promptly that obligation, incumbent upon *all States*, to report (to the Secretary-General) on their compliance with the resolutions at issue. There are, notably, other paragraphs in those resolutions that are specifically directed at nuclear-weapon States, or make specific references to the NPT. In sum, references to *all States* are deliberate, and in the absence of any references to a treaty or other specifically-imposed international obligation, this thus points towards a customary law obligation to negotiate and achieve nuclear disarmament.

IV   U.N. Security Council Resolutions and *Opinio Juris*

56. Like the U.N. General Assembly, the U.N. Security Council has also often dwelt upon the matter at issue. May I refer, *inter alia*, to Security Council

resolutions S/23500, of 31.01.1992; S/RES/984, of 11.04.1995; S/RES/1540, of 28.04.2004; S/RES/1673, of 27.04.2006; S/RES/1810, of 25.04.2008; S/RES/1887, of 24.09.2009; and S/RES/1997, of 20.04.2011, – to which others can be added.[33] May I at first recall that, at a Security Council's meeting at the level of Heads of State and Government, held on 31.01.1992, the President of the U.N. Security Council made a statement on behalf of the members of the Security Council that called upon all member States to fulfil their obligations on matters of arms control and disarmament, and to prevent the proliferation of all weapons of mass destruction[34] (encompassing nuclear, chemical, and biological weapons).

57. The statement expressed the feeling prevailing at the time that the end of the Cold War "has raised hopes for a safer, more equitable and more humane world", giving now to the world "the best chance of achieving international peace and security since the foundation of the United Nations".[35] The members of the Security Council then warned against the threat to international peace and security of all weapons of mass destruction, and expressed their commitment to take appropriate action to prevent "the spread of technology related to the research for or production of such weapons".[36] They further stressed the importance of "the integral role in the implementation" of the NPT of "fully effective IAEA safeguards", and of "effective export controls"; they added that they would take "appropriate measures in the case of any violations notified to them by the IAEA".[37]

58. The proliferation of all weapons of mass destruction is defined in the aforementioned Security Council statement, notably, as a threat to international peace and security, – a point which was to be referred to, in subsequent resolutions of the Security Council, to justify its action under Chapter VII of the U.N. Charter. In three of its subsequent resolutions, in a preambular paragraph

---

33   Cf. also Security Council resolutions S/RES/1695 of 15.07.2006; S/RES/1718 of 14.10.2006; S/RES/1874 of 12.06.2009; S/RES/1928 of 07.06.2010; S/RES/2094 of 07.03.2013; S/RES/2141 of 05.03.2014; S/RES/2159 of 09.06.2014; S/RES/2224 of 09.06.2015; S/RES/2270 of 02.03.2016. In preambular paragraphs of all these Security Council resolutions, the Security Council reaffirms, time and time again, that the proliferation of nuclear, chemical and biological weapons, and their means of delivery, constitutes a threat to international peace and security.

34   U.N. doc. S/23500, of 31.01.1992, pp. 1–5.
35   Ibid., pp. 2 and 5.
36   Ibid., p. 4.
37   Ibid., p. 4.

(resolutions 1540, of 28.04.2004, para. 2; 1810, of 25.04.2008, para. 3; and 1887, of 24.09.2009, para. 2), the Security Council reaffirms the statement of its President (adopted on 31.01.1992), and, also in other resolutions, further asserts (also in preambular paragraphs) that the proliferation of nuclear, chemical and biological weapons is a threat to international peace and security[38] and that all States need to take measures to prevent such proliferation.

59. In resolution 1540/2004 of 28.04.2004, adopted by the Security Council acting under Chapter VII of the U.N. Charter, it sets forth legally binding obligations on all U.N. member States to set up and enforce appropriate and effective measures against the proliferation of nuclear, chemical, and biological weapons, – including the adoption of controls and a reporting procedure for U.N. member States to a Committee of the Security Council (sometimes referred to as the "1540 Committee"). Subsequent Security Council resolutions reaffirm resolution 1540/2004 and call upon U.N. member States to implement it.

60. The U.N. Security Council refers, in particular, in two of its resolutions (984/1995, of 11.04.1995; and 1887/2009 of 24.09.2009), to the obligation to pursue negotiations in good faith in relation to nuclear disarmament. In its preamble, Security Council resolution 984/1995 affirms the need for all States Parties to the NPT "to comply fully with all their obligations"; in its operative part, it further "[u]rges all States, as provided for in Article VI of the Treaty on the Non-Proliferation of Nuclear Weapons, to pursue negotiations in good faith on effective measures relating to nuclear disarmament and on a treaty on general and complete disarmament under strict and effective international control which remains a universal goal" (para. 8). It should not pass unnoticed that Security Council resolution 984/1995 pre-dates the ICJ's 1996 Advisory Opinion on the *Threat or Use of Nuclear Weapons*.

61. And Security Council resolution 1887/2009 of 24.09.2009, in its operative part, again calls upon States Parties to the NPT "to comply fully with all their obligations and fulfil their commitments under the Treaty" (para. 2), and, in particular, "pursuant to Article VI of the Treaty, to undertake to pursue negotiations in good faith on effective measures relating to nuclear arms reduction and disarmament"; furthermore, it calls upon "all other States to join in this

---

38   Cf. e.g. Security Council resolutions 1540, of 28.04.2004; 1673, of 27.04.2006; 1810, of 25.04.2008; 1977, of 20.04.2011. And cf. also resolutions 1695, of 15.07.2006; 1718, of 14.10.2006; 1874, of 12.06.2009; 1928, of 07.06.2010; 2094, of 07.03.2013; 2141, of 05.03.2014; 2159, of 09.06.2014; 2224, of 09.06.2015; and 2270, of 02.03.2016.

endeavour" (para. 5). It should not pass unnoticed that it is a general call, upon all U.N. member States, whether or not Parties to the NPT.

62. In my perception, the aforementioned resolutions of the Security Council, like those of the General Assembly (cf. *supra*), addressing all U.N. member States, provide significant elements of the emergence of an *opinio juris*, in support of the gradual formation of an obligation of customary international law, corresponding to the conventional obligation under Article VI of the NPT. In particular, the fact that the Security Council calls upon *all States*, and not only States Parties to the NPT, to pursue negotiations towards nuclear disarmament in good faith (or to join the NPT State Parties in this endeavour) is significant. It is an indication that the obligation is incumbent on all U.N. member States, irrespectively of their being or not Parties to the NPT.

V The Saga of the United Nations in the Condemnation of Nuclear Weapons

63. The U.N. resolutions (of the General Assembly and the Security Council) that I have just reviewed (*supra*) portray the United Nations' longstanding saga in the condemnation of nuclear weapons. This saga goes back to the birth and earlier years of the United Nations. In fact, nuclear weapons were not in the minds of the Delegates to the San Francisco Conference of June 1945, at the time when the United Nations Charter was adopted on 26.06.1945. The U.S. dropping of atomic bombs over Hiroshima and Nagasaki, heralding the nuclear age, occurred on 06 and 09 August 1945, respectively, over ten weeks before the U.N. Charter's entry into force, on 24.10.1945.

64. As soon as the United Nations Organization came into being, it promptly sought to equip itself to face the new challenges of the nuclear age: the General Assembly's very first resolution, – resolution 1(I) of 24.01.1946, – thus, established a Commission to deal with the matter, entrusted with submitting reports to the Security Council "in the interest of peace and security" (para. 2(a)), as well as with making proposals for "control of atomic energy to the extent necessary to ensure its use only for peaceful purposes", and for "the elimination from national armaments of atomic weapons and of all other major weapons adaptable to mass destruction" (para. 5(b)(c)).

65. One decade later, in 1956, the International Atomic Energy Agency (IAEA) was established. And half a decade later, in 1961, the General Assembly adopted

a ground-breaking resolution: it would be proper here to recall the precise terms of the historical General Assembly resolution 1653 (XVI), of 24.11.1961, titled "Declaration on the Prohibition of the Use of Nuclear and Thermo-Nuclear Weapons". That célèbre resolution 1653 (1961) remains contemporary today, and, 55 years later, continues to require close attention; in it, the General Assembly

> *Mindful* of its responsibility under the Charter of the United Nations in the maintenance of international peace and security, as well as in the consideration of principles governing disarmament,
>
> *Gravely concerned* that, while negotiations on disarmament have not so far achieved satisfactory results, the armaments race, particularly in the nuclear and thermo-nuclear fields, has reached a dangerous stage requiring all possible precautionary measures to protect humanity and civilization from the hazard of nuclear and thermo-nuclear catastrophe,
>
> *Recalling* that the use of weapons of mass destruction, causing unnecessary human suffering, was in the past prohibited, as being contrary to the laws of humanity and to the principles of international law, by international declarations and binding agreements, such as the Declaration of St. Petersburg of 1868, the Declaration of the Brussels Conference of 1874, the Conventions of The Hague Peace Conferences of 1899 and 1907, and the Geneva Protocol of 1925, to which the majority of nations are still parties,
>
> *Considering* that the use of nuclear and thermo-nuclear weapons would bring about indiscriminate suffering and destruction to mankind and civilization to an even greater extent than the use of those weapons declared by the aforementioned international declarations and agreements to be contrary to the laws of humanity and a crime under international law,
>
> *Believing* that the use of weapons of mass destruction, such as nuclear and thermo-nuclear weapons, is a direct negation of the high ideals and objectives which the United Nations has been established to achieve through the protection of succeeding generations from the scourge of war and through the preservation and promotion of their cultures,
>
> 1. *Declares* that:
>   (a) The use of nuclear and thermo-nuclear weapons is contrary to the spirit, letter and aims of the United Nations and, as such, a direct violation of the Charter of the United Nations;
>   (b) The use of nuclear and thermo-nuclear weapons would exceed even the scope of war and cause indiscriminate suffering and destruction to mankind and civilization and, as such, is contrary to the rules of international law and to the laws of humanity;

(c) The use of nuclear and thermo-nuclear weapons is a war directed not against an enemy or enemies alone but also against mankind in general, since the peoples of the world not involved in such a war will be subjected to all the evils generated by the use of such weapons;

(d) Any State using nuclear and thermo-nuclear weapons is to be considered as violating the Charter of the United Nations, as acting contrary to the laws of humanity and as committing a crime against mankind and civilization;

2. *Requests* the Secretary-General to consult the Governments of Member States to ascertain their views on the possibility of convening a Special Conference for signing a Convention on the prohibition of the use of nuclear and thermo-nuclear weapons for war purposes and to report on the results of such consultation to the General Assembly at its XVIIth session.

66. Over half a century later, the lucid and poignant declaration contained in General Assembly resolution 1653 (1961) appears endowed with permanent topicality, as the whole international community remains still awaiting for the conclusion of the propounded general Convention on the prohibition of nuclear and thermo-nuclear weapons: nuclear disarmament remains still a goal to be achieved by the United Nations today, as it was in 1961. The Comprehensive Nuclear-Test-Ban Treaty (CTBT), adopted on 24.09.1996, has not yet entered into force, although 164 States have ratified it to date.

67. It is beyond the scope of the present Dissenting Opinion to dwell upon the reasons why, already for two decades, one remains awaiting for the CTBT's entry into force.[39] Suffice it here to recall that the CTBT provides (Article XIV) that for it to enter into force, the 44 States specified in its Annex 2 need to ratify it;[40] a number of these States have not yet ratified the CTBT, including some NWS, like India and Pakistan. NWS have invoked distinct reasons for their positions conditioning nuclear disarmament (cf. *infra*). The entry into force of the CTBT has thus been delayed.

---

39 For a historical account and the perspectives of the CTBT, cf., e.g., K.A. Hansen, *The Comprehensive Nuclear Test Ban Treaty*, Stanford, Stanford University Press, 2006, pp. 1–84; [Various Authors,] *Nuclear Weapons after the Comprehensive Test Ban Treaty* (ed. E. Arnett), Stockholm-Solna/Oxford, SIPRI/Oxford University Press, 1996, pp. 1–141; J. Ramaker, J. Mackby, P.D. Marshall and R. Geil, *The Final Test – A History of the Comprehensive Nuclear-Test-Ban Treaty Negotiations*, Vienna, Ed. Prep. Comm. of CTBTO, 2003, pp. 1–265.

40 Those 44 States, named in Annex 2, participated in the CTBT negotiations at the Conference on Disarmament, from 1994 to 1996, and possessed nuclear reactors at that time.

68. Recently, in a panel in Vienna (on 27.04.2016) in commemoration of the 20th anniversary of the CTBT, the U.N. Secretary-General (Ban Ki-moon) pondered that there have been advances in the matter, but there remains a long way to go, in the determination "to bring into force a legally binding prohibition against all nuclear tests". He recalled to have

> repeatedly pointed to the toxic legacy that some 2,000 tests left on people and the environment in parts of Central Asia, North Africa, North America and the South Pacific. Nuclear testing poisons water, causes cancers, and pollutes the area with radioactive fall-out for generations and generations to come. We are here to honour the victims. The best tribute to them is action to ban and to stop nuclear testing. Their sufferings should teach the world to end this madness.[41]

He then called on the (eight) remaining CTBT Annex 2 States "to sign and ratify the Treaty without further delay", so as to strengthen its goal of universality; in this way, – he concluded, – "we can leave a safer world, free of nuclear tests, to our children and to succeeding generations of this world".[42]

69. To this one may add the unaccomplished endeavours of the U.N. General Assembly Special Sessions on Disarmament. Of the three Special Sessions held so far (in 1978, 10th Special Session; in 1982, 12th Special Session; and in 1988, 15th Special Session),[43] the first one appears to have been the most significant one so far. The Final Document adopted unanimously (without a vote) by the 1st Special Session on Disarmament sets up a programme of action on disarmament and the corresponding mechanism in its current form.

70. That Final Document of the first General Assembly Special Session on Disarmament (1978) addresses nuclear disarmament in its distinct aspects. In this respect, the General Assembly begins by observing that the accumulation of nuclear weapons constitutes a threat to the future of humankind (para. 1), in effect "the greatest danger" to humankind and to "the survival of civilization" (para. 47). It adds that the arms race, particularly in its nuclear aspect, is incompatible with the principles enshrined in the United Nations Charter (para. 12).

---

41 U.N. doc. SG/SM/17709-DC/3628, of 27.04.2016, pp. 1–2.
42 *Ibid.*, p. 2.
43 Ever since, several G.A. resolutions have called for a 4th Special Session on Disarmament, but it has not yet taken place.

In its view, the most effective guarantee against the dangers of nuclear war is the complete elimination of nuclear weapons (paras. 8 and 56).[44]

71. While disarmament is the responsibility of all States, the General Assembly asserts that NWS have the primary responsibility for nuclear disarmament. There is pressing need of "urgent negotiations of agreements" to that end, and in particular to conclude "a treaty prohibiting nuclear-weapon tests" (paras. 50–51). It further stresses the importance of nuclear-weapon-free zones that have been established or are the subject of negotiations in various parts of the globe (paras. 60–64).

72. The Conference on Disarmament, – since 1979 the sole multilateral disarmament-negotiating forum of the international community, – has helped to negotiate multilateral arms-limitation and disarmament agreements.[45] It has focused its work on four main issues, namely: nuclear disarmament, prohibition of the production of fissile material for weapon use, prevention of arms race in outer space, and negative security assurances. Yet, since the adoption of the CTBT in 1996, the Conference on Disarmament has been largely deadlocked, in face of the invocation of divergent security interests, added to the understanding that nuclear weapons require mutuality; furthermore, the Rules of Procedure of the Conference provide that all decisions must be adopted by consensus. In sum, some States blame political factors for causing its longstanding stalemate, while others attribute it to outdated procedural rules.

73. After all, in historical perspective, some advances have been attained in the last decades in respect of other weapons of mass destruction, as illustrated by the adoption of the Convention on the Prohibition of the Development, Production and Stockpiling of Bacteriological (Biological) and Toxin Weapons and on their Destruction (on 10.04.1972), as well as the Convention on the Prohibition of the Development, Production, Stockpiling and Use of Chemical Weapons and on their Destruction (on 13.01.1993); distinctly from the CTBT (*supra*), these two Conventions have already entered into force (on 26.03.1975, and on 29.04.1997, respectively).

---

44 And cf. also paras. 18 and 20.
45 E.g., the aforementioned NPT, CTBT, the Biological Weapons Convention, and the Chemical Weapons Convention, in addition to the seabed treaties, and the Convention on the Prohibition of Military or Any Other Hostile Use of Environmental Modification Techniques.

74. If we look at conventional international law only, weapons of mass destruction (poisonous gases, biological and chemical weapons) have been outlawed; yet, nuclear weapons, far more destructive, have not been banned yet. This juridical absurdity nourishes the positivist myopia, or blindness, in inferring therefrom that there is no customary international obligation of nuclear disarmament. Positivists only have eyes for treaty law, for individual State consent, revolving in vicious circles, unable to see the pressing needs and aspirations of the international community as a whole, and to grasp the *universality* of contemporary international law – as envisaged by its "founding fathers", already in the XVIth–XVIIth centuries, – with its underlying fundamental principles (cf. *infra*).

75. The truth is that, in our times, the obligation of nuclear disarmament has emerged and crystallized, in both conventional and customary international law, and the United Nations has been giving a most valuable contribution to this along the decades. The matter at issue, the United Nations saga in this domain, was brought to the attention of the ICJ, two decades ago, in the advisory proceedings that led to its Advisory Opinion of 1996 on the *Threat or Use of Nuclear Weapons*, and now again, two decades later, in the present contentious proceedings in the cases of *Obligations Concerning Negotiations Relating to Cessation of the Nuclear Arms Race and to Nuclear Disarmament*, opposing the Marshall Islands to India, Pakistan and the United Kingdom, respectively.

76. The aforementioned U.N. resolutions were in effect object of attention on the part of the contending parties before the Court (Marshall Islands, India, Pakistan and the United Kingdom). In the oral phase of their arguments, they were dealt with by the participating States (Marshall Islands, India and the United Kingdom), and, extensively so, in particular, by the Marshall Islands and India. The key point is the relation of those resolutions with the emergence of *opinio juris*, of relevance to the identification of a customary international law obligation in the present domain. May I turn, then, to the positions sustained by the contending parties, in the written phase of the proceedings in the *cas d'espèce*.

VI   U.N. Resolutions and the Emergence of *Opinio Juris*: The Positions of the Contending Parties

77. In its written submissions and oral arguments before the Court in the present case(s) of *Obligations Concerning Negotiations Relating to Cessation of the Nuclear Arms Race and to Nuclear Disarmament*, the Marshall Islands

addresses General Assembly resolutions on nuclear disarmament, in relation to the development of customary international law;[46] it also refers to Security Council resolutions.[47] Quoting the ICJ's Advisory Opinion of 1996, it contends (perhaps not as clearly as it could have done) that although General Assembly resolutions lack binding force, they may "sometimes have normative value", and thus contribute to the emergence of an *opinio juris*.[48]

78. In its written submissions and oral arguments before the Court, India addresses U.N. General Assembly resolutions on follow-up to the ICJ's Advisory Opinion of 1996, pointing out that it is the only nuclear weapon State that has co-sponsored and voted in favour of such resolutions.[49] India supports nuclear disarmament "in a time-bound, universal, non-discriminatory, phased and verifiable manner".[50] And it criticizes the M.I. for not supporting the General Assembly follow-up resolutions in its own voting pattern (having voted against one of them, in favour once, and all other times abstained).[51]

79. In its *Preliminary Objections* (of 15.06.2015), the United Kingdom, for its part, after recalling the Marshall Islands' position on earlier U.N. General Assembly resolutions, in the sixties and seventies (paras. 21 and 98(c) and (h)), then refers to its own position thereon (paras. 84 and 99(c)). It also refers to U.N. Security Council resolutions (para. 92). It then recalls the Marshall Islands' arguments – e.g., that "the U.K. has always voted against" General Assembly resolutions on the follow-up of the ICJ Advisory Opinion of 1996, and of the U.N. High Level Meetings in 2013 and 2014 (paras. 98(e) and (h)), – in order to rebut them (paras. 99–103).

80. As for Pakistan, though it informed the Court of its decision not to participate in the oral phase of the present proceedings (letter of 02.03.2016), in the submissions in its *Counter-Memorial* it argues that the ICJ 1996 Advisory Opinion nowhere stated that the obligation under Article VI of the NPT was a general obligation or that it was opposable *erga omnes*; in its view, there was no *prima facie* evidence to this effect *erga omnes*.[52] As to the U.N. General Assembly resolutions following up the ICJ's 1996 Advisory Opinion, Pakistan notes

---

46   ICJ, doc. CR 2016/1, of 07.03.2016, para. 7.
47   *Ibid.*, para. 8.
48   *Ibid.*, para. 7.
49   ICJ, doc. CR 2016/4, of 10.03.2016, para. 1, p. 19.
50   *Counter-Memorial* of India, p. 9, para. 13.
51   *Ibid.*, p. 8, para. 12.
52   *Counter-Memorial* of Pakistan., p. 8, para. 2.3.

that it has voted in favour of these resolutions from 1997 to 2015, and by contrast, – it adds, – the Marshall Islands abstained from voting in 2002 and 2003 and again from 2005 to 2012.[53]

81. After recalling that it is not a Party to the NPT,[54] Pakistan further argues that General Assembly resolutions do not have binding force and cannot thus, in its view, give rise to obligations enforceable against a State.[55] Pakistan concludes that the General Assembly resolutions do not support the proposition that there exists a customary international law obligation "rooted" in Article VI of the NPT. Rather, it is the NPT that underpins the Marshall Islands' claims.[56]

82. In sum, the United Kingdom has voted against such resolutions, the Marshall Islands has abstained in most of them, India and Pakistan have voted in favour of them. Despite these distinct patterns of voting, in my view the U.N. General Assembly resolutions reviewed in the present Dissenting Opinion, taken altogether, are not at all deprived of their contribution to the conformation of *opinio juris* as to the formation of a customary international law obligation of nuclear denuclearization. After all, they are resolutions of the U.N. General Assembly itself (and not only of the large majority of U.N. member States which voted in their favour); they are resolutions of the United Nations Organization itself, addressing a matter of common concern of humankind as a whole (cf. Part XIX, *infra*).

VII Human Wickedness: From the XXIst Century Back to the Book of *Genesis*

83. Since the beginning of the nuclear age in August 1945, some of the great thinkers of the XXth century started inquiring whether humankind has a future. Indeed, this is a question which cannot be eluded. Thus, already in 1946, for example, deeply shocked by the U.S. atomic bombings of Hiroshima and Nagasaki (on 06 and 09 August 1945, respectively),[57] Mahatma Gandhi, in

---

53 *Ibid.*, p. 8, para. 2.4.
54 *Ibid.*, p. 14, para. 4.4; p. 30, para. 7.55.
55 *Ibid.*, p. 38, paras. 7.95–7.97.
56 *Ibid.*, p. 38, para. 7.97.
57 Preceded by a nuclear test undertaken by the United States at Alamagordo, New Mexico, on 16.07.1945.

promptly expressing his worry about the future of human society, wrote, in the Journal *Harijan*, on 07.07.1946, that

> So far as I can see, the atomic bomb has deadened the finest feeling that has sustained mankind for ages. There used to be the so-called laws of war which made it tolerable. Now we know the naked truth. War knows no law except that of might.[58]

84. And M. Gandhi, denouncing its brutality, added that the "atom bomb is the weapon of ultimate force and destruction", evidencing the "futility" of such violence; the development of the atom bomb "represents the most sinful and diabolical use of science".[59] In the same Journal *Harijan*, M. Gandhi further wrote, on 29.09.1946, that non-violence is "the only thing the atom bomb cannot destroy"; and he further warned that "unless now the world adopts non-violence, it will spell certain suicide for mankind".[60]

85. Over a decade later, in the late fifties, Karl Jaspers, in his book *La bombe atomique et l'avenir de l'homme* (1958), regretted that the existence of nuclear weapons seemed to have been taken for granted, despite their capacity to destroy humankind and all life on the surface of earth.[61] One has thus to admit, – he added, – that "cette terre, qui est née d'une explosion de l'atome, soit anéantie aussi par les bombes atomiques".[62] K. Jaspers further regretted that progress had occurred in technological knowledge, but there had been "no progress of ethics nor of reason". Human nature has not changed: "ou l'homme se transforme ou il disparaît".[63]

86. In the early sixties, for his part, Bertrand Russell, in his book *Has Man a Future?* (1961), likewise regretted that people seemed to have got used to the

---

[58] M. Gandhi, "Atom Bomb and Ahimsa", *Harijan* (07.07.1946), reproduced *in*: *Journalist Gandhi – Selected Writings of Gandhi* (org. S. Sharma), 1st ed., Mumbai, Ed. Gandhi Book Center, 1994, p. 104; also *cit. in*: P.F. Power, *Gandhi on World Affairs*, London, Allen & Unwin, 1961, pp. 63–64.

[59] *Cit. in*: *What Mahatma Gandhi Said about the Atom Bomb* (org. Y.P. Anand), New Delhi, National Gandhi Museum, 1998, p. 5.

[60] From the Journal *Harijan* (29.09.1946), *cit. in*: Faisal Devji, *The Impossible Indian – Gandhi and the Temptation of Violence*, London, Hurst & Co., 2012, p. 150.

[61] K. Jaspers, *La bombe atomique et l'avenir de l'homme* [1958], Paris, Buchet/Chastel, 1963, pp. 22 and 336.

[62] *Ibid.*, p. 576.

[63] *Ibid.*, pp. 621 and 640.

existence of nuclear weapons, in a world dominated by a "will towards death", prevailing over sanity.[64] Unfortunately, – he proceeded, – "love for power" has enticed States "to pursue irrational policies"; and he added:

> Those who regard *Genesis* as authentic history, may take Cain as the first example: he may well have thought that, with Abel out of the way, he could rule over coming generations.[65]

To B. Russell, it is "in the hearts of men that the evil lies", it is in their minds that "the cure must be sought".[66] He further regretted the discouraging results of disarmament Conferences, and even wrote that ICJ pronouncements on the issue should be authoritative, and it was not "optional" for States "to respect or not international law".[67]

87. For his part, Karl Popper, at the end of his life, in his book (in the form of an interview) *The Lesson of This Century* (1997), in assembling his recollections of the XXth century, expressed the anguish, for example, at the time of the 1962 Cuban missiles crisis, with the finding that each of the 38 warheads at issue had three thousand times more power than the atomic bomb dropped over Hiroshima.[68] Once again, the constatation: human nature has not changed. K. Popper, like other great thinkers of the XXth century, regretted that no lessons seemed to have been learned from the past; this increased the concern they shared, in successive decades, with the future of humankind, in the presence of arsenals of nuclear weapons.

88. A contemporary writer, Max Gallo, in his recent novel *Caïn et Abel – Le premier crime*, has written that the presence of evil is within everyone; "le Mal est au coeur du Bien, et cette réalité ambiguë est le propre des affaires humaines".[69] Writers of the past, – he went on, – "eux aussi – toi Dante, toi

---

64   B. Russell, *Has Man a Future?*, [London], Penguin Books, 1962 [reprint], pp. 27 and 37.
65   *Ibid.*, p. 45.
66   *Ibid.*, pp. 45–46, and cf. 69.
67   *Ibid.*, pp. 97 and 79.
68   K. Popper, *The Lesson of This Century* (interview with G. Bosetti), London/N.Y., Routledge, 1997, pp. 24 and 28. And cf. also, earlier on, K. Popper, *La Responsabilidad de Vivir – Escritos sobre Política, Historia y Conocimiento* [1994], Barcelona, Paidós, 2012 [reed.], p. 242, and cf. p. 274.
69   M. Gallo, *Caïn et Abel – Le premier crime*, [Paris], Fayard, 2011, pp. 112 and 141.

Dostoïevski, et ceux qui vous ont inspiré, Eschyle, Sophocle – attisent le brasier du châtiment et de la culpabilité".[70] And he added:

> Partout, Caïn poignarde ou étrangle Abel. (...) Et personne ne semble voir (...) la mort prochaine de toute humanité. Elle tient entre ses mains l'arme de sa destruction. Ce ne sont plus seulement des villes entières qui seront incendiées, rasées: toute vie sera alors consumée, et la terre vitrifiée.
>
> Deux villes ont déjà connu ce sort, et l'ombre des corps de leurs habitants est à jamais encrustée dans la pierre sous l'effet d'une chaleur de lave solaire.
>
> (...) [P]artout Caïn poursuivra Abel. (...) Les villes vulnérables seront ensanglantées. Les tours les plus hautes seront détruites, leurs habitants ensevelis sous les décombres.[71]

89. As well captured by those and other thinkers, in the Book of *Genesis*, the episode of the brothers Cain and Abel portraying the first murder ever, came to be seen, along the centuries, as disclosing the presence of evil and guilt in the world everyone lives. This called for care, prudence and reflection, as it became possible to realize that human beings were gradually distancing themselves from their Creator. The fragility of civilizations soon became visible. That distancing became manifest in the subsequent episode of the Tower of Babel (*Genesis*, Ch. 11: 9). As they were built, civilizations could be destroyed. History was to provide many examples of that (as singled out, in the XXth century, by Arnold Toynbee). Along the centuries, with the growth of scientific-technological knowledge, the human capacity of self-destruction increased considerably, having become limitless in the present nuclear age.

90. Turning back to the aforementioned book by B. Russell, also in its French edition (*L'homme survivra-t-il?*, 1963), he further warned therein that

> "il faut que nous nous rendions compte que la haine, la perte de temps, d'argent et d'habilité intellectuelle en vue de la création d'engins de destruction, la crainte du mal que nous pouvons nous faire mutuellement, le risque quotidien et permanent de voir la fin de tout ce que l'homme a réalisé, sont le produit de la folie humaine. (...) C'est dans nos

---

70   *Ibid.*, p. 174.
71   *Ibid.*, pp. 236–237.

cœurs que réside le mal, c'est de nos cœurs qu'il doit être extirpé".[72] ["we must become aware that the hatred, the expenditure of time and money and intellectual hability upon weapons of destruction, the fear of what we may do to each other, and the imminent daily and hourly risk of an end to all that man has achieved, (...) all this is a product of human folly. (...) It is in our hearts that the evil lies, and it is from our hearts that it must be plucked out"[73]].

91. Some other great thinkers of the XXth century (from distinct branches of knowledge), expressed their grave common concern with the increased human capacity of destruction coupled with the development of scientific-technological knowledge. Thus, the historian Arnold Toynbee (*A Study in History*, 1934–1954; and *Civilization on Trial*, 1948), regretted precisely the modern tragedy that human iniquity was not eliminated with the development of scientific-technological knowledge, but widely enlarged, without a concomitant advance at spiritual level.[74] And the increase in armaments and in the capacity of destruction, – he added, – became a symptom of the fall of civilizations.[75]

92. For his part, the writer Hermann Hesse, in a posthumous book of essays (*Guerre et paix*, 1946), originally published shortly after the II world war, warned that with the mass killings, not only do we keep on killing ourselves, but also our present and perhaps also our future.[76] The worst destruction, – he added, – was the one organized by the State itself, with its corollary, "the philosophy of the State", accompanied by capital and industry.[77] The philosopher and theologian Jacques Maritain (*Oeuvres Complètes*, 1961–1967), in turn, wrote that the atrocities perpetrated in the XXth century had "une importance plus

---

72 B. Russell, *L'homme survivra-t-il?*, Paris, Éd. J. Didier, 1963, pp. 162–163.
73 B. Russell, *Has Man a Future?*, op. cit. supra n. (85), pp. 109–110. Towards the end of his life, Bertrand Russell again warned against the extreme danger of atomic and hydrogen bombs, and expressed his concern that people seemed to get used to their existence; cf. B. Russell, *Autobiography* [1967], London, Unwin, 1985 [reed.], pp. 554–555.
74 Cf. A.J. Toynbee, *A Study in History*, Oxford, Oxford University Press, 1970 [3rd reprint], pp. 48–558, 559–701, 702–718 and 826–850; A.J. Toynbee, *Civilization on Trial*, Oxford/N.Y., Oxford University Press, 1948, pp. 3–263.
75 A.J. Toynbee, *Guerra e Civilização* [*War and Civilization*], Lisbon, Edit. Presença, 1963, pp. 29, 129 and 178.
76 H. Hesse, *Sobre la Guerra y la Paz* [1946], 5th ed., Barcelona, Edit. Noguer, 1986, pp. 119 and 122.
77 H. Hesse, *Guerre et Paix*, Paris, L'Arche Éd., 2003 [reed.], pp. 127 and 133.

tragique pour la conscience humaine".[78] In calling for an "integral humanism", he warned that the human person transcends the State, and the realisation of the common good is to be pursued keeping in mind human dignity.[79] In his criticism of the "realists", he stressed the imperatives of ethics and justice, and the importance of general principles of law, in the line of jusnaturalist thinking.[80]

93. Another writer, the humanist Stefan Zweig, remained always concerned with the fate of humankind. He was impressed with the Scripture's legend of the Tower of Babel, having written an essay on it in 1916, and kept it in mind along the years, as shown in successive essays written in more than the two following decades,[81] taking it as a symbol of the perennial yearning for a unified humanity. In his own words,

> The history of tomorrow must be a history of all humanity and the conflicts between individual conflicts must be seen as redundant alongside the common good of the community. History must then be transformed from the current woeful State to a completely new position; (...) it must clearly contrast the old ideal of victory with the new one of unity and the old glorification of war with a new contempt for it. (...) [T]he only important thing is to push forward under the banner of a community of nations, the mentality of mankind (...).[82]

94. Yet, in his dense and thoughtful intellectual autobiography (*Le monde d'hier*, 1944), written shortly before putting an end to his own life, Stefan Zweig

---

[78] J. Maritain, "Dieu et la permission du mal", in *Œuvres de Jacques Maritain – 1961–1967 (Jacques et Raissa Maritain – Oeuvres Complètes)*, vol. XII, Fribourg/Paris, Éd. Universitaires/Éd. Saint-Paul, 1992, p. 17, and cf. p. 41.

[79] Cf. J. Maritain, *Humanisme intégral*, Paris, Aubier, 2000 (reed.), pp. 18, 37, 137 and 230–232; J. Maritain, *The Person and the Common Good*, Notre Dame, University of Notre Dame Press, 2002 (reed.), pp. 29, 49–50, 92–93 and 104; J. Maritain, *O Homem e o Estado*, 4th ed., Rio de Janeiro, Livr. Agir Ed., 1966, pp. 96–102; J. Maritain, *Los Derechos del Hombre y la Ley Natural*, Buenos Aires, Ed. Leviatan, 1982, pp. 38, 44, 50, 69 and 94–95, and cf. pp. 79–82; J. Maritain, *Para una Filosofía de la Persona Humana*, Buenos Aires, Ed. Club de Lectores, 1984, pp. 164, 176–178, 196–197, 221 and 231.

[80] J. Maritain, *De la justice politique – Notes sur la présente guerre*, Paris, Libr. Plon, 1940, pp. 88, 90–91, 106–107 and 112–114.

[81] As shown in his posthumous book of essays: S. Zweig, *Messages from a Lost World*, London, Pushkin Press, 2016, pp. 55, 88–90, 97, 107 and 176.

[82] *Ibid.*, pp. 170 and 175.

expressed his deep concern with the fading away of conscience, disclosed by the fact that the world got used to the "dehumanisation, injustice and brutality, as never before in hundreds of centuries";[83] persons had been transformed into simple objects.[84] Earlier on, – before the nuclear age, – his friend the psychologist Sigmund Freud, in a well-known essay (*Civilization and Its Discontents*, 1930), expressed his deep preoccupation with what he perceived as an impulse to barbarism and destruction, which could not be expelled from the human psyche.[85] In face of human hostility and the threat of self-disintegration, – he added, – there is a consequent loss of happiness.[86]

95. Another psychologist, Carl Jung, referring, in his book *Aspects du drame contemporain* (1948), to events of contemporary history of his epoch, warned against subsuming individuals under the State; in his view, collective evil and culpability contaminate everyone everywhere.[87] He further warned against the tragic dehumanization of others[88] and the psychic exteriorizations of mass movements (of the collective inconscient) conducive to destruction.[89]

96. To the writer and theologian Albert Schweitzer (who wrote his *Kulturphilosophie* in 1923), the essence of civilization lies in the respect for life, to the benefit of each person and of humankind.[90] He rejected the "illness" of *Realpolitik*, having stated that good consists in the preservation and exaltation of life, and evil lies in its destruction; nowadays more than ever, – he added, – we need an "ethics of reverence for life", what requires responsibility.[91] He insisted, in his book *La civilisation et l'éthique* (1923), that respect for life started as from "une prise de conscience" of one's responsibility *vis-à-vis* the life of others.[92]

---

83 S. Zweig, *O Mundo que Eu Vi* [1944, *Die Welt von Gestern*], Rio de Janeiro, Edit. Record, 1999, p. 483, and cf. 272–274, 278, 462, 467, 474, 490 and 503–505.

84 *Ibid.*, p. 490.

85 Sigmund Freud, *Civilization and Its Discontents* [1930], N.Y., Norton & Cia., 1962 [reed.], pp. 7–9, 26, 36–37 and 59–63.

86 Cf. *ibid.*, pp. 23 and 67–92.

87 C.G. Jung, *Aspects du drame contemporain*, Genève/Paris, Libr. de l'Univ. Georg/Éd. de la Colonne Vendôme, 1948, pp. 99 and 145.

88 *Ibid.*, pp. 173 and 179.

89 *Ibid.*, pp. 198–200, 208, 218–219 and 223.

90 A. Schweitzer, *Filosofia da Civilização* [1923], São Paulo, Edit. Unesp, 2011 [reed.], pp. 80, 304, 311 and 315.

91 A. Schweitzer, *Pilgrimage to Humanity* [*Weg zur Humanität*], N.Y., Philosophical Library, 1961, pp. 87–88, 99 and 101.

92 M. Arnold, *Albert Schweitzer – La compassion et la raison*, Lyon, Éd. Olivétan, 2015, pp. 74–75 and 77.

97. Later on in his life, then in the nuclear age, in his series of lectures *Paix ou guerre atomique* (1958), A. Schweitzer called for an end to nuclear weapons, with their "destructions et anéantissements inimaginables".[93] In his own words,

> La guerre atomique ne connaît pas de vainqueurs, mais uniquement des vaincus. Chaque belligérant subit par les bombes et les projectiles atomiques de l'adversaire les mêmes dégâts qu'il lui inflige par les siens. Il en résulte un anéantissement continu (...). Il peut seulement dire: allons-nous nous suicider tous les deux par une extermination réciproque?[94]

98. Well before them, by the turn of the XIXth to the XXth century, the writer Leo Tolstoi warned (*The Slavery of Our Times*, 1900) against the undue use of the State monopoly of "organized violence", conforming a new form of slavery of the vulnerable ones;[95] he criticized the recruitment of personnel to be sent to war to kill defenseless persons, perpetrating acts of extreme violence.[96] On his turn, the physician Georges Duhamel warned (in his account *Civilisation – 1914–1917*) against the fact that war had become an industry of killing, with a "barbaric ideology", destroying civilization with its "lack of humanity"; yet, he still cherished the hope that the spirit of humanism could flourish from the ashes.[97]

99. The historian of ideas Isaiah Berlin, for his part, warned (*The Proper Study of Mankind*) against the dangers of the *raison d'État*, and stressed the relevance of *values*, in the search of knowledge, of cultures, and of the *recta ratio*.[98] On his turn, the writer Erich Fromm upheld human life in insisting that there could only exist a truly "civilized" society if based on humanist values.[99] Towards

---

93   *Cit. in ibid.*, p. 111.
94   Extract from his book *Paix ou guerre atomique* (1958), reproduced in his posthumous book of essays: A. Schweitzer, *Respect de la vie* (org. B. Kaempf), Paris, Éd. Arfuyen/CIAL, 1990, p. 98.
95   L. Tolstoi, *La Esclavitud de Nuestro Tiempo* [1900], Barcelona, Littera, 2000 [reed.], pp. 86–87, 89, 91 and 97.
96   *Ibid.*, pp. 101, 103–104 and 121.
97   G. Duhamel, *Civilisation – 1914–1917*, Paris, Mercure de France, 1944, pp. 53 and 274–275; G. Duhamel, *Mémorial de la guerre blanche – 1938*, Paris, Mercure de France, 1945, pp. 41, 95, 100, 102 and 170.
98   I. Berlin, *The Proper Study of Mankind*, N.Y., Farrar & Straus & Giroux, 2000 (reed.), pp. 78, 135, 155, 217, 235–236, 242, 247, 311 and 334; I. Berlin, "Return of the *Volksgeist*: Nationalism, Good and Bad", *in At Century's End* (ed. N.P. Gardels), San Diego/Cal., Alti Publ., 1995, p. 94.
99   Cf. E. Fromm, *Las Cadenas de la Ilusión – Una Autobiografía Intelectual* [1962], Barcelona, Paidós, 2008 [reed.], pp. 78 and 234–239.

the end of his life, in his book *The Anatomy of Human Destructivity* (1974), he warned against destruction and propounded the prevalence of love for life.[100]

100. E. Fromm further warned that the devastation of wars (including the contemporary ones) have led to the loss of hope and to brutalization, amidst the tension of the co-existence or ambivalence between civilization and barbarism, which requires all our endeavours towards the revival of humanism.[101] Likewise, in our days, the philosopher Edgar Morin has also warned that the advances of scientific knowledge disclosed an ambivalence, in that they provided, on the one hand, the means to improve the knowledge of the world, and, on the other hand, with the production (and proliferation) of nuclear weapons, in addition to other weapons (biological and chemical) of mass destruction, the means to destroy the world.[102]

101. Future has thus become unpredictable, and unknown, in face of the confrontation between the forces of life and the forces of death. Yet, – he added, – human beings are endowed with conscience, and are aware that civilizations, as well as the whole of humankind, are mortal.[103] E. Morin further contended the tragic experiences lived in recent times should lead to the repentance of barbarism and the return to humanism; in effect, to think about, and resist to, barbarism, amounts to contributing to recreate humanism.[104]

102. For his part, in the late eighties, in his book of essays *Silences et mémoires d'hommes* (1989), Elie Wiesel stressed the need of memory and attention to the world wherein we live, so as to combat the indifference to violence and evil.[105] Looking back to the Book of *Genesis*, he saw it fit to recall that "Caïn et Abel – les premiers enfants sur terre, – se découvrirent ennemis. Bien que frères, l'un devin l'assassin ou la victime de l'autre. L'enseignement que nous devrions en tirer? Deux hommes peuvent être frères et néanmoins désireux de

---

100 Cf. E. Fromm, *Anatomía de la Destructividad Humana* [1974], Mexico/Madrid/Buenos Aires, 2009 [reed.], pp. 16–468; and cf. also E. Fromm, *El Amor a la Vida* [1983 – *Über die Liebe zum Leben*], Barcelona, Paidós, 2016 (4th reprint), pp. 15–250.
101 E. Fromm, *Las Cadenas de la Ilusión...*, op. cit. supra n. (120), pp. 240 and 250–251.
102 E. Morin, *Vers l'abîme?*, Paris, L'Herne, 2012, pp. 9, 24–25 and 40–41.
103 *Ibid.*, pp. 27, 30, 59, 85, 89, 126 and 181.
104 E. Morin, *Breve Historia de la Barbarie en Occidente*, Barcelona, Paidós, 2009, p. 94, and cf. pp. 60 and 92–93.
105 E. Wiesel, *Silences et mémoires d'hommes*, Paris, Éd. Seuil, 1989, pp. 166, 173 and 175.

s'entre-tuer. Et aussi: quiconque tue, tue son frère. Seulement cela, on l'apprend plus tard".[106]

103. Turning attention to the threat of nuclear weapons, E. Wiesel sharply criticized the already prevailing attitude of indifference to it: "le monde, aujourd'hui, nous paraît étonnamment indifférent vis-à-vis de la question nucléaire", – an attitude which he found ununderstandable.[107] And he added that

> L'indifférence (...) peut elle aussi devenir contagieuse. (...) L'indifférence permet également de mesurer la progression du mal que mine la société. (...) Là encore, la mémoire seule peut nous réveiller. Si nous nous souvenons de ce qui s'est passé il y a quarante ans, nous avons une possibilité d'empêcher de nouvelles catastrophes. Sinon, nous risquons d'être les victimes de notre propre indifférence. Car si nous sommes indifférents aux leçons de notre passé, nous le serons aux espoirs inhérents à notre avenir. (...) Voici mon angoisse: si nous oublions, nous serons oubliés. (...) Si nous restons indifférents à notre sort, (...) il ne restera personne pour raconter notre histoire.[108]

104. In effect, already in the early XXth century, Henri Bergson, in his monograph *La conscience et la vie* (1911), devoted attention to the search for meaning in life: to him, to live with conscience is to remember the past (memory) in the present, and to anticipate the future.[109] In his own words,

> Retenir ce qui n'est déjà plus, anticiper sur ce qui n'est pas encore, voilà donc la première fonction de la conscience. (...) [L]a conscience est un trait d'union entre ce qui a été et ce qui sera, un pont jeté entre le passé et l'avenir.[110]

105. Also in international legal doctrine, there have been those who have felt the need to move away from State voluntarism and acknowledge the prevalence of conscience over the "will". It is not my intention to dwell upon this

---

106   *Ibid.*, pp. 167–168.
107   *Ibid.*, p. 174, and cf. p. 170.
108   *Ibid.*, pp. 175–176.
109   H. Bergson, *La conscience et la vie* [1911], Paris, PUF, 2012 [reprint], pp. 10–11, 13 and 26.
110   *Ibid.*, pp. 5–6.

point here, as I have dealt with it elsewhere.[111] For the purposes of the present Dissenting Opinion, suffice it to recall a couple of examples. The jurist Gustav Radbruch, at the end of his life, forcefully discarded legal positivism, always subservient to power and the established order, and formulated his moving conversion and profession of faith in jusnaturalism.[112] His lucid message was preserved and has been projected in time,[113] thanks to the devotion of his students and disciples of the School of Heidelberg.

106. There are further examples of doctrinal endeavours to put limits to State voluntarism, such as the jusnaturalist construction of, e.g., Alfred Verdross, – as from the *idée du droit*, – of an objective law finding expression in the general principles of law, preceding positive international law;[114] or else the conception of the *droit spontanée*, of Roberto Ago, upholding the spontaneous formation (emanating from human conscience, well beyond the "will" of individual States) of new rules of international law.[115]

107. In the view of Albert de La Pradelle, the conception of the formation of international law on the strict basis of reciprocal rights and duties only of States is "extremely grave and dangerous".[116] International law is a "droit de la communauté humaine", encompassing, besides States, also peoples and human beings; it is the "droit de toute l'humanité", on the foundations of which are the general principles of law.[117] To A. de La Pradelle, this "droit de l'humanité" is not static, but rather dynamic, attentive to human values, in the line of jusnaturalist thinking.[118]

111 Cf. A.A. Cançado Trindade, *International Law for Humankind – Towards a New Jus Gentium*, 2nd rev. ed., Leiden/The Hague, Nijhoff/The Hague Academy of International Law, 2013, pp. 141–147 and 153–161.

112 Cf. G. Radbruch, *Introducción a la Filosofía del Derecho*, 3rd ed., Mexico/Buenos Aires, Fondo de Cultura Económica, 1965, pp. 9–180.

113 Cf., e.g., R. Alexy, *The Argument from Injustice – A Reply to Legal Positivism*, Oxford, Oxford University Press, 2010, pp. 3–130.

114 A. Verdross, *Derecho Internacional Público*, 5th ed., Madrid, Aguilar, 1969 [reprint], pp. 15–19.

115 R. Ago, "Nouvelles réflexions sur la codification du droit international", 92 *Revue générale de droit international public* (1988) p. 540, and cf. p. 541 on "la nature non volontaire de l'origine du droit coutumier".

116 A. de La Pradelle, *Droit international public* (cours sténographié), Paris, Institut des Hautes Études Internationales/Centre Européen de la Dotation Carnegie, November 1932/May 1933, p. 33, and cf. pp. 36–37.

117 *Ibid.*, pp. 49–59, 149, 222 and 264.

118 Cf. *ibid.*, pp. 412–413.

108. "Juridical conscience" is invoked in lucid criticisms of legal positivism.[119] Thus, in his monograph-plea (of 1964) against nuclear weapons, for example, Stefan Glaser sustained that customary international norms are those that, "according to universal conscience", ought to regulate the international community, for fulfilling common interest and responding to the demands of justice; and he added that

> C'est sur cette conscience universelle que repose la principale caractéristique du droit international: la conviction que ses normes sont indispensables pour le bien commun explique leur reconnaissance en tant que règles obligatoires.[120]

109. This is the position that I also uphold; in my own understanding, it is the universal juridical conscience that is the ultimate material source of international law.[121] In my view, one cannot face the new challenges confronting the whole international community keeping in mind only State susceptibilities; such is the case with the obligation to render the world free of nuclear weapons, an imperative of *recta ratio* and not a derivative of the "will" of States. In effect, to keep hope alive it is necessary to bear always in mind humankind as a whole.

110. For my part, within the ICJ, I have deemed it fit to ponder, in my Dissenting Opinion (paras. 488–489) in the case concerning the *Application of the Convention against Genocide* (Croatia *versus* Serbia, Judgment of 03.02.2015), that, from Homer's *Iliad* (late VIIIth or early VIIth century b.C.) to date, individuals, indoctrinated and conditioned for war and destruction, have become objects of the struggle for domination. I recalled that this has been lucidly warned by Simone Weil, in a penetrating essay (of 1934), to whom this ends up victimizing everyone, there occurring "the substitution of the ends by the means", transforming human life into a simple means, which can be sacrificed; individuals become unable to think, in face of the "social machine" of destruction of the spirit and fabrication of the inconscience.[122]

---

119   Such as, e.g., those of Antonio Gómez Robledo, *Meditación sobre la Justicia* [1963], Mexico/Buenos Aires, Fondo de Cultura Económica, 1963, pp. 179 and 185; R. Quadri, "Cours général de droit international public", 113 *Recueil des Cours de l'Académie de Droit International de La Haye* (1964) pp. 326, 332, 336–337, 339 and 350–351.

120   S. Glaser, *L'arme nucléaire à la lumière du droit international*, Paris, Pédone, 1964, p. 18.

121   Cf. A.A. Cançado Trindade, *op. cit. supra* (132), Ch. VI, pp. 139–161.

122   S. Weil, *Reflexiones sobre las Causas de la Libertad y de la Opresión Social*, Barcelona, Ed. Paidós/Universidad Autónoma de Barcelona, 1995, pp. 81–82, 84 and 130–131; S. Weil,

111. The presence of evil has accompanied and marked human existence along the centuries. In the same aforementioned Dissenting Opinion in the case concerning the *Application of the Convention against Genocide* (2015), after drawing attention to "the ever-lasting presence of evil, which appears proper to the human condition, in all times", I added:

> It is thus understandable that it has attracted the concern of, and has presented challenges to, legal thinking, in our times and previous centuries, as well as other branches of knowledge (such as, e.g., history, psychology, anthropology, sociology, philosophy and theology, among others). It has marked presence in literature as well. This long-standing concern, along centuries, has not, however, succeeded to provide an explanation for evil.
>
> Despite the endeavours of human thinking, along history, it has not been able to rid humankind of it. Like the passing of time, the ever-lasting presence of evil is yet another mystery surrounding human beings, wherever and while they live. Whenever individuals purport to subject their fellow human beings to their 'will', placing this latter above conscience, evil is bound to manifest itself. In one of the most learned writings on the problem of evil, R.P. Sertillanges ponders that the awareness of evil and the anguish emanated therefrom have marked presence in all civilizations. The ensuing threat to the future of human kind has accounted for the continuous presence of that concern throughout the history of human thinking.[123]
>
> Religions were the first to dwell upon the problem of evil, which came also to be considered by philosophy, history, psychology, social sciences, and literature. Along the centuries, human thinking has always acknowledged the need to examine the problem of evil, its incidence in human relations, in the world wherein we live, without losing faith in human values.[124] Despite the perennial quest of human thinking to find answers to the problem of evil, – going as far back as the *Book of Job*, or even further back, to the *Genesis* itself,[125] – not even theology has found an explanation for it, satisfactory to all (paras. 472–474).

Réflexions sur les causes de la liberté et de l'oppression sociale, Paris, Gallimard, 1955, pp. 124–125, and cf. pp. 114–115 and 144.

123 R.P. Sertillanges, *Le problème du mal – l'histoire*, Paris, Aubier, 1948, pp. 5–412.

124 *Ibid.*, pp. 5–412.

125 Cf., *inter alia*, e.g., M. Neusch, *L'énigme du mal*, Paris, Bayard, 2007, pp. 7–193; J. Maritain, *Dio e la Permissione del Male*, 6th ed., Brescia, Edit. Morcelliana, 2000, pp. 9–100; E. Fromm, *Anatomía de la Destructividad Humana*, Mexico/Madrid/Buenos Aires, Siglo XXI

112. The Scripture's account of Cain and Abel (*Genesis*, Ch. 4: 8–10) along the centuries came to be regarded as the aetiology of the fragmentation of humankind, as from the indifference of an individual to the fate of another. The increasing disregard for human life was fostered by growing, generalized and uncontrolled violence in search of domination. This was further aggravated by ideological manipulations, and even the dehumanization of the others, the ones to be victimized. The problem of evil continues to be studied, in face of the human capacity for extreme violence and self-destruction on a large scale.[126] The tragic message of the Book of *Genesis*, in my perception, seems perennial, as contemporary as ever, in the current nuclear age.

VIII   The Attention of the United Nations Charter to Peoples

113. It should be kept in mind that the United Nations Charter was adopted on 26.06.1945 on behalf of "we, the peoples of the United Nations". In several provisions it expresses its concern with the living conditions of all peoples (preamble, Articles 55, 73(a), 76, 80), and calls for the promotion of, and universal respect for, human rights (Articles 55(c), 62(2), 68, 76(c)). It invokes the "principles of justice and international law" (Article 1(1)), and refers to "justice and respect for the obligations arising from treaties and other sources of international law" (preamble). It further states that the Statute of the ICJ, "the principal judicial organ of the United Nations", forms "an integral part" of the U.N. Charter itself (Article 92).

Edit., 2009 [reprint.], pp. 11–468; P. Ricoeur, *Evil – A Challenge to Philosophy and Theology*, London, Continuum, 2007, pp. 33–72; P. Ricoeur, *Le mal – Un défi à la philosophie et à la théologie*, Genève, Éd. Labor et Fides, 2004, pp. 19–65; C.S. Nino, *Juicio al Mal Absoluto*, Buenos Aires, Emecé Edit., 1997, pp. 7–292; A. Morton, *On Evil*, N.Y./London, Routledge, 2004, pp. 1–148; T. Eagleton, *On Evil*, New Haven/London, Yale University Press, 2010, pp. 1–163; P. Dews, *The Idea of Evil*, Oxford, Wiley-Blackwell, 2013, pp. 1–234.

126   Cf., moreover, *inter alia*, e.g., [Various Authors,] *Le Mal* (ed. C. Crignon), Paris, Flammarion, 2000, pp. 11–232; J. Waller, *Becoming Evil*, 2nd ed., Oxford, Oxford University Press, 2007, pp. 3–330; S. Baron-Cohen, *The Science of Evil – On Empathy and the Origins of Cruelty*, N.Y., Basic Books, 2012, pp. 1–243; L. Svendsen, *A Philsophy of Evil*, Champaign/London, Dalkey Archive Press, 2011 [reprint], pp. 9–282; M. Salvioli, *Bene e Male – Variazioni sul Tema*, Bologna, Ed. Studio Domenicano (ESD), 2012, pp. 11–185; D. Livingstone Smith, *Less than Human*, N.Y., St. Martin's Press, 2011, pp. 1–316; R. Safranski, *El Mal, o el Drama de la Libertad*, 4th ed., Barcelona, Tusquets Edit., 2014, pp. 15–281; S. Neiman, *Evil in Modern Thought*, 2nd ed., Princeton/Oxford, Princeton University Press, 2015, pp. 1–359; J.-C. Guillebaud, *Le tourment de la guerre*, Paris, Éd. de l'Iconoclaste, 2016, pp. 9–390.

114. In the mid-fifties, Max Huber, a former Judge of the PCIJ, wrote that international law has to protect also values common to humankind, attentive to respect for life and human dignity, in the line of the jusnaturalist conception of *the jus gentium*; the U.N. Charter, in incorporating human rights into this *droit de l'humanité*, initiated a new era in the development of international law, in a way rescuing the idea of the *civitas maxima*, which marked presence already in the historical origins of the law of nations. The U.N. Charter's attention to peoples, its principled position for the protection of the human person, much transcend positive domestic law and politics.[127]

115. The new vision advanced by the U.N. Charter, and espoused by the Law of the United Nations, has, in my perception, an incidence upon judicial settlement of international disputes. Thus, the fact that the ICJ's mechanism for the handling of contentious cases is an inter-State one, does not mean that its reasoning should also pursue a strictly inter-State dimension; that will depend on the nature and substance of the cases lodged with it. And there have been several cases lodged with the Court that required a reasoning going well beyond the inter-State dimension.[128] Such reasoning beyond the inter-State dimension

---

127 Max Huber, *La pensée et l'action de la Croix-Rouge*, Genève, CICR, 1954, pp. 26, 247, 270, 286 and 291.

128 Cf., e.g., the case of *Nottebohm* (1955, pertaining to double nationality); the cases of the *Trial of Pakistani Prisoners of War* (1973), of the *Hostages (U.S. Diplomatic and Consular Staff) in Teheran* case (1980); of the *Application of the Convention against Genocide* (Bosnia *versus* Serbia, 1996 and 2007); of the *Frontier Dispute between Burkina Faso and Mali* (1998); the triad of cases concerning consular assistance – namely, the cases *Breard* (Paraguay *versus* United States,1998), the case *LaGrand* (Germany *versus* United States, 2001), the case *Avena and Others* (Mexico *versus* United States, 2004); the cases of *Armed Activities in the Territory of Congo* (D.R. Congo *versus* Uganda, 2000, concerning grave violations of human rights and of International Humanitarian Law); of the *Land and Maritime Boundary between Cameroon and Nigeria* (1996); of *Questions Relating to the Obligation to Prosecute or Extradite* (Belgium *versus* Senegal, 2009–2013, pertaining to the principle of universal jurisdiction under the U.N. Convention against Torture); of *A.S. Diallo* (Guinea *versus* D.R. Congo, 2010, on detention and expulsion of a foreigner), of the *Jurisdictional Immunities of the State* (Germany *versus* Italy, Greece intervening, 2010–2012); of the *Application of the International Convention on the Elimination of All Forms of Racial Discrimination* (Georgia *versus* Russian Federation, 2011); of the *Temple of Preah Vihear* (Cambodia *versus* Thailand, provisional measures, 2011); of the *Application of the Convention against Genocide* (Croatia *versus* Serbia, 2015). To those cases one can add the two most recent Advisory Opinions of the ICJ, on the *Declaration of Independence of Kosovo* (2010); and on a *Judgment of the ILO Administrative Tribunal upon a Complaint Filed against the IFAD* (2012).

is faithful to the U.N. Charter, the ICJ being "the principal judicial organ of the United Nations" (Article 92).

116. Recently, in one of such cases, that of the *Application of the Convention against Genocide* (Croatia *versus* Serbia, 2015), in my extensive Dissenting Opinion appended thereto, I have deemed it fit, *inter alia*, to warn that

> The present case concerning the *Application of the Convention against Genocide* (Croatia *versus* Serbia) provides yet another illustration of the pressing need to overcome and move away from the dogmatic and strict inter-State outlook, even more cogently. In effect, the 1948 Convention against Genocide, – adopted on the eve of the Universal Declaration of Human Rights, – is not State-centered, but rather *people-centred*. The Convention against Genocide cannot be properly interpreted and applied with a strict State-centered outlook, with attention turned to inter-State susceptibilities. Attention is to be kept on the *justiciables*, on the victims, – real and potential victims, – so as to impart justice under the Genocide Convention (para. 496).

117. In a report in the early nineties, a former U.N. Secretary-General, calling for a "concerted effort" towards complete disarmament, rightly pondered that "[d]ans le monde d'aujourd'hui, les nations ne peuvent plus se permettre de résoudre les problèmes par la force. (...) Le désarmement est l'un des moyens les plus importants de réduire la violence dans les relations entre États".[129] There followed the cycle of World Conferences of the United Nations along the nineties, in a commendable endeavour of the United Nations *to go beyond and transcend the purely inter-State dimension*, imbued of a spirit of solidarity, so as to consider the challenges for the future of humankind.

118. Those U.N. World Conferences disclosed a growing awareness of the international community as a whole, and entered into a continuing universal dialogue between U.N. member States and entities of the civil societies, – which I well remember, having participated in it,[130] – so as to devise the new

---

129 B. Boutros-Ghali, *Nouvelles dimensions de la réglementation des armements et du désarmement dans la période de l'après-guerre froide – Rapport du Secrétaire Général*, N.Y., Nations Unies, 1993, pp. 21–22.

130 E.g., in the U.N. Conference on Environment and Development (Rio de Janeiro, 1992, in its World NGO Forum) and in the II World Conference on Human Rights (Vienna, 1993, in the same Forum and in its Drafting Committee).

international agenda in the search of common solutions for the new challenges affecting humankind as a whole. In focusing attention on vulnerable segments of the populations, the immediate concern has been with meeting basic human needs, that memorable cycle of World Conferences disclosed a common concern with the deterioration of living conditions, dramatically affecting increasingly greater segments of the population in many parts of the world nowadays.[131]

119. The common denominator in those U.N. World Conferences – as I have pointed out on distinct occasions along the last two decades[132] – can be found in the recognition of the legitimacy of the concern of the international community as a whole with the conditions of living of all human beings everywhere. The placing of the well-being of peoples and human beings, of the improvement of their conditions of living, at the centre of the concerns of the international community, is remindful of the historical origins of the *droit des gens*.[133]

120. At the end of the decade and the dawn of the new millennium, the United Nations Millennium Declaration (adopted by General Assembly's resolution 55/2, of 08.09.2000) stated the determination "to eliminate the dangers posed by weapons of mass destruction" (para. II(8)), and, noticeably,

---

131   A growing call was formed for the pursuance of social justice *among* and *within* nations.
132   A.A. Cançado Trindade, *A Proteção dos Vulneráveis como Legado da II Conferência Mundial de Direitos Humanos (1993–2013)*, Fortaleza/Brazil, IBDH/IIDH/SLADI, 2014, pp. 13–356; A.A. Cançado Trindade, "Sustainable Human Development and Conditions of Life as a Matter of Legitimate International Concern: The Legacy of the U.N. World Conferences", *in Japan and International Law – Past, Present and Future* (International Symposium to Mark the Centennial of the Japanese Association of International Law), The Hague, Kluwer, 1999, pp. 285–309; A.A. Cançado Trindade, "The Contribution of Recent World Conferences of the United Nations to the Relations between Sustainable Development and Economic, Social and Cultural Rights", *in Les hommes et l'environnement: Quels droits pour le vingt-et-unième siècle? – Études en hommage à Alexandre Kiss* (eds. M. Prieur and C. Lambrechts), Paris, Éd. Frison-Roche, 1998, pp. 119–146; A.A. Cançado Trindade, "Memória da Conferência Mundial de Direitos Humanos (Viena, 1993)", 87/90 *Boletim da Sociedade Brasileira de Direito Internacional* (1993–1994) pp. 9–57.
133   Those Conferences acknowledged that human rights do in fact permeate all areas of human activity, and contributed decisively to the reestablishment of the central position of human beings in the conceptual universe of the law of nations (*droit des gens*). Cf., on the matter, A.A. Cançado Trindade, *Évolution du Droit international au droit des gens – L'accès des particuliers à la justice internationale: le regard d'un juge*, Paris, Pédone, 2008, pp. 1–187.

> To strive for the elimination of weapons of mass destruction, particularly nuclear weapons, and to keep all options open for achieving this aim, including the possibility of convening and international conference to identify ways of eliminating nuclear dangers (para. II(9)).

121. In addition to our responsibilities to our individual societies, – the U.N. Millennium Declaration added, –

> we have a collective responsibility to uphold the principles of human dignity, equality and equity at the global level. (...) [W]e have a duty therefore to all the world's people, especially the most vulnerable and, in particular, the children of the world, to whom the future belongs.
>
> We reaffirm our commitment to the purposes and principles of the Charter of the United Nations, which have proved timeless and universal. Indeed, their relevance and capacity to inspire have increased, as nations and peoples have become increasingly interconnected and interdependent (paras. I(2–3)).

IX Impertinence of the So-Called *Monetary Gold* "Principle"

122. The distortions generated by the obsession with the strict inter-State paradigm are not hard to detect. An example is afforded, in this connection, by the ICJ's handling of the *East Timor* case (1995): the East Timorese people had no *locus standi* to request intervention in the proceedings, not even to present an *amicus curiae*, although the crucial point under consideration was that of sovereignty over their own territory. Worse still, the interests of a third State (which had not even accepted the Court's jurisdiction) were taken for granted and promptly safeguarded by the Court, by means of the application of the so-called *Monetary Gold* "principle", – an assumed "principle" also invoked now, two decades later, in the present case concerning the obligation of elimination of nuclear weapons!

123. Attention has to be turned to the *nature* of the case at issue, which may well require a reasoning – as the *cas d'espèce* does – moving away from "a strict State-centred voluntarist perspective" and from the "exaltation of State consent", and seeking guidance in fundamental principles (*prima principia*), such as the principle of humanity. This is what I pointed out in my extensive Dissenting Opinion in the case concerning the *Application of the Convention against Genocide* (Croatia *versus* Serbia, Judgment of 03.02.2015), where I pondered

inter alia that such *prima principia* confer to the international legal order "its ineluctable axiological dimension"; they "conform its *substratum*, and convey the idea of an *objective* justice, in the line of jusnaturalist thinking" (para. 517).

124. That was not the first time I made such ponderation: I had done the same, in another extensive Dissenting Opinion (para. 213), in the case concerning the *Application of the International Convention on the Elimination of All Forms of Racial Discrimination – CERD* (Georgia *versus* Russian Federation, Judgment of 01.04.2011). In my subsequent aforementioned Dissenting Opinion in the case concerning the *Application of the Convention against Genocide* I expressed my dissatisfaction that in a case pertaining to the interpretation and application of the Convention against Genocide, the ICJ even made recourse to the so-called *Monetary Gold* "principle",[134] which had no place in a case like that, and "which does not belong to the realm of the *prima principia*, being nothing more than a concession to State consent, within an outdated State voluntarist framework" (para. 519).

125. May I, in the present Dissenting Opinion, this time in the case of *Obligations Concerning Negotiations Relating to Cessation of the Nuclear Arms Race and to Nuclear Disarmament*, again leave on the records my dissatisfaction for the same reason. Once again, may I stress that the adjudication of a case like the present one shows the need to go beyond the strict inter-State outlook. The fact that the mechanism for the adjudication of contentious cases before the ICJ is an inter-State one, does not at all imply that the Court's reasoning should likewise be strictly inter State. In the present case concerning nuclear weapons and the obligation of nuclear disarmament, it is necessary to focus attention on peoples, rather than on inter-State susceptibilities. It is imperative to keep in mind the world population, in pursuance of a humanist outlook, in the light of the *principle of humanity*.

X   The Fundamental Principle of the Juridical Equality of States

126. The present case of *Obligations Concerning Negotiations Relating to Cessation of the Nuclear Arms Race and to Nuclear Disarmament* stresses the utmost importance of the principle of the juridical equality of States. The importance attributed to fundamental principles, the idea of an objective justice, and its incidence upon the laws, go back in time, being deeply-rooted in jusnaturalist

---

134   Even if only to dismiss it (para. 116).

thinking. If laws are deprived of justice, they no longer oblige in conscience. Ethics cannot be dissociated from law; in the international scenario, each one is responsible for all the others. To the "founding fathers" of the law of nations (*droit des gens*), like F. de Vitoria and F. Suárez, the principle of equality was fundamental, in the relations among individuals, as well as among nations. Their teachings have survived the erosion of time: today, four and a half centuries later, the basic principle of equality and non-discrimination is in the foundations of the Law of the United Nations itself.

127. The present case of *Obligations Concerning Negotiations Relating to Cessation of the Nuclear Arms Race and to Nuclear Disarmament* is surely not the first one before the ICJ that brings to the fore the relevance of the principle of the juridical equality of States. In the ICJ's Order (of Provisional Measures of Protection) of 03.03.2014, I have deemed it fit to point out, in my Separate Opinion appended thereto, that the case concerning *Questions Relating to the Seizure and Detention of Certain Documents and Data*

> bears witness of the relevance of the principle of the juridical equality of States. The prevalence of this fundamental principle has marked a long-standing presence in the realm of international law, ever since the times of the II Hague Peace Conference of 1907, and then of the drafting of the Statute of the Permanent Court of International Justice by the Advisory Committee of Jurists, in June–July 1920. Recourse was then made, by that Committee, *inter alia*, to general principles of law, as these latter embodied the objective idea of justice. A general principle such as that of the juridical equality of States, enshrined a quarter of a century later in the United Nations Charter (Article 2(1)), is ineluctably intermingled with the quest for justice.
>
> Subsequently, throughout the drafting of the 1970 U.N. Declaration on Principles of International Law concerning Friendly Relations and Cooperation among States in accordance with the Charter of the United Nations (1964–1970), the need was felt to make it clear that stronger States cannot impose their will upon the weak, and that *de facto* inequalities among States cannot affect the weaker in the vindication of their rights. The principle of the juridical equality of States gave expression to this concern, embodying the *idée de justice*, emanated from the universal juridical conscience (paras. 44–45).

128. And one decade earlier, in my General Course on Public International Law delivered at the Hague Academy of International Law (2005), I pondered that

On successive occasions the principles of international law have proved to be of fundamental importance to humankind's quest for justice. This is clearly illustrated by the role played, *inter alia*, by the principle of juridical equality of States. This fundamental principle, – the historical roots of which go back to the II Hague Peace Conference of 1907, – proclaimed in the U.N. Charter and enunciated also in the 1970 Declaration of Principles, means ultimately that all States, – factually strong and weak, great and small, – are equal before international law, are entitled to the same protection under the law and before the organs of international justice, and to equality in the exercise of international rights and duties.

Despite successive attempts to undermine it, the principle of juridical equality of States has remained, from the II Hague Peace Conference of 1907 to date, one of the basic pillars of International Law. It has withstood the onslaught of time, and shown itself salutary for the peaceful conduction of international relations, being ineluctably associated – as it stands – with the foundations of International Law. It has been very important for the international legal system itself, and has proven to be a cornerstone of international law in the United Nations era. In fact, the U.N. Charter gave it a new dimension, and the principle developments such as that of the system of collective security, within the ambit of the law of the United Nations.[135]

129. By the turn of the century, the General Assembly's resolution 55/2, of 08.09.2000, adopted the United Nations Millennium Declaration, which *inter alia* upheld the "sovereign equality of all States", in conformity with "the principles of justice and international law" (para. I(4)). Half a decade later, the General Assembly's resolution 60/1, of 16.09.2005, adopted the *World Summit Outcome*, which *inter alia* expressed the determination "to establish a just and lasting peace all over the world in accordance with the purposes and principles of the [U.N.] Charter", as well as "to uphold the sovereign equality of all States" (para. I(5)). In stressing therein the "vital importance of an effective multilateral system" to face current challenges to international peace and security (paras. 6–7), the international community reiterated its profession of faith in the general principles of international law.

---

135 A.A. Cançado Trindade, *International Law for Humankind – Towards a New Jus Gentium*, op. cit. supra n. (132), pp. 84–85, and cf. pp. 62–63, 65 and 73.

XI Unfoundedness of the Strategy of "Deterrence"

130. In effect, the strategy of "deterrence", pursued by NWS in the present context of nuclear disarmament in order to attempt to justify their own position, makes abstraction of the fundamental principle of the juridical equality of States, enshrined into the U.N. Charter. Factual inequalities cannot be made to prevail over the juridical equality of States. All U.N. member States are juridically equal. The strategy of a few States pursuing their own "national security interests" cannot be made to prevail over a fundamental principle of international law set forth in the U.N. Charter: factual inequalities between States cannot, and do not prevail over the juridical equality of States.

131. In its 1996 Advisory Opinion on the *Threat or Use of Nuclear Weapons*, permeated with ambiguity, the ICJ gave undue weight to "the still strong adherence to the practice of deterrence" (paras. 67 and 73) by a few NWS, to the point of beholding in it an obstacle to the formation and consolidation of *opinio juris* and a customary rule as to the illegality of nuclear weapons, leading to "a specific and express prohibition" of their use (para. 73). Here the Court assumed its usual positivist posture: in its view, the prohibition must be express, stated in positive law, even if those weapons are capable of destroying all life on earth, the whole of humankind...

132. The ICJ, in its Advisory Opinion of 1996, gave too much weight to the opposition of NWS as to the existence of an *opinio juris* on the unlawfulness of nuclear weapons. And this, despite the fact that, in their overwhelming majority, member States of the United Nations stand clearly against nuclear weapons, and in favour of nuclear disarmament. The 1996 Advisory Opinion, notwithstanding, appears unduly influenced by the lack of logic of "deterrence".[136] One cannot conceive, – as the 1996 Advisory Opinion did, – of recourse to nuclear weapons by a hypothetical State in "self-defence" at the unbearable cost of the devastating effects and sufferings inflicted upon humankind as a whole, in an "escalade vers l'apocalypse".[137]

---

136 Cf. criticisms of such posture in, e.g., A. Sayed, *Quand le droit est face à son néant – Le droit à l'épreuve de l'emploi de l'arme nucléaire*, Bruxelles, Bruylant, 1998, pp. 79–80, 84, 88–89, 96 and 113.

137 Cf. *ibid.*, p. 147, and cf. pp. 129, 133, 151, 160, 174–175, 197 and 199–200.

133. The infliction of such devastation and suffering is in flagrant breach of international law, – of the ILHR, IHL and the Law of the United Nations (cf. Part XII, *infra*). It is, furthermore, in flagrant breach of norms of *jus cogens*.[138] The strategy of "deterrence" seems to make abstraction of all that. The ICJ, as the International Court *of Justice*, should have given, on all occasions when it has been called upon to pronounce on nuclear weapons (in the exercise of its jurisdiction on contentious and advisory matters), far greater weight to the *raison d'humanité*,[139] rather than to the *raison d'État* nourishing "deterrence". We have to keep in mind the human person and the peoples, for which States were created, instead of relying only on what one assumes to be the *raison d'État*. The *raison d'humanité*, in my understanding, prevails surely over considerations of *Realpolitik*.

134. In its 1996 Advisory Opinion, the ICJ, however, at the same time, rightly acknowledged the importance of complete nuclear disarmament, asserted in the series of General Assembly resolutions, and the relevance of the corresponding obligation under Article VI of the NPT to the international community as a whole (paras. 99 and 102). To the Court, this is an obligation of result, and not of mere conduct (para. 99). Yet, it did not extract the consequences of that. Had it done so, it would have reached the conclusion that nuclear disarmament cannot be hampered by the conduct of a few States – the NWS – which maintain and modernize their own arsenals of nuclear weapons, pursuant to their strategy of "deterrence".

135. The strategy of "deterrence" has a suicidal component. Nowadays, in 2016, twenty years after the 1996 ICJ Advisory Opinion, and with the subsequent reiteration of the conventional and customary international legal obligation of nuclear disarmament, there is no longer any room for ambiguity. There is an *opinio juris communis* as to the illegality of nuclear weapons, and as to the well-established obligation of nuclear disarmament, which is an obligation of result and not of mere conduct. Such *opinio juris* cannot be erased by the dogmatic positivist insistence on an express prohibition of nuclear weapons; on

---

138   On the expansion of the material content of this latter, cf. A.A. Cançado Trindade, "*Jus Cogens*: The Determination and the Gradual Expansion of Its Material Content in Contemporary International Case-Law", *in* XXXV *Curso de Derecho Internacional Organizado por el Comité Jurídico Interamericano – 2008*, Washington D.C., OAS General Secretariat, 2009, pp. 3–29.

139   A.A. Cançado Trindade, "La Humanización del Derecho Internacional y los Límites de la Razón de Estado", *in* 40 *Revista da Faculdade de Direito da Universidade Federal de Minas Gerais* – Belo Horizonte/Brazil (2001), pp. 11–23.

the contrary, that *opinio juris* discloses that the invocation of the absence of an express prohibition is nonsensical, in relying upon the destructive and suicidal strategy of "deterrence".

136. Such strategy is incompatible with jusnaturalist thinking, always attentive to ethical considerations (cf. Part XIV, *infra*). Over half a century ago (precisely 55 years ago), the U.N. General Assembly had already stated, in its seminal resolution 1653 (XVI) of 1961, that the use of nuclear weapons was "contrary to the spirit, letter and aims of the United Nations", a "direct violation" of the U.N. Charter, a breach of international law and of "the laws of humanity", and "a crime against mankind and civilization" (operative para. 1). Several subsequent General Assembly resolutions upheld the same understanding of resolution 1653(XVI) of 1961 (cf. Part III, *supra*), leaving thus no room at all for ambiguity or hesitation, or to any concession.

137. Two decades ago, in the advisory proceedings of late 1995 before the ICJ, conducive to its 1996 Advisory Opinion on *Threat or Use of Nuclear Weapons*, fierce criticisms were voiced of the strategy of "deterrence", keeping in mind the inhumane sufferings of victims of nuclear detonation, radiation and contamination.[140] Attention was drawn, on the occasion, to the "distortion of logic" in "deterrence", in trying to rely on so immensely destructive weapons to keep peace, and in further trying to persuade others "to accept that for the last 50 or so years this new and more dangerous and potentially genocidal level or armaments should be credited with keeping peace".[141]

138. In the aforementioned advisory proceedings, "nuclear deterrence" was dismissed as being "simply the maintenance of a balance of fear";[142] it was criticized as seeking to ground itself on a "highly questionable" premise, whereby a handful of NWS feel free to "arrogate to themselves" the faculty "to determine what is world peace and security, exclusive in the context of their own" national strategies and interests.[143] It was contended that nuclear weapons are in breach of international law by their own nature, as weapons of catastrophic mass destruction; "nuclear deterrence" wrongfully assumes that States and individuals act rationally, leaving the world "under the nuclear sword of Damocles", stimulating "the nuclear ambitions of their countries, thereby increasing

---

140 Cf., e.g., the testimonies of the Mayors of Hiroshima and Nagasaki, in Part XII, *infra*.
141 ICJ, doc. CR 95/35, of 15.11.1995, p. 32 (statement of Zimbabwe).
142 ICJ, doc. CR 95/27, of 07.11.1995, p. 37 (statement of the Mayor of Nagasaki).
143 *Ibid.*, p. 45, para. 14 (statement of Malaysia).

overall instability", and also increasing the danger of their being used "intentionally or accidentally".[144]

139. The NWS, in persisting to rely on the strategy of "deterrence", seem to overlook the above-reviewed distinct series of U.N. General Assembly resolutions (cf. Part III, *supra*) condemning nuclear weapons and calling for their elimination. The strategy of "deterrence" has come under strong criticism along the years, for the serious risks it carries with it, and for its indifference to the goal – supported by the United Nations, – of achieving a world free of nuclear weapons. Very recently, e.g., participants in the series of Conferences on the Humanitarian Impact of Nuclear Weapons (2013–2014) have strongly criticized the strategy of nuclear "deterrence". In a statement sent to the 2014 Vienna Conference, for example, the U.N. Secretary-General warned against the dangers of nuclear "deterrence", undermining world stability (cf. Part XVIII, *infra*).

140. There is here, in effect, clearly formed, an *opinio juris communis* as to the illegality and prohibition of nuclear weapons. The use or threat of use of nuclear weapons being a clear breach of international law, of International Humanitarian Law and of the International Law of Human Rights, and of the U.N. Charter, renders unsustainable and unfounded any invocation of the strategy of "deterrence". In my view, a few States cannot keep on insisting on "national security interests" to arrogate to themselves indefinitely the prerogative to determine by themselves the conditions of world peace, and to impose them upon all others, the overwhelming majority of the international community. The survival of humankind cannot be made to depend on the "will" of a handful of privileged States. The universal juridical conscience stands well above the "will" of individual States.

XII   The Illegality of Nuclear Weapons and the Obligation of Nuclear Disarmament

1   *The Condemnation of All Weapons of Mass Destruction*

141. Since the beginning of the nuclear age, it became clear that the effects of nuclear weapons (such as heat and radiation) cannot be limited to military targets only, being thus by nature indiscriminate and disproportionate in their long-term devastation, disclosing the utmost cruelty. The *opinio juris communis* as to the prohibition of nuclear weapons, and of all weapons of mass

---

144   *Ibid.*, p. 55, para. 8; and cf. pp. 60–61 and 63, paras. 17–20 (statement of Malaysia).

destruction, has gradually been formed, along the last decades.[145] If weapons less destructive than nuclear weapons have already been expressly prohibited (as is the case of biological and chemical weapons), it would be nonsensical to argue that, those which have not, by positive conventional international law, like nuclear weapons, would not likewise be illicit; after all, they have far greater and long-lasting devastating effects, threatening the existence of the international community as a whole.

142. It may be recalled that, already in 1969, *all* weapons of mass destruction were condemned by the *Institut de Droit International* (I.D.I.). In the debates of its Edinburgh session on the matter, emphasis was placed on the need to respect the principle of distinction (between military and non-military objectives), and the terrifying effects of the use of nuclear weapons were pointed out, – the example of the atomic bombing of Hiroshima and Nagasaki having been expressly recalled.[146] In its resolution of September 1969 on the matter, the *Institut* began by restating, in the preamble, the *prohibition of recourse to force* in international law, and the duty of protection of civilian populations in any armed conflict; it further recalled the general principles of international law, customary rules and conventions, – supported by international case-law and practice, – which "clearly restrict" the extent to which the parties engaged in a conflict may harm the adversary, and warned against

> the consequences which the indiscriminate conduct of hostilities and particularly the use of nuclear, chemical and bacteriological weapons, may involve for civilian populations and for mankind as a whole.[147]

143. In its operative part, the aforementioned resolution of the *Institut* stressed the importance of the principle of distinction (between military and non-military objectives) as a "fundamental principle of international law" and the pressing need to protect civilian populations in armed conflicts,[148] and added, in paragraphs 4 and 7, that:

---

145 Cf., e.g., G.E. do Nascimento e Silva, "A Proliferação Nuclear e o Direito Internacional", *in Pensamiento Jurídico y Sociedad Internacional – Libro-Homenaje al Prof. A. Truyol y Serra*, vol. II, Madrid, Universidad Complutense, 1986, pp. 877–886; C.A. Dunshee de Abranches, *Proscrição das Armas Nucleares*, Rio de Janeiro, Livr. Freitas Bastos, 1964, pp. 114–179.

146 Cf. *Annuaire de l'Institut de Droit International* – Session d'Edimbourg (1969)-II, pp. 49–50, 53, 55, 60, 62–63, 66, 88–90 and 99.

147 Text *in: Annuaire de l'Institut de Droit International* – Session d'Edimbourg (1969) II, pp. 375–376.

148 Paras. 1–3, 5–6 and 8, *in ibid.*, pp. 376–377.

Existing international law prohibits all armed attacks on the civilian population as such, as well as on non-military objects, notably dwellings or other buildings sheltering the civilian population, so long as these are not used for military purposes (...).

Existing international law prohibits the use of all weapons which, by their nature, affect indiscriminately both military objectives and non-military objects, or both armed forces and civilian populations. In particular, it prohibits the use of weapons the destructive effect of which is so great that it cannot be limited to specific military objectives or is otherwise uncontrollable (self-generating weapons), as well as of 'blind' weapons.[149]

144. For its part, the International Law Association (I.L.A.), in its more recent work (in 2014) on nuclear disarmament, after referring to Article VI of the NPT, was of the view that it was not only conventional, but also an evolving customary international obligation with an *erga omnes* character, affecting "the international community as a whole", and not only the States Parties to the NPT.[150] It also referred to the "world-wide public opinion" pointing to "the catastrophic consequences for humankind of any use or detonation of nuclear weapons", and added that reliance on nuclear weapons for "deterrence" was thus unsustainable.[151]

145. In its view, "nuclear" deterrence is not a global "umbrella", but rather a threat to international peace and security, and NWS are still far from implementing Article VI of the NPT.[152] To the International Law Association, the provisions of Article VI are not limited to States Parties to the NPT, "they are part of customary international law or at least evolving custom"; they are valid *erga omnes*, as they affect "the international community as a whole", and not only a group of States or a particular State.[153] Thus, as just seen, learned institutions in international law, such as the I.D.I. and the I.L.A., have also sustained the prohibition in international law of all weapons of mass destruction, starting with nuclear weapons, the most devastating of all.

---

149   Text *in ibid.*, pp. 376–377.
150   International Law Association (I.L.A.), Committee: *Nuclear Weapons, Non-Proliferation and Contemporary International Law* (2nd Report: *Legal Aspects of Nuclear Disarmament*), I.L.A. Washington Conference, 2014, pp. 2–4.
151   *Ibid.*, pp. 5–6.
152   *Ibid.*, pp. 8–9.
153   *Ibid.*, p. 18.

146. A single use of nuclear weapons, irrespective of the circumstances, may today ultimately mean the end of humankind itself.[154] All weapons of mass destruction are illegal, and are prohibited: this is what ineluctably ensues from an international legal order of which the ultimate material source is the *universal juridical conscience*.[155] This is the position I have consistently sustained along the years, including in a lecture I delivered at the University of Hiroshima, Japan, on 20.12.2004.[156] I have done so in the line of jusnaturalist thinking, faithful to the lessons of the "founding fathers" of the law of nations, keeping in mind not only States, but also peoples and individuals, and humankind as a whole.

2 *The Prohibition of Nuclear Weapons: The Need of a People-Centred Approach*

147. In effect, the nuclear age itself, from its very beginning (the atomic blasts of Hiroshima and Nagasaki in August 1945) can be properly studied from a people-centred approach. There are moving testimonies and historical accounts of the devastating effects of nuclear weapons, from surviving victims and witnesses.[157] Yet, even with the eruption of the nuclear age, attention remained focused largely on State strategies: it took some time for them gradually to shift to the devastating effects of nuclear weapons on peoples.

148. As recalled in one of the historical accounts, only at the first Conference against Atomic and Hydrogen Bombs (1955), "the victims had their first

---

154 Nagendra Singh, *Nuclear Weapons and International Law*, London, Stevens, 1959, p. 242.

155 A.A. Cançado Trindade, *International Law for Humankind – Towards a New Jus Gentium*, op. cit. supra n. (132), Ch. VI ("The Material Source of International Law: Manifestations of the Universal Juridical Conscience"), pp. 139–161.

156 Text of my lecture reproduced *in*: A.A. Cançado Trindade, *Le Droit international pour la personne humaine*, Paris, Pédone, 2012, Ch. I ("L'illicéité de toutes les armes de destruction massive au regard du droit international contemporain"), pp. 61–90; A.A. Cançado Trindade, *A Humanização do Direito Internacional*, 2nd ed., Belo Horizonte/Brazil, Edit. Del Rey, 2015, Ch. XVII ("The Illegality under Contemporary International Law of All Weapons of Mass Destruction"), pp. 361–390.

157 Michihiko Hachiya, *Journal d'Hiroshima – 6 août-30 septembre 1945* [1955], Paris, Éd. Tallandier, 2015 [reed.], pp. 25–281; Toyofumi Ogura, *Letters from the End of the World – A Firsthand Account of the Bombing of Hiroshima* [1948], Tokyo/N.Y./London, Kodansha International, 2001 [reed.], pp. 15–173; Naomi Shohno, *The Legacy of Hiroshima – Its Past, Our Future*, Tokyo, Kösei Publ. Co., 1987 [reed.], pp. 13–140; Kenzaburo Oe, *Notes de Hiroshima* [1965], [Paris,] Gallimard, 1996 [reed.], pp. 17–230; J. Hersey, *Hiroshima* [1946], London, Penguin, 2015 [reprint], pp. 1–98.

opportunity, after ten years of silence, to make themselves heard", in that forum.[158] Along the last decades, there have been endeavours to shift attention from State strategies to the numerous victims and enormous damages caused by nuclear weapons, focusing on "human misery and human dignity".[159] Recently, one significant initiative to this effect has been the series of Conferences on the Humanitarian Impact of Nuclear Weapons (2013–2014), which I shall survey later on in this Dissenting Opinion (cf. Part XVIII, *infra*).

149. There has been a chorus of voices of those who have been personally victimized by nuclear weapons in distinct circumstances, – either in the atomic bombings of Hiroshima and Nagasaki (1945), or in nuclear testing (during the cold-war era) in regions such as Central Asia and the Pacific. Focusing on their intensive suffering (e.g., ensuing from radioactive contamination and forced displacement),[160] affecting successive generations, they have drawn attention to the humanitarian consequences of nuclear weapon detonations.

150. In addressing the issue of nuclear weapons, on four successive occasions (cf. *infra*), the ICJ appears, however, to have always suffered from inter-State myopia. Despite the clarity of the formidable threat that nuclear weapons represent, the treatment of the issue of their prohibition under international law has most regrettably remained permeated by ambiguities. The present case of *Obligations Concerning Negotiations Relating to Cessation of the Nuclear Arms Race and to Nuclear Disarmament* is the third time that attempts were made, by means of the lodging of contentious cases with the ICJ, to obtain its pronouncement thereon. On two prior occasions – in the *Nuclear Tests* cases (1974 and 1995),[161] the Court assumed, in both of them, a rather evasive posture, avoiding to pronounce clearly on the substance of a matter pertaining to the very survival of humankind.

151. May I here briefly single out one aspect of those earlier contentious proceedings, given its significance in historical perspective. It should not pass unnoticed that, in the first *Nuclear Tests* case (Australia and New Zealand

---

158   Kenzaburo Oe, *Hiroshima Notes* [1965], N.Y./London, Marion Boyars, 1997 [reed.], pp. 72 and 159.
159   *Ibid.*, pp. 149 and 162.
160   Cf. J. Borrie, "Humanitarian Reframing of Nuclear Weapons and the Logic of a Ban", 90 *International Affairs* (2014) p. 633, and cf. pp. 637, 643–644 and 646.
161   Cf. *I.C.J. Reports 1974*, pp. 63–455; and cf. *I.C.J. Reports 1995*, pp. 4–23, and the position of three dissenting Judges in *ibid.*, pp. 317–421.

versus France), one of the applicant States contended, *inter alia*, that the nuclear testing undertaken by the French government in the South Pacific region violated not only the right of New Zealand that no radioactive material enter its territory, air space and territorial waters *and* those of other Pacific territories but *also* "the rights of all members of the international community, including New Zealand, that no nuclear tests that give rise to radioactive fall-out be conducted".[162]

152. For its part, the other applicant State contended that it was seeking protection to the life, health and well-being of Australia's population, in common with the populations of other States, against atmospheric nuclear tests by any State.[163] Thus, over three decades ago, the perspective of the *Applications Instituting Proceedings* of both New Zealand and Australia (of 1973) went clearly – and correctly so – beyond the purely inter-State dimension, as the problem at issue concerned the international community as a whole.

153. Both Australia and New Zealand insisted on the people-centred approach throughout the legal proceedings (written and oral phases). New Zealand, for example, in its *Memorial*, invoked the obligation *erga omnes* not to undertake nuclear testing "owed to the international community as a whole" (paras. 207–208), adding that non-compliance with it aroused "the keenest sense of alarm and antagonism among the peoples" and States of the region wherein the tests were conducted (para. 212). In its oral arguments in the public sitting of 10.07.1974 in the same *Nuclear Tests* case, New Zealand again invoked "the rights of all members of the international community", and the obligations *erga omnes* owed to the international community as a whole.[164] And Australia, for example, in its oral arguments in the public sitting of 08.07.1974, referring to the 1963 Partial Test Ban Treaty, underlined the concern of "the whole international community" for "the future of mankind" and the responsibility imposed by "the principles of international law" upon "all States to refrain from testing nuclear weapons in the atmosphere".[165]

---

162 ICJ, *Application Instituting Proceedings* (of 09.05.1973), *Nuclear Tests* case (New Zealand *versus* France), pp. 8 and 15–16, cf. pp. 4–16.

163 ICJ, *Application Instituting Proceedings* (of 09.05.1973), *Nuclear Tests* case (Australia *versus* France), pp. 12 and 14, paras. 40, 47 and 49(1).

164 ICJ, *Pleadings, Oral Arguments, Documents – Nuclear Tests cases* (vol. II: New Zealand *versus* France, 1973–1974), pp. 256–257 and 264–266.

165 ICJ, *Pleadings, Oral Arguments, Documents – Nuclear Tests cases* (vol. I: Australia *versus* France, 1973–1974), p. 503.

154. The outcome of the *Nuclear Test* cases, however, was rather disappointing: even though the ICJ issued orders of Provisional Measures of Protection in the cases in June 1973 (requiring the respondent State to cease testing), subsequently, in its Judgments of 1974,[166] in view of the announcement of France's voluntary discontinuance of its atmospheric tests, the ICJ found, yielding to State voluntarism, that the claims of Australia and New Zealand no longer had "any object" and that it was thus not called upon to give a decision thereon.[167] The dissenting Judges in the case rightly pointed out that the legal dispute between the contending parties, far from having ceased, still persisted, since what Australia and New Zealand sought was a declaratory judgment of the ICJ stating that atmospheric nuclear tests were contrary to international law.[168]

155. The reticent position of the ICJ in that case was even more regrettable if one recalls that the applicants, in referring to the "psychological injury" caused to the peoples of the South Pacific region through their "anxiety as to the possible effects of radioactive fall-out on the well-being of themselves and their descendants", as a result of the atmospheric nuclear tests, ironically invoked the notion of *erga omnes* obligations (as propounded by the ICJ itself in its *obiter dicta* in the *Barcelona Traction* case only four years earlier).[169] As the ICJ reserved itself the right, in certain circumstances, to reopen the case decided in 1974, it did so two decades later, upon an application instituted by New Zealand *versus* France. But in its Order of 22.09.1995, the ICJ dismissed the complaint, as it did not fit into the *caveat* of the 1974 Judgment, which concerned

---

166 For a critical parallel between the 1973 Orders and the 1974 Judgments, cf. P. Lellouche, "The *Nuclear Tests* Cases: Judicial Silence *versus* Atomic Blasts", 16 *Harvard International Law Journal* (1975) pp. 615–627 and 635; and, for further criticisms, cf. *ibid.*, pp. 614–637.

167 *I.C.J. Reports 1974*, pp. 272 and 478, respectively.

168 ICJ, *Nuclear Tests* case, Joint Dissenting Opinion of Judges Onyeama, Dillard, Jiménez de Aréchaga and Waldock, *I.C.J. Reports 1974*, pp. 319–322, 367–369, 496, 500, 502–504, 514 and 520–521; and cf. Dissenting Opinion of Judge De Castro, *ibid.*, pp. 386–390; and Dissenting Opinion of Judge Barwick, *ibid.*, pp. 392–394, 404–405, 436–437 and 525–528. It was further pointed out that the ICJ should thus have dwelt upon the question of the existence of rules of *customary* international law prohibiting States from causing, through atmospheric nuclear tests, the deposit of radio-active fall-out on the territory of other States; ICJ, *Nuclear Tests* case, Separate Opinion of Judge Petrén, *I.C.J. Reports 1974*, pp. 303–306 and 488–489. It was the existence or otherwise of such customary rules that had to be determined, – a question which unfortunately was left largely unanswered by the Court in that case.

169 As recalled in the Joint Dissenting Opinion of Judges Onyeama, Dillard, Jiménez de Aréchaga and Waldock, *I.C.J. Reports 1974*, pp. 362, 368–369 and 520–521; as well as in the Dissenting Opinion of Judge Barwick, *ibid.*, pp. 436–437.

atmospheric nuclear tests; here, the complaint was directed against the underground nuclear tests conducted by France since 1974.[170]

156. The ICJ thus lost two historical opportunities, in both contentious cases (1974 and 1995), to clarify the key point at issue (nuclear tests). And now, with the decision it has just rendered today, 05.10.2016, it has lost a third occasion, this time to pronounce on the *Obligations Concerning Negotiations Relating to Cessation of the Nuclear Arms Race and to Nuclear Disarmament*, at the request of the Marshall Islands. This time the Court has found that the existence of a legal dispute has not been established before it and that it has no jurisdiction to consider the Application lodged with it by the Marshall Islands on 24.04.2014.

157. Furthermore, in the mid-nineties, the Court was called upon to exercise its advisory function, in respect of a directly related issue, that of nuclear weapons: both the U.N. General Assembly and the World Health Organization (WHO) opened those proceedings before the ICJ, by means of requests for an Advisory Opinion. Such requests no longer referred to nuclear tests, but rather to the question of the threat or use of nuclear weapons in the light of international law, for the determination of their illegality or otherwise.

158. In response to only one of the applications, that of the U.N. General Assembly,[171] the Court, in the Advisory Opinion of 08.07.1996 on the *Threat or Use of Nuclear Weapons*, affirmed that neither customary international law nor conventional international law authorizes specifically the threat or use of nuclear weapons; neither one, nor the other, contains a complete and universal prohibition of the threat or use of nuclear weapons as such; it added that such threat or use which is contrary to Article 2(4) of the U.N. Charter and does not fulfil the requisites of its Article 51, is illicit; moreover, the conduct in armed conflicts should be compatible with the norms applicable in them, including those of International Humanitarian Law; it also affirmed the obligation to

---

170 Cf. *I.C.J. Reports 1995*, pp. 288–308; once again, there were Dissenting Opinions (cf. *ibid.*, pp. 317–421). Furthermore, petitions against the French nuclear tests in the atoll of Mururoa and in that of Fangataufa, in French Polinesia, were lodged with the European Commission of Human Rights (EComHR); cf. EComHR, case *N.N. Tauira and 18 Others versus France* (appl. n. 28204/95), decision of 04.12.1995, 83-A *Decisions and Reports* (1995) p. 130.

171 As the ICJ understood, as to the other application, that the WHO was not competent to deal with the question at issue, – despite the purposes of that U.N. specialized agency at issue and the devastating effects of nuclear weapons over human health and the environment...

undertake in good will negotiations conducive to nuclear disarmament in all its aspects.[172]

159. In the most controversial part of its Advisory Opinion (resolutory point 2E), the ICJ stated that the threat or use of nuclear weapons "would be generally contrary to the rules of international law applicable in armed conflict", mainly those of International Humanitarian Law; however, the Court added that, at the present stage of international law "it cannot conclude definitively if the threat or use of nuclear weapons would be lawful or unlawful in an extreme circumstance of self defence in which the very survival of a State would be at stake".[173] The Court therein limited itself to record the existence of a legal uncertainty.

160. In fact, it did not go further than that, and the Advisory Opinion was permeated with evasive ambiguities, not avoiding the shadow of the *non liquet*, in relation to a question which affects, more than each State individually, the whole of humankind. The Advisory Opinion made abstraction of the fact that International Humanitarian Law applies likewise in case of self-defence, always safeguarding the principles of distinction and proportionality (which nuclear weapons simply ignore),[174] and upholding the prohibition of infliction of unnecessary suffering.

161. The Advisory Opinion could and should have given greater weight to a point made before the ICJ in the oral arguments of November 1995, namely, that of the need of a people-centred approach in the present domain. Thus, it was stated, for example, that the "experience of the Marshallese people confirms that unnecessary suffering is an unavoidable consequence of the detonation

---

172   *I.C.J. Reports 1996*, pp. 266–267.
173   *Ibid.*, p. 266.
174   L. Doswald-Beck, "International Humanitarian Law and the Advisory Opinion of the International Court of Justice on the Legality of the Threat or Use of Nuclear Weapons", 316 *International Review of the Red Cross* (1997) pp. 35–55; H. Fujita, "The Advisory Opinion of the International Court of Justice on the Legality of Nuclear Weapons", *in ibid.*, pp. 56–64. International Humanitarian Law prevails also over self-defence; cf. M.-P. Lanfranchi and Th. Christakis, *La licéité de l'emploi d'armes nucléaires devant la Cour Internationale de Justice*, Aix-Marseille/Paris, Université d'Aix-Marseille III/Economica, 1997, pp. 111, 121 and 123; S. Mahmoudi, "The International Court of Justice and Nuclear Weapons", 66 *Nordic Journal of International Law* (1997) pp. 77–100; E. David, "The Opinion of the International Court of Justice on the Legality of the Use of Nuclear Weapons", 316 *International Review of the Red Cross* (1997) pp. 21–34.

of nuclear weapons";[175] the effects of nuclear weapons, by their nature, are widespread, adverse and indiscriminate, affecting also future generations.[176] It was further stated that the "horrifying evidence" of the use of atomic bombs in Hiroshima and Nagasaki, followed by the experience and the aftermath of the nuclear tests carried out in the region of the Pacific Island States in the 1950s and the 1960s, have alerted to "the much graver risks to which mankind is exposed by the use of nuclear weapons".[177]

162. The 1996 Opinion, on the one hand, recognized that nuclear weapons cause indiscriminate and durable suffering, and have an enormous destructive effect (para. 35), and that the principles of humanitarian law (encompassing customary law) are "intransgressible" (para. 79); nevertheless, these considerations did not appear sufficient to the Court to discard the use of such weapons also in self-defence, thus eluding to tell what the Law is in all circumstances. It is clear to me that States are bound to respect, and to ensure respect, for International Humanitarian Law (IHL) and the International Law of Human Rights (ILHR) in *any circumstances*; their fundamental principles belong to the domain of *jus cogens*, in prohibition of nuclear weapons.

163. Again, in the 1996 Opinion, it were the dissenting Judges, and not the Court's split majority, who drew attention to this,[178] and to the relevance of the Martens clause in the present context[179] (cf. Part XIII, *infra*). Moreover, the 1996 Opinion also minimized (para. 71) the resolutions of the U.N. General Assembly which affirm the illegality of nuclear weapons[180] and condemn their use as a violation of the U.N. Charter and as a crime against humanity. Instead, it took note of the "policy of deterrence", which led it to find that the members of the international community continued "profoundly divided" on the matter, rendering it impossible to determine the existence of an *opinio juris* in this respect (para. 67).

---

175 ICJ, doc. CR 95/32, of 14.11.1995, p. 22 (statement of the Marshall Islands).
176 *Ibid.*, p. 23.
177 ICJ, doc. CR 95/32, of 14.11.1995, p. 31 (statement of Solomon Islands). Customary international law and general principles of international law have an incidence in this domain; *ibid.*, pp. 36 and 39–40.
178 ICJ Advisory Opinion on *Threat or Use of Nuclear Weapons, I.C.J. Reports 1996*, Dissenting Opinion of Judge Koroma, pp. 573–574 and 578.
179 Cf. *ibid.*, Dissenting Opinions of Judge Shahabuddeen, pp. 386–387, 406, 408, 410–411 and 425; and of Judge Weeramantry, pp. 477–478, 481, 483, 486–487, 490–491, 494, 508 and 553–554.
180 Notably, the ground-breaking General Assembly resolution 1653(XVI), of 24.11.1961.

164. It was not incumbent upon the Court to resort to the unfounded strategy of "deterrence" (cf. Part XI, *supra*), devoid of any legal value for the determination of the formation of a customary international law obligation of prohibition of the use of nuclear weapons. The Court did not contribute on this matter. In unduly relying on "deterrence" (para. 73), it singled out a division, in its view "profound", between an extremely reduced group of nuclear powers on the one hand, and the vast majority of the countries of the world on the other; it ended up by favouring the former, by means of an inadmissible *non liquet*.[181]

165. The Court, thus, lost yet another opportunity, – in the exercise of its advisory function as well, – to contribute to the consolidation of the *opinio juris communis* in condemnation of nuclear weapons. Its 1996 Advisory Opinion considered the survival of a hypothetical State (in its resolutory point 2E), rather than that of peoples and individuals, and ultimately of humankind as a whole. It seemed to have overlooked that the survival of a State cannot have primacy over the right to survival of humankind as a whole.

3   *The Prohibition of Nuclear Weapons: The Fundamental Right to Life*

166. There is yet another related point to keep in mind. The ICJ's 1996 Advisory Opinion erroneously took IHL as *lex specialis* (para. 25), overstepping the ILHR, oblivious that the maxim *lex specialis derogat generalis*, thus understood, has no application in the present context: in face of the immense threat of nuclear weapons to human life on earth, both IHL and the ILHR apply in a converging way,[182] so as to enhance the much-needed protection of human life. In any circumstances, the norms which best protect are the ones which apply, be them of IHL or of the ILHR, or any other branch of international protection of the human person (such as the International Law of Refugees – ILR). They are all equally important. Regrettably, the 1996 Advisory Opinion unduly minimized

---

181   A.A. Cançado Trindade, *International Law for Humankind – Towards a New Jus Gentium*, *op. cit. supra* n. (132), pp. 415–418; L. Condorelli, "Nuclear Weapons: A Weighty Matter for the International Court of Justice – *Jura Novit Curia*?", 316 *International Review of the Red Cross* (1997) pp. 9–20; M. Mohr, "Advisory Opinion of the International Court of Justice on the Legality of the Use of Nuclear Weapons under International Law – A Few Thoughts on Its Strengths and Weaknesses", 316 *International Review of the Red Cross* (1997) pp. 92–102. The Opinion is not conclusive and provides no guidance; J.-P. Queneudec, "E.T. à la C.I.J.: méditations d'un extra-terrestre sur deux avis consultatifs", 100 *Revue générale de Droit international public* (1996) 907–914, esp. p. 912.

182   Cf. A.A. Cançado Trindade, *Derecho Internacional de los Derechos Humanos, Derecho Internacional de los Refugiados y Derecho Internacional Humanitario – Aproximaciones y Convergencias*, Geneva, ICRC, [2000], pp. 1–66.

the international case-law and the whole doctrinal construction on the right to life in the ambit of the ILHR.

167. It should not pass unnoticed, in this connection, that contemporary international human rights tribunals, such as the European (ECtHR) and the Inter-American (IACtHR) Courts of Human Rights, in the adjudication of successive cases in recent years, have taken into account the relevant principles and norms of both the ILHR and IHL (conventional and customary). For its part, the African Commission of Human and Peoples' Rights (AfComHPR), in its long-standing practice, has likewise acknowledged the approximations and convergences between the ILHR and IHL, and drawn attention to the principles underlying both branches of protection (such as, e.g., the principle of humanity).

168. This has been done, in distinct continents, so as to seek to secure the most effective safeguard of the protected rights, in all circumstances (including in times of armed conflict). Contrary to what was held in the ICJ's 1996 Advisory Opinion, there is no *lex specialis* here, but rather a concerted endeavour to apply the relevant norms (be them of the ILHR or of IHL) that best protect human beings. This is particularly important when they find themselves in a situation of utmost vulnerability, – such as in the present context of threat or use of nuclear weapons. In their case-law, international human rights tribunals (like the ECtHR and the IACtHR) have focused attention on the imperative of securing protection, e.g., to the fundamental right to life, of persons in great vulnerability (potential victims).[183]

169. In the course of the proceedings before the ICJ in the present cases of *Obligations* Concerning Negotiations Relating to Cessation of the Nuclear Arms Race and to Nuclear Disarmament, the applicant State draws attention reiteratedly to the devastating effects upon human life of nuclear weapons detonations. Thus, in the case opposing the Marshall Islands to the United Kingdom, the applicant State draws attention, in its Memorial, to the destructive effects of nuclear weapons (testing) in space and time (pp. 12–14). In its oral arguments of 11.03.2016, the Marshall Islands addresses the "tragic losses to the Marshallese", the "dire health consequences suffered by the Marshallese following nuclear contamination, including extreme birth defects and cancers".[184]

---

[183] Cf. A.A. Cançado Trindade, *The Access of Individuals to International Justice*, Oxford, Oxford University Press, 2012 [reprint], Chs. II–III and VII, pp. 17–62 and 125–131.
[184] ICJ, doc. CR 2016/5, of 11.03.2016, p. 9, para. 10.

170. In the case opposing the Marshall Islands to India, the applicant State, in its *Memorial*, refers to the grave "health and environmental consequences of nuclear testing" upon the Marshallese (pp. 5–6). In its oral arguments of 07.03.2016, the Marshall Islands stated:

> The Marshall Islands has a unique and devastating history with nuclear weapons. While it was designated as a Trust Territory by the United Nations, no fewer than 67 atomic and thermonuclear weapons were deliberately exploded as 'tests' in the Marshall Islands, by the United States. (...) Several islands in my country were vaporized and others are estimated to remain uninhabitable for thousands of years. Many, many Marshallese died, suffered birth defects never before seen and battled cancers resulting from the contamination. Tragically the Marshall Islands thus bears *eyewitness* to the horrific and indiscriminate lethal capacity of these weapons, and the intergenerational and continuing effects that they perpetuate even 60 years later.
>
> One 'test' in particular, called the 'Bravo' test [in March 1954], was one thousand times stronger than the bombs dropped on Hiroshima and Nagasaki.[185]

171. And in the case opposing the Marshall Islands to Pakistan, the applicant State, in its *Memorial*, likewise addresses the serious "health and environmental consequences of nuclear testing" upon the Marshallese (pp. 5–6). In its oral arguments of 08.03.2016, the Marshall Islands recalls the 67 atomic and thermonuclear weapons "tests" that it had to endure (since it became a U.N. Trust Territory); it further recalls the reference, in the U.N. Charter, to nations "large and small" having "equal rights" (preamble), and to the assertion in its Article 2 that the United Nations is "based on the principle of the sovereign equality of all its Members".[186]

172. Two decades earlier, in the course of the advisory proceedings before the ICJ of late 1995 preceding the 1996 Advisory Opinion on the *Threat or Use of Nuclear Weapons*, the devastating effects upon human life of nuclear weapons detonations were likewise brought to the Court's attention. It is beyond the purposes of the present Dissenting Opinion to review all statements to this effect; suffice it here to recall two of the most moving statements, from the Mayors of Hiroshima and Nagasaki, who appeared before the Court as

---

185 ICJ, doc. CR 2016/1, of 07.03.2016, p. 16, paras. 4–5.
186 ICJ, doc. CR 2016/2, of 08.03.2016, p. 10, paras. 5–7.

members of the Delegation of Japan. The Mayor of Hiroshima (Mr. Takashi Hiraoka) thus began his statement of 07.11.1995 before the ICJ:

> I am here today representing Hiroshima citizens, who desire the abolition of nuclear weapons. More particularly, I represent the hundreds of thousands of victims whose lives were cut short, and survivors who are still suffering the effects of radiation, 50 years later. On their behalf, I am here to testify to the cruel, inhuman nature of nuclear weapons. (...)
>
> The development of the atomic bomb was the product of cooperation among politicians, military and scientists. The nuclear age began the moment the bombs were dropped on human beings.
>
> Their enormous destructive power reduced utterly innocent civilian populations to ashes. Women, the elderly, and the newborn were bathed in deadly radiation and slaughtered.[187]

173. After stressing that the mass killing was "utterly indiscriminate", he added that, even today, "thousands of people struggle daily with the curse of illness caused by that radiation", there being until then "no truly accurate casualty figures".[188] The exposure in Hiroshima to high levels of radiation, – he proceeded, – "was the first in human history", generating leukemia, distinct kinds of cancer (of breast, lung, stomach, thyroid, and other), extending for "years or decades", with all the fear generated by such continuing killing "across years or decades".[189]

174. Even half a century later, – added the Mayor of Hiroshima, – "the effects of radiation on human bodies are not thoroughly understood. Medically, we do know that radiation destroys cells in the human body, which can lead to many forms of pathology".[190] The victimized segments of the population have continued suffering "psychologically, physically, and socially from the atomic bomb's after-effects".[191] He further stated that

> The horror of nuclear weapons (...) derives (...) from the tremendous destructive power, but equally from radiation, the effects of which reach across generations. (...) What could be more cruel? Nuclear weapons are

---

187 ICJ, doc. CR 95/27, of 07.11.1995, pp. 22–23.
188 Ibid., pp. 24–25.
189 Ibid., pp. 25–27.
190 Ibid., p. 25.
191 Ibid., pp. 27–28.

more cruel and inhumane than any weapon banned thus far by international law.[192]

175. After singling out the significance of U.N. General Assembly resolution 1653 (XVI) of 1961, the Mayor of Hiroshima warned that "[t]he stockpiles of nuclear weapons on earth today are enough to annihilate the entire human race several times over. These weapons are possessed on the assumption that they can be used".[193] He concluded with a strong criticism of the strategy of "deterrence"; in his own words,

> As long as nuclear weapons exist, the human race faces a real and present danger of self-extermination. The idea based on nuclear deterrence that nuclear war can be controlled and won exhibits a failure of human intelligence to comprehend the human tragedy and global environmental destruction brought about by nuclear war. (...) [O]nly through a treaty that clearly stipulates the abolition of nuclear weapons can the world step toward the future (...).[194]

176. For his part, the Mayor of Nagasaki (Mr. Iccho Itoh), in his statement before the ICJ, also of 07.11.1995, likewise warned that "nuclear weapons bring enormous, indiscriminate devastation to civilian populations"; thus, five decades ago, in Hiroshima and Nagasaki, "a single aircraft dropped a single bomb and snuffed out the lives of 140.000 and 74.000 people, respectively. And that is not all. Even the people who were lucky enough to survive continue to this day to suffer from the late effects unique to nuclear weapons. In this way, nuclear weapons bring enormous, indiscriminate devastation to civilian populations".[195]

177. He added that "the most fundamental difference between nuclear and conventional weapons is that the former release radioactive rays at the time of explosion", and the exposure to large doses of radiation generates a "high incidence of disease" and mortality (such as leukaemia and cancer). Descendants of atomic bomb survivors will have, amidst anxiety, "to be monitored for several generations to clarify the genetic impact"; "nuclear weapons are inhuman tools for mass slaughter and destruction", their use "violates international

---

192 *Ibid.*, p. 30.
193 *Ibid.*, pp. 30–31.
194 *Ibid.*, p. 31.
195 ICJ, doc. CR 95/27, of 07.11.1995, p. 33.

law".¹⁹⁶ The Mayor of Nagasaki concluded with a strong criticism of "nuclear deterrence", characterizing it as "simply the maintenance of a balance of fear" (p. 37), always threatening peace, with its "psychology of suspicion and intimidation"; the Nagasaki survivors of the atomic bombing of 50 years ago, "continue to live in fear of late effects".¹⁹⁷

178. Those testimonies before the ICJ, in the course of contentious proceedings (in 2016) as well as advisory proceedings (two decades earlier, in 1995), leave it quite clear that the threat or use (including "testing") of nuclear weapons entails an arbitrary deprivation of human life, and is in flagrant breach of the fundamental right to life. It is in manifest breach of the ILHR, of IHL, as well as the Law of the United Nations, and hand an incidence also on the ILR. There are, furthermore, in such grave breach, aggravating circumstances: the harm caused by radiation from nuclear weapons cannot be contained in space, nor can it be contained in time, it is a true inter-generational harm.

179. As pointed out in the pleadings before the ICJ of late 1995, the use of nuclear weapons thus violates the right to life (and the right to health) of "not only people currently living, but also of the unborn, of those to be born, of subsequent generations".¹⁹⁸ Is there anything quintessentially more cruel? To use nuclear weapons appears like condemning innocent persons to hell on earth, even *before* they are born. That seems to go even further than the Book of *Genesis*'s story of the original sin. In reaction to such extreme cruelty, the consciousness of the rights inherent to the human person has always marked a central presence in endeavours towards complete nuclear disarmament.

4 The Absolute Prohibitions of *Jus* Cogens and the Humanization of International Law

180. The absolute prohibition of arbitrary deprivation of human life (*supra*) is one of *jus cogens*, originating in the ILHR, and with an incidence also on IHL and the ILR, and marking presence also in the Law of the United Nations. The absolute prohibition of inflicting cruel, inhuman or degrading treatment is one of *jus cogens*, originating likewise in the ILHR, and with an incidence also on IHL and the ILR. The absolute prohibition of inflicting unnecessary suffering is one of *jus cogens*, originating in IHL, and with an incidence also on the ILHR and the ILR.

---

196 *Ibid.*, pp. 36–37.
197 *Ibid.*, p. 39.
198 ICJ, doc. CR 95/35, of 15.11.1995, p. 28 (statement of Zimbabwe).

181. In addition to those converging trends (ILHR, IHL, ILR) of international protection of the rights of the human person, those prohibitions of *jus cogens* mark presence also in contemporary International Criminal Law (ICL), as well as in the *corpus juris gentium* of condemnation of all weapons of mass destruction. The absolute prohibitions of *jus cogens* nowadays encompass the threat or use of nuclear weapons, for all the human suffering they entail: in the case of their use, a suffering without limits in space or in time, and extending to succeeding generations.

182. I have been characterizing, along the years, the doctrinal and jurisprudential construction of international *jus cogens* as proper of the new *jus gentium* of our times, the International Law for Humankind. I have been sustaining, moreover, that, by definition, international *jus cogens* goes beyond the law of treaties, extending itself to the law of the international responsibility of the State, and to the whole *corpus juris* of contemporary International Law, and reaching, ultimately, any juridical act.[199]

183. In my lectures in an OAS Course of International Law delivered in Rio de Janeiro almost a decade ago, e.g., I have deemed it fit to ponder that

> The fact that the concepts both of the *jus cogens*, and of the obligations (and rights) *erga omnes* ensuing therefrom, already integrate the conceptual universe of contemporary international law, the new *jus gentium* of our days, discloses the reassuring and necessary opening of this latter, in the last decades, to certain superior and fundamental values. This significant evolution of the recognition and assertion of norms of *jus cogens* and obligations *erga omnes* of protection is to be fostered, seeking to secure its full practical application, to the benefit of all human beings. In this way the universalist vision of the founding fathers of the *droit des gens* is being duly rescued. New conceptions of the kind impose themselves in our days, and, of their faithful observance, will depend to a large extent the future evolution of contemporary international law.
>
> This latter does not emanate from the inscrutable 'will' of the States, but rather, in my view, from human conscience. General or customary international law emanates not so much from the practice of States (not devoid of ambiguities and contradictions), but rather from the *opinio juris communis* of all the subjects of international law (States, international

---

[199] A.A. Cançado Trindade, *International Law for Humankind – Towards a New Jus Gentium*, op. cit. supra n. (132), Ch. XII, pp. 291–326.

organizations, human beings, and humankind as a whole). Above the will stands the conscience. (...)

The current process of the necessary *humanization* of international law stands in reaction to that state of affairs. It bears in mind the universality and unity of the human kind, which inspired, more than four and a half centuries ago, the historical process of formation of the *droit des gens*. In rescuing the universalist vision which marked the origins of the most lucid doctrine of international law, the aforementioned process of humanization contributes to the construction of the new *jus gentium* of the XXIst century, oriented by the general principles of law. This process is enhanced by its own conceptual achievements, such as, to start with, the acknowledgement and recognition of *jus cogens* and the consequent obligations *erga omnes* of protection, followed by other concepts disclosing likewise a universalist perspective of the law of nations.

(...) The emergence and assertion of *jus cogens* in contemporary international law fulfill the necessity of a minimum of verticalization in the international legal order, erected upon pillars in which the juridical and the ethical are merged. The evolution of the concept of *jus cogens* transcends nowadays the ambit of both the law of treaties and the law of the international responsibility of the States, so as to reach general international law and the very foundations of the international legal order.[200]

5   *The Pitfalls of Legal Positivism: A Rebuttal of the So-Called Lotus "Principle"*

184. A matter which concerns the whole of humankind, such as that of the existence of nuclear weapons, can no longer be appropriately dealt with from a purely inter-State outlook of international law, which is wholly surpassed in our days. After all, without humankind there is no State whatsoever; one cannot simply have in mind States, apparently overlooking humankind. In its 1996 Advisory Opinion, the ICJ took note of the treaties which nowadays prohibit, e.g., biological and chemical weapons,[201] and weapons which cause excessive damages or have indiscriminate effects (para. 76).[202]

---

200   A.A. Cançado Trindade, "*Jus Cogens*: The Determination and the Gradual Expansion of Its Material Content in Contemporary International Case-Law", *in XXXV Curso de Derecho Internacional Organizado por el Comité Jurídico Interamericano – 2008*, Washington D.C., OAS General Secretariat, 2009, pp. 3–29.

201   The Geneva Protocol of 1925, and the Conventions of 1972 and 1993 against Biological and Chemical Weapons, respectively.

202   E.g., the 1980 Convention on Prohibitions or Restrictions on the Use of Certain Conventional Weapons Which May Be Deemed to Be Excessively Injurious or to Have Indiscriminate Effects.

185. But the fact that nowadays, in 2016, there does not yet exist a similar general treaty, of specific prohibition of nuclear weapons, does not mean that these latter are permissible (in certain circumstances, even in self defence).[203] In my understanding, it cannot be sustained, in a matter which concerns the future of humankind, that which is not expressly prohibited is thereby permitted (a classic postulate of positivism). This posture would amount to the traditional – and surpassed – attitude of the *laisser-faire, laisser-passer*, proper of an international legal order fragmented by State voluntarist subjectivism, which in the history of international law has invariably favoured the most powerful ones. *Ubi societas, ibi jus...*

186. Legal positivists, together with the so-called "realists" of *Realpolitik*, have always been sensitive to the established power, rather than to values. They overlook the time dimension, and are incapable to behold a universalist perspective. They are static, in time and space. Nowadays, in the second decade of the XXIst century, in an international legal order which purports to assert common superior values, amidst considerations of international *ordre public*, and basic considerations of humanity, it is precisely the reverse logic which is to prevail: *that which is not permitted, is prohibited.*[204]

187. Even in the days of the *Lotus* case (1927), the view endorsed by the old PCIJ whereby under international law everything that was not expressly prohibited would thereby be permitted, was object of severe criticisms, not only of a compelling Dissenting Opinion in the case itself[205] but also on the part of expert writing of the time.[206] Such conception could only have flourished in an epoch "politically secure" in global terms, certainly quite different from that of the current nuclear age, in face of the recurrent threat of nuclear weapons

---

203   The Roman-privatist influence – with its emphasis on the autonomy of the will had harmful consequences in traditional international law; in the public domain, quite on the contrary, conscience stands above the "will", also in the determination of competences.
204   A.A. Cançado Trindade, *O Direito Internacional em um Mundo em Transformação*, Rio de Janeiro, Edit. Renovar, 2002, p. 1099.
205   Cf. Dissenting Opinion of Judge Loder, PCIJ, *Lotus* case (France *versus* Turkey), Series A, n. 10, Judgment of 07.09.1927, p. 34 (such conception was not in accordance with the "spirit of international law").
206   Cf. J.L. Brierly, *The Basis of Obligation in International Law and Other Papers*, Oxford, Clarendon Press, 1958, p. 144; H. Lauterpacht, *The Function of Law in the International Community*, Oxford, Clarendon Press, 1933, pp. 409–412 and 94–96; and cf., subsequently, e.g., G. Herczegh, "Sociology of International Relations and International Law", *in Questions of International Law* (ed. G. Haraszti), Budapest, Progresprint, 1971, pp. 69–71 and 77.

and other weapons of mass destruction, the growing vulnerability of territorial States and indeed of the world population, and the increasing complexity in the conduction of international relations. In our days, in face of such terrifying threat, it is the logic opposite to that of the *Lotus* case which imposes itself: all that is not expressly permitted is surely prohibited.[207] All weapons of mass destruction, including nuclear weapons, are illegal and prohibited under contemporary international law.

188. The case of *Shimoda and Others* (District Court of Tokyo, decision of 07.12.1963), with the dismissed claims of five injured survivors of the atomic bombings of Hiroshima and Nagasaki, stands as a grave illustration of the veracity of the maxim *summum jus, summa injuria*, when one proceeds on the basis of an allegedly absolute submission of the human person to a degenerated international legal order built on an exclusively inter-State basis. May I here reiterate what I wrote in 1981, regarding the *Shimoda and Others* case, namely,

> (...) The whole arguments in the case reflect the insufficiencies of an international legal order being conceived and erected on the basis of an exclusive inter-State system, leaving individual human beings impotent in the absence of express treaty provisions granting them procedural status at international level. Even in such a matter directly affecting fundamental human rights, the arguments were conducted in the case in the classical lines of the conceptual apparatus of the so-called law on diplomatic protection, in a further illustration of international legal reasoning still being haunted by the old Vattelian fiction.[208]

189. There exists nowadays an *opinio juris communis* as to the illegality of all weapons of mass destruction, including nuclear weapons, and the obligation of nuclear disarmament, under contemporary international law. There is no "gap" concerning nuclear weapons; given the indiscriminate, lasting and indescribable suffering they inflict, they are outlawed, as much as other weapons

---

207 A.A. Cançado Trindade, *O Direito Internacional em um Mundo em Transformação*, op. cit. supra n. (225), p. 1099.

208 A.A. Cançado Trindade, "The Voluntarist Conception of International Law: A Re-Assessment", 59 *Revue de droit international de sciences diplomatiques et politiques* – Geneva (1981) p. 214, and cf. pp. 212–213. On the need of a universalist perspective, cf. also Cf. K. Tanaka, "The Character or World Law in the International Court of Justice" [translated from Japanese into English by S. Murase], 15 *Japanese Annual of International Law* (1971) pp. 1–22.

of mass destruction (biological and chemical weapons) are. The positivist outlook purporting to challenge this prohibition of contemporary general international law has long been surpassed. Nor can this matter be approached from a strictly inter-State outlook, without taking into account the condition of peoples and human beings as subjects of international law.

190. All weapons of mass destruction are illegal under contemporary international law. The threat or use of such weapons is condemned in any circumstances by the universal juridical conscience, which in my view constitutes the ultimate material source of International Law, as of all Law. This is in keeping with the conception of the formation and evolution of International Law which I have been sustaining for many years; it transcends the limitations of legal positivism, seeking to respond effectively to the needs and aspirations of the international community as a whole, and, ultimately, of all humankind.

XIII   Recourse to the "Martens Clause" as an Expression of the *Raison d'Humanité*

191. Even if there was a "gap" in the law of nations in relation to nuclear weapons, – which there is not, – it is possible to fill it by resorting to general principles of law. In its 1996 Advisory Opinion, the ICJ preferred to focus on self-defence of a hypothetical individual State, instead of developing the rationale of the *Martens clause*, the purpose of which is precisely that of filling gaps[209] in the light of the principles of the law of nations, the "laws of humanity" and the "dictates of public conscience" (terms of the wise premonition of Fyodor Fyodorovich von Martens,[210] originally formulated in the I Hague Peace Conference of 1899).

192. Yet, continuing recourse to the *Martens clause*, from 1899 to our days, consolidates it as an expression of the strength of human conscience. Its historical

---

209   J. Salmon, "Le problème des lacunes à la lumière de l'avis 'Licéité de la menace ou de l'emploi d'armes nucléaires' rendu le 8 juillet 1996 par la Cour Internationale de Justice", *in Mélanges en l'honneur de N. Valticos – Droit et justice* (ed. R.-J. Dupuy), Paris, Pédone, 1999, pp. 197–214, esp. pp. 208–209; R. Ticehurst, "The Martens Clause and the Laws of Armed Conflict", 317 *International Review of the Red Cross* (1997) pp. 125–134, esp. pp. 133–134; A. Azar, *Les opinions des juges dans l'Avis consultatif sur la licéité de la menace ou de l'emploi d'armes nucléaires*, Bruxelles, Bruylant, 1998, p. 61.

210   Which was intended to extend juridically the protection to the civilians and combatants in all situations, even if not contemplated by the conventional norms.

trajectory of more than one century has sought to extend protection juridically to human beings in all circumstances (even if not contemplated by conventional norms). Its reiteration for over a century in successive international instruments, besides showing that conventional and customary international law in the domain of protection of the human person go together, reveals the Martens clause as an emanation of the *material* source *par excellence* of the whole law of nations (the universal juridical conscience), giving expression to the *raison d'humanité* and imposing limits to the *raison d'État*.[211]

193. It cannot be denied that nuclear weapons are intrinsically indiscriminate, incontrollable, that they cause severe and durable damage and in a wide scale in space and time, that they are prohibited by International Humanitarian Law (Articles 35, 48 and 51 of the Additional Protocol I of 1977 to the 1949 Geneva Conventions on International Humanitarian Law), and are inhuman as weapons of mass destruction.[212] Early in the present nuclear age, the four Geneva Conventions established the *grave violations* of international law (Convention I, Article 49(3); Convention II, Article 50(3); Convention III, Article 129(3); and Convention IV, Article 146(3)). Such *grave violations*, when involving nuclear weapons, victimize not only States, but all other subjects of international law as well, individuals and groups of individuals, peoples, and humankind as a whole.

194. The absence of conventional norms stating specifically that nuclear weapons are prohibited in all circumstances does not mean that they would be allowed in a given circumstance. Two decades ago, in the course of the advisory proceedings of late 1995 before the ICJ leading to its 1996 Advisory Opinion on the *Threat or Use of Nuclear Weapons*, some of the participating States drew attention to the incidence of the Martens clause in the present domain.[213] It was pointed out, on the occasion, that the argument that international instruments do not specifically contain an express prohibition of use of nuclear weapons seems to overlook the Martens clause.[214]

---

211 A.A. Cançado Trindade, *Tratado de Direito Internacional dos Direitos Humanos*, vol. II, Porto Alegre/Brazil, S.A. Fabris Ed., 1999, pp. 497–509.
212 Cf. comments *in Commentary on the Additional Protocols of 8 June 1977 to the Geneva Conventions of 12 August 1949* (eds. Y. Sandoz, C. Swinarski and B. Zimmermann), Geneva, ICRC/Nijhoff, 1987, pp. 389–420 and 597–600.
213 Cf. ICJ, doc. CR 95/31, of 13.11.1995, pp. 45–46(statement of Samoa); ICJ, doc. CR 95/25, of 03.11.1995, p. 55 (statement of Mexico); ICJ, doc. CR 95/27, of 07.11.1995, p. 60 (statement of Malaysia).
214 ICJ, doc. 95/26, of 06.11.1995, p. 32 (statement of Iran).

195. Also in rebuttal of that argument, – typical of legal positivism, in its futile search for an express prohibition, – it was further observed that the "principles of humanity" and the "dictates of public conscience", evoked by the Martens clause, permeate not only the law of armed conflict, but "the whole of international law"; they are essentially dynamic, pointing to conduct which may nowadays be condemned as inhumane by the international community,[215] such as recourse to the threat or use of nuclear weapons. It was further stated, in the light of the Martens clause, that the "threat and use of nuclear weapons violate both customary international law and the dictates of public conscience".[216]

196. The Martens clause safeguards the integrity of Law (against the undue permissiveness of a *non liquet*) by invoking the principles of the law of nations, the "laws of humanity" and the "dictates of the public conscience". Thus, that absence of a conventional norm is not conclusive, and is by no means the end of the matter, – bearing in mind also customary international law. Such absence of a conventional provision expressly prohibiting nuclear weapons does not at all mean that they are legal or legitimate.[217] The evolution of international law[218] points, in our days, in my understanding, towards the construction of the International Law for humankind[219] and, within the framework of this latter, to the outlawing by general international law of all weapons of mass destruction.

197. Had the ICJ, in its 1996 Advisory Opinion on the *Threat or Use of Nuclear Weapons*, made decidedly recourse in great depth to the Martens clause, it would not have lost itself in a sterile exercise, proper of a legal positivism *déjà vu*, of a hopeless search of conventional norms, frustrated by the finding of what it understood to be a lack of these latter as to nuclear weapons specifically, for the purposes of its analysis. The existing arsenals of nuclear weapons, and of other weapons of mass destruction, are to be characterized by what

---

215   ICJ, doc. 95/22, of 30.10.1995, p. 39 (statement of Australia).
216   ICJ, doc. 95/35, of 15.11.1995, p. 33 (statement of Zimbabwe).
217   Stefan Glaser, *L'arme nucléaire à la lumière du Droit international*, Paris, Pédone, 1964, pp. 15, 21, 24–27, 32, 36–37, 41, 43–44 and 62–63, and cf. pp. 18 and 53.
218   If, in other epochs, the ICJ had likewise limited itself to verify a situation of "legal uncertainty" (which, anyway, does not apply in the present context), most likely it would not have issued its *célèbres* Advisory Opinions on *Reparations for Injuries* (1949), on *Reservations to the Convention on the Prevention and Punishment of the Crime of Genocide* (1951), and on *Namibia* (1971), which have so much contributed to the evolution of international law.
219   Cf. A.A. Cançado Trindade, *International Law for Humankind – Towards a New Jus Gentium, op. cit. supra* n. (132), pp. 1–726.

they really are: a scorn and the ultimate insult to human reason, and an affront to the juridical conscience of humankind.

198. The aforementioned evolution of international law, – of which the Martens clause is a significant manifestation, – has gradually moved from an international into a universal dimension, on the basis of fundamental values, and in the sense of an *objective justice*,[220] which has always been present in jusnaturalist thinking. Human conscience stands above the "will" of individual States. This evolution has, in my perception, significantly contributed to the formation of an *opinio juris communis* in recent decades, in condemnation of nuclear weapons.

199. This *opinio juris communis* is clearly conformed in our days: the overwhelming majority of member States of the United Nations, the NNWS, have been sustaining for years the series of General Assembly resolutions in condemnation of the use of nuclear weapons as illegal under general international law. To this we can add other developments, reviewed in the present Dissenting Opinion, such as, e.g., the NPT Review Conferences, the establishment of regional nuclear-weapon-free zones, and the Conferences on the Humanitarian Impact of Nuclear Weapons (cf. parts XVI–XVIII, *infra*).

XIV   Nuclear Disarmament: Jusnaturalism, the Humanist Conception and the Universality of International Law

200. The existence of nuclear weapons, – maintained by the strategy of "deterrence" and "mutually assured destruction" ("MAD", as it became adequately called, since it was devised in the cold-war era), is the contemporary global tragedy of the nuclear age. Death, or self-destruction, haunts everyone everywhere, propelled by human madness. Human beings need protection from themselves, today more than ever,[221] – and this brings our minds to other

---

220   A.A. Cançado Trindade, *Los Tribunales Internacionales Contemporáneos y la Humanización del Derecho Internacional*, Buenos Aires, Ed. Ad-Hoc, 2013, pp. 166–167; and cf. C. Husson-Rochcongar, *Droit international des droits de l'homme et valeurs – Le recours aux valeurs dans la jurisprudence des organes spécialisés*, Bruxelles, Bruylant, 2012, pp. 309–311, 451–452, 578–580, 744–745 and 771–772.

221   In another international jurisdiction, in my Separate Opinion in the IACtHR's case of the *Massacres of Ituango versus Colombia* (Judgment of 01.07.2006), I devoted part of my reflections to "human cruelty in its distinct manifestations in the execution of State policies" (Part II, paras. 9–13).

domains of human knowledge. Law by itself cannot provide answers to this challenge to humankind as a whole.

201. In the domain of nuclear disarmament, we are faced today, within the conceptual universe of international law, with unexplainable insufficiencies, or anomalies, if not absurdities. For example, there are fortunately in our times Conventions prohibiting biological and chemical weapons (of 1972 and 1993), but there is to date no such comprehensive conventional prohibition of nuclear weapons, which are far more destructive. There is no such prohibition despite the fact that they are in clear breach of international law, of IHL and the ILHR, as well as of the Law of the United Nations.

202. Does this make any sense? Can international law prescind from ethics? In my understanding, not at all. Just as law and ethics go together (in the line of jusnaturalist thinking), scientific knowledge itself cannot be dissociated from ethics. The production of nuclear weapons is an illustration of the divorce between ethical considerations and scientific and technological progress. Otherwise, weapons which can destroy millions of innocent civilians, and the whole of humankind, would not have been conceived and produced.

203. The principles of *recta ratio*, orienting the *lex praeceptiva*, emanate from human conscience, affirming the ineluctable relationship between law and ethics. Ethical considerations are to guide the debates on nuclear disarmament. Nuclear weapons, capable of destroying humankind as a whole, carry evil in themselves. They ignore civilian populations, they make abstraction of the principles of necessity, of distinction and of proportionality. They overlook the principle of humanity. They have no respect for the fundamental right to life. They are wholly illegal and illegitimate, rejected by the *recta ratio*, which endowed *jus gentium*, in its historical evolution, with ethical foundations, and its character of universality.

204. Already in 1984, in its *general comment* n. 14 (on the right to life), the U.N. Human Rights Committee (HRC – under the Covenant on Civil and Political Rights), for example, began by warning that war and mass violence continue to be "a scourge of humanity", taking the lives of thousands of innocent human beings every year (para. 2). In successive sessions of the General Assembly, – it added, – representatives of States from all geographical regions have expressed their growing concern at the development and proliferation of "increasingly awesome weapons of mass destruction" (para. 3). Associating itself with this concern, the HRC stated that

(...) It is evident that the designing, testing, manufacture, possession and deployment of nuclear weapons are among the greatest threats to the right to life which confront mankind today. This threat is compounded by the danger that the actual use of such weapons may be brought about, not only in the event of war, but even through human or mechanical error or failure.

Furthermore, the very existence and gravity of this threat generates a climate of suspicion and fear between States, which is in itself antagonistic to the promotion of universal respect for and observance of human rights and fundamental freedoms in accordance with the Charter of the United Nations and the International Covenants on Human Rights.

The production, testing, possession, deployment and use of nuclear weapons should be prohibited and recognized as crimes against humanity.

The Committee, accordingly, in the interest of mankind, calls upon all States (...) to take urgent steps (...) to rid the world of this menace (paras. 4–7).[222]

205. The absence in contemporary international law of a comprehensive conventional prohibition of nuclear weapons is incomprehensible. Contrary to what legal positivists think, law is not self-sufficient, it needs inputs from other branches of human knowledge for the realisation of justice. Contrary to what legal positivists think, norms and values go together, the former cannot prescind from the latter. Contrary to legal positivism, – may I add, – jusnaturalism, taking into account ethical considerations, pursues a universalist outlook (which legal positivists are incapable of doing), and beholds humankind as entitled to protection.[223]

---

[222] "*General Comment*" n. 14 (of 1984) of the HRC, text *in*: United Nations, *Compilation of General Comments and General Recommendations Adopted by Human Rights Treaty Bodies*, doc. HRI/GEN/1/Rev.3, of 15.08.1997, pp. 18–19. The HRC, further stressing that the right to life is a fundamental right which does not admit any derogation not even in time of public emergency, related the current proliferation of weapons of mass destruction to "the supreme duty of States to prevent wars". Cf. also U.N. *Report of the Human Rights Committee*, G.A.O.R. – 40th Session (1985), suppl. n. 40 (A/40/40), p. 162.

[223] A.A. Cançado Trindade, *International Law for Humankind – Towards a New Jus Gentium*, *op. cit. supra* n. (120), pp. 1–726. *Recta ratio* and universalism, present in the jusnaturalist thinking of the "founding fathers" of international law (F. de Vitoria, F. Suárez, H. Grotius, among others), go far back in time to the legacies of Cicero, in his characterization of *recta ratio* in the foundations of *jus gentium* itself, and of Thomas Aquinas, in his conception

206. Humankind is subject of rights, in the realm of the new *jus gentium*.[224] As this cannot be visualized from the optics of the State, contemporary international law has reckoned the limits of the State as from the optics of humankind. Natural law thinking has always been attentive to justice, which much transcends positive law. The present case of *Obligations Concerning Negotiations Relating to Cessation of the Nuclear Arms Race and to Nuclear Disarmament* has been lodged with the International Court *of Justice*, and not with an International Court of Positive Law. The contemporary tragedy of nuclear weapons cannot be addressed from the myopic outlook of positive law alone.

207. Nuclear weapons, and other weapons of mass destruction, have no ethics, have no ground on the law of nations (*le droit des gens*): they are in flagrant breach of its fundamental principles, and those of IHL, the ILHR, as well as the Law of the United Nations. They are a contemporary manifestation of evil, in its perennial trajectory going back to the Book of *Genesis* (cf. Part VII, *supra*). Jusnaturalist thinking, always open to ethical considerations, identifies and discards the disrupting effects of the strategy of "deterrence" of fear creation and infliction[225] (cf. Part XI, *supra*). Humankind is victimized by this.

208. In effect, humankind has been, already for a long time, a *potential victim* of nuclear weapons. To establish such condition of potential victim, one does not need to wait for the actual destruction of life on earth. Humankind has, for the last decades, been suffering psychological harm caused by the existence itself of arsenals of nuclear weapons. And there are peoples, and segments of

---

of *synderesis*, as predisposition of human reason to be guided by principles in the search of the common good; *ibid.*, pp. 10–14.

224   *Ibid.*, Ch. XI, pp. 275–288; A.A. Cançado Trindade, "Quelques réflexions sur l'humanité comme sujet du droit international", *in Unité et diversité du Droit international – Écrits en l'honneur du Prof. P.-M. Dupuy* (eds. D. Alland, V. Chetail, O. de Frouville and J.E. Viñuales), Leiden, Nijhoff, 2014, pp. 157–173.

225   Cf., to this effect, C.A.J. Coady, "Natural Law and Weapons of Mass Destruction", *in Ethics and Weapons of Mass Destruction – Religious and Secular Perspectives* (eds. S.H. Hashmi and S.P. Lee), Cambridge, Cambridge University Press, 2004, p. 122, and cf. p. 113; and cf. also J. Finnis, J.M. Boyle Jr. and G. Grisez, *Nuclear Deterrence, Morality and Realism*, Oxford, Clarendon Press, 1987, pp. 77–103, 207–237, 275–319 and 367–390. In effect, contemporary expert writing has become, at last, very critical of the "failed strategy" of "deterrence"; cf., *inter alia*, e.g., [Various Authors,] *At the Nuclear Precipice – Catastrophe or Transformation?* (eds. R. Falk and D. Krieger), London, Palgrave/MacMillan, 2008, pp. 162, 209, 218 and 229; A.C. Alves Pereira, *Os Impérios Nucleares e Seus Reféns: Relações Internacionais Contemporâneas*, Rio de Janeiro, Ed. Graal, 1984, pp. 87–88, and cf. pp. 154, 209 and 217.

populations, who have been *actual victims* of the vast and harmful effects of nuclear tests. The existence of *actual and potential victims* is acknowledged in international case-law in the domain of the International Law of Human Rights.[226] To address this danger from a strict inter-State outlook is to miss the point, to blind oneself. States were created and exist for human beings, and not *vice-versa*.

209. The NPT has a universalist vocation, and counts on everyone, as shown by its three basic principled pillars together. In effect, as soon as it was adopted, the 1968 NPT came to be seen as having been devised and concluded on the basis of those principled pillars, namely: non-proliferation of nuclear weapons (preamble and Articles I–III), peaceful use of nuclear energy (preamble and Articles IV–V), and nuclear disarmament (preamble and Article VI).[227] The antecedents of the NPT go back to the work of the U.N. General Assembly in 1953.[228] The NPT's three-pillar framework came to be reckoned as the "grand bargain" between its parties, NWS and NNWS. But soon it became a constant point of debate between NWS and NNWS parties to the NPT. In effect, the "grand bargain" came to be seen as "asymmetrical",[229] and NNWS began to criticize the very slow pace of achieving nuclear disarmament as one of the three basic principled pillars of the NPT (Article VI).[230]

---

226 For an early study on this issue, cf. A.A. Cançado Trindade, "Co-Existence and Co-Ordination of Mechanisms of International Protection of Human Rights (At Global and Regional Levels)", 202 *Recueil des Cours de l'Académie de Droit International de La Haye* (1987), Ch. XI, pp. 271–283. And for subsequent developments on the notion of *potential victims*, cf. A.A. Cançado Trindade, *The Access of Individuals to International Justice*, Oxford, Oxford University Press, 2012 [reprint], Ch. VII, pp. 125–131.
227 Articles VIII–XI, in turn, are procedural in nature.
228 In particular the speech of President D.D. Eisenhower (U.S.) to the U.N. General Assembly in 1953, as part of his plan "Atoms for Peace"; cf., e.g., I. Chernus, *Eisenhower's Atoms for Peace*, [Austin,] Texas A&M University Press, 2002, pp. 3–154.
229 J. Burroughs, *The Legal Framework for Non-Use and Elimination of Nuclear Weapons*, [N.Y.], Greenpeace International, 2006, p. 13.
230 H. Williams, P. Lewis and S. Aghlani, *The Humanitarian Impacts of Nuclear Weapons Initiative: The "Big Tent" in Disarmament*, London, Chatam House, 2015, p. 7; D.H. Joyner, "The Legal Meaning and Implications of Article VI of the Non-Proliferation Treaty", in: *Nuclear Weapons and International Law* (eds. G. Nystuen, S. Casey-Maslen and A.G. Bersagel), Cambridge, Cambridge University Press, 2014, pp. 397, 404 and 417, and cf. pp. 398–399 and 408; and cf. D.H. Joyner, *Interpreting the Nuclear Non-Proliferation Treaty*, Oxford, Oxford University Press, 2013 [reprint], pp. 2, 104 and 126, and cf. pp. 20, 26–29, 31, 97 and 124.

210. Under the NPT, each State is required to do its due. NWS are no exception to that, if the NPT is not to become dead letter. To achieve the three interrelated goals (non-proliferation of nuclear weapons, peaceful use of nuclear energy, and nuclear disarmament) is a duty of each and every State towards humankind as a whole. It is a universal duty of conventional and customary international law in the nuclear age. There is an *opinio juris communis* to this effect, sedimented along the recent decades, and evidenced in the successive establishment, in distinct continents, of nuclear-weapon-free zones, and nowadays in the Conferences on the Humanitarian Impact of Nuclear Weapons (cf. parts XVII–XVIII, *infra*).

XV The Principle of Humanity and the Universalist Approach: *Jus Necessarium* Transcending the Limitations of *Jus Voluntarium*

211. In my understanding, there is no point in keeping attached to an outdated and reductionist inter-State outlook, particularly in view of the revival of the conception of the law of nations (*droit des gens*) encompassing humankind as a whole, as foreseen and propounded by the "founding fathers" of international law[231] (in the XVIth–XVIIth centuries). It would be nonsensical to try to cling to the unduly reductionist inter-State outlook in the international adjudication of a case concerning the contending parties and affecting all States, all peoples and humankind as a whole.

212. An artificial, if not fossilized, strictly inter-State mechanism of dispute-settlement cannot pretend to entail or require a (likewise) entirely inadequate and groundless inter-State reasoning. The law of nations cannot be interpreted and applied in a mechanical way, as from an exclusively inter-State paradigm. To start with, the humane ends of States cannot be overlooked. In relation to nuclear weapons, the *potential victims* are the human beings and peoples, beyond their respective States, for whom these latter were created and exist.

213. As I had the occasion to point out in another international jurisdiction, the law of nations (*droit des gens*), since its historical origins in the XVIth century, was seen as comprising not only States (emerging as they were), but also peoples, the human person (individually and in groups), and humankind as a

---

[231] A.A. Cançado Trindade, *Évolution du Droit international au droit des gens – L'accès des particuliers à la justice internationale: le regard d'un juge*, Paris, Pédone, 2008, pp. 1–187.

whole.²³² The strictly inter-State outlook was devised much later on, as from the Vattelian reductionism of the mid-XVIIIth century, which became *en vogue* by the end of the XIXth century and beginning of the XXth century, with the well-known disastrous consequences – the successive atrocities victimizing human beings and peoples in distinct regions of world, – along the whole XXth century.²³³ In the present nuclear age, extending for the last seven decades, humankind as a whole is threatened.

214. Within the ICJ as well, I have had also the occasion to stress the need to go beyond the inter-State outlook. Thus, in my Dissenting Opinion in the recent case of the *Application of the Convention against Genocide* (Croatia *versus* Serbia, Judgment of 03.02.2015), I have pointed out, *inter alia*, that the 1948 Convention against Genocide is not State-centric, but is rather oriented towards groups of persons, towards the victims, whom it seeks to protect (paras. 59 and 529). The humanist vision of the international legal order pursues an outlook centred on the peoples, keeping in mind the humane ends of States.

215. I have further underlined that the *principle of humanity* is deeply-rooted in the long-standing thinking of natural law (para. 69).

> Humaneness came to the fore even more forcefully in the treatment of persons in *situation of vulnerability, or even defencelessness*, such as those deprived of their personal freedom, for whatever reason. The *jus gentium*, when it emerged as amounting to the law of nations, came then to be conceived by its 'founding fathers' (F. de Vitoria, A. Gentili, F. Suárez, H. Grotius, S. Pufendorf, C. Wolff) as regulating the international community constituted by human beings socially organized in the (emerging) States and co-extensive with humankind, thus conforming the *necessary* law of the *societas gentium*.
>
> The *jus gentium*, thus conceived, was inspired by the principle of humanity *lato sensu*. Human conscience prevails over the will of individual States. Respect for the human person is to the benefit of the common good. This humanist vision of the international legal order pursued – as it does nowadays – a *people-centered outlook*, keeping in mind the *humane ends of the State*. The precious legacy of natural law thinking, evoking the right human reason (*recta ratio*), has never faded away; (paras. 73–74).

---

232 IACtHR, case of the *Community Moiwana versus Suriname* (Judgment of 15.06.2005), Separate Opinion of Judge Cançado Trindade, paras. 6–7.

233 *Ibid.*, paras. 6–7.

The precious legacy of natural law thinking has never vanished; despite the indifference and pragmatism of the "strategic" *droit d'étatistes* (so numerous in the legal profession nowadays), the *principle of humanity* emerged and remained in international legal thinking as an expression of the *raison d'humanité* imposing limits to the *raison d'État* (para. 74).

216. This is the position I have always taken, within the ICJ and, earlier on, the IACtHR. For example, in the ICJ's Advisory Opinion on *Judgment n. 2867 of the ILO Administrative Tribunal upon a Complaint Filed against IFAD* (of 01.02.2012), I devoted one entire part (n. XI) of my Separate Opinion to the erosion – as I perceive it – of the inter-State outlook of adjudication by the ICJ (paras. 76–81). I warned likewise in my Separate Opinion (paras. 21–23) in the case of *Whaling in the Antarctic* (Australia *versus* Japan, Order of 06.02.2013, on New Zealand's intervention), as well as in my recent Separate Opinion (paras. 16–21 and 28–41) in the case of *Alleged Violations of Sovereign Rights and Maritime Spaces in the Caribbean Sea* (Nicaragua *versus* Colombia, Preliminary Objections, Judgment of 17.03. 2016).

217. Earlier on, within the IACtHR, I took the same position: for example, *inter alia*, in my Concurring Opinions in both the Advisory Opinion n. 16, on the *Right to Information on Consular Assistance in the Framework of the Due Process of Law* (of 01.10.1999), and the Advisory Opinion n. 18, on the *Juridical Condition and Rights of Undocumented Migrants* (of 17.09.2003), of the IACtHR, I deemed it fit to point out, – going beyond the strict inter-State dimension, – that, if non-compliance with Article 36(1)(b) of the 1963 Vienna Convention on Consular Relations takes place, it occurs to the detriment not only of a State Party but also of the human beings at issue. Such pioneering jurisprudential construction, in the line of jusnaturalist thinking, rested upon the evolving concepts of *jus cogens* and obligations *erga omnes* of protection.[234]

218. *Recta ratio* stands firmly above the "will". Human conscience, – the *recta ratio* so cultivated in jusnaturalism, – clearly prevails over the "will" and the strategies of individual States. It points to a universalist conception of the *droit des gens* (the *lex praeceptiva* for the *totus orbis*), applicable to all (States as well as peoples and individuals), given the unity of the human kind. Legal positivism, centred on State power and "will", has never been able to develop such universalist outlook, so essential and necessary to address issues of concern to

---

[234] Cf. comments of A.A. Cançado Trindade, *Os Tribunais Internacionais e a Realização da Justiça*, Rio de Janeiro, Edit. Renovar, 2015, pp. 463–468.

humankind as a whole, such as that of the obligation of nuclear disarmament. The universal juridical conscience prevails over the "will" of individual States.

219. The "founding fathers" of the law of nations (such as, *inter alii*, F. de Vitoria, F. Suárez and H. Grotius) had in mind humankind as a whole. They conceived a universal *jus gentium* for the *totus orbis*, securing the unity of the *societas gentium*; based on a *lex praeceptiva*, the *jus gentium* was apprehended by the *recta ratio*, and conformed a true *jus necessarium*, much transcending the limitations of the *jus voluntarium*. Law ultimately emanates from the common conscience of what is juridically necessary (*opinio juris communis necessitatis*).[235] The contribution of the "founding fathers" of *jus gentium* found inspiration largely in the scholastic philosophy of natural law (in particular in the stoic and Thomist conception of *recta ratio* and justice), which recognized the human being as endowed with intrinsic dignity.

220. Moreover, in face of the unity of the human kind, they conceived a truly *universal* law of nations, applicable to all – States as well as peoples and individuals – everywhere (*totus orbis*). In thus contributing to the emergence of the *jus humanae societatis*, thinkers like F. de Vitoria and D. de Soto, among others, permeated their lessons with the humanist thinking that preceded them. Four and a half centuries later, their lessons remain contemporary, endowed with perennial validity and aptitude to face, e.g., the contemporary and dangerous problem of the existing arsenals of nuclear weapons. Those thinkers went well beyond the "will" of States, and rested upon the much safer foundation of human conscience (*recta ratio* and justice).

221. The conventional and customary obligation of nuclear disarmament brings to the fore another aspect: the issue of the *validity* of international legal norms is, after all, metajuridical. International law cannot simply remain indifferent to values, general principles of law and ethical considerations; it has, to start with, to identify what is *necessary*, – such as a world free of nuclear weapons, – in order to secure the survival of humankind. This *idée du droit* precedes positive international law, and is in line with jusnaturalist thinking.

222. *Opinio juris communis necessitatis* upholds a customary international law obligation to secure the survival of humankind. Conventional and customary obligations go here together. Just as customary rules may eventually

---

235   A.A. Cançado Trindade, *International Law for Humankind – Towards a New Jus Gentium*, op. cit. supra n. (120), pp. 137–138.

be incorporated into a convention, treaty provisions may likewise eventually enter into the *corpus* of general international law. Customary obligations can either precede, or come after, conventional obligations. They evolve *pari passu*. This being so, the search for an express legal prohibition of nuclear weapons (such as the one undertaken in the ICJ's Advisory Opinion of 1996 on the *Threat or Use of Nuclear Weapons*) becomes a futile, if not senseless, exercise of legal positivism.

223. It is clear to human conscience that those weapons, which can destroy the whole of humankind, are unlawful and prohibited. They are in clear breach of *jus cogens*. And *jus cogens* was reckoned by human conscience well before it was incorporated into the two Vienna Conventions on the Law of Treaties (of 1969 and 1986). As I had the occasion to warn, three decades ago, at the 1986 U.N. Conference on the Law of Treaties between States and International Organizations or between International Organizations, *jus cogens* is "incompatible with the voluntarist conception of international law, because that conception failed to explain the formation of rules of general international law".[236]

XVI   NPT Review Conferences

224. In fact, in the course of the written phase of the proceedings before the Court in the present case of *Obligations Concerning Negotiations Relating to Cessation of the Nuclear Arms Race and to Nuclear Disarmament*, both the Marshall Islands[237] and the United Kingdom[238] addressed, in their distinct arguments, the series of NPT Review Conferences. For its part, India also addressed the Review Conferences,[239] in particular to leave on the records its position on the matter, as explained in a statement made on 09.05.2000.

225. Likewise, in the course of the oral phase of the present proceedings before the Court in *cas d'espèce*, the applicant State, the Marshall Islands, referred to

---

236   U.N., *United Nations Conference on the Law of Treaties between States and International Organizations or between International Organizations – Official Records*, vol. I (statement by the Representative of Brazil, A.A. Cançado Trindade, of 12.03.1986), pp. 187–188, para. 18.

237   *Application Instituting Proceedings*, p. 24, para. 66; and *Memorial*, pp. 29, 56–60, 61, 63, 68–69, 71 and 73, paras. 50, 123–128, 130, 136, 150, 153, 154, 161–162 and 168; and *Statement of Observations on [U.K.'s] Preliminary Objections*, pp. 15 and 47, paras. 32 and 126.

238   *Preliminary Objections*, pp. 1–2, 10 and 23, paras. 2–3, 21 and 50.

239   *Counter-Memorial*, p. 15, para. 23 n. 49, and Annex 23.

the NPT Review Conferences in its oral arguments in two of the three cases it lodged with the Court against India,[240] and the United Kingdom;[241] references to the Review Conferences were also made, for their part, in their oral arguments, by the two respondent States which participated in the public sittings before the Court, namely, India[242] and the United Kingdom.[243] Those Review Conferences conform the factual context of the *cas d'espèce*, and cannot pass unnoticed. May I thus proceed to a brief review of them.

226. The NPT Review Conferences, held every five years, started in 1975. The following three Conferences of the kind were held, respectively, in 1980, 1985 and 1990, respectively.[244] The fifth of such Conferences took place in 1995, the same year that the Marshall Islands became a party to the NPT (on 30.01.1995). In one of its decisions, the 1995 NPT Conference singled out the vital role of the NPT in preventing the proliferation of nuclear weapons, and warned that the proliferation of nuclear weapons would seriously increase the danger of nuclear war.[245] For their part, NWS reaffirmed their commitment, under Article VI of the NPT, to pursue in good faith negotiations on effective measures relating to nuclear disarmament.

227. The 1995 Review Conference prolonged indefinitely the NPT, and adopted its decision on "Principles and Objectives for Nuclear Non-Proliferation and Disarmament". Yet, in its *report*, the Main Committee I (charged with the implementation of the provisions of the NPT) observed with regret that Article VI and preambular paragraphs 8–12 of the NPT had not been wholly fulfilled,[246] with the number of nuclear weapons then existing being greater than the one existing when the NPT entered into force; it further regretted "the continuing lack of progress" on relevant items of the Conference on Disarmament, and urged a commitment on the part of NWS on "no-first use and non-use of nuclear weapons with immediate effect".[247]

---

240 ICJ. doc. CR 2016/1, of 07.03.2016, pp. 26–27 and 50, paras. 9 and 17 (M.I.); ICJ. doc. CR 2016/6, of 14.03.2016, p. 32, para. 10 (M.I.).
241 ICJ. doc. CR 2016/5, of 11.03.2016, p. 47, para. 8 (M.I.).
242 ICJ. doc. CR 2016/4, of 10.03.2016, p. 14, para. 3 (India).
243 ICJ. doc. CR 2016/7, of 09.03.2016, pp. 14–16 and 18–19, paras. 20, 22, 24, 32 and 37 (United Kingdom).
244 For an assessment of these earlier NPT Review Conferences, cf. H. Müller, D. Fischer and W. Kötter, *Nuclear Non-Proliferation and Global Order*, Stockholm–Solna/Oxford, SIPRI/Oxford University Press, 1994, pp. 31–108.
245 Decision 2, NPT/CONF.1995/32 (Part I), Annex, p. 2.
246 *Final Document*, Part II, p. 257, paras. 3–3*ter*., and cf. pp. 258 and 260, paras. 4 and 9.
247 *Ibid.*, pp. 271–273, paras. 36–39.

228. Between the fifth and the sixth Review Conferences, India and Pakistan carried out nuclear tests in 1998. For its part, on several occasions, the Movement of Non-Aligned Countries called for "urgent" measures of nuclear disarmament.[248] To this effect, the 2000 Review Conference agreed to a document containing the "13 Practical Steps" in order to meet the commitments of States Parties under Article VI of the NPT.[249] The "13 Practical Steps" stress the relevance and urgency of ratifications of the CTBT so as to achieve its entry into force, and of setting up a moratorium on nuclear-weapon tests pending such entry into force. Furthermore, they call for the commencement of negotiations on a treaty banning the production of fissile material for nuclear weapons and also call upon NWS to accomplish the total elimination of nuclear arsenals.[250]

229. At the 2005 Review Conference, no substantive decision was adopted, amidst continuing disappointment at the lack of progress on implementation of Article VI of the NPT, particularly in view of the "13 Practical Steps" agreed to at the 2000 Review Conference. Concerns were expressed that new nuclear weapon systems were being developed, and strategic doctrines were being adopted lowering the threshold for the use of nuclear weapons; moreover, regret was also expressed that States whose ratification was needed for the CTBT's entry into force had not yet ratified the CTBT.[251]

230. Between the 2005 and the 2010 Review Conferences, there were warnings that the NPT was "now in danger" and "under strain", as the process of disarmament had "stagnated" and needed to be "revived" in order to prevent the spread of weapons of mass destruction. The concerns addressed what was regarded as the unsatisfactory stalemate in the Conference on Disarmament in Geneva, which had been "unable to adopt an agenda for almost a decade" to identify substantive issues to be discussed and negotiated in the Conference.[252]

---

248   NPT/CONF.2000/4, paras. 12–13.
249   *Final Document*, Part I, pp. 14–15.
250   The "13 Practical Steps", moreover, affirm that the principle of irreversibility should apply to all nuclear disarmament and reduction measures. At last, the 13 practical steps reaffirm the objective of general and complete disarmament under effective international control, and stress the importance of both regular reports on the implementation of NPT's Article VI obligations, and the further development of verification capabilities.
251   NPT/CONF.2005/57, Part I, and cf. report on the 2005 Review Conference *in*: 30 *U.N. Disarmament Yearbook* (2005) Ch. I, p. 23.
252   Hans Blix, *Why Disarmament Matters*, Cambridge, Mass./London, Boston Review/MIT, 2008, pp. 6 and 63.

231. The "Five-Point Proposal on Nuclear Disarmament", announced by the Secretary-General in an address of 24.10.2008,[253] began by urging all NPT States Parties, in particular the NWS, to fulfil their obligations under the Treaty "to undertake negotiations on effective measures leading to nuclear disarmament" (para. 1).[254] It called upon the permanent members of the Security Council to commence discussions on security issues in the nuclear disarmament process, including by giving NNWS assurances against the use or threat of use of nuclear weapons (para. 5). It stressed the need of "new efforts to bring the CTBT into force", and encouraged NWS to ratify all the Protocols to the Treaties which established Nuclear-Weapon-Free Zones (para. 6). Moreover, it also stressed "the need for greater transparency" in relation to arsenals of nuclear weapons and disarmament achievements (para. 7). And it further called for the elimination also of other types of weapons of mass destruction (para. 8).

232. The "Five-Point Proposal on Nuclear Disarmament" was reiterated by the U.N. Secretary-General in two subsequent addresses in the following three years.[255] In one of them, before the Security Council on 24.09.2009, he stressed the need of an "early entry into force" of the CTBT, and pondered that "disarmament and non-proliferation must proceed together"; he urged "a divided international community" to start moving ahead towards achieving "a nuclear-weapon-free world", and, at last, he expressed his hope in the forthcoming 2010 NPT Review Conference.[256]

233. Both the 2000 and the 2010 Review Conferences made an interpretation of nuclear disarmament under Article VI of the NPT as a "positive disarmament obligation", in line with the *dictum* in the ICJ's 1996 Advisory Opinion

---

253   Cf. U.N. Secretary-General (Ban Ki-moon), Address (at a conference at the East–West Institute): "The United Nations and Security in a Nuclear-Weapon-Free World", *in U.N. News Centre*, of 24.10.2008, pp. 1–3.

254   It added that this could be pursued either by an agreement on "a framework of separate, mutually reinforcing instruments", or else by negotiating "a nuclear-weapons convention, backed by a strong system of verification, as has long been proposed at the United Nations" (para. 2).

255   On two other occasions, namely, during a Security Council Summit on Nuclear Non-Proliferation on 24.09.2009, and at a Conference organized by the East–West Institute on 24.10.2011.

256   U.N. Secretary-General (Ban Ki-moon), "Opening Remarks to the Security Council Summit on Nuclear Non-Proliferation and Nuclear Disarmament", *in U.N. News Centre*, of 24.09.2009, pp. 1–2.

of nuclear disarmament in good faith as an obligation of result.[257] The 2010 Review Conference expressed its deep concern that there remained the continued risk for humankind put by the possibility that nuclear weapons could be used, and the catastrophic humanitarian consequences that would result therefrom.

234. The 2010 Review Conference, keeping in mind the 1995 decision on "Principles and Objectives for Nuclear Non-Proliferation and Disarmament" as well as the 2000 agreement on the "13 Practical Steps", affirmed the vital importance of the universality of the NPT,[258] and, furthermore, took note of the "Five-Point Proposal on Nuclear Disarmament" of the U.N. Secretary-General, of 2008. For the first time in the present series of Review Conferences, the *Final Document* of the 2010 Review Conference recognized "the catastrophic humanitarian consequences that would result from the use of nuclear weapons".[259]

235. The Final Document welcomed the creation of successive nuclear-weapon-free zones,[260] and, in its conclusions, it endorsed the "legitimate interest" of NNWS to receive "unequivocal and legally binding security assurances" from NWS on the matter at issue; it asserted and recognized that "the total elimination of nuclear weapons is the only absolute guarantee against the use or threat of use of nuclear weapons".[261] The aforementioned Final Document reiterated the 2010 Review Conference's "deep concern at the catastrophic humanitarian consequences of any use of nuclear weapons", and "the need for all States at all times to comply with applicable international law, including international humanitarian law".[262] This key message of the 2010 Review Conference triggered the initiative, three years later, of the new series of Conferences on the Humanitarian Impact of Nuclear Weapons (cf. *infra*).

236. The "historic acknowledgement" of "the catastrophic humanitarian consequences of any use of nuclear weapons" was duly singled out by the ICRC, in its

---

257 D.H. Joyner, "The Legal Meaning and Implications of Article VI of the Non-Proliferation Treaty", in: *Nuclear Weapons and International Law* (eds. G. Nystuen, S. Casey-Maslen and A.G. Bersagel), Cambridge, Cambridge University Press, 2014, pp. 413 and 417.
258 NPT/CONF.2010/50, vol. I, pp. 12–14 and 19–20.
259 Cf. *2010 Review Conference – Final Document*, vol. I, doc. NPT/CONF.2010/50, of 18.06.2010, p. 12, para. 80.
260 Cf. *ibid.*, p. 15, para. 99.
261 *Ibid.*, p. 21, point (i).
262 *Ibid.*, p. 19, point (v).

statement in the more recent 2015 Review Conference;²⁶³ the ICRC pointed out that that new series of Conferences (2013–2014, in Oslo, Nayarit and Vienna) has given the international community "a much clearer grasp" of the effects of nuclear detonations on peoples around the world. It then warned that, 45 years after the NPT's entry into force, "there has been little or no concrete progress" in fulfilling the goal of elimination of nuclear weapons. As nuclear weapons remain the only weapons of mass destruction not prohibited by a treaty, "filling this gap is a humanitarian imperative", as the "immediate risks of intentional or accidental nuclear detonations" are "too high and the dangers too real".²⁶⁴

237. The 2015 Review Conference displayed frustration over the very slow pace of action on nuclear disarmament, in addition to current nuclear modernization programs and reiteration of dangerous nuclear strategies, apparently oblivious of the catastrophic humanitarian consequences of nuclear weapons. At the 2015 Review Conference, the Main Committee I, charged with addressing Article VI of the NPT, stressed the importance of "the ultimate goal" of elimination of nuclear weapons, so as to achieve "general and complete disarmament under effective international control".²⁶⁵

238. The 2015 Review Conference reaffirmed that "the total elimination of nuclear weapons is the only absolute guarantee against the use or threat of use of nuclear weapons, including the risk of their unauthorized, unintentional or accidental detonation".²⁶⁶ It expressed its "deep concern" that, during the period 2010–2015, the Conference on Disarmament did not commence negotiations of an instrument on such nuclear disarmament,²⁶⁷ and then stressed the "urgency for the Conference on Disarmament" to achieve "an internationally legally binding instrument" to that effect, so as "to assure" NNWS against the use or threat of use of nuclear weapons by all NWS.²⁶⁸

239. After welcoming "the increased and positive interaction with civil society" during the cycle of Review Conferences, the most recent 2015 Review Conference stated that

---

263   ICRC, "Eliminating Nuclear Weapons", *Statement – 2015 Review Conference of the Parties to the NPT*, of 01.05.2015, p. 1.
264   *Ibid.*, pp. 2–3.
265   *2015 Review Conference – Working Paper of the Chair of Main Committee* I, doc. NPT/CONF.2015/MC.I/WP.1, of 18.05.2015, p. 3, para. 17.
266   *Ibid.*, p. 5, para. 27.
267   *Ibid.*, p. 5, para. 35.
268   *Ibid.*, p. 6, para. 43.

understandings and concerns pertaining to the catastrophic humanitarian consequences of any nuclear weapon detonation underpin and should compel urgent efforts by all States leading to a world without nuclear weapons. The Conference affirms that, pending the realization of this objective, it is in the interest of the very survival of humanity that nuclear weapons never be used again.[269]

XVII The Establishment of Nuclear-Weapon-Free Zones

240. In addition to the aforementioned NPT Review Conferences, the *opinio juris communis* on the illegality of nuclear weapons finds expression also in the establishment, along the last half century, of nuclear-weapon-free zones, which has responded to the needs and aspirations of humankind, so as to rid the world of the threat of nuclear weapons. The establishment of those zones has, in effect, given expression to the growing disapproval of nuclear weapons by the international community as a whole. There are, in effect, references to nuclear-weapon-free zones in the arguments, in the written phase of the present proceedings, of the Marshall Islands[270] and of the United Kingdom[271] in the present case *of Obligations Concerning Negotiations Relating to Cessation of the Nuclear Arms Race and to Nuclear Disarmament.*

241. I originally come from the part of the world, Latin America, which, together with the Caribbean, form the first region of the world to have prohibited nuclear weapons, and to have proclaimed itself as a nuclear-weapon-free zone. The pioneering initiative in this domain, of Latin America and the Caribbean,[272] resulted in the adoption of the 1967 Treaty for the Prohibition of Nuclear Weapons in Latin America and the Caribbean and its two Additional Protocols. Its reach transcended Latin America and the Caribbean, as evidenced by its two Additional Protocols,[273] and the obligations set forth in its legal regime were wide in scope:

---

269   *Ibid.*, p. 7, paras. 45–46(1).
270   *Application Instituting Proceedings* of the M.I., p. 26, para. 73; and *Memorial* of the M.I., pp. 40, 53 and 56, paras. 84, 117 and 122.
271   *Preliminary Objections* of the U.K., p. 2, para. 4.
272   On the initial moves in the U.N. to this effect, by Brazil (in 1962) and Mexico (taking up the leading role from 1963 onwards), cf. Naciones Unidas, *Las Zonas Libres de Armas Nucleares en el Siglo XXI, op. cit. infra* n. (298), pp. 116, 20 and 139.
273   The first one concerning the States internationally responsible for territories located within the limits of the zone of application of the Treaty, and the second one pertaining to the nuclear-weapon States.

> Le régime consacré dans le Traité n'est pas simplement celui de non-prolifération: c'est un régime d'absence totale d'armes nucléaires, ce qui veut dire que ces armes seront interdites à perpétuité dans les territoires auxquels s'applique le Traité, quel que soit l'État sous le contrôle duquel pourraient se trouver ces terribles instruments de destruction massive.[274]

242. By the time of the creation of that first nuclear-weapon-free zone by the 1967 Treaty of Tlatelolco, it was pointed out that it came as a response to humanity's concern with its own future (given the threat of nuclear weapons), and in particular with "the survival of the humankind".[275] That initiative[276] was followed by four others of the kind, in distinct regions of the world, conducive to the adoption of the 1985 South Pacific (Rarotonga) Nuclear-Free Zone Treaty, the 1995 Southeast Asia (Bangkok) Nuclear-Weapon-Free Zone Treaty, the 1996 African (Pelindaba) Nuclear Weapon-Free Zone Treaty,[277] as well as the 2006 Central Asian (Semipalatinsk) Nuclear-Weapon-Free Zone Treaty. Basic considerations of humanity have surely been taken into account for the establishment of those nuclear-weapon-free zones.

243. In fact, besides the Treaty of Tlatelolco, also the Rarotonga, Bangkok, Pelindaba, and Semipalatinsk Treaties purport to extend the obligations enshrined therein, by means of their respective Protocols, not only to the States of the regions at issue, but also to nuclear States,[278] as well as States which are internationally responsible, *de jure* or *de facto*, for territories located in the respective regions. The verification of compliance with the obligations regularly engages the IAEA.[279] Each of the five aforementioned treaties (Tlatelolco, Rarotonga, Bangkok, Pelindaba and Semipalatinsk) creating nuclear-weapon-free zones has distinctive features, as to the kinds and extent of obligations and methods of verification,[280] but they share the common ultimate goal of preserving humankind from the threat or use of nuclear weapons.

---

274   A. García Robles, "Mesures de désarmement dans des zones particulières: le Traité visant l'interdiction des armes nucléaires en Amérique Latine", 133 *Recueil des Cours de l'Académie de Droit International de La Haye* [RCADI] (1971) p. 103, and cf. p. 71.

275   *Ibid.*, p. 99, and cf. p. 102.

276   Which was originally prompted by a reaction to the *Cuban missiles crisis* of 1962.

277   Naciones Unidas, *Las Zonas Libres de Armas Nucleares en el Siglo XXI*, N.Y./Geneva, U.N.-OPANAL/UNIDIR, 1997, pp. 9, 25, 39 and 153.

278   Those Protocols contain the undertaking not only not to use nuclear weapons, but also not to threaten their use; cf. M. Roscini, *op. cit. infra* (n. 307), pp. 617–618.

279   The Treaty of Tlatelolco has in addition counted on its own regional organism to that end, the Organism for the Prohibition of Nuclear Weapons in Latin America (OPANAL).

280   Cf., in general, M. Roscini, *Le Zone Denuclearizzate*, Torino, Giappichelli Ed., 2003, pp. 1–410; J. Goldblat, "Zones exemptes d'armes nucléaires: une vue d'ensemble", *in Le*

244. The second nuclear-weapon-free zone, established by the Treaty of Rarotonga (1985), with its three Protocols, came as a response[281] to long-sustained regional aspirations, and increasing frustration of the populations of the countries of the South Pacific with incursions of NWS in the region.[282] The Rarotonga Treaty encouraged the negotiation of a similar zone, – by means of the 1995 Bangkok Treaty, – in the neighbouring region of Southeast Asia, and confirmed the "continued relevance of zonal approaches" to the goal of disarmament and the safeguard of humankind from the menace of nuclear weapons.[283]

245. The third of those treaties, that of Bangkok, of 1995 (with its Protocol), was prompted by the initiative of the Association of South–East Asian Nations (ASEAN) to insulate the region from the policies and rivalries of the nuclear powers. The Bangkok Treaty, besides covering the land territories of all ten Southeast Asian States, is the first treaty of the kind also to encompass their territorial sea, 200-mile exclusive economic zone and continental shelf.[284] The fourth such treaty, that of Pelindaba, of 1996, in its turn, was prompted by the continent's reaction to nuclear tests in the region (as from the French nuclear tests in the Sahara in 1961), and the aspiration – deeply-rooted in African thinking – to keep nuclear weapons out of the region.[285] The Pelindaba Treaty (with its three Protocols) appears to have served the purpose to eradicate nuclear weapons from the African continent.

246. The fifth such treaty, that of Semipalatinsk, of 2006, contains, like the other treaties creating nuclear weapon-free zones (*supra*), the basic prohibitions to

---

  droit international des armes nucléaires (Journée d'études, ed. S. Sur), Paris, Pédone, 1998, pp. 35–55.
281   Upon the initiative of Australia.
282   M. Hamel-Green, "The South Pacific – The Treaty of Rarotonga", *in Nuclear Weapons-Free Zones* (ed. R. Thakur), London/N.Y., MacMillan/St. Martin's Press, 1998, p. 59, and cf. p. 62.
283   *Ibid.*, pp. 77 and 71.
284   This extended territorial scope has generated resistance on the part of nuclear-weapon States to accept its present form; A. Acharya and S. Ogunbanwo, "The Nuclear-Weapon-Free Zones in South–East Asia and Africa", *in Armaments, Disarmament and International Security – SIPRI Yearbook* (1998) pp. 444 and 448.
285   Naciones Unidas, *Las Zonas Libres de Armas Nucleares en el Siglo XXI, op. cit. supra* n. (298), pp. 60–61; and cf. J.O. Ihonvbere, "Africa – The Treaty of Pelindaba", *in Nuclear Weapons-Free Zones, op. cit. supra* n. (303), pp. 98–99 and 109. And, for a general study, cf. O. Adeniji, *The Treaty of Pelindaba on the African Nuclear-Weapon-Free Zone*, Geneva, UNIDIR, 2002, pp. 1–169.

manufacture, acquire, possess, station or control nuclear explosive devices within the zones.[286] The five treaties at issue, though containing loopholes (e.g., with regard to the transit of nuclear weapons),[287] have as common denominator the practical value of arrangements that transcend the non-proliferation of nuclear weapons.[288]

247. Each of the five treaties (of Tlatelolco, Rarotonga, Bangkok, Pelindaba and Semipalatinsk) reflects the characteristics of each of the five regions, and they all pursue the same cause. The establishment of the nuclear weapon-free zones has been fulfilling the needs and aspirations of peoples living under the fear of nuclear victimization.[289] Their purpose is being served, also in withholding or containing nuclear ambitions, to the ultimate benefit of humankind as a whole.

248. Nowadays, the five aforementioned nuclear weapon-free zones are firmly established in densely populated areas, covering most (almost all) of the landmass of the southern hemisphere land areas (while excluding most sea areas).[290] The adoption of the 1967 Tlatelolco Treaty, the 1985 Rarotonga Treaty, the 1995 Bangkok Treaty, the 1996 Pelindaba Treaty, and the 2006 Semipalatinsk Treaty, have disclosed the shortcomings and artificiality of the posture of the so-called political "realists",[291] which insisted on the suicidal strategy of nuclear "deterrence", in their characteristic subservience to power politics.

---

286 M. Roscini, "Something Old, Something New: The 2006 Semipalatinsk Treaty on a Nuclear Weapon-Free Zone in Central Asia", 7 *Chinese Journal of International Law* (2008) p. 597.

287 As to their shortcomings, cf., e.g., J. Goldblat, "The Nuclear Non-Proliferation Régime: Assessment and Prospects", 256 *Recueil des Cours de l'Académie de Droit International de La Haye* (1995) pp. 137–138; M. Roscini, *op. cit. supra* n. (286), pp. 603–604.

288 J. Enkhsaikhan, "Nuclear-Weapon-Free Zones: Prospects and Problems", 20 *Disarmament – Periodic Review by the United Nations* (1997) n. 1, p. 74.

289 Cf., e.g., H. Fujita, "The Changing Role of International Law in the Nuclear Age: from Freedom of the High Seas to Nuclear-Free Zones", *in Humanitarian Law of Armed Conflict: Challenges Ahead – Essays in Honour of F. Kalshoven* (eds. A.J.M. Delissen and G.J. Tanja), Dordrecht, Nijhoff, 1991, p. 350, and cf. pp. 327–349.

290 J. Prawitz, "Nuclear-Weapon-Free Zones: Their Added Value in a Strengthened International Safeguards System", *in Tightening the Reins – Towards a Strengthened International Nuclear Safeguards System* (eds. E. Häckel and G. Stein), Berlin/Heidelberg, Springer-Verlag, 2000, p. 166.

291 Cf. Naciones Unidas, *Las Zonas Libres de Armas Nucleares en el Siglo XXI, op. cit. supra* n. (298), pp. 27, 33–38 and 134.

249. The substantial *Final Report* of 1999 of the U.N. Disarmament Commission underlined the relevance of nuclear-weapon-free zones and of their contribution to the achievement of nuclear disarmament,[292] "expressing and promoting common values" and constituting "important complementary" instruments to the NPT and the "international regime for the prohibition" of any nuclear-weapon explosions.[293] Drawing attention to the central role of the United Nations in the field of disarmament,[294] the aforementioned *Report* added:

> Nuclear-weapon-free zones have ceased to be exceptional in the global strategic environment. To date, 107 States have signed or become parties to treaties establishing existing nuclear-weapon-free zones. With the addition of Antarctica, which was demilitarized pursuant to the Antarctic Treaty, nuclear-weapon-free zones now cover more than 50 per cent of the Earth's land mass. (...)
>
> The establishment of further nuclear-weapon-free zones reaffirms the commitment of the States that belong to such zones to honour their legal obligations deriving from other international instruments in force in the area of nuclear non-proliferation and disarmament to which they are parties.[295]

250. Moreover, the 1999 *Final Report* of the U.N. Disarmament Commission further stated that, for their part, NWS should fully comply with their obligations, under the ratified Protocols to the Treaties of treaties on nuclear-weapon-free zones, "not to use or threaten to use nuclear weapons".[296] It went on to encourage member States of those zones "to share experiences" with States of other regions, so as "to establish further nuclear-weapon-free zones".[297] It concluded that the international community, by means of "the creation of nuclear-weapon-free zones around the globe", should aim at "general and complete disarmament under strict and effective international control, so that future generations can live in a more stable and peaceful atmosphere".[298]

---

292 U.N., *Report of the Disarmament Commission – General Assembly Official Records* (54th Session, supplement n. 42), U.N. doc. A/54/42, of 06.05.1999, Annex I, pp. 6–7, paras. 1, 6 and 9.
293 *Ibid.*, p. 7, paras. 10–11 and 13.
294 *Ibid.*, Annex II, p. 11 3rd preambular paragraph.
295 *Ibid.*, Annex I, p. 7, para. 5; and p. 8, para. 28.
296 *Ibid.*, p. 9, para. 36.
297 *Ibid.*, p. 9, para. 41.
298 *Ibid.*, p. 9, para. 45.

251. To the establishment of aforementioned five nuclear-weapon-free zones other initiatives against nuclear weapons are to be added, such as the prohibitions of placement of nuclear weapons, and other kinds of weapons of mass destruction, in outer space, on the seabed, on the ocean floor and in the subsoil beyond the outer limit of the territorial seabed zone, – "denuclearized" by the Treaties of Antarctica (1959), Outer Space (1967) and the Deep Sea Bed (1971), respectively, to which can be added the Treaty on the Moon and Other Celestial Bodies (1979), established a complete demilitarization thereon.[299]

252. The fact that the international community counts today on five nuclear-weapon-free zones, in relation to which States that possess nuclear weapons do have a particular responsibility, reveals an undeniable advance of right reason, of the *recta ratio* in the foundations of contemporary international law. Moreover, the initiative of nuclear-weapon-free zones keeps on clearly gaining ground. In recent years, proposals are being examined for the setting up of new denuclearized zones of the kind,[300] as well as of the so-called single-State zone (e.g., Mongolia).[301] That initiative further reflects the increasing disapproval, by the international community as a whole, of nuclear weapons, which, in view of their hugely destructive capability, constitute an affront to right reason (*recta ratio*).

XVIII Conferences on the Humanitarian Impact of Nuclear Weapons (2013–2014)

253. In the course of the proceedings in the present case of *Obligations Concerning Negotiations Relating to Cessation of the Nuclear Arms Race and to Nuclear Disarmament*, several references were made to the more recent series of Conferences on the Humanitarian Impact of Nuclear Weapons (2013–2014), and in particular to the statement made therein (in the second of those Conferences)

---

299 Cf. G. Venturini, "Control and Verification of Multilateral Treaties on Disarmament and Non-Proliferation of Weapons of Mass Destruction", 17 *University of California Davis Journal of International Law and Policy* (2011) pp. 359–360.

300 E.g., in Central and Eastern Europe, in the Middle East, in Central and North–East and South Asia, and in the whole of the southern hemisphere.

301 Cf. A. Acharya and S. Ogunbanwo, *op. cit. supra* n. (284), p. 443; J. Enkhsaikhan, *op. cit. supra* n. (288), pp. 79–80. Mongolia in effect declared its territory as a nuclear-weapon-free zone (in 1992), and in February 2000 adopted national legislation defining its status as a nuclear-weapon-free State. This was acknowledged by U.N. General Assembly resolution 55/33S of 20.11.2000.

by the Marshall Islands, asserting that NWS should fulfill their obligation, "long overdue", of negotiation to achieve complete nuclear disarmament (cf. *infra*). The Marshall Islands promptly referred to its own statement in the Nayarit Conference (2014) in its *Memorial* in the *cas d'espèce*, as well as in its oral arguments before the ICJ.

254. In effect, the Conferences on the Humanitarian Impact of Nuclear Weapons (a series initiated in 2013) were intended to provide a forum for dialogue on, and a better understanding of, the humanitarian consequences of use of nuclear weapons for human beings, societies, and the environment, rather than a substitute of bilateral and multilateral fora for disarmament negotiations. This forum for dialogue and better understanding of the matter has counted on three Conferences to date, held, respectively, in Oslo in March 2013, in Nayarit in February 2014, and in Vienna in December 2014.

255. This recent series of Conferences has drawn attention to the humanitarian effects of nuclear weapons, restoring the central position of the concern for human beings and peoples. It has thus stressed the importance of the human dimension of the whole matter, and has endeavoured to awaken the conscience of the whole international community as well as to enhance the needed humanitarian coordination in the present domain. May I next proceed to a survey of their work and results so far.

1 *First Conference on the Humanitarian Impact of Nuclear Weapons*

256. The first Conference on the Humanitarian Impact of Nuclear Weapons took place in Oslo, Norway, on 04–05 March 2013, having counted on the participation of Delegations representing 127 States, United Nations agencies, the International Committee of the Red Cross (ICRC), the Red Cross and the Red Crescent movement, international organizations, and civil society entities. It should not pass unnoticed that only two of the NWS, India and Pakistan, were present at this Conference (and only India made a statement).[302] On the other hand, neither the Marshall Islands, nor the permanent members of the U.N. Security Council, attended it.

257. The Oslo Conference addressed three key issues, namely: (a) the immediate human impact of a nuclear weapon detonation; (b) the wider economic, developmental and environmental consequences of a nuclear weapon detonation; and (c) the preparedness of States, international organizations, civil

---

302 *In*: https://www.regjeringen.no/globalassets/upload/ud/vedlegg/hum/hum_india.pdf.

THE UNIVERSAL JURIDICAL CONSCIENCE, HUMANENESS 591

society and the general public to deal with the predictable humanitarian consequences that would follow from a nuclear weapon detonation. A wide range of experts made presentations during the Conference.

258. Attention was drawn, e.g., to the nuclear testing's impact during the cold-war period, in particular to the detonation of not less than 456 nuclear bombs in the four decades (between 1949 and 1989) in the testing ground of Semipalatinsk, in eastern Kazakhstan. It was reported (by UNDP) that, according to the Kazakh authorities, up to 1.5 million people were affected by fall-out from the blasts at Semipalatinsk; the nuclear test site was shut down in mid-1991. Other aspects were examined, all from a humanitarian outlook.[303] References were made, e.g., to General Assembly resolutions (such as resolution 63/279, of 25.04.2009), on humanitarian rehabilitation of the region. Such a humanitarian approach proved necessary, as the "historical experience from the use and testing of nuclear weapons has demonstrated their devastating immediate and long-term effects".[304]

259. The key conclusions of the Oslo Conference, as highlighted by Norway's Minister of Foreign Affairs in his closing statement,[305] can be summarized as follows. First, it is unlikely that any state or international body (such as U.N. relief agencies and the ICRC) could address the immediate humanitarian emergency caused by a nuclear weapon detonation in an adequate manner and provide sufficient assistance to those affected. Thus, the ICRC called for the abolition of nuclear weapons as the only effective preventive measure, and several participating States stressed that elimination of nuclear weapons is the only way to prevent their use; some States called for a ban on those weapons.

260. Secondly, the historical experience from the use and testing of nuclear weapons has demonstrated their devastating immediate and long-term effects. While the international scenario and circumstances surrounding it have changed, the destructive potential of nuclear weapons remains. And thirdly, the effects of a nuclear weapon detonation, irrespective of its cause, will not be

---

303   For accounts of the work of the 2013 Oslo Conference, cf., e.g., *Viewing Nuclear Weapons through a Humanitarian Lens* (eds. J. Borrie and T. Caughley), Geneva/N.Y., U.N./UNIDIR, 2013, pp. 81–82, 87, 90–91, 93–96, 99, 105–108 and 115–116.
304   Norway/Ministry of Foreign Affairs, *Chair's Summary – Humanitarian Impact of Nuclear Weapons*, Oslo, 05.03.2013, p. 2.
305   *In*: https://www.regjeringen.no/en/aktuelt/nuclear_summary/id716343/.

constrained by national borders, and will affect States and peoples in significant ways, in a trans-frontier dimension, regionally as well as globally.

2   Second Conference on the Humanitarian Impact of Nuclear Weapons

261. The second Conference on the Humanitarian Impact of Nuclear Weapons took place in Nayarit, Mexico, on 13–14 February 2014, having counted on the participation of Delegations representing 146 States. The Marshall Islands, India and Pakistan attended it, whereas the United Kingdom did not. In addition to States, other participants included the ICRC, the Red Cross and the Red Crescent movement, international organizations, and civil society entities. During the Nayarit Conference, the Delegate of the Marshall Islands stated that NWS States were failing to fulfill their obligations, under Article VI of the NPT and customary international law, to commence and conclude multilateral negotiations on nuclear disarmament; in his words:

> the Marshall Islands is convinced that multilateral negotiations on achieving and sustaining a world free of nuclear weapons are long overdue. Indeed we believe that states possessing nuclear arsenals are failing to fulfill their legal obligations in this regard. Immediate commencement and conclusion of such negotiations is required by legal obligation of nuclear disarmament resting upon each and every state under Article VI of the Non Proliferation Treaty and customary international law. It also would achieve the objective of nuclear disarmament long and consistently set by the United Nations, and fulfill our responsibilities to present and future generations while honouring the past ones.[306]

262. Earlier on, the Minister of Foreign Affairs of the Marshall Islands stated, at the U.N. High-Level Meeting on Nuclear Disarmament, on 26.09.2013, that the Marshall Islands "has a unique and compelling reason" to urge nuclear disarmament, namely,

> The Marshall Islands, during its time as a UN Trust Territory, experienced 67 large-scale tests of nuclear weapons. At the time of testing, and at every possible occasion in the intervening years, the Marshall Islands

---

[306]   Marshall Islands' Statement, Second Conference on the Humanitarian Impact of Nuclear Weapons, Nayarit, Mexico, 13–14 February 2014 (*in:* http://www.reachingcriticalwill.org/images/documents/Disarmament-fora/nayarit-2014/statements/MarshallIslands.pdf). The text is also quoted by the Marshall Islands in its *Memorial* in Marshall Islands *versus* United Kingdom, Annex 72.

has informed UN members of the devastating impacts of these tests – of the deliberate use of our people as unwilling scientific experiments, of ongoing health impacts inherited through generations, of our displaced populations who still live in exile or who were resettled under unsafe circumstances, and then had to be removed. Even today, science remains a moving target and our exiled local communities are still struggling with resettlement.

(...) Perhaps we [the Marshallese] have one of the most important stories to tell regarding the need to avert the use of nuclear weapons, and a compelling story to spur greater efforts for nuclear disarmament (pp. 1–2).[307]

263. The Marshall Islands' statement in the 2014 Nayarit Conference was thus one of a few statements in which the Marshall Islands has articulated its claim, whereon they rely in the *cas d'espèce, inter alia*, to substantiate the existence of a dispute, including with the United Kingdom, which was not present at the Conference.[308] The Nayarit Conference participants also heard the poignant testimonies of five *Hibakusha*, – survivors of the atomic bombings of Hiroshima and Nagasaki, – who presented their accounts of the overwhelming devastation inflicted on those cities and their inhabitants by the atomic blasts (including the victims' burning alive, and carbonized or vaporized, as well as the long-term effects of radiation, killing survivors along seven decades).

264. They stressed the "moral imperative" of abolition of nuclear weapons, as humanity and nuclear weapons cannot coexist. A group of Delegations of no less than 20 States called expressly for a ban of nuclear weapons, already long overdue; this was the sword of Damocles hanging over everyone's heads. The "mere existence" of nuclear weapons was regarded as "absurd"; attention was

---

307   In: http://www.un.org/en/ga/68/meetings/nucleardisarmament/pdf/MH_en.pdf. And the Marshall Islands' Minister of Foreign Affairs (Ph. Muller) added that

"It should be our collective goal as the United Nations to not only stop the spread of nuclear weapons, but also to pursue the peace and security of a world without them. Further, the Republic of the Marshall Islands has recently ratified the Comprehensive Test Ban Treaty and urges other member states to work towards bringing this important agreement into force.

The Marshall Islands is not the only nation in the Pacific to be touched by the devastation of nuclear weapon testing. (...) We express again our eventual aspirations to join with our Pacific neighbours in supporting a Pacific free of nuclear weapons in a manner consistent with international security" (pp. 1–2).

308   *Memorial* of the M.I. in Marshall Islands *versus* United Kingdom, para. 99.

also drawn to the 2013 U.N. General Assembly High-Level Meeting on Disarmament, and to the obligations under international law, including those deriving from the NPT as well as common Article 1 of the Geneva Conventions on IHL.[309]

265. Furthermore, an association of over 60 entities of the civil society, from more than 50 countries, stated[310] that their own engagement was essential, as responsibilities fell on everyone to prevent the use of nuclear weapons; and prevention required the prohibition and ban of nuclear weapons, in the same way as those of biological and chemical weapons, landmines, and cluster munitions. Both the association, and the *Hibakusha*, condemned the dangerous strategy of nuclear "deterrence".

266. The 2014 Nayarit Conference's conclusions, building on the conclusions of the previous Oslo Conference, can be summarized as follows. First, the immediate and long-term effects of a single nuclear weapon detonation, let alone a nuclear exchange, would be catastrophic. The mere existence of nuclear weapons generates great risks, because the military doctrines of the NWS envisage preparations for the deliberate use of nuclear weapons. Nuclear weapons could be detonated by accident, miscalculation, or deliberately.

267. Delegations of over 50 States from every region of the world made statements unequivocally calling for the total elimination of nuclear weapons and the achievement of a world free of nuclear weapons. At least 20 Delegations of participating States in the Conference (*supra*) expressed the view that the way forward would be a ban on nuclear weapons. Others were equally clear in their calls for a Convention on the elimination of nuclear weapons or a new legally binding instrument.[311]

268. Secondly, some Delegations pointed out the security implications of nuclear weapons, or else expressed skepticism about the possibility of banning

---

309 Mexico/Gobierno de la República, *Chair's Summary – Second Conference on the Humanitarian Impact of Nuclear Weapons*, Mexico, 14.02.2014, pp. 2–3.
310 On behalf of the International Campaign to Abolish Nuclear Weapons (ICAN), a coalition of over 350 entities in 90 countries.
311 For example, for its part, India favoured a step-by-step approach towards the elimination of nuclear weapons, ultimately leading to "a universal, non-discriminatory Convention on prohibition and elimination of nuclear weapons"; cf. www.reachingcriticalwill.org/images/documents/Disarmament-fora/nayarit-2014/statements/India.pdf.

nuclear weapons as such. There were those which favoured a "step-by-step" approach to nuclear disarmament (within the framework of the NPT Action Plan), and called for the participation of NWS in this process. For their part, the nuclear-weapon-free States, in their majority, were however of the view that the step-by-step approach had failed to achieve its goal; they thus called for a new approach to nuclear disarmament.

269. Thirdly, for the Chairman of the Conference, a ban on nuclear weapons would be the first step towards their elimination; such a ban would also rectify the anomaly that nuclear weapons are the only weapons of mass destruction that are not subject to an explicit legal prohibition. He added that achieving a world free of nuclear weapons is consistent with States' obligations under international law, including under the NPT and common Article 1 to the Geneva Conventions on IHL. He at last called for the development of new international standards on nuclear weapons, including a legally binding instrument, to be concluded by the 70th anniversary of the atomic bombings of Hiroshima and Nagasaki.[312]

3   *Third Conference on the Humanitarian Impact of Nuclear Weapons*

270. The third Conference on the Humanitarian Impact of Nuclear Weapons took place in Vienna, Austria, on 08–09 December 2014, having carried forward the momentum created by the previous Conference in Mexico. It counted on the participation of Delegations of 158 States, as well as the U.N., the ICRC, the Red Cross and Red Crescent movement, civil society entities and representatives of the academic world. For the first time, of the NWS, the United Kingdom attended the Conference; Delegates from India, Pakistan, and the Marshall Islands were present as well.

271. Once again, the Conference participants heard the testimonies of survivors, the *Hibakusha*. Speaking of the "hell on earth" experienced in Hiroshima and Nagasaki; the "indiscriminate massacre of the atomic bombing" showed "the illegality and ultimate evil of nuclear weapons".[313] In its statement, the Marshall Islands, addressing the testing in the region of 67 atomic and hydrogen bombs, between 1946 and 1958, – the strongest one having been the Bravo

---

312   Cf.   http://www.reachingcriticalwill.org/images/documents/Disarmament-fora/nayarit-2014/chairs-summary.pdf.

313   Cf. *Vienna Conference on the Humanitarian Impact of Nuclear Weapons (08–09 December 2014)*, Vienna, Austria's Federal Ministry for Europe, Integration and Foreign Affairs, 2015, p. 19.

test (of 01.03.1954) of a hydrogen bomb, 1000 times more powerful than the atomic bomb dropped over Hiroshima, – referred to their harmful impacts, such as the birth of "monster-like babies", the continuous suffering from "thyroid cancer, liver cancer and all types of radiogenic cancerous illnesses", extending over the years.[314]

272. For its part, the ICRC stated that nuclear weapons ignore the principle of proportionality, and stand in breach of IHL (both conventional and customary) by causing unnecessary suffering to civilians; it expressed "significant concerns about the eventual spread of radiation to civilian areas and the radiological contamination of the environment" and everyone.[315] The ICRC further observed that, after "decades of focusing on nuclear weapons primarily in technical-military terms and as symbols of power", a fundamental and reassuring change has occurred, as debates on the matter now shift attention to what those weapons "would mean for people and the environment, indeed for humanity".[316]

273. The U.N. Secretary-General (Ban Ki-moon) sent a statement, read at the Conference, wherein he condemned expenditures in the modernization of weapons of mass destruction (instead of meeting the challenges of poverty and climate change). Recalling that the obligation of nuclear disarmament was one of both conventional and customary international law, he further condemned the strategy of nuclear "deterrence"; in his own words,

> Upholding doctrines of nuclear deterrence does not counter proliferation, but it makes the weapons more desirable. Growing ranks of nuclear-armed States does not ensure global stability, but instead undermines it. (…) The more we understand about the humanitarian impacts, the more it becomes clear that we must pursue disarmament as an urgent imperative.[317]

274. The Vienna Conference contributed to a deeper understanding of the consequences and risks of a nuclear detonation, having focused to a larger extent on the legal framework (and gaps therein) with regard to nuclear weapons.[318]

---

314   *Ibid.*, p. 34.
315   *Ibid.*, p. 58.
316   *Ibid.*, p. 17.
317   Statement reproduced *in ibid.*, p. 16.
318   Cf. *ibid.* pp. 1–88.

It was reckoned that the impact of nuclear weapons detonation, irrespective of the cause, would go well beyond national borders, and could have regional and even global consequences, causing destruction, death, diseases and displacement on a very large scale, as well as profound and long-term damage to the environment, climate, human health and well-being, socioeconomic development and social order. They could, in sum, threaten the very survival of humankind. It was acknowledged that the scope, scale and interrelationship of the humanitarian consequences caused by nuclear weapon detonation are catastrophic, and more complex than commonly understood; these consequences can be large scale and potentially irreversible.

275. States expressed various views regarding the ways and means of advancing the nuclear disarmament agenda. The Delegations of 29 States called for negotiations of a legally-binding instrument to prohibit or ban nuclear weapons. A number of Delegations considered that the inability to make progress on any particular step was no reason not to pursue negotiations in good faith on other effective measures to achieve and maintain a nuclear-weapon-free world. Such steps have been taken very effectively in regional contexts in the past, as evidenced by nuclear-weapon-free zones.

276. As the general report of the Vienna Conference observed, the three Conferences on the Humanitarian Impact of Nuclear Weapons (of Oslo, Nayarit and then Vienna), have contributed to a "deeper understanding" of the "actual risks" posed by nuclear weapons, and the "unspeakable suffering", devastating effects, and "catastrophic humanitarian consequences" caused by their use. As "nuclear deterrence entails preparing for nuclear war, the risk of nuclear weapon use is real. (...) The only assurance against the risk of a nuclear weapon detonation is the total elimination of nuclear weapons", in "the interest of the very survival of humanity"; hence the importance of Article VI of the NPT, and of the entry into force of the CTBT.[319]

277. The 2014 Vienna Conference's conclusions can be summarized as follows. First, the use and testing of nuclear weapons have demonstrated their devastating immediate, mid- and long-term effects. Nuclear testing in several parts of the world has left a legacy of serious health and environmental consequences. Radioactive contamination from these tests disproportionately affects women and children. It contaminated food supplies and continues to be measurable in the atmosphere to this day.

---

319   Ibid., pp. 5–7.

278. Secondly, as long as nuclear weapons exist, there remains the possibility of a nuclear weapon explosion. The risks of accidental, mistaken, unauthorized or intentional use of nuclear weapons are evident due to the vulnerability of nuclear command and control networks to human error and cyber-attacks, the maintaining of nuclear arsenals on high levels of alert, forward deployment and their modernization. The dangers of access to nuclear weapons and related materials by non-state actors, particularly terrorist groups, persist. All such risks, which increase over time, are unacceptable.

279. Thirdly, as nuclear deterrence entails preparing for nuclear war, the risk of the use of nuclear weapons is real. Opportunities to reduce this risk must be taken now, such as de-alerting and reducing the role of nuclear weapons in security doctrines. Limiting the role of nuclear weapons to deterrence does not remove the possibility of their use, nor does it address the risks stemming from accidental use. The only assurance against the risk of a nuclear weapon detonation is the total elimination of nuclear weapons.

280. Fourthly, the existence itself of nuclear weapons raises serious ethical questions, – well beyond legal discussions and interpretations, – which should be kept in mind. Several Delegations asserted that, in the interest of the survival of humankind, nuclear weapons must never be used again, under any circumstances. Fifthly, no State or international organ could adequately address the immediate humanitarian emergency or long-term consequences caused by a nuclear weapon detonation in a populated area, nor provide adequate assistance to those affected. The imperative of prevention as the only guarantee against the humanitarian consequences of nuclear weapons use is thus to be highlighted. Sixthly, participating Delegations reiterated the importance of the entry into force of the CTBT as a key element of the international nuclear disarmament and non-proliferation regime.

281. Seventhly, it is clear that there is no comprehensive legal norm universally prohibiting the possession, transfer, production and use of nuclear weapons, that is, international law does not address today nuclear weapons in the way it addresses biological and chemical weapons. This is generally regarded as an anomaly – or rather, a nonsense, – as nuclear weapons are far more destructive. In any case, international environmental law remains applicable in armed conflict and can pertain to nuclear weapons, even if not specifically regulating these latter. Likewise, international health regulations would cover effects of nuclear weapons. In the light of the new evidence produced in those two

years (2013–2014) about the humanitarian impact of nuclear weapons, it is very doubtful whether such weapons could ever be used in conformity with IHL.

4   Aftermath: The "Humanitarian Pledge"

282. At the 2014 Vienna Conference, although a handful of States expressed scepticism about the effectiveness of a ban on nuclear weapons, the overwhelming majority of NPT States Parties expected the forthcoming 2015 NPT Review Conference to take stock of all relevant developments, including the outcomes of the Conferences on the Humanitarian Impact of Nuclear Weapons (*supra*), and determine the next steps for the achievement and maintenance of a nuclear-weapon-free world. At the end of the Vienna Conference, the host State, Austria, presented a "Pledge" calling upon States parties to the NPT to renew their commitment to the urgent and full implementation of existing obligations under Article VI, and to this end, to identify and pursue effective measures to fill the legal gap for the prohibition and elimination of nuclear weapons.[320]

283. The Pledge further called upon NWS to take concrete interim measures to reduce the risk of nuclear weapons detonations, including by diminishing the role of nuclear weapons in military doctrines. The Pledge also recognised that: (a) the rights and needs of the victims of nuclear weapon use and testing have not yet been adequately addressed; (b) all States share the responsibility to prevent any use of nuclear weapons; and (c) the consequences of nuclear weapons use raise profound moral and ethical questions going beyond debates about the legality of these weapons.

284. Shortly before the Vienna Conference, 66 States had already endorsed the Pledge; by the end of the Conference, 107 States had endorsed it, thus "internationalizing" it and naming it at the end as the "Humanitarian Pledge".[321] On 07.12. 2015, the U.N. General Assembly adopted the substance of the Humanitarian Pledge in the form of its resolution 70/48. As of April 2016, 127 States have formally endorsed the Humanitarian Pledge; unsurprisingly, none of the NWS has done so.

---

320   *In*: http://www.bmeia.gv.at/fileadmin/user_upload/Zentrale/Aussenpolitik/Abruestung/-HINW14/HINW14Vienna_Pledge_Document.pdf. The Pledge only refers to States' obligations under the NPT and makes no mention of customary international law.

321   http://www.bmeia.gv.at/fileadmin/user_upload/Zentrale/Aussenpolitik/Abruestung/-HINW14/HINW14.

285. Recent endeavours, such as the ones just reviewed of the Conferences on the Humanitarian Impact of Nuclear Weapons have been rightly drawing attention to the grave humanitarian consequences of nuclear weapons detonations. The reframing of the whole matter in a people-centred outlook appears to me particularly lucid, and necessary, keeping in mind the unfoundedness of the strategy of "deterrence" and the catastrophic consequences of the use of nuclear weapons. The "step-by-step" approach, pursued by the NWS in respect to the obligation under Article VI of the NPT, appears essentially State-centric, having led to an apparent standstill or deadlock.

286. The obligation of nuclear disarmament being one of result, the "step-by-step" approach cannot be extended indefinitely in time, with its insistence on the maintenance of the nuclear sword of Damocles. The "step-by-step" approach has produced no significantly concrete results to date, seeming to make abstraction of the numerous pronouncements of the United Nations upholding the obligation of nuclear disarmament (cf. *supra*). After all, the absolute prohibition of nuclear weapons, – which is multifaceted,[322] is one of *jus cogens* (cf. *supra*). Such weapons, as the Conferences on the Humanitarian Impact of Nuclear Weapons have evidenced, are essentially inhumane, rendering the strategy of "deterrence" unfounded and unsustainable (cf. *supra*).

287. Ever since those Conferences (2013–2014), there has been a tendency (in 2014–2016) of slight reduction of nuclear warheads,[323] though NWS have kept on modernizing their respective nuclear armament programs, in an indication that nuclear weapons are likely to remain in the foreseeable future.[324] Yet, the growing awareness of the humanitarian impact of nuclear weapons has raised the question of the possibility of developing "a deontological position according to which the uniquely inhumane suffering that nuclear weapons inflict on their victims makes it inherently wrongful to use them".[325]

288. *Tempus fugit*. There remains a long way to go to achieve a nuclear-weapon-free world. The United Nations itself has been drawing attention to the urgency

---

322 Encompassing measures relating to any use, threat of use, development, production, acquisition, possession, stockpiling and transfer of nuclear weapons.
323 From around 16.300 nuclear warheads in 2014 to 15,850 in 2015, and to 15,395 in early 2016.
324 Cf. SIPRI *Yearbook 2016: Armaments, Disarmament and International Security*, Stockholm-Solna, SIPRI, 2016, Ch. 16, pp. 609–667.
325 ILPI, *Evidence of Catastrophe – A Summary of the Facts Presented at the Three Conferences on the Humanitarian Impact of Nuclear Weapons*, Oslo, ILPI, 2015, p. 15.

of nuclear disarmament. It has done so time and time again, and, quite recently, in the convocation in October 2015, of a new Open-Ended Working Group (OEWG), as a subsidiary body of the U.N. General Assembly, to address concrete and effective legal measures to attain and maintain a world without nuclear weapons.[326] It draws attention therein to the importance of multilateralism, to the relevance of "inclusiveness" (participation of all U.N. member States) and of the contribution, in addition to that of States, also of international organizations, of entities of the civil society, and of the academia.[327] And it reaffirms "the urgency of securing substantive progress in multilateral nuclear disarmament negotiations", in order "to attain and maintain a world without nuclear weapons".[328]

289. It should not pass unnoticed that all the initiatives that I have just reviewed in the present Dissenting Opinion (NPT Review Conferences, the establishment of nuclear-weapon-free zones, and the Conferences on the Humanitarian Impact of Nuclear Weapons), referred to by the contending parties in the course of the proceedings before the ICJ in the present case of *Obligations Concerning Negotiations Relating to Cessation of the Nuclear Arms Race and to Nuclear Disarmament*, have gone beyond the inter-State outlook. In my perception, there is great need, in the present domain, to keep on looking beyond States, so as to behold peoples' and humankind's quest for survival in our times.

XIX Final Considerations: *Opinio Juris Communis* Emanating from Conscience (*Recta Ratio*), Well above the "Will"

290. Nuclear weapons, as from their conception, have been associated with overwhelming destruction. It may be recalled that the first atomic bombs were fabricated in an epoch of destruction and devastation, – the II world war, – of the abominable "total war", in flagrant breach of IHL and of the ILHR.[329] The fabrication of nuclear weapons, followed by their use, made abstraction of the fundamental principles of international law, moving the world into lawlessness

---

326   U.N. General Assembly, doc. A/C.1/70/L.13/Rev.1, of 29.10.2015, pp. 1–3.
327   Preamble, paras. 8 and 14–15.
328   Operative part, para. 2.
329   For an account, cf., e.g., *inter alia*, J. Lukacs, *L'héritage de la Seconde Guerre Mondiale*, Paris, Ed. F.-X. de Guibert, 2011, pp. 38–39, 55, 111 and 125–148; and cf. I. Kershaw, *To Hell and Back – Europe 1914–1949*, London, Penguin, 2016, pp. 7, 356, 407, 418, 518 and 521.

in the current nuclear age. The strategy of "deterrence", in a "dialectics of suspicion", leads to an unforeseeable outcome, amidst complete destruction. Hence the utmost importance of negotiations conducive to general disarmament, which, – as warned by Raymond Aron [already] in the early sixties, – had "never been taken seriously" by the super-powers.[330]

291. Last but not least, may I come back to a key point which I have dwelt upon in the present Dissenting Opinion pertaining to the *opinio juris communis* as to the obligation of nuclear disarmament (cf. Part XV, *supra*). In the evolving law of nations, basic considerations of humanity have an important role to play. Such considerations nourish *opinio juris* on matters going well beyond the interests of individual States. The ICJ has, on more than one occasion, taken into account resolutions of the United Nations (in distinct contexts) as a means whereby international law manifests itself.

292. In its *célèbre* Advisory Opinion (of 21.06.1971) on *Namibia*, for example, the ICJ dwelt upon, in particular, two U.N. General Assembly resolutions relevant to the formation of *opinio juris*.[331] Likewise, in its Advisory Opinion (of 16.10.1975) on the *Western Sahara*, the ICJ considered and discussed in detail some U.N. General Assembly resolutions.[332] In this respect, references can further be made to the ICJ's Advisory Opinions on *Legal Consequences of the Construction of a Wall in the Occupied Palestinian Territory* (of 09.07.2004),[333] and on the *Declaration of Independence of Kosovo* (of 22.07.2010).[334] In its 1996 Advisory Opinion on the *Threat or Use of Nuclear Weapons*, the ICJ admitted, – even if in a rather restrictive way, – the emergence and gradual evolution of an *opinio juris* as reflected in a series of resolutions of the U.N. General Assembly (para. 70). But the ICJ could have gone (much) further than that.

---

330   R. Aron, *Paz e Guerra entre as Nações* [1962], Brasília, Edit. Universidade de Brasília, 1979, pp. 413, 415, 421–422 and 610. R. Aron's book contains his reflections on the new age of nuclear weapons, amidst the tensions of the cold-war era, and the new challenges and dangers it imposed, – persisting to date, – for the future of humankind; cf., for the French edition, R. Aron, *Paix et guerre entre les nations*, 8th ed., Paris, Éd. Calmann-Lévy, 2015, pp. 13–770.

331   On the principle of self-determination of peoples, namely, G.A. resolutions 1514(XV) of 14.12.1960, and 2145(XXI) of 27.10.1966; cf. *I.C.J. Reports 1971*, pp. 31, 45 and 49–51.

332   Cf. *I.C.J. Reports 1975*, pp. 20, 23, 26–37, 40, 57 and 67–68.

333   Cf. *I.C.J. Reports 1975*, pp. 171–172, paras. 86–88.

334   Cf. *I.C.J. Reports 2010*, p. 437, para. 80 (addressing a General Assembly resolution "which reflects customary international law").

293. After all, *opinio juris* has already had a long trajectory in legal thinking, being today endowed with a wide dimension. Thus, already in the XIXth century, the so-called "historical school" of legal thinking and jurisprudence (of F.K. von Savigny and G.F. Puchta) in reaction to the voluntarist conception, gradually discarded the "will" of the States by shifting attention to *opinio juris*, requiring practice to be an authentic expression of the "juridical conscience" of nations and peoples. With the passing of time, the acknowledgment of conscience standing above the "will" developed further, as a reaction against the reluctance of some States to abide by norms addressing matters of general or common interest of the international community.

294. This had an influence on the formation of rules of customary international law, a much wider process than the application of one of its formal "sources". *Opinio juris communis* came thus to assume "a considerably broader dimension than that of the subjective element constitutive of custom".[335] *Opinio juris* became a key element in the *formation* itself of international law, a *law of conscience*. This diminished the unilateral influence of the most powerful States, fostering international law-making in fulfilment of the public interest and in pursuance of the common good of the international community as a whole.

295. The foundations of the international legal order came to be reckoned as independent from, and transcending, the "will" of individual States; *opinio juris communis* came to give expression to the "juridical conscience", no longer only of nations and peoples – sustained in the past by the "historical school" – but of the international community as a whole, heading towards the universalization of international law. It is, in my perception, this international law of conscience that turns in particular towards nuclear disarmament, for the sake of the survival of humankind.

---

335 A.A. Cançado Trindade, *International Law for Humankind – Towards a New Jus Gentium*, op. cit. supra n. (120), p. 137, and cf. p. 138; and cf. R. Huesa Vinaixa, *El Nuevo Alcance de la "Opinio Juris" en el Derecho Internacional Contemporáneo*, Valencia, Tirant lo Blanch, 1991, pp. 30–31 and 36–38, and cf. pp. 76–77, 173, 192, 194, 199 and 204–205; R.E. Piza Escalante, "La '*Opinio Juris*' como Fuente Autónoma del Derecho Internacional ('*Opinio Juris*' y '*Jus Cogens*')", 39 *Relaciones Internacionales* – Heredia/C.R. (1992) pp. 61–74; J.I. Charney, "International Lawmaking – Article 38 of the ICJ Statute Reconsidered", *in New Trends in International Lawmaking – International "Legislation" in the Public Interest* (Proceedings of the Kiel Symposium, March 1996), Berlin, Duncker & Humblot, 1997, pp. 180–183 and 189–190.

296. In 1983, Wang Tieya wrote against minimizing the legal significance of resolutions of General Assembly, in particular the declaratory ones. As they clarify principles and rules of international law, he contended that they "cannot be said to have no law-making effect at all merely because they are not binding in the strict sense. At the very least, since they embody the convictions of a majority of States, General Assembly resolutions can indicate the general direction in which international law is developing".[336] He added that those General Assembly resolutions, reflecting the position of "an overwhelming majority of States", have "accelerated the development of international law", in helping to crystallize emerging rules into "clearly defined norms".[337] In the same decade, it was further pointed out that General Assembly resolutions have been giving expression, along the years, to "basic concepts of equity and justice, or of the underlining spirit and aims" of the United Nations.[338]

297. Still in the eighties, in the course I delivered at the Institute of Public International Law and International Relations of Thessaloniki, in 1988, I began by pondering that customary and conventional international law are interrelated, – as acknowledged by the ICJ itself[339] – and U.N. General Assembly resolutions contribute to the emergence of *opinio juris communis*.[340] I stood against the "strictly voluntarist position" underlying the unacceptable concept

---

336   Wang Tieya, "The Third World and International Law", *in The Structure and Process of International Law: Essays in Legal Philosophy Doctrine and Theory* (eds. R.St.J. Macdonald and D.M. Johnston), The Hague, M. Nijhoff, 1983, p. 964.
337   *Ibid.*, pp. 964–965.
338   B. Sloan, "General Assembly Resolutions Revisited (Forty Years Later)", 58 *British Year Book of International Law* (1987) p. 80, and cf. pp. 116, 137 and 141.
339   For example, in the course of the proceedings in the *Nuclear Tests* cases (1973–1974), one of the applicant States (Australia) recalled, in the public sitting of 08.07.1974, that the ICJ had held, in the *North Sea Continental Shelf* cases (*I.C.J. Reports 1969*, p. 41), that a conventional norm can pass into the general *corpus* of international law thus becoming also a rule of customary international law; cf. ICJ, *Pleadings, Oral Arguments, Documents – Nuclear Tests cases* (vol. I: Australia *versus* France, 1973–1974), p. 503. In effect, – may I add, – just as a customary rule may later crystallize into a conventional norm, this latter can likewise generate a customary rule. International law is not static (as legal positivists wrongfully assume); it is essentially dynamic.
340   A.A. Cançado Trindade, "Contemporary International Law-Making: Customary International Law and the Systematization of the Practice of States", *in Sources of International Law* (Thesaurus Acroasium, vol. XIX), Thessaloniki, Institute of Public International Law and International Relations, 1992, pp. 68 and 71.

of so-called "persistent objector", and added that dissent from "one or another State individually cannot prevent the creation of new customary rules" or obligations, ensuing from *opinio juris communis* and not from *voluntas*.[341]

298. In the evolution of international law in time, – I proceeded, – voluntarist positivism has shown itself "entirely incapable" of explaining the consensual formation of customary international obligations; contrary to "the pretensions of positivist voluntarism" (with its stubborn emphasis on the consent of individual States), "freedom of spirit is the first to rebel" against immobilism, in devising responses to new challenges affecting the international community as a whole, and acknowledging obligations incumbent upon all States.[342]

299. In my "repudiation of voluntarist positivism", I concluded on this point that the attention to customary international law ("incomparably less vulnerable" than conventional international law to voluntarist temptations) is in line with the progressive development (moved by conscience) of international law, so as to provide a common basis for the fulfilment of the needs and aspirations of all peoples.[343] Today, almost three decades later, I firmly restate, in the present Dissenting Opinion, my own position on the matter, in respect of the customary and conventional international obligation to put an end to nuclear weapons, so as to rid the world of their inhuman threat.

300. May I here, furthermore, ponder that U.N. General Assembly or Security Council resolutions are adopted on behalf not of the States which voted in favour of them, but more precisely on behalf of the United Nations Organization itself (its respective organs), being thus *valid for all U.N. member States*. This applies to the resolutions surveyed in the present Dissenting Opinion. It should be kept in mind that the U.N. is endowed with an international legal personality of its own, which enables it to act at international level as a distinct entity, independently of individual member States; in this way, it upholds the juridical equality of all States, and mitigates the worrisome vulnerability of factually weaker States, such as the NNWS; in doing so, it aims – by

---

341   *Ibid.*, pp. 78–79.
342   *Ibid.*, pp. 126–129.
343   *Ibid.*, pp. 128–129. And cf., more recently, in general, A.A. Cançado Trindade, "The Contribution of Latin American Legal Doctrine to the Progressive Development of International Law", 376 *Recueil des Cours de l'Académie de Droit International de La Haye* (2014) pp. 9–92, esp. pp. 75–76.

multilateralism – at the common good, at the realization of common goals of the international community as a whole,[344] such as nuclear disarmament.

301. A small group of States – such as the NWS – cannot overlook or minimize those reiterated resolutions, extended in time, simply because they voted against them, or abstained. Once adopted, they are valid for all U.N. member States. They are resolutions of the United Nations Organization itself, and not only of the large majority of U.N. member States which voted in favour of them. U.N. General Assembly resolutions, reiteratedly addressing matters of concern to humankind as a whole (such as existing nuclear weapons), are in my view endowed with normative value. They cannot be properly considered from a State voluntarist perspective; they call for another approach, away from the strict voluntarist-positivist one.

302. Conscience stands above the "will". The universal juridical conscience stands well above the "will" of individual States, and resonates in resolutions of the U.N. General Assembly, which find inspiration in general principles of international law, which, for their part, give expression to values and aspirations of the international community as a whole, of all humankind.[345] This – may I reiterate – is the case of General Assembly resolutions surveyed in the present Dissenting Opinion (cf. *supra*). The values which find expression in those *prima principia* inspire every legal order and, ultimately, lie in the foundations of this latter.

303. The general principles of law (*prima principia*), in my perception, confer upon the (national and international) legal order its ineluctable axiological dimension. Notwithstanding, legal positivism and political "realism", in their characteristic subservience to power, incur into their basic mistake of minimizing those principles, which lie in the foundations of any legal system, and which inform and conform the norms and the action pursuant to them, in the search for the realization of justice. Whenever that minimization of principles has prevailed the consequences have been disastrous.[346]

---

344 Cf., in this sense, A.A. Cançado Trindade, *Direito das Organizações Internacionais*, 6th rev. ed., Belo Horizonte/Brazil, Edit. Del Rey, 2014, pp. 51 and 530–531.

345 A.A. Cançado Trindade, *International Law for Humankind – Towards a New Jus Gentium*, op. cit. supra n. (132), pp. 129–138.

346 A.A. Cançado Trindade, *A Humanização do Direito Internacional*, 2nd rev. ed., Belo Horizonte/Brazil, 2015, pp. 6–24; A.A. Cançado Trindade, *Os Tribunais Internacionais e a Realização da Justiça*, op. cit. supra n. (255), pp. 410–418.

304. They have been contributing, in the last decades, to a vast *corpus juris* on matters of concern to the international community as a whole, such as nuclear disarmament. Their contribution to this effect has overcome the traditional inter-State paradigm of the international legal order.[347] This can no longer be overlooked in our days. The inter-State mechanism of the *contentieux* before the ICJ cannot be invoked in justification for an inter-State reasoning. As "the principal judicial organ" of the United Nations (U.N. Charter, Article 92), the ICJ has to bear in mind not only States, but also "we, the peoples", on whose behalf the U.N. Charter was adopted. In its international adjudication of contentious cases, like the present one of *Obligations Concerning Negotiations Relating to Cessation of the Nuclear Arms Race and to Nuclear Disarmament*, the ICJ has to bear in mind basic considerations of humanity, with their incidence on questions of admissibility and jurisdiction, as well as of substantive law.

XX   Epilogue: A Recapitulation

305. Coming to the end of the present Dissenting Opinion, I feel in peace with my conscience: from all the preceding considerations, I trust to have made it crystal clear that my own position, in respect of all the points which form the object of the present Judgment on the case of *Obligations Concerning Negotiations Relating to Cessation of the Nuclear Arms Race and to Nuclear Disarmament*, stands in clear and entire opposition to the view espoused by the Court's majority that the existence of a legal dispute has not been established before it, and that the Court has no jurisdiction to consider the Application lodged with it by the Marshall Islands, and cannot thus proceed to the merits of the case. Not at all: in my understanding, there is a dispute before the Court, which has jurisdiction to decide the case. There is a conventional and customary international law obligation of nuclear disarmament. Whether there has been a concrete breach of this obligation, the Court could only decide on the merits phase of the present case.

306. My dissenting position is grounded not only on the assessment of the arguments produced before the Court by the contending parties, but above all on issues of principle and on fundamental values, to which I attach even greater importance. As my dissenting position covers all points addressed in the present Judgment, in its reasoning as well as in its conclusion, I have thus

---

347   A.A. Cançado Trindade, *Direito das Organizações Internacionais*, op. cit. supra n. (344), pp. 530–537.

felt obliged, in the faithful exercise of the international judicial function, to lay on the records, in the present Dissenting Opinion, the foundations of my dissenting position thereon. I deem it fit, at this last stage, to recapitulate all the points of my dissenting position, expressed herein, for the sake of clarity, and in order to stress their interrelatedness.

307. *Primus*: According to the *jurisprudence constante* of the Court, a dispute is a disagreement on a point of law or fact, a conflict of legal views or interests; The existence of an international dispute (at the time of lodging a claim) is a matter for the objective determination of the Court. The existence of a dispute may be inferred. *Secundus*: The objective determination of a dispute by the Court is not intended to protect respondent States, but rather and more precisely to secure the proper exercise of the Court's judicial function. *Tertius*: There is no requirement of prior notice of the applicant State's intention to initiate proceedings before the ICJ, nor of prior "exhaustion" of diplomatic negotiations, nor of prior notification of the claim; it is, in sum, a matter for objective determination of the Court itself.

308. *Quartus*: The Marshall Islands and the United Kingdom/India/Pakistan have pursued distinct arguments and courses of conduct on the matter at issue, evidencing their distinct legal positions, which suffice for the Court's objective determination of the existence of a dispute. *Quintus*: There is no legal ground for attempting to heighten the threshold for the determination of the existence of a dispute; in its *jurisprudence constante*, the Court has expressly avoided a formalistic approach on this issue, which would affect access to justice itself. The Court has, instead, in its *jurisprudence constante*, upheld its own *objective determination* of the existence of a dispute, rather than relying – as it does in the present case – on the subjective criterion of "awareness" of the respondent States.

309. *Sextus*: The distinct series of U.N. General Assembly resolutions on nuclear disarmament along the years (namely, warning against nuclear weapons, 1961–1981; on freeze of nuclear weapons, 1982–1992; condemning nuclear weapons, 1982 2015; following-up the ICJ's 1996 Advisory Opinion, 1996–2015) are endowed with authority and legal value. *Septimus*: Their authority and legal value have been duly acknowledged before the ICJ in its advisory proceedings in 1995. *Octavus*: Like the General Assembly, the Security Council has also expressed its concern on the matter at issue, in its work and its resolutions on nuclear disarmament.

310. *Nonus*: The aforementioned United Nations resolutions, in addition to other initiatives, portray the longstanding saga of the United Nations in the condemnation of nuclear weapons. *Decimus*: The fact that weapons of mass destruction (poisonous gases, biological and chemical weapons) have been outlawed, and nuclear weapons, far more destructive, have not been banned yet, is a juridical absurdity. The obligation of nuclear disarmament has emerged and crystallized nowadays in both conventional and customary international law, and the United Nations has, along the decades, been giving a most valuable contribution to this effect.

311. *Undecimus*: In the *cas d'espèce*, the issue of United Nations resolutions and the emergence of *opinio juris communis* in the present domain of the obligation of nuclear disarmament has grasped the attention of the contending parties in submitting their distinct arguments before the Court. *Duodecimus*: The presence of evil has marked human existence along the centuries. Ever since the eruption of the nuclear age in August 1945, some of the world's great thinkers have been inquiring whether humankind has a future, and have been drawing attention to the imperative of respect for life and the relevance of humanist values. *Tertius decimus*: Also in international legal doctrine there have been those who have been stressing the needed prevalence of human conscience, the universal juridical conscience, over State voluntarism.

312. *Quartus decimus*: The U.N. Charter is attentive to peoples; the recent cycle of World Conferences of the United Nations has had, as a common denominator, the recognition of the legitimacy of the concern of the international community as a whole with the conditions of living and the well-being of peoples everywhere. *Quintus decimus*: General principles of law (*prima principia*) rest in the foundations of any legal system. They inform and conform its norms, guide their application, and draw attention to the prevalence of *jus necessarium* over *jus voluntarium*.

313. *Sextus decimus*: The nature of a case before the Court may well require a reasoning going beyond the strictly inter-State outlook; the present case concerning the obligation of nuclear disarmament requires attention to be focused on peoples, in pursuance of a humanist outlook, rather than on inter-State susceptibilities. *Septimus decimus*: The inter-State mechanism of adjudication of contentious cases before the ICJ does not at all imply that the Court's reasoning should likewise be strictly inter-State. Nuclear disarmament is a matter of concern to humankind as a whole.

314. *Duodevicesimus*: The present case stresses the utmost importance of fundamental principles, such as that of the juridical equality of States, following the principle of humanity, and of the idea of an objective justice. *Undevicesimus*: Factual inequalities and the strategy of "deterrence" cannot be made to prevail over the juridical equality of States. *Vicesimus*: "Deterrence" cannot keep on overlooking the distinct series of U.N. General Assembly resolutions, expressing an *opinio juris communis* in condemnation of nuclear weapons. *Vicesimus primus*: As also sustained by general principles of international law and international legal doctrine, nuclear weapons are in breach of international law, of IHL and the ILHR, and of the U.N. Charter.

315. *Vicesimus secundus*: There is need of a people-centred approach in this domain, keeping in mind the fundamental right to life; the *raison d'humanité* prevails over the *raison d'État*. Attention is to be kept on the devastating and catastrophic consequences of the use of nuclear weapons. *Vicesimus tertius*: In the path towards nuclear disarmament, the peoples of the world cannot remain hostage of individual State consent. The universal juridical conscience stands well above the "will" of the State. *Vicesimus quartus*: The absolute prohibitions of arbitrary deprivation of human life, of infliction of cruel, inhuman or degrading treatment, and of infliction of unnecessary suffering, are prohibitions of *jus cogens*, which have and incidence on ILHR and IHL and ILR, and foster the current historical process of humanization of international law.

316. *Vicesimus quintus*: The positivist outlook unduly overlooks the *opinio juris communis* as to the illegality of all weapons of mass destruction, including [and starting with] nuclear weapons, and the obligation of nuclear disarmament, under contemporary international law. *Vicesimus sextus*: Conventional and customary international law go together, in the domain of the protection of the human person, as disclosed by the Martens clause, with an incidence on the prohibition of nuclear weapons. *Vicesimus septimus*: The existence of nuclear weapons is the contemporary tragedy of the nuclear age; today, more than ever, human beings need protection from themselves. Nuclear weapons have no ethics, and ethics cannot be separated from law, as taught by jusnaturalist thinking.

317. *Vicesimus octavus*: Humankind, a subject of rights, has been a potential victim of nuclear weapons already for a long time. *Vicesimus nonus*: The law of nations encompasses, among its subjects, humankind as a whole (as propounded by the "founding fathers" of international law). *Trigesimus*: This humanist vision is centred on peoples, keeping in mind the humane ends of

States. *Trigesimus primus*: *Opinio juris communis necessitatis*, upholding a customary and conventional obligation of nuclear disarmament, has been finding expression in the NPT Review Conferences, in the relevant establishment of nuclear-weapon-free zones, and in the recent Conferences of Humanitarian Impact of Nuclear Weapons, – in their common cause of achieving and maintaining a nuclear-weapon-free world. *Trigesimus secundus*: Those initiatives have gone beyond the State-centric outlook, duly attentive to peoples' and humankind's quest for survival in our times.

318. *Trigesimus tertius*: *Opinio juris communis* – to which U.N. General Assembly resolutions have contributed – has a much broader dimension than the subjective element of custom, being a key element in the formation of a law of conscience, so as to rid the world of the inhuman threat of nuclear weapons. *Trigesimus quartus*: U.N. (General Assembly and Security Council) resolutions are adopted on behalf of the United Nations Organization itself (and not only of the States which voted in their favour); they are thus valid for *all* U.N. member States.

319. *Trigesimus quintus*: The United Nations Organization, endowed with an international legal personality of its own, upholds the juridical equality of States, in striving for the realization of common goals such as nuclear disarmament. *Trigesimus sextus*: Of the main organs of the United Nations, the contributions of the General Assembly, the Security Council and the Secretary-General to nuclear disarmament have been consistent and remarkable along the years.

320. *Trigesimus septimus*: United Nations resolutions in this domain address a matter of concern to humankind as a whole, which cannot thus be properly approached from a State voluntarist perspective. The universal juridical conscience stands well above the "will" of individual States. *Trigesimus octavus*: The ICJ, as the principal judicial organ of the United Nations, is to keep in mind basic considerations of humanity, with their incidence on questions of admissibility and jurisdiction, as well as of substantive law. *Trigesimus nonus*: In sum, the ICJ has jurisdiction to consider the *cas d'espèce*, and there is a conventional and customary international law obligation of nuclear disarmament; whether there has been a breach of this obligation, the Court could only decide on the merits phase of the present case.

321. *Quadragesimus*: A world with arsenals of nuclear weapons, like ours, is bound to destroy its past, dangerously threatens the present, and has no future

at all. Nuclear weapons pave the way into nothingness. In my understanding, the International Court *of Justice*, as the principal judicial organ of the United Nations, should, in the present Judgment, have shown sensitivity in this respect, and should have given its contribution to a matter which is a major concern of the vulnerable international community, and indeed of humankind as a whole.

(Signed) *Antônio Augusto* CANÇADO TRINDADE
Judge

CHAPTER 4

Victims' Right to Reparations for War Damages

1 Declaration in the case of *Armed Activities on the Territory of the Congo* (D.R. Congo *versus* Uganda, Order [Reparations] of 01.07.2015)

1. I have voted in favour of the adoption – by unanimity – of the present Order, whereby the International Court of Justice (ICJ) has found that the proper course to take, in the present case of *Armed Activities on the Territory of the Congo* (D.R. Congo *versus* Uganda), is to resume the proceedings on reparations. Yet I think the ICJ, in support of its own Order just adopted today, 01 July 2015, should have given a more thorough account of the facts brought to its attention by the two contending Parties. In effect, D.R. Congo and Uganda have, for a couple of years, been forwarding correspondence to the Court concerning the ongoing negotiations between them for reparations for damages,[1] in pursuance of resolutory point n. 14 of the *dispositif* of the Court's Judgment of 19.12.2005 in the present case.

2. Thus, two years after the Court's Judgment of 2005, the two contending parties, D.R. Congo and Uganda, in their meeting in Ngurdoto (Tanzania), agreed (on 08.09.2007) to constitute an *ad hoc* Committee, *inter alia* to consider the implementation of the ICJ Judgment of 2005 as to reparations (Article 8 of the Agreement). After the bilateral Agreement of Ngurdoto, D.R. Congo and Uganda held four inter-ministerial Meetings in South Africa. The persistent difficulties in negotiations were reported to the Court,[2] as well as their endeavours in their production of evidence, e.g., in the Meeting of Kinshasa (of 10-14.12.2012) of the aforementioned *ad hoc* Committee, held in a spirit of "fraternity and friendship" (*fraternité et amitié*).[3] In the most recent inter-ministerial Meeting, which took place in Pretoria, on 17-19.03.2015, they concluded that, despite their endeavours, in a "spirit of brotherhood and good neighbourliness", they

---

[1] Namely, the correspondence with the Court from D.R. Congo (of 10.03.2015, of 07.05.2015) as well as from Uganda (of 25.03.2015, and of 10.04.2015). I can add, to this correspondence, that of previous years, namely: of 04.09.2014 and 19.02.2014 (from Uganda), of 25.03.2014 (from D.R. Congo); of 16.10.2013 (from Uganda), of 06.02.2013 (from D.R. Congo); of 07.11.2012 and of 19.04.2012 (from Uganda), and of 23.09.2011, of 05.07.2011 and 13.06.2011 (from D.R. Congo); of 25.08.2010 (from D.R. Congo), and of 06.09.2010 (from Uganda).

[2] As in, e.g., the Agreed Minutes of the ministerial Meeting in Johannesburg, on 13–14.09.2012.

[3] As reported in the *Procès-Verbal* of the Kinshasa Meeting, of 14.12.2012.

had not succeeded to reach a consensus in their negotiations, which had thus come to an end "at technical and ministerial level".[4]

3. Looking back in time, the Court, almost a decade ago, in its aforementioned Judgment of 19.12.2005, set forth the duty of the contending parties to make reparation (Uganda, resolutory point n. 5; and D.R. Congo, resolutory point n. 13) in the *dispositif* of its Judgment on the merits in the *cas d'espèce*. The absence in resolutory points ns. 5 and 13 of time-limits to that effect, in my view did not imply that negotiations (to reach an agreement on reparations) could continue indefinitely, as they have done. On the contrary, having extended for almost a decade, they have already far exceeded a reasonable time, bearing in mind the situation of the victims, still waiting for justice. The acknowledgment of the great suffering of the local population in the conflicts in the Great Lakes region[5] should have been accompanied by the determination of a reasonable time for the provision of reparations for damages inflicted upon the victims.

4. The lesson to be drawn from this decade of waiting for reparations is clear to me: in a case like the present one, of *Armed Activities on the Territory of the Congo*, involving grave violations (as established by the Court[6]) of the International Law of Human Rights and of International Humanitarian Law, the Court should not have left the question of reparations, as it did in its Judgment of 19.12.2005, open to negotiations between the Parties without a time-limit, without a reasonable time. I hope the Court has learned this lesson and no longer does what it did in its 2005 Judgment as to the timing of reparations for damages, in cases of this kind. After all, in the present case of *Armed Activities on the Territory of the Congo*, the members of the affected segments of the population keep on waiting, for almost a decade, for the reparations due to them for the damages they suffered.

5. In this connection, three years ago, in the case of *A.S. Diallo* (Guinea *versus* D.R Congo, Judgment on reparations, of 19.06.2012), I observed, in my Separate Opinion, that this "victim-centred outlook has entailed implications for the reparations due, has clarified their forms, has fostered the progressive

---

4 Paragraphs 6 and 8 of the Agreed Minutes of the Pretoria Meeting on the Implementation of the 2005 Judgment of the ICJ, of 17–19.03.2015.
5 As acknowledged by the ICJ in its Judgment of 19.12.2005, paras. 26 and 221.
6 ICJ Judgment of 19.12.2005, paras. 207, 209–211 and 219–221, and resolutory point n. (3) of the *dispositif*.

development of international law in the present domain" (para. 94). I further pondered that,

> Within this humanized outlook, the *reparatio* (from the Latin *reparare*, "to dispose again") ceases all the effects of the breaches of international law (the violations of human rights) at issue, and provides satisfaction (as a form of reparation) to the victims; by means of the reparations, the Law reestablishes the legal order broken by those violations, – a legal order erected on the basis of the full respect for the rights inherent to the human person. The full *reparatio* does not "erase" the human rights violations perpetrated, but rather ceases all its effects, thus at least avoiding the aggravation of the harm already done, besides restoring the integrity of the legal order, as well as that of the victims.
>
> One has to be aware that it has become commonplace in legal circles (...) to repeat that the duty of reparation, conforming a "secondary obligation", comes after the breach of international law. This is not my conception (...). In my own conception, breach and reparation go together, conforming an indissoluble whole: the latter is the indispensable consequence or complement of the former. The duty of reparation is a *fundamental* obligation, and this becomes clearer if we look into it from the perspective of the centrality of the victims, which is my own. (...) (paras. 39–40).

6. In the present case of *Armed Activities on the Territory of the Congo*, the Court, as the master of its procedure, was, in my understanding, fully entitled, in the proper exercise of its judicial function and in the interest of the sound administration of justice (*la bonne administration de la justice*), by means of the present Order, to resume the proceedings on reparations in the *cas d'espèce*, so as to avoid further delays, and to give effect to resolutory point n. 14 of its Judgment on the merits of 19.12.2005. The Court now knows that it is necessary to bridge the regrettable gap between the time of human justice and the time of human beings.

7. Reparations, in cases involving grave breaches of the International Law of Human Rights and of International Humanitarian Law, cannot simply be left over for "negotiations" without time-limits between the States concerned, as contending parties. Reparations in such cases are to be resolved by the Court itself, within a reasonable time, bearing in mind not State susceptibilities, but rather the suffering of human beings, – the surviving victims, and their close relatives, – prolonged in time, and the need to alleviate it. The aforementioned

breaches and prompt compliance with the duty of reparation for damages, are not be separated in time: they form an indissoluble whole.

(Signed) *Antônio Augusto* CANÇADO TRINDADE
Judge

2 Declaration in the case of *Armed Activities on the Territory of the Congo* (D.R. Congo *versus* Uganda, Order [Reparations], of 11.04.2016)

1. In concurring with the adoption of the present Order (of 11.04.2016) of the International Court of Justice (ICJ) in the case of *Armed Activities on the Territory of the Congo* (D.R. Congo *versus* Uganda), in which the Court discloses its prudence as to the length of the requested extension of time, I feel obliged, at the same time, to lay on the records, in this Declaration, my concern at the continuing prolongation of the proceedings as to reparations in the *cas d'espèce*.

2. Looking back in time, it took almost a decade, since the Court's Judgment of 19.12.2005 (on the merits) in the present case, for the contending parties to come to the conclusion, in their inter-ministerial Meeting held in Pretoria, on 17-19.03.2015, that they had not succeeded to reach a consensus in their negotiations. The aforementioned Judgment of 19.12.2005, – over a decade ago, – set forth the duty of the contending parties to provide reparations for damages.

3. In effect, the D.R. Congo and Uganda have both shown their awareness that the proceedings in the present case of the *Armed Activities on the Territory of the Congo* have consumed far too long a time. The D.R. Congo did so, when asking the Court (Application of 08.05.2015) "to reopen proceedings" for determination of the reparations due. In its Order of 01.07.2015, the ICJ decided to resume the proceedings on reparations.

4. In my Declaration appended to that Order, I pondered that the lesson to be learned was that "the Court should not have left the question of reparations, as it did in its Judgment of 19.12.2005, open to negotiations between the parties without a time-limit, without a reasonable time" (para. 4). After all, – I added, – the members of the segments of the population victimized in the present case of *Armed Activities on the Territory of the Congo* have kept on waiting, for more than one decade, for "the reparations due to them for the damages they suffered" (para. 4).

5. Yet, shortly afterwards, upon a new request of the D.R. Congo (not objected to by Uganda), the ICJ issued a new Order in the *cas d'espèce*, of 10.12.2015, this time granting a further extension of the time-limit for the filing of the

Memorials (on reparations) of the two contending parties.[1] And now, once again, in the more recent correspondence presented to the Court, the D.R. Congo requests (letter of 31.03.2016) another extension of time,[2] given the large scale of the damages and the complexity of the fact-finding.

6. In its letter of response (of 08.04.2016), Uganda, for its part, states that it is prepared to agree with a much shorter extension of time.[3] The Court, in the Order it has just adopted today, has found an intermediary solution, in between the time-extension requested by the D.R. Congo and the one agreed upon by Uganda. In the resolutory point of the present Order of the ICJ, it extends to 28.04.2016 the time-limit for the filing by the two parties of their respective *Memorials* on reparations.

7. It is understandable that both contending parties seek to prepare and substantiate their arguments as to reparations, and this is commendable, but this should not entail further prorogations or delays in the proceedings. *Tempus fugit*. In their more recent correspondence addressed to the Court, the contending parties have shown their awareness of this. Thus, in its letter of 31.03.2016, the D.R. Congo stated that it felt obliged to request this new extension of time-limit "with reluctance" (p. 1), given the "unprecedented complexity" of this dispute (a five-year conflict), in which "for the first time in its history the Court will be faced with the question of reparation for war damages on such an unusual scale" (p. 1).

8. Yet, other contemporary international tribunals have for some time been constructing their case-law on this matter;[4] a study of it could prove useful

---

[1] The time-limit was extended by the Court from 06.01.2016 to 28.04.2016. The D.R. Congo had asked for an extension until "late April or mid–May 2016").

[2] Now an additional extension of time of ten months.

[3] Namely, an extension of three months.

[4] Cf. A.A. Cançado Trindade, *The Access of Individuals to International Justice*, Oxford, Oxford University Press, 2011, pp. 151–191; A.A. Cançado Trindade, *Évolution du Droit international au droit des gens – L'accès des particuliers à la justice internationale: le regard d'un juge*, Paris, Pédone, 2008, pp. 132–146 and 151–184; A.A. Cançado Trindade, *El Ejercicio de la Función Judicial Internacional – Memorias de la Corte Interamericana de Derechos Humanos*, 3rd. ed., Belo Horizonte/Brazil, Edit. Del Rey, 2013, pp. 59–74 and 336–342; A.A. Cançado Trindade, *El Derecho de Acceso a la Justicia en Su Amplia Dimensión*, 2nd. ed., Santiago de Chile, Ed. Librotecnia, 2012, pp. 367–396 and 423–559; A.A. Cançado Trindade, *State Responsibility in Cases of Massacres: Contemporary Advances in International Justice*, Utrecht, Universiteit

to the contending parties in the *cas d'espèce*, as well as to the ICJ itself. In any case, as to the time-length, in their latest arguments before the ICJ, the contending parties disclosed their awareness of the need to avoid further delays in the present proceedings on reparations. Thus, still in its letter of 31.03.2016, the D.R. Congo announced that "this request for postponement will be the last of the kind" (p. 2).

9. For its part, in its letter of 06.04.2016, Uganda considered the time-extension requested "excessive" and "disproportionate" (pp. 1–2): as considerable time has already lapsed (since the 2005 Judgment on the merits), this case being "the second oldest on the Court's docket", – it proceeded, – the applicant State "has already had considerable time to collect evidence relating to its reparations claim" (p. 1). Uganda added that this matter should be now "resolved on a timely basis" (p. 2).

10. Over a decade ago, in delivering its Judgment of 19.12.2005 on the merits in the present case, the ICJ was aware that the particularisation of the damages inflicted by the parties was, at that stage, of course not sufficient: such account of damages had been addressed by the D.R. Congo mainly in its *Reply* of 29.05.2002, and by Uganda in its *Counter-Memorial* of 21.04.2001, but in rather general terms, and not set out in great detail. In its 2005 Judgment, the Court made it clear that, in order to decide on reparations, though it was not necessary to embark on findings of fact with regard to each individual incident (paras. 205 and 237), the whole matter had to be addressed in greater detail at the following stage of reparations (para. 345(6) and (14)), when it would need to be particularised.

11. The complexity of the case is widely known. Yet, as years go by, the history of the conflict at issue is gradually being written.[5] The needed particularisation of

---

Utrecht, 2011, pp. 1–71. And cf. also: [Various Authors,] *Réparer les violations graves et massives des droits de l'homme: La Cour Interaméricaine, pionnière et modèle?* (eds. E. Lambert Abdelgawad and K. Martin-Chenut), Paris, Éd. Société de Législation Comparée, 2010, pp. 17–334; I. Bottigliero, *Redress for Victims of Crimes under International Law*, Leiden, Nijhoff, 2004, pp. 1–253; [Various Authors,] *Reparations for Victims of Genocide, War Crimes and Crimes against Humanity* (eds. C. Ferstman, M. Goetz and A. Stephens), Leiden, Nijhoff, 2009, pp. 7–566; L. Moffett, *Justice for Victims before the International Criminal Court*, London/N.Y., Routledge, 2014, pp. 1–289; J.-B. Jeangène Vilmer, *Réparer l'irréparable – Les réparations aux victimes devant la Cour Pénale Internationale*, Paris, PUF, 2009, pp. 1–182.

5 Cf., *inter alia*, e.g., N. Nzereka Mughendi, *Guerres récurrentes en République Démocratique du Congo – Entre fatalité et responsabilité*, Paris, L'Harmattan, 2010, pp. 15–199; P. Mbeko and H. Ngbanda-Nzambo, *Stratégie du chaos et du mensonge – Poker Menteur en Afrique des*

the damages is possible, in particular for the purpose of collective reparations to the victims, and it should not entail further delays in the proceedings. After more of a decade, the time has now come for a prompt determination of the reparations for damages inflicted upon the numerous victims.

12. According to a *célèbre* maxim, *justice delayed is justice denied.* This point was object of meditation already in Seneca's *Letters to Lucilius* (circa 62–64 A.D.). In the search for the realization of justice, undue delays are indeed to be avoided. The victims (in armed conflicts) of grave breaches of the International Law of Human Rights and of International Humanitarian Law have a *right to reparations,* – most likely collective reparations, and in their distinct forms, – within a reasonable time.

13. The more time passes, the more difficult fact-finding and investigations *in loco* become. I have addressed this point, among others, in my recent and extensive Dissenting Opinion (Paras. 149–179, 195, 287, 321, 497–499, 533–535 and 538–539) in the case of the *Application of the Convention against Genocide* (Croatia *versus* Serbia, Judgment of 03.02.2015). Furthermore, as life-time is rather brief, and passes fast, many victims of those grave violations cross the final threshold of their lives without finding justice, or else having lost any hope in it.

14. Ancient Stoic thinking was already conscious of the perennial mystery surrounding human existence, that of the passing of time. Stoicism, in its perennial wisdom, recommended (as in, e.g., Seneca's *De Brevitate Vitae,* circa 40 A.D.) to keep always in mind all times – past, present and future – jointly: time past, by means of remembrance; time present, so as to make the best use of it (in search of justice); and time future, so as to anticipate and prevent all one can, thus seeking to make life longer.

15. The duty of reparation is firmly-rooted in the history of the law of nations. The acknowledgment of such duty goes back to its origins, to the perennial lessons of the "founding fathers" of international law. In this connection, four years ago, in my lengthy Separate Opinion in the case of *A.S. Diallo* (Guinea *versus* D.R Congo, Judgment on reparations, of 19.06.2012), I deemed it fit to

---

Grands Lacs, Québec, Édit. de l'Érablière, 2014, pp. 9–643; Lwamba Katansi, *Crimes et châtiments dans la région des Grands Lacs,* Paris, L'Harmattan, 2007, Ch. 7, pp. 41–72; G. Prunier, *Africa's World War – Congo, the Rwandan Genocide, and the Making of a Continental Catastrophe,* Oxford, Oxford University Press, 2010, pp. 113–368 and 396–468; Th. Turner, *The Congo Wars: Conflict, Myth and Reality,* London/N.Y., Zed Books, 2008 (reimpr.), pp. 1–233.

recall the lessons and writings of the "founding fathers" that expressly referred to it (paras. 12 and 15–19), in the light of the principle *neminem laedere*.

16. I thus recalled the relevant passages in the classic works of, e.g., Francisco de Vitoria (Second *Relectio – De Indis*, 1538–1539); Hugo Grotius (*De Jure Belli ac Pacis*, 1625, book II, Ch. 17); Samuel Pufendorf (*Elementorum Jurisprudentiae Universalis – Libri Duo*, 1672; and *On the Duty of Man and Citizen According to Natural Law*, 1673); Christian Wolff (*Jus Gentium Methodo Scientifica Pertractatum*, 1764; and *Principes du droit de la nature et des gens*, 1758); among others, such as the pertinent considerations also of Alberico Gentili (*De Jure Belli*, 1598); Francisco Suárez (*De Legibus ac Deo Legislatore*, 1612); Cornelius van Bynkershoek (*De Foro Legatorum*, 1721; and *Questiones Juris Publici – Libri Duo*, 1737).

17. There is nothing new under the sun. The more we do research on the classics of international law (largely forgotten in our hectic days), the more we find reflections on the victims' right to reparations for injuries, – also present in the writings of, e.g., Juan de la Peña (*De Bello contra Insulanos*, 1545); Bartolomé de Las Casas (*De Regia Potestate*, 1571); Juan Roa Dávila (*De Regnorum Justitia*, 1591); Juan Zapata y Sandoval (*De Justitia Distributiva et Acceptione Personarum ei Opposita Disceptatio*, 1609).

18. In sum, since the origins of the law of nations, there was acknowledgment of the duty to provide redress to those who suffered damages caused by wrongful acts, in distinct circumstances. The realm of the evolving *jus gentium*, the law of nations, was conceived as encompassing the international community of (emerging) States, as well as all peoples, groups and individuals: *jus gentium* was regarded as coextensive with humanity.

19. The duty of reparation for injuries was clearly seen as a response to an *international need*,[6] in conformity with the *recta ratio*, – whether the beneficiaries were (emerging) States, peoples, groups or individuals. The *recta ratio* provided the basis for the regulation of human relations with the due respect for each

---

6 J. Brown Scott, *The Spanish Origin of International Law – Francisco de Vitoria and His Law of Nations*, Oxford/London, Clarendon Press/H. Milford, 1934, pp. 140, 150, 163, 165, 172, 210–211 and 282–283; and cf. also, Association Internationale Vitoria-Suarez, *Vitoria et Suarez: Contribution des théologiens au Droit international moderne*, Paris, Pédone, 1939, pp. 73–74, and cf. pp. 169–170; A.A. Cançado Trindade, "Prefacio", *in Escuela Ibérica de la Paz (1511–1694) – La Conciencia Crítica de la Conquista y Colonización de América* (eds. P. Calafate and R.E. Mandado Gutiérrez), Santander, Ed. Universidad de Cantabria, 2014, pp. 40–109.

other's rights.[7] As I have pondered in my earlier Declaration appended to the Court's previous Order of 01.07.2015 in the present case of the *Armed Activities on the Territory of the Congo*, and I here reiterate in the ICJ's new Order just adopted today (11.04.2016),

> Reparations, in cases involving grave breaches of the International Law of Human Rights and of International Humanitarian Law (...) are to be resolved by the Court itself within a reasonable time, bearing in mind not State susceptibilities, but rather the suffering of human beings, – the surviving victims, and their close relatives, – prolonged in time, and the need to alleviate it. The aforementioned breaches and prompt compliance with the duty of reparation for damages, are not be separated in time: they form an indissoluble whole (para. 7).

20. In the present case of the *Armed Activities on the Territory of the Congo*, the ultimate beneficiaries of reparations for damages resulting from grave breaches of the International Law of Human Rights and International Humanitarian Law (as determined by the ICJ) are the human beings victimized. They are the *titulaires* of the right to reparations, as subjects of the law of nations, as conceived and sustained, in historical perspective, by the "founding fathers" of international law. This is deeply-rooted in the historical trajectory of our discipline. As *titulaires* of that right, they have, in the *cas d'espèce*, been waiting for reparations for a far too long a time; many of them have already passed away. *Justitia longa, vita brevis*.

(Signed) Antônio Augusto CANÇADO TRINDADE
Judge

---

[7] The *right reason* lies at the basis of the law of nations, being the spirit of justice in the line of natural law thinking; this trend of international legal thinking has always much valued the *realization of justice*, pursuant to a "superior value of justice". P. Foriers, *L'organisation de la paix chez Grotius et l'école de droit naturel* [1961], Paris, J. Vrin, 1987, pp. 293, 333, 373 and 375 [reed. of study originally published *in*: *Recueil de la Société Jean Bodin pour l'histoire comparative des institutions*, vol. 15-Part II, Bruxelles, Libr. Encyclopédique, 1961].

3 Separate Opinion in the Case of *Armed Activities in the Territory of the Congo* (D.R. Congo *versus* Uganda, Order [Reparations], of 06.12.2016)

1. In the course of the handling of proceedings on reparations in the present case of *Armed Activities on the Territory of the Congo* (D.R. Congo *versus* Uganda), I have been having concerns, – as already expressed on the occasion of two previous Orders (of 01.07.2015 and 11.04.2016), – which I deem it fit again to lay on the records in today's Order (of 06.12.2016), in the present Separate Opinion in the *cas d'espèce*.

2. This time, I shall summarize my concerns in four interrelated points, namely: (a) the undue prolongation of time in the adjudication of cases of grave violations of international law; (b) breach and reparation conforming an indissoluble whole; (c) the fundamental duty of prompt reparation; and (d) reparations in distinct forms. May I turn to each of them in sequence; the path will then be paved for the presentation of my concluding observations.

I Undue Prolongation of Time in the Adjudication of Cases of Grave Violations of International Law

3. It is most regrettable to find that, the graver the breaches of international law appear to be, the more time-consuming and difficult it becomes to impart justice. Last year, in its Judgment of 03.02.2015 in the case concerning the *Application of the Convention against Genocide* (Croatia *versus* Serbia), the ICJ rejected the claim (and counter-claim) after a virtually unprecedented prolongation of 16 years of the process, despite the *vita brevis* of victimized human beings. In my extensive Dissenting Opinion appended thereto, I devoted a whole section of it to the "regrettable delays in the adjudication" of the case (paras. 6–18). And this is not the only example to this effect.

4. It was preceded by the Court's Judgment (of 26.02.2007) of the *Bosnian Genocide* case (Bosnia and Herzegovina *versus* Serbia and Montenegro), after 14 years of process. In another case, the one concerning the *Obligation to Prosecute or Extradite* (Belgium *versus* Senegal), the numerous victims of the occurrences at issue had to wait a long time until finding justice in the ICJ Judgment on the merits (of 20.07.2012). Yet, the surviving victims of the occurrences at

issue in the case of *Jurisdictional Immunities of the State* (Germany *versus* Italy, with Greece intervening), lost all hope in human justice after the delivery of the ICJ Judgment of 03.02.2012, upholding the prevalence of State immunities over the right of access to justice *lato sensu*, in particular in face of international crimes.

5. In the handling by the ICJ of the present case concerning *Armed Activities on the Territory of the Congo* (reparations), there are already 11 years since the ICJ delivered its Judgment (of 19.12.2005) on the merits, wherein grave breaches were established by the Court; yet, the numerous victims still wait for reparations. And this is the third time, in the ongoing proceedings on reparations, that I deem it fit to leave on the records my concerns as to the continuing and undue prolongation of time, to the detriment of the victims themselves.[1] *Tempus fugit*.

6. In its aforementioned Judgment of 2005, the ICJ was particularly attentive to those grave breaches (massacres of civilians, incitement of ethnic conflicts among groups, forced displacement of persons, among others), having drawn attention to the need of reparation, though unfortunately without setting up a reasonable time-limit for that. In the current written phase of proceedings on reparations in the *cas d'espèce*, special attention has again been devoted to those grave breaches (e.g., in the region of Ituri and the city of Kisangani),[2] including an express cross-reference to a resolution of the Security Council (on the occurrences in Kisangani) in that respect,[3] and references to recent proceedings on reparations before the International Criminal Court (ICC) in the case of *Th. Lubanga Dyilo*.[4]

7. The Security Council resolution just mentioned, – SC resolution 1304 (of 16.06.2000), – upheld, over one and a half decades ago, *inter alia*, the duty to "make reparations" for damages (loss of life and others) "inflicted on the civilian population in Kisangani", and requested the Secretary-General to "submit an assessment of the damage[s] as a basis for such reparations" (para. 14).

---

1 Cf., earlier on, ICJ, case of *Armed Activities on the Territory of the Congo* (D.R. Congo *versus* Uganda, Order of 01.07.2015), Declaration of Judge Cançado Trindade, paras. 1–7; ICJ, case of *Armed Activities on the Territory of the Congo* (D.R. Congo *versus* Uganda, Order of 11.04.2016), Declaration of Judge Cançado Trindade, paras. 1–20.
2 Cf. D.R. Congo, *Mémoire – Réparations*, of 26.09.2016, chs. 3–4, pp. 72–133, paras. 3.01–4.76.
3 Cf. *ibid.*, p. 109, para. 4.04.
4 Cf. *ibid.*, pp. 77 and 96, paras. 3.10 and 3.37, respectively.

A report to that effect was forwarded to the President of the Security Council, appended to a letter from the Secretary General of 04.12.2000.[5]

8. That report (resulting from an assessment mission to Kisangani), which did not have the pretension to address at length or to exhaust the issue of reparations (para. 1), nonetheless singled out programmes of rehabilitation of victims (paras. 33–34). The report pointed out that the "recent war" in the D.R. Congo "involved seven neighbouring countries", creating a situation that "resulted in a major humanitarian crisis": the war-affected people rose "by around 7 to 20 million", including "1.8 million internally displaced people and over 400 thousand refugees", with "serious repercussions on the stability of the entire central African region" (paras. 13 and 44).[6]

9. So, in view of the virtual impossibility to provide *restitutio in integrum* in cases of mass crimes, reparations were seen, already one and a half decades ago, in 2000, to include not only compensation and satisfaction, but also rehabilitation of the victims (medical and social services), apologies (as satisfaction), guarantees of non-repetition of the grave breaches (occurred in the armed conflicts of the Great Lakes), among other forms of reparation. Half a decade later, the ICJ delivered its Judgment on the merits in the case of *Armed Activities on the Territory of the Congo* (2005), and now, over a decade later, we are still in the written phase of the proceedings on reparations for damages. *Justitia longa, vita brevis*.

II Breach and Reparation Conforming an Indissoluble Whole

10. May I recall that the duty of reparation is deeply and firmly-rooted in the history of the law of nations, going back to its origins, when it marked presence in the writings of the "founding fathers" of our discipline, who expressly referred to it in the light of the principle *neminem laedere*. I had the occasion to review their writings in my extensive Separate Opinion in the case of *A.S. Diallo* (reparations, Guinea *versus* D.R. Congo, Judgment of 19.06.2012). May I herein single out and stress an important point.

---

5 Cf. U.N./Security Council doc. S/2000/1153, of 04.12.2000, pp. 1–12.
6 As I pointed out in my Declaration (para. 11 n. 5) appended to the Court's Order of 11.04.2016, the great proportions and complexity of the armed conflicts in the Great Lakes are gradually being written in historical bibliography.

11. Thus, already in the first half of the XVIth century, Francisco de Vitoria held, in his celebrated Second *Relectio – De Indis* (1538–1539), that "the enemy who has done the wrong is bound to give all this redress";[7] there is a duty, even amidst armed hostilities, to make restitution (of losses) and to provide reparation for "all damages".[8] F. de Vitoria found inspiration in the much earlier writings of Thomas Aquinas (from the XIIIth century), and pursued an anthropocentric outlook in his lectures at the University of Salamanca.[9]

12. The new humanist thinking came thus to mark presence in the emerging law of nations. In the second half of the XVIth century, Bartolomé de Las Casas, in his *De Regia Potestate* (1571), after invoking the lessons of Thomas Aquinas, also asserted the duty of *restitutio* and reparation for damages.[10] In one of his best-known works, *Brevísima Relación de la Destrucción de las Indias* (1552), B. de Las Casas not only denounced the numerous massacres of native people, but also asserted the duty of reparations for damages.[11] Still in the XVIth century, the duty of *restitutio* and reparation for damages was Juan Roa Dávila, in his *De Regnorum Iusticia* (1591), also referring to Thomas Aquinas.[12]

13. Later on, in the XVIIth century, Hugo Grotius, in his well-known *De Jure Belli ac Pacis* (1625), dedicated a whole chapter to the obligation of reparation for damages (Book II, Chapter 17).[13] He kept in mind the dictates of *recta ratio*. To him, the "injured party" was not necessarily a State; he referred to

---

7   Franciscus de Victoria, *Second Relectio – On the Indians* [*De Indis*] [1538–1539], Oxford/London, Clarendon Press/H. Milford, 1934 [reed.], p. LV.
8   *Ibid.*, p. LV; and cf. Francisco de Vitoria, "Relección Segunda – De los Indios" [1538–1539], in *Obras de Francisco de Vitoria – Relecciones Teológicas* (ed. T. Urdañoz), Madrid, BAC, 1955, p. 827.
9   As from his first lecture; cf. Francisco de Vitoria, *Sobre el Poder Civil* [*Relectio de Potestate Civili*, 1528] (ed. J. Cordero Pando), Salamanca, Edit. San Estéban, 2009 [reed.], pp. 22 and 44.
10 Bartolomé de Las Casas, *De Regia Potestate o Derecho de Autodeterminación* [1571] (eds. L. Pereña, J.M. Pérez-Prendes, V. Abril and J. Azcárraga), CSIC, Madrid, 1969, p. 72.
11 Bartolomé de Las Casas, *Brevísima Relación de la Destrucción de las Indias* [1552], Barcelona, Ediciones 29, 2004 [reed.], pp. 14, 17, 23, 27, 31, 45, 50, 72–73, 87 and 89–90 (massacres), Bartolomé de Las Casas, *Brevísima Relación de la Destruición de las Indias* [1552], Barcelona, Ed. Galaxia Gutenberg / Universidad de Alicante, 2009, pp. 91–92 and 116–117.
12 Juan Roa Dávila, *De Regnorum Iusticia o El Control Democrático* [1591] (eds. L. Pereña, J.M. Pérez-Prendes and V. Abril), Madrid, CSIC/Instituto Francisco de Vitoria, 1970, pp. 59 and 63.
13 Hugonis Grotii, *De Iure Belli Ac Pacis* [1625], Book II, Ch. XVII, The Hague, M. Nijhoff, 1948, pp. 79–82.

distinct kinds of damage caused by breaches of "rights resulting to us", or from "losses suffered by negligence"; such damages or losses created an obligation of reparation.[14]

14. Also in the XVIIth century, Samuel Pufendorf, in his thoughtful book *On the Duty of Man and Citizen According to Natural Law* (1673), stressed the need to provide reparation for damages at the same time that condemned by natural law vengeance, so as to secure peace. He warned that, without providing *restitutio*,

> men in their wickedness will not refrain from harming each other; and the one who has suffered loss will not readily bring himself to make peace with the other as long as he has not obtained compensation. (...) The obligation to make restitution for loss arises not only from harm done with intentional malice but also from harm done by negligence or by easily avoidable fault, without direct intention.[15]

15. Subsequently, in the XVIIIth century, also in the line of jusnaturalist thinking, Christian Wolff, in his book *Principes du droit de la nature et des gens* (1758), also asserted the duty of appropriate reparation for damages.[16] Other examples could be added, but the aforementioned suffice for the purpose of the present Separate Opinion. It is not surprising to find that the "founding fathers" of international law were particularly attentive to the duty of reparation for damages. They addressed reparations in respect of distinct sorts of disputes, concerning distinct subjects, – States as well as nations, peoples, groups and individuals.

16. Already in the XVIth century, F. de Vitoria viewed the international community of emerging States as "co-extensive with humanity", and the provision of redress corresponded to "an international need"[17] in conformity with *recta*

---

14   *Ibid.*, pp. 79–80, paras. I and VIII-IX; and cf. H. Grotius, *Le droit de la guerre et de la paix* [1625] (eds. D. Alland and S. Goyard-Fabre), Paris, PUF, 2005 [reed.], pp. 415–416 and 418, paras. I and VIII-IX.

15   Samuel Pufendorf, *On the Duty of Man and Citizen According to Natural Law* [1673] (eds. J. Tully and M. Silverthorne), Cambridge, Cambridge University Press, 2003 [reprint], pp. 57–58, and cf. pp. 59–60.

16   Christian Wolff, *Principes du droit de la nature et des gens* [1758], vol. III, Caen, Ed. Université de Caen, 2011 [reed.], Ch. VI, pp. 293–294, 296–297 and 306.

17   Cf. Association Internationale Vitoria-Suarez, *Vitoria et Suarez: Contribution des théologiens au Droit international moderne*, Paris, Pédone, 1939, pp. 73–74, and cf. pp. 169–170;

ratio. The emerging *jus naturae et gentium* was universalist, directed to all peoples; law and ethics went together, in the search for justice.[18] Reminiscent of Cicero's ideal of *societas hominum*,[19] the "founding fathers" of international law conceived a "universal society of the human kind" (*commune humani generis societas*) encompassing all the aforementioned subjects of the law of nations (*droit des gens*).

17. The reductionist outlook of the international legal order, which came to prevail in the XIXth and early XXth centuries, beholding only absolute State sovereignties and subsuming human beings thereunder, led reparations into a standstill and blocked their conceptual development. This latter has been retaken in current times, contributing to the historical process of humanization of contemporary international law.

18. The legacy of the "founding fathers" of international law has been preserved in the most lucid international legal doctrine, from the XVIth-XVIIth centuries to date. It marks its presence in the universality of the law of nations, in the acknowledgment of the importance of general principles of law, in the relevance attributed to *recta ratio*. It also marks its presence in the acknowledgment of the indissoluble whole conformed by breach and prompt reparation.

19. Reparations – in particular collective reparations – are at last attracting growing attention of international legal doctrine in our days, as well as in case-law. This should not pass unnoticed; to recall just one example, the ICC (Appeals Chamber), e.g., in its recent Judgment on reparations (of 03.03.2015)

J. Brown Scott, *The Spanish Origin of International Law – Francisco de Vitoria and His Law of Nations*, Oxford/London, Clarendon Press/H. Milford, 1934, pp. 282–283.

18 [Various Authors,] *Alberico Gentili – Giustizia, Guerra, Imperio* (Atti del Convegno di San Ginesio, sett. 2010), Milano, Giuffrè Edit., 2014, pp. 275 and 320, and cf. pp. 299–300 and 327.

19 Cf., *inter alia*, e.g., M. Luque Frías, *Vigencia del Pensamiento Ciceroniano en las Relecciones Jurídico-Teológicas del Maestro Francisco de Vitoria*, Granada, Edit. Comares, 2012, pp. 70, 95, 164, 272–273, 275, 278–279, 284, 398–399 and 418–419; A.A. Cançado Trindade and V.F.D. Cançado Trindade, "A Pré-História do Princípio de Humanidade Consagrado no Direito das Gentes: O Legado Perene do Pensamento Estóico", *in O Princípio de Humanidade e a Salvaguarda da Pessoa Humana* (eds. A.A. Cançado Trindade and C. Barros Leal), Fortaleza/Brazil, IBDH/IIDH, 2016, pp. 49–84.

in the case of *Th. Lubanga Dyilo*, has drawn particular attention to *collective* reparations, in the factual context of the case.[20]

III   The Fundamental Duty of Prompt Reparation

20. When damages ensuing from grave violations of the International Law of Human Rights and International Humanitarian Law have occurred, – as some of those found by the ICJ (2005 Judgment) in the present case concerning *Armed Activities on the Territory of the Congo*, the ultimate beneficiaries of the reparations due are the victims, human beings as subjects of international law. The duty of reparation is not only a "secondary obligation" (as conventional wisdom tries to make one believe in current times). Not at all: it is, in my perception, a truly fundamental obligation. Such breaches entail the duty of prompt reparation, conforming an indissoluble whole.

21. Breach and reparation, in my understanding, cannot be separated in time, as the latter is to cease promptly all the effects of the former. The harmful effects of wrongdoing cannot be allowed to prolong indefinitely in time, without reparations to the victims. The duty of reparation does not come, as a "secondary obligation", after the breach, to be complied when the States concerned deem feasible. The duty of reparation, a fundamental obligation, arises immediately with the breach, to be promptly complied with, so as to avoid the aggravation of the harm already done, and restore the integrity of the legal order.

22. Hence its fundamental importance, especially if we approach it from the perspective of the centrality of the victims, which is my own. The indissoluble whole conformed by breach and reparation admits no disruption by means of undue and indefinite prolongation of time. In the *cas d'espèce*, the present Order discloses that the contending parties are aware of the passing of time without reparation and its negative impact upon the victims individually or in groups.

23. And the Court, reassuringly, for the first time, expresses in the present Order, just before its resolutory points, its own consciousness of the need, at this stage, "to rule on the question of reparations without undue delay", so as to avoid further undue prolongation of time. After all, only with reparation (from the Latin *reparare*, "to dispose again") will the effects of the breaches be made

---

20   Paragraphs 7, 52–53, 126, 133, 147, 152–153, 155–156, 165–166, 177, 180, 207 and 212.

to cease: an international tribunal should keep in mind that it is unreasonable and unjust to spend years and years to determine reparations. Only the prompt compliance with the fundamental duty of full reparation will cease the consequences ensuing from the breaches, thus restoring the integrity of the international legal order.

IV Reparations in Distinct Forms

24. There is a remaining point to be made here. In the course of the current proceedings on reparations in the present case concerning *Armed Activities on the Territory of the Congo*, reparations in distinct forms are to be kept in mind. The contending parties, D.R. Congo and Uganda, have shown awareness also of that, in their respective *Memorials* on reparations. Each of them refers to reparations, in the forms, in particular, of *compensation* and *satisfaction*, – even though, as already pointed out, there are still other forms of reparations,[21] so as to alleviate human suffering and also to foster reconciliation.

25. For example, in its *Memorial*, dated 26.09.2016, the D.R. Congo refers to reparation in its distinct forms.[22] Under the heading of *compensation*, the D.R. Congo claims reparation for damage caused to people, to property, to natural resources, as well as macro-economic damage.[23] Under the heading of *satisfaction*, the D.R. Congo claims reparation in the form of the initiation of criminal investigations and prosecutions of officers and soldiers of Uganda's People's Defence Force, the creation of a fund to promote reconciliation between the Hema and Lendu peoples in Ituri, and the payment of a lump sum to repair non-material damage suffered by the Congolese State and population.[24]

26. For its part, in its *Memorial*, dated 28.09.2016, Uganda likewise refers to reparation in its distinct forms.[25] Under the heading of *compensation*, Uganda claims reparation for damage caused to its Chancery buildings. Under the heading of *satisfaction*, Uganda refers to damage caused to Ugandan diplomats

---

21 Cf. paragraph 9, *supra*, of the present Separate Opinion.
22 D.R. Congo, *Mémoire – Réparations*, Ch. 7, Section 1, pp. 224–247, paras. 7.02–7.64 (compensation); and Ch. 7, Section 2, pp. 248–255, paras. 7.65–7.84 (satisfaction).
23 *Ibid.*, Ch. 7, Section I, pp. 226–244.
24 *Ibid.*, Ch. 7, Section 2, pp. 249–255.
25 Uganda, *Memorial on Reparation*, Ch. 2, Section III, pp. 31–53, paras. 2.23–2.69 (compensation); and Ch. 2, Section II, pp. 24–31, paras. 2.7–2.22 (satisfaction).

and other persons, and to diplomatic premises and property; it expresses its understanding that the responsibility findings in the ICJ 2005 Judgment constitute an "appropriate form of satisfaction", providing reparation for the damages suffered.[26]

27. The attention of the contending parties to reparations in its distinct forms may help to avoid further undue prolongations of time in the current proceedings in the *cas d'espèce*. In my Dissenting Opinion in the ICJ Order of 28.05.2009 in the case concerning the *Obligation to Prosecute or Extradite*, I devoted special attention to the need to bridge or reduce the *décalage* between the time of human beings and the time of human justice (paras. 46–64), pondering that it is "indeed imperative" to do so (para. 49).

V   Concluding Observations

28. In my understanding, the Court is not conditioned or limited by what the parties request or want, not even in the fixing of time-limits. As I have been pointing out within the ICJ time and time again, – and I reiterate it herein, – the Court is not an arbitral tribunal.[27] The Court is master of its own procedure, also in the fixing of time-limits, in the path towards the realization of justice, avoiding the undue prolongation of time.

29. *Justitia longa, vita brevis*; the time of human justice is not the time of human beings. If we care to seek new and forward-looking ideas to endeavour to overcome this *décalage*, we are likely to find them in the lessons of the "founding fathers" of international law. Although the world has entirely changed from the times of the "founding fathers" of the law of nations (*droit des gens*) to our own, the fulfilment of human aspirations and the search for the realization of

---

26   Cf. *ibid.*, Ch. 3, Section II, p. 62, para. 3.11; Ch. 3, Section III, p. 65, para. 3.21; and Ch. 3, Section IV, p. 70, para. 3.33.

27   Cf., e,g., to this effect, ICJ, case of the *Obligation to Prosecute or Extradite* (Order of 28.05.2009), Dissenting Opinion of Judge Cançado Trindade, para. 88; ICJ, case of the *Application of the International Convention on the Elimination of All Forms of Racial Discrimination* [CERD] (Judgment of 01.04.2011), Dissenting Opinion of Judge Cançado Trindade, paras. 205–206; ICJ, [merged] cases of the *Certain Activities Carried out by Nicaragua in the Border Area / Construction of a Road in Costa Rica along the San Juan River* (Judgment of 16.12.2015), Separate Opinion of Judge Cançado Trindade, paras. 39–41; ICJ, case of *Alleged Violations of Sovereign Rights and Maritime Spaces in the Caribbean Sea*, Judgment of 17.03.2016, Separate Opinion of Judge Cançado Trindade, para. 25.

justice are a-temporal, remain always present, as imperatives of the human condition itself.

30. The lessons of the "founding fathers" of the law of nations (*droit des gens*) remain thus as contemporary as ever, and forward-looking in our days. The duty of prompt reparation forms part of their perennial legacy. That legacy is to keep being cultivated,[28] so as to face new challenges that contemporary international tribunals face in our days, from an essentially humanist approach.

31. One is to move beyond the unsatisfactory inter-State outlook, if one is to foster the progressive development of international law in the domain of reparations, in particular collective reparations. Prolonged delays are most regrettable, particularly from the perspective of the victims. As already seen, the "founding fathers" of international law went well beyond the strict inter-State outlook, and were particularly attentive to the duty of prompt reparation for damages (cf. *supra*).

32. It is in jusnaturalist thinking – as from the XVIth century – that the goal of prompt reparation was properly pursued. Legal positivist thinking – as from the late XIXth century – unduly placed the "will" of States above *recta ratio*. It is in jusnaturalist thinking – revived as it is nowadays[29] – that the notion of *justice* has always occupied a central position, orienting *law* as a whole; *justice*, in sum, is at the beginning of all *law*, being, moreover, its ultimate end.

(Signed) *Antônio Augusto* CANÇADO TRINDADE
Judge

---

28 On that legacy, cf., recently, A.A. Cançado Trindade, *A Humanização do Direito Internacional*, 2nd. rev. ed., Belo Horizonte/Brazil, Edit. Del Rey, 2015, Ch. XXIX ("A Perenidade dos Ensinamentos dos 'Pais Fundadores' do Direito Internacional") ["The Perennity of the Teachings of the 'Founding Fathers' of International Law"], 2015, pp. 647–676.

29 Cf., in the last decades, e.g., *inter alii*, A.A. Cançado Trindade, *O Direito Internacional em um Mundo em Transformação*, Rio de Janeiro, Edit. Renovar, 2002, pp. 1028–1029, 1051–1052 and 1075–1094 (universal values underlying the new *jus gentium*, common to the whole of humankind, to all human beings – *civitas maxima gentium*); J. Maritain, *Los Derechos del Hombre y la Ley Natural*, Buenos Aires, Ed. Leviatán, 1982 [reimpr.], pp. 79–80, and cf. p. 104 (the human person transcending the State, and having a destiny superior to time). Cf. also, e.g., [Various Authors,] *Droit naturel et droits de l'homme – Actes des Journées internationales de la Société d'Histoire du Droit* (Grenoble-Vizille, mai 2009 – ed. M. Mathieu), Grenoble, Presses Universitaires de Grenoble, 2011, pp. 40–43, 52–53, 336–337 and 342.

CHAPTER 5

The Evolving Law on Conservation of Living Species

Separate Opinion in the case of *Whaling in the Antarctic* (Australia *versus* Japan, New Zealand intervening, Judgment of 31.03.2014)

Table of Contents — Paragraphs

I. The Object and Purpose of the ICRW Convention 2
   1. The Teleological Approach 4
   2. Response of New Zealand to Questions from the Bench 8
II. Collective Guarantee and Collective Regulation 10
   1. Collective Decision-Making under the ICRW Convention 10
   2. Review of Proposed Special Permits under the Schedule 13
III. The Limited Scope of Article VIII(1) of the ICRW Convention 20
IV. The Evolving Law Relating to Conservation: Interactions between Systems 25
V. The ICRW Convention as a "Living Instrument": The Evolving *Opinio Juris Communis* 27
VI. Inter-Generational Equity 41
VII. Conservation of Living Species (Marine Mammals) 48
   1. The Tension between Conservation and Exploitation: Arguments of the Parties 48
   2. Whale Stocks – Conservation and Development: Responses of the Parties and the Intervenor to Questions from the Bench 52
   3. General Assessment 57
VIII. Principle of Prevention and the Precautionary Principle: Arguments of the Parties and the Intervenor 60
IX. Responses from the Experts, and Remaining Uncertainties around "Scientific Research" (under Jarpa-II) 72
X. Reiterated Calls under the ICRW Convention for Non-Lethal Use of Cetaceans 75
XI. Concluding Observations, on Jarpa-II Programme and the Requirements of the ICRW Convention and Its Schedule 80

1. I have accompanied the Court's majority, in voting in favour of the adoption of the present Judgment in the case *Whaling in the Antarctic*. Yet, I would have wished certain points to be further developed by the Court. I feel thus obliged to leave on the records, in the present Separate Opinion, the foundations of my

personal position thereon. To this effect, I shall address the following points: (a) the object and purpose of the International Convention on the Regulation of Whaling (the teleological approach); (b) collective guarantee and collective regulation; (c) the limited scope of Article VIII(1) of the ICRW Convention; (d) the evolving law relating to conservation: interactions between systems; (e) the ICRW Convention as a "living instrument": the evolving *opinio juris communis*; (f) inter-generational equity; (g) conservation of living species (marine mammals); (h) principle of prevention and the precautionary principle; (i) remaining uncertainties around "scientific research" (under Jarpa-II programme). The way will then be paved for my concluding observations, on Jarpa-II programme and the requirements of the ICRW Convention and its Schedule.

I   The Object and Purpose of the ICRW Convention

2. I find it necessary, to start with, to dwell upon the *object and purpose* of the International Convention on Regulation of Whaling (ICRW Convention), so as to set the context for the consideration of the interpretation of Article VIII of the ICRW Convention, and of the question whether Japan complied with its obligations under the ICRW Convention and its Schedule (cf. *infra*). Both contending Parties, Australia and Japan, and the intervenor, New Zealand, have in fact dedicated some attention to the object and purpose of the ICRW Convention. The adoption of a Convention like the ICRW, endowed with a supervisory organ of its own, evidences that the goal of conservation integrates its object and purpose, certainly not limited to the development of the whaling industry.

3. To try to reduce the object and purpose of the ICRW Convention to the protection or development of the whaling industry would be at odds with the rationale and structure of the ICRW Convention as a whole. If the main goal of the ICRW Convention were only to protect and develop the whaling industry, the entire framework of the ICRW Convention would have been structured differently. Moreover, the fact that the ICRW Convention is a multilateral treaty, encompassing member States that do not practice whaling, also speaks to the understanding that the ICRW Convention's object and purpose cannot be limited to the development of the whaling industry. Furthermore, in the same line of reasoning, the adoption of a moratorium on commercial whaling within the framework of the ICRW Convention also seems to indicate that the conservation of whale stocks is an important component of the object and purpose of the ICRW Convention.

1 The Teleological Approach

4. May I turn briefly to the preamble of the ICRW Convention, which contains indications as to the object and purpose of the Convention. First, the preamble recognizes "the interest of the nations of the world in safeguarding for future generations the great natural resources represented by the whale stocks"; this seems, in my view, to be in line with the purpose of conserving and protecting whales. Secondly, other preambular paragraphs mention "regulation" of whaling to ensure conservation and development of whale stocks. Then, the preamble also posits that the States Parties "decided to conclude a convention to provide for the proper conservation of whale stocks and thus make possible the orderly development of the whaling industry".

5. It appears that the primary object and purpose of the ICRW Convention can be found in the conservation and recovery of whale populations. The ICRW Convention provides for a mechanism to ensure its own evolution in face of changing conditions and new challenges. The International Whaling Commission (IWC) has a specific role (under Article VI) to make recommendations to States Parties, in the form of resolutions, to which they are to give consideration in good faith. The practice of the IWC, conformed by its successive resolutions, seems to indicate that conservation of whale stocks is an important objective of the ICRW: for example, in a number of resolutions, the IWC has focused on non-lethal methods of research concerning whales, disclosing a concern with the conservation of whale stocks.[1] Thus, in my perception, the use of whales cannot take place to the detriment of the conservation of whale stocks.

6. The Schedule of regulations annexed to the ICRW Convention is an integral part of it, with equal legal force; amendments have regularly been made to the Schedule, so as to cope with international environmental developments. States Parties thus count on a scheme to act together in the common interest, setting a proper balance between conservation and the use of whale resources. The ICRW Convention, adopted in 1946 to stop the over-exploitation of whales, presented thus two novelties in comparison with the first treaties on whaling: the creation of the IWC (under Article III), and the inclusion of the Schedule, controlling whaling so as to achieve conservation and recovery of whale stocks. It became a multilateral scheme, seeking to avoid unilateral action so as to foster conservation.

---

[1] E.g., Resolution 2007–3 (*Resolution on the Non-Lethal Use of Cetaceans*); Resolution 2007–1 (Resolution on Jarpa).

7. The object and purpose of the ICRW Convention are to be construed in light of its text, its supervisory mechanism, and its nature as a multilateral treaty encompassing both whaling and non-whaling States. The object and purpose of the Convention point to, as a guiding principle, the conservation and recovery of whale stocks, – not to be seen on an equal footing with the sustainable development of the whaling industry or the protection of commercial whaling. A State Party – Japan or any other – cannot act unilaterally to decide whether its programme is fulfilling the object and purpose of the ICRW Convention, or the objective of conservation.

2   Response of New Zealand to Questions from the Bench

8. In this connection, in the course of the oral pleadings before the Court (on 08.07.2013), I deemed it fit to put the following questions to the intervenor, New Zealand:

> 1. In your view, does the fact that the International Convention for the Regulation of Whaling is a multilateral treaty, with a supervisory organ of its own, have an impact on the interpretation of its object and purpose?
> 2. You have stated in your Written Observations (of 4 April 2013) that the object and purpose of the International Convention for the Regulation of Whaling is: "to replace unregulated, unilateral whaling by States with collective regulation as a mechanism to provide for the interests of the parties in the proper conservation and management of whales" (p. 16, para. 33). In your view, is this a widely accepted interpretation nowadays of the object and purpose of the International Convention for the Regulation of Whaling?[2]

9. As to these questions, New Zealand at first recalled that, distinctly from the 1937 International Agreement for the Regulation of Whaling, the 1946 ICRW Convention counts on a permanent Commission (the IWC) endowed with a supervisory role, evidencing a "collective enterprise", and acknowledging that whale conservation "must be an international endeavour". In sum, in New Zealand's view, the object and purpose of the ICRW Convention ought to be approached in the light of the *collective interest* of States Parties in the conservation and management of whale stocks.[3] Secondly, New Zealand argued that the IWC had recognizedly become the appropriate organ for the conservation

---

[2] ICJ doc. CR 2013/17, of 08.07.2013, pp. 49–50.
[3] Cf. ICJ, *Responses of New Zealand to the Questions Put by Judge Cançado Trindade at the End of the Public Sitting Held on 8 July 2013*, of 12.07.2013, pp. 6–7, paras. 1–3.

and management of whales. Such role of collective regulation of the IWC, – New Zealand added, – was in the line of the U.N. Convention on the Law of the Sea, which requires States (Article 65) to cooperate with a view to the conservation of marine mammals and to work through the appropriate international organs. Such endeavours of conservation have become a "collective responsibility", and the IWC – New Zealand added – would "work co-operatively to improve the conservation and management of whale populations and stocks on a scientific basis and through agreed policy measures".[4]

II   Collective Guarantee and Collective Regulation

1   *Collective Decision-Making under the ICRW Convention*

10. The collective system established by the ICRW Convention is crucial to the understanding and proper handling of the present case of *Whaling in the Antarctic*. In my view, the system created by the Convention aims at replacing a system of unilateral unregulated whaling, with a system of collective guarantee and regulation so as to provide for the interests of the States Parties in the proper conservation and management of whales. To my mind, the structure of the Convention evidences that one of its aims is to achieve collective guarantee through collective regulation, in relation to all activities associated with whaling. This collective regulation is achieved through a process of collective decision-making by the IWC, which adopts regulations and resolutions (*supra*).

11. In addition, it may be recalled that the IWC may also adopt recommendations addressed to any or all of the States Parties on any matters which relate to whales or whaling and to the objective and purpose of the Convention. These recommendations and resolutions, in my understanding, express the collective views of the Parties under the Convention concerning the protection of their interests in the proper conservation and management of whales. Furthermore, membership of the IWC has grown along the years, with many members having no whaling industry or history of whaling activities; their common interest would arguably be the conservation and management of whales themselves, rather than solely the preservation of the whaling industry.

12. Thus, the nature and structure of the ICRW Convention, the fact that it is a multilateral Convention (comprising both whaling and non-whaling States) with a supervisory organ of its own, which adopts resolutions and

---

4   *Ibid.*, pp. 8–9, paras. 1–4.

recommendations, highlights the collective decision-making process under the Convention and the collective guarantee provided thereunder. In the light of the object and purpose of the ICRW Convention, clearly a system of collective guarantee and collective regulation operates thereunder.

2   Review of Proposed Special Permits under the Schedule

13. In fact, in numerous resolutions, the IWC has provided guidance to the Scientific Committee for its review of Special Permits under Paragraph 30 of the Schedule. This is aimed at amending proposed special permit programmes that do not meet the conditions. The expectation ensues therefrom that, e.g., non-lethal methods will be used whenever possible, on the basis of successive resolutions of the IWC stressing the relevance of obtaining scientific information without needing to kill whales for "scientific research". In accordance with the IWC resolutions, the Scientific Committee has, for its part, elaborated a series of *Guidelines* to enable it to undertake its function of review of Special Permits (under Paragraph 30 of the Schedule).

14. In the present proceedings before the ICJ, this practice has been brought to the attention of the Court, in particular by New Zealand,[5] who has further pointed out that over 25 resolutions of the IWC, issued after the Scientific Committee's review of proposed special permits (under Article VIII of the ICRW Convention), have been consistently requesting the States Parties concerned "not to proceed where the Scientific Committee had determined that the proposed activity did not satisfy the Scientific Committee's criteria".[6] Such is the case of IWC resolutions 1987–1, 1987–2, 1987–3, 1987–4, 1989–1, 1989–2, 1989–3, 1990–1, 1990–2, 1991–2, 1991–3, 1993–7, 1993–8, 1994–9, 1994–10, 1994–11, 1995–9, 1996–7, 1997–5, 1997–6, 2000–4, 2000–5, 2001–7, 2001–8, 2003–2, 2003–3, 2005–1, and 2007–1.[7] Hence, it is clear that one counts nowadays on a system of collective guarantee and collective regulation under the ICRW Convention (cf. also *infra*).

15. Bearing the IWC resolutions in mind, the Scientific Committee's Guidelines have endeavoured to assist it in undertaking adequately its function of review of special permit proposals and of research results from existing and

---

5   Both in its *Written Observations*, of 04.04.2013, and in its *oral arguments*; cf. ICJ, *Written Observations of New Zealand*, of 04.04.2013, pp. 30–33, paras. 55–60; and ICJ, doc. CR 2013/17, of 08.07.2013, pp. 30–31 and 39, paras. 50–54 and 14.
6   ICJ, *Written Observations of New Zealand*, of 04.04.2013, p. 56, para. 98.
7   *Cit. in ibid.*, p. 56, para. 98, n. 195.

completed special permits. In its most recent *Guidelines*, adopted in 2008 (Annex P), the Scientific Committee's review process focuses on, *inter alia*, the possibility of using non-lethal research methods, the aims and the methodology and the sample size, the point whether the catches will have an adverse effect on the stocks (paras. 2–3). Moreover, the proposed activity is to be subject to periodic and final reviews. It is clear that there is here not much room for State unilateral action and free-will.

16. It clearly appears, from Paragraph 30 of the Schedule,[8] that a State Party issuing a Special Permit is under the obligation to provide the IWC Secretary with proposed scientific permits *before* they are issued, and in sufficient time so as to allow the Scientific Committee to review and comment on them. Paragraph 30 of the Schedule thus plays an important role in the overall structure of the ICRW Convention and in the pursuit of the fulfilment of its object and purpose. It establishes a review procedure that must be followed in relation to the granting of special permits, and that serves as a mechanism through which the granting of special permits may be monitored by the IWC. Accordingly, States granting Special Permits do not have an unfettered freedom to issue such permits.

17. It follows therefrom that, even if the recommendations of the Scientific Committee and the IWC are not *per se* legally binding on States, States willing to issue Special Permits should consider the comments of the IWC and the recommendations of the Scientific Committee in good faith (principle of *bona fides*). The terms of Paragraph 30 make it clear that the particular duty to provide proposed Special Permits in advance to the IWC is set forth so as to enable the Scientific Committee to "review and comment" on them. It seems that, if States were to decide, at their free will, whether or not to take into account the comments and recommendations of the IWC and the Scientific

---

8   Paragraph 30 of the Schedule states that a State Party shall provide the IWC Secretary with proposed scientific permits "before they are issued and in sufficient time to allow the Scientific Committee to review and comment on them". The proposed permits should specify: "(a) objectives of the research; (b) number, sex, size and stock of the animals to be taken; (c) opportunities for participation in the research by scientists of other nations; and (d) possible effect on conservation of stock". Paragraph 30 adds that proposed permits "shall be reviewed and commented on by the Scientific Committee at Annual Meetings when possible. When permits would be granted prior to the next Annual Meeting, the Secretary shall send the proposed permits to members of the Scientific Committee by mail for their comment and review. Preliminary results of any research resulting from the permits should be made available at the next Annual Meeting of the Scientific Committee".

Committee, that provision would be rendered meaningless, dead letter; the review procedure would then become a sort of unacceptable "rubber stamp" mechanism, whereby States issuing permits would be able to disregard completely the comments and recommendations whenever they wished.

18. Paragraph 30 thus creates a *positive* (procedural) obligation[9] of the State willing to issue a special permit to cooperate with the IWC and the Scientific Committee. It would seem inconsistent with the purpose of Paragraph 30 if a State Party would feel entitled to issue a special permit without having cooperated with the IWC and the Scientific Committee, or without having given any consideration whatsoever to the views of other States Parties expressed through the comments of the IWC and the recommendations of the Scientific Committee.

19. In its 2006 *Report* (p. 50), the Scientific Committee was of the view that the Jarpa-II proposed programme provided the specifications required by Paragraph 30 of the Schedule. One has here, as already indicated, a system of collective guarantee and collective regulation under the ICRW Convention. In the framework of this latter, the Court has determined, on distinct points, that the respondent State has not acted in conformity with Paragraph 10(d) and (e), and Paragraph 7(b), of the Schedule[10] to the ICRW Convention (resolutory points 3–5).

III   The Limited Scope of Article VIII(1) of the ICRW Convention

20. Keeping the review system in mind, and given the arguments of the contending Parties and of the intervenor as to the scope of Article VIII[11] within

---

[9]   On the conceptualization of positive obligations in a distinct context, cf., e.g., D. Xenos, *The Positive Obligations of the State under the European Convention of Human Rights*, London/N.Y., Routledge, 2012, pp. 57–141.

[10] Paragraph 10(d) of the Schedule establishes a moratorium on the taking, killing or treating of (sperm, killer and baleen) whales, except minke whales, by factory ships or whale catchers attached to factory ships. And paragraph 10(e) provides in addition for a "comprehensive assessment" of the effects of catches on whale stocks and the establishment of new catch limits. And paragraph 7(b) of the Schedule prohibits commercial whaling in the Southern Ocean Sanctuary (a prohibition to be reviewed every ten years).

[11] Article VIII(1) of the ICRW Convention reads as follows:
      "Notwithstanding anything contained in this Convention any Contracting Government may grant to any of its nationals a special permit authorizing that national to kill, take and treat whales for purposes of scientific research subject to such restrictions as to

the ICRW Convention as a whole, a point to be addressed is that of the requirements for a whaling programme to be considered "for purposes of scientific research". The key point seems to be whether a whaling programme carried out under a Special Permit must be exclusively for scientific research and not for any other purpose. In other words, the question is whether the same programme may be carried out under a Special Permit for the purpose of "scientific research" and, e.g., for purpose of selling the whale meat.

21. In my understanding, Article VIII(1) of the ICRW Convention is not to be interpreted broadly, so as to go against the object and purpose of the normative framework of the Convention as a whole. Article VIII(1) appears as an *exception* to the normative framework of the ICRW Convention, to be thus interpreted restrictively. The purpose, in particular, of granting Special Permits, is, to my mind, to allow for scientific research to be undertaken; other purposes do not seem to be allowed under Article VIII, and should not fall under the exception of Article VIII(1), which, in my understanding, applies solely and specifically to scientific research programmes. If a programme with multiple purposes (including a "scientific research" purpose) could be qualified for a Special Permit under Article VIII(1), the provision would not have been drafted in the way it was. Article VIII(1) is phrased in terms ("for purposes of") which seem to make it clear that the sole purpose for which a Special Permit shall be granted is the conduct of scientific research. Otherwise, it could be expected that the expression "or other purposes" would also have been included.

22. The Court has determined that the Special Permits granted by Japan in connection with Jarpa-II "do not fall within the provisions of Article VIII(1)" of the ICRW Convention (resolutory point 2). As to whether a State issuing a Special Permit under Article VIII(1) has the discretion to determine whether a whaling programme is "for purposes of scientific research", such question can only be properly considered within the whole framework of the ICRW Convention as a multilateral treaty, nowadays endowed with a supervisory mechanism of its own. Accordingly, a State issuing a permit does not have *carte blanche* to dictate that a given programme is "for purposes of scientific research". It is not

---

number and subject to such other conditions as the Contracting Government thinks fit, and the killing, taking, and treating of whales in accordance with the provisions of this Article shall be exempt from the operation of this Convention. Each Contracting Government shall report at once to the Commission all such authorizations which it has granted. Each Contracting Government may at any time revoke any such special permit which it has granted."

sufficient for a State Party to describe its whaling programme as "for purposes of scientific research", without demonstrating it.

23. In my view, such an unfettered discretion would not be in line with the object and purpose of the ICRW Convention, nor with the idea of multilateral regulation. The State issuing a Special Permit should take into consideration the resolutions of the IWC which provide the views of other States Parties as to what constitutes "scientific research". There is no point in seeking to define "scientific research" for all purposes. When deciding whether a programme is "for purposes of scientific research" so as to issue a special permit under Article VIII(1), the State Party concerned has, in my understanding, a duty to abide by the principle of prevention and the precautionary principle (cf. *infra*).

24. In my perception, Article VIII, part and parcel of the ICRW Convention as a whole, is to be interpreted taking into account its object and purpose. This discards any pretence of devising in it a so-called "self-contained" regime or system, which would go unduly against the ICRW Convention's object and purpose. In sum, in my understanding, in line with the object and purpose of the ICRW Convention (*supra*), a State Party does not have an unfettered discretion to decide the meaning of "scientific research" and whether a given whaling programme is "for purposes of scientific research". The interpretation and application of the ICRW Convention in recent decades bear witness of a gradual move away from unilateralism and towards multilateral conservation of living marine resources, thus clarifying the limited scope of Article VIII(1) of the ICRW Convention.

IV The Evolving Law Relating to Conservation: Interactions between Systems

25. With the growth in recent decades of international instruments related to conservation, not one single of them is approached in isolation from the others: not surprisingly, the co-existence of international treaties of the kind has called for a *systemic outlook*, which has been pursued in recent years. Reference can here be made, e.g., to the 1973 Convention on International Trade in Endangered Species of Wild Fauna and Flora (CITES Convention), the 1979 Convention on Migratory Species of Wild Animals, the 1980 Convention on the Conservation of Antarctic Marine Living Resources, the 1982 U.N. Convention on the Law of the Sea, the 1992 U.N. Convention on Biological Diversity (CBD Convention).

26. The systemic outlook seems to be flourishing in recent years. For example, at its fifth meeting, in 2000, the Conference of States Parties to the CBD Convention referred to "the interactions between climate change and the conservation and sustainable use of biological diversity in a number of thematic and cross-cutting areas", including, *inter alia*, marine and coastal biodiversity.[12] As for the ICRW Convention, the most complete academic work produced to date, on its legal regime, that of Patricia Birnie, supports the teleological interpretation of the ICRW Convention, stressing the growing importance of *conservation* in the evolving interpretation and application of the ICRW Convention; she further points out that related treaties (e.g., the CITES Convention) have helped to identify the wide range of matters of concern to the international community as a whole, such as, e.g., *inter alia*, the protection of wild fauna and flora.[13]

V   The ICRW Convention as a "Living Instrument": The Evolving *Opinio Juris Communis*

27. The interpretation and application of the aforementioned treaties, in the light of the systemic outlook, have been contributing to the gradual formation of an *opinio juris communis* in the present domain of contemporary international law. The present Judgment of the ICJ in the *Whaling in the Antarctic* case has recalled the establishment, in 1950, by the IWC, of the Scientific Committee to assist it in discharging its functions; as from the mid-eighties, the Scientific Committee has conducted its review of Special Permits on the basis of *Guidelines*, issued or endorsed by the IWC (para. 47). Moreover, the IWC is entitled to adopt *recommendations* (under Article VI of the ICRW Convention), which may be relevant (when adopted by consensus or unanimity) for the interpretation of the Convention or its Schedule (para. 46). As the ICJ itself has put it, the functions conferred upon the IWC "have made the Convention an evolving instrument" (para. 45).

---

12   CBD, *Scientific Assessments – Note by the Executive Secretary*, doc. UNEP/CBD/SBSTTA/10/7, of 05.11.2004, p. 8, para. 29.

13   P. Birnie, *International Regulation of Whaling: From Conservation of Whaling to Conservation of Whales and Regulation of Whale-Watching*, vol. II, N.Y./London/Rome, Oceana Publs., 1985, pp. 583 and 635. She further singles out the continuing work of the IWC, with several resolutions addressing "a wide variety of new issues", such as, *inter alia*, criteria for aboriginal subsistence whaling, small cetaceans, creation of sanctuary areas, preservation of habitats, "humane killing", discouragement of whaling, among others; cf. *ibid.*, vol. II, p. 641.

28. The present Judgment of the ICJ proceeds to assert that States Parties to the ICRW Convention "have a duty to co-operate with the IWC and the Scientific Committee" and to "give due regard to recommendations calling for an assessment of the feasibility of non-lethal" research methods (para. 83). In this respect, it further recalls, *inter alia*, that "the two experts called by Australia referred to significant advances in a wide range of non-lethal research techniques over the past 20 years" (para. 137). The Judgment the Court has just adopted today, 31.03.2014, is likely to be of importance to the future of the IWC, and to secure the survival of the ICRW Convention itself, as a "living instrument" capable of keeping on responding to needs of the international community and new challenges that it faces nowadays in the present domain.

29. This is not the first time that the Court acknowledges that international treaties and conventions are "living instruments". In its *célèbre* Advisory Opinion (of 21.06.1971) on *Namibia*, for example, the ICJ referring to the mandates system of the League of Nations era, stated that

> the concepts embodied in Article 22 of the Covenant (...) were not static, but were by definition evolutionary (...). [V]iewing the institutions of 1919, the Court must take into consideration the changes which have occurred in the supervening half-century, and its interpretation cannot remain unaffected by the subsequent development of law, through the Charter of the United Nations or by way of customary law. Moreover, an international instrument has to be interpreted and applied within the framework of the entire legal system prevailing at the time of its interpretation. In the domain to which the present proceedings relate, the last fifty years, as indicated above, have brought important developments. (...) In this domain, as elsewhere, the *corpus juris gentium* has been considerably enriched, and this the Court, if it is faithfully to discharge its functions, may not ignore (para. 53).

30. Subsequently, in its Judgment (of 25.09.1997) in the case concerning the *Gabčíkovo-Nagymaros Project* (Hungary *versus* Slovakia), the ICJ pondered that "newly developed norms of environmental law are relevant for the implementation of the [1977] Treaty" in force between Hungary and Slovakia, that was the object of the dispute. The Court proceeded that the contending Parties are required, "in carrying out their obligations to ensure that the quality of water in the Danube is not impaired and that nature is protected, to take new environmental norms into consideration". Accordingly, – the Court added, – the

1977 Treaty "is not static, and is open to adapt to emerging norms of international law" (para. 112).

31. Other contemporary international tribunals have pursued the same evolutionary interpretation. For example, the European Court of Human Rights, in its Judgment (of 25.04.1978) in the *Tyrer versus United Kingdom* case, asserted that the European Convention on Human Rights "is a living instrument", to be "interpreted in the light of present-day conditions" (para. 31). Subsequently, the European Court reiterated, *expressis verbis*, this *obitur dictum*, in its Judgment (on preliminary objections, of 23.03.1995) in the case of *Loizidou versus Turkey*, wherein it added that, accordingly, the provisions of the European Convention, as a "living instrument",

> cannot be interpreted solely in accordance with the intentions of their authors as expressed more than forty years ago. (...)
>
> In addition, the object and purpose of the Convention as an instrument for the protection of individual human beings requires that its provisions be interpreted and applied so as to make its safeguards practical and effective (paras. 71–72).

32. Likewise, the Inter-American Court of Human Rights, in its Judgment (of 31.08.2001) in the case of the *Mayagna (Sumo) Awas Tingni Community versus Nicaragua*, stated that "human rights treaties are living instruments, the interpretation of which ought to adapt to the evolution of times, and, in particular, to current living conditions" (para. 146). In the same line of thinking, in its earlier Advisory Opinion (of 01.10.1999) on *The Right to Information on Consular Assistance in the Framework of the Guarantees of the Due Process of Law*, the Inter-American Court observed that the International Law of Human Rights

> has much advanced by means of the evolutionary interpretation of the international instruments of protection. Such evolutive interpretation is in conformity with the general rules of interpretation of treaties set forth in the Vienna Convention of 1969. (...) [H]uman rights treaties are living instruments, the interpretation of which has to follow the evolution of times and current living conditions (para. 114).

33. The experience of supervisory organs of various international treaties and conventions points to this direction as well. Not seldom they have been faced with new challenges, requiring new responses from them, which could never

have been anticipated, not even imagined, by the draftsmen of the respective treaties and conventions. In sum, international treaties and conventions are a product of their time, being also *living instruments*. They evolve with time; otherwise, they fall into *desuetude*. The ICRW Convention is no exception to that. Those treaties are endowed with supervisory organs of their own (like the ICRW Convention) disclose more aptitude to face changing circumstances.

34. Moreover, in distinct domains of international law, treaties endowed with a supervisory mechanism of their own have pursued a hermeneutics of their own,[14] facing the corresponding treaties and conventions as *living instruments*. International treaties and conventions are products of their time, and their interpretation and application *in time*, with a temporal dimension, bears witness that they are indeed living instruments. This happens not only in the present domain of conservation and management of living marine resources, but likewise in other areas of international law.[15]

35. By the time of the adoption of the 1946 ICRW Convention, in the mid-xxth century, there did not yet exist an awareness that the living marine resources were not inexhaustible. Three and a half decades later, the adoption of the 1982 U.N. Convention on the Law of the Sea (UNCLOS) – a major international law achievement in the xxth century – contributed to the public order of the oceans, and to the growing awareness that their living resources were not inexhaustible. Unilateralism gradually yielded to collective regulation towards conservation. An example to this effect is provided, under the 1946 ICRW Convention, by the 1982 general moratorium on commercial whaling.

36. Another example can be found in the establishment by the IWC of whale sanctuaries (under Article V(1) of the ICRW Convention) (*infra*). The IWC has so far adopted three whale sanctuaries: first, the Southern Ocean Sanctuary (1948–1955); secondly, the Indian Ocean Sanctuary (1979, renewed in 1989, and indefinitely as from 1992); thirdly, the new Southern Ocean Sanctuary (from 1994 onwards). Moreover, in its meetings of 2001–2004, the IWC was lodged

---

14 Cf., for example, in the domain of the international protection of the rights of the human person, e.g., A.A. Cançado Trindade, *Tratado de Direito Internacional dos Direitos Humanos*, vol. II, Porto Alegre/Brazil, S.A. Fabris Ed., 1999, Ch. XI, pp. 23–200.

15 Cf. A.A. Cançado Trindade, *International Law for Humankind – Towards a New Jus Gentium*, 2nd. rev. ed., Leiden/The Hague, Nijhoff, 2013, ch. II ("Time and Law Revisited: International Law and the Temporal Dimension"), pp. 31–51.

with a proposal (revised in 2005) of a new sanctuary, the South Atlantic Sanctuary,[16] so as to reassert the need of conservation of whales.

37. Along the last three decades, the IWC has repeatedly made clear that lethal research methods are not in line with the aforementioned moratorium. In its *Resolution 2003–2*, for example, the IWC calls for a limitation of "scientific research" to "non-lethal methods only", and expresses its opposition to commercial whaling, "contrary to the spirit of the moratorium", and presents an annotated compilation of its "Conservation Work", with a systematization of resolutions to this effect (Annexes I–II). It is nowadays reckoned that States Parties to the ICRW Convention that wish to issue special permits are bound to cooperate with the IWC and the Scientific Committee, and to give consideration to the views of other States Parties expressed through the comments of the IWC and the recommendations of the Scientific Committee.

38. Parallel to this, multilateral Conventions (such as UNCLOS and CBD) have established a framework for the conservation and management of living marine resources. The UNCLOS Convention contains a series of provisions to that effect.[17] As to the CBD Convention, the Conference of the Parties held in Jakarta in 1995, for example, adopted the *Jakarta Mandate on Coastal and Marine Biodiversity*, reasserting the relevance of conservation and ecologically sustainable use of coastal and marine biodiversity, and, in particular, linking conservation, sustainable use of biodiversity, and fishing activities.

39. Furthermore, in its meeting of 2002, the States Parties to the Convention on Migratory Species (CMS) pointed out the need to give greater protection to six species of whales (including the Antarctic minke whales) and their habitats, breeding grounds and migratory routes. These are clear illustrations of the evolving *opinio juris communis* on the matter. In its 2010 meeting, held in Agadir, Morocco, the "Buenos Aires Group"[18] reiterated support for the creation of a new South Atlantic Sanctuary for whales, and positioned itself in favour of conservation and non-lethal use of whales,[19] and against so-called "scientific whaling" (in particular in case of endangered or severely depleted species).

---

16   Propounded mainly by Brazil, Argentina, South Africa and Uruguay in the ambit of the IWC. On the proposal, cf. Chair's Report of the 57th Annual Meeting of the International Whaling Commission, pp. 33–34.
17   Such as Articles 61, 64–67, 192, 194 and 204(2).
18   Formed by Argentina, Brazil, Chile, Colombia, Costa Rica, Dominican Republic, Ecuador, Mexico, Panama, Peru and Uruguay.
19   Cf. Chair's Report of the 62nd Annual Meeting of the International Whaling Commission, pp. 7–8.

40. The "Buenos Aires Group" stressed the needed implementation of the moratorium, and recalled the achievements of the IWC since the early eighties. It further called for a reform of Articles V (whaling under objection) and VIII (scientific whaling) of the ICRW Convention, so that their interpretation and application do not go against the principle of conservation of whales underlying the Convention. More recently, on 04.02.2013, the same "Buenos Aires Group" expressed its "strongest rejection" of the ongoing whale hunting (including species classified as endangered) in the Southern Ocean Sanctuary (para. 1), with catches pointing to "an operation of a commercial nature which lacks any scientific justification" (para. 2). After calling for non-lethal methods and "the maintenance of the commercial moratorium in place since 1986", the "Buenos Aires Group" stated that the ongoing whale hunting was in breach of "the spirit and the text" of the 1946 ICRW Convention, and failed to respect "the integrity of the whale sanctuaries recognized by the IWC" (paras. 3–4).

VI   Inter-Generational Equity

41. The 1946 ICRW Convention was indeed pioneering, in acknowledging, in its preamble, "the interest of the nations of the world in safeguarding for future generations the great natural resources represented by the whale stocks". At that time, shortly after the II world war, its draftsmen could hardly have anticipated that this concern would achieve the dimension it did, in the international agenda and in international law-making (in particular in the domain of international environmental law) in the decades that followed. The long-term temporal dimension, underlying the inter-generational equity, was properly acknowledged. And the conceptual construction of *inter-generational equity* (in the process of which I had the privilege to take part) was to take place, in international legal doctrine, four decades later, from the mid-eighties onwards.

42. Within this Court, I had in fact the occasion to address the long-term temporal dimension, in relation to *inter-generational equity*, in my Separate Opinion in the case of the *Pulp Mills on the River Uruguay* (Argentina *versus* Uruguay, Judgment of 20.04.2010). I pondered therein that

> (…) The long-term temporal dimension marks its presence, in a notorious way, in the domain of environmental protection. The concern for the prevalence of the element of *conservation* (over the simple exploitation of natural resources) reflects a cultural manifestation of the integration of the human being with nature and the world wherein he or she lives. Such understanding is, in my view, projected both in space and in time,

as human beings relate themselves, in the space, with the natural system of which they form part (and ought to treat with diligence and care), and, in time, with other generations (past and future),[20] in respect of which they have obligations. (...)

In fact, concern with future generations underlies some environmental law conventions.[21] In addition, in the same line of reasoning, the 1997 UNESCO Declaration on the Responsibilities of the Present Generations Towards Future Generations, after invoking, *inter alia*, the 1948 Universal Declaration of Human Rights and the two 1966 U.N. Covenants on Human Rights, recalls the responsibilities of the present generations to ensure that "the needs and interests of present and future generations are fully safeguarded" (Article 1, and preamble). The 1997 Declaration added, *inter alia*, that "the present generations should strive to ensure the maintenance and perpetuation of humankind with due respect for the dignity of the human person" (Article 3). Almost two decades earlier, the U.N. General Assembly adopted, on 30.10.1980, its resolution proclaiming "the historical responsibility of States for the preservation of nature for present and future generations" (para. 1); it further called upon States, in "the interests of present and future generations", to take "measures (...) necessary for preserving nature" (para. 3). (...).

May I recall that the subject at issue was originally taken up by the Advisory Committee to the United Nations University on a project on the matter, in early 1988, so as to provide an innovative response to rising

---

20 Future generations promptly began to attract the attention of the contemporary doctrine of international law: cf., e.g., A.-Ch. Kiss, "La notion de patrimoine commun de l'humanité", 175 *Recueil des Cours de l'Académie de Droit International de La Haye* (1982) pp. 109–253; E. Brown Weiss, *In Fairness to Future Generations: International Law, Common Patrimony and Intergenerational Equity*, Tokyo/Dobbs Ferry N.Y., United Nations University/Transnational Publs., 1989, pp. 1–351; A.-Ch. Kiss, "The Rights and Interests of Future Generations and the Precautionary Principle", *in The Precautionary Principle and International Law – The Challenge of Implementation* (eds. D. Freestone and E. Hey), The Hague, Kluwer, 1996, pp. 19–28; [Various Authors,] *Future Generations and International Law* (eds. E. Agius and S. Busuttil *et alii*), London, Earthscan, 1998, pp. 3–197; [Various Authors,] *Human Rights: New Dimensions and Challenges* (ed. J. Symonides), Paris/Aldershot, UNESCO/Dartmouth, 1998, pp. 1–153; [Various Authors,] *Handbook of Intergenerational Justice* (ed. J.C. Tremmel), Cheltenham, E. Elgar Publ., 2006, pp. 23–332.

21 E.g., the 1992 U.N. Framework Convention on Climate Change, the 1997 Kyoto Protocol to the U.N. Framework Convention on Climate Change, the 1985 Vienna Convention for the Protection of the Ozone Layer, the 1987 Montreal Protocol on Substances that Deplete the Ozone Layer, among others.

and growing concerns over the depletion of natural resources and the degradation of environmental quality and the recognition of the need to conserve the natural and cultural heritage (at all levels, national, regional and international; and governmental as well as non-governmental). The Advisory Committee, composed of Professors from distinct continents,[22] met in Goa, India,[23] and issued, on 15 February 1988, a final document titled "*Goa Guidelines on Intergenerational Equity*",[24] which stated:

> Th[e] temporal dimension is articulated through the formulation of the theory of "intergenerational equity"; all members of each generation of human beings, as a species, inherit a natural and cultural patrimony from past generations, both as beneficiaries and as custodians under the duty to pass on this heritage to future generations. As a central point of this theory the right of each generation to benefit from this natural and cultural heritage is inseparably coupled with the obligation to use this heritage in such a manner that it can be passed on to future generations in no worse condition that it was received from past generations. This requires conservation and, as appropriate, enhancement of the quality and of the diversity of this heritage. The conservation of cultural diversity is as important as the conservation of environmental diversity to ensure options for future generations.
>
> Specifically, the principle of intergenerational equity requires conserving the diversity and the quality of biological resources (...).
>
> (...) The principles of equity governing the relationship between generations (...) pertain to valued interests of past, present and future generations, covering natural and cultural resources. (...) There is a complementarity between recognized human rights and the proposed intergenerational rights. (...).[25]

---

[22] Namely, Professors E. Brown Weiss, A.A. Cançado Trindade, A.-Ch. Kiss, R.S. Pathak, Lai Peng Cheng, and E.W. Ploman.

[23] In the meeting held in Goa, India, convened by the United Nations University (U.N.U.), the members of the U.N.U. Advisory Committee acted in their own personal capacity.

[24] These Guidelines, adopted on 15 February 1988, were the outcome of prolonged discussions, which formed part of a major study sponsored by the U.N.U. It is not my intention to recall, in the present Separate Opinion, the points raised in those discussions, annotated in the unpublished U.N.U. *dossiers* and working documents, on file with me since February 1988.

[25] The full text of the "*Goa Guidelines on Intergenerational Equity*" is reproduced in Annexes to the two following books, whose authors participated in the elaboration of the document: E. Brown Weiss, *In Fairness to Future Generations: International Law, Common Patrimony and Intergenerational Equity*, op. cit. supra n. (12), Appendix A, pp. 293-295;

And the aforementioned U.N.U. document moved on to propose strategies to implement inter-generational rights and obligations. From then onwards, the first studies on this specific topic of inter-generational equity, in the framework of the conceptual universe of International Environmental Law, began to flourish.²⁶ From the late eighties onwards, inter-generational equity has been articulated amidst the growing awareness of the vulnerability of the environment, of the threat and gravity of sudden and global changes, and, ultimately, of one's own mortality.²⁷

43. Inter-generational equity comes again to the fore in the present case of *Whaling in the Antarctic*. The factual context of the *cas d'espèce* is of course quite distinct from that of the *Pulp Mills* case; yet, significantly, in one and the other, *inter-generational equity* (with its long-term temporal dimension) marks its presence. It does so in distinct international instruments of international environmental law, and in its domain as a whole. And this cannot pass unnoticed here.

44. In this respect, the 1973 CITES Convention, e.g., states in its preamble that wild fauna and flora "must be protected for this and the generations to come", and adds that "peoples and States are and should be the best protectors of their own wild fauna and flora". The CITES Convention provides for control of trade, and prevention or restriction of exploitation of species (Article II). The 1979 Convention on the Conservation of Migratory Species of Wild Animals asserts in its preamble the awareness that each generation "holds the resources of the earth for future generations and has an obligation to ensure that this legacy is conserved and, where utilized, is used wisely". Furthermore, it recognizes in the preamble that "wild animals in their innumerable forms are an irreplaceable part of the earth's natural system which must be conserved for the good of mankind".

45. The 1992 CBD Convention expresses, in its preamble, the determination "to conserve and sustainably use biological diversity for the benefit of present and future generations". It further assert in its preamble that "the conservation of biological diversity is a common concern of humankind", and calls for "the conservation of biological diversity and the sustainable use of its components", also to "contribute to peace for humankind". In its operative part, the CBD

A.A. Cançado Trindade, *Direitos Humanos e Meio Ambiente: Paralelo dos Sistemas de Proteção Internacional*, Porto Alegre/Brazil, S.A. Fabris Ed., 1993, Annex IX, pp. 296–298.

26 Cf., *inter alia*, note (18), *supra*.
27 Paragraphs 114, 118, 120 and 121 of my aforementioned Separate Opinion.

Convention then proceeds, in detail, to provide for conservation of biological diversity and its sustainable use (Articles 1, 6–10, 11–13, and 17–18).

46. In the course of a meeting of a UNEP Group of Legal Experts, – of which I keep a good memory, – which took place in Malta, before the holding of the 1992 UNCED Conference in Rio de Janeiro, – in the period of the *travaux préparatoires* of the CBD Convention, – the need was stressed of relating "preventive with corrective measures", with preventive measures seeming "to lend themselves more easily to an inter-generational perspective".[28] The Group of Legal Experts then identified "the constitutive elements" of common concern of humankind, namely: "involvement of all countries, all societies, and all classes of people within countries and societies; long-term temporal dimension, encompassing present as well as future generations; and some sort of sharing of burdens of environmental protection".[29]

47. In effect, inter-generational equity marks presence nowadays in a wide range of instruments of international environmental law, and indeed of contemporary public international law. It goes beyond the scope of the present Separate Opinion to dwell extensively upon them. Suffice it here to refer to yet another illustration. The 2001 UNESCO Universal Declaration on Cultural Diversity, e.g., after expressing, in its preamble, the aspiration to "greater solidarity" on the basis of "recognition of cultural diversity, of awareness of the unity of humankind, and of the development of intercultural exchanges", adds, in Article 1, that "cultural diversity is as necessary for humankind as biodiversity is for nature"; in this sense, "it is the common heritage of humanity and should be recognized and affirmed for the benefit of present and future generations".

VII Conservation of Living Species (Marine Mammals)

1 *The Tension between Conservation and Exploitation: Arguments of the Parties*

48. In the course of the proceedings (written phase) of the present case *Whaling in the Antarctic*, both Australia and Japan referred, in distinct terms to the

---

28 UNEP, "Report on the Proceedings of the Meeting Prepared by the *Co-Rapporteurs*, Prof. A.A. Cançado Trindade and Prof. D.J. Attard", *in The Meeting of the Group of Legal Experts to Examine the Concept of the Common Concern of Mankind in Relation to Global Environmental Issues* (ed. D.J. Attard – Malta, University of Malta, 13-15.12.1990), Nairobi, UNEP, 1991, p. 22, para. 6.

29 *Ibid.* p. 21, para. 4.

conservation of marine mammals. To start with, Australia's *Memorial* devoted some attention to the development, from the mid-seventies onwards, of a treaty-based regime for the conservation of marine mammals. It observed that, from then onwards, "the international community has adopted an increasingly conservation-oriented approach in the development of treaty regimes, including those covering marine mammals" (para. 4.84). This, in its view, has led to "significant developments in the law relating to conservation" (para. 4.85).

49. In Australia's view, those international instruments recognise "the intrinsic value" of all living species, and "the importance of conservation of migratory species and biological diversity as common concerns of mankind". They are directly relevant to the conservation and management of whales, and support an interpretation of Article VIII of the ICRW Convention that "contributes to, rather than undermines, the conservation of whales" (para. 4.86). Australia then advances "a restrictive interpretation of the Article VIII exception, and a stringent limitation on the use of lethal methods of scientific research if non-lethal means are available" (para. 4.86). Australia further refers to the recognition of the "precautionary approach" in several "international environmental agreements, concerning both broader environmental matters, and, more particularly, the conservation and protection of marine mammals" (para. 4.89).

50. For its part, Japan, in its *Counter-Memorial*, argued that, in its view, there is "no contradiction" between the conservation and the exploitation of whales, not even under the ICRW Convention (para. 6.15). In the same line of thinking, – Japan added, – the U.N. Convention on Biological Diversity (CBD) "permits the use of biological resources" in a manner that avoids or minimizes "adverse impacts" on biological diversity (para. 6.17). In Japan's view, the term "use" includes "both commercial exploitation and use for the purposes of scientific research" (para. 6.18). Japan then recalled that the concept of "sustainable use" has been further developed by the Conference of the States Parties to the CBD, which, in 2004, adopted the *Addis Ababa Principles and Guidelines on the Sustainable Use of Biodiversity*, recognizing that:

> Sustainable use is a valuable tool to promote conservation of biological diversity, since in many instances it provides incentives for conservation and restoration because of social, cultural and economic benefits that people derive from that use. In turn, sustainable use cannot be achieved without effective conservation measures. In this context, and as recognized in the Plan of Implementation of the World Summit on Sustainable Development, sustainable use is an effective tool to combat poverty, and consequently, to achieve sustainable development (*cit. in* para. 6.19).

51. Japan further argued that the policy of "combination of conservation and sustainable use" under the CBD has been a "matter of practical necessity", and "what types and levels of utilization are sustainable will depend on the status of the species and the demands upon it at any particular time" (para. 6.20). As the "level of exploitation" would depend on "the conservation status of the species in question", – Japan added, – it followed that "the measures adopted to promote sustainable use of biological resources should be adjusted according to the information available about a species, bearing in mind the precautionary approach" (para. 6.22).

2 Whale Stocks – Conservation and Development: Responses of the Parties and the Intervenor to Questions from the Bench

52. There has been growing awareness in recent years that the ICRW Convention does not allow the use of whales to take place to the detriment of the conservation of whale stocks. The general membership of the ICRW Convention (encompassing both whaling and non-whaling States) has been attentive to the growing emphasis on conservation, with more protective measures (by the IWC), and the gradual crystallization of the precautionary principle (cf. *infra*). In the present case of *Whaling in the Antarctic*, in the course of the oral pleadings before the Court (on 08.07.2013), I deemed it fit to put the following questions to Japan, Australia and New Zealand together:

> 1. How do you interpret the terms "conservation and development" of whale stocks under the International Convention for the Regulation of Whaling?
> 2. In your view, can a programme that utilizes lethal methods be considered "scientific research", in line with the object and purpose of the International Convention for the Regulation of Whaling?[30]

And then, I addressed the following additional questions only to Japan:

> 1. To what extent would the use of alternative non-lethal methods affect the objectives of the JARPA-II programme?
> 2. What would happen to whale stocks if many, or even all States Parties to the International Convention for the Regulation of Whaling, decide to undertake "scientific research" using lethal methods, upon their own initiative, similarly to the *modus operandi* of JARPA-II?[31]

---

30   ICJ, doc. CR 2013/17, of 08.07.2013, p. 49.
31   ICJ, doc. CR 2013/17, of 08.07.2013, p. 49.

53. The questions I put to Australia, Japan and New Zealand together pertained to the interpretation of the terms "conservation and development" of whale stocks under the ICRW, and to the methods to be used in "scientific research" in the light of the object and purpose of the ICRW Convention. In its answer, Australia drew attention to quotas for "aboriginal subsistence whaling", and to measures for purposes other than consumption (e.g., whale watching).[32] For its part, Japan referred to the co-existence between "conservationist measures" (e.g., moratorium and sanctuaries) and "scientific whaling" under Article VIII of the ICRW Convention.[33]

54. In its response, the intervenor, New Zealand, warned against the excesses of commercial whaling (also referring to the sustainable use of whale stocks), invoking the preamble of the ICRW Convention's provision, to the effect that whale capture cannot endanger those "natural resources". New Zealand further referred to the duty of cooperation and "the needs of conservation for the benefit of all". Invoking the precautionary approach, New Zealand ascribed a limited role to Article VIII for the conduct of scientific research, adding that lethal methods could only be used when they created no risk of an adverse effect on the whales stock.[34]

55. As to one of the questions I addressed to Japan, pertaining to the objectives of a programme (*supra*), the argument advanced by Japan was that the research objectives (of Jarpa-II) dictated the methods, and not *vice-versa*. If certain data could only be collected by using lethal methods, in its view there would be no alternative non-lethal methods. Japan then added that there were limitations to the use of non-lethal methods of biopsy sampling and satellite tagging.[35]

56. Australia retorted that the objectives of Jarpa-II were, in its view, rather vague and general, and seemed to have been adopted and applied so as to allow the killing of whales; thus, the methods (of Jarpa-II) dictated the objectives, and not *vice-versa*. After criticizing the stated objectives of Jarpa-II, Australia advocated the use of non-lethal methods under that programme. And it added that, if many of the States Parties to the ICRW Convention felt entirely free, – as Japan does, – to decide for itself to issue Special Permits under Article

---

32   ICJ, doc. CR 2013/19, of 10.07.2013, p. 54, para. 79.
33   ICJ, doc. CR 2013/21, of 15.07.2013, pp. 40–41, paras. 20–21.
34   ICJ, *Responses of New Zealand...*, op. cit. supra n. (3), pp. 4–5, paras. 1–4.
35   ICJ, doc. CR 2013/22, of 15.07.2013, p. 48, para. 20.

VIII for the taking of any number of whales, this would certainly have adverse effects on the fin, humpback and other whale stocks.[36] Australia expressed its concern that, as the situation stands at present, "an unknown and indefinite number of whales will be taken under Jarpa-II".[37]

3 General Assessment

57. It has been made clear, in recent decades, that the international community has adopted a conservation-oriented approach in treaty regimes, including treaties covering marine mammals. The ICRW Convention is to be properly interpreted in this context; it does not stand alone as a single international Convention aimed at conservation and management of marine mammals. The ICRW Convention is part of a plethora of international instruments adopted in recent years, aiming at conservation with a precautionary approach. Amongst these instruments stands the U.N. Convention on Biological Diversity (CBD), adopted at the U.N. Conference on Environment and Development (UNCED), in Rio de Janeiro, on 05.06.1992, which can here be recalled as an international instrument aiming at conservation of living species.

58. The CBD is directly pertinent to conservation and management of whales. For example, in its preamble, it asserts *inter alia* its determination "to conserve and sustainably use biological diversity for the benefit of present and future generations". In this respect, the ICRW Convention should be read in the light of other international instruments that follow a conservation-oriented approach and the precautionary principle. The existence of the ICRW Convention in relation to Conventions aimed at conservation of living resources supports a narrow interpretation of Article VIII of the ICRW Convention.

59. Accordingly, Article VIII(1), as already pointed out, cannot be broadly interpreted, and cannot at all be taken as a so-called "self-contained" regime or system. It is not a free-standing platform, not a *carte blanche* given to States to do as they freely wish. It is part and parcel of a system of collective guarantee and collective regulation oriented towards the conservation of living species. Thus, Article VIII(1) can only be interpreted in a restrictive way; all States Parties to the ICRW Convention have recognizedly a common interest in the conservation and in the long-term future of whale stocks.

---

36 ICJ, *Written Comments of Australia on Japan's Responses to Questions Put by Judges during the Oral Proceedings*, of 22.07.2013, pp. 8–13.
37 ICJ, doc. CR 2013/20, of 10.07.2013, p. 16, para. 37.

VIII Principle of Prevention and the Precautionary Principle: Arguments of the Parties and the Intervenor

60. Although the Court does not dwell upon the precautionary principle or approach in the present Judgment in the case of *Whaling in the Antarctic*, I deem it fit to recall and point out herein that, in the course of the proceedings in the present case, the two contending Parties as well as New Zealand addressed the principle of prevention and the precautionary principle as related to the *cas d'espèce*. In its *oral arguments*, Australia stressed *conservation* under contemporary international environmental law, invoking its "three main legal pillars", namely, "intergenerational equity, the principle of prevention and the precautionary approach", – principles that are to "govern the interpretation and the application of the 1946 Convention régime, as they make it possible for its object and purpose to be achieved".[38]

61. In the same line of thinking, in its *Memorial* Australia upheld the precautionary principle, asserting that, for example, "[t]he establishment of sanctuaries reflects also the increasing importance of the precautionary approach in the IWC's management and conservation of whales" (p. 42, para. 2.80). It has then added that

> The IWC now pursues conservation of whales as an end itself. In so doing, it places greater reliance on a precautionary approach to conservation and management combined with a focus on non-consumptive use (p. 52, para. 2.99).

62. Australia, in sum, identified an "increasingly conservation-oriented approach" (p. 172, para. 4.83). This is so in view of the growing pursuance of the precautionary approach. In Australia's perception,

> This development, which has been recognised by the IWC, must be taken into account in interpreting the Article VIII exception. In practical terms, and in the face of uncertainty as to the status of whale stocks and the effect of any lethal take, precaution directs an interpretation of Article VIII that limits the killing of whales.
>
> The precautionary approach specifically is intended to provide guidance in the development and application of international environmental

---

38   ICJ, doc. CR 2013/7, of 26.06.2013, pp. 56–58, paras. 50, 55 and 57–58.

law where there is scientific uncertainty. The core of this approach is reflected in Principle 15 of the Rio Declaration (...). The approach requires caution and vigilance in decision-making in the face of such uncertainty.

The precautionary approach has been recognised in a number of international policy documents and international environmental agreements, concerning both broader environmental matters and, more particularly, the conservation and protection of marine mammals.

The Contracting Governments to the ICRW have agreed to the adoption of a precautionary approach in a wide range of matters. As applied to Article VIII, this means that the uncertainty regarding the status of whale stocks requires Contracting Governments to act with prudence and caution by strictly limiting the grant of special permits under Article VIII (pp. 173–176, paras. 4.87–4.91).[39]

63. In sum, in Australia's understanding, developments in international law confirm that "Article VIII is to be interpreted as an exception that is only available in limited circumstances"; Article VIII "is not self-judging", and its application is to be "determined by reference to objective criteria, consistent with those adopted by the Commission established under the ICRW" Convention. Such an approach, – Australia added, – is consistent with "the broader international legal framework in which the ICRW now rests", which promotes a "conservation-oriented focus" that is consistent with the precautionary approach (pp. 173–176, paras. 4.87–4.91). Australia concluded on this point that "the Article VIII exception" had a "strictly limited application", in particular where there is "uncertainty regarding the status of the relevant whale stocks" (p. 187, para. 4.119). Also in its *oral arguments*, Australia insisted that "the aim of the precautionary approach is conservation (...)", and this latter applies in particular "where there is scientific uncertainty".[40]

---

39 Australia recalled, still in its *Memorial*, not only the incorporation of the precautionary approach (as propounded in Principle 15 of the Rio Declaration on Environment and Development) in "a growing number of international treaties", but also the contemporary case-law on the subject, of the ICJ (case of the *Pulp Mills on the River Uruguay*), as well as of the International Tribunal for the Law of the Sea (ITLOS – the *Southern Bluefin Tuna* cases, and the Advisory Opinion of its Seabed Disputes Chamber, on the *Responsibilities and Obligations of States Sponsoring Persons and Entities with Respect to Activities in the Area*) (pp. 173–176, paras. 4.87–4.91).

40 ICJ, doc. CR 2013/7, of 26.06.2013, p. 47, paras. 53–54.

64. For its part, in its arguments (in the written and oral phases) Japan did not elaborate on the principle of prevention. Furthermore, in its Counter-Memorial, it somehow minimized the precautionary approach,[41] but it conceded that such approach entailed "the conduct of further special permit whaling for scientific purposes as a means of improving understanding of marine ecosystems and the sustainability of whale stocks"; it was on that basis, – Japan added, – "that Jarpa and Jarpa-II" "have been designed and carried out", in a "prudent and cautious" way, posing "no risk to the survival of abundant minke whale stocks".[42]

65. In its *oral arguments*, Japan further stated that it was conducting "scientific research" in such a way that "no harm to stocks" would occur "in full application of the precautionary approach". It added that "[l]ittle is known of the ecosystem in the Antarctic Ocean", and it was "precisely to supply the Scientific Committee with necessary scientific data that Japan is pursuing research whaling", and, together with "other nations' contribution, conservation and management based on science under the IWC has been making progress".[43] In invoking the precautionary approach (as expressed in Principle 15 of the Rio Declaration on Environment and Development), Japan asserted that the Jarpa-II programme was "consistent" with its requirements; Japan then called for "a permissive interpretation and application of Article VIII of the ICRW Convention, so as to render it effective".[44]

66. For its part, New Zealand, in its *oral arguments*, in addressing the *principle of prevention*, stated that "consultations and negotiations" – in pursuance of the duty of co-operation – are to be "meaningful",[45] also taking into account "the views and legitimate interests of others".[46] Turning to the precautionary

---

41   Cf. ICJ, *Counter-Memorial [of Japan]*, p. 132, para. 3.92.
42   Japan added that "possible effects of Jarpa-II catches on whale stocks were analysed and submitted to the IWC Scientific Committee in 2005", and those analyses concluded that "there would be no adverse effects on the long-term status of any of the targeted whale species in the Antarctic". Japan concluded that, if there was "scientific uncertainty about the conservation status and population dynamics of whale stocks", then further research would become necessary, and it would keep on "acting prudently in continuing to conduct Jarpa-II". ICJ, *Counter-Memorial [of Japan]*, pp. 424–426, paras. 9.33–9.36.
43   ICJ, doc. CR 2013/12, of 02.07.2013, pp. 15–16, para. 9.
44   ICJ, doc. CR 2013/16, of 04.07.2013, pp. 29–35, para. 19, and cf. also paras. 11–12, 15–16, and 20–21.
45   ICJ, doc. CR 2013/17, of 08.07.2013, p. 45, para. 30.
46   *Ibid.*, p. 46, para. 33.

principle or approach, New Zealand argued, in its *Written Observations*, that States Parties to the ICRW Convention do not have full discretion, in the form of a "blank cheque", to "determine the number of whales to be killed under Special Permit under Article VIII"; they have to proceed reasonably, so as to achieve the object and purpose of the Convention as a whole.[47]

67. That number of whales, – New Zealand proceeded in its *Written Observations*, – ought to be "necessary and proportionate to the objectives of the scientific research", pursuant to the precautionary approach as related to "the conservation and management of living marine resources". New Zealand added, in its *Written Observations*, that States Parties are required to act with "prudence and caution", particularly when "information is uncertain, unreliable or inadequate", so as to avoid "any harm" (pp. 40–41, paras 73–74). In issuing a Special Permit, a State Party to the ICRW Convention is to demonstrate that it "will avoid any adverse effect on the conservation of the stock" (p. 41, para. 75).

68. Again in its *oral arguments*, New Zealand sustained that the issue here in contention is the number of whales to be killed, which, in its view, cannot be "entirely self-judging", nor completely without review.[48] In its view, the determination of that number should take into account certain factors, namely:

(a) first, the number of whales killed must be the lowest necessary for, and proportionate to, the purposes of scientific research;
(b) as a consequence, there is an expectation that non-lethal methods of research will be used;
(c) third, the number of whales to be killed must be set at a level which takes into account the precautionary approach; and
(d) finally, the discretion to set the number of whales to be killed must be exercised reasonably and consistent with the object and purpose of the Convention.[49]

69. Insisting on the relevance of the precautionary approach, New Zealand added that States Parties to the ICRW Convention "should act with prudence and caution when applying provisions, such as Article VIII, which may have

---

47   Ibid., pp. 25–27, paras. 34–38.
48   ICJ, doc. CR 2013/17, of 08.07.2013, p. 35, para. 3.
49   ICJ, doc. CR 2013/17, of 08.07.2013, pp. 35–36, para. 3.

an effect on the conservation of natural resources". Such "prudence and caution" are even more needed "when the information is uncertain, unreliable or inadequate" (para. 15). A "prudent and cautious" approach would ensure that the number of whales to be taken "is necessary and proportionate", and would "give preference to the conduct of non-lethal methods of research. (...) [U]ncertainty is the very reason for acting with caution".[50]

70. Even if the Court, in the present Judgment in the *Whaling in the Antarctic* case, has not seen it fit to pronounce on the principle of prevention and the precautionary principle, it is, in my view, significant that the contending parties, Australia and Japan, and the intervenor, New Zealand, have cared to refer to these principles, in general, in their arguments as to whether or not Japan's whaling practices under Special Permits conform to them. Such principles are to inform and conform any programmes under Special Permits within the limited scope of Article VIII of the ICRW Convention. Furthermore, the principles of prevention and precaution appear interrelated in the present case of *Whaling in the Antarctic*.

71. May I add just one final remark in this respect. Despite the hesitation of the ICJ (and of other international tribunals in general) to pronounce and dwell upon the precautionary principle, expert writing increasingly examines it, drawing attention to its incidence when there is need to take protective measures in face of risks, even in the absence of corresponding scientific proof. The precautionary principle, in turn, draws attention to the time factor, the temporal dimension, which marks a noticeable presence in the interpretation and application of treaties and instruments of international environmental law.[51] In this domain in general, and in respect of the ICRW Convention in particular, there has occurred, with the passing of time, a move towards conservation of living marine resources as a common interest, prevailing over State unilateral action in search of commercial profitability.[52] This move has taken place by the operation of the system of collective guarantee, collective decision-making and collective regulation under the ICRW Convention (cf. item II, *supra*).

---

50 ICJ, doc. CR 2013/17, of 08.07.2013, p. 40, para. 17.
51 Cf., generally, e.g., Y. Tanaka, "Reflections on Time Elements in the International Law of the Environment", 73 *Zeitschrift für ausländisches öffentliches Recht und Völkerrecht* (2013) pp. 143–147, 150–156, 165–167 and 170–175.
52 Cf. M. Bowman, "'Normalizing' the International Convention for the Regulation of Whaling", 29 *Michigan Journal of International Law* (2008) pp. 139, 163, 175–177 and 199.

IX Responses from the Experts, and Remaining Uncertainties around "Scientific Research" (under Jarpa-II)

72. During the public sittings of the Court, I deemed it fit to put several questions to the experts of Australia and Japan. In response to my five questions put to him, the expert of Australia (M. Mangel) addressed the availability of non-lethal research techniques to States Parties to the 1946 ICRW Convention in the context of conservation and management of whales, pointing out that their use (so as to replace lethal methods) would depend on "having a relevant question", as there is "always a tension in the scientific community about the exact question".[53] Satellite tagging, e.g., has become a non-lethal tool, with the technological development as from the early nineties, for the collection of information (e.g., on the movement of whales).[54]

73. In response to my three questions put to him, the expert of Japan (L. Walloe) compared biopsy sampling with lethal sampling. He admitted that he could not determine the total of whales to be killed to attain the objectives of "scientific research" (as under Jarpa-II), as that, in his view, would depend on the question one would be focusing on; but, "for the time being", he added, and "for some years", it would "be justified to kill 850".[55] He submitted that, for certain purposes, "lethal research" (e.g., on the amount of stomach contents) continued to be necessary.[56] Yet, despite these responses, there remained, in my perception, the impression of a lack of general criteria for the determination of the total whales to be killed, and for how long, for the purposes of so-called "scientific research".

74. "Scientific research" is surrounded by uncertainties; it is undertaken on the basis of uncertainties. Suffice it here to recall the legacy of Karl Popper, who used to ponder wisely that scientific knowledge can only be uncertain or conjectural, while ignorance is infinite. Scientific research is a search for truth, amidst conjectures, and, given one's fallibility, one has to learn with mistakes incurred into. One can hope to be coming closer to truth, but without knowing for sure whether one is distant from, or near it. Without the ineluctable refutations, science would fall into stagnation, losing its empirical character. Conjectures and refutations are needed, for science to keep on advancing in

---

53 ICJ, doc. CR 2013/9, of 27.06.2013, pp. 64–66.
54 *Ibid.*, pp. 66–67.
55 ICJ, doc. CR 2013/14, of 03.07.2013, pp. 50–51.
56 *Ibid.*, pp. 51–52.

its empirical path.⁵⁷ As to the *cas d'espèce*, would this mean that whales could keep on being killed, and increasingly so, for "scientific purposes" and amidst scientific uncertainty? I do not think so; there are also non-lethal methods, and, after all, living marine resources are not inexhaustible.

X Reiterated Calls under the ICRW Convention for Non-lethal Use of Cetaceans

75. The reiterated calls for non-lethal use of cetaceans, under the ICRW Convention, cannot pass unnoticed here. In its Resolution 1995-9, on whaling under special permit, the IWC recommended that "scientific research" intended to assist the comprehensive assessment of whale stocks should be undertaken by non-lethal means; furthermore, it recalled that the ICRW Convention recognizes the common interest of all "the nations of the world" in safeguarding the "great natural resources" of whale stocks "for future generations". Subsequently, in its Resolution 2005-1, on Jarpa-II, the IWC began by recalling (second preambular paragraph) that

> since the moratorium on commercial whaling came into force in 1985–1986, the IWC has adopted over 30 resolutions on Special Permit whaling in which it has generally expressed its opinion that Special Permit whaling should: be terminated and scientific research limited to non-lethal methods only (2003–2); refrain from involving the killing of cetaceans in sanctuaries (1998–4); ensure that the recovery of populations is not impeded (1987); and take account of the comments of the Scientific Committee (1987).

76. Resolution 2005-1 of the IWC proceeded to express concern (sixth preambular paragraph) that "more than 6,800 Antarctic minke whales (*Balaenoptera bonaerensis*) have been killed in Antarctic waters under the 18 years of Jarpa, compared with a total of 840 whales killed globally by Japan for scientific research in the 31-year period prior to the moratorium". It then noted (tenth preambular paragraph) that "some humpback whales which will be targeted by Jarpa-II belong to small, vulnerable breeding populations around small island States in the South Pacific", and "even small takes could have a detrimental

---

57 Cf. K.R. Popper, *Conjecturas e Refutações – O Progresso do Conhecimento Científico* [*Conjectures and Refutations – The Growth of Scientific Knowledge*], 5th ed., Brasília, Editora Universidade de Brasília, 2008, pp. 255, 257, 260, 269 and 271.

effect on the recovery and survival of such populations". The IWC further expressed concern (eleventh preambular paragraph) that "Jarpa-II may have an adverse impact on established long-term whale research projects involving humpback whales". At last, the operative part of Resolution 2005-1 "strongly" urged Japan to withdraw its Jarpa-II proposal, or else to revise it to consider using non-lethal means.

77. Two years later, the IWC adopted two new Resolutions on the non-lethal use of whale resources. In Resolution 2007–1, the IWC recalled that Paragraph 7(b) of the Schedule establishes the Southern Ocean sanctuary; it further recalled its repeated requests to States Parties to refrain from issuing special permits for research involving the killing of whales within the Southern Ocean Sanctuary. It then expressed concern at continuing lethal "research" within the Southern Ocean Sanctuary. In relation to Jarpa-II in particular, the IWC noted that, thereunder, "the take of minke whales has been more than doubled, and fin whales and humpback whales have been added to the list of targeted species" (fourth preambular paragraph). Convinced that "the aims of Jarpa-II do not address critically important research needs" (six preambular paragraph), Resolution 2007-I, in its operative part, called upon Japan 31 recommendations of the Scientific Committee and "to suspend indefinitely the lethal aspects of Jarpa-II conducted within the Southern Ocean Whale Sanctuary".

78. In addition, the IWC recalled, in Resolution 2007–3 (on *Non-Lethal Use of Cetaceans*), the ICRW Convention's aim to safeguard "the natural resources represented by whale stocks for the benefit of future generations" (first preambular paragraph). It noted that many coastal States adopted policies of non-lethal use of cetaceans in the waters under their jurisdiction, in the light of relevant provisions of the 1982 U.N. Convention on the Law of the Sea and the 1992 Rio Declaration on Environment and Development (second preambular paragraph). It pondered that "most whale species are highly migratory" and are "thus shared biodiversity resources" (third preambular paragraph). Calling for the non-lethal use of whales, it further noted that "the moratorium on commercial whaling has been in effect since 1986 and has contributed to the recovery of some cetacean populations essential for the promotion of non-lethal uses in many countries" (sixth preambular paragraph).

79. Next, in the same Resolution 2007–3, the IWC expressed its concern that whales in the XXIst century "face a wider range of threats than those envisaged when the ICRW was concluded in 1946" (seventh preambular paragraph). The IWC further notes that the *Buenos Aires Declaration* states that "high quality

and well managed implementation of whale watching tourism promotes economic growth and social and cultural development of local communities, bringing educational and scientific benefits, whilst contributing to the protection of cetacean populations" (eighth preambular paragraph). Accordingly, in the operative part of Resolution 2007–3, the IWC recognized, first, the valuable benefits to be derived from "the non-lethal uses of cetaceans as a resource, both in terms of socio-economic and scientific development", and secondly, the non-lethal use as "a legitimate management strategy". Thus, the IWC encouraged member States "to work constructively" towards "the incorporation" of the needs of non-lethal uses of whale resources in "any future decisions and agreements".

XI Concluding Observations, on Jarpa-II Programme and the Requirements of the ICRW Convention and Its Schedule

80. Last but not least, as to the central question of the present case, that is, whether Jarpa-II is in conformity with the ICRW Convention and its Schedule, – object of the main controversy between Australia and Japan, – in my perception Jarpa-II does not meet the requirements of a programme "for purposes of scientific research" and does not fall under the exception contained in Article VIII of the ICRW Convention. There are a few characteristics of Jarpa-II which do not allow it to qualify under the exception of Article VIII, to be restrictively interpreted; in effect, the programme at issue does not seem to be genuinely and *solely* motivated by the purpose of conducting scientific research.

81. This is so, keeping in mind the relation between Jarpa-II's stated objectives and the methods used to achieve these objectives: lethal methods, which Jarpa-II widely applies in its operations, are, in my view, only to be used, first, where it is unavoidable to achieve a crucial objective of the scientific research; secondly, where no other methods would be available; and thirdly, where the number of whales killed corresponds to those necessary to conduct the research. In practice, the use of lethal methods by Jarpa-II in relation to what seems to be a large number of whales does not appear justifiable as "scientific research".

82. Furthermore, the fact that Jarpa-II runs for an indefinite duration also militates against its professed purpose of "scientific research". To my mind, a scientific programme, when being devised, should have objectives which go along a specific time-frame for their achievement. To prolong the killing whales

indefinitely does not seem to be in line with scientific research, nor justifiable. In addition, there subsists the concern with the possible adverse effects of Jarpa-II on whale stocks. As just indicated, Jarpa-II utilises lethal methods and runs for an indefinite time. It is not entirely convincing that, under these parameters, whale stocks subject to the programme will not be adversely affected. This is exacerbated in the hypothesis that other States Parties to the ICRW Convention decide to follow the same approach and methodology of Japan, and start likewise killing whales allegedly for similar purposes of "scientific research".

83. There could be an adverse impact on whale stocks if other States Parties to the ICRW Convention decided to kill as many whales as Japan, within an unlimited timeframe, for purposes of "scientific research". Jarpa-II, in the manner it is being currently conducted, can have adverse effects on whale stocks. Even if there is a minor scientific purpose in the Jarpa-II programme, it is clearly not the main purpose of the programme. In my view, given the methodologies used (widely employing lethal methods – cf. *supra*), the structure of the programme and its duration, "scientific research" is not the sole purpose of the programme, nor the main one.

84. As to the question whether commercial aspects are permissible under Article VIII(2) of the Convention,[58] the text of this provision seems clear: it does not seem expressly to allow for commercial aspects of a whaling programme under special permit. Article VIII(2) is aimed, in my perception, solely to avoid waste. The commercialisation of whale meat does not seem to be in line with the purpose of granting Special Permits and should not be validated under this provision. Permitting commercial aspects of a special permit whaling programme under this provision would go against Article VIII as a whole, and the object and purpose of the ICRW Convention (cf. *supra*). Commercial whaling, pure and simple, is not permissible under Article VIII(2).

85. As to the Schedule, Paragraph 30 sets forth a *positive* procedural obligations of States Parties to the ICRW Convention, whereby Japan's co-operation with the IWC and the Scientific Committee is expected. The Court has found, in the present Judgment in the *Whaling in the Antarctic* case, that Japan has not acted in conformity with paragraph 10(d) and (e) (whaling moratorium, and assessment of effects of whale catches on stocks), and paragraph 7(b) (prohibition

---

58   Which reads as follows: – "Any whales taken under these special permits shall so far as practicable be processed and the proceeds shall be dealt with in accordance with directions issued by the Government by which the permit was granted".

of commercial whaling in the Southern Ocean Sanctuary), of the Schedule (resolutory points 3–5). Japan does not appear to have fulfilled this obligation to take into account comments, resolutions and recommendations of the IWC and the Scientific Committee.

86. For example, I note that many resolutions[59] have been issued along the years concerning Jarpa-II and its use of lethal methods, which Japan does not seem to have fully taken into account, given its continued use of lethal methods. The Court itself has drawn attention, in the present Judgment (para. 144), to the paucity of analysis by Japan of the feasibility of non-lethal methods to achieve Jarpa-II objectives; and it has added that

> Given the expanded use of lethal methods in Jarpa-II, as compared to Jarpa, this is difficult to reconcile with Japan's duty to give due regard to IWC resolutions and Guidelines and its statement that Jarpa-II uses lethal methods only to the extent necessary to meet its scientific objectives (para. 139).

87. Moreover, it could hardly be claimed that the sole purpose of programme Jarpa-II is "scientific research", as it appears that some commercial aspects permeate the programme. Jarpa-II programme does not seem to fall under the exception of Article VIII of the ICRW Convention. In the present Judgment,

---

59   Cf., e.g., *Resolution on Japanese Proposal for Special Permits*, App. 4, Chairman's Report of the 39th Annual Meeting, *Rep. IWC* 38, 1988, 29 (Resolution 1987–4); *Resolution on the Proposed Take by Japan of Whales in the Southern Hemisphere under Special Permit*, App. 3, Chairman's Report of the 41st Annual Meeting, *Rep. IWC* 40, 1990, 36 (Resolution 1989–3); *Resolution on Special Permit Catches by Japan in the Southern Hemisphere*, App. 2, Chairman's Report of the 42nd Meeting, *Rep. IWC* 41, 1991, 47–48 (Resolution 1990–2); *Resolution on Special Permit Catches by Japan in the Southern Hemisphere*, App. 2, Chairman's Report of the 43rd Meeting, *Rep. IWC* 42, 1992, 46 (Resolution 1991–2); *Resolution on Special Permit Catches by Japan in the Southern Hemisphere*, App. 5, Chairman's Report of the 44th Meeting, *Rep. IWC* 43, 1993, 71 (Resolution 1992–5); Resolution on Special Permit Catches by Japan in the Southern Hemisphere, App. 7, Chairman's Report of the 45th Annual Meeting, *Rep. IWC* 44, 1994, 33 (Resolution 1993–7); *Resolution on Special Permit Catches by Japan in the North Pacific*, Resolution 1994–9, App. 15, Chairman's Report of the 46th Annual Meeting, *Rep. IWC* 45, 1995, 47 (Resolution 1994–9); Resolution on Special Permit Catches by Japan in the Southern Hemisphere, Resolution 1994–10, App. 15, Chairman's Report of the 46th Annual Meeting, *Rep. IWC* 45, 1995, 47 (Resolution 1994–10); *Resolution on Special Permit Catches by Japan*, Resolution 1996–7, App. 7, Chairman's Report of the 48th Meeting, *Rep. IWC* 47, 1997, 51–52 (Resolution 1996–7); *cit. in* ICJ, doc. CR 2013/8, of 26.06.2013, pp. 34–35.

the Court has found that the special permits granted by Japan in connection with Jarpa-II do not fall under Article VIII(1) of the ICRW Convention (resolutory point 2). The present case has provided a unique occasion for the Court to pronounce upon a system of collective regulation of the environment for the benefit of future generations. The notion of *collective guarantee* has been developed, and put in practice, to date in distinct domains of contemporary international law. The Court's present Judgment in the *Whaling in the Antarctic* case may have wider implications than solely the peaceful settlement of the present dispute between the contending Parties, to the benefit of all.

88. Last but not least, may I observe that international treaties and conventions are a product of their time; yet, they have an aptitude to face changing conditions, and their interpretation and application in time bears witness that they are *living* instruments. They evolve with time, otherwise they would fall into *desuetude*. The 1946 ICRW Convention is no exception to that, and, endowed with a mechanism of supervision of its own, it has proven to be a *living* instrument. Moreover, in distinct domains of international law, treaties and conventions – especially those setting forth a mechanism of protection – have required the pursuance of a hermeneutics of their own, as *living* instruments. This happens not only in the present domain of conservation and sustainable use of living marine resources, but likewise in other areas of international law.

89. The present case on *Whaling in the Antarctic* has brought to the fore the evolving law on the conservation and sustainable use of living marine resources, which, in turn, has disclosed what I perceive as its contribution to the gradual formation of an *opinio juris communis* in the present domain of contemporary international law. *Opinio juris*, in my conception, becomes a key factor in the formation itself of international law (here, conservation and sustainable use of living marine resources); its incidence is no longer that of only one of the constitutive elements of one of its "formal" sources.[60] The formation of international law in domains of public or common interest, such as that of conservation and sustainable use of living marine resources, is a much wider process than the formulation of its "formal sources", above all in seeking the legitimacy of norms to govern international life.[61]

---

60   These latter being only means or vehicles for the formation of international legal norms.
61   For the conceptualization of this outlook, cf. A.A. Cançado Trindade, *International Law for Humankind...*, op. cit. supra n. (15), pp. 134–138, esp. p. 137.

90. *Opinio juris communis*, in this way, comes to assume a considerably broader dimension than that of the subjective element constitutive of custom, and to exert a key role in the emergence and gradual evolution of international legal norms. After all, juridical conscience of what is necessary (*jus necessarium*) stands above the "free-will" of individual States (*jus voluntarium*), rendering possible the evolution of international law governing conservation and sustainable use of living marine resources. In this domain, State voluntarism yields to the *jus necessarium*, and notably so in the present era of international tribunals, amidst increasing endeavours to secure the long-awaited primacy of the *jus necessarium* over the *jus voluntarium*. Ultimately, this becomes of key importance to the realization of the pursued common good.

(Signed) *Antônio Augusto* Cançado Trindade
Judge

CHAPTER 6

The Relevance of General Principles of International Law

1 Separate Opinion in the case concerning the *Obligation to Negotiate Access to the Pacific Ocean* (Bolivia *versus* Chile, Preliminary Objections, Judgment of 24.09.2015)

Table of Contents — Paragraphs

I. *Prolegomena* 1-5
II. Preliminary Objections and Merits: Reasoning in Search of Justice 6-11
III. Jurisdictional Basis and the Merits: Case-Law of the PCIJ and ICJ
   1. Joinder of Preliminary Objections to the Merits 12-15
   2. Not Exclusively "Preliminary" Character of Objections to Jurisdiction (and Admissibility) 16-22
IV. Relevance of General Principles of International Procedural Law
   1. General Principles and the Foundations of the International Legal Order 23-25
   2. General Principles in Distinct Incidental Proceedings 26-31
   3. General Principles in the Joinder of Proceedings 32-35
   4. General Principles in Advisory Proceedings 36-38
   5. General Assessment 39-40
V. General Principles of International Law, Latin American International Legal Doctrine, and the Significance of the Pact of Bogotá 41-53
VI. The Pact of Bogotá and Judicial Settlement by the ICJ 54-58
VII. Concluding Observations: The Third Way (*Troisième Voie/Tercera Vía*) under Article 79(9) of the Rules of Court – Objection Not of an Exclusively Preliminary Character 59-67

I Prolegomena

1. I have voted in favour of the adoption today, 24 September 2015, of the present Judgment on Preliminary Objection in the case concerning the *Obligation to Negotiate Access to the Pacific Ocean*, between Bolivia and Chile, whereby the International Court of Justice (ICJ) has found that it has jurisdiction to consider the claim lodged with it under Article XXXI of the 1948 American Treaty

on Pacific Settlement (Pact of Bogotá). Yet, there are certain aspects of the question decided by the Court, to which I attribute importance for its proper understanding, which are not properly reflected in the reasoning of the present Judgment. I feel thus obliged to dwell upon them, in the present Separate Opinion.

2. In particular, I find the treatment dispensed by the ICJ in the present Judgment, to the jurisdictional regime of the Pact of Bogotá, and in particular to the basis of its own jurisdiction (Article XXXI of the Pact) (paras. 37 and 54) as well as to the relevant provision (Article 79(9)) of the Rules of Court (paras. 52–53), far too succinct. In order to rest on a more solid ground, the Court should, in my perception, have dwelt further upon those provisions, faced as it was with the contention that the respondent State's characterization of the subject-matter of the present dispute would amount to a refutation of the applicant State's case on the merits (para. 52).

3. The ICJ should, in my perception, have devoted as much attention to Article XXXI of the Pact and Article 79(9) of the Rules of Court as it did as to Article VI of the Pact (paras. 24 and 38–50). In the present Separate Opinion, I deem it fit to stress the importance of the aforementioned provisions, in relation to the factual context of the *cas d'espèce* and the handling of the question lodged with the Court. To that effect I shall develop my considerations that follow. I shall begin by addressing the reasoning, in search of justice, as to preliminary objections and the merits.

4. I shall next consider the relation between the jurisdictional basis and the merits in the case-law of the Hague Court (PCIJ and ICJ), focusing, earlier on, on the joinder of preliminary objections to the merits, and then on the not exclusively "preliminary" character of objections to jurisdiction (and admissibility). I shall then dwell upon the relevance of general principles of international procedural law, as related to the foundations of the international legal order, and on their incidence, in contentious cases, on distinct incidental proceedings (preliminary objections, provisional measures, counter-claims and intervention), on the joinder of proceedings, as well as on advisory proceedings.

5. After an assessment of the matter, I shall proceed to consider the general principles of international law, Latin American doctrine and the significance of the 1948 Pact of Bogotá. Last but not least, the way will then be paved for the presentation of my concluding observations on the third way (*troisième*

voie/tercera vía) devised by Article 79(9) of the Rules of Court, namely, that of the determination of an objection not of an exclusively preliminary character, leading to the opening of further proceedings and moving into the merits of the case.

II   Preliminary Objections and Merits: Reasoning in Search of Justice

6. In effect, may I begin by pointing out that a clear cut separation between the procedural stages of preliminary objections and merits reflects the old voluntarist-positivist conception of international justice subjected to State consent. Yet, despite the prevalence of the positivist approach in the era of the Permanent Court of International Justice (PCIJ), soon the old Hague Court reckoned the need to join a preliminary objection to the merits (cf. *infra*). A preliminary objection to jurisdiction *ratione materiae* is more likely to appear related to the merits of a case than an objection to jurisdiction *ratione personae* or *ratione temporis*.[1] I shall seek to clarify this in my considerations that follow.

7. In effect, to start with, the search for justice transcends any straight-jacket conception of international legal procedure. In my Dissenting Opinion in the ICJ's Judgment on Preliminary Objections of 01.04.2011 in the case concerning the *Application of the Convention on the Elimination of All Forms of Racial Discrimination* (Georgia *versus* Russian Federation), I laid down in depth my criticisms of the voluntarist approach to the Court's jurisdiction. As I do not purport to retake here the consideration of this particular issue, I limit myself to refer to the pertinent passages of my aforementioned Dissenting Opinion (paras. 37–63, 79–87, 140, 167 and 181) in this respect.

8. Moreover, in the handling of this issue, the Hague Court (PCIJ and ICJ) has, throughout its history, been attentive to the interests of the parties and the preservation of the equilibrium between them in the course of the procedure. Hence the constant recourse by the Court to the principle of the sound administration of justice (*la bonne administration de la justice*); the acknowledgment

---

1   Cf., to this effect, F. Ammoun, "La jonction des exceptions préliminaires au fond en Droit international public", *in Il processo internazionale – Studi in onore di G. Morelli*, 14 *Comunicazioni e Studi* (1975) pp. 34 and 38, and cf. p. 21.

of this principle, in the course of incidental proceedings of the ICJ, has further had repercussion in contemporary expert writing.²

9. There are successive examples in the case-law of the Hague Court disclosing its reliance on the principle of the sound administration of justice (*la bonne administration de la justice*). Early in its life, the PCIJ, in the *Panevezys-Saldutiskis Railway* (Order of 30.06.1938), in deciding to join Lithuania's preliminary objections to the merits, expressly stated that

> the Court may order the joinder of preliminary objections to the merits, whenever the interests of the good administration of justice require it (p. 56).

10. This *célèbre obiter dictum* was kept in mind, along the years, by the ICJ as well (cf. *infra*). In the course of its prolonged handling of the *Barcelona Traction* case, it was repeatedly pointed out, in expert writing in the mid-sixties, that, even if the joinder to the merits appeared as an exceptional measure, there were situations in which the clear-cut separation of a preliminary objection from the merits could raise much difficulty, the solution thus being the joinder. Given the straight connection between the preliminary objection and the merits, the joinder would correspond to a necessity, in the interests of the sound administration of justice (*la bonne administration de la justice*).³

11. In all its historical trajectory, the PCIJ, and later on the ICJ from the very beginning of its operation, made it clear that *the Court is master of its procedure*. It does not and cannot accept straight-jacket conceptions of its own procedure; reasoning is essential to its mission of realization of justice. The path followed has been a long one: for decades the idea of a "joinder" of a preliminary objection to the merits found expression in the then Rules of Court; from

---

2 Cf., *inter alia*, e.g., Hironobu Sakai, "*La bonne administration de la justice* in the Incidental Proceedings of the International Court of Justice", 55 *Japanese Yearbook of International Law* (2012) pp. 110–133; R. Kolb, "La maxime de la 'bonne administration de la justice' dans la jurisprudence internationale", *in*: *La bonne administration de la justice internationale*, 27 *L'Observateur des Nations Unies* (2009)-II, pp. 5–21.

3 Cf. M. Mabrouk, *Les exceptions de procédure devant les juridictions internationales*, Paris, LGDJ, 1966, pp. 286–289; G. Abi-Saab, *Les exceptions préliminaires dans la procédure de la Cour Internationale*, Paris, Pédone, 1967, pp. 194–198; E. Grisel, *Les exceptions d'incompétence et d'irrecevabilité dans la procédure de la Cour Internationale de Justice*, Berne, Éd. H. Lang & Cie., 1968, pp. 175–180 and 182.

the early seventies onwards, the Rules of Court began to provide for further proceedings in the cases, given the fact that the objections at issue did not disclose an exclusively "preliminary" character (*infra*).

III   Jurisdictional Basis and the Merits: Case-Law of the PCIJ and ICJ

1   *Joinder of Preliminary Objections to the Merits*

12. Early in its history, the old PCIJ decided to join preliminary objections to the merits of the cases. It did so, for the first time, in the *Administration of the Prince von Pless* case (Order of 04.02.1933), wherein it stated that the question before it concerned the merits of the case, and thus it could not pass upon "the question of jurisdiction until the case ha[d] been argued upon the merits" (p. 15); it decided to join Poland's preliminary objection to the merits (p. 16).

13. In the same decade, the PCIJ, in the cases *Pajzs, Csáky and Esterházy* (Order of 23.05.1936), having found the questions raised in Yugoslavia's objections "too intimately" and "too closely interconnected" with Hungary's submissions on the merits, ordered likewise the joinder of those objections to the merits (p. 9). Likewise, shortly afterwards, in the *Losinger* (Order of 27.06.1936), the PCIJ again ordered the joinder, having found that the plea to the jurisdiction appeared as a "defence on the merits" (pp. 23–24). And the PCIJ, once more, ordered the joinder of preliminary objections to the merits in the aforementioned *Panevezys-Saldutiskis Railway* case (Order of 30.06.1938, pp. 55–56).

14. For its part, the ICJ, in the handling of subsequent cases, was soon also faced with circumstances which led it to determine the joinder of a preliminary objection of the merits. Thus, in the case of *Certain Norwegian Loans* (28.09.1956), the ICJ decided, on the basis of an understanding between the parties, to join the preliminary objections to the merits (p. 74). Shortly afterwards, in the case of the *Right of Passage over Indian Territory* (Judgment on Preliminary Objections, of 26.11.1957), the ICJ pointed out that any evaluation of India's fifth and sixth preliminary objections would risk prejudging the merits; accordingly, it decided to join those objections to the merits (pp. 150 and 152).

15. Later on, in the case of *Barcelona Traction* (Judgment on Preliminary Objections, of 24.07.1964), the Hague Court, recalling its case-law (PCIJ and ICJ) on the matter (pp. 41–42), decided likewise to join Spain's third and fourth preliminary objections to the merits (p. 46). In the aftermath of its prolonged and cumbersome handling of the *Barcelona Traction* case (1964–1970), the ICJ

deemed it fit to introduce, in 1972, a change in the wording of the provision at issue of the Rules of Court. The PCIJ Rules of Court (dating back to 1936) referred to the Court's deciding on the preliminary objection or joining it to the merits.[4] That provision survived in the ICJ Rules of Court of 1946, and until the amendments introduced into the Rules in 1972 (cf. *infra*). The provision then adopted in 1972 has been passed on to the Rules of Court of 1978 and 2000 (*infra*), and remains the same to date.

2 Not Exclusively "Preliminary" Character of Objections to Jurisdiction (and Admissibility)

16. The change in the Rules of Court adopted in 1972,[5] and subsequently maintained in the Rules of 1978,[6] and of 2000,[7] was object of attention in the Court's Judgments on Jurisdiction and Admissibility (of 26.11.1984) and on the Merits (of 27.06.1986) in the *Nicaragua versus United States* case. In the 1984 Judgment the ICJ, having found that the issue before it concerned "matters of substance relating to the merits of the case", then acknowledged that "the procedural technique formerly available of joinder of preliminary objections to the merits has been done away with since the 1972 revision of the Rules of Court" (para. 76).

17. Then, in its 1986 Judgment on the same case (merits), the ICJ explained the reason of the change introduced in the relevant provision of the Rules of Court, in the following terms:

> The present case is the first in which the Court has had occasion to exercise the power first provided for in the 1972 Rules of Court to declare that a preliminary objection "does not possess, in the circumstances of the

---

[4] Paragraph 5 of Article 62 of the Rules of Court (of 1936) provided that: – "After hearing the Parties the Court shall give its decision on the objection or shall join the objection to the merits. If the Court overrules the objection or joins it to the merits, it shall once more fix time-limits for the further proceedings".

[5] Paragraph 7 of Article 69 of the Rules of Court (of 1972) provided that: – "After hearing the parties, the Court shall give its decision in the form of a judgment, but which it shall either uphold the objection, reject it, or declare that the objection does not possess, in the circumstances of the case, an exclusively preliminary character. If the Court rejects the objection or declares that it does not possess an exclusively preliminary character, it shall fix time-limits for the further proceedings".

[6] Paragraph 7 of Article 79 of the Rules of Court (of 1978) had exactly the same content and phraseology of Article 69(7) of the previous Rules of Court (of 1972).

[7] Paragraph 9 of Article 79 of the current Rules of Court (of 2000) has likewise the same content and phraseology of Article 79(7) of the previous Rules of Court (of 1978).

case, an exclusively preliminary character". It may therefore be appropriate to take this opportunity to comment briefly on the rationale of this provision of the Rules, in the light of the problems to which the handling of preliminary objections has given rise. In exercising its rule-making power under Article 30 of the Statute, and generally in approaching the complex issues which may be raised by the determination of appropriate procedures for the settlement of disputes, the Court has kept in view an approach defined by the [PCIJ]. That Court found that it was at liberty to adopt

> the principle which it considers best calculated to ensure the administration of justice, most suited to procedure before an international tribunal and most in conformity with the fundamental principles of international law (*Mavrommatis Palestine Concessions* [case], P.C.I.J., [Judgment of 30.08.1924,] p. 16).

Under the Rules of Court dating back to 1936 (which on this point reflected still earlier practice), the Court had the power to join an objection to the merits "whenever the interests of the good administration of justice require it" (*Panevezys-Saldutiskis Railway* [case, Order of 30.06.1938, p. 56]), and in particular where the Court, if it were to decide on the objection, "would run the risk of adjudicating on questions which appertain to the merits of the case or of prejudging their solution" (*ibid.*). If this power was exercised, there was always a risk, namely that the Court would ultimately decide the case on the preliminary objection, after requiring the parties fully to plead the merits, – and this did in fact occur ([in the] *Barcelona Traction* [case, Judgment of 1970, p. 3]). The result was regarded in some quarters as an unnecessary prolongation of an expensive and time-consuming procedure.

Taking into account the wide range of issues which might be presented as preliminary objections, the question which the Court faced was whether to revise the Rules so as to exclude for the future the possibility of joinder to the merits, so that every objection would have to be resolved at the preliminary stage, or to seek a solution which would be more flexible. The solution of considering all preliminary objections immediately and rejecting all possibility of a joinder to the merits had many advocates and presented many advantages. (...) However, that does not solve all questions of preliminary objections, which may, as experience has shown, be to some extent bound up with the merits. The final solution adopted in 1972, and maintained in the 1978 Rules, concerning preliminary objections is the following: the Court is to give its decision by which it shall either uphold the objection, reject it, or declare that the objection does not possess, in the circumstances of the case, an exclusively preliminary character. If the Court rejects the objection, or declares that it does not possess an exclusively preliminary character, it shall fix time-limits for the further proceedings (Art. 79, para. 7).

(...) The new rule (...) thus presents one clear advantage: that it qualifies certain objections as preliminary, making it quite clear that when they are exclusively of that character they will have to be decided upon immediately, but if they are not, especially when the character of the objections is not exclusively preliminary because they contain both preliminary aspects and other aspects relating to the merits, they will have to be dealt with at the stage of the merits. This approach also tends to discourage the unnecessary prolongation of proceedings at the jurisdictional stage (paras. 38–41).

18. In this respect, at the time of change in 1972 of the Rules of Court, a former Latin American Judge of the ICJ observed that, in face of the provision in Article 62(5) of the 1946 Rules of Court as to the possible joinder of a preliminary objection to the merits, the ICJ was worried with procedural delays, with "duplication of work" and "repetition of arguments".[8] Hence the amendments introduced the new provision of the Rules of Court, deleting the express reference to the joinder, so as "to provide greater flexibility" and to avoid procedural delays, in sum, to achieve a more orderly and expeditious and "a less onerous administration of international justice".[9]

19. From the Court's decision in the *Nicaragua versus United States* case (1984–1986, *supra*) onwards, the ICJ has pursued this new outlook to the point at issue in its case-law. The Court has thus moved on to further proceedings (on the merits) when the objections lodged before it do not show to have a "preliminary" character. Thus, in its two Judgments on Preliminary Objections (of 27.02.1998) in the *Lockerbie* cases, the Court saw it fit again to explain the changes effected (in 1972) in its Rules of Court (the new Article 79). Article 79(9) of the current Rules of Court is clear, in that, if an objection seems to touch on the merits of the case, the Court may declare that it does not possess an "exclusively preliminary character", and move on to further proceedings

---

8 E. Jiménez de Aréchaga, "The Amendments to the Rules of Procedure of the International Court of Justice", 67 *American Journal of International Law* (1973) pp. 11 and 13.

9 *Ibid.*, pp. 21–22.

(on the merits). This amounted to a new outlook of what was earlier referred to[10] as joining the preliminary objection to the merits. In the *Lockerbie* cases, the Court pondered that

> The solution adopted in 1972 was ultimately not to exclude the power to examine a preliminary objection in the merits phase, but to limit the exercise of that power, by laying down the conditions more strictly (paras. 48 and 49, respectively, of the two Judgments of 27.02.1998).

20. This new outlook, – the ICJ proceeded, – presented the "clear advantage" of, once finding that the character of the objections at issue was "not exclusively preliminary", discouraging the "unnecessary prolongation of proceedings at the jurisdictional stage". The ICJ then found, in the *Lockerbie* cases, that the respective objections of the United States and the United Kingdom did not have "an exclusively preliminary character" within the meaning of Article 79 of the Rules, and could only be considered when the Court reached the merits of the case (paras. 50 and 51, respectively, of the two Judgments of 27.02.1998).

21. In the same line of thinking, shortly afterwards, in the case of the *Land and Maritime Boundary between Cameroon and Nigeria* (Judgment on Preliminary Objections, of 11.06.1998), the ICJ found that it could not give a decision on Nigeria's eighth preliminary objection "as a preliminary matter", and that it had "of necessity (...) to deal with the merits of Cameroon's request" (para. 116). The Court concluded and declared that the eighth preliminary objection did not have, in the circumstances of the case, "an exclusively preliminary character" (paras. 117–118).

22. One decade later, in its Judgment on Preliminary Objections (of 18.11.2008) in the case of the *Application of the Convention against Genocide* (Croatia *versus* Serbia), the ICJ, found that Serbia's second preliminary objection did not possess, in the circumstances of the case, "an exclusively preliminary character" (paras. 130 and 146). Very recently, in its Judgment of 03.02.2015, the ICJ at last delivered its Judgment on the merits of that case. We are here in a domain wherein general principles of law play an important role, whether they are substantive principles (such as those of *pacta sunt servanda*, or of *bona fides*), or procedural principles, to which I turn attention now.

---

10 Article 62(5) of the previous Rules of Court.

IV Relevance of General Principles of International Procedural Law

1 *General Principles and the Foundations of the International Legal Order*

23. In my perception, recourse to general principles of international procedural law is in effect ineluctable, in the realization of justice. General principles are always present and relevant, at substantive and procedural levels. Such principles orient the interpretation and application of legal norms. They rest on the foundations of any legal system, which is made to operate on the basis of fundamental principles. Ultimately, without principles there is truly no legal system. Fundamental principles form the *substratum* of the legal order itself.[11]

24. May it here be recalled that, in another case, like the present one, opposing two other Latin American States (Argentina and Uruguay), the case concerning *Pulp Mills on the River Uruguay* (Judgment of 20.04.2010), I deemed it fit to call the Court's attention, in my Separate Opinion, to the fact that *both* contending parties, Argentina and Uruguay, had expressly invoked general principles of law in the course of the contentious proceedings (para. 46). In doing so, I added, they were both

> being faithful to the long-standing tradition of Latin American international legal thinking, which has always been particularly attentive and

---

11   A.A. Cançado Trindade, *International Law for Humankind – Towards a New Jus Gentium*, 2nd. rev. ed., Leiden/The Hague, Nijhoff/The Hague Academy of International Law, 2013, pp. 58–61; and cf. A.A. Cançado Trindade, "Foundations of International Law: The Role and Importance of Its Basic Principles", *in* XXX *Curso de Derecho Internacional Organizado por el Comité Jurídico Interamericano* – OEA (2003) pp. 359–415.

12   Andrés Bello, *Princípios de Derecho Internacional* (1832), 3rd. ed., Paris, Libr. Garnier Hermanos, 1873, pp. 3 *et seq.*; C. Calvo, *Manuel de droit international public et privé*, 3rd. rev. ed., Paris, A. Rousseau Ed., 1892, Ch. I, pp. 69–83; L.M. Drago, *La República Argentina y el Caso de Venezuela*, Buenos Aires, Impr. Coni Hermanos, 1903, pp. 1–18; L.M. Drago, *La Doctrina Drago – Colección de Documentos* (pres. S. Pérez Triana), London, Impr. Wertheimer, 1908, pp. 115–127 and 205; A.N. Vivot, *La Doctrina Drago*, Buenos Aires, Edit. Coni Hermanos, 1911, pp. 39–279; II Conférence de la Paix, *Actes et discours de M. Ruy Barbosa*, La Haye, W.P. Van Stockum, 1907, pp. 60–81, 116–126, 208–223 and 315–330; Ruy Barbosa, *Obras Completas*, vol. XXXIV (1907)-II: *A Segunda Conferência da Paz*, Rio de Janeiro, MEC, 1966, pp. 65, 163, 252, 327 and 393–395; Ruy Barbosa, *Conceptos Modernos del Derecho Internacional*, Buenos Aires, Impr. Coni Hermanos, 1916, pp. 28–29 and 47–49; Clovis Bevilaqua, *Direito Público Internacional* (A Synthese dos Princípios e a Contribuição do Brazil), vol. I, Rio de Janeiro, Livr. Francisco Alves, 1910, pp. 11–15, 21–26, 90–95, 179–180 and 239–240; Raul Fernandes, *Le principe de l'égalité juridique des États dans l'activité internationale*

devoted to general principles of law, in the contexts of both the formal "sources" of international law[12] as well of codification of international law.[13]

---

de l'après-guerre, Geneva, Impr. A. Kundig, 1921, pp. 18–22 and 33; J.-M. Yepes, "La contribution de l'Amérique Latine au développement du Droit international public et privé", 32 *Recueil des Cours de l'Académie de Droit International de La Haye* [RCADI] (1930) pp. 731–751; J.-M. Yepes, "Les problèmes fondamentaux du droit des gens en Amérique", 47 RCADI (1934) p. 8; Alejandro Álvarez, *Exposé de motifs et Déclaration des grands principes du Droit international moderne*, 2nd. ed., Paris, Éds. Internationales, 1938, pp. 8–9, 13–23 and 51; C. Saavedra Lamas, *Por la Paz de las Américas*, Buenos Aires, M. Gleizer Ed., 1937, pp. 69–70, 125–126 and 393; Alberto Ulloa, *Derecho Internacional Público*, vol. I, 2nd. ed., Lima, Impr. Torres Aguirre, 1939, pp. 4, 20–21, 29–30, 34, 60, 62 and 74; Alejandro Álvarez, *La Reconstrucción del Derecho de Gentes – El Nuevo Orden y la Renovación Social*, Santiago de Chile, Ed. Nascimento, 1944, pp. 19–25 and 86–87; Ph. Azevedo, *A Justiça Internacional*, Rio de Janeiro, MRE, 1949, pp. 24–26, and cf. pp. 9–10; J.-C. Puig, *Les principes du Droit international public américain*, Paris, Pédone, 1954, p. 39; H. Accioly, *Tratado de Direito Internacional Público*, 2nd. ed., vol. I, Rio de Janeiro, IBGE, 1956, pp. 32–40; Alejandro Alvarez, *El Nuevo Derecho Internacional en Sus Relaciones con la Vida Actual de los Pueblos*, Santiago, Edit. Jurídica de Chile, 1961, pp. 155–157, 304 and 356–357; A. Gómez Robledo, *Meditación sobre la Justicia*, México, Fondo de Cultura Económica, 1963, p. 9; R. Fernandes, *Nonagésimo Aniversário – Conferências e Trabalhos Esparsos*, vol. I, Rio de Janeiro, M.R.E., 1967, pp. 174–175; A.A. Conil Paz, *Historia de la Doctrina Drago*, Buenos Aires, Abeledo-Perrot, 1975, pp. 125–131; E. Jiménez de Aréchaga, "International Law in the Past Third of a Century", 159 RCADI (1978) pp. 87 and 111–113; L.A. Podestá Costa and J.M. Ruda, *Derecho Internacional Público*, 5th. rev. ed., vol. I, Buenos Aires, Tip. Ed. Argentina, 1979, pp. 17–18 and 119–139; E. Jiménez de Aréchaga, *El Derecho Internacional Contemporáneo*, Madrid, Ed. Tecnos, 1980, pp. 107–141; A.A. Cançado Trindade, *Princípios do Direito Internacional Contemporâneo*, Brasília, Edit. University of Brasília, 1981, pp. 1–102 and 244–248; Jorge Castañeda, *Obras Completas* – vol. I: *Naciones Unidas*, Mexico, S.R.E./El Colegio de México, 1995, pp. 63–65, 113–125, 459, 509–510, 515, 527–543 and 565–586; [Various Authors,] *Andrés Bello y el Derecho* (Colloquy of Santiago de Chile of July 1981), Santiago, Edit. Jurídica de Chile, 1982, pp. 41–49 and 63–76; D. Uribe Vargas, *La Paz es una Trégua – Solución Pacífica de Conflictos Internacionales*, 3rd. ed., Bogotá, Universidad Nacional de Colombia, 1999, p. 109; A.A. Cançado Trindade, *O Direito Internacional em um Mundo em Transformação*, Rio de Janeiro, Edit. Renovar, 2002, pp. 91–140 and 863–889 and 1039–1071.

13 Lafayette Rodrigues Pereira, *Princípios de Direito Internacional*, vols. I–II, Rio de Janeiro, J. Ribeiro dos Santos Ed., 1902–1903, pp. 1 *et seq.*; A.S. de Bustamante y Sirvén, *La II Conferencia de la Paz Reunida en La Haya en 1907*, vol. II, Madrid, Libr. Gen. de V. Suárez, 1908, pp. 133, 137–141, 145–147, 157–159, and cf. also vol. I, pp. 43, 80–81 and 96; Epitacio Pessôa, *Projecto de Código de Direito Internacional Público*, Rio de Janeiro, Imprensa Nacional, 1911, pp. 5–323; F.-J. Urrutia, "La codification du droit international en Amérique", 22 RCADI (1928) pp. 113, 116–117 and 162–163; G. Guerrero, *La codification du droit*

25. The ICJ has remained attentive to general principles (cf. *supra*) in the exercise of the international judicial function. As master of its procedure, as well as of its jurisdiction, the Court is fully entitled to determine freely the order in which it will resolve the issues raised by the contending parties. And, in doing so, it is not limited by the arguments raised by the contending parties, as indicated by the principle *jura novit curia*. The Court knows the Law, and, in settling disputes, attentive to the equality of parties, it also says what the Law is (*juris dictio, jus dicere*).

2   General Principles in Distinct Incidental Proceedings

26. Along the years, as one would expect, the principle of the sound administration of justice (*la bonne administration de la justice*) has been resorted to in respect of distinct kinds of incidental proceedings (Rules of Court, Articles 73–86), namely, *preliminary objections, provisional measures of protection, counter-claims* and *intervention*. The aforementioned principle has marked its presence, as already seen in the present Separate Opinion, in the handling of the incidental proceedings of preliminary objections (cf. *supra*). Recourse has likewise been made to that principle, in recent years, in the other incidental proceedings of provisional measures, counter-claims and intervention. May I briefly refer to its incidence, as I perceive it, in these other incidental proceedings.

27. In so far as *provisional measures of protection* are concerned, in my Dissenting Opinion in the case of *Questions Relating to the Obligation to Prosecute or to Extradite* (Belgium *versus* Senegal, Order of 28.05.2009), I deemed it fit to

---

international, Paris, Pédone, 1930, pp. 11, 13, 16, 152, 182 and 175; J.-M. Yepes, "La contribution de l'Amérique Latine au développement du Droit international public et privé", 32 RCADI (1930) pp. 714–730 and 753–756; Alejandro Álvarez, "Méthodes de la codification du droit international public – Rapport", in *Annuaire de l'Institut de Droit International* (1947) pp. 38, 46–47, 50–51, 54, 64 and 69; J.-M. Yepes, *Del Congreso de Panama a la Conferencia de Caracas (1826–1954)*, Caracas, M.R.E., 1955, pp. 143, 177–178, 193 and 203–208; R.J. Alfaro, "The Rights and Duties of States", 97 RCADI (1959) pp. 138–139, 145–154, 159 and 167–172; G.E. do Nascimento e Silva, "A Codificação do Direito Internacional", 55/60 *Boletim da Sociedade Brasileira de Direito Internacional* (1972–1974) pp. 83–84 and 103; R.P. Anand, "Sovereign Equality of States in International Law", 197 RCADI (1986) pp. 73–74; A.A. Cançado Trindade, "The Presence and Participation of Latin America at the II Hague Peace Conference of 1907", *in Actualité de la Conférence de La Haye de 1907, II Conférence de la Paix* (Colloque du centenaire, 2007 – ed. Yves Daudet), La Haye/Leiden, Académie de Droit International de La Haye / Nijhoff, 2008, pp. 51–84.

recall that, in its case-law, the ICJ has ordered provisional measures so as to contribute "to secure *la bonne administration de la justice*" (para. 28). I pondered that "in the case-law itself of the ICJ there are already elements disclosing the concern of the Court, when issuing Orders of provisional measures, *to strive towards achieving a good administration of justice*" (para. 29). I further warned that, in the consideration of the *cas d'espèce*, the Court should keep in mind that "the *right to the realization of justice* assumes a central place, and a paramount importance, and becomes thus deserving of particular attention" (para. 29).

28. As to *counter-claims*, in my Dissenting Opinion in the case of *Jurisdictional Immunities of the State* (Germany *versus* Italy, Order of 06.07.2010), I felt obliged to stress that

> (...) Without Italy's counter claim of reparations for damages arising of war crimes, the Court will now have a much narrower horizon to pronounce on Germany's (original) claim of State immunity. The present decision of the Court made *tabula rasa* of its own previous reasonings, and of 70 years of the more enlightened legal doctrine on the matter, to the effect that counter-claims do assist in achieving the sound administration of justice (*la bonne administration de la justice*) and in securing the needed equilibrium between the procedural rights of the contending parties.
>
> In any case, as the Court's majority decided summarily to discard the counter-claim as "inadmissible as such", – with my firm dissent, – it should at least have instructed itself properly by holding, first, public hearings to obtain further clarifications from the contending parties. It should not have taken the present decision without first having heard the contending parties in a public sitting, for five reasons, namely: (a) first, as a basic requirement ensuing from the principle of international procedural law of the sound administration of justice (*la bonne administration de la justice*); (b) secondly, because counter-claims are ontologically endowed with *autonomy*, and ought to be treated on the same footing as the original claims, that they intend to neutralize (*supra*); (c) thirdly, claims and counter-claims, "directly connected" as they ought to be, require a strict observance of the *principe du contradictoire* in their handling altogether; (d) fourthly, only with the faithful observance of the *principe du contradictoire* can the *procedural equality* of the parties (applicant and respondent, rendered respondent and applicant by the counter-claim) be

secured; and (e) fifthly, last but not least, the issues raised by the original claim and the counter-claim before the Court are far too important – for the settlement of the case as well as for the present and the future of International Law, – to have been dealt with by the Court in the way it did, summarily rejecting the counter-claim (paras. 29–30).

29. And in so far as *intervention* is concerned, again in the case in the case of *Jurisdictional Immunities of the State* (Germany *versus* Italy, intervention of Greece, Order of 04.07.2011), I developed my reflections on the importance of sound reasoning in that respect (paras. 1–61). More recently, in the *Whaling in the Antarctic* case (Australia *versus* Japan, intervention of New Zealand, Order of 06.02.2013), I pondered, in my Separate Opinion, that

> The *resurgere* of intervention is thus most welcome, propitiating the sound administration of justice (*la bonne administration de la justice*), attentive to the needs not only of all States concerned but of the international community as a whole, in the conceptual universe of the *jus gentium* of our times (para. 68).

30. In sum, the principle of the sound administration of justice (*la bonne administration de la justice*) permeates the considerations of all the aforementioned incidental proceedings before the Court, namely, preliminary objections, provisional measures of protection, counter-claims and intervention. As expected, general principles mark their presence, and guide, all Court proceedings. The factual contexts of the cases vary, but the incidence of those principles always takes place. Other illustrations, which abound, can be here referred to.

31. A very recent example, of less than three months ago, can be found in the Court's Order of 01.07.2015, in the case of *Armed Activities on the Territory of the Congo* (D.R. Congo *versus* Uganda) wherein the Court took account of "the requirements of the sound administration of justice" (para. 7) in order to resume the proceedings in the case as to reparations (para. 8). In my Declaration appended to that Order, I have stressed the relevance of the application of the principle of the sound administration of justice (*la bonne administration de la justice*) for the proper exercise of the international judicial function (para. 6). Yet another illustration in the case-law of the ICJ is provided by the incidence – as I perceive it – of the principle of the sound administration of justice (*la bonne administration de la justice*) in the Court's handling of joinder of proceedings in two recent (joined) cases, to which I now briefly turn.

3 General Principles in the Joinder of Proceedings

32. The joinder of proceedings (regulated by Article 47 of the Rules of Court) has found application by the Court in the recent cases of *Certain Activities Carried out by Nicaragua in the Border Area* (Costa Rica *versus* Nicaragua) and *Construction of a Road in Costa Rica along the San Juan River* (Nicaragua *versus* Costa Rica) (two Court's Orders of 17.04.2013). In both Orders of joinder, the ICJ stated that the joinders previously effected by it, and before it by its predecessor, were "consonant" with "the principle of the sound administration of justice" and also with "the need for judicial economy".[14] Likewise, in those two cases, the Court deemed it appropriate to join their proceedings, "in conformity with the principle of the sound administration of justice and with the need for judicial economy".[15]

33. In my Separate Opinions in each of the Orders in the two cases, I devoted special attention to the incidence of the principle of the sound administration of justice in respect of joinders of proceedings.[16] I pointed out that, even if *la bonne administration de la justice* flourished initially as a maxim, it later gave expression to a principle. In my perception, the proper exercise of the international judicial function "requires the blend of logic and experience (*la sagesse et l'expérience*), deeply-rooted in legal thinking (of comparative domestic law and of international law)", so as to endeavour "to secure the sound administration of justice". And I added:

> Positivists try in vain to subsume this latter under the *interna corporis* of the international tribunal at issue, in their well-known incapacity to explain anything that transcends the regulatory texts. (...)
>
> The sound administration of justice enables the international tribunal at issue to tackle questions of procedure even if these latter have "escaped" the regulations of its *interna corporis*. It is, in my perception, the idea of an objective justice that, ultimately, guides the sound administration of justice (*la bonne administration de la justice*), in the line of jusnaturalist thinking. The proper pursuit of justice is in conformity with the general principles of law. With the reassuring evolution and expansion of judicial settlement in recent decades, there has been, not surprisingly, an increasing recourse to the maxim *la bonne administration de la*

---

14   Paras. 18 and 12, respectively.
15   Paras. 24 and 18.
16   Paras. 10–23 and 25–27.

justice, – which gives expression to a general principle of law, captured by human conscience[17] (paras. 13 and 15).

34. Hence the relevance of the proper handling of international procedure, for the sake of the realization of justice (para. 17). In this connection, already in the late thirties, Maurice Bourquin deemed it fit to single out the relevance of the "qualité des procédures". To him,

> Une bonne procédure facilite la solution des difficultés. Une mauvaise procédure fait, en revanche, plus de mal que de bien. Mais ce n'est pas un mécanisme, même admirablement agencé, qui pourrait régler à lui seul une pareille matière. Ce qu'il faut ici, par-dessus tout, c'est un certain état d'esprit, (...) le calme de la raison; c'est cette chose si simple et pourtant si rare qu'on appelle le bon sens.[18]

35. Common sense is indeed the least common of all senses, it cannot simply be assumed. Hence the need to keep always in mind the principle of *la bonne administration de la justice*. It is not the only principle of the kind. The maxim *audiatur et altera pars* (or *audi alteram partem*) gave expression to the general principle of law providing for *procedural equality* between the contending parties in the course of judicial proceedings.[19] Another principle of international procedural law, that of *jura novit curia* (going back to Roman law), acknowledges the freedom and autonomy of the judge in searching for and determining the law applicable to a given dispute, without being restrained by the arguments of the parties.[20]

4   *General Principles in Advisory Proceedings*

36. The principle of the sound administration of justice (*la bonne administration de la justice*) has been resorted to not only in the proceedings of contentious cases, but in the Court's advisory proceedings as well. May I turn briefly to these latter now. On successive occasions the Court, by resorting to *la bonne*

---

17   On human conscience – the universal juridical conscience – as the ultimate material source of international law, cf. A.A. Cançado Trindade, *International Law for Humankind...*, *op. cit supra* n. (15), ch. VI, pp. 139–161.

18   M. Bourquin, "Stabilité et mouvement dans l'ordre juridique international", 64 *Recueil des Cours de l'Académie de Droit International de La Haye* (1938) p. 472.

19   Bin Cheng, *General Principles of Law as Applied by International Courts and Tribunals*, London, Stevens, 1953, p. 291.

20   Cf. my Separate Opinions in the two Orders of joinder of the ICJ in the aforementioned cases of *Certain Activities* and *Construction of a Road*, para. 19.

administration de la justice, has endeavoured to secure the observance of the principle of *procedural equality* of the parties. Already in the mid-fifties, the ICJ expressed its attention to general principles of international procedural law.

37. Thus, in its Advisory Opinion (of 23.10.1956) on the *Judgments of the ILO Administrative Tribunal upon Complaints Made against UNESCO*, the ICJ, after having noted the "absence of equality" (in its advisory proceedings) ensuing from the Statute of the Court itself, pondered that "[t]he principle of equality of the parties follows from the requirements of good administration of justice" (p. 86). The Court would better have stated, more precisely, that the principle of equality of the parties *orients* or *guides* the requirements of good administration of justice. In my understanding, principles (*prima principia*) stand higher than rules or requirements, and orient them.

38. Two and a half decades later, the ICJ again stressed the relevance of "the principle of equality of the parties" in its Advisory Opinion of 20.07.1982, concerning an *Application for Review of a Judgment of the U.N. Administrative Tribunal* (paras. 29–32 and 79). In its most recent Advisory Opinion (of 01.02.2012), on a *Judgment of the ILO Administrative Tribunal upon a Complaint Filed against IFAD*, the ICJ insisted on "the right to equality in the proceedings" (para. 30), on "the principle of equality before the Court" as "a central aspect of the good administration of justice" (paras. 35 and 44), and on "the principle of equality in the proceedings before the Court, required by its inherent judicial character and by the good administration of justice" (para. 47).[21] In my Separate Opinion (paras. 28–51 and 82–118) appended to this recent Advisory Opinion of the ICJ of 2012, I have dwelt in depth (paras. 20–56 and 82–118) upon the imperative of securing the equality of parties in the international legal process.

5   *General Assessment*

39. As seen in the preceding paragraphs, fundamental principles, forming the *substratum* of the legal order itself, are always present, at substantive and procedural levels. They orient the interpretation and application of legal norms, and recourse to them is ineluctable in the realization of justice. I have reviewed their incidence in distinct incidental proceedings of contentious cases (of preliminary objections, provisional measures, counter-claims and intervention),

---

21   It further insisted on "equality of access" to justice (paras. 37, 39, 43 and 48), on "the concept of equality before courts and tribunals" (paras. 38 and 40), and on the guarantee of "equal access and equality of arms" (para. 39).

in addition to the joinder of proceedings, as well as in advisory proceedings (cf. *supra*).

40. The ICJ, explaining the reasons to decide the way it did, for example, in its two aforementioned Orders (of 17.04.2013) of joinder of the proceedings in the cases concerning *Certain Activities Carried out by Nicaragua in the Border Area* (Costa Rica *versus* Nicaragua) and *Construction of a Road in Costa Rica along the San Juan River* (Nicaragua *versus* Costa Rica), pondered that its decision to join the proceedings would allow it "to address simultaneously the totality of the various interrelated and contested issues raised by the Parties" (para. 23). In my Separate Opinions appended to those two Orders, I deemed it fit to state:

> In my perception, the presence of the idea of justice, guiding the sound administration of justice, is ineluctable. Not seldom the text of the Court's *interna corporis* does not suffice; in order to impart justice, in circumstances of this kind, an international tribunal such as the ICJ is guided by the *prima principia*. To attempt to offer a definition of the sound administration of justice that would encompass all possible situations that could arise would be far too pretentious, and fruitless. An endless diversity of situations may be faced by the ICJ, leading it – in its pursuit of the realization of justice – to deem it fit to have recourse to the principle of the sound administration of justice (*la bonne administration de la justice*); this general principle, in sum, finds application in the most diverse circumstances. (...)
>
> (...) The idea of justice guides the sound administration of justice (*la bonne administration de la justice*), as manifested, e.g., in decisions aiming at securing the *procedural equality* of the contending parties.
>
> General principles of law have always marked presence in the pursuit of the realization of justice. In my understanding, they comprise not only those principles acknowledged in national legal systems, but likewise the general principles of international law. They have been repeatedly reaffirmed, time and time again, and, – even if regrettably neglected by segments of contemporary legal doctrine, – they retain their full validity in our days. An international tribunal like the ICJ has consistently had recourse to them in its *jurisprudence constante*. Despite the characteristic attitude of legal positivism to attempt, in vain, to minimize their role, the truth remains that, without principles, there is no legal system at all, at either national or international level.
>
> General principles of law inform and conform the norms and rules of legal systems. In my understanding, sedimented along the years, general

principles of law form the *substratum* of the national and international legal orders, they are indispensable (forming the *jus necessarium*, going well beyond the mere *jus voluntarium*), and they give expression to the idea of an *objective* justice (proper of jusnaturalist thinking), of universal scope. Last but not least, it is the general principles of law that inspire the interpretation and application of legal norms, and also the law making process itself[22] (paras. 20 and 25–27).

V General Principles of International Law, Latin American International Legal Doctrine, and the Significance of the Pact of Bogotá

41. In this connection, may I now turn to the Pact of Bogotá, Article XXXI of which provides the jurisdictional basis for the Court's present Judgment in the case concerning the *Obligation to Negotiate Access to the Pacific Ocean*. May I briefly recall how the Pact of Bogotá was envisaged in the epoch it came to see the light of the day. As soon as the Pact of Bogotá was adopted in 1948, it was reckoned that, among the solutions in the domain of peaceful settlement of international disputes, stress needed to be laid by the Pact in particular upon the importance of judicial settlement. Article XXXI of the Pact, in providing for the compulsory jurisdiction of the ICJ for the settlement of "all disputes of a juridical nature", was regarded as being in line with Latin American doctrine as to the primacy of law and justice over recourse to force.[23] Already in 1948, it was pointed out that

> La finalidad evidente de todo el sistema creado en [el Pacto de] Bogotá es la de asegurar que ningún conflicto ni ninguna controversia susceptible de poner en peligro la paz de América, quede sin solución pacífica. Para ésto, el Pacto generalizó, en un compromiso colectivo, la jurisdicción obligatoria de la Corte Internacional de Justicia.[24]

---

22   A.A. Cançado Trindade, *International Law for Humankind: Towards a New Jus Gentium*, op. cit. supra n. (15), Ch. III, pp. 85–121, esp. pp. 90–92.

23   Cf. R. Cordova, "El Tratado Americano de Soluciones Pacíficas – Pacto de Bogotá", 1 *Anuario Jurídico Interamericano* – Pan American Union (1948) pp. 11–15 and 17.

24   *Ibid.*, p. 11 – "The clear aim of the whole system created in [the Pact of] Bogotá is that of securing that no conflict nor any controversy susceptible of putting in risk the peace of America, is to remain without peaceful settlement. To that end, the Pact generalized, in a collective engagement, the compulsory jurisdiction of the International Court of Justice". [My own translation].

42. This brings us closer to the object and purpose of the Pact itself, taken as a whole. In effect, the 1948 Pact of Bogotá was promptly regarded as a work of codification of peaceful settlement in international law, moving beyond the arbitral solution (deeply-rooted in Latin American experience) into judicial settlement itself, without the need of a special agreement to that effect.[25] Without imposing any specific means of peaceful settlement, the Pact of Bogotá took a step forward in rendering obligatory peaceful settlement itself, and enhanced recourse to the ICJ.[26]

43. The adoption of the Pact of Bogotá, with this advance in dispute-settlement, was the culminating point of the evolution, starting in the XIXth century, of the commitment of Latin American countries with peaceful settlement of international disputes, moving towards compulsory jurisdiction of the Hague Court. This feature of Latin American international legal thinking arose out of the concertation of the countries of the region in two series of Conferences, namely: (a) the Latin American Conferences (1826–1889);[27] and (b) the Pan American Conferences (1889–1948),[28] leading to the adoption, in 1948, of the OAS Charter and the Pact of Bogotá. The gradual outcome of this concertation echoed at the II Hague Peace Conference (1907), and in the drafting process of the Statute of the PCIJ (1920) and the ICJ (1945).[29]

---

25   J.M. Yepes, "El Tratado Americano de Soluciones Pacíficas (Pacto de Bogotá)", 9 *Universitas* – Pontificia Universidad Católica Javeniana (1955) pp. 23–25 and 40.

26   *Ibid.*, pp. 34 and 36.

27   Starting with the Conference (*Congreso Anfictiónico*) of Panama of 1826, followed by the Conferences (with small groups of States) of Lima (1847–1848), Santiago de Chile (1856), Lima (1864–1865 and 1877–1880) and Montevideo (1888–1889).

28   Starting with the Conference of Washington (1889), followed by the International Conferences of American States of Mexico (1901–1902), Rio de Janeiro (1906), Buenos Aires (1910), Santiago de Chile (1923), Havana (1928), Montevideo (1933), Lima (1938), and Bogotá (1948, wherein the OAS Charter and the Pact of Bogotá were adopted, initiating the era of the OAS).

29   For an account and examination of those historical antecedents, cf. F.V. García-Amador (coord.), *Sistema Interamericano a través de Tratados, Convenciones y Otros Documentos*, vol. I: Asuntos Jurídico-Políticos, Washington D.C., OAS General Secretariat, 1981, pp. 1–67; A.A. Cançado Trindade, "The Presence and Participation of Latin America at the II Hague Peace Conference of 1907", *in Actualité de la Conférence de La Haye de 1907, II Conférence de la Paix (Colloque de 2007)* (ed. Y. Daudet), The Hague/Leiden, The Hague Academy of International Law/Nijhoff, 2008, pp. 51–84; H. Gros Espiell, "La doctrine du Droit international en Amérique Latine avant la Première Conférence Panaméricaine (Washington, 1889)", 3 *Journal of the History of International Law/Revue d'histoire du droit international* (2001) pp. 1–17.

44. The adoption of the Pact of Bogotá in 1948 was the culmination of the sustained and enduring posture of Latin American States in support of peaceful settlement of disputes, and of the compulsory jurisdiction of the Hague Court over disputes of a "juridical nature". In effect, three years after the adoption of the U.N. Charter in 1945, Latin American States did in Bogotá in 1948 what they had announced in San Francisco as a goal: the recourse, under Article XXXI of the Pact of Bogotá, to the compulsory jurisdiction of the ICJ, for the settlement of disputes of a "juridical nature", irrespective of the position that States Parties to the Pact might have taken under the optional clause (Article 36(2)) of the ICJ Statute. That was a significant step ahead.

45. As it was adopted, the Pact of Bogotá was promptly regarded by its contemporaries as a landmark in the development of this chapter of international law:

> Hasta la reunión de la IX Conferencia [Internacional Americana (Bogotá, 1948)] no existía en América lo que podríamos llamar el estatuto de la *pax americana*. Había habido sólo una multitud de convenciones que reglamentaban fragmentariamente los distintos medios de solución pacífica. (...) De ahí la necesidad (...) de elaborar un instrumento único que (...) coordinase el conjunto para que constituyesen un cuerpo armónico, tanto en la parte substantiva como en la procedimental. Puede decirse que el Pacto de Bogotá ha alcanzado ese objetivo. Un sólo tratado, bien estructurado, como éste, que prevea todos los casos posibles de conflictos entre los Estados americanos y que estipule de una manera ineludible la solución pacífica obligatoria de todas las controversias, implica sin duda un progreso real del Derecho internacional americano. (...)
>
> (...) Nos referimos especialmente (...) a la disposición que confiere, *ipso facto* y sin necesidad de ningún convenio especial, jurisdicción obligatoria a la Corte Internacional de Justicia para todas las diferencias de carácter jurídico entre los Estados signatarios.[30]

---

30   *Ibid.*, pp. 24–25 – "Until the meeting of the IX [International American] Conference [(Bogotá, 1948)] there did not exist in America what we could call the statute of the *pax americana*. There was only a multitude of conventions which regulated in a fragmented way the distinct means of peaceful settlement (...) Hence the necessity (...) to elaborate one sole instrument which (...) would coordinate the whole matter so as to render it a harmonious *corpus*, as substantive as well as procedural level. One may say that the Pact of Bogotá has achieved that aim. One sole treaty, well structured, like this one, which foresees all possible cases of conflicts among the American States and which stipulates in an ineluctable way the compulsory peaceful settlement of all controversies, implies undoubtedly a real progress of the American International Law. (...)

46. There was, in the Pact of Bogotá, a combination of the obligation to submit disputes of a juridical nature (i.e., those based on claims of legal rights) to judicial or arbitral settlement, – with the free choice of means of peaceful settlement as to other types of controversies; in this way, the 1948 Pact innovated in providing for peaceful settlement of all disputes.[31] In adopting the 1948 Pact of Bogotá, Latin American States made a point of expressing their "spirit of confidence", added to their "feeling of common interest", in judicial settlement (more perfected than arbitral settlement), in particular the compulsory jurisdiction of the ICJ.[32] Hence the relevance of Article XXXI of the Pact, also in relation to Article VI.

47. Moreover, the 1948 Charter of the Organization of American States (OAS) relied upon the adoption of a "special treaty" for the peaceful settlement of international disputes among States of the region, and the Pact of Bogotá was intended to be that "special treaty". Yet, despite the achievement, in historical perspective,[33] of the adoption of the 1948 American Treaty on Pacific Settlement (Pact of Bogotá), and the fact that it had been elaborated in a conceptual framework which best reflected Latin American international law doctrine, – as time went on, not so many States became Parties to it. For those which did not ratify it, earlier treaties continue to operate, providing a diversity of bases for the peaceful settlement of international disputes, which the Pact of Bogotá sought to overcome and systematize.

48. This may explain why, already in the mid-fifties, the possibility of its future revision was already admitted.[34] The 1948 Pact of Bogotá, as just seen,

      (...) We refer especially (...) to the provision which confers, *ipso facto* and without the need of any special agreement, compulsory jurisdiction to the International Court of Justice for all disputes of a juridical nature among the signatory States" [My own translation].

31 W. Sanders, "The Organization of American States – Summary of the Conclusions of the Ninth International Conference of American States (Bogotá, Colombia, March 30–May 2, 1948)", 442 *International Conciliation* (June 1948) p. 400.

32 Ch.G. Fenwick, "The Pact of Bogotá and Other Juridical Decisions of the Ninth Conference", 82 *Bulletin of the Pan American Union* (August 1948) n. 8, pp. 424–425.

33 Cf., for a general study, J.M. Yepes, *Del Congreso de Panamá a la Conferencia de Caracas (1826–1954)*, Caracas, [Ed. Concurso M.R.E. de Venezuela], 1955, pp. 29–208.

34 Cf. Ch.G. Fenwick, "The Revision of the Pact of Bogotá", 48 *American Journal of International Law* (1954) pp. 123–126. It was pointed out, *inter alia*, that, e.g., Bolivia and Ecuador had both made reservations to Article VI of the Pact (excluding its application to matters already settled by treaty), bearing in mind "treaties which they believe were entered into under compulsion"; *ibid.*, p. 124.

has already a long history, during which the question of its reform was more than once envisaged. From the early seventies onwards, the idea of its reassessment or revision was in effect contemplated, though without effects. Thus, in an Opinion of 16.09.1971, the OAS Inter-American Juridical Committee, having examined the matter, was of the view that its key provisions (such as Articles XXXI and VI) could not be modified or suppressed.[35] The Committee concluded that the Pact of Bogotá rightly regulates all procedures (including compulsory judicial or arbitral ones) of peaceful settlement, and should not be opened to modifications;[36] it finally urged OAS member States to ratify the Pact of Bogotá.[37]

49. In the mid-eighties the idea of its revision was again brought to the fore, – in the 1984 OAS General Assembly, held in Brasília, – in the wider context of the OAS reforms as a whole (1985 Protocol of Cartagena de Indias); concern was expressed in the Committee with the relatively small number of ratifications (13 at that time) and the fact that it had been rarely resorted to in practice until then.[38] The OAS Inter-American Juridical Committee issued a new Opinion on 29.08.1985, and, once again, the idea of reforming the Pact of Bogotá did not prosper. The Committee pondered, in its Opinion of 1985, that the Pact, – the special treaty foreseen under Article 26 of the OAS Charter, – amounted to a codification of the existing treaties on peaceful settlement of disputes in the inter-American system.[39]

50. The Committee decided, in the same Opinion, that Article XXXI of the Pact was to remain unaltered, as it constituted one of its key features, in setting forth the recourse to the ICJ, by means of the recognition of its jurisdiction as "compulsory *ipso facto*, without the necessity of any special agreement", so long as the treaty remains in force for the settlement of "disputes of a juridical nature" specified in the Pact itself.[40] The Committee thus dismissed any amendments that purported to put an end to the automatism of recourse to the compulsory

---

35   Cf. Comité Jurídico Interamericano, "Dictamen", *in*: 10 *Recomendaciones e Informes* (1967–1973) pp. 402–403.
36   *Ibid.*, pp. 402–403.
37   *Ibid.*, p. 406 – Subsequently, in the mid-seventies, the OAS Permanent Council took note that no recommendations had been presented of reforms of the Pact of Bogotá; cf. OEA/Consejo Permanente, doc. OEA/Ser.G-CP/CG-628/75, of 21.11.1975, p. XI.
38   Cf. Comité Jurídico Interamericano, 16 *Informes y Recomendaciones* (1984) p. 59; Comité Jurídico Interamericano, 17 *Informes y Recomendaciones* (1985) pp. 62–63.
39   Listed in Article LVIII of the Pact itself; cf. "Dictamen", *in*: Comité Jurídico Interamericano, 17 *Informes y Recomendaciones* (1985), pp. 65 and 95.
40   *In ibid.*, pp. 66, 74–75 and 81.

jurisdiction of the ICJ under the Pact of Bogotá (Article XXXI).[41] The Committee's Opinion of 1985 was followed by a project presented by Colombia to the OAS in 1986–1987,[42] which sought an adjustment of the Pact with the provisions of the OAS Charter as amended by the Protocol of Cartagena de Indias.[43]

51. In this respect, in 1987, the OAS Committee on Juridical and Political Affairs (subsidiary organ of the OAS Permanent Council) found the existence of differences of opinion within the OAS as to an eventual revision of the Pact of Bogotá. In the lack of any consensus to amend the Pact, this latter, accordingly, subsisted as it stood, and as it stands today. The OAS General Secretariat, for its part, likewise studied the matter in 1985–1987,[44] and concluded that the Pact of Bogotá is the "special treaty" adopted in compliance with Article 26 of the OAS Charter, and could only be changed if all States Parties to it so decided,[45] – which was not the case. The Pact remained unchanged.

52. Throughout these exercises, from 1971 to the late eighties, although an argument was made in favour of a reform of the Pact of Bogotá,[46] this latter remained unchanged, and the main trend of expert writing leaned in support of the preservation of its provisions, stressing, in particular, the historical relevance of Article XXXI of the Pact, for ascribing the utmost importance to judicial settlement of "disputes of a juridical nature", by means of automatic acceptance of the compulsory jurisdiction of the ICJ, thus overriding obligations ensuing from optional clause declarations.[47]

---

41   Cf. *ibid.*, p. 75.
42   Cf. OAS, doc. AG/doc.2030/86, pp. 1–19; OAS/Permanent Council, doc. OEA/Ser.G-CP/CAJP-662/87, of 03.05.1987, pp. 1–5; OAS/Permanent Council, doc. OEA/Ser.G-CP/CAJP-666/87, of 11.05.1987, pp. 1–6.
43   Cf. doc. OEA/Ser.G-CP/CAJP-666/87, *cit. supra* n. (42), of 11.05.1987, p. 3.
44   Cf. OEA/Consejo Permanente, doc. OEA/Ser.G-CP/doc.1560/85-Part II, of 09.04.1985, pp. 13–23.
45   Cf. OEA/Consejo Permanente, doc. OEA/Ser.G-CP/CAJP-676/87, of 02.06.1987, pp. 13–15, and cf. pp. 1–12.
46   Cf. G. Leoro F., "La Reforma del Tratado Americano de Soluciones Pacíficas o Pacto de Bogotá", *in*: OEA, *Anuario Jurídico Interamericano* (1981) pp. 43 and 77–79.
47   Cf. A. Herrarte, "Solución Pacífica de las Controversias en el Sistema Interamericano", *in*: OEA, VI *Curso de Derecho Internacional Organizado por el Comité Jurídico Interamericano* (1979) pp. 220 and 225; E. Valencia-Ospina, "The Role of the International Court of Justice in the Pact of Bogotá", *in Liber Amicorum In Memoriam of Judge J.M. Ruda* (eds. C.A. Armas Barea, J. Barberis *et alii*), The Hague, Kluwer, 2000, pp. 296–297, 301 and 305–306; A. Bazán Jiménez, "Tratado Americano de Soluciones Pacíficas – Pacto de Bogotá", 57 *Revista Peruana de Derecho Internacional* (2007) pp. 21, 36 and 47–48.

53. This was a significant contribution of Latin American international legal thinking to the matter, enhancing compulsory judicial settlement. Article XXXI of the Pact of Bogotá had the legal effect of transforming the "loose relationship" ensuing from optional clause declarations under Article 36(2) of the ICJ Statute into a "treaty relationship", endowed with

> the binding force and the stability which is characteristic of a conventional link, and not of the regime of the optional clause. In this way, the Latin American States which have accepted the Pact of Bogotá have established, in their mutual relations, and in view of the close historical and cultural ties between them, the compulsory jurisdiction of the Court on much stronger terms than those resulting from the network of declarations made under Article 36(2) of the Statute.[48]

VI   The Pact of Bogotá and Judicial Settlement by the ICJ

54. The Pact of Bogotá served as basis of the ICJ's jurisdiction in the case of the 1906 Arbitral Award by the King of Spain (Honduras versus Nicaragua, 1960), – but ever since, until the mid-eighties, the Pact laid dormant, in so far as the ICJ jurisdiction is concerned. Furthermore, the Pact of Bogotá, despite its few ratifications (only [fourteen]),[49] was to be considered in the context of regional arrangements for conflict resolution in Latin America, given the importance ascribed by Latin American States to the general principle of peaceful settlement of international disputes.[50]

55. After the aforementioned dismissed initiatives as to its eventual amendment (*supra*), there occurred, from the late eighties onwards, a gradual revival of the Pact of Bogotá, as basis of the ICJ's jurisdiction, in disputes – like the one

---

48 E. Jiménez de Aréchaga, "The Compulsory Jurisdiction of the International Court of Justice under the Pact of Bogotá and the Optional Clause", *in International Law at a Time of Perplexity – Essays in Honour of S. Rosenne* (eds. Y. Dinstein and M. Tabory), Dordrecht, Nijhoff, 1989, pp. 356–357.

49 Currently (September 2015): Bolivia, Brazil, Chile, Costa Rica, Dominican Republic, Ecuador, Haiti, Honduras, Mexico, Nicaragua, Panama, Paraguay, Peru, Uruguay. (Denunciations: Colombia, El Salvador).

50 Cf. A.A. Cançado Trindade, "Regional Arrangements and Conflict Resolution in Latin America", *in Conflict Resolution: New Approaches and Methods*, Paris, UNESCO, 2000, pp. 141–162; A.A. Cançado Trindade, "Mécanismes de règlement pacifique des différends en Amérique Centrale: de Contadora à Esquipulas-II", 33 *Annuaire français de Droit international* (1987) pp. 798–822.

in the present case – opposing Latin American States. Reference can be made to the Court's Judgments in the cases, e.g., of *Border and Transborder Armed Actions* (Nicaragua *versus* Honduras, 1988), *Territorial and Maritime Dispute between Nicaragua and Honduras in the Caribbean Sea* (2007), *Dispute regarding Navigational and Related Rights* (Costa Rica *versus* Nicaragua, 2009), *Pulp Mills on the River Uruguay* (Argentina *versus* Uruguay, 2010), *Territorial and Maritime Dispute* (Nicaragua *versus* Colombia, 2013), *Maritime Dispute* (Peru *versus* Chile, 2014). To these, one may add five other cases, currently pending before the Court.[51] Yet, despite this recent revival of the Pact of Bogotá, I suppose no one would dare to predict, or to hazard a guess, as to further developments in its application in the future. After all, despite advances made, experience shows, within a larger context, that the *parcours* towards compulsory jurisdiction is a particularly long one, there still remains a long path to follow[52]...

56. It should not pass unnoticed that, significantly, the legacy of Latin American doctrine (*supra*) as to the enhancement of judicial settlement of international disputes was well captured and sustained by the ICJ, e.g., in its Judgment of 20.12.1988 in the case concerning *Border and Transborder Armed Actions* (Nicaragua *versus* Honduras). The ICJ held therein that Article XXXI of the Pact of Bogotá enshrines an engagement which can in no way be amended by a subsequent unilateral declaration. In the words of the Court itself, whenever such declaration is made, "it has no effect on the commitment" resulting from Article XXXI of the Pact (para. 36). The States Parties to the Pact have not linked together Article XXXI and such declarations (para. 40); that commitment "is independent of such declarations" (para. 41).

---

51 Such as the (merged) cases of *Certain Activities Carried out by Nicaragua in the Border Area* (Costa Rica *versus* Nicaragua), and of *Construction of a Road in Costa Rica along the San Juan River* (Nicaragua *versus* Costa Rica), – as well as the cases of *Maritime Delimitation in the Caribbean Sea and the Pacific Ocean* (Costa Rica *versus* Nicaragua), *Alleged Violations of Sovereign Rights and Maritime Spaces in the Caribbean Sea* (Nicaragua *versus* Colombia), *Question of the Delimitation of the Continental Shelf between Nicaragua and Colombia beyond 200 Nautical Miles from the Nicaraguan Coast* (Nicaragua *versus* Colombia).

52 For a recent study, cf. A.A. Cançado Trindade, "Towards Compulsory Jurisdiction: Contemporary International Tribunals and Developments in the International Rule of Law – Part I", *in* XXXVII *Curso de Derecho Internacional Organizado por el Comité Jurídico Interamericano – 2010*, Washington D.C., OAS General Secretariat, 2011, pp. 233–259; A.A. Cançado Trindade, "Towards Compulsory Jurisdiction: Contemporary International Tribunals and Developments in the International Rule of Law – Part II", *in* XXXVIII *Curso de Derecho Internacional Organizado por el Comité Jurídico Interamericano – 2011*, Washington D.C., OAS General Secretariat, 2012, pp. 285–366.

57. In sum, the Court's jurisdiction is grounded on the provision of a treaty (the Pact of Bogotá), and not on a unilateral declaration, as under the optional clause of Article 36(2) of the ICJ Statute. Article XXXI was intended to enhance the jurisdiction of the Court, *ratione materiae* and *ratione temporis* (not admitting subsequent restrictions, while the Pact remains in force), as well as *ratione personae* (concerning all States Parties to the Pact). In my own perception, the traditional voluntarist conception (a derivative of anachronical legal positivism) yielded to the reassuring conception of the *jus necessarium*, to the benefit of the realization of international justice.

58. It was made clear by the ICJ, already in the case of *Border and Transborder Armed Actions*, that Article XXXI amounts to a compromissory clause which sets forth the engagement, by the States Parties to the Pact, as to the conventional basis of the jurisdiction of the ICJ, to settle all "disputes of a juridical nature", independently of the optional clause (Article 36(2) of the ICJ Statute). The Court stressed that it was "quite clear from the Pact that the purpose of the American States in drafting it was to reinforce their mutual commitments with regard to the judicial settlement. This is also confirmed by the *travaux préparatoires*" of the Pact, during which the judicial procedure before the ICJ was regarded as "the principal procedure for the peaceful settlement of conflicts between the American States" (para. 46). Furthermore, expert writing has likewise acknowledged that Article XXXI of the Pact of Bogotá enhanced the procedure of judicial settlement by the ICJ.[53]

VII Concluding Observations: The Third Way (*Troisième Voie/Tercera Vía*) under Article 79(9) of the Rules of Court – Objection Not of an Exclusively Preliminary Character

59. May I come to the remaining aspect that I purport to address in the present Separate Opinion. In its Judgment of today, 24.09.2015, in the case concerning the *Obligation to Negotiate Access to the Pacific Ocean*, the Court – as I have already pointed out (cf. paras. 2–3, *supra*) – has very briefly referred to Article

---

[53] Cf., e.g., R. Casado Raigón, "La Sentencia de la CIJ de 20 de Diciembre de 1988 (Competencia y Admisibilidad de la Demanda) en el Asunto Relativo a Acciones Armadas Fronterizas y Transfronterizas (Nicarágua c. Honduras)", 41 *Revista Española de Derecho Internacional* (1989) pp. 402–405 and 407; E. Orihuela Calatayud, "El Pacto de Bogotá y la Corte Internacional de Justicia", 42 *Revista Española de Derecho Internacional* (1990) pp. 430–431, 433, 436 and 438.

XXXI of the Pact of Bogotá and to Article 79(9) of the Rules of Court, in comparison with the attention it devoted to Article VI of the Pact. May it here be recalled that, in the case of *Nicaragua versus United States* (merits, Judgment of 27.06.1986), the ICJ elaborated on the scope of Article 79 of the Rules of Court, to the effect that the provision

> presents one clear advantage: that it qualifies certain objections as preliminary, making it quite clear that when they are exclusively of that character they will have to be decided upon immediately, but if they are not, especially when the character of the objections is not exclusively preliminary because they contain both preliminary aspects and other aspects relating to the merits, they will have to be dealt with at the stage of the merits. This approach also tends to discourage the unnecessary prolongation of proceedings at the jurisdictional stage (para. 41).

60. This point was later reiterated by the ICJ in the *Lockerbie* cases (preliminary objections, Libya *versus* United Kingdom and United States, Judgments of 27.02.1998, paras. 49 and 48, respectively). Moreover, in the aforementioned case of *Territorial and Maritime Dispute* (Nicaragua *versus* Colombia, preliminary objections, Judgment of 13.12.2007), it was also clarified by the Court that, in principle, a party raising a preliminary objection (to jurisdiction or admissibility) is entitled to have that objection answered at the preliminary stage of the proceedings unless the Court "does not have before it all facts necessary" to decide the question raised, or else the Court, in answering that objection, would prejudge the dispute, or some elements thereof, on the merits (para. 51).

61. Article 79(9) of the Rules of Court is not limited to the ICJ deciding in one way or another (upholding or rejecting) the objection raised before it in the course of the proceedings. Article 79(9) in effect contemplates a third way (*troisième voie/tercera vía*), namely, in its terms:

> declare that the objection does not possess, in the circumstances of the case, an exclusively preliminary character. If the Court rejects the objection or declares that it does not possess an exclusively preliminary character, it shall fix time-limits for the further proceedings.

62. This being so, the ICJ, moving into the merits, asserts its jurisdiction; this happens because the character of the objection contains aspects relating to the merits, and thus requires an examination of the merits. This is so in the present case concerning the *Obligation to Negotiate Access to the Pacific Ocean*,

as to the dispute arisen between Bolivia and Chile, as to whether their practice subsequent to the 1904 Peace Treaty substantiates an obligation to negotiate on the part of the respondent State. Such negotiations have given rise to a dispute, not settled by the 1904 Peace Treaty. Chile's objection cannot be properly decided without deciding the merits of the dispute, as it does not have an exclusively preliminary character, appearing rather as a defence as to the merits of Bolivia's claim.

63. There have been negotiations, extending well after the adoption of the 1948 Pact of Bogotá, in which both contending parties were actively engaged; although in the present Judgment there is no express reference to any of such negotiations specifically, the ICJ takes note of arguments made in the course of the proceedings of the *cas d'espèce* to the effect that negotiations took place subsequently to the 1904 Peace Treaty (para. 19)[54] on unsettled issues, well beyond the date of the adoption of the Pact of Bogotá (on 30.04.1948), until 2012. The present case relating to the *Obligation to Negotiate Access to the Pacific Ocean* concerns such process of negotiations, and the issue whether there is a duty to pursue them further.

64. To assert the duty to negotiate is not the same as to assert the duty to negotiate an agreement, or a given result. The former does not imply the latter. This is a matter for consideration at the merits stage. The Court is here concerned only with the former, the claimed duty to negotiate. The objection raised by the respondent State does not appear as one of an exclusively preliminary character. The substance of it can only be properly addressed in the course of the consideration of the merits of the *cas d'espèce*, not as a "preliminary objection". The Court is thus right in proceeding – for this particular reason – to fix time-limits for further proceedings (Article 79(9) *in fine*), moving into the merits phase. The contending parties' post-1904 exchanges and declarations appear to substantiate an obligation to negotiate, beyond and irrespective of the 1904 Peace Treaty. The Court has thus to move into the merits, in order to examine, and pronounce upon, the *punctum pruriens* of the *cas d'espèce*.

65. May it here be further pointed out that, in the case of the *Territorial and Maritime Dispute* (Nicaragua *versus* Colombia, preliminary objections, Judgment of 13.12.2007), the ICJ, after recalling the *rationale* of Article VI of the Pact of Bogotá, found that the dispute had not been settled by the treaty at issue (of 1938, and Protocol of 1930), nor by a judicial decision, and thus found it had

---

54   And cf. paras. 49–50.

jurisdiction under Article XXXI of the Pact (paras. 77 and 120). The ICJ deemed it fit further to recall that Article 79(9) of its Rules of Court establishes three ways in which it may dispose of a preliminary objection: either to uphold or to reject it, or else to declare that it does not possess an exclusively preliminary character (para. 48).

66. This would have been, in my perception, the proper and more prudent way for the Court to dispose of the preliminary objection raised by Chile in the present case opposing it to Bolivia. In any case, the ICJ would move into the merits. The first and third ways foreseen by Article 79(9) of the Rules of Court lead, on the basis of distinct reasonings, to a consideration of the merits of the case. In the previous case of the *Territorial and Maritime Dispute*, opposing Nicaragua to Colombia (*supra*), the ICJ further stressed that the commitment under Article XXXI of the Pact of Bogotá is an "autonomous one" (independent from an optional clause declaration), which enhances the access to the Court (paras. 134–135) and the judicial settlement of "disputes of a juridical nature" under the Pact of Bogotá. Article XXXI cannot be unduly limited by optional clause declarations, nor by preliminary objections which do not possess an exclusively preliminary character.

67. May I conclude that the objection raised by Chile appears as a defence to Bolivia's claim as to the merits, inextricably interwoven with this latter. And the Court, anyway, does not count on all the necessary information to render a decision on it as a "preliminary" issue. It is, in my view, more in line with the good administration of justice (*la bonne administration de la justice*) that the Court should keep the issue to be resolved at the merits stage, when the contending parties will have had the opportunity to plead their case in full. This would entail no delays at all for the forthcoming proceedings as to the merits. Last but not least, Article VI of the Pact of Bogotá does not exclude the Court's jurisdiction in respect of disputes arisen after 1948: to hold otherwise would deprive the Pact of its *effet utile*. The Pact of Bogotá, in line with the mainstream of Latin American international legal doctrine, ascribes great importance to the judicial settlement of disputes, – its main or central achievement, – on the basis of its Article XXXI, a milestone in the conceptual development of this domain of international law.

(Signed) *Antônio Augusto* CANÇADO TRINDADE
Judge

2 Separate Opinion in the case of *Questions Relating to the Seizure and Detention of Certain Documents and Data* (Timor-Leste *versus* Australia, Order, Provisional Measures, of 03.03.2014)

Table Of Contents — Paragraphs

I. *Prolegomena* 1
II. The Centrality of the Quest for Justice 3
    1. Impertinence of Reliance on Local Remedies in the Circumstances of the Present Case 4
    2. Impertinence of Reliance on Avoidance of "Concurrent Jurisdiction" in the Circumstances of the Present Case 6
    3. General Assessment 11
III. Impertinence of Reliance upon Unilateral Acts of States in the Course of International Legal Proceedings 13
IV. *Ex Conscientia Jus Oritur* 26
V. The Question of the Ownership of the Seized Documents and Data 29
VI. The Relevance of General Principles of International Law 33
    1. Responses of the Parties to a Question from the Bench 34
    2. General Assessment 37
VII. The Prevalence of the Juridical Equality of States 44
VIII. Provisional Measures of Protection Independently of Unilateral "Undertakings" or Assurances 46
IX. The Autonomous Legal Regime of Provisional Measures of Protection 59
X. Epilogue: A Recapitulation 63

I   *Prolegomena*

1. Destiny has wished that the judicial year of 2014 of the International Court of Justice (ICJ) was to start with the consideration of the present case concerning *Questions Relating to the Seizure and Detention of Certain Documents and Data*, lodged with the Court on 17.12.2013, which once again shows that the factual context of disputes lodged with an international tribunal like the ICJ may well cross the threshold of human imagination. In effect, I have concurred with my

vote to the adoption of the present Order of 03.03.2014, as I consider that the provisional measures of protection ordered by the Court are better than nothing, better than not having ordered any such measures at all. Yet, given the circumstances of the *cas d'espèce*, I think that the Court should have gone further, and should have ordered the measure requested by Timor-Leste, to the effect of having the documents and data (containing information belonging to it) seized by Australia immediately sealed and delivered into the *custody of the Court itself* here at its *siège* at the Peace Palace at The Hague.

2. I feel thus obliged to leave on the records the foundations of my personal position on the matter. To that effect, I shall address, first, the centrality of the quest for justice (disclosing the impertinence of the invocation of the local remedies rule, and of reliance on avoidance of so-called "concurrent jurisdiction"). Secondly, I shall dwell on the impertinence of reliance upon unilateral acts of States in the course of international legal proceedings. Thirdly, I shall address the prevalence of human values and the idea of objective justice over facts (*ex conscientia jus oritur*). Fourthly, I shall address the question of the ownership of the seized documents and data. Fifthly, I shall focus on the relevance of general principles of international law. Sixthly, I shall dwell upon the prevalence of the juridical equality of States. I shall then move to my last line of considerations, on provisional measures of protection independently of unilateral "undertakings" or assurances, and on what I deem it fit to characterize as the *autonomous* legal regime of provisional measures of protection. Last by not least, I shall proceed to a recapitulation of all the points made in the present Separate Opinion.

II The Centrality of the Quest for Justice

3. To start with, in the course of the present proceedings the Court was faced with arguments, advanced in particular by the respondent State, which required from it clarification so as to address properly the request for provisional measures of protection. Those arguments pertained to Australia's reliance on: (a) local remedies to be allegedly exhausted (by the applicant State) in national courts; and (b) avoidance of concurrent jurisdiction (the ICJ and the Arbitral Tribunal of the Permanent Court of Arbitration [PCA]). Those arguments were advanced by counsel for Australia as alleged impediments to Timor-Leste to seek provisional measures of protection from the ICJ itself, as it has done. Yet, it promptly became clear that, in the circumstances of the *cas d'espèce*, reliance on local remedies and on avoidance of "concurrent jurisdiction" (judicial

and arbitral procedures) were impertinent, and missed the central point of the quest for justice in the circumstances of the *cas d'espèce*.

1 Impertinence of Reliance on Local Remedies in the Circumstances of the Present Case

4. At the public sitting before the Court of 21.01.2014, counsel for Australia contended that Timor-Leste was to pursue "remedies in an Australian court", even though it conceded that this was not a "diplomatic protection claim".[1] For its part, Timor-Leste contended that the rule of exhaustion of local remedies had no application here, in a case like the present one, "where a State asserts its own right against the State that has harmed it".[2] It was made clear that, in such circumstances, it would be impertinent to insist on recourse to local remedies.

5. In effect, the rule of exhaustion of local remedies surely does not apply here. First, this is a public complaint, a State claim with public – not private – origin. Secondly, this is a complaint of a *direct* injury to the State itself, fundamentally distinct from one of diplomatic protection. Thirdly, the State is, clearly, not only pursuing its own interests, but vindicating what it regards as its own right. Fourthly, in so doing, the State is acting on its own behalf. *In such circumstances*, a State cannot be compelled to subject itself to appear before national tribunals. As widely reckoned in international case-law and legal doctrine, in these circumstances the local remedies rule does not apply: *par in parem non habet imperium, non habet jurisdictionem*.[3]

2 Impertinence of Reliance on Avoidance of "Concurrent Jurisdiction" in the Circumstances of the Present Case

6. Counsel for Australia then drew attention to the pending arbitral proceedings opposing it to Timor-Leste, adding that the ICJ, depending in its view on State consent, had "no inherent priority" over "other forums specially consented to by States", nor review authority over them, unless "such priority or authority have been expressly conferred".[4] This argument was laid down on a strict State voluntarist outlook, privileging State's will. Counsel of Australia proceeded that concurrent jurisdiction (ICJ and PCA Arbitral Tribunal) should

---

[1] ICJ, doc. CR 2014/2, of 21.01.2014, pp. 19–20, para. 37.
[2] ICJ, doc. CR 2014/1, of 20.01.2014, p. 26, para. 20.
[3] A.A. Cançado Trindade, *The Application of the Rule of Exhaustion of Local Remedies in International Law*, Cambridge, Cambridge University Press, 1983, pp. 173–174.
[4] ICJ, CR 2014/2, of 21.01.2014, pp. 43–44, paras. 21–22.

be avoided, as "[a] rigid adherence to the parallelism of jurisdictions will only encourage forum shopping, conflict and fragmentation, unduly favouring successive claimants".[5] In Australia's Counsel's view, in order to avoid one international tribunal affecting "parallel proceedings" before another, and also to avoid "two conflicting decisions on the same issue" (25–26), in his view the PCA Arbitral Tribunal, and not the ICJ, was a "more appropriate forum" for dealing with provisional measures in the present case (31–33).[6]

7. The ICJ has promptly and rightly disposed of these arguments in the present Order of 03.03.2014. From the start, it recalled that, in its previous Order, of 28.01.2014, in the present case, it

> decided not to accede to Australia's request for a stay of the proceedings, considering, *inter alia*, that the dispute before it between Timor-Leste and Australia was [is] sufficiently distinct from the dispute being adjudicated upon by the Arbitral Tribunal in the Timor Sea Treaty Arbitration (para. 17).

The arguments that it rejected unduly shifted attention from the quest for justice and the imperative of the realization of justice, into alleged needs of delimitation of competences between international tribunals.

8. Furthermore, it so happens that the Rules of Procedure of the PCA Arbitral Tribunal, in charge of the arbitration under the Timor Sea Treaty, provide that "[a] request for interim measures addressed by any party to a judicial authority shall not be deemed incompatible with the agreement to arbitrate, or as a waiver of that agreement". The *interna corporis* of the PCA Arbitral Tribunal itself see no need of avoiding "forum shopping", or "parallelism of jurisdictions", or "fragmentation of international law", or the like. It is duly focused on the quest for justice.

9. In the present case, there is clearly no impediment to resort to another judicial instance in order to obtain provisional measures of protection, quite on the contrary. The contending Parties are expressly allowed to do so, in case such provisional measures are needed. And, contrary to what Australia's Counsel says, the ICJ, and not the PCA Arbitral Tribunal, is surely the "more appropriate forum" for dealing with provisional measures of protection in the case

---

5   *Ibid.*, pp. 44–45, para. 24.
6   *Ibid.*, pp. 45–47, paras. 25–26 and 31–33.

of which it has been seized. Moreover, it is my feeling that a word of caution is here needed as to the aforementioned euphemisms (the empty rhetoric of "forum shopping", "parallelism", avoidance of "fragmentation" of international law and of "proliferation" of international tribunals) with which a trend of contemporary legal doctrine (*en vogue* in the north of the equator) has in recent years tried in vain to brain-wash scholars of our discipline of the younger generations, unduly diverting attention from the quest for justice to alleged "problems" of "delimitation" of competences.

10. In this respect, destiny has wished (once again) that, shortly before the present case was lodged with the ICJ, in the centennial celebrations of the Peace Palace (ICJ Seminar of 23.09.2013) I had the occasion to ponder that

> In our days, the more lucid international legal doctrine has at last discarded empty euphemistic expressions used some years ago, – such as so-called "proliferation" of international tribunals, so-called "fragmentation" of international law, so-called "forum-shopping", – which diverted attention to false issues of delimitation of competences, oblivious of the need to focus it on the imperative of an enlarged access to justice. Those expressions, narrow-minded and unelegant and derogatory, and devoid of any meaning, paid a disservice to our discipline; they missed the key point of the considerable advances of the old ideal of international justice in the contemporary world.[7]

3 *General Assessment*

11. Not surprisingly, the argument of the respondent State invoking the rule of exhaustion of local remedies (*supra*) did not survive in the circumstances of the present case. After all, *par in parem non habet imperium, non habet jurisdictionem*. Nor did its other argument, invoking the alleged risks of so-called "parallelism", or "concurrent jurisdiction", or "forum shopping", or "fragmentation" of international law, or the like. Such "neologisms", so much *en vogue* in international legal practice in our days, seem devoid of any meaning, besides diverting attention from the crucial point of the *quest for justice* to the false issue of "delimitation" of competences. It is about time to stop referring to so-called

---

[7] A.A. Cançado Trindade, "A Century of International Justice and Prospects for the Future", in *A Century of International Justice and Prospects for the Future / Rétrospective d'un siècle de justice internationale et perspectives d'avenir* (eds. A.A. Cançado Trindade and D. Spielmann), Oisterwijk, Wolf Legal Publs., 2013, p. 21.

"fragmentation" of international law.[8] The current enlargement of access to justice to the *justiciables* is reassuring. International courts and tribunals have a *common mission* to impart justice, which brings their endeavours together, in a harmonious way, and well above zeals of so-called "delimitation" of competences, much to the liking of the international legal profession.

12. In the present case concerning *Questions Relating to the Seizure and Detention of Certain Documents and Data*, the ICJ has put the issue in the right perspective. In the Order it has just adopted today, 03.03.2014, it has pointed out (para. 17) that, one month ago, in its previous Order of 28.01.2014 in the *cas d'espèce*, it has

> decided not to accede to Australia's request for a stay of the proceedings, considering, *inter alia*, that the dispute before it between Timor-Leste and Australia is sufficiently distinct from the dispute being adjudicated upon by the Arbitral Tribunal in the Timor Sea Treaty Arbitration.

III   Impertinence of Reliance upon Unilateral Acts of States in the Course of International Legal Proceedings

13. In the present case concerning *Questions Relating to the Seizure and Detention of Certain Documents and Data*, the ICJ has thus rightly discarded the empty and misleading rhetoric of "fragmentation" of international law. The multiplicity in international courts and tribunals simply reflects the way international law has evolved in our times. Yet, turning now to a distinct point, the ICJ has insisted on relying upon unilateral acts of States (such as promise, in the form of assurances or "undertakings"), thus failing, once again, to extract the lessons from its own practice in recent cases.

14. Promises or assurances or "undertakings" have been relied upon in a distinct context, that of diplomatic relations. When they are unduly brought into the domain of international legal procedure, they cannot serve as basis for a decision of the international tribunal at issue, even less so when they ensue from an original act of arbitrariness. The posture of an international tribunal

---

8   As it is surely not at all a topic for codification or progressive development of international law, it should never have been retained in the agenda of the U.N. International Law Commission, as it did in 2002–2006. It is, at most, a topic for a University thesis (for a LL.M, rather than a Ph.D. degree).

cannot be equated to that of an organ of conciliation. Judicial settlement was conceived as the most perfected means of dispute-settlement; if it starts relying upon unilateral acts of States, as basis for the reasoning of the decisions to be rendered, it will undermine its own foundations, and there will be no reason for hope in the improvement of judicial settlement to secure the prevalence of the rule of law.

15. Reliance upon unilateral acts of promise or assurances has been the source of uncertainties and apprehension in the course of international legal proceedings. Suffice it here to recall, for example, that, in the case concerning *Questions Relating to the Obligation to Prosecute or Extradite* (Belgium *versus* Senegal), the ICJ, instead of ordering provisional measures of protection, preferred to rely on a pledge on the part of the respondent State. In my Separate Opinion in the Judgment on the merits of 20.07.2012 in that case, after reiterating my dissent in the Court's Order of 28.05.2009 in the *cas d'espèce*, I recalled (paras. 73–78) all the uncertainties that followed and the apprehension undergone by the Court (which I see no need to reiterate here) for its reliance on assurances.

16. Had the Court ordered the requested provisional measures in that case, this would have saved the Court from those uncertainties which put at greater risk the outcome of the international legal proceedings. As I concluded in my aforementioned Separate Opinion,

> Unilateral acts of States – such as, *inter alia*, promise – were conceptualized in the traditional framework of the inter-State relations, so as to extract their legal effects, given the "decentralization" of the international legal order. Here, in the present case, we are in an entirely distinct context, that of *objective* obligations (...). In the ambit of these obligations, a pledge or promise made in the course of legal proceedings before the Court does not remove the prerequisites (of urgency and of probability of irreparable damage) for the indication of provisional measures by the Court (para. 79).

17. In the present case concerning *Questions Relating to the Seizure and Detention of Certain Documents and Data*, the ICJ, distinctly, has indicated provisional measures, but not in the terms they were requested by Timor-Leste: it has preferred to rely on unilateral assurances or "undertakings" on the part of the State which seized the documents and data at issue. The Court has thus disclosed its unwillingness to learn the lessons to be extracted from its own experience in recent cases. It has preferred, seemingly oblivious of its own

authority, to keep on acting as a sort of "diplomatic court", rather than rigorously as a court of law. To my mind, *ex factis jus non oritur*.

18. The aforementioned case of *Hissène Habré*, opposing Belgium to Senegal, is not an isolated illustration of the point I am addressing here. In its recent Order (of 22.11.2013) in the merged cases of *Certain Activities Carried out by Nicaragua in the Border Area* and of the *Construction of a Road in Costa Rica along the San Juan River*, the ICJ conceded:

> The Court (...) takes note of the assurances of Nicaragua (...) that it considers itself bound not to undertake activities likely to connect any of the two *caños* with the sea and to prevent any person or group of persons from doing so. However, the Court is not convinced that these instructions and assurances remove the imminent risk of irreparable prejudice, since, as Nicaragua recognized, persons under its jurisdiction have engaged in activities in the disputed territory, namely, the construction of the two new *caños*, which are inconsistent with the Court's Order of 8 March 2011 (para. 50).

19. In my Separate Opinion appended to the Court's more recent Order of 22.11.2013, I again made the point of the need to devote greater attention to the *legal nature* of provisional measures of protection, and their *legal effects*, particularly those endowed with a *conventional* basis such as the provisional measures ordered by the ICJ (paras. 22–23 and 27–28). Only in this way they will contribute to the progressive development of international law. Persistent reliance on unilateral "undertakings" or assurances or promises formulated in the context of provisional measures in no way contributes to the proper understanding of the expanding legal institute of provisional measures of protection in contemporary international law.

20. Expert writing on unilateral acts of States has been very careful to avoid the pitfalls of "contractual" theories in international law, as well as the dangers of unfettered State voluntarism underlying unilateralist manifestations in the decentralized international legal order. Unilateral acts, as manifestations of a subject of International Law to which this latter may attach certain consequences, do not pass without qualifications. Proposed enumerations of unilateral acts in International Law have not purported to be exhaustive,[9] or

---

9 J. Dehaussy, "Les actes juridiques unilatéraux en Droit international public: à propos d'une théorie restrictive", 92 *Journal du droit international* – Clunet (1965) pp. 55–56, and cf. p. 63;

conclusive as to their legal effects. It is not surprising to find that expert writing on the matter has thus endeavoured to single out those unilateral acts to which legal effects can be ascribed,[10] – and all this in the domain of diplomatic relations, *certainly not in the realm of international legal procedure*.

21. Other contemporary international tribunals have likewise been faced with uncertainties and apprehension deriving from unilateral assurances by contending parties. For example, in its Judgment (of 17.01.2012) in the case of *Othman (Abu Qatada) versus United Kingdom*, the European Court of Human Rights (ECtHR – Fourth Section) took account of the expressions of "grave concern" as to diplomatic assurances, manifested in the course of the legal proceedings (para. 175): first, such assurances "were unable to detect abuse"; secondly, "the monitoring regimes provided for by assurances were unsatisfactory"; thirdly, "frequently local monitors lacked the necessary independence"; and fourthly, "assurances also suffered from a lack of incentives to reveal breaches" (paras. 176–179). States, in their relations with each other, can take into account diplomatic assurances, and extract consequences therefrom. International tribunals, for their part, are not bound to base their decisions (on provisional measures or others) on diplomatic assurances: they are bound to identify the applicable law, to interpret and apply it, in sum, to say what the law is (*juris dictio*).

22. International legal procedure has a logic of its own, which is not to be equated to that of diplomatic relations. International legal procedure is not properly served with the insistence on reliance on unilateral acts proper of diplomatic relations, – even less so in face of the perceived need of assertion

---

and cf. also, generally, A. Miaja de la Muela, "Los Actos Unilaterales en las Relaciones Internacionales", 20 *Revista Española de Derecho Internacional* (1967) pp. 456–459; J. Charpentier, "Engagements unilatéraux et engagements conventionnels: différences et convergences", *in Theory of International Law at the Threshold of the 21st Century – Essays in Honour of K. Skubiszewski* (ed. J. Makarczyk), The Hague, Kluwer, 1996, pp. 367–380.

10 Cf., in particular, Eric Suy, *Les actes juridiques unilatéraux en Droit international public*, Paris, LGDJ, 1962, pp. 1–271; K. Skubiszewski, "Les actes unilatéraux des États", *in: Droit international – Bilan et perspectives* (ed. M. Bedjaoui), vol. 1, Paris, Pédone, 1991, pp. 231–250; G. Venturini, "La portée et les effets juridiques des attitudes et des actes unilatéraux des États", 112 *Recueil des Cours de l'Académie de Droit International de La Haye* (1964) pp. 63–467. And cf. also: A.P. Rubin, "The International Legal Effects of Unilateral Declarations", 71 *American Journal of International Law* (1977) pp. 1–30; C. Chinkin, "A Mirage in the Sand? Distinguishing Binding and Non-Binding Relations between States", 10 *Leiden Journal of International Law* (1997) pp. 223–247.

that *ex injuria jus non oritur*. Even if an international tribunal takes note of unilateral acts of States, it is not to take such acts as the basis for the reasoning of its own decisions.

23. In this connection, may I recall that, in the course of the advisory proceedings of the ICJ concerning the *Declaration of Independence of Kosovo* (Advisory Opinion of 22.07.2010), a couple of participants invoked the principle *ex injuria jus non oritur*. In my Separate Opinion appended to the Court's Advisory Opinion, I asserted that

> According to a well-established general principle of international law, a wrongful act cannot become a source of advantages, benefits or else rights for the wrongdoer: *ex injuria jus non oritur* (para. 132).

24. After considering the application of this principle in the factual context of the matter then before the ICJ (paras. 133–135), I added:

> This general principle, well-established as it is, has at times been counterbalanced by the maxim *ex factis jus oritur*. (...) In the conceptual universe of international law, as of Law in general, one is in the domain of *Sollen*, not of *Sein*, or at least in that of the tension between *Sollen* and *Sein*. (...)
>
> [T]he maxim *ex factis jus oritur* does not amount to a *carte blanche*, as Law plays its role also in the emergence of rights out of the tension between *Sollen* and *Sein*. (...) (paras. 136–137).

25. In effect, to allow unilateral acts to be performed (in the course of international legal proceedings), irrespectively of their discretionary – if not arbitrary – character, and to accept subsequent assurances or "undertakings" ensuing therefrom, is to pave the way to uncertainties and unpredictability, to the possibility of creation of *faits accomplis* to one's own advantage and to the other party's disadvantage. The certainty of the application of the law would be reduced to a mere probability. As the lucid writer Machado de Assis remarked in the XIXth century,

> Se esse mundo não fosse uma região de espíritos desatentos, era escusado lembrar ao leitor que eu só afirmo certas leis quando as possuo deveras; em relação a outras restrinjo-me à admissão da probabilidade.[11]

---

11   Machado de Assis, *Memórias Póstumas de Brás Cubas* [1881]: – "If this world would not be a region of unattentive spirits, there would be no need to remind the reader that I only

IV   Ex Conscientia Jus Oritur

26. Already in the late forties, – at a time when international legal doctrine was far more cultivated than it seems to be nowadays, – it was observed that modern international law is not prepared to admit that "la légère validation d'actes nuls et illicites".[12] In effect, – as pointed out one decade earlier, in the late thirties, – even if international law finds itself in presence "d'actes, d'engagements et de situations qui se prétendent à tort créateurs de droit", such acts, undertakings and situations

> sont nuls (...), pour la raison que, tirant origine d'un acte illégal, ils ne sauraient produire de résultats avantageux pour le coupable. *Ex injuria jus non oritur* est un principe général de droit. (...) [L']essence du droit, c'est à dire (...), l'efficacité juridique et la validité de ses obligations, ne peuvent être affectées par des actes individuels d'illégalité.[13]

27. No State is entitled to rely itself upon an arbitrary act in order to vindicate what it regards as a right of its own, ensuing therefrom. May I further recall, in this respect, that, in the past, a trend of legal doctrine – favoured by so-called "realists" – attempted to deprive some of the strength of the general principle *ex injuria jus non oritur* by invoking the maxim *ex factis jus oritur*. In doing so, it confused the validity of norms with the required coercion (at times missing in the international legal order) to implement them. The validity of norms is not dependent on coercion (for implementation); they are binding as such (objective obligations).

28. The maxim *ex factis jus oritur* wrongfully attributes to facts law-creating effects which facts *per se* cannot generate. Not surprisingly, the *"fait accompli"* is very much to the liking of those who feel strong or powerful enough to try to impose their will upon others. It so happens that contemporary international law is grounded on some fundamental general principles, such as the principle of the *juridical equality of States*, which points in the opposite direction.

---

affirm certain laws when I truly possess them; in relation to others I limit myself to the admission of the probability" [my own translation].

12   P. Guggenheim, "La validité et la nullité des actes juridiques internationaux", 74 *Recueil des Cours de l'Académie de Droit International de La Haye* (1949) pp. 230–233, and cf. pp. 226–227.

13   H. Lauterpacht, "Règles générales du droit de la paix", 62 *Recueil des Cours de l'Académie de Droit International de La Haye* (1937) pp. 287–288.

Factual inequalities between States are immaterial, as all States are juridically equal, with all the consequences ensuing therefrom. Definitively, *ex factis jus non oritur*. Human values and the idea of objective justice stand above facts. *Ex conscientia jus oritur*.

V   The Question of the Ownership of the Seized Documents and Data

29. Another issue, addressed by the contending Parties in the course of the present proceedings, was that of the ownership of the documents and data seized by Australia. From the start, Timor-Leste asserted, in its oral arguments, that the present case "is one in which Timor-Leste is complaining of the seizure of its property and is seeking the recovery of the documents that were held on its behalf by Mr. Collaery".[14] Counsel for Timor-Leste then stated that its lawyer (Mr. Collaery), through his office,

> conducts his legal activities covering a number of matters for the Government of Timor-Leste, as well as for other clients. In that office, Mr. Collaery regularly keeps, on behalf of the Government of Timor-Leste, many confidential documents relating to the international legal affairs of Timor-Leste. Some cover such very important and delicate matters as the negotiations between the two countries regarding access to the maritime resources of the Timor Sea.[15]

30. The applicant State then asserted that it was clear that among the documents and data seized

> were many files relating to matters on which Mr. Collaery's office was working on behalf of the Government of Timor-Leste. All these files are thus the property of the Government of Timor-Leste and were held as such by Mr. Collaery in the course of his duties on behalf of the Government of Timor-Leste. [T]he client (in this case, the Government) has proprietary ownership of documents that have been brought into existence, or received, by a lawyer acting as agent on behalf of the client, or that have been prepared for the benefit of the client and at the client's expense, such as, letters of advice, memoranda and briefs to counsel.[16]

---

14   ICJ, doc. CR 2014/1, of 20.01.2014, p. 24, para. 16.
15   ICJ, doc. CR 2014/1, of 20.01.2014, p. 19, para. 8.
16   ICJ, doc. CR 2014/1, of 20.01.2014, p. 21, para. 11.

31. For its part, Australia preferred not to dwell upon the issue of the ownership of the seized documents and data. It argued that

> Questions of ownership cannot be answered in the absence of a proper examination of the documents in question. That examination has not occurred because we have not inspected the documents. We therefore cannot accept the proposition that the documents are necessarily the property of Timor-Leste, nor can we put you a full submission on where ownership might lie.[17]

32. Timor-Leste insisted on its position, affirming categorically that "documents in the hands of lawyers on behalf of their clients belong to the clients, in this case, Timor-Leste. That applies to most of the items seized".[18] From the aforementioned, it is clear that Australia did not clarify its position as to who owns the seized documents and data, having preferred not to respond to Timor-Leste's arguments that those documents and data are its property. This is another point to be kept in mind, in the proper consideration of the requested provisional measures in the *cas d'espèce*.

VI   The Relevance of General Principles of International Law

33. In the course of the public sitting of the Court of 21.01.2014, I deemed it fit to put the following question to both contending Parties, Timor-Leste and Australia:

> What is the impact of a State's measures of alleged national security upon the conduction of arbitral proceedings between the Parties? In particular, what is the effect or impact of seizure of documents and data, in the circumstances of the present case, upon the settlement of an international dispute by negotiation and arbitration?[19]

1   *Responses of the Parties to a Question from the Bench*

34. In his prompt answer to my question, counsel for Timor-Leste, remarking that he would try to respond it "both as a matter of principle, and as it applies to this case", stated that

---

17   ICJ, doc. CR 2014/4, of 22.01.2014, p. 19, para. 41.
18   ICJ, doc. CR 2014/3, of 22.01.2014, p. 19, para. 33.
19   ICJ, doc. CR 2014/2, of 21.01.2014, p. 48.

States should refrain from allowing national interests, including national security interests – important though they may be – adversely to affect international proceedings between sovereign States, and the ability of sovereign States to obtain legal advice. Nothing should be done which would infringe the principles of the sovereign equality of States, non-intervention, and the peaceful settlement of disputes, which are at the core of the international legal order as reflected in the United Nations Charter and other key documents, such as the [1970] Declaration on Principles of International Law concerning Friendly Relations.[20]

Applying this approach to the case in hand, we look to the Court to ensure that Australia does not secure an unfair advantage, either in the context of litigation or in the context of future negotiations concerning the maritime boundary.

While it would appear that both Parties agree that legal privilege is a general principle of law, and that it is not without limitations, the Parties seem to disagree as to the scope of these limitations. In response to Judge Cançado Trindade's question, I would point to the difference between such limitations under domestic law, as argued for by Australia, and limitations under international law. The domestic limitations argued for by Australia cannot apply when a sovereign State seeks legal advice. Australia is not entitled to restrict Timor-Leste's ability freely to communicate with its lawyers for reasons that are at the end of the day entirely domestic in nature. There is no limit on immunity in respect of diplomatic documents on Australian soil, and there is no reason of principle why the same should not apply to a State's claim to privilege in respect of legal advice.

In any case, any assertion of limitation to privilege should not hinder Timor-Leste's preparations for international proceedings or negotiations. This principle was expressly recognized in the *Libananco* case.[21] Contrary to what Mr. Burmester said yesterday,[22] recognition of this principle should not preclude Australia from continuing its criminal investigation; it would just ensure that Timor-Leste's documents remain inviolable as part of that process.

---

20   U.N. doc. A/RES/25/2625, *Declaration on Principles in International Law concerning Friendly Relations and Co-operation among States in accordance with the Charter of the United Nations*, of 24.10.1970.

21   Case *Libananco Holdings Co. Ltd. versus Turkey*, ICSID case ARB/06/8, Decision on Preliminary Issues, of 23.06.2008, p. 42, para. 2.

22   Cf. ICJ doc. CR 2014/2, of 21.01.2014, p. 32, para. 17.

Mr Campbell began by asking you to keep in mind the alleged general principles applying to provisional measures set out in their *Written Observations*. (...) [W]e do not regard as convincing what they had to say on that matter. The *Written Observations* take a very narrow view of the scope of provisional measures. Yet the institution of provisional measures is an essential one to the judicial process. It is one the importance of which is increasingly recognized by international courts and tribunals (paras. 3–7).[23]

35. For its part, in his response to my question, counsel for Australia, like that of East Timor (*supra*), began saying that it would endeavour to answer it "first at the level of principle and then at the level of application"; and then he added that

At the level of principle, we would accept that, if a State engages in arbitration with another State, and finds it necessary to take measures of national security which may bear on the arbitration, the State should, as a matter of prudence, if not strict law, take such steps as are reasonable to limit the impact of national security measures on the arbitration. We accept, as was put this morning, that to do otherwise would interfere with arbitration as a peaceful method of resolving inter-State disputes. I emphasize, the principle is qualified by reasonableness. The circumstances may not always provide a perfect accommodation between the two interests in conflict and a State could not be asked absolutely to put on hold measures of national security merely because it is brought to arbitration (para. 4).

36. This was the "general answer"; moving then to the "specific answer", counsel for Australia proceeded:

[I]n the present case the measures of national security will have no adverse impact on this Arbitration, for three reasons. Firstly, Timor-Leste's

---

23   Counsel for Timor-Leste added: – "Of course, like any other judicial proceeding it can be abused, but courts know how to deal with that. We reject any insinuation by Australia that Timor-Leste is acting abusively in seeking provisional measures. In particular, we reject the unworthy suggestion by Professor Crawford that we are using these proceedings 'to skirt around the confidentiality provisions and maximise the opportunity for publicity and comment prejudicial to Australia'. We are not"; ICJ doc. CR 2014/3, of 22.01.2014, pp. 12–14. And, for Australia's argument, cf. ICJ doc. CR 2014/2, of 21.01.2014, p. 39, para. 8.

counsel in the Arbitration, on 5 December [2013], accepted they have copies of the key removed documents, including an *affidavit* from the person they describe as "Witness K" which they have lodged with the PCA. No case of disadvantage has been made before you. Second[ly], the Attorney-General acted reasonably from the outset – from the Ministerial Statement of 4 December [2013], supplemented by undertakings – to ensure there would be no illegitimate advantage to Australia by way of documents being made available to the legal team in the Arbitration. Wisely, with hindsight, he anticipated this problem might arise and he acted in advance to prevent it. The third part of the practical answer is that there is not a skerrick of evidence pointed to by Timor-Leste to suggest the undertakings have not been honoured to date or will not be honoured in the future. (...) [T]he documents have been kept under seal (...).

(...) Timor-Leste has the documents it needs for the arbitration; it has adequate undertakings to protect the integrity of the arbitration; and the undertakings are being honoured (paras. 5–6).

2 *General Assessment*

37. In sum, and as pointed out by the ICJ in the present Order, Australia has clearly relied on its solemn "undertakings" that the documents of Timor-Leste's legal adviser that it has seized in Canberra will be kept sealed and inaccessible, safeguarding their confidentiality, so as not to be used to the disadvantage of Timor-Leste in the proceedings of the Timor Sea Treaty Arbitral Tribunal (paras. 35–39). Timor-Leste, in turn, has challenged such arguments (paras. 40–41), and has held that it seeks to protect the ownership and property rights it holds over the seized material (inviolability and immunity of its property) as a sovereign State (para. 24), and has added that the seized documents and data concern its position on matters pertaining to the Timor Sea Treaty Arbitration and in the context of future negotiations; such matters, – it has added, – are "crucial to the future of Timor-Leste as a State and to the well-being of its people" (para. 33).

38. Arguments of alleged "national security", such as raised by Australia in the *cas d'espèce*, cannot be made the concern of an international tribunal, in a case like the present one. The Court has before itself general principles of international law (*supra*), and cannot be obfuscated by allegations of "national security", which fall outside the scope of the applicable law here. In any case, an international tribunal cannot pay lip-service to allegations of "national security" made by one of the parties in the course of legal proceedings.

39. This particular point was made by Timor Leste in the *cas d'espèce*. In this respect, the *ad hoc* International Tribunal for the Former Yugoslavia (ICTFY – Appeals Chamber), in its decision (of 29.10.1997)[24] in the *Blaškić* case, confronted with a plea that documents sought from Croatian State officials were protected by "national security", pondered:

> [T]o grant States a blanket right to withhold, for security purposes, documents necessary for trial might jeopardise the very function of the International Tribunal, and "defeat its essential object and purpose". The International Tribunal was established for the prosecution of persons responsible for war crimes, crimes against humanity and genocide; these are crimes related to armed conflict and military operations. It is, therefore, evident that military documents or other evidentiary material connected with military operations may be of crucial importance, either for the Prosecutor or the defence, to prove or disprove the alleged culpability of an indictee, particularly when command responsibility is involved (in this case military documents may be needed to establish or disprove the chain of command, the degree of control over the troops exercised by a military commander, the extent to which he was cognisant of the actions undertaken by his subordinates, etc.). To admit that a State holding such documents may unilaterally assert national security claims and refuse to surrender those documents could lead to the stultification of international criminal proceedings: those documents might prove crucial for deciding whether the accused is innocent or guilty. The very *raison d'être* of the International Tribunal would then be undermined (para. 65).

40. The due process of law cannot be undermined by the behaviour of one of the parties dictated by reasons of alleged "national security". Equality of arms (*égalité des armes*) in arbitral and judicial proceedings is to be preserved. International tribunals know how to handle confidential matters in the course of legal procedure, and this cannot be intermingled with one of the parties' concerns with its own "national security". In the experience of contemporary international tribunals, there have been occasions of hearings of testimonies in special sittings, so as to, e.g., duly instruct the case and protect witnesses; to evoke but one illustration, the Inter-American Court of Human Rights (IACtHR), in the course of the proceedings culminating in its Judgment of

---

24 Appeal's Chamber's Decision of 29.10.1997, of review of the Decision of Trial Chamber II of 18.07.1997, para. 65.

25.11.2000 (merits) in the case of *Bámaca Velásquez versus Guatemala*, deemed it necessary to collect the testimony of a witness, and commissioned three of its members to do so, in a sitting held outside its *siège* in Central America;[25] the sitting took place at the headquarters of the Organization of American States (OAS) in Washington D.C., as the witness concerned was still defining its migratory status as a refugee.

41. As to the handling of confidentiality, international tribunals know their respective applicable law, and do not yield to considerations of domestic law as to "national security"; they keep in mind the imperative of due process of law in the course of international legal proceedings, and preserve the equality of arms (*égalité des armes*), in the light of the principle of the proper administration of justice (*la bonne administration de la justice*). Allegations of State secrecy or "national security" cannot at all interfere with the work of an international tribunal, in judicial settlement or arbitration.

42. In my perception, Timor-Leste has made its case that the documents seized from its legal adviser's office in Canberra, containing confidential information concerning its positions in the Timor Sea Treaty Arbitration, are not to be used to its disadvantage in that PCA arbitration. Timor-Leste's preoccupation has its *raison d'être*, and, in my view, the ICJ has taken the right decision to order the provisional measures; however, it should have done so in the terms requested by Timor-Leste, namely, to have the documents seized by Australia immediately sealed and delivered into the custody of the ICJ itself, here in its *siège* at the Peace Palace at The Hague. The present proceedings in the case concerning *Questions Relating to the Seizure and Detention of Certain Documents and Data*, suggest, once again, in the light of the arguments advanced by both Timor-Leste and Australia, that States appear far more sensitive than human beings. Even more so in a delicate matter such as the one of the present case. As the learned Antônio Vieira observed in the XVIIth century,

> Não há dúvida que todas as coisas são mais estimadas e de maior gosto quando se recuperam depois de perdidas, que quando se possuem sem se perderem.[26]

---

25   In the host State, in San José of Costa Rica.
26   Antônio Vieira, *Sermão de Santo Antônio* [1657]: – "There is no doubt that all things are more esteemed and of greater taste when recovered after having been lost, than when possessed without being lost" [my own translation].

43. It is clear that the concern of an international tribunal is with properly imparting justice, rather than with assessing measures of alleged "national security", entirely alien to its function. International tribunals are concerned with the prevalence of international law; national governments (their secret or so-called "intelligence" services) occupy themselves with issues they regard as affecting alleged "national security". The international legal positions of one State cannot be subjected to measures of alleged "national security" of another State, even less so when they are contending Parties in a same contentious case before an international tribunal. In this connection, an international tribunal such as the ICJ is to make sure that the principle of the *juridical equality* of States prevails, so as to discard eventual repercussions in the international legal procedure of *factual inequalities* between States.

VII   The Prevalence of the Juridical Equality of States

44. The present case concerning *Questions Relating to the Seizure and Detention of Certain Documents and Data*, bears witness of the relevance of the principle of the juridical equality of States. The prevalence of this fundamental principle has marked a longstanding presence in the realm of international law, ever since the times of the II Hague Peace Conference of 1907, and then of the drafting of the Statute of the Permanent Court of International Justice by the Advisory Committee of Jurists, in June-July 1920. Recourse was then made, by that Committee, *inter alia*, to general principles of law, as these latter embodied the objective idea of justice. A general principle such as that of the juridical equality of States, enshrined a quarter of a century later in the United Nations Charter (Article 2(1)), is ineluctably intermingled with the quest for justice.

45. Subsequently, throughout the drafting of the 1970 U.N. Declaration on Principles of International Law concerning Friendly Relations and Co-operation among States in accordance with the Charter of the United Nations (1964–1970), the need was felt to make it clear that stronger States cannot impose their will upon the weak, and that *de facto* inequalities among States cannot affect the weaker in the vindication of their rights. The principle of the juridical equality of States gave expression to this concern, embodying the *idée de justice*, emanated from the universal juridical conscience. I have had the occasion to dwell upon this point elsewhere, having pondered that

> On successive occasions the principles of international law have proved to be of fundamental importance to humankind's quest for justice. This is

clearly illustrated by the role played, *inter alia*, by the principle of juridical equality of States. This fundamental principle, – the historical roots of which go back to the II Hague Peace Conference of 1907, – proclaimed in the U.N. Charter and enunciated also in the 1970 Declaration of Principles, means ultimately that all States, – factually strong and weak, great and small, – are equal before International Law, are entitled to the same protection under the law and before the organs of international justice, and to equality in the exercise of international rights and duties.

Despite successive attempts to undermine it, the principle of juridical equality of States has remained, from the II Hague Peace Conference of 1907 to date, one of the basic pillars of International Law. It has withstood the onslaught of time, and shown itself salutary for the peaceful conduction of international relations, being ineluctably associated – as it stands – with the foundations of International Law. It has been very important for the international legal system itself, and has proven to be a cornerstone of International Law in the United Nations era. In fact, the U.N. Charter gave it a new dimension, and the principle of juridical equality of States, in turn, paved the way for, and contributed to, new developments such as that of the system of collective security, within the ambit of the law of the United Nations.[27]

VIII Provisional Measures of Protection Independently of Unilateral "Undertakings" or Assurances

46. As from the characterizations by the ICJ itself of the essence and main features of the dispute lodged with it in the *cas d'espèce*, one would legitimately expect that the Court would not proceed to ground the Provisional Measures of Protection that it has indicated in the present Order on a unilateral "undertaking" or assurance by one of the contending Parties, precisely the one that has caused a damage – by the seizure and detention of the documents and data at issue – to the applicant State. In effect, in the present Order, the ICJ, after taking note of the principal claim of Timor-Leste that "a violation has occurred of its right to communicate with its counsel and lawyers in a confidential manner with regard to issues forming the subject-matter of pending arbitral proceedings and future negotiations between the Parties", recalled that

---

27 A.A. Cançado Trindade, *International Law for Humankind – Towards a New Jus Gentium*, 2nd. rev. ed., Leiden/The Hague, Nijhoff, 2013, pp. 84–85, and cf. pp. 62–63, 65 and 73.

this right derives from the fundamental principle of the juridical equality of States, enshrined into Article 2(1) of the U.N. Charter (para. 27).

47. The ICJ then proceeded that "equality of the parties must be preserved" when they are engaged – pursuant to Article 2(3) of the U.N. Charter – in the process of peaceful settlement of an international dispute (another general principle of international law). Once a State is engaged therein, it is entitled to undertake arbitral proceedings or negotiations "without interference by the other party in the preparation and conduct of its case" (para. 27). It follows, – the Court added, – that

> in such a situation, a State has a plausible right to the protection of its communications with counsel relating to an arbitration or to negotiations, in particular, to the protection of the correspondence between them, as well as to the protection of confidentiality of any documents and data prepared by counsel to advise the State in such a context (para. 27).

48. The Court concluded, on this issue, that at least some of the rights for which Timor-Leste seeks protection are "plausible", – in particular, "the right to conduct arbitration proceedings or negotiations without interference by Australia", and "the correlative right of confidentiality of and non-interference in its communications with its legal advisers" (para. 28). I would take even a step further, in acknowledging that a *right is a right*, irrespective of its so-called "plausibility" (whatever that might concretely mean).[28] In any case, having reached such conclusion, one would expect the Court to order its own provisional measures of protection independently of any promise or unilateral "undertaking" on the part of the State which has breached that "plausible" right.

49. For reasons which escape my comprehension, the Court did not do so, and, from then onwards, embarked on a distinct line of reasoning, on the basis of the "undertaking" or assurance by Australia to secure the confidentiality of the material seized by its agents in Canberra on 03.12.2013. The Court was aware of the imminent risk of irreparable harm (para. 42), and insisted that there remained a risk of further disclosure of the seized material (para. 46) to the additional disadvantage of Timor-Leste. The Court considered that

---

28 "Plausibility", as understood nowadays, has its etymological origins traced back to the XVI–XVII centuries, meaning something which is worth of approval or applause (from *plaudere*).

there could be a very serious detrimental effect on Timor-Leste's position in the Timor Sea Treaty Arbitration and in future maritime negotiations with Australia should the seized material be divulged to any person or persons involved or likely to be involved in that Arbitration or in negotiations on behalf of Australia. Any breach of confidentiality may not be capable of remedy or reparation as it might not be possible to revert to the *status quo ante* following disclosure of the confidential information (para. 42).

50. How can the Court assume that such breach of confidentiality has not already occurred, to the detriment of Timor-Leste? On what basis can the Court assume that the material seized by Australia has not yet been divulged, or was not divulged on the days following its seizure, and before the "undertaking" or assurance by Australia? How can the Court be sure that Timor-Leste has not yet suffered an irreparable harm? How can the Court proceed, on the basis of the seizure undertaken by the Australian Security Intelligence Organisation (ASIO), to ground in the present Order its own provisional measures of protection, instead of taking the custody of the seized material? From this point of the present Order (of reliance on the seizure of documents and data for alleged "national security" reasons) onwards, it is difficult to avoid the sensation of entering into the realm of surrealism.

51. The fact is that it cannot be denied with certainty that, with the seizure of the documents and data containing its privileged information, Timor-Leste has *already* suffered an irreparable harm. Six and a half decades ago (in 1949), in his last book, *Nineteen Eighty-Four*, George Orwell repeatedly warned: – "Big Brother is Watching You".[29] Modern history is permeated with examples of the undue exercise of search and seizure, on the part of those who felt powerful enough to exercise unreasonable surveillance of others. Modern history has also plenty of examples of the proper reaction on the part of those who felt victimized by such exercise of search and seizure. In so reacting, the latter felt that, though lacking in factual power, they had Law on their side, as all are equal before the law. If G. Orwell would rise from his tomb today, I imagine he would probably contemplate writing *Two Thousand Eighty-Four*, updating his perennial and topical warning, so as to encompass surveillance not only at *intra-State* level, but also at *inter-State* level; nowadays, "Big Brother is

---

29 Part I, Chapter I; and Part III, Chapter VI.

Watching You", on a much wider geographical scale, also in the relations across nations.

52. If the Court were sensitive to that, it would have ordered – as in my view it should have done its provisional measures of protection independently of any unilateral "undertaking" or assurance on the part of the State which exercised search and seizure (Australia) of documents and data containing privileged information belonging to the applicant State (Timor-Leste). The Court would have ordered – as in my view it should have done – the seized documents and data to be promptly sealed and delivered into its custody here at its *siège* at the Peace Palace at The Hague. In any case, the provisional measures of protection indicated in the present Order of the Court, concerning a situation of urgency, purports to prevent *further* irreparable harm to Timor-Leste.

53. The Court did not at all need to have relied, in its present Order, factually upon Australia's seizure of the documents and data containing information belonging to Timor-Leste, so as to order Australia to "keep under seal the seized documents and electronic data and any copies thereof" (resolutory point 2). The Court should have itself taken custody of those documents and data (and any copies thereof) from now on. Instead of that, the Court ordered the State which seized them to ensure that no *further* damage is done to Timor-Leste by further disclosure for use by any person(s), of the seized material (resolutory point 1).

54. Ironically, in the present Order the Court itself admits (para. 30) that the provisional measures of protection requested by Timor-Leste are aimed at preventing *further* damage to it. It is clear that damage has already been made to Timor-Leste. Yet the Court orders provisional measures of protection to be taken by the State – as from its unilateral "undertaking" – that has seized the documents and data for alleged reasons of "national security". In this connection, in the mid-fifties, the poet Vinicius de Moraes pitied the ungrateful task of those who worked in archives (and I would here add, in secret archives, amidst documents allegedly concerning "national security"); in his own words,

> Antes não classificásseis
> Os maços pelos assuntos
> Criando a luta de classes
> Num mundo de anseios juntos! (...)
> Ah, ver-vos em primavera
> Sobre papéis de ocasião

Na melancólica espera
De uma eterna certidão! (...).³⁰

55. In distinct contexts, the inviolability of State papers and documents has been an old concern in diplomatic relations. The 1946 U.N. Convention on the Privileges and Immunities of the United Nations refers to the "inviolability for all papers and documents" of member States participating in the work of its main and subsidiary organs, or in conferences convened by the United Nations (Article IV). In the same year, a resolution of the U.N General Assembly asserted that such inviolability of all State papers and documents was granted by the 1946 Convention "in the interests of the good administration of justice".³¹ Thus, already in 1946, the U.N. General Assembly had given expression in a resolution to the presumption of the inviolability of the correspondence between member States and their legal advisers. This is an international law obligation, not one derived from a unilateral "undertaking" or assurance by a State following its seizure of documents and data containing information belonging to another State.

56. In my perception, there is no room, in provisional measures of protection, for indulging into an exercise of balancing of the interests of the contending parties. For example, in the present Order, the Court refers to the "significant contribution" of Australia's unilateral "undertaking" or promise (of 21.01.2014) towards "mitigating the imminent risk of irreparable prejudice" to Timor-Leste (para. 47). Yet, immediately afterwards, the Court goes on to say that, despite that unilateral "undertaking" by Australia, "there is still an imminent risk of irreparable prejudice" to Timor-Leste (para. 48). This being so, what is the "significant contribution" of the unilateral "undertaking" or assurance to mitigate the "imminent risk of irreparable prejudice" to Timor Leste? The Court provides no explanation for its assertion. What is so "significant" about that

---

30   Vinicius de Moraes, "Balada das Arquivistas", *in Antologia Poética* (1954):
      Better if you would not classify
      The files by the subjects
      Creating class struggle
      In a world plenty of anguish! (...)
      Ah, to see you all in the springtime
      Over occasional papers
      In the melancholic expectation
      Of an eternal certificate! (...) [my own translation].
31   U.N., G.A. resolution 90(I), of 1946, para. 5(b).

unilateral act? The Court does not demonstrate its "significance", only takes the promise at its face value.

57. Can a unilateral assurance or promise provide a basis for the Court's reasoning in Orders of binding provisional measures of protection? Not at all, – as I sustained half a decade ago in my Dissenting Opinion in the case concerning *Questions Relating to the Obligation to Prosecute or Extradite* (Belgium versus Senegal, Order of 28.05.2009), and as I once again sustain in this Separate Opinion in present Order of 03.03.2014 in the case concerning *Questions Relating to the Seizure and Detention of Certain Documents and Data*. Like Ionesco's *Rhinocéros* (1960), *je ne capitule pas…*

58. The ICJ is not a simple *amiable compositeur*, it is a court of law, the principal judicial organ of the United Nations (Article 92 of the U.N. Charter). In the exercise of its judicial function, it is not to ground its reasoning on unilateral "undertakings" or assurances or promises formulated in the course of the international legal proceedings. Precepts of law provide a much safer ground for its reasoning in the exercise of its judicial function. Those precepts are of a perennial value, such as the ones (Ulpian's) opening book I (item I, para. 3) of Justinian's *Institutes* (early VIth century): *honeste vivere, alterum non laedere, suum cuique tribuere* (to live honestly, not to harm anyone, to give each one his/her due).

IX   The Autonomous Legal Regime of Provisional Measures of Protection

59. This brings me to my last point in the present Separate Opinion. The present legal proceedings, in my perception, bring to the fore, once again, what I have for some time been characterizing as *the autonomous legal regime of provisional measures of protection*. In this respect, as I have pointed out, e.g., in my Dissenting Opinion in the merged cases of *Certain Activities Carried out by Nicaragua in the Border Area* and of the *Construction of a Road in Costa Rica along the San Juan River* (Order of 16.07.2013), opposing Costa Rica to Nicaragua (and *vice-versa*), the object of requests for provisional measures of protection is different from the object of applications lodged with international tribunals, as to the merits.

60. Furthermore, the rights to be protected are not necessarily the same in the two respective proceedings. Compliance with provisional measures runs

parallel to the course of proceedings as to the merits of the case at issue. The obligations concerning provisional measures ordered and decisions as to the merits (and reparations) are not the same, being autonomous from each other. The same can be said of the legal consequences of non-compliance (with provisional measures, or else with judgments as to the merits), the breaches (of ones and the others) being distinct from each other (paras. 70–71).

61. What ensues herefrom is the pressing need to dwell upon, and to develop conceptually, the *autonomous legal regime* of provisional measures of protection, particularly in view of the expansion of these latter in our days (para. 75). This is the point which I have made not only in my Dissenting Opinion in the two aforementioned merged cases opposing Costa Rica to Nicaragua, but also in my earlier Dissenting Opinion (paras. 80–81) in the case of *Questions Relating to the Obligation to Prosecute or Extradite* (Belgium *versus* Senegal, Order of 28.05.2009), and which I see it fit to reiterate here, in the present case on *Questions relating to the Seizure and Detention of Certain Documents and Data* (Timor-Leste *versus* Australia). It should not pass unnoticed that this point has marked presence in these recent cases, surrounded by entirely distinct circumstances. This, in my view, discloses the importance of the acknowledgment of the *autonomous legal regime* of provisional measures of protection, irrespective of the circumstances of the cases at issue.

62. I deem it a privilege to be able to serve the cause of international justice here at the Peace Palace at The Hague. With all that is going on here at the Peace Palace, – at the ICJ and at the PCA next door, – as well illustrated herein, the present case concerning *Questions Relating to the Seizure and Detention of Certain Documents and Data*, since its lodging with the ICJ last December 2013 up to now, marks a proper closing of the celebrations of the centenary of the Peace Palace. This emblematic centenary would have been more remarkable if the ICJ had ordered today, 03.03.2014, what in my view it should have done, i.e., the adoption of an Order of provisional measures of protection to the effect of, from now on, keeping custody itself, as master of its own jurisdiction, of the seized documents and data containing information belonging to Timor-Leste, here in its premises in the Peace Palace at The Hague.

X   Epilogue: A Recapitulation

63. From the preceding considerations, I hope it has become crystal clear why I consider that the provisional measures of protection indicated by the Court

in the present Order of 03.03.2014, in the case concerning *Questions Relating to the Seizure and Detention of Certain Documents and Data*, are better than nothing, better than not having ordered any such measures at all, though I find that the Court should have gone further, and have ordered provisional measures of protection independently of any unilateral "undertaking" or assurance by one of the parties, and should have kept custody of the seized documents and data itself, at its *siège* here at the Peace Palace at The Hague. I have thus felt obliged, in the faithful exercise of the international judicial function, to lay the foundations of my own position in the *cas d'espèce* in the present Separate Opinion. I deem it fit, at this stage, to recapitulate all the points of my personal position, expressed herein, for the sake of clarity, and in order to stress their interrelatedness.

64. *Primus*: When a State pursues the safeguard of its own right, acting on its own behalf, it cannot be compelled to appear before the national tribunals of another State, its contending Party. The local remedies rule does not apply in cases of this kind; *par in parem non habet imperium, non habet jurisdictionem*. *Secundus*: The centrality of the search for justice prevails over concerns to avoid "concurrent jurisdiction". *Tertius*: The imperative of the realization of justice prevails over manifestations of a State's will. *Quartus*: Euphemisms *en vogue* – like the empty and misleading rhetoric of "proliferation" of international tribunals, and "fragmentation" of international law, among others, – are devoid of any meaning, and divert attention to false issues of "delimitation" of competences, oblivious of the need to secure an enlarged access to justice to the *justiciables*.

65. *Quintus*: International courts and tribunals share a *common mission* to impart justice, which stands above zeals of "delimitation" of competences. *Sextus*: Unilateral "undertakings" or assurances by a contending party cannot serve as basis for provisional measures of protection. *Septimus*: Reliance on unilateral "undertakings" or assurances has been the source of uncertainties and apprehension; they are proper to the realm of inter-State (diplomatic) relations, and reliance upon such unilateral acts is to be avoided in the course of international legal proceedings; *ex factis jus non oritur*.

66. *Octavus*: International legal procedure has a logic of its own, which is not to be equated to that of diplomatic relations, even less so in face of the perceived need of assertion that *ex injuria jus non oritur*. *Nonus*: To allow unilateral acts to be performed with the acceptance of subsequent "undertakings" or assurances ensuing therefrom would not only generate uncertainties, but also

create *faits accomplis* threatening the certainty of the application of the law. *Decimus*: Facts only do not *per se* generate law-creating effects. Human values and the idea of objective justice stand above facts; *ex conscientia jus oritur*.

67. *Undecimus*: Arguments of alleged "national security", as raised in the *cas d'espèce*, cannot be made the concern of an international tribunal. Measures of alleged "national security", as raised in the *cas d'espèce*, are alien to the exercise of the international judicial function. *Duodecimus*: General principles of international law, such as the juridical equality of States (enshrined into Article 2(1) of the U.N. Charter), cannot be obfuscated by allegations of "national security". *Tertius decimus*: The basic principle of the juridical equality of States, embodying the *idée de justice*, is to prevail, so as to discard eventual repercussions in international legal procedure of factual inequalities among States.

68. *Quartus decimus*: Due process of law, and the equality of arms (*égalité des armes*), cannot be undermined by recourse by a contending party to alleged measures of "national security". *Quintus decimus*: Allegations of State secrecy or "national security" cannot interfere in the work of an international tribunal (in judicial or arbitral proceedings), carried out in the light of the principle of the proper administration of justice (*la bonne administration de la justice*).

69. *Sextus decimus*: Provisional measures of protection cannot be erected upon unilateral "undertakings" or assurances ensuing from alleged "national security" measures; provisional measures of protection cannot rely on such unilateral acts, they are independent from them, they carry the authority of the international tribunal which ordered them. *Septimus decimus*: In the circumstances of the *cas d'espèce*, it is the Court itself that should keep custody of the documents and data seized and detained by a contending party; the Court should do so as master of its own jurisdiction, so as to prevent further irreparable harm.

70. *Duodevicesimus*: The inviolability of State papers and documents is recognized by international law, in the interests of the good administration of justice. *Undevicesimus*: The inviolability of the correspondence between States and their legal advisers is an international law obligation, not one derived from a unilateral "undertaking" or assurance by a State following its seizure of documents and data containing information belonging to another State.

71. *Vicesimus*: There is an autonomous legal regime of provisional measures of protection, in expansion in our times. This autonomous legal regime

comprises: (a) the rights to be protected, not necessarily the same as in the proceedings on the merits of the concrete case; (b) the corresponding obligations of the States concerned; (c) the legal consequences of non-compliance with provisional measures, distinct from those ensuing from breaches as to the merits. The acknowledgment of such autonomous legal regime is endowed with growing importance in our days.

(Signed) *Antônio Augusto Cançado Trindade*
Judge

CHAPTER 7

The Autonomous Legal Regime of Provisional Measures of Protection

1 Separate Opinion in the joined cases of *Certain Activities Carried out by Nicaragua in the Border Area* (Costa Rica *versus* Nicaragua) and *Construction of a Road in Costa Rica along the San Juan River* (Nicaragua *versus* Costa Rica) (Judgment of 16.12.2015)

Table of Contents — Paragraphs

I. *Prolegomena* 1–3
II. Manifestations of the Preventive Dimension in Contemporary International Law 4–5
III. The Autonomous Legal Regime of Provisional Measures of Protection 6
    1. The Evolution of Provisional Measures of Protection 7–12
    2. The Conformation of Their Autonomous Legal Regime 13–16
IV. Provisional Measures: The Enlargement of the Scope of Protection 17–23
V. Breach of Provisional Measures of Protection as an Autonomous Breach, Engaging State Responsibility by Itself 24–25
VI. The ICJ's Determination of Breaches of Obligations under Provisional Measures of Protection 26–33
VII. A Plea for the Prompt Determination of Breaches of Provisional Measures of Protection: Some Reflections 34–44
VIII. Supervision of Compliance with Provisional Measures of Protection 45–46
IX. Breach of Provisional Measures and Reparation for Damages 47–52
X. Due Diligence, and the Interrelatedness between the Principle of Prevention and the Precautionary Principle 53–57
XI. The Path towards the Progressive Development of Provisional Measures of Protection 58–66
XII. Epilogue: A Recapitulation 67–73

I *Prolegomena*

1. I have accompanied the majority in voting in favour of the adoption today, 16 December 2015, of the present Judgment of the International Court of

Justice (ICJ) in the two joined cases of *Certain Activities Carried out by Nicaragua in the Border Area* (Costa Rica *versus* Nicaragua) and of the *Construction of a Road in Costa Rica along the San Juan River* (Nicaragua *versus* Costa Rica). Yet, there are certain points ensuing from the Court's decision which, though not dwelt upon at depth by the Court in its reasoning, are in my view endowed with importance, related as they are to the proper exercise of the international judicial function. I feel thus obliged to dwell upon them, in the present Separate Opinion, nourishing the hope that the considerations that follow may be useful for the handling of this matter by the ICJ in future cases.

2. I start drawing attention to the manifestations, in the *cas d'espèce*, of the preventive dimension in contemporary international law. I then turn attention to the key point, which I have been sustaining in the adjudication of successive cases in this Court, namely, that of the conformation of the *autonomous legal regime* of provisional measures of protection, in the course of their evolution (after their transposition from comparative domestic procedural law into international law). Next, I consider the widening of the scope of protection by means of provisional measures, and the breach of these latter as an autonomous breach, engaging State responsibility by itself. I then proceed to examine the determination by the ICJ of breaches of obligations under Provisional Measures of Protection.

3. In sequence, I present a plea for the prompt determination by the Court of breaches of Provisional Measures of Protection. My next line of considerations is on the supervision of compliance with Provisional Measures of Protection. Following that, I examine the interrelationship between the breach of provisional measures and the duty of reparation (in its distinct forms) for damages. I then turn attention to due diligence, and the interrelatedness between the principle of prevention and the precautionary principle. Next, I purport to detect the path towards the progressive development of Provisional Measures of Protection. Last but not least, I present, in an epilogue, my final considerations on the matter, in the form of a recapitulation of the main points sustained herein, in the course of the present Separate Opinion.

II   Manifestations of the Preventive Dimension in Contemporary International Law

4. May I begin by observing that the two joined cases of *Certain Activities Carried out by Nicaragua in the Border Area* and of the *Construction of a Road in Costa Rica along the San Juan River* bring to the fore the relevance of the

preventive dimension in contemporary international law, as reflected in the present Judgment, of 16 December 2015, in the finding and legal consequences of breaches of Provisional Measures of Protection (in the *Certain Activities* case), as well as in the acknowledgment of the obligation of conducting an environmental impact assessment (EIA) (in the *Construction of a Road* case as well). This preventive dimension grows in importance in the framework of regimes of protection (such as those, e.g., of the human person, and of the environment). Moreover, it brings us particularly close to general principles of law. Such preventive dimension stands out clearly in the succession of the Court's Orders of Provisional Measures of Protection of 08.03.2011, 16.07.2013 and 22.11.2013.[1]

5. The question of the non-compliance with, or of breaches of, the aforementioned Orders of Provisional Measures of Protection, was carefully addressed by the two contending parties in the course not only of the Court's proceedings pertaining to such Orders,[2] but also in the course of its proceedings (written and oral phases) as to the merits of the *Certain Activities* case. Concern with the issue of non-compliance with, or breaches of the Court's Order of 08.03.2011, for example, was in effect expressed in Costa Rica's *Memorial*[3] – a whole chapter, – as well as in its oral arguments;[4] Nicaragua, likewise, devoted a chapter of its *Counter-Memorial*,[5] as well as its oral arguments,[6] to the issue. The same concern was expressed, in respect of the Court's subsequent Order of Provisional Measures of 16.07.2013, – and of events following it, – in the oral arguments of Costa Rica[7] and of Nicaragua.[8] Again, in respect of the Court's third Order of Provisional Measures, of 22.11.2013, reference can further be made to the oral arguments of both Costa Rica[9] and Nicaragua.[10]

1   Reference can further be made to the Court's subsequent Order of 13.12.2013.
2   Cf., as to Costa Rica's oral arguments, ICJ, docs. CR 2013/24, of 14.10.2013, pp. 12–61; and CR 2013/26, of 16.10.2013, pp. 8–35; and, as to Nicaragua's oral arguments, ICJ, docs. CR 2013/25, of 15.10.2013, pp. 8–57; and CR 2013/27, of 17.10.2013, pp. 8–44.
3   Cf. *Memorial*, Chapter VI, paras. 6.1–6.63.
4   Cf. ICJ, docs. CR 2015/2, of 14.04.2015, pp. 17 and 23–25; CR 2015/4, of 15.04.2015, pp. 23–32; and CR 2015/14, of 28.04.2015, pp. 39–42 and 65–66.
5   Cf. *Counter-Memorial*, Chapter 7, paras. 7.4–7.46.
6   Cf. ICJ, docs. CR 2015/5, of 16.04.2015, p. 18; CR 2015/7, of 17.04.2015, pp. 46–50; and CR 2015/15, of 29.04.2015, pp. 43–44.
7   Cf. ICJ, docs. CR 2015/2, of 14.04.2015, pp. 24–25; CR 2015/4, of 15.04.2015, pp. 31–32.
8   Cf. ICJ, doc. CR 2015/7, of 17.04.2015, pp. 48–50.
9   Cf. ICJ, docs. CR 2015/4, of 15.04.2015, pp. 31–34; and CR 2015/14, of 28.04.2015, pp. 65–66.
10 Cf. ICJ, doc. CR 2015/7, of 17.04.2015, pp. 41–45.

III The Autonomous Legal Regime of Provisional Measures of Protection

6. The *autonomous legal regime* of Provisional Measures of Protection has been quite discernible to me: I have been drawing attention to it, in the way I conceive such autonomous legal regime, in successive Dissenting and Individual Opinions in this Court. The present Judgment of the ICJ in the two joined cases of *Certain Activities* and of the *Construction of a Road* is a proper occasion to dwell further upon it. The Court has duly considered the submissions of the parties, Costa Rica and Nicaragua (paras. 121–129), and has found that the respondent State incurred into a breach of the obligations under its Order of Provisional Measures of Protection of 08.03.2011 by the excavation of two *caños* in 2013 and the establishment of a military presence in the disputed territory (paras. 127 and 129, and resolutory point n. 3 of the *dispositif*). The ICJ has pointed out that the respondent State itself had acknowledged, in the course of the oral hearings, that "the excavation of the second and third *caños* represented an infringement of its obligations under the 2011 Order" (para. 125).[11]

1 *The Evolution of Provisional Measures of Protection*

7. There are, as from this finding of the Court of a breach of provisional measures in the *cas d'espèce*, several points that come to my mind, all relating to what I have been conceptualizing, along the years, as the autonomous legal regime of Provisional Measures of Protection.[12] This regime can be better

---

11 In the oral hearing of 16.04.2015, the agent of the respondent State asserted that "Nicaragua deeply regrets the actions following the 2011 Order on Provisional Measures that led the Court to determine, in November 2013, that a new Order was required"; ICJ, doc. 2015/5, of 16.04.2015, p. 18, para. 42. On the following day counsel recalled this (ICJ, doc. 2015/7, of 17.04.2015, p. 45, para. 14), and again it did so in the hearing of 29.04.2015, adding that there was thus "no need for future remedial measures"; ICJ, doc. 2015/15, of 29.04.2015, p. 44, paras. 23–24.

12 Cf. A.A. Cançado Trindade, *Évolution du Droit international au droit des gens – L'accès des particuliers à la justice internationale: le regard d'un juge*, Paris, Pédone, 2008, pp. 64–70; A.A. Cançado Trindade, "La Expansión y la Consolidación de las Medidas Provisionales de Protección en la Jurisdicción Internacional Contemporánea", *in Retos de la Jurisdicción Internacional* (eds. S. Sanz Caballero and R. Abril Stoffels), Cizur Menor/Navarra, Cedri/CEU/Thomson Reuters, 2012, pp. 99–117; A.A. Cançado Trindade, *El Ejercicio de la Función Judicial Internacional – Memorias de la Corte Interamericana de Derechos Humanos*, 3rd. ed., Belo Horizonte/Brazil, Edit. Del Rey, 2013, Chapters V and XXI (Provisional Measures), pp. 47–52 and 177–186; A.A. Cançado Trindade, "Les mesures provisoires de protection dans la jurisprudence de la Cour Interaméricaine des Droits de l'Homme", *in Mesures*

appreciated if we consider provisional measures in their historical evolution. May I recall that, in their origins, in domestic procedural law doctrine of over a century ago, provisional measures were considered, and evolved, in order to safeguard the effectiveness of the jurisdictional function itself.

8. They thus emerged, in the domestic legal systems, in the form of a *precautionary legal action* (*mesure conservatoire* / *acción cautelar* / *ação cautelar*), aiming at guaranteeing, not directly subjective rights *per se*, but rather the jurisdictional process itself. They had not yet freed themselves from a certain juridical formalism, conveying the impression of taking the legal process as an end in itself, rather than as a means for the realization of justice. With the gradual transposition of provisional measures from domestic into international law level, they came to be increasingly resorted to, in face of the most diverse circumstances disclosing the probability or imminence of an irreparable damage, to be prevented or avoided.

9. Their transposition into international legal procedure, and the increasing recourse to them within the framework of domains of protection (e.g., of the human person or of the environment), had the effect, in my perception, of enlarging the scope of international jurisdiction, and of refining their conceptualization. International case-law on Provisional Measures of Protection expanded considerably along the last three decades, making it clear to the contending parties that they are to abstain from any action which may aggravate the dispute *pendente lite*, or may have a prejudicial effect on the compliance with the subsequent judgment as to the merits.

10. Their *rationale* stood out clearer, turning to the protection of rights, of the equality of arms (*égalité des armes*), and not only of the legal process itself. Along the last three decades, Provisional Measures of Protection have freed themselves from the juridical formalism of the procedural doctrine of over a century ago, and have, in my perception, come closer to reaching their plenitude. They have become endowed with a character, more than precautionary, truly *tutelary*. When their basic requisites, – of gravity and urgency, and the needed prevention of irreparable harm, – are met, they have been ordered, in the light of the needs of protection, and have thus conformed a true *jurisdictional guarantee of a preventive character*.

---

conservatoires et droits fondamentaux (eds. G. Cohen-Jonathan and J.-F. Flauss), Bruxelles, Bruylant/Nemesis, 2005, pp. 145–163.

11. For many years I have been insisting on this particular point. To recall but one example, already by the turn of the century, in another international jurisdiction, in my Concurring Opinion appended to the Order of 25.05.1999 of the Inter-American Court of Human Rights (IACtHR) in the case of *James and Others*, concerning Trinidad and Tobago, I deemed it fit to draw attention to the configuration, in provisional measures of protection of our times, of a true *jurisdictional guarantee of a preventive character* (para. 10). I further drew attention to the inherent power or *faculté* of an international tribunal to determine the *scope* of the provisional measures that it decided to order (para. 7). All this comes to reinforce the preventive dimension, proper of those measures.

12. In the case of the ICJ (like in that of the IACtHR), such provisional measures do have a conventional basis (Article 41 of the ICJ's Statute). But even if an international tribunal does not count on such a conventional basis, it has, in my understanding, inherent powers to indicate such measures, so as to secure the sound administration of justice (*la bonne administration de la justice*). Contemporary international tribunals have the *compétence de la compétence* (*Kompetenz-Kompetenz*) in the domain of provisional measures as well, so as to safeguard the respective rights of the contending parties in the course of the legal process. The grant of those measures is a significant manifestation of the preventive dimension in contemporary international law.

2   *The Conformation of Their Autonomous Legal Regime*

13. In effect, the evolution of provisional measures in recent years has, in my perception, made very clear that they operate within an autonomous legal regime of their own, encompassing their juridical nature, the rights and obligations at issue, their legal effects, and the duty of compliance with them. It is now the duty of contemporary international tribunals to elaborate on such autonomous legal regime, and to extract the legal consequences ensuing therefrom. In order to do so, it is necessary, in my understanding, to keep in mind – may I reiterate – their juridical nature, the rights to be preserved and the corresponding obligations in their wide scope, and their legal effects (cf. *infra*).

14. In my Dissenting Opinion in the Court's Order (of 28.05.2009) in the case of *Questions Relating to the Obligation to Prosecute or Extradite* (Belgium versus Senegal), wherein the Court decided not to indicate or order provisional measures, I pondered that Provisional Measures of Protection have lately much evolved, and appear nowadays as being "endowed with a character, more than precautionary, truly *tutelary*" (para. 13). Their development – I added – has led

the Court gradually to overcome the strictly inter-State outlook in the acknowledgment of the rights to be preserved (paras. 21, 25 and 72). Such rights to be protected by Provisional Measures have encompassed, in the *cas d'espèce*, the *right to the realisation of justice*, – i.e., the right to see to it that justice is done, – "ineluctably linked to the rule of law at both national and international levels" (paras. 92–95 and 101).

15. Four years later, in my Dissenting Opinion in the Court's Order (of 16.07.2013) in the joined cases of *Certain Activities Carried out by Nicaragua in the Border Area* (Costa Rica *versus* Nicaragua) and *Construction of a Road in Costa Rica along the San Juan River* (Nicaragua *versus* Costa Rica), wherein the Court simply reaffirmed a previous Order (of 08.03.2011) and decided not to indicate or order new provisional measures or modify the previous Order, I drew attention to the overcoming of the inter-State outlook in the present domain of provisional measures (para. 49), given that they came to extend protection also to the human person (paras. 39–42). I further warned that non-compliance with Provisional Measures of Protection amounts to a breach of an international obligation, engaging State responsibility *per se* (paras. 70–72). Provisional measures have an *autonomous legal regime* of their own, – I concluded, – and they have grown in importance, – with their preventive dimension underlined by their juridical nature, – "in respect of regimes of *protection*, such as those of the human person as well as of the environment" (paras. 73 and 75).

16. Shortly afterwards, in my subsequent Separate Opinion in the Court's following Order of Provisional Measures (of 22.11.2013) in the same two joined cases opposing the two Central American countries, Nicaragua and Costa Rica, wherein the Court decided to indicate or order new provisional measures, I observed that the duty of compliance with Provisional Measures of Protection outlines their *autonomous legal regime* (paras. 23–24). Provisional Measures – I proceeded – generate *per se* obligations, irrespective of, or independently from, those ensuing from the Court's Judgments on the merits or on reparations (para. 29). I insisted that Provisional Measures of Protection, in their evolution, have become, more than precautionary, truly *tutelary* (para. 26), and I then added, moving into their effects, that non-compliance with Provisional Measures of Protection engages autonomously the international responsibility of the State (paras. 24 and 39–40). Such non-compliance is "an autonomous breach of a conventional obligation (concerning provisional measures), without prejudice to what will later be decided by the Court as to the merits" (para. 37).

IV Provisional Measures: The Enlargement of the Scope of Protection

17. In the present Judgment in the two joined cases of *Certain Activities* and of the *Construction of a Road*, the Court has found, – in Section III.C concerning the *Certain Activities* case, – that the excavation of the second and the third *caños* and the establishment of a military presence in the disputed territory breached the obligations of the provisional measures of protection it had ordered (on 08.03.2011), and constituted "a violation of the territorial sovereignty" of the applicant State (para. 129). Beyond that, provisional measures, in my perception, do widen the scope of protection; it is not only a matter of State sovereignty. Protection extends to the environment, and the right to life; their safeguard is also necessary to avoid aggravating the dispute or rendering it more difficult to resolve (cf. para. 123).

18. The enlargement, by provisional measures, of the scope of protection, is deserving of attention and praise. It is reassuring that prevention and precaution have found their place in the conceptual universe of the law of nations, the *droit des gens*, – and a prominent place in international environmental law. It could not have been otherwise. From the days of the U.N. Conference on Environment and Development (Rio de Janeiro, 1992) up to the present, this has occurred amidst the acknowledgment of risks and the limitations of human knowledge. Prevention and precaution have enforced each other, and the new awareness of their need has paved the way to the aforementioned expansion of Provisional Measures of Protection along the last three decades.

19. It is not casual that they came to be conceived as precautionary measures (*mesures provisoires / medidas cautelares*), prevention and precaution underlying them all. Precaution, in effect, takes prevention further, in face of the uncertainty of risks, so as to avoid irreparable damages. And here, again, in the domain of Provisional Measures of Protection, the relationship between international law and time becomes manifest. The inter-temporal dimension is here ineluctable, overcoming the constraints of legal positivism. International law endeavours to be *anticipatory* in the regulation of social facts, so as to avoid irreparable harm; Provisional Measures of Protection expand the protection they pursue, as a true international *jurisdictional guarantee* of a preventive character.[13]

---

13   Cf., in this sense, A.A. Cançado Trindade, *International Law for Humankind – Towards a New Jus Gentium*, 2nd rev. ed., Leiden/The Hague, Nijhoff/The Hague Academy of International Law, 2013, pp. 40–47.

20. In order to avoid irreparable harm, one cannot remain closed in the fugacious present, but rather look back in time and learn the lessons of the past, as much as, at the same time, look into the future, to see how to avoid irreparable harm. We – or survive – surrounded by uncertainties, which call for precaution. As Seneca warned in his *De Brevitate Vitae* (circa 49 A.D.), it is wise to keep in mind all times – past, present and future – together: time past, by recollection; time present, by making the best use of it; and time future, by anticipating whatever one can, and thus making one's life meaningful, safer and longer.[14] In his late years, in his *Letters to Lucilius* (circa 62–64 A.D.), Seneca, in his Stoic search for some means of reconciliation with the frailty of human nature, stated:

> We are tormented alike by what is past and what is to come. (...) [M]emory brings back the agony of fear while foresight brings it on prematurely. No one confines his unhappiness to the present.[15]

21. Back to our times, in this XXIst century, in yet another case before this Court, on the request for interpretation in the case of the *Temple of Préah Vihéar* (Cambodia *versus* Thailand), the ICJ, in its Order of Provisional Measures of Protection of 18.07.2011, took the unprecedented and correct decision to order, *inter alia*, the creation of a provisional "demilitarized zone" around the Temple and in the proximities of the border between the two countries, which contributed to put an end to the armed hostilities around the Temple in the border region between Cambodia and Thailand. In my Separate Opinion appended to that Order, I supported the Court's correct decision, which, in my understanding, extended protection not only to the territory at issue, but also to the populations living thereon, as well as to the monuments conforming the Temple which, by decision of UNESCO (of 2008), integrate the cultural and spiritual world heritage (paras. 66–95).

22. In the same Separate Opinion, I dwelt upon the temporal dimension in international law, this latter being also *anticipatory* in the regulation of social facts (paras. 64–65). In the context of the *cas d'espèce*, Provisional Measures rightly extended protection also to cultural or spiritual heritage, upholding a universal value (para. 93). They brought *"territory, people and human values together"*, well beyond State territorial sovereignty (para. 100), – as shown by the establishment, in the Order, of the aforementioned demilitarized zone

---

14   L.A. Seneca, *On the Shortness of Life* (*De Brevitate Vitae*) [circa 49 A.D.], Part XV.
15   L.A. Seneca, "Letter V", *in Letters to Lucilius* [circa 62–64 A.D.].

(para. 117). I further observed that rights of States and rights of individuals evolve *pari passu* in contemporary *jus gentium*, and added:

> Cultural and spiritual heritage appears more closely related to a *human context*, rather than to the traditional State-centric context; it appears to transcend the purely inter-State dimension (...) (para. 113).

23. Beyond the classic territorialist outlook is the "human factor"; protection by means of provisional measures extended itself to local populations as well as to the cultural and spiritual world heritage (paras. 96–113), in the light of the *principle of humanity*, orienting the *societas gentium* towards the realization of the common good (paras. 114–115 and 117). After all, – I added, – one cannot consider territory (whereon hostilities were taking place) in isolation (as in the past), making abstraction of the population (or the local populations), which form the most precious component of statehood. One is to consider people on territory (cf. paras. 67, 81, 97, 100, 114), – I concluded, – there being epistemologically no inadequacy to extend protection, by means of provisional measures, also to human life and cultural and spiritual world heritage.

V   Breach of Provisional Measures of Protection as an Autonomous Breach, Engaging State Responsibility by Itself

24. The breach of a provisional measure of protection is *additional* to the breach which comes, or may come, later to be determined as to the merits of the case at issue. The factual context may be the same, but State responsibility is engaged not only with the occurrence and determination of a breach of an international obligation as to the merits, but also earlier on, with the occurrence and determination of a breach of an obligation under an Order of provisional measures of protection. The latter is an autonomous breach. State responsibility is thus engaged time and time again, in respect of the breaches of obligations as to provisional measures (prevention) and as to the merits.

25. The breach of a provisional measure of protection is an autonomous breach, added to the one which comes, or may come, later to be determined as to the merits. As such, it can be promptly determined, with its legal consequences, without any need to wait for the conclusion of the proceedings as to the merits. Although in the Order of 22.11.2013 the Court did not expressly determine the occurrence of a breach of the earlier Order of 08.03.2011, it implicitly held so, in reiterating the earlier Order and indicating new provisional measures.

In my view, the Court should have done so already in its Order of 16.07.2013, as explained in my Dissenting Opinion appended thereto.

VI   The ICJ's Determination of Breaches of Obligations under Provisional Measures of Protection

26. In its practice, the ICJ has come to determine, on a few occasions so far, breaches of obligations under provisional measures of protection it had ordered; it has done so at the end of the proceedings as to the merits of the corresponding cases. This has occurred, until the Judgment the Court has just delivered today, 16 December 2015, in the joined cases of *Certain Activities* and of the *Construction of a Road*, in its Judgments as to the merits in the three cases of *LaGrand* (of 27.06.2001), of *Armed Activities on the Territory of the Congo* (of 19.12.2005), and of the *Bosnian Genocide* (of 26.02.2007).

27. Earlier on, in the case of the *Hostages in Tehran* (United States *versus* Iran, Judgment of 24.05.1980), the ICJ stated that its Order of Provisional Measures of 15.12.1979 had been either "rejected" or "ignored" by the authorities of the respondent State (paras. 75 and 93); the Court expressed its concern with the aggravation of the "tension between the two countries" (para. 93), but, in the *dispositif* of the Judgment, it did not expressly assert that the aforementioned Order of Provisional Measures had been breached. No consequences from non-compliance with its provisional measures were drawn by the Court.

28. The ICJ only started doing so in the course of the last 15 years, i.e., in the XXIst century, – although, in my view, nothing hindered it from doing so well before, in earlier cases. Thus, in its Judgment of 27.06.2001 in the *LaGrand* case (Germany *versus* United States), the ICJ, after holding that its Order of Provisional Measures of 03.03.1999 had not been complied with (para. 115), stated, in resolutory point n. 5 of the *dispositif*, that the respondent State had breached the obligation incumbent upon it under the aforementioned Order of Provisional Measures. Yet, once again the Court did not draw any consequences from the conduct in breach of its provisional measures.

29. Four years later, in its Judgment of 19.12.2005 in the case concerning *Armed Activities on the Territory of the Congo* (D.R. Congo *versus* Uganda), the ICJ, dwelling again on the matter, first recalled its finding that the respondent State was "responsible for acts in violation of international human rights law and international humanitarian law carried out by its military forces" in the

territory of the D.R. Congo (para. 264), committed in the period between the issue of its Order of Provisional Measures (of 01.07.2000) and the withdrawal of Ugandan troops in June 2003. Turning to its Order of Provisional Measures adopted half a decade earlier, the ICJ found that the respondent State had not complied with it (para. 264), and reiterated its finding in resolutory point n. 7 of the *dispositif*.

30. Another case of determination by the ICJ of a breach of its Orders of Provisional Measures of Protection was that of the *Application of the Convention against Genocide* (Bosnia and Herzegovina *versus* Serbia and Montenegro): the Court held so in its Judgment of 26.02.2007, while the Orders of Provisional Measures had been adopted 14 years earlier, on 08.04.1993 and 13.09.1993. They were intended to cease the atrocities that were already being perpetrated. The Court found, only in its Judgement of 2007 (para. 456), that the respondent State had failed to "take all measures within its power to prevent commission of the crime of genocide", as indicated in its Order of 08.04.1993 (para. 52.A(1)) and reaffirmed in its Order of 13.09.1993, nor did it comply with the measure of ensuring that "any (...) organizations and persons which may be subject to its (...) influence (...) do not commit any acts of genocide", as also indicated in its Order of 08.04.1993 (para. 52.A(2)) and reiterated in its Order of 13.09.1993.[16]

31. Two years after the first Order (of 08.04.1993), the U.N. safe-area of Srebrenica collapsed, and the mass-killings of July 1995 in Srebrenica occurred, in a flagrant breach of the provisional measures ordered by the ICJ. In the meantime, the proceedings in the case before the ICJ prolonged in time: as to preliminary objections until 1996; as to counter-claims until 1997, and again until 2001; and as to the merits until 2007. Along these years, much criticism was expressed in expert writing that the manifest breaches of the ICJ's Orders of Provisional Measures of Protection of 1993 (*supra*) passed for a long time without determination, and without any legal consequences.

32. As to the ICJ's Judgment on the merits of the aforementioned case of *Application of the Convention against Genocide* (2007), the Court was requested by the applicant State to hold the respondent State to be under an obligation to

---

16   Bosnia and Herzegovina promptly brought the matter before the U.N. Security Council, to have the Court's Orders enforced; the Security Council promptly adopted its Resolution 819 (of 16.04.1993), which, after expressly invoking the ICJ's Order (of 08.04.1993), ordered the immediate cessation of the armed attacks and several other measures to protect persons in Srebrenica and its surrounding areas.

provide "symbolic compensation" (para. 458) for the massacres at Srebrenica in July 1995. The Court, however, considered that, for the purposes of reparation, the respondent State's non-compliance with its Orders of 08.04.1993 and 13.09.1993 "is an aspect of, or merges with, its breaches of the substantive obligations of prevention and punishment laid upon it by the Convention" (para. 469). Thus, instead of ordering symbolic compensation, the Court deemed it fit to "include in the operative clause of the present Judgment, by way of satisfaction, a declaration that the Respondent has failed to comply with the Court's Orders indicating provisional measures" (para. 469).

33. The ICJ then found, in resolutory point n. 7 of the *dispositif*, that the respondent State had "violated its obligations to comply with the provisional measures ordered by the Court on 8 April and 13 September 1993 in this case, inasmuch as it failed to take all measures within its power to prevent genocide in Srebrenica in July 1995". It took 14 years for the Court to determine the breach of its Provisional Measures of Protection in the *cas d'espèce*. In my understanding, there was no need to wait such a long time to determine the breach of such measures; on the contrary, they should have been promptly determined by the ICJ, will all legal consequences. This tragic case shows that we are still in the infancy of the development of the legal regime of provisional measures of protection in contemporary international law. A proper understanding of the *autonomous legal regime* of those measures may foster their development at conceptual level.

VII   A Plea for the Prompt Determination of Breaches of Provisional Measures of Protection: Some Reflections

34. In the *cas d'espèce* (*Certain Activities* case), the breaches of provisional measures have been determined by the Court within a reasonably short lapse of time, – unlike in the case of *Armed Activities on the Territory of the Congo* (half a decade later) and in the *Bosnian Genocide* case (almost one and a half decade later). In the *cas d'espèce*, the damages caused by the breaches of provisional measures have not been irreparable, – unlike in the *LaGrand* case, – and with their determination by the Court in the present Judgment its effects can be made to cease. This brings to the fore, in my perception, an important point related to the autonomous legal regime of provisional measures of protection.

35. In effect, in my understanding, the determination of a breach of a provisional measure of protection is not – should not be – conditioned by the

completion of subsequent proceedings as to the merits of the case at issue. The legal effects of a breach of a provisional measure of protection should in my view be promptly determined, with all its legal consequences. In this way, its anticipatory rationale would be better served. There is no room for raising here alleged difficulties as to evidence, as for the ordering of provisional measures of protection, and the determination of non-compliance with them, it suffices to rely on *prima facie* evidence (*commencement de preuve*). And it could not be otherwise.

36. Furthermore, the rights that one seeks to protect under provisional measures are set forth in the case of the *Temple of Préah Vihéar* (cf. *supra*). Likewise, the obligations (of prevention) are new or additional ones, in relation to those ensuing from the judgment on the merits. There is yet another point which I deem it fit to single out here, namely, contemporary international tribunals have, in my understanding, an inherent power or *faculté* to order provisional measures of protection, whenever needed, and to determine, *ex officio*, the occurrence of a breach of provisional measures, with its legal consequences. Having pointed this out, my concern here is now turned to a distinct, and very concrete point.

37. The fact that, in its practice, the ICJ has only indicated provisional measures *at the request* of a State party, in my view does not mean that it cannot order such measures *sponte sua*, *ex officio*. The ICJ Statute endows the Court with "the power to indicate, if it considers that circumstances so require, any provisional measures which ought to be taken to preserve the respective rights of either party" (Article 41(1)). The Rules of Court provide for request by a party for the indication of provisional measures (Article 73(1)); yet they add that, irrespective of such request, the Court may indicate provisional measures that, in its view, "are in whole or in part other than those requested" (Article 75(2)).

38. For example, in the case concerning the *Land and Maritime Boundary between Cameroon and Nigeria*, the ICJ indicated, in its Order of 15.03.1996 (paras. 20 and 49), provisional measures that were distinct from, and broader than, those requested by the applicant State.[17] It expressly stated, in that Order, that it was entitled to do so, that it had the power to indicate measures "in whole or in part other than those requested / *totalement ou partiellement*

---

17 The Court then found, six years later, in its Judgment of 10.10.2002, that the applicant State had not established that there had been a breach by the respondent State (para. 322) of the provisional measures indicated in its Order of 15.03.1996.

différentes de celles qui sont sollicités" (para. 48). Furthermore, the Rules of Court provide that

> The Court may at any time decide to examine *proprio motu* whether the circumstances of the case require the indication of provisional measures which ought to be taken or complied with by any or all of the parties (Article 75(1)).

The Rules of Court moreover set forth that it "may request information from the parties on any matter connected with the implementation of any provisional measures it has indicated" (Article 78).

39. The Court, thus, is not conditioned by what a party, or the parties, request(s), nor – in my view – even by the existence of the request itself. Here, in the realm of Provisional Measures of Protection, once again the constraints of voluntarist legal positivism are, in my view, overcome.[18] The Court is not limited to what the contending parties want (in the terms they express their wish), or so request. The Court is not an arbitral tribunal, it stands above the will of the contending parties. This is an important point that I have been making on successive occasions within the ICJ, in its work of international adjudication.

40. In effect, there have lately been cases lodged with it, where the ICJ has been called upon to reason beyond the inter-State dimension, not being limited by the contentions or interests of the litigating States: this is the point I deemed it fit to stress in my Separate Opinion (paras. 227–228) in the Court's Judgment (merits) of 30.11.2010 in the case of *A.S. Diallo* (Guinea *versus* D.R. Congo). Earlier on, in the Court's Order (provisional measures) of 28.05.2009 in the case of *Questions Relating to the Obligation to Prosecute or Extradite* (Belgium *versus* Senegal), I stated, in my Dissenting Opinion appended thereto, that the Court is not to relinquish its jurisdiction in respect of Provisional Measures of Protection in face of what appears to be the professed intentions of the parties; on the contrary, the Court is to assume the role of guarantor of compliance with conventional obligations, beyond the professed intention or will of the parties (para. 88).

---

18   For my criticisms of the voluntarist conception of international law, cf. A.A. Cançado Trindade, "The Voluntarist Conception of International Law: A Re-Assessment", 59 *Revue de droit international de sciences diplomatiques et politiques* – Sottile (1981) pp. 201–240.

41. In the same line of thinking, in the ICJ's Judgment (preliminary objections) of 01.04.2011 in the case concerning the *Application of the International Convention on the Elimination of All Forms of Racial Discrimination* (CERD – Georgia *versus* Russian Federation), I asserted, in my Dissenting Opinion appended thereto, that the ICJ cannot "keep on embarking on a literal or grammatical and static interpretation of the terms of compromissory clauses" enshrined in human rights treaties (such as the CERD Convention), "drawing 'preconditions' therefrom for the exercise of its jurisdiction, in an attitude remindful of traditional international arbitral practice" (para. 206). On the contrary, – I added, – "[w]hen human rights treaties are at stake, there is need, in my perception, to overcome the force of inertia, and to assert and develop the compulsory jurisdiction of the ICJ on the basis of the compromissory clauses contained in those treaties" (para. 206).

42. The Court, – may I reiterate, – is not an arbitral tribunal, it stands above the will of the contending parties. It is not conditioned by requests or professed intentions of the contending parties. It has an inherent power or *faculté* to proceed promptly to the determination of a breach of provisional measures, in the interests of the sound administration of justice. And *recta ratio* guides the sound administration of justice (*la bonne administration de la justice*). *Recta ratio* stands above the will. It guides international adjudication and secures its contribution to the rule of law (*prééminence du droit*) at international level.

43. The Court is entirely free to order the provisional measures that it considers necessary, so as to prevent the aggravation of the dispute or the occurrence of irreparable harm, even if the measures it decides to order are quite different from those requested by the contending parties. The ICJ has in fact done so, not surprisingly, also in relation to situations of armed conflicts; the Court has been faced, in such situations (surrounded by complexity), with the imperative of *protection* of human life. Thus, in its Order of Provisional Measures of Protection, of 01.07.2000, in the case concerning *Armed Activities on the Territory of the Congo* (D.R. Congo *versus* Uganda), the ICJ, invoking Article 75(2) of the Rules of Court, once again asserted its power to order measures that are "in whole or in part other than those requested / *totalement ou partiellement différentes de celles qui sont sollicités*" (para. 43).

44. The Court, in my view, after examining the circumstances of the *cas d'espèce*, may proceed to order, *sponte sua*, provisional measures of protection. And it may, in my conception, proceed *motu proprio*, – thus avoiding the aggravation

of a situation, – to determine *ex officio*, the occurrence of a breach of an Order of Provisional Measures of Protection. Keeping in mind the preventive dimension in contemporary international law (cf. *supra*), and the need to prevent further irreparable harm, the Court does not have to wait until the completion of the proceedings as to the merits, especially if such proceedings are unreasonably prolonged, as, e.g., in the case of the *Bosnian Genocide* (cf. *supra*).

VIII Supervision of Compliance with Provisional Measures of Protection

45. The fact that the ICJ has, so far, very seldom proceeded to the determination of a breach of provisional measures in the subsequent proceedings as to the merits of the respective cases, in my view does not mean that it cannot do so promptly, by means of another Order of Provisional Measures. Furthermore, the Court has monitoring powers as to *compliance* with provisional measures. If any unforeseeable circumstance may arise, the ICJ is, in my understanding, endowed with inherent powers or *facultés* to take the decision that ensures compliance with the provisional measures it has ordered, and thus the safeguard of the rights at stake.

46. All the aforesaid enhances the preventive dimension of Provisional Measures of Protection. These latter have experienced a remarkable development in recent years, in contemporary international law on the matter. Such measures now call for further development at conceptual level. They have an autonomous legal regime of their own, which encompasses supervision of compliance with them. The Court is endowed with monitoring powers to this effect. This is yet another element which comes to enforce the rule of law (*prééminence du droit*) at international level.

IX Breach of Provisional Measures and Reparation for Damages

47. May I now turn to yet another relevant point pertaining to the autonomous legal regime of Provisional Measures of Protection, namely, the legal consequences of the finding of a breach of such provisional measures. In addressing those consequences, the Court is likely to face the need to consider remedies, reparations in their distinct forms, and costs. This point has not passed unperceived in the present Judgment of the ICJ in the two joined cases of *Certain*

Activities and of the *Construction of a Road*. The Court has addressed reparations in the two joined cases.[19]

48. Reparations are here contemplated in all their forms, – namely, e.g., compensation, satisfaction, guarantee of non-repetition, among others. In the *cas d'espèce*, – the *Certain Activities* case, – the ICJ has determined the respondent's duty of *compensation* for the material damage (para. 142); it has further determined that, in the circumstances of the case, given its finding of a breach of provisional measures (by the excavation of the *caños* and the establishment of a military presence in the disputed territory), the declaration by the Court to this effect provides adequate *satisfaction* to the applicant for the non-material damage (para. 139), without the need to award costs (para. 144).

49. The ICJ has found that it has thereby afforded "adequate satisfaction" (para. 139) to the applicant, by its declaration, in the *Certain Activities* case,[20] of a breach of obligations ensuing from the Order of provisional measures of 08.03.2011. Furthermore, the ICJ indicated new provisional measures in its Order of 22.11.2013, so as to cease the effects of the harmful activities and to remedy that breach. In the joined case of *Construction of a Road*, the ICJ declined to award *compensation* (para. 226), but determined – even if not here referring specifically to a breach of provisional measures – that its declaration of wrongful conduct for the respondent's breach of the obligation to conduct an environmental impact assessment provides adequate *satisfaction* to the applicant (para. 224).

50. The grant of this form of reparation (satisfaction) in the two joined cases is necessary and reassuring. The fact that the ICJ did not establish a breach of provisional measures nor did it indicate new provisional measures *already* in its Order of 16.07.2013 (as it should, for the reasons explained in my Dissenting Opinion appended thereto), and only did so in its subsequent Order of 22.11.2013, gives weight to its decision not to award costs.[21] After all, the prolongation of the proceedings (as to provisional measures)[22] was due to the

---

19 Paras. 137–144 and 224–228, respectively.
20 Paras. 127 and 129, and resolutory point n. 3.
21 Para. 144 (*Certain Activities* case) of the present Judgment.
22 After the hearings of 11-13.01.2011 (following Costa Rica's initial request for the indication of provisional measures in the *Certain Activities* case), those of 14-17.10.2013 (following Costa Rica's further request for the indication of provisional measures in the *Certain*

hesitation of the Court itself. Accordingly, the relevant issue here is, thus, reparation (rather than costs of hearings) for breach of Provisional Measures of Protection.

51. In effect, breach and duty of reparation come together. As I pointed out in my Separate Opinion in the *A.S. Diallo* case (Guinea *versus* D.R. Congo, reparations, Judgment of 19.06.2012), the duty of reparation has deep historical roots, going back to the origins of the law of nations, and marking presence in the legacy of the "founding fathers" of our discipline (paras. 14–21). The duty of reparation is widely acknowledged as one of general or customary international law (para. 25). I stressed that

> The duty of full reparation is the prompt and indispensable complement of an international wrongful act, so as to cease all the consequences ensuing therefrom, and to secure respect for the international legal order. (...) The breach of international law and the ensuing compliance with the duty of reparation for injuries are two sides of the same coin; they form an *indissoluble whole* (...).
>
> (...) [T]he *reparatio* (from the Latin *reparare*, "to dispose again") ceases all the effects of the breaches of international law (...) at issue, and provides satisfaction (as a form of reparation) to the victims; by means of the reparations, the Law re-establishes the legal order broken by those violations (...).
>
> One has to be aware that it has become commonplace in legal circles – as is the conventional wisdom of the legal profession – to repeat that the duty of reparation, conforming a "secondary obligation", comes after the breach of international law. This is not my conception; when everyone seems to be thinking alike, no one is actually thinking at all. In my own conception, breach and reparation go together, conforming an indissoluble whole: the latter is the indispensable consequence or complement of the former. The duty of reparation is a *fundamental* obligation (...). The indissoluble whole that violation and reparation conform admits no disruption (...), so as to evade the indispensable consequence of the international breaches incurred into: the reparations due to the victims (paras. 32, 35 and 39–40).

Activities case), and those of 05-08.11.2013 (following Nicaragua's request for the indication of provisional measures in the *Construction of a Road* case).

52. The interrelationship between breach and duty of reparation marks presence also in the realm of the autonomous legal regime of Provisional Measures of Protection. A breach of a provisional measure promptly generates the duty to provide reparation for it. It is important, for provisional measures to achieve their plenitude (within their legal regime), to remain attentive to reparations – in their distinct forms – for their breach. Reparations (to a greater extent than costs) for the autonomous breach of Provisional Measures of Protection are a key element for the consolidation of the autonomous legal regime of Provisional Measures of Protection.

X   Due Diligence, and the Interrelatedness between the Principle of Prevention and the Precautionary Principle

53. Now that I approach the conclusion of the present Separate Opinion, may I come back to its point of departure, namely, the relevance of the preventive dimension in contemporary international law. Such preventive dimension marks presence in the Judgment the ICJ has just adopted, in the two joined cases of *Certain Activities Carried out by Nicaragua in the Border Area* and of the *Construction of a Road in Costa Rica along the San Juan River*. It is significant that, in the course of the proceedings in the present joined cases, the duty of *due diligence* has been invoked, just as it was in an earlier Latin American case, that of the *Pulp Mills on the River Uruguay* (2010), opposing Argentina to Uruguay.

54. In respect of the *cas d'espèce* (and specifically of the *Construction of a Road* case), it has been asserted that the populations of both countries, Nicaragua and Costa Rica, "deserve to benefit from the highest possible standards of environmental protection", and that the States of Central America have adopted and applied environmental and related laws to secure "high standards of protection".[23] Due diligence has thus been duly acknowledged, once again, in a Latin American case before the ICJ. There are other related aspects in the preventive dimension. The duty to conduct an environmental impact assessment, for example, as determined by the Court in the present Judgment, in the case of the *Construction of a Road* (paras. 153–162), brings to the fore, in my

---

23   ICJ, doc. CR 2015/15, of 29.04.2015, pp. 44–45, paras. 26–27 (statement of counsel of Nicaragua).

perception, the interrelatedness between the *principle of prevention* and the *precautionary principle*.

55. I had the occasion to dwell upon this particular point in the other aforementioned Latin American case, of half a decade ago, concerning *Pulp Mills on the River Uruguay* (Argentina *versus* Uruguay). In my Separate Opinion appended to the ICJ's Judgment of 20.04.2010 in the *Pulp Mills* case, I pondered that, while the principle of prevention assumes that risks can be objectively assessed so as to avoid damage, the precautionary principle assesses risks in face of uncertainties, taking into account the vulnerability of human beings and the environment, and the possibility of irreversible harm (paras. 72–73).

56. Unlike the positivist belief in the certainties of scientific knowledge, – I proceeded, – the precautionary principle is geared to the duty of *due diligence*, in face of scientific uncertainties;[24] precaution is thus, nowadays, more than ever, needed (paras. 83 and 89). It is not surprising that some environmental law Conventions give expression to both the principle of prevention and the precautionary principle, acknowledging the link between them, providing the foundation of the duty to conduct an environmental impact assessment (paras. 94–96), – as upheld by the ICJ in the joined case of the *Construction of a Road*.

57. In the present Judgment, the Court, recalling its earlier decision in the *Pulp Mills* case (2010), referred in a reiterated way to the requirement of due diligence in order to prevent significant transboundary environmental harm (para. 104). It focused on the undertaking of an environmental impact assessment in the wider realm of general international law (paras. 104–105). And it then stated that

> If the environmental impact assessment confirms that there is a risk of significant transboundary harm, the State planning to undertake the activity is required, in conformity with its due diligence obligation, to notify and consult in good faith with the potentially affected State, where that is necessary to determine the appropriate measures to prevent or mitigate that risk (para. 104).

---

24   For a recent reassessment of the precautionary principle, cf. A.A. Cançado Trindade, "Principle 15 – Precaution", *in The Rio Declaration on Environment and Development – A Commentary* (ed. J.E. Viñuales), Oxford, Oxford University Press, 2015, pp. 403–428.

XI The Path towards the Progressive Development of Provisional Measures of Protection

58. Having pointed that out, the main lesson learned from the adjudication of the *cas d'espèce*, that I deem it fit to leave on the records, in the present Separate Opinion, under the umbrella of the preventive dimension in contemporary international law, as developed in the preceding paragraphs, pertains to what I conceptualize as the conformation of an *autonomous legal regime* of provisional measures of protection, with all its elements and implications, as related to the Court's finding in the joined case of *Certain Activities*.

59. Thus, in my Dissenting Opinion in the ICJ's Order of 16.07.2013 in the present two joined cases of *Certain Activities* and of the *Construction of a Road*, wherein the Court decided not to indicate new provisional measures, nor to modify the provisional measures indicated in its previous Order of 08.03.2011, I asserted, and deem it fit here to reiterate:

> My thesis, in sum, is that provisional measures, endowed with a conventional basis – such as those of the ICJ (under Article 41 of the Statute) – are also endowed with autonomy, have a legal regime of their own, and non-compliance with them generates the responsibility of the State, entails legal consequences, without prejudice of the examination and resolution of the concrete cases as to the merits. This discloses their important preventive dimension, in their wide scope. The proper treatment of this subject-matter is the task before this Court, now and in the years to come.
>
> (...) Provisional measures of protection generate obligations (of prevention) for the States concerned, which are distinct from the obligations which emanate from the Judgments of the Court as to the merits (and reparations) of the respective cases. This ensues from their autonomous legal regime, as I conceive it. There is, in my perception, pressing need nowadays to refine and to develop conceptually this autonomous legal regime, – focused, in particular, on the contemporary expansion of provisional measures, the means to secure due and prompt compliance with them, and the legal consequences of non-compliance – to the benefit of those protected thereunder.
>
> (...) [T]he matter before the Court calls for a more pro-active posture on its part, so as not only to settle the controversies filed with it, but also to tell what the Law is (*juris dictio*), and thus to contribute effectively to the avoidance or prevention of irreparable harm in situations of urgency,

to the ultimate benefit of *all* subjects of international law – States as well as groups of individuals, and *simples particuliers*. After all, the human person (living in harmony in her natural habitat) occupies a central place in the new *jus gentium* of our times (paras. 72 and 75–76).

60. Provisional Measures of Protection have grown in importance, and have expanded and have much developed in recent years, particularly in the framework of regimes of protection (such as those, e.g., of the human person and of the environment). Provisional Measures of Protection have become, more than precautionary, truly *tutelary*, enlarging the scope of protection. The autonomous legal regime of Provisional Measures of Protection, in conclusion, is conformed, in my conception, by the juridical nature of such measures, the rights at issue and the obligations derived therefrom, their legal effects, and the duty of compliance with them, – all running parallel to the proceedings as to the merits of the *cas d'espèce*. It also encompasses the legal consequences ensuing therefrom.

61. The rights protected by Provisional Measures of Protection are not the same as those pertaining to the merits of the case at issue. The obligations ensuing from Provisional Measures of Protection are distinct from, and additional to, the ones that may derive later from the Court's subsequent decision as to the merits. In case of a breach of a provisional measure of protection, the notion of victim of a harm emerges also in the framework of such provisional measures; irreparable damages can, by that breach, occur in the present context of prevention.

62. In order to avoid or prevent those damages, provisional measures of protection set forth obligations of their own,[25] distinct from the obligations emanating later from the respective Judgments as to the merits of the corresponding cases.[26] As I pondered, one decade ago, in another international jurisdiction, an international tribunal has the inherent power or *faculté* to supervise *motu proprio* the compliance or otherwise, on the part of the State concerned, with the provisional measures of protection it ordered; this is "even more necessary

---

25 Cf., in this sense, IACtHR, case of *Eloísa Barrios and Others*, concerning Venezuela, Order of 29.06.2005, Concurring Opinion of Judge Cançado Trindade, paras. 5–6.
26 Cf., in this sense, IACtHR, case of the *Communities of Jiguamiandó and Curbaradó*, concerning Colombia, Order of 07.02.2006, Concurring Opinion of Judge Cançado Trindade, paras. 5–6.

and pressing in a situation of extreme gravity and urgency", so as to prevent or avoid irreparable damage.²⁷

63. In such circumstances, an international tribunal cannot abstain from exercising its inherent power or *faculté* of supervision of compliance with its own Orders, in the interests of the sound administration of justice (*la bonne administration de la justice*). Non-compliance with Provisional Measures of Protection amounts to a breach of international obligations deriving from such measures. This being so, the determination of their breach, in my understanding, does not need to wait for the conclusion of the proceedings as to the merits of the case at issue, particularly if such proceedings are unduly prolonged.

64. Furthermore, the determination of their breach is not conditioned by the existence of a request to this effect by the State concerned; the Court, in my view, is fully entitled to proceed promptly to the determination of their breach *sponte sua, ex officio*, in the interests of the sound administration of justice (*la bonne administration de la justice*). The determination of a breach of provisional measures entails legal consequences; this paves the way for the granting of remedies, of distinct forms of reparation, and eventually costs.

65. In the present Judgment of the ICJ in the two joined cases of *Certain Activities* and of the *Construction of a Road*, the ICJ was attentive to this point, having found that, by its own determination of a breach of obligations ensuing from the Order of provisional measures of 08.03.2011 – in the *Certain Activities* case,²⁸ – it has afforded "adequate satisfaction" to the applicant State (para. 139). For all the aforesaid, it is high time to refine, at conceptual level, the autonomous legal regime of Provisional Measures of Protection.

66. Such refinement can clarify further this domain of international law marked by prevention and the duty of due diligence, and can thus foster the progressive development of those measures in the contemporary law of nations, faithful to their preventive dimension, to the benefit of all the *justiciables*. The progressive development of Provisional Measures of Protection is a domain in respect of which international case-law seems to be preceding legal doctrine, and it is a source of satisfaction to me to endeavour to contribute to that.

---

27 Cf., in this sense, IACtHR, case of *Eloísa Barrios and Others*, Order of 22.09.2005, concerning Venezuela, Concurring Opinion of Judge Cançado Trindade, para. 6.
28 Paras. 127 and 129, and resolutory point n. 3.

XII Epilogue: A Recapitulation

67. Provisional measures of protection provide, as we can see, a fertile ground for reflection at the juridico-epistemological level. Time and law are here ineluctably together, as in other domains of international law. Provisional measures underline the preventive dimension, growing in clarity, in contemporary international law. Provisional measures have undergone a significant evolution, but there remains a long way to go for them to reach their plenitude. In order to endeavour to pave this way, may I, last but not least, proceed to a brief recapitulation of the main points I deemed it fit to make, particularly in respect of Provisional Measures of Protection, in the course of the present Separate Opinion.

68. *Primus*: The preventive dimension in contemporary international law is clearly manifested in the formation of what I conceive as the autonomous legal regime of Provisional Measures of Protection. *Secundus*: Such preventive dimension grows in importance in the framework of regimes of protection (e.g., of the human person and of the environment), bringing us closer to general principles of law. *Tertius*: Provisional measures, historically emerged in comparative domestic law as a precautionary legal action, had their scope enlarged in international jurisdiction, becoming endowed with a tutelary – rather than only precautionary – character, as a true jurisdictional guarantee of a preventive nature. *Quartus*: Prevention and precaution underlie provisional measures, anticipatory in nature, so as to avoid the aggravation of the dispute and irreparable damage.

69. *Quintus*: In the framework of their autonomous legal regime, provisional measures guarantee rights which are not necessarily the same as those invoked in the proceedings as to the merits. *Sextus*: In the framework of their autonomous legal regime, provisional measures generate *per se* obligations, independently from those ensuing from the Court's subsequent judgment on the merits or on reparations. *Septimus*: The Court is fully entitled to order Provisional Measures of Protection, and to order *motu proprio*, any measure which it deems necessary.

70. *Octavus*: The Court is fully entitled to order *motu proprio* provisional measures which are totally or partially different from those requested by the contending parties. *Nonus*: The Court is fully entitled to order further provisional measures *motu proprio*; it does not need to wait for a request by a party to do so. *Decimus*: The Court has inherent powers or *facultés* to supervise *ex officio*

compliance with Provisional Measures of Protection and thus to enhance their preventive dimension.

71. *Undecimus*: Non-compliance amounts to an autonomous breach of provisional measures, irrespective of what will later be decided (any other breach) by the Court as to the merits. *Duodecimus*: A breach of a Provisional Measure of Protection engages by itself State responsibility, being additional to any other breach will may come later to be determined by the Court as to the merits. *Tertius decimus*: The notion of victim marks presence also in the realm of Provisional Measures of Protection.

72. *Quartus decimus*: The determination by the Court of a breach of a provisional measure should not be conditioned by the completion of subsequent proceedings as to the merits; the legal effects of such breach should be promptly determined by the Court, in the interests of the sound administration of justice (*la bonne administration de la justice*). *Quintus decimus*: Contemporary international tribunals have an inherent power or *faculté* to determine promptly such breach, with all its legal consequences (remedies, satisfaction as a form of reparation, and eventually costs). *Sextus decimus*: The duty to provide reparation (in its distinct forms) is promptly generated by the breach of Provisional Measures of Protection.

73. *Septimus decimus*: The interrelationship between breach and duty of reparation marks presence also in the realm of the autonomous legal regime of Provisional Measures of Protection. *Duodevicesimus*: The autonomous legal regime of their own, with all its elements (cf. *supra*), contributes to the prevalence of the rule of law (*prééminence du droit*) at international level. *Undevicesimus*: Provisional Measures of Protection have much evolved in recent decades, but there remain a long way to go so as to reach their plenitude. *Vicesimus*: Contemporary international tribunals are to refine the autonomous legal regime of Provisional Measures of Protection, and to foster their progressive development, to the benefit of all the *justiciables*.

(Signed) *Antônio Augusto* CANÇADO TRINDADE
Judge

2 Separate Opinion in the case of *Questions Relating to the Seizure and Detention of Certain Documents and Data* (Timor-Leste *versus* Australia, Order, Provisional Measures [Modification], of 22.04.2015)

1. Although I have concurred in the adoption today, 22 April 2015, of the present Order of Provisional Measures of Protection in the case of *Questions Relating to the Seizure and Detention of Certain Documents and Data* (Timor-Leste *versus* Australia), for standing in agreement with the resolutory points of its *dispositif*, I do not entirely share the reasoning of the Court which has led to its decision. I feel thus obliged, in the faithful exercise of the international judicial function, to lay on the records, in the present Separate Opinion, the foundations of my own personal position on the relevant issues, raised herein, pertaining to provisional measures of protection. Such measures, in my understanding, are endowed with an autonomous legal regime of their own.

2. The present Order of Provisional Measures of Protection should, in my view, have been adopted by the Court *proprio motu*, on the basis of Article 75(1) of its Rules, upon its own initiative and in its own terms, and not in the terms of an initiative of request by a contending Party, on the basis of Article 76(1) of its Rules. In any case, the International Court of Justice (ICJ) does not need to abide by the request itself of a provisional measure of protection, in the terms that the request is made. It may indicate or order provisional measures of protection that go beyond what was requested, in terms wholly or partly distinct from those of the request (Article 75(2) of its Rules).[1]

3. After all, the Court is master of its own competence in matters of provisional measures of protection. It can indicate or order them *sponte sua*. The ICJ is master of its own procedure and jurisdiction, and it can perfectly act *ex officio* in the domain of what I have been conceptualizing, in the adjudication of successive cases before the ICJ, as the *autonomous legal regime* of provisional

---

[1] And it may *proprio motu* request information from the contending Parties on "any matter" connected with the implementation of any provisional measures it has indicated or ordered (Article 78 of its Rules).

measures of protection.² Within this legal regime, the Court is well entitled to take a more proactive posture (under Article 75(1) and (2) of its Rules), in the light also of the principle of the juridical equality of States.

4. As I stated in my earlier Separate Opinion (paras. 14–15, 17, 19 and 25) in the ICJ's Order of 03.03.2014 in the present case of *Questions Relating to the Seizure and Detention of Certain Documents and Data*, the Court is on safer ground if it does not rely, in its decisions, only on unilateral assurances or "undertakings" on the part of States, which can prove to be "the source of uncertainties and apprehension in the course of international legal proceedings" (para. 15). In my perception, the Court is on safer ground if it acts on its own initiative and terms, attentive to the *legal nature* and the *effects* of provisional measures of protection.

5. As these latter purport to prevent irreparable harm – or, like in the present case, to prevent *further* irreparable harm to Timor-Leste, – there is no room for indulging into an exercise of balancing the interests of the contending parties, as anyway the ICJ is not an *amiable compositeur*, but rather a court of law. Another word of attention is called for at this stage. The Agent for Australia, in its letter to the ICJ of 25.03.2015, while expressing Australia's preparedness now to return the documents and materials (belonging to Timor-Leste) that it seized on 03.12.2013, again refers – as it had done earlier on – to its alleged "serious national security concerns" (p. 1). Yet, as I deemed it fit to warn in my previous Separate Opinion (paras. 38–41) in the Court's Order of 03.03.2014 in

---

2   Cf. to this effect, the considerations developed in my Dissenting Opinion in the Court's Order of 28.05.2009 in the case concerning *Questions Relating to the Obligation to Prosecute or Extradite* (Belgium *versus* Senegal), paras. 26–27, 29, 84, 88, 90–91; in my Separate Opinion in the Court's Order of 18.07.2011 in the case of the *Temple of Préah Vihéar* (Cambodia *versus* Thailand), paras. 65 and 74; in my Dissenting Opinion in the Court's Order of 16.07.2013 in the merged cases of *Certain Activities Carried out by Nicaragua in the Border Area* (Costa Rica *versus* Nicaragua) and of *Construction of a Road in Costa Rica along the San Juan River* (Nicaragua *versus* Costa Rica), paras. 40–42, 46–47, 50–53, 59–60 and 69–76; in my Separate Opinion in the Court's Order of 22.11.2013 in the merged cases of *Certain Activities Carried out by Nicaragua in the Border Area* (Costa Rica *versus* Nicaragua) and of *Construction of a Road in Costa Rica along the San Juan River* (Nicaragua *versus* Costa Rica), paras. 20–40; and in my Separate Opinion in the Court's Order of 03.03.2014, case of *Questions Relating to the Seizure and Detention of Certain Documents and Data* (Timor-Leste versus Australia), paras. 59–62 and 71.

the present case, arguments of alleged "national security", such as the ones in the present case, cannot be made the concern of an international tribunal.

6. The ICJ is attentive, instead, to the general principles of law, to the prevalence of the due process of law, to the preservation of equality of arms (*égalité des armes*). Initiatives of ordering new provisional measures of protection should, in my understanding, rest on the ICJ itself, rather than on requests of the contending parties to that effect. Moreover, as I sustained in my previous Separate Opinion (paras. 53 and 62) in the ICJ's Order of 03.03.2014 in the *cas d'espèce*, the Court should have taken and kept custody itself of Timor-Leste's seized documents, here in its premises in the Peace Palace at The Hague, so as to have them promptly returned, duly sealed, to Timor-Leste, whom they belong to.

7. The ICJ should have thus proceeded, as master of its own jurisdiction, without leaving space and time to abide later by the (respondent) State's "will". In my perception, contrary to what the Court says in the present Order (paras. 12, 14, 15 and 18), the situation itself has not at present changed. *Animus* is not a synonym of *factum*. What has now changed, is not the objective situation in the present case, but rather the state of mind, the attitude or predisposition of the respondent State, as it now realizes that the seized documents and data should be returned, – it can be added, – properly sealed, to Timor-Leste, whom they belong to. In any case, in the present Order, the Court rightly determines that the documents are kept sealed until thus returned by Australia to Timor-Leste's lawyers (resolutory points 1–2).

8. Already in 1931, it was pondered with insight that provisional measures are bound to assist the development of international law, as they, after all, contribute to the realization of justice in a given legal situation.[3] At that time, the old Permanent Court of International Justice (PCIJ) already admitted its prerogative to indicate or modify *ex officio* provisional measures of protection, in terms other than the ones requested by the contending Parties.[4] The ICJ, for its part, in revising the relevant provisions of its Rules of Court and bringing

---

3   P. Guggenheim, *Les mesures provisoires de procédure internationale et leur influence sur le développement du droit des gens*, Paris, Libr. Rec. Sirey, 1931, pp. 14–15 and 62.
4   G. Guyomar, *Commentaire du Règlement de la Cour Internationale de Justice – Interprétation et pratique*, Paris, Pédone, 1973, pp. 348.

them closer to its Statute (Article 41(1)),[5] sought to enhance the authority of its initiative to indicate or order provisional measures of protection.[6]

9. The ICJ is entitled to do so *in its own terms*, as it deems appropriate, even more so to prevent an aggravation of a dispute.[7] This Court has already disclosed its preparedness to do so: an example to this effect lies in the decision of the ICJ, – which I keep in grateful memory, – in its Order of 18.07.2011 in the case of the *Temple of Préah Vihéar* (Cambodia *versus* Thailand), to establish a "provisional demilitarized zone", so as to prevent further irreparable harm.

10. Nowadays, with eight and a half decades of sedimentation of experience, looking back in time, we can realize that steps ahead have been taken, but the move towards the progressive development of international law in this domain has been rather slow. In our days, in early 2015, such progressive development requires an awareness of the autonomous legal regime of provisional measures of protection, as well as judicial decisions which reflect it accordingly, with all its implications.

11. In my perception, the way is paved and the time is ripe for the ordering by the ICJ of provisional measures of protection *proprio motu*, on the basis of Article 75(1) and (2) of the Rules of Court. Advances in this domain cannot be achieved in pursuance of a voluntarist conception of international law in

---

[5] From the start, Article 41(1) of the Statute of the ICJ – and of its predecessor, the PCIJ – set forth the power of the Court to indicate provisional measures; the doctrinal debates that followed (as to their effects) did not hinder the development of a vast case-law (of the PCIJ and the ICJ) on the matter; cf., e.g., J. Sztucki, *Interim Measures in the Hague Court – An Attempt at a Scrutiny*, Deventer, Kluwer, 1983, pp. 35–60 and 270–280; J.B. Elkind, *Interim Protection – A Functional Approach*, The Hague, Nijhoff, 1981, pp. 88–152.

[6] Cf. S. Rosenne, *Provisional Measures in International Law – The International Court of Justice and the International Tribunal for the Law of the Sea*, Oxford, Oxford University Press, 2005, pp. 73–74. The ICJ can do so *proprio motu*, whenever, in its assessment, the circumstances of the case so require; cf. K. Oellers-Frahm, "Article 41", in *The Statute of the International Court of Justice – A Commentary* (eds. A. Zimmermann *et alii*), 2nd. ed., Oxford, Oxford University Press, 2012, pp. 1050 and 1053.

[7] Cf. H. Thirlway, *The Law and Practice of the International Court of Justice – Fifty Years of Jurisprudence*, Oxford, Oxford University Press, 2013, vol. I, pp. 953–955; and vol. II, pp. 1805–1806.

general, and of international legal procedure in particular.[8] The requirements of objective justice stand above the options of litigation strategies. These latter rest in the hands of the contending Parties, while the former constitute the essentials whereby an international tribunal accomplishes its mission to impart justice.

12. The autonomous legal regime (as I perceive it) of provisional measures of protection has been formed after a long evolution. The traditional precautionary legal actions, as they originally flourished in comparative domestic procedural law, were transposed into the international legal order, and evolved in both of them,[9] appearing nowadays with a character, more than precautionary, truly *tutelary*. Provisional measures of protection constitute nowadays a true jurisdictional guarantee of a preventive character, corresponding to an evolutionary legal conception.

13. In my conception, the *autonomous* (not simply "accessory") legal regime of provisional measures of protection, in expansion in our times, disclosing the relevant preventive dimension in international law, comprises the *rights* to be protected (which are not necessarily the same as in the proceedings on the merits of the concrete case), the corresponding *obligations* of the States concerned, and the *legal consequences of non-compliance* with provisional measures (which are distinct from those ensuing from breaches as to the merits of the case). And the Court is fully entitled to decide thereon, without waiting for the manifestations of the "will" of a contending State party. It is human conscience, standing above the "will", that accounts for the progressive development of international law. *Ex conscientia jus oritur*.

(Signed) *Antônio Augusto* CANÇADO TRINDADE
Judge

---

8 For my criticisms of the voluntarist conception, cf. A.A. Cançado Trindade, *Le Droit international pour la personne humaine*, Paris, Pédone, 2012, pp. 115–136; A.A. Cançado Trindade, *Los Tribunales Internacionales Contemporáneos y la Humanización del Derecho Internacional*, Buenos Aires, Ed. Ad-Hoc, 2013, pp. 69–77; A.A. Cançado Trindade, *Os Tribunais Internacionais e a Realização da Justiça*, Rio de Janeiro, Edit. Renovar, 2015, pp. 197–198 and 352–354.

9 Cf., on the case-law of national tribunals, e.g., E. García de Enterria, *La Batalla por las Medidas Cautelares*, 2nd. rev. ed., Madrid, Civitas, 1995, pp. 25–385; and cf., on the case-law of international tribunals, e.g., R. Bernhardt (ed.), *Interim Measures Indicated by International Courts*, Berlin/Heidelberg, Springer-Verlag, 1994, pp. 1–152.

Index

access to justice   95, 503, 708, 730
actus reus   45, 191, 197, 202, 209, 224, 233
Aeschylus   275, 401, 525
affidavits   188, 193
Ago, Roberto   282, 409, 532
Álvarez, Alejandro   23
Anouilh, J.   175
Aquinas, Thomas   455, 627
arbitration   707, 709, 718–721, 725, 749
Aron, Raymond   353, 602

Bergson, Henri   281, 408, 531
Berlin, Isaiah   279, 406
biodiversity   650, 654–656, 659
Bourquin, Maurice   689
Boutros-Ghali, B.   101
burden of proof   81, 84, 157, 223, 230–231
Bynkershoek, Cornelius van   622

codification   684
collective guarantee   55, 225, 637, 641, 664
common good   357, 481, 654
compétence de la compétence   11, 14, 16, 26–27, 37, 739
conciliation   710
Cóndor, Operation   83
continuing violations   148, 152, 156, 231
corpus juris gentium   65–67, 69, 74, 224, 230, 233, 312, 439, 484, 562, 607
crime of State   164
crimes against humanity   74, 79, 95, 114, 124, 154, 193–194, 263, 295, 322, 506, 720
customary international law   225, 233–234, 244–245, 248–250, 259, 261, 267, 260, 271, 319, 329, 343, 358, 360, 362, 377, 395, 398–399, 422, 440, 447, 451, 455, 474, 486, 502–503, 520, 522, 544, 547–548, 555–556, 568, 578, 592, 596, 604–605, 611

Dante   274, 402, 524
deportations   105, 113, 125, 130, 159, 192, 206
de Soto, Domingo   328, 455, 577
"deterrence"   238, 293–296, 298, 306, 311, 320, 323, 345, 349, 353, 361, 366, 384, 420–423, 433, 447, 476–477, 479, 487, 543–546, 555–556, 596, 600, 602, 610
disappearances, enforced   49, 83, 99–100, 102, 148, 151–153, 155–156, 213, 231
displacement, forced   104, 121, 130, 158–159, 191, 213, 222, 232–233
Dostoïevski   274, 402, 525
due diligence   754, 757
due process of law   720
Duhamel, Georges   279, 406, 529

effet utile   19, 26, 65, 224, 227, 233
equality of arms / *égalité des armes*   87, 686, 690–691, 720–721, 762
"ethnic cleansing"   62, 99, 101, 103, 105, 131
Euripides   140

fact-finding   102–103, 213, 231, 619, 621
Freud, Sigmund   278, 405, 528
Fromm, Erich   280, 407, 529–530

Gallo, Max   274, 402, 524
Gandhi, Mahatma   272–273, 400, 522–523
general principles of law   282, 291, 293, 313, 487, 541, 577, 606, 610 682–685, 698, 722, 731
Genesis, Book of   214, 272, 274–275, 281, 285, 312, 323, 400–401, 408, 412, 438, 450, 522, 524–525, 530, 534–535, 561,
genocide   45, 54, 65, 74–75, 79–80, 89, 91, 94–95, 106, 114, 120, 122, 127–128, 131, 145–147, 160, 164, 185, 191, 193–194, 197, 215, 222–225, 227–228, 720, 745
Gentili, Alberico   71, 326, 453, 575, 622
Glaser, Stefan   24, 283, 533
Grotius, Hugo   22, 72, 178–179, 326, 328, 453–454, 575, 577, 622, 627

Hague Peace Conference, I   317, 516, 566
Hague Peace Conference, II   291–292, 419, 516, 541–542, 693, 722
heritage, natural and cultural   653
Hesse, Hermann   276, 403, 526
Hibakusha   344–345, 471–473, 593–595

historiography   96
Homer   48–49, 283, 410, 533
Huber, Max   23, 286, 413, 536
humanization of international law   75, 238, 312–313, 366, 439–440, 488, 492, 563, 610, 629
human rights, grave violations of   84, 87, 89

inherent powers   10–13, 16, 27–31, 35–36, 383, 749–750, 756–759
Institut de Droit International   297–299, 424–426, 547
Inter-American Juridical Committee   696
inter-generational equity   637, 651–654, 660, 666
International Committee of the Red Cross   179, 343, 590, 592
International Criminal Law   101, 151, 224–226, 228, 230, 233, 312, 439 562
International Environmental Law   664
International Humanitarian Law   66, 69, 73, 75, 93, 97, 101, 103, 151–152, 158, 179, 219, 224–226, 228, 230–231, 233, 254, 258, 294, 296, 304–305, 307, 311–312, 318, 321, 323, 361, 386, 431–434, 438–439, 444, 447, 450, 487–488, 544, 546, 553–557, 561, 567, 570, 572, 601, 610, 615, 621, 623, 630, 744
International Law Association   298–299, 425–426, 548
International Law of Human Rights   66, 68–69, 73, 75, 93, 101, 151, 224–226, 228, 230, 233, 294, 296, 305, 307, 311–312, 321, 323–324, 361, 432–434, 438–439, 447, 450, 487–488, 544, 546, 555–557, 561, 570, 572–573, 601, 610, 615, 621, 623, 630, 648, 744
International Law of Refugees   66, 69, 75, 93, 101, 224–226, 228, 230, 233, 307, 311–312, 361, 434, 438–439, 488, 556, 561, 610
international law, progressive development of   633, 711, 762–764
international legal personality   57
international tribunals   27–28, 30, 32–33, 35, 44, 72, 80–81, 87–88, 94, 152, 156, 209, 211, 224, 230, 434, 557, 619, 648, 664, 707, 720, 731

Jaspers, Karl   273, 400–401, 523
Job, Book of   214, 285, 534
Jung, Carl   278, 405, 528
jura novit curia   32, 685, 689
juridical equality of States   238, 240, 291–293, 418–420, 487, 540–543, 605, 611, 714, 717, 722–724, 761
jus cogens   125, 155, 158, 231, 238, 294, 305, 312–313, 327, 329, 351, 361, 366, 432, 439–440, 454–455, 488, 492, 561–563, 576, 578
jus gentium   23, 66, 70, 225, 286, 313, 323, 326, 328, 439, 448, 449, 454, 536, 562–563, 570, 575, 577, 622, 687, 743
jusnaturalism   226, 230, 277, 282–283, 290–291, 320, 322–323, 361, 367, 417–418, 454, 493, 532, 569–570, 576, 633, 688

La Pradelle, Albert de   282, 409–410, 532
Las Casas, Bartolomé de   128, 622, 627
Lemkin, Raphael   127–128
local remedies, exhaustion of   706, 708, 730

Machado de Assis   713
marine resources, living   664, 671
Maritain, Jacques   276–277, 404, 526–527
Martens clause   74, 238, 317–319, 367, 443, 443–446, 566–568, 610
Martens, Fyodor F. von   317, 444, 566
massacres   82–83, 110, 119, 199, 221, 228
mass graves   99, 102–103, 119, 146, 180–181, 183–184, 232
mens rea   45, 191, 197–198, 209–210, 212–213, 224, 232–233
missing persons   145–149, 152, 156, 177, 231
Moraes, Vinicius de   726
Morin, Edgar   280, 407, 530

natural law   158, 231, 326, 449, 453, 455, 475, 575, 577, 628
natural resources   664, 666
non-derogable rights   153
nuclear disarmament   238, 244–245, 252–253, 256–262, 264, 266–267, 270–272, 287, 290, 293–294, 297, 304, 316, 320, 327–328, 332–334, 341, 343, 351, 355, 357, 359–360, 362, 366, 373, 377, 379, 387, 392, 394–395,

INDEX

399, 417, 421, 451, 454, 459–463, 470, 472, 475, 485–487, 489, 498–499, 501, 504, 506, 509–511, 513, 515, 520, 537, 543–544, 561, 565, 574, 581, 583, 592, 601–602, 606, 608–611
nuclear-weapon-free zones 239, 253, 257–258, 266, 320, 324, 332, 335–336, 338–340, 362, 377, 386, 394, 461–466, 506, 519, 569, 581, 584–585, 588–590, 601, 611

obligations *erga omnes* 155, 268, 298–299, 301–302, 313, 327, 425, 428–430, 439–440, 454, 499, 521, 548, 552, 563, 576
opinio juris communis 238–239, 250, 255, 259, 261, 268, 270–272, 293, 295–297, 306, 316, 320, 325, 328, 335, 352–356, 361–362, 366–367, 378, 383, 390, 395, 397, 399, 420, 422–424, 433, 446, 454–455, 479–482, 487–488, 492–493, 508, 520–522, 544, 546, 555, 562, 565, 569, 574, 577, 584, 601–605, 610, 637, 650, 671–672
ordre public 25, 315, 441
Organization of American States (OAS) 695–697, 721
Orwell, George 725

pacta sunt servanda 682
Pact of Bogotá 675, 692–700, 703
Peña, Juan de la 622
Politis, Nicolas 22
Popper, Karl 274, 401, 524, 665–666
positivism, legal 238, 267, 282, 314, 322, 395, 410, 443, 446, 449, 455, 482–483, 492, 532–533, 563, 566, 568, 571, 633, 688, 721, 748
precautionary principle 657, 659–664, 735, 741, 754, 758
prima principia 21, 226–227, 234, 290, 357, 360, 417, 484, 487, 539–540, 606, 609, 690–691
principle neminem laedere 626
principle of equality and non-discrimination 139, 156, 291, 541
principle of humanity 44, 67–73, 75, 104, 220, 228, 230, 233–234, 239 290, 326–327, 361, 417, 453, 487, 493, 539–540, 570, 575–576, 610, 743

principles of international law 292, 298, 361, 418–419, 481, 540, 542, 547, 601, 675, 690, 716–717
principle of prevention 660, 662, 664, 735, 741, 754, 758
provisional measures of protection, autonomous legal regime of 728–729, 731–732, 735, 737, 740, 743, 746, 750, 753, 755, 759–760, 763–764
Puchta, G.F. 354, 480, 603
Pufendorf, Samuel 71, 326, 453, 575, 622, 628

Radbruch, Gustav 282, 408
recta ratio 21, 25, 37, 158, 230–231, 234, 239, 283, 321, 326, 328, 340, 352, 367, 410, 448, 454–455, 467, 493, 529, 570, 575–577, 601, 622, 627–629, 633, 749
refugees 121, 189–191
reparations 158, 214–217, 233, 614, 616–618, 623–626, 628–631, 633, 687, 735, 750–753, 759
Roa Dávila, Juan 622, 627
Roman law 689
rule of law 35, 37, 62, 95, 749–750, 759
Russell, Bertrand 274–275, 401–402, 523–525

Savigny, F.K. von 354, 480, 603
Schweitzer, Albert 278–279, 405–406, 528–529
Seneca 47, 621, 742
Sertillanges, R.P. 213, 284, 411, 534
Sophocles 174–175, 275, 401, 525
sound administration of justice 17, 37, 616
standard of proof 80–81, 85–86, 91, 94, 157, 195, 209, 213, 222, 230
State responsibility 55, 75–81, 83, 86, 107, 153, 195, 223–225, 233, 440, 652, 735
State succession 53, 56–57, 61, 64, 229–230
Suárez, Francisco 22, 71, 291, 326, 328, 418, 453–454, 541, 575, 577, 622

Tieya, Wang 355, 481, 604
Tolstoi, Leo 279, 406, 529
torture 123–125, 153, 195, 201, 203, 222, 231
Toynbee, Arnold 275–276, 402–403, 526
Truth Commissions 152

unilateral acts   711
United Nations Charter   68, 151, 230, 254, 262–263, 265, 285–287, 289, 291–293, 296, 361, 382, 390, 392, 412–414, 418–420, 423, 435, 448, 484, 487, 507, 509, 516–518, 535–536, 539, 541–543, 546, 555, 571, 607, 610, 722–723, 731
United Nations University   652
Universal Declaration of Human Rights   151, 221, 287, 414, 537, 652
universal juridical conscience   66, 106, 283, 292, 296, 299, 316–317, 319, 327, 354, 357, 360, 410, 419, 443–444, 446, 481, 484, 487, 489, 533, 541, 546, 549, 566, 569, 722
ut res magis valeat quam pereat   11

Vattel, E. de   326, 443, 452, 465, 575
Verdross, Alfred   282, 409, 532

Vienna Conventions on the Law of Treaties   20, 455–456
Vieira, Antônio   721
Vitoria, Francisco de   21–22, 71, 128, 291, 326, 328, 418, 453–455, 541, 575, 577, 622, 627–628

war crimes   114, 124, 720
Weil, Simone   218, 283, 410, 533
Wiesel, Elie   280–281, 407–408, 530–531
witnesses   185–186, 188, 193, 205, 208
Wolff, Christian   71, 326, 453, 575, 622, 628
World Conference on Human Rights, II   60–62, 92, 106–107, 231
World Conferences, U.N.   288, 415, 537–538, 741

Zapata y Sandoval, Juan   622
Zweig, Stefan   277–278, 404–405, 527

Printed in the United States
By Bookmasters